D1481416

LET THE EARTH HEAR HIS VOICE

LET THE EARTH HEAR HIS VOICE

International Congress on World Evangelization Lausanne, Switzerland

OFFICIAL REFERENCE VOLUME:

Papers and Responses

Edited by J.D. Douglas

1313 Hennepin Avenue
Minneapolis, Minnesota, 55403
U.S.A.

*The opinions expressed in this
book are those of the
contributing authors and not
necessarily of the International
Congress on World
Evangelization.*

Library of Congress Catalog
Card Number: 74-24847

Printed in the U.S.A.

FOREWORD

To those who were there Lausanne '74 was an unforgettable experience. God called us to repentance for our failures and lack of vision. He encouraged us through a heightened awareness of the work of the Holy Spirit in fruitful evangelization all over the world. He sobered us and called us to prayer as we considered the hard places of the world and the many yet unreached with the Gospel. He enabled us to hear and appreciate points of view other than our own—even those with which we disagreed. Our vision was expanded, our hearts were melted together in love, our minds were stimulated to face issues squarely in the light of his Word, and our wills were moved to enter into a solemn covenant to be instruments in the hand of our Sovereign Lord so that the Congress theme, "Let the Earth Hear His Voice," might become a reality.

Even those who were at Lausanne were able to share in only a fraction of the program. Here for all to study and digest and act on are the varied study papers and summaries of discussion groups.

Our prayer as this volume is released is that all who read it will experience the same movement of the Spirit to love and obedience we who were at Lausanne '74 sensed in those days.

A. JACK DAIN
BILLY GRAHAM

INTRODUCTION

From the beginning the International Congress on World Evangelization was marked by involvement. Participants sent in requests for subjects to be covered. These suggestions are evident in the wide range of topics included. Plenary papers were sent in advance of the Congress and participants' questions, observations and criticisms were sent directly to the speaker involved. At the Congress he did not read his paper but responded to this information. Involvement continued at the Congress in National Strategy and Theology Study papers. Each participant was in one of each of these groups. The fruit of these extended discussions follows each paper.

Realism characterized the Congress papers and discussion. This helped to lead to the vital characteristic of action. Many National Strategy Groups crystallized plans for evangelization which may be instructive to others. They were asked to answer basically two questions: How can we best evangelize our own nation together? And, what contribution can we make to cross-cultural evangelization so that the two billion who have never heard may be reached with the Good News? Practical implications for action came out of the theology and strategy groups. The material here also has the great advantage of wide cross-cultural interaction from all six continents. The Church at the Congress learned from all of its parts.

As you dip into these materials at the point of your particular interest, it is our prayer that the same Spirit who met us in Lausanne, Switzerland, from July 16-25, 1974, will meet you as well—melting and molding you to crystallize the part he wants you to have in world evangelization.

DONALD HOKE
PAUL LITTLE

CONTENTS

Section I:
Opening Convocation

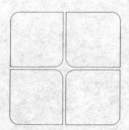

INTRODUCTION TO COVENANT
John Stott

The Lausanne Covenant is a very solemn personal commitment. It commits us to concrete and sacrificial action. It can be signed with integrity only after careful thought and prayer. Some of you may need longer in which to consider it and will send in your signed card within the next few days after you've left. Others may not feel able to sign it at all. Each of us must make his own conscientious decision before God and each who signs it signs not in any representative capacity but as an individual member of the body of Christ. Nevertheless, it expresses, so far as we have been able to secure, the consensus of the Congress. It is, therefore, now my privilege to invite you, indeed to encourage you, if the Holy Spirit so directs your conscience, to add your signature to the Lausanne Covenant which binds us to pray together, to plan together, to work together for the evangelization of the whole world. And first, Dr. Billy Graham as honorary chairman of the Congress and Bishop Jack Dain as chairman of the planning committee, who have themselves reached a conscientious decision in this matter, will affix their signatures to the Covenant.

In that same spirit, we now invite those of you who have your Covenants with you and who wish to, to sign and we will maintain silence for one minute for this purpose.

I would now pray in the closing words of the Covenant in the conclusion that God may help us, each one, by his grace and for his glory to be faithful to this, our Covenant. Amen. Alleluia.

THE LAUSANNE COVENANT

Introduction

We, members of the Church of Jesus Christ, from more than 150 nations, participants in the International Congress on World Evangelization at Lausanne, praise God for his great salvation and rejoice in the fellowship he has given us with himself and with each other. We are deeply stirred by what God is doing in our day, moved to penitence by our failures and challenged by the unfinished task of evangelization. We believe the Gospel is God's good news for the whole world, and we are determined by his grace to obey Christ's commission to proclaim it to all mankind and to make disciples of every nation. We desire, therefore, to affirm our faith and our resolve, and to make public our covenant.

1. The Purpose of God

We affirm our belief in the one eternal God, Creator and Lord of the world, Father, Son and Holy Spirit, who governs all things according to the purpose of his will. He has been calling out from the world a people for himself, and sending his people back into the world to be his servants and his witnesses, for the extension of his kingdom, the building up of Christ's body, and the glory of his name. We confess with shame that we have often denied our calling and failed in our mission, by becoming conformed to the world or by withdrawing from it. Yet we rejoice that even when borne by earthen vessels the Gospel is still a precious treasure. To the task of making that treasure known in the power of the Holy Spirit we desire to dedicate ourselves anew.

(Isa. 40:28; Matt. 28:19; Eph. 1:11; Acts 15:14; John 17:6, 18; Eph. 4:12; I Cor. 5:10; Rom. 12:2; II Cor. 4:7)

2. The Authority and Power of The Bible

We affirm the divine inspiration, truthfulness and authority of both Old and New Testament Scriptures in their entirety as the only written Word of God, without error in all that it affirms, and the only infallible rule of faith and practice. We also affirm the power of God's Word to accomplish his purpose of salvation. The message of the Bible is addressed to all mankind. For God's revelation in Christ and in Scripture is unchangeable. Through it the Holy Spirit still speaks today. He illumines the minds of God's people in every culture to perceive its truth freshly through their own eyes and thus discloses to the whole church ever more of the many-colored wisdom of God.

(II Tim. 3:16; II Pet. 1:21; John 10:35; Isa. 55:11; I Cor. 1:21; Rom. 1:16; Matt. 5:17,18; Jude 3; Eph. 1:17,18; 3:10,18)

3. The Uniqueness and Universality of Christ

We affirm that there is only one Savior and only one Gospel, although there is a wide diversity of evangelistic approaches. We recognize that all men have some knowledge of God through his general revelation in nature. But we deny that this can save, for men suppress the truth by their unrighteousness. We also reject as derogatory to Christ and the Gospel every kind of syncretism and dialogue which implies that Christ speaks equally through all religions and ideologies. Jesus Christ, being himself the only God-man, who gave himself as the only ransom for sinners, is the only mediator between God and man. There is no other name by which we must be saved. All men are perishing because of sin, but God loves all men, not wishing that any should perish but that all should repent. Yet those who reject Christ repudiate the joy of salvation and condemn themselves to eternal separation from God. To proclaim Jesus as "the Savior of the world" is not to affirm that all men are either automatically or ultimately saved, still less to affirm that all religions offer salvation in Christ. Rather it is to proclaim God's love for a world of sinners and to invite all men to respond to him as Savior and Lord in the wholehearted personal commitment of repentance and faith. Jesus Christ has been exalted above every other name; we long for the day when every knee shall bow to him and every tongue shall confess him Lord.

(Gal. 1:6-9; Rom. 1:18-32; I Tim. 2:5,6; Acts 4:12; John 3:16-19; II Pet. 3:9; II Thess. 1:7-9; John 4:42; Matt. 11:28; Eph. 1:20,21; Phil. 2:9-11)

4. The Nature of Evangelism

To evangelize is to spread the good news that Jesus Christ died for our sins and was raised from the dead according to the Scriptures, and that as the reigning Lord he now offers the forgiveness of sins and the liberating gift of the Spirit to all who repent and believe. Our Christian presence in the world is indispensable to evangelism, and so is that kind of dialogue whose purpose is to listen sensitively in order to understand. But evangelism itself is the proclamation of the historical, biblical Christ as Savior and Lord, with a view to persuading people to come to him personally and so be reconciled to God. In issuing the Gospel invitation we have no liberty to conceal the cost of discipleship. Jesus still calls all who would follow him to deny themselves, take up their cross, and identify themselves with his new community. The results of evangelism include obedience to Christ, incorporation into his church and responsible service in the world.

(I Cor. 15:3,4; Acts 2:32-39; John 20:21; I Cor. 1:23; II Cor. 4:5; 5:11,20; Luke 14:25-33; Mark 8:34; Acts 2:40,47; Mark 10:43-45)

5. Christian Social Responsibility

We affirm that God is both the Creator and the Judge of all men. We therefore should share his concern for justice and reconciliation throughout human society and for the liberation of men from every kind of oppression. Because mankind is made in the image of God, every person, regardless of race, religion, color, culture, class, sex or age, has an intrinsic dignity because of which he should be respected and served, not exploited. Here too we express penitence both for our neglect and for having sometimes regarded evangelism and social concern as mutually exclusive. Although reconciliation with man is not reconciliation with God, nor is social action evangelism, nor is political liberation salvation, nevertheless we affirm that evangelism and socio-political involvement are both part of our Christian duty. For both are necessary expressions of our doctrines of God and man, our love for our neighbor and our obedience to Jesus Christ. The message of salvation implies also a message of judgment upon every form of alienation, oppression and discrimination, and we should not be afraid to denounce evil and injustice wherever they exist. When people receive Christ they are born again into his kingdom and must seek not only to exhibit but also to spread its righteousness in the midst of an unrighteous world. The salvation we claim should be transforming us in the totality of our personal and social responsibilities. Faith without works is dead.

(Acts 17:26,31; Gen. 18:25; Isa. 1:17; Psa. 45:7; Gen. 1:26,27; Jas. 3:9; Lev. 19:18; Luke 6:27,35; Jas. 2:14-26; John 3:3,5; Matt. 5:20; 6:33; II Cor. 3:18; Jas. 2:20)

6. The Church and Evangelism

We affirm that Christ sends his redeemed people into the world as the Father sent him, and that this calls for a similar deep and costly penetration of the world. We need to break out of our ecclesiastical ghettos and permeate non-Christian society. In the church's mission of sacrificial service evangelism is primary. World evangelization requires the whole church to take the whole Gospel to the whole world. The church is at the very center of God's cosmic purpose and is his appointed means of spreading the Gospel. But a church which preaches the Cross must itself be marked by the Cross. It becomes a stumbling block to evangelism when it betrays the Gospel or lacks a living faith in God, a genuine love for people, or scrupulous honesty in all things including promotion and finance. The church is the community of God's people rather than an institution, and must not be identified with any particular culture, social or political system, or human ideology.

(John 17:18; 20:21; Matt. 28:19,20; Acts 1:8; 20:27; Eph. 1:9,10; 3:9-11; Gal. 6:14,17; II Cor. 6:3,4; II Tim. 2:19-21; Phil. 1:27)

7. Cooperation in Evangelism

We affirm that the church's visible unity in truth is God's purpose. Evangelism also summons us to unity, because our oneness strengthens our witness, just as our disunity undermines our gospel of reconciliation. We recognize, however, that organizational unity may take many forms and does not necessarily forward evangelism. Yet we who share the same biblical faith should be closely united in fellowship, work and witness. We confess that our testimony has sometimes been marred by sinful individualism and needless duplication. We pledge ourselves to seek a deeper unity in truth, worship, holiness and mission. We urge the development of regional and functional cooperation for the furtherance of the church's mission, for strategic planning, for mutual encouragement, and for the sharing of resources and experience.

(John 17:21,23; Eph. 4:3,4; John 13:35; Phil. 1:27; John 17:11-23)

8. Churches in Evangelistic Partnership

We rejoice that a new missionary era has dawned. The dominant role of western missions is fast disappearing. God is raising up from the younger churches a great new resource for world evangelization, and is thus demonstrating that the responsibility to evangelize belongs to the whole body of Christ. All churches should therefore be asking God and themselves what they should be doing both to reach their own area and to send missionaries to other parts of the world. A re-evaluation of our missionary responsibility and role should be continuous. Thus a growing partnership of churches will develop and the universal character of Christ's Church will be more clearly exhibited. We also thank God for agencies which labor in Bible translation, theological education, the mass media, Christian literature, evangelism, missions, church renewal, and other specialist fields. They too should engage in constant self-examination to evaluate their effectiveness as part of the Church's mission.

(Rom. 1:8; Phil. 1:5; 4:15; Acts 13:1-3; I Thess. 1:6-8)

9. The Urgency of the Evangelistic Task

More than 2,700 million people, which is more than two-thirds of mankind, have yet to be evangelized. We are ashamed that so many have been neglected; it is a standing rebuke to us and to the whole church. There is now, however, in many parts of the world an unprecedented receptivity to the Lord Jesus Christ. We are convinced that this is the time for churches and para-church agencies to pray earnestly for the salvation of the unreached and to launch new efforts to achieve world evangelization. A reduction of foreign missionaries and money in an evangelized country may sometimes be necessary to facilitate the national church's growth in self-reliance and to release resources for unevangelized areas. Missionaries should flow ever more freely from and to all six continents in a spirit of humble service. The goal should be, by all available means and at the earliest possible time, that every person will have the opportunity to hear, understand, and receive the good news. We cannot hope to attain this goal without sacrifice. All of us are shocked by the poverty of millions and disturbed by the injustices which cause it. Those of us who live in affluent circumstances accept our duty to develop a simple life-style in order to contribute more generously to both relief and evangelism.

(John 9:4; Matt. 9:35-38; Rom. 9:1-3; I Cor. 9:19-23; Mark 16:15;
Isa. 58:6,7; Jas. 1:27; 2:1-9; Matt. 25:31-46; Acts 2:44,45; 4:34,35)

10. Evangelism and Culture

The development of strategies for world evangelization calls for imaginative pioneering methods. Under God, the result will be the rise of churches deeply rooted in Christ and closely related to their culture. Culture must always be tested and judged by Scripture. Because man is God's creature, some of his culture is rich in beauty and goodness. Because he has fallen, all of it is tainted with sin and some of it is demonic. The Gospel does not presuppose the superiority of any culture to another, but evaluates all cultures according to its own criteria of truth and righteousness, and insists on moral absolutes in every culture. Missions have all too frequently exported with the Gospel an alien culture, and churches have sometimes been in bondage to culture rather than to the Scripture. Christ's evangelists must humbly seek to empty themselves of all but their personal authenticity in order to become the servants of others, and churches must seek to transform and enrich culture, all for the glory of God.

(Mark 7:8,9,13; Gen. 4:21,22; I Cor. 9:19-23; Phil. 2:5-7; II Cor. 4:5)

11. Education and Leadership

We confess that we have sometimes pursued church growth at the expense of church depth, and divorced evangelism from Christian nurture. We also acknowledge that some of our missions have been too slow to equip and encourage national leaders to assume their rightful responsibilities. Yet we are committed to indigenous principles, and long that every church will have national leaders who manifest a Christian style of leadership in terms not of domination but of service. We recognize that there is a great need to improve theological education, especially for church leaders. In every nation and culture there should be an effective training program for pastors and laymen in doctrine, discipleship, evangelism, nurture and service. Such training programs should not rely on any stereotyped methodology but should be developed by creative local initiatives according to biblical standards.

(Col. 1:27,28; Acts 14:23; Tit. 1:5,9; Mark 10:42-45; Eph. 4:11,12)

12. Spiritual Conflict

We believe that we are engaged in constant spiritual warfare with the principalities and powers of evil, who are seeking to overthrow the church and frustrate its task of world evangelization. We know our need to equip ourselves with God's armor and to fight this battle with the spiritual weapons of truth and prayer. For we detect the activity of our enemy, not only in false ideologies outside the church, but also inside it in false gospels which twist Scripture and put man in the place of God. We need both watchfulness and discernment to safeguard the biblical Gospel. We acknowledge that we ourselves are not immune to worldliness of thought and action, that is, to a surrender to secularism. For example, although careful studies of church growth, both numerical and spiritual, are right and valuable, we have sometimes neglected them. At other times, desirous to insure a response to the Gospel, we have compromised our message, manipulated our hearers through pressure techniques, and become unduly preoccupied with statistics or even dishonest in our use of them. All this is worldly. The church must be in the world; the world must not be in the church.

(Eph. 6:12; II Cor. 4:3,4; Eph. 6:11,13-18; II Cor. 10:3-5; I John 2:18-26, 4:1-3; Gal. 1:6-9; II Cor. 2:17, 4:2; John 17:15)

13. *Freedom and Persecution*

It is the God-appointed duty of every government to secure conditions of peace, justice, and liberty in which the church may obey God, serve the Lord Christ, and preach the Gospel without interference. We, therefore, pray for the leaders of the nations and call upon them to guarantee freedom of thought and conscience, and freedom to practice and propagate religion in accordance with the will of God and as set forth in The Universal Declaration of Human Rights. We also express our deep concern for all who have been unjustly imprisoned, and especially for our brethren who are suffering for their testimony to the Lord Jesus. We promise to pray and work for their freedom. At the same time we refuse to be intimidated by their fate. God helping us, we too will seek to stand against injustice and to remain faithful to the Gospel, whatever the cost. We do not forget the warnings of Jesus that persecution is inevitable.

(I Tim. 1:1-4; Acts 4:19, 5:29; Col. 3:24; Heb. 13:1-3; Luke 4:18;
Gal. 5:11, 6:12; Matt. 5:10-12; John 15:18-21)

14. *The Power of The Holy Spirit*

We believe in the power of the Holy Spirit. The Father sent his Spirit to bear witness to his Son; without his witness ours is futile. Conviction of sin, faith in Christ, new birth, and Christian growth are all his work. Further, the Holy Spirit is a missionary spirit; thus evangelism should arise spontaneously from a Spirit-filled church. A church that is not a missionary church is contradicting itself and quenching the Spirit. Worldwide evangelization will become a realistic possibility only when the Spirit renews the church in truth and wisdom, faith, holiness, love, and power. We, therefore, call upon all Christians to pray for such a visitation of the sovereign Spirit of God that all his fruit may appear in all his people and that all his gifts may enrich the body of Christ. Only then will the whole church become a fit instrument in his hands, that the whole earth may hear his voice.

(I Cor. 2:4; John 15:26,27, 16:8-11; I Cor. 12:3; John 3:6-8;
II Cor. 3:18; John 7:37-39; I Thess. 5:19; Acts 1:8; Psa. 85:4-7;
67:1-3; Gal. 5:22,23; I Cor. 12:4-31; Rom. 12:3-8)

15. *The Return of Christ*

We believe that Jesus Christ will return personally and visibly, in power and glory, to consummate his salvation and his judgment. This promise of his coming is a further spur to our evangelism, for we remember his words that the Gospel must first be preached to all nations. We believe that the interim period between Christ's ascension and return is to be filled with the mission of the people of God, who have no liberty to stop before the end. We also remember his warning that false Christs and false prophets will arise as precursors of the final Antichrist. We, therefore, reject as a proud, self-confident dream the notion that man can ever build a utopia on earth. Our Christian confidence is that God will perfect his kingdom, and we look forward with eager anticipation to that day, and to the new heaven and earth in which righteousness will dwell and God will reign forever. Meanwhile, we rededicate ourselves to the service of Christ and of men in joyful submission to his authority over the whole of our lives.

(Mark 14:62; Heb. 9:28; Mark 13:10; Acts 1:8-11; Matt. 28:20;
Mark 13:21-23; John 2:18, 4:1-3; Luke 12:32; Rev. 21:1-5;
II Pet. 3:13; Matt. 28:18)

Conclusion

Therefore, in the light of this our faith and our resolve, we enter into a solemn covenant with God and with each other, to pray, to plan, and to work together for the evangelization of the whole world. We call upon others to join us. May God help us by his grace and for his glory to be faithful to this our covenant! Amen, Alleluia!

OPENING GREETINGS
Georges-Andre Chevallaz

In our day, the world is growing smaller. Distances have been shortened. Highways, railways, and airlines take us long distances to great sports events, music festivals, and congresses in a few hours. By radio or TV we can be observers instantly to events which happen thousands of miles away. International games find millions of people joining the excitement simultaneously.

Never before has the world known such unparalleled exchange. However, in reality, this interaction is only an illusion. It is only a dream, a bubble. Its presence magnifies the discordancies, the distortions, the basic flaws from which the world's tensions stem. Instead of uniting, the technology which abolished distance and brought physical unity increases conflicts in geometric proportions in relation to the concentration of the people in large masses.

In such a time as this, when we are all so accessible to each other, when research and creativity have reached such peaks, one would expect that our intellectual achievements would overcome prejudices and passions. Instead, divisions and dissensions reign. Didn't Nietzsche announce in his strange prediction "a twentieth century in which a nationalism of animals with horns would demand the selection of virile virtues"?

We have already had experiences from which we have not learned, but rather collective self-destruction has been stimulated. One cannot get rid of the impression that many of the diplomatic colloquies are nothing less than elegant dances with the polite purpose of deferring the brutal shock which is stubbornly approaching.

Therefore we appreciate the calling which gathers you here, the will of one spirit and of one new heart, a fraternity based on the evangelical teaching.

Surely we could not fail to notice that the Gospel has served as pretext, as excuse, as alibi for many varied secular causes, for contestable confrontation, for partisan intransigences springing violently from one side or the other, heavier loaded with intolerance than the purely political options.

But we have also the certainty, that clinging to its essence, its purity, its simplicity of teaching, its concern for the welfare of others, its awareness of the relativity of human concepts, Christianity goes beyond ideological quarrels, interests, and partisan loyalties. It can unite men in a spirit of mutual respect, consideration, and love for our neighbor, even though he may be very different from ourselves.

It is in this hope that I bring greetings and best wishes to your meeting from the Federal Council.

INTERNATIONAL CONGRESS ON WORLD EVANGELIZATION
Bishop A. J. Dain

The Right Rev. Dain, Sydney, Australia,
is the Assistant Bishop of the Anglican
Diocese of Sidney

Those who have been responsible for drawing up the program of this Congress have asked specifically that at this point in the opening service we should face the spiritual challenge and implications of our presence in this hall. We have come vast distances, we have incurred considerable expense — either ourselves or through the sacrificial generosity of others — and we are utilizing at least two weeks of valuable time.

Onlookers may well ask, "For what purpose?" In a few minutes we are going to take part in a solemn act of personal dedication and commitment. May I, however inadequately, try to suggest how we may make our presence at this Congress spiritually effective so that our act of dedication is more meaningful.

The Congress has from the outset been planned not as an isolated event, but as a working Congress involving a continuing process. This process began many months ago with the arrival of the first major papers, has continued and will continue during these days together and will reach forward to the days and months that lie ahead when we have returned to our homes and we seek to utilize the inspiration and insight which we have acquired.

May I first express a very genuine word of gratitude on behalf of the Congress committees for the magnificent response from participants to the circulated papers, for this has assured us of your deep involvement in the Congress. I would now plead for this same degree of involvement to continue during our days together here in Lausanne. You are here, most of you, as participants. You are not delegates. This word "participant" was chosen with great care for two major reasons. First, to avoid any suggestion that this was a legislative body of elected delegates. It is no such thing. Secondly, because if you are participants and you are true to your title, then you must participate. The Congress has no legislative mandate. It depends upon the spiritual, moral and personal influence of each individual participant. And the effectiveness of the Congress, under God, depends upon the deep personal participation of every participant and observer.

The Apostle Paul in his epistle to the Ephesians speaks of the vital subject of the growth of the Body of Christ. He points out here and elsewhere that this growth depends upon three vital facts. First, *a right relationship with the head of the Body,* that is Christ. Second, *a right relationship with the other members of the Body,* for he speaks of these members being fitly joined together. This, incidentally, Paul reminds us in the previous verse involves "speaking the truth in love" and I would plead that we would always seek to do this during our days together. The third vital truth, however, and the one that I want to emphasize at this moment is *the personal responsibility of each member of the Body* for the growth of the Body. The authorized version speaks in that passage of "that which *every joint* supplieth." We each one are joints and parts in this Congress. The growth of the Body of Christ in these days as we consider the vital task of world evangelization will depend primarily not upon the Congress as a whole, but upon each and every one of us. We each one have a vital contribution to make and I would ask that you, by God's grace, will seek to be a true participant by making your own personal contribution to the Congress.

You may rightly ask, "How can I best fulfill all that is required of me as a participant?" and I would like to make a few practical suggestions.

First, in your own life, I would urge a deliberate discipline. Insure an adequate pattern of sleep. There will be every temptation to stay up late, talk with your friends, and the Congress itself with its own program will make very heavy physical demands upon you. The meal breaks will give you ample time for fellowship, so I would urge that you guard your sleep, remembering that your body is the temple of the Holy Ghost.

Two, I would urge that you maintain your own life of personal communion with God. It will be all too easy to let it slide during days when you are involved in so many meetings and there are so many corporate acts of prayer. These, however, do not replace your own walk with God and this will mean an earlier rising so that you can also enter into the corporate times of prayer with fellow participants in your hotels and dormitories.

Three, I would ask that you would seek to arrive at all sessions of the Congress slightly ahead of the time when they commence so that you can have that quiet moment of spiritual reflection as a preparation of heart and mind for all that follows. In this connection I would, however, point out that you need exercise and, where possible, I would suggest that you utilize the opportunities of walking to the Congress or walking through the Congress grounds after the meals.

Four, I would further plead that you would accept the disciplines of involvement in the whole of the program as far as this is physically possible. This will involve your meeting in the small groups such as the national strategy groups, and I would hope that you would each one feel that you are able to contribute in these groups. It would be profitable in this connection if each evening participants could read the papers which will be discussed the following day.

Five, throughout the Congress, I would urge you to be alert, looking for those lessons which the Holy Spirit has to teach you personally in the whole task of the fulfillment of world evangelization. Try constantly to be thinking of what action you and others associated with you can take for the achievement of the spiritual goals of the Congress in your own church and organization. Action should always be the goal of our thinking and discussion, while always recognizing our total dependence upon the Holy Spirit.

Six, finally, I would plead that we all recognize that Lausanne's impression of this World Congress on evangelization is going to be formulated not by the words we speak here in the Congress, but by the lives which we live in our hotels and dormitories, in the buses and trains, as we buy our papers and stamps. It is my hope and prayer that each one of us will reflect something of the beauty of Jesus.

I have already made it clear that this is not a legislative Congress of delegates, but it is anticipated that the Holy Spirit will guide and lead us into ways and means of translating our vision, our hopes and our goals into concrete action.

A small group of those with special skills will be working from the outset on a Congress statement — it will probably take the form of a "Lausanne Covenant" which you will all be able to sign if you so wish. It is planned that draft copies of this statement will be prepared during the early days of the Congress and put into your hands, probably on Friday or Saturday so that you can make appropriate comments which can be returned and studied by the drafting committee before the printing of the final statement. This will be put into your hands on Wednesday evening for signature before you leave. This will have personal implications for each one of us as we commit ourselves afresh to our Lord in the task of world evangelization. The statement will also carry our message to the wider world.

It is anticipated that in several of the functional groups concerned with theological training, evangelism, cross-cultural missions, mass communications, relief and Christian aid, there may well come new initiatives for closer cooperation and coordination. We shall await with keen interest the reports which come to us from these areas and also from the regional groups at the end of the Congress.

Thus far, I have mainly dealt with the practical aspects of our involvement in the life of the Congress and I close by sharing this spiritual burden which lies upon my own heart. Our preparation and response is not only one of mind and of body, but it must be from the heart. Two of the early disciples said, "Did not our hearts burn within us while he talked with us in the way?" And I long that our hearts, here in Lausanne, may burn within us during these days as the risen Christ walks and talks with us in the way. There are four distinct emphases that have been laid upon my own heart which I can only share with you as we now move into the Congress.

The first is the basic need for what the Berlin Congress hymn called "the vision of a dying world." There must be a note of urgency in all that we do, not only because we are acting in direct response to our Lord's command, but because of the vastness of the task which confronts us and the shortage of the time.

Millions have never even heard — and we need to ponder whether we have been seized with the urgency of the task and the spiritual plight of the lost. Whenever our Lord saw men and women in all their need, we read that he was moved with compassion. One longs that we too may meet here with hearts that are touched with that same compassion. While serving in the Navy, I was introduced to the writings of Miss Amy Wilson Carmichael of Dohnavur and a story she told in one of her early books was one of the strong motivating influences which took me out of the Navy and sent me as a missionary to the India of which she wrote. I have never forgotten the words and the picture which she conjures in her writing.

Miss Carmichael, lying in her bed and hearing the constant clanging of the temple bells, saw in her mind a vivid picture. At her feet a precipice broke sheer down into space. Flowing over the precipice were streams of people from every direction. All were totally blind and they made straight for the precipice edge. Some screamed as they suddenly realized themselves falling. Others went quietly without a sound.

Along the edge of the precipice, there were a few sentries set at intervals, but the intervals were far too great to be effective. The people fell in their blindness unwarned, and the grass around them seemed blood red.

Then she saw, as it were, in the background a group of people sitting in a lovely garden beneath the trees and they were making chains of little flowers — daisy chains. They seemed occasionally disturbed by the piercing cries. When one of their number wanted to go and help, they held him back and said, "Why get so excited? You must wait for a definite call. You haven't finished your daisy chains." One girl stood alone at the edge of the precipice waving people back — her parents' call reminded her that furlough was due, but no one was sent to fill her gap and over the precipice flowed a veritable waterfall of humanity. And then the people in the garden sang a hymn.

And then came the sound of a million broken hearts crying out in one full drop — one sob — and a horror of darkness was upon me, for I knew what it was — the cry of blood.

I heard the voice of the Lord, "What hast thou done? The voice of thy brother's blood calls out unto me from the ground." So wrote Miss Carmichael.

The vision of a dying world. This is something that must be in our minds and hearts as we together face the whole task of world evangelization. Are we prepared to ask God to give us in these days such a vision of a dying world?

My next three points of emphasis are all found in the short but remarkable account of the birth of the missionary movement as recorded in the 13th chapter of Acts. I find much food for thought as I note what happened in the church at Antioch when this very significant missionary outreach took place in the early church. There were three component parts in that happening.

The first — as at Pentecost itself, was *the divine activity of the Holy Spirit*. Verse 2, "As they ministered to the Lord and fasted, the *Holy Spirit* said, 'Separate me Barnabas and Saul for the work to which I have called them.'"

Verse 4, "So they, being sent by *the Holy Spirit* went down to Seleucia." Note, it was *the Holy Spirit* who spoke to the Church. It was *the Holy Spirit* who called Barnabas and Saul. It was *the Holy Spirit* who sent Barnabas and Saul.

I thank God for every insight, every lesson, every example, every statistic that will better enable us to achieve our God-given task more effectively. But I say without hesitation, these alone will not suffice. We, as the church at Antioch, must above all else hear the voice of the Spirit.

"He that hath ears to hear, let him hear what the Spirit saith unto the churches."

We, like Barnabas and Saul, need to be both called and sent by that same Holy Spirit as we personally become involved in varying ways and in varying degrees in this task of evangelization. The sovereignty of the Holy Spirit in every heart and life, in every church and organization, is the paramount need of the hour.

Secondly, there was right in the heart of that remarkable incident *worship and prayer.* "While they were worshipping the Lord, the Holy Spirit said . . ." "After fasting and *prayer,* they sent them off." This first missionary church was a church in which worship and prayer were absolute essentials. Can we seek personally and corporately over these ten days to emulate the church at Antioch and seek to be found in that spirit of worship and prayer? Can I specifically suggest that you, each one, seek to pray with at least one other person daily?

Thirdly, and finally, there was one further factor present which the divine author of Scripture has not only included but repeated twice in the space of two verses.

Verse 2. "While they ministered to the Lord *and fasted.* . . ."

Verse 3. "*After fasting* and praying, they laid their hands on them and sent them off . . ."

I believe firmly that at certain times and under certain circumstances, fasting has a legitimate place in the life of the believer.

But here, I am much more concerned with the spiritual principle which is illustrated, namely *sacrifice.* The church at Antioch meant business. They were prepared to go without that to which they were legitimately entitled, be it leisure or food or recreation, in the interest of the Gospel. The first missionary church was characterized by sacrifice and every missionary church since has, in some measure, carried the same authenticating marks.

Do we imagine for one moment that we can come here and share in a Congress on world evangelization and ever be quite the same again? The sovereign operation of the Holy Spirit in our lives over these days may and almost certainly will involve unexpected and costly demands. What price am I, what price are you, prepared to pay? Do you recall the words of Thomas when he said, "Except I shall see in his hands the print of the nails, I will not believe"? There is a sense in which the world is saying the same thing. Is there the equivalent of the print of the nails in my hands, in yours, or are our hands soft and clean because they have never grappled with sin and suffering? Our task of world evangelization is nothing less than spiritual warfare as we seek, under God, to turn man from darkness to light and from the power of Satan unto God. It was our Lord who, confronted with just such a situation, said, "This kind goeth not out, but by prayer and fasting."

LET THE EARTH HEAR HIS VOICE
Billy Graham

Dr. Graham, Montreat, North Carolina, USA, is an internationally-known evangelist.

Greetings, grace and peace be unto you from God our Father and the Lord Jesus Christ. On behalf of our executive planning committee and the convening committee that has already been introduced, it is my privilege to join Bishop Jack Dain in welcoming you to this International Congress on World Evangelization. In one sense, this Congress has been fourteen years in planning. It was here in nearby Montreux, Switzerland, fourteen years ago that a small group of us met for several days of prayer and discussion about the task of world evangelization. Partly as a result of that meeting the Berlin Congress was held in 1966 under the auspices of the religious journal, *Christianity Today,* whose editor, Dr. Carl Henry, was chairman of that Congress. Since Berlin a number of regional congresses have been held — at Singapore, Bogotá, Minneapolis, Amsterdam, and other places. Almost all of the major countries of the world have had a congress on evangelism in the last eight years. Three years of intense prayer and careful planning have brought us to this moment and in the providence of God I believe that this could be one of the most significant gatherings, not only in this century, but in the history of the Christian Church. During the last few years we have heard many voices. We have heard the voice of the philosopher who often raises more doubts than certainties, who would rather seek than find, who doubts life's meaning. We are gathered in Lausanne to let the earth hear his voice.

We have heard the voices of the psychologists and the psychiatrists with their commendable attempts to unravel the mysteries of human behavior and the human mind. We are gathered in Lausanne to let the earth hear his voice.

We have heard the voice of the men of war, the military, the defense ministers, telling us that the path to peace and safety lies in the missile silos, nuclear submarines, orbiting satellites, and laser beams. We are gathered in Lausanne to let the earth hear his voice.

We have heard the voice of the diplomat shouting peace one day and warning of war the next day. We are gathered in Lausanne to let the earth hear his voice.

We have heard the uncertain voices of modern theologies that speak of a dead God and point us to the wandering stars of moral relativism, linguistic analysts who shred the biblical faith, and religious syncretists who take Christ from his solitary throne and deny his uniqueness and place him in the pantheon of popular deities. We are gathered in Lausanne to let the earth hear his voice.

We've often heard the voice of the politician with his all-too-often false promises. We are gathered in Lausanne to let the earth hear his voice.

We've heard the voice of the economists with their dire predictions of inflation, depression, and world famine. We are gathered in Lausanne to let the earth hear his voice.

We have heard the anguished voice of history, crying out from a crucible of pain, telling us lessons that we never seem able to learn. We are gathered in Lausanne to let the earth hear his voice.

We have heard the voice of Satan himself, lying, flattering, oppressing, afflicting, influencing, destroying, sowing discord, spreading false doctrines, and gathering his forces for another massive assault against the kingdom of God. We are gathered in Lausanne to let the earth hear his voice.

Perhaps the Apostle John foresaw such a day as this: "And they sang a new song saying, You were slain and have redeemed us to God by your blood out of every kindred, and tongue, and people, and nation; and you have made us unto our God kings and priests." We are gathered to hear his voice.

THE TASK BEFORE US

Waldron Scott

Introduction:

Only a few thousand people first heard the Gospel of Jesus Christ on the shores of the Mediterranean Sea nineteen centuries ago. Today, a thousand million people profess Christianity, making it the first truly worldwide faith. William Temple, the late Archbishop of Canterbury, referred to this as "the great, new fact of our time." This achievement, of course, is not to *our* credit — it is the *Lord's* doing, the work of *his* Spirit, in accordance with his eternal plan. As Ephesians 1:10 says, "a plan for the fullness of time, to unite all things in him, things in heaven and things on earth." So we have not gathered to congratulate *ourselves*. We are here to celebrate *God's* glory and grace.

Lausanne reflects this great, new fact of our time. We participate together as members of a *worldwide* Church. From thirty countries of Asia and Australia 660 of us have come. From Africa 370 of us are here representing forty-seven different countries. From Latin America another 219 of us have come from twenty-nine countries. 560 are here from North America. Our hosts are the 562 participants representing thirty-five nations of Europe.

During the first 500 years of Christian history believers were just a small fraction of the world's population. During the second 500 years Europe was evangelized but North Africa and the Middle East were lost to Islam — so there was little net gain. During the third period also there was little church growth. After the misguided attempt of the Crusades, European Christians concentrated on inward renewal and reform. But God had not abandoned his great plan to disciple the nations. During the past 500 years, and particularly in the last two centuries, the world has witnessed a dramatic upsurge of the Christian community.

Some of the fastest growing churches in the world are in *Asia*. Men's response to the Gospel there has thrilled us all. There are now approximately seventy million Christians in Asia. Half of these are in the Philippine Republic. It is true that seventy million is only a tiny percentage of Asia's total population; but a more important statistic than absolute numbers must be considered — namely, the rate of growth; that is, the *percentage* of increase of a group over a given period.

During the first three-quarters of our century Christians in Asia have increased at a rate nearly three times that of non-Christians. At the beginning of the twentieth century there were 75 non-Christians in Asia for every Christian. Today, this ratio has dropped to twenty-two to one — one-third of the previous proportion! And it appears that this trend will continue throughout the remainder of this century — clear evidence that the Spirit of God is moving mightily in Asia in our time.

But God's power has been even more dramatically evident in *Africa* during the twentieth century. At the beginning of this century only 7½ per cent of Africa's peoples professed the name of Christ. Today, the proportion of Africans who have indicated their allegiance to Jesus has risen to 33 per cent. And by the year 2000, just twenty-five years from now, nearly half of the continent will have come under the banner of the Cross!

A few moments ago we noted that Christians in Asia are increasing at a rate nearly three times that of non-Christians. In *Africa* during the same period the rate has been almost *four times* faster! That is, whereas the population of Africa generally is increasing at a rate of 1.2 per cent per year, the Christian community is expanding by 4.6 per cent annually. At the beginning of our century there were twenty-eight non-Christians in Africa for every Christian. Today, there are only 2½ — a ten-fold drop! And, as we saw with respect to Asia, in Africa also this trend will persist for at least the next twenty-five years.

Thus, it is probable that by the year 2000 there will be more *non-Western* Christians in the world than Western! Also, by that date the center of gravity of Christendom will have shifted from *north* of the equator to *south*.

Part of this shift can be traced to the growing number of evangelicals in *Latin America*. Latin America has been a Christian continent for over 400 years. Brazil, for example, is the world's largest Catholic country. Within Latin America during the twentieth century overall church growth has resulted not merely from normal population increases but from the multiplication of evangelical communities. The current population growth rate in Latin America is about 3 per cent — the highest in the world. Among evangelicals, however, the growth rate in recent years has been 10 per cent! In other words, evangelicals are expanding three times faster than the population at large!

In contrast with Latin America, *North* America is predominantly Protestant, though with a significant Catholic element. North American church membership increased steadily for more than a hundred years. But, as pointed out in the book, *Why Conservative Churches are Growing*, some of the largest denominations in America have experienced declines in membership since 1965. In contrast, such declines are not apparent in Bible-centered churches. It is also worth noting that the number of missionaries affiliated with North American *evangelical* societies has increased by 60 per cent in recent years.

Up to this point we have been considering the amazing expansion of Christianity through the centuries — and for this we praise God. *Now* we turn our attention to the task that remains before us — the more than two billion *unreached* people on our planet.

In doing so we look first at Europe, the center of Christian faith for the past 1500 years — the home of the Protestant Reformation — and the home base for much of the modern global missionary movement. Within this century European Christendom has experienced steady secularization combined with intense opposition from atheistic materialism — so much so that contemporary European culture is frequently said to be "post Christian." Christian expansion in Europe in recent decades has not kept pace with the continent's population growth. Church attendance has decreased significantly during the past half-century.

Less than 3 per cent of those now living in Europe are members of *non-Christian* religions such as Judaism, Islam and Hinduism. Over 25 per cent are avowedly atheist, though living in countries which are historically Christian. Nearly two-thirds are Christian, the majority being Roman Catholic and Eastern Orthodox.

It is impossible, of course, to estimate the precise number of *committed* Christians. But in most European countries regular church attendance does not exceed 5 per cent. It is apparent, then, that the task of evangelizing Europe consists as much in reaching those who are Christian in name only as in persuading atheists or members of non-Christian religions.

The situation in North America is similar to that in Europe in that there are relatively few adherents of non-Christian religions to win — Eskimos, Indians, and members of the Jewish faith being the main exceptions. One difference is that North America is almost totally Christian — at least formally. Militant atheism is not a major factor as in Europe. *Another* difference is that the evangelical sector is somewhat larger than in Europe — or at least more visible! Yet America's pervasive materialism presents a formidable challenge to evangelism.

Again, in *Latin America* the challenge is not only the aboriginal tribes — though it is imperative that they be reached — it is also the great mass of nominal Christians who combine various mixtures of pagan and Christian practices.

In some respects, therefore, the evangelistic challenge presented by Europe, North America, and Latin America is similar. When we look at the challenge of *Africa,* however, we see something quite different. Here the percentage of adherents of traditional tribal religions — and Islam — is much higher than in Europe, North America, and Latin America.

From the standpoint of sheer numbers, however, *Asia,* even more than Africa, presents the greatest challenge of all to our generation. Members of non-Christian religions constitute fully 95 per cent of the population of this vast continent! The significance of this strikes home when we realize that Asia, though only one of six continents, contains more than half of the world's population — that is, more than half of all those for whom Christ died.

Within this circle, which has a radius of less than 2000 miles, lives 45 per cent — nearly half — of our planet's peoples. We are not suggesting, of course, that the entire evangelistic and missionary resources of the Christian church be projected into this area — we have already indicated the special challenges of the other continents — but it is imperative that we recognize that almost half of the fulfillment of the Great Commission in our time *will* be decided in *this* small area. It is reasonable to assume that the greatest part of the task of world evangelization in the immediate future lies in *Asia.*

Yes, something new. A worldwide Church! Christians in every land! And yet, so much remains to be done! Hindus, Muslims, Chinese — these three groups alone constitute 83 per cent of all non-Christians in Asia and Africa. And note how they are growing! Moreover, they are beyond the reach of ordinary near-neighbor evangelism. Consequently Lausanne emphasizes the importance of both local evangelism *and* missionary outreach.

Missionaries — that is, disciple-makers sent out across cultural frontiers — are needed more than ever. Even Western missionaries are required in many places in greater numbers than ever, in spite of some voices to the contrary. Yet these three groups — Hindus, Muslims, Chinese —

nearly two billion strong — are the object of only 5 per cent of today's Protestant missionary force! The other 95 per cent of our missionaries are directing their efforts toward that much *smaller* group of unreached peoples which, though admittedly important, nevertheless comprises only 17 per cent of the unreached citizens of Asia and Africa.

One reason for this, of course, is that Hinduism, Islam, and Buddhism, as well as Chinese communism, present special obstacles to Western evangelistic agencies. Realistic strategy for the coming quarter-century, therefore, calls for many more *Third World* missionaries. Indeed, this strategy appears to have been inaugurated already by the Holy Spirit, for one of the most exciting developments in our time is the emergence of Third World missions. The authors of this book, *Missions from the Third World,* report that more than 200 agencies from forty-six Western countries have *already* sent out more than 3,000 missionaries.

Nigeria, India, and Brazil lead the way, followed by the Philippines, Japan, Mexico, and Third World ethnic missions from the United States. But these are only the vanguard. Thousands more are needed! Surely one of the most significant things we can do here at Lausanne is to give prayerful consideration to how missionaries from the Third World can be multiplied.

It may appear that too much emphasis has been placed on statistics in this presentation. We recognize the dangers inherent in working with figures — and it is perfectly true that our Lord is as much concerned with quality as with quantity. However, statistics are useful in revealing something of the *dimensions* of the task before us. For every person in our world today who professes the name of Jesus, there are *two* who have never *heard* his name. And, in the words of the Apostle Paul, "How are they to believe in him of whom they have never heard? And how are they to hear without a preacher? And how can they preach unless they be sent?" To these sharp questions we may add a fourth: "And how are they to go if they do not have the facts?"

Now that we have considered some relevant facts — if each of us were to return home from Lausanne and bend every effort to mobilize our fellow Christians first, for the evangelization of our own nation, and then for the whole world — what wonders might God do? May Isaiah's prayer be each of ours: "Here am I, Lord; send me!"

WHY LAUSANNE?
Billy Graham

Greetings in the Name of our Lord Jesus Christ.

The Planning Committee has invited participants from every possible nation and nearly every evangelical denomination and para-church organization in the world.

Never before have so many representatives of so many evangelical Christian churches in so many nations and from so many tribal and language groups gathered to worship, pray, and plan together for world evangelization.

Assembled here tonight are more responsible leaders, from more growing national churches of Asia, Africa, and Latin America, than have ever met before.

Here in Lausanne tonight are participants from areas where the Gospel had not been preached until recent decades.

This Lausanne Congress is also significant because representatives are here from older churches that have witnessed and evangelized for centuries, and younger churches in Africa, Asia, and Latin America who have taken up the torch and are sending missionaries to other nations as well. In recent years, teams of Christians from Indonesia have gone to Pakistan. Koreans are sending evangelists to Thailand. Japanese are going to Indonesia, Taiwanese are going to Africa, and Africans are going to the United States! And we need them — and welcome them! It is a new day for world evangelization when the whole church can go into much of the world.

Almost 20 per cent of you here are engaged in cross-cultural overseas evangelism. Others of you represent every conceivable type of evangelistic effort within your nations.

The evangelistic cutting edge of the Church of Jesus Christ worldwide is here to seek how we can work together to fulfill Christ's last commission as quickly and thoroughly as possible. Therefore, I have come to Lausanne with great hope, even as you have.

Since we met in Berlin eight years ago, tremendous developments have been taking place in the religious world. We are all aware of the startling changes in the Roman Catholic world. I also detect a wistful longing on the part of a small, but growing, number of ecumenical leaders for a greater emphasis on orthodox biblical theology and a re-evaluation of some of the pronouncements in theological, sociological, and political areas.

Then there has been the phenomenal development of the Charismatic movement.

We have met at a time marked by signposts of both promise and danger. Promise — in that God is at work in a remarkable way. Never have so many people been so open to the Gospel.

In parts of Asia, there are evidences of the outpourings of God's Spirit in evangelism. In Korea, the church is increasing at a rate four times faster than the population.

In certain parts of North-East India, Christians now form a majority of the population and are bringing about a whole new dimension of civic righteousness.

In Papua, New Guinea, a land where the Gospel was virtually unknown before this generation, a large percentage of the people now profess faith in Christ.

Latin Americans are responding to the Gospel in unprecedented numbers. Evangelical churches in many parts of Latin America are multiplying vigorously.

In North America, especially the United States, there has been a remarkable upsurge of interest in the Gospel in the last decade — especially among the youth.

It is true that old traditional denominations with theologically liberal tendencies are declining, yet it is interesting to note the more evangelical denominations such as the Southern Baptist Convention (America's largest Protestant denomination) are showing a steady growth.

Another interesting phenomenon in America is that the evangelical theological seminaries and Bible schools are overflowing and the more liberal schools are seeing a dramatic drop in enrollment. At the same time scores of para-church evangelistic organizations are flourishing as never before.

In 1945, Christians in Africa numbered about twenty million. Today they number at least 70 million.

Africa, south of the Sahara, could become substantially Christian by the end of the century, in spite of many dangers, obstacles, and even persecutions in some areas.

Europe, which has contributed so much to the evangelization of the world in centuries past is very difficult to evaluate. Yet there are signs of awakening. I have held almost as many crusades in Europe as in America, if we include Britain.

During Euro '70, four years ago, we connected thirty-seven cities by closed-circuit television. In many areas there was an overwhelming response to the Gospel.

Next year, thousands of Christian young people will be gathering in Brussels for "Eurofest," a week of Bible study and evangelism.

In both Eastern and Western Europe there are thousands of dedicated, committed believers. Unfortunately, the overwhelming majority of the people of Europe never darken the doors of a church.

A Danish clergyman recently said, "Europe is one vast mission field." But there are encouraging signs almost everywhere that God is also at work here.

In the Eastern socialist world there are evidences of a quiet but real work of the Spirit. In one country the Baptists, for example, have doubled in numbers in the last decade. Belief in God is indestructible — even in the Soviet Union; among workers and intellectuals alike, there is a growing awareness of God.

One reporter states that East European students are looking wistfully over their shoulder to Moses and to Christ for a reason to live.

In these days, God is giving his people an opportunity for worldwide witness — perhaps a last chance!

But with the promise, there are many dangers. As we meet here, world problems press upon us. Inflation is sweeping the world; but even worse, the world stands on the very brink of famine.

Droughts, floods, and other calamities have destroyed, or drastically diminished grain stocks not only in Africa, but in the Philippines, India, Bangladesh, and Pakistan.

The world food shortage is seen in the dry and dusty countries of sandal-shod farmers and nomads, in exposed ribs and swollen bellies.

At the present time we are seeing a dramatic shift in the world monetary situation. In ten years the Middle-Eastern oil-producing countries will totally dominate the entire international monetary market.

By 1980, just six years from now, a Lebanese banker estimates these Middle Eastern countries will have nearly two-thirds of all the monetary reserves in the world.

The wealth of the West accumulated since World War II is draining away. The European Common Market will have a balance of payments deficit of about 35 billion dollars this year alone and this is only the beginning. All of this will most certainly affect those missionary agencies that depend on financial support in the West. Even smaller and underdeveloped nations are working on the atomic bomb.

Millions of people have a mood of deep pessimism. Men's hearts are indeed failing them for fear as our Lord predicted.

Absence of a fear of God, loss of moral absolutes, sin accepted and glorified, breakdown in the home, disregard for authority, lawlessness, anxiety, hatred, and despair — these are signs of a culture in decay.

In the West we are witnessing societies in trauma, shaken by war, scandals, inflation, surfeited and bored with materialism, turned off by lifeless religion.

Thousands are turning to perversions, the occult, with its Satan worship, mind control, astrology, and various ploys of the devil to lure men to turn from the truth.

We read about whole villages in the Soviet Union dominated by witches.

It is right that we look for answers and solutions but we must look in the right place, and that place is the Lord Jesus Christ who can bring spiritual renewal and liberation.

We meet at a time when the world longs for reassurance, peace, hope, and purpose. Isaiah, the prophet, said centuries ago, "And when they shall say unto you, Seek unto them that have familiar spirits and unto wizards that peep, and that mutter: should not a people seek unto their God?" (Isaiah 8:19)

Most of us hold the view of Scripture that teaches that as we approach the end of history things will get worse — that our Lord predicted in Matthew 24, false prophets, earthquakes, famines, wars, betrayals, moral permissiveness, persecution, apostasy, would precede his return.

We know the whole world will not be converted to Christ — the whole world is not going to become permanently peaceful, but our Lord did promise, "And this Gospel of the kingdom shall be preached in all the world for a witness unto all nations; and then shall the end come."

God is calling out a people for his name — a Christian community in the midst of the ruins of man's sins, a bride from all races, tongues, and nations for the coming bridegroom. It is an exciting and thrilling time to be witnesses to this Gospel.

However, 64 years ago, the delegates to the historic Edinburgh Conference in Edinburgh with an overwhelming optimism about the future of evangelism, missions, and its impact on what was already being called "The Christian Century." They never dreamed they were less than four years from the devastation of World War I and only thirty years away from World War II.

But we here at this Congress have an unparalled opportunity as the world may be standing at the very brink of Armageddon.

Let us unite in proclaiming Jesus Christ as God and only Savior and persuading men to become his disciples at this fateful hour. It is my prayer that we will return from Lausanne to carry the Gospel of Christ throughout the world.

As this Congress convenes, four basic presuppositions should undergird our labors. These four foundation stones have guided our planning and should underlie everything we do at this Congress.

First, this Congress stands in the tradition of many movements of evangelism throughout the history of the Church.

From the time of the early Apostles to the present, evangelism has been the lifeblood of the Church.

When the Spirit fell on the Church at Pentecost, 120 believers soon became 3,000. The 3,000 soon multiplied to 5,000. And so the fire of Christ spread throughout the Roman Empire to Britain, France, Germany, and Spain, into the Caucasus, into India, and to the islands of the sea.

This Congress is the most recent link in a long chain of evangelism conferences stretching back into the last century, which Latourette called "The great century of missionary advance."

At that time, sparked by thousands of young people, the Student Volunteer Movement set as its goal, "The evangelization of the world in this generation." It is one of the tragedies of the missionary movement that today, over 60 years after Edinburgh, many Christians not only doubt that the goal is possible but even question whether it is desirable.

Dr. Arthur Johnston has done considerable research in this area and received his doctorate on this subject; I, along with him, have asked myself two questions.

First: What characterized the great missionary and evangelistic movements of the last century?

Second: How have these movements lost their zeal for evangelism?

The missionary and evangelistic movements of the last century were based on the authority of the Scriptures as the Word of God.

Because these people were biblically oriented, they had a definite view of salvation. They took seriously what the Bible says about man's lostness and his need for redemption.

They also believed strongly in "conversion," convinced that by the regenerating power of the Holy Spirit, men could be forgiven and changed.

They believed that evangelism was not an option but an imperative. They were convinced that the primary mission of the Church is to declare the Good News of Jesus Christ. They were preoccupied with obedience not obstacles.

But, somehow, as time went on, many of these movements lost their zeal. Why?

Evangelism always faces two dangers. First, there are external bar-

riers to effective evangelism. Many of these we will be exam... ...ce left F...
Congress. The dangers experienced did not dampen their zeal. T... ...left F...
evangelism thrives on dangers. I believe, however, an even greater danger
comes from *within missionary and evangelistic agencies — the internal
danger.*

The reason that the great missionary movements of the nineteenth
century were able to make a lasting impact on the world was because *internally* they were strong. They knew what they believed and they determined to proclaim it to the world. We need to pray for that kind of faith
and urgency today.

But they gradually lost their strength. How? In the nineteenth century
there was little disagreement about "the message" of evangelism.

Holding to a high view of Scripture, Christians preached the unique
Gospel of Christ to a lost humanity. In a series of conferences — not unlike this one — Christians sought to examine and reaffirm the evangelistic
task of the Church.

One of those important conferences was convened in New York in 1900.

At that conference, John R. Mott, who has been called the architect
of the ecumenical movement, saw in the command of Christ the responsibility of each generation to preach Christ to its own known and accessible
world. The spoken message was to be supported by education, literacy
programs, and medicine. "The goal of the church," he said, "was the conversion of souls and the edification of the infant churches."

Ten years later, the most historic conference on evangelism and missions of this century was held in Edinburgh, Scotland. But something
happened after Edinburgh in 1910. It was only a small cloud on the horizon, but it became a cyclone that swept the world.

Even before Edinburgh, theological changes were subtly infiltrating
Christian youth movements causing some to weaken their ties to orthodox faith. The authority of evangelism began to shift from the Scriptures
to the organized church. They focused attention on the materialistic
salvation of the *community* rather than the individual. This became known
as the "social Gospel." Emphasis turned to man "in this world," rather
than "in this *and* the next world."

It is my hope and prayer that Lausanne 1974 will take us back "theologically" though not politically or sociologically to the visions and concepts of those great conferences in the early part of this century.

Since then, the world church has floundered. It has lost much of the
vision and zeal of those days, for three primary reasons:

1. The loss of the authority of the message of the Gospel.
2. The preoccupation with social and political problems.
3. The equal preoccupation with organizational unity.

From Edinburgh came *two major streams* of the modern missionary
movement.

*The first was the evangelical. A second stream might be termed the
ecumenical.*

In one important respect, however, New York and Edinburgh were
prototypes of this 1974 Congress on World Evangelization. The delegates
to New York and Edinburgh were chosen very largely from leaders in
evangelism and mission. Leaders of churches, *as churches,* were not pre-

dominantly there. Hence, participants could single-mindedly consider
world evangelization rather than *"everything"* the Church ought to do.

The succeeding world missionary gatherings at Jerusalem, Tambaram,
Mexico City, and Bangkok were made up not only of evangelists and
missionaries, but more and more of eminent leaders of the churches who
were there in their capacity as *churchmen* — not as evangelists or
missionaries.

Delegates of the young churches in Asia, Africa, and Latin America
were asking primarily at these conferences, "How can the missionary
movement help *us* in our social and political problems?"

The delegates did not necessarily always faithfully represent their more
evangelical constituents at home. The majority at home were far more
evangelically, theologically oriented. Thus, the spotlight gradually shifted
from evangelism to social and political action. Finally, guidelines were
drawn up which called almost entirely for humanization — the reconciliation of man with man, rather than of man with God.

This is a Congress of World Evangelization. Now we are enthusiastic
about all the many things churches properly do, from worship to social
concern.

But our calling is to a specific sector of the Church's responsibility —
evangelism. We believe our point of view has not been adequately represented at some of the other world Church gatherings. Therefore, we
are met to pray, talk, plan and — please God — to advance the work
of evangelism.

This is a conference of evangelicals. The participants were asked to
come because you are evangelical — concerned with evangelism and
missions. We here tonight stand firmly in the evangelical tradition of
biblical faith.

*Second, this Congress convenes as one body, obeying one Lord, facing
one world, with one task.*

The following words to the Ephesians could have been written specifically for the Lausanne Congress on Evangelization. Let us listen to
them . . . and this is my text tonight: "In Christ, ye who sometimes were
far off are made nigh by the blood of Christ. For he is our peace, who
hath made both one, and hath broken down the middle wall of partition
between us; . . . for through him we both have access by one Spirit unto
the Father. Now, therefore, ye are no more strangers and foreigners, but
fellow citizens with the saints and of the household of God; and are built
upon the foundation of the apostles and prophets, Jesus Christ himself
being the chief cornerstone" (Eph. 2:13-20).

This Congress should not stress older and younger churches. We see
the Church as one.

Some churches are older, some are younger. Cultures and circumstances differ, but our mission is the same, our spiritual resources are the
same — one body, one Lord, one task.

Salvation is by faith in Jesus Christ alone. Therefore, we come to
the task of evangelism as one Church, one body, one company of the redeemed, proclaiming the Lord Jesus Christ.

We assemble not as strangers, but as members of the household of God,
to find out more perfectly his will for evangelism in our critical time.

We hold that we are already "one body" — already unified by "the head" which is Christ. Whatever our cultural, racial or linguistic background, we are brothers and sisters in Christ.

Certainly we have some doctrinal differences. We have cultural and political differences, but we are one in the Spirit. We shout with one voice, "Jesus *alone* saves."

We have one task — to proclaim the message of salvation in Jesus Christ.

In rich countries and in poor, among the educated and uneducated, in freedom or oppression, we are determined to proclaim Jesus Christ in the power of the Holy Spirit that men may put their trust in him as Savior, follow him obediently, and serve him in the fellowship of the Church of which he alone is King and head.

Here in Lausanne, let's make sure that *evangelization* is the one task which we are unitedly determined to do.

Third, this Congress convenes to re-emphasize those biblical concepts which are essential to evangelism.

There are at least *five concepts* that both the evangelical and the non-evangelical world have been studying and debating during the past few years — concepts which we believe to be essential to true evangelism and which I expect we will reaffirm in this Congress.

Each of these is crucial, and yet each has been drastically reinterpreted or diluted in some parts of the organized church.

Each, though, re-examined in the light of our times, must be reaffirmed by those committed to biblical evangelism.

First, we are committed to the authority of Scripture.

We hold that the entire Bible is the infallible Word of God. Many years ago I had to accept this position by faith.

Even though I myself cannot understand it all, it is taken by the Holy Spirit and made inerrant to my spirit. It is an "everlasting body of revealed truth" that is authoritative. It demands faith and obedience today as well as yesterday.

If there is one thing that the history of the Church should teach us, it is the importance of a theology of evangelism derived from the Scriptures.

A second concept we expect to reaffirm is "the lostness" of man apart from Jesus Christ.

The Bible portrays man as originally created by God for fellowship with him. However, *sin* intervened in the Garden of Eden. Man is now born alienated from God. Without Jesus Christ, he is lost and without hope in this world or the next.

It was Jesus who spoke most pointedly about the reality of heaven and hell. Notice the terms Jesus used to describe the state of the lost, "a place of wailing"; "a place of weeping"; "a furnace of fire"; "a place of torment"; "a place of outer darkness"; "a place of everlasting punishment"; "a place prepared for the devil and his angels."

These descriptions of our Lord are terrible enough without even trying to interpret them.

Our Lord further said, "He that believeth on the Son hath everlasting life: and he that believeth not the Son shall not see life; but the wrath of God abideth on him" (John 3:36).

Many years ago, a man in England on his way to the gallows was being warned by the Anglican chaplain of the "wrath to come" unless he repented. He turned to the chaplain and said, "If I believed the way you believe, I would crawl across England on broken glass to warn people."

My fellow evangelists and missionaries, if men are lost as Jesus clearly thought they are, then we have no greater priority than to lift up a saving Christ to them as Moses did the brazen serpent in the wilderness.

Thirdly, we expect to reaffirm at this Conference that "salvation" is in Jesus Christ alone. There is a narrowness to the Gospel that is unpopular with the world.

The early Apostles declared, "Neither is there salvation in any other: for there is none other name under heaven given among men, whereby we must be saved" (Acts 4:12).

Again, however, there has been a steady erosion of belief in this clear scriptural teaching. Some have openly taught that there are many ways to God and that ultimately no one is lost. The vast permissiveness of our day has left its stain on the Church. Not Christ "the one way," according to God's revelation, but "many ways," according to one's culture and inclination. To this, evangelicals must return a resounding *NO.*

There may be many roads to Jesus Christ, but only one to God and that is *through* Jesus Christ, who said, "I am the Way, the Truth, and the Life."

When Sadhu Sundar Singh was asked what the Christian faith had to offer India that the other religions of India did not already possess, he replied, without a moment's hesitation, "Jesus Christ."

Fourthly, at this Congress we expect to reaffirm that our witness must be by both word and deed. You cannot separate the two. Our lives, both individually and collectively, must reflect clearly the truths we proclaim. Faith without works is dead.

The source of salvation is grace. The ground of our salvation is the Atonement. The means of our salvation is faith. The evidence of salvation is works.

Many today are debating the question of the proper place of social action in the overall program of the Church. Much will be said at this Congress concerning this matter.

Perhaps we will not find all the answers, but we here reaffirm the fact that our words and our deeds must both reflect the Gospel.

Historically, evangelicals have changed society, influencing men everywhere in the battle against slavery and in the quest for social justice. We should be proud of this tradition.

At the same time, we must squarely face the challenges of our own age. We must be sensitive to human need wherever it is found.

We must confess, in all honesty, that we have not always been true to our tradition. At times we have not been consistent, or we have failed to appreciate the implications of the truths we have proclaimed.

It seems to me that we are always in danger of falling into at least three or four errors on social action.

The *first* is to deny that we have any social responsibility as Christians. It is true that this is not our priority mission. However, it is equally true that Scripture calls us time and again to do all in our power to alleviate human suffering and to correct injustice.

The *second* error is to let social concern become our all consuming mission.

Jesus said, "What shall it profit a man if he gain the whole world and lose his own soul?" What if we developed a materialistic Utopia (which sinful man never will) in which every inhabitant of the planet would be fed, clothed, housed and cared for in every way? Man still would not find the "purpose," the "happiness," the "peace," and the "joy" that his heart craves for, apart from God.

This hopelessness has been articulated by such writers as Simon Bolivar, Jean-Paul Sartre, Heidegger, and Jaspers.

In a modern play, the playwright imagines everybody getting in a room and having everything that should satisfy modern man, such as sex, food, drink, drugs, money, pleasure, entertainment — but *nothing satisfies.*

The writer has no answer. He suggests that life has no significance, coherence, integrity, or meaning and that there is no way out of the human dilemma.

This comes from a man who had everything materially. Some of the unhappiest people I know are millionaires, apart from Christ.

Without a personal relationship with Christ, man is "lost" in this world and the next. The rich man that Jesus told about was materially rich, but spiritually poor. God called him a fool. Man is a spiritual being. He is never "satisfied" or "fulfilled" until his soul is at peace with God.

A *third* error is to identify the Gospel with any one particular political program or culture. This has been my own danger.

When I go to preach the Gospel, I go as an ambassador for the Kingdom of God — not America. To tie the Gospel to any political system, secular program, or society is dangerous and will only serve to divert the Gospel. The Gospel transcends the goals and methods of any political system or any society, however good it may be. Jesus touched on this in his conversation with Pilate. In answering Pilate he said, "My kingdom is not of this world."

Perhaps there is a *fourth danger* for us and that is the danger of trying to make all Christians act alike, regardless of where God may have placed them. Some, by the nature of your societies, are able to have a fair degree of influence.

Others of you come from countries in which this is very difficult. We should each recognize the others' problems, dilemmas, or opportunities as the case may be.

Our situations are radically different. For example, the social, cultural, and political problems are totally different for the Christian in Uganda than in Great Britain, or for the Christian in Australia and in Czechoslovakia. But, thank God, our spiritual resources are the same.

These four things all point to the last concept which we must reaffirm at this Congress — the necessity of evangelism.

In certain circles today, evangelism is spoken of only as the "Christian presence." Almost total emphasis is placed on living a consistently moral life in one's environment. This is as it should be — it is good — but I maintain that evangelism is much more than nonverbal — "faith cometh by hearing and hearing by the Word of God."

After all humanists may heal, feed, and help, but this social presence isn't Gospel proclamation.

The Gospel is an announcement of the Good News. But what Good News? It is the thrilling proclamation that Jesus Christ, very God and very man, died for my sins on the cross, was buried, and rose the third day.

The Son has made full atonement for my sins. If I reach forth by faith to receive Christ as my personal Savior, I am declared forgiven by God, not through any merit of mine, but through the merits of Christ's shed blood. I rejoice in pardon for the past, the indwelling presence of the Holy Spirit for the present and the living hope for the future.

The great philosophical questions concerning where I came from, why I am here and where I am going are answered; and in grateful obedience my life should be "rich in good works."

Evangelism has been reinterpreted in some circles to mean primarily "changing the structures of society in the direction of justice, righteousness and peace."

Industrial evangelism, for example, is held to be *not* bringing workers to redemptive faith in Jesus Christ, but improving the conditions under which men work.

Don't get me wrong. We evangelicals should believe that improving working conditions is something each individual believer should be concerned about, but this is not primarily "evangelism." Evangelicals should reject all such devaluation of the concept of the meaning of the "evangel" — the evangelist cannot ignore social injustice.

I believe in political freedom, changing unjust political and social structures where needed and where possible — equal justice for all. But this is not strictly "evangelism" — this has often historically come as the fruit of missions and evangelism.

In the early part of this century, Robert E. Speer, one of the key figures in the beginnings of the ecumenical movement, gave an address entitled "The Supreme and Determining Aim."

He said "We must not confuse *the aim* of foreign missions with *the results* of foreign missions. Wherever the Gospel goes, it plants in the hearts of men forces that produce new lives. It plants among communities of men forces that create new social combinations. It is impossible that any human tyranny should live where Jesus Christ is King.

"It is a dangerous thing to charge ourselves openly before the world with the aim of reorganizing states and reconstructing society. Missions are powerful to transform the face of society because they ignore the face of society and deal with it at its heart."

In perspective, we may not agree with all of this statement; yet the basic truth is there.

Biblically, evangelism can mean nothing else than proclaiming Jesus Christ by presence and by trusting the Holy Spirit to use the Scriptures to persuade men to become his disciples and responsible members of his Church.

Furthermore, *evangelism* and the *salvation of souls* is the *vital mission* of the Church. The whole Church must be mobilized to bring the whole Gospel to the whole world.

This is our calling. These are our orders. Thus, while we may discuss social and political problems, our priority for discussion here is *the salvation of souls.*

Christians must regain the sense of direction, the feeling of urgency, and the depth of conviction which gave birth to the powerful slogan "The Evangelization of the World in this Generation."

It is true we live in different days from those of the nineteenth century. And new days demand new methods.

Our evangelistic methods differ in many ways from those of D. L. Moody. Even at this hour, there are scores of different methods of evangelism being effectively used. The method we use may be among the least effective.

No evangelism is effective unless it is "personal." But some things never change. The Word of God never changes. Christ never changes. The power of the Spirit to transform lives never changes. The demand for obedience never changes. Our commission to go to the ends of the earth never changes. And Christ's promise to be with us to the end never changes.

In other words, the "message" we proclaim never changes — only "methods" change! The task of this Congress therefore is to relate the changless Gospel to a changing world.

Fourthly, this Congress convenes to consider honestly and carefully both the unevangelized world and the Church's resources to evangelize the world.

Here, we will study together such questions as *where* are the unevangelized, *when* can a person, a village, a city, or a country be said to be evangelized.

In the last quarter of the twentieth century, the *unevangelized world consists of two main blocs of people.*

First, are the superficially Christian populations. If you ask them their religion, they more than likely reply, "Christian," but they do not personally know Christ.

Second, the *"unevangelized world"* consists of large "unreached" populations which can be found in almost every country. For example, the Turks, Algerians, and the Vietnamese in Europe constitute large unreached populations in the heart of Europe itself.

There are tens of millions who live in areas that never hear the Gospel. Some countries of the world are almost completely closed to the Gospel except by radio. We should give a great deal of thought and prayer to ways and means of reaching these lost millions. At this Congress we should pray for the faithful, unknown, and unheralded witnesses in these areas of the world — there were believers in Caesar's household.

In these unreached populations, Christians of any sort, "born again" or in name only, constitute only a tiny fraction . . . sometimes one in a hundred; often one in a thousand.

This Congress will be shocked to learn of the magnitude of the unreached populations on every continent.

The Planning Committee of this Congress asked the School of Missions at Fuller Theological Seminary and Missions Advance Research Center to assemble hard facts on unreached populations. The two agencies appointed a "work team" which enlisted the aid of hundreds around the world to gather data. I shall not anticipate their report, but I must say that the situation revealed in their report is sobering.

We *must evangelize* in "the world" which this data reveals. Our evangelistic strategy should be formed in view of this *actual* situation. There may be some places in the world where the Church would actually be stronger if missionaries were withdrawn and sent to areas of great need.

While some people can be evangelized by their neighbors, others and greater multitudes are cut off from their Christian neighbors by deep linguistic, political, and cultural chasms. They will never be reached by "near neighbor" evangelism. To build our evangelistic policies on "near neighbor" evangelism alone is to shut out at least a billion from any possibility of knowing the Savior.

Churches *of every land,* therefore must deliberately send out evangelists and missionaries to master other languages, learn other cultures, live in them perhaps for life, and thus evangelize these multitudes. Thus, we should reject the idea of a moratorium on sending missionaries.

At the first meeting of the Executive Planning Committee for the Congress when the name was debated, it was decided to call it *"The International Congress on World Evangelization,"* not just evangelism. Many sincere Christians around the world are concerned for evangelism.

They are diligent at evangelizing in their own communities and even in their own countries. But they do not see *God's big picture* of "world need" and the "global responsibility" that he has put upon the church in his Word.

The Christians in Nigeria are not just to evangelize Nigeria, nor the Christians in Peru just the people of Peru. God's heartbeat is for the world.

Christ commissioned us not only to make disciples in every nation, but to preach the Gospel to every creature.

In this connection, we would do well to bear in mind, as we gather for the Congress on World Evangelization, that by our attitude and conduct in our individual daily contacts with the people of this great city, we either confirm or contradict the message we seek to proclaim.

What a tragedy if, in the midst of our deliberations on how to reach the world for Christ, we should fail to evangelize by word and life the very city in which we meet.

But, let us pray that here at Lausanne God will help us to the big picture of the whole world for which Christ died and for which he made us responsible to preach the Gospel.

Let our hearts echo his words, "O earth, earth, earth, hear ye the word of the Lord!"

When Wesley was shut off from the established church of his day, he proclaimed, "The world will be my parish," and he kept a map of the world before him. Carey put up a map of the world in his shoe shop.

When I see the world from the moon on television, I want to reach out and grab it for Christ. As Isaiah said, "Look unto me, and be ye saved, all the ends of the earth: for I am God, and there is none else" (Isa. 45:22).

World evangelization means continued and increasing sendings of missionaries and evangelists from every church in every land to the unreached billions. The Church must learn to utilize every technological and spiritual resource at its command for the spreading of the Gospel of Jesus Christ.

Finally, what do we hope will be accomplished at this Congress? Let me share four of my hopes with you.

1. *I would like to see the Congress frame a biblical declaration on evangelism.* The time has come again for the evangelical world to speak with a strong clear voice as to the biblical definition of evangelism. I would challenge the World Council of Churches Assembly next year planned for Djakarta to study such a statement carefully and prayerfully with the idea of adopting more evangelical concepts of evangelism and missions.

2. *I would like to see the Church challenged to complete the task of world evangelization.* Never has the Church been stronger, more deeply entrenched in more countries, more truly a world Church, and more able to evangelize than it is today.

Our Lord said, "Look unto the fields for they are white unto harvest." Never has the grain been thicker than it is today.

The world population by the end of this century, at the present rate of increase, will be seven billion. But never have the instruments been sharper.

We have the manpower in the thousands of keen young Christians God has been calling to himself in recent years.

The time has come for action! Effective methods of evangelism, developed in various parts of the world during the past decades, both by denominations and by para-church organizations, should be studied and developed. Participants of this Congress should take back suggestions and ideas and share them and apply them in their own lands.

3. *I trust we can state what the relationship is between evangelism and social responsibility.* Let us rejoice in social action, and yet insist that it alone is not evangelism and cannot be substituted for evangelism. This relationship disturbs many believers. Perhaps Lausanne can help clarify it.

4. *I hope that a new "koinonia" or fellowship among evangelicals of all persuasions will be developed throughout the world.* I hope there will develop here what I like to call "The Spirit of Lausanne." The time has come for evangelicals to move forward, to encourage, challenge and bring hope to the World Church.

Evangelicals are rapidly gaining recognition and momentum! From this Congress can come a *new love,* a *new fellowship,* a *new slogan,* and a *new song,* but most of all, a *new commitment.*

I believe the Lord is saying to us, "Let's go forward together in a worldwide fellowship in evangelism, in missions, in Bible translation, in literature distribution, in meeting world social needs, in evangelical theological training, etc."

There are two basic needs if we are to leave with the spirit of Lausanne. *The first has to do with prayer.* For the ten days prior to Pentecost, the disciples "continued with one accord in prayer and supplications" (Acts 1:14). Their prayers were heard. The Spirit descended. The power abounded. Weak men became strong, faithless men became faithful. Speechless men spoke the Word with strength and, most glorious of all, sinners who listened became saints through faith in the risen Christ.

It is my hope that there will be a tremendous emphasis on prayer during this Congress. Evangelism is always in danger of succumbing to a humanistic activity. With all the emphasis on crowds and our thrill and excitement about church growth, we should remember that Jesus sometimes fled from the crowds.

In discussions of evangelism, too little is often made of the spiritual life and prayer.

It is foolish and vain to try to do God's work without God's power.

But there is no way for Christians to have God's power except by prayer. I have learned from many years of evangelistic experience that successful evangelism, whatever method may be used, must be saturated in prayer.

The second need is to leave the Congress filled with the power of the Holy Spirit. Only a Spirit-filled people can finish the job of world evangelization.

We will be here for ten days, even as the disciples of our Lord tarried for ten days before Pentecost. They did this in obedience to the command of Jesus, "Tarry ye in Jerusalem until ye are endued with power from on high" (Luke 24:49).

The power they needed is the power we need. There can be no adequate evangelism without the Holy Spirit. It is the Holy Spirit who convicts of sin, righteousness and judgment. It is the Holy Spirit who performs the work of regeneration.

It is the Holy Spirit who indwells believers. It is the Holy Spirit who guides, teaches, instructs, and fills the new believer.

The great communicator of the Gospel is the Holy Spirit. He uses ordinary people such as us as instruments — but it is his work!

Thus, when the Gospel is faithfully declared, it is the Holy Spirit who sends it like a fiery dart into the hearts of those who have been prepared.

Thus, it is my hope that during this Congress there will be a constant recognition of the person and work of the Holy Spirit in evangelism.

God has gathered us here at a time of great opportunity, but also at a time of unprecedented danger. The harvest is ripe! But harvest time only lasts a short time. What we do we must do with urgency.

Storm clouds are gathering. Satan is marshalling his forces for his fiercest attack in history. Ours is a cosmic struggle both in the "seen" and the "unseen" world. Satan will do everything he can to discourage, divide and defeat us as we seek to carry out the Great Commission of our Lord.

But we follow the Son of God who has already "nullified" the power of death, hell and Satan. The final victory is certain.

The night before he was assassinated, Dr. Martin Luther King spoke in Memphis about how he had climbed the mountain. When he had scaled the heights of the mountain he said that he was able to look over into the Promised Land. He said, "Mine eyes have seen the glory of the coming of the Lord."

You and I have climbed the mountain that separated us from the Living God. We have scaled its heights. We have looked into the Promised Land. Our eyes have seen the glory of God.

He has given us the vision to see, the faith to believe, and the courage to act. But we have not yet entered the Promised Land.

Down below us on the plains of the world are the millions of men and woman who do not know there is a mountain to climb; they do not know there is a Promised Land to enter.

They have not seen, believed nor acted. We who have seen the Promised Land must go down into the valley when Lausanne is over and tell the multitudes there is a mountain to climb and a Promised Land to enter.

God has cut the pathway to the top of that mountain with the blood of his Son. God has prepared a Promised Land where there is no night, no sin, no suffering, no hunger, no sorrow, no tears, and no death.

And to us has been given the task and the privilege to tell all men everywhere that if they follow the blood-stained trail to the Son of God, they will climb the mountain, they will see the Promised Land, and they will know the glory of the coming of the Lord.

Why Lausanne?

That the earth may hear his voice!

Section II:
Devotional Bible Studies

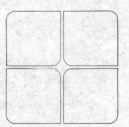

GOD AT WORK THROUGH MEN: STEPHEN (ACTS 6)

Nilson A. Fanini

*Dr. Fanini, Estado do Rio, Brazil,
is Pastor of the First Baptist
Church of Niteroi.*

The text which was given me to make a biblical study is, I believe, one of the richest in all of the Word of God. We are *not* going to study the institution of the deacon itself, but the life of one of the first seven deacons — which teaches us the principles of a life full of the Holy Spirit. No one can be an efficient, effective evangelist if he is not full of the Holy Spirit. In Acts 6:5, Stephen is described as "a man full of faith and of the Holy Spirit. . . ." Let us then examine the seven characteristics that distinguish a man full of the Holy Spirit.

1. *One who is a channel through whom God performs his signs and miracles here on earth*

Acts 6:8 says: "Stephen, full of grace and power, was performing great wonders and signs among the people." Then a man full of the Holy Spirit is the bed of the river through which flows the power of God to do his works. And thus full of the Holy Spirit it becomes possible for God to do his great signs among the people. The Bible is very clear on this — what he did and had the capacity to do was because he was full of the Holy Spirit. We, too, can be channels to be used in the hands of this powerful God. The method may change, but the power is always the same. I have seen in my own life such great miracles as those described in the Bible.

Here there is no reference to how Stephen looked, how he dressed, combed his hair, etc. — it only says one thing: that he had the power of God. Any person, any man who puts himself at God's disposition, can become a channel for the all-powerful God to do miracles in his life. It is not right that we ask God for the Holy Spirit. The Holy Spirit already lives in us, since we were saved. This body is called the temple of the Holy Spirit. Then what we must pray is: "Lord, help me surrender myself as the temple of the Holy Spirit." We must pray to be his temple. We must pray that God will punish us and that he will take from within us everything which is impeding the manifestation.

2. *One who reacts graciously when provoked*

"And fixing their gaze on him, all who were sitting in the Council saw his face like the face of an angel" (Acts 6:15). Note what they felt in respect to Stephen.

Verse 13 indicates false witnesses, saying: "This man incessantly speaks against this holy place, and the law. . . ." He had neither spoken against the holy place, nor had he blasphemed. Read verse 11 ("Then they secretly induced men to say, 'We have heard him speak blasphemous words against Moses and against God'"), and see that they suborned the men to speak against poor Stephen. If you were to be taken before a tribunal and there would be bribed witnesses to speak and lie against you, how would you react toward such a provocation? Now if you were full of the Holy Spirit in such a situation — as was Stephen — you also would remain with a face like that of an angel. It is difficult for us to have such a comportment when it is our natural reaction to react against such an accusation. Then, reemphasizing, the man full of the Holy Spirit always reacts with grace — that is, he is fully clothed in grace, in the midst of such provocations.

3. *One who is powerful in the Scriptures*

No man can be fuller of the Holy Spirit than he is full of the Scriptures. Then, if you want to be full of the Holy Spirit, first fill yourself with Scriptures. After they faced Stephen and said everything against him, they asked: "Are all these things true? What do you have to say now that you have heard these witnesses?" He, being full of the Holy Spirit, did not reply, "You're lying!" He did not try to hit them. He did not become upset. He only opened his mouth and began to cite Scriptures. My brothers, nothing must take the place of the Word of God. There is neither enough time nor words to emphasize sufficiently the necessity to study the Word of God. Any man who becomes educated and cultured, but is without the Word of God, will feel less and less used of God. God has used many men who have little education, but who have power in the Scriptures. You must not fail; you must preach to yourselves and — through a baptism by immersion — baptize yourselves in the world of the Scriptures. Should they lie and say numerous things against you, you can only tolerate it if you are full of the Holy Spirit. For when they asked Stephen, "Are these things they are saying against you the truth?" he began citing Scripture (see Acts 7:2).

"Hear me brethren and fathers! The God of glory appeared to our father Abraham when he was in Mesopotamia, before he lived in Haran..." Then the best lawyer in the world is the Word of God. He traced the story of how God had led the people of Israel. He then showed his listeners that he was the end of that which God had begun long ago with Abraham. He believed and was ready to die for the belief. Man is ready to die only when he is full of the Holy Spirit. He knew that with his answer he was signing his own death warrant. Could it be that God had abandoned him? Could it be that God had turned his back on him? No. He was full of the Holy Spirit and God was sustaining him. Do you have the courage to preach like Stephen? Only a man full of the Holy Spirit is one who has that courage of Stephen to preach. And without being full of the Holy Spirit, it is crazy to even want to preach with the courage of Stephen. Full of the Holy Spirit, your message can be accepted and have the beneficent acceptance of the Holy Spirit; but without being full of the Holy Spirit, your message preached in the manner of Stephen is even dangerous to the point of losing your head. He really accused even us in verse 52 of chapter 7: "Which one of the prophets did your fathers not persecute? And they even killed those who had previously announced the coming of the Righteous One, whose betrayers and murderers you have now become." And when one of you says such a thing as this to a judge, it is indeed best that the Holy Spirit be with you.

4. One who is sustained by God

In verse 55 of chapter 7, we see this image in front of us: "Being full of the Holy Spirit, he gazed intently into heaven and saw the glory of God, and Jesus standing at the right hand of God . . ." Note that he saw the glory of God, and Jesus, because he was full of the Holy Spirit. When the crisis came, God gave him a glorious vision. Therefore, a person who sees Jesus, sees God, sees the glory of God and Jesus at the right hand of God, is automatically immunized against pain. Which of us would fear man or what man could do if he is seeing God face to face?

5. One who is equal to Jesus in the days of his flesh

Stephen was similar to Jesus in his actions as well as in his attitude. Note in chapter 7 that Paul was there. You see in verse 59 that when they were stoning Stephen, two things happened. Are you already aware how much Stephen was like Jesus at the hour of death? On the Cross Jesus said: "Receive my spirit. . . . Forgive them, Father, for they know not what they do. . . ." The Bible itself says that he offered himself by the eternal Spirit. Stephen then was also full of the same eternal Spirit because he acted as Jesus did. When they began to stone him, he fell down on his knees and said: "Receive my spirit," and shouted in a loud voice: "Lord, do not hold this sin against them!" Only a man full of the Holy Spirit is to have the capacity to be supernatural. To be full of the Holy Spirit is to be equal to Jesus in life as well as in death. To be full of the Holy Spirit has nothing to do with the manner in which one dresses, or cuts his hair, or how one looks, or whether one has a large or small Bible under his arm — but it has to do with what is on the inside of a person.

6. One whose death is greatly lamented

In verse 2, chapter 8, we read: "And some devout men buried Stephen and made loud lamentation over him." If you want to be grievously lamented after death, you must be full of the Holy Spirit when you are alive. And the memory of what Stephen was gave a great encouragement to the preaching in the primitive Church. Stephen left a great spiritual legacy for those who were to come after him. What more can we say about a man full of the Holy Spirit? Now that we have mentioned all of these aspects, one more point is still missing.

7. One who not only is full of power, but also is ready to do things for God

For example, in the beginning when it says that Stephen was full of the Holy Spirit, it also says that he was ready to do *any* work for God. No one, then, can be full of the Holy Spirit if he also is not ready to do as God orders. Each day when I get up, I first ask God to correct my spirit, to use me, saying as a soldier: *"I am ready; use me; command me what I shall do."* Then many times when God places his power within you, he will use that very power against your own will. God does not throw away his power.

I have heard of a pastor who was directing a series of conferences and was hurrying to catch a plane afterwards in order to attend a convention. When he arrived at the airport, he noticed they had changed his passage. This made him extremely irritated; he became angrier and angrier and even red in the face as he discussed the matter with the airline agent. What really happened was the following: He had bought a ticket for economy class and they had given him a ticket in first class. (As you know, that would mean he would have to pay the difference between the less expensive economy class and first class.) It was because of this difference in price that he became so upset. Finally, when he was seated in the plane, he bowed his head and began to pray. In a little while someone sat down at his side. He turned to see a soldier. Then a steward approached and asked what he would like to drink. He said, "I don't want anything"; while the soldier answered, "Bring two whiskeys and put them here." They then began conversing and he asked the soldier where he was going. "I'm going to Vietnam to die!" He then began to witness to the soldier and asked him, "Are you a Christian?" He said, "No." "Do you know Christ?" "No." "May I speak about Jesus?" "I am dying to hear!" And the soldier continued: "This morning I went to church to find an answer for my hungry heart. I participated in all of the worship service, I listened to all of the message, but there was nothing to help me." Never be guilty of not preaching to souls in your sermons. Think about the guilt of that pastor who preached on that morning in such a manner that the young man went away as hungry as he had entered.

Then that pastor picked up his New Testament and began presenting the plan of salvation to the soldier. And right there the soldier lowered his head and prayed and gave his heart to Jesus. Then he did what every Christian should do. His eyes filled with tears and he returned the whiskey to the steward. Shortly thereafter, they opened the curtain that separates economy from first class and the pastor saw that the economy class was full of other pastors bound for the convention. And they shouted: "Hey, what are you doing there?" He understood that he had been sent by the Holy Spirit. Only a man full of the Holy Spirit could be a powerful evangelist.

GOD AT WORK THROUGH MEN: ANANIAS AND PAUL

Philip Teng

Dr. Teng, Hong Kong, is Vice –
President and Professor of the Alliance
Bible Seminary.

In the passage of Scripture for this morning, we have two people whom God used in carrying out his plan — Paul and Ananias. These two persons form a sharp contrast. Ananias was hardly known to Christians, yet God chose to use him. In fact Paul, who was going to be a famous and great Christian leader, needed his prayer and counseling. In these two persons we find a most significant combination in evangelism. Ananias represents Christians who are nobodies, engaged in personal evangelism. They are not known to the Christian public but known of God and greatly valued by God. They are absolutely indispensable. Personal evangelism is still the foundation of all types of evangelism. Paul represents the other type — the great leaders in evangelism whom God raises up for the need of the times and to whom God gives special talents and vision. They are also indispensable in the hand of God.

Our meditation this morning will concentrate on Paul — a man raised and used by God in evangelism. God used him to turn the world upside down because he himself was first turned upside down by God. Or, to use a modern word, God used Paul to revolutionize the world because he himself was first revolutionized by God. Here we have a basic principle in evangelism: God revolutionizes the world through people who are revolutionized by God first.

How was Paul revolutionized? We find the answer in the third chapter of Philippians.

In the first place, Paul was revolutionized in his concept of salvation. In the past, he tried hard to attain to righteousness by keeping the Law of God, but now he rejoices in receiving the righteousness of God through faith in Jesus Christ. He has great joy in passing on to others this great news of salvation through Jesus Christ. In reading through Paul's epistles, we often find him suddenly bursting into a song or a shout in great excitement and exultation about God's unfathomable grace and wisdom in Jesus Christ. There is glorious salvation in Christ! There is freedom, and peace, and joy, and hope in Christ! May we, too, have the same joy and assurance in proclaiming the unsearchable riches of the Gospel of Christ.

In the second place, Paul was revolutionized in his sense of value. In the past, he was bent on gain for himself, but now, he counts all gain as loss and all loss as gain for Christ. Not only that, but also he had joy in sacrificing everything for Christ. He says in Phil. 2:17, "If I be offered upon the sacrifice and service of your faith, I joy and rejoice with you all." Paul indeed followed the steps of his Lord of whom it was said, "Though he was rich, yet for your sakes he became poor that ye through his poverty might be rich." It is certainly true to speak of Paul as "poor, yet making many rich; as having nothing and yet possessing all things."

When he came to the end of his earthly journey, he could only speak of his overcoat and his books (II Tim. 4:13), yet he was so rich in Christ, and he made many people rich in Christ. This reminds us of John Wesley whose autographed will was discovered in 1768 in which only his clerical gowns, his watch, and his books were mentioned. That was all that he had in material things but many people were enriched through his ministry. Gandhi of India said to a missionary, "Sing me the deepest hymn of Christianity." "Which one?" the missionary asked. Gandhi said, "When I Survey the Wondrous Cross." All of us are familiar with the lines of this hymn: "My richest gain I count but loss. . . . All the vain things that charm me most, I sacrifice to his blood. . . . Love so amazing, so divine, demands my soul, my life, my all."

In the third place, Paul was revolutionized in his concept of life. There are two things that stand out in Paul's new understanding of life:

First, abundant life through death. Paul says, "Always bearing about in the body the dying of the Lord Jesus that the life also of Jesus might be made manifest in our body" (II Cor. 4:10). One phase of the rich meaning of these words is that when Paul died to his self-life, others were brought to have life in Christ. Probably Paul also had something else in mind when he said these words which could be illustrated by his experience in the city of Lystra. Paul was stoned by the angry Jews and he was thought to be dead, and it was possible that he was dead, and they pulled him out of the city. But God healed him. Shortly afterwards, Paul again went to Lystra to preach the Gospel — what dedication and bravery! This time, we read of Christians in Lystra who evidently had been brought to life in Christ through Paul's reported death.

Second, Paul had only one goal in his life which is the "one thing" in his life — "I press toward the mark for the prize of the high calling of God in Christ Jesus" (Phil. 3:14). This is the center of all Paul's efforts. This concentration creates a focus which generates dynamic power in Paul's life. A life without a focus can never achieve anything. A Christian or a Christian worker without a focus in his life or service cannot accomplish things for Christ. Dedication brings concentration, and concentration brings fruitfulness. When Paul was warned by the Holy Spirit of dangers that were waiting for him at Jerusalem (Acts 21:11), he would not listen to those who tried to persuade him not to go to that city. He understood the real intention of the Holy Spirit in revealing dangers to him, and he took them as challenge and went ahead. And he said, "And now I go bound in the spirit unto Jerusalem; not knowing the things that shall befall me there, save that the Holy Spirit witnesseth in every city, saying that bonds and afflictions await me. But none of these things move me, neither count I my life dear unto myself so that I might finish my course with joy and the ministry which I have received of the Lord Jesus to testify the Gospel of the grace of God" (Acts 20:22-24).

When Mary Slessor passed into higher service, her mission had to send twenty men to take over her work. That shows the power that is generated by full dedication.

We pray that God will raise up more fully dedicated Christians and Christian workers all over the world who will have Paul's "one thing" in their lives.

GOD AT WORK THROUGH MEN: PETER AND THE ROMAN OFFICER (ACTS 10:9-48)
Branko Lovrec

Dr. Lovrec, Zagreb, Yugoslavia,
is the Founder of Duhovna Starnost
(Spiritual Reality), a Christian publishing firm.

The historical occurrence recounted in this passage is of great significance to the church and Christianity, because the account of God's opening the door of the Gospel to the Gentiles is repeated three times.

Who was Cornelius? A Roman officer serving in Israel, he accepted faith in the living God and submitted to the religious laws and practices of the Jews. This was, however, inadequate for his salvation. But God still heard this devout man's prayer and wanted to bring him into the fellowship of Christians, and perfectly arranged a meeting with Peter who had to open the door of Christianity to him.

What can we learn from this account and apply to ourselves? The contemporary world is religiously inclined and exerts every effort in an attempt to achieve salvation. However, despite its religiosity, the world does not know Jesus and consequently cannot find that only way to God.

But to return to the text. Here God prepares Peter for a specific mission. He is charged with announcing the saving message of Jesus Christ, the Good News of Salvation, without works. As a devout Jew who had received the commandment from Jesus not to go among the pagans (Matt. 10:5), he could not comprehend the opportunity arising for Gentiles to be saved as well. Therefore, God prepared him in a graphic way and in a manner which he could understand. God uses various means to assert his will in history, and in this instance he resorted to a special vision to give Peter his commandment about the necessity of going to a pagan's house.

Peter's faithfulness in prayer was a prerequisite to this special revelation from God. We cannot, however, conclude that just because Peter prayed at a special time, God used him as an agent to deliver the Gospel to a pagan. God had him in his plan, so that Peter really opened the door to Christianity for the Gentiles with the keys which Christ, in a figurative way, had given him. It is interesting to note that through the prayers of Cornelius and Peter, God was able to adapt perfectly the time and place to complete the work of salvation in a pagan.

Peter was astonished by this divine proclamation and summons, so that initially he rejected God's command. In his prejudicial devotion he answered God: "Not so, Lord!" and in so doing uttered a paradox, for while he called God his Lord he could not reject him simultaneously. Still, God did not withdraw his command but repeated it three times so that Peter would be radically changed.

God's timing and placing of events are perfect, but we are more concerned about particulars and childish details than in unquestioningly obeying God's commands and acting on them. It is God's problem how to bring people to hear the truth which he has revealed to me. I must be careful not to alter the truth while being faithful to my vision.

The meeting of Peter and Cornelius is extremely significant since God had prepared both of these men. We must always remember that God is the prime mover in the work of evangelism, much more than we are. If we believe that he has given us a message, then we also believe that he will give us people who need to hear that message. God will arrange a time and place for us to meet those who need salvation. Frequently we are too occupied with the organization of places to meet, and the gathering of people, and too little concerned about studying God's proclamation and the content of the message we need to share.

People are interested in hearing what God has revealed to us. The proclamation is given to us in the Bible. We don't need others! It is perfect and complete! We need only to understand it and share it with others.

The most wonderful words a minister of the Gospel can hear are those which Peter heard when Cornelius told him, ". . . therefore we are all here present before God, to hear all things that are commanded thee of God" (v. 33).

And Peter did not hesitate to give a complete account of Jesus Christ, the one about whom we need to speak. He presented the heart of the Gospel in a very brief interval and in just a few sentences, but sufficient that a man who had been prepared by God could understand and accept it. How many times have our sermons concentrated on everything except Jesus, and then we are surprised at the lack of results!

The Good News for Cornelius and his house was this: salvation is possible through Jesus Christ (v. 36). This should be the content of our Good News.

Peter thus described Christ as the Lord of all. He was a historical personage and the fulfillment of prophecy. He was the God-man, of supernatural capabilities. Peter witnessed to this, because he saw and experienced it all.

Christ, the one about whom he spoke, died on the Cross and rose again — this is basic to the message — and revealed himself to his chosen ones.

Subsequently Christ commanded them to announce this to *the people* (this is what Peter says), however, Christ said in Matt. 28:19, "to *all peoples* in the world." Due to the prejudices of Jewish customs and orthodox Judaism, God had to intervene in a special way to change Peter and compel him to speak to a pagan. The result was forthcoming.

This account can serve as an example for us in our work, but we dare not anticipate God's repeating in detail every move he made with Peter. The lesson is clear. We must preach the Good News to everyone, without regard to racial, cultural, and national differences, not only to those we find pleasant and likeable, and those who are wealthy and influential because they can be more useful to us in our work, but to everyone. We dare not limit God's message and the Gospel, for then we will make the same mistake as Peter did. Then God had to intervene. Let us never say to God, "Not so, Lord," for he can punish us.

May we let God do the organizing and let us remain faithful to the message which is revealed to us!

GOD AT WORK THROUGH MEN: PAUL AND THE GREEK PHILOSOPHERS (ACTS 17:22-34)

Samuel Kamaleson

Dr. Kamaleson, Madras,
India, is the District Superintendent for
the Methodist Church in Southern Asia.

Easter set the earliest believers on a path of effective communication. Easter released them from being frozen around non-living issues of the past to life-giving relationships because of, and around, the risen Jesus. Paul was among these effective communicators.

In the 15th and 16th chapters of the book of Acts, the Holy Spirit reveals some cardinal principles in the ways in which he leads Paul to become this effective communicator. The believer *lives by faith*. And the leading of the Holy Spirit in the total mechanics of communicating the resurrection of Jesus Christ may not be *explicit*. In fact, if "science is proof without certainty," then, "faith is certainty without proof." God leads as Paul follows his nudgings and the thoughts that he had dropped. In Acts 15:36-41 we read about the *Jerusalem Conference* with the issue of the Gentile Christians and the law. Paul along with Barnabas decides to revisit the churches to tell them about the decisions of the council. They violently disagree over John Mark (vs. 39). These saints of the early church do not seem to have any special guidance up to this point. Paul takes Silas and Timothy and moves out. This *move of faith* is then honored and clarified by a series of doors being closed while others are opened.

In Acts 16:4-9 there is trouble over the itinerary. The Holy Spirit shuts doors and prevents them from the wrong entry. In their *move of faith* they were not afraid of action or closed doors. They sought God more earnestly rather than stop. "How" the Holy Spirit gave his guidance is not as important as that he did guide. God gave the Macedonian call to the servants who had proved their submissiveness to him by accepting his course corrections while in the act of obedience. He could trust only such with the *vision of the lost*. While Paul refused to be either afraid or to sit inactive beside a closed door, he was used by the Holy Spirit to fulfill the *goal that God had for him to fulfill*. Since full knowledge of what lies ahead may cause us to be "afraid," God does not give all the details right at the beginning.

In Acts 16:9-15 the action begins. Now there is a team. Luke has joined them. While visiting the established churches they watch the genesis of new churches. They find a home to live in and a congregation to preach to while there are those who are being saved! In Acts 16:16-24 the whole picture changes. But in verses 25-34, Paul and Silas come into victory instead of despair. And quickly after the jailer and his family are baptized God removes his servants from Philippi through Thessalonica and Berea to Athens. And by this time Paul has understood the plan of God in terms of the compulsion to communicate the truth of the resurrection effectively, followed by the inevitable stirring up of trouble as well as the conversion of some.

To Mars Hill (vs. 16-21) While waiting for his teammates to arrive, Paul does not wait to be told about the need for the message of the resurrection to be told in Athens. The Resurrected One was Paul's absolute now. And all other absolutes of life that regulated his life prior to the Damascus road experience were now only relative absolutes to this "Absolute-Absolute!" This risen Jesus kept him from becoming frozen around any personal hang-ups that would prevent him from being alive to the crying needs of his environment by casting his soul on ice. So Paul obeyed this inner prompting in terms of the external need.

Paul used the (vs. 17) already structured situation (synagogue) as well as the unorthodox situation (public square) to fulfill God's purposes through making effective contact with the people of Athens. Thus, to the one who moved by faith in response to his inner awareness as well as the sensitivity of the external needs, the opportunity was given. Paul made contact with the Epicurean and Stoic philosophers (vs. 18). Paul's personal qualifications won him a place among the intellectuals. Paul's knowledge of the risen Jesus as his absolute among absolutes — his "new place to stand" — gave him the "message" that he was to give. Paul's knowledge of the Holy Spirit's guidance in fulfilling this "mission" made him the "messenger" with the sense of purpose and urgency.

The philosophers were interested in what Paul had to say. The phrase that they used to describe him and the situation indicates "this new teaching which you present" (vs. 19). But Paul had preached "Jesus and the resurrection" (vs. 18). This was much more than words and phrases. This was event with content. The philosophers wanted to "know" this "new teaching" and to "know . . . what these things mean." Could it be that the Holy Spirit had already drawn their initial interest to come to focus upon Paul's message?

Luke says that Athenians and the foreigners who wanted to be "like the Athenians spent their time in nothing except telling or hearing something new" (vs. 21). Life's frustrations force men to intellectual speculations. But if life does not extend beyond "telling and hearing something new" — never into creative and redemptive action — would it not be falling short of its ultimate possibilities? So Paul was brought to the Areopagus not to defend himself but to explain his philosophy.

At Mars Hill (vs. 22-31) Basing his cue on the words of the prophet as found in Zech. 9:13, "Thy sons, O Zion, against thy sons, O Greece," J.S. Stewart calls this moment a moment of prophetic fulfillment. The words of the apostle in vs. 22 concerning the interests of the Athenians in religion are not to be taken as complimentary in intention. Such compliments were not only condemned in the Areopagus, but this was not the intended meaning of the words of the apostle. According to F.F. Bruce, "What was piety to the Greeks was superstition in the eyes of the apostle." He then proceeds to instruct them on the basis of their ignorance (vs. 23). To Paul, meaning for existence now depended upon the personal knowledge of Jesus Christ as the Risen Lord. If men lacked this knowledge of the Absolute-Absolute, then Paul found it necessary to "set (him) forth unto (them)."

In the passage covered within vs. 24-30, Paul sets forth the God of biblical revelation. The philosophical distinctions are ignored and "proc-

lamation" takes place. Since God made everything he is the Lord of all
and hence cannot be limited to man-made temples (vs. 24). It is not God
who is dependent upon man for his needs, for he has no needs. But he
supplies all of the needs of all creatures — including man. How necessary
this proclamation seems to be in the midst of the "modern culture" wherein the secularistic views create the craving within man for the transcendent
God whom they have sought to exclude (vs. 25)! This God has already
determined the boundaries within which man will function. God controls
human history. God has also determined limits within which man can be
"man" by forming him out of the materials that he had spoken into existence and "breathing" into him his breath of life. Thus, man retains his
humanity by being submissive to God and realizing that he is not just animal, but made to have "dominion" over all other creatures. In all this
God's purpose is that man "might feel after him and find him" (vs. 27).

In vs. 28, Paul illustrates by quoting from Greek poets. This is very
effective in communicating the truth of Revelation to an audience that
is well versed in their own pre-Christian heritage. Even in India the concept of the "Prajapathi" suffering for the sins of the "praja" is a readily
understood concept among those who are the intellectuals within the
non-Christian communities. "That man is merely the material is always a
philosophical possibility, is it not? Have not your own poets sung about
this?" — this was Paul's thrust. Then, according to Paul's line of thought,
it will not be proper to reduce such a God to images. He could have based
his argument about the passage in Isa. 44:9 ff. God might have overlooked
these acts of ignorance in times past. But now he is calling for "repentance"
and as a fruit of repentance to worship him alone (vs. 30). God cannot
overlook man's idolatrous actions any longer because he has made himself plainly known through a man. He has spoken in words and deeds that
man can understand through this man. He has set up a day for judgment
when he will judge the whole world by this man. Hence it is mandatory
that every man obey this man. God made his appointment of this man
known to all by "bringing him back to life again" after he had died (vs. 31).
Paul is referring to John 5:27 and the thought of a fixed day of final judgment is from the biblical Revelation.

In the entire presentation Paul does not stop with mere words and
statements. He moves into the importance of "events" — when these are
"events" that are attested to by God himself then they judge us and our
actions. In Jesus Christ, God has broken into human history. Thus by our
responses to Jesus Christ we are judged.

Now the congregation at Mars Hill comes alive!

After Mars Hill. For the three verses that follow this is not an apt
title. Verse 32 still indicates the same geographical location. But the
passage now speaks about the response to the Mars Hill proclamation.
As long as Paul spoke about a "philosophy of life" or "another option
among many others" they were willing to hear and even enjoy. But Jesus
Christ the person demanded action in the form of commitment. Incarnation, resurrection, judgment, the close of history as predetermined event,
demand more than aesthetic enjoyment. They demand obedience in faith.

"When they heard Paul speak of the resurrection of a person who had
been dead, some laughed" (vs. 32). This is not an unknown reaction. It

still sounds clearly modern. The demand of faith seems to mock the basic premise of the pride of man's reasoning capacity. And still they who declare this have to say, "That which we have seen and heard we proclaim also to you" (I John 1:1-4).

"But others said, 'We want to hear more about this later'" — so there were others! And there still are "others." We can never treat them as merely people who want to avoid the issue of commitment and faith. They wanted to hear again because they were eager that this message should be true. To them there were no other options worthwhile. They had not found the answers in them. It is this thinking group that we encounter as a fruitful possibility in modern times. They are inquisitive. They refuse to be made to conform to the popular patterns of thoughts around them. Could this be the effect of the "God-shaped vacuum in man"? Could these who refuse to be conformed to a pattern of thinking, be the "true" intellectuals? How often one meets these in ancient cultures that have resisted the Christian faith until recent times, when, due to irresistible desire to look beyond what they have known they are willing to look even at Jesus Christ! Could there be a fear of the unanswered questions about the future? Jesus Christ himself never turned away from the honest "doubter" and the real "quester."

"But a few joined him and became believers" (vs. 34). And there are always these few. For them the quest has ended. Perhaps the Holy Spirit will use these "new creation(s)" to mock the mockers! Perhaps when man has calculated in terms of numbers God had accomplished his goal! After all, did he not lead Paul and Silas to the prison to gather to himself the family of a jailer? Praise be to his Name!!

GOD AT WORK IN CIRCUMSTANCES: PERSONAL MEETINGS (ACTS 8:26-40)
F.E. Accad

Rev. Accad, Beirut, Lebanon,
is the Executive Secretary of the Bible
Societies in the Near East.

This passage tells us about a meeting between two persons. The encounter would have been impossible had not God intervened to reduce the gap existing between the two people in question.

The first person was the minister of the Queen of Ethiopia. He came from a far country and seemed to have been traveling alone. He was not a Jew, but a Gentile. He was, meanwhile, a eunuch; and (according to Ex. 29:33, Lev. 26:20, Lev. 22:10-16, and Deut. 23:1) he was not allowed to have anything to do with the God of Israel. He could not offer actual worship as he was not able to come near any altar nor present any offering. And yet he was a pious man and was even reading the Old Testament in the Septuagint (LXX) translation, understood by the learned people of his time.

The second person was Philip, a Jew of good reputation, full of the Spirit of God and wisdom. He was chosen to serve in material things (to feed the widows and look after them). But God sent him to Samaria, and his ministry started a real revival among the people — where, in the midst of his great work, sinners were saved in great numbers, a multitude of sick people were healed, and where many Jews possessed by demons were delivered. And so there was much joy in that city (Acts 8:5-8).

In the middle of this great success and rewarding revival, the angel of the Lord said to Philip (v. 26): "Rise and go toward the *south* . . . to Gaza. This is a *desert* road . . ." The original text says: "This is a desert," probably referring to Gaza itself also. Philip obeyed, putting aside immediately all his plans and the revival in which he was ministering. He changed his direction from northbound to southbound, from a fertile and densely populated country to a desert and lonely area. He followed the guidance of the Lord.

No wonder that God was, under these conditions, able to plan such an encounter to take place between Philip and this "very important official" and to make this encounter bring forth eternal fruit. The high position of this official should have prevented him from having anything to do with a modest man such as Philip. On the other hand, it would have been very normal also for Philip, as a Jew, to shrink from having anything to do with a stranger — especially when he discovered that he was a eunuch (as this was considered taboo by the religious people of his time).

The tool of the contact in this important encounter was the Scripture from which Philip built up his conversation that led his newly-met friend to accept Christ as his personal Savior and to be baptized in his Name.

Do things happen in this same way today? In similar situations, the results should always be similar . . . where the Lord's servant is guided by him; when he is ready to change his plans in order to obey his Lord's guidance, and as long as he takes the Word of God as his sure and infallible tool — God's Word shall not return unto him void.

Is this true also in hard places and impossible lands where everything seems so tightly closed and where so many precious lives and so much money have been wasted for so many years, and where it seems that no results (or very little) have been achieved?

Through working for nearly forty-two years in such a barren and difficult field, I can testify to the faithfulness of God to scores of people I have met and whose situations are similar to that of this Ethiopian — and could be typified by the following incident (which I select from many similar ones because it took place just recently):

A few months ago, I was visiting a small but very rich place in the Arabian Peninsula with a missionary friend. The guiding angel of the Lord spoke also to my heart about the ex-ruler of this place, whom I had known for several years and with whom I had visited quite often, but had never brought him to face a decision for Christ. I had asked the friends with whom I was staying to join with me in a time of prayer for guidance and boldness in my visit to him the next day. In the morning two friends, the missionary who was with me and the native secretary of the hospital there, came with me for a visit. His Highness received us in a very friendly way, as usual; and, as he sat beside me, I immediately started to talk to him about the things I had on my heart for him — namely, the salvation of his soul through Christ's atoning sacrifice and death on the Cross for him.

At this point his Highness opened his heart and told us how his late father believed in Christ and in his sacrifice to save him. "Moreover," he said, "my father used to tell our mother in front of us all that he hoped to be still alive when Christ returns to this world, as he would then never die but would be in Christ's kingdom where peace would be paramount, the deserts would flourish and be full of water, and the people would live happily together without wars, sufferings, diseases, hunger, etc., according to the Bible." Then he added, "Father did not see the fulfillment of these prophecies, as we did not have — then — the present revenue from the oil to change the desert; but now everything is changed and I wish that my father was still living to see it."

As I asked him how his father got a copy of the Bible and how he learned about Christ, he answered, "Every time my father was sick, he went to a Mission Hospital near us. There the doctor gave him a copy of the Bible and the missionaries visited him quite often during his stay in the hospital and also later, here in our home, in order to explain these things to him. This is how he became a faithful believer in Christ."

"Allow me a question, your Highness," I said, "What about you? Are you also a believer like your Father?"

"Inshallah" [as God wills], he answered.

"No," said I, "this will never do because you do not have two souls, so that you can gamble with one of them. You have only one soul, and you cannot afford to lose it by not taking utmost care of it."

"What shall I do, then?" asked his Highness.

"Exactly as your father did," I answered. "Believe on the Lord Jesus Christ and you will be saved."

"How can I do this?" asked he.

"Just by trusting in the Lord's love for you and in his willingness to save you from your sins; and by asking him in prayer to be with you henceforth and always, by his Holy Spirit," was my answer.

"Yes, I want to do this," said his Highness, "but I do not know how to pray for it. Will you do it for me?"

"Yes," said I, "on the condition that you join with me with all your heart in the prayer and by saying 'Amen' to my request for you."

This we immediately did. His Highness stood in the midst of his large sitting room and before all his astonished visitors put his hands into mine as I prayed for him. He also said, "Amen" several times; and as I finished my prayer, I noticed that his face was wet with tears.

I visited his Highness two months ago with the secretary of the Mission Hospital who had accompanied me on the previous visit and whose name is George. His Highness' vast sitting room, where he received us again, was full of people. Several of them were bankers, others religious leaders, and some of them were reading to him from some religious books they had brought with them. But he left them all and took us into one side of the sitting room where again we had a long talk with him about the Bible and its message. He then looked at my companion saying, "George, you tell the doctor in your hospital (and he mentioned the doctor's name) that when Accad visits us the next time he is to live with me here in the palace as I have many things to study with him." This he repeated several times as he accompanied us to the car to bid us goodbye.

As I have already said, this is only one case among scores of other similar cases. It is a person-to-person meeting guided by the Spirit of God and based on his Holy Word. There all prejudices disappear and the Word of God accomplishes its blessed purpose in saving the souls of lost people.

I would like to close with the following striking statement from Dr. Samuel Zwemer's many sayings during his long ministry in the Muslim world, "At Christ's return, we shall be astonished at the huge number of people who will rise from all the Muslim cemeteries of the world to welcome him as their friend and Savior." May all the people hear soon his voice!

GOD AT WORK IN AREAS OF UNKNOWN POSSIBILITIES (ACTS 16:5-15)
Manuel Scott

Rev. Scott, Los Angeles,
California, USA, is the Pastor of Calvary
Baptist Church.

A minister is said to have called on an elderly member. The woman was past ninety, blind, half deaf, and unable to walk. Nevertheless, she was radiant and responsive, all aglow with contagious poise and power. The minister was moved to inquire as to the secret of her apparent grace and charm. In answering she said that in early childhood she was a regular participant in the Sunday school. She confessed, however, that she was the black sheep of the class, a troublemaker for her teacher, and a distraction to the learning process. Obviously, the classroom session was much improved in her absence. Notwithstanding, far from what anyone might suppose, she concluded, "It is what went on in that Sunday school class that keeps me glowing and going now."

Here is an illustration of the fact that we do not know how much good we do nor how much God is getting done in bleak, barren, and burdensome situations. We do not know what eternal thread of purpose and program runs through these tangled webs of dismay, disappointment, and disillusionment. We do not know what spiritual achievements are accomplished through stress, strain, and seemingly senseless struggle. We do not know how, time and again, failure, frustration, and fear bring forth much fruit.

The sixteenth chapter of Acts records that Paul and his company made plans to spend time in Asia, but were prevented. They set their sights on Bithynia, but the Spirit set up roadblocks. Contrary to the course they had charted they touched down at Troas. It was here that Paul heard the momentous Macedonia call: "Come over into Macedonia and help us." In responding to the summons the Gospel entered the continent of Europe, a watershed and landmark in the establishment of churches and the expansion of Christianity. The Greek-Roman world with its mind and machine and roads and regimes was an unequaled facility for the furtherance of the Gospel. More often than seldom the Christian evangelist aspires for Asia, but is compelled another way; and has his hopes on Bithynia, but is hindered.

To the end that this veto of ventures will not drive us to desertion and despair, we must undergird ourselves with nerving theological affirmations and formulations. When our dreams are tossed and blown, and when success eludes us, and stress enfeebles us, authentic ideas of God serve as a bulwark of defense and a source of comfort and counsel.

One such idea is that God is at work in the world with an agenda to which he allocates priority. God never abdicates his throne or abandons history. Jesus has his signature on this sentiment: "My Father worketh hitherto," he said, "and I work" (John 5:17).

Rene Descartes, the philosopher, as pointed out in a plenary paper, is monstrously mistaken in supposing that the totality of reality is represented in man (the thinking subject) and the natural world (the object man thinks upon). The existence of which we are a part involves God, the transcendent power and imminent presence, who initiates conditions and introduces changes in the time-space continuum in keeping with his ultimate intentions. God acts in spite of man's sins or Satan's might.

"Behold, he taketh away, who can hinder him? Who will
say unto him, what doest thou?" (Job 9:12).

A second theological formulation is that man, unlike God, has an epistemological disability. We know a little and God knows everything.

Well over two decades ago George Buttrick told us that a part of man's dilemma is his constitutional and invincible ignorance. From this dilemma not even the mature Christian is delivered. As the Scripture says, "We know in part," "We prophesy in part," "We see through a glass darkly." Until that "which is perfect is come" our perspective and penetration are partial; only fragments are in focus. We will understand it better by and by. Someone has defined religion as "awe in the presence of the unknown."

In no system of truth or branch of knowledge is human ignorance so immense and man's I.Q. so low as in theology. Our ideas of God involve us with incomparable and incomprehensible infinity. Two questions in the book of Job remind us of this.

"Canst thou by searching find out God?
Canst thou find out the Almighty unto perfection?" (Job 11:7).

We have to do with a God about whom thick clouds and great darkness gather. We have to do with a God whose ways are not our ways and whose thoughts are not our thoughts. We have to do with a God whose understanding advances beyond man's as a mind of an Einstein surpasses that of an ant. We have to do with a deity whose designs include not just cultures and countries, but the cosmos; not just the hour, but the ages; not just individuals, but the family of man; and not just the space-time context, but the trans-temporal and trans-spatial. We have to do with a monarch and master who "moves in mysterious ways" and manipulates with ambivalent actions. He supports us, but he also sacrifices us. He gives us the pleasure of experiencing his presence, but he also pains us with an experience of his absence. He knows the way we take, but veils in secrecy the way he takes. He opens doors that no man can shut and shuts doors that no man can open. He helps, but he also hinders. He heals, but he also hurts. He blesses, but he also bleeds. He answers prayer, but the answers are often denials and delays. He promises a crown, but he constrains us to bear a cross.

Moreover, when we are caught in confining and oppressive circumstances we should console and counsel ourselves with the idea that God's relationship with us is one in which he not only does things for us, but he gets things done by us and through us. God chooses us in order to use us. We are slowly coming to appreciate in the Christ family that in the God-man relationship there is a "God for us" side and a "God by us" side. This utilitarian motif and method of God unfolds in a single verse in John's Gospel. John spotlights the summit scenario in the Bible salvation story. "For the law was given *by* Moses, but grace and truth came *by* Jesus Christ" (John 1:17). We are not simply God's sheep, fed and tended by him, we are his servants, running errands and doing chores. We are not just his allies. We are his agents and ambassadors. We are not merely his dependents, we are also his disciples to whom he gives tough assignments. We are not just God's guest; we are his host. We are more than his creation; we are his channels. We are not merely members of Christ's body; we are means to his ends. We are holders of both a sonship and a servantship. We have a charge to keep, a race to run, and a course to finish.

In many maiming and mean situations God often makes his goal while our goal is missed. Moses misses the promised land but God plants his "peculiar people" there. David's dream to build God a house is denied, but God gets it done through his son. Paul did not make his journey into Spain, but the Gospel did.

Finally, when the areas in which we work are unpromising and the possibilities unknown, we can be refreshed in remembering that the best is yet to come. God has prepared for us some better things. When at a wedding in Cana Jesus turned water to wine, the governor of the feast remarked to the bridegroom essentially this: "You have saved the best for the last" (John 2:10).

This is a fitting parable and prophecy of what our Lord has done for his laborers. Golden streets, pearly gates, jasper walls, and trees bearing twelve manners of fruit with leaves which are good for the healing of the nations are symbols and metaphors used by the Seer of Patmos (John) to say that the best is yet to come.

New Testament evangelism is inseparable from New Testament eschatology. Evangelism stipulates the imperative (go make disciples). Eschatology supplies the incentive (I will give thee a crown of life). The New Testament church bore the "bitter now and now" by beholding the "sweet by and by." They did not stagger at the promise: "In my Father's house are many mansions. If it were not so I would have told you. I go to prepare a place for you" (John 14:2). They felt intensely the inscrutable desirable destiny for the Christian pilgrim that Paul expresses: "Eye hath not seen, nor ear heard, neither have entered into the heart of man, the things which God hath prepared for them that love him" (I Cor. 2:9).

GOD AT WORK IN TIMES OF PERSECUTION (ACTS 7:54-8:8)
Billy Kim

Rev. Kim, Suwon,
Korea, is the Director of Far East Broadcasting
Company in Korea and National
Director of Youth for Christ, Korea.

Most of us have witnessed God at work in normal circumstances in a given country. Some have experienced adverse situations and even severe persecution. In these portions of Scripture we will try to analyze how God worked in the early church in times of persecution, and also how God is working in this modern day in times of stress and persecution of the Christian church.

Persecution is a storm that is permitted to scatter the seed of the Word, dispurse the sower and reaper over many fields. It is God's way of extending his kingdom; bringing good out of evil and making the wrath of men to praise him. "All things work together for good. . . ." "There is that scattereth and yet increaseth," we are told. So it was when the Huguenots were driven from France, the Protestants from Spain, the Puritans from England, and the North Koreans to South Korea.

Persecution brings about growth. Through persecution Daniel, Shadrach, Meshach, and Abednego were able to bring a heathen and adulterous nation to recognize the fact that there is one true God. Because of persecution upon Elijah's ministry, the people of Israel realized who their true and living God was.

As we study the book of Acts, these facts stand out:
first impressions produced in Jerusalem
first pentecostal message
first opposition
first true communism
first discipline
first persecution
first church organization
first Christian martyr

Usually we are fearful when we hear of great persecution of a church or a group of Christians. But the church's greatest danger has never been created by persecution or opposition. When she has been opposed and persecuted she has been made pure and strong. Wherever the church is patronized and admired by the world she becomes weak. How shall we safeguard against this? We must obey God. If the church is obeying God she can never be weakened by patronage, and she can never be paralyzed by compromise. She must forevermore stand alone bearing her testimony, opening her portals to receive the wounded in order that they may be healed. A great church stands ready to take the wanderers back again, and lead them to health and blessedness; never permitting the standard of her ideals to be lowered or her message of righteousness to be silenced.

Persecution of Christians and the church has been one of the greatest factors in the propagation and evangelization of the Gospel of our Lord Jesus Christ.

As we read the book of Acts we find that the persecution of Stephen was so intense that they literally gnashed him with their teeth. The reasons for persecuting him were probably many, but these three seem to be very evident: (1) they claimed that since the Apostles were untrained they were causing confusion by performing miracles; (2) the Sadducees particularly objected to the fact that they were proclaiming the resurrection; (3) all of this was associated with Jesus for it represented a real blow to their authority.

During the conflict with the Koreans, Communist soldiers moved into a peaceful farm village of South Korea. Some time before this, a faithful missionary brought the Gospel to this village. Those who were converted soon were witnessing to friends. It wasn't long until most of the folks in this village had turned to Jesus Christ in simple faith. One day the Communist soldiers made all of the people of this particular village gather at the village church. They told them that they were to renounce their faith in Christ or face certain death. The soldiers jerked a picture of Christ off the wall and ordered each person to come down in front and spit upon the picture of Christ. The first man to walk down the aisle was a deacon. He looked at the picture for a few seconds, then quickly spat, and walked to one side. The man who followed him did the same thing. The third and fourth men imitated the first two men's actions. The fifth person to walk forward was a young teen-age girl. She looked at the picture of Christ and then bent down and wiped the spit off with her skirt. She hugged the picture of Christ to her heart and said, "Shoot me, I am ready to die." The soldier couldn't shoot. He ordered everyone to get out. Shortly afterwards four shots were fired. The people overheard the Communist soldiers say, "You are not fit to live. If you had a chance to renounce Communism, you would do the same thing." Because of the strong faith of one young girl, the rest of the village was saved. "Whoever shall save his life shall lose it . . ." When severe persecution comes, people are gnashed at with teeth, cried out at, they who are doing the persecuting stop their ears and refuse to listen to reason. All sense of direction is gone and men act inhumanly.

In verse four we find that the Christians were scattered abroad. At the time of Stephen's death there was a crisis in the history of the church. Now Jerusalem ceases to be the center of interest. It almost fades from the pages of history until recent years. Because of persecution, the church now moves out upon the pathway of her victorious business, independent of Jerusalem. This is the supreme revelation of the book of Acts. Whenever the church is governed from Jerusalem or Rome, or any place other than Heaven, it is hindered and hampered and prevented from fulfilling the Great Commission.

Recently a Christian historian told me that in 1945 North Korea had approximately eighteen per cent of her population Christian, and South Korea only claimed three per cent to be Christian. Five years later, when the Korean War broke out several million people evacuated from the North to the South as refugees. Many of these were Christians who could not survive under Communism and were forced to move to the South. They brought with them their vigorous Christian faith and caused the church in the South to grow and spread like wildfire. Persecution during adverse circumstances caused the evangelization of South Korea. Those who came from the North went everywhere preaching the Word and establishing a place of worship and witness. Today in South Korea, the church growth is four times faster than the population growth.

One of my dear pastor friends was forced to leave his parents and two children in North Korea. He came south with his wife and two babies. He has personally won thousands of souls to Christ. God works mightily during times of persecution.

Great joy was in the city, we are told in Acts, chapter eight, verse eight. Through tremendous persecution and hardship and suffering and even the bitter experience of losing all their earthly goods, yet there was great joy!

Korea, and particularly the Christians, have suffered much persecution. Still, in God's infinite grace, Christianity has made a greater impact upon our national life than in any other country in Asia. Severe persecution came to Korea when she was occupied for a number of years by a neighboring country. Many of the churches were closed and missionaries told to leave. Christians were jailed and some gave their lives for their faith. A small Methodist church, located thirteen miles from my home in the village of Jae-am, was opened up without explanation one Sunday morning. The Christians came joyfully to the church. Then the doors were locked from the outside, gasoline was poured around the church and it was set on fire. A squad of police surrounded the building, ready to shoot any who might try to escape through a window. Twenty-nine people died inside the burning church. They died singing the hymn that Korean Christians still love to sing,

"Nearer my God to thee, nearer to thee
E'en though it be a cross
Nearer to thee."

After the second World War, a group of Christians erected a monument and engraved the names of those twenty-nine people who gave their lives for Christ in the church that Sunday. A few years ago, a group of pastors came from the country that had occupied Korea. They visited this village and saw the monument and heard the story behind it. They returned to their home country and raised $25,000. They used this money to erect a church in the place where the old one had burned down. On September 27, 1970, at 3:00 p.m. the beautiful church was dedicated. It was my privilege to attend this dedication service. The church was packed out. The group of pastors who had raised the money were there too. As we sang the final hymn, automatically men got up from their seats and embraced one another. They were proving that the past had been forgiven and forgotten. Only Jesus Christ could reunite two enemy peoples like this. Since then many of the people in that village and the surrounding area have turned to Christ in faith. Do not be discouraged. Let us go on. We are more than conquerors through Christ. Amen.

GOD AT WORK IN TIMES OF DRAMATIC CHURCH GROWTH
Isabelo F. Magalit

Dr. Magalit, Manila,
Philippines, is the Associate General
Secretary of the International Fellow-
ship of Evangelical Students in East Asia.

We have heard in this Congress how the church is growing in certain parts of the world — in Korea and Indonesia for instance, and in Brazil and Kenya. We rejoice over what God is doing and the 'rest of us have much to learn from our brothers and sisters whose churches are growing so quickly.

The most dramatic example of rapid church growth, however, is found in the New Testament. Luke tells us in Acts, chapter two, that the body of believers grew from 120 to 3,120 in one day. That's twenty-six times, or 2,600 per cent, and the figure does not even include those who were won day by day thereafter.

What is the explanation for this remarkable growth? The Holy Spirit coming in great power upon God's people on the day of Pentecost. The "greater works" which the Lord Jesus had promised his followers in John 14 (verse 12) have now been fulfilled. (Incidentally, that promise is for us also.) God himself had set the stage for this great event. Only weeks before, the earthly ministry of Jesus had ended in Jerusalem amid great excitement and he was now the talk of the town. He had not only been tried and crucified but his followers now claimed that he had come back from the dead and had made several personal appearances to them. His tomb was empty! And now, on the day of Pentecost, while Jews from all over the known world gathered in Jerusalem for a religious festival, the Holy Spirit came in power upon his people!

It is God who is at work in times of dramatic church growth. It is God who is at work. Look at the last phrase in our passage, verse 47: "And the Lord added to their number day by day those who were being saved."

Now, numerical growth is not always a measure of true spiritual effectiveness. For instance, I am told that one reason some Indonesians have flocked to the Christian church is the risk of being presumed a Communist if one were neither a Muslim nor a Christian. Again, we are all familiar with the phenomenon we may call "many decisions but few disciples." By lowering the demands of the Gospel we can persuade many more adherents but only end up with a form of nominal Christianity. Then again, in the Philippines we have a fast-growing unitarian sect that is noted for its aggressive and indoctrinating methods. We would hardly ascribe its growth to God at work!

My professor in statistics used to warn us: there are three kinds of liars — simple liars, wicked liars, and then statisticians! Statistics do not always lie, of course. It all depends on the statistician. Who is the statistician? Who is doing the adding?

"And the Lord added to their number day by day those who were being saved." There is numerical growth which comes because God is at work.

It takes place when the Lord Jesus adds to his church. He saves them first, and then he adds them to his church. Don't miss his double work: he does not add them to his church without saving them first, but neither does he save them without adding them to his church. In both instances, it is the Lord who is at work.

He did this work daily. Every day, the Lord saved people and every day he added them to his church. Church growth in this book of Acts was not an occasional, sporadic, specially organized campaign. It was normal, natural, continuous, and compelling!

And it takes place when the Holy Spirit comes in power upon the people of God. But what does it mean for the Holy Spirit to be present among his people in power? Our passage tells us two things. First there is Spirit-filled preaching, and second there is Spirit-filled community.

Spirit-filled preaching

Let me just list four characteristics of Peter's Spirit-filled preaching. First, Peter's sermon was arresting. He caught the attention of his audience. Second, Peter builds upon the interest and understanding of his listeners. He was aware that he was speaking to Jews. Third, Peter centered his preaching on Christ. The crucified Jesus is now both Lord and Christ, in fulfillment of prophecy. Fourth, Peter clearly set forth the need for decisive response. His hearers must repent and be baptized.

Spirit-filled community

There are also four things that characterized the Spirit-filled community.

Notice first that they were not a loose association with easy membership. They were the company of the committed. Only those who believed the Good News and repented of their sins as signified by being baptized were admitted.

Second, notice the things that preoccupied them: first — apostolic teaching, second — life sharing, and third — common worship.

Teaching by the apostles was not an occasional special event but something they devoted themselves to. When numerical growth does not produce "Bible addicts" it is wise to ask if the Holy Spirit is present in power. Apostolic teaching is a pre-occupation of every Spirit-filled church.

Look also at the quality of their fellowship and life sharing. Goods were communal and people received according to their need. While the particular pattern did not persist, surely the principle is abiding, namely, that all my goods, all my money, my time, my energy, my gifts, are not mine. They belong to God and to the people of God.

Look at the combination of joy and reverence in their worship as they gathered for prayer and the Lord's table. Reverence and joy together can only be produced by the presence of the Holy Spirit in power.

Third, notice the other supernatural evidences of God's presence among them: signs and wonders. I believe that miracles are given by

God primarily to authenticate his messengers (see verse 22). Therefore God's presence among his people is shown not only by spectacular
phenomena but also by the unmistakable change in our character as the
Holy Spirit produces love, joy, peace, and the rest of his fruit.

Fourth, and finally, notice their reputation with outsiders. They
had favor with all the people. There was no question of confusing the
church and the world: the church was so distinctive. And yet, we are
sure that because the church was so distinctive in its common life, in its
worship, and in its witness, it was attractive to outsiders. "And day by
day the Lord added to their number those who were being saved."

God grant that we in our churches and Christian fellowships may
become like them. Then the earth will hear his voice.

Section III:
Plenary Papers and Responses

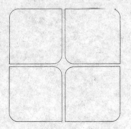

THE BIBLICAL BASIS OF EVANGELISM
John R. W. Stott

Dr. Stott, London, England,
is on the staff of All Souls Church,
Langham Place, and is President of the
Evangelical Alliance.

Introduction

It may seem crazy, in a cross-cultural Congress like this, that I should begin by quoting from those two peculiarly English characters of fiction, Alice in Wonderland and Humpty Dumpty! For it is more than possible that some of you have never heard of them. Never mind: I still think you will appreciate this part of their conversation.

"When *I* use a word," Humpty Dumpty said in a rather scornful tone, "it means just what I choose it to mean, neither more nor less."

"The question is," said Alice," whether you *can* make words mean different things."

"The question is," said Humpty Dumpty, "which is to be master — that's all."

The issue between Alice and Humpty Dumpty — whether man can manipulate the meaning of words or whether words have an autonomy which cannot be infringed — is still a contemporary issue. The modern church sometimes seems like a kind of theological wonderland in which numerous Humpty Dumptys enjoy playing with words and making them mean what they want them to mean.

The task assigned to me is to take a cluster of related words in the forefront of recent debate — mission, evangelism, dialogue, salvation and conversion — and attempt to define them biblically.

Please do not misunderstand my purpose. I do not propose to put up a few ecumenical skittles in order to knock them down with well-aimed evangelical balls, so that we can all applaud our easy victory! We all know that during the last few years, especially between Uppsala and Bangkok, ecumenical-evangelical relations hardened into something like a confrontation. I have no wish to worsen this situation. Mind you, I believe some ecumenical thinking is mistaken. But then, frankly, I believe some of our evangelical formulations are mistaken also. Many ecumenical Christians seem hardly to have begun to learn to live under the authority of Scripture. We evangelicals think we have — and there is no doubt we sincerely want to — but at times we are very selective in our submission, and the traditions of the evangelical elders sometimes owe more to culture than to Scripture.

So I hope in my paper to strike a note of evangelical repentance, and indeed I hope we shall continue to hear this note throughout the Congress. Both our profession and our performance are far from perfect. We have some important lessons to learn from our ecumenical critics. Some of their rejection of our position is not a repudiation of biblical truth, but rather of our evangelical caricatures of it.

Since I have been invited to speak on "the nature of biblical evangelism" I shall try to define it according to Scripture and so bring both ecumenical and evangelical thinking to the same independent and objective test. If both sides are willing for this, then neither of us need copy Humpty Dumpty and twist words to suit our own pleasure.

1. *Mission*

The first word is "mission," for it is here that we have to begin.

In the past — at least until the IMC conference at Willingen in 1952 — it was taken for granted that mission and evangelism, missions and evangelistic programs, missionaries and evangelists were more or less synonymous. "The place of missions in the life of the church," said Archbishop Randall Davidson on the first night of Edinburgh 1910, "must be the central place, and none other." I do not think he was using the word "missions" in any special or technical sense, any more than when the Division of World Mission and Evangelism was brought into being the expressions "world mission" and "evangelism" were neatly distinguished from one another.

Recently, however, the word "mission" has come to be used in a wider and more general sense, to include evangelism but not to be identical with it, and I see no reason why we should resist this development. "Mission" is an activity of God arising out of the very nature of God. The living God of the Bible is a sending God, which is what "mission" means. He sent the prophets to Israel. He sent his Son into the world. His Son sent out the apostles, and the seventy, and the church. He also sent the Spirit to the church and sends him into our hearts today.

So the mission of the church arises from the mission of God and is to be modeled on it. "As the Father has sent me," Jesus said, "even so I send you" (John 20:21 cf. 17:18). If, then, we are to understand the nature of the church's mission, we have to understand the nature of the Son's! Not, of course, that his church can copy him in all things, for he came to die for the sins of the world. Nevertheless, in at least two major respects, he sends us as he was himself sent.

First, he sends us *into the world*. For he was sent into the world and enter the world he did. He did not touch down like a visitor from outer space, or arrive like an alien bringing his own alien culture with him. No. He took to himself our humanity, our flesh and blood. He actually became one of us and experienced our frailty, our suffering, our temptations. He even bore our sin and died our death.

And now he sends us "into the world," to identify with others as he identified with us, to become vulnerable as he did. It is surely one of our most characteristic evangelical failures that we have seldom taken seriously this principle of the Incarnation. "As our Lord took on our flesh," runs the report from Mexico City 1963, "so he calls his church to take on the secular world. This is easy to say and sacrificial to do." But it comes more natural to us to shout the Gospel at people from a distance than to involve ourselves deeply in their lives, to think ourselves into their problems, and to feel with them in their pains.

Secondly, Christ sends us into the world to *serve*. For he came to serve. Not just to seek and to save, nor just to preach, but more generally to serve. He said so. His contemporaries were familiar with Daniel's picture of the Son of man receiving dominion and being served by all

(7:14). But Jesus knew he had to serve before he would be served, and to endure suffering before he could receive dominion. So he fused two apparently incompatible Old Testament images, Daniel's Son of man and Isaiah's suffering servant, and said, "The Son of man....came not to be served but to serve, and to give his life a ransom for many" (Mark 10:45). What is unique is that he came to "give his life," to die. But this supreme atoning sacrifice was the climax of a life of service. In his public ministry he proclaimed the Kingdom of God and taught its implications, he fed hungry mouths and washed dirty feet, he healed the sick, comforted the sad, and raised the dead. He gave himself in selfless service for others.

Now he tells us that as the Father sent him into the world, so he sends us. Our mission, like his, is to be one of service. He emptied himself of status and took the form of a servant (Phil. 2:7). So must we. He supplies us with the perfect model of service and sends his church into the world to be a servant church. Is it not important for us to recover this biblical emphasis? In many of our attitudes and enterprises, we (especially those of us who come from Europe and North America) have tended to be more bosses than servants. Yet is it not in a servant role that we can find the right synthesis of evangelism and social action? For both should be authentic expressions of the service we are sent into the world to give. How then, someone may ask, are we to reconcile this concept of mission as service with the Great Commission of the risen Lord? Often, perhaps because it is the last instruction Jesus gave before returning to the Father, I venture to say that we give it too prominent a place in our Christian thinking. I beg you not to misunderstand me. I believe the whole Church is under obligation to obey its Lord's commission to take the Gospel to all nations. But I am also concerned that we should not regard it as the only instruction Jesus left us. He also quoted Lev. 19:18, "You shall love your neighbor as yourself," called it "the second and great commandment" (second in importance only to the supreme command to love God with all our being), and elaborated it in the Sermon on the Mount. He insisted that in God's vocabulary our neighbor includes our enemy, and that to love is to "do good," to give ourselves to serve his welfare.

Here then are two instructions, "love your neighbor" and "go and make disciples." What is the relation between the two? Some of us behave as if we thought them identical, so that if we have shared the Gospel with somebody, we consider we have completed our responsibility to love him. But no. The Great Commission neither explains, nor exhausts, nor supersedes the Great Commandment. What it does is to add to the command of neighbor-love and neighbor-service a new and urgent Christian dimension. If we truly love our neighbor we shall without doubt tell him the Good News of Jesus. But equally if we truly love our neighbor we shall not stop there.

So we are sent into the world, like Jesus, to serve. For this will be the natural expression of our love for our neighbor. We love. We go. We serve. And in this we have (or should have) no ulterior motive. True, the Gospel lacks credibility if we who preach it are interested only in souls, and have no concern about the welfare of people's bodies, situations, and community. Yet the reason for an acceptance of social responsibility is not in order to give the Gospel a credibility it would otherwise lack, but simple uncomplicated compassion. Love does not need to justify itself. It just expresses itself in service wherever it sees need.

"Mission," then, is not a word for everything the church does (including, for example, worship). "The church is mission" sounds fine, but it's an overstatement. Nor does "mission" cover everything God does in the world. For God is the Creator and is constantly active in the world in providence and in common grace, quite apart from the purposes for which he sent his Son, his Spirit, his apostles, and his church into the world. "Mission" rather describes everything the church is sent into the world to do. "Mission" embraces the church's double vocation to be "the salt of the earth" and "the light of the world." For Christ *sends* the church into the earth to be its salt, and *sends* the church into the world to be its light.

There are important lessons for us evangelicals to learn from those two controversial ecumenical reports on the missionary structure of the congregation published in 1968 under the title *The Church for Others*. A good deal in it we would not be able to accept, but much is stimulating and challenging. In particular, relating to our present theme of "mission," there is the call to the church to live "ex-centredly," to find its center not in itself but outside itself, "to turn itself outwards to the world" and to be truly a "church for others." Such an inside-out revolution would lead to a radical change in our church structures. The book is right to brand many of them "heretical structures" because they deny the Gospel and impede the mission of God. Too often we are "waiting churches" into which the people are expected to come. We must replace our "come-structures" by "go-structures" (pages 17-19). All this is implicit in "mission."

2. *Evangelism*

Evangelism is an essential part of the church's mission. What is it?

Euangelizomai is to bring or to announce the *euangelion*, the good news. Once or twice in the New Testament it is used of secular news items, as when Timothy brought Paul the good news of the Thessalonians' faith and love (I Thess. 3:6) and when the angel Gabriel told Zechariah the good news that his wife Elizabeth was to have a son (Luke 1:19). But the regular use of the verb relates to the Christian Good News. It is the spread of this which constitutes evangelism. This fact has important consequences.

First, evangelism must not be defined in terms of its *results*, for this is not how the word is used in the New Testament. Normally the verb is in the middle voice. Occasionally it is used absolutely, for example "there they evangelized," meaning "there they preached the Gospel" (Acts 14:7, cf. Rom. 15:20). Usually, however, something is added: either the message preached (e.g., they "went about evangelizing the word," Acts 8:4), or the people to whom or places in which the Gospel is preached (e.g., the apostles "evangelized many villages of the Samaritans" and Philip "evangelized all the towns" along the coast, Acts 8:25, 40). There is no mention whether the word which was "evangelized" was believed, or whether the inhabitants of the towns and villages "evangelized" were converted. To "evangelize" in biblical usage does not mean to win converts (as it usually does when we use the word) but simply to announce the good news, irrespective of the results.

You may recall that the famous watchword of the Student Volunteer Movement, "the evangelization of the world in this generation," was criticized for this reason. Professor Gustav Warneck attacked it at the ninth Continental Missions Conference at Bremen in May, 1897, on the ground that it was a naively optimistic and rather man-confident forecast that the world would be won for Christ in that generation. But John Mott rallied to the watchword's defense. He maintained that "the evangelization of the world" meant neither its conversion nor its Christianization, that it did not encourage superficial preaching, and that it was not to be regarded as a prophecy. As William Richey Hogg writes, the watchword was "a call to obligation, not a prophecy of fact!"

In a somewhat similar way J. I. Packer in his *Evangelism and the Sovereignty of God* has justly criticized the famous definition of evangelism first formulated in England in 1919 by the Archbishops' "Committee of Enquiry into the Evangelistic Work of the Church." It begins: "To evangelize is so to present Christ Jesus in the power of the Holy Spirit that men shall come to put their trust in God through him. . . ." Dr. Packer draws attention to the form of the sentence "*so* to present Christ Jesus . . . that men *shall* . . ." This is to define evangelism in terms of success. But to evangelize is not *so* to preach that something happens. Of course the objective is that something will happen, namely that people will respond and believe. Nevertheless, biblically speaking, to evangelize is to proclaim the Gospel, whether anything happens or not.

Second, evangelism must not be defined in terms of *methods*. To evangelize is to announce the good news, however the announcement is made, or to bring good news, by whatever means it is brought. We can evangelize by word of mouth (whether to individuals, groups, or crowds); by print, picture, and screen; by drama (whether what is dramatized is fact or fiction); by good works of love; by a Christ-centered home; by a transformed life; and even by a speechless excitement about Jesus.

Third, evangelism may and must be defined only in terms of the *message*. Therefore biblical evangelism makes the biblical evangel indispensable. Nothing hinders evangelism today more than the widespread loss of confidence in the truth, relevance, and power of the Gospel. When this ceases to be good news from God and becomes instead "rumors of God," we can hardly expect the church to exhibit much evangelistic enthusiasm!

If we agree that the Gospel is God's good news and that, despite all the rich diversity of its formulation in the New Testament, this was only one basic apostolic tradition of the Gospel (as Paul claims, I Cor. 15:11), we should be able to reconstruct it. Indeed, many have done so. All concur that, in a single word, God's good news is Jesus. He is the heart and soul of the Gospel. Thus, what Philip told the Ethiopian was simply "the good news of Jesus" (Acts 8:35), and Paul began his great manifesto of the Gospel — his letter to the Romans — by describing himself as "set apart for the Gospel of God . . . concerning his Son . . . Jesus Christ our Lord" (Rom. 1:1-4).

But how did the apostles present Jesus? If we compare the early sermons recorded in the Acts with each other and with Paul's statement of the Gospel at the beginning of I Corinthians 15, it becomes clear that the good news contained at least the following four elements.

First, there were *the gospel events,* primarily the death and resurrection of Jesus. Sometimes the apostles began with a reference to the life and ministry of the man Jesus, and usually they went on to his enthronement as Lord and his return as Judge. But their message focused on his death and resurrection. Nor did they proclaim these (as some say) as non-theological history, just "you killed him, but God raised him." Already they had a doctrine of both. His death was "according to the definite plan and foreknowledge of God" (Acts 2:23), and the Cross on which it took place they deliberately called a "tree" to indicate the divine curse under which he died (Acts 5:30, 10:39, 13:29; Deut. 21:22, 23; Gal. 3:10, 13; I Pet. 2:24), while the resurrection was a divine vindication, snatching him from the place of a curse to the place of honor and authority at God's right hand (e.g., Acts 2:32, 33).

Second, there were *the gospel witnesses.* That is, the apostles proclaimed the death and resurrection of Jesus both "according to the Scriptures" (Acts 2:25ff, 3:18, 24; cf. I Cor. 15:3, 4) and according to the evidence of their own eyes. "We are witnesses of these things," they kept saying (e.g., Acts 2:32, 5:32). So we today have no liberty to preach Christ crucified and risen according to our own fancy or even according to our own experience. The only Christ there is to preach is the biblical Christ, the objective historical Jesus attested by the joint witness of the prophets of the Old Testament and the apostles of the New (cf. Acts 10:39-43). Our witness is always secondary to theirs.

Third, there were *the gospel promises.* The apostles did not proclaim the death and resurrection of Jesus merely as events, even when enriched by doctrinal significance and biblical witness. For the good news concerns not just the historic but the contemporary Christ, not just what he once did but what he now offers on the basis of what he did. What is this? In Peter's Pentecost address, the very first Christian sermon ever preached, he was able to promise them with complete assurance that they could receive both "the forgiveness of sins" and "the gift of the Holy Spirit" (Acts 2:38). Salvation is more than this, but it is certainly not less. It includes the remission of past guilt and the gift of an entirely new life through the regenerating and indwelling Holy Spirit.

Fourth, there were *the gospel demands,* namely repentance and faith. "Repent," Peter said (Acts 2:38, 3:19), but also declared that "everyone who believes in him (Jesus) receives forgiveness of sins through his name" (Acts 10:43 cf. 13:38, 39). In addition he commanded, "Be baptized every one of you in the name of Jesus Christ." The apostles certainly never held a mechanical view of baptism, for they always set it in its context of repentance and faith. On the day of Pentecost those Jews were being required to submit to baptism in the name of the very Jesus whom they had previously repudiated and killed. Whatever else baptism may signify, it certainly was and is a public token of repentance and faith in Jesus.

It is true, of course, that salvation is by grace alone through faith alone, and we must be careful never to define faith in such a way as to ascribe to it any merit. The whole value of faith lies in its object (Jesus Christ), not in itself. Nevertheless, faith is a total, penitent, and submissive commitment to Christ, and it would have been inconceivable to the apostles that anybody could believe in Jesus as Savior without submitting to him as Lord. We cannot chop Jesus Christ up into bits and then respond to only one of the bits. The object of saving faith is the whole and undivided person of our Lord and Savior, Jesus Christ.

Evangelism, then, is sharing this Gospel with others. The good news is Jesus, and the good news about Jesus which we announce is that he died for our sins and was raised from death by the Father, according to the Scriptures of the Old and New Testaments, and that on the basis of his death and resurrection he offers forgiveness of sins and the gift of the Spirit to all those who repent, believe, and are baptized.

3. *Dialogue*

The next question about evangelism brings us to our third word. Is there any room in the proclamation of the good news for "dialogue"? It is well known that during the past decade or two the concept of "dialogue with men of other faiths" has become the ecumenical fashion, and that we evangelicals have tended to react rather sharply against it. Is our negative reaction justified?

We could begin our answer by realizing that the word "dialogue" is derived from the Greek verb *dialegomai*, to "discuss" or "argue," which Luke used some nine times in the Acts to describe Paul's preaching, e.g., "For three weeks he argued with them from the Scriptures, explaining and proving that it was necessary for the Christ to suffer and to rise from the dead . . ." (Acts 17:2, 3, 17, 18:4, 19, 19:8, 9, 20:7, 9, 24:25). This at least shows that Paul was not afraid in his evangelistic preaching to use the massive reasoning powers which God had given him. He did not only "proclaim," Luke says; he also "reasoned," "persuaded," and "proved." At the same time, this is not the sort of dialogue which people envisage today, for Paul's dialogue was part of his Christ-centered proclamation.

James A. Scherer, in his contribution to *Protestant Crosscurrents in Mission* (1968), traces the popularity of dialogue back to the 1928 IMC conference at Jerusalem. "Jerusalem had seen a momentary flirtation with religious sophistry," he writes, but ten years later at the Tambaram conference "Christ became once again the Word made flesh in whom God had acted for men's salvation." One of the most influential figures at Tambaram was Hendrik Kraemer. He called the church to repossess its faith "in all its uniqueness and adequacy and power," and added, "We are bold enough to call men out from them (sc., other religions) to the feet of Christ. We do so because we believe that in him alone is the full salvation which man needs."

It is precisely this emphasis on the uniqueness and finality of Christ which tends to be muted by those who are calling the church to dialogue. Evangelism gives way to syncretism, and the proclamation of the truth is replaced by a common search for truth. The most extreme ecumenical statement I have read comes from the pen of Professor J. G. Davies, who insists on openness as a prerequisite of the dialogue. "Complete openness means that every time we enter into dialogue our faith is at stake. If I engage in dialogue with a Buddhist and do so with openness I must recognize that the outcome cannot be predetermined either for him or for me. The Buddhist may come to accept Jesus as Lord, but I may come to accept the authority of the Buddha, or even both of us may end up as agnostics. Unless these are *real* possibilities, neither of us is being fully open to the other. . . .To live dialogically is to live dangerously."

No evangelical Christian could accept this kind of uncommitted openness. On the contrary, if we enter into dialogue with a non-Christian, whether a person of some other faith or of no faith, we enter it as committed men, men unashamedly committed to Christ. The paragraph on dialogue in the Uppsala report expressed this point well, "A Christian's dialogue with another implies neither a denial of the uniqueness of Christ, nor any loss of his own commitment to Christ."

Why, then, should Christians engage in dialogue with non-Christians? Here are some words from the report of the CWME conference in Mexico City in 1963, "True dialogue with a man of another faith requires a concern both for the Gospel and for the other man. Without the first, dialogue becomes a pleasant conversation. Without the second, it becomes irrelevant, unconvincing or arrogant." Or, as Uppsala put it, "A genuinely Christian approach to others must be human, personal, relevant and humble." It is these qualities which, I fear, are sometimes missing in our evangelical evangelism. We often give the impression of being glib and brash, and our critics accuse us of a wide variety of horrid attitudes like "paternalism," "imperialism," and "triumphalism."

If dialogue is a serious conversation in which we are prepared to listen as well as speak, is it not an indispensable aspect of true evangelism? Although the Gospel is invariable in its substance, the way we approach people and explain things to them is bound to vary, unless we are totally lacking in sensitivity. Dialogue, writes Canon Max Warren, "is in its very essence an attempt at mutual listening, listening in order to understand. Understanding is its reward."

So dialogue becomes a token of Christian humility and love, because it indicates our resolve to rid our minds of the prejudices and caricatures we may entertain about the other man; to struggle to listen through his ears and see through his eyes so as to grasp what prevents him from hearing the Gospel and seeing Christ; to sympathize with him in all his doubts and fears and "hang-ups." No one has expressed this better than Archbishop Michael Ramsey who tells us that we are to "go out and put ourselves with loving sympathy inside the doubts of the doubting, the questions of the questioners, and the loneliness of those who have lost their way." It is once more the challenge of the Incarnation, to renounce evangelism by inflexible slogans and instead to involve ourselves in the real dilemmas of other men.

4. Salvation

Having talked about "mission" and "evangelism," it is natural to take the word "salvation" next. For the Gospel is "the power of God for salvation to every one who has faith" and it is through the *kerygma* that God chooses "to save those who believe" (Rom. 1:16; I Cor. 1:21).

But many people are embarrassed by salvation terminology, while others reject it as a meaningless inheritance from the traditional religion of the past. So there are not wanting those who are seeking to translate the word "salvation" into a more modern idiom. This is fine and necessary, provided that they remain loyal to the biblical revelation. For a translation is one thing (the old message in new words); a fresh composition is something quite different.

First, some say that "salvation" means psycho-physical health or "wholeness." They point out that Jesus said to the woman with the issue of blood, to blind Bartimaeus, and to a leprosy sufferer, "Your faith has saved you," which in each case the Authorized Version renders "your faith has made you whole" (Mark 5:34, 10:52; Luke 17:19), while we are also told that as many as touched Christ's garment "were made well," which in the Greek is *esozonto* "were saved" (Mark 6:56). But Jesus spoke to the fallen woman the same words, "Your faith has saved you" (Luke 7:48-50), and "salvation" words are also used of deliverance from drowning and from death (e.g., Matt. 8:25; Mark 15:30, 31). Are we then to argue from these uses of the verb "to save" that the salvation Christ offers is a composite rescue from physical ills of every kind, including disease, drowning, and death? It would be impossible to reconstruct the biblical doctrine of salvation in these terms. Salvation by faith in Christ crucified and risen is moral not material, a deliverance from *sin*, not from *harm*, and the reason Jesus said "your faith has saved you" to both categories is that his works of physical rescue (from disease, drowning, and death) were intentional "signs" of his salvation, and were understood by the early Church to be such.

In saying this I do not deny that disease and death are alien intrusions into God's good world; nor that God heals both through natural means and sometimes supernaturally, for all healing is divine healing; nor that our new life in Christ can bring a new physical and emotional well-being as psychosomatic conditions due to stress, resentment, and anxiety are cured; nor that at the consummation when we are given new bodies and enter a new society we shall be rid of disease and death forever. What I am saying is that the salvation offered in and through Jesus Christ today is not a complete psycho-physical wholeness; to maintain that it is to anticipate the Resurrection.

Second, others are saying that "salvation" means, or at least includes, socio-political liberation. It is not now health, but justice for the community.

The Mexico City Conference in 1963 had asked, "What is the form and content of the salvation which Christ offers men in the secular world?" but left their question unanswered.

At Uppsala in 1968, "the goal of mission" was defined in terms of "humanization." The influence of the report *The Church For Others* was strong. It had affirmed that "wherever men and women are led to restored relationships in love of neighbor, in service and suffering for the sake of greater justice and freedom," these things must be recognized as "signs of the fullness of humanity" which Christ is providing. After Uppsala at the ecumenical "Consultation on Development" at Montreux (1970) it was said that "God's salvation of mankind in Christ encompasses the development of all of man's faith, institutions and structures. . . . True development is the battle for the wholeness of man both individual and corporate." The reference to man's "wholeness" is again significant, although it was conceived now more in social than in physical terms. It was taken up again at Bangkok. Here there was certainly the recognition that "salvation is Jesus Christ's liberation of individuals from sin and all its consequences," but the Assembly concentrated on a different kind of liberation, "The salvation which Christ brought, and in which we participate, offers a comprehensive wholeness in this divided life . . . God's liberating power changes both persons and structures . . . Therefore we see the struggles for economic justice, political freedom and cultural renewal as elements in the total liberation of the world through the mission of God."

Humanization, development, wholeness, liberation, justice: let me say at once that all these are not only desirable goals, but that Christians should be actively involved in pursuing them, and that we evangelicals have often been guilty of opting out of such social and political responsibilities. We are to blame for this neglect. We should repent of it and not be afraid to challenge ourselves and each other that God may be calling many more of us than hear his call to immerse ourselves in the secular world of politics, economics, sociology, race relations, preventive medicine, development, and a host of other such spheres for Christ.

But these things do not constitute the "salvation" which God is offering the world in and through Christ. They could be included in "the mission of God," insofar as Christians are giving themselves to serve in these fields. But to call socio-political liberation "salvation" is to be guilty of a gross theological confusion. It is to mix what Scripture keeps distinct — God the Creator and God the Redeemer, justice and justification, common grace and saving grace, the reformation of society and the regeneration of man. It is significant that the main biblical argument with which Bangkok tried to buttress its position was the liberation of Israel from the oppression of Egypt, which is not only an embarrassing topic for residents in the Middle East, but a misuse of Scripture. The Exodus was the redemption of God's covenant people. It is used in Scripture as a foreshadowing of redemption from sin through Christ. It offers no conceivable justification or pattern of national liberation movements today.

Third, if biblical "salvation" is neither psycho-physical wholeness nor socio-political liberation, it is a personal freedom from sin and its consequences, which brings many wholesome consequences in terms both of health and of social responsibility (as we have seen). In many ways "liberation" (personal, not economic or political) is a good modern word for "salvation" because it not only alludes to the rescue we sinners need but also hints at the "liberty" into which the liberated are brought.

Freedom is as popular a word today as salvation is unpopular. But unfortunately too many people think and talk of freedom in purely negative terms. One of the Christian's best contributions to the debate about freedom is to insist that we think of it *positively,* in terms not only of what we are set free *from* but of what we are set free *for.* This is what Scriptures does, as I would like now to demonstrate while touching briefly on the familiar three phases or "tenses" of salvation.

First, we have been saved from the wrath of God, from his just judgment upon our sins. It is not merely that we had guilt feelings and a guilty conscience, and found relief from these in Christ. It is that we were actually objectively guilty before God, and that Christ bore our guilt and was condemned in our place in order that we might be justified. The argument of Romans 1 to 8 is so familiar to us that I do not need to elaborate it. The point I emphasize is that salvation does not stop with justification and must not therefore be equated with it. For with justification comes adoption. We were "slaves" under the curse of the law, but now we are "sons," enjoying free and happy access to our heavenly Father. And the Holy Spirit constantly witnesses with our Spirit that we are indeed his children (Rom. 8:14-17; Gal. 4:4-7). Now we are to live as free men.

Second, we are being saved. Salvation in the New Testament is as much a present process as a gift or possession received in the past. If you ask me if I am saved, and if I think biblically before I answer, I could just as well reply "no" as "yes." I have been saved by the grace of God, yes, from his wrath, from my guilt and condemnation. But no, I am not yet saved, for sin still dwells within me and my body is not yet redeemed. It is the common tension in the New Testament between the "now" and the "not yet." Nevertheless, during this present time, gradually but surely, the indwelling Spirit of Christ is subduing the flesh within me and is transforming me into the image of Christ, "from one degree of glory to another" (II Cor. 3:18; Gal. 5:16-26).

In this present salvation too we should emphasize the positive. We are being set free from the bondage of our own self-centeredness. Why? In order to give ourselves in service to God and man. We exchange one slavery for another. We are no longer the slaves of sin and self, but we are the willing slaves of God, yes, and you are slaves too for Jesus' sake (Rom. 6:22; II Cor. 4:5). I wonder if it is our evangelical concentration on the negative aspect of salvation which has often brought our doctrine into disrepute? Should we not emphasize far more than we usually do that we cannot claim to be saved from self if we do not go on to abandon our liberated self in selfless service?

Third, our final salvation lies in the future. It is the object of our hope, for Christian hope is precisely "the hope of salvation" (I Thess. 5:8; cf. Rom. 8:24). It is not only that we shall be delivered from "the wrath of God," but also from the whole process of decay in creation and from evil whether in ourselves or in our society. For we are to have new bodies, and there is to be a new heaven and a new earth (e.g., Rom. 8:

18-25; II Pet. 3:13). Then we shall experience, and the whole creation will experience with us, what Paul calls "the liberty of the glory of the children of God" (Rom. 8:21).

Thus in each phase of our salvation Scripture lays its emphasis not on our rescue (from wrath, from self, from decay) but on the freedom which this rescue will bring — freedom to approach God as our Father, freedom to give ourselves in service, and finally the "freedom of glory" when, rid of all the limitations of our flesh-and-blood existence, we can devote ourselves without reserve to God and to each other. Are we saved? Yes, and "we rejoice" (Rom. 5:2, 3, 11). Are we saved? No, and in this body and with the whole creation "we groan inwardly" as we wait for the consummation. We rejoice and we groan: this is the paradoxical experience of Christians who have been saved and are being saved, and at the same time are not yet saved.

5. *Conversion*

The fifth word we have to consider is "conversion." It indicates that the announcement of the good news of salvation requires a response. We must reject as hopelessly unbiblical the notion that all men have been saved by Christ and that the only function of "evangelism" is to acquaint the ignorant of this good news. It is true that "God . . . through Christ reconciled us to himself," but this does not mean that all men are reconciled to God. For now he commits to us the ministry and the message of reconciliation, and bids us beg people on behalf of Christ, "Be reconciled to God." What validity would such an appeal have if those who hear it are already reconciled to God but simply do not know it? (II Cor. 5:18-20). No. God was indeed "in Christ" reconciling the world to himself, but now we must be "in Christ" ourselves if we are to receive the reconciliation and to become a new creation (II Cor. 5:19, 21, 17).

Solemnly we have to affirm that those to whom we announce the Gospel and address our appeal are still "perishing." We proclaim to them the good news of Christ not because they are saved already but in order that they may be saved. It is impossible to be a biblical Christian and a universalist simultaneously. We may (and I think should) preserve a certain humble and reverent agnosticism about the precise nature of hell, as about the precise nature of heaven. But clear and dogmatic we must be that hell is an awful, eternal reality. It is not dogmatism that is unbecoming in speaking about the fact of hell; it is glibness and frivolity. How can we even think about hell without tears?

If, then, a response to the Gospel is necessary, this response is called "conversion." *Epistrepho,* though usually in the middle or passive voice and therefore commonly translated to "be converted," really has an active sense, to "turn." When used in secular contexts in the New Testament it means either to "turn around" (as when Jesus turned around to see who had touched him, Mark 5:30) or to "return" (as when an unwanted greeting of peace returns to its giver, Matt. 10:13. Note that the usual word for "return" is *hapostrepho,* e.g., Luke 2:20, 43). And when the word is used theologically it also means to turn from one direction to another, or return from one place to another. Thus, Christians can be described as having "turned to God from idols" (I Thess.

1:9) and, after "straying like sheep," as having "now returned to the Shepherd and Guardian of your souls" (I Pet. 2:25). Since the turn from idols and sin is usually called "repentance," and the turn to God and Christ "faith," we reach the interesting biblical equation that "repentance + faith = conversion."

As we consider the call to conversion in the contemporary world, it may be appropriate to issue three warnings.

First, conversion is not a work which man can do by himself. True, men are described as "turning to the Lord" (e.g., Acts 9:35, 11:21), and conversion is something we do in contrast to regeneration which is something God does, a new birth "from above." True also, evangelists are sometimes described in the New Testament as themselves "converting" people, like John the Baptist who would "turn many . . . to the Lord their God" (Luke 1:16, 17) and like the brother who "brings back a sinner from the error of his way" (Jas. 5:19, 20). Nevertheless, neither could the sinner turn nor could the evangelist turn him but for the work of the Holy Spirit (see, e.g., Acts 26:18). So repentance and faith are plainly declared in the New Testament to be both the duty of men (e.g., Acts 2:38, 16:31, 17:30) and the gift of God (e.g., Acts 11:18; Eph. 2:8; Phil. 1:29). And however perplexing this antinomy may be, it is necessary in our man-centered, self-confident age to assert it, so that we may humble ourselves before God.

Second, conversion is not the renunciation of all our inherited culture. Conversion involves repentance, and repentance is renunciation. But what needs to be renounced? Too often we expect conversion to take place in a vacuum, without helping the convert to grasp in precise concrete terms what he is having to turn from. Or, worse still, we expect the convert to step right out of his former culture into a Christian subculture which is totally distinctive. Sometimes, we seem to call him to withdraw from the real world altogether. It is probably in reaction to this kind of "conversion" that the DWME study "Conversion in a Secular Age" said, "Conversion . . . is not, in the first place, either saving one's own soul or joining a society." The pre-Uppsala booklet, All Things New (p. 43), added that, though it is both these things secondarily, yet "fundamentally conversion means commitment, in penitence and faith, to what God himself is doing in human history." Candidly, this is over-stated, for conversion is turning to God and not to anything God is doing. Nevertheless, the emphasis is understandable. Conversion must not take the convert out of the world but send him back into it, the same person in the same world, and yet a new person with new convictions and new standards. Christ says, "Come," but then immediately adds, "Go," that is, go back into the world for me.

In both West and East it is vital for us to distinguish between Scripture and culture, and between those things in culture which are inherently evil and must be renounced for Christ's sake, and those things which are good or indifferent and may be retained, even perhaps transformed and enriched. In the West, according to the authors of God's Lively People (1971), we seem to expect new converts to abandon their contemporary behavior and adopt a new life-style which turns out to be not new but old. "The new Christian has to learn the old hymns and appreciate them. He has to learn the language of the pulpit. He has to share in some conservative political opinions. He has to dress a bit old-fashioned. In brief, he has to step back two generations and undergo what one may call a painful cultural circumcision" (p. 206). In the East too and wherever a non-Christian religion dominates a country's culture, we need great wisdom to discern between what can be retained and what must be renounced. We cannot agree with Dr. M.M. Thomas' call for "a Christ-centered fellowship of faith and ethics in the Hindu religious community." Bishop Lesslie Newbigin is right to call this proposal "quite unrealistic" and to insist that "a man who is religiously, culturally and socially part of the Hindu community is a Hindu." But I think we can agree with Bishop Kenneth Cragg who, against a Muslim rather than a Hindu background, writes that "baptism . . . does not, properly understood, deculturalize the new believer; it enchurches him . . . conversion is not 'migration'; it is the personal discovery of the meaning of the universal Christ within the old framework of race, language and tradition."

Third, conversion is not the end. On the contrary, it is a new beginning. It is to be followed by the life of discipleship, by a growth into Christian maturity, by membership in the church (see Acts 2:40, 47) and by involvement in the world.

Such is the nature of biblical evangelism. It is part of God's mission through God's church in God's world. It is the spreading by any and every means of the good news of Jesus, crucified, risen, and reigning. It includes the kind of dialogue in which we listen humbly and sensitively in order to understand the other person and to learn how to present Christ to him meaningfully. It is the offer, on the ground of the work of Christ, of a salvation which is both present possession and future prospect, both liberation from self and liberation for God and man. And it invites a total response of repentance and faith which is called "conversion," the beginning of an altogether new life in Christ, in the church and in the world.

BIBLICAL AUTHORITY AND EVANGELISM
Susumu Uda

*Dr. Uda, Tokyo, Japan, is a Professor
in the Japan Christian Theological
Seminary and pastor of the Kugayama
Presbyterian Church.*

Introduction

The problem of authority is the most fundamental problem that the Christian Church always faces. This is because Christianity is built upon the truth mediated by God's revelation. Without revelation there would be no foundation for Christian faith and action. Therefore, it is no exaggeration to say that with the reality of revelation Christianity stands or falls.

However, today the very concept of revelation is under attack. Is there such a thing as what the church calls "the revelation of God"? asks modern man living in the present age of mass atheism and a completely secular culture. Usually his reaction to this question is quite sceptical or strongly negative. He believes a "modern myth" that all that lies beyond the world of senses, the conclusions of logic, and all that cannot be proved scientifically, is purely incredible. Hence, the Christian claim to have the revelation of the transcendent God stands in the sharpest possible antithesis to the claim of our age. The sense of transcendence and the consciousness of divine revelation has disappeared almost completely. What is allowed at most by modern man is a kind of religion of this world only, in which the very concept of revelation has no place.

But if there is a divine revelation as the church has believed through the centuries, what is its mode or form? Is it discoverable in all existing things or only in some? If in some, then in which? And by what criteria are they selected as its media? Where are they found? What is their authority? (cf. W. Temple: "Revelation" in *Revelation,* ed., J. Baillie and H. Martin, 1937). The church has to face all these questions, and it is certainly the duty of the church, both to itself and to the world, to make a clear theological statement about the fundamental issue of revelation on which her life rests.

General revelation and evangelism

The opening verses of the epistle to the Hebrews inform us that it has pleased God to reveal himself in "diverse manners." In the course of the church's history God's revelation thus given in diverse manners came to be commonly understood under two categories, namely, *general* and *special* revelation. Down through the centuries it has been an integral part of the teaching of the church that the Scripture teaches the revelation of God in his works of creation. On the basis of the so-called "nature psalms" (Psa. 8, 19, 65, 104) as well as other passages such as John 1:4-9, Acts 14:17, 17:22ff., Rom. 1:18ff. and 2:14ff., the church has proclaimed that God always surrounds all mankind "like a theater"

(J. Calvin) (i) in the constitution of human existence, (ii) in the whole structure of nature, and (iii) in God's providential government of human history. And this general revelation has long been taken as the basis of the church's assertion of the responsibility of the whole human race and also as the *point of contact* for the evangelistic call to repentance. However, to-day, as we attempt to understand the exact *nature* and *meaning* of this general revelation, opinions differ and we find the situation isn't so simple.

The "knowing God" of the natural man

The first chapter of Romans has been regarded as good material for the confession of general revelation, but one must take care how he uses it. Romans 1:19 explains how it can be said that men suppress the truth in unrighteousness; they suppress the truth because there is a manifestation of truth to them (v. 18), and the truth manifested to them is described as "what can be known about God" (v. 19). The content of this knowledge is defined in v. 20 as "his invisible nature, namely, his eternal power and deity." That is, the eternity of God and the divine attributes are manifest to men (i) *since* the creation of the world and (ii) *through* the works of creation. The cognitive perception elicited from the manifestation of divine glory in the visible creation is spoken of as "knowing God" in v. 21.

What does all this mean to us today? Roman Catholicism, by means of direct appeal to Romans 1:20, concludes that a *true* though incomplete knowledge of God is possible with certainty *through the natural light of reason,* apart from the revelation in Christ. According to this, we can know the one, only, true God, our Creator and Lord, from created reality by means of human reason. But, is this what Paul really meant by the "knowing God" of the natural man? Didn't Christ say, "And this is life eternal, that they should know thee the only true God, and him whom thou didst send, even Jesus Christ" (John 17:3)? Although we ought to appreciate its apologetic intent to seek to answer all forms of modern agnosticism and irrationalism, there are serious problems with this view. *First,* it is clear that a specific anthropology is involved here, a view of man that the ability of human reason is neither sin-depraved nor disturbed, so that reason can still function rightly and therefore reach God. But, isn't it a biblical fact that sin works a destructive effect not only in our moral motives but also *in our minds,* so that the things of God cannot be known by the natural man (I Cor. 2:14)? *Second,* this view of Rome is in conflict with the Pauline doctrine that the Gentiles are estranged from the life of God by the emptiness of mind and ignor-norance (Gal. 4:8; I Thess. 4:5; II Thess. 1:8). And it is in line with the teaching of the Old Testament that the heathen do not know the true God (Ps. 97:6). *Third,* in Romans 1 general revelation is placed in a specific context: Man — sinful and fallen man — is still surrounded by the light of general revelation, but this same man pollutes and misunder-stands this light and suppresses it in unrighteousness (v. 18). This same man substitutes the image of a perishable man for the majesty of the eternal God (v. 23). This same man honors and worships the creature above the real Creator (v. 25). Because of this, therefore, man stands under the wrath of God, in the state of guilt (v. 18). Thus the context in which Romans 1 is placed shows that it is not permissible to separate the knowing God of the natural man from the dark side of his exchange of gods, and it is not right to talk about the value of general revelation without considering the anger of God, which condemns man's holding back the truth in unrighteousness. What Romans 1 makes clear is that the light of general revelation does not lead man to the knowledge of the true God and the kind of knowledge which the natural man has is a knowledge which, as a fatal consequence of sin, is transformed into the illusion of idolatry!

Today in our evangelistic and apologetic effort the matter of how we view natural man is becoming more and more important. The Christian as God's prophet interprets the world according to his mind; as his priest he dedicates the meaning of the world to God; and as his king he rules over the world for his glory (II Cor. 5:17). In sharp contrast to this, the natural man, allowing no authority to stand over him, thinks of himself as the ultimate judge of what can or cannot be. And the facts of man's environment are not created or controlled by the providence of God. The universe is a *chance*-controlled universe! So as soon as there is any discussion between the Christian and the non-Christian about something which involves principle the radical difference between them immediately appears, as clearly pointed out by even a secular thinker, "If by religion one refers to an explanation of the universe and a derivation of moral norms from theological premises, then indeed there is logical incompatibility with the results, methods, and general outlook of science" (cf. C. Van Til: *The Protestant Doctrine of Scripture*, 1967, pp. 12ff.). Any evangelistic effort which does not reckon with this decisive difference will be routed, and concessions to please the mind of the natural man can be no part of real Christian strategy.

The law written on man's heart

In Romans 1 Paul makes clear that man even in his sinful state does not stand outside of any connection with the light of God's revelation. In chapter 2 he states that this same man in his practical life still has some discernment with respect to that which is contained in God's law and his ordinances for the preservation of human life.

In Romans 2:14 it is stated that the Gentiles are "without the law" and "have not the law" in the sense of specially revealed law (i.e., the Law of Moses), nevertheless, (i) they are confronted by the law of God in their consciousness by reason of what they natively and constitutionally are; (ii) they do things which this law prescribes; (iii) this doing is not external constraint but by natural impulse. In v. 15 it is further stated that not only does the doing of the things of the law prove the work of the law written in their hearts, but the witness of *conscience* does also. This conscience is certainly not to be viewed as an ever unchanging something (II Tim. 3:1f.), but Paul saw that even in the Gentile world people in one way or another are preserved from the full consequences of their alienation from God. In other words, there is still a witnessing of the law written in the hearts of men who neither know God nor serve him. And man, being compelled to take note of this, cannot escape from the goodness of the preserving and ruling God and his holy law.

Today, talk about nihilism is widespread. It seems to be a common thing to talk about the death of God and the subsequent disappearance of absolute moral standards. But it must be noted that human life even in its present radical estrangement from God has not completely passed into meaninglessness and lawlessness. By God's preserving grace some acceptance still stands for right and justice, for punishing evil and rewarding good (Rom. 13:3-4). There is still appreciation for community, love, and social welfare. There is still a searching for a new humanism (cf. R. Shinn: *Man: The New Humanism*, 1967). In Japan the fact that new religious sects have mushroomed to a remarkable extent since the war strongly witnesses to the unrest of peoples' hearts, which do not come to rest until they rest in God (Augustine). It also shows the fact of their searching for a way to truer humanness and more dependable values on the other. Hence, in the midst of the ongoing secularism and pluralism in our society, the church must use the doctrine of general revelation as a reminder of God who still holds fast human life and who does not abandon the world because of his love towards this world (John 3:16, cf. also Col. 1:17).

The Gospel and other religions

In connection with the matter of general revelation, today, the question of the relation between the Christian Gospel and other religions is becoming more and more urgent. This is because: (i) As an external impulse the extension of communication and the worldwide exchange of ideas have resulted in a general intermingling of various religions; (ii) Inside some parts of the church contemporary ecumenical theology, strongly influenced by the idea of one broad, universal revelation of God in the background of the various religions, tends to press the matter of interreligious cooperation and even interpenetration (in this "syncretism" is the key issue); (iii) An energetic effort on the part of the Third World churches to formulate an indigenous theology lead them to use their native religious sources as in equal standing with the Word of God and even to admit the possibility of salvation in their traditional religions. Might it not be possible for non-Christian religions to point to Christ in the same way as the Old Testament does? Is there anyone who comes to the Father except through him? (John 14:6). On these questions Paul's address at Athens seems to furnish some biblical guidelines.

At the beginning of his address Paul's attention is focused upon the religious devotion of the Athenians, "I perceive that in every way you are very religious" (Acts 17:22). What was prominently in view in Paul's mind was their *religiousness*. And his grappling with their religiousness was mainly due to his view of the nature of man as created in the image of God and therefore made to respond to his Creator (Gen. 1:26-27). According to Paul's understanding, however inadequate and even false the Gentile religion might be as a consequence of sin, its very existence is nevertheless a confirmation of the fact that man still retains his fundamental character as a religiously responsible being and man even in his most extreme aberrations does not release himself from the light of God's revelation. That is, in terms of a Reformer John Calvin, man possesses as man an indelible "sense of deity," so that no man might shelter himself under the pretext of ignorance.

Then it is tremendously important to note that Paul evaluates the religion of the Athenians as one of *ignorance* (v. 23). Here Paul says in effect, "That which you worship acknowledging openly your ignorance, I proclaim unto you." In saying so he does not mean to complete what the Athenians already possess of true religion. On the contrary, what they acknowledge as ignorance has a far deeper meaning for Paul. He clearly makes contact with the Greek mind by way of the altar and the unknown God; but his point of contact is the ignorance of the Greeks. He sees this ignorance more profoundly than the Athenians' own acknowledgment of it allows for. He calls them to repentance and conversion from this ignorance. Thus Paul maintains a clear-cut distinction between the Christian Gospel and pagan idolatry (cf. his same consistent attitude at Lystra in Acts 14:14f). In reality, Paul is neither accommodating his Gospel to the Hellenistic religiosity of his day, nor saying that the peculiarities of each religion are simply special forms of the common essence as the science of comparative religion teaches Today.

Perhaps the most controversial part of Paul's address is 17:24-29. His proclamation of God as Creator and Ruler of the world is viewed by some as an affirmation of the Greek monotheism and consequently as an affirmation of a common ground with the religious outlook of the Greeks. Is this Paul's real intention? Was there really commonness in the view of God? As pointed out above, Paul proclaims this God as one who is fundamentally unknown to them. Paul well knows that the tendency to create gods in man's own image, as had occurred in the idol worship of the Old Testament, lies in all of the so-called religions of men. And what man achieves by religion is never the true knowledge of God, but only a fiction that has nothing to do with reality. As man cannot, dare not, see himself as he is, he cannot and will not see God as he really is. Rather, what underlies Paul's whole presentation in this section is the light of God's special revelation associated with his own apostolic authority and reinforced by his direct dependence upon the teaching of the Old Testament. Paul here is thoroughly on biblical ground when he speaks of God as the one "who made the world and everything in it" (v. 24), for this statement is a virtual quotation from Exodus 20:11 and has found expression repeatedly in both the Old and New Testament (Ps. 146:6; Isa. 37:16; Acts 4:24, 14-15). Likewise, the declaration that God is "Lord of heaven and earth," and "does not live in shrines made by man" (v. 24) is a reflection of I Kings 8:27 and is the very point which Stephen affirmed (Acts 7:48). Being keenly aware of the Greek's *monistic* view of the cosmos, that is, the cosmos as basically one without a clear distinction between the Creator-God and the creature, Paul here witnesses to the important fact that only in the biblical outlook the doctrine of the sovereign Creator and Ruler comes to the fullest expression without any compromise (cf. N. Stonehouse: *Paul Before the Areopagus and other New Testament Studies*, 1957).

Isn't it often the case that whenever sight is lost of the biblical revelation of the God of the Bible and man's creatureliness and his abnormality, man's religious imagination will eventually end up either in blending God and nature (i.e., Shinto's polytheistic finite gods) or blending God and the self (i.e., self-deification in Buddhism)?

The Bible is "most necessary"

Hitherto the church has derived all her doctrines from the Bible. Whenever in the course of her long history the question, "What is to be believed?" arose, it was to the Bible that the church turned. Before we take up the question of the authority of the Bible, we ought to be clear about the fundamental factors which make the Bible, God's written special revelation, "most necessary" (cf. the first paragraph of the Westminster Confession). (i) Whence do we know our misery and the love of God in Jesus Christ? The answer which the Heidelberg Catechism gives is very simple, but also very penetrating. It simply says, "Out of the law of God" (Q.3). Since man has sinned, he has become a "willing slave" of sin and thereby totally incapable spiritually. But from the moment man sinned God began to manifest his saving grace. In order that men, thus blinded by sin, may learn correctly his will, works and ways with respect to this saving, restorative work, God's special communication to them became a necessity (II Tim. 3:17). (ii) The necessity of God's written special revelation appears also with respect to man's inability to interpret *nature* aright. I Kings 20:28 presents before us man's typical case that the attraction of nature, with its fascinating and terrifying aspects, leads to nature-worship when sight is lost of God's interpretative light. And we may listen to the "harmony of the spheres" as Pythagoras, and still not understand God's revelation in nature. Now we as sinners are in a position of need of a "glass" through which we understand again the real meaning and purpose of the creation of God. It should be remembered that with the so-called "nature-psalms" we touch upon the songs of praise of *the Lord's people.* For instance, Psalm 19 deals with nature, but also with the *law* of God. Psalm 93 deals with nature, but also with *the holiness of God's house* (cf. G. C. Berkouwer: *General Revelation,* 1955). (iii) The necessity of God's written special revelation must also be considered from the fact that since God is transcendent man cannot adequately think of God and properly describe him in human language (Job 36:26, I Tim. 6:15-16). Only in this revelation is God authentically known. (iv) The Christian view of *God as a person* or the personal God points to the necessity of God's special communication. Ramm describes as follows, "As man stands before this Person, the Person of God, he discovers that he cannot open up the discussion. Under what terms could such a conversation be opened up? . . . What are the connecting ligaments between the human and the divine mind? . . . If we are ready to converse, is God ready to listen? Perhaps God has called to us and we have not heard? If we call, must God answer? Here man stands before the sovereign Person, the transcendent Person! *If there is to be a conversation this Person must initiate it . . .* In the divine readiness this sovereign Person does speak! He does open up the conversation! *And this conversation springing from the readiness of this Person is special revelation" (Special Revelation and the Word of God,* 1961, p. 25). And we simply add that this conversation is now embodied in the Bible. (v) The church on the earth often comes under the temptation of evil forces to degenerate forms of faith and worship, and therefore renewal is constantly needed. But by what could it be possible? Psalm 119:50 informs us that the way the Spirit of God renews the very life of the church is by applying to us the Word of God.

All Scripture is "God-breathed"

The real issue before the entire church and every individual Christian today is: What is to be our view of and attitude toward the Bible? The most popular approach to this question today is to submit the Bible to the so-called scientific examination of the "experts" and then abide by that testimony, or to judge the Bible by the standards of whether modern man thinks it relevant to his day. What is to be the evangelical approach to this question? To be sure, the evangelical approach should not be the one which precludes scholarly research and serious discussions about the contemporary relevancy of the Bible. But the evangelical approach will give to the *self-testimony* of the Bible the first priority over any other considerations. As every man has a right to speak for himself and testimony to oneself ought not be ruled out as improper, so it is with the Bible. And if men were not liars or deceivers, their own testimony about themselves would be sufficient. This same principle should be applied in our approach to the Bible. If the Bible is not to be depended upon when it speaks of itself, how do we know that it is trustworthy when it speaks about anything else?

It has been the faith of the people of God from the very foundation of the church until today that the Bible is the Word of God in such a sense that whatever it says God says. The biblical warrant for this attitude of entire trust in the Bible is the *inspiration* of God the Holy Spirit. In the well-known passage, II Timothy 3:16, Paul says, "All Scripture is given by inspiration of God." The word which calls for our special attention is the Greek word for "inspiration." It is *"theopneustos."* What this word says of Scripture is, not that it is "breathed into by God" or is the product of the divine "inbreathing" into its human authors, but it is breathed out by God, "God-breathed," the product of the creative breath of God. The "breath of God" is in the Bible a symbol of the almighty and irresistible outflow of his power (Psa. 33:4). In a word, the text explicitly teaches the divine origin of "all Scripture." This same truth is expressed also by Peter. In II Peter: 1-16 Peter is assuring his readers that what had been made known to them of "the power and coming of our Lord Jesus Christ" did not come through "cleverly devised myths." He presents to them the testimony of eyewitnesses (vvs. 16-18). And then he says that they have better testimony than that of eyewitnesses. It is "the prophetic word" which is "more sure" (v. 19). Peter, of course, refers to Scripture. In v. 20 he emphatically states that Scripture does not owe its origin to "the impulse of man," but its origin lies in God, "Men moved by the Holy Spirit spoke from God." The Greek word, *"pheromenoi,"* for "moved" is a remarkable word. It means "brought," "borne," or "carried along." That is, the Holy Spirit actually lifted them up and carried them along, and thus they spoke. They were borne or carried along under the determining influence of the Spirit and not by their own power. As a result of the inspiration by the Holy Spirit, the church has believed, the Bible possesses divine authority and trustworthiness. Further, we hear the most definitive word about the authority of the Bible from the lips of our Lord himself. In Matthew 5:18 Christ says, "Not an iota, not a dot, will pass from the law until all is accomplished." As the previous verse shows, Christ is here referring to the sacred writings of the Jews as a unit. But he says very positively that this book is perfect to the smallest detail. John's Gospel also gives many witnesses of Jesus' complete trust toward the Bible. One of the most striking cases is John 10:35, "The Scripture cannot be broken." The concept of breaking a law was well understood by the people of that day. If a man breaks a law, he is guilty and so liable to punishment. When one breaks the law, he treats the law as nonexistent, and in effect annuls it. The Scripture, however, possesses an authority so great that it cannot be broken. What the Scripture says will stand steadfast (cf. Heb. 2:2) and cannot be annulled. If the Scripture speaks, the issue is settled once and for all.

This high view of the Bible is not merely the creation of late Judaism nor the invention of the post-Reformation period. It was indeed held by the Jews, by the early Church, and through the centuries. Standing on the promises of God found in the revealed Word of God has certainly been the essential characteristic of the faith of God's people. And the prophets and the apostles could back their proclamation with a "thus saith the Lord" and could boldly say, "I declare unto you" (Acts 17:23), simply because they were sure that they stood on the Book in which divine authority resides.

In his recent book, *Why Conservative Churches are Growing*, 1972, Dean Kelly warns concerning the dying churches, in which what he calls "strictness" of belief and practice are out of favor, and the qualities which are popularly esteemed are those that conduce, not to the strength of the quest for meaning, but to its weakening: relativism, diversity, dialogue, and leniency. And it is not accidental that a sociologist Peter Berger came up with the conslusion in *The Sacred Canopy*, 1967, that the loss of authority in the churches is fundamental to the process of decline!

"Sanctify them in the truth; thy word is truth"

In recent discussion the subject of the authority of the Bible and its role in evangelism is one about which there has been much confusion. The Bangkok Conference on "Salvation Today," for instance, revealed a crisis situation within the WCC-related churches. The Bible is viewed by many as merely a collection of fallible human witnesses to the experience of the so-called "authentic way of human existence" (a mode of living with true humanness). And correlative to this relativistic view of the Bible, it must be noted, is a strongly humanistic and socialistic view of the church's message and her mission. This is clearly demonstrated by the "political theology" which is now becoming one of the most influential voices in the ecumenical movement. In this, the newly discovered social and political dimension of the Gospel becomes its sole and entire content. All Christian elements tend to be swallowed up by incorporation into certain political thought and action such as the Marxist idea of social revolution. And this, as Heinz Zahrnt aptly points out, makes society the factor which determines everything, so that society itself becomes God — following the phenomenon of the "death of God." The Bible then is considered only from the point of view of what it has to contribute to the carrying out of current social and political tasks *(What Kind of God?,* 1970, pp. 222-3). Thus, instead of the church changing the world, the world is changing the church and her message! All this reminds us that the choice the church makes regarding the foundation of her faith determines the road to be traveled all the way.

In the midst of the world in a mess and the "searching generation" now is the time for the Church of Jesus Christ to give heed to the truth expressed in the words of Christ's priestly prayer, "Sanctify them in the truth; thy word is truth" (John 17:17). Unless the church turns to the authoritative Word of the sovereign God as supreme authority, she will soon cease to be the church of the living God.

BIBLICAL AUTHORITY AND EVANGELISM
Susumu Uda

Introduction

I believe many of you know already that Dean M. Kelley, one of the U.S. National Council of Churches leaders, who is a Methodist minister, recently published an extremely interesting book called, *Why Conservative Churches Are Growing* (1972). This analyzes the churches of the United States and presents their problems from the standpoint of religious sociology. This book points out the fact that the ecumenical churches have been rapidly decreasing in membership, while attendance of evangelical churches, on the other hand, has been growing.

For example, the Southern Baptist Convention grew by 2.26 per cent per annum; the Christian Reformed by 2.2 per cent; and the Assemblies of God by 2.1 per cent, respectively. One of the important reasons is that the ecumenical churches opened the door to dialogue, leniency, diversity, and relativism.

On the other hand, the author observes that the evangelical churches are practicing "strictness" in the teaching of doctrine, in the matter of requirements for baptism, and in church discipline. Now, the practice of such a "strictness" seems to be closely related with the matter of "authority" in faith. Peter Berger, a religious sociologist, rightly suggests that the fundamental cause for the decline of the churches today lies in the loss of authority.

Now, I believe, it is appropriate to take up the subject of "Biblical Authority" as the first session of this Congress. I'd like to consider the subject initially from the aspect of general revelation of God — then proceed to relate it to the view of the Bible.

Never has there been such an age as today when "authority" sounds hollow. Never has there been such an age as today when "authority" is fundamentally questioned. Claims have been made — even in the church — as follows: "This world is destined to dip and fall into chaos, so that the light of God is not even found in it." "God's revelation comes through our neighbor." Or, "Today, almost nothing is known about the historical Jesus." Another claim is, "Since the Bible as a whole is an ancient myth, we must demythologize it and translate it into the words and thinking of modern man." As we see these claims being made in the church, we must make sure once again that we have the clear understanding and confidence when it comes to "biblical authority," the foundation of faith and evangelism.

1. *General revelation and evangelism*

Today, an accurate understanding of God's general revelation is an important factor in formulating the theory of evangelism. Currently there are three different views: (i) that all religions are partially enlightened by the light of God's revelation. With this emphasis, rejecting the claim of the absoluteness of Christianity, it aims at a universal *world religion.* (ii) That revelation comes only through Christ, and that nature, reason, and history do not convey the light of revelation at all. (iii) That natural man is still able to lead man to true knowledge of God — though incomplete — by the light of his own reason or nature. How should we consider the subject of general revelation in the area of evangelism?

a. *Possibility of the knowledge of God by the natural man.* According to Psalm 19:1-6, the light of God is shown to all the people just as the benefit of the sun covers all the people of the earth. Romans 1:20 says, "For the invisible things of (God) from the creation of the world are clearly seen, being understood by the things that are made, even his eternal power and Godhead." Both Roman Catholicism and a certain segment of the evangelical churches — by means of direct appeal to Romans 1:20 — conclude that even the natural man can come to the true knowledge of God. If it is true, it means that we in Japan (a country full of paganism) can easily teach the triune God of the Bible without too much difficulty simply by adding Christ on top of the national view of gods and then pouring the Holy Spirit on them. Is it really true?

Romans 1:18 ff. testify that the natural man is not only surrounded by the light of the general revelation of God, but — simultaneously — he is trying to hold back the light "in unrighteousness" (v. 18). In other words, he is trying hard to suppress the light and dispel the light. And the wrath of God is revealed on such a natural man.

Furthermore, practically, "his foolish heart was darkened" (v. 21) and "he worshipped and served corruptible man, birds, beasts, and creeping things more than the Creator" (vs. 22, 23, 25). Here, the natural man — though being confronted with the light of God's revelation — has not reached the point of discovering the true God because of his sin; but has actually fallen into an illusion of idolatry. This has been pointed out by Paul, a man of rich experience in evangelism. As a matter of fact, Japan might serve as an illustration to prove that point. Anything from the sun, the Emperor, feudal lords, a mountain, river, monkey (the Sanno god), dove (the Hachiman god), deer (the Kasuga god), fox (the Inari god), and even the "salt heating pan" (a Shiogama shrine) — as well as mentally abnormal persons — have been worshiped as gods; and people have served them. A lukewarm attitude against the power of paganism will not make evangelism fruitful.

Another thing I have learned from the recent experience of evangelism is the anti-Christian and the Satanic nature which is expressed by the natural man's reasoning. The reasoning of natural man works and is based on its own presuppositions, and this reasoning is diametrically opposed to Christian presuppositions.

The primary presuppositions of the natural man are: (i) man does not recognize any authority that stands over him; and (ii) this world is ultimately a "chance-controlled" world which is basically irrationalistic. And based upon these presuppositions, man with his natural reasoning is actually saying, "Curse to the Lord." This we have to remember.

Under such circumstances, in an effort to seek contact with unbelievers for the purpose of winning them for the Lord, if we allow any compromise with the natural man, this amounts to digging the grave of the evangelist.

Today, the conversion experience *(metanoia)* is not regarded as merely an emotional thing or the matter of will, but as the conversion of the whole man, including his reasoning, which is under the serious effect of sin. Unless we reconfirm this definition, we will not see the realization of deep-rooted evangelism in a true sense of the word. The fact that we in Japan have so many so-called "Christians" who have "graduated" has a definite relationship to these situations.

b. *"Image of God" and God's common grace.* The cognitive nature of the natural man is — as has been said previously — "ignorance" and "darkness" (see Gal. 4:8; I Thess. 4:5; II Thess. 1:8). Romans 2:14-15 teaches that the things contained in the law of God are written in their hearts and that their conscience is also bearing witness of it.

We are seeing "man's dehumanizing acts against man" in every area of present-day society. Because of the avarice for wealth, a man destroys himself and his fellow workers as if nothing were the matter. However, Paul claimed that — even in such a state — man is confronted with the light of God's general revelation at the depth of his existence and in the midst of social activities.

As we study this subject, we come to notice two things that the Bible is saying: (i) God created man in his own image (Gen. 1:27); and (ii) God is giving all the people of the world his preserving grace (Acts 17:25b). Paul here seems to be saying that with the law and conscience written in the hearts of men, "the image of God" is preserved even now. Then, how shall we understand the import of his description?

Generally, man is different from all other creatures — sinner or not; that is, a man is absolutely unique (Psalm 8). Man is a sinner; he is a being with rational power. Another aspect is the consciousness of his responsibility to respond to his Creator; that is, a man knows the law of God in one way or another. Thus, he is in a position to become aware of responsibility. Therefore man is protected from falling into a completely unlawful state, morally and socially.

According to Ruth Benedict, the Japanese culture is said to be the "Culture of Shame." In it also, that which makes a man a human being is preserved in some form. Talk about nihilism is being spread today into the daily lives of the public. But the Christian churches must rightly realize that morality, responsibility to social justice, community awareness, and the pursuit of humanism are made possible because of the "image of God" as well as God's preserving grace. At the same time, we must have a clear conviction as we stand at the place of evangelism that God keeps on loving us even now without giving up this world (John 3:16; Col. 1:17).

2. Relationship between the Gospel and other religions

When it comes to the question of the relationship between the Gospel and other religions, it is an extremely difficult question for the churches of Asia and Africa for the following reasons:

(i) The extension of communication and the worldwide exchange of ideas have been promoting mutual contact among various religions.

(ii) Ecumenical theology, which strongly emphasizes the dialogue and cooperation with other religions, is heading toward a syncretistic world religion, somewhat similar to that which was advocated by Toynbee.

(iii) The "indigenous theology" in the Third World is headed toward universalism from the standpoint of "Bible only" and "Christ only"; and this trend is making the issue more complicated.

Paul's address at Areopagus (Acts 17) gives us necessary guiding principles concerning this subject. *First,* according to Acts 17:22, Paul considers faith and religiousness of the Greek as a clue to evangelism. There, Paul saw the "Seed of Religion," "God awareness" (Calvin calls it), as an element of God's image; and he seems to have taken it as a contact point for evangelism. *Second,* Paul evaluated their faith and religion as one of "ignorance" (v. 23); and it is important to note that he calls them to repentance and conversion from the ignorance of verse 30 (see Acts 26:18). Such a clear-cut point of view is seen even at Lystra, and it is typical of Paul (Acts 14:14 ff). *Third,* through verses 24 29, Paul is proclaiming God as the Creator and Ruler of the world. In the past, it was viewed that Paul was affirming common ground for both the Gospel and the Greek religion in the matter of monotheism. Such a view has been adopted in actual evangelism.

However, if you consider the following points, it becomes doubtful that Paul actually held such a view. (i) The God of the Bible was unknown to the Greek, Paul claimed. (ii) Paul's address was based upon the Old Testament and the revelation he received from the Risen Lord. That is, "God that made the world and all things therein" (v. 24) is virtually the quotation from Exodus 20:11 and is found repeatedly in the Bible. "Lord of heaven and earth . . ." that "dwelleth not in temples made with hands . . ." is the reflection of I Kings 8:27 and is strongly emphasized by Stephen in Acts 7:48. (iii) The Greek view of the cosmos in those days was *monism* and was based upon the concept of cosmos as basically one. It is entirely different from the evangelical view of cosmos where the Creator and the creatures are basically different. Of this, Paul was evidently fully aware.

Paul's faith in the Creator-God was not contradictory to his faith in resurrection. But we have to remember that the resurrection was not acceptable to those who were listening to Paul (vs. 31-33).

When man as a human being in his fallen state loses sight of the Revelation of the true God, then man's religious imagination will eventually end up either in blending God and nature (as is the case with the gods in Shintoism), or he will end up blending God and self (as is the case with self-deification in Buddhism).

3. Bible and evangelism

a. *The Bible is most necessary.* So far, we have touched on a few points concerning general revelation and evangelism. My next point will show you that general revelation is insufficient and that the Bible, which is the written revelation, is "most necessary." (The first paragraph of the Westminster Confession)

(i) Concerning the misery of self and God's salvation through

Christ, man does not have any other way but the Word of God (II Tim. 3:17, "Heidelberg Catechism, Q. 3").

(ii) I Kings 20:28 illustrates the case of a man without the light of God's special revelation. When he is attracted by nature with its fascinating and terrifying aspects, he tends to be led to nature worship. And he may listen to the "harmony of spheres" claimed by Pythagoras; still he interprets it according to his premises and does not reach the point of discovering the true God and the true meaning of his creation.

(iii) The central core of Christian life is to believe in the eternal promises of God (Romans 4:3). Abraham and those who were living in those days were led to take it through the direct revelation of God.

Today, our faith is not based upon anything like "I feel" or "I think." In reality, it is possible for us to know it only through the testimony of the promise of God contained in the Bible.

(iv) The driving force of renewal and reform of the church which is sought for in each era is the Word of God, as Psalm 119:50 indicates. Amos 8:11 tells us that "the failure to listen to the Word of the Lord" meant death to Israel.

b. *Evangelical approach to the Bible.* The greatest point at issue for Christianity — the dividing point of every issue — is the Bible. That is because the Bible alone is the only source of information.

Today, the most popular method to determine the view of the Bible is to submit the Bible to the so-called "scientific examination of the experts" and then to abide by that testimony — to judge the Bible by the standards of whether modern man thinks it relevant for his day. In other words, precisely speaking, the Bible is subjected to man's assessment.

On the contrary, the fundamental characteristic of evangelical approach is the *self-testimony* of the Bible — the first priority over any other consideration. Even in the legal world, testimony to oneself ought not be ruled out as improper. If he is not a swindler — and if he testifies to truth — a man has a right to be heard.

As Ramm indicated, if the appearance of the Bible is simply the extension of the mode of God's revelational activity, the attitude of man as a creature should be, "I will listen; Lord, speak to me." And to establish a mediator between God who speaks and us should be considered a Satanic concept (Job. 9:32-33).

Furthermore, as Young pointed out, if the Bible is not trusted when it testifies of itself, how and where can we find the guarantee that the Bible is to be trusted when it speaks of other things, such as salvation by Christ or the Great Commission for world evangelization?

c. *The Bible as the Word of God.* From the very beginning of the church, the people of God have been confessing that the Bible is the trustworthy Word of God — and the only criterion of faith and practice. The basis of this confession has been regarded as the work called the "inspiration" of God the Holy Spirit.

Today, there is a theory that "inspiration" related to the central thought of the Bible writers. Others say that the inspiration is the existential illumination that readers have. Furthermore, there are those who emphasize greatly the humanistic aspect of inspiration.

The Bible says, "It is breathed by God" — (the product of the creative breath of God — "*theopneustos*" of II Tim. 3:16). Bible writers were "carried along" by the Holy Spirit and they wrote (II Pet. 1:16 "*pheromenoi*").

The lips of our Lord himself testified to the authority and trustworthiness of the Bible (Matt. 5:18; John 10:35). Today, in many liberal churches, we see the phenomenon of the "disappearance of the Holy Spirit." Then it is by no means by chance that the works of the Holy Spirit — including inspiration and regeneration — have been rationally reinterpreted in the modern churches.

I believe that, under such circumstances — before liberals talk about inspiration — there is one thing that they seriously question on the subject of the Bible; namely, the faith in the Holy Spirit.

Conclusion

In recent discussions, the subject of the authority of the Bible and its role in evangelism is the one about which there has been much confusion. The WCC Bangkok Conference held last year on "Salvation Today" revealed it very clearly. There the Bible was viewed by many as merely a collection of human witnesses to the experiences of the so-called "mode of life with true humanness." Along with this a strongly humanistic and socialistic view of the church's mission was adopted. It should be noted that behind such a trend, there is a great influence of "political theology" which is trying to make *social change* — and not the Bible — the foundation of everything.

As Zahrnt pointed out, society is the factor that determines everything. And as Schaeffer indicated, the church is full of "the theology of the echo of this world."

In the early church, the Christians were changing the world. But now the world is turning the church upside down and throwing it into confusion. This is a fact.

As we consider seriously that we are "God's remnant," sent to the suffering world where signs of the last day are evident, once again we must humble ourselves before God and give heed to the truth expressed in the words of Christ's high priestly prayer: "Sanctify them in the truth; thy word is truth" (John 17:17).

THE DIMENSIONS OF WORLD EVANGELIZATION
Donald A. McGavran

*Dr. McGavran, Pasadena, California, USA,
is Senior Professor of Missions, School of
World Mission, Fuller Theological Seminary.*

Introduction

The task of this Issue Strategy Paper is to depict, in bold outline the main dimensions of world evangelism and the major issues confronting it, and to suggest strategies called for by these epoch-making times. I speak of three divine, four human, and three methodological dimensions.

By *evangelism,* I mean proclaiming Jesus Christ as God and Savior and persuading men to become his disciples and responsible members of his church. This distinguishes evangelism from philanthropy, from "everything God wants done," and from bringing about desirable changes in the structures of society. Those are good things to do, but are not evangelism. Evangelism is the duty and privilege of all Christians, whether baptized yesterday or long ago. Churches organized in Bangladesh in 1973 should engage in evangelism just as fervently as those organized in Norway a thousand years ago.

By *world* evangelism, I mean that carried on across linguistic, cultural, and geographic boundaries. Huge numbers of men and women will never be reached by Christian neighbors. They have no Christian neighbors. They seldom if ever see Christians. They often live in other countries and speak other languages. They consider themselves different and live behind cultural walls which shut them off from ordinary evangelism. World evangelism stressing cooperating strategies toward reaching all men for Christ, presents Christ Jesus to these teeming multitudes. World evangelism, also, is the duty and privilege of all Christians from every land, every language, and every culture, and prepares the way for our Lord's triumphant return.

Facing the enormous range and complexity of world evangelism and world mission, I confine myself to main aspects and bare outlines. Even some of these, I leave to later papers.

I shall stress *new* dimensions for we live in a new world. Eurican[1] empires have collapsed and the vehicle they provided evangelism lies on the scrap heap. Numerous, though often small, Christian denominations are found all across Latfricasia[2]. Large numbers of travelers tour all nations for study, business, or just to see the country. Tremendous differences in productivity, knowledge, wealth, and resources divide the nations into haves and have-nots. This Congress must think in *new* dimensions.

FOOTNOTES

[1] *Eurica . Europe and North America.*

[2] *Latfricasia . Latin America, Africa, and Asia.*

Readers will kindly forgive the inconvenience caused by these contractions. Where it is necessary, as in this paper, to repeatedly refer to all these geographic areas, much time is saved by the contractions. They will commend themselves to you.

I shall also stress *continuing* dimensions, for biblical truth applies everywhere, human nature remains the same, and man's alienation from God continues unabated. Since two billion, rapidly becoming three billion, do not know Jesus Christ, world evangelism must continue. Churches and Christians are not free to divert to other causes the sacred resources gathered to make Christ known, loved, and obeyed everywhere. Christians minister to men's needs — and men have no greater needs than to be reconciled to their Father and to walk in the Light. Lausanne must think in *continuing* dimensions.

Before the Congress, participants will receive a definitive account of hundreds of populations of the world unreached or alienated from the Gospel. Readers will therefore be vividly aware of them. The main dimensions of world evangelism I present will be best seen if the unreached peoples are held sharply in mind. Evangelism concerns *people* — men and women, fathers and mothers, sons and daughters, students and laborers, farmers and mechanics, striving, thinking, fighting, sinning, dreaming, bleeding and dying *people*. Generalizations and numbers (shorthand symbols) help us see the multitudes on whom Christ looked with compassion.

PART I: Divine Dimensions
Divine dimension — God's will and world evangelization
The most important dimension of world evangelism is God's will: Christ's act on Calvary, his Resurrection, the sanctifying sending Holy Spirit and the authoritative infallible Bible. I heartily endorse what Dr. Stott has so well said. I need say no more, except perhaps at three points which bear especially upon world evangelism.

a. Nothing affects world evangelism more than what the Bible teaches concerning the possibility of salvation of men through their adherence to various ideologies and religions. Today it has become popular in some sections of the church to affirm that men can be saved through sincere adherence to the best they know. God is savingly at work, we are told, in the whole range of human experience. All Christians have to do is to dialogue with men of other religions and move amiably forward in joint search for God. All such argument, biblical evangelism holds, is erroneous. The only salvation of which the apostles speak is that which comes through faith in Jesus Christ. To our own children, and to those of our Jewish, Buddhist, Marxist, Hindu, Muslim and Secularist friends alike, we declare that there is "no other Name." Christ alone is the Door. He alone is the Truth. He alone has Life. As ambassadors appointed by Christ, we beseech them all (our children and theirs) to be reconciled to God and become active members of the Body of Christ.

b. Similarly, while the scriptures of men and the writings of their philosophers and teachers certainly contain many good things, we hold that the Bible alone, relating all that can be known about the earthly life of Jesus Christ, is the inspired Word of God. It alone is a sufficient rule of faith and practice. It is the standard, the perfect yardstick, by which all other writings about salvation and morals are to be judged.

As world evangelism proceeds in charity toward all men, truth compels Christians to be clear on this point.

c. Because of the tremendous drive to replace evangelism with social action pressing toward righteousness, mercy and peace, Lausanne must speak clearly on social action. There *is*, indeed, a crying need in the world for brotherhood, righteousness, and peace. Christians are doing much to bring these about, and *will do more*. Make no mistake about that. But horizontal reconciliation of man with man is not vertical reconciliation of man with God. Social action is good; but it must neither be called evangelism nor substituted for it. The *temporal* welfare of mankind demands clarity at these points. We must not deny to men, struggling to build a righteous, peaceful society, the most potent element in that struggle, namely multitudes of Christian cells (churches) where men meet around the Bible to seek the will of God and to open themselves to his righteousness and his power. The *eternal* welfare of men also demands clarity. We must not deceive men by giving them "the bread which perishes" in place of the Bread of Heaven.

Divine dimension 2 — God accepts world cultures

A pernicious notion that world evangelism is a concealed form of Eurican imperialism and will destroy the beautiful cultures of Asia, Africa, and Latin America has recently been retarding world evangelism. The idea is false and must be cleared out of the way. It is not in harmony with the revealed will of God. World evangelism has nothing to do with Eurican imperialism, past or present. This Congress does not believe that Eurican culture is God's chosen culture. English, German, and French, though useful on occasion, are not God's only languages. He is fluent in thousands! Eurican culture is not God's model for all the world. Indeed, myriads of Eurican Christians work constantly to make their cultures more biblical. They teach that many aspects of Eurican cultures are highly displeasing to God and must be eliminated.

According to the Bible, God has no favorites among cultures. He accepts them all. We read in Rev. 21:26: "The wealth and splendor of the nations shall be brought into the Holy City."

The kings of earth bring in all their splendor, in stream the beautiful cultures of mankind. Hour after hour, day after day, the glories of the nations march in.

But there is one condition. The inspired writer continues in verse 27, "But nothing unclean shall enter." No oppression, no injustice, no pornography, no idolatry, no corruption, no lust, no drunkenness, no lies, no racial arrogance. The cultures of the earth, purged of the sins, weaknesses, and uglinesses which now afflict all of them, redeemed and made more beautiful by the blood of the Lamb, will troop in to the New Jerusalem, and *the Lord God will accept all of them* as part of the brilliance and the glory of the Holy City. And they shall dwell forever before his face.

That city is nothing that man can make. Its maker and builder is God. But, till the Lord's return, Christians set their faces toward that city, which shines with the glory of God. As they press on toward the radiance of perfect goodness, justice, and love, Christians strive to make their camp grounds conform to the heavenly pattern. Since in the New Jerusalem, God will accept all the glories of the redeemed nations, surely in the visible church, God does now accept the myriad cultures of redeemed mankind, each so well adapted to the circumstances under which he has appointed it to live.

The cultures as they stand are incredibly varied and rich. Yet every one is a mixture of good and bad components. As the adherents of each culture become Christians, the vast majority of its component parts will be little affected — Chinese will continue eating with chopsticks and Russians with forks. But components which work against human welfare and are contrary to God's revealed will, will be either modified or eliminated.

Evangelism redeems each culture whose adherents believe the Gospel, and *makes each more beautiful while it remains itself.* Evangelization is the greatest benefit possible to confer on any culture. Far from destroying it, evangelization brings out its latent goodnesses, which Christianity, the world religion, rapidly disseminates to all men. Witness the worldwide use — in hundreds of languages — of Negro spirituals, and the remarkable popularity of Indian ashrams.

Divine dimension 3: God creates a great new resource for world evangelism

In view of the two billion who have yet to hear of the Savior, and of the strange sickness which currently afflicts Christian mission, God has created a great new resource for world evangelism.

Everyone knows of the hundreds of *Eurican* missionary societies, but few know that God has raised up two hundred missionary societies in *Latfricasia.* The 200 Latfricasian missionary sending agencies and their 3,400 missionaries, reported in 1972, are only a part of the whole. Furthermore, if God has done this in the grey dawn, what will he not do as the sun rises higher in the heavens? As dedicated Christians of Eurica begin cooperating with Latfricasians in global propagation of the Gospel, very great disciplings are sure to happen.

Three main results of this great new resource stand out. *First, the numbers out there, evangelizing across cultural and linguistic barriers, have been materially augmented.* They are about to be increased still more. In Japan, a movement is afoot to send out 1,000 Japanese missionaries. In Korea, two seminaries are establishing specialized schools to prepare Korean evangelists to spread the Gospel outside Korea. It is well within the range of possibility that Korea should by 1984 send 2,000 missionaries abroad.

To date, many Latfricasian missionaries evangelize *within* their countries but in tribes and languages other than their own. Many go to other countries one by one and fit into Christian institutions there. This is a wise first step. But the evangelist is *a herald to those who have not heard.* He is not a fraternal worker to existing churches. His primary function is not to demonstrate brotherhood, but to reconcile unbelievers to God in the Church of Jesus Christ. So we may confidently expect that as numbers of Latfricasian missionaries increase, their evangelistic function will be emphasized.

The second main result of the great new resource is that it separates world evangelism from Eurican dominance. Part of the strange sickness which has afflicted world evangelism is that evangelism has appeared to be "Euricans spreading their religion." "Evangelism" and "missionary" appeared synonymous with "Eurican imperialism." No one wanted this. It was not true. But nevertheless this was — in some places more than others — a common impression. Naturally, nationalist Christians exclaimed, "Let us have no more religious imperialism." Some even believed that the word "missionary" was too mixed up with Eurican bossiness to be useful again.

The rise of Latfricasian missionary societies counters all this. Latfricasian missionary societies (multiplying year by year, sending out thousands of missionaries, creating missionary training institutions, praying for their evangelists overseas, developing theologies which require world evangelism) are acting as if Eurican dominance did not exist. *God* is speaking directly to them and they — like Barnabas and Saul — are going, "sent out by *the Holy Spirit.*" God is pouring out his Spirit on his people in *all* nations. World evangelism is being seen again as simple obedience to the divine call, as God's great answer to desperate human need.

The third result of Latfricasian missionary societies *is that by them world evangelism has been separated from the dominance of Latfricasian churches.* Let me speak plainly. Most "missionary" gatherings of the last fifty years have been attended by national leaders who represented the church, not the mission. Their concerns were the concerns of their national churches, not primarily of world evangelism. Thus the missionary movement, with the best intentions in the world, has been giving places of great power to good Christians who were *not* primarily interested in world evangelism. They were churchmen, principals of Christian colleges, heads of seminaries, prominent lawyers, government officials, and the like. Quite naturally they saw the needs of their churches more vividly than the needs of the unconverted. They correctly dominated Latfricasian *churches.* They unfortunately also dominated *world evangelism* in Latfricasian lands — and have retarded it.

As Latfricasian *missionary* societies are founded and multiply, it is going to become more and more possible for Euricans engaged in world evangelism to work with *Latfricasians to whom God has given the same obedience.* Evangelistic resources will be expended by persons *passionately interested in evangelism.* World evangelism is going to be freed from the dominance of good Christians, to whom God has given other obediences. The surge of power thus released will build a world evangelism commensurate with today's spiritual need and opportunity.

In addition to these three results, a fascinating *possibility* opens before us here at Lausanne — that part of the evangelistic power of Eurica be given to Latfricasian missionary societies engaged in conversion evangelism outside their own culture areas. Latfricasia is rich in man power. Its churches are culturally close to the peoples of Asia, Africa, and Latin America, but do not have the large resources needed to transport their evangelists across the oceans. Some cooperative arrangement with Eurican missionary societies would seem to be mutually profitable. (The largest part of Eurican missionary resources will, of course, continue to be spent in sending Eurica's own sons and daughters to areas where the Christ of Calvary is neither known nor loved. Evangelism to be valid must be the testimony of a church's own life blood, the witness of its own sons and daughters. But cooperation in great commission missions should be mutually fulfilling to Eurican and Latfricasian missionary societies.)

PART II: Human Dimensions

Human dimension 1 — The two billion with no knowledge of Christ

The huge numbers of the unevangelized constitute a most important human dimension of world evangelism.

More than two-thirds of mankind has yet to hear of Jesus Christ. C. Peter Wagner calls this two-thirds the "Fourth World." A small part of the Fourth World is in Switzerland, Europe, and North America, where maybe ninety million have never really heard the words "Jesus Christ," and consequently have never thought of accepting him as Savior and Lord. The overwhelming majority of the Fourth World, however, lives in Latfricasia. The missionary movement of the last two hundred years has established many churches there, but in most Latfricasian countries, all of the baptized put together (real Christians and nominal) are only a tiny minority of the total population. Often only one in a hundred is a Christian. Often less than one in a thousand is.

Furthermore, while the Gospel has been widely proclaimed, it has *not* been widely received. A few units of population have become heavily Christian. Most have not become heavily Christian. Most have not become Christian at all. As a result, congregations in each geographical unit of Latfricasia are usually made up of Christians predominately of one or two tribes, castes, or levels of economic or educational advancement. For example, in South India, where there are hundreds of castes, most Christians come from five castes only — Nadar, Pariah, Mala, Madiga, and Syrian. In Bolivia, most evangelical Christians come from *one* ethnic unit — the Aymara people. In Fiji, 98 per cent of the church comes from the aboriginal tribes and less than two per cent from the 200,000 East Indian immigrants. Endless other examples could be given.

These "pockets" of Christians have the same difficulty evangelizing outside their linguistic and ethnic boundaries as black Baptists would have in Lausanne evangelizing white Marxists. Outside their own ethnic units, the evangelizing power of churches is usually small.

Let us think of the little clusters of churches in most Latfricasian countries as existing on ethnic islands, surrounded by oceans of men and women who have never heard of Jesus Christ, never seen a Bible and never talked to a Christian. This is the brutal fact confronting world evangelism. This is the basic evangelistic problem faced by the World Church.

The policy advocated by some — that each cluster of congregations evangelize where it is, and the World Church de-emphasize sending evangelists from one land to another — is no solution. If carried out, it would deny the Gospel to huge populations, growing hungrier every year. That way lies disobedience and spiritual death.

The right way is for the whole church in the whole world to undertake the whole task as commanded by the Lord himself. The Christians on the islands will do their part in the evangelization of the oceans, but the tremendous reaches of humanity (which the islands are not evangelizing) *must be evangelized.* God will send in obedient servants from India, Africa, Korea, Nagaland, Mexico, United States, Brazil, Norway, and Scotland, in short, from every section of Eurica and Latfricasia. The Christians on the islands will welcome them as comrades in the urgent task of carrying the bread of life to the hungry multitudes.

Two billion of our brothers and sisters are living and dying with no allegiance to, and usually no knowledge of, the Savior of the world who "offered for all time one sacrifice for sins and took his seat at the right hand of God" (Heb. 10:12). The church must not betray the two billion. This Congress on Evangelism has no more important duty than to gaze on the plight of these multitudes, pour out before God earnest prayer for their salvation, and call on churches and missionary societies to launch programs of world evangelism of a magnitude commensurate with the herculean task. This is the first human dimension of World Evangelism.

Human dimension 2 — The magnificent and intricate mosaic of mankind

Mankind does not exist as one homogeneous whole, through which the Christian faith can readily run, given only the desire of existing Christians to evangelize. On the contrary, mankind exists as an incredibly intricate mosaic. Men are divided into thousands of linguistic divisions — if dialects are added, then tens of thousands! Ethnic units (racial blocks, castes, tribes, clans, extended families) are exceedingly numerous and divide all populations into segments psychologically closed to the rest of the world. Consider, for example, the exclusiveness of orthodox Jews, Chinese merchants, Masai tribesmen, or the landed aristocracy of Colombia. Let us now sub-divide each linguistic and ethnic unit into social and economic segments — rich and poor orthodox Jews, educated and illiterate Masai tribesmen, Brahmans who own factories and those who own nothing! We now begin to see the extensiveness and complexity of the magnificent mosaic which is the second human dimension of world evangelism. It is this mosaic which Christ commands us to evangelize. World evangelism, if it is to measure up to today's task and opportunity, means precisely kinds of communication of the Gospel which will carry across the hard little walls which so effectively separate each piece of the mosaic from the next.

The Christian faith — once in and abundant — flows well within each piece of the mosaic, but tends to stop at linguistic and ethnic barriers. Most existing congregations are shut up to one language, one ethnic unit, and frequently to one social or economic class. Since men like to become Christians without crossing barriers, the first task among the two billion is an evangelism designed to multiply churches in each new piece of the magnificent mosaic. Only after numerous indigenous churches exist in each piece, has spontaneous evangelism much chance of succeeding.

Tremendously important parts of the mosaic are the cities, growing greater each day. Cities exist in all lands, and to date have proved somewhat resistant to the Christian message. Urban churches are growing more by influx of rural Christians than by conversion of the city masses. World evangelism must reverse this and start multitudes of thriving congregations in the great commerical, manufacturing, educational, and communication centers of the modern world.

Adaptation of Christianity to the culture of each piece of the mosaic is crucially important. Tens of thousands of adaptations must be made. Christianity must be freed from the tyranny of Eurican patterns of worship and of church. It must also be freed from the tyranny of Latfricasian patterns. For example, Christianity in India is not likely to flow into the middle castes until it shakes itself free from the tyranny both of Eurican patterns and of Indian patterns developed while it grew strong among the lowest of the hundreds of castes. Evangelical Christianity in Mexico is not likely to thrive among the Maya Indians as long as it approaches them in the patterns of the Spanish-speaking evangelical churches.

Thus, the goal of world evangelism is not merely "a church of Jesus Christ" in every nation. To state the task that way is to misunderstand it. The true goal is to multiply, *in every piece of the magnificent mosaic, truly Christian churches which fit that piece,* are closely adapted to *its* culture, and recognized by *its* non-Christians as "our kind of show." Doing *that* is the second human dimension of world evangelism.

Human dimension 3 — Unprecedented receptivity

The third broad stroke in the human picture of world evangelism is today's unprecedented receptivity to the Christian religion. Consider a few facts.

Taiwan in 1946 had only 33,000 Christians. Twenty-five years later, in 1971, it had 650,000. Perhaps 50,000 of these were Christians who in 1948 came over with Generalissimo Chiang Kai Shek from the mainland; but the vast majority were converts won in Taiwan. In these twenty-five years, the church in Taiwan *multiplied twenty times.*

In India, in the newly created States of Meghalaya and Nagaland, Christians are now either in the majority or soon will be.

In 1952, Africa south of the Sahara had, I calculated, 20 million Christians. In 1968, sixteen years later, a second careful calculation showed 50 million. In less than twenty years, the Christian population had increased by 30 million. Nothing like it has been seen in Christian history. The church continues to grow apace. Dr. Barrett, the Anglican authority, has made a careful demographic forecast that if present trends continue, there will be 357 million Christians in Africa by the year 2000. I have no reason to doubt his estimate; but if it is only half right, there will still be 180 million Christians in Africa *twenty-six years from now.*

I could easily mention Korea, Indonesia, Brazil, Chile, and a dozen other lands where notable ingathering is going on.

How does it happen that so many Christians in high places have failed to see this unprecedented receptivity? The wave of pessimism which swept over the churches following World War II triggered a hasty — and unsound — reinterpretation of Christian objectives and an accompanying withdrawal from world evangelism. In the climate thus created, the tremendous receptivity of many of the world's populations was obscured and — by a few die-hards — is still denied. But like Mt. Everest, unprecedented receptivity is *there* and constitutes a major dimension of world evangelism.

Pessimists can, of course, rivet their gaze on resistant areas, of which there are still many. But provedly responsive populations are so huge that we are not yet adequately harvesting *them*. We can almost thank God that the resistant fields have *not* yet ripened! The resistant peoples of the world — make no mistake — must also hear the Gospel. The Bible straightly charges us to preach to all the world — and that means resistant as well as receptive. We should obey that command. But we should also answer all Macedonian calls and baptize all the responsive, so that none holds out his hands in vain, begging for the Gospel.

This Congress must beware of pessimistic generalizations to the effect that evangelism is passé, missionaries are not wanted, modern man demands bread not God, and a pluralistic world simply cannot conceive of one way to God and one revelation of his will. Some of these gloomy generalizations are the fruit of the Eurican guilt complex. Some Europeans' good news consists in beating their breasts and proclaiming their guilt! Other pessimism is caused by decades of defeat in resistant populations and is set forth as universal truth concerning world evangelism. Much negativism is the outcome of eroded faith, non-biblical presuppositions, and heretical opinions, phrased in seemingly objective judgments about "the modern mind" and "current trends." This Congress must reject sub-Christian philosophies and theologies masquerading as scientific assessment of the situation.

The facts support a far different assessment — unprecedented receptivity! Facts call for evangelism on a greater scale. Churches from more nations than ever before must thrust out more ambassadors of Christ. Latfricasian churches are beginning to send significant numbers. They must be helped to send still more and guided so that their missionaries and evangelists take advantage of two hundred years' experience when Euricans had to initiate world evangelization alone. Eurica also must increase the quantity and improve the quality of her sendings. The church in all six continents must surge forward in evangelism.

Receptivity is a human dimension. It consists of responsive persons. But it is also a divine dimension. God has spoken to these multitudes. The Holy Spirit has turned them receptive. They hear the voice of the Great Shepherd and seek to follow him. Christ's church in all six continents must look to her Master and follow his lead in proclaiming the Good News of salvation and incorporating believers in multiplying thousands of Christian cells, churches of Christ, congregations of the redeemed.

Human dimension 4 — The suddenly important masses
World evangelism must evangelize the masses.

The day of the common man has dawned. An irreversible tide is sweeping the voiceless multitudes to positions of tremendous power.

Illiterate peasants, country serfs, factory laborers, poverty-stricken miners, cannon fodder, the poor, the hewers of wood and drawers of water have been given the vote in nation after nation. They are the court of last appeal. This is the fruit partly of Christian conviction and partly of western democracy, fertilized of late by Russian and Chinese Communism.

There have always been enormous numbers of common people; but today they have become aware of their importance, and their *power*. They are demanding equal pay, equal educational opportunity, equal leisure — in short, social justice. The roar of their demands testifies eloquently to the titanic force of the revolutionary dynamic. Monseigneur Cardijn, founder of the Young Christian Workers, recently wrote: "These proletarian masses, which today are powerless, will tomorrow become the arbiters of order, progress and peace. Only the blind are unaware of this. No technological power can prevent these populations from deciding tomorrow the future of the world" (Retif: 1962: 154).

Awakening multitudes are often basically receptive to the Gospel. In the past, despite the fact that Eurican missionaries and Latfricasian ministers, being educated middle class people, have usually approached the middle classes first, the huge majority of those accepting Jesus Christ and becoming Christians have been common people. Currently also tremendous growth of Pentecostal and other churches is taking place among the masses. The masses have a built-in receptivity to the Good News. Oppressed and ground down, they, like ancient Israel, are "looking for a Savior." Their ears are atune to him who cries, "Come unto me all you who labor and are heavy laden." For the foreseeable future, the masses will continue receptive.

Furthermore, the Christian church has good news for the awakening masses — that God the Father Almighty is just and intends to have a just world. The revolutionary impact of this simple statement should be grasped. It affirms that the very structure of the universe favors the common man. It proclaims that God intends an order of society in which each man can and will receive justice. This meets the deepest needs of the proletariat. Contrary to paternalistic thinking, the greatest need of the masses is neither aid nor kindness. Their greatest need is neither handouts nor social action; but a religion which gives them bedrock on which to stand as they battle for justice.

The highly valuable gifts of the Christian religion are: God the Father Almighty who hates injustice, God the Son who died for each man of the masses, and the Bible which demands justice for the common man. The Christian religion endows every human being with infinite value. "Making people Christian," along with other things, means giving them a world view and a Bible which irresistibly, though often slowly, create equality of opportunity and undergird all strivings against entrenched privilege. With *this* wealth in hand, the masses can conquer secondary poverties.

Evangelistic policies should be determined not on the aristocratic feudal social orders which dominated the world a few years ago; but on the forms which society is taking and is going to take. In the new social orders being born today, the comman man is going to play a determining role. Hence the common man must be *effectively evangelized now.* This is the fourth human dimension in world evangelism.

PART III: METHODOLOGICAL DIMENSIONS
Methodological dimension 1 — Kinds of evangelism

The kinds of evangelism needed today have been used through the centuries; but seeing them as different kinds, giving them different names, and planning for adequate amounts of each is a new dimension of world evangelism.

Let us, following Dr. Ralph Winter, distinguish three kinds of evangelism — E-1, E-2, and E-3.

E-1 evangelizes people in one's own language and culture.

E-2 evangelizes people of a similar language and culture.

E-3 evangelizes people of radically different languages and cultures. These distinctions will help us understand world evangelism.

Most local evangelism which Christians and churches do in their own neighborhoods, is E-1, many "home missionaries" are carrying out E-1. When the early Christians fled from Jerusalem, they "went about preaching the Gospel." Since they "spake the word to none but Jews" they were engaged in E-1 evangelism. E-1 is excellent for reaching one's own people, but stops at cultural and linguistic barriers. It does not reach "the Gentiles." We must recruit and train millions of E-1s — unpaid volunteer evangelists. They play a most important role. However, in today's bewildering pluralism, with thousands of languages, cultures, classes, occupations, economic levels, and residential groupings, E-1 has serious limitations. It seldom carries the Gospel from one piece of the mosaic into the next.

E-2 is needed. E-2 resolutely evangelizes men of other but similar cultures and languages. For example, were the Lutheran Church of Germany to multiply churches among Greek immigrants working in German factories it would be carrying out E-2 evangelism. The Karen churches of South Burma sent E-2s to evangelize the Kachins of North Burma. Since Spanish culture and language are similar to the British, British Christians send E-2 missionaries to evangelize Spanish speakers of Bolivia. Tremendous multiplication of E-2 evangelism is urgent.

E-3 evangelism seeks out men of radically different cultures and languages. St. Paul was an E-1 and an E-2 missionary in Mediterranean lands, but had he gone to the Chinese, the Bantus, or the philosophers of India he would have been doing E-3 evangelism. Huge blocks of humanity lie beyond the reach of E-1 *and E-2* evangelism. Only evangelists who learn a radically different language and a radically different culture can communicate Christ to awaiting hundreds of millions.

For example, while in Europe out of every thousand citizens, at least 900 have been baptized, in China out of every thousand, less than one has been. Obviously, if the evangelization of China is left to this one man (i.e., to E-1 and E-2 evangelism) the vast majority of the 800 million Chinese will never even hear the name of Jesus. Multitudes of E-3s are essential. They go to other countries and evangelize men of other languages, religions, and cultures, who do not yet know the Savior.

Tremendous need for E-3 evangelism surges round us at Lausanne.

That in the foreseeable future, E-1 can reach most people in most nations is an irresponsible daydream. Only the deliberate, costly sending of E-2 and E-3 evangelists across cultural, linguistic, and national frontiers can possibly accomplish world evangelization.

Professor Jack Shepherd has recently defined "a missionary" as a Christian of any culture or nation who is *sent, across cultural and linguistic frontiers, to win men to Christ and incorporate them in Christian churches. Missionaries* are carrying out E-2 and E-3 evangelism. That is their basic function.

In this paper, to mean men and women engaged in Evangelism 2 and 3, I shall use the words "Missionary," "Evangelist 2," and "Evangelist 3" interchangeably.

Distinguishing three kinds of evangelism is essential to clear thinking. Each variety is needed — E-1, E-2 and E-3 — *and in great quantity*. To think solely in terms of E-1 is to misunderstand evangelism, to doom millions to live without Christ, and to condemn to failure societies pressing on to justice and brotherhood. To think in terms of three varieties, however, is to understand global evangelism and to take a long step toward meeting basic human needs and liberating societies.

Methodological dimension 2 — modes of church growth

In answering our basic question, "What does carrying out the great commission mean today?", we must consider modes of church growth. Evangelism is not shouting "the right words" whether anything happens or not. Evangelism always longs for the salvation of those who hear. Evangelism proclaims Jesus Christ as God and Savior and persuades men to become his disciples and responsible members of his church. Evangelism prays for church growth. Lausanne must therefore consider the *modes of church growth* being blessed of God to the salvation of millions. These constitute the normal outcomes of evangelism.

The first mode of growth is *"one-by-one-against-the-family."* In this, converts come to Christ one by one, regardless of what other members of their families do. Often the family tries to prevent the person becoming a Christian. When he accepts Christ he does so alone, against the family. On new ground, lone persons are often the first fruit of evangelism. This form of growth has taken place across all lands of earth. God uses it to begin the process, but he blesses other modes to better and greater growth.

The second mode of church growth is *the family movement to Christ.* In this, several members of a family accept the Lord at the same time. The New Testament tells of many family conversions. "He and his household" accepted the Lord, is frequently recorded. "One by one against the family" should normally progress to where decisions are being made family by family. The church grows better when this happens.

The third mode of church growth is *the people movement to Christ.* In this, chains of families, all within the same segment of populations (the same caste, tribe, or culture unit) become Christians. "A people movement results from the joint decision of a number of individuals — whether five or five hundred — all from the same people, which enables them to become Christian without social dislocation, while remaining in full contact with their non-Christian relatives, thus enabling other groups of families across the years, after suitable instruction to come to similar decisions and form Christian churches made up exclusively of members of that people" (p. 297, *Understanding Church Growth*).

The great advances of the Christian religion on new ground have come very largely by people movements. These are today bringing multitudes to Christian faith in all the continents. Tomorrow, the great surges of church growth are likely to come from people movements of which there are many different varieties. *World evangelism should constantly be praying for and planning for family movements and people movements to Christ.*

The fourth mode of church growth being blessed of God is the multiplication in cities and villages of *house churches*. Tens of thousands can now be established. Evangelism will be more effective as it finds ways to organize converts into small congregations in homes.

As the Gospel is proclaimed on new ground, much seed-sowing evangelism is in order. Nevertheless we must constantly aim at church growth and seek modes of evangelism God has blessed to the multiplication of churches.

Measurement of outcomes also is essential. The shepherd must count his sheep to know that one is lost. Measurement must, of course, be undertaken with due sensitivity to imponderable values. Yet churches consist of countable members and there is nothing particularly spiritual in not counting them. All worthwhile enterprises set goals and estimate advance by degrees of achievement. The men who set up this Congress knew exactly how many hotel rooms and how many seats they would require. Measurement is essential. Recently the cause of world evangelism has been materially advanced by Dr. Vergil Gerber's delightfully clear procedures for helping pastors and church leaders measure their evangelistic effectiveness. His *Manual for Evangelism/Church Growth* should be widely used in all countries. It is already available in fourteen languages.

Methodological dimension 3 — Multiplying evangelists

Global evangelism in the modern world means multiplying evangelists — E-1s, E-2s, and E-3s. *Multiplying E-1s* means promoting spontaneous evangelism, mobilizing churches for outreach, and equipping lay Christians with spiritual gifts sufficient to multiply churches in their own cultures. Significant extension in each piece of the mosaic where the church is now strong has become abundantly possible today and must be pressed.

Multiplying E-2s and E-3s means creating specialized messengers — apostles equipped to operate across linguistic and cultural barriers, who will face the unprecedented receptivity of many pieces of the magnificent mosaic.

God is calling for thousands of Latfricasian and Eurican evangelists. The hugely responsive pieces of the mosaic can be discipled only as churches from *every* land send their best sons to carry the Gospel across cultural frontiers. The task is international in scope. "Sending churches" are now everywhere. Christ calls messengers across culture barriers to hundreds of thousands of villages, towns and cities where tremendous numbers have not heard the Gospel. He says, "Find and feed my sheep."

Large numbers are needed — it makes no difference whether these are called E-2 and E-3 evangelists or missionaries, or are Euricans or Latfricasians! The day is too urgent to quibble over words.

Wisdom is demanded in their deployment. Their recruitment and support are challenging enterprises. Instructing sending churches in every nation in missionary duties and privileges should become at once an important function of every theological training school and denominational headquarters.

These multiplied thousands of evangelists should maintain the servant image and, in Pauline fashion, soon turn the direction of new churches over to new Christians. The cultural integrity of each cluster of churches must be preserved and each, as soon as it is formed, encouraged to join in the evangelism of the "yet-to-believe."

Multiplying evangelists is a costly dimension. Lausanne must resist the shoddy idea that world evangelism can be achieved cheaply without sending missionaries. Sacrifice is demanded. Life must be poured out. But if that is done, never in the history of the world have the prospects been brighter for the Water of Life flowing freely to thirsty men. Let there be no failure of nerve, no faltering of faith. These are years when, with John on Patmos, we must see *every creature in heaven* and *on earth* and *under the earth* and *in the sea* crying, 'Praise and honor and glory and power to him who sits on the throne and to the Lamb for ever and ever.'"

CONCLUSION

In the first letter of Paul to the Corinthians in chapter one we read, "For the preaching of the Cross is folly to those who are perishing, but to us who are being saved it is the power of God. . . . For since, in the wisdom of God, the world did not know God through wisdom, it pleased God through the folly of what we preach to save those who believe. For Jews demand signs and Greeks seek wisdom, but we preach Christ crucified, a stumbling block to Jews and folly to the Gentiles, but to those who are called, both Jews and Greeks, Christ the power of God and the wisdom of God."

World evangelism goes forward, not in the power of men, but in the power of God; not in the wisdom of men, but in the wisdom of God, not by philosophy but by the Cross of Christ. This is the ultimate dimension of world evangelism.

Tremendous forces are arrayed against world evangelism; but in the sign of the Cross, the mission of healing and redeeming sinful, alienated men and their societies will overcome all adversaries. The Cross is the dynamic of renewal and revival and awakening within the church. The Cross is also the dynamic of evangelization across cultural barriers outside the church. Evangelism continues till there is a cell of committed Christians in every community in every city and every countryside throughout the whole wide world. This will prepare the way for our Lord's triumphant return.

THE DIMENSIONS OF WORLD EVANGELIZATION

Donald McGavran

Christian Friends:

We have all studied the strategy paper on "The Vast Dimensions of World Evangelism." More than a thousand of you sent in responses and Mr. Little has asked me to prepare this address in their light. I am assuming that the paper forms the foundation of our thoughts, and I shall interact with your responses which greatly enriched my thinking, and talk to you in a quite informal way. I wish I could answer every one of your questions, but there are *thousands* of them! I shall speak to representative questions and in that way touch on most of your concerns.

Before I do that, let me very briefly recapitulate the main stream of my thought. I presented ten dimensions of world evangelization.

I stressed, *first*, that Christ commands world evangelization, salvation comes only through faith in Jesus Christ, the only inspired Scripture is the Bible, and while horizontal reconciliation of man with man is good, it is no substitute for vertical reconciliation of man with God. *Second*, comes the biblical fact that God accepts all cultures as equally valid vehicles for the Gospel. *Third*, the cheering news that God has recently created a great new resource for world evangelism — hundreds of Latfricasian missionary societies whose sendings total thousands of cross-cultural missionary-evangelists.

Fourth comes the awesome challenge to evangelize three billion, living with no knowledge of Jesus. *Fifth*, these billions exist as an intricate mosaic of tribes, castes, peoples, and languages, and this mosaic demands many kinds of evangelism. *Sixth*, unprecedented receptivity reveals attainable multitudes in many lands. *Seventh*, the tremendously important masses await the Gospel with outstretched hands.

Eighth, I placed "Recognizing and Using Three Evangelisms" — E-1 with men of our own cultures, E-2 with men of slightly different cultures, and E-3 with men of radically different cultures. *Ninth*, I discussed the four kinds of church growth which mark our day — one by one, family by family, people movements and the formation of house churches. *Tenth*, I stressed the costly multiplying of evangelists and missionaries. Thousands of full-time evangelists who work across cultures, and literally millions of unpaid lay evangelists who work in their own neighborhoods must be *prayed* for, *recruited, trained,* and *deployed.*

Such in *barest* outline are the global dimensions of world evangelism. Please remember them. The immense task is worldwide. It touches every tribe and tongue and people and nation. Each of us knows well a small part of the whole; we must try to see the other parts. We cannot exaggerate the significance of seeing the big picture. The huge dimensions of the task to which God calls us should occupy the center of our consciousness and be the subject of our prayers. We are gathered on the King's business. And the King is coming!

Now let me turn to some of the questions and comments which

formed in your minds as you studied and prayed about the exciting dimensions of world evangelization.

Dimension one

You agreed heartily to most matters treated under the first dimension; but wanted two points discussed. First, several asked the searching question, "When has a man or a society been evangelized? When is the job complete?" The biblical answer is clear. A man has been evangelized *when becoming a disciple of Jesus Christ becomes a real possibility to him.* Not when he has heard the Gospel once, not when he has been fed or taught, not when he joins a liberation movement, or passes the doors of a church; but when becoming a Christian appears to him as a genuine option. He has then truly "heard" the Gospel. Most men will be evangelized when some of their kith and kin become Christian and they hear the Gospel from and see it lived out by *their own kind of people.* It then becomes understandable. Scripture is clear that many will still reject the Good News, but at least they have really heard it. In short, evangelization is complete when the multitudinous *neighborhoods* of mankind have in each of them a believing obedient congregation. All the other good things I mentioned are steps in the process, but the goal is an ongoing believing congregation in each neighborhood — each thousand, let us say, of the sons of men.

Second, about a tenth of you asked questions like these: Can we evangelize in today's world without vigorously engaging in social action? Can men be saved as individuals, if the social order is bad? Must not evangelism aim to change evil social structures? These questions deserve careful answers.

Of course, Christians engage in social action. Social structures, when evil, must be changed. Christians have always done this, are doing it, and always will. Ethical improvements, both personal and social, are the fruit of salvation. They issue naturally from sound conversion. The Holy Spirit leads Christians into all righteousness — both individual and corporate. Biblically well-instructed Christians are the world's greatest reformers. The most potent forces for social change are Bible-reading, Bible-obeying churches.

But first, my friends, you must have some Christians and some churches!! First you must have reborn men. Evangelism is persuading men to accept Christ and his gift of forgiveness, new power, and new righteousness. Evangelism is not proclaiming the desirability of a liquor-less world and persuading people to vote for prohibition. Evangelism is not proclaiming the desirability of sharing the wealth and persuading people to take political action to achieve it. Christians who judge these and others like them to be good ends will of course work for them, pray for them and fight for them. And I will enthusiastically back such Christians. Make no mistake about that!

But evangelism is something else. Evangelism is proclaiming Jesus Christ as God and only Savior and persuading men to become his disciples and responsible members of his church. That is the first and basic task. Calling people to repent and to become disciples of the Son of Righteousness is the most important political act that anyone can perform. Until politicized Christians realize that, our politics will be terribly inadequate.

Then too we must remember that the biblical conditions for conversion are only three — repentance, belief on the Lord Jesus, and baptism. Christians like to add to these biblical requirements ethical improvements of many kinds — quit drinking, stop smoking, start tithing, attack slavery, renounce child labor, stop segregation, and on and on. The wise evangelist adds such of these good things as he can; but never "loads on the law" so greatly that becoming a Christian is seen merely as a matter of ethical improvement. On the contrary, he intends that "becoming a Christian" should always be seen as — quite simply — trusting Jesus and being arrayed in his righteousness. Once that is done, once the new Christians feed on the Divine Word, ethical improvement follows. When, through belief on Jesus Christ, men's sins have been nailed to the Cross and his blood has cleansed them, they can be, ought to be, and are being led into and indeed pushed into as much righteousness and beneficial social change as possible. The Bible is full of examples.

Dimension two

Most of you rejoiced in the thought that "God accepts world cultures"; but many asked me to explain what this means. Let me try. You see, European cultures and languages are in no sense favorites of God. He speaks every language fluently. *People can become good Christians in every culture.* To be sure, each culture is a mixture of many good and a few bad components. As its adherents become Christians, bad components must be cleansed or eliminated, but most components will come in as they are. Men will continue to speak the same language, live in the same kind of houses, wear the same kind of clothes. Factory workers will continue to work in factories and field workers in fields.

Evangelism redeems each culture whose adherents believe the Good News and makes each more beautiful while it remains itself. Evangelization is the greatest benefit possible to confer on any culture. Far from destroying it, evangelization brings out its latent beauties. All this is what we mean by saying that "God accepts world cultures."

Dimension three

No section of this strategy paper excited more comment than that which described the new resource which God is creating for world evangelization. The multiplication of Latfricasian missionary societies sending out Asians, Africans, and Latin Americans was news to many of you. More than 200 sending agencies are now in existence and their number is increasing. I reported 3,400 Latfricasian missionaries and church-planting evangelists, but when all the facts are known, the numbers are sure to be greater.

This Congress does well to rejoice in the sending of these Latfricasian evangelists. As sister missionary societies multiply and hundreds of thousands of congregations — did you hear me? — hundreds of thousands of Latfricasian congregations catch the vision of world evangelization and send out their sons and daughters to announce "release to captives and recovery of sight to the blind, preach to the poor and proclaim the acceptable year of the Lord," *the magnitude of the resource which God has raised up will become apparent.* Think of what praying for "our missionaries at work in the South Sudan" will do for thousands of *Christian congregations in Uganda!* Think of what sacrificial giving to "our missionaries in Andhra Pradesh" will do for thousands of *churches in Tamilnadu!* Think of what a burden for the evangelization of Asian millions will do for the churches of Korea, Japan, Philippines, and North-east India!

Hundreds of you commented favorably on my suggestion that, while Latricasians will give sacrificially to their own missions, and while Euricans will continue to send thousands of their best sons and daughters to evangelize the three billion, "some cooperative arrangement between Eurican and Latfricasian missionary societies would be mutually profitable." You want this fascinating possibility explored. I hope it will be explored in the working groups here at Lausanne. As you explore and implement the plan, let me suggest that the key is *conversion evangelism.* Any responsible Latfricasian missionary society, engaged in church-multiplying evangelism, could to advantage use substantial aid from sister missionary societies in Eurica. I believe these in turn would look with favor on cooperating with Asian, African, and Latin American colleagues who are evangelizing and planting new churches.

An infilling of the Holy Spirit which sends out bands of evangelists to the lost is what we should pray for. Then all missionary societies in all six continents will multiply their sendings.

Dimension four

Please remember that in January, 1975, the population of the world will pass the four billion mark. This means that instead of two billion, there are now close to *three* billion with no knowledge of the Christ of Calvary. We must make sure that Lausanne does not betray the three billion. The task of evangelism is greater than it has ever been — but so are our resources. Huge numbers of the "yet to believe" and "yet to be saved" tug at our hearts.

In many Latfricasian lands, little clusters of congregations are surrounded by multitudes who have never heard of Jesus Christ and never seen or read a Bible. As you Latfricasian delegates face this brutal fact, many of you said substantially this, "We will do our part. We will stretch every nerve. We will send our sons and our money. But it is impossible for us to evangelize these multitudes alone. Missionary societies and churches from all six continents must *do* more, *pray* more, *give* more, and *send* more. Only a vast outpouring of witness will meet the world need." A typical comment is this, "In this country, our unreached population is so big and our church so small that, unless Lausanne arouses the World Church to evangelize as it has never done before, most people are going to die in their sins."

Dimension five

Many kinds of evangelism are required. Most of you knew of the thousands of pieces in the mosaic of mankind — language groups, religion groups, castes, tribes, classes, occupational groups, fishermen, peasants, elite, students, and on and on. Some of you, however, had *not* realized that each piece of the mosaic demands an evangelism specially suited to itself. *Many kinds* of evangelism are required. Each must be tailored — to fit perhaps the elite, perhaps the proletariat, perhaps the peasants — in short, tailored to suit one particular piece of the mosaic.

A perceptive delegate asked, "My fellow Christians gladly evangelize their own tribesmen, but how can I get them to care about the salvation of the people down on the plains who have raided us for hundreds of years?" Multiply that question by thousands and you see one most important dimension of the mosaic.

But there is another. Many of you called attention to the fact that evangelizing our own social context, our own piece of the mosaic, is both possible and urgent. You asked me to emphasize it. I do so gladly. "Perhaps the most immediately practical response to Lausanne," you said, "is *neighborhood evangelism.* That everyone can do. That everyone should do." I thoroughly agree.

Dimension six

Unprecedented receptivity reveals winnable multitudes. Most of you were surprised at this; yet the facts are beyond dispute. Renewal and evangelism and church growth surge through North America and Europe. Evangelical movements of power are seen in Brazil, Chile, Bolivia, Ecuador, and other countries of Latin America. Notable church growth has occurred in Taiwan, Korea, the Philippines, Indonesia, and parts of India. All Africa south of the Sahara is in process of becoming substantially Christian. Twenty-five thousand of the hundred thousand gypsies in France have become Christian in recent years.

True, as some of you pointed out, there still are many resistant populations where evangelists and missionaries can preach and preach and heal and heal, and men dully turn away from the Savior. In such lands, seed-sowing evangelism is still greatly needed. Missionary societies will, of course, continue it.

But these resistant populations must not hide from us the numerous winnable multitudes. We sometimes hear that evangelism is old-fashioned and outmoded, no one wants to become a Christian, modern man needs bread, not God, and the era of church-planting is past. What utter nonsense! We must denounce the Satanic word that when men choose God, he will deny them bread. Our Lord clearly said, "Seek first the Kingdom of God and all these things *shall* be added unto you." As one of you said so truly, "Loss of empire dulled our vision and diminished our faith; but thank God we do not have to live in the past." Another wrote, "After Willengen, we expected defeat and retreat, but God had other things in store for us. He has marvelously advanced the Gospel. The churches here, though they face terrific problems, are growing as they have never done." The sober truth is, as one of you wrote, "God is opening more and more doors to evangelism today."

Dimension seven

Suddenly important masses await the Gospel. Several of you urged me to "emphasize above all else the evangelization of ordinary men." A typical response reads, "It is high time we gave more emphasis to reaching the masses — in Eurica as well as in Latfricasia. In Eurica the church and its evangelism have become middle class institutions and do little to reach working men." Our Lord declared that one of the marks of the coming of his Kingdom was that *the poor* had the Gospel preached to them. The masses are crucially important in God's program of evangelism.

Dimension eight

Three kinds of evangelism — E-1, E-2, and E-2 — are needed to reach the four billion who inhabit the globe. Since my colleague, Dr. Ralph Winter, will devote his whole address to this subject, I call attention to only one of your comments. Stressing that E-1 is good, but not enough, one thoughtful church leader wrote, "Turning global evangelization over to each church where it stands and expecting thus to complete the evangelization of the world is an utterly inadequate policy based on a simplistic understanding of the situation." That is a true word.

Dimension nine

The world church is today liberating men by four great modes of church growth — one by one *out* of the family, and often, alas, *against* it; family by family; people movements to Christ; and multiplication of house and hamlet churches. This section of the strategy paper elicited hundreds of comments and requests for information. Many of you knew by experience one of these modes and wanted to know about the others. You asked for information about people movements and how to start them. You were fascinated by the idea of house churches, but not sure they were possible. You asked me to tell you how to win families. You questioned the desirability of people movements. One of you wrote indignantly, "Why does any conversion ever have to be 'against the family'?" Your important questions would require hours to answer — and I have minutes. The best I can do is to make four brief suggestions.

First, read extensively on church growth. Many have written on the subject. Available books deal with church growth in Africa, Asia, Europe, Latin America, North America, and Oceania. Read voraciously. Subscribe to a magazine on church growth.

Second, when necessary, translate materials on the growth of churches into your language.

Third, teach all four modes of church growth to your fellow workers and to seminary students. Introduce church growth into your seminary or Bible school curriculum. Often evangelism is unfruitful because it plans for response according to a mode which does not suit the population being evangelized. Evangelism must call for a mode of church growth possible to that population.

Fourth, observe and study the modes which, in your land, God is blessing to the multiplication of his churches and the extension of his Kingdom. The world church needs the light which *your* research can shed on this vital outcome of evangelism.

A number of you felt that urban church growth had been slighted. I plead guilty at this point. I devoted a paragraph to it, but should have said *much* more about multiplying congregations in towns and cities. Evangelism must win the *urban* world. Urban evangelism should establish great numbers of vigorous Christian cells, house churches, small churches, large churches, mono-ethnic churches, multi-ethnic churches, and cathedrals. Organizational forms are essential and should be multitudinous. Urban men desperately need Christian churches.

God has recently given us, through sociology and the science of management and social control, new understanding of the city. As redeemed men use these, they will begin to solve the horrendous problems and repel the demonic forces which blight and curse the rapidly growing cities. Solving the problems will not be easy, but God has given Christians two tools — evangelism and the sciences of man — which can make cities better places in which to live. Cities must have redeemed men, filled with the Holy Spirit. Urban church growth must harness the sciences of man to divine ends and direct the enterprise according to God's revelation in the Bible and in Jesus Christ.

Dimension ten

The last dimension I stress is *costly multiplying of evangelists and missionaries.* Expending what treasure is necessary, we must multiply lay Christians for outreach and train *unpaid* leaders who go out among their fellows to find the lost. We must equip lay Christians with spiritual gifts sufficient to witness in their own cultures, strengthen existing congregations, and multiply new congregations. Significant extension in each piece of the mosaic where the church is now strong must be pressed. Tremendous increase of glad volunteer near-neighbor evangelists is now abundantly possible.

We must also multiply Latfricasian and Eurican culture-crossing evangelists and missionaries — life-time people. Several of you pointed out that this means "creating specialized messengers, equipped to operate, for many years, across linguistic and cultural barriers." One man wrote, "The many responsive segments of the population can be discipled only as churches from every land send their best sons to carry the Gospel across cultural frontiers. The task is international in scope." Sending missionaries is everybody's task. Every congregation should be a sending congregation! Christ calls messengers across culture barriers to hundreds of thousands of villages, towns and cities where millions have not heard the Gospel.

Multiplying evangelists is *costly.* Lausanne must resist the shoddy idea that world evangelization can be achieved cheaply. Sacrifice is demanded. Life must be poured out. But if that is done, never have the prospects been brighter for the Water of Life flowing freely to thirsty men. Let there be no failure of nerve, no faltering of faith.

Our conversation about the ten dimensions of world evangelization draws to a close. As we, coming from every part of the world, have studied these dimensions, I trust we have seen the vast, varied, and exciting tasks to which God calls us. I trust our plans are big plans — as big as the needs of men, as big as the purposes of God.

We meet at a time of unique opportunity. European empires have ended. The brotherhood of nations has begun. Evangelization means all Christian churches and all missionary societies (Latfricasian and Eurican) directed by the Risen and Reigning King, streaming out to evangelize, liberate, and bless every corner of the world. He commands us to saturate our neighborhoods with the Gospel. He directs us to carry the Bread of Heaven to hungry multitudes across every chasm of language, culture, and class. Our Lord wants sure foundations built, redeemed men and women, on which a more just, more peaceful and brotherly world can be built.

And he marches on before us into every city, every village, every plain, and every mountain — loving and serving, saving and blessing all who will believe in him and be made whole. Evangelization means, very simply, following in his bloodstained footprints and inviting men to believe on him — till he comes.

EVANGELISM AND THE WORLD
Rene'Padilla

*Dr. Padilla is Associate General
Secretary for Latin America of the
International Fellowship of Evangelical
Students with headquarters in Buenos Aires.*

The Gospel of Jesus Christ is a personal message — it reveals a God who calls each of his own by name. But it is also a cosmic message — it reveals a God whose purpose includes the whole world. It is not addressed to the individual *per se,* but to the individual as a member of the old humanity in Adam, marked by sin and death, whom God calls to be integrated into the new humanity in Christ, marked by righteousness and eternal life.

The lack of appreciation of the wider dimensions of the Gospel leads inevitably to a misunderstanding of the mission of the church. The result is an evangelism that regards the individual as a self-contained unit — a Robinson Crusoe to whom God's call is addressed as on an island — whose salvation takes place exclusively in terms of a relationship to God. It is not seen that the individual does not exist in isolation, and consequently that it is not possible to speak of salvation with no reference to the world of which he is a part.

In his high priestly prayer Jesus Christ pleaded thus for his disciples: "I am no more in the world, but they are in the world, and I am coming to thee. . . . I do not pray that thou shouldst take them out of the world, but that thou shouldst keep them from the evil one. They are not of the world, even as I am not of the world" (John 17:11, 15-16). The paradox of Christian discipleship in relation to the world is placed before us — to be *in* the world, but not to be *of* the world. The present paper may be regarded as an attempt to explain the meaning of that paradox in its bearing on evangelism. The study is divided into three parts. The first is an analysis of the various usages of the term "world" in the New Testament. The second shows in what sense evangelism deals with a separation from the world, inasmuch as the disciples of Christ are not *of* the world. The third, finally, views evangelism from the perspective of involvement with the world, an involvement which reflects the fact that the disciples of Christ are *in* the world.

PART ONE: THE WORLD IN BIBLICAL PERSPECTIVE

A simple observation of the important place that the term *world* (Greek: *cosmos*) has in the New Testament (especially in the Johannine and Pauline writings, and passages relating to the history of salvation) should suffice to demonstrate the cosmic dimension of the Gospel. God's work in Jesus Christ deals directly with the world as a whole, not simply with the individual. Thus, a soteriology that does not take into account the relationship between the Gospel and the world, does not do justice to the teaching of the Bible.

But, what is the world?

I cannot here attempt an exhaustive study of the topic, but by way of introduction will briefly try to sort out the various strands of meaning of the complex term *cosmos* in the New Testament.

1. *The world is the sum total of creation, the universe, "the heavens and the earth" that God created in the beginning and that one day he will recreate.*[1]

What is most distinctive in the New Testament concept of the universe is its christological emphasis. The world was created by God through the Word (John 1:10), and without him nothing that has been made was made (John 1:3). The Christ whom the Gospel proclaims as the agent of redemption is also the agent of God's creation. And he is at the same time the goal toward which all creation is directed (Col. 1:16) and the principle of coherence of all reality, material and spiritual (Col. 1:17).

In the light of the universal significance of Jesus Christ, the Christian cannot be pessimistic concerning the final destiny of the world. In the midst of the changes of history, he knows that God has not abdicated his throne and that at the proper time all things will be placed under the rule of Christ (Eph. 1:10; cf. I Cor. 15:24ff.). The Gospel implies the hope of "a new heaven and a new earth" (Rev. 21; cf. II Pet. 3:13)[2]. Consequently, the only true evangelism is that which is oriented toward that final goal of "the restoration of all things" in Christ Jesus, promised by the prophets and proclaimed by the apostles (Acts 3:21). Eschatology centered in the future salvation of the soul turns out to be too limited in the face of secular eschatologies of our day, the most important of which — the Marxist — looks forward to the establishment of the ideal society and the creation of a new man. Today more than ever the Christian hope in its fullest dimensions must be proclaimed with such conviction and with such force that the falseness of every other hope should not need to be demonstrated.

2. *In a more limited sense, the world is the present order of human existence, the space-time context of man's life.*[3]

This is the world of material possessions, where men are concerned for "things" that are necessary but that easily become an end in themselves (Luke 12:30). "Anxiety" for these things is incompatible with seeking the Kingdom of God (Luke 12:22-31). The treasures that man can store up on earth are perishable (Matt. 6:19). It is useless for him to gain "the whole world" and lose or forfeit his own self (Luke 9:25; cf. John 12:25). There is a Christian realism that demands that we take seriously that "we brought nothing into the world, and we cannot take anything out of the world" (I Tim. 6:7). All material possessions lie under the sign of the transitoriness of a world that advances inexorably toward the end. In the light of the end everything that belongs solely to the present order becomes relative; it cannot be considered the totality of human existence (I Cor. 7:29-31; cf. I John 2:17). On the contrary, it forms part of that system of man's rebellion against God that will be discussed later in this study.

To proclaim the Gospel is to proclaim the message of a Kingdom that is not of this world (John 18:36) and whose politics therefore cannot conform to the politics of the kingdoms of this world. This is a Kingdom whose sovereign rejected "the kingdoms of the world and their glory" (Matt. 4:8; cf. Luke 4:5), in order to establish his own kingdom on the basis of love. It is a kingdom that is made present among men, here and now (Matt. 12:28), in the person of one who does not come from *this world (tou cosmou toutou),* but "from above," from an order beyond the transitory scene of human existence (John 8:23).

3. *The world is humanity, claimed by the Gospel, but hostile to God and enslaved by the powers of darkness.*[4]

Occasionally *cosmos* denotes humanity, with no reference to its position before God.[5] Much more frequently, though, it denotes humanity in its relation to the history of salvation that culminates in Jesus Christ, by whom it is judged.

a. *The world claimed by the Gospel.* The most categorical affirmation of God's will to save the world is made in the person and work of his Son Jesus Christ. Our difficulties in explaining how it is possible that, in spite of the fact that God's will is that his salvation reach all men (I Tim. 2:4), not all are actually saved, should not lead us to deny the universal scope of New Testament soteriology. According to the New Testament, Jesus Christ is not the Savior of a sect, but rather "the Savior of the world" (John 4:42; I John 4:14; I Tim. 4:10). The world is the object of God's love (John 3:16). Jesus Christ is the Lamb of God that takes away the sin of the world (John 1:29), the light of the world (John 1:9, 8:12, 9:5), the propitiation not only for the sins of his own people but "also for the sins of the whole world" (I John 2:2; cf. II Cor. 5:19). To this end he was sent by the Father — not to condemn the world, but "that the world might be saved through him" (John 3:17).

Obviously, God's salvation in Christ Jesus is universal in scope. But the universality of the Gospel must not be confused with the universalism of contemporary theologians who hold that, on the basis of the work of Christ, all men have received eternal life, whatever their position before Christ. The benefits obtained by Christ are inseparable from the Gospel and, consequently, can only be received *in* and *through* the Gospel. To preach the Gospel is not only to proclaim an accomplished fact, but rather to proclaim the accomplished fact and, *simultaneously,* to make a call to faith. The proclamation of Jesus as "the Savior of the world" is not an affirmation that all men are automatically saved, but rather an invitation to all men to put their confidence in the one who gave his life for the sin of the world. "Christ does not save us apart from faith, faith does not restore us apart from Christ. He became one with us, we have to become one with him. Without the affirmation of this double process of self-identification and of the results that follow it, there is no complete exposition of the Gospel."[6]

From the universality of the Gospel is derived the universality of the evangelizing mission of the church. The Gospel's claim on the world, initiated in Jesus Christ, is continued through his followers. As the Father sent him, so he has sent them into the world (John 17:18). Repentance and forgiveness of sin in his name must be announced to all nations (Luke 24:47; cf. Matt. 28:19; Mark. 16:15). And it is this demand of the Gospel that gives meaning to history until the end of the present era (Matt 24:14).

b. *The world hostile to God and enslaved by the powers of darkness.* The most distinctive usage of *cosmos* in the New Testament is predominately negative. It refers to humanity, but to humanity in open hostility against God, personified as the enemy of Jesus Christ and his followers. The Word through whom all things were made came into the world, but "the world knew him not" (John 1:10). He came as the light of the world (John 8:12, 9:5), to bear witness to the truth (John 18:37), but "men loved darkness rather than light, because their deeds were evil" (John 3:19). It was collective rejection. But it was the only attitude consistent with the nature of the world alienated from God — the world *cannot* receive the Spirit of truth (John 14:17), the carnal mind *cannot* submit to God's law (Rom. 8:7). This is the tragedy of the world — it is caught up in the vicious circle of a rejection that leads it to hate Christ and his followers (John 15:18, 24; I John 3:1, 13) and that at the same time leaves it incapable of recognizing the truth of the Gospel (John 9:39-41). The condition of the world in its rebellion against God is such that Jesus Christ does not even pray for it (John 17:9).

But if we dig a bit deeper in our analysis of the concept of the world in the Johannine and Pauline writings, it becomes obvious that behind this rejection of Jesus Christ lies the influence of spiritual powers hostile to man and to God. "The whole world is in the power of the evil one" (I John 5:19). The "wisdom of the world," characterized by its ignorance of God, reflects the wisdom of "the rulers of this age" — the powers of darkness — that crucified Christ (I Cor. 1:20, 2:6, 8). Unbelievers' blindness to the Gospel is the result of the action of Satan, "the god of this world" (II Cor. 4:4). Apart from faith, men are in subjection to the spirit of the age (the *zeitgeist*) controlled by the "prince of the power of the air (Eph. 2:2). The world is under the domination of the "elemental spirits" (Gal. 4:3, 9; Col. 2:8, 20), the principalities and powers (Rom. 8:38f.; I Cor. 15:24, 26; Eph. 1:21, 3:10, 6:12; Col. 1:16, 2:10, 15).

The picture of the world that emerges from the texts mentioned is confirmed by the rest of the New Testament. In it, as in first-century Judaism, the present age is conceived of as the period in which Satan and his hosts have received the authority to rule the world. The universe is not a closed universe, in which everything can be explained by an appeal to natural causes. It is, rather, the arena in which God — a God who acts in history — is engaged in a battle with the spiritual powers that enslave men and hinder their perception of the truth revealed in Jesus Christ.

This diagnosis of man's plight in the world cannot simply be thrown into the wastebasket as stemming out of the apocalyptic speculation that was common among the Jews of New Testament times. As E. Stauffer says, "In primitive Christianity there is no theology without demonology." And without demonology the answer to the problem of sin must be found exclusively in man, without giving due attention to the fact that man himself is the victim of an order that transcends him and imposes on him a detrimental way of life. Sin (singular) is not the sum total of the individual sins (plural) of man. It is, on the contrary, an objective situation that conditions men and forces them to commit sin: "Every one who commits sin is a slave to sin" (John 8:34). The essence of sin is the lie ("You will be like God" — Gen. 3:5), and lying has its origin in the devil, the "liar and the father of lies (John 8:44). Sin, then, is a social and even a cosmic, not merely an individual, problem. Personal sins — those that according to Jesus come "from within, out of the heart of man" (Mark 7:21-22) — are the echo of a voice that comes from the creation, the creation that "was subjected to futility" and that will be "set free from its bondage to decay" (Rom. 8:20-21).

Unfortunately, much too frequently it has been taken for granted that the concrete manifestation of satanic action among men takes place primarily or even exclusively in those phenomena that fall within the sphere of demonic possession or the occult. Thus we have lost sight of the demonic nature of the whole spiritual environment that conditions man's thought and conduct. The individualistic concept of redemption is the logical consequence of an individualistic concept of sin which ignores "all that is in the world" (not simply in the heart of man), namely, "the lust of the flesh and the lust of the eyes and the pride of life" (I John 2:15-16). In one word, it ignores the reality of *materialism*, that is, the absolutization of the present age in all it offers — consumer goods, money, political power, philosophy, science, social class, race, nationality, sex, religion, tradition, etc.; the "collective egoism" (to borrow Niebuhr's phrase) that conditions man to seek his realization in "the desirable things" of life; the Great Lie that man derives his meaning from "being like God," in independence from God.

Under the domination of the powers of darkness, the world stands at the same time under the judgment of God. Though God did not send his Son to condemn the world, but that the world through him might be saved (John 3:17, cf. 12:47), the world is judged by its own rejection of the light of life that has made its appearance among men. "This is the judgment, that the light has come into the world, and men loved darkness rather than light, because their deeds were evil" (John 3:19, cf. 12:48).

In conclusion, man's problem in the world is not simply that he commits isolated sins or gives in to the temptation of particular vices. It is, rather, that he is imprisoned within a closed system of rebellion against God, a system that conditions him to absolutize the relative and to relativize the absolute, a system whose mechanism of self-sufficiency deprives him of eternal life and subjects him to the judgment of God. This is one of the reasons why evangelism cannot be reduced to the verbal communication of doctrinal content, with no reference to specific forms of man's involvement in the world. It is also one of the reasons why the evangelist's confidence cannot rest in the efficiency of his methods. As the Apostle Paul taught, "We are not contending against flesh and blood, but against the principalities, against the powers, against the world rulers of this present darkness, against the spiritual hosts of wickedness in the heavenly places" (Eph. 6:12). The proclamation of the Gospel does take seriously the necessity of divine resources for the battle.

PART TWO: EVANGELISM AND SEPARATION FROM THE WORLD

The Gospel does not come from man, but from God. Its entrance into the world necessarily leads to conflict, because it questions the absolute nature of "the desirable things" of the old era. Its presence alone means crisis, because it demands that man discern between God and the false gods, between light and darkness, between truth and error. Those who bear the Gospel, then, are "the aroma of Christ to God among those who are being saved and among those who are perishing, to one a fragrance from death to death, to the other a fragrance from life to life" (II Cor. 2:15-16). The Gospel unites, but it also separates. And out of this separation created by the Gospel springs the church as a community called to be not *of* the world but to be *in* the world.

The concept of the church as an entity "separated" from the world lends itself to all kinds of false interpretations. At the one extreme is the position which holds that there is no real separation but only a simple epistemological difference; the church knows — that it has been reconciled to God, while the world does not know — and that is all[7]. At the other extreme is the position which holds that the separation is an impassable chasm between two cities that only communicate with each other as the one sets out on a crusade to conquer the other. Our concept of the nature of the separation between the church and the world inevitably influences our definition of the Gospel and our methods of evangelism. We urgently need to recover an evangelism that takes seriously the distinction between the church and the world, seen from the perspective of the Gospel; an evangelism that is oriented toward breaking man's slavery in the world and does not itself become an expression of the church's enslavement to the world.

1. Evangelism and the proclamation of Jesus Christ as Lord of all

A brief study of the New Testament is sufficient to show that the essentials of its message are summarized in the oldest creed of the church: "Jesus Christ is the *Kyrios*." Though it is true that only after the resurrection were the disciples able to grasp the importance of this title as applied to Jesus Christ, there is no doubt that for them the one whom God had *made* "Lord and Christ" was none other than the Jesus who had been crucified (Acts 2:36). To say that Jesus Christ is Lord is to say that the same Jesus whom God put forward "as a propitiatory offering by his blood" (Rom. 3:25) is now "Lord of all " (Rom. 10:12). Having provided the basis for the forgiveness of sin through the sacrifice of himself, he has occupied the place that is rightly his as mediator in the government of the world (Heb. 1:4).

On the basis of the texts mentioned, to which several others could be added, it is obvious that it is impossible to separate the priestly ministry of Jesus Christ from his kingly ministry. From the New Testament perspective the work of God in his Son cannot be limited to cleansing from the guilt of sin; it is also a liberation from the powers of darkness, a transference to the Messianic Kingdom which, in anticipation of the end, has been made present in Christ (Col. 1:13). The Christ who wrought forgiveness of sins is also the Christ who wrought liberation from slavery to the world. The hour of the Cross was the hour of the judgment of this world and of its "ruler" (John

12:31, 16:11); the hour in which Christ disarmed the principalities and powers and proclaimed their defeat, leading them as prisoners in a triumphal parade (Col. 2:15). Jesus Christ has been exalted as the *Kyrios* of all the universe (Eph. 1:20-22; Phil. 2 9-11; I Pet. 3:22) and it is as such that he is able to save all those who call on his name (Rom. 10:12-13). Salvation in Christ involves both forgiveness of sin (I John 1:9) and victory over the world (John 5:4), by faith.

To evangelize, then, is not to offer an experience of freedom from feelings of guilt, as if Christ were a super-psychiatrist and his saving power could be separated from his Lordship. To evangelize is to proclaim Christ Jesus as Lord and Savior, by whose work man is delivered from both the guilt and the power of sin and integrated into God's plans to put all things under the rule of Christ. As Walter Kunneth[8] has pointed out, an individualistic Christology — a Christology that views Christ only in his relation to the individual — leaves the door open to a denial of creation, for the world must then be understood as if it existed apart from the Word of God which gives it meaning. The Christ proclaimed by the Gospel is the Lord of all, in whom God has acted decisively in history in order to form a new humanity. The one who places his confidence *in him* is delivered from "the present evil age" (Gal. 1:4) and from the powers by which it is characterized; the world is crucified to him, and he to the world (Gal. 6:14); he cannot submit to false gods, as if he still belonged to the sphere of their influence (Col. 2:20).

Obviously, the separation of the church from the world can only take place from a theological, eschatological perspective. It is *before God* that the church takes shape as a community that belongs, not to the present age, but to the coming age. By vocation, it is not *of* the world in the sense that it has rejected the Great Lie implicit in materialsim, with its absolutization of "the desirable things" that the world offers. Though the old era is under the dominion of idols that set themselves up as gods and lords, for the church there is only one God, the Father, and one Lord, Jesus Christ, the mediator of creation and of redemption (I Cor. 8:5, 6). Here and now, in anticipation of the universal recognition of Jesus Christ as Lord of all creation (Phil. 2:9-11), the church has received him (Eph. 1:22) and lives by virtue of the blessings and gifts which he as Lord bestows (Eph. 1:3-14, 4:7-16). This is the basic difference between the church and the world.

Without the proclamation of Jesus Christ as Lord of all, in the light of whose universal authority all values of the present age become relative, there is no true evangelism. To evangelize is to proclaim Jesus Christ as the one who is reigning today and who will continue to reign "until he has put all his enemies under his feet." (I Cor. 15:25). New Testament cosmic Christology is an essential element of the Gospel proclamation.

2. Evangelism and worldliness

On the Cross Jesus Christ inflicted a decisive defeat on the prince of this world. The enemy has been mortally wounded. The resurrection has demonstrated that the futility to which creation is subjected does not mean that God has abdicated his rule over it. All creation will be delivered from its bondage to decay (Rom. 8:20-21); the whole universe will be placed under the rule of Christ (Eph. 1:10).

Hope in the final triumph of Jesus Christ belongs to the essence of the Christian faith; what God did through the death and resurrection of his Son, he will complete at the end of time.

We cannot, however, fool ourselves about the actual historic situation of the church in relation to the world. A rapid reading of the New Testament points out the crude reality of the conditioning that the world and "the things that are in the world" exercise over man, whether Christian or not. The victory of Christ over the world and the powers is not a mere doctrine requiring intellectual assent; it is a fact that must become concrete reality in Christian experience through faith. To Jesus' claim "I have overcome the world" (John 16:33) corresponds the believer's "victory that overcomes the world, our faith" (I John 5:4). In other words, the Christian is called to *become* what he already *is*. The imperative of the evangelical ethic forms an indissoluble whole with the indicative of the Gospel.

As long as the present age endures, the battle against the powers of darkness continues. Worldliness never ceases to be a threat to the church and its evangelizing mission. In spite of having been delivered from the present evil age (Gal. 1:4), Christians run the risk of returning to the "weak and beggarly elemental spirits" to which this age is subject (Gal. 4:9), the risk of submitting themselves to slavery to human regulations ("Do not handle, do not taste, do not touch") as if they were still *of* the world (Col. 2:20-22). For this reason, Christians need to be reminded of the liberty that has been given them in Christ. Because he died and rose again, the way has been opened to live here and now in the liberty of the children of God that belongs to the new era. All legalism is, therefore, worldliness — a return to slavery to the powers of darkness. And this is applicable to the prohibitions and taboos that today in many places in the world are part of the "evangelical subculture" and that are often so confused with the Gospel that evangelism becomes a call to observe certain religious rules and practices and loses its meaning as proclamation of the message of liberty.

Another form in which worldliness enters the life and mission of the church today is the adaptation of the Gospel to the "spirit of the times." Because of the limits of space, I will cite only two examples:

a. *"Secular Christianity."* Already in the first century an attempt was made to accommodate the Gospel to the dualism between *spirit* and *matter* that was part of the ideological atmosphere of the day. Thus developed what in the history of Christian thought is known as "Docetism" — in the face of a dualistic interpretation of the world, a *new* Christology was proposed that would make the Gospel acceptable to those who could not conceive of the possibility that God (good by nature) should enter into direct relation with matter (evil by nature). Such seems to be the heresy to which the Epistles of John refer.

The problem today is not the dualism between spirit and matter, but rather secularism — the concept that the natural world represents the totality of reality and therefore the only possible knowledge is the "scientific." It is the logical consequence of another type of dualism derived from the philosophy of Descartes — the dualism between *man* (the thinking subject) and the world (the object of thought)[9] There is no place for God as the transcendent being who has the power to act in history and in nature. All that exists or happens in the universe can be explained by the laws of cause and effect; what cannot be investigated by empirical methods cannot be real.

All the versions of "secular Christianity" advocated by modern theologians assume the validity of secularism, sometimes under the garb of mere "secularity." They all take as their starting point a world in which man has supposedly come of age (as seen by Dietrich Bonhoeffer) and has no need for supernatural reality, the basic premise of religion. Their purpose is a "re-statement" of the Gospel for this modern man who has learned to get along in the world and now he has no need of supernatural help. The end of "supernaturalism," the end of that old doctrine of transcendence which is part and parcel of a pre-scientific concept of the universe, has arrived. If the Christian faith is to survive, it must be brought up to date; it must throw off every residue of "transcendentalism" and express itself in secular terms, so that no thinking man has to reject it together with the accompanying pre-scientific ideas. Far from being an enemy of the Christian faith, secularism is an ally, since (as Friedrich Gogarten argued) man's responsibility for the world is the very essence of the Gospel.

Thus the foundation is laid for man to concentrate *all* his effort in building the earthly city, without having to concern himself with reality "beyond" or "above" the natural realm. Man is the author of his own destiny and his vocation is exclusively historical.

Robert J. Blaikie[10] has demonstrated in detail that in the Cartesian system of reality that underlies "secular Christianity" there really is no place for the concept of man as an "agent" — a person capable of acting freely and introducing intentional changes in the world. Action is the basic characteristic of personal reality. But if man is no more than the thinking subject and the world only the object of his thought, completely determined within a closed system of causes and effects, it follows that man is not personal reality and cannot be considered an active agent. Common sense tells us, nevertheless, that we are in effect beings living and acting in the world and that the concept of reality as something that can only be known "objectively" by means of the scientific method, is an incomplete view of reality based on philosophical premises that, as such, cannot be proven scientifically. In conclusion, "secular Christianity" is not a mere "re-statement" of the Gospel, but rather a capitulation in favor of a distorted concept of reality that is part of modern secularism.

Man's responsibility for creation is an essential aspect of his vocation, according to the biblical definition; the exclusion of God, as the personal God who acts in nature and in human history, is a compromise with "the spirit of the age." It is a form of worldliness. "Secular Christianity" is a man-centered religion that says man hears only what he wants to hear — that he is his own boss, that the future is in his hands, that God can only be tolerated as something impersonal that he can manipulate. It is a denial of the biblical message whose basic presupposition is that God transcends the universe and acts freely within it.

In the final analysis, what "secular Christianity" does is to sanctify the secular, replacing God's love manifested in Jesus Christ by love for *the things* of the secular city, as if the present order, to which they belong, had absolute value. John's admonition to a first-century church threatened by Docetism is relevant today, "Do not love the world or the things in the world. If any one loves the world, love for the Father is not in him" (I John 2:15).

b. *"Culture Christianity."* No less harmful to the cause of the Gospel than "secular Christianity" is the identification of Christianity with a culture or a cultural expression. In the sixteenth century, Latin America was conquered in the name of the Catholic king and queen of Spain. This conquest was not only military but religious as well. It was concerned with implanting not merely Spanish culture, but a "Christian culture." Only in recent years has Rome become aware that the Christianity of the people of Latin America is almost purely nominal. In the nineteenth century, the Christian missionary outreach was so closely connected with European colonialism that in Africa and Asia Christianity would become identified as the white man's religion.

Today, however, there is another form of "culture Christianity" that has come to dominate the world scene — the "American Way of Life." This phenomenon is described by a North American Christian writer in these terms, "A major source of the rigid equation of socio-political conservatism with evangelicalism is conformity with the world. We have equated 'Americanism' with Christianity to such an extent that we are tempted to believe that people in other cultures must adopt American institutional patterns when they are converted. We are led through natural psychological processes to an unconscious belief that the essence of our American Way of Life is basically, if not entirely, Christian."[11]. This equation in the United States insures the presence of a large number of middle class whites in the church. But the price the church has had to pay for quantity is to forfeit its prophetic role in society. What Tillich called "the Protestant principle," that is, the capacity to denounce every historic absolutization, is impossible for "culture Christianity." And this explains the confusion of Christian orthodoxy with socio-economic and political conservatism present in Evangelicalism in the United States.

In the light of the powerful influence that this type of Christianity has had in what is known as "the mission field," the Gospel that is preached today in the majority of countries of the world bears the marks of "the American Way of Life." It is not surprising that at least in Latin America today the evangelist often has to face innumerable prejudices that reflect the identification of Americanism with the Gospel in the minds of his listeners. The image of a Christian that has been projected by some forms of United States Christianity is that of a successful businessman who has found the formula for happiness, a formula he wants to share with others freely. The basic problem is that, in a market of "free consumers" of religion in which the church has no possibility of maintaining its monopoly on religion, this Christianity has resorted to reducing its message to a minimum in order to make all men *want* to become Christians. The Gospel thus becomes a type of merchandise, the acquisition of which guarantees to the consumer the highest values — *success* in life and personal *happiness* now and forever. The act of "accepting Christ" is the means to reach the ideal of "the good life," at no cost. The Cross has lost its offense, since it simply points to the sacrifice of Jesus Christ for us, but it is not a call to discipleship. The God of this type of Christianity is the God of "cheap grace," the God who constantly gives but never demands, the God fashioned expressly for mass-man, who is controlled by the law of least possible effort and seeks easy solutions, the God who gives his attention to those who will not reject him because they need him as an analgesic.

In order to gain the greatest possible number of followers, it is not enough for "culture Christianity" to turn the Gospel into a product; it also has to distribute it among the greatest number of consumers of religion. For this, the twentieth century has provided it with the perfect tool — technology. The strategy for the evangelization of the world thus becomes a question of mathematical calculation. The problem is to produce the greatest number of Christians at the least possible cost in the shortest possible time, and for this the strategists can depend on the work of the computer. Thanks to computers, never in the modern era have we been closer to the reestablishment of one culture unified by the Christian faith — the *Corpus Christianum.* The "culture Christianity" of our day has at its disposal the most sophisticated technological resources to propagate its message of success throughout the world and to do it *efficiently!*

Obviously, what is objectionable in this approach to evangelism is not the use of technology in itself. Viewed alone, technology, like science or money, is morally neutral. Nor is the concern that there be more Christians in the world to be questioned. God "desires all men to be saved and to come to the knowledge of the truth" (I Tim. 2:4). The problem with this "culture Christianity" lies in that it reduces the Gospel to a formula for success and equates the triumph of Christ with obtaining the highest number of "conversions." This is a man-centered Christianity that clearly shows itself to be conditioned by the "technological mentality" — that mentality that, as Jacques Ellul has pointed out,[12] regards efficiency as the absolute criterion and on this basis seeks, in all areas of human life, the systematization of methods and resources to obtain preestablished results. It is the "religious" product of a civilization in which *nothing,* not even man himself, escapes technology — a civilization obsessed with its search for the "one best way" that inevitably leads to automation. This is another form of worldliness. The manipulation of the Gospel to achieve successful results inevitably leads to slavery to the world and its powers.

As is the case with "secular Christianity," the basic question in relation to "culture Christianity" is the very significance of the Gospel. I am afraid, nevertheless, that the proponents of this type of Christianity are those least able to see the problem, since the majority of them live in the land where the technological mentality exerts its greatest influence. It is not surprising that any criticism of this approach to evangelism should fall on deaf ears or be interpreted as a lack of interest in the propagation of the Gospel. At this rate we may ask if the day is not close when missionary strategists employ B.F. Skinner's "behavior conditioning"[13] and "Christianize" the world through the scientific control of environmental conditions and human genetics.

The proclamation of Jesus Christ as Lord of all is a call to turn to God from idols, to serve a living and true God (I Thess. 1:9). Where there is no concept of the universal sovereignty of God there is no repentance; and where there is no repentance there is no salvation. Christian salvation is, among other things, liberation *from* the world as a closed system, *from* the world that has room only for a god bound by sociology, *from* the "consistent" world that rules out God's free, unpredictable action. One cannot be a friend of this world without being an enemy of God (Jas. 4:4). To love this world is to reject the love of God (I John 2:15). The Gospel, then, is a call not only to faith, but also to repentance, to break with the world. And it is only in the extent to which we are free from this world that we are able to serve our fellowmen.

PART THREE:
EVANGELISM AND INVOLVEMENT WITH THE WORLD
The Kingdom of God has arrived in the person of Jesus Christ. Eschatology has invaded history. God has clearly expressed his plan to place all things under the rule of Christ. The powers of darkness have been defeated. Here and now, in union with Jesus Christ, man has within his reach the blessings of the new era.

However, the Kingdom of God has not yet arrived in all its fullness. Our salvation is "in hope" (Rom. 8:24). According to God's promise, "we wait for new heavens and a new earth in which righteousness dwells" (II Pet. 3:13). Ours is the time of the patience of God, who does not wish "that any should perish, but that all should reach repentance" (II Pet. 3:9).

1. Evangelism and repentance ethics
The Gospel is always proclaimed in opposition to an organized lie — the Great Lie that man realizes himself by pretending to be God, in autonomy from God; that his life consists in the things he possesses; that he lives for himself alone and is the owner of his destiny. All history is the history of this Lie and of the destruction it has brought upon man — the history of how man (as C.S. Lewis would aptly express it) has enjoyed the horrible liberty he has demanded and consequently has been enslaved.

The Gospel involves a call to repentance from this Lie. The relation between the Gospel and repentance is such that preaching the Gospel is equivalent to preaching "repentance and forgiveness of sins" (Luke 24:47), or to testifying "of repentance to God and of faith in our Lord Jesus Christ" (Acts 20:21). Without this call to repentance there is no Gospel. And repentance is not merely a bad conscience — the "worldly grief" that produces death (II Cor. 7:10) — but a change of attitude, a restructuring of one's scale of values, a reorientation of the whole personality. It is not simply giving up habits condemned by a moralistic ethic, but rather laying down the weapons of rebellion against God, to return to him. It is not simply recognizing a psychological necessity, but rather accepting the Cross of Christ as death to the world in order to live before God.

This call to repentance throws into relief the social dimension of the Gospel. It comes to man enslaved by sin in a specific social situation, not to a "sinner," in the abstract. It is a change of attitude that becomes concrete in history. It is a turning from sin to God, not only in the individual's subjective consciousness, but *in the world.* This truth is clearly illustrated in John the Baptist's proclamation of the Kingdom (Matt. 3:1-12, Luke 3:7-14), concerning which I will simply make the following observations: (i) It has a strong eschatological note. The time of fulfillment of God's promises given through his prophets has come. The presence of Jesus Christ among men is the evidence that God is active in history to accomplish his purposes: "The kingdom of heaven is at hand" (Matt. 3:2). (ii) This new reality places men in a position of crisis — they cannot continue to live as if nothing had happened; the Kingdom of God demands a new mentality, a reorientation of all their values, repentance (Matt. 3:2). Repentance has an eschatological significance — it marks the boundary between the old age and the new, between judgment and promise. (iii) The change imposed involves a new life-style: "Bear fruits that befit repentance" (Luke 3:8). Without ethics there is no real repentance. (iv) Repentance ethics is more than generalizations — it has to do with specific acts of self-sacrifice in concrete situations. To each one who becomes convicted by his message, John the Baptist has a fitting word, and in each case his ethical demand touches the point at which the man is enslaved to the powers of the old age and closed to God's action. To the people in general he says, "He who has two coats, let him share with him who has none; and he who has food, let him do likewise." To the tax collectors, "Collect no more than is appointed you." To the soldiers, "Rob no one by violence or by false accusation, and be content with your wages" (Luke 3:11-14). The crisis created by the Kingdom cannot be resolved by accepting concepts handed down by tradition ("We are descendants of Abraham"), but rather by obedience to the ethics of the Kingdom.

Where there is no concrete obedience there is no repentance. And without repentance there is no salvation (Mark 1:4; Luke 13:3; Matt. 21:32; Acts 2:38, 3:19, 5:31). Salvation is man's return to God, but it is at the same time *also* man's return to his neighbor. In the presence of Jesus Christ, Zacchaeus the publican renounces the materialism that has enslaved him and accepts responsibility for his neighbor ("Behold, Lord, the half of my goods I give to the poor; and if I have defrauded any one of anything, I restore it fourfold" — Luke 19:8). This renunciation and this commitment Jesus calls "salvation" ("Today salvation has come to this house" — Luke 19:9). Zacchaeus' response to the Gospel call could not be expressed in more concrete or "worldly" terms. It is not merely a subjective, but a moral experience — an experience that affects his life precisely at that point at which the Great Lie had taken root; an experience that brings him out of himself and turns him toward his neighbor.

The Gospel message, since it was first proclaimed by Jesus Christ, involves a call to repentance (Matt. 4:17). Repentance is much more than a private affair between the individual and God. It is the complete reorientation of life in the world — among men — in response to the work of God in Jesus Christ. When evangelism does not take repentance seriously, it is because it does not take the world seriously, and when it does not take the world seriously it does not take God seriously. The Gospel is not a call to social quietism. Its goal is not to take a man out of the world, but to put him into it, no longer as a slave but as a son of God and a member of the body of Christ.

If Jesus Christ is Lord, men must be confronted with his authority over the totality of life. Evangelism is not, and cannot be, a mere offer of benefits achieved by Jesus Christ. Christ's work is inseparable from his person; the Jesus who died for our sins is the Lord of the whole universe, and the announcement of forgiveness in his name is inseparable from the call to repentance, the call to turn from "the rulers of this world" to the Lord of glory. But "no one can say Jesus is Lord except by the Holy Spirit" (I Cor. 12:3).

2. Evangelism and "otherworldliness"

To "secular Christianity," obsessed with the life of this world, the only salvation possible is one which fits within the limits of this present age. It is essentially an economic, social and political salvation, although sometimes (as in the case of the Latin American "theology of liberation") an attempt is made to extend the concept to include "the making of a new man," author of his own destiny[14]. Eschatology is absorbed by the Utopia and the Christian hope becomes confused with the worldly hope proclaimed by Marxism.

At the other extreme is the concept of salvation as the future salvation of the soul, in which present life has meaning only as a preparation for the "hereafter." History is assimilated by a futurist eschatology and religion becomes a means of escape from present reality. The result is a total withdrawal from the problems of society in the name of "separation from the world." It is this misunderstanding of the Gospel which has given rise to the Marxist criticism of Christian eschatology as the "opiate of the people."

That this concept of salvation is a misunderstanding of biblical soteriology should not need to be demonstrated. Unfortunately, it is a concept so deep-rooted in the preaching of so many evangelical churches that we must stop to analyze the question.

In the first place, for Jesus Christ himself the mission entrusted to him by the Father was not limited to preaching the Gospel. Matthew, for example, summarizes Jesus' earthly ministry in these words, "And he went about all Galilee, *teaching* in their synagogues and *preaching* the gospel of the kingdom and *healing* every disease and every infirmity among the people" (Matt. 4:23; cf. 9:35). Even if evangelism is defined solely in terms of *verbal* communication — a definition that would leave much to be desired in the light of the psychology of communication — we still must add, on the basis of the text, that evangelism was only one of the elements of Jesus' mission. Together with the *kerygma* went the *diaconia* and the *didache*. This presupposes a concept of salvation that includes the whole man and cannot be reduced to the simple forgiveness of sins and assurance of unending life with God in heaven. A comprehensive mission corresponds to a comprehensive view of salvation. Salvation is wholeness. Salvation is total humanization. Salvation is eternal life — the life of the Kingdom of God — life that begins here and now (and this is the meaning of the present tense of the verb "*has* eternal life" in the Gospel and the letters of John) and touches all aspects of man's being.

In the second place, Jesus' work had a social and political dimension. The individualism of "culture Christianity" to which I have referred above sees the Lord with only one eye and consequently sees him as an individualistic Jesus who is concerned with the salvation of individuals. An unprejudiced reading of the Gospels shows us a Jesus who, in the midst of many political alternatives (Pharisaism, Sadduceeism, Zealotism, Essenism) personifies and proclaims a new alternative — the Kingdom of God. To say that Jesus is the Christ is to describe him in political terms, to affirm that he is *king*. His kingdom is not of this world, not in the sense that it has nothing to do with the world, but in the sense that it does not adapt itself to human politics. It is a kingdom with its own politics, marked by sacrifice. Jesus is a king who "came not to be served but to serve, and to give his life as a ransom for many" (Mark 10:45). This service to the point of sacrifice belongs to the very essence of his mission. And this must be the distinctive sign of the community that acknowledges him as king. According to the politics of man, "those who are supposed to rule over the Gentiles lord it over them, and their great men exercise authority over them"; in the politics of the Kingdom of God, he who wants to be great "must be slave of all" (Mark 10:43-44). Thus Jesus confronts the power structures by denouncing their deep-seated ambition to rule, and by proclaiming another alternative, based on love, service, self-dedication to others. He does not take refuge in "religion" or "spiritual things," as if his kingdom had nothing to do with political and social life, but he demythologizes the politics of man and presents himself as the Servant-King, the creator and model of a community that submits to him as Lord and commits itself to live as he lived. The concrete result of Jesus' sacrifice for the sake of others, whose culmination was reached in the Cross, is this community patterned after the Servant-King: a community in which each member gives according to his means and receives according to his needs, since "it is more blessed to give than to receive" (Acts 2:45, 4:34-35, 20:35); a community in which racial, cultural, social, and even sexual barriers disappear, since "Christ is all, and in all" (Col. 3:11; Gal. 3:28); a community of reconciliation with God and reconciliation among men (Eph. 2:11-22); and a community, finally, that serves as a base for the resistance against the conditioning by "the present evil age" and makes it possible for Jesus' disciples to live *in* the world without being *of* the world.

In the third place, the new creation in Jesus Christ becomes history in terms of good works. In Paul's words, God has "created [us] in Christ Jesus for good works, which God prepared beforehand, that we should walk in them" (Eph. 2:10). Jesus Christ "gave himself for us to redeem us from all iniquity and to purify for himself a people of his own who are *zealous for good deeds*" (Tit. 2:14). The New Testament knows nothing of a Gospel that makes a divorce between soteriology and ethics, between communion with God and communion with one's neighbor, between faith and works. The Cross is not only the negation of the validity of every human effort to gain God's favor by works of the law; it is *also* the demand for a new quality of life characterized by love — the opposite of an individualistic life, centered on personal ambitions, indifferent to the needs of others. The significance of the Cross is both soteriological and ethical. This is so because in choosing the Cross Jesus not only created the indicative of the Gospel ("By this we know love, that he laid down his life for us" — I John 3:16a), but also *simultaneously* provided the pattern for human life here and now ("And we ought to lay down our lives for the brethren" — I John 3:16b). Just as the Word became man, so also must love become good works if it is to be intelligible to men. This is what gives meaning to "worldly goods" — they can be converted into instruments through which the life of the new age expresses itself. This is what John means when he says, "If any one has the world's goods and sees his brother in need, yet closes his heart against him, how does God's love abide in him? Little children, let us not love in word or speech but *in deed and in truth*" (I John 3:17). God's love expressed in the Cross must be made *visible* in the world through the church. The evidence of eternal life is not the simple confession of Jesus Christ as Lord, but "faith working through love" (Gal. 5:6). Jesus said, "Not every one who says to me 'Lord, Lord,' shall enter the kingdom of heaven, but he who does the will of my Father who is in heaven" (Matt. 7:21).

In the light of the biblical teaching there is no place for an "other-worldliness" that does not result in the Christian's commitment to his neighbor, rooted in the Gospel. There is no room for "eschatological paralysis" nor for a "social strike." There is no place for statistics on "how many souls die without Christ every minute," if they do not take into account how many of those who die, die victims of hunger. There is no place for evangelism that, as it goes by the man who was assaulted by thieves on the road from Jerusalem to Jericho, sees in him only a soul that must be saved and ignores the man. "What does it profit, my brethren, if a man says he has faith but has not works? Can his faith save him? If a brother or sister is ill-clad and in lack of daily food, and one of you says to them, 'Go in peace, be warmed and filled,' without giving them the things needed for the body, what does it profit? So faith by itself, if it has no works, is dead" (Jas. 2:14-17).

Only in the context of a soteriology that takes the world seriously is it possible to speak of the *oral* proclamation of the Gospel. If men are to call on the name of the Lord, they must believe in him; "and how are they to believe in him of whom they have never heard?" (Rom. 10:14). But the "word of reconciliation" entrusted to the church is the prolongation of the act of reconciliation in Jesus Christ. "For our sake he made him to be sin who knew no sin, so that in him we might become the righteousness of God" (II Cor. 5:21). It was thus — from within the situation of sinners, in an identification with them which he carried to its final consequences — that God in Christ reconciled the world to himself, once and for all. This was the vertical movement of the Gospel, the movement that in the Cross reached its darkest point. This is the heart of the Gospel. But it is also the standard for evangelism. If God worked out reconciliation from within the human situation, the only fitting evangelism is that in which the Word becomes flesh in the world and the evangelist becomes "the slave of all" in order to win them to Christ (I Cor. 9:19-23). The first condition for genuine evangelism is the crucifixion of the evangelist. Without it the Gospel becomes empty talk and evangelism becomes proselytism.

The church is not an otherworldly religious club that organizes forays into the world in order to gain followers through persuasive techniques. It is the sign of the Kingdom of God; it lives and proclaims the Gospel here and now, *among men,* and waits for the consummation of God's plan to place all things under the rule of Christ. It has been freed *from* the world, but it is *in* the world; it has been sent by Christ into the world *just as Christ* was sent by the Father (John 17:11-18). In other words, it has been given a mission oriented toward the building of a new humanity in which God's plan for man is accomplished, a mission that can be performed only through sacrifice. Its highest ambition cannot and should not be to achieve the success that leads to triumphalism, but rather faithfulness to its Lord, which leads it to confess, "We are unworthy servants; we have only done what was our duty" (Luke 17:10). The confession can be made only by those who live by God's grace and desire that all their works result in the glory of the one who died for all, "that those who live might live no longer for themselves but for him who for their sake died and was raised" (II Cor. 5:15).

FOOTNOTES

[1]. Matt. 24:21; John 1:9, 10, 17:5, 24; Acts 17:24; Rom. 1:20; I Cor. 4:9, 8:4; Eph. 1:4; Phil. 2:15; Heb. 4:3, 9:26.

[2]. It is noteworthy that the New Testament never uses the term *cosmos* to refer to the eschatological world of the Christian hope, for which other expressions are used.

[3]. Matt. 4:8; John 8:23, 12:25, 16:33, 18:30; I Cor. 7:31; I John 3:17; I Tim. 6:7.

[4]. The texts in which *cosmos* with this connotation appears are numerous in Johannine and Pauline writtings. The usage of the term with this meaning is peculiar to the New Testament.

[5]. Matt. 5:14, 13:38, 18:7; I Cor. 1:27f., 3:22, 4:13; II Pet. 2:5, 3:6; Heb. 11:7, 38.

[6]. Vincent Taylor, *Forgiveness and Reconciliation,* 1941, p. 273.

[7].This position is illustrated by Oscar Cullmann's affirmation that "the fundamental distinction . . . between all the members of the lordship of Christ and the members of the Church is that the former do not know that they belong to this lordship, whereas the latter do know it" *The Christology of the New Testament,* 1963, p. 231.

[8]. *The Theology of the Resurrection,* 1965, pp. 161-62.

[9]. René Descartes' formula, "I think, therefore I am" failed to take

into account that man is not a mind, but a mind/body (a psychosomatic being), living and acting in the world, and that the "subjective" and "objective" aspects of reality are therefore inseparable in knowledge. The failure resulted in the split of reality into two levels: the upper level of the "subjective" (feelings and religion) and the lower level of the "objective" (facts and science). This split is behind much of modern thinking in the fields of science, philosophy, and theology.

10. *Secular Christianity and the God Who Acts*, 1970.
11. David O. Moberg, *The Great Reversal*, 1972, p. 42.
12. *The Technological Society*, 1970.
13. Cf. *Beyond Freedom and Dignity*, 1971.
14. Cf. Gustavo Gutierrez, *Teologia de la liberacion*, 1973, p. 132.

EVANGELISM AND THE WORLD
René Padilla

As I begin I would like to express my deep appreciation to those of you who have sent your questions and comments in response to my paper. It has been a great encouragement to me to see that many of you do in fact share my concern for an evangelization which is more faithful to the Gospel and less bound to worldly ideologies. Only one of my readers has said that he doesn't understand why my paper was ever written. Others may feel the same way, but they kindly remained silent about it, and that has led me to believe that on the whole I have before me a rather sympathetic audience. I am therefore going to put all the cards on the table with the prayer that God lead us during these days to a clearer understanding of all that he expects of us as disciples of our Lord Jesus Christ in the twentieth century.

The task of answering all the questions that have been asked and amplifying all the points that have been said to need amplification is an impossible task. May I plead for your forbearance if it looks as if I'm not taking into account a question or comment you feel very strongly about. I've done my best to select themes that are not only closely related to my topic, but also of the widest interest among those attending this meeting.

In the first section of my paper I take a look at the use of the term *cosmos* (world) in the New Testament. My purpose is to show that according to Scriptures the Gospel is addressed not to man as an isolated being called to respond to God with no reference to his life context, but rather to man in relation to the world. The Gospel always comes to man in relation to the world of creation, the world that was made through Jesus Christ and that is to be re-created through him. It comes to man within the present order of existence, immersed in the transient world of material possessions. It comes to man as a member of humanity — the world for which Christ died but, at the same time, the world hostile to God and enslaved to the powers of darkness. The aim of evangelization is, therefore, to lead man, not merely to a subjective experience of the future salvation of his soul, but to a radical reorientation of his life, including his deliverance from slavery to the world and its powers on the one hand, and his integration into God's purpose of placing all things under the rule of Christ on the other hand. The Gospel is not addressed to man in a vacuum. It has to do with man's movement from the old humanity in Adam, which belongs to this age that is passing away, into the new humanity in Christ, which belongs to the age to come.

In the second section of my study I attempt to bring out the significance of evangelization in relation to separation from the world. Because Jesus has been made Lord and King over all things through his death and resurrection, here and now, in anticipation of the deliverance of the whole creation from its bondage to decay, those who believe in him are delivered from slavery to the world and its powers.

Salvation is not exclusively forgiveness of sins, but also transference from the dominion of darkness to a realm where Jesus is recognized as *Kyrios* of all the universe — the Kingdom of God's beloved Son (Col. 1:13).

May I here make a parenthesis to say that the whole question of repentance could well have been considered in this second section, rather than under the section dealing with evangelization and involvement with the world. Repentance does often have a negative connotation — it is a "turning away from" according to Scripture. If I have preferred to deal with it in the following section, it is simply because I want to emphasize not the act of repentance as such, but the positive ethical implications of repentance for man's life in the world.

Going back to section II, I illustrate the problem of worldliness in evangelization by referring first to the confusion of the Gospel with moralistic rules and practices. In reaction to this, one of my critics asks, "Why is legalism considered worldliness? The Bible is full of negative commands." Biblical negative injunctions taken in the context of salvation history — that is one thing. They are included in the law that the New Testament describes as "holy and just and good" (Rom. 7:12). Rules and practices derived from "the tradition of the elders" — that is something else. I am not defending a new (antinomian) morality. What I am doing is pointing out the danger of reducing the Christian ethic to a set of rules and regulations that "have indeed an appearance of wisdom . . . but have no value in checking the indulgence of the flesh" (Col. 2:23).

That there is a place for the use of the law in the Christian life (which in theology is known as "the third use of the law"), no Christian should deny. The problem comes when the Christian life is turned into outward conformity to prohibitions and taboos that have no relation to the Gospel. This, according to Paul, is a return to "the weak and beggarly elemental spirits" — it's a slavery to the world. But, then, "Aren't some of the negatives necessary safeguards for unstable Christians?" I see the need to raise up fences for the protection of small children. What concerns me is that these fences are often turned into cement walls within which there grows an "evangelical subculture," isolated from the real issues of life in the world.

If we think that by legalism we are in fact fostering separation from the world, let us take into account that one may conform to regulations such as "Do not smoke" or "Do not drink beer" and still remain in slavery to the "collective egoism" that conditions man's life in the world. Whenever we concentrate on "microethics" and slight the problems of "macroethics," we place ourselves under the Lord's judgment, "Woe to you, scribes and Pharisees, hypocrites; for you tithe mint and dill and cummin, and have neglected the weightier matters of the law, justice and mercy and faith; these you ought to have done without neglecting the others. You blind guides, straining at a gnat and swallowing a camel!" (Matt. 23:23-24).

As a second illustration of the way in which worldliness can affect evangelization I briefly discuss the question of the adaptation of the Gospel to the "spirit of the times." I cite two examples of such an accommodation: "Secular Christianity," and "Culture Christianity." As was to be expected, no one in this Congress really seems to disagree with my basic conclusion that "secular Christianity" is "not a mere 're-statement' of the Gospel, but rather a capitulation in favor of a distorted concept of reality that is part of modern secularism." The situation is entirely different when it comes to the question of culture Christianity. For one of my critics my description of this type of Christianity is "so patently a caricature as to create static that cannot but block" the transmission of "many insights which people attending the conference will need"; for another one, "What America is sharing with the world today is a parody of Christianity, tied to a materialistic philosophy and a truncated theology," and I come close to saying it, but "have not gone far enough." Whether my description is an overstatement or an understatement, it is not for me to decide. In view of the conflicting opinions, however, it does seem extremely important for this Congress to come to grips during these days with the theological and practical issues related to the problem of culture Christianity. I, for one, believe that it would be a great pity if by the end of our time together we have done little more than pat our backs and tell each other that we have the right theology, that the evangelical churches are on the right track, and that all we need now is the right strategy and the most efficient methods for the evangelization of the world.

Please allow me to clarify that I have no intention of judging the motives of the propounders of American culture Christianity. It is the Lord who judges; when he comes he will disclose the purposes of the heart and "if any one builds on the foundation with gold, silver, precious stones, wood, hay, straw — each man's work will become manifest; for the day will disclose it" (I Cor. 3:12-13).

My duty before God this morning is rather to try to make, with as much objectivity and fairness as I can, a theological evaluation of a type of Christianity which, having as its center the United States, has however spread widely throughout the world.

Granted, I could have chosen a variety of "culture Christianity" other than "the American Way of Life," as some of you have suggested.

I do not wish to imply that American Christians are the only ones who may fall into the trap of confusing Scripture and culture. The fact, however, is that, because of the role that the United States has had to play in world affairs as well as in the spread of the Gospel, this particular form of Christianity, as no other today, has a powerful influence far beyond the borders of that nation. So, for those of you who wonder why I condemn the identification of Christianity with "the American Way of Life" but not with other national cultures, this is my answer. Behind my condemnation of this variety of culture Christianity lies a principle to any other kind of culture Christianity, namely, that the church must be delivered from anything and everything in its culture that would prevent it from being faithful to the Lord in the fulfillment of its mission within and beyond its own culture. The big question that we Christians always have to ask ourselves with regard to our culture is, "Which elements of it should be retained and utilized and which ones should go for the sake of the Gospel?"

When the church lets itself be squeezed into the mold of the world, it loses the capacity to see and, even more, to denounce, the social evils in its own situation. Like the color-blind person who is able to distinguish certain colors, but not others, the worldly church recognizes the personal vices traditionally condemned within its ranks, but is unable to see the evil features of its surrounding culture. In my understanding, this is the only way one can explain, for example, how it is possible for American culture Christianity to integrate racial and class segregation into its strategy for world evangelization. The idea is that people *like* to be with those of their own race and class and we must therefore plant segregated churches, which will undoubtedly grow faster. We are told that race prejudice "can be understood and should be made an aid to Christianization." No amount of exegetical maneuvering can ever bring this approach in line with the explicit teaching of the New Testament regarding the unity of men in the body of Christ, "Here there cannot be Greek and Jews, circumcised and uncircumcised, barbarian, Scythian, slave, free man, but Christ is all, and in all" (Col. 3:11); "There is neither Jew nor Greek, there is neither slave nor free, there is neither male nor female; for you are all one in Christ Jesus" (Gal. 3:28). How can a church that, for the sake of numerical expansion, deliberately opts for segregation, speak to a divided world? By what authority can it preach man's reconciliation with God through the death of Christ, which is one aspect of the Gospel, when in fact it has denied man's reconciliation with man through the same death, which is another aspect of the Gospel (Eph. 21:14-18)? As Dr. Samuel Moffett put it at the Berlin Congress, "When racial discrimination enters the churches, it is something more than a crime against humanity; it is an act of defiance against God himself."

It is perhaps in this context that I should say a word on the prophetic ministry today, as I have been asked to do. For it is only in the measure in which the church itself is the incarnation of God's purpose to put all things under the Lordship of Christ, that it can denounce the evils in society which are a denial of God's original purpose for men. There is an internal connection between the life of the church and its prophetic ministry, and between the prophetic ministry of the church and its evangelization. The church is called to be here and now what God intends the whole of society to be. In its prophetic ministry it lays open the evils that frustrate the purpose of God in society; in its evangelization it seeks to integrate men into that purpose of God whose full realization is to take place in the Kingdom to come. Consequently, wherever the church fails as a prophet it also fails as an evangelist.

A church that is not faithful to the Gospel in all its dimensions inevitably becomes an instrument of the status quo. The Gospel is meant to place the totality of life under the universal Lordship of Jesus Christ, not to produce cultic sects; it is an open break with the status quo of the world. Therefore a Gospel that leaves untouched our life in the world — in relationship to the world of men as well as in relationship to the world of creation — is not the Christian Gospel, but culture Christianity, adjusted to the mood of the day.

This kind of Gospel has no teeth — it is a Gospel that the "free-consumers" of religion will want to receive because it is cheap and it demands nothing of them. The Gospel in the first century was, according to Canon Michael Green, "politically suspect, socially disruptive." The Gospel of culture-Christianity today is a message of conformism, a message that, if not accepted, can at least be easily tolerated because it doesn't disturb anybody. The racist can continue to be a racist, the exploiter can continue to be an exploiter. Christianity will be something that runs along life, but will not cut through it.

A truncated Gospel is utterly insufficient as a basis for churches that will be able "to generate their own Calvins, Wesleys, Wiberforces and Martin Luther Kings." It can only be the basis for unfaithful churches, for strongholds of racial and class discrimination, for religious clubs with a message that has no relevance to practical life in the social the economic and the political spheres.

Now, perhaps, I'm in a position to explain my reservations about the emphasis on numbers in relation to the Christian mission. One of my readers has commented, "I hope the author is not saying that those who advocate church growth and who think that the number of converts is important necessarily fall into the category of those who opt for superficial conversion. Some of us believe that both quality and quantity are important." My answer is that the numerical expansion of the church is a legitimate concern for anyone who takes the Scriptures seriously. As I have stated in my paper, this concern as such should not be questioned. "God desires that all men be saved and come to the knowledge of the truth." John R. Mott's concern to bring the Gospel "within the reach of every creature within this generation" is a biblical concern and should be a part of our Christian commitment.

Furthermore, there is nothing to insure that those who win fewer people for Christ will be able to show forth a higher quality of Christians as a result of their work. The point, however, is that quality is at least as important as quantity, if not more, and that, therefore, faithfulness to the Gospel should never be sacrificed for the sake of quantity. When the Gospel is truncated in order to make it easy for all men to become Christians, from the very outset the basis is laid for an unfaithful church. As the seed, so the tree, and as the tree, so its fruit. It follows that the real question with regard to the growth of the church is not successful numerical expansion — a success patterned after worldly standards — but faithfulness to the Gospel, which will surely lead us to pray and work for more people to become Christians. I am for quantity, but for quantity in the context of faithfulness to the Gospel. I am for numbers, but for numbers of people who have heard a presentation of the Gospel in which the issues of faith and unbelief have been made clear and the choice between grace and judgment has been a *free choice*.

In contrast with the "gospel of the sword," the Gospel of the Cross leaves open the possibility for people to reject Christ because of finding his claims too costly and admits that there are cases when it is better not to have certain people in the church, even though that means a smaller membership. Was not that Jesus' attitude in dealing with the rich young ruler (Mark 10:17-22) or with the multitudes at the peak of his popularity (Luke 14:25-32)? Furthermore, if a truncated Gospel necessarily results in churches that are themselves a denial of the Gospel, in speaking of the numerical expansion of the church it is not out of place to ask what kind of church it is that is being multiplied. It may be that such multiplication turns out to be a multiplication of apostasy! Obviously, then, the real question is not numerical growth per se, but faithfulness to the Gospel.

In my paper, I state that culture-Christianity not only has turned the Gospel into a cheap product, but has, also, turned the strategy for the evangelization of the world into a problem of technology. One of my critics describes my reservations with regard to this approach to world evangelization as "a Latin American hangup." This is an *ad hominem* argument. Latin Americans have not made any particular contribution to the definition of the limitations of technology when it comes to man. In fact, it is to a Frenchman, Jacques Ellul, that I appeal when I refer to the "technological mentality" which conditions American culture-Christianity – the mentality according to which *efficiency* is an absolute criterion on the basis of which one should seek, in all areas of human life, the systematization of methods and resources to obtain pre-established results. It is to this absolutization of efficiency, at the expense of the integrity of the Gospel, that I object. Technology has its place in evangelization; it would be foolish for me to deny that. The problem comes when technology is made a substitute for Scripture under the assumption that what we need is a better strategy, not a more biblical Gospel and a more faithful Church. The picture of the church that one derives from the New Testament is certainly not that of a powerful organization that has achieved success in its conquest of the world by the masterly use of human devices and techniques. It is rather the picture of a community experiencing a new (supernatural) reality — the Kingdom of God — to which "the Lord called day by day those who were being saved." As Michael Green has put it, "in the early church the maximum impact was made by the changed lives and quality of community among the Christians." "Changed lives and quality of community" — that is, faithfulness to the Gospel in practical life — do not come through technology, but through the Word and the Spirit of God. Technology will never make up for our failure to let the Gospel mold our lives!

Furthermore, if the strategy for world evangelization is tied up to technology, then obviously the ones who have the final word on the strategy that the church is to follow in the future are those who have the technical know-how as well as the resources to make the necessary investigations. The church in the Third World has nothing to say on the matter. Isn't this again a way to identify the Gospel with worldly power, a way to perpetuate the dominion/dependence patterns that have often characterized missionary work for the last hundred years? What becomes of the universal character and the unity of the Church of Christ? But perhaps these things don't matter, after all — the real problem is to produce the greatest number of Christians at the least possible cost in the shortest possible time!

If I have dealt with American culture-Christianity, it is not because I am unaware of the fact that in other situations Christians may fall into the trap of accommodating the Gospel to their own culture. It is rather because of the wide influence of *this* variety of culture-Christianity in evangelical circles around the world. But I have no difficulty in accepting that, as someone has put it, "there is a parallel danger in developing countries where national goals and leaders are idolized by mass cult"; or that, as someone else has expressed it, "it is questionable whether we can accept in the Christian context some of the cultural aspects of other nations." There is, then, the place for the question, "How do we non-Americans avoid creating our own version of culture-Christianity?" I will, however, attempt to kill two birds with one stone by taking up that question in connection with a similar one raised by an American who acknowledges the problem of culture-Christianity in his own situation, "How can I overcome culture-Christianity, since I cannot get out of my own culture?"

In the *first place*, let us recognize the conditioning that the world and "the things that are in the world" exercise over us, even in relation to our service to God. All too often we are ready to condemn the distortions that others have openly allowed to come into their theology through the front door, but remain impervious of the distortions that have come into our evangelization through the back door. The orthodoxy of our creed is no guarantee of our own faithfulness to the Gospel in either our life or service. The key word here is *humility*.

In the *second place*, let us be aware of the need to place our lives and activities continually under the judgment of the Word of God. We cannot simply assume that we have the truth and that everything else, including our evangelization and our ethics, will just fall in line with that truth. The purpose of theology is not merely to reaffirm what previous generations have said in the past, but to bring the whole life and mission of the church into line with God's revelation. All our assumptions and methods must therefore be examined in the light of Scripture. The Gospel itself, not success, is the criterion to evaluate our work. The key word here is *theological renewal*.

In *the third place*, let us take seriously the unity of the body of Christ throughout the world. If the church is really one, then there is no place for the assumption that one section of the church has the monopoly on the interpretation of the Gospel and the definition of the Christian mission. Those of us who live in the Third World cannot and should not be satisfied with the rote repetition of doctrinal formulas or the indiscriminate application of canned methods of evangelization imported from the West.

I am not advocating here a relativistic approach to theology. I am calling for the recognition of a problem and a change of attitude with regard to the making of theology and the planning of world evangelization. The problem is that one version of culture-Christianity, with an inadequate theological foundation and conditioned by "fierce pragmatism" — the kind of pragmatism that in the political sphere has produced Watergate — should be regarded as the official evangelical position and the measure of orthodoxy around the world. The change of attitude is the renunciation to ethnocentrism and the promotion of theological cross-fertilization among different cultures. Under the Spirit of God, each culture has something to contribute in connection with the understanding of the Gospel and its implications for the life and mission of the church. American culture-Christianity should not be allowed to deprive us of the possibility that we *all* — whatever our race, nationality, language, or culture — as equal members in the one body of Christ, "attain the unity of the faith and of the knowledge of the Son of God, to mature manhood, to the measure of the stature of the fullness of Christ" (Eph. 4:13). The key word here is *cross-fertilization.*

I believe with all my heart that if with a humble spirit, recognizing our need of deliverance from the world, we come to the Word of God and are willing to learn from one another, the Spirit of God will work in us that we may be, not a mere reflection of society with its materialism, but "the salt of the earth" and "the light of the world."

The third section of my paper deals with evangelization and involvement with the world. Here I first propose that repentance, conceived as a reorientation of one's whole personality, throws into relief the social dimension of the Gospel, for it involves a turning from sin to God, not only in the individual subjective consciousness, but *in the world.* Without ethics, I say, there is no repentance. Am I slighting the personal aspect of evangelization, as I have been accused of doing? I don't think I am. What I am doing is recognizing that man is a social being and that, therefore, there is no possibility for him to be converted to Christ and to grow as a Christian except as a social being. Man never turns to God as a sinner in the abstract — he always turns to God in a specific social situation.

A first objection to my emphasis on repentance is that the call to repentance is not an essential aspect of the Gospel. Jesus' summons to repent, "for the kingdom of heaven is at hand," we are told, "is addressed to the Jews." We cannot, however, confuse Jesus' approach to the Jews with what would apply in the age of grace. "The Jews rejected Jesus' proposals, and he then offered, through his apostles and the Holy Spirit, the salvation to all by grace." When we come to the preaching of the Gospel in the Gentile world — so this argument goes — the emphasis is on faith, not on repentance.

What we have before us is a very serious question, indeed. The argument has to do with nothing less than the very content of the message we are to proclaim to the world. There is no use in taking for granted that we all agree on the Gospel that has been entrusted to us and that all we need now is more efficient methods to communicate it. If we think so, we deceive ourselves. The Gospel of repentance is one thing; the gospel of cheap grace is something else. Time doesn't allow me to discuss the question in full. Let me limit myself to the following observations:

1. In the Great Commission, as it appears in Luke 24:47, Jesus himself defined the content of the message that his disciples were to proclaim to the nations as "repentance and forgiveness of sins. . . in his name." That the early heralds of the message faithfully followed his instructions is ratified by the book of Acts. Repentance was an integral part not only of Peter's and the other early apostles' preaching among the Jews

(Acts 2:38, 3:19, 5:31), but also of Paul's preaching among the Gentiles (Acts 17:30, 20:21, 26:18). To those who would use Acts 16:31 ("Believe in the Lord Jesus, and you will be saved, you and your household"), let me point out that verse 31 is followed by verse 32, "And they spoke the word of the Lord to him and to all that were in the home." To those who call my attention to I Corinthians 15:1-5 as a passage that contains a full synthesis of Paul's message and yet makes no reference to repentance, let me point out that the passage doesn't make explicit reference to faith either — the emphasis is on the facts of the Gospel, not on the appropriation of it.

2. It is true that the words "repentance" or "repent" are not commonly found in the Pauline epistles (cf. Rom. 2:4, II Cor. 7:9, II Tim. 2:25). This must not lead us, however, to contrast his emphasis on justification by faith with Jesus' call to repentance. No more can justification be separated from regeneration than forgiveness from repentance. For Paul, as well as for all the writers of the New Testament, the God who justifies or forgives is also the God who delivers from slavery to sin. As J. Jeremias puts it, "God's acquittal is not only forensic, it is not 'as if,' not a mere word, but it is God's word that works and creates life. God's word is always an effective word. As an antedonation of God's final acquittal, justification is pardon in the fullest sense. It is the beginning of a new life, a new existence, a new creation through the gift of the Holy Spirit." Justification, therefore, cannot be separated from the fruits of justification, even as faith cannot be separated from works. We do great disservice to Paul if we do not see that the same moral transformation to which the Gospels and Acts point by the term "repentance" is assumed by his teaching on dying to sin and being raised to life (Rom. 6), or on the new creation in which the old has passed away and the new is come (I Cor. 5:17), or on the contrast between gratifying the desires of the flesh and walking by the Spirit (Gal. 5).

3. Faith without repentance is not saving faith but presumptuous believism. The aim of the Gospel is to produce in us faith, but faith that works through love. Without the works of love there is no genuine faith. If it is true that we are not saved by works, it is also true that the faith that saves is the faith that works. As Luther put it, "Faith alone justifies, but faith is never alone." The indicative of the Gospel and the imperative of Christian ethics may be distinguished but must never be separated.

It is hard to avoid the conclusion that the basis for the denial of repentance as an essential aspect of the Gospel is not the result of a careful study of Scripture, but another expression of the attempt to accommodate the Gospel to the world for the sake of numbers — the message must be reduced to a minimum in order to make it possible for all men to want to become Christian. As a matter of fact, easy salvation (what Bonhoeffer called "cheap grace") is part and parcel of the variety of culture-Christianity to which I referred before. A question that my emphasis on repentance naturally raises in that context is, "Is not repentance, as you define it, asking too much of a new convert?" May I ask, in response, how much is *too much*? The most that man can give either to the living God or to the false gods of this world is his own life. But is that not precisely what God demands of man? Granted that following conversion there is a process of growth in which one comes to an increasing understanding of the implications of his commitment to Christ. The point, however, is that a conversion without repentance — which is a spurious conversion — can only lead to a Christian life without repentance — which is a spurious Christian life. Birth and growth form an organic unity — the only faith that will *grow* in obedience is the faith that is *born* in obedience to God's command to repent. Becoming a Christian is not a religious change, in which one becomes the adherent of a cult, but a reorientation of the whole man in relation to God, to men and to creation. It is not the mere addition of new patterns imposed on the old — such as church attendance, Bible reading, and prayer — but a restructuring of one's whole personality, a reorientation of one's whole life in the world. If a person doesn't see that with Christ this is what he is in for, he is not in. Thas task of the evangelist in communicating the Gospel is not to make it easier, so that people will respond positively, but to make it clear. Neither Jesus nor his apostles ever reduced the demands of the Gospel in order to make converts. No cheap grace, but God's kindness which is meant to lead to repentance, provides the only solid basis for discipleship. He who accommodates the Gospel to the mood of the day, in order to make it more palatable, does so because he has forgotten the nature of Christian salvation — it is not man's work, but God's. "With men it is impossible, but not with God, for all things are possible with God" (Mark 10:27).

The future of the church does not depend on our ability to persuade people to give intellectual assent to a truncated Gospel, but on our faithfulness to the full Gospel of our Lord Jesus Christ and God's faithfulness to his Word. "Half gospels have no dignity and no future. Like the famous mule, they have neither pride of ancestry nor hope of posterity" (P.T. Forsyth).

Under the subtitle "evangelism and other-worldliness" I speak of two extreme positions with regard to the present world. The one is that which conceives of salvation as something that fits within the limits of the present age, in terms of social, economic, and political liberation. The personal dimensions of salvation are eliminated or minimized. The individual is lost in society. There is little or no place for forgiveness from guilt and sin, or for the resurrection of the body and immortality. *This world* is all that there is and the fundamental mission of the church must therefore be conceived in terms of the transformation of *this world* through politics. At the other end of the scale is the view according to which salvation is reduced to the future salvation of the soul and the present world is nothing more than a preparatory stage for life in the hereafter. The social dimensions of salvation are completely, or almost completely, disregarded and the church becomes a redeemed ghetto charged with the mission of rescuing souls from the present evil world. Didn't Jesus say, "My kingdom is not of this world?" Why should the church be concerned for the poor and the needy? Didn't he say, "The poor you always have with you?" The only responsibility that the church has toward the world is, then, the preaching of the Gospel and the planting of churches, "There are many goods the church *may* do, of course; but they do not belong to its essential mission."

I maintain that both of these views are incomplete gospels and that the greatest need of the church today is the recovery of the full Gospel of our Lord Jesus Christ — the whole Gospel for the whole man for the whole world.

On the one hand, the Gospel cannot be reduced to social, economic and political categories, nor the church to an agency for human improvement. Even less can the Gospel be confused with a political ideology or the church with a political party. As Christians we are called to witness to the transcendental, other-worldly Christ, through whose work we have received forgiveness of sins and reconciliation to God. We believe in man's need of a new birth through a personal encounter with God in Jesus Christ, by the action of the Holy Spirit, through the proclamation of the Word of God. And we maintain that nothing can take the place of spiritual regeneration in the making of new men. This is biblical soteriology and we are fully committed to it. We cannot accept the equation of salvation with the satisfaction of bodily needs, social amelioration, or political liberation.

On the other hand, there is no biblical warrant to view the church as an other-worldly community dedicated to the salvation of souls, or to limit its mission to the preaching of man's reconciliation to God through Jesus Christ. As Elton Trueblood has put it, "A genuine Gospel will always be concerned with human justice rather than with the mere cultivation of a warm inner glow." The responsibility of defining that relation between the Gospel and the concern for human justice falls within the province of another paper — the one by my colleague Samuel Escobar. I will limit myself to answering a few key questions out of the many that have been sent to me in response to my own paper:

1. *"How involved should we be in justice and economics?"* The fact is that, whether we like it or not, we are already involved. Politics and economics are unavoidable — they are a part of the reality that surrounds us while we are in the world. The real question, therefore, is, "Since we are in fact involved, how can we make sure that our involvement is faithful to the Gospel of our Lord Jesus Christ?" Even though we may try not to take any notice of politics and economics, *they* always take notice of us.

2. *"Is the change of the structure of society a part of the evangelistic mandate?"* The same question, in essence, is asked in other words: *"Are you not confusing the two kingdoms?"* Here I can only insist that "the imperative of the evangelical ethic forms an indissoluble whole with the indicative of the Gospel." Another way to say it would be that the two tables of the law belong together, or that concern for man's reconciliation with God cannot be separated from concern for social justice, or that the evangelistic mandate has to be fulfilled in the context of obedience to the cultural mandate, or that the Kingdom of God manifests itself in the midst of the kingdoms of men, or simply that the mission of the church is indivisible from its life. I refuse, therefore, to drive a wedge between a primary task, namely the proclamation of the Gospel, and a secondary (at best) or even optional (at worst) task of the church. In order to be obedient to its Lord the church should never do

anything that is not essential; therefore, nothing that the church does in obedience to its Lord is unessential. Why? Because love to God is inseparable from love to men; because faith without works is dead; because hope includes the restoration of all things to the Kingdom of God. I am not confusing the two kingdoms — I do not expect the ultimate salvation of man or society through good works or political action. I am merely asking that we take seriously the relevance of the Gospel to the totality of man's life in the world. The only other possible alternative is to say that God is interested in our calling him "Lord, Lord," but not in our obedience to his will in relation to such crucial issues as social injustice and oppression, famine, war, racism, illiteracy, and the like.

3. *"Is it legitimate to say that Jesus was a political king? Are you not defining politics in your own terms?"* When I say that in describing Jesus as the Christ we are in fact describing him in political terms I do not mean that he involved himself in what we today consider political action in a narrow sense, but that *Messiah (king) is* a political description. He did not come in order to create a religion, but in order to accomplish God's purpose of placing all things under his government. Those who acknowledge him as Lord are not only reconciled to God but also given in him a model for human life, life in the *polis.* Here and now, in this world, his disciples are called to bring their personal and corporate life into line with the will of God expressed in the ethics of the Kingdom, whose central principle is love.

4. *"In emphasizing the ethical, how do we avoid moralism and legalism in our teaching?"* By teaching the true nature of Christian morality, i.e., that morality is not outward subjection to rules and norms, but heart obedience in response to God; that the essence of Christian morality is gratitude. The way to avoid the danger of falling into moralism and legalism is not to eliminate the ethical demands of the Gospel, but to see that obedience is an essential aspect of faith's response to the Gospel and is always obedience by the power of God who works in us through the Spirit.

5. *"What can the church do, when the problems are so staggering?"* The church has not been called to solve all the problems, but to be faithful to God with what it has. The greatest contribution that the church can make to the world is to be all that she is supposed to be. Among other things: (a) A community of *reconciliation.* In the midst of a fragmented world, here is a community where all barriers that divide disappear, where men learn to welcome one another as Christ has welcomed them, for the glory of God. (b) A community of *personal authenticity.* In the midst of a world in which each man has to fit into the mold imposed on him by his society, here is a community where each one is accepted as he is and encouraged to develop fully as a man made in the image of God. (c) A community of *serving and giving.* In the midst of a world where man lives to be served and to receive, here is a community where man lives to serve and to give.

This brings me to a conclusion. Our greatest need is a more biblical Gospel and a more faithful church. We may go away from this Congress with a nice set of papers and statements that will be filed away and forgotten, and with the memories of a big, impressive world meeting. Or we may go away with the conviction that we have magic formulas for the conversion of people. My own hope and prayer is that we go away with a repentant attitude with regard to our enslavement to the world and our arrogant triumphalism, with a sense of our helplessness to break away from our bonds, and yet also with a great confidence in God, the Father of our Lord Jesus Christ, who "by the power at work within us is able to do far more abundantly than all we ask or think. To him be glory in the church and in Christ Jesus, to all generations for ever and ever. Amen."

EVANGELISM IN ASIA
I. Ben Wati

Dr. Ben Wati, New Delhi,
India, is Executive Secretary of the Evangelical Fellowship of India.

Introduction

2000 years ago Dr. Luke reported, "All they which dwelt in Asia heard the Word of the Lord" (Acts 19:10).

In his epistle to the Corinthians Paul said, "The churches of Asia salute you" (I Cor. 16:19).

There are twenty-one references to Asia in the New Testament, and we know that the first Christian churches were planted in Asia.

However, the New Testament geography of Asia was very limited. Today it is the largest continent with a vast land mass which extends from the Pacific Ocean to the Black Sea. In fact there appears to be a strong geographical argument for considering Europe as a peninsula of Asia!

Asia is an explosive continent, a struggling giant, with a solid mass of humanity in a pluralistic society. Asia gave birth to all the eight major religions of the world plus all the sects, and their scriptures are written in seven Asian languages.

According to Dr. Monier Williams of Oxford University, "Asian religious literature varies from the most exuberant verbosity to the most obscure brevity, from subtle reasoning to transparent sophistry, from high morality — often expressed in impressive language worthy of Christianity itself — to precepts implying a social condition scarcely compatible with the lowest grade of culture and civilization" (*Indian Wisdom*, 1875).

Asia has the largest number of adherents to the major world religions except Christianity; for, after two millennia, only 2 per cent of Asians have accepted Christianity. Therefore we are challenged by a Himalayan task to evangelize 98 per cent of Asian peoples.

The church in almost every land of Asia is a tiny David confronting a giant Goliath of non-Christian religions and cultures, of communism and increasing secularism. And the emerging Asian churches have to operate in the midst of passionate nationalsim, international tensions, social and economic struggles, and amid resurgent religions.

In this Congress there are statistics galore to impress upon us the urgency to evangelize the various areas of the globe. From one point of view one could say that if it has taken 2,000 years to reach only 2 per cent of Asians for Christ, it would take 98,000 years to evangelize Asia! However, we need not rely too much on this type of statistics.

The other day, on the walls of Sat Tal Ashram (founded by Dr. E. Stanley Jones), I was intrigued by a printed poster which reads:
God's Word and Statistics
God's Word says: what we should do
Statistics show: what we are doing.

God's Word says: "Go into all the world."
Statistics show: Less than one-half of the world is reached.
God's Word says: "Unto every creature."
Statistics show: The Westerner has a 95 per cent priority on the Gospel ministry.
God's Word says: "The uttermost parts."
Statistics show: The comfortably situated and civilized parts.
God's Word says: "Every tongue."
Statistics show: Over 1,000 tongues are still without the Gospel.
God's Word says: "We have this ministry."
Statistics show: Less than 1 per cent of Christians are engaged in the ministry.
God's Word says: "Sow (that is, scatter) the seed."
Statistics show: The seed is heaped up in a few centers.

Let us, therefore, mobilize the total membership.

Main Report: In this Congress it is my great joy and privilege to report that despite many roadblocks, evangelism in Asia is gaining ground. Asia is open to the Good News as never before. Our Sovereign Lord God is at work everywhere and we see great opportunities to present Jesus Christ as the only Savior of Asia. Asian evangelicals have caught a new vision not only to evangelize their people but also to send missionaries to the ends of the earth.

It may be in war-torn Cambodia and Vietnam; it may be in the so-called closed countries like Afghanistan, Bhutan, or Nepal; it may be in Muslim countries like Indonesia, Pakistan, or Bangladesh; it may be in developed countries like Israel or Japan; it may be in bustling and prosperous Singapore or Hong Kong; in every country and island of Asia the gospel witness is increasing.

Every day radio evangelism in major languages and in tribal dialects of Asia has responses from thousands upon thousands of people. Prayer cells and evangelistic cells are multiplying. Ministry among students and youth gains momentum everywhere. In some countries like India, Bible correspondence courses are very popular: at least 100,000 Hindus, Muslims and Sikhs are studying the Bible in any given day.

There are new patterns of evangelism as in the Philippines where Christ the Only Way and the Lay Evangelistic Groups movements have made an impact in the last few years. India Penetration Plan is poised for a bold thrust into the future outreach in the Indian subcontinent.

Even in the great mainland of Communist China, though the church buildings are deserted, the believers are maintaining their faith and a suffering, worshiping, and witnessing church exists.

We hear thrilling reports of people being baptized in the name of Jesus Christ in different parts of Asia. In one day, on July 3, 1973, there was a baptism of 1,060 people in a river in South India. Dr. Wesley Duewel, President of OMS International, mentioned in a letter that in Korea 300 were baptized in one day and nearly 2,000 on the next day, and 700 on the third day. In a two-week period there were over 5,000 baptized among the armed forces in Korea last year.

We hear of Gurkha soldiers who were converted in Hong Kong and who continue their fellowship in Nepal, their homeland. I know of people who were baptized at midnight in New Delhi, and others baptized in the swimming pool of a posh hotel. We praise God for what happened in one part of Indonesia and what may transpire in a new nation like Bangladesh. God is at work and we know that the Word of God is not bound.

Most of all, there is a new missionary vision among Asians in many countries. According to *Mission for a Third World* (James Wong, editor) 211 Asian missionary agencies send some 2,994 missionaries. In the first All-Asia Mission Consultation held in Seoul, Korea (August 27-30, 1973), the following was included in a statement:

"Having had factual reports from representatives of many Asian countries where the Gospel of Jesus Christ has not been effectively preached; and realizing that the unfinished task is so tremendous . . . We appeal to the Christian churches in Asia to be involved in the preaching of the Gospel, specially through sending and receiving Asian missionaries to strengthen the witness to the saving power of Christ.

"We are compelled by the Holy Spirit to declare that we shall work towards the placing of at least two hundred new Asian missionaries by the end of 1974.

"These missionaries will be involved primarily in evangelism in the power of the Holy Spirit in order that men and women may come to believe God's work of grace through Jesus Christ and in turn be agents of evangelism in the fellowship of his church, the body of Christ. These missionaries will also be sent to plant evangelistic churches where they do not already exist."

Rev. David J. Cho, Secretary of the Continuation Committee of the All-Asia Mission Consultation, hopes that the Holy Spirit will enable 10,000 Asian missionaries to be trained and sent into the world by A.D. 2000. We praise God for this new venture among Asian evangelicals.

Some Problems: However, the church lacks spiritual life. The life of many a nominal Christian is canceling out the witness of the Gospel. In many places rural congregations are like sheep without a shepherd, deprived of pastoral care, Bible reading, prayer, fellowship, and regular worship. For years they do not see the Lord's Table.

The church lacks evangelistic concern because it is inward looking. So much so that the energies of the church in some places are utilized in litigation, dividing churches, and weakening the witness.

Perhaps basic to this are theological delusions which hinder evangelism in Asia. An inadequate view of the Holy Scriptures, universalism, syncretism, secularism, static concepts of the church; all this hinders evangelism in many parts of Asia.

We see churchless Christians in some countries where there is no freedom of religion. We know of pockets in India where the new converts cannot join the established churches and they have their own Koinonia groups.

There is also the fear of dialogue with men of other faiths. The present structure of the church in some parts of Asia prevents laymen from having any ministry; all is left to the clergy. There is also a lack of cultural expression, which shows that a church is a foreign tree not rooted in the culture of the land. All these are problems which we must face and overcome if there is to be church growth in Asia. But the future prospects are bright.

While writing this report, I received a news release from the OMS International Inc. in Greenwood, Indiana, USA. It is dated June 1, 1974. I was so thrilled that I want to share it all:

ONE MILLION KOREANS RECEIVE WITNESS.

"Approximately 1,000,000 people were reached with a direct soul-winning witness on Good Friday, April 12. The preparation began months in advance. Each of the 200,000 members, believers, and youth of the OMS-founded churches across Korea shared in the prayer preparation. Each selected five individuals as his personal prayer target. For these he prayed daily until he witnessed to them on Good Friday. In the 750 local OMS churches, where 4:30 or 5:00 a.m. prayer meetings have been held for years, intercession focused on this intensive soul-winning campaign.

"For further preparation, each local church was supplied with a special manual on soul winning, flip-charts to use in soul-winning classes, and instruction on how to use the specially prepared six-page tract, "Invitation to Abundant Life." Bible Literature International furnished 200,000 Heart of Pak tracts. At least 465,000 OMS tracts were used. New York Bible Society International and Pocket Testament League sent a total of 300,000 Gospels of John for the campaign.

"Good Friday became 'one great day of witness,' with more than 965,000 pieces of literature used in an outreach to approximately one million prayer-prepared individuals. Reports continue to come in, but already total 16,068 adults and 11,100 children who professed to accept Christ as Savior. These were all introduced to the local church congregations on Easter Sunday. Christian workers wept for joy. One pastor said he had waited 20 years to see this day. Some churches made the whole month of April a time of witness. Many individuals plan to continue witnessing to five new persons each day. Other denominations have said they would like to join in a similar witness next year. This can only be the beginning." Praise the Lord for what is happening.

Conclusion:

Politically and outwardly, the temper of the times in Asia may not look very favorable for evangelism. Socially and culturally, the peoples of Asia may be all tangled up in ancient knots or mixed up with modern distractions. But millions are in sincere search for inner peace which only the Prince of Peace can provide. Therefore pray that the Lord's message will spread rapidly and triumph wherever it goes, winning converts everywhere in Asia.

2,000 years ago "all they which dwelt in Asia heard the Word of the Lord." As we near A.D. 2000 we must unite in prayer and close our ranks so that the tribals in the mountains, the dwellers in the remotest islands, the Hindus, Muslims, and Buddhists, students, youth, children and all others, yes, all Asia may hear his voice, follow Jesus Christ and worship the only true and living God.

WESTERN EUROPE IN THE SEVENTIES:

Jan van Capelleveen

The two most significant developments on the religious scene of Western Europe are the almost total collapse of institutional church leadership and a completely new interest in the Bible. This has been described with the words: The church is out and the Bible is in.

The church is out, institutionally speaking. The tremendous interest in church unity, evident in the sixties, has petered out. Instead a polarization, a disunity is noticeable in almost every church — liberal or conservative. A result is that people show little interest in what the church is doing and hardly any interest in official proclamations and synodical decisions. Big city churches almost all over Western Europe had to reduce the number of pastors for financial reasons, often by more than fifty per cent.

Yet, the Bible seems to be in. Just last night I received the annual report of the United Bible Societies. For the first time European countries show a remarkable growth in Bible distribution, and countries like Austria, Western Germany, the Netherlands and Norway claim record sales. New too is the fact that the Bible Societies have added a new phrase to their vocabulary: Missionary Bible translation and Bible distribution. It has been discovered that the Bible translations used by the churches, and usually made for use by the churches are incomprehensible for people outside. Since special translations for them were made, like *Good News for Modern Man* and similar translations in German, Dutch, Spanish, Portuguese and French, people outside the church have rediscovered the Bible. The Netherlands Bible Society recently held an opinion poll on possession and the use of the Bible. It has now become evident that lately many people outside the church have started to read the Bible.

But the Bible Societies of Europe want to reach more groups which have heretofore been forgotten. In their working plan for Europe they plan Bible distribution through special selections for migrant workers. They are beginning to reach the people who have lost the art of reading with Listeners' Bibles, Bibles on cassettes. The Bible Societies not only want to publish the Bible as a book but want to translate it into the other media of radio, television, cassettes, cartoons, posters and slide presentations. For years the Bible Societies were the handmaiden of the church. Now they want to serve also as the messenger boys of the world.

Another important development in Western Europe must have our attention. The Dutch poll gave a lot of older Christians a jolt. It proved that the Bible is read least by people between 50 and 65 years of age. It also showed that their children between the ages of fifteen and twenty-five belong to the group of the best Bible readers. This news was published on the day the hippy underground paper, "Aloha," ceased existence. In the sixties it was the leading voice of the hippy movement. It died, however, because of lack of interest. A new and different generation has come upon the scene in the seventies. New movements have taken over the limelight of publicity.

One of these new movements is the reborn Youth for Christ. In 1968 it discovered coffeebar evangelism by accident. Soon this organization owned at least a score of buildings in which coffeebars were held and where young people could find a home away from home. It was discovered that young people not only want to wear their own clothes and listen to their own music, but they also need their own youthful atmosphere. They want informality. They sit on the ground. They search for what the Dutch call "gezelligheid," a warm, cozy togetherness, which went out of the homes when the television came in. Now this movement reaches at least 2000 teenagers per day.

At the same time that Youth for Christ was born, a Navigator tried to reach students in the city of Delft. After one year he had gathered thirteen students; after two years, some forty. Now this has become the largest student Christian movement in the country and it is branching out to high school young people with brand new captain clubs.

About the same time a young Dutch fellow decided to do something about the hippies sleeping in the Amsterdam parks. He took a few of them into his home to help them break the drug bondage. Now some forty of these people live and work together in The Hague. On Sunday afternoons often three to 400 people attend the meetings. This work of the Jesus People has spread all over Holland into Germany and Belgium. The central theme of their theology is Jesus. They read the Bible as a guide for everyday life. They may show little interest in historical studies, but they want to practice what they preach. They are radicals, but not rebels. These movements hardly relate to the existing churches. They do not oppress them. They hardly criticize them. Often they speak warmly about them, like one speaks about his own grandmother who spends her last days in a room full of portraits of the past. It is wonderful to visit her for just a short time, it would be impossible to live with her. The churches themselves seem to be flabbergasted by this new revival among young people. They hardly criticize them; they look upon them as something exotic.

This is the situation at this moment. Will these movements and the churches be able to find one another? I'm afraid they are, for the moment, going around in different orbits. Perhaps they will meet in the future, when teenagers have outgrown their jeans and the churches change their high-button shoes for footwear which will give them a new readiness to announce the Good News of peace, as Paul says in the letter to the Ephesians.

THE EVANGEL IN
LATIN AMERICA TODAY

Robinson Cavalcanti

Dr. Cavalcanti, Rio de Janeiro,
Brazil, is Professor of Political
Science for the Federal University,
Recife, and Area Director for the University
Biblical Alliance of Brazil (ABUB).

Evangelical Christianity in Latin America is divided into two distinct eras and is entering now its third phase. The first era was the heroic one of the pioneers living in an atmosphere of intolerance and persecution. Thanks to the Lord for all those who survived and transmitted the faith to the coming generations! The second era in most recent years, was the era of creation of the roots, which had a decisive influence in many parts of the world, being one of the relevant expansion periods of the church history. Thanks to the Lord for this era and these blessings! The third era, I think is starting the opportunities today.

I don't know whether in any other part of the world there are so many possibilities to propagate the Gospel. We are living in an atmosphere of great religious freedom. Reunions and divine services — as long as they do not interfere with the laws and morals — are admitted in any place, even in the square. We can use — sometimes even free of charge — press, radio, and television. The evangelicals are becoming respectable persons who are listened to, consulted, and who are getting, more and more, greater financial possibilities and more personnel. The place of the Bible is no more the stake, but the bookcase, the library and the bookshop. Xenophobia — a factor of perturbation for the missionaries — dying down. Nevertheless, the most relevant factor is that, from the slums to the universities, wherever there is a preacher and a message, there will be listeners.

All of it, however, is not a carpet of roses. There are still some foci of traditional Roman-Catholic resistance, even though hidden by a smile. The ecumenism has entailed a most dangerous notion of relativism ("now we are all brothers") which constitutes a difficult obstacle to the evangelization. The mysticism of Afro-American, spirito-Kardecist, syncretistical or Oriental origin attracts more and more people at present. To a smaller extent than in the past, Marxists and radicals represent an open provocation. The elite continues to be sensitive to the rationalistic philosophies of European origin. The urban individualism of a competitive society underlines the idea that "there is no time to waste with these kinds of things" and that "religion is something individual." Hedonism, practical materialism, and indifference characterize most of the members of a new-growing society. Finding the Gospel insufficiently rational, mystic, practical, or relevant, our new listeners say "no" or delay an option, while the adherents seem to be inferior compared with the previous decade.

If things do not go well, if despite all possibilities we do not obtain success in proportion to our efforts, we have to ask if the answer lies in the Christian community itself. We can watch — with the exception of a few groups or persons — conformism grow, striving for material comfort and the acceptance by many people of a cheap salvation without any real committment. There are nominal evangelists, non-converted descendants, or the "decided" in a hurry in front of a simplified message. These are the groups geared to violent political contestation and to a neo-herodian adhesion with the loss of sense of a critical participation. These are preoccupying symptoms! The breath of the new theology, as well as the "siren's song" of the new Rome, have dangerously touched most prophets' houses. The ecclesiastical policy and the promotion or worship of personality has shocked the new generation. The biggest scandal is the denominational sectarianism, the non-cooperative mind, the lack of love, the mutual complaints on the part of leading people. Let us add to all this a narrow mind and poor missionary action by our potential, the lack of an up-to-date apologetic, of an autochthonous theological mind and a mental methodological alienation to the culture we live in.

If half-heartedness and failing reign, it is time for the Latin American Christians to repent and to change. It is time to join the hands, the hearts, the talents and the resources. It is time to open churches where they do not yet exist, and not where our denomination is absent. It is time for us to strive for the Divine Spirit whose power and manifestations seem to be, to some people, their exclusive property. Whereas others, who worship him with their lips and credos, are afraid that he may upset their inflexible doctrines, their lives, and their ministries. It is time to re-study and to proclaim, courageously, the whole Bible, or else history will classify us as being of a decadent era. And the Lord will not wait with his judgment.

EVANGELISM OPPORTUNITIES AND OBSTACLES IN AFRICA
Byang H. Kato

*Dr. Kato, Nairobi, Kenya, is General
Secretary of the Association of
Evangelicals of Africa and Madagascar.*

Introduction

"But I will stay in Ephesus until Pentecost, for a wide door for effective work has opened to me, and there are many adversaries" (I Cor. 16: 8, 9). RSV.

The Apostle Paul uttered this joyous and challenging statement at the peak of his successful ministry in Ephesus. Behind him was a dynamic church consisting of well-taught and consolidated believers with assurance of salvation (Acts 19:1-16). Within the same church were radiant Christians who had come out of utter darkness, having cut loose the cords that bound them with the pagan past to follow unreservedly the Lord who had bought them (Acts 19:7-20). "So mightily grew the Word of God and prevailed" (Acts. 19:20).

In the midst of this tremendous success was a strong opposition. Demetrius raised the public conscience against Christianity through the use of economic (v. 25), religious (v. 26), cultural (v. 27), and political (v. 34) arguments. Their business was in jeopardy as the Christians refused to engage themselves any more in the art of making charms. The prestigious temple of Diana, one of the seven wonders of the ancient world, was losing its reputation.

The Ephesian situation is repeating itself in Africa today. The tremendous success of Christianity is being matched with religious, economic, cultural and political challenges.

With the exciting past of the first and second generation of Christians in Africa, we are now thrown into the adolescent third generation Christianity. Effective doors of opportunity continue to expand. Tools for the effective ministry increase at the rate of the technological and economic development of Africa. The rapid growth of population at 2.3 per cent adds to the door of opportunity. But the enemy of souls is not asleep.

1. Opportunities in Africa

Let us look more closely at the factors favorable to the evangelization of Africa, before surveying the obstacles.

a. *Religious factors.* While in a man-made religious system the worshiper paradoxically presents a barricade between himself and the triune God, nevertheless it shows man's craving for reality which Christianity alone can satisfy. The religious situation in Africa may be summed up this way:

(i) *Islam.* It is estimated that there are 70 million Muslims in black Africa. The strength of Islam, however, is many times exaggerated. Apart from an inflation of figures by statisticians, there are many nominal Muslims, perhaps at a higher rate than that of nominal Christians. Villages are known to have been declared Muslim whereas only the village head has made a conscientious decision. With a careful and enduring "friendship" evangelism, many of these superficial Muslims can be brought to Christ. Islamic Project for Africa has shown that this can be done without compromising the Christian principles.

(ii) *African traditional religions.* While there are certain areas in which these traditional religions are remaining, on the whole the pagan worship is losing its grip. The old men who have clung to the ancestor gods are passing away. The younger generation hates to be associated with pagan practices. Thus not a few Africans are left without a faith. Some attach themselves to either Islam or Christianity. The field is truly ready for rich harvest.

(iii) *Independent movements.* The estimated figure of 6,000 semi-Christian sects in Africa, growing at a rate of 100 new sects each year is alarming. Certainly there can be born-again Christians in some of these independent movements. But the legalistic and syncretistic approach of most of them makes it difficult for an average adherent to see clearly the way of salvation by faith in Christ. It is a problem to know what to do with some of the sects. Should well-instructed, born-again believers become immersed in their midst to guide individuals to salvation? Should we attract their leaders to the established Bible schools and cause a spiritual revolution that way? Whatever we do, here is a vast segment of African society running to several millions which has been touched by the Gospel yet in which the evidence of transformation remains dubious.

(iv) *Other sects and religions.* Buddhism, theosophy, and materialism are taking toll of Africans and expatriates. Jehovah's Witnesses have been outlawed in at least three countries but their number continues to grow elsewhere.

b. *Social factors favoring evangelism.*

(i) *Political atmosphere.* More than two-thirds of Africa's heads of states are professing Christians. I am not aware of any state in Africa where freedom of worship is outlawed.

(ii) *Family system.* The extended family system in Africa provides a great opportunity for reaching many people with the Gospel. The breadwinner of a family is quickly becoming the decision-maker. In the case of a committed Christian breadwinner, the whole family unit could be brought to Christ. African Christians should in a Cornelius fashion, share Christ, and not only material possessions, with their kinsmen.

(iii) *Urbanization.* While the movement into the cities creates countless problems, it also presents a wonderful opportunity for evangelism. Young people from well-sheltered Muslim homes become open to Gospel witness. Many single ladies in apartments present a wonderful opportunity for organized Bible study groups. Many young graduates have plenty of time after work for Christian ministry.

(iv) *Children's ministry.* Probably more than two-thirds of Africa's 300 million population are children under fifteen.

(v) *Church attendance.* In some parts of Africa today 70 per cent of the population go to church. This presents a great opportunity for discipling the adherents into full involvement in the body of Christ.

c. *Academic Factors*

(i) *Religious knowledge in schools.* A popular adage in Africa today is "knowledge is power." This is a line with Solomon's wise counsel, "And with all thy getting, get understanding" (Prov. 4:7). Although the prevailing trend is the transfer of schools to the states, in most countries religious instruction is a part of the curriculum. Bible as a subject is very popular with many students. Correspondence courses appeal to thousands of ambitious youths.

(ii) *Literacy.* The average percentage of literacy in black Africa is less than 20 per cent. Almost every government sees illiteracy as an obstacle to progress. Every movement that seeks to promote literacy is not only welcomed, but may even receive government subsidy. Christians can utilize this method through the literature produced and the personal friendship established. The Women's Fellowship of the Evangelical Churches of West Africa (ECWA) in Nigeria has chosen for its theme in 1974 "Everyone teach one." This is worthy of emulation by women in other countries.

(iii) *Mass Media.* The Voice of Kenya (VOK) radio and television provides an opportunity for fourteen hours free religious broadcasting each week. The New Life for All in Nigeria is sometimes paid for the Christian programs it provides for radio and television stations in Nigeria. In Zambia the Southern Baptists cannot cope with the opportunities for free-time religious broadcasts.

Opportunities for the use of literature arc even greater. Each copy of the well-known *African Challenge,* now *Today's Challenge,* published by ECWA Productions Ltd., in Nigeria is shared by ten readers. But non-Christian literature is more easily obtainable by the public as it is distributed free in many cases.

2. *Obstacles to evangelism in Africa*

When the church is at its peak of success, the enemy of souls emerges with greater animosity to swallow up the baby child.

a. *External obstacles.*

(i) *Islam.* The traditional methods of education, medicine, and mass media devised by Christian missions are now tools in the hands of Muslims. There are now many Muslim schools and colleges in Nigeria, and possibly in other countries too. For several years Al-azhar University in Cairo provided top-level Islamic education for Africa. But Bayero College in Nigeria today can boast of turning out scores of Islamic theologians each year.

The use of radio, television and literature is becoming more and more popular. Muslim councils have been formed in Uganda and Nigeria as a counterpart of National Councils of Churches. This united effort consolidates and promotes Islamic faith, making it relevant and appealing to the intelligent youths of Africa. The World Muslim Congress has made traumatic gains in Africa as a result of the Middle East situation.

(ii) *African traditional religions.* Syncretism is a realistic threat to biblical Christianity in Africa. "Pagan" worship is increasingly considered a part of African culture which must be preserved. Idols are considered wonderful works of art that must not be destroyed. Missionaries are constantly attacked for "having destroyed our culture" even though some of the destruction might have been the burning of charms. In Kenya there is even a society for the promotion of "pagan" worship which is called "Waganga wa Miti Shamba Society."

(iii) *Goverment attitudes*. Some African governments are so sold on cultural revolution and the philosophy of authenticity that to stand for the uniqueness of the Christian faith is considered unpatriotic. There are, in fact, reports of persecution and intimidation of Christians in some countries.

b. *Internal obstacles*.

(i) *Liberal ecumenism*. A recent meeting of African church leaders, while advocating evangelism of frontier regions of Africa, did not provide the atmosphere that would promote evangelism. The traditional understanding of biblical salvation is now reduced to political and economic liberation. The primary task of the church now becomes a fight for liberation from political oppression rather than liberation from the bondage of sin. The spiritual atmosphere that should characterize a Christian leaders' conference was conspicuously missing. Such a secularization of Christianity cannot enhance biblical evangelism.

c. *Neutral obstacles*. Christian organizations working in Africa can be an instrument for evangelism or a hindrance. One sad thing with some Christian organizations working in Africa is that they know too much. They come to Africa with a packaged deal which must not be tampered with. Such an approach will not help evangelism. There is a great need of cooperation among evangelical organizations operating in Africa.

3. *Conclusion*

In closing, I want to emphasize that these are exciting days in Africa. The opportunities are unlimited. We are on the verge of either an unprecedented harvest of souls and a major breakthrough in discipling of thousands of believers, or Christianity is about to face its darkest hour in Black Africa. It depends on how sensitive and obedient Bible-believing Christians are to the Holy Spirit. May the Lord of the Church give us sufficient grace to face the challenge that is ahead of the Christians in Africa in particular, and in the world in general.

METHODS AND STRATEGY IN THE EVANGELISM OF THE EARLY CHURCH
Michael Green

*Mr. Green is Principal of St. John's
College, Nottingham, England. He has
written several books, including
EVANGELISM IN THE EARLY CHURCH
and RUNAWAY WORLD.*

When a movement grows from a dozen peasants in an unimportant corner of the world, to be the official religion of the civilized world inside 300 years; when it is sufficiently independent of that civilization to survive its fall, and indeed the fall of every successive civilization since; when it is universal enough in its appeal to win millions of converts in all sectors of the globe, among all types of men, belonging to every race, culture, and personality type — then it is arguable that such a movement has got something. It is also arguable that we have a good deal to learn from its strategy and tactics, its methods and approaches.

That movement is Christianity. The church of today is heir to the revolutionary forces which changed the face of the world in the decades following the death and resurrection of Jesus. And yet, one would never guess it. The idea of the modern church being a revolutionary, invading force is laughable in the West though readily understandable in Indonesia, Korea, Latin America, and many parts of Africa. Certainly a Western Christian such as myself can only hang his head in shame when comparing our own approach to evangelism with that of the early Christians, and with that of contemporary Christians in many developing countries. Let us just set out some of the more obvious contrasts.

The early church made evangelism their number one priority. Today it comes far down the list. It is widely agreed that one of the best reports ever prepared and presented in the Church of England was that entitled, *Towards the Conversion of England*, thirty years ago. It was masterly, but the trouble is that it has never been implemented. The matter is not deemed sufficiently important. The same can be said of most plans formulated in many denominations in many nations.

The early church had a deep compassion for men without Christ. Many sections of the modern church are far from convinced that it much matters whether you have Christ or not. Other religions are nearly, if not quite, as good a way to God; humanists live blameless lives; and in any case, it will all come right in the end — God is far too nice to damn anyone.

The early church was very flexible in its preaching of the Good News, but utterly opposed to syncretism (mixing other elements with the Gospel) of any sort. Many parts of the modern church tend to be rigid in their evangelistic categories, but are inclined to play a great deal with syncretism, as Lesslie Newbigin has forcefully pointed out in *The Finality of Christ*.

The early church was very open to the leading of the Holy Spirit;

in every evangelistic advance recorded in Acts it is the Spirit who is the motivator and energizer. In the modern church of the West, managerial skills, committee meetings, and endless discussion are thought essential for evangelism; prayer and dependence on the Spirit seem often to be optional extras.

The early church was not unduly minister-conscious. There is notorious difficulty in attempting to read back any modern ministerial pattern into the New Testament records. Today, everything tends to center around the minister. The paid servant of the church is expected to engage in God-talk, but not others.

In the early church, every man was expected to be a witness to Christ. Today witness is at a discount compared with dialogue; and it is only expected of certain gifted clergy at best, not of run-of-the mill Christians.

In the early church, buildings were unimportant; they did not have any during the period of their greatest advance. Today they seem all-important to many Christians; their upkeep consumes the money and interest of the members, often plunges them into debt, and isolates them from those who do not go to church. Indeed, even the word has changed meaning. "Church" no longer means a company of people, as it did in New Testament times. These days it means a building.

In the early church, evangelism was a natural, spontaneous "chattering" of good news. It was engaged in continuously by all types of Christians as a matter of course and of privilege. Today, it is spasmodic, heavily organized, and usually dependent on the skills and enthusiasm of the visiting specialist.

In the early church, the policy was to go out to where people were, and make disciples of them. Today it is to invite people along to churches, where they do not feel at home, and get them to hear the preaching of the Gospel. Today's church attempts suction, invitation, "in-drag"; the early church practiced explosion, invasion, outreach.

In the early church, the Gospel was frequently argued about in the philosophical schools, discussed in the streets, talked over in the laundry. Today it is not discussed very much at all, and certainly not on "secular" ground. It belongs in church, on a Sunday, and a properly ordained minister should do all the talking.

In the early church, whole communities seem to have been converted at once. In the atomized church of the West, individualism has run riot, and evangelism, like much else, tends to come to its climax in a one-to-one encounter.

In the early church the maximum impact was made by the changed lives and quality of community among the Christians. Today, much Christian life-style is almost indistinguishable from that of non-Christians, and much church fellowship is conspicuous for its coolness.

These are just some of the contrasts between the church of yesterday and the church of today in the matter of evangelism — contrasts which encourage us to examine afresh the message of the early Christians and the methods they adopted.

1. *The message*

I shall not expand too much on the pattern of the New Testament proclamation, because so much work has been done on it in recent years, since the publication of C.H. Dodd's *The Apostolic Preaching and its Development*. Throughout the Gospel of Mark, Hebrews, the Pauline Letters, I Peter, and Acts, it is possible to discern the main bones of much early Christian preaching. The age of fulfillment has dawned. God has at last sent his Messiah, Jesus. He died in shame upon a Cross. He rose again from the tomb and is even now Lord, seated at the Father's right hand. The proof of his vindication lies in the gift of the Holy Spirit. And he will come again to judge the world at the conclusion of human history. Therefore, repent, believe, and be baptized into Christ and joined to the church. Such would be a rough summary of a pattern of proclamation which can be found, explicit or implicit, in a broad variety of strands within the New Testament. This was the Good News that they told men (our "evangelism" comes from the Greek word "martyr" which meant "witness" before it came to denote the witness who sealed his testimony with his blood). They varied a great deal in the stress they laid on different elements in the story. But they were all convinced that in Jesus, God's final act of deliverance, the climax of all his saving and revealing activity throughout Israel's history had begun. In particular, it was the death and resurrection (never the one without the other) of Jesus that formed the focus of their message. This Jesus, who had tasted death for every man, and himself had taken responsibility for human wrongdoing, was alive — indeed he was enthroned in the universe. As such, he offered both pardon and power to those who committed themselves to him. The long-awaited Spirit of God was his gift to believers.

Thus God's law was no longer something exterior to man, threatening him. The longings of Jeremiah and Ezekiel were fulfilled in the inauguration of this New Covenant, wherein the Spirit of God became resident within the very hearts of his people, as the pledge of their acceptance, the helper in their prayers, the compass in their morals, the power for godly living, and the first installment of heaven.

This is the general gist of the message preached by those early evangelists. It was not an easy one for Jews to accept — no circumcision, no Torah, no sabbath, a crucified Messiah (contradiction in terms!), a church which included Gentiles, and was entered by baptism: all this was anathema to the Jew. It was no easier for the Greek world to accept — for it was Eastern, exclusive, new, of doubtful morality, politically suspect, socially disruptive, and intellectually ridiculous. Yet this was the message which the Christians continued to preach. When addressing Gentile believers they added three introductory themes: you can see them in the Acts sermons at Lystra and Athens, to backward and to intellectual alike. They were, first, an exposition of the one true God; second, an exposure of idolatry; and third, the story of Jesus, through whom alone this invisible God can be made known to us without any shred of idolatry.

There are three aspects of their message to which we might profitably pay attention.

a. It was Christ-centered. Jesus was the center of what they proclaimed. It might be Paul at Athens proclaiming, "Jesus and resurrection,"
or Philip in the desert, "telling him the Good News of Jesus," but always
Christ was the kernel of their message. God had made Jesus both Messiah (Christ) and Lord (a name used both for heathen gods, and for
Yahweh in the Old Testament). So central was "Christ" (Messiah —
God's ultimate deliverer) to their interpretation of who Jesus was,
that they earned themselves a nickname — *Christians.* Is this centrality
of Jesus not something that the contemporary evangelist could well
ponder? He might be interpreted as Son of Man, the High Priest accord-
ing to the Melchizedek order, the Suffering Servant, the Prophet like
Moses, or the author, sustainer, and goal of the whole universe (as in
Colossians I and Ephesians I). No matter. It was to Jesus they returned,
Jesus whom they announced. Incidentally it is interesting to notice, in
view of the current radical divide between the Jesus of history and the
Christ of faith, and the supposed irrelevance of the story of Jesus to
the proclamation of the Gospel of the living Christ, that the early
Christians would have none of it. They wrote and used the Gospel
stories, the parables and miracles, to preach the historical Jesus as the
Lord, the Christ, whom they worshiped.

b. It was flexible. This is where Dodd's book falls short: he does not
sufficiently allow for the flexibility in preaching the Gospel which
marked those early Christians. When studying the approaches of Christians to Jews and Gentiles, rich and poor, clever and unintelligent,
over the first two centuries I was amazed at the variety in their proclamation. The Gospel was born, of course, in a Palestinian milieu. Old
Testament models came readily enough to hand. Jesus was seen as the
fulfillment of Daniel's Son of Man, Isaiah's Suffering Servant, the
anointed prophet, priest, and king of various Old Testament strands:
he was the exalted Lord of Psa. 110:1, the prophet like Moses, and the
ultimate successor to David.

But on Gentile soil it was different. The first evangelists engaged
on extensive retranslation work, not so much of words, as of concepts.
They did not begin by quoting Old Testament texts; they started from
the felt needs of the hearers, and used imagery that would communicate
with them. Thus we find Paul at Athens proceeding inductively from
what he sees around him; the altar to an unknown God. In Romans
we find him speaking of adoption, a concept as familiar among the
pagans as it was alien to Hebrew culture. In I Cor. 15:3-5 we find the
core of the primitive preaching to the Jews: Jesus died for our sins,
and was raised the third day. Given the background of the profoundly
ethical God of the Old Testament, "How shall a man be right with
God?" was the critical question for any thoughtful Jew. Paul shows how
it is answered in Christ crucified and risen. But he gives a very different
interpretation of that Cross and resurrection to the Gentiles in Col.
2:15, I Tim. 3:16. Here it is not so much sin which oppresses (conviction of sin is rarely found outside a monotheistic culture) but bondage;
bondage to the various demonic powers which hold men in control,
particularly Fate *(heimarmene)* and Necessity *(ananche).* To men with

such a problem, the incarnation of Jesus and his triumphant resurrection were the key points to stress. Indeed, a whole theological emphasis depicting Christ as conqueror springs from looking at the resurrection in this light. And it certainly brought deliverance to pagan men, obsessed as they were with the sense of the demonic. "We are above Fate," cries Tatian, "and instead of the demons which deceive we have learned one Master who does not deceive." The very word, "Lord," so often attached to Jesus in the Pauline letters, is meant to distinguish him sharply from the "many lords" mentioned in I Cor. 8:5, who had held his readers in thralldom. Similarly, the accent shifts from the Kingdom of God, which Jesus himself heralded so consistently, to "eternal life" or "salvation," words which conveyed the sense of Jesus' message more clearly to Gentile hearers. To a world which, under Stoic influence, conceived of a universal Reason (Logos) underlying the universe, a Reason in which all men naturally had part, Jesus is proclaimed in John I (and similarly in Col. 1:15ff; Heb. 1:1ff) as *the* universal Reason underlying all there is; this Reason was God himself, active since the creation of the world. But all men do not naturally partake of the eternal Logos; they are rebels, and only those who receive him have the right to call themselves sons of God. And thus the idea, common in Stoic circles, is made the vehicle of Christian preaching.

There were other men in antiquity who would have latched on immediately to this Logos idea; men of the neo-Platonist school, who conceived of it as the eternal order of pure reality, somehow copied, however inadequately, in all things that are good and true in this world of space and time. "Well," says St. John, "if that is how you think, let me tell you something: there is one single area in the universe where the ideal has become real, where the archetype has broken through, where the Word has become flesh. And that is in the life, death, and resurrection of Jesus Christ." John 1:14 is in fact, a powerful philosophical claim for the absoluteness of Jesus of Nazareth.

Clearly, there was nothing inflexible about these early Christians in the New Testament period. Nor was there in the succeeding century or two, as the Gospel spread. You find philosophers like Justin and Tatian retaining their philosopher's robe and arguing the truth of the Christian philosophy against all comers. You find them looking not only to the Old Testament but to the myths of Homer and Hesiod for truths that would help to illuminate the person and work of Jesus. They were convinced that all truth is God's truth. Therefore they rejoiced when they found that some of the ancient heathen poets or philosophers had spoken true things which were endorsed in the Gospel of Christ.

I used to think it was odd (if not worse!) of Clement of Rome in the nineties of the first century, to use the mythical bird, the phoenix, before I had seen the picture of the phoenix at Pompeii (a city destroyed in A.D. 79) and read what the painter, hungering for immortality, had written below it. "O phoenix, you are a lucky thing!" Then I realized how wise an apologist Clement had been in relating the resurrection of the Lord to the very symbol of need which the painter of the phoenix had revealed. Like Paul, Clement had become all things to all men, so that by all means he might save some.

Of course, the early Christians made two types of mistakes in this attempt to preach the Gospel meaningfully into their situation. Gnosticism which was a way of salvation through knowledge, was the fruit of uncritically accepting pagan frames of reference, just as syncretism is today. And Ebionism, which stressed the humanity of Jesus to the exclusion of his deity, was the fruit of rigid determination to preach Jesus as "Son of God" to Jews who could not possibly hear those words without the feeling that it was blasphemy (though other christological formulations, just as absolute, could have been acceptable to them). These two Christian heresies of the second century were the direct result in the one case of uncritical cross-cultural relativism, and in the other of soldiering obstinately on using the language of Zion and expecting people to understand it if they were not gospel hardened. The implications for today are obvious. *Honest to God,* by Bishop John Robinson, was a genuine attempt to communicate the Christian faith to men who were alienated by the way most clergy preached it: the fantastic sales of the book show what a vast number of people were touched by such an approach; unfortunately, it was no longer the Gospel of Jesus Christ that was communicated. (Robinson attempts to communicate the Gospel to the so-called "modern man come of age" by removing what are believed to be unpalatable supernatural elements.) Surely we are called back to that daring flexibility of the early Christians, letting the world set the agenda, and answering it imaginatively in the light of the New Testament witness to Jesus. If we take the variety of the New Testament itself as our model, we shall never be monochrome or dull; if we submit our retranslated message to the judgment of the New Testament we shall not erode the Gospel in the process of translating it. This is a perilously knife-edge operation, but every evangelist must undertake it if he is to be faithful both to Christ and to his own generation.

c. It was definite. Christianity took root in unwelcoming pagan soil. The old pantheon of gods was receiving constant additions as the Roman Empire expanded, and new deities were absorbed. It would have been easy enough to get Jesus accepted on these terms. Alternatively, there were the mystery religions; remarkably Christian in a way, with their stress on a dying and rising god — the year deity, the fertility god. Jesus could have been identified with such a deity. Alternatively, there was the imperial cult: Caesar was Lord, and if only Christians had been willing to accord him divine honors, they would not have been persecuted for the loyalty they gave to Jesus. Again, there were the philosophical schools, coming together a good deal by the first century, and having a more religious flavor about them, as Platonic idealism, mixed with high Stoic ethics, sought not only the Absolute but God.

Now it is interesting that the Christians used all these paths in order to bring men to Christ, but they did not surrender to any of them. Paul was willing to be misunderstood as adding two new deities to the pantheon when preaching "Jesus and Resurrection" at Athens, so long as he had the opportunity to explain to the assembled multitude that he was doing no such thing! In that same address he used concepts familiar to both the Epicureans and the Stoics, and yet he was unfashionable enough to tell them both that the one thing they needed to do was to repent! And when Christians said, "Jesus is Lord," though it sounded rather like the imperial acclamations, in fact it was assigning exclusive divine honors to Jesus.

So while the early Christians would use any pathway to Christ, it was to Christ that these pathways unambiguously led. There was no hint of compromise, of syncretism. Paul addressed the Colossians when a syncretizing heresy was under way. *"Jesus and...*a variety of mediators" was their cry. Paul used much of their language. But he claimed an utterly exclusive position for his Lord. Whatever other "principalities and powers" there might be, Jesus was their creator and their Lord. He was the origin, the goal, and the principle of coherence in the whole universe, and his death on the Cross the only way of access to God. Did the false teachers speak of *pleroma,* the supposed habitat of these inter-mediating powers? Fine, says Paul, so long as you are clear about one thing. "In Christ lives all the fullness *(pleroma)* of the Godhead in bodily form." Great flexibility in presentation, then, but great firmness on content was his emphasis. And the content was Jesus, Creator, Savior, and Lord. To be sure they realized that other faiths contain much that is true. It would be strange if they did not. But they do not contain any truth about God that is not to be found in the Judaeo-Christian revelation, and they certainly contain a great deal of error. What is more, they do not provide any means of access to God whatsoever. That is provided uniquely by the One who came from God to reveal and to save.

The point is that no *man* can bridge the divide between the Holy and the sinful, between the Infinite and the finite, between God and man. The early Christians were convinced that God had visited his people in person, and accordingly were prepared to be martyred for their assertion that "there is salvation in no other; for there is no other name under heaven given to men whereby we must be saved" (Acts 4:12). Despite the flexibility of their message, it was always Christ-centered and always carried the implication of decision in repentance, faith, and baptism. Whether we look at the appeals to commitment in Acts, or turn to *2 Clement* (an early church document about A.D. 150) or the *Protrepticus* (an address to the Greeks by Clement of Alexandria, who wrote towards the end of the second century, seeking to win them over to Christianity), or to Gregory's fascinating account of the way in which that wise fisher of men and massive intellectual, Origen, hunted him out, taught him, intrigued him, and eventually brought him to Christ, the picture is uniform. The apostolic kerygma demanded a response. This was not something shallow or emotional, but touched the conscience, illuminated the understanding, brought the will into submission, and transformed the subsequent life. It was nothing less than a new birth.

2. The methods

There does not seem to have been anything very remarkable in the strategy and tactics of the early Christian mission. Indeed, it is doubtful if they had one. I do not believe they set out with any blueprint. They had an unquenchable conviction that Jesus was the key to life and death, happiness and purpose, and they simply could not keep quiet about him. The Spirit of Jesus within them drove them into mission. The tandem relationship between the Spirit bearing witness to Jesus and the believers bearing that witness (John 15:26f, Acts 1:7, 8) was well understood among them, and the initiatives in evangelism which we read of in Acts are consistently laid at the door of the Lord the Spirit himself: effective mission does not spring from human blueprints. No, the nearest to a strategy those early Christians had was, perhaps, as follows:

a. They worked from the center outwards. "Beginning from Jerusalem" was the key word in Jesus' farewell charge to his disciples. And beginning from where they were, those twelve men swiftly grew by means of prayer, fellowship, a deep experience of the Spirit, and fearless preaching even in the face of persecution, into a body to whom God was adding fresh converts daily, and who filled the whole of Jerusalem with their teaching. Acts then traces, briefly, the spread of the Gospel into Judaea, then to Samaria, and from there to the uttermost parts of the earth. But always the policy seems to be to get the heart of the group hot, for only then will it be ready for fresh additions. The policy of so much modern evangelism is to drag people from the outside inwards; their policy was the opposite — to move from the inside outwards, and to evangelize, not on their own ground, but on other people's.

b. They were involved, yet mobile. They were indeed involved, totally involved. It is fascinating to find that in the early centuries of the church there was no division between those who told the good news and those who only listened to it. All were involved in the mission. You see this graphically portrayed in the spontaneous evangelistic sortie of nameless amateur evangelists from Jerusalem when Stephen had been killed and the remaining leaders were caught up in the city. The believers scattered, and "those that were scattered abroad went everywhere preaching the message." Celsus, in the second century, complains of the Christians at work, in the laundry, in the schoolroom, at the street corner, who were always jabbering away about their Jesus. Could any leading critic of Christianity today make the same charge?

Indeed, if one were to put it in a single sentence, the Early Church succeeded because every man was a missionary; the modern church fails because "missionary" has become a dirty word. These early Christians were all involved in the mission; and they were deeply involved in their communities as well. We read of doctors, teachers, agriculturalists, and others in normal jobs really caring for the communities in which they worked. Several times we have moving accounts of the way in which Christians tended victims in a plague at the risk of their own lives; and the love and self-sacrifice of Christians for their townsfolk even in the face of fierce opposition and martyrdom, won grudging praise from the pagans.

But with this sense of commitment to the local community, and

involvement with its life, went a remarkable mobility. You got bishops
like Irenaeus moving all around the known world. You got top intellectuals like Pantaenus leaving the Christian University at Alexandria
of which he was the head, and going off to spread the Gospel among
the "Indians." You got farmers moving from village to village to win
fresh converts to their Lord. And you only need to glance back to the
Acts, and look at Philip, Peter, Paul, or Aquila and Priscilla, to see how
readily these early Christians were prepared to abandon home comforts
for the sake of the Good News.

The question arises, are we? It would seem to me that the church
today throughout the West at any rate, is paralyzed by a crippling lack
of mobility. Granted that patterns of community, education and employment are so different, is there not, I wonder, a growing materialism that
saps our total dedication to Christ and willingness to go anywhere and
do anything for him if the Spirit should so lead?

c. They used their influence. It seems to me that many of these men
planned their time with some care, conscious that they had but one life,
and that they were determined to use it to the full for God. So they
entered spheres where their influence would be felt to the maximum.
That, presumably, helped to dictate the direction of the Pauline Missionary Journeys. Antioch was the third city in the empire; Philippi
was a Roman colony and administrative capital; Thessalonica was the
administrative center of Macedonia; Athens was the cultural center
of the world; Corinth was the capital of the province of Achaea; Eph
esus, where he spent three years, was the largest city in Asia; and
Rome, his goal in the west, was mistress of the world.

It is hard to escape the conclusion that Paul, for one, was determined to use his talents to the full in the places where they would do
the most good. Of course, such planning can degenerate into worldly
ambition, but it need not, if the guidance of the Spirit is sought. Perhaps we should look for more of it today?

d. They exercised oversight. This is one of the intriguing factors in
ancient evangelism which is not always looked after so well today. They
were out from the start to consolidate gains. New disciples needed to
be strengthened. Converts needed to be added to the church as well
as to the Lord. They continued in the fellowship of the apostles, in
their teaching, in their worship, and in their evangelism. There was,
at least in some circles, some communalism of goods and life-style which
may have been economic madness but bore eloquent testimony to the
oneness in Christ which they talked about. That unity was maintained
even as the church grew. The ancient splits between Jew and Samaritan,
between Jew and Gentile, between bond and free, between male and
female were not allowed to spoil the unity given by the Spirit. To this
end, the apostles revisited their converts, they set up presbyters to look
after them, they wrote letters to them, they sent messengers to them,
and they prayed for them. Their unity so impressed the pagans of antiquity that they gradually began to call Christians "The Third Race" —
not pagans, not Jews, but something radically different. From the most

diverse backgrounds they had come together to form one new humanity in Christ. And wise diligent Christian oversight had been largely instrumental in maintaining this God-given unity.

e. *They produced witnesses.* This has already been touched on. It was the normal thing, not the pleasurable exception, for a Christian to become so thrilled with Christ that he had to find ways of expressing it to his non-Christian neighbors. Indeed, in contrast to much of our own effort these days, the early evangelists seem to have set themselves to increase the numbers of witnesses to Christ, not the number of those they could persuade to listen to addresses about Christ. They were out not to gather hearers, but to equip missionaries. This may not have been very self-conscious on their part, but it was a strategic decision of the utmost importance, and one which the modern church has scarcely begun to appreciate, unlike some of the sects, such as the Jehovah's Witnesses.

If these five factors seem to have been influential in determining the overall strategy of the early Christians, we may conclude by pointing out some of their tactical approaches which might prove suggestive for us today.

Their methods on the whole, while varied, were unremarkable. There is no key to instant success to be found by ransacking the methods used by the early church. Like us, they spoke in church. Like us, they spoke in the open air, though more frequently and with more directness, humor, and comeback from the audience than is common in the West. I believe that the rise and strength of the Pentecostals in South America is due, partly at least, to their insistence that members should bear witness to Christ upon the streets. After all, that is how it all began; and I am not persuaded that the day of the open air is over.

Like us, they visited. Ananias' visit to Saul of Tarsus is perhaps the classic case in the Acts. This again is a method that has fallen on evil days, and ministers persuade themselves that in this busy television-addicted age, it cannot be done, by themselves or laymen. It can be done and it must. I have led people to Christ simply by visiting them in their homes without any exposure to preaching, and many of you have done the same. It is an important method of evangelism.

Like us, they made use of literary evangelism. The written word was not so easy and cheap to produce in the days of handwritten books, but they did use this method; what, after all, are the Gospels intended for? But in particular they employed the Old Testament Scriptures. Just as Philip used verses in Isaiah 53 to open the eyes of the Ethiopian eunuch, so countless missionaries of the next two centuries followed suit. Men like Justin, Tatian, Pantaenus, and Athenagoras in the second century were won to the faith through reading the Scriptures of the Old Testament. We would be foolish to underestimate the converting power of the Word of God even in the absence of any human interpreter.

But if you asked me to name a few of the main methods used in evangelism then which are not given sufficient weight now, I should want to isolate four:

(i) The impact of *fellowship.* Whether you look at Jerusalem or Antioch; whether you read between the lines of the Epistles to the

Philippians or Thessalonians; whether you pin your attention on Ephesus in the days of Paul and John, or Carthage in the days of Tertullian, the decisive importance of Christian fellowship is plain to see. These Christians embraced all the colors, all the classes, and all the untouchables of ancient society into one. They gave the impression of perpetual celebration, even in the face of death. Their services for worship gave rein for various spiritually gifted people to use their gift for the good of the whole. Their caring for each other in need became proverbial in antiquity. When people saw how these Christians loved one another; when they saw that in this society of Jesus the powers of the age to come were really exercised (prophecy, tongues, healing, alongside teaching, administration, and works of mercy), then they listened to the message of Jesus, who alone accounted for such a remarkable situation. Protestants for far too long have failed to recognize what the Catholics have appropriated, that the church is in a very real sense part of the Gospel. Unless the fellowship in the Christian assembly is far superior to that which can be found anywhere else in society, then the Christians can talk about the transforming love and power of Jesus till they are hoarse, but people are not going to listen very hard. There are a few churches in Britain that have learned this lesson. Their common life is so attractive and warm that outsiders are drawn to Jesus, and come to him whether or not the minister happens to be in residence. The work goes on without constant injections of life from the leadership. Because it is the life of the Body of Christ flowing out to folks in their need and loneliness. In churches like that men are daily added to the number of the believers just as they were in the first century. But let none of us think that we can "run" a church like that. It can only come as the Lord the Spirit is in control of ministers and people alike, as mutual trust grows among the members, and as the gifts of different members are recognized and given full play. Above all, Christians must be prepared to be honest with each other, and not keep up a facade of goodness. After all, we are accepted by God while we are sinners, and should not need to pretend to each other that we are anything different. When that costly "body life" is characteristic of modern Christianity, it may well have the same success as it did in the early centuries.

(ii) The value of *homes*. To be sure, the early Christians were driven to make a great deal of use of the home, because they were not allowed to possess any property until the end of the second century. They were not allowed to have large public meetings under the rule of a number of the emperors because of the possible political implications. In other words, the church in the first three centuries grew without the aid of two of our most prized tools: mass evangelism and evangelism in church. Instead, they used the home. In Acts we read of homes being used extensively, such as the homes of Jason and of Justus, of Philip and of Mark's mother. Sometimes it is a prayer meeting, sometimes an evening for fellowship and instruction, sometimes a Communion service, sometimes a meeting for new converts, sometimes a houseful of seekers, sometimes an impromptu gathering.

The value of the home as opposed to, or rather complementary to, the more formal worship in church, is obvious. It enables people to

question (and check) the leader. It promotes dialogue. It enables difficulties to be sorted out. It facilitates fellowship. It can so easily issue in
corporate action and service in which all the different limbs in the body
can play their part. Of course, some clergy don't like it. It takes the power
out of their hands; it can fragment the congregation; the groups can
become introverted. All of these dangers are real. But they are dangers
the early church managed to overcome, for the most part. And so can
we . . . if we will trust the people of God to be the people of God in
and through the home. The growing use of homes in Christian work the
world over is one of the most encouraging signs of a breakthrough in
evangelism in the future.

(iii) The use of *apologetic*. A marked feature of the early evangelists
is that they used their minds to relate the Gospel to the intellectual and
cultural concerns of their day. I am greatly impressed by the way the
apologists of the second century continued as teachers of philosophy,
convinced that they had found the true philosophy that would avail for
all men anywhere. They related Christ to the intellectual world of their
day, in terms which made sense to those who started with no Christian
presuppositions. They set out to demonstrate the existence of the one
God from whom everything derived. They laughed at the foolish polytheism of the Greek and Roman pantheon. They showed the folly of
Homer and Hesiod in their popular epics, attributing human sins writ
large to the gods, and instead pointed to the holiness of God, a holiness
which struck a chord in every man's conscience. They argued the reality
of the resurrection: Tertullian in his *de Resurrectione* maintains with
good reason that if God could fashion a human body out of the fusion
of sperm and egg, it is not in the least difficult to suppose that he could
fashion a spiritual body for Christians in heaven, which would combine
the continuity of the ego with a new and far more wonderful form for
its expression. Origen's famous catechetical school at Alexandria was
not only a training ground for Christian intellectuals, but a place where
the faith was debated, argued over, and pressed home to sceptics and
inquirers. It was the same 150 years earlier when Paul argued the Christian way against all comers at Tyrannus' school in Ephesus. The very
words used in the New Testament to express the Christian preaching
denote a high intellectual endeavor: words such as *didaskein*, "to instruct"
kerussein, "to proclaim like a herald," *euangelizesthai*, "to proclaim good
news," *katangellein*, "to make careful announcement," *diamarturesthai*,
"to testify," *katelenchein*, "to convince by argument," *dialegesthai*, "to
argue," and so forth. They spent a lot of time on this intellectual com-
mendation of the Good News. They were prepared to argue, to go out
on to neutral or hostile ground. They gave testimony, they had constant reference to the facts of the Gospel and the teaching of the Old
Testament (words like *sunzetein* and *sumbibazein* indicate this serious
searching of the Scriptures). Sometimes this took a day or even a week.
Sometimes they returned to the attack again and again. But of the
serious intellectual content of the proclamation in the early days, there
can be no doubt. They would have gotten nowhere without such an
apologetic. Both the Jewish and Gentile cultures were thoroughly opposed to what they had to tell. And if their position could be undermined

by argument, they would soon have been driven off the streets. But it could not. It was the truth. And because it is the truth, followers of Christ need fear no truth, for it all belongs to him, and sheds some light on the truth made personal in Christ. It seems to me, therefore, that if we are to learn from the early Christians, we shall not be content with repeating louder and more often the "simple Gospel"; there is actually no such thing. For the truth is both so simple that a child can understand the bones of the matter, and so profound that no intellectual can ever plumb its depths. It is, of course, true that argument will never get a man into the Kingdom of God. The fact remains that many a man will never face up to the personal challenge of Jesus upon his life until he both sees an acceptable intellectual framework for belief, and has had his intellectual escape routes destroyed by a patient, efficient, convincing Christian apologetic. Men like Schaeffer, Guinness, and a few others are notable within our generation for attempting this most demanding intellectual and spiritual discipline of providing a Christian apologetic as a framework for proclaiming the Christian Gospel. We need a more widespread determination to follow their example if the Gospel is to be seen to be relevant to the intellectual as well as the cultural and moral needs of men. Personally, I always have a time for debate and questions in evangelistic work in universities throughout the world. I love meeting people in town halls, lecture theaters, dance halls, and pubs to debate the truth and the relevance of the Christian faith. I believe it is high time for us to emerge from the ghetto of intellectual obscurantism, just as we are beginning to emerge from the ghetto of evangelical shibboleths and church-building-centered ministry, on to the common ground, the neutral places, the places where men debate and congregate and argue. That is where the battle was won in the early days. Today, most of us have hardly begun to fight on this sort of ground.

(iv) I notice the priority of *personal conversation* among the early Christians. It was a method Jesus employed a great deal. St. John's Gospel has a particular interest in these personal encounters of Jesus with individuals, and the variety of approach he took with each of them, in every case finding a way to them through their felt need, and never bound to a system. It was Philip's way when he led the Ethiopian eunuch to Christ, Paul's way when he brought Onesimus to the faith. And so it continued. The personal witness of an old man who met him in the fields and brought the conversation around to Jesus marked the beginning of Justin's conversion, early in the second century. Cyprian was won through the personal conversation of a presbyter who visited him, Gregory through the personal work of Origen. There is a lovely passage at the beginning of Minucius Felix's *Octavius* which sheds a lot of light on the way these conversations might begin and be carried on, in this instance, along the seashore as two friends go for a walk.

Perhaps this is the greatest lesson we can learn from the early church in the very changed situation of our own day. The most effective method of evangelism and the most widespread, in the long run, in its results, is conversation evangelism, where one who has found Jesus shares his discovery, his problems, his joys and his sorrows with one who is still groping in the dark. There is no joy like introducing a friend to Christ

in this way. You do not need to be clever or experienced. You do not
need to be an eloquent speaker, or capable of arranging your material
in an orderly fashion. You just need to love the Lord, love your friend,
and talk to the one about the other, in prayerful dependence on the
Spirit, and then to the other about the one whom you have found to
be alive and able to transform you. If all Christians set about doing this,
they would not need much other methodology from the early church.
The Gospel would once more spread like wildfire.

EVANGELISM IN THE EARLY CHURCH
Michael Green

If I were an Englishman I would mumble, "Good morning." As I am half Welsh and half Australian, I will use the greeting that the Orthodox Church gives to one another at Easter. "Christ is risen," to which everyone replies, "He is risen indeed." That greeting captures the conviction of the early Christians. Jesus is alive. That is the key to their evangelism.

Before taking up some of the points you raised in your response to my paper, I would like to remind you of the main bones of what I wrote. I began by pointing out a dozen contrasts in evangelistic priorities, attitudes and methods between the early Christians and ourselves. These alone, if taken seriously, could transform the world Christian scene. Just imagine what could happen if even half the Christians in the world were happy, loving, bold witnesses to Jesus; if we really cared for those without Christ; if our church life was so loving and warm that men wanted to know our secret; if we chattered the good news as naturally as the English talk about the weather and the South Africans about rugby football!

Second, I spoke about the message of these early Christians. There was nothing dull and repetitive about it. It was expressed in everyday language. It was clear and simple. But it was profound and thoughtful, too, providing a firm basis for understanding the world and God and man. They did not rely on slogans; no three quick points or four spiritual laws to make you a Christian. Their approach was varied and flexible, but it always centered on Jesus, through whom the world will be judged. Jesus Christ is the same yesterday, today, and forever, but the roads to him are infinitely varied. Those early Christians bent their minds to understand Jesus in all his many-sidedness; they took pains to understand the fears and needs and hunger of the folk they lived among; and then they tried to bring men with all their varied needs, and Jesus with all his varied resources together, as they urged people in no uncertain terms to repent, believe, and be baptized into the church of Christ.

Third, I spoke of the methods of the early Christians in evangelism. Their strategy was largely unselfconscious, but they certainly worked outwards in ever-widening circles from a live, warm center. They certainly conserved the resultant conversions with great pastoral care into a worldwide church; and they set out to enable spontaneous evangelism to occur by building up not merely disciples but witnesses.

I ought to have made more clear my distinction between these broad stragetic aims, and the methods or tactics they used to achieve them. These were varied — preaching in synagogue and open air, visitation, literature work, and so forth. I laid particular stress on four areas which I believe have a great deal to teach us today: first, the sheer impact of a vital Christian fellowship; second, the incalculable importance of open Christian homes; third, the determination of these early Christians to relate their faith to the culture in which they lived; and fourth, the immense value they set on personal conversation about Jesus as the prime way of winning others to him.

So much for my paper. Thank you so much for your comments and most helpful criticisms. I think it is best if I concentrate on four

main areas in reply: strategy, message, methods, and motivation.
1. Strategy

Many of you commented that my paper was thin on the strategy of the early Christians. You are right. You see, I don't believe they had much of a strategy. It has been argued by some theologians that the Jewish Christians stayed working in Palestine because they hoped that the Gentiles would flow to Mount Zion when Israel responded to her Messiah; and that the Gentile mission of the Pauline church believed that it would work the other way round, and if they concentrated on evangelizing the world Israel would then turn to Christ within their lifetimes, and the Lord would return. If Jewish and Gentile missions had those strategies, then both were wrong! But I believe it was much less cut and dried than this. Just think: which of the advances in mission sprang from the planners in Jerusalem? The Gospel spread out in an apparently haphazard way as men obeyed the leading of the Spirit, and went through the doors he opened. Nobody among the apostolic circle said, "Let's evangelize those horrid Samaritans down the road." They never thought of it: and when one of their chief cooks, a Greek-speaking fellow called Philip, got on with the job, they were so surprised that they sent a commission of top people to make sure that it was all OK. Nobody among the apostolic circle thought it would be a good idea to tell the Good News to a colored eunuch from Ethiopia, or run a crusade in the third city of the empire, Antioch, or start a mission to Europe. All these developments are specifically attributed in Acts to the Holy Spirit who led men, usually very ordinary men, little men, sometimes against their will even — and certainly without the planning of their leaders, to break fresh ground in this way. So while it is right to set our sights high, and aim to spread the Gospel throughout the globe in this generation, we must remember that it is Christ, not Lausanne, that holds the key of David. It is he alone who shuts and no man opens; who opens, and no man shuts. We must not organize him out of the picture.

I sense two real dangers in this Congress in the whole area of strategy, areas on which the early church can supply a corrective:

a. The danger of triumphalism. The impression that we alone among Christians have the right message and the right know-how: let's finish the job. The sense that efficiency on the evangelistic production lines will inevitably produce results. The preoccupation with numbers. Are we not dangerously activist, even Arminian? Have we forgotten the appalling fall-out from shallow evangelism which is all too often man-centered and need-oriented? Have we reflected that by success-measurement techniques the Cross would be rated the greatest failure in history? I fear we evangelicals often look arrogant, self-confident in our strategy and techniques. If so, we shall rightly incur the judgment of God.

The church at Corinth was rather triumphalist. They thought they had already arrived. And Paul uncompromisingly reminds them of the Cross, not merely in their message but as a way of life. Sarcastically he chides this arrogant triumphalism of theirs. "Already full! Already rich! Already entered upon your kingdom! I wish you had — so that we might share it with you . . . We are fools for Christ's sake, but you are such wise Christians. You are held in honor, but we in disrepute. Right up till now we are hungry, thirsty, ill-clothed, buffeted about, homeless. We have become the refuse of the world, the off-scouring of all things" (I Cor. 4:8 ff.).

The theology of crucifixion (of the messengers no less than the message) must never be elbowed out by the theology of triumph — this side of heaven. Let us beware of this subtle danger.

b. The danger of isolating evangelism. Don't misunderstand me. Evangelism is the church's first priority. I pray that Lausanne will recall evangelism to the top of the church's agenda. But you cannot isolate the preaching of Good News, without destroying the Good News itself. You cannot remain true to the New Testament and say, "Evangelism is primary: fellowship, worship, and service are quite distinct and nothing to do with it." No. What God has joined together we are not at liberty to put asunder. We are called to be the church as well as proclaim the Good News: the two are inextricably connected. It was when the worship, the teaching, the prayer, the fellowship of the earliest church at Jerusalem was so hot, that God added daily to their number. The end of Acts 5 brings us almost to a revival situation in Jerusalem . . . and then comes Acts 6, with a little matter of social justice and fellowship.

They could so easily have brushed it aside and said, "Don't fuss about the widows: let's get on with the preaching. That is what matters." If they had done that, God's Spirit would have been grieved, the fellowship would have been ruined, and the outreach would have ceased to be effective. People would no longer have been converted into an unjust, unloving church. Or think of the church at Antioch. The church which launched the first missionary journey overseas, the church which first won the nickname "Christian" because its members were always talking about Christ — this church made such an impact because of the quality of its life.

Bishop Dain has already reminded us of the reality of their worship and their sacrifices. Notice also two other things about that church. It has a remarkable fellowship. Master and slave ate together. Jew and Greek ate together: unparalleled in the ancient world. Their fellowship was so vital that their leadership could be drawn from different races and cultures and colors and classes. Here was a fellowship in Christ which transcended all natural groupings and barriers. There was nothing like it anywhere — and there still isn't.

Don't tell me that fellowship is not in itself an evangelistic agency! Of course it is. And the same applies to the social concern at Antioch. It was so lively that they had a collection for Christians hundreds of miles away in Jerusalem who had used up their capital by pooling it in community living. They might have said, "We are not sure they are sound. They are deplorably High Church in their practices, their circumcision, their law-keeping." But they said nothing of the sort. They gave instead. This church at Antioch which is the fountain-head of Christian mission combined gossiping Jesus at home and backing missions overseas with a freedom in worship, a depth in fellowship, and a practical social concern which embodied the message they proclaimed. So, you see, it is not enough to say that social action should be the fruit of Gospel preaching: sometimes it is not, as Latin America knows all too well. But in a profound sense the church's social concern, worship, and fellowship either demonstrate or deny the message that is preached. We cannot escape from the fact that the church is itself part of the kerygma.

Let me put this another way. We see the danger of isolating the proclamation when we look at the work and the influence of Rudolf Bultmann. He is not interested in the life, the healings, the teaching of Jesus, for that, he thinks, is not the Gospel. The Gospel has been shrunk to a formula of justification, proclaimed with authority and to be believed in faith — then a man will find authentic existence. Not many here would go along with that. But are we not in danger of doing the very same thing? We tend to isolate what we call the Gospel from what Jesus called the Kingdom of God. How much have we heard here about the Kingdom of God? Not much. It is not our language. But it was Jesus' prime concern. He came to show that God's kingly rule had broken in to our world: it no longer lay entirely in the future, but was partly realized in him and those who followed him. The Good News of the Kingdom was both preached by Jesus and embodied by him. Both were essential. Neither was secondary. So it must be with us. Our life-style, our attitudes, our concern for the sick and the suffering, the under-privileged and the hungry, either confirm or deny the message of salvation, of wholeness, which we proclaim. Let us beware of separating proclamation from life. Remember that the church is the sign of God's Kingdom in our world, not just the body of folk who talk about it!

2. Message

There are a couple of points I must briefly touch on in the area of the message of these early Christians.

a. The place of the Creator. Often in current evangelism we present Jesus almost as a washing powder who washes whiter, or as a trip to end all trips. We isolate experience from truth. We leave a holy Creator God out of the picture. We must not do it: or our shallow converts will keep their religious faith carefully insulated from their thinking about daily life. We must not do it: for this would be untrue to the Gospel and its early preachers. Remember how in atheistic and polytheistic situations, at Lystra, at Athens, at Rome, they prefaced their preaching about Jesus by establishing the reality of the infinite, personal, holy God who created both the world and man, the God who is our sustainer and our goal. God is Creator no less than Redeemer. Daily work is as much his concern as Sunday worship. Creation at the beginning, redemption at the middle, and the new creation at the end are three aspects of the Gospel of salvation which hang together. Yet we leave out creation, and wonder why Christians don't integrate their faith with their daily, workday lives. We leave out the end, heaven and hell, and wonder why Christians are so earthbound and pagans so unmoved.

b. The place of flexibility. There was the fear in some of your responses that I was opening the door to syncretism. Not at all. I simply mean that there are hundreds of roads to Jesus Christ. Don't confine yourself to one. The New Testament writers used masses of pictures — new birth, new vision, wholeness, joining up in a new army, liberation, marriage with Christ, being drowned in Christ, welcoming Christ into the life. They used fear, love, faith, and hope — four of the classic attitudes to life they found in different types of people, as avenues to Jesus. Jesus himself did not begin with heavy texts from the Old Testament, much as he respected its authority. He started where people were, with their concerns about ploughing, cooking, fishing, farming, and so on in order to lead them to the place where they would face up to the mystery of the Kingdom of God. We need equal flexibility.

Now I am a fly fisherman. I love the March Brown fly. There is nothing to compare with it on a Welsh river in March. But it is useless in September. If I flog the water in September with my March Brown fly, and catch nothing, I could conclude that the fish were all hardened against my offering, that they would never respond. Or I could change my fly! That is what I mean by flexibility. This is what I mean by translating the Gospel into thought-forms people use. That is what I mean by letting the world set the agenda. You have to find out where a man lives, mentally and spiritually, before you can show him how Jesus relates to his life. It is not much good talking to a schizophrenic about pardon — what he needs is to be integrated. It is not much good showing a man plagued with demonic forces that Christ is his substitute on the Cross. True, but not that part of the truth which will help him at that point. He needs to know that Christ is the conqueror, that he stripped off principalities and powers and triumphed over them in the Cross. In a word, be totally committed to the biblical Christ in your message; and for the way you present him, be totally flexible. Personally, I have found that I can get in very easily to many modern men by a discussion of "What is the point of living?" "What is freedom and how do you get it?" "Is violence inescapable?" "What does it mean to be human?" "What is the meaning of love?" All these are questions of our age, at any rate in my country, and they all lead straight to Jesus.

3. Methods

I do not want to say much about methods. The early Christians were very varied in the methods they used. We should be equally varied. We get hung up on methods and techniques — but quite wrongly. Once there is a burning passion to share Jesus with others inside your heart, you'll find a way of doing it all right, without reading a manual on the subject. I would like to underline five, however:

a. *Personal conversation.* Philip running after the eunuch in his chariot, Paul chatting up the jailors who were chained to him, that is the way it spread. You have done it, I have done it, in cafes, airplanes, television studios, cars, on roadsides, and so on. But when this chattering the Gospel becomes a *habit* for Christians, it will make a powerful impact, as it did in the early Church.

On the flight out here, a police inspector told me of one of his Christian colleagues who has recently been killed in Northern Ireland. As he lay dying from a bomb, the sergeant came up to him. "Sarge," he said, "I've often talked to you about Jesus. I'm going to meet him now. Will I see you there one day?" Those were his dying words, and they led that sergeant to Christ. This was the method most used in the ancient world. It is effective as no other method is. For it hits the individual need. Yet we evangelicals prefer to go to endless congresses on evangelism rather than do it! Or we kid ourselves that careful training is needed.

I have recently helped in a mission near Heathrow Airport. Well over 100 people have come to Christ, and they are busy chatting to their friends about the Lord.

Often the vicar gets rung up by a young Christian who is actually talking at that moment to a non-Christian friend. He says, "Hey, vicar, what do I say to a chap who says this?" Is it surprising that in that congregation people are coming to the Lord every day?

b. Open air work. This is largely discredited in the main-line churches of the West these days, but why? The Pentecostals know its power. So did the ancient church. There is a lovely description of an open air in a third century writing, the *Clementine Recognitions.* I think you would enjoy it. (I shall now read parts of p. 198 and 199 of *Evangelism in the Early Church.*) Let us develop this method again. When people see us coming out of the church into the street they will begin to sit up and take notice.

c. Body life. Do you recall how in the Corinthian assembly everyone brought his hymn, his prophecy, his prayer? Well, I was preaching in an Anglican church like that recently. It was very full. The worship was lovely — led not by an organ but by an orchestra of new converts. Overhead screens were used for the choruses; two contrasting and carefully prepared testimonies were given; praise came up from all over the building; the prayers were based on cuttings from the newspaper; and at the end, after the call to repentance and faith, coffee came round the pews and I asked every Christian to counsel the person sitting next to him. It went on for about two hours, and many people came to the Lord. Even more important, the whole body of Christ in that church was mobilized. They expect, and they get, converts daily.

d. Home meetings. This was a prime way in the early Church: it still is. I must tell you about the development of one I've been involved in recently.

It began last Christmas when a couple came to church on their annual visit. I happened to be preaching, and God must have used it to them. They wrote and asked me to come and discuss God with them. I found that Brian, the man, had invited his adult brother and sister. It was a ready-made home meeting. We had four hours, starting with the existence of God and ending on commitment to Christ. We agreed to meet again. By the next time, Brian, a builder, had asked Christ into his life. His wife and accountant brother did so soon afterwards. The sister is still not there yet. We have had several Bible studies in the past weeks, and then three days ago they threw open their home and gave a supper party for their friends to meet me and hear about Jesus. Three from that supper are now interested and the Bible study going which will now include his mother who came to the Lord about two weeks ago. The value of the house meeting, the chance for dialogue, the friendly atmosphere, the joy of discovery, the chain reaction is clear to see. That's what they realized in the early Church.

e. *Neutral ground.* How can we come out of the ghetto and be seen on neutral ground? How can we be a Paul in the school of Tyrannus, a Justin outside the baths of Rome? I do not know. I love taking a public hall for a debate with a local atheist, and giving plenty of chance for the Christians on the floor to bear testimony. I love holding dialogue with university students outside on the grass, or in the bar of the student union. The lunch break in a factory sometimes gives opportunities. What I do know is that we must, like the early Christians, find ways of coming out into the neutral ground, and let our Gospel be heard, discussed, and argued over by those who at present dismiss it or are ignorant of it.

I would like to dwell on other facets of the early Church in evangelism — their joyful sense of discovery, their expectation that the Holy Spirit would really change lives, their self-sacrifice and willingness for persecution, their dependence on the message of the Scriptures and prayer. I would like to speak of the need for research centers in different parts of the world, such as they already have in India, to help Christians in the area think through the perilous but necessary task of translating the Gospel without diluting it. But time does not allow. I end with a few words on:

4. *Motivation*

I neglected this vital area in my paper, and some of you asked how we could motivate Christians to share the Gospel. Make no mistake about it. This is the key to the problem of continuous outreach. If this could be burnt in on our souls, a Congress like this would not be necessary. I think the early Christians would answer something like this if we asked them why they did not lose heart.

a. The example of God who cared so much that he sent his Son to be a missionary to our world.

b. The love of Christ that grips us. He went to the Cross for us. He tells us to go and pass it on. Evangelism is the obedient response to the love of Christ which has gripped us.

c. The gift of the Spirit, who is specifically given us for witness bearing. The task of world evangelization and the equipment of the Holy Spirit are the two characteristics Jesus gave of the time between his ascension and his return.

So the early Christians would ground their evangelism fairly and squarely in the nature of the triune God. At his heart lies mission. But they had three other reasons which drove them on.

a. The privilege of being Christ's ambassador, the representative of the King of Kings. *We* have received this ministry. Amazing privilege!

b. The need of those without Christ. This rings through the New Testament and the early fathers. Like Bishop Dain, it was when I realized that men without God were lost now and would be lost forever — even nice folk, even my family and friends — that I vowed that I would burn up my one life in telling others of the fabulous Good News that Jesus has brought to our world.

c. Lastly, there is the sheer joy of it. It radiates out from the New Testament. It is infectious. You could put these Christians in prison, and they sang praises. You could tell them to shut up, and they talked all the more. Persecute them, and they spread their message in the next town. Kill them, and they went to their deaths with joy, and called down blessings on their murderers. That is why I would not exchange this business of spreading the Gospel for any occupation on earth. It is an enormous privilege. It is desperately needed. And it is utterly fulfilling. It is what we were made for.

CONTEMPORARY PRACTICES OF EVANGELISM
G. W. Peters

*Dr. Peters is Professor of World
Missions at Dallas Theological
Seminary, Dallas, Texas, USA, and is the
author of "Saturation Evangelism,"
and other books.*

It is readily admitted that the evangel — the Gospel — is the central message of the New Testament. Historically, the church has believed with considerable consistency and fervor that God has dealt effectively and adequately in Christ Jesus — his life, death, resurrection and enthronement — with the sins and sin of mankind and provided an eternal salvation for all who will believe.

The Gospel is God-wrought in history. It is revelation-given for history. It is absolute, perfect, and final. Therefore the Gospel message is one and abiding. The method of the dissemination of the Gospel and the practices of proclamation are man-related and therefore are relative. They are conditioned by the messenger and the psychology and sociology of the people to whom the Gospel is being proclaimed. The methods of operation and the patterns of communication vary greatly. Methods are people-related. The Bible therefore does not lay down absolute patterns and methods in evangelism.

Because of this, a method which may be very effective at one time, at one place, among one people, may not be effective at another time, another place, another people. In fact, it may prove disadvantageous if not disastrous. Therefore, a method-bound movement cannot become an effective *world* movement. Neither can it last very long. It will soon be relegated to the outdated and the outworn. We do not need renewal of the Gospel, but we do need continuous renewal of methodology to communicate the age-old Gospel in an intelligible, meaningful, and purposeful manner.

Methodology must also be distinguished from abiding principles and ideals in evangelism. The Gospel must be orally communicated, the Gospel must be demonstrated in life and action, the Gospel appeal must be made personal, it must be made intelligible, meaningful, attractive, persuasive, and inviting. Man must be confronted. Gospel communication must be preaching and speaking for a verdict. These are principles of Gospel communication. They are qualities of communication and are biblically constant.

Whether such communication is in the *form* of private conversation, public proclamation, group teaching, or door-to-door witnessing is not the important question. There is a quality which rings out the genuineness of the Gospel, reality of experience, and depth of conviction and concern.

In contrast to this, methodology is only a quantitative vehicle to make known the Gospel relevantly, effectively, and attractively. There is therefore no method which is universal and abiding. It must also be realized that no method is so inclusive that it becomes a sufficient method for all people. While one method may be more efficient than another method, no method is all-sufficient to communicate the Gospel to all people even in the same time and at the same place. Flexibility, variability, and openness become important virtues if evangelism is to be comprehensive and effective.

With these introductory remarks we turn to a survey of the main contemporary patterns of evangelism. Next I present New Testament ideals in evangelism, considering the criteria for evaluating evangelism and the realization of the ideals. Finally we briefly assess the present-day evangelism scene.

Crusade evangelism

Crusade evangelism is a serious and organized attempt to communicate in an intelligible and meaningful manner the Gospel of Jesus Christ to the masses of people in public gatherings. The supreme objective is to expose as many people as possible to the Gospel of Jesus Christ and to persuade them to accept the gracious offer of God in Christ Jesus and thus find forgivenss of sins and eternal life in Christ as Savior and Lord; become followers of the Master and learning, fellowshipping and serving members in a local church.

It must be emphasized, however, that crusade evangelism is also God's prophetic voice to the people and the nation. Crusade evangelism does not address itself *solely* to the individual and his sins and for salvation. It must become the voice of God to the people and nation, speaking boldly about the binding, blinding, and blighting sins of the nation, society and institutions and calling all men to repentance. There is a broader scope to evangelism than only the conversion of the individual. Evangelism must penetrate society with the message of salvation and judgment.

Patterns of crusade evangelism

Crusade evangelism may take on various patterns. It may be *national in scope* and advance a program of evangelism that encompasses a whole nation. Such programs have been designed and are being sponsored by the Latin American Mission in various Latin American countries. The programs are known as in-depth evangelism. A similar program known as New Life for All originated in Jos, Nigeria. The latter is gradually and progressively spreading into a number of countries in Africa. These programs were interdenominational in complexion, design, and organization.

Denominational campaigns of national scope have been conducted mainly by the Southern Baptists. After attempts in several countries, concerted efforts were made in Japan in 1963 and Brazil in 1965. These were followed by similar crusades in other countries but not in the same dimensions, enthusiasm, or success. In recent years the Western Hemisphere Crusade put forth great efforts to present the Gospel to the people in several countries in South, Central, and North America. A special feature of the Southern Baptist campaigns have been "simultaneous city-wide crusades."

An effective national campaign was carried through in Korea by the joint Korean churches in 1965.

At present a national campaign of note is in progress in the Philippines. It is less a campaign of crusades in the ordinary sense of the word, but rather a crusade to plant thousands of evangelism and Bible study cells throughout the Republic.

United city-wide and area-wide campaigns have become a part of the heritage of the evangelical churches. In recent decades they have become a world-wide phenomenon through the efforts of such instruments as the "Billy Graham Team," the "World Vision" endeavors, the "Good News Crusades" of the Assemblies of God, and others. In more recent years evangelists of renown from the Third World have left indelible imprints upon their countries and beyond them.

Local church evangelism campaigns are growing less and less in the established churches. This includes both the public evangelistic crusade and "enlistment evangelism." This is tragic, to say the least.

Fellowship-evangelism

The report of Luke on the life and ministry of the apostolic church is very sketchy, yet most meaningful and helpful for our orientation. He tells us that "they continuing daily with one accord in the temple, and breaking bread *from house to house . . ."* and again "And daily in the temple, and *in every house* they ceased not to teach and preach Jesus Christ (evangelized)" (Acts 2:46, 5:42). Somewhat later Paul reminds the Ephesians: "I kept back nothing that was profitable unto you, but have showed you and have taught you publicly, and from *house to house"* (Acts 20:20).

Two facts stand out clearly. The early church practiced both large gatherings in public places and small assemblies in the homes of believers. Again, the house meetings or small group encounters had a threefold purpose: first, *fellowship* of the saints, second, *teaching,* and third, *evangelism* of the neighborhood or community.

Fellowship or small group evangelism is not a modern invention or an accommodation to the conveniences of the non-churchgoer. It is an apostolic pattern that is being discovered and revived in our days. It is practiced with great effectiveness in Korea by numerous Presbyterian churches and other groups, by the Pentecostals in Latin America, by the evangelical churches in Great Britain and in several cities in the U.S.A., notably Dallas, Texas.

It should be noted that we are speaking of *fellowship-evangelism* in an atmosphere of friendship and neighborliness. I purposely hyphenate the fellowship-evangelism. It is not fellowship and evangelism, not even fellowship for the purpose of evangelism, but evangelism in and through fellowship. It needs to be recognized that biblical fellowship has evangelizing effects and powers. Evangelism is implicit in fellowship as fellowship is implicit in being in Christ. Fellowship-evangelism seeks to correlate two of the most dynamic New Testament concepts. This does not just happen. It is an art that will be achieved only when the Holy Spirit is truly in control and when it becomes a fellowship *in* the Spirit. The strength of the small group meeting will depend to a great extent upon the success in keeping the two concepts of fellowship and evangelism in proper balance, continuous tension and beautiful correlation. Fellowship must constitute the *quality* and evangelism must be the *purpose*, while friendship and neighborliness born out of spiritual concern for the welfare of others must create the *atmosphere* of the total setting.

Fellowship-evangelism, therefore, is less formal and more personal than crusade evangelism; it is less structured and more functional than public evangelism. It is not, however, as individual and confronting as personal evangelism usually is. It seems to be a happy and very effective mediation between crusade and personal evangelism if efficiently administered and properly conducted.

Levels of fellowship-evangelism

First, *household evangelism.* Household evangelism seldom appears in the vocabulary of books on evangelism. This seems peculiar for at least four reasons. (i) The family or household is a universally appearing social phenomenon. (ii) It is the first and most significant social institution created by God and the only institution that belongs to man in his original and sinless state. (iii) Family or household life is carefully ordered in the Bible and experiences of blessings and judgments are vividly portrayed. Again, household evangelism, household conversions, household baptisms, and household churches are quite prominent in the New Testament. (iv) The family or household is the basic and foundational social unit from which all other social units arise. The preservation and building of this unit ought to be a primary concern of Christianity and it ought to constitute the foundational unit of the Christian church.

Few examples of present-day practices in household evangelism can be cited. It is being practiced with considerable success in India by the Oriental Missionary Society and some related patterns do emerge in Japan and Zaire. It resulted in record conversions in Egypt before the wars interrupted the work. At present it is more a *"concept"* than a practice, program or movement. It ought to and can be fanned into a worldwide movement because the family is universal, household evangelism is a crying need, and household evangelism and household conversions have tremendous advantages. Household evangelism must be returned to its rightful place among the practices of evangelism.

Second, *small group evangelism.* Small group evangelism has proliferated considerably and has taken on various designations and forms. They are in part a revival of an apostolic pattern and in part a modernizing of the Methodist class meetings of the eighteenth century. It has ardent advocates and defenders. *D. H. Adeney* vigorously promotes "Cell Groups" through a specialized institute which he has founded in Singapore for this purpose. The institute is known as Discipleship Training Center. A pamphlet entitled "Cell Groups" explains the program. Michael Skinner of Wesley House, Cambridge, England, tells us: "For twenty-five years I have been an unashamed fanatic about house groups. This book makes no apology for such fanaticism but seeks to justify it on biblical grounds, as well as on the score of temporary needs and practical politics." His book, *House Groups,* is inspirational, instructional and provocative.

Speaking of the Methodist class meetings, Mr. Skinner comments: "The good things in the class meeting are plain. It practiced Christian fellowship of the New Testament patterns, it consolidated the gains of preaching and nurtured the spiritually awakened, it made people articulate about their faith and able witnesses to it in the world" (p. 106).

Dr. Matthew S. Prince of Knoxville, Tennessee, has founded the "New Life" movement which he introduces with the following words: "New Life is a Christian mission whose only purpose is to make Jesus Christ known by the best means available . . .

"New Life works through Christians who care for their fellow man. Four meetings for guests follow once a week . . .

"We make every effort to be sensitive to people, remain flexible, and communicate Christ in the most effective way possible. Therefore, the length of the series may vary. However, the format remains basically the same — discussion designed to answer questions about firming up a personal relationship with God through faith in Jesus Christ."

Dr. Howard Hendricks, Dallas, Texas, outlines home Bible classes according to pattern, purpose, and procedure. Under *pattern* he prescribes three characteristics if home Bible study groups are to be effective:
1. They must be community-centered.
2. They must be home-centered.
3. They must be evangelism-centered.

He continues on the *purpose:*
1. To provide the opportunity for Christians to reach the unsaved.
2. Present the Gospel to the unsaved (the main purpose).
3. To provide a feeder for the local church.

He sees the *procedure* under three headings:
1. Personnel — the host and/or the hostess and the teacher.
2. Program.
3. Promotion.

Third, specialized group evangelism. In the last decades numerous specialized group ministries have developed. *Child Evangelism Fellowship, International* (U.S.A.) and *Children's Special Service Mission,* now known as Scripture Union (Great Britain), specialize in reaching children with the Gospel.

Youth For Christ, International; Young Life Movement; Teen Evangelism, all U.S.A.-based, are penetrating youth with the message of the Gospel in an effective manner.

Inter-Varsity Christian Fellowship, Campus Crusade International Students, Inc., and *Navigators* are concentrating on the college and university campuses with relevant messages and relevant methods.

The impressive tri-annual "Urbana" conferences of the Inter-Varsity Christian Fellowship U.S., have attracted world attention and influenced thousands of young people for Christ. No less notable have been some of the gatherings under the auspices of Campus Crusade. Expo '72 will long be remembered by Dallas people and thousands of youth.

The Christian Business Men's Committee is directing its energy towards winning business men for Christ.

The *Christian Academies,* a German movement of great significance, are designed to acquaint, to dialogue with and to confront professionals with the Gospel and the claims of Christ.

Among Armed Forces

Evangelism has found much emphasis in the last decades and has been very successful in Korea. *Christian Service Men's Centers* organization is doing fine work in many cities in military evangelism.

All these organizations have worthy and vigorous programs. Fellowship-evangelism has almost unlimited possibilities and opportunities.

Personal evangelism

Personal evangelism is well illustrated and its effectiveness is demonstrated in the New Testament. Christ is our foremost example, instructor and inspiration in personal evangelism.

Personal evangelism today presents itself in three particular forms.

First, direct confrontation evangelism. Here the Gospel is being offered to the individual and the claims of Christ are made known in a face to face meeting and without lengthy introductions. This type has been popularized and schematized by R.A. Torrey in his famous book *"Personal Evangelism."* Various modifications of the same direct approach have been advanced by numerous authors and organizations. The best known today perhaps are the "Four Spiritual Laws" and their usage by Campus Crusade, and Dr. D. James Kennedy's (Fort Lauderdale) "Explosion Evangelism."

Second, friendship personal evangelism. The purpose of friendship personal evangelism is as definite as that of direct confrontation evangelism. The procedure, however, differs greatly. The cultivation of genuine and concerned friendship constitutes an integral part in the presentation of the Gospel and the claims of Christ. It seems a more natural approach than the direct confrontation. However, it is beset with some difficulties. It is admitted that to gain the confidence and friendship of unsaved people is not easy as it is often imagined. To make the transition from friendship to actual personal evangelism demands a good measure of tact and divine wisdom.

Yet, friendship personal evangelism is a sound approach. The art of being a friend and a soul winner can be acquired in the school of Christ and experience. It is an effective method not only to elicit decisions but also to lead individuals on into a life of Christian discipleship.

Third, dialogue personal evangelism. Dialogue is the opposite from monologue. It is a two-way conversation rather than a one-way presentation or proclamation. The meeting of Christ and Nicodemus may be taken as a biblical pattern of dialogue personal evangelism. The *purpose* is evangelism, the *procedure* is dialogue — the friendly exchange of views and convictions, the intimate sharing of experiences, needs, aspirations, and frustrations, with a view of dissolving the difficulties, obstacles, and prejudices in the heart and mind of the unsaved person. It is a gentle attempt to persuade the individual to accept the offer of God in Christ Jesus and to commit himself to Christ for salvation and life.

Life-style evangelism

Life-style evangelism as a program is a recent phenomenon. In reality and practice it is as old as Christianity. Much of the evangelism of Christ was life-style evangelism, that is, it grew out of ordinary life situations and experiences and was conducted in a life-style manner without having been planned or being programmed.

Life-style evangelism has become institutionalized and popularized in our days. The governing concepts of life-style evangelism are informality, familiarity, belongingness, friendliness, helpfulness, non-offensiveness, life-relatedness and non-programmed behavior and conversation.

Life-style evangelism has proliferated and has taken on many forms. I mention only three patterns.

Camp evangelism. Camp life is nothing new. Camp life is known in the Bible and has been known in Europe for many years. It is a part of vacation experiences. However, camp life for evangelism purposes is not as ancient. In the sense of modern camps, it is a relatively late comer.

Today camp and campers abound and facilities have been modernized and are made commodious. Many camps are being used to a tremendous advantage in evangelism. The family-style camp is increasing in numbers, popularity, and effectiveness. The fame of camp style evangelism has spread around the world and is greatly honored by the Lord in bringing people to the knowledge of salvation and the fellowship of believers.

Dinner evangelism. Dinner evangelism is both biblical and social. It is a pleasant and open approach to introduce friends and neighbors, colleagues and business associates, servants and masters to the Gospel of Jesus Christ. Its social setting allows for an atmosphere of relaxation, friendship and neighborliness. Such dinners may be held in church facilities, restaurants, or social and entertainment places. The choice of the place is important. Most people prefer a religiously neutral place.

Dinner evangelism has proven very effective in numerous places and is today a popular method of evangelism in many churches and associations in U.S.A. It is much appreciated among the ladies in Japan in several large metropolitan areas.

Coffeehouse evangelism. Coffeehouse evangelism is a late comer in the Western world. It gained fame and popularity during the tide of the "hippy" movement. It is still serving large numbers of people, particularly the university and college population. While it seems like a modified and modernized rescue mission on a college or university level, it is not that at all. It is rather an adaptation of evangelism to the mood and life-style of the times. It should not be considered a rescue mission operation in the ordinary sense of the word. It seeks to reach the hearts of youth by means of meeting their social needs rather than their physical needs, providing for them a haven of friendship in a hostile, depersonalized, and mechanized world of tensions, loneliness, pressures, competition, and chilling, individualistic society. At the same time it seeks to convince and to demonstrate to youth that the Gospel of Jesus Christ and the salvation in him are not bound to institutions and establishments. Christ can be found in the informal setting of a coffeehouse over a "cup of coffee" with a concerned friend.

Life-style evangelism has its place in a mechanistic and institutionalized world.

Mass media evangelism

Mass media evangelism is the most difficult part to present. It has taken on the form of Bible distribution evangelism, Christian literature evangelism, radio evangelism, television evangelism, press evangelism, film evangelism, recording evangelism, cassette tape evangelism, etc. No doubt there are other forms of mass media evangelism. From this listing it is evident that mass media evangelism is a most fascinating and a most challenging aspect of the Christian ministry and Gospel outreach. Yet, to describe and evaluate it becomes most difficult. In its scope it is so vast as to encompass the whole globe; in its possibilities it is so measureless as to defy our imagination; in its claims it is so overwhelming as to make objectivity almost impossible. In its presentation of concrete evidences it must remain general and vague because of the very nature of the work.

Whatever our position on mass media evangelism may be, mass media in communication has come to stay. It is today one of the greatest social molding forces in the world of humanity and one of the most rapidly expanding industries and institutions of the world. The Christian church simply cannot ignore it.

At present millions of dollars are being spent in Christian mass communication of the Gospel message in all the different forms mentioned above. The more than fifty Christian radio stations in the non-Western world make the Gospel available to countless multitudes. At the same time they reach into areas otherwise unreachable. It is my impression that money prayerfully given and honestly spent by reputable agencies is money well invested in Gospel proclamation.

New Testament ideals in evangelism

The remarkable proliferation of evangelism patterns is evidence of the vitality and the flexibility, adaptability, and creativity of evangelical Christianity. The impulse of evangelism in the last two decades is one of the deepest renewals of the living church of Jesus Christ in this century. It is a new pulsation of the Holy Spirit; it is the swelling of a wave which could crest in our generation. By the gracious operation of the Holy Spirit it could bring spiritual renewal through the Gospel of Jesus Christ to multitudes in our century.

No less significant is the new "age of anticipation" which presents to the church of Jesus Christ an unprecedented opportunity to proclaim the good news of God's gift in Christ Jesus. Never before has the world been more impatient with the status quo; never before has the world demanded such drastic, almost revolutionary changes, never before has the world been more open to "news" about a new hope, a new way, a new life, a new future. This is a time of crusading for Christ.

In the midst of these opportunities and challenges in the world and the renewal and proliferation of evangelism patterns, it behooves the church of Jesus Christ and particularly the leadership of evangelism endeavors and organizations to remain sober and vigilant. Two principles must govern us. *First,* no one method or pattern is sufficient to do the whole job. *Second,* enthusiasm and mighty pulsations are constructive only if they are guided by New Testament ideals. There are *qualities* in biblical evangelism which evangelical evangelism must not fail to build into its efforts.

It is therefore of utmost importance that evangelism continuously evaluate itself carefully against New Testament ideals and criteria. Here is our safe guide, our sure standard, and unfailing judge in all our activities and endeavors. Evangelism is no exception. Evaluation of evangelism, therefore must become an integral part of every evangelism endeavor.

Criteria in evaluating evangelism

This is not the place for a biblical discourse on the nature of evangelism. Here we are more interested in the effectiveness of evangelism. In the light of the New Testament what can we expect of biblically ideal evangelism? What are some of the New Testament ideals in evangelism that constitute our criteria? Every New Testament evangelism endeavor ought to face at least four basic issues.

a. The first issue is: *Has the evangelism effort and endeavor brought renewal, revitalization, a new pulsation of the Holy Spirit to the local church communities?* Has the effort reached into the lives of the people of God as well as reached out into the world? Has it kindled a new fire in the hearts and lives of God's people? Has the concern of the church deepened, broadened and been intensified over the lostness of mankind without the Gospel and over the people held in bondage of sin which is entrenched in the lives of the masses, in society, and institutions?

I am fully aware of the distinction that must be made between revival and evangelism. I can well see that the emphasis can be on the one or on the other, but I cannot see that they can exclude each other. Wherever a real revival takes place, evangelism will burst forth and where there is real evangelism revival must accompany it.

b. The second issue is: *Has the evangelism effort added new converts to the local churches?* Has the Gospel message penetrated sufficiently to actually convert and change the direction and relationships of the individual? Or has the conversion (?) stopped short in a profession or decision?

There are three elements closely related in the New Testament, in fact so closely that they often have been fused in theology into one theological concept. They are the three concepts of profession of faith, baptism, and being added to the local church of believers. According to the New Testament a true conversion holds these three concepts together in one "great New Testament experience" without sacramentally fusing these into a unit (Acts 2:41). If a breakdown occurs in this chain of events, serious consequences may follow.

Therefore, has the evangelism effort resulted in adding new converts to local congregations?

c. The third issue is: *Has the evangelism effort eventuated in a movement or has it remained one great event in the community?* It is not too difficult to bring a great and impressive event to pass. Organization, finances, and promotion enable us to accomplish this. It is however a different matter to bring about an event that will continue to generate sufficient dynamic to transmute the event into a movement that will increase in strength and intensity, and enlarge in scope and dimension. Such an event was Pentecost. It eventuated in a movement of tremendous dynamic and proportions which progressively encompassed all of Palestine.

It was evangelism released and relayed. And so it was in Antioch, in Syria, in Thessalonica, in Rome (Acts 13:1-4; I Thess. 1:8; Rom. 1:8, 15:18, 19). By the end of the Apostolic Age Christianity had become a movement which was spreading throughout the entire Roman Empire. Evangelism had become contagious rather than programmed. It had become the life-style of the Christian churches.

d. The fourth issue evangelism must face is: *Has the evangelism effort facilitated the continued ministry of the local churches in the community?* It is possible for evangelism efforts of the right pattern to unlock the community and environs for and to facilitate the continued Gospel ministry of the local congregations. Such was the ministry of the Apostles and the church at Jerusalem and lay people were able to establish churches throughout Judea, Samaria, and Galilee. Such was the ministry of Paul in the churches in and about Lystra and Iconium (Acts 16:5), in Ephesus (Acts 19:10, 26), and in Thessalonica (I Thess. 1:8), and throughout the Near East and Greece (Rom. 15:18, 19). Somehow Paul's practices and patterns of evangelism were of such a nature that they unlocked total areas and communities for the Gospel ministry into which others were able to enter and effectively evangelize. This must be accepted as a biblical norm in evangelism strategy.

In summary then, I conclude that ideal New Testament evangelism must build into its efforts dynamic factors that will bring renewal to the churches, that will add new converts to local congregations, that will transmute the event into a movement, and that will facilitate the continued Gospel ministry of the local congregations in the communities.

This brings us to the heart of the discussion. How can the ideals of the New Testament be achieved? Three basic statements will be made.

Realizing New Testament ideals in evangelism

First, ideal New Testament evangelism is achievable. Our best evidence is the New Testament itself. The book of Acts demonstrates and illustrates it. Here is our basic pattern. Historical evidences can be found in the churches of the second and third centuries and in present-day Korea where the ground-swell of evangelism, while it has fluctuated in intensity, has never subsided to the degree that it was endangered to be lost completely. In a somewhat different manner it is evident in the East Africa Revival. It has been progressing for some forty years, has penetrated some seventy different tribal areas, and left no church and community untouched in large sections of five or six countries and several denominations. Evangelism can become the way of life for the churches.

Second, ideal New Testament evangelism while flexible and adaptable is undergirded by a firm structure which rests upon definite principles. These principles can be outlined in a simple way as:

Step one: *mechanics* — strategy, organization,
Step two: *dynamics* — mobilization, cooperation,
Step three: *bridges* — surveys, publicity, relationships,
Step four: *operation* — presentation, penetration, permeation, confrontation,
Step five: *evaluation*.

Two facts must be emphasized.

(i) *The role of preparation.* From the above outline it is evident that preparation takes a great deal of time and energy. If we fail here, we fail. A German student of revivals and evangelism (Dr. W. Dilger) makes the observation that from the historical perspective every major religious event and movement of significance has had at least thirty years of preparation. This is not too difficult to document. Therefore I conclude that every great and effective evangelism endeavor demands much time and energy to prepare. In fact, it can be and has been established that the retention power of the churches is practically proportionate to the time and energy expended in preparation.

(ii) *The significance of the chain of steps.* It should be noted that in building an evangelism program which is to evaluate in a dynamic evangelistic movement no "step" can be neglected. The effectiveness of the program can be weakened considerably on any one of these levels. No chain is stronger than its weakest link. Careful ministry must go into each one of the steps.

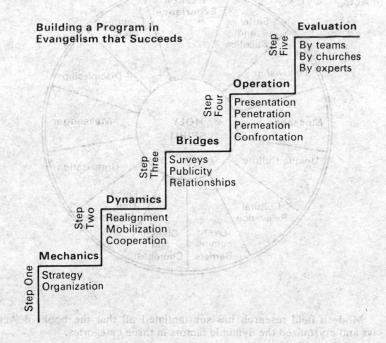

Building a Program in Evangelism that Succeeds

Evaluation
Step Five
By teams
By churches
By experts

Operation
Step Four
Presentation
Penetration
Permeation
Confrontation

Bridges
Step Three
Surveys
Publicity
Relationships

Dynamics
Step Two
Realignment
Mobilization
Cooperation

Mechanics
Step One
Strategy
Organization

Third, ideal New Testament evangelism revolves around clusters and constellations of dynamic factors which the Holy Spirit uses to energize evangelism. There is no single factor and no simple explanation of any dynamic program of evangelism. It is a combination, coordination, and integration of series of factors. Such factors must be discovered, defined, released, channeled and directed towards desirable goals and purposes. *They can be built into a program of evangelism.*

All Christians would agree that ultimately all Christian ministries of the Gospel in their effectiveness are dependent upon the Holy Spirit. He alone is the efficient, sufficient and effective cause. Dynamic movements and programs ultimately are the result of the gracious and sovereign operations of the Holy Spirit. It is, however, a fact of revelation and experience that the Holy Spirit does not operate in a vacuum. He involves men and means. Therefore measurable and definable factors become discernable which the Holy Spirit utilizes to make his power operative.

Let me illustrate this from the book of Acts and from modern field research. A diagrammatical presentation of the book of Acts would appear somewhat as portrayed on this page.

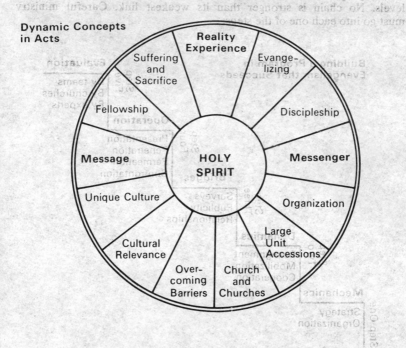

Dynamic Concepts in Acts

Reality Experience · Evangelizing · Discipleship · Messenger · Organization · Large Unit Accessions · Church and Churches · Overcoming Barriers · Cultural Relevance · Unique Culture · Message · Fellowship · Suffering and Sacrifice

HOLY SPIRIT

Modern field research has substantiated all that the book of Acts says and crystalized the dynamic factors in three categories.

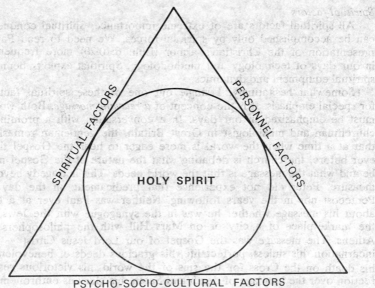

This three-dimensional diagram of spiritual, personnel, and psycho-socio-cultural factors, may be filled in as follows.

Spiritual factors:
- Victorious prayer
- Triumphant faith
- Dynamic fellowship
- Reality experience
- Fervor of evangelism
- Relevant message
- Attitude of expectation
- Membership involvement

Personnel factors:
- Men of God (with all its biblical implications)
- Men of the world
- Men of the people
- Men of the church
- Men of evangelism passion

Psycho-socio-cultural factors:

It is too often forgotten that man is mercilessly molded by his culture and that his personality make-up reflects his culture at least in three ways:
- In his mentality
- In his society
- In his structures

A few comments on the above outline are apropos.

Spiritual factors

All spiritual factors are of extreme importance. Spiritual conquests can be accomplished only by spiritual forces. We need to read Paul's presentation of the Christian's armor (Eph. 6:10-20) more frequently in our days of technology and methodology. Spiritual exploits demand spiritual equipment and dynamics.

Somewhat hesitatingly, I single out one of these spiritual factors for special emphasis. It is the concept of *a relevant message.* Both words must be emphasized in our days. In a conversation with a prominent churchman and missiologist in Great Britain, the gentleman remarked that at a time when the world is more eager to hear the Gospel than ever before, the church is debating what the nature of the Gospel may be and what the message is that the world needs. This is tragedy beyond measure. Peter did not experience that predicament on the day of Pentecost nor in the years following. Neither was Paul ever at a loss about his message whether he was in the synagogue with the Jews, in the marketplace of a city or on Mars Hill with the philosophers of Athens. The message was the Gospel of our Lord Jesus Christ — his incarnation, his sinless, perfect life, his gracious deeds of benevolence, his death on the Cross for the sins of the world, his victorious resurrection over the bondage of death and Satan, his glorious enthronement at the right hand of God as the Paraclete of his own. Thus the Saviorhood of Christ in his substitutionary work for mankind and his present Lordship in the universe were boldly and joyfully declared. The apostles confronted men with a divine offer of forgiveness of sin and the gift of eternal life and called upon men everywhere to repent and believe in the Lord Jesus Christ for their salvation.

There is a theological framework without which proclamation ceases to be evangelism and evangelical preaching. Evangelistic preaching cannot be divorced from a specific content which constitutes the nature of the Christian Gospel.

There is, however, a peculiar note of emphasis in the various messages of the apostles in the book of Acts, an emphasis that relates that message uniquely to that particular people and that situation. *It is a relevant message that did not miss the mark.* It won a hearing and it hit the target because it met man in his struggle with sin, his thirst for salvation, and brought assurance for eternity.

There is an emphasis of the Gospel that is peculiarly relevant to the different generations, the different peoples, the different cultural molds, the different situations. *It is a fact that the effectiveness of evangelism depends to a great extend upon our ability to make the Gospel message relevant to the religious needs and hopes, the aspirations and anticipations, the yearnings and strivings, the fears and frustrations of the people.* Only so will we win a hearing. Here is our initial and effective point of contact and departure to the deeper and full needs of the spiritual nature of man in his sin and guilt, bondage and lostness. Man will hear when he can expect that a need will be met, a hope will be fulfilled, an anticipation will be realized. The Gospel must earn its own hearing and receiving.

Personnel factor

God's supreme method is man, man regenerated, sanctified, committed, mobilized, trained, and equipped. God's chief instrument is the church, the church as a body of dedicated people. Spiritual leadership and a mobilized, trained membership are God's demand for the advancement of his cause. *Evangelism will be perennial and effective to the degree that it will succeed to mobilize, train and actively involve the total "priesthood" of God, the total "body" of Christ.* This is an axiom of the Scriptures that can be neglected only at the peril of the church.

Psycho-socio-cultural factors

While all men think and have an equal capacity to think, not all men think alike. There is a difference in the *mentality* of the people of the world. East and West, North and South are equal, but they are not alike. They are equally endowed by God but they are not molded alike by their cultures in their way of thinking. They are equally created in the image of God, but they are not sculptured alike in the "image of mentality, society and structure." There are differences. Culture has cast the mind into a certain mold of thinking. Some cultures are more rational-logical, others meditative-intuitive, still others imaginative-mythological. Our generation is rapidly becoming existential. *And it is this cultural mold of mentality that determines principles and practices of communication.* Communication does not take place *in the same way* everywhere. It differs considerably. *It is a fact, however, that the effectiveness of evangelism depends upon our ability to communicate the content of the Gospel in an intelligible, attractive, meaningful, persuasive and consistent manner and demonstrate its value and workability in a manner and way of life.*

Again, culture molds man *socially.* Socialization is a life-long process and shapes man in all his relationships and roles, values and priorities, behavior and vocation. Man lives in a social web of relationships from which he cannot remove himself without serious harm to his personality. Therefore, there are different types of society in this world — individuals, family, tribe, community, etc.

It must be kept in mind that *man's social mold and pattern determine the methods of operations* which are most effective in reaching him with the Gospel of Jesus Christ. Thus in many areas of Indonesia people will respond best in families and communities, in India by castes and sections of villages, in other areas as tribes and in Mexico students are most open to the Gospel in groups of five to eight. If the Muslim world is ever to be reached with the Gospel we will need to devise methods of penetrating total communities.

Thus methods of evangelism ought to vary as we enter and encounter the different societies. Therefore, one method which may work well at one time and with one people may not be appropriate and effective at another time and with other people. *Consequently, the effectiveness of evangelism depends upon our ability to design and apply methods of evangelism that will integrate and utilize the social web of relationships of people as natural "bridges to God" between individuals, families, tribes, and communities. Such relationships serve most effectively*

as channels for the flow of dynamics in evangelism and Gospel expansion.
Such evangelism may be less conspicuous but it will be more effective.
We need new patterns of household and community evangelism that
will garner in total areas in communities as well as individuals into the
kingdom of God.

Similarly we must think about *structures.* Though there is no totally
unstructured society, people differ greatly in their social and cultural
structuring. An effective evangelism program and organization must
take the structure of the people into consideration.

It must be stated that American aggressive activism in organization
and promotion often overwhelms and frustrates the people of other
lands and cultures and paralyzes the flow of dynamics which would
generate and flow freely if the organization and structure of the program
were to take the "local" structure and organization more into consideration. Latin American Pentecostalism, in Africa New Life for All
and "indigenous" evangelism movements in India are our best evidence
of the workability of "local" structuring of dynamic movements. The
Holy Spirit uses all kinds of structures. *Therefore, the effectiveness of*
evangelism depends on the degree to which the Holy Spirit is permitted
to operate freely and unshackled by traditional or idealized structuralism
and allowed to develop a relevant, native and dynamic functionalism with
an appropriate but subordinate structure.

The psycho-socio-cultural factors call for much wisdom, grace,
humility, patience, adaptability, flexibility, and creativity. It simply
is a fact of history that cultural accommodation or adaptability is a
tremendously dynamic factor in man's way of life and ministry. *The*
dynamics of an evangelism program will depend to a considerable degree
upon our ability to discover, harness, and utilize the psychological, social,
and cultural forces and patterns of the people and environment in the
communication and propagation of the Gospel and building up the saints
into an effective evangelizing congregation in their own community.

Assessing the present-day evangelism scene

Permit me to assess the present-day evangelism scene very briefly.
We are living in a time of greatest resurgence in evangelism. There
is a marvelous renewal of evangelism on deep levels within certain
strata of the church of Jesus Christ. Great evangelistic efforts are
being witnessed on various levels and in various patterns. Evangelism
is coming into its own. Evangelistic movements are seen around the
world. This is a great day for those who have been praying for and
laboring in behalf of evangelism. We must not permit the present mood
and momentum to suffer for want of support and action. We humbly
attribute the renewal in evangelism to the gracious operation of the
Holy Spirit and are grateful for this experience.

We are in the midst of unprecedented opportunities and challenges
in a world open to the "good news" and with overwhelming response
to the Gospel in many areas of the world. Indeed, the world seems more
eager to hear and to respond than the Christian church is prepared to
tell and to accommodate. In many places churches are overcrowded
with new converts who need a spiritual home, spiritual nurture, and

biblical instruction. This is a time of unparalleled harvest for the kingdom of God. We may well apply the angelic call to ourselves and our time: "Thrust in thy sickle and reap: for the time is come for thee to reap; for the harvest of the earth is ripe" (Rev. 14:16). The call for reapers is more urgent today than ever before. More souls are being born into the kingdom of God than ever before and bewildered, depressed, eager, and searching multitudes are pressing at the gates of the church. This is the day of evangelism.

We are experiencing a never-before-witnessed proliferation of patterns of evangelism. Novel and original ways are being designed and practiced which for the moment attract and appeal to varied people. Some, no doubt, will soon fall by the wayside and new ones will take their place. There is flexibility and creativity evident at least on a superficial level.

It must be confessed, however, that a great segment of the church of Jesus Christ remains relatively neutral and some even critical towards the great evangelism pulsation that is being experienced today and which we believe to have originated with the Holy Spirit. With others evangelism in the biblical sense is not central. It is an almost unknown factor to them. A renewal of greater dimensions is needed.

It must also be admitted that much of evangelism today seemingly lacks the real dynamic of the Holy Spirit because the dynamic spiritual factors have not been built into the program and efforts. We are in a great haste to get moving. As a result the ideals of New Testament evangelism are only slightly in evidence in spite of tremendous efforts, great organizations, and strong promotions. The churches are not truly renewed, comparatively few members are added to local congregations of believers, relatively few dynamic movements of evangelism are in evidence, and the local congregations are sagging in their relations to the communities. They are not potent and transforming factors in life, culture, and society.

It must also be conceded that evangelism as a way of life in the churches has practically disappeared. To an overwhelming degree evangelism has become the effort of "teams of specialists" and less the initiative and activity of the churches and the membership. This has made much of evangelism a grandstand experience with a few mighty giants of God facing the world and Satan in the arena and the multitude of Christians as the spectators in the comfortable and walled-off grandstand. It remains a fact that the main resources in manpower for evangelism have thus far not been tapped. The great assets of the church are frozen in beautiful cathedrals and churches. Mobilization of all Christians for evangelism is heard as an occasional slogan but is not seen in general practice. The priesthood of all believers has remained a dogma few take seriously, a church of "we the people" is little believed and experienced. Evangelism as a ground-swell and "people movement" is little known since the close of the third century.

It must also be acknowledged that much of evangelism is relatively ineffective because it has become westernized and stereotyped in program, procedures, and methodology. It has remained unrelated in communication to the psychology of the people to whom it was addressed. It has often violated in its methodology the basic principles of indigenous sociology and ruthlessly cut across social ties and the web of relationships thus blocking the natural channels of the free flow of dynamics. It has set up structures that were strange to the people and "David was unable to go to war in the armor of Saul." Therefore evangelism remained relatively impotent, often became offensive, not necessarily because of the "Cross" or the "Crucified One" but because of the impositions of strange elements upon the psychology, sociology, and structures of the people.

God is the God of all mankind. He wants all men to come to the knowledge of his dear Son and our blessed Savior. Therefore evangelism must always remain supremely a message and not a method. Methodology and structure must always remain subordinate and subservient. They must not be permitted to become master.

I therefore conclude that:

Evangelism is a message
Evangelism must be central
Evangelism must be governed by New Testament ideals
Evangelism can be dynamic
Evangelism must become perennial
Evangelism must become the way of life of the church of Jesus Christ.
World evangelism can become a reality in our generation if . . . .

CONTEMPORARY PRACTICES OF EVANGELISM

G.W. Peters

Honored chairman, participants, observers and guests, I consider it a privilege to have had the opportunity to address you through my paper on "Contemporary Practices of Evangelism."

I realize that the paper is quite incomplete and that is so for a number of reasons.

First, because of the vast amount of material that had to be crowded into a few pages. The proliferation of patterns of evangelism in our days demonstrates the vitality of evangelical Christianity and the incarnation of the Gospel message in the "new man" that is emerging in our age. It ought to bring rejoicing into our hearts and courage into our work.

Second, the paper is incomplete because it limited itself almost exclusively in the selection of material for the first part to the North American scene. This was done on purpose. There is no thought in me to present North America as an example of innovation. The idea was more to present North America as a "case study." I am quite well acquainted with the evangelistic movements around the world, but it is practically impossible to mention all of them. New patterns are emerging almost daily somewhere in the world. Why each one must "brand" his by a unique name and form an organization around it remains a human riddle.

Third, the paper will seem very incomplete to some because in it I have held to my understanding of the biblical meaning of the concept of evangelism.

I have deliberately and consciously held to a somewhat narrow interpretation of evangelization. I have distinguished the concept from *conversion.* I fully agree that all evangelism aims at conversion. We make no secret of our deliberate intention of turning people to the living God from their idols whether such idols are images, nationalism, secularism or even "Kultur-Christentum" (culture-Christianity). We preach for a verdict and confront people everywhere with Jesus Christ — God incarnated, crucified, risen, enthroned, and coming again. We do not believe that Jesus Christ may be a good substitute for other saviors or an addition to them. We believe that he is the *only* Savior of the world and that men everywhere must make a deliberate choice to accept Christ, enter the Kingdom of God through the new birth and by divine adoption become members of the household of God. Having received such from God, man is to become a disciple of Christ and a servant of mankind.

The above is the conscious *purpose* of evangelization. However, evangelization may take place without such radical moral and spiritual conversion. Man may refuse to repent of his sins and believe in the Lord Jesus Christ. He thus remains under the wrath of God. Therefore evangelization and conversion are not synonymous. The concepts must not be fused or confused.

I have also distinguished evangelization from *Christianization.* Christianization refers to the *process* of gradual transformation, of growth *from* faith *to* faith, *from* knowledge *to* knowledge, *from* glory *to* glory. It is the progressive realization in our lives of the hope whereunto we are called. It is the maturing, perfecting, and enriching process in the life of the believer. It is the processing of the vine to produce fruit, more fruit, much fruit, abiding fruit. It is the training of the citizen in the Kingdom of God to serve man and God well. It is the equipping of the Christian to play his role in the family, church, and society according to the purpose and will of God.

A distinction has also been made in the concept of evangelization and *social action.* Social action has become a vague and "hiding" concept. It may mean many different things to many different people. It must be admitted that it is our extra-biblical word. The Bible knows the word *"service"* and evangelicals would do well to return to this *word* and to search its meaning. Certainly Christ is the supreme example as servant and also in the type of service. Paul is a servant for Jesus' sake and the church must serve as its Master served.

I fully appreciate the meaning of all four concepts — evangelization, conversion, Christianization, service. They are firmly routed in the Bible. To interrelate them, however, essentially and experimentally and fuse them conceptually, results in nebulous thinking and inconsistent action. While it may be difficult and even unwise to separate them too rigidly, to fuse them conceptually is biblically unwarranted, historically disadvantageous, and practically confusing.

With these preliminary clarifications I turn to the paper. Three main points are made:

First, contemporary practices of evangelism are presented under five main families.

Second, I present "New Testament Ideals in Evangelism" with two sub-points. (i) Criteria in evaluating evangelism. (ii) Realizing New Testament ideals in evangelism.

Third, assessing present-day evangelism.

Your response to my paper was overwhelming and gratifying. I thank you for it. There was little criticism but there were many questions. From the more than 1,600 responses, I have gleaned the following most frequently repeated, impressive, and urgent issues as they relate to my paper. I present them to you for your consideration:

One — Where can we find information and helpful material on the different patterns of evangelism?

Two — What can we do that evangelism will become once again the way of life (the life-style) of the church? How can we motivate, mobilize and train the membership to become active and effective in evangelism?

Three — Why is present-day evangelism not more effective? What hinders evangelical Christianity from becoming a marching army in evangelism? Does God bypass the established, historical churches and work mainly through special groups?

Four — How can we best discover the most appropriate methods for "our" culture? And, how do we best communicate to "our" people?

Five — Because the Holy Spirit is sovereign, can he be programmed in evangelism? Is programmed evangelism really Spirit-directed evangelism? Is not true Spirit-directed evangelism spontaneous evangelism? This is somewhat of a summary of the *burdens* expressed in the responses. To fully respond to them would require a book and a Congress in itself. The best answers will be found in smaller, local study conferences.

One — Information is not difficult to get if you read the English language. A central information center for each country, however, seems important to assist pastors and churches in this vital question.

Two — There is a remarkable moving of the Spirit and a renewal in evangelism taking place in our days. However, it seemingly touches the young people and the laymen more than the ministry, clergy, theologians, and ecclesiastical and theological institutions.

According to the divine order, however, the key to church renewal of any kind is the leadership and the pastor. Here the fire ought to begin to burn, from here it most rapidly and most progressively spreads.

There is another divine ideal. The church is God's supreme agent of evangelism. This will be presented in a paper somewhat later. Permit me to say something here with all caution and serious hesitation. Hesitation, not because I am saying a half-truth, but because I could be misunderstood. Yet it must be said. We are all deeply concerned about and committed to the evangelization of the world. This is a divine burden. How is this to be accomplished? Automatically we are thinking of mission societies and missionaries. This we ought to think. Mission societies and missionaries will be demanded for years to come. They must *send,* they must *go!*

However, it must be emphasized with equal force that the world will not be evangelized solely or mainly by mission agencies and professional missionaries. The biblical and main key is the local church mobilized and trained in evangelism. The mission agency and the missionary are the *advance guard to establish an outpost.* They are the supplement of the church in world evangelism. This is a principle that must be taught and preached until it will sink into the fibre of the life of the church.

Ideally this will be accepted with ease. Practically it is one of the most difficult truths for the present-day church to achieve. There are many theological, historical, structural, and psychological barriers that must be overcome to practice a general priesthood of all believers in the full sense of the word.

In a most concrete manner, permit me to say that a local congregation will be motivated and mobilized when the pastor is motivated by a consuming passion in evangelism, when he in action demonstrates such passion, and when he patiently and diligently by word and example will train his membership in evangelism. Let no one think that it is easy to move a congregation into evangelism and maintain it there until evangelism becomes a part of the way of life of the church. It will take toil and tears, prayer and patience, example and encouragement. But it can be done. It has been done. Sooner or later the church *becomes* what the pastor *is.* The church takes on the image and the life-style of the pastor. If evangelism is the way of life of the pastor, the church will sooner or later and by degrees turn into the same way of life or get rid of the pastor.

Let us keep it firmly in mind, *a major key* to world evangelization is the mobilization of every local congregation in the task. And the major key to the local church according to the divine order is the leadership and the pastor.

Here is our awesome responsibility as leaders, teachers, and pastors.

As we mobilize the church in evangelism, we will soon discover that a three-winged pattern will evolve. In general we will find that some 10 to 15 per cent can be mobilized for active confrontation evangelism. An additional 20-30 per cent can be trained in friendship evangelism. The remainder must be trained in prayer-evangelism, prayer which undergirds the other two efforts. Thus the total church becomes involved. This is God's ideal and this must be our endeavor. Let us make it clear that evangelization is not a gift but a biblical duty.

Three — Question three relates to present-day ineffectiveness in evangelism. This is a most crucial issue. In a day when the opportunities are unprecedented and the tide of evangelism is swelling, ineffectiveness discourages many a servant of God. Certainly the fault does not lie with God. God is not willing that any should perish. Neither can it be said that the Gospel is not relevant. It is God's message to man in all his needs. It is relevant to every man and to every age. The problem must lie elsewhere.

Of course, we draw the conclusion that we are not as spiritual as we ought to be. This I readily admit. The spiritual quality of many churches is lamentable. The Holy Spirit is little recognized, little feared, and little obeyed. This is tragedy multiplied.

To correct this indispensable qualification, however, does not assure effectiveness. Beyond the spiritual qualification are at least four other road-blocks. They are theological, ideological, methodological, and structural.

Theologically evangelism may be weakened because of the nature of the message. The central message in evangelism must be two-pronged. *Objectively* we preach Jesus Christ as the God-man-crucified, risen, enthroned, and coming again. The Saviorhood of Christ must ring true and through. There must be no uncertain tone about it. It is somewhat disturbing that even in evangelical proclamation the Lordship of Christ is beginning to over-ride the emphasis of the Saviorhood of Jesus Christ. That is contrary to the divine order. While it is dangerous to separate the Lordship from the Saviorhood, it is perilous to precede the Saviorhood with the Lordship or make the latter dominant in evangelism. The demands of God must always be preceded or at least definitely prefaced by the gifts of God, or else conversion becomes a reformation without spiritual regeneration.

Subjectively much evangelism fails to preach repentance and faith on the part of man. Therefore "conversion" becomes a "believiani" or a professing without possessing.

The objective and subjective must be kept in a proper balance. *Idealogically* many churches are introspective and introverted. There is a fair degree of concern and service, but such concern and service is consumed by its own constituency. There is much inreach but little outreach! There is much fellowship but little evangelism, there is much teaching but little discipleship, there is much performance but little accomplishment. There is much programming but little mission. The church is self-consuming because it is self-centered and it is not focused upon the world.

Methodologically evangelism weakens itself when it insists on a "four-square" method (ready-tailored method) that can be transported and imported from age to age, generation to generation, culture to culture. No method is universally applicable in detail and form, though there are certain methods which are more normative than others.

Without hesitation I recommend household or family evangelism anywhere in the world. The family is a universal sociological unit. However, it is more than a sociological unit. It is a divinely ordained unit. As such it must always be included in our plans and program of evangelism.

In general, however, methods are determined by three factors — the evangelist, the mood of the time, and psycho-cultural existence of the people.

Structurally evangelism can be bound very easily. I urge the readers to study carefully the message of Howard Snyder. It deserves our attention.

It is too often forgotten that two power structures pervade every institution and every movement. These are the organizational power structure or *form*, and the functional power structure or *purpose*.

Let us keep in mind that the purpose of the church and evangelism is divinely ordained. Not so is the form. Here we have freedom to change adapt, modify, and create.

It is often forgotten that the church of Jesus Christ has experienced two periods when it was uniquely formed. In the first three centuries Episcopalianism in its Eastern and Western appearances and variations was formed. And, again in the sixteenth and seventeenth centuries the new forms which have characterized the modern denominations were constituted.

It must be realized that both these periods in the history of the church were times when the church was on the *defensive*. Thus the times demanded *a relevant form. It is a form for defensive positions.* Seriously we must ask: is a structure built for *defensive purposes* also the most effective and efficient structure for *an offensive warfare?* This is the crucial question about structure.

There is nothing uniquely sacred (though to us it may be) about our structures. Are they relevant? Or have we come to the time and place in history where structure dominates function, form enslaves purpose, and we are unable to move ahead aggressively?

Let us be open to God, and under the guidance of the Holy Spirit liberate purpose within form and foundation within structure, organism within organization, life within the body.

Such an attitude will also answer the question whether the Holy Spirit can be programmed. No, he cannot be programmed. But as a Spirit of order he operates according to *his order* but not without an order.

Let us claim the power of God and walk and work in the power, liberty, and order of God, and world evangelization will become a reality.

RESPONSE TO: CONTEMPORARY PRACTICES OF EVANGELISM
Nene Ramientos

Dr. Ramientos, Philippines, is the Coordinating
Director of Christ the Only Way Movement,
a nationwide evangelistic effort.

Under the subject of *Crusade evangelism,* Dr. George Peters refers to a crusade evangelism that is going on in the Philippines which he calls a crusade to plant thousands of evangelism and Bible study cells throughout the Republic.

This is exactly what we are trying to do in the Philippines in our national program of saturation evangelism and church growth known as the Christ the Only Way Movement. The Movement started as a vision at the World Congress on Evangelism in Berlin in 1966, formulated as a mission at the Asia-South Pacific Congress on Evangelism in Singapore in 1968, and finally launched as a united action of Philippine evangelical churches at the All Philippines Congress on Evangelism in 1970.

We have just concluded a six-month city-wide evangelistic campaign all over the Philippines where as many people as possible have been exposed to the preaching of the Gospel of Jesus Christ. The many hundreds of inquirers in these campaigns have been organized into home Bible study groups, while others have already joined local churches. Our follow-up strategy in the Christ the Only Way Movement for our city-wide evangelistic campaigns and other mass Gospel meetings is these home Bible study groups which we call the Lay Evangelistic Group Studies. As a rule, we do not bring our inquirers into the fellowship of existing Lay Evangelistic Group Studies, or LEGS for short, where they study the Word of God at least one hour each week. And in the absence of any LEGS unit in the area, we form these inquirers into new LEGS groups.

It is obvious from this strategy that our immediate goal of crusade evangelism in the Philippines through the Christ the Only Way Movement is the establishment of new groups of believers or new congregations. We are not content with the mere expansion of membership of existing local churches. We feel that since our goal is to disciple the Filipino nation, we must have churches or groups of believers meeting regularly for worship in every conceivable cultural and homogeneous group of people throughout the Philippine archipelago.

Spain ruled the Philippines for more than three centuries, and it was when there was already a Catholic church in every town and a Catholic chapel in every barrio that Spain could lay claim that the Philippines was already Christianized. Perhaps when we shall have already established a group or groups of believers in every city, town, and barrio throughout the Philippines, we might also be able to claim that we have already discipled the entire Filipino nation for Christ.

We feel it is not enough to set as the goal of evangelism the winning of souls to Jesus Christ, or that the ultimate goal of evangelism is the establishment or growth of churches. Indeed, evangelism must result in the conversion of people to Jesus Christ and the growth of the Christian community. But this must be done within the context of the Great Commission of God for the church, which is the *discipling of a nation.*

It is possible for a country to have a population of believers in Christ much larger than the Christian population of another country, and still remain undiscipled as a nation. On the other hand, the country with a much smaller population of believers in Christ may be the one that has already met the requirements of being discipled as a nation. On the basis of our own cultural understanding of bringing an entire nation within the psychological influence of religion as Spain did in the Philippines in the latter part of the sixteenth century, we feel it is not so much the number of people won to Christ and the number of churches established or the increase of membership in churches, as in the strategic establishment of these hundreds of groups of believers or house churches within psychological distance between each other that determines whether a nation is already discipled for Jesus Christ.

There are 52,048 barrios, 1,433 towns, and 61 cities in the Philippines. This means that about 55,000 churches or groups of believers are needed to bring the entire Philippine population within psychological distance of Christian communities. There are already more than 3,000 Christian churches in the Philippines. Most of these are in the cities and towns. This means therefore that we need about 50,000 more new groups of believers or churches, most of which will be in the barrios and towns. This is the only way to bring the entire Filipino nation within psychological distance of groups of believers in Christ.

This is what we are striving to do in the Philippines through the Christ the Only Way Movement. We have set as our goal the establishment of groups of believers in all the barrios and towns of the country where there are yet no groups of believers or Christian churches. Based on our survey, we will need at least 50,000 more new groups of believers or Bible-believing churches to reach our goal of discipling the Philippines for Christ in our generation.

Right now, we have about 10,000 of these Lay Evangelistic Group Studies throughout the country. We hope to convert these 10,000 LEGS into groups of believers meeting regularly for worship in strategic areas of the communities where they are located. Added to these 10,000 LEGS are more than 6,000 cells of believers which we call in the Christ the Only Way Movement, Core groups. These Cores are groups of believers in Christ meeting regularly once a week for sharing, teaching, and praying. These are already believers in Christ and from these groups come those who lead in the Lay Evangelistic Group Studies. We also hope to convert these Core groups into new congregations or house churches. Like the LEGS which are convertible to groups of believers, the Core groups are potential new congregations or house churches.

This is what we believe the Lord of the harvest is asking us to do in the Philippines today. Our timetable to reach our goal is set towards the end of the present century. We believe the Lord has given us the program to disciple the Philippines in our time. We believe the Lord has given us the people who can do the task of fulfilling the Great Commission in our land. We believe the Lord will provide us the means to teach, train, and mobilize our churches in the Philippines for the task of discipling our nation in our generation.

THE NATIONAL CAMPAIGN OF EVANGELISM — NEW LIFE FOR ALL IN CAMEROON
Elias N.G. Cheng

*Rev. Cheng, Bamenda, Cameroon, is Evangelism
Secretary in the Northwest and Southwest
Provinces for the New Life for All movement.*

Introduction: In the fifties and the early sixties most of the churches in Cameroon became independent from missionary influence. Few local leaders had been prepared to cope with the administrative pattern inherited from the foreign missions. As a result, some of the best preachers were put into administrative posts. As a matter of fact, in the first decade of "independence" the young churches spent most of their energy for administrative purposes.

Why a National Campaign of Evangelism in Cameroon?

From 5.8 million people in 1970 it is estimated that the total population of Cameroon will reach 6.4 million in 1975, at an annual growth rate of 2.1 per cent. There is a huge number of people who have not accepted Christ crowded in Cameroonian cities. There are still villages in rural areas which are isolated and far removed from all economic and technical development. There are groups and whole tribes who have barely been touched by the Gospel. An expanding Muslim community in North Cameroon represents a challenge to the Christian church.

In September, 1969, representatives from most of the Protestant churches and missions in Cameroon met, and unanimously decided to launch what would be known as the National Campaign of Evangelism — new life for all. It was decided that the material and methods that had proved successful in Nigeria should be used in the initial phase.

The National Campaign of Evangelism was launched under the auspices of the Federation of Evangelical Churches and Missions in Cameroon (Federation des Eglises et Missions Evangeliques du Cameroun, FEMEC). Apart from one denomination, all major churches in the country have been supporting the movement.

Mobilization by Retreats

It became evident that a total evangelization of the country could be achieved only by a total mobilization of all born-again Christians, not leaving the responsibility to pastors and paid church workers only.

Interdenominational Retreats

At the forefront of the planning were the following objectives: a) Mobilization of all Christians to become witnesses. b) The involvement of the *local churches,* because only an evangelization which starts with the renewal of the local church has any hope for success. c) *The unity of the body of Christ.* All denominations in Cameroon were invited to join the movement if they could agree to its aims. They were asked not to hunt for converts for their own church, but to proclaim Christ's rule over all the earth. d) *Systematic matching of needs and resources.* The National

Campaign in Cameroon systematically wanted to reach all people in
Cameroon by a coordinated program. The Campaign incorporated social
aspects of witnessing through preaching, teaching, and medical care. God
is opening the way not only into homes but into hearts. Thousands are
hungry for the Good News and only changed men and women who fill
the churches can bring it to them.

Outreach

A team is composed as follows: a) a preacher — pastor or evangelist.
b) a medical worker — doctor or nurse. c) an agent for rural development
— teacher or agriculturalist.

All team workers are supposed to participate in personal witnessing.
Service is given to people in all aspects of life.

This has been a thrilling and blessed ministry. The population in vast
rural areas has been confronted with the claims of Christ, in areas where
evangelists rarely or never reach by foot.

Campus Crusade For Christ International

In 1972 cooperation was established with Campus Crusade for Christ
International, and CCC staff held the first Lay Institute for Evangelism
in Cameroon in October, 1972. Other efforts are going forward in literature and mass media. The periodical, "Onward" has the largest circulation of any Protestant paper in Cameroon.

What about statistics?

In general we have not stressed the importance of statistics. When
over-emphasizing statistics of new converts, the Christians may be interested in getting a great number of "converts" and forget to follow
through with the new Christians, leading them into a Christian community
and helping them grow in their faith.

Furthermore, the National Campaign of Evangelism is not a "campaign" in the traditional meaning of the word. It is not a specific effort
for harvesting in a limited period. Rather it is an evangelistic movement
helping the churches to keep up the flame of evangelism. Thus the central
office for NCE does not keep any records of statistical results. The fruits
are registered in the local congregations.

The national secretary for evangelism reported, "We have just finished a week of NLFA meetings here in Poli. I was astonished to see the
crowds of people. During my twenty-three years of missionary service I
have not seen anything like it.

"During the visit of the Gospel teams at the Tikar plain many people
were touched by the Word of God and threw away their fetishes and left
their witchcraft practices demonstrating that they would trust their lives
entirely to Jesus Christ."

God has set an open door for the churches in Cameroon. Political
stability and peace leave a golden opportunity to preach the Gospel in
every corner of the country. The National Campaign of Evangelism is
not bound to follow only one specific type of evangelistic program. The
national center for evangelism will be a continuing resource, and a strategy center for the mobilization of churches and missions in Cameroon.
Other world evangelistic programs will be studied. We are open for the

use of any material and methods that can be adapted and effectively used in our country. Above all we rely upon the power of the Holy Spirit as the only force to change men and empower persons and churches for effective evangelism.

Let the earth hear his voice. Amen!

IN-DEPTH EVANGELISM
IN LATIN AMERICA

Orlando E. Costas

After a decade of Evangelism-In-Depth programs, Latin America has witnessed in the last three years a theoretical and practical expansion of the In-Depth Evangelism strategy. Firmly grounded on the concept of the mobilization of the church for the evangelization of the world, In-Depth Evangelism has moved away from the traditional one year program to a more comprehensive and multiphase approach to the church's fulfillment of the Great Commission. Let us briefly consider some of the main traits of In-Depth Evangelism as it is currently being carried out in Latin America.

First of all, In-Depth Evangelism in Latin America is attempting to awaken the church to the complicated nature of the world and the imperative of reaching every inch of it with the Gospel. This means pointing to the different dimensions of the world which together form the stage of human life: the geographic, the cultural, the structural, to mention just three. It implies calling attention to the fact that the church must take seriously the totality of the world and thus be concerned not only about the geographical penetration of the Gospel, but also about its cultural and sociological impact. Above all, this means helping the church to develop a matching comprehensiveness in resources, methods and strategic action in order to effectively meet the challenge of a world rightly characterized as a complicated conglomerate of peoples, places and relationships.

Secondly, In-Depth Evangelism in Latin America is attempting to recover the fullness of the evangelistic message by calling attention to the comprehensive reality which it announces. *If* the Kingdom of God, which the Gospel proclaims, is a new order of life characterized by the sovereign rule of God in Christ and his reconciling action in behalf of mankind, *if* this reality affects, as Scripture says, the personal present and future of the peoples of the earth as well as their collective present and future; *if* God's Kingdom manifests itself both in the personal life of those who enter therein, through the regenerating power of the Holy Spirit, as well as in the structures of society and the dynamics of culture, through the leavening function of the Gospel; *and if* in calling men and women to submit their lives to Christ, the King, it also addresses itself to their cultural ties and structural realities and calls them to repentance and obedience — *then* the communication of this message demands integrity. We need to recover in evangelism the biblical and dynamic fullness of the Gospel so that those who are invited to come into the Kingdom may have a clear perspective of what it is all about. And *this* is precisely one of the things that In-Depth Evangelism is trying to do in Latin America in this decade.

Beyond this, it is trying to call the church to the imperative of the mobilization of its *entire* constituency in order that she might experience *integral* growth. Such growth must involve the experience of the ingathering of new believers, the development of the church's internal structures, the deepening of her understanding of God's Word and an ever-greater participation in the afflictions of the world. This four-fold typology of church growth, which we have identified as four-dimensional growth, (numerical, organic, conceptual and incarnational), has led In-Depth Evangelism in Latin America to a multiplicity of interrelated programs. Some of them are geared for pastors and church leaders.

They are instructional and inspirational in scope. Others are research-oriented. They are analytical, diagnostical and evaluative and are meant to help the church take a good look at herself and at the world to which God sends her to evangelize, in order to develop the most effective means of accomplishing this task. Yet others are demonstrational. They are meant to provide concrete opportunities for organized efforts of evangelistic mobilization and involve as many activities as there are needs, opportunities and resources.

All of these types of In-Depth programs are being carried out in different parts of the Continent at different intervals and through different channels. They all have the same end: to help the entire Latin American evangelical church be what God wants her to be, that is, a *dynamic organism* and a *community* which is at once a living worshiping fellowship (God's people in action), a dynamic training center, and an effective evangelistic team involved in a continuous worldwide and deep outreach.

This is why I must disagree with Professor Peters' reference to In-Depth Evangelism as a national crusade. To be sure, there are crusades in demonstrational in-depth evangelistic programs. But to say that this is all there is to In-Depth Evangelism is to reflect a lack of up-to-date information as to its unique thrust. At least in Latin America, In-Depth Evangelism is fundamentally aiming at the mobilization of the whole church with all of her resources for *a comprehensive* approach to the evangelization of the whole world. It is not just a campaign to enlist as many believers as possible to do house-to-house visitation, to "saturate" their community with the Gospel, to establish house churches, or to gather great crowds for a series of public meetings. It involves this, of course, but it goes much farther — as far as stirring up the church to put all of her time, manpower and financial resources and all of her organizational and programmatic structures at the service of the Gospel of the Kingdom of God, to the end that evangelism be liberated from the tragedy which it has fallen into in many contemporary circles, namely, that of being a commercial, manipulative whitewash, and become, instead, a comprehensive enterprise where the Gospel is shared in depth and out of the depth of man's needs and life situations, so that the knowledge of Christ may one day truly cover the earth as the waters cover the sea.

THE HIGHEST PRIORITY: CROSS—CULTURAL EVANGELISM

Ralph D. Winter

Dr. Winter is Professor of
the History of the Christian Movement
in the School of World Mission at
Fuller Seminary, Pasadena, California
and Director of the William Carey
Library.

In recent years, a serious misunderstanding has crept into the thinking of many evangelicals. Curiously, it is based on a number of wonderful facts: the Gospel has now gone to the ends of the earth. Christians have now fulfilled the Great Commission in at least a geographical sense. At this moment of history, we can acknowledge with great respect and pride those evangelists of every nation who have gone before us and whose sacrificial efforts and heroic accomplishments have made Christianity by far the world's largest and most widespread religion, with a Christian church on every continent and in practically every country. This is no hollow victory. Now more than at any time since Jesus walked the shores of Galilee, we know with complete confidence that the Gospel is for all men, that it makes sense in any language, and that it is not merely a religion of the Mediterranean or of the West.

This is all true. On the other hand, many Christians as a result have the impression that the job is now nearly done and that to finish it we need only to forge ahead in local evangelism on the part of the now world-wide church, reaching out wherever it has already been planted. Many Christian organizations, ranging widely from the World Council of Churches to many U.S. denominations, even some evangelical groups, have rushed to the conclusion that we may now abandon traditional missionary strategy and count on local Christians everywhere to finish the job.

This is why *evangelism* is the one great password to evangelical unity today. Not everyone can agree on foreign mission strategies, but more people than ever agree on *evangelism,* because that seems to be the one obvious job that remains to be done. All right! There is nothing wrong with evangelism. Most conversions must inevitably take place as the result of some Christian witnessing to a near neighbor, and that is evangelism. The awesome problem is the additional truth that most non-Christians in the world today are not culturally near neighbors of any Christians, and that it will take a special kind of "cross-cultural" evangelism to reach them.

Cross-cultural evangelism: The crucial need.

Let us approach this subject with some graphic illustrations. I am thinking, for example, of the hundreds of thousands of Christians in Pakistan. Almost all of them are people who have never been Muslims and do not have the kind of relationship with the Muslim community that encourages witnessing. Yet they live in a country that is 97 per cent Muslim! The Muslims, on their part, have bad attitudes toward the stratum of society represented by the Christians. One group of Christians has boldly called itself *The Church of Pakistan*. Another group of Christians goes by the name, *The Presbyterian Church of Pakistan*. While these are "national" churches in the sense that they are part of the nation, they can hardly be called national churches if this phrase implies that they are culturally related to that vast bloc of people who constitute the other 97 per cent of the country, namely, the Muslims. Thus, although the Muslims are geographically near neighbors of these Christians, normal evangelism will not do the job.

Or take the Church of South India, a large church which has brought together the significant missionary efforts of many churches over the last century. But while it is called *The Church of South India*, 95 per cent of its members come from only five out of the more than 100 social classes (castes) in South India. Ordinary evangelism on the part of existing Christians will persuade men and women of those same five social classes. It would be much more difficult — it is in fact another kind of evangelism — for this church to make great gains within the 95 other social classes, which make up the vast bulk of the population.

Or take the great Batak church in Northern Sumatra. Here is one of the famous churches of Indonesia. Its members have been doing much evangelism among fellow Bataks, of whom there are still many thousands whom they can reach without learning a foreign language, and among whom they can work with maximum efficiency of direct contact and understanding. But at the same time, the vast majority of all the people in Indonesia speak other languages, and are of other ethnic units. For the Batak Christians of Northern Sumatra to win people to Christ from other parts of Indonesia will be a distinctly different kind of task. It is another kind of evangelism.

Or take the great church of Nagaland in Northeast India. Years ago, American missionaries from the plains of Assam reached up into the Naga hills and won some of the Ao Nagas. Then these Ao Nagas won practically their whole tribe to Christ. Next thing, Ao Nagas won members of the nearby Santdam Naga tribe, that spoke a sister language. These new Santdam Naga Christians then proceeded to win almost the whole of their tribe. This process went on until the majority of all fourteen Naga tribes became Christian. Now that most of Nagaland is Christian — even the officials of the state government are Christian — there is the desire to witness elsewhere in India. But for these Nagaland Christians to win other people in India is as much a foreign mission task as it is for Englishmen, Koreans, or Brazilians to evangelize in India. This is one reason why so far the Nagas have made no significant attempt to evangelize the rest of India. Indian citizenship is one advantage the Naga Christians have as compared to people from other countries, but citizenship does not make it easier for them to learn any of the hundreds of totally foreign languages in the rest of India.

In other words, for Nagas to evangelize other peoples in India, they will need to employ a radically different kind of evangelism. The easiest kind of evangelism, when they used their own language to win their own people, is now mainly in the past. The second kind of evangelism was not a great deal more difficult — where they won people of neighboring Naga tribes, whose languages were sister languages. The third kind of evangelism, needed to win people in far-off parts of India, will be much more difficult.

Let's give labels to these different kinds of evangelism. Where an Ao Naga won another Ao, let us call that *E-1 evangelism*. Where an Ao went across a tribal language boundary to a sister language and won the *Santdam*, we'll call it *E-2 evangelism*. (The E-2 task is not as easy and requires different techniques.) But then if an Ao Naga goes to another region of India, to a totally strange language, for example, Telegu, Korhu or Bhili, his task will be considerably more difficult than E-1 or even E-2 evangelism. We will call it *E-3 evangelism*.

Let us try out this terminology in another country. Take Taiwan. There also there are different kinds of people. The majority are Minnans, who were there before a flood of Mandarin-speaking people came across from the mainland. Then there is the huge bloc of Hakka-speaking people who came from the mainland much earlier. Up in the mountains, however a few hundred thousand aboriginal peoples speak Malayo-Polynesian dialects entirely different from Chinese. Now if a Mainlander Chinese Christian wins others from the mainland, that's E-1 evangelism. If he wins a Minnan Taiwanese or a Hakka, that's E-2 evangelism. If he wins someone from the hill tribes, that's E-3 evangelism, and remember, E-3 is a much more complex task, performed at a greater *cultural* distance.

Thus far we have only referred to language differences, but for the purpose of defining evangelistic strategy, any kind of obstacle, any kind of communication barrier affecting evangelism is significant. In Japan, for example, practically everybody speaks Japanese, and there aren't radically different dialects of Japanese comparable to the different dialects of Chinese. But there are social differences which make it very difficult for people from one group to win others of a different social class. In Japan, as in India, social differences often turn out to be more important in evangelism than language differences. Japanese Christians thus have not only an E-1 sphere of contact, but also E-2 spheres that are harder to reach. Missionaries going from Japan to other parts of the world to work with non-Japanese with totally different languages are doing an evangelistic task on the E-3 basis.

Lastly, let me give an example from my own experience. I speak English as a native language. For ten years, I lived and worked in Central America, for most of the time in Guatemala, where Spanish is the official language, but where a majority of the people speak some dialect of the Mayan family of aboriginal languages. I had two languages to learn. Spanish has a 60 per cent overlap in vocabulary with English, so I had no trouble learning that language. Along with the learning of Spanish, I became familiar with the extension of European culture into the New World, and it was not particularly difficult to understand the lifeways of the kind of people who spoke Spanish. However, because Spanish was so easy by comparison, learning the Mayan language in our area was, I found, enormously more difficult. In our daily work, switching from English to Spanish to a Mayan language made me quite aware of the three different "cultural distances." When I spoke of Christ to a

Peace Corpsman in English, I was doing E-1 evangelism. When I spoke to a Guatemalan in Spanish, it was E-2 evangelism. When I spoke to an Indian in the Mayan language, it was the much more difficult E-3 evangelism.

Now where I live in Southern California, most of my contacts are in the E-1 sphere, but if I evangelize among the million who speak Spanish, I must use E-2 evangelism. Were I to learn the Navajo language and speak of Christ to some of the 30,000 Navajo Indians who live in Los Angeles, I would be doing E-3 evangelism. Reaching Cantonese-speaking refugees from Hong Kong with the Good News of Christ would also be, for me, an E-3 task. Note, however, that what for me is E-3 could be only E-2 for someone else. American-born Chinese would find Hong Kong refugees only an E-2 task.

Everyone who is here in this Congress has his own E-1 sphere in which he speaks his own language and builds on all the intuition which derives from his experience within his own culture. Then perhaps for almost all of us there is an E-2 sphere — groups of people who speak languages that are a little different, or who are involved in culture patterns sufficiently in contrast with our own as to make communication more difficult. Such people can be reached with a little extra trouble and with sincere attempts, but it will take us out of our way to reach them. More important, they are people who, once converted, will not feel at home in the church which we attend. In fact, they may grow faster spiritually if they can find Christian fellowship among people of their own kind. More significant to evangelism: it is quite possible that with their own fellowship, they are more likely to win others of their own social grouping. Finally, each of us here in Lausanne has an E-3 sphere: most languages and cultures of the world are totally strange to us; they are at the maximum cultural distance. If we attempt to evangelize at this E-3 distance, we have a long uphill climb in order to be able to make sense to anyone.

In summary, the master pattern of the expansion of the Christian movement is first for special E-2 and E-3 efforts to cross cultural barriers into new communities and to establish strong, on-going, vigorously evangelizing denominations, and then for that national church to carry the work forward on the really high-powered E-1 level. We are thus forced to believe that until every tribe and tongue has a strong, powerfully evangelizing church in it, and thus, an E-1 witness within it, E-2 and E-3 efforts coming from outside are still essential and highly urgent.

Cross-cultural evangelism: The Biblical mandate

At this point, let us ask what the Bible says about all this. Are these cultural differences something the Bible takes note of? Is this something which ought to occupy our time and attention? Is this matter of cultural distance something which is so important that it fits into a Congress like this? Let us turn to the Bible and see what it has to say.

Let us go to that vital passage in the first chapter of Acts, so central to this whole Congress, where Jesus refers his disciples to the worldwide scope of God's concern — "in Jerusalem, in all Judea, and in Samaria, and into the uttermost part of the earth." If it were not for this passage (and all the other passages in the Bible which support it) we would not even be gathered here today. Without this biblical mandate, there could not have been a Congress on World Evangelization. It is precisely this task — the task of discipling all the nations — which includes all of us and unifies all of us in a single, common endeavor. Notice, however, that Jesus does not merely include the whole world. He distinguishes between different parts of that world and does so according to the relative distance of those people from his hearers. On another occasion he simply said, "Go ye into all the world," but in this passage he has divided that task into significant components.

At first glance you might think that he is merely speaking geographically, but with more careful study, it seems clear that he is not talking merely about *geographical* distance, but about *cultural* distance. The clue is the appearance of the word *Samaria* in this sequence. Fortunately, we have special insight into what Jesus meant by *Samaria,* since the New Testament records in an extended passage the precise nature of the evangelistic problem Jews faced in trying to reach the Samaritans. I speak of the well-known story of Jesus and the woman at the well. Samaria was not far away in the geographical sense. Jesus had to pass there whenever he went from Galilee to Jerusalem. Yet when Jesus spoke to this Samaritan woman, it was immediately obvious that he faced a special cultural obstacle. While she was apparently close enough linguistically for him to be able to understand her speech, her very first reply focused on the significant difference between the Jews and the Samaritans — they worshiped in different places. Jesus did not deny this profound difference, but accepted it and transcended it by pointing out the human, cultural limitations of both the Jewish and the Samaritan modes of worship. He spoke to her heart and by-passed the cultural differences.

Meanwhile, the disciples looking on were mystified and troubled. Even had they understood that God was interested in Samaritans, they probably would have had difficulty grappling with the cultural differences. Even if they had tried to do so, they might not have been sensitive enough to by-pass certain differences and go directly to the heart of the matter — which was the heart of the woman.

Paul acted on the same principle when he sought to evangelize the Greeks, who were at an even greater cultural distance. Just imagine how shocked some of the faithful Jewish Christians were when they heard rumors that Paul by-passed circumcision, one of the most important cultural differences to the Jews, even Christian Jews, and went to the heart of the matter. He was reported to them as saying, "Neither circumcision nor uncircumcision is worth anything in comparison to being in Christ, believing in him, being baptized in his name, being filled with his Spirit, belonging to his body."

At this point we must pause long enough to distinguish between cultural distance and walls of prejudice. There may have been high *walls of prejudice* involved where Jews encountered Samaritans, but it is obvious that the Greeks, who did not even worship the same God, were at a far greater *cultural distance* from the Jews than were the Samaritans, who were close cousins by comparison. It is curious to note that sometimes those who are closest to us are hardest to reach. For example, a Jewish Christian trying to evangelize would understand a Samaritan more easily than he would understand a Greek, but he would be more likely to be hated or detested by a Samaritan than by a Greek. In Belfast today, for example, the problem is not so much cultural distance as prejudice. Suppose a Protestant who had grown up in Belfast were to witness for Christ to a nominal Belfast Catholic and an East Indian. He would more easily understand his Catholic compatriot, but would face less prejudice from the East Indian. Generally speaking, then, cultural distance is more readily traversed than high walls of prejudice are climbed.

But, returning to our central passage, it is clear that Jesus is referring primarily neither to geography nor walls of prejudice when he lists *Judea, Samaria,* and *the ends of the earth.* Had he been talking about prejudice, Samaria would have come last. He would have said, "in Judea, in all the world, and *even in Samaria."* It seems likely he is taking into account cultural distance as the primary factor. Thus, as we today endeavor to fulfill Jesus' ancient command, we do well to be sensitive to *cultural distance.* His distinctions must underlie our strategic thinking about the evangelization of the whole world.

Evangelism in the Jerusalem and Judea sphere would seem to be what we have called *E-1 evangelism,* where the only barrier his listeners had to cross in their proposed evangelistic efforts was the boundary between the Christian community and the world immediately outside, involving the same language and culture. This is "near neighbor" evangelism. Whoever we are, wherever we live in the world, we all have some near neighbors to whom we can witness without learning any foreign language or taking into account any special cultural differences. This is the kind of evangelism we usually talk about. This is the kind of evangelism most meetings on evangelism talk about. One of the great differences between this Congress and all previous congresses on evangelism is its determined stress on *crossing cultural frontiers where necessary* in order to evangelize the whole earth. The mandate of this Congress does not allow us to focus merely on Jerusalem and Judea.

The second sphere to which Jesus referred is that of the Samaritan. The Bible account shows that although it was relatively easy for Jesus and his disciples to make themselves understood to the Samaritans, the Jew and the Samaritan were divided from each other by a frontier consisting of dialectal distinctions and some other very significant cultural differences. This was *E-2 evangelism,* because it involved crossing a *second* frontier. First, it involved crossing the frontier we have referred to in describing E-1 evangelism, the frontier between the church and the world. Secondly, it involved crossing a frontier constituted by significant (but not monumental) differences of language and culture. Thus we call it *E-2 evangelism.*

E-3 evangelism, as we have used the phrase, involves even greater cultural distance. This is the kind of evangelism that is necessary in the third sphere of Jesus' statement, "to the uttermost part of the earth." The people needing to be reached in this third sphere live, work, talk, and think in languages and cultural patterns utterly different from those native to the evangelist. The average Jewish Christian, for example, would have had no head start at all in dealing with people beyond Samaria. If reaching Samaritans seemed like crossing two frontiers (thus called E-2 evangelism), reaching totally different people must have seemed like crossing three, and it is reasonable to call such a task *E-3 evangelism.*

It is very important to understand the full significance of the distinctions Jesus is making. Since he was not talking about geographical, but cultural distance, the general value of what he said has striking strategic application today. Jesus did not mean that all down through history Samaria specifically would be an object of special attention. One Christian's Judea might be another Christian's Samaria. Take Paul, for example. Although he was basically a Jew, he no doubt found it much easier to traverse the cultural distance to the Greeks than did Peter, because unlike Peter, Paul was much better acquainted with the Greek world. Using the terminology we have employed, where an E-1 task is near, E-2 is close, and E-3 is far (in *cultural*, not geographical distance), we can say that reaching Greeks meant working at an E-2 distance for Paul; but for Peter it meant working at an E-3 distance. For Luke, who was himself a Greek, reaching Greeks was to work only at an E-1 distance. Thus what was distant for Peter was near for Luke. And vice versa: reaching Jews would have been E-1 for Peter, but more likely E-3 for Luke. It may well be that God sent Paul rather than Peter to the Gentiles partially because Paul was closer culturally. By the same token, Paul, working among the Greeks at an E-2 distance, was handicapped by comparison with E-1 "nationals" like Luke, Titus, and Epaphroditus; and, as a matter of evangelistic strategy, he wisely turned things over to "national" workers as soon as he possibly could. Paul himself, being a Jew, often began his work in a new city in the Jewish synagogue where he himself was on an E-1 basis and where, with the maximum power of E-1 communication, he was able to speak forcefully without any non-Jewish accent.

Let us straightforwardly concede right here that, all other things being equal, the national leader always has a communication advantage over the foreigner. When the evangelists went from the plains of Assam up into the Naga hills, it must have been very much harder for them to win Ao Nagas than it was for Ao Naga Christians to do so, once a start had been made. When the first German missionaries preached to the Bataks, they must have had a far greater problem than when the faith, once planted, was transmitted from Batak to Batak. E-1 evangelism — where a person communicates to his own people — is obviously the most potent kind of evangelism. People need to hear the Gospel in their own language. Can we believe God intends for them to hear it from people who speak without a trace of accent? The foreign missionary communicator may be good, but he is not good enough. If it is so important for Americans to have thirty translations of the New Testament to choose from, and even a "Living Bible," which allows the Bible to speak in colloquial English, then why must many peoples around the world suffer along with a Bible that was translated for them by a foreigner, and thus almost inevitably speaks to them in halting phrases?

This is why the easiest, most obvious surge forward in evangelism in the world today will come if Christian believers in every part of the world are moved to reach outside their churches and win their cultural near neighbors to Christ. They are better able to do that than any foreign missionary. It is tragic perversion of Jesus' strategy if we continue to send missionaries to do the job that local Christians can do better. There is no excuse for a missionary in the pulpit when a national can do the job better. There is no excuse for a missionary to be doing evangelism on an E-3 basis, at an E-3 distance from people, when there are local Christians who are effectively winning the same people as part of their E-1 sphere.

In view of the profound truth that (other things being equal) E-1 evangelism is more powerful than E-2 or E-3 evangelism, it is easy to see how some people have erroneously concluded that E-3 evangelism is therefore out-of-date, due to the wonderful fact that there are now Christians throughout the whole world. It is with this perspective that major denominations in the U.S. have at some points acted on the premise that there is no more need for missionaries of the kind who leave home to go to a foreign country and struggle with a totally strange language and culture. Their premise is that "there are Christians over there already." With the drastic fall-off in the value of the U.S. dollar and the tragic shrinking of U.S. church budgets, some U.S. denominations have had to curtail their missionary activity to an unbelievable extent, and they have in part tried to console themselves by saying that it is time for the national church to take over. In our response to this situation, we must happily agree that wherever there are local Christians effectively evangelizing, there is nothing more potent than E-1 evangelism.

However, the truth about the superior power of E-1 evangelism must not obscure the obvious fact that E-1 evangelism is literally *impossible* where there are no witnesses within a given language or cultural group. Jesus, as a Jew, would not have had to witness directly to that Samaritan woman had there been a local Samaritan Christian who had already reached her. In the case of the Ethiopian eunuch, we can conjecture that it might have been better for an Ethiopian Christian than for Philip to do the witnessing, but there had to be an initial contact by a non-Ethiopian in order for the E-1 process to be set in motion. This kind of initial, multiplying work is the primary task of the missionary when he rightly understands his job. He must decrease and the national leader must increase. Hopefully Jesus' E-2 witness set in motion E-1 witnessing in that Samaritan town. Hopefully Philip's E-2 witness to the Ethiopian set in motion E-1 witnessing back in Ethiopia. If that Ethiopian was an Ethiopian Jew, the E-1 community back in Ethiopia might not have been very large, and might not have effectively reached the non-Jewish Ethiopians. As a matter of fact, scholars believe that the Ethiopian church today is the result of a much later missionary thrust that reached, by E-3 evangelism, clear through to the ethnic Ethiopians.

Thus, in the Bible as in our earlier illustrations from modern mission history, we arrive at the same summary:

The master pattern of the expansion of the Christian movement is first for special E-2 and E-3 efforts to cross cultural barriers into new communities and to establish strong, on-going, vigorously evangelizing denominations, and then for that national church to carry the work forward on the really high-powered E-1 level. We are thus forced to believe that until every tribe and tongue has a strong, powerfully evangelizing church in it, and thus an E-1 witness within it, E-2 and E-3 efforts coming from outside are still essential and highly urgent. From this perspective, how big is the remaining task?

Cross-cultural evangelism:
The immensity of the task

Unfortunately, most Christians have only a very foggy idea of just how many peoples there are in the world among whom there is no E-1 witness. But fortunately, preparatory studies for this Congress have seriously raised this question: Are there any tribal tongues and linguistic units which have not yet been penetrated by the Gospel? If so, where? How many? Who can reach them? Even these preliminary studies indicate that cross-cultural evangelism must still be the highest priority. Far from being a task that is now out-of-date, the shattering truth is that at least four out of five non-Christians in the world today are beyond the reach of *any* Christian's E-1 evangelism.

Why is this fact not more widely known? I'm afraid that all our exultation about the fact that every *country* of the world has been penetrated has allowed many to suppose that every *culture* has by now been penetrated. This misunderstanding is a malady so widespread that it deserves a special name. Let us call it "people blindness" that is, blindness to the existence of separate *peoples* within *countries;* a blindness, I might add, which seems more prevalent in the U.S. and among U.S. missionaries than anywhere else. The Bible rightly translated could have made this plain to us. The "nations" to which Jesus often referred were mainly ethnic groups within the single political structure of the Roman government. The various nations represented on the day of Pentecost were for the most part not *countries* but *peoples*. In the Great Commission as it is found in Matthew, the phrase "make disciples of all *ethne* (peoples)" does not let us off the hook once we have a church in every country — God wants a strong church within every people!

"People blindness" is what prevents us from noticing the sub-groups within a country which are significant to development of effective evangelistic strategy. Society will be seen as a complex mosaic, to use McGavran's phrase, once we recover from "people blindness." But until we all recover from this kind of blindness, we may confuse the legitimate desire for church or national unity with the illegitimate goal of uniformity. God apparently loves diversity of certain kinds. But in any case this diversity means evangelists have to work harder. The little ethnic and cultural pieces of the complex mosaic which is human society are the very subdivisions which isolate four out of five non-Christians in the world today from an E-1 contact by existing Christians. The immensity of the cross-cultural task is thus seen in the fact that in Africa and Asia alone, one calculation has it that there are 1,993 million people virtually without a witness. The immensity of the task, however, lies not only in its bigness.

The problem is more serious than retranslating the Great Commission in such a way that the peoples, not the countries, become the targets for evangelism. The immensity of the task is further underscored by the far greater complexity of the E-2 and E-3 task. Are we in America, for example, prepared for the fact that most non-Christians yet to be won to Christ (even in our country) will not fit readily into the kinds of churches we now have? The bulk of American churches in the North are middle-class, and the blue-collar worker won't go near them. Evangelistic crusades may attract thousands to big auditoriums and win people in their homes through television, but a large proportion of the newly converted, unless already familiar with the church, may drift away simply because there is no church where they will feel at home. Present-day American Christians can wait forever in their cozy, middle-class pews for the world to come to Christ and join them. But unless they adopt E-2 methods and both *go out after these people and help them found their own churches,* evangelism in America will face, and is already facing, steadily diminishing returns. You may say that there are still plenty of people who don't go to church who are of the same cultural background as those in church. This is true. But there are many, many more people of differing cultural backgrounds who, even if they were to become fervent Christians, would not feel comfortable in existing churches.

If the U.S. — where you can drive 3,000 miles and still speak the same language — is nevertheless a veritable cultural mosaic viewed evangelistically, then surely most other countries face similar problems. Even in the U.S., local radio stations employ more than forty different languages. In addition to these language differences, there are many equally significant social and cultural differences. Language differences are by no means the highest barriers to communication.

The need, in E-2 evangelism, for whole new worshiping groups is underscored by the phenomenon of the Jesus People, who have founded hundreds of new congregations. The vast Jesus People Movement in the U.S. does not speak a different language so much as it involves a very different life-style and thus a different style of worship. Many American churches have attempted to employ the guitar music and many of the informal characteristics of the Jesus Movement, but there is a limit to which a single congregation can go with regard to speaking many languages and employing many life-styles. Who knows what has happened to many of the "mods" and "rockers" who were won as a result of Billy Graham's London Crusades? On the one hand, the existing churches were understandably culturally distant from such people, and on the other hand, there may not have been adequate E-2 methods employed so as to form those converts into whole new congregations. It is this aspect of E-2 evangelism which makes the cross-cultural task immensely harder. Yet it is essential. Let us take one more well-known example.

When John Wesley evangelized the miners of England, the results were conserved in whole new worshiping congregations. There probably would never have been a Methodist movement had he not encouraged these lower-class people to meet in their own Christian gatherings, sing their own kind of songs, and associate with their own kind of people. Furthermore, apart from this E-2 technique, such people would not have been able to win others and expand the Christian movement in this new level of society at such an astonishing rate of speed. The results rocked and permanently changed England. It rocked the existing churches, too. Not very many people favored Wesley's contact with the miners. Fewer still agreed that miners should have separate churches!

At this point we may do well to make a clear procedural distinction between E-1 and E-2 evangelism. We have observed that the E-2 sphere begins where the people you have reached are of sufficiently different backgrounds from those of people in existing churches that they need to form their own worshiping congregations in order best to win others of their own kind. John, chapter four, tells us that "many Samaritans from that city believed in him (Jesus) because of the woman's testimony." Jesus evangelized the woman by working with great sensitivity as an E-2 witness; she turned around and reached others in her town by efficient E-1 communication. Suppose Jesus had told her she had to go and worship with the Jews. Even if she had obeyed him and gone to worship with the Jews, she would on that basis have been terribly handicapped in winning others in her city. Jesus may actually have avoided the issue of where to worship and with what distant Christians to associate. That would come up later. Thus the Samaritans who believed the woman's testimony then made the additional step of inviting a Jew to be with them for two days. He still did not try to make them into Jews. He knew he was working at an E-2 distance, and that the fruits could best be conserved (and additional people best be won) if they were allowed to build *their own fellowship of faith.*

A further distinction might be drawn between the kind of cultural differences Jesus was working with in Samaria and the kind of differences resulting from the so-called "generation gap." But it really does not matter, in evangelism, whether the distance is cultural, linguistic, or an age difference. No matter what the reason for the difference or the permanence of the difference, or the perceived rightness or the wrongness of the difference, the procedural dynamics of E-2 evangelism techniques are quite similar. The E-2 sphere begins whenever it is necessary to found a new congregation. In the Philippines we hear of youth founding churches. In Singapore we know of ten recently established youth break-away congregations. Hopefully, eventually, age-focused congregations will draw closer to existing churches, but as long as there is a generation gap of serious proportions, such specialized fellowships are able to win many more alienated youth by being allowed to function considerably on their own. It is a good place to begin.

Whatever we may decide about the kind of E-2 evangelism that allows people to meet separately who are different due to temporary *age differences,* the chief factors in the immensity of the cross-cultural task are the much more profound and possibly permanent *cultural differences.* Here too some will always say that true cross-cultural evangelism is going too far. At this point we must risk being misunderstood in order to be absolutely honest. All around the world, special evangelistic efforts continue to be made which often break across culture barriers. People from these other cultures are won, sometimes only one at a time, sometimes in small groups. The problem is not in winning them; it is in the cultural obstacles to proper follow-up. Existing churches may cooperate up to a point with evangelistic campaigns, but they do not contemplate allowing the evangelistic organizations to stay long enough to gather these people together in churches of their own. They mistakenly think that being joined to Christ ought to include joining existing churches. Yet if proper E-2 methods were employed, these few converts, who would merely be considered somewhat odd additions to existing congregations, *could* be infusions of new life into whole new pockets of society where the church does not now exist at all!

A discussion of the best ways to organize for cross-cultural evangelism is beyond the scope of this paper. It would entail a great deal of space to chart the successes and failures of different approaches by churches and by para-church organizations. It may well be that E-2 and E-3 methods are best launched by specialized agencies and societies working loyally and harmoniously with the churches. Here we must focus on the nature of cross-cultural evangelism and its high priority in the face of the immensity of the task. Aside from the Chinese mainland sector, the two greatest spheres in which there is a tragic paucity of effective cross-cultural evangelism are the Muslim and the Hindu. Our concluding words will center on these two groups, which in aggregate number well over one billion (1,000,000,000) people.

As we have earlier mentioned, a converted Muslim will not feel welcome in the usual Presbyterian Church in Pakistan. Centuries-old suspicions on both sides of the Muslim-Hindu fence make it almost impossible for Muslims, even converted Muslims, to be welcomed into the churches of former Hindu peoples. The present Christians of Pakistan (almost all formerly Hindu) have not been at all successful in integrating converted Muslims into their congregations. Furthermore, it is not likely to occur to them that Muslims can be converted and form their own separate congregations. The enormous tragedy is that this kind of impasse postpones serious evangelism along E-2 lines wherever in the world there are any of the 664 million Muslims. Far to the east of Mecca, in certain parts of Indonesia enough Muslims have become Christians that they have not been forced one by one to join Christian congregations of another culture. Far to the west of Mecca, in the middle of Africa on some of the islands of Lake Chad we have reports that a few former Muslims, now Christians, still pray to Christ five times a day and worship in Christian churches on Friday, the Muslim day of worship. These two isolated examples suggest that Muslims can become Christians without necessarily undergoing serious and arbitrary cultural dislocation. There may be a wide, new, open door to the Muslims if we will be as cross-culturally alert as Paul was, who did not require the Greeks to become Jews in order to become acceptable to God.

Vast *new* realms of opportunity may exist in India, too, where local prejudice in many cases may forestall effective "near-neighbor" evangelism. Indians coming from a greater distance might by E-2 or E-3 methods be able to escape the local stigmas and establish churches within the 100 or so social classes as yet untouched. It is folly for evangelists to ignore such factors of prejudice, and their existence greatly increases the immensity of our task. Prejudice of this kind adds to cultural distance such obstacles that E-2 evangelism where prejudice is deep is often more difficult than E-3 evangelism. In other words, scholarly, well-educated Christians from Nagaland or Kerala might possibly be more successful in reaching middle-class Hindus in South India with the Gospel than Christians from humble classes who have grown up in that area and speak the same language, but are stigmatized in local relationships. But who dares to point this out? It is ironic that national Christians all over the non-Western world are increasingly aware that they do not need to be Westernized to be Christian, yet they may in some cases be slow to sense that the challenge of cross-cultural evangelism requires them to allow other people in their own areas to have the same liberty of self-determination in establishing culturally divergent churches of their own.

In any case, the opportunities are just as immense as the task. If 600 million Muslims await a more enlightened evangelism, there are also 500 million Hindus who today face monumental obstacles to becoming Christians other than the profound spiritual factors inherent in the Gospel. One keen observer is convinced that 100 million middle-class Hindus await the opportunity to become Christians — but there are no churches for them to join which respect their dietary habits and customs. Is the kingdom of God meat and drink? To go to the special efforts required by E-2 and E-3 evangelism is not to let down the standards and make the Gospel easy — it is to disentangle the irrelevant elements and to make the Gospel clear. Perhaps everyone is not able to do this special kind of work. True, many more E-1 evangelists will eventually be necessary to finish the task. But the highest priority in evangelism today is to develop the cross-cultural knowledge and sensitivities involved in E-2 and E-3 evangelism. Where necessary, evangelists from a distance must be called into the task. Nothing must blind us to the immensely important fact that at least *four fifths* of the non-Christians in the world today will never have any straightforward opportunity to become Christians unless the Christians themselves go more than halfway in the specialized tasks of cross-cultural evangelism. Here is our highest priority.

THE HIGHEST PRIORITY:
CROSS-CULTURAL EVANGELISM
Ralph D. Winter

I am deeply grateful to each of these men who have preceded me and for the time they have spent reading my paper and responding to it. I cannot blame them if they did not always understand what I meant. I am sure what I wrote was not entirely clear. In almost no case am I in any disagreement with their emphases. Often they have added things which I would have put in myself had I had more space.

In particular, may I say how very grateful I am to Pablo Pérez and Philip Hogan for their emphasis upon the spiritual factors, which in many cases override all others in importance. However, I am sure that they are not trying to say that the presence of the Holy Spirit in our lives does away with the need for any active intellectual analysis. In the headquarters of Dr. Hogan's church in Springfield, Missouri, the Holy Spirit has superintended them in an immense amount of tough thinking and analysis, or they would not be operating the largest printing establishment in the state of Missouri, nor would they have been one of the very first of the mission agencics in the United States to make extensive use of computer facilities. Quite obviously, there is no conflict, rightly understood, between the guidance of the Holy Spirit and the need for careful, patient, analytical thinking.

It is evident that we must not fail to distinguish between what we may expect *God* to do and what God may legitimately expect *us* to do. For example, I feel sure that God, if he wished to, would be able by his Holy Spirit to eliminate language differences and merge everyone into a single congregation. But we must respect the fact that the outpouring of the Holy Spirit in the New Testament did not eliminate the Greek language, nor the Greek culture, but in fact allowed an additional Greek-speaking church tradition where there was only a Jewish church before. There may have been many Jewish Christians who fervently wished the Greeks would follow their form of worship, but God apparently had other plans.

Dr. Pérez has helpfully stressed the fact that the Gospel changes human cultures; it does not merely yield to them. He, of course, is speaking *within* a culture as an E-1 evangelist. This is the proper attitude. But if Dr. Pérez were to go to a foreign country to a new situation, he would then be in a different situation, and would have to be very respectful of the culture and not fight against it as he knows how to do within his own culture. I, for example, in my own ministry in a foreign situation, had to learn to respect and not to fight much of the aboriginal culture lest I myself confuse *my* culture with the Gospel.

Now in regard to Dr. Loewen's paper, one of the misunderstandings which we discovered only yesterday afternoon is that my use of the phrase "near-neighbor evangelism" is confined to the E-1 sphere, whereas he is taking it to mean E-1 *and E-2.* If I were to mean what he meant by the phrase, then I would come out with the same statements that he has, which naturally reduces the proposal that "four out of five non-Christians are beyond the reach of near-neighbor evangelism." I also appreciate very much the fact that he has underscored the great complexity of E-3 evangelism. As an anthropologist, he seems almost to say that witnessing to totally strange people is so difficult that it ought not to be attempted. I would agree except to add the provision that E-3 evangelism, however difficult it may be, must be attempted at all costs where there is no reasonable possibility of effective E-1 and E-2 evangelism. There are, as an example, hundreds of thousands of Christians in Ethiopia today who would not know Christ, and who would not have the Bible, had evangelical Christians from other lands stayed home and simply insisted that the local Coptic church should do the job. In Ethiopia and in countless other situations, both in the past and in the future, E-1 and E-2 evangelism is not a viable option, and in that case the extraordinarily difficult E-3 distance must be traversed by someone who is obedient to that level of hazard and difficulty which Dr. Loewen so rightly underscores.

For these reasons, therefore, I feel I must applaud the plans being laid by David Cho and others in Asia for 100 Asian missionaries to go to that great island of Kalimantan. This will surely speed up, not hinder, world evangelization. And there is still another island, the world's largest, once called New Guinea. In the western half alone, indeed in just the immense swampy southern section of the western half — a swamp so large that someone said the largest swamp in Florida looks like a phone booth by comparison — there are 380 tribal languages in which the Gospel is not yet preached. Only with bold planning and prayerful obedience will these people soon be reached for Christ, but we cannot expect near-neighbor evangelism of any type to reach them in this century. If Korean E-3 missionaries can join forces there with the present tiny crew of Western agencies, this will be a splendid example of East-West partnership in a new modern era of cross-cultural evangelism.

I might add that there are other reasons for E-3 contacts being maintained even after a church is born. One is the need we all have for what René Padilla called "cross-fertilization." E-3 is maximally tough, but it is maximally stimulating. God has not meant for his world family to persist in cultural ghettos. He has not intended, on the one hand, to merge the whole family into a single culture. On the other hand, he does not want ghettos. The body of Christ can be healthy only if there are separate organs, *and* the separate organs serve each other. The two-way flow of E-3 personnel is a most important phenomenon which must increase not decrease in the life of the world Christian family.

Let me now turn to the many hundreds of responses I have received from other participants in the Congress. I deeply value and intend to save every one of your papers that came to me. Practically all the questions either concerned the statistical *scope* of the task or the theological *nature* of the task.

Questions about the statistical scope of the task

Let us consider first the *scope* of the task. Figure 1 is an attempt to sum it up. Jesus said that no man builds a tower without first sitting down and calculating the cost. Here at this Congress we must sit down and assess the task of world evangelization.

CHRISTIANS	Western	Africa	Asia	TOTAL	
Nurture	120	40	40	200	
E-0 Renewal	845	76	58	979	
	965	116	98	1179	
NON-CHRISTIANS					
E-1 Ord. Ev.	180	82	74	336	----13%
E-2, E-3, CC Ev.	147	200	2040	2387	----87%
	327	282	2114	2723	
GRAND TOTAL	1292	398	2212	3902	

Figure 1

Note that the numbers above are all in *millions* of people in the world today. You will see I have first divided between those who call themselves Christians and those who do not call themselves Christians, and you will see in the column on the far right that the total number of Christians is 1179 million, and the total number of non-Christians is 2723 million.

I want you to think for a moment about this latter number — 2700 million. Do you notice that this is about one million people for each participant in this Congress? (This means that if each of you all had been busy and had won a million people on your way here, we would have been able to disband the Congress!) These two numbers, 1179 and 2723, are, of course, not precise counts except at a certain date — since the population clock tells us such numbers are constantly changing. For example, the number of Christians, 1179 million, is increasing by 70,000 each day we are gathered here. If we had an evangelism clock in addition to a population clock, it would register the number of additional Christians each minute. For example, from the opening of this Congress until now, four days later, the number of Christians in the world has grown more than a quarter of a million. If we had a really sophisticated clock, we could even record the fact that each day in practically every country of the world, the *percentage* of Christians is also increasing. I add these comments lest anyone shrink from the task of evangelizing the massive numbers of non-Christians in Figure 1. I don't want you to wonder if there is any hope of being successful in world evangelization. Dear brothers and sisters, we *are* being successful right now, and we surely have no *statistical* reason not to make definite plans here at this Congress to move ahead with Jesus Christ, Lord of History, to finish the task of world evangelization.

In other words, the numbers in the last column are only apparently static. They do not show the fact that we are constantly gaining in the Christian percentage in all columns, that is, in the Western World, in Africa, and in Asia. (Australia and Latin America are included in the Western World; the Pacific I am including in the Asia column.)

You will now note that both the Christian and the non-Christian populations have been further divided. The Christian group is divided into the committed Christians, who need nurture; and nominal Christians, who need renewal. Then the non-Christians are also divided in two groups,

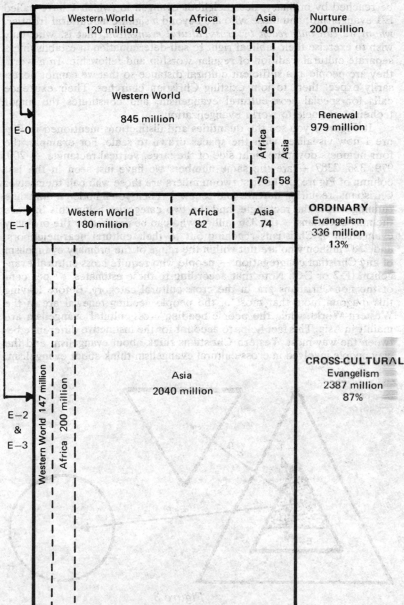

Figure 2.

this distinction being the heart of my whole presentation: those who can be reached by ordinary, near-neighbor evangelism (which I have called E-1 evangelism); and those who are beyond a significant cultural frontier, *whom we can only reach by cross-cultural evangelism,* that is, who may wish to exercise their biblical right to self-determination in establishing a separate cultural tradition of regular worship and fellowship. In a word, they are people at a sufficient cultural distance so that we cannot necessarily expect them to join existing Christian churches. Their existence calls for special cross-cultural evangelism, and constitutes the major technical obstacle to world evangelization.

In Figure 2 you see the quantities and distinctions mentioned in Figure 1 now visualized with the spaces drawn to scale. For example, the four numbers down the right side of the large, vertical rectangle — 200, 979, 336, 2387 — are the same numbers we have just seen in the last column of Figure 1. The first two numbers are those who call themselves Christians, requiring nurture and renewal. Then you'll notice a dark line running across the rectangle, and the two categories below this line are the non-Christians — the 336 million who can be reached by the ordinary evangelism of Christians reaching out to their cultural near-neighbors, and 2387 million who are not within the range of the ordinary evangelism of any Christian congregation — people who require cross-cultural evangelism (E-2 or E-3). Note that according to these estimates, 87 per cent of the non-Christians are in the cross-cultural category. Before leaving this diagram, note that most of the people needing renewal are in the Western World, while the people needing cross-cultural evangelism are mainly in Asia. This fact helps to account for the instinctive difference between the way most Western Christians think about evangelism and the way people involved in cross-cultural evangelism think about evangelism.

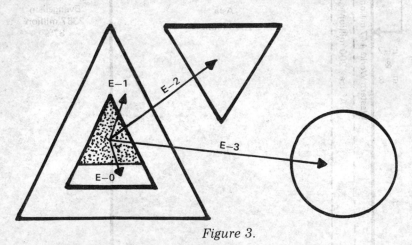

Figure 3.

Now let's look at Figure 3. Here you see a small triangle representing the Christian community, from which four arrows emerge. One arrow, labeled E-0, is aimed into a sector within the Christian community. This is the winning of nominal Christians to personal faith and commitment — the "evangelical experience." This E-0 evangelism involves just as much a spiritual experience as E-1, E-2, or E-3 evangelism, but there is no cultural distance involved — hence the zero. The arrow labeled E-1 goes out of the church into the culture within which the church is at home, the only barrier being the "stained-glass barrier" between the church and the world. People in this area, if converted, will feel at home in existing churches. However, the E-2 arrow reaches outside this culture into a similar culture that is nevertheless sufficiently different to make the founding of separate congregations desirable to act as a base for effective outreach to others in that same culture. The E-3 arrow involves similar church-planting implications, but reaches out to a totally strange culture (the circle).

I hope this doesn't seem too complicated. It is a help when looking at any country or region of the world to size up the situation by making a rough estimate of the number of people in each of these five categories which the diagram in Figure 3 gives us: First, there are the committed Christians (shaded area) who are the only active agents you can count on to do the work. Next there are the four kinds of people who are not committed Christians and who are either at a 0, 1, 2, or 3 cultural distance away from the committed Christians. Following this scheme, you can divide the people in a small town into these five categories. Or you can make estimates of the number of people in these five categories for a whole country. This seems to be helpful to size up the task.

I have done this by way of example in the diagrams in Figure 4. The first three diagrams are for three different sections of the non-Western world, where from left to right there is a progressively greater number of committed Christians. (In these diagrams I have not distinguished between the E-2 and E-3 areas because they are both cross-cultural evangelism and therefore usually require founding new churches.) The fourth diagram — the Western World — shows the close comparison between the South Pacific and Western World. In both cases a high proportion of the people are at least nominal Christians, and this means the need for cross-cultural evangelism internal to the regions may not seem so important to people in these areas.

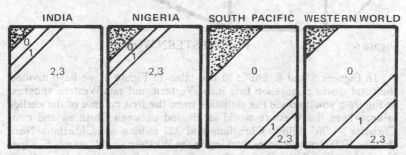

| INDIA | NIGERIA | SOUTH PACIFIC | WESTERN WORLD |

Figure 4.

On the other hand, India and Nigeria are more typical of all the rest of the world, and that is why cross-cultural evangelism is of the highest priority in the non-Western world. Let me repeat that although there are a lot of Christians in India, this must not obscure the fact that most of the people in India are at a *cross-cultural* distance from any Christian congregation whatsoever.

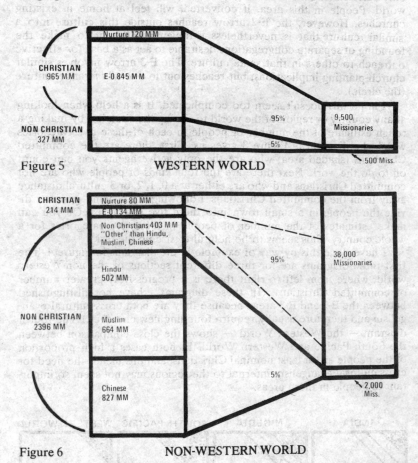

Figure 5   WESTERN WORLD

Figure 6   NON-WESTERN WORLD

In Figures 5 and 6, unlike in the table in Figure 1, we have divided the total world population first into Western and non-Western spheres. In Figure 5 you'll notice the statistics from the first column of the earlier table, where the Western world is divided between Christian and non-Christian — 965 million Christians and 327 million non-Christians. Note that the 10,000 missionaries working in the Western world (mainly Europe, North America, Latin America) are focusing almost all of their efforts on the nominal Christian sphere while only a fairly small percentage, according to my estimates, are really concentrating on people who do not consider themselves Christians (E-1, E-2, and E-3). This is not surprising, because the majority of Westerners are nominal Christians. Things are very different in the non-Western world, as we see in Figure 6. There for simplicity we have divided all the non-Christians into four groups — Chinese, Muslim, Hindu and "other." The bottom three layers represent three virtually untouched blocs of humanity, amounting to 1933 million people.

Let us think prayerfully for a moment about these three groups. A few minutes ago we noted that there are roughly one million non-Christians in the world for each participant here. If our Congress participants consisted of people whose gifts and calling were focused proportionately on all non-Christians in the world, would we not have to have here one participant for each million in each of these groups? This means we would have to have 502 people here specializing on reaching the 502 million non-Christian Hindus. These would have to be cross-cultural specialists, on the whole. We would also have to have 664 people here specializing on reaching the 664 million Muslims. They too would have to be almost entirely cross-cultural specialists, since only tiny numbers of Muslims can be won by local Christians living in their areas who try to reach them by ordinary evangelism. (Parenthetically, let me observe that the Muslim group, which is already immense, is growing at a biological rate almost double that of the Chinese, and that if present rates continue, there will be more Muslims than Chinese within about ten years.) Moving on to the Chinese, proportionately to represent the 827 million non-Christian Chinese would require at this Congress 827 people specializing on the task of reaching them. In the case of the Chinese there are millions of Christian Chinese to help in the task, but even so, the Chinese are so split up by dialects, social distinctions, and highly significant clan differences that most of this task is E-2 rather than E-1, and thus mainly a cross cultural problem as with the other two major blocs.

Now note something very significant. As in the case of the Western world, most of the cross-cultural workers are focusing their efforts on nurture and E-0 evangelism connected with the Christian community. The number of Christians in the non-Western world (214 million) is the sum of the Africa and Asia columns in the previous table, that is 116 + 98. Again by merging the columns, there are 80 million committed Christians in the non-Western world, whose nurture soaks up a very large proportion of the energies of both Christian missionaries and national church leaders; there are also 134 million nominal Christians who take up practically all of the rest of the efforts. It is only a guess, but it is safe to say that 95 per cent of all missionaries deployed in the non-Western world are focusing their efforts either on communities that claim to be Christian or upon non-Christian peoples in the immediate environment of the Christians, these latter probably being mainly the 403 million non-Christians in the "other" category in this chart. That leaves only a tiny percentage of cross-cultural workers to deal with the three major blocs of non-Western non-Christians. Brothers and sisters, this is a grim picture. The task to be done on the left is big enough, but precisely where the cross-cultural task is the largest, the cross-cultural workers are the fewest.

For example, the number of effective evangelists winning middle caste and upper caste Hindus (well over 400 million people) are very few indeed, and the number of effective cross-cultural evangelists winning Muslims are very few indeed. While there may be proportionately more cross-cultural workers who are reaching out to non-Christian Chinese, these would mainly be in Taiwan. But even in Taiwan most missionaries and national leaders are absorbed with the needs of the Christian community. This is not to begrudge the "interchurch" exchange of E-3 workers. *The danger is that we may easily deceive ourselves concerning the proportionate weight of personnel that is going to the evangelism of non-Christians.* This is so important to understand that we must use an extended illustration of this whole matter of the statistical scope of the task of cross-cultural evangelism. Since I have already said a good deal in my original paper about Pakistan, let me build on that situation.

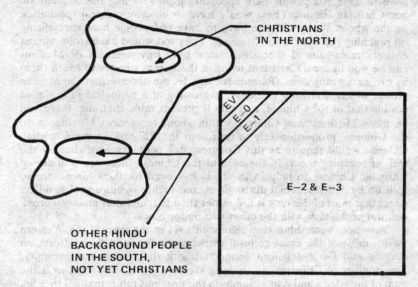

Figure 7. PAKISTAN

The rough proportions in Pakistan are similar to the diagram in Figure 4 for India. In Pakistan there are proportionately fewer Christians than in India, but they number well over one-half million (out of 70 million). The Christian community today is the product of a great people movement and spiritual revival over a half-century ago, but there are very few people living today who were brought to Christ in that movement, and the churches of Pakistan by now have a sizeable proportion of their own members who need to be won by E-0 evangelism to personal spiritual obedience to Christ. The really surprising thing is why the E-1 sphere is so small. A country of 70 million people where there are 500,000 Christians does not on the face of it seem likely to be a place where near-neighbor evangelism would have relatively small significance. Why can't the 500,000 Christians just reach out to their near neighbors and win them to

Christ? This is the crucial question. The answer is that 99 per cent of the Christians have a Hindu (not Muslim) cultural background, whereas 97 per cent of the non-Christians in Pakistan are Muslim. In the north you have scattered communities of Christians (just as in India, most Christians are in separated, isolated areas, almost like ghettos), but their *physical* separation from so many of their countrymen does not remotely approach the significance of their *cultural* isolation.

Thus, from the beginning of the revival movement in the north over fifty years ago until the present time, almost never has a Muslim joined a Christian church, while hundreds of thousands of former Hindus have become Christians. Although the church in Pakistan has a large E-0 population of nominal Christians, it is continuing to win some remaining Hindus to Christ through E-1 evangelism. On this basis, how soon will the church run out of Hindus to convert? In the northern part of the country, where most of the Christians are, practically all of the non-Muslim people of Pakistan are already at least nominally Christian. Curiously, there are almost a million people of Hindu background yet to win, but they are in the South, hundreds of miles from the main body of Christians. While it would be relatively simple for these Christians to do evangelism in the South (only a geographical distance away), the Christians are very, very distant from their Muslim neighbors. Why? Because there is a very pronounced cultural distance between the cultural tradition represented by the church and the cultural tradition represented by the Muslims.

Let us be more specific. Both Muslims and the (Hindu-background) Christians in the North speak Urdu. But they don't speak exactly the same kind of Urdu. A Muslim can tell either by listening or by reading that the religious language of the Christians comes from the originally Hindu minority in his country, and he has monumental prejudices about this difference. The Christians, on the other hand, while they don't hate the Muslims, don't feel it is necessary to make a special translation of the New Testament into the religious language of the Urdu-speaking Muslims, even though there are more than 30 million Urdu-speaking Muslims alone! Feelings of suspicion between the two communities are so great that an occasional Muslim convert does not feel at home in any of the Christian congregations. Christians have not yet made an effective effort nor even drawn up speculative plans for the development of worshiping communities drawn wholly from the Muslim tradition. This is only natural, in a way, because the Christians come from a stratum of society which has for centuries been impoverished and virtually enslaved. The Christians even yet are barely struggling to their feet economically. Their resources, their education, their evangelistic imagination does not readily stretch to radically new ways of evangelizing the Muslims — especially not to ways that will allow the Muslims the kind of liberty in Christ which the Gospel guarantees them.

The situation in Pakistan both illustrates the immense scope of the need for cross-cultural evangelism, and also moves us into the theological dimension of the problem. To that dimension we must now turn.

Questions about the theological nature of the task
    First briefly let me say a word to those who asked, in effect, "Will not the allowance of indigenous life ways lead us into syncretism?" Michael

Green has already answered this for us in his excellent discussion of flexibility without syncretism. I might add a personal note that as a Western Christian, I grew up without realizing that Easter Sunrise services could easily revert to their original paganism if Christians attending them do not see and sense a Christian meaning in them. The very word *Easter* comes from a Teutonic spring goddess of fertility called *Eostre*. The same is true of Christmas. We have all fought to maintain Christ in Christmas, since Christmas is also originally a pagan holiday that was taken over by the early church. (Romans gave gifts to each other on December 25th long before Jesus was born, and for that matter, Jesus may have been born in June, not in December.) Briefly, in employing pagan words and customs, we must be careful to make sure that the whole counsel of God is constantly taught and understood.

The main theological question, raised more often than any other, is so profound that I feel I must devote my remaining time to it. The question was stated in many ways in your response papers, but is basically this: "Will not our unity in Christ be destroyed if we follow a concept of cross-cultural evangelization which is willing to set up separate churches for different cultural groups within the same geographical area?" It is only with humble dependence upon the Holy Spirit to honor the Word of God above the secular influences to which we all are subject that I dare to proceed with a perspective which I myself could not understand nor accept until several years ago. I was brought up in the United States, where for many people integration is almost like a civil religion, where such people almost automatically assume that eventually everyone will speak English and really shouldn't speak any other language. To me cultural diversity between countries was a nuisance, but cultural diversity within a country was simply an evil to be overcome. I had no thought of excluding anyone from *any* church, (and I still do not), but I did unconsciously assume that the best thing that could happen to Black, White, Chicano, etc., was that they all would eventually come to the White, Anglo-Saxon, Protestant church and learn to do things the way that I felt was most proper.

Following this kind of American culture-Christianity, many missionaries have assumed that there ought to be just one national church in a country — even if this means none at all for certain sub-groups? Such missionaries, in all earnestness, have assumed that the denominational pluralism in their own home country is simply a sin to be avoided. They have assumed that *Southern* Baptists aren't necessary in *Northern* India, even though, as a matter of fact, in Boston today most of the Anglo churches have been sitting around waiting for the Arabs and the Japanese to come to their churches, and it has taken Southern Baptists to go into Northern United States and plan Arab churches, and Japanese churches, and Portuguese churches, and Greek churches, and Polish churches, right under the nose of hundreds of good-willed Anglo churches which have been patiently waiting for these people to assimilate to the Anglo way of life. With one or two fine exceptions, the Anglo churches, with all their evangelistic zeal, simply did not have the insight to do this kind of E-2 and E-3 evangelism.

For my own part, after many years of struggling with this question, I am now no less concerned than before about the unity and fellowship of the Christian movement across all ethnic and cultural lines, but I realize now that Christian unity cannot be healthy if it infringes upon Christian liberty. In terms of evangelism, we must ask whether the attempt to extend, for example in Pakistan, an external form into the Muslim culture is more important than making the Gospel clear to such peoples within their own culture. Can we not condition our desire for uniformity by an even greater desire for effective preaching of the Gospel? I personally have come to believe that unity does not have to require uniformity, and I believe that there must be such a thing as healthy diversity in human society *and in the Christian world church.* I see the world church as the gathering together of a great symphony orchestra where we don't make every new person coming in play a violin in order to fit in with the rest. We invite the people to come in to play the same score — the Word of God — but to play their own instruments, and in this way there will issue forth a heavenly sound that will grow in the splendor and glory of God as each new instrument is added.

But some of you have said, "OK, if that is what you mean, what about the Apostle Paul? Did he set up separate congregations for masters and slaves?" I really don't know. I don't think so. But that does not mean that didn't happen. In a recent monograph by Paul Minear entitled *The Obedience of Faith,* the author suggests that in Rome there were probably five separate congregations of Christians, who numbered a total 3000, and that Paul's letter to the Romans was written actually to a cluster of churches in the city of Rome. He also suggests that these churches were very different from each other, some being composed almost entirely of Jewish Christians, and others (the majority) almost entirely of Gentile Christians. "Instead of visualizing a single Christian congregation, therefore, we should constantly reckon with the probability that within the urban area were to be found forms of Christian community which were as diverse, and probably also as alien, as the churches of Galatia and those of Judea." But whatever the case in Rome, Paul in his travels was usually dealing with the phenomenon of house churches, where whole households, masters and slaves, quite likely worshiped together. We cannot believe he ever separated people. However, we do know that he was willing to adopt in different places a radically different approach, as he put it, "for those under the law and for those not under the law." When, for example, he established an apparently non-Jewish congregation among the Galatians, it was obviously different, perhaps radically different from that of the Jewish congregations elsewhere. We know this because Jewish Christians followed Paul to the Galatians and tried to make them conform to the Jewish Christian pattern. Galatia is a clear case where it was impossible for Paul to submit simultaneously both to the provisions of the Jewish Christian way of life and at the same time to the patterns of an evidently Greek (or perhaps Celtic) congregation.

Paul's letter to the Galatians, furthermore, shows us how determined he was to allow the Galatian Christians to follow a different Christian life-style. Thus while we do not have any record of his forcing people to meet separately, we do encounter all of Paul's holy boldness set in opposition to anyone who would try to *preserve a single normative pattern* of Christian life through a cultural imperialism that would *prevent* people from employing their own language and culture as a vehicle for worship and witness. Here, then, is a clear case of a man with cross-cultural evangelistic perspective doing everything within his power to guarantee liberty in Christ to converts who were different from his own social background.

This same thing is seen when Paul opposed Peter in Antioch. Peter was a Galilean Jew who was perhaps to some extent bi-cultural. He could have at least been able to understand the predominantly Greek life-style of the Antioch church. Indeed, he did seem to fit in until the moment other Jewish Christians came to the door. At this point Peter also discovered that in a given situation he had to choose between following Jewish or Greek customs. At this point he wavered. Did he lack the Spirit of God? Did he lack the love of God? Or did he fail to understand the way of God's love? Peter did not question the validity of a Greek congregation. Peter had already acknowledged this before his Jewish compatriots walked in the door. The point was that Peter was pained for others to know him as one who could shift from one community to the other. What this means to us today is quite clear. There were in fact in the New Testament period two significantly different communities of believers. Peter was regarded the apostle to the circumcision and Paul to the uncircumcision. Peter identified more easily with the Jews, and no doubt had a hard time explaining to Jews his experience at Cornelius' household, namely his discovery that Greek congregations were to be considered legitimate. Paul, on the other hand, was able to identify more closely with the Greek congregations. They were perhaps eventually his primary missionary target, even though in a given locality he always began with the Jews.

One clue for today is the fact that where Paul found some Christians to be overscrupulous about certain foods, he counseled people in those situations to abide by the stricter sensibilities of the majority. However, it is always difficult to make exact parallels to a modern situation. The New Testament situation would compare more easily to modern India today were it the case that the only Christians in India were Brahmins (and other members of the middle castes) with their highly restrictive diet. Then we would envision Brahmin Christians finding it hard to allow the less restrictive meat-eating groups to become Christian; but the actual situation is very nearly the reverse. In India today it is those who eat meat who are Christians, and the problem is how to apply Paul's missionary strategy to this situation. In regard to food restrictions, it is as though the Brahmins are "under the law," not the present Christians. In this situation can we imagine Paul saying, "To those under the law I will go as under the law if by all means I may win some"? Can we hear him say as an E-2 or E-3 evangelist, "If meat makes my brother offended, I will eat no meat"? Can we hear him defending worshiping groups among the Brahmins against the suggestion *or expectation* that they should change their diet or join congregations of very different life-style in order to be accepted as Christians? Against the accusation that he was dividing the church of Christ, can we hear Paul insist that "in Christ there is neither Jew nor

Greek, low caste nor high caste"? Is this not the actual force of his oft-repeated statement that these different kinds of people, following their different cultural patterns, are all equally acceptable to God? Was he really announcing a policy of local integration, or was he insisting on the equality of diversity?

Note very carefully that this perspective does not enforce (nor even allow) a policy of segregation, nor any kind of ranking of Christians in first- and second-class categories. It rather guarantees equal acceptability of different traditions. It is a clear-cut apostolic policy against forcing Christians of one life-style to be proselytized to the cultural patterns of another. This is not a peripheral matter in the New Testament. True circumcision is of the heart. True baptism is of the heart. It is a matter of faith, not works, or customs, or rites. In Christ there is freedom and liberty in this regard — people must be free either to retain or abandon their native language and life-style. Paul would not allow anyone to glory either in circumcision or in uncircumcision. He was absolutely impartial. He was also widely misunderstood. Paul's problem ultimately was in gaining acceptance by the Jews, and it was Asian Jews, possibly Christians, who pointed him out in the temple and thus finally caused his martyrdom for his belief in the separate liberty of the Greek Christian tradition. Let no one who seeks to be a missionary in the tradition of the Apostle Paul expect that working between two cultures will be easy to do. But he can take heart in the fact that the hazards of the profession are more than justified by the urgent missionary purposes of the cross-cultural evangelist.

If, for example, a cross-cultural evangelist encourages members of a Brahmin family to begin worship services in their own home, does he insist that they invite people from across town to their very first meeting? On the other hand, any Brahmin who becomes a Christian and who begins to understand the Bible will soon realize, whether it was entirely clear before or not, that he now belongs to a world family within which there are many tribes and tongues — indeed, according to the Book of Revelation (Rev. 7:9), this kind of diversity will continue right down to the end of time. When the cross-cultural evangelist allows the development of a Brahmin congregation, he is not thereby proposing Brahmin segregation from the world church. He is not suggesting that the Brahmin Christians shun other Christians, but that Brahmins be included within the world church. He is merely affirming their liberty in Christ to retain those elements of their life-style that are not inimical to the Gospel of Christ. He is not increasing their alienation. He is giving them the Word of God which is the passkey to the ultimate elimination of all manner of prejudices, and is already signing them into a world Christian family which embraces all peoples, tribes and tongues as equals.

Now, I regret that this subject is so delicate, and I would not embark upon it if it were not so urgently significant for the practical evangelistic strategies which we must have if we are going to win the world for Christ. I would not even bring it up. Yet I must say I believe this issue is the most important single issue in evangelism today.

Many people asked me what I meant by the strategic value of the establishment of youth churches. It is important to realize the youth situation is highly parallel to the situation we have just discussed. It is by no means a case where we are suggesting that young people not be allowed in adult services. We are not suggesting segregation of the youth. Youth churches are not ends, but means. We are not abandoning the thought that young people and older people should often be in the same service together. We are merely insisting, with what I pray is apostolic intuition, that young people have the freedom in Christ to meet together by themselves if they choose to, and *especially if this allows them to attract other young people who would likely* not come to Christ in an age-integrated service.

I will, however, freely admit that this strategy may unintentionally make it appear that we are setting aside goals of unity for goals of evangelism. This in fact is not the case. It is quite the opposite: we are willing to do evangelism in the highly divided world in which we live, believing wholeheartedly that in the long run the working of the Holy Spirit through true evangelism is the only way to melt down the high walls of prejudice and thus produce unity where none at all existed before.

Some have warned that this kind of culturally sensitive evangelism will lead to ghetto churches. I suggest rather that it will go to ghetto situations and eventually bring those isolated people into contact with others in a rewarding and enriching way. Where there are already ghetto churches all around the world that are isolated from their neighbors, this may not be the fault of the original evangelists, but of the nurture in succeeding years. If the Gospel begins in a ghetto, it should not end there. Rival street gangs may more easily be brought together by being brought to Christ separately. The initial evangelist does not add a ghetto to the church; he takes the church to the ghetto. People from that ghetto are then automatically present at the next city-wide Christian meeting. The efforts of the Billy Graham Crusades must be seen in this light not as an optional, but as an essential, beautiful, and permanent part of God's ultimate uniting strategy. There must, in fact, be annual city-wide and regional Christian festivals whether or not Billy Graham can personally be there. There must be many other contacts between Christians of all kinds between such annual meetings. Yet we must yield to the fact that God allows the family and the local congregation and even whole denominations to speak different languages and to express their faith in different linguistic and cultural traditions. But woe to such self-determining Christians if this liberty in Christ becomes understood as a basis for superiority or isolation. Why? Because, as Paul said, "In Christ there is neither Greek nor Jew, nor Barbarian, nor Scythian, nor bond nor free, nor male nor female."

It is a curious fact that the kind of culturally sensitive evangelism I have been talking about has always been acceptable wherever people are geographically isolated. No one minds if Japanese Christians gather by themselves in Tokyo, or Spanish-speaking Christians gather by themselves in Mexico, or Chinese-speaking Christians gather by themselves in Hong Kong. But there is considerable confusion in many people's minds as to whether Japanese, Spanish and Chinese Christians should be allowed or encouraged to gather by themselves in Los Angeles. Very specifically, is it good evangelistic strategy to found separate congregations in Los Angeles in order to attract such people? Do Cantonese-speaking non-Christians need a Cantonese-speaking congregation to attract them to Christian faith and fellowship? If you talk to different people, you will get different answers. In my opinion, this question about evangelistic strategy in the forming of separate congregations must be considered an area of Christian liberty, and is to be decided purely on the basis of whether or not it allows the Gospel to be presented effectively to more people — that is, whether it is evangelistically strategic. Some go as far as granting separate *language* congregations, but hesitate when the differences between people are social and non-linguistic. Somehow they feel that people may be excused for meeting separately if their language is different, but that the Gospel urges us to ignore all other cultural differences. Many people are literally outraged at the thought that a local congregation would deliberately seek to attract people of a certain social level. And yet, while no one should be excluded from any church under any circumstances, it is a fact that where people can choose their church associations voluntarily, they tend to sort themselves out according to their own way of life pretty consistently. But this absolutely must be their own free choice. We are never suggesting an enforced segregation. Granting that we have this rich diversity, let us foster unity and fellowship between *congregations* just as we now do between *families* rather than to teach everyone to worship like Anglo-Americans. Let us glory in the fact that the *world* Christian family now already includes representatives of more different languages and cultures than any other organization or movement in human history. Americans may be baffled and perplexed by world diversity. God is not. Let us glory in the fact that God has allowed different life-styles to exist in different forms, and that this flexibility has been exercised throughout history. Let us never be content with mere isolation, but let us everlastingly emphasize that the great richness of our Christian tradition can only be realized as these differing life ways maintain creative contact. But let us be cautious about hastening to uniformity. If the whole world church could be gathered into a single congregation, Sunday after Sunday, there would eventually and inevitably be a loss of a great deal of the rich diversity of the present Christian traditions. Does God want this? Do we want this?

Jesus *died* for these people around the world. He did not die to preserve our Western way of life. He did not die to make Muslims stop praying five times a day. He did not die to make Brahmins eat meat. Can't you hear Paul the Evangelist saying we must go to these people within the systems in which they operate? True, this is the cry of a cross-cultural evangelist, not a pastor. We can't make every local church fit the pattern of every other local church. But we must have radically new efforts of cross-cultural evangelism in order to effectively witness to 2387 million people, and we cannot believe that we can continue virtually to ignore this highest priority.

RESPONSE TO DR. RALPH WINTER'S PAPER
Philip Hogan

Dr. Hogan, Springfield, Missouri, USA, is the Executive Director for Foreign Missions of the General Council of the Assemblies of God.

In responding to the excellent paper by Dr. Ralph Winter, one cannot help but worship at the shrine of his tremendous grasp of the remaining world missionary challenge and his inimitable way of categorizing these challenges into neat little categories so that they can be easily grasped by those of us whose minds are not nearly so methodical.

While it is true that spiritual factors seldom ever reduce themselves into human equations, there is a dangerous tendency to be over-idealistic when we attempt to analyze in human terms the great spiritual challenges of our times. Yet we can be grateful to Dr. Winter and his paper because it is a kind of a prism which brings into focus many views and serves to get all the issues out before us very clearly.

It is well that Dr. Winter, in his first paragraph reviews the heroic accomplishments made by Christianity in the world today. This is worthy of emphasis. This is, thank God, no hollow victory and we need not gather here as a council of despair.

Dr. Winter further acknowledges that the real frontier is not geographical but cultural. Modern ingenuity of this twentieth century has bequeathed us communication and transportation possibilities that change the "Go ye" in the Great Commission, from one of geography to one of cultural and sociological distances.

Dr. Winter makes a further excellent point when he reminds us that it is people and not political groupings that should concern the evangelist and the church-planter.

This brings us to the main presuppositions of Dr. Winter's paper, that is, the E-1, E-2, and E-3 concept of spheres for the purpose of gospel witnessing.

If Dr. Winter's premise is correct that the easiest and most successful evangelism is done at the shortest cultural distance, that is, in the E-1 sphere, then we should by all means take every opportunity to reach people from the great Hindu-Muslim-Chinese block who for study or business or any other reason, leave their cultural surroundings and expose themselves to the outside.

For instance, what about the great world of foreign students which constantly invades the campuses of the West. For certain, a great deal of splendid effort is being put forth to reach these people, yet, it is only reasonable to conclude that much more prayer and spiritual focus should be beamed their way if they, indeed, can come to the saving knowledge of Jesus Christ outside of the cultural block of which they are a part, and then go back to be E-1 emissaries.

With respect to Dr. Winter's further observations that successful

E-2 evangelism must look towards gathering the results into local units of the Body of Christ, which are formed around the cultural milieu in which they are converted: while one cannot deny that practically this seems like the proper thing to do, actually pressed to its final conclusion it would mean a very great proliferation further within the Body of Jesus Christ. Must we forever remain divided on the basis of culture, language, or color? Is it not possible to believe that newly-won Christians can be so obsessed with the object of their new love that the expulsive power of this new affection will overcome human dividing lines? Is it too much to believe that the sovereign Lord of the harvest can so revive the existing structure until it lowers the prejudice barrier to include all true-born sons of God into a warm fellowship?

Perhaps this is the proper moment to inject into this brief response what I hope will be my main contribution. That is, simply an appeal to all of us to recognize the sovereignty of the Holy Spirit and to emphasize once again the truth of Acts 5:32, "And we are his witnesses of these things and so is also the Holy Ghost whom God has given to them that obey Him." Truly the task of worldwide witnessing is a joint task. It is the cooperative endeavor between the Lord of the harvest and his church, made up of human vessels. Sometimes in the very act of analyzing, we rule out, on the basis of human categories, the overriding factor of our times that we are witnessing worldwide, an outpouring of the Spirit of God upon persons and in places for which there is no human design and in which there is not one shred of human planning. The inscrutable ways and origins of the Spirit, indeed, add a strange and fiction-like quality to serving God in these days.

A few years ago Hendrik Kraemer, the noted missions professor, spoke to a group of missions administrators in Chicago. At the conclusion of his address, the subject of Japan and its recent history came into discussion.

It was observed by different participants in the discussion that immediately following World War II, when the emperor had renounced his deity, the inevitable spiritual vacuum created by this act afforded one of the greatest opportunities any nation has ever known for evangelism.

Further observations were made concerning how propitious it would have been if the churches in the rest of the world had focused their attention on the emperor himself. If he had accepted the claims of Jesus Christ, perhaps a whole nation could have been won in a day!

The venerable Dr. Kraemer listened to this for some time, then remarked "I never did agree with you Americans. You seem to have the idea that by getting together and using the proper methods you can do anything. You leave out of consideration the operation of the Holy Spirit." This blunt Dutch professor indeed said it all and said it well. Some of us who are privileged to travel widely and see much in this twentieth century must be overwhelmed and humbled before the moving of the Spirit's own sovereign presence in the world.

Make no mistake, the missionary venture of the church, no matter how well planned, how finely administered, or how fully supported, would fail like every other vast human enterprise were it not that where human instrumentality leaves off, a blessed ally takes over. It is the Holy Spirit

who calls, it is the Holy Spirit who inspires, it is the Holy Spirit who reveals, and it is the Holy Spirit who administers.

The very promise of the coming of the Holy Spirit is connected with
worldwide witnessing. "But you shall receive power, after that the Holy
Ghost is come upon you: and ye shall be witnesses unto me both in
Jerusalem, and in all Judea, and in Samaria, and unto the uttermost part
of the earth" (Acts 1:8).

I am persuaded to believe that after taking advantage of every tool,
pursuing every possible human plan, all one needs to do to find plenty of
service is simply to follow the leading of the Spirit. When one engages
this truth and begins to live by its principle, there will be whole communities, whole cities, whole nations, whole cultures, and whole segments
of pagan religions that will suddenly be thrust open to the Gospel witness.

Who would have thought in 1964 that Indonesia would be one of the
ripest mission fields in the world today. Yet on the turn of events that
happened around the stroke of midnight, the whole political and spiritual complexion of a vast nation has been changed. All the charts, plans,
and maps of all the missiologists of the world could not have designed
these moments.

Today we are witnessing an outpouring of the Spirit upon groups and
individuals that our prejudices and our provincialism are sometimes
slow to accept.

The essential optimism of Christianity is that the Holy Spirit is a
force capable of bursting into the hardest paganism, discomfiting the most
rigid dogmatism, electrifying the most suffocating organization, and
bringing the glory of Pentecost.

Dare we stand in awe, my friends, and witness in these days the wonder
of the ages? The Spirit of God is being outpoured upon persons and in
places for which there is no human design and not one shred of human
planning.

Indeed, if we will be alert, we can be like a spectator with a box seat,
watching the greatest drama of all times unfold before us through which
the sovereign Lord of the harvest, through his Spirit, is presenting the
claims of Jesus Christ and calling out a people for his Name.

In Mark, the fourth chapter, there is a parable which is peculiar to
Mark. He alone relates it to us. It says, "This is what the kingdom of God
is like. It is like what happens when a man casts seed upon the earth.
He sleeps and he wakes night and day, and the seed sprouts and grows
and he does not know how it does it. The earth produces fruit with help
from no one, first the shoot, then the ear, then the full corn of the ear.
When the time allows it, immediately he dispatches the sickle for the time
of the harvest is come." The earth produces fruit with help from no one,
or as it is stated in the King James Version, simply, "The earth bringeth
forth fruit of itself."

Please understand me, I am not pleading for a kind of "sitting where
they sit and letting God happen" kind of attitude. But what I am pleading
for is that at the end of every human endeavor there must be a simple
dependence upon the Holy Spirit who, beyond the shadow of any doubt,
is at work in his world in an unprecedented way and if we sow in faith,
believing in the magic power of the seed, we must, as well, believe that

there will be receptive soil, sometimes suddenly and beyond the power of any human reasoning. When the wind of God truly blows, E-3 evangelism becomes as easy and successful as E-1 or E-2, and perhaps one of the major concerns of this conference should be that we discover where God walks and get into stride with him in his march through time and eternity.

> God is working his purpose out as year succeeds
> to year,
> God is working his purpose out and the time is
> drawing near,
> Nearer and nearer draws the time, the time that
> shall surely be,
> When the earth shall be filled with the glory
> of God, as the waters cover the sea.

RESPONSE TO DR. RALPH D. WINTER'S PAPER

Jacob Loewen

*Dr. Loewen, Zambia, is a translation
consultant for the Bible Society. He
formerly worked in South America
in a similar capacity.*

When I received the request to respond as a Christian anthropologist to Dr. Ralph Winter's paper, "The Highest Priority — Cross-cultural Evangelism," I looked at the title and cabled: "Yes, I'll be delighted," I responded so enthusiastically because I also strongly believe that one of the greatest habitual problems of evangelization and church growth on a worldwide scale is that the church, once established, is again and again tempted to stabilize within a specific homogeneous group, be that a tribe, a culture, a social group or social class in larger stratified societies, and in the process it loses its zeal to witness across cultural boundaries.

When I tried to enter into the reasoning of Dr. Winter's paper, however, ever-increasing inner struggles took hold of me. It grew so acute that I finally telephoned long-distance from Africa to California to discuss my concerns with Dr. Winter. For this reason I could base my reaction not only on the paper itself, which you presumably have all read, but also on the telephone dialogue. Since you did not all share in this dialogue, however, and have had only the original paper, I feel that I must limit myself largely to it. Nevertheless, where it is especially pertinent I will make reference to the telephone dialogue.

Before I begin my response proper, however, it seems wise for me to try to summarize briefly the theses of Dr. Winter's paper, because some of you have read it some time ago and its contents may be somewhat hazy in your own minds. Furthermore, I want you to be aware of what I personally extracted from the paper, because you may not have understood it precisely that way.

As the title correctly indicates, the central thrust of Dr. Winter's paper is the high priority need for the Gospel to be carried across cultural boundaries. In developing this theme he stresses the following points:

a. The task of world evangelism is the timeless biblical mandate of the church, and as such must be a central concern of this Congress — a Congress on World Evangelization (pp. 1-2, 7, 10).

b. That certain Christian groups and churches have erroneously been lulled to believe that the Gospel has now reached the "uttermost parts of the earth" and so it is up to the local Christians to finish the task by local evangelism (p. 1).

c. That the task of evangelism, on the basis of the differing cultural distances to be bridged between the myriad of tribes and peoples in the world, can be classified into three categories:

E-1: evangelism within homogeneous groups.

E-2: evangelism of geographically close and culturally or linguistically related groups.

E-3: evangelism of culturally distant groups in which the evangelist is separated from the people to be evangelized by monumental (Winter's own term) cultural distances (pp. 4-5ff).

d. That for the Gospel to reach all societies or all segments of socially complex societies, it will be necessary for E-2 or E-3 to cross the cultural gap and to spark the development of the church in each culturally definable social group, which, once reached, can then complete the task of evangelism by powerful and effective E-1 (p. 6).

e. That in the unfinished task of reaching the still-unreached, E-3 evangelism stands out "head and shoulders" above all other forms of evangelism because:

(i) At least four out of five people in the largely unevangelized blocks of humanity do not have any near Christian neighbors (pp. 2, 14).

(ii) Where there are Christian neighbors, local prejudice frequently makes E-2 all but impossible. An E-3 outsider, not sharing in the E-2 prejudice system, can often do much more effective evangelism (pp. 8-9, 20).

f. That every evangelist must be deeply aware of what kind of cultural gap there is to be bridged, and that the foreigner of E-3 distance should never attempt to do what a national of E-1 or E-2 distance can do (pp. 11-12). Now to the response proper.

As a Christian anthropologist I can wholeheartedly endorse Dr. Winter's thrust that our evangelism must not be short-circuited by cultural distance, but I do have a number of concerns about the emphases his paper places on E-3 evangelism. (Here it needs to be pointed out that during the telephone conversation Dr. Winter already stated that he saw E-2 and E-3 as a single continuum, and that if they are to be separated, they are to be preferred in that order. E-3 should be employed only when E-2 is impossible.)

Secondly, I cannot share his view that 87 per cent of all non-Christians have no near neighbors.

Before I state my concerns, I feel that I should also remind the delegates that:

1. I am deeply aware that I am stressing my personal point of view over against Dr. Winter's point of view in some aspects, and that the Congress participants will have to help both of us to sort out which of these emphases, if either, contains the greatest degree of relevant truth for their particular situation.

2. I myself treasure among my most sacred memories as a missionary a whole series of E-3 experiences that God saw fit to bless with church growth. I cannot detail them individually here so I merely refer to some of them by name: the Choco church in Panama, the Waunana in Colombia, and the group conversion of the Chulupi in the village of Sandhorst in the Paraguayan Chaco.

3. The Bible provides us with several most wonderful examples of E-3 evangelism, like Jonah going to Nineveh. In fact, the incarnation, when God in the form of his Son emptied himself of his divine prerogatives (Phil. 2:6-7) and became a human being (John 1:1), is to me the supreme example of E-3 and the very foundation of all subsequent evangelism.

4. As God has used E-3 in the past, I am convinced that he will also use it in the future. However, as Dr. Winter says, it is extraordinary evangelism (pp. 2, 6, 10), and therefore it also carries with it some extraordinary requirements and limitations. These are:

a. That the would-be evangelist must follow Christ's example and knowingly empty himself of his own culture and be identified with the people in the culture to be evangelized — few of us E-3 missionaries have achieved this.

b. Because of this weakness on our part, God usually uses the E-3 evangelist only as a catalyst, and not as a long-time leader. In fact, when Jonah proclaimed the judgment of God on Nineveh, it was the king who took the initiative and called his people to repentance, leaving the frustrated E-3 missionary to mope under a juniper bush. Sometimes the contact will be only an "accidental" encounter in passing, like Philip and the eunuch who met briefly on the deserted Gaza road under the Holy Spirit's guidance. Then before the eunuch could become attached to his spiritual father, the same Spirit of God snatched him away.

c. For E-3 evangelism to be effective, the recipient culture must be able to separate the true message content from the cultural wrapper in which it comes and then be aware of congenial models for the new life in Christ that will permit healthy spiritual development. Otherwise it may fall back on syncretistic models of its own old life, or more likely it will try to pattern itself according to the cultural models of the E-3 evangelist's culture.

I want to divide the statement of my concerns about E-3 into three categories which I will, for the sake of easy reference, label biblical, anthropological, and practical, respectively.

1. *Biblical concerns*

a. To my understanding, Acts 1:8 obviously stresses E-1 evangelism for Jerusalem and Judea, and E-2 for Samaria, but not necessarily E-3 for the rest of the world. I say this because I feel that the world, as the early Christians saw it, was the then-known Greco-Roman world of which Jerusalem, Judea, and Samaria were integral parts. Hence we are dealing with E-2 distances throughout rather than with E-3 distances.

b. I find the prejudice reason for using E-3 over against E-2 very questionable, because Christ, Paul plainly tells us, has torn down the walls of separation (Eph. 2:13-16), and in Christ there is no distinction between Jews or Gentiles, slave or free man, etc. (Col. 3:10-11). Thus when a person of E-3 distance must evangelize in a situation where prejudice keeps the church of E-2 distance from doing the job, I fear that the converts are really being taught to accept an inferior kind of Christianity — a Christianity that is not strong enough to break down the walls of prejudice. I have serious question whether this kind of Christianity is worth "selling."

c. The biblical model which I personally see throughout the book of Acts involves only an alternation of E-1 and E-2. After the Holy Spirit came and the disciples lost their fear and began to witness boldly, earth-shaking demonstrations of God's power in the lives of men rocked the very foundations of the Jewish society in Jerusalem, and soon not only Jerusalem, but also all of Judea was blanketed with the good news: "The

Messiah has come! He is Jesus who was crucified, but whom God raised from the dead, to be the Savior and healer of all men." When a group has such a powerful E-1 experience, E-2 is the inevitable, direct result. In fact, E-2, as the book of Acts shows, can take on a variety of forms.

(i) People whose lives have been transformed by the power of God cannot help but share this wonderful experience with others. Thus Philip (with the help of a little bit of persecution in Jerusalem) goes to Samaria where Jesus had already sown the good seed and sparks a wonderful conversion movement. But at the height of this movement, before Philip himself can become a "permanent fixture" there, the Spirit of God sends him away to a second form of E-2 evangelism.

(ii) When people from neighboring groups hear that a good thing has happened to people they are acquainted with, they often come from a considerable distance to get more information or to see first-hand this good thing God is doing. Thus we can report the conversion of the Ethiopian eunuch to whom Philip ministered on the Gaza road.

(iii) A third form of E-2 evangelism is seen in Acts 10 in the account of Cornelius, the Roman officer, who sent messengers to Peter asking him to bring him and his family the good news of Jesus Christ. Here is an alien resident in a foreign land. He sees what God does for the Jews and he as a Gentile wants to experience the same for himself and his family, so he calls the Christians for help.

(iv) And finally, in Acts 13 and 23 we see a fourth form of E-2. Here the Spirit of God asks the churches to send several bi-cultural men from their midst to do E-2 evangelism in the length and breadth of the Roman Empire, and thus the church at Antioch sends Paul and Barnabas to do the job for which God had prepared them and to which he had called them.

2. *Anthropological concerns*

From the anthropological perspective, I think Dr. Winter is correct when he states that great cultural distance spells even greater communication problems. The reason is that effective cross-cultural communication can happen only when the new recipient can separate the message content from its cultural form; or we could say, when the meaning of a message is separated from its cultural wrapper. In the E-1 situation both the message and the wrapper are understood and are meaningful to both the evangelist and the convert. At the E-2 level the two different peoples in contact usually have an awareness of the cultural differences that separate them, and so the alien wrapper of the message is easily distinguished from its true content. For example, I once asked a South American Indian, who was seeing immersion baptism for the first time, "What in the world are those people doing?"

"They're head-pouring," he answered casually.

"Head-pouring!" I said. "Why, they're putting the people under water all the way. There's no pouring going on there."

"I know," he responded, "but it means the same thing as when the priest pours water on the baby's head."

Frequently at the E-3 level the wrapper, no matter how incongruous, has been accepted as part of the message. Often this wrapper has effectively choked the real life out of the message.

Again, when we look at effective movements of cultural change that have blanketed many tribes and cultures, we find that like church growth in Acts, they are spread by an alternation of E-1 and E-2. Effective E-1 in a given society leads to E-2 (in some or all of its forms). Once having taken root in a new setting, the change grows until the resulting excitement again bursts its cultural seams and goes E-2. This can be seen in the spread of peyote as a religious experience in North America. Peyote, the cactus drug, was first used as a substitute for white man's Holy Spirit by the Indians in Northern Mexico; but then it rapidly spread northward through many tribes of the United States into Canada, often reaching into tribes who had formerly been bitterest enemies.

The same can be said about Muchape, the anti-witch medicine of East-Central Africa. It had its origin somewhere in Central Mozambique and moved north as far as Tanzania and Kenya, east to Angola and Zaire, and south into South Africa — all in the course of one generation. The pattern of its spread was effective E-1 which became E-2, which again became E-1, which having changed the new society again, goes E-2 to reach its neighbors.

3. *Practical considerations* At the practical level there again are several points to underscore.

a. James Scherer in his book, *Missionary Go Home,* has already pointed out very effectively that for all their self-sacrifice and dedication, E-3 missionaries almost universally have not been able to pass on their zeal for evangelism to their converts. At least one reason seems to be that too much of the foreign wrapper was imported and this prevented healthy, meaningful E-1 evangelism from developing in the local situation.

b. When the E-3 foreign missionary's own cultural models for conversion, church, and Christian living become the one and only model God requires, the evangelized people are pushed to become imitation Europeans rather than spiritually reborn nationals. At a recent conference at which I spoke about indigenous and foreign conversion models, one of the leading nationals got up and said, "Sir, what you have said about conversion deeply moves me, because, I must confess, I have not been converted that way. My deeper African values have not been changed. I have merely become an imitation European on the outside. I have not learned to listen to the Holy Spirit, but I have been trained to listen very carefully to what the missionary wants." Furthermore, the denominational nature of most mission work, or even the distance between supposedly non-denominational faith missions, has often helped to create support for local prejudice systems rather than helping to eliminate them. In fact, very frequently Christianity has helped to provide the new sanctified rationale for the continuing prejudice, as Dr. Winter's paper already points out.

c. Because missionaries often developed the feeling that their work was somehow lacking in depth, they opted to stay longer and to try harder to get better results. But the result they really achieved, as Claude Stipe has already pointed out, is that they tended to usurp the place of the Holy Spirit in the lives of the believers. I cannot think of a more painful experience than when I myself had to confess to the young Choco church in Panama that I had kept one of their men from doing what the Spirit of God had told him to do because of my public pronouncements.

d. When the Asia Conference of Churches some time ago, and the All Africa Council of Churches recently, called for a moratorium on the missionary personnel and foreign funds, there were, of course, some anti-Western sentiments coloring the proposal, but as I listened to the Lusaka discussions I became convinced that African leaders were really saying: "We need that moratorium so that we can let what is 'rice Christian' in our midst die. We need time to peel off the foreign wrapper and to find what the real message of God for us is. Then we need to translate this message into life and action so that we can do effective E-1 evangelism in our midst. Once we have achieved this, then we will again be ready to join hands with the rest of the churches in the world to complete the task of world evangelism."

Now a few remarks in the second area of concern: I am afraid that I have to confess that I do not share Dr. Winter's view that the so-called non-Christian world has no near neighbors. In fact, I feel that we as evangelists often fail to see and to utilize the cultural links of near-neighbor relationships which God in his providence forges. Look at China for exampe: right now in Tanzania and Zambia there are some 30-40,000 working together with Africans to build a new railroad. Could it not be that God has called African believers to share the Good News with these Chinese workers? Then could not these transformed by the power of God become God's tools to spark a Good-News revolution in China?

Before I conclude, I want to sound a personal testimony with which I hope you can identify. Dr. Graham underscored the fact that as the Scriptures lost their authority in the lives of believers and in the work of the church in the West, evangelistic fervor declined accordingly. I want to testify that we are on the verge of a possible reversal of this trend as the result of two new developments in Bible translation.

a. The Bible societies have accepted the principle that all new translation shall be done by mother-tongue speakers of these languages. This makes nationals responsible for the quality of the translation.

b. The second is a growing awareness that most languages have obligatory grammatical or semantic categories for which there is no help in the Greek or Hebrew text. In order for these translations to be equally authentic, it is essential that the Spirit of God who spoke in the original, speak today to clarify God's intent.

The result is that in an ever-increasing number of languages, mother-tongue speakers as translators are appealing to the entire community to pray: God if you had said this only in our language, how would you have said it? The startling result of the answer to these prayers is that in these African contexts the Bible no longer is a message of the white-man's God, to white people, said to be valid also for Africans, but it is the authoritative message of God to the specific group since he has now spoken to them specifically in the clarification of the demands of their language. The resulting authority of the Bible is reminiscent of the power of the Word in the early chapters of Acts.

In conclusion I want to say that it is my genuine desire that this conference and my small part in it can help set our own hearts on fire so that each one of us returning home may bring that "spark" from God which will start an evangelistic fire in our home community to give our people a deep experience of the power and Spirit of God in such a dynamic way that movements like the one described in Acts will begin in many places in the world, and that the fire of E-1 becoming E-2 evangelism will sweep the world like the great grass fires that race across the vast, African grasslands in the dry season.

RESPONSE TO RALPH D. WINTER AND DR. JACOB LOEWEN
David J. Cho

1. Generally, I agree with Dr. Winter's position. As to Dr. Loewen's, while I admit that there are a number of good points, I cannot agree with his negative judgment upon the necessity or effectiveness of cross-cultural evangelism.

2. An honest criticism on the failures of Western missions is praiseworthy. Yet, it should aim at correcting the past mistakes for constructing a right mission strategy for today. It should not aim merely to deny the effectiveness of cross-cultural evangelism.

3. The claim that the days of world mission are gone is mistaken. Without a burning zeal for mission to the enormous, unreached area, the concern for the E-1 evangelism would itself die.

4. Dr. Winter places the highest priority on E-3 while placing E-3 at the third place in order after E-1 and E-2. The order should be reversed. The evangelism of the highest priority, i.e., E-3 should be placed at the first, even in order. Dr. Winter's E-3 should be E-1 and his E-1 should be E-3.

5. Geographical ordering from the nearest area to the farthest is the measurement of a human-centered perspective. With mission and evangelism seen and understood in terms of divine mandate, there is no difference between "home" and "abroad." There simply is "a world." All of the E-1, E-2, E-3 should be equally and simultaneously stressed. When one of the three is neglected, the evangelical enterprises in other areas are bound to fail.

6. As a response to the negative position toward the cross-cultural evangelism, I present my views as the following: The failure of the Euro-American missions was not as much due to the problem of communication gap as to the problem of life-style and posture of missionaries. The failures were rather due to the lack of right motivation and dedication. Here is an example of the case. In Korea there are two opposite kinds of missionaries.

> 1. Mr. A is a second-generation missionary. He is not yet able to preach in Korean. He still has difficulties with Korean foods. He cannot read Korean newspapers or magazines. Even though he works hard, he is not willing to break through the cultural gap.

> 2. Mr. B has been a missionary in Korea only about five years. He is, however, fluent in the Korean language. He contributes quite a number of articles to magazines and newspapers. He spends much time in the bookstores on the street and tries to read as many newly published books as possible. He is well accustomed to the

Korean way of life and places himself in the current of Korean culture.

Mr. A belongs to a well-financed mission board. Mr. B is poorly supported for his living. As for the success and effectiveness of the two kinds of missionaries, you do not have to ask me to answer further.

7. We have to realize another fact, that the Western mission is entering its fourth stage. I describe the first stage as the planting stage, the second as the cultivating stage, the third as the growing stage, and the fourth as the maturing stage.

8. Accordingly, the cross-cultural evangelism has entered the stage of East-West cross-cultural evangelism. Mission should not be used as an instrument for the denominational expansion or territorial expansion of colonialism. The mission today should be Gospel-centered and multi-nationally structured.

9. The world mission is a divine imperative and mandate. We cannot say more or less of the importance of it. We can only respond to his love and dedicate ourselves for the task.

10. The Tunisian Church in North Africa has vanished with her glory from the earth. The churches in Asia Minor disappeared. Wasn't it due to the exclusiveness on the cross-cultural matters and to the loss of missionary vision?

11. The secular world continues to engage in cross-cultural enterprises: international funds, international research organizations, international monetary circulations, etc. If mission and evangelism do not engage in cross-cultural enterprises, there will come a crisis for mission and evangelism.

RESPONSE TO DR. RALPH D. WINTER'S PAPER
Pablo M. Pérez

Dr. Pérez, Mexico City,
Mexico, is Visiting Professor of World
Missions at Dallas Theological Seminary.

Culture as a most vital factor in the effective communication of the Gospel of Jesus Christ can no longer be ignored or passed off lightly. In today's world when a new sense of self-awareness and pride has arisen in all quarters, when different peoples are asserting themselves with increased dignity, and when no apology needs to be made concerning one's particular heritage, the Church of Jesus Christ cannot afford to overlook the validity of these cultural distinctions.

And Dr. Ralph Winter has challenged us not only to accept the fact of, as he calls it, "cultural distance," but to enter into a frank and intelligent discussion and understanding of the implications related to it. Such statements as "the awesome problem is...that most non-Christians in the world today are not culturally near neighbors of any Christians," and that it will "take a special kind of cross-cultural evangelism to reach them," are rather compelling. No believer who is identified with his Master can dismiss it, nor should he fail to be moved to take the adequate steps to turn the tide. By the same token, no one can dare to stress a highly nationalistic spirit which bows to local pressures rather than gives way to the innermost desires of God's heart.

Also the very fact that there are distinct peoples within any given country in the world today who are isolated from a Christian witness — four out of every five people in the world — shows us both the immensity of the task and the grief our Savior must still be experiencing. Clearly, something drastic has to be done if his redeeming power is to be known and understood by those who are lost in their trespasses and sins.

For reasons of clarity Dr. Winter has grouped these differences under the three main headings which he has designated as E-1, E-2, and E-3. This is a handy formula in many respects, for it opens our eyes to the complexity of human cultures. However, I believe he would be the first one to admit that it is by far an over-simplification of the situation. This is evidenced by the complication posed simply by the different sub-groups that he mentioned.

Closely related to this is the need to establish a clear-cut distinction between the different items which constitute any given culture and those elements which cut across cultures and have now become a feature in several latitudes regardless of cultural backgrounds. Prejudice is but one of them, and they all seem to present a common front which results in a rather formidable barrier to effective evangelism. For instance, young people today are showing their distrust for their elders in many ways across the world; oppressed peoples, who have arbitrarily been classified as minorities, are discovering new means of rejecting the Gospel; intellectuals have not relented in their almost uniform appeal to science over faith. These and many more have produced appealing arguments and somewhat predictable reactions which are not completely controlled by the culture of a particular locality. Call it guilt by association, differences of interpretation of the same basic truth — the case of the Samaritans in John 4, as mentioned by Dr. Winter — or call it any other way, these obstacles and features of our present civilization evidence supracultural characteristics which have to be confronted and dealt with adequately.

Along the same lines one can find that Dr. Winter's initial emphasis on evangelism as being effective communication is later expanded to mean the establishing of "strong, on-going, vigorously evangelizing denominations, and then for that national church to carry the work forward on the really high-powered E-1 level." While it is true that communication implies a follow-up process, and that any evangelistic effort cannot stop when a person becomes a new person in Christ and leave him there, the subject of a "national" church raises a different issue. In other words, whereas there is an urgent need to conduct E-2 and E-3 type evangelism to communicate initially the Gospel simply because there are not enough E-1 people to do the task in many areas, it does not follow that the churches into which these people will have to be incorporated must necessarily be made up exclusively of people of common background and/ or likes or dislikes. This may be pragmatically defensible, and even temporarily tolerated, but it will also tend to perpetuate adverse existing conditions and prejudices simply because they can be labeled as culturally determined.

But this is neither the biblical pattern nor intention, particularly in the book of Acts. Even cursory reading of the first verses in chapter 13 will tell us that Simon called Niger, Lucius of Cyrene, and Manaen "who had been brought up with Herod the tetrarch" were a part of the church in Antioch not so much because that was where they "felt at home," but because this is where the Holy Spirit had appointed them to be. Social and cultural considerations must have played a key role, as will be pointed out later on, but there was another compelling force to gather them together in the same place at that time. Just the same, the church in Ephesus, both as it is introduced to us in its early stages in Acts 17 and as it was further maturing in the letter addressed to it — to say nothing about the apostolic guidelines given to Timothy in the first letter he received from Paul, and the divine observations found in Revelation 2:1-7 — exhibits a true and determined effort to bring both Jew and Asian together. It is stated not only that Paul preached indiscriminately to both Jews and Greeks in Asia for two years (Acts 19:10), but that Christ had brought down the wall of partition that separated Jew from Gentile, "for he himself is our peace" (Eph. 2:14), as a climax to his argument for the unity within the church of Jesus Christ. Thus we "are no longer strangers and aliens, but . . . fellow-citizens with the saints, and are of God's household" (Eph. 2:19). This Christ accomplished by his blood (v. 13), and is thus not to be taken lightly.

This does have a bearing today, especially in the Third World where social stratification is much more visible than in North America and where, I am convinced, this very feature has to be recognized and even used initially for the communication of the Gospel, but should never be allowed to remain as a permanent distinctive of the church of Jesus Christ any place in the world.

This brings us to a consideration of the relationship between culture and Christianity, especially with respect to the stages of maturity which are beyond the initial communication. To say that for the church to work effectively in evangelization on the E-1 sphere may mean that a culture is to be accepted as it is, and a church to be established by its guidelines, poses new problems. For one thing, even the implied thought behind this reasoning will tend to absolutize culture and make the newly-established and maturing church so basically affected by its environment as to be somewhat unable to affect it. True, as Latourette constantly points out in his works, the world to which Christianity comes affects the church powerfully, but at the same time the church by its very presence, if nothing else, must definitely affect the world which surrounds it.

This means, as has already been mentioned, that cultural differences are not to be perpetuated in the churches, but also that the counter-cultural characteristic of Christianity cannot, again, be ignored. This is because for many centuries the church has been subjected to all kinds of modifications and adaptations with different degrees of syncretism which in many places has produced an almost unrecognizable type of Christianity, be it Christo-paganism or present-day Constantinianism. But the words of Jesus, "You are the salt of the earth," and those of a similar nature, were not simply nice-sounding figures of speech, much less pious platitudes, but serious injunctions to cause a veritable revolution in the world.

The observation made by the Thessalonian unbelieving Jews that "these men (meaning not only Paul and Silas, but Christians in general) who have upset the world have come here also," is no mild comment on the radical effect of the Gospel message. In other words, the Gospel is supposed to act as an agent of change both individually and corporately to improve existing cultures. This does not mean that one should envision or work for the establishment of a "Christian culture" which will then be the prototype for everyone else to copy, but that it should so transform the individuals in any given culture as to have them act as constant correctives of the unbiblical patterns of that culture. This is because churches are to be established in order to fulfill the purpose of God as revealed in his Word through human agents, who will remain in need of correction even though they are members of Christ's body, but not to serve the purposes of any given culture.

This leads us to the last observation, that is, of the relative place of culture in God's plan. While culture is a most important and vital factor of human life, it is not the determinant one. At best, it is a conditioning factor since it is in constant flux and at the mercy of many changing patterns and circumstances. Thus it should not be allowed to set down the rules, not even those within its own sphere of influence, which will eventually result in the configuration of the church in a local area. It is my conviction that the Holy Spirit is the determining factor in any strategy of evangelism at any stage of its implementation. It is he who compels both believer and unbeliever to obey the Word of God and to act upon its claims by meeting them where they are culturally, but imposing his guidelines within God's ultimate plan for man.

This is borne out in many passages of Scripture, but perhaps we should go to the believers in Samaria in order to keep within the example used by Dr. Winter. He pointed out that the woman at the well "reached others in her town by efficient E-1 communication," and that "hopefully Jesus' E-2 witness set in motion E-1 witnessing in that Samaritan town." In other words, that while they had needed to be reached by an E-2 intervention in the person of our Lord himself, another E-2 visit should have been unnecessary, if not altogether unlikely. However, we see in Acts 8 that Philip did go again — whether it was to Sychar or not the Scriptures do not tell us — and that there is every evidence that the E-1 type of evangelization started by the woman never did amount to much. Furthermore, it is to be noted that the apostles in Jerusalem, in what could be construed as in keeping with true paternalistic fashion, thought it wise to send Peter and John to Samaria to give some kind of sanction to what was going on there. To put it differently, there was not only a repetition of E-2 evangelistic effort, but of E-2 intervention in the internal affairs of that fellowship of faith.

But, is that what really took place? Should we not take a second look at the situation and see that whereas Samaria might have represented a cultural distance of sorts, cultural distance was no obstacle for the Holy Spirit to impose his strategy even though there had been a rather convincing E-1 type of evangelistic communication? What I am trying to say is that the Holy Spirit does want us to see and be sensitive to cultural differences, but that he neither wants us to be controlled by them to the extent that we do not step into places where there may be some kind of E-1 type evangelism and thus fail to accomplish the task that is still formidable, nor that he allows us to set guidelines for his church that are dictated exclusively by circumstances.

Thus while cross-cultural evangelism may be the highest priority — and I am convinced that it is — it does not exist for its own sake, nor is it based on cultural differences themselves as much as on the compulsion and guidelines determined by the Holy Spirit. We should not, therefore, commit ourselves to patterns of action or strategy which may make sense, humanly speaking, but rather let him work in us, through us, and even in spite of us, for his own purpose and the glory of God.

THE HOLY SPIRIT IN WORLD EVANGELIZATION
Gottfried Osei-Mensah

Rev. Osei-Mensah, Nairobi, Kenya,
is Pastor of the Nairobi Baptist Church.

Introduction
We all admit, as Christians, our need for divine help in the task of evangelizing the world. We also acknowledge that the help we need is available through the Holy Spirit, Christ's gift to his people for the fulfillment of their mission (Acts 1:8). However, considerable confusion exists among Christians today, both in thought and practice, concerning the nature of the Spirit's power and how it can be appropriated in evangelism.

1. His part and ours
"You shall receive power when the Holy Spirit has come upon you . . ." (Acts 1:8)

a. *The Spirit came as Lord.* If you received a package of explosives you would have to decide what to do with it. But if you were favored with the visit of a dignitary, he more or less decides what to do with you! You are at his disposal. The Lord Jesus promises his people, not "parcels of power," but the powerful personage of the Holy Spirit to stay with them. The coming of the Holy Spirit was proof that God had exalted Jesus Christ to the position of highest authority, honor, and rule. God had thereby vindicated Jesus' claim to be the Son of God and the Savior of mankind (see Acts 2:33, 36). The supreme work of the Holy Spirit is to witness to this reality on earth; and he does so in and through Christians (John 15:26). For this end, we must consistently submit to him as our Teacher, our Master, and our Helper.

b. *The Spirit is our Teacher.* It is the work of the Holy Spirit to reveal truths previously hidden from human search and understanding, and to enlighten men's minds to know and understand them (I Cor. 2:9, 10). In this way, he led the apostles to fully understand our Lord Jesus Christ, and the work for salvation which God has done through him for all mankind. They saw in their Savior, raised to the position of honor by the Father, infinite riches and merits to meet the needs of all who trust in him. Life took on new meaning in the light of God's revelation. Creation, they understood, had a purpose and goal. Man's problems in life were understood in reference to his rebellion and estrangement from God. They knew, by personal experience, that God had provided in Jesus the basis for pardon and reconciliation for all mankind. And so they preached the Good News to people everywhere.

What the Holy Spirit taught the apostles is embodied in the Scriptures for us. When we come to the Bible with open minds and humble hearts, the same Spirit illumines the written Word and enlightens our minds to know and to obey the truth.

If the role of the Holy Spirit is to teach, ours is to be diligent students of the Word. Our churches everywhere are full of Christians who possess sufficient truth for salvation but not enough to make them confident in sharing their faith with other people. One of the first steps in mobilizing Christians for world evangelization should be the promotion of personal and group Bible studies in our churches, in addition to expository preaching from our pulpits. We must aim to make every Christian "a workman who has no need to be ashamed, rightly handling the word of truth" (II Tim. 2:15).

We must also be diligent students of the different cultures in which we are called to serve. Paul's language and thought-patterns were chosen to suit his Jewish audience in Acts 22, and his Athenian audience in Acts 17:16ff. Unless this is done, our relevant Good News will be lost in the process of communication. One practical application of this to world evangelization is to promote first-class translation of the Scriptures into every language. The revival and growth of the churches in Korea and in East Africa have been attributed largely to the availability and faithful teaching of the Bible in the vernacular of the people.

c. *The Spirit is our Master.* It is the work of the Holy Spirit, living in us, to free us from the rule of sin in our daily lives, and to help us live the new life we share with Christ. In this process he may use the strong attraction of Christ's love to help us live the new life we share with Christ. In this process, he may use the strong attraction of Christ's love to help us aspire to a greater devotion to him. He may also use a painful discipline of some trial to return us to submission and obedience. There is no better witness to the authority, honor, and rule of our Savior among men than to see us gladly and thankfully subject to his authority and rule, thereby upholding his honor. If they see us free from the rule of sin in our lives, they have the evidence that Jesus Christ is powerful to save.

Submission to the rule of Christ's Holy Spirit is no easy matter in this permissive and materialistic age. Every Christian must make a conscious effort to "lay aside every weight, and sin which clings too closely," and refuse to be "conformed to this world" (Heb. 12:1; Rom. 12:2). The practical discipline of regular fasting and stricter stewardship of our resources of time, money, and materials may be salutary in our age. Somehow or other, the evangelical Christian's reverence and submission to Christ's authority in every aspect of life needs to be more evident than it is today.

d. *The Spirit is our Helper.* Obedience and submission to the Holy Spirit lead us to consciously enjoy the presence of our Lord in our lives (John 14:21,23). We all know the deep peace of being in the center of the Lord's will for us at a particular time. Then, whatever else is true, we enjoy the knowledge of being the objects of his love and care.

The consciousness of the Lord's presence enabled the disciples to face alienation in a world that could not understand them; and hatred from people who crucified their Lord (John 15:18-20).

We need the Holy Spirit's help as we approach modern, self-sufficient men and women with the Good News; to bear their antagonism cheerfully; to challenge their apathy boldly; and to plead with them lovingly to quit their sinful way of life and return to the Lord who is ready to pardon them, and give them a fulfilling purpose in life.

Twentieth-century evangelicals have paid lip service to the Holy

Spirit as our Helper for too long. Prayer meetings are the poorest attended church meetings everywhere. As we have imbibed the self-confident spirit of our age, prayer has become a meaningless postscript to our plans and programs. Yet the Lord knows we are utterly weak in ourselves, and incapable of bearing lasting spiritual fruit without him. In the Holy Spirit, there is "power to the tired and worn out, and strength to the weak" (Isa. 40:29). The confidence which the Spirit gives to praying Christians can lead to far more imaginative planning, and a fruitful result. For example, in the early 1960s the Christian Union of Ibadan University, Nigeria, had an idea. They concentrated prayer on students in each hall of residence for a whole week in turn, followed by a week of personal visit and witness to every student in the hall by the Christians. God honored their practical dependence on him and a steady flow of converted students were added to the Christian Union every term.

When you speak of an incident to someone who does not want to believe you, his attitude makes you feel helpless. But if another person is present who witnessed the same incident, the whole situation is different. The nods of your fellow-witness give you confidence in speaking, and add weight to what you say. In the same way, the Holy Spirit is our fellow-witness to Christ in a sceptical world (John 15:26,27). His presence and help gives authority to what we tell people about our Savior, and challenges them to some decisive action. In his presence, men and women who have heard and resisted God's truth for a long time, suddenly break down under the conviction of his love for them personally, through Jesus Christ. The conversion experience is the crowning of the Spirit's convincing and convicting work in a person's life.

Summary

We have considered the nature of the Holy Spirit's power and how it relates to evangelism. In all that has been said so far, emphasis has been put on the Spirit's work in and through the individual. This is primary. But the Holy Spirit may also move on a large scale in different communities and cultural groups.

Ephesus is a biblical example of the impact of the Good News on every aspect of community life (see Acts 19). Paul made a few converts there, trained them in discipleship for two years; and the result was that "all the residents of Asia (modern Turkey) heard the word of the Lord, both Jews and Greeks" (v. 10). The word of the Lord converted deficient, nominal Christianity (vs. 1-7); challenged Jewish traditionalism (vs. 8,9); condemned religious syncretism (vs. 11-17); conquered occultism (vs. 18-20); and undermined questionable trade and industry at Ephesus (vs. 23-27). Individuals entered a deep spiritual experience; the name of the Lord Jesus was extolled, and the Word of the Lord took root and prevailed in that cultural setting.

Men and women filled with the Holy Spirit have "turned the world upside down" many times since those apostolic days. Tribe after tribe has become disenchanted with the unjust, immoral, and wasteful aspects of their traditional beliefs and practices. Through the activities of Christian educators, Bible translators, medical missionaries, literature and radio evangelists, as well as the changed lives of their own people who have believed, they have been attracted to the Christian faith. True conviction has led many of them to turn to God from idols to serve a living and true God (I Thess. 1:9).

Authentic Christianity is engaged in a serious confrontation with the forces of syncretism in Africa today. The search for the "authentic African" by nationalist leaders is tending to the revival of heathenism everywhere. The phenomenal growth of the African Independent churches already show syncretistic signs, perhaps unintentionally at present, due to lack of biblical teaching. The third factor is the quest for African theology which is gathering momentum among liberal theologians all over tropical Africa. Evangelization of Africa in the next decade will depend on the victory authentic Christianity wins in the present conflict, and its justification to be truly African because truly rooted in Africa.

In practical terms, this means the provision of facilities for training Africans in biblical theology, Christian education, and expository preaching, in the context of Africa. This, I believe, is a matter of urgency, if God's Word is to grow and prevail mightily in Africa tomorrow.

2. *Appropriating the Spirit's power*

We pointed out at the beginning that the Holy Spirit is sovereign Lord, and that we are at his disposal. Moreover, there is no reluctance on his part to release his power in and through us. "He it is who awakens in the hearts of believers the jealousy for the honor of their Lord, the compassion for the souls of the perishing, the faith in his promise, the willing obedience to his commands, in which mission takes its rise."

To be his effective instruments in the task of world evangelization we must be in a right relationship with him, namely, submissive to his teaching and rule in our lives, and dependent on his leading and help in our plans to carry out the Lord's command to preach the Good News to all mankind.

There are two main schools of thought today with regard to how a Christian enters and maintains this right relationship with the Holy Spirit.

a. *The fullness of the Holy Spirit.* A life of moral and spiritual victory begins for the Christian when he comes to realize, through faith, that his old self was crucified with Christ, and that he now shares with Christ the new life in the Spirit (Rom. 6:4, 8:2). From then onward his joy and fruitfulness in service depend on his obedience to the Holy Spirit living in him — the condition for remaining "filled with the Spirit" (Eph. 5:18). If he grieves the Holy Spirit through disobedience, selfishness, or apathy, spiritual and moral defeat, powerlessness and barrenness result. The way back into fellowship with the Spirit is via repentance, confession of the sin, and faith in God through Christ's work on the Cross to forgive, accept us back, and fill us afresh with the Holy Spirit.

The East African revival has followed this path of repentance, forgiveness, cleansing, and fullness. It all began about forty years ago with a growing dissatisfaction with defeat in the spiritual life of individuals, and dismay at the coldness in the common life of the church. God met their need; and ten years later, it was said of the growing numbers of the "saved ones":

"They had one and all been through 'the valley of humiliation' to a deep and even agonizing sense of sin; they had been driven to painful and costly repentance, often with its exacting demands of open confession and restitution; and they had seen and found cleansing in the precious blood of Christ, and victory over sin through his indwelling Spirit. They were marked men: joy shone in their faces and everywhere they went they had a testimony."

It remains true today that the movement is characterized by joy and praise to the Lord; mutual care and fellowship transcending the barriers of class, tribe or race; and concern for the unsaved. True, in fellowships where the evangelistic concern has been lost, "the brethren" have become inward looking, and love has given place to legalism.

b. *The baptism with the Spirit.* The baptism with the Holy Spirit has been variously understood and interpreted by Christians. The Holiness Movement (late nineteenth century) identified it with "entire sanctification" as a second blessing subsequent to conversion. The early Pentecostals understood it as a third, distinctive experience — "a gift of power upon the sanctified life." Today, most people use the phrase to describe "a second encounter with God (the first being conversion) in which the Christian begins to receive the supernatural power of the Holy Spirit into his life." The preparation for experiencing the power of the Holy Spirit in this way is generally given as: repentance of every known sin, specific request for the baptism with the Spirit, yielding of the entire being to the Lord Jesus Christ, and expectant faith awaiting the fulfillment of God's promised blessing. The fellowship, prayer, and laying on of hands by those who have had the experience may be a boost for the faith of the candidate, but they are not essential for receiving the baptism. For most people who seek this experience, the undisputed sign of its fulfillment is to speak in tongues. Don Basham, a prominent leader in the charismatic movement, insists that, "something is missing in your spiritual life if you have received the Holy Spirit yet have not spoken in tongues." However, there are other leaders in the movement who dismiss this sentiment as unnecessary, unbiblical, and divisive.

It is true that not all the claims of the "exploding power for evangelism" resulting from the "baptism with the Holy Spirit" can be justified in my part of the world. On the contrary, considerable zeal has been spent in attempts to "evangelize" Christians! The resulting confusion has done much damage to a fine work of the Holy Spirit in many schools and colleges of tropical Africa. At the same time, there are some who have found a spiritual and psychological release through this experience, and are serving the Lord effectively. Some of them are exercising spiritual gifts they were not aware of having before.

A full discussion of the baptism with the Holy Spirit is beyond the scope and purpose of this paper. Those evangelicals who understand the baptism with the Spirit as an initial, and therefore universal Christian experience make a strong biblical case for their position. They see in the New Testament the Holy Spirit's norm for most Christian people, which is one initiatory baptism and a continuous and increasing fullness or repeated fillings. They admit that, "sometimes the bestowing of certain spiritual gifts seems to be accompanied by a quickening, an enriching, a deepening of the recipient's spiritual life; sometimes a Christian worker is given supernatural power for the particular work to which God has called him." But they would insist that "those to whom the sovereign Spirit grants such experiences should not, if they are true to Scripture, refer to any of them as the baptism of the Spirit; nor should they urge the same experiences upon others as if they were the spiritual norm."

We could wish that all Christians were of one mind concerning the doctrine of the Holy Spirit. But this is not necessary before we can look to him together to empower us for the task of world evangelization. Our differences are basically in the area of Christian experience rather than that of Christian belief. As we face together the mammoth task of making Christ known to men and women for salvation, and the sense of our utter inadequacy, three things should unite us — whatever our particular understanding of the teaching on the Holy Spirit:

(i) A common thirst for the Spirit's fullness — to cleanse, fill, and rule our lives with the authority of our Lord Jesus Christ.

(ii) A common faith in our exalted Lord Jesus Christ to make good in our experience his promise that, "he who believes in me . . . out of his heart shall flow rivers of living water" (John 7:38,39). The evangelistic implication of this promise is inescapable.

(iii) A common heart-cry, uniting us together at the feet of the Lord Jesus Christ in response to his loving invitation to all who thirst to come to him and drink (see John 7:37). By faith, we must thank him for his power which perfectly matches our weakness; and we must acknowledge our constant dependence on him.

Paul's word of exhortation seems relevant here: "Let those of us who are mature be thus minded; and if in anything you are otherwise minded, God will reveal that also to you. Only let us hold true to what we have attained" (Phil. 3:15,16).

3. *Our planning and his leading*

The words of Dr. Andrew Murray quoted earlier seem fitting: "It is the Holy Spirit who awakens in the hearts of believers the jealousy for the honor of their Lord, compassion for the souls of the perishing, the faith in his promise, the willing obedience to his commands in which the mission takes its rise. He it is who draws together to united effort, who calls forth suitable men to go out, who opens the door and prepares the hearts of the heathen to desire or to receive the Lord."

The Holy Spirit leads by inspiring us with a life and disposition out of which right purposes and decisions come forth. In the context of world evangelization, the "right purpose" may be defined as the spreading of the saving rule of the Lord Jesus Christ in the lives of men and women. The "right decisions" have to do with the most effective way we may do this in our own generation.

a. *Leading by inspiring.* A life of submission and habitual fellowship with the Holy Spirit in the Word of God, meditation, and prayer is the context in which we should expect spiritual vision. The secret (friendship) of the Lord is for those who fear him (Psa. 25:14). Movements and associations which have counted for God in world evangelization have been born as God has found individuals or small bands of committed men and women to share his plans and movements for their time. God matches our commitment to his will with an adventurous faith. Then, he causes to blossom in the obedient Christian, potentials and abilities he has himself placed in us to realize the vision. He also gives new powers and abilities where necessary. No sharp distinction should be made between a Christian's so-called natural abilities and the more supernatural abilities the Holy Spirit enables us to exercise either regularly or on specific occasions. The Christian existed in the creative imagination of God long before he was born or regenerated (Gal. 1:15; Eph. 1:4). Therefore, his abilities and potentials, when consecrated to the Lord, are no less the gifts of his grace than the supernatural endowments he may be given to exercise to confirm the Good News in a frontier situation. Both gifts may be abused for selfish purposes; but when dedicated to the glory of Christ, they are equally channels for the Holy Spirit's use. The tendency in some quarters to oppose the Spirit's immediacy to his working through the renewed minds and committed wills of Christians is neither biblical nor spiritual. It frustrates the very first commandment of the Lord; namely, to love God with all our heart, soul, and mind (Matt. 22:37).

b. *Right purposes.* To keep a spiritual vision in focus, and to use wisely our God-given resources (be it of time, money, spiritual gifts, or personnel) require careful planning and some degree of organization. The invisible church of Jesus Christ is an organism, but every local representation of it functions as an organization (Eph. 4:11-16). There are dangers with every human organization, including Christian ones. The chief danger with every Christian organization is the loss of spiritual vision. But the alternative is not the abolition of organization, but the setting of wise and spiritual goals and objectives: wise because biblical, and spiritual because the Holy Spirit's help (rather than human techniques) is counted on as the dynamic for their achievement. Nothing is more calculated to check our tendency to sloth than a clear spiritual vision articulated in concrete objectives and well-defined principles for action. Spiritual goals give meaning to commitment, inspire perseverance in prayer, and promote self-discipline for their realization.

The Apostle Paul taught these things by precept and example: "Do you not know that in a race all the runners compete, but only one receives the prize? So run that you may obtain it. Every athlete exercises self-control in all things. They do it to obtain a perishable wreath, but we an imperishable . . . I do not run aimlessly, I do not box as one beating the air" (I Cor. 9:24-26).

Underlying Paul's missionary effort was a definite plan and strategy:

(i) He gave priority to pioneer areas where Christ had not yet been preached (Rom. 15:20,22).

(ii) He used the Roman highways and aimed for centers of influence (refer to his missionary routes).

(iii) He moved in widening circles from established bases (refer to his missionary routes and his letters, e.g., Rom. 15:24; I Cor. 16:5-9).

(iv) He involved the churches he planted in all aspects of outreach: prayer, giving, co-workers and apprentices (Acts 20:4; Eph. 6:19; Phil. 1:5,7, 4:14-16).

(v) He did not expose himself irresponsibly to danger, but was not afraid to face it when he knew he was in the Lord's will (Acts 14:5,6, 17:10,13,14, 18:9-11; I Cor. 16:8,9).

(vi) Paul's plans were open-ended and completely available to the Holy Spirit's intervention at any point. If anyone showed that there was no conflict between sound spiritual planning and the immediacy of the Holy Spirit's working, it was the Apostle Paul (Acts 16:6-10). When the Holy Spirit intervenes sovereignly in our plans, he helps us achieve more than we had hoped for, not less. Through his intervention referred to above, the Good News reached Europe, and Asia and Bithynia were not ultimately forgotten (I Pet. 1:1). However, that was Paul's strategy. We have the responsibility to work out our own, under the inspiration, guidance, and fellowship of the same Spirit.

c. *Right decisions.* Our overall purpose as evangelical Christians is not difficult to state: to tell the Good News that Jesus Christ saves to everybody everywhere in our generation. We share this purpose with the Holy Spirit, our co-witness to Christ. However, to make right decisions at Lausanne (or after) as to how we may do this most effectively, we need to ask other questions: how is the Holy Spirit moving today? What is the prophetic vision for now? How do we interpret our generation and its events? What points of contact has the Good News with the struggles, hopes, and fears of mankind today?

The world can be divided roughly into three areas, based on current response to the Christian message:

(i) *Areas of rapid growth.* Roughly, this comprises the "Third World," non-Islam countries. For these, the right decision would seem to be the provision of facilities for teaching and training new Christians for more outreach and productive service.

(ii) *Areas of hostile resistance.* Areas dominated by hostile faiths and ideologies. The decision here must include the concentration of prayer to break down the power of sin, and achieve a break-through with the Good News. Meanwhile, full advantage should be taken of legitimate contacts available, such as radio broadcasts, correspondence courses, and Christians in educational, medical, and other secular employments overseas.

(iii) *Areas of apathy.* Roughly, countries formerly identified with Christianity. We need the unashamed witness of the many who have found reality in the Lord Jesus in the midst of much formalism in the churches. We need also fresh, imaginative approaches to the generation who do not go to church, and who do not see any relevance in Christianity.

In a shrinking world of jet travel and satellite communication, evangelical cooperation is not only desirable, but would seem to be vital for the goal of world evangelization. Our evident oneness is a powerful witness to Christ as Son of God and Savior of mankind (John 17:21, 23). We owe it also to our Lord, as good stewards of his resources, in a world of rising costs. Duplication and even competition among evangelicals, on the other hand, contradicts our message and confuses those we seek to reach for Christ. Whenever the Holy Spirit revives Christians and makes them jealous for the honor of their Lord, sectional and parochial interests lose much of their importance, and are ready to be set aside for higher objectives. May the Holy Spirit therefore revive and unite us so that mankind may hear its Savior's voice.

THE HOLY SPIRIT IN EVANGELISM
A testimony by Tom Houston

Rev. Houston, London, England,
is Communication Director for the
British and Foreign Bible Society.

I have had problems with the Holy Spirit. These have not been so much when I have been at the receiving end of the work of the Holy Spirit. That has been all right. From the time I was converted as a boy he took the initiative and brought me to Jesus without programs or follow up or any of the things I keep hearing are so necessary. Since then he has not let me go and has always taken new initiatives to develop me as a person who wants to be like Jesus. No, I have as much as I can cope with in the working of the Holy Spirit in my own life before God. There is no great problem there other than keeping up with what he seems to want me to do.

The problems arise when it is a question of my being a channel through whom he works in other people. I am rather ashamed about some of this because I have done some stupid things in my time in the name of the Holy Spirit. I'm afraid it was years before I realized that the Holy Spirit could be the most effective cover-up device for my getting what I wanted. Everybody kept talking about Acts 2 and I fell for it. It was a long time and after quite a lot of damage was done that I realized that the chapter I needed to go to sleep and get up on was Acts 8. There that big-head Simon Magus acted out for all to see the role that was most natural to me. Do you remember what he said? "Give me this power too, so that anyone I place my hands on will receive the Holy Spirit." You will recall that Peter did not use the most polite language in telling him what he thought of that. Peter was not around to deal with me like that or it might have saved a lot of heartache. For, you see, I got the message that somehow I could be used by God in a much greater way than I had been; a greater way than anybody I knew until then; perhaps even a greater way than Billy Graham or John Wesley or Hudson Taylor or Charles Grandison Finney or quite a few others. After all did Jesus not say, "Whoever believes in me will do the works I do — yes, he will do even greater ones, for I am going to the Father"?

It's a long story. It took a long time and I cannot tell you it all in ten minutes. Suffice it to say that I sought God for the fullness of the Spirit in nearly every way that has been written and talked about. I have had quite a number of the experiences that are described as being important and I have made claims and statements that I am ashamed to remember. But because the Holy Spirit was faithful and in his sovereignty would not let me go or be put off by my insufferable self-centeredness, I lasted until I saw that I was like Simon Magus in the eighth chapter of Acts and had better not be. The work of the Spirit is not to build me up but to reduce me to size so that Jesus could be seen. I have had to settle for certain options that I see to be part of the package that the New Testament offers me in connection with the Holy Spirit. You see,

I get two sets of signals from my Bible. I get pictures about rushing mighty winds, floods, baptisms by fire, places shaking and so on — all symbols of power, force, violence, coercion, crashing, breaking, burning, overwhelming — all big and great and grand. On the other hand, I get signals about God's not being in the wind and the fire and the earthquake but in the still small voice. I get signals about it not being by "might" and "power" but — strange to say — "by my Spirit."

Now being the kind of person I am, I cannot stand the grand. It goes to my head and that will not do. So I have to want the Spirit of Truth rather than the Spirit of Power, for in my hands the Spirit of Power would do violence to the voluntariness that is the very essence of the Good News of Jesus.

I have to avoid in my thinking the grand metaphors of fullness and baptism because they swamp me and like their counterparts in nature cause erosion instead of fertility. Instead I have to have a modest checklist approach. There is no doubt, I cannot deny it, that the Holy Spirit has me. He is in me — wonder of wonders!

I can deal with most of my difficulties by going through my New Testament checklist:

1. Am I lying to the Holy Spirit by being dishonest and professing more than is true like Ananias and Sapphira?
2. Am I resisting the Holy Spirit by refusing the truth like the Jerusalem Jews?
3. Am I grieving the Holy Spirit by having a bad relationship with others like the Ephesians?
4. Am I quenching the Holy Spirit by cramping the development and use of God's gifts in other people or in myself like the Thessalonians?

This practical approach helps me more than the undefined metaphors of fullness, etc. They cover all the aspects of my life and the Spirit's work — my character, knowledge, relationship, and service.

Oh yes, and about the gifts. It was a great relief to me when I saw the point of the "nothings" in I Cor. 13: "Though I have the gift . . . nothing." Those three zeros in verses 1, 2, and 3. It was so simple, yet for years I never saw it. You get no marks for gifts! Why should you? They are just your basic equipment. That took a lot of the heat out of my striving. The other thing that helped me was this "feelings are a bonus." If you get them, fine. If you don't, you won't starve.

Another important landmark in my experience and understanding of the Holy Spirit again had to do with his being the Spirit of Truth. John put it perfectly when he said, "When the Spirit of Truth comes he will lead you into *all* the truth" (John 16:13). When through seeking the fullness of the Spirit in a self-centered way I was in the wilderness, it dawned on me that if a baptism or new infilling of the Spirit was the answer to every problem that arose, as I was being told and was saying myself, I could do without most of the New Testament. There was little use for the pages and pages of moral and doctrinal instruction that make up so much of the Bible. I sensed there was something wrong then, and the fact that the Spirit of truth leads into *all* the truth has been of vital importance to me. The only special emphasis that I can live with is the whole Word of God for the whole life of man. The Spirit of Truth can only operate healthily when he is communicating within the context of the whole counsel of God. The Spirit and the Word cannot be separated or be in conflict at any point.

What has all this to do with evangelism? Well, it's saying that for Tom Houston much of what was going around about the Holy Spirit would have left him operating in the first half of the parable of the sower only. The good seed of the Word would have been scattered where it had no chance of germinating, where it would have germinated under artificial heat in shallow soil, or where because of haste it would have been sown among thorns. All such seed is ultimately lost for lack of understanding the message. But since the Spirit of Truth has had to be my emphasis rather than the Spirit of Power, I have learned slowly to work in evangelism so that as far as in me lies the seed of the Word that germinates through my ministry will last till it bears fruit, some more than others — but fruit none the less.

You may have guessed by now, that I have had what was called "the baptism of the Spirit" and did not find it helpful. I have spoken with tongues and it put me back in my spiritual life. Yet I know that others have been greatly helped by experiences like this. How do I live with this?

I believe that the way to resolve the differences we have about the Holy Spirit is in a more honest understanding of what the Bible teaches. I have come to see two things.

1. I began by assuming that "the baptism of the Spirit" is a technical term which always means the same thing. I have not seen this demonstrated to be true. I am open to the view that it may in fact be a metaphor or a picture which describes notable experiences of the Spirit.

2. I also assumed that the experience of the Holy Spirit came in the same ways everywhere in the New Testament. This again is an assumption that I have never seen demonstrated to be true. In fact the textual evidence is to the contrary. I believe that God brings out the range of gifts and experiences that are needed for each situation and each person. If there is *not* adequate help or "edification" by normal means then perhaps tongues are needed to help build up. On the other hand, if, as is true, I am built up adequately by other means of grace, what need do I have of tongues?

I genuinely accept that there is a stated variety in the way the Spirit works in individuals and different places in the New Testament and that it is the same today. This helps me to live with and love those whose experience is different from mine.

Now I was asked to make a personal statement. This I have done as honestly as I know how. I hope it has come through to you that I am not trying to do more than that. I do not suggest that what has been my experience should in any sense be standardized and applied to others. This I think is often our trouble that what has been precious to us we have tried to force on others. David's rejection of Saul's armor should have cured us of that. No, this is a personal statement. If it helps use it. If it does not, then leave it and find your own way with the Spirit for as Jesus says, he is quite unpredictable. "The wind blows wherever it wishes: you hear the sound it makes but you do not know where it comes from or where it is going. It is the same way with everyone who is born of the Spirit" (John 3:8).

I believe in the Holy Spirit who brought me to Jesus when I was not looking for him, who has kept me alive when the odds were that I should die as a Christian, who consistently reduces me to size, who seems still to work in other lives through me, sovereignly as he chooses for the glory of Jesus.

THE WORK OF THE HOLY SPIRIT IN EVANGELIZATION, INDIVIDUALLY AND THROUGH THE CHURCH.

A testimony by Rev. Juan Carlos Ortiz

The Holy Spirit in these last days is doing a new thing among the people of God. He is regrouping his people. Regrouping. Perhaps you ask, "What do you mean by 'regrouping'?" We were grouped, up to now, in different worlds by denominations, by races, by different types of groups. But in these last days the Holy Spirit is doing a new thing in Argentina and in all of Latin America and in many other parts of the world. The Holy Spirit is starting to regroup us into only two groups: those who love one another and those who *do not* love one another. Just two groups. And this is what the Lord Jesus Christ meant when he said, "That by this shall all men know that ye are my disciples." No, not by the good philosophical definition of our doctrine but the way we live together, the way we love one another. "By *this* shall all men know that ye have love one to another." And even in the last of time when everything will be finished, there are going to be only two groups, the sheep and the goats.

The sheep are those who love one another, that help each other, that feed the hungered, that dress and clothe those who have nothing; those who love one another. And the goats are those who do not love one another. And it is very easy to know who is in the sheep group and who is in the goat group because the sheep usually go all together, they put head to head and they go in one unit; but the goats, they go butting one another, continually butting. So if you want to know to which group any person belongs, you don't have to have the gift of discernment. If he butts, he is a goat. When we get together, when we love one another, even if you are premillennialist or postmillennialist or anything you have to say about your doctrine, the Holy Spirit today is renewing the fruit of the Spirit. Love, joy, peace — all those things are going to be the elements that show the world that we are his people. So God is regrouping his people and this is starting among the leaders. The Lord has not 400 churches in one city, in one locality; he has only one church divided in 400 pieces. All the pastors and leaders of that locality are the elders of the one church God has in that city. We should get together not only for a united campaign. We should get together because Jesus Christ wants us to be together. In every city we have pastors, leaders, Bible school teachers, seminary teachers, theologians. If we could have fellowship in the city we would grow because the knowledge that everybody has would be shared with the others and the whole church would be renewed and strengthened by the joint ministry of all the leaders of a certain location. And this is what is happening in our country.

A group of pastors of Buenos Aires is meeting two or three times a week. Monthly or every two months we go out for retreats. We have started to love one another — Baptists, Methodists, Anglicans, even Roman Catholic priests and Pentecostals — all types of ministers. The only base we have to get together is that we love one another. We have been enriched by the ministry of the others and the renewal that is taking over our countries. Happening there and going through all Latin America, and other parts of the world, is because a group of ministers are gathering together, loving one another, and sharing the things the Lord is revealing.

Jesus once asked that we be one. To be one. As the Trinity is One — Father, Son and the Holy Spirit are one, so he wants us to be one. To be one. And that means that we should be one not only in the evangelistic efforts, not only in the fellowship meeting, but we should love one another of the family in every city. We are like potatoes. Potatoes when they are planted are grouped by two, three or four in each plant. Then comes the harvest; they take the potatoes and put all of them in one box. But that is not unity yet; that's only regrouping, that's only confraternity, that's only fellowship but not unity. Those potatoes have yet to be peeled. When they are peeled and put together, they say, "Ah, now we are one." Not yet. They must be cut. Because cut ones are mashed potatoes. Hallelujah. Many potatoes but *one* mashed potato. When the potatoes are mashed not one of the potatoes can say, "This is me, ah?" And this is what the Holy Spirit, hallelujah, is starting to do today. The whole world is renewing this love that the same Spirit gives. Let's love one another, let's love with all our hearts. This is the key for evangelization because Jesus said, "That they may be one."

THE HOLY SPIRIT IN EVANGELISM
A testimony by Larry Christenson

Dr. Christenson, San Pedro, California,
USA, is Pastor of Trinity Lutheran Church.

For more than forty years I have been a Christian. And yet, as recently as twelve months ago, I have been evangelized. I go back to my earliest childhood memories, and there I discover, firmly implanted, a belief in Jesus as my personal Lord and Savior. And yet, in recent years, I have been evangelized.

The Apostle Paul wrote to believers in Ephesus who had faith in the Lord Jesus, and demonstrated that faith in love toward all the saints (Eph. 1:15). Yet he goes on to pray for them in essentially the same terms that he would use to pray for unbelievers: That the "eyes of their hearts may be enlightened" to see the truth that is in Jesus (Eph. 1:18, 5:8-14).

In Samaria, under the preaching of Philip the evangelist, many believed and were baptized. Yet their eyes were opened to a major new dimension of their life in Christ when Peter and John came down and prayed for them that they might receive the Holy Spirit (Acts 8:9-17).

The need to be evangelized, the need to be brought from darkness to light, is not a one-time need, but an ongoing need. If time permitted, we could trace this theme, with its clear evangelistic imagery, through Old Testament types, New Testament Scriptures, and myriad examples in the history of the church.

The Evangel, or Gospel, is the Good News about Jesus. When someone shows me something about Jesus which I have not known or experienced before, and the Holy Spirit awakens in me the expectation that this is going to become real in my own life, then I have been evangelized. I am not evangelized one time only, when I have an initial, saving encounter with Jesus. Nor am I evangelized every moment of every day, so that evangelism, as a term, becomes simply equivalent with the totality of Christian experience, and thereby, for all practical purposes, takes on another meaning. But I am evangelized at those moments when God determines to make known to me some major dimension of the person and work of his Son, which hitherto I have not known or experienced.

The writer to the Hebrews recounts how those to whom he is writing had laid hold on the foundational doctrines of the faith, and demonstrated great "work and love in serving the saints." But then he goes on to say that he "desires each one to show the same earnestness in realizing the full assurance of hope until the end" (Heb. 6:10-11).

If I live to be twice my forty-six years, I hope to go on being evangelized right up to the end.

Now I have discovered, as I am sure you also have discovered, that you can most readily lead others into those dimensions of the Christian life which the Holy Spirit has made particularly real to you. Hans Nielsen Hauge, the great Norwegian evangelist, had a vivid sense of the urgency of the Gospel message. It is told how he could fall into conversation with a stranger on the road, and within ten minutes have him on his knees, praying for forgiveness and assurance of salvation. Samuel Morris, the young man who came from Africa to the United States in the last century, knew the power of prayer. Barely educated, living in a strange culture, of another race, and dying before he had reached his twenty-second birthday, he nevertheless evangelized a university and became the fountainhead of a whole missionary movement because he knew God to be a prayer-answering God. When he simply closed his eyes and began to speak to his heavenly Father, whole congregations went to their knees, weeping.

One of the miracles of divine providence is the way in which God matches our need to be evangelized in some particular area, with a person or a group that has a lively faith for exactly that dimension of the Christian life. That is surely one of the fringe benefits of a great Congress like this: We are exposed to many possibilities for being evangelized!

The ministry which God has given me, as a parish pastor, has been mostly among Christians. At my ordination, my bishop laid upon me, as my chief charge, the work of "equipping the saints" (Eph. 4:12). While some of my experience has been in evangelizing those with no previous relationship to Jesus, more of it has been in evangelizing those who, like myself, already had at least an initial encounter with Christ. In the fourteen years that I have been pastor at Trinity Lutheran Church in San Pedro, California, I and my congregation have been evangelized. We have had opened to us dimensions of the Christian life which before we had not known or experienced.

As I look back over these years, one thing in particular stands out, and that is the way in which the Holy Spirit works in the process of evangelism. It is commonplace to say that evangelism depends upon the working of the Holy Spirit. But I believe that when I am evangelized, the working of the Holy Spirit has a precise focus, and that to know this is of critical importance when I make the transition from being the evangelized to being the evangelist. If I want to share with others what God has made real to me, I must not only know, but I must expect and depend upon this precise working of the Holy Spirit. This is what I would like to share with you, today, by way of testimony.

About two months after I came as pastor to San Pedro, we had a family retreat, the theme of which was *prayer* — the purpose of prayer, the promises connected with prayer, the centrality of prayer in the Christian life. The result of this retreat was that a fair number of people in the congregation were evangelized. This dimension of the Christian life opened up to them.

Now certainly prayer was not a new word to them. They were not utterly without previous experience in prayer. But you could talk to any of them today, and they would tell you that from that time prayer became a reality in their life which it was not before.

What made the difference? The difference was that there was quickened within them the expectation that God was going to act in response to their prayers. This was the working of the Holy Spirit. The words and ideas they heard were not new, as such. They may have heard much the same teaching years earlier, but it was only words and ideas, or at best an historical record of how some people had experienced the reality of prayer. But they themselves remained unevangelized until the Holy Spirit gave them the expectation that this was something that was about to happen in their own experience. He had ignited this expectation in my wife and myself some time earlier, and now it spread into the congregation.

Later on, when we undertook a considered study of Christian family life, this dimension of prayer formed a major part of it. People have come to us and remarked how some people have read this study of family life, and as a result have come to faith in Jesus. They think this somewhat strange, for it is not an "evangelistic" book. But really, it is not strange, because that study is the fruit of an expectation which the Holy Spirit quickened in us, that God's grace would be experienced in the everyday action and interaction of families which took seriously his plan for family life, and undergirded it with a life of prayer.

About thirteen years ago, we found ourselves involved in the charismatic renewal — before it even had a name, or had become a movement. It began with an interest in healing, then with speaking in tongues, prophecy, and other gifts of the Spirit. I suppose I had studied some of these things in the seminary, but it cannot have made much of an impression on me. I certainly never expected any such things to happen in my own life. But then, partly through reading, partly through personal contacts, but mostly through a study of Scripture, I was evangelized. The Holy Spirit quickened in me the expectation that these gifts of the Holy Spirit were available for us today.

It is certainly none of my purpose to rehearse controversies that have sometimes surrounded this subject. I simply share my testimony. After having lived in this dimension of Christian experience for nearly a third of my life, together with the people of my congregation, I have come to see in it this same precise working of the Holy Spirit: he has quickened an expectation that God is going to do something, and God has done it. A new dimension of Christian experience has opened up, a dimension promised by Jesus and practiced by the Apostles.

We have been told that modern man cannot believe in miracles and the supernatural. He is scientific, logical, realistic. If we are to gain the ear of modern man, we must de-mythologize the Gospel. But we have found almost the opposite to be the case. Precisely because modern man is realistic, he will not buy a de-mythologized Gospel. You cannot put a Bible in a man's hand, which tells about a Jesus who did mighty works and wonders and overcame the power of the devil, and commissioned his followers to do the same, and then offer him a church which has only words and a flurry of human activity.

San Pedro lies close to the center of the aero-space industry in California, so in our congregation we have a number of scientists and engineers. They are virtual stereotypes of the "modern man" that theologians write about; men who hurl satellites into space, and land the Apollo on the moon. Are men like this resistant to the miraculous and the supernatural? Not at all. In many ways they remind me of the centurion who came to Jesus, asking Jesus to heal his servant (Matt. 8:5-13). The centurion exercised power and authority in his own sphere as a soldier. He recognized in Jesus a similar capacity to exercise power and authority in the spiritual realm. It is not uncommon on a Sunday evening to see one of these men at the altar of our church, praying for the sick, or exercising a gift of clear prophetic insight, this same man who, on Monday morning, may fly to Texas to confer with other scientists about a new landing system for a space vehicle.

The Holy Spirit is quickening an expectation for spiritual gifts in our day, to remind the church that Jesus' ministry of power is both her heritage and her calling.

"The miracle-workers in the church," said a forerunner of the charismatic movement in England more than a century ago, "are Christ's hands, to show the strength that is in him. The healers of diseases are his touch, to show what pity and compassion are in him. The faith-administrators are his lion-heart, to show how mighty and fearless he is. The utterances of wisdom and knowledge are his mind, to show how rich and capacious it is."

In this cold and skeptical age, in this age which has been taught to disbelieve in the miraculous and the supernatural, we have found that this dimension of the Christian faith speaks to a deep need in the heart of man, a need which I would call the need to be *touched*. Not only to hear and think about the love and power and reality of God, but to experience it in concrete ways.

Our theme, then, is this: That in evangelism the Holy Spirit quickens an expectation that God is going to do something. His focus is not upon what God has done, but upon what he is going to do. The evangelist may tell me what Jesus has done for me. He may explain to me the whole process of salvation. But it remains history and theory until the Holy Spirit awakens in me the expectation that this reality is about to lay hold on my own life, now.

What, then, is our part? It is to "prepare the way of the Lord," to go before him, like John the Baptist, or like the seventy, and announce his coming,

"This Jesus, who forgives sin; this Jesus who answers prayer; this Jesus who gives the Holy Spirit; this Jesus who draws us into community with other believers — this Jesus is coming. He is coming to us. He is coming now. Prepare to receive him."

THE WORK OF THE HOLY SPIRIT IN EVANGELIZATION, INDIVIDUALLY AND THROUGH THE CHURCH
A testimony by Bishop Festo Kivengere

I hope as you clap after these testimonies you mean the clap is to Jesus, not to the testifier.

I want to invite a number of people from Tanzania, Uganda and Kenya, to come forward and stand around here. Men, women, bishops, archbishops, laymen, nobility, come right around here. They are going to sing to this crowd of brethren as a testimony when I am through.

I want to praise the Lord for the testimony. All I want to share with you in this short time is the glorious work of the Holy Spirit in bringing new life to a dead church which you traditionally call "revival." You can call it renewal, coming to life or whatever you choose. I want therefore to take a few moments to praise the Lord Jesus for Miss Kim's song. As she sang that wonderful song from the bottom of her heart, she was actually singing the theme of the East African revival because that is how it all began. The Lord Jesus in his risen power through the power of the Holy Spirit began to visit a church which was scattered like bones. Each member of the church was in his own little corner, and utterly lonely. Men and women were separated from each other because of tribes, because of race, because of doctrine. And there was no life, no testimony, no movement, no doors. It was a miserable existence in a church with a name of being a Christian church. Particularly, my church was very evangelical and very dry.

It may surprise some of you evangelicals that you can be evangelical and dry, but you can. And then Jesus Christ came. How? And why? It all began through the love as Miss Kim sang it. The attraction, the growing power came through a simple presentation of the New Testament and the Holy Spirit took men and women, including myself, from our isolation and drew us to the center, the Cross. The theme of East African revival was the Cross and we needed it. There was no medicine to heal our tribal separations and resentment. There was no possibility of uniting the black and the pink. There was no possibility of bringing men and women together — Africans are *chiefs* by nature and the husband is a chief at home (many of them were polygamists, of course). Therefore, there was no fellowship; there was a name but there was no fellowship. The Holy Spirit drew men and women from their isolation, and changed us — sins were sins in the glare of God's love and hearts were melted.

My brother talked about mashed potatoes. It takes the wounded hand to mash human life. There is no other way of softening, melting, and drawing together except through the love of Jesus on Calvary. And when that happens, do you know, may I use a simple expression? Each man was like a balloon — a pastor, a balloon in his ministry; laymen, all over there. And, of course, laymen in the congregation became little balloons, and you cannot have fellowship. You simply bounce from each other and fly away. You should have balloons, big ones you see. Husbands with big, big balloons controlling and ruling by force. The black man became a balloon in his particular culture and the white man was a balloon in his superiority. You never have fellowship that way.

Then, the message of God and the love of Jesus Christ, by the power of the Holy Spirit, drew us to Jesus. And in discovering Jesus we discovered ourselves and our miserable separations and our mean attitudes and we began to repent. Repent. That worked. A pastor standing before his congregation weeping — a very embarrassing experience for a man who wants a reputation in the ministry. A husband kneeling before his wife repenting. What came out of this? A fellowship, a song of joy. Even in the Anglican Church people began to clap like Pentecostals! And people began to love each other, Thank you, Pentecostals, for clapping.

Things were moving but in the center was Jesus Christ and out of this came a fellowship of love. The bleeding Savior united these men and women and out of isolated balloons he got a broken group of men and women who love each other deeply. Then, the Holy Spirit began his tremendous work of baptizing us all in the love of Jesus Christ. He filled us with that love and in that love we saw the world. Men went out like fire, evangelizing their neighbors, evangelizing the business men, talking to uncles and aunts; it became one huge crowd of evangelists. We praise the Lord.

That is what has happened in East Africa and out of this has grown a fellowship which knows no color, no race, no denominational barrier. The people who are going to come and sing with me here belong to this thing. Brethren, come along.

PERSONAL TESTIMONY
Corrie ten Boom

Miss ten Boom, Baarn, Holland,
is a traveling evangelist and author of
nine books including The Hiding Place.

And it's what you heard has taught me to obey the Lord. In the Bible we read in Col. 1:11, "As you live this new life with Jesus Christ, we pray that you will be strengthened from God's boundless resources, so that you will find yourselves able to pass through any experience and endure it with courage."

God's boundless resources we find when we obey the commandment, "Be filled with the Spirit." This is not a suggestion; the Bible has no suggestions, only commandments, and this is the most happy commandment of the whole Bible.

When the Lord told us to witness and make the disciples over the whole world, he promised, "You will receive power after the Holy Spirit has come upon you."

To me, a little story of a bird, a woodpecker, has helped in this. A woodpecker picked with his beak against the stem of a tree like they are used to do. At that very moment, the lightning struck the tree and destroyed it and the woodpecker flew away and said, "I didn't know that there was so much power in my beak." I don't ask you, have you the Holy Spirit, but has the Holy Spirit you?

When I was a little girl, I remember that I talked with my father and I said, "Daddy, I will never be strong enough to be a real witness and a martyr for Jesus." And father said, "When you go to travel, when do I give you the train ticket, or the money for it — three weeks before?" I said, "No, daddy, the day that I go to travel." And father said, "That is what God does. You don't need to have the power to suffer for Jesus at this moment, but the moment that you will have the great honor to be a martyr for Jesus, the Lord will give you everything." And I've experienced that we have not a "spirit of fear but of power and love and a sound mind" and the Holy Spirit is there always to do the job, to make us ready.

We live in a time that we can expect the good Lord, Jesus, coming very soon. Many of the signs of the time are very clear and it's very important that we are ready for Jesus' coming. Peter writes, "Because you have a hope like this before you, I urge you to make certain that such a day would find you at peace with God and with men, clear and blameless in his sight." Sometimes I tremble when I think that is necessary — to be right with God and right with men.

In Russia once I got great comfort by a story. A Russian said, "There was a big apartment house; many people lived there and they all put their junk in the basement. But there was in the basement also a beautiful harp. It was broken and nobody could repair it. Once there came a drunk who said, 'May I sleep this night in your house? There is such a terrible snowstorm.' And they said, 'We have no guest rooms but you can sleep in the basement.' After some hours they suddenly heard beautiful music in the basement and the owner of the harp came down and said, 'How could you repair that harp?' And the man said, 'I have made this harp and when you have made something, you can also repair it.'"

Who has made you? Wasn't it God? Wasn't it that nothing has been made without Jesus? Do you think he is able to make you good, blameless, and right with God and men so that you will be ready for Jesus' coming? He is able and he will do it for it is written that Paul prayed, "May the God of peace make you holy through and through. May you be kept in spirit, soul, and body in spotless integrity until the coming of the Lord Jesus Christ." Is that possible? A spotless integrity — you and I? Yes! For the rest of the text is, "He who calls you is utterly faithful and he will finish what he has set out to do."

The Holy Spirit shows us many things, as it were, from God's point of view. The Holy Spirit gives you wisdom to cast your burdens on the Lord because he gives us spiritual insight and understanding.

I was in Vietnam and I was there not as thermometer but as thermostat. Do you know what I mean? The thermometer goes with the heat and the cold up and down. A thermostat brings a cold room immediately in contact with the source of heat and so restores the temperature. I carried the load of suffering that I saw in the hospital, in the tribes, in the front lines, and the Holy Spirit showed me that I had to cast my burden on the Lord. We are not called to be burden-bearers but cross-bearers and fruit-bearers, so I could be used as an open channel of streams of living water. In my work to bring the Gospel in many places I sometimes feel weak and old, not adequate to speak in so many different meetings, but I trust what we heard today, again and again, "You shall receive power after the Holy Spirit has come upon you." The Holy Spirit gives power and we can never expect too much from him. He points to the Cross where Jesus finished all for our redemption, and obedience and surrender is the answer.

I was comforted by a story told in New Zealand. A little boy went with his father over a bridge. It was a very small bridge and he was scared, and he said, "Daddy, I'm afraid. Do you see this water underneath us?" And the father said, "Boy, give me your hand." Then he was not afraid any longer but in the evening he had to go again over the bridge and now it was pitch dark. He said, "Daddy, I'm more scared than this morning," and then the father took the little boy in his arms and immediately the boy fell asleep and awakened in his own little bed. That is surrender to the Lord Jesus and that is what the Holy Spirit teaches us how that we are safe in Jesus' hands.

When I was in prison where my sister died and 95,000 women were killed or died, I experienced this saying, what Paul has written to the Philippians when he was in a terrible prison. The Holy Spirit had pointed him to Jesus and he did with me, and I can say with him that he wrote in the text, "I count everything as lost compared with the priceless privilege " (I read it from the Amplified New Testament), "the overwhelming preciousness, the unsurpassable worth, and the supreme advantage of knowing Jesus Christ, my Lord, and of progressively, more intimately, getting acquainted with him." That happened when I was in that terrible prison. That can happen with you when you let the Holy Spirit turn your eyes more and more to the Lord Jesus even when we are perhaps entering a time of very great darkness and suffering over the world.

The world is very sick, very ill. Who is it that overcomes the world? He who believes that Jesus is the Son of God. I am sure that all of us believe that Jesus is the Son of God. That means that you and I, that we all have to overcome the world and that is hope for the world. The best is yet to be. Jesus is coming and he has said, "I will make everything new" and that this world, yes, this sick, ill world will be covered with the knowledge of God, like the waters cover the bottom of the sea. What a joy to know from the Word of God that God has no problems, only plans. There's never a panic in heaven, and we have to be right with God and we know it. That is because of the finished work of Jesus at the Cross. And we have to be right with men also because of Jesus' presence. The love of God, he will bring into our hearts through the Holy Spirit who is given to us (Rom. 5:5).

I love the Germans. There is not a country where I work with such a great joy. My greatest friends live in that country, but sometimes I find people who have been cruel to me in the concentration camp. Once I saw a lady in the meeting and suddenly I thought, "That woman was the nurse who was so cruel to my dying sister," and there came hatred and bitterness in my heart; but when I felt that there was hatred and bitterness in my heart, I knew I had not forgiven her. And I know and you know that Jesus has said (you can read it in Matt. 5), "If you do not forgive those who have sinned against you, my heavenly Father will not forgive you your sins." But I said, "Oh Lord, I cannot, I am not able." And suddenly I saw it. I cashed the check of Rom. 5:5. I said, "Thank you, Lord Jesus, that you have brought into my heart God's love through the Holy Spirit who is given to me and thank you, Father, that your love in me is stronger than my bitterness and hatred." I could go to that nurse and I could shake hands with her, and I had the joy to be used by the Lord to bring her to this decision for the Lord Jesus. What a joy.

It is so good to know that it is not a trying and trying heart. John Bunyan made a very good little poem:

> Run, John, run, the law commands,
> But gives us neither feet nor hands.
> Far better news the Gospel brings,
> It bids us fly and gives us wings.

Isn't that good? I like that. When the Lord says, "Love your enemies," he gives you the love that he demands from you. There is an ocean of God's love and that love is available for you, and that can make us love our enemies and then we'll really become mashed potatoes. Hallelujah!

One of the most cruel things I have suffered was when in the concentration camp, we had to stand naked. They stripped us of all our clothing and I said to Betsie, my sister, "I cannot bear this. This is so terrible." But it was suddenly as if I saw Jesus at the Cross. It was the Holy Spirit who turned my eyes to Jesus and the Bible tells that he hung there naked, they stripped him of all his garments and he hung there for me. By my suffering I could understand a fraction of the suffering of Jesus and it made me so happy, so thankful, that I could bear my suffering.

> Love so amazing, so divine,
> Demands my life, my soul, my all.

The Holy Spirit will turn your eyes to Jesus, whatever happens and then we are ready, we are even willing, and we are able to suffer. Amy Carmichael has written, "We have a scarred captain. Should not we have scars? Under his mighty banners, we are going to the wars. Lest we forget, Lord, when we meet, show us your hands and feet."

And may the love, mercy, and power of Jesus Christ be multiplied to you during this time of titanic spiritual warfare. The Lord wins and is able to hold us up and cause us to triumph in all situations that we may have to face. Hallelujah!

Jesus *was* victor, he *is* victor, and he *will be* victor. Amen.

WORLD EVANGELIZATION AND THE KINGDOM OF GOD

Peter Beyerhaus

Dr. Beyerhaus, Tubingen, Germany,
is Professor of Mission Studies and Ecumenical
Theology at the University of Tubingen.

Introduction

What is our inspiring vision when we at this Congress again set our minds to evangelize the world in our generation? It is that this troubled earth finally will see the Kingdom of God.

But what exactly do we *mean* if we speak of the Kingdom of God as the goal of evangelism? Do we think mainly of a spiritual event which takes place hiddenly in the hearts of men, or do we refer to a new order of the world? Would such a new world order become realized here and now, or do we see it as a future event, which we only can hope for? In which way can our evangelistic action contribute to the establishment of God's Kingdom?

The purpose of this paper is first, in a number of propositions, to *redefine* on biblical grounds the nature of evangelism in relation to the Kingdom of God; second, to *clarify* this biblical concept over against its present-day distortions; and, third, to indicate the *practical consequences* which follow for our evangelistic actions in the present situation.

PART ONE: Evangelization: Inviting into the kingdom of grace
1. *The Gospel which Jesus preached to the Jews was the "glad tidings" to them as it announced the fulfillment of Israel's central hope, the final establishment of God's messianic rule.*

The proclamation of the Kingdom of God (the Kingdom of Heaven) forms the heart of the evangelistic ministry of Jesus (Matt. 4:17) and his apostles. Jesus points to the Kingdom as the very reason for his coming: "I must evangelize about the Kingdom of God in the other cities also; for I was sent for this purpose" (Luke 4:43).

Why did Jesus choose this idea of God's Kingdom as his favorite theme? The German scholar Wilhelm Bousset has rightly stated, "The sum total of everything which Israel expected of the future was the Kingdom of God." Jesus, therefore, did not introduce a new idea when speaking about the Kingdom. Rather he referred to the most important concept of Israel's belief and hope. The Old Testament had left the Jews with one basic problem: *On the one hand* Israel had always believed and confessed that her God *is* already the sovereign ruler over his whole creation. More especially he had chosen Israel to participate in his Lordship by becoming a kingdom of priests among all nations (Exod. 19:5-6). — *On the other hand* Israel also experienced that the nations did not recognize God's rule. At times God did not even seem to be able to protect his own people from the attacks of its heathen enemies. Was God a king without a kingdom?

The answer which was given to Israel through the prophets was this: it is on account of Israel's own disobedience against God's holy commandments that the special Covenant was broken. Therefore God has delivered the Israelites into the hands of the Gentile nations. But God does not give up his intention to make the whole earth the place of his glory and to use Israel to establish his rulership over all nations. The day will come when God again will demonstrate his power and manifest himself as the supreme king of the earth. He will interfere in the course of history and change the lot of his people. This will be on the so-called *Day of the Lord*. The Day of the Lord stands for the great series of eschatological events, where God finally will restore his people Israel both spiritually and physically. God will pour out his *Spirit* on his people to bring about a spiritual regeneration (Ezk. 37:9-10; 39:29; Joel 2:28-29; Zech. 12:10). He will send the *Messiah* to be the agent of salvation. Through him God will establish his reign of peace on Mount Zion. This rule will extend to all nations on earth (Isa. 2:1-5; 9:1-7; 11:1-16). Voluntarily the kings will come to Jerusalem to worship the God of Israel and to accept his laws. And thus they will live in peace, justice and prosperity. This is what the words "Malkut Jaweh," i.e., the Kingdom of the Lord, meant to the Israelites.

And now we make two important observations:

The *first observation* is that it is exactly in connection with the prophetic announcement of the "Day of the Lord" where the concept of evangelism is born already in Old Testament times. The word "evangelize" is used for the first time in its typically biblical meaning in the 52nd and the 61st chapters of Isaiah. The prophet receives a vision which he is urged to proclaim to his people. He sees the Lord return to Zion and take up his universal reign (Isa. 52:7-8). The office of the evangelist himself assumes messianic character. He becomes spiritually identified with the expected Messiah, whose ministry again is described as a prophetic function. It is a marvelous message of eschatological salvation which forms the content of this evangelism: "The Spirit of the Lord is upon me, because the Lord has anointed me to evangelize (i.e., to bring good tidings to) the afflicted; he has sent me to bind up the brokenhearted, to proclaim liberty to the captives . . . to proclaim the year of the Lord's favor, the day of vengeance of our Lord; to comfort all who mourn" (Isa. 61:1-2).

Our *second observation* is this: The same prophetic understanding of evangelism as announcing the Kingdom of God breaking liberatingly into history is taken up in the New Testament Gospels again. But there are some decisive new elements in the New Testament understanding of the kingdom. Jesus himself called the new elements the mysteries (or secrets) of the kingdom (Matt. 13:11), which he unfolded in his own teaching.

2. *The Kingdom which is proclaimed in New Testament evangelism is centered in Jesus Christ.*

In the first sermon in the synagogue of Nazareth Jesus identifies himself with the messianic prophet of Isaiah 61:1, "The Spirit of the Lord God is upon me, because the Lord anointed me to evangelize the afflicted." His startling comment on this famous text is:

"Today the scripture has been fulfilled in your hearing!"

This does not mean that the Kingdom as it was expected so anxiously by the Jews is already totally established by the work of Jesus (realized eschatology). There is not that drastic change in history and nature yet which will mark the shalom, the peace, of the messianic kingdom. But his proclamation and his works demonstrate vital elements of it. They are not the kingdom in full, but they are *signs* which point to Jesus himself as the bringer of this kingdom. In fact he is the most important and central element of the kingdom. All the gifts of the messianic kingdom are contained in the person of Jesus Christ and mediated through his messianic ministry. It is a ministry rather different from the spectacular political expectations of the contemporary Jews, especially of the Pharisees and the Zealots for it culminates in the vicarious death of the Messiah (Matt. 16:21-27). This appears scandalous even to his own disciples, although it was already predicted in the Servant Songs of Isaiah (especially chapter 53). But this is the peculiar way in which the Kingdom of God was to be ushered in according to the plan of God.

Therefore all evangelism which is carried out by the apostles and the early church is Christ-centered. In fact, it has rightly been observed that in the writings of Paul and John the very place which Jesus in his evangelism gave to the kingdom, is now filled by Jesus himself (2 Cor. 1:20). It is Christ's coming, his atoning death, his victorious resurrection and his glorious return which now form the main pillar of evangelistic preaching both to the Jews and Gentiles. "For Jews demand signs and Greeks wisdom, but we preach Christ crucified" (I Cor. 1:22).

Christ must, therefore, remain the center of *our* evangelism as well. And it must be the authentic Christ, as he is proclaimed and taught in the apostolic writings of the New Testament.

The great danger in the churches' mission today is that they reverse God's way from the Old to the New Testament. The Old Testament descriptions of the gifts of the kingdom, liberation, and eschatological "shalom" are rediscovered. But often they are isolated from Christ as the bringer and the Lord of the Kingdom and from the way in which he accomplished the restoration of God's rule over men. This is the nature of a post-Christian ideology. It is shocking to discover, how today some theologians and church leaders even draw parallels between New Testament salvation and that salvation which is brought or promised by present-day ideologies and religions. Jesus, as far as he still is referred to by them, is reduced to the type of liberator who from Cyrus to Mao Tsetung has many important parallels. This is a terrible distortion of the biblical Gospel of the kingdom. For even if the kingdom as promised by the prophets were already realized visibly, it would be of no avail to us, if Jesus were not to be found in it (Psa. 73:25).

3. *Christian evangelism preaches a kingdom that is realized now by spiritual regeneration.*

The second distinct mark in the New Testament understanding of the Kingdom is that its deepest nature is *spiritual*. This does not renounce the expectation that it one day also will come with visible force, "with power and great glory" (Matt. 24:30), and that it will reshape the whole physical world as well. But its basic structure is not physical (Rom. 14:17). We may *define* the New Testament understanding of the kingdom as follows:

The kingdom of God is God's redeeming Lordship successively winning such liberating power over the hearts of men, that their lives and thereby finally the whole creation (Rom. 8:21) become transformed into childlike harmony with his divine will.

This is the reason why the kingdom of God could never be established by political action. And since sinful man by nature is opposed to the will of God, it can not even be brought about by moral education. The acknowledgment of God's rule presupposes a miraculous change of heart which can be achieved only by an intervention of God himself.

At the Cross of Jesus Christ, God has made peace between the sinful world and himself. Through the gifts of the Holy Spirit poured out on the day of Pentecost and henceforth bestowed on each repentant believer (Acts 2:38), God makes it possible for men to accept his offer of reconciliation and to live a victorious new life in childlike communion with God (Rom. 8:1-27).

The invitation to receive this wonderful offer is the *basic function of Christian evangelism.* The evangelist on the commission of Christ himself offers God's grace to a mankind whose essential misery is its righteous condemnation by God (II Cor. 5:17-21). And those who aided by the Holy Spirit accept the message of reconciliation are already entering the kingdom of God (Matt. 10:15; 21:31). Having become members of the invisible kingdom of grace now, they will, if they endure, most surely be partakers in the messianic rule when the kingdom comes in power and glory.

This spiritual nature of the kingdom has always been stressed by evangelicals, even in view of the demands for its social realization. The suffering under the injustice and oppression in the present state of world affairs and the cry for liberation and peace are needs which burn in the hearts of conscientious people at all times and in all cultures. In response to this, new religions and ideologies have emerged, and social and political movements for drastic changes in society have been founded. Today the quest for total *renewal* is resounding with even greater vigor than before. Some churches are responding to it through so-called Church Renewal movements. But the crucial question is: "Renewal which way?" Is it through a return to the Word of God or through group dynamics and ideological indoctrination?

More and more influential Christians today are inclined to side with the Marxists who believe that the reason for all oppression and violence is to be found in the economic laws inherent in our present capitalistic system and the wrong distribution of power in the established world society, especially in Europe and North America. Revolutionary change of all social and political structures would then be the answer. In Bangkok 1973 even the churches were called upon to become "renewed" by ridding themselves of the "captivity of power in the North Atlantic Community."

Evangelicals will agree that the concentration of executive power and finances can corrupt. Far too often they have not been aware of the social and political side of moral evil and its institutional perpetuation. But the basic fallacy of Marxism and any other kind of humanistic ideology of salvation is that it believes in the inherent goodness of human nature. Therefore the results accomplished by such types of revolutionary renewal are very often the appearance of the same selfish and heartless oppression now shifted into the hands of the revolutionaries of yesterday.

The "renewal" which God has to offer is a far more radical one. It is the renewal of our mind by being regenerated and transformed to the mind of Jesus Christ (Rom. 12:2). This offer by far exceeds all other human solutions. This offer is made in evangelism. The total ministry of Jesus consisted in teaching, evangelizing, and healing (Matt. 5:23, 9:35, 10:7-8). Evangelism has one specific function in this total missionary ministry: it is decisively to ignite the desire for new life in Christ. But as soon as this life is born, it will express itself in the works of love (Gal. 5:6). We should never allow ourselves to distrust the worth of God's offer through our evangelistic ministry, and secretly exchange our birthright for an ideological pottage of lentils.

Neither should it be argued that such spiritual renewal remains merely internal or individualistic. Perhaps sometimes evangelicals have been tempted to reduce the gifts of renewal to this dimension. But this is a caricature of true evangelical understanding of the gifts of the kingdom. If a man is really renewed in Christ, this renewal will start internally in him. This is and remains true.

But if this new spiritual life develops in a healthy way, it will make itself felt in all spheres of a man's life and social involvement. The inter-human relations of the Christians are the links between personal regeneration and the transformation of society through the forces of the Kingdom (Matt. 5:13-16). Truly regenerated Christians are better citizens. For their Christian life also generates in them a new spontaneousness and creativity in moral action, a new responsibility in public positions entrusted to them, and the desire to bring about reconciliation, solidarity, and mutual participation. This has already been proved many times in history. I am thinking of the evangelical contribution to the abolition of slavery and the social reforms for the protection of widows and orphans, or the institution of the diaconate of charity.

What practical conclusions should we draw from this insight? There are two:

First, the offer of regenerating spiritual power is to be authenticated by the messenger's own spiritual life. The whole Christian community needs a new awakening and strengthening of its life by the Holy Spirit. Only then can we be joyful witnesses of the good news of salvation. The Holy Spirit came into our hearts when we were born again; but often we block his working by disobeying God and by neglecting to foster our spiritual lives. Such an inner blockage is broken when the Word of God preached to us drives us to repentance and new dedication. Let us, therefore, conduct "missions to missions." Small cells and regular gatherings like the Keswick conferences should be encouraged which concentrate on the task of reviving the worker's inner life by Bible messages, counseling, and prayer.

Second, evangelical missions ought to develop convincing models of social and political involvement which are generated and directed by Christ's redeeming love. The personal contact with the people with whom we share the new life will unveil both their spiritual and their bodily needs. If we approach the latter ones, we should show that the physical, social, economic, and political problems too, are rooted in fallen man's thirst for God as the fountain of life. On the other hand true evangelism will show that no single aspect of human life and suffering lies outside the concern of Christ and his church. Here the doctrine of the different gifts and assignments of the members of Christ's body should be developed practically. This leads us to our next biblical proposition:

4. *Evangelism leads into the church as the new messianic community of the Kingdom.*

One of the intricate questions of New Testament theology is the *relation* between the *Kingdom of God* and the *church.* There are two extremes in answering this question. The *high-church* tradition on the one side has tended to equate the Kingdom with the church. Everything a mission does should contribute to establishing and developing the church. On the other side there are those *liberal theologians* who with Loisy maintain that Jesus was so obsessed by the belief in the imminent coming of the Kingdom that he never intended to establish a church.

The church is not identical with the Kingdom of God. But she is Kingdom of God is neither identical with the doctrine of the Church, nor does it exclude it. The truth is that the messianic Kingdom presupposes a messianic community. It is the specific people of God, destined to exercise the messianic ministry to the rest of the nations.

The Church is not identical with the Kingdom of God. But she is the transitory communal form of it in the present age, and through his church Christ exercises a most important ministry towards the visible coming of the Kingdom. She is the new Israel, the messianic community of the New Covenant: "You are a chosen race, a royal priesthood, a holy nation, God's own people, that you may declare the wonderful deeds of him who called you out of darkness into his marvelous light" (I Pet. 2:9).

This is of tremendous importance for our understanding of evangelism. The *goal of evangelism* is not only to make individual believers. The goal of evangelism is to persuade these believers to be incorporated as responsible members into the church as God's messianic community. In the total task of *mission* the work of evangelism is continued by the planting of local churches in each nation. Even as a small minority such a church is to be regarded as the first fruit of Christ's saving love for the whole people and shall, therefore, be established on a self-multiplying basis (Church Growth).

This brings us to the task of *church education.* The task of mission is not only to gather new converts into the churches, but to help these churches to grow into their full maturity. This means both to develop the internal life of the church by deepening their spiritual knowledge and fellowship, and to relate the church to the needs of the environment. Bible Classes, Bible Schools, Christian Academies, and Leadership Training Centers will have to fulfill a decisive role in educating

Christians to become responsible members of their churches rather than sheep who simply are attended to.

New insistence on the role of the priesthood of all believers must not divert our concern for improving *theological education* for the ministry of the younger churches. Within the next ten years the process of complete nationalization of the ordinary ministry of Third World churches will have to be concluded. This means that they must have a fully indigenous leadership on all levels, shepherds and teachers, who are able to uphold, defend and spread the Christian faith both in genuine continuity with the historic tradition and in relevant relation to the specific environment of these churches.

PART TWO: Evangelization preparing the kingdom of glory

Genuine Christian faith in the Kingdom has always been marked by an awareness which is joyful and painful at the same time. It is the *joy* that the Kingdom of grace has already come with the first arrival of Christ. And it is the *pain* that Christ has not yet come again to establish his kingdom in power and glory by demonstrating his victory before the eyes of all mankind. There is still something which contradicts the lordship of Jesus Christ:

1. *The opposition between the Kingdom of God and the kingdom of Satan involves the evangelist in warfare.*

When we see the role of evangelism within the framework of God's coming Kingdom, we must still consider the existence of that opposing metaphysical force which the Gospel of John calls the *"prince of this world"* (John 12:31, 14:30, 16:11). The world which is to be won for the Kingdom of Christ through evangelism is no neutral territory. It is in a state of active rebellion. The idolatrous religions of men are ways in which Satan seduces the heathen to worship him (1 Cor. 10:20; 11 Cor. 6:16). Their personal, cultural, and social life is under demonic captivity, where love of God and one's neighbor is replaced by suspicion and hostility (Rom. 1:24-30). This grim fact gives a dramatic notion to the concepts both of the Kingdom of Christ and of evangelism. The advancement of the Kingdom of Christ takes place by a successive dethronement of Satan (Luke 10:17-19). The decisive victory has already been won on the Cross, where Satan lost his legal rights over mankind (John 12:31). Evangelism, therefore, is accompanied by the fight with satanic forces (Matt. 10:1,8). It is to proclaim over them the victory of Christ and to command them to depart.

But according to the testimony of the New Testament the power of Satan on earth has not been totally annihilated yet, nor will it be, before the glorious return of Christ; nor will the totality of mankind be won over from Satan's dominion to the Kingdom of Christ. Evangelism calls for a *decision*. The Holy Spirit gives us the freedom to say "yes," but he also leaves to us the liberty to say "no." Therefore the final result of evangelism is not the unification of mankind under the rule of Christ, but on the contrary a growing polarization between the Kingdom of God and the kingdom of Satan.

One of the most fatal errors in mission work is the idea that it is our task in this present age — before the visible reappearance of Christ —

to Christianize the world and thereby to establish the messianic Kingdom by our own power. Such mistaken Christians are directed by the utopian vision of a unified mankind in which perfect peace and justice have become a universal reality now. They are however, frustrated by the fact that a great part of mankind simply refuses to accept the Gospel and to live according to the new law of Christ's Kingdom. Therefore they despair of the efficiency of purely spiritual means, i.e., an evangelistic method which relies wholly on the challenging impression of the Word of God on the human conscience.

Two dangerous alternatives are offered to an eschatologically oriented evangelism. The *first* one is the development of a misdirected form of evangelism which in order to achieve striking visible results resorts to psychological methods like mass hypnosis, group dynamic experiments, personality cults or even the radiation of para-psychological forces disguised as the work of the Holy Spirit. Some people try to attract their listeners by material benefits or by the promise of spectacular healing or earthly prosperity which will follow their conversion. There is no real blessing in such work. It might even drive the evangelist himself into secret cynicism and loss of his faith.

The other equally mistaken alternative is offered by Christians who replace the messianic Kingdom by a utopian vision to be realized by political means. They repeat the error of the Zealots at the time of Jesus, who wanted to force the Kingdom of God to come by ejecting the Romans by the sword. The physical resources of the Christian churches do not, of course, suffice to remove all forces of oppression. Therefore some even advocate an alliance with the liberation movements within all non-Christian religions and ideologies. This new concept of "mission" is today's greatest menace to the worldwide church; I would call it the *Mission of Barabbas.* It has no promise of the Lord. It might, however, reach at least a transitory success. But such a worldwide kingdom which is achieved by the combined spirits, concepts, and methods of the dynamic movements of this age would be a Kingdom without Christ. It would be the anti-Christian kingdom.

And this is what we, in fact, have to expect. The New Testament clearly predicts that in spite of great victories of the Gospel amongst all nations the resistance of Satan will continue. Towards the end it will even increase so much that Satan, incarnated in the human person of Antichrist, will assume once more an almost total control over disobedient mankind (II Thess. 2:3-12; Rev. 13). It is important to notice the religious appearance of the reign of Antichrist. He will gain his strong hold over mankind not only by military or political force alone, but also through the magic enchantments of his false prophet (Rev. 13:11-17).

But God has given us a weapon with which to resist. It is the sword of the Spirit (Eph. 6:17), the Word of God. It is the damaging testimony of the martyrs that through Christ's victory on the Cross Satan has lost his dominion (Rev. 12:11-12).

I am afraid that many evangelical Christians are neither prepared nor equipped yet to fight this battle. We need new *biblical clarity* in order to get reassured of our evangelistic motivation and to be able to discern the spirits. Today Satan attacks churches, missions, and individual Christians all over the world by heretical movements which threaten them with spiritual confusion. The Declarations of Wheaton and Frankfurt have undertaken to penetrate this smoke-screen theologically. The issues mentioned in these historic statements ought to be taken up on all levels of the worldwide mission. They must be answered by way of affirmation and refutation in clear-cut confessional statements which are binding to our evangelistic activities and identify us in the eyes of our Christian supporters.

2. *Evangelism is inspired by the vision of the Kingdom in glory which will be established through the return of Christ.*

Evangelism comes to men with a present *offer* based upon Christ's victory on the Cross, and with an eschatological *promise* based on his final victory by his return. This dialectical tension within the historical movement of God's Kingdom is the driving dynamic of evangelism.

It *offers* God's grace in Christ and new life in the Holy Spirit now. It *promises* total redemption of our bodies and of the whole creation in the Kingdom of Glory to come. Paul says that the whole "creation waits with eager longing for the revealing of the Son of God . . . because the creation itself will be set free from its bondage and obtain the glorious liberty of the children of God" (Rom. 8:19, 20). This will take place at the return of Christ. He will transform his militant church into his triumphant church, which will reign together with him in his messianic Kingdom of universal peace (Matt. 19:28-29; Luke 22:28-30; I Cor. 6:2; Rom. 20:4).

This eschatological notion has always been the distinct mark of a truly biblical understanding of evangelism. It has inspired many missionaries with a holy restlessness. But there is one question which is controversial even amongst evangelicals. What will be the exact nature of the Kingdom which Christ will establish by his return? Will it be the totally new heaven and the new earth which John describes in Revelation 21 and 22 (Amillennialism)? Or will it be the Millennium which he mysteriously speaks about in Revelation 20:1-6 (Premillennialism)? The biblical texts give us material support, but also difficulty for both of these views.

Amillennarians understand Rev. 20:1-6 not literally but symbolically. They hold that we live in the Millennium now, or rather at the end of it, when Satan is loosed again. The risen saints would be those who after their victorious death are united with Christ now in heaven, although their bodies are not resurrected yet.

Premillennarians conceive the *Kingdom in power*, which the returning Christ will establish, as an anticipation of the final *Kingdom in glory*, which will only come when even death has been swallowed up into victory (I Cor. 15:24-26).

Still another attempt to solve the apparent tension between the different eschatological texts like Revelation 20:1-6 and 2 Peter 3:10 is *Postmillennialism.* Here the Millennium would be the last victorious phase of church history before the return of Christ. It brings an almost universal recognition of the Gospel amongst the nations through a new outpouring of the Holy Spirit. But it is difficult to reconcile such a view with the clear biblical prediction of the numerical shrinkage and tribulation of the church at the close of this age. Jesus himself prophesies that the very survival of the elect will be threatened (Matt. 24:21-31). The persecutor is Antichrist, whom "the Lord Jesus will slay with the breath of his mouth and destroy by his appearing and his coming" (II Thess. 2:8). In fact, are not these apocalyptical features becoming visible even before our own eyes? Is not the shadow of Antichrist falling on us already? Where do Postmillenarians place his appearance? If they have no answer to this question, their view of the Millennium can hardly be called biblical.

Personally I am inclined to agree with a modified premillenarian view which meets the confessional criticism directed against Chiliasm a materialistic form of the Millennium. The *parousia,* i.e., the appearance of Christ, is not a plain melting of the invisible and the visible realms of Christ's reign into a political theocracy where he and his saints permanently reside on our old earth again. Rather we should understand the parousia as the climactic encounter of the yet invisible Lordship of Christ with present world history. Thereby the dividing world between here and beyond, between now and then will become transparent for a definite period, until all cosmic power has been subdued to Christ (I Cor. 15:25-26), and world history is swallowed up by new creation.

Only God's final fulfillment of the biblical prophecies will bring us the solution to all exegetical problems. In any case the controversy between Amillenarians and Premillenarians need not affect our understanding of evangelism as urgently oriented toward the appearance of Christ's coming with his Kingdom in power and glory. Absolute agreement is necessary only on two points: First, that Christ will establish this Kingdom only after we have carried out faithfully his commission to evangelize all nations (Matt. 24:14; Mark 13:10; Acts 1:6-8): second, that churches and missions have to be watchful against the antichristian temptation (Matt. 24:4, 11, 23-26).

3. *The crowning link between the evangelization of the world and the establishment of the messianic Kingdom will be the restitution of Israel.*

Why do I believe that the Millennium is an intervening period between the return of Christ and the creation of a new heaven and a new earth? It is because of the specific role which the Old Testament has assigned to the people of Israel within the messianic Kingdom. These prophecies have neither been fulfilled yet, nor have they been obliterated by the creation of the church as the new spiritual Israel (Acts 1:6). Paul, in Romans 11:29 very definitely states that the gifts and the call of God to Israel are irrevocable. He clearly predicts the final conversion of the historic Israel. This reinclusion into the olive tree of the people of God, will mean great riches for the Gentile nations (v. 12).

Now there is an important threefold relationship between the Church's world-evangelism to the Gentile nations and the final acceptance of the people of Israel:

First, Paul states that one vital purpose in his ministry to the Gentiles is to make his fellow Jews jealous of their salvation in Christ (Rom. 11:11-14). This means that our evangelistic work should always be done with an eye cast desirously on the promised salvation of the Jews as well.

This Christian *witness to Israel* must *always* accompany mission to the Gentiles.

The *second* connection is the mystery that the present hardening of Israel will cease when the full number of the Gentiles has come in (v. 25). This actually means that the *time of world-evangelism is limited.* The times of grace for the Gentiles are exactly the interval between the hardening of Israel which followed their rejection of their Messiah and his Gospel, and their eschatological restitution, which will, according to Ezekiel 37:8-10, be first physical and thereafter spiritual.

The *third* connection between the church's mission to the Gentiles and the restitution of Israel is of vital importance to our understanding of the *limitation of our task* in world evangelism. Israel's conversion will mark the transformation from world-evangelization to world-christianization. The church's assignment in the present dispensation is not to take the world of nations politically under the law of Christ as expressed in the Sermon on the Mount. Under the present conditions where Satan still is unbound this is simply not possible. But in the messianic reign Satan will be bound and not be able to deceive the nations any more (Rev. 20:3). Therefore the rule of peace exercised through the ministry of Israel from Mount Zion will also establish a long-lasting political peace. Meanwhile, however, world-evangelism has only one direct purpose. It is to call and to gather the eschatological community of the elect out of all nations.

That Israel forms the decisive eschatological linkage between world-evangelism and the establishment of the messianic Kingdom is a prophetic insight especially exciting to our present generation. Jesus has said to the Jews: "Jerusalem will be trodden down by the Gentiles, until the (appointed) times (of grace-kairoi) of the Gentiles will be fulfilled" (Luke 21:24). This is exciting. For in the year 1967 our very generation became witness to how Jerusalem in an amazing war was recaptured by the Jews. For the first time since its destruction in A.D. 70 the capital of Israel is not trodden down by the Gentiles any more. But the Yom Kippur war in 1973 brought about a new turn. Because of the oil boycott of the Arab States nearly all peoples of the earth are turning against Israel, as predicted by the Old Testament prophets (Ezk. 38; Zech. 12:3). Does this mean that the times of grace for the heathen, i.e., the appointed times for world-evangelization are drawing to their end as well? I believe so. In fact we are observing this already in many parts of the world. Is there then no point any more in convening this International Congress on World Evangelization? On the contrary!

4. *Re-enforced evangelism is the erected sign of victory in the final battle of the Kingdom of Christ with the powers of Antichrist.*

In his apocalyptic sermon on the Mount of Olives about the fate of Jerusalem and the end of world history Jesus answers a question which is equally burning to our generation (Matt. 24:3): "When will this be, and what will be the sign of your coming and the close of the age?" Jesus mentions a number of striking signs. They appear in nature and in world history as well as in the life of the Christian church: wars, famines, earthquakes, false prophets. They all signalize that the end is approaching; but they are not the end yet. Then Jesus comes to the dramatic last phase; the great apostasy, where most men's love will grow cold, (Matt. 24:10-12), precedes the great tribulation (vv. 21-22). The final phase of church history will not be marked by great revival movements or by the complete christianization of the nations. On the contrary: only a minority of elect will endure and be saved (Matt. 24:22, 25). yet one basic function of the church will go on even under these circumstances. Nobody will stop it until it has reached its target: "And this Gospel of the Kingdom will be preached throughout the whole earth, as a testimony to all nations, and then the end will come" (Matt. 24:14). This prophecy puts Christ's commission to evangelize the world into an apocalyptic context. Evangelism is the chief contribution of the church to hasten the visible establishment of Christ's Kingdom on earth. Only when this work is complete, will Christ come to redeem the groaning creation from its present bondage.

The purpose of such eschatological evangelism is not only to make as many converts as possible. In that case statistics would decide the meaning of world-evangelization. Our task is not to boast in numerical results (although we may rejoice at them!), for the full number of those who will be saved is known to God alone (John 10:16; Rom. 11:25). It must be assumed that the majority of the listeners will not receive our offer of grace. Still Jesus insists that the Gospel of the Kingdom will and must be preached throughout the world until the end. Why? Because each nation on earth must have heard the testimony of Christ as the Lord and Redeemer of the world in order to recognize him when he comes in glory (Matt. 24:30; Rev. 1:7). Then people will either be accepted or be judged according to their obedience or disobedience to the Word. But all knees in heaven and on earth and under the earth will bow, and every tongue will confess that Christ is the Lord, to the glory of God (Phil. 2:10).

What does this mean for our task here and now? Let me conclude by putting a threefold challenge to this Congress:

a. The still-open doors for the Gospel call for an all-out effort to evangelize all six continents. Churches and missions should make it their target to reach every living person with the good news within the next ten years. It is clear that we thereby should make the best use of all modern means of communication and prepare excellent programs for radio and TV. But wherever it is legally possible, our evangelistic outreach should culminate in personal visitation and in a face-to-face encounter. This means that the whole believerhood in a given locality ought to be involved: evangelism in depth!

b. All such efforts would benefit greatly if they could draw from the experiences of fellow Christians in other parts of the world, and if they would be co-ordinated in a worldwide strategy. It should include all churches, mission societies, Christian groups, and individuals who sincerely believe that the proclamation of the undiluted Gospel to the unreached two billion is our most important task in this decisive hour of world history. I fully trust that this Lausanne Congress will result in a new spiritual awareness of evangelical unity. But if we want this to be more than a transitory emotional upheaval as experienced by people in so many previous conferences, this feeling should become visible.

What we are called to at this hour is to make a decisive step to form a worldwide association for the evangelization of the world in our generation.

c. We do not know, however, how much time we still have to prepare such bold plans for world evangelization. God's mission can express itself in our plans, but he is not bound by them. On the contrary, his mission can proceed even in a situation of persecution, where any organized mission is no longer possible. There he uses instead the confessing testimony of individual Christians and small groups. This is already the situation in most countries behind the iron curtain. Let us support these our brethren and sisters by our intercessions. And let us prepare ourselves and our constituencies for such time as such martyrdom may be expected of us, too.

For it is "through many tribulations we must enter the Kingdom of God" (Acts 14:22).

WORLD EVANGELIZATION AND THE KINGDOM OF GOD

Peter Beyerhaus

"World Evangelization and the Kingdom of God!" Seldom in my life has a work been assigned to me which was so inspiring to myself as this biblical foundation paper. Why? Firstly, because this task has forced me to rethink my own mission theology in the light of one of the Bible's most central themes. This has led me to new insights and clarified my total view. Above all it has filled me with deeper joy about the richness of God's wonderful counsel of salvation!

This joy was greatly increased, secondly, by the discovery how much agreement there exists between evangelical Christians on all six continents on the basic principles of world evangelization. This has been a genuine surprise to me. I spent several days in studying the more than 2000 responses to this paper. There were, to be sure, many details that were questioned from various positions. A few writers even outrightly rejected the whole conception as irrelevant. But the overwhelming response was a cordial consent to the main thrust of the presentation. I believe the reason for this worldwide agreement is this: we evangelicals have one authoritative frame of reference which is shared by us all. The Bible is the infallible source and rule of our faith, teaching and practice. Where this frame of reference, however, becomes shaky, our understanding and practice of evangelism, too, will diverge into most bewildering directions.

I. The Distinction between the Kingdom of Grace and of Glory

Let me briefly summarize the main points of our paper. World evangelization — more than any enterprise — needs a strong, inspiring motivation. We have chosen to express this motivation by the key message of the greatest of all evangelists, Jesus Christ himself: "Repent, for the Kingdom of God is at hand."

The Kingdom of God has always been central in the history of Christian missions. Today it has become the watch-cry again to missions of rather different theological assumptions. Accordingly, the same term "Kingdom of God" may mean something totally different to them. Therefore, we must redefine it on the basis of biblical theology. The concept "Kingdom of the Lord" originates in the Old Testament. The final coming of the "Malkuth Jahweh," the universal rule of the Lord, was the sum total of the great promises, which God had given to his chosen people Israel. It meant, first of all, liberation and a state of spiritual and physical well-being — shalom — through an unbroken covenantal relationship between Israel and her God. But much more, it also meant Jahweh's universal reign of peace from Mt. Zion over all the nations on earth. The visible bearer of this eschatological rule would be the royal Messiah whose law is administered to the rest of mankind by his royal priesthood Israel. Therefore the expectation of the Kingdom of the Lord was concentrated in the hope for the coming Messiah.

The great and decisive message of the New Testament Gospel is, that this expectation is fulfilled through the coming of Jesus. But at once a great paradox was presented to the minds of the Jews. Jesus clearly indicated that in his person and ministry the Kingdom had come. His miracles caused many of his hearers to believe in him. But still the great event, the turning of all historical and even cosmic conditions, did not take place. This was a riddle which became a real stumbling block to the Jews. It finally caused them to deliver their Messiah over to the Gentile governor to be executed.

Yet there was an answer to the mystery of the Kingdom as presented by Jesus. This answer was that the establishment of the Kingdom is not one single event, but a sequence of decisive stages. My paper is based upon the clear distinction between two decisive stages. We have called them the *Kingdom of Grace* and the *Kingdom of Glory.*

I believe that it is crucial for our understanding of evangelism to keep this distinction in mind. The conflict between two completely different understandings of mission today originates in the confusion about the difference between the present and the future stage of the Kingdom. This is why we had to bring in so much eschatology into our argument.

The coming of the Kingdom is just one way of describing God's redemptive work with his fallen creation. God has created the world, and especially man, to be the object of his love and to reflect his eternal glory. But the original harmony was broken by the double rebellion in the spirit world and in the human world. Therefore all creation has fallen into the slavery of corruption and death. The misery of the present physical world is just the visible expression of the broken inner harmony in the spiritual world. The two are interrelated. But since the structure of God's creation is spiritual, it is necessary that the redemption *starts from within.*

The gift which is brought to us by Jesus under the term "Kingdom of God" is basically the restoration of the broken relationship between God and fallen mankind. Our sins, which separate us from God, are forgiven, and through the Holy Spirit our mind is renewed into child-like trust and obedience to God our heavenly Father. This gift is based upon the redemptive work of Christ, his death and resurrection. The gift is enjoyed within the fellowship of the believers in Christ, the church, which is the Kingdom of Grace. The gift is mediated through the preaching of the Gospel and sealed by baptism. Administering the means of grace, therefore, is the main task of evangelism.

This insistence on the spiritual nature of the Kingdom in its present state, does not mean that its working is merely internal and invisible. Where God rules over man anew, new life flows into his heart, but also into his society, and finally also into his whole environment. Through renewed people God really starts to renew the structures of our physical world. The evangelistic work of Jesus, too, was accompanied by his visible signs of healing, feeding, and exorcising the demons.

Yet we must insist that in its present state as a Kingdom of Grace, God's Kingdom is not complete yet. Neither by a history of evolution nor by violent revolutions will this present world of ours be changed into the ideal state of the Kingdom of God as promised through the prophets. Physically, man and all creation are still under the laws of the old age of corruption. The Kingdom of Grace is still counteracted by the three ancient enemies sin, devil and death, although they are, in principle, already defeated by Christ. We are still longing for the redemption of our bodies and of the physical world. This will take place in the apocalyptical event when Christ returns and establishes his Kingdom in power and glory. This will mean the complete transformation of the present structures of fallen creation into structures that without resistance function in accordance with the will of God.

What, then, is the meaning of the present phase between the first and the second coming of Christ? The meaning is that the saving Lordship of Jesus Christ is proclaimed to all the nations on earth. It is to invite people everywhere to join the Kingdom of Grace now and thereby to become partakers of the forthcoming Kingdom of Glory. Scripture tells us that Jesus will not come again before all nations have heard the Gospel and the full number of the elect has been gathered into the messianic community.

Evangelism, therefore, is the one basic function which gives meaning to the present interval between the establishment of the Kingdom of Grace and its consummation into the Kingdom of Glory.

But here one more distinction must be observed: world evangelization is not identical with world Christianization. We have both the command and the promise to complete the evangelization of the world before Christ's return. But we have no promise that we will achieve the conversion of all people whom we reach. We hope and pray that the harvest will be abundant.

Perhaps here my paper sounded a little different in comparison with the optimism of my friend and colleague, Dr. McGavran. Basically we are in agreement. I do trust that Christ will bless our evangelistic testimony. With my own eyes I have seen in East Africa, in India and in Korea and even in Germany that he is just now doing so. But still I do not expect finally all mankind will join the church and thereby transform the world into the Kingdom of Glory.

Such a mistaken view — sometimes called post-millennialism — is contradicted by the clear prediction of Jesus Christ and his apostles. I am especially referring to Christ's Sermon on the Mt. of Olives (Matt. 24) and to the Revelation of St. John. Therefore I endorse the statement of my paper: "The final phase of church history will not be marked by great revival movements or by the complete Christianization of the nations. On the contrary: only a minority of elect will endure and be saved."

Now I do not want to take up the quarrel of the three conflicting eschatological views of a-millennialism, pre-millennialism and post-millennialism again. I have been justly warned not to wreck this Congress by introducing the one topic on which evangelicals are most passionately divided. Many other correspondents have pointed out that my own position in Part Two, statement two, was not really clear. I don't agree. Scripture itself by its seemingly contradicting statements has drawn a veil over the exact sequence of the apocalyptic mysteries. This veil will only be removed as the prophecies are fulfilled.

But there are two points where a certain amount of eschatological agreement is absolutely indispensable for Christian mission.

The *one* is that worldwide evangelization is the most important and joyful task which is to be fulfilled by the church before Christ will come to erect his Kingdom in power and glory.

The *other* point is that the whole history of mankind is heading for the forthcoming clash between Christ and Antichrist. We are — in this phase of history — not facing the unification of mankind under one head, Christ. Rather we are torn apart by two opposing unification movements: the gathering of the messianic community, that is the church of Christ on the one hand, and the great union movement of the worshipers of the "beast." Finally, each human being will find himself involved on one side of this war. Therefore the words of Christ to the last generation are very solemn: "He who endures till the end shall be saved!" (Matt. 24:13).

II. Three Conflicting Views on World Evangelism

The clear apprehension of the eschatological nature of the Kingdom is not only decisive for our theological understanding of world evangelism. It also determines the adoption of evangelistic methods. Let me first restate and develop what I called the "two dangerous alternatives":

A) One is current within the *conciliar movement*. It is inspired by the "utopian vision" of a united world community. It is developed without proper regard to the biblical prophecies of the return of Christ, his victory over Antichrist and the great judgment, which must precede such a state of eschatological universal shalom. People of all denominations, classes, religions and ideologies are seen as already now being drawn together into one society which is ruled by justice, peace and continuous development. It is not the Gospel, but the ideals of a new humanism which brings them together. One way to overcome the present resistance to such development is to overthrow all oppressive systems by violent liberation movements. This is really advocated today as a new form of world mission, and I have called it the *"Mission of Barabbas."*

Barabbas was probably a member of the political party of the Zealots. He wanted to hasten the coming of a national Messianic Kingdom by throwing out the Roman oppressors. Therefore he joined the guerrilla movement. And we remember: he was much more attractive to the Jews than a Savior decorated with a crown of thorns.

An additional way toward worldwide unification is to pull down the dividing walls between Christianity and other religions. This is done by engaging in dialogue and thereby establishing the alleged spiritual unity of all religions. This will necessarily result in a new form of syncretism, where the different ways of separation of the religions are seen as leading to the same goal.

These two concepts of liberation and unity are evident distortions of the biblical understanding of true freedom and fellowship in Christ. Yet the "utopian vision" is spreading with an alarming speed in world Christianity. Many Christians — even evangelicals — are attracted by it. For they regard it as the only alternative to the imminent destruction of our world by a collective suicide of mankind.

Indeed, it would be the only alternative, *if we had no hope* in the *return of Christ*. But the Bible gives us a different, yet much more reliable answer to our present anxieties. Therefore it is imperative that we reaffirm the authentic prophecies of the coming Kingdom and refute the "utopian vision." This has been done quite recently by an International Convention of Confessing Christians. It was held in Berlin on the Day of Ascension this year. We issued a biblical document which tackles exactly these issues. It is, therefore, called the *"Berlin Declaration on Ecumenism 1974. Freedom and Fellowship in Christ."* Already now it has been acclaimed and signed by evangelical Christians from all parts of the world.

B) But there is another dangerous alternative. It has originated within evangelical Christianity itself. Here the mistaken idea which corresponds to the "utopian vision" of the present Ecumenical Movement is the enthusiastic expectation of an imminent "second Pentecost." Through its power, it is believed, all mankind will be converted and thus the kingdom will be ushered in, in glory.

In response to hundreds of questions let me briefly develop this point. The type of evangelism which is based on such an enthusiastic expectation puts exceeding trust in a new occurrence of an abundance of signs and miracles, attributed to the power of the Holy Spirit. This induces the evangelist to try to get hold of such extraordinary power by getting into physical touch with other persons who are laden with it already. Then the minds of the listeners are attracted to the promised manifestation of that extraordinary force. If they actually do not see real miracles happen, they are at least caught by the suggestive spell of the evangelist.

This mistaken concept of evangelism is tempting especially Bible-believing Christians. For it is a subtle imitation of the true gifts of the Holy Spirit as we find them especially in the book of Acts, and as they are found, in exceptional cases, also amongst genuine Christians today.

But the difference is a double one.

Firstly this concept replaces the biblical hope for the returning Christ by the unbiblical expectation of a second Pentecost. Neither Jesus nor his apostles promised this to the church.

Secondly the main evangelistic impact is no longer the convincing force of the Gospel on the conscience of man. Rather it is the irresistible pull of an anonymously radiating soul-force not entirely different from the demonic spirit forces in non-Christian religions. I have, indeed, come across the work of such pseudo-evangelists who have attracted many Christians. They were left behind in a state of spiritual confusion and anxiety.

The reason was that those evangelists did not really work in the power of the Holy Spirit. Instead they used the charm of their personality and a parapsychological force which is also exemplified by Hindu gurus and African diviners. Therefore it is most important to exercise the discernment of the spirits. Usually a biblical examination of their teaching is quite sufficient. For seldom is Christ as crucified for our sins the center of their message. Instead the whole emphasis is on the extraordinary gifts ascribed to the Holy Spirit quite apart from the true redemption of the sinner.

As Christians are approaching the final stage of history, they must increasingly become aware of the working of such spirits of imitation. For Christ tells us that shortly before the end false Christs and false prophets will arise and show great signs and wonders, so as to lead astray, if possible, even the elect (Matt. 24:24).

C) What, then, are the main features of a world evangelization which is determined by the biblical concept of the kingdom? The eschatological notion of the kingdom, we said, implies two basic affirmations:

One is that evangelization is heading for the victorious return of Jesus Christ, the Conqueror of Calvary.

The other is, that this final victory is preceded by the increasing confrontation with Antichrist.

These two affirmations must determine our attitude and our methods in evangelization. What does this mean?

1. World evangelization is expectant of great victories. Let us, like Paul, be assured that we have the one message which has the power radically to renew the life of every human being and even to turn the course of world history. It is the message that the crucified Savior is the Lord, and that in Jesus alone there is salvation now and on the coming Day of Judgment. This unchangeable message is meant for people at all times, in all parts of the world, in every sphere of society, for people of every religious or secular conviction, for man in every spiritual and moral condition. If faithfully communicated, God's Word will never return in vain. It will accomplish the purpose for which he has sent it.

2. Christ is already the Lord of the universe invisibly. His Lordship will be revealed at his return, when all knees will bow in his name. Therefore in evangelism we have to claim for him the totality of man's life — first of all, his life as an individual, and then, also, his corporate life as a social and political being. Therefore the oral witness must be accompanied by deeds of love that manifest the capacity of the Gospel to give new life to the whole man.

3. If evangelism is heading for the climax of world history, Christ's coming in glory, only total mobilization for evangelism can befit such a great cause. If we believe that this event is very near, no half-hearted solutions will be acceptable. This is the reason why I have pleaded, and why I am pleading again today:

Let us evangelicals all over the world line up in an international fellowship in world evangelization! The reason is not the joy to found another organization, as some have thought. The reason is that today only evangelicals are fully aware of the real need of the desperate unevangelized billions, their need of the saving Gospel. But up to now there is not enough wise coordination and mutual encouragement between the ten thousands of scattered evangelical enterprises which are serving this purpose. Therefore we run into the risk of functional and sometimes even theological disorientation. This may prove to be disastrous in our present spiritual conflict in world Christianity.

But total mobilization for evangelism starts on the local level. I have also pleaded for the nationalization of the indigenous ministry within the next ten years. I did not mean the voluntary withdrawal of foreign missionaries, but their change in function. There are still needs — also in the West! — for mutual inspiration and for breaking new grounds. The cry for a "moratorium" issued at Bangkok can not be justified on a biblical basis. But I mean that evangelism will unfold its full force only if it is carried by fully responsible local churches which are growing spiritually and numerically.

Now let us turn to our second eschatological affirmation: the growing polarization between Christ and Antichrist. Satan uses his remaining time before the glorious return of Christ to disturb his growing Kingdom of Grace both from outside and from within. This means:

4. We have to guard the biblical Gospel which alone can bring salvation to the world. The greatest menace to world evangelization today does not come from *outside* but from inside the church. It is Satan's dissemination of a spirit of doctrinal confusion amongst the laborers of the kingdom. I believe that even the efforts of this costly Congress will be totally frustrated if we do not give an unmistakable direction to the forces of world evangelization, a direction which enables them clearly to discern the spirits. Therefore I have referred to the Declaration of Wheaton 1966, Frankfurt 1970 and now Lausanne 1974. These are documents which do not simply restate the well-known evangelical position. They clearly take issue with the actual heresies which undermine this position, although they make use of evangelical words.

5. True evangelism always implies the risk of *persecution* both of the preacher and of the converts. If our churches and missions live in perfect peace with the world, we must be alarmed. Most likely we have conformed ourselves and our message to the humanistic spirit of our age which finally will bring forth the Antichrist. Therefore it is most essential that in our deliberations about world evangelization we fully bring in the experience of our brethren who already today are rendering their witness in view of open persecution. Their situation can be ours tomorrow. This will be the actual test whether our evangelical conviction is genuine.

6. Satan's tenacious resistance cruelly reminds us that it is not our human efforts — not even our evangelistic efforts — which establish the Kingdom of God. In every moment we are wholly dependent on the concurrence by our heavenly King and the sending of his Spirit.

Therefore the top priority for fruitful evangelism is the daily renewal of our personal relation with Christ. Several of my correspondents have rightly stressed the central place of *prayer* in evangelism. I regret that I have not pointed out this sufficiently in my paper. But it is central to my own view of evangelism:

"Did we in our own strength confide,
    Our striving would be losing,
    Were not the right man on our side,
    The man of God's own choosing." (Martin Luther)

What then is the first and the last decisive contribution to our topic: "World Evangelization and the Kingdom of God"? It is the fervent prayer: "Thy Kingdom come!"

EVANGELISM AND MAN'S SEARCH FOR FREEDOM, JUSTICE AND FULFILLMENT

Samuel Escobar

Mr. Escobar, Toronto, Ontario, Canada,
is General Secretary of the Inter-Varsity
Christian Fellowship of Canada.

1. The world in which we live

"Imagine that all the population of the world were condensed to the size of one village of 100 people. In this village 67 of that 100 people would be poor; the other 33 would be in varying degrees well off. Of the total population, only 7 would be North Americans. The other 93 people would watch the 7 North Americans spend one-half of all the money, eat one-seventh of all the food, and use one-half of all the bathtubs. These 7 people would have ten times more doctors than the other 93. Meanwhile the 7 would continue to get more and more and the 93 less and less."[1]

This dramatic account of the disparity of wealth in the world becomes more significant for Christians today because it can be said that Christianity at the moment is concentrated in that part of the world where the privileged 33 per cent live. Moreover, the average income in the opulent Christian West is about $2,400, while the average income for the non-Christian underdeveloped world is $180. This gap is widening, and it is expected that in the next ten years another $1,100 will be added to the difference.[2] What are the consequences for Christians in the developed countries — North America, for example — who have an evangelistic concern?

"As part of the wealthy seven we are trying to reach as many of the other 93 for Christ as we can. We tell them about Jesus and they watch us throw away more food than they ever hope to eat. We are busy building beautiful church buildings, and they scrounge to find shelter for their families. We have money in the bank and they do not have enough to buy food for their children. All the while we tell them that our Master was the Servant of men, the Savior who gave his all for us and bids us give all for him . . . We are the rich minority in the world. We may be able to forget about that or consider it unimportant. The question is, can the 93 forget?"[3]

Our situation is quite different from that of New Testament days. Then the developed world and the powerful metropolis were pagan lands, and the message of salvation spread from a poor obscure province subjugated under colonial rule. In those days, the mother church in the undeveloped province went through a famine and was helped by offerings gathered in the young churches of the rich Greek cities.[4] As we think of evangelism in a world dimension, we cannot forget the facts that surround our task these days, the reality that overpopulation, hunger, oppression, war, torture, violence, pollution, and the extreme forms of wealth and poverty are not disappearing, but rather growing at an astonishing pace.

2. A new attitude in missions: the "Plot" theories

As the great missionary leader, Leslie Lyall, points out, there has also been a radical change in the mood of those involved in the task of evangelism around the world:

"At the historic worldwide missionary conference held in Edinburgh in 1910, in the heyday of western colonial expansion and before the first of two tragic world wars had shattered the imperial dream, missionary statesmen looked out from their Christian citadel in the West over a pagan world, but a world which their optimism expected soon to become Christian through the influence of Christian colonization in Asia and Africa. (They ignored Latin America which many of them regarded as already 'Christian.') . . . Sixty years later the picture is profoundly different. The imperial dream has been finally shattered. Imperialism and colonialism instead of proving to be the allies of evangelism, came to be regarded after the Second World War as its enemies. The church in the Third World is today acutely embarrassed by any past association with either and is trying to live down and out-live the commonly held view that Christianity was in some way a part of the 'imperialist plot' to dominate the world — 'the spearhead of cultural imperialism.'"[5]

If we put together the growing imbalance of development and affluence in the world, with the past relationship between the "Christian" Western powers and the missionary enterprise to the Third World, we can understand why the suspicion that the whole task of evangelization in its three dimensions is only an "imperialist plot," a Western way of manipulating people. It would be like selling opiate to keep the masses of the Third World quiet in the midst of their misery and suffering, just as in some so-called "Christian" countries, religion is used as a way of keeping some social classes humble and subject to the powerful dominant classes. Those who advocate this view can well point to the way in which Christians, evangelicals in particular, oppose the violence of revolution but not the violence of war; they condemn the totalitarianism of the left but not that of the right; they speak openly in favor of Israel, but very seldom speak or do anything about the Palestinian refugees; they condemn all the sins that well-behaved middle class people condemn but say nothing about exploitation, intrigue, and dirty political maneuvering done by great multi-national corporations around the world.

Of course, all this insistence on hunger, suffering, violence, pollution, unbalanced trade and development and the growing gap between rich and poor nations could be easily dismissed as part of a great plot against Christianity, as part of a Communist or Humanist plan to subvert the good Christian West. Some think that evangelism and missions have nothing to do with all this, that it is for liberals to mention these facts, that we should close our eyes to such ugly facts and give ourselves entirely to the task of propagating verbal summaries of the Gospel adapted for mass consumption, by all the available means.

3. Traditional attitudes among evangelicals: Constantinism and indifference

Two attitudes share this position. The first is that of commitment to the West. Because Marxism represents the official ideology in the so-called Communist world, and because some ethnic religions try to be the ideology of emerging nationalisms, the great temptation for some western Christians is to make Christianity the official ideology of the West. The greatest temptation these days for the Christian who wants to evangelize or do missionary work is to take Christianity as the official religion that explains, justifies, and backs whatever the Western nations do.

The other attitude is indifference to the issues: the Gospel is a spiritual message that has nothing to say about social problems. The task of evangelism and missions is to snatch up souls from perdition and hell. Though not always expressed, the implication is that the social behavior of the convert is not vitally and visibly affected by the message. If he is a rich exploiter he is never asked to leave his possessions. If he is poor, he is told to be content with his status. If he lives in a nation built upon the principle of the superiority of one race, he is asked to wait for heaven where probably there will be no color barrier.

Are there groups with strong racist tendencies? Well, we should not bother their prejudice with teaching about equality before God. Any reference in the Bible to race can be interpreted in a way that does not disturb the established law and order.

This attitude of indifference to the non-spiritual dimensions of the reality of man reminds me of how Spaniard missionaries "evangelized" Latin America. They came in the wake of the Conquest. They came with the sword in one hand and the cross in the other. Indian chiefs that did not submit were burned alive, but if they accepted the Spanish version of the Gospel and were baptized, they had a less painful death: killed on a scaffold, strangled by an iron collar. But, of course, they were told first that because of their baptism they were going to heaven. This is an extreme form of an evangelization concerned only with the souls of the people.

4. *Recent evangelical thinking about the social dimensions of life in relation to evangelism*

One interesting development of the Congresses on Evangelism that were held around the world after Berlin 1966, has been the rediscovery of the social dimensions of the Gospel. In Berlin itself some areas of responsibility were explored in the sections on "Hindrances to Evangelism in the Church" and "Obstacles to Evangelism in the World."[6]

For instance, in the first section Walter Kunneth's basic paper stated:

"Correct doctrine and proper proclamation do not guarantee the penetrating power of the Gospel, since various personal and very real circumstances can hover over the Gospel like a dismal smoke screen and thus make its clarity difficult to understand." [7]

In one of the papers for the same section, Samuel H. Moffett touched a very delicate but crucial area of self-containment in the church: racism and social discrimination. He argued that the fact that the church would accept racial segregation and political conservatism from the social structure in which it lives was a hindrance to evangelism in certain nations and in the world.[8]

Nationalism was a vital issue in the section on obstacles to evangelism in the world. In his basic paper Harold Kuhn had said:

"It takes no political radicalism to suggest that God's providence may be working in those movements whereby peoples historically disadvantaged by cultural, economic, or religious factors try to share the freedoms and comforts achieved by the more prosperous societies . . . Christians can applaud movements that erase the feelings of fatalism from the under-privileged and that recognize such infusion or restoration of a sense of self-worth as 'the Lord's doing.'"[9]

Heini Germann Edey and Michael Cassidy provided two shorter papers on the subject of nationalism, and the very fact that the second became controversial shows that he had been too explicit in his condemnation of evils that affected the church in some areas of the world.[10] In any case, as this writer's paper on totalitarianism[11] tried to show, neither commitment to the West nor indifference is an attitude that necessarily follows an evangelical stand.

After Berlin, the national and regional Congresses rediscovered an articulated evangelical social concern with a surprising coincidence in contents and tone. Here we have some examples:

This is a voice from Asia:

"There is no such thing as a separate individual Gospel and a separate social gospel. There is only one Gospel — a redeemed man in a reformed society . . . Social problems assume greater importance in Christianity than in Buddhism or Hinduism. The theory of Karma and rebirth gives a fairly reasonable explanation for social inequalities of this life which on the one hand are consequences of the previous life and on the other hand can be compensated for in the next life. But to a Christian there is only one earthly life and so social problems have to be dealt with now or never . . . Part of the tragedy of our time is that evangelical Christians are avoiding the revolution that they themselves caused (by their earlier biblical social witness) and so others have stepped in. The result is that many changes that could have been effected peacefully have become violent. While the means may not justify the end, they do determine it. While man cannot be saved by the good society, he can be destroyed by the bad one".[12]

Here we have a voice from Europe:

"The principle of evangelism has been that the renewal of the individual also reforms society. It is not possible to reform society without renewing the individual. First the individual then the community. It is clearly to be seen in many big communities that this is true. But especially in many mission fields, it has been noticed that the separating of spiritual and physical needs, or individual and social effects of evangelism is impossible. Our Lord Jesus Christ is the solution, and the creation and the redemption are united in an inseparable unity . . .

"If we make Christ a political Messiah we have misunderstood his Gospel. But the Gospel is also misunderstood if we shut our eyes totally to the social implications of our faith. Perhaps our attitudes and norms have been bearing more the ideals of the Christian faith . . . We must realize that we do not preach only by speaking, but also by being silent. According to the faith and the light that has been given to me, I believe that Christian attitudes are needed in relation to big social issues. There is no call for cautious reactionaries in these matters but for brave people who carry out God's will in various fields".[13]

Here we have a voice from the U.S.A.:

"As Christians we have to be concerned both for love and justice. Love goes beyond justice, and only the saving power of Jesus Christ can produce real love. But love is not a substitute for justice, and since not all men are or will be converted to Christ and since even we Christians have imperfect love, we have a responsibility to seek justice in society. A Christian politician who seeks to pass laws that create guidelines for justice is doing God's work just as truly as a Christian pastor who seeks to win the lost to Christ." [14]

Here we have a voice from Latin America:

"Christian service is not optional. It is not something we can do if we want to. It is the mark of the new life. 'You will know them by their fruits.' 'If you love me, you will keep my commandments.' If we are in Christ we have the spirit of service of Christ. So to discuss whether we should evangelize or promote social action is worthless. They go together. They are inseparable. One without the other is evidence of a deficient Christian life. So we must not try to justify service for our neighbor by claiming that it will 'help us' in our evangelism. God is equally interested in our service and in our evangelistic task. Let us not have a guilty conscience over our schools, hospitals, health centers, student centers, and so on. If they are also used for evangelism, splendid! But let us not use them as a medium of coercion to force the Gospel on others. It is not necessary. In themselves they are an expression of Christian maturity . . . it is fundamental to recognize that society is more than just the sum of a number of individuals. It is naive to affirm that all that is needed is new men in order to have a new society. Certainly every man should do whatever he is able to do to get the transforming message of Christ to his fellow citizens. But it is also true that it is precisely these new men who sometimes need to transform the structures of society so that there may be less injustice, less opportunity for man to do evil to man, for exploitation."[15]

An interesting coincidence in this effort to rediscover the social implication of the Gospel is the reference to what evangelicals did in the past. Several papers in these Congresses mentioned the work of Wilberforce and the abolitionists of slavery as well as other evangelical social reformers in England. It was clearly stated almost in every paper on the issue that an evangelical stance in relation to the fundamentals of the faith had as a logical consequence an involvement in social service and social action.

A similar lesson comes from the history of missions. When the history of the missionary enterprise is seen without the ideological lens of the right or the left it becomes evident that the missionary work of proclamation of the Gospel has always been accompanied by results that affected social and political structures. It is recognized today that many of those who fought for independence in the anti-colonial movements that followed the Second World War, were people that had been educated, and probably motivated in their love for freedom, by the missionary schools established during the last century and the first part of this century in Asia and Africa. In Latin America, on the other hand, the presence of evangelical missionaries in countries like Mexico, Peru, Argentina, Guatemala, and Ecuador, was welcomed by those who were fighting for freedom and justice in society. The reason was that the old social structure with its feudalistic organization was blessed by the Roman Catholic church. So the presence of these missionaries who preached a gospel of freedom from the burden of a semi-pagan religiosity was going to produce people that would also fight for freedom in society. And it happened that way. Pablo Besson, a Swiss Baptist missionary in Argentina, was a fighter for religious and civil freedom, and his battles took him to the Argentinian Parliament. Evangelical missionaries were active in the fight for religious and civil freedom in Peru. Also in several Latin American countries, evangelicals have been champions of the rights of the Indian majorities enslaved by centuries of white domination.

It might be well to point out that the intention of these evangelicals was basically evangelistic and their missionary zeal had a deep spiritual dimension, but the evils of society were such that out of their Christian vocation they could not but become involved in the fight for social change. What the Finnish evangelical, Benjamin Fernando, said in Amsterdam then is true: "Part of the tragedy of our time is that evangelical Christians are avoiding the revolution that they themselves caused (by their earlier biblical social witness) and so others have stepped in."

5. The biblical model of evangelism

The Primitive church was not perfect, but evidently it was a community that called the attention of men because of the qualitative differences of its life. The message was not only heard from them, it was also seen in the way they lived. Consequently, in the evangelistic and missionary process as we see it in the Bible, there is a reality to be seen and experienced by men, as well as a Gospel that is proclaimed. If we read the Epistles we see that the emphasis is not so much on exhortations to evangelize as on the qualities of the new life in Christ. Christ has commissioned us to be his messengers by word and deed, by a way of being and by a way of speaking. George Duncan said in Berlin:

"In evangelism we are so eager to have people listen that we fail to recognize that they want also to look. They want to look as they listen, and what they see with their eyes should confirm visually the truth of what they hear with their ears. Evangelism has been defined as the offering of a whole Christ for the whole man by the whole church to the whole world. If this is indeed evangelism then it will require the three channels of communication . . . there must be the declaration; there must be the illustration of the Gospel; and finally the products of the Gospel must be able to stand the closest examination."[16]

What we observe in the history of missions as to the way evangelicals have sparked social change by the proclamation of the Gospel and the establishing of new churches, corresponds to what we observe in the biblical pattern of evangelism. This has also been rediscovered by modern evangelical scholarship and reflection about evangelical practice. Again, a very eloquent example comes from the Berlin Congress, where the first three Bible studies dealt with the Great Commission. In his exposition about the Great Commission in the Gospel of John, the R·v. John Stott struck a basic note by stating:

"'As my Father hath sent me, even so send I you' (John 20:21). I venture to say that although these words represent the simplest form of the Great Commission, it is at the same time its most profound form, its most challenging and therefore its most neglected. In these words Jesus gave us not only a command to evangelize ('The Father sent me, I send you'), but also a pattern of evangelism ('As the Father sent me, so I send you'). The church's mission in the world is to be like Christ's. Jesus Christ was the first missionary, and all our mission is derived from his."[17]

Jesus Christ, our model of missionary, was not only the carrier of a message, but he himself was the message, by his way of being among men, by the qualities of his character, by his compassion and his readiness to come close to men in their need. The New Testament is clear in the demand for the Christian and the church to be also a living expression of the message, "living letters" as Paul put it in I Cor. 3:1-3.

To emphasize the communication of the message at the expense of the qualities that must characterize the messengers is not a biblical pattern. The concern with the maturity of the church and the Christian goes hand in hand with the concern for the extension and numerical growth of the church. That is the only way to be faithful to the Word of God. Jesus Christ and Paul were as concerned as we could ever be with the evangelization of the world, with the needs of the masses for the Gospel. However, every page of the New Testament is permeated with their concern for the growth in quality of the disciples and the community.

This concern with the quality of the new life in Christ is precisely relevant to the discussion of the relation between evangelism and social evils. The sinfulness of man is visible in the way every dimension of his life has been distorted from the original design of the Creator. Oppression and injustice, as they become visible in the structures of community life and nations, are the results of disobedience to God and idolatry. When men turn to God and are transformed by the Spirit, their individual lives as well as the structures in which they live are affected. This is evident in the book of Acts where the end of idolatry is a danger for the business structure of a city (Acts 19), where the spiritual liberation of a girl also affects the social and financial life of a group of people and brings political accusations against the apostles (Acts 16:16-23). The individual and the world in which he lives cannot be the same after the Gospel has entered in (II Cor. 5:17).

It is this transforming power of the Gospel that distinguishes it from mere religion. In many religions "salvation" is conceived as a way out of the realities of social, political, and material life. It might be compared to a drug that helps people to have an imaginary flight out of reality. But Christ creates a new man within reality, and through the new man transforms reality. God had a purpose in creation and when men turn to Christ, a process begins in them by which they grow in the fulfillment of the original purpose of God. This fulfillment involves every area of life through which man can love God. It has to do with his whole being: heart, soul, strength and mind (Luke 10:27).

But not only does the message of the Gospel have a transforming content; a study of the Bible shows that it also has a context. The people who hear the Gospel have certain expectations, hopes and needs for which Christ provides an answer. The message "makes sense" as it touches deep-seated needs which are felt in a different way in every person. Jesus Christ comes to preach the message of the Kingdom of God to a nation where there are many expectations about the Kingdom (Luke 2:25,26,38, 3:15, 4:20-22). In other nations the need takes a different shape (Acts 14:8-17, 17:16-23). Jesus Christ and the apostles take their context seriously and communicate the message in such a way that it will touch the need of their listeners. One thing that they refuse, of course, is to change the message in order to get a better hearing or more quantitative results (John 6:60-69; Gal. 1:6-10).

6. A warning to evangelicals

Evangelicals, seriously concerned with the integrity of the Gospel as well as with the proclamation of it unto the ends of the earth, must keep in mind the biblical pattern of evangelism and the biblical content of the Gospel. Several times through the history of the church, Christians have fallen into the temptation of adapting their message, twisting and distorting it. Such was the case with liberalism, an effort to make the Gospel more palatable to the rationalist mind of the nineteenth and early twentieth centuries. We were presented with the social gospel of a wrathless God who was going to save a sinless man through a crossless Christ. The ethical demands of Christ were presented as separate from the saving power of his Cross and resurrection. He was presented as a model to be followed, but there was no transforming power that would help men to follow in his steps.

The temptation for evangelicals today is to reduce the Gospel, to mutilate it, to eliminate any demands for the fruit of repentance and any aspect that would make it unpalatable to a nominally Christian society, even any demands that would make it unpalatable to an idolatrous society. The church must, by all means, keep constantly alert to the needs of the millions who have not heard the Gospel. But with equal zeal it must stress the need for the whole Gospel of Jesus Christ as Savior and Lord whose demands cannot be cheapened. No eagerness for quantitative growth of the church should render us silent about the whole counsel of God.

The danger of evangelicalism is that it will present a saving work of Christ without the consequent ethical demands, that it will present a Savior who delivers from the bondage of spiritual slavery but not a model of the life that the Christians should live in the world. A spirituality without discipleship in the daily social, economic, and political aspects of life is religiosity and not Christianity. The love of God and his plan for the life of a man who is exploiting others and swindling them is not only that he should become an active member of a church giving good offerings to the cause. It is also that he should repent and show the signs of a new life in his business (Luke 19:1-10).

Once and for all we should get rid of the false notion that concern for the social implications of the Gospel and the social dimensions of witnessing comes from false doctrine or lack of evangelical conviction. Contrariwise, it is concern for the integrity of the Gospel that motivates us to stress its social dimension. This is what a contender for the faith said in 1911, in one of the volumes of *The Fundamentals:*

"A true gospel of grace is inseparable from a gospel of good works. Christian doctrines and Christian duties cannot be divorced. The New Testament no more clearly defines the relation of the believer to Christ than to the members of one's family, to his neighbors in society and to his fellow-citizens in the state. These social teachings of the Gospel need a new emphasis today by those who accept the whole Gospel, and should not be left to be interpreted and applied by those alone who deny essential Christianity . . . Some are quite comfortable under what they regard as orthodox preaching, even though they know their wealth has come from the watering of stocks and from wrecking railroads, and from grinding the faces of the poor. The supposed orthodoxy of such preaching is probably defective in its statements of the social teaching of the Gospels. One might be a social bandit and buccaneer and yet believe in the virgin birth and the resurrection of Christ."[18]

Another contender for the faith, precisely the architect of the Berlin Congress, warns evangelicals not to fall in the trap into which fundamentalism fell, thus becoming a "perversion of the biblical spirit." What was the mistake of fundamentalism that we should avoid?

"The Gospel was often narrowed to personal and pietistic religious experience, in which the spiritual role of the intellect is disparaged, and the social and cultural imperative of Christianity evaded."[19]

7. *Elements for outlining a strategy of obedience to the Lord and concern for freedom, justice, and fulfillment*

Oppression, injustice and frustration of God's design for man's life are characteristic of the world in which we live. We found them in varying degrees in every human society. Underdeveloped societies have sometimes vast segments of their population living in sub-human conditions while some privileged elites enjoy power and the best products of human development. Well-developed societies sometimes have minorities which do not share in the benefits of human progress made available to the average citizen by material and institutional development after the industrial revolution. Revolutions against exploitation in some nations have become institutionalized forms of exploitation of the revolution. Though the influence of biblical principles and a Christian way of life can be traced in both material and social development in some regions of the world, no society has ever achieved the balance of authority and freedom, justice, and peace, fulfillment and joy that even the most modest social theorists have imagined. The words of the prophets of Israel condemning misery and injustice that go hand-in-hand with affluence and waste (Amos, Isaiah), could be applied with very little adaptation to several areas of the world and to the universal human family. Oppression, injustice, and the frustration of God's design are visible in relationships inside nations and also between nation and nation.

God's call to his people to be a different people — salt, light, a holy nation — was given in a world that was like ours, an imperfect world torn apart by sin and its consequences. And God's call to witness and to the proclamation of his name demands immediate obedience. There is no indication that God's people have to wait until the world becomes better in order to obey his call and demands. For those who have heard the call of the Lord and live under his Lordship, obedience is unavoidable, whatever the circumstances. Consequently, when Christians gather to think again in the mission of the people of God today, a strategy has to be developed that will help us to visualize the task and give content to our obedience.

First axiom. The Gospel is the message of God's salvation for man accomplished by Jesus Christ in the Cross and the resurrection. Man's sinfulness is evident in the totality of his life as an individual and as a member of the human race. Evil is a reality in the intellectual as well as in the physical and social dimension of man's life and human structures. God's salvation transforms man in the totality of his life and in that way affects man's life and human structures. To give only a spiritual content to God's action in man or to give only a social and physical dimension to God's salvation are both unbiblical heresies, and as such evangelicals should reject them.

Second axiom. God calls those who become his people to be part of a community. So the new humanity that Christ is creating becomes visible in communities that have a quality of life that reflects Christ's example. The message of salvation is not only heard in verbal propositions but visible in a group of people that live by it and are ready to die by it. The church, the community of those called by God, is a signpost for the Kingdom and it shows what God can do with man as an individual and as a member of the human race. Salvation and evangelization considered only in individualistic terms or in verbal terms are also heresies that fall short of the totality of biblical revelation.

Third axiom. The church is not a perfect society while it is in the world. Made up of imperfect men, it shows the marks of Christ's work but it also has shortcomings and defeats. But God has provided means by which the church can be ministered to grow continually to the stature of Christ: his Word, prayer, fellowship, the ministry. Because the church is not perfect, it carries on her task of witness and proclamation in an imperfect way, subject to the limitations and conditioning of history. The Gospel is a treasure that is carried by earthen vessels. The history of missions shows, however, that God's design is not hindered by these imperfections and that his Word has advanced in spite of them. Any boasting of perfection in discipleship or missionary methodology falls short of the biblical teaching and the historical experience. Part of this human limitation is the fact that sometimes the message of Christ advances in the wake of an imperial advance or parallel to it.

Fourth axiom. Because of man's sinfulness and imperfection, even the best dreams of building a just, free world fail, and have failed historically. Those who are called by God in Christ share the aspirations that mankind everywhere has for a better society. As transformed people they are salt and light, and because of that they sometimes even spark a change. However, their expectation is not for a utopia that man will achieve in this age, but rather for the new earth and new heaven that Christ will bring in a definitive way when he comes again. Consequently, though faithfulness to Christ demands from Christian individuals and churches service and involvement in the good of other fellow human beings, Christians know that perfection never comes completely before Christ's return. They also know that the future of God's church and God's mission does not depend on the rise or fall of this or that civilization, of this or that race or nation, of this or that social and political system.

Besides these principles, the strategy of obedience should also take into account the different situations in which the Christian community lives in society. Through the centuries there have been variations in the position of Christians in society and in the ways open to their action and influence. These variations correspond to the different mechanisms of social and political action and to the different qualitative presence of Christians. At least three possibilities can be considered.

First situation. Societies where Christians are a small minority and their presence is felt on a small scale. To the extent to which these Christians are faithful to the integrity of the Gospel, their way of life usually provides a vivid contrast with that of society around. This is the situation of the first centuries of our era and of several countries where missionaries go today.

A variation of this situation comes in societies where though there is a nominal allegiance to Christianity, social structures and institutions as well as everyday life do not show the signs of Christian influence. For example, modern Roman Catholic observers recognize in Latin America that:

"Though Latin America presents itself to the world as a Catholic continent, and has some tradition, some forms, institutions, and structures apparently Catholic . . . it is not Catholic, but it is everyday more pagan and paganizing."[20]

Living Christian communities in this situation become distinct minorities. Though their number and influence are limited in terms of social or political action, their dynamism as a model of social relationships, reconciliation, and coexistence under the Lordship of Christ is very powerful as we can see from reading the book of Acts.

Another variation of this situation is that in which the Christian missionary brings with himself the technological developments of a different society and even in spite of his minority status becomes influential and powerful. This type of situation is disappearing as colonialism in the nineteenth century way disappears also. Quite differently from the New Testament situation, however, in this case there is the temptation of using technology as a means of coercion, giving way to the type of follower that in China was called "rice Christian."

Second situation. Societies where there is a long tradition of definite Christian influence in government, legislation, politics and social action. To the extent to which society has been permeated by some Christian principles the vivid contrast between the Christian community and society around has disappeared. It is not always possible to say to what degree Christians have "christianized society" or to what degree society has "paganized the church." But it cannot be denied that responsible Christians have access to public office, to decision-making positions and to a saying and action in the shaping of the social structures. In these cases there are many ways open to Christian action and the contribution of Christians to the continuous reform of society is visible.

To the extent to which these societies abandon their Christian roots, obedience to the Lord and the Word of God becomes a radical position. When the real spirit of Christ has been left out of a so-called "Christian" way of life, those who advocate commitment to Christ and obedience to his Lordship, sound like revolutionaries, and sometimes become aligned with political radicalism in their criticism of society, though, of course, they act out of a completely different motivation. This would be the case in the so-called Western world, where secularism is rapidly replacing Christian influence, while Christians — especially evangelicals — watch indifferently in the name of commitment to evangelism, not realizing the degree to which their version of the Gospel is also secularized and paganized by their passive acceptance of their society's pagan value system.

Third situation. Societies (perhaps post-Christian) where power has been achieved by a definitely anti-Christian force. In these cases, an ideology or a religion becomes the "official creed" of society and Christians are reduced to a passive fight for survival, and are treated as second-class citizens. Persecution and even martyrdom for the faith are a constant threat and Christians are forced to observe the maximum neutrality in political and social affairs.

This is the situation of Christians in some countries where Islam or Marxism is the official creed, and it is aggravated in those cases in which relations of the churches with a condemned historical past are used as embarrassing arguments against the faithful. We could say that an example of this situation was seen at the height of persecution from the imperial power in the second and third centuries. Christians also lived in this type of situation under Nazi Germany and some other forms of totalitarianism. Faithfulness, courage, and the disposition to suffer for the Lord are the elements of a strategy for the Christians here. The avenue of personal evangelism and communal worship is always open at that cost. Daily life in those circumstances may be for the people of God the avenue through which his power operates quietly, when the noise of public activism is not allowed.

8. Outline of a strategy for these situations

If we can recall statements that have been made before, it is fundamental for evangelicals that the message we preach be really the pure Gospel and the whole Gospel. No strategy can mean a change of the Gospel to adapt it and make it palatable. It is also fundamental that willingly or unwillingly, if we are followers of Christ, we have been called to be witnesses. We might choose to be silent witnesses but if our life is really being transformed by God's Spirit, sooner or later we will be called to give an account of our hope. We might choose to close our eyes to the needs of the world around us and beyond our borders, but the command to be always ready in case the King sends us, has not changed. In the face of difficulties and hardships, the command of Christ cannot be changed: "You will be my witnesses."

For Christians living in the first situation, *service* is the main avenue of obedience to the social and political demands of the Gospel. Service first in the context of the Christian community. No measure of exegetical acrobatics can take us to the conclusion that the concern of the Jerusalem Christians that "each would have according to his need" (Acts 4:35) was motivated by wrong eschatological dating or was a serious mistake in light of modern capitalistic principles. Through the book of Acts, and also in the epistles, that is a constant concern.

This is the basis for the almost natural way in which enthusiastic commitment to obeying the Lord in the missionary enterprise has created so many service agencies also. The Wesleyan revival of piety and evangelism was accompanied by the participation of evangelicals in some of the most imaginative philanthropic enterprises. Evangelism In Depth has gone hand in hand with the "good-will caravans" in Latin America. One of the most missionary-minded churches in Korea is also a church that has shown outstanding concern for the poor and needy. The linguistic and literacy work of the Wycliffe Bible translators has many service avenues that have open doors to the Gospel. And all these forms of service should continue hand in hand with concern for the announcement of the Gospel. Service provided in the name of Christ must point to the transforming power of Christ's work. The social impact of committed people is the demonstration of the truth of the biblical teaching about growth. The numerical growth of the church in the New Testament is linked to the growth in Christ that makes the disciples a transforming fellowship.

Some service agencies have to re-evaluate their aims in light of developments in the areas where they work. If there was a time when the only education available for poor classes or oppressed races was that provided by Christians, and if the situation has changed so that those societies are giving better attention to them, Christians should find new ways of service to accompany their missionary endeavor. What they should not accept is a missionary strategy that in its concern for numerical growth reduced evangelism to the transmission of verbal summaries of the Gospel from the distance of non-involvement.

The other way open for Christians in situation one is that of *personal excellency*. The operative principle behind the witness of Joseph in Egypt, Esther in Persia, and Daniel in Babylon is that one individual member of a small minority under God can achieve a position of power and be used as a witness in that situation for the sake of God's glory and for the sake of his people. Minority churches should not be closed to this possibility, and should sustain in prayer and fellowship those who are called this way. The faithfulness of these biblical characters is linked to their knowledge of God and his Word. With the spirtual diet of isolated biblical verses from here and there, no one will survive the tensions of that position. Deep teaching of the Word and prayer become vital for sustaining a person with such calling. And no measure of interest in the "masses" can excuse us from definite commitment to teaching the whole counsel of God in his church whatever the society in which we live.

Discipleship and biblical instruction become also very important when the growth of the Christian community gives an increasing number of new avenues of social service and political action. Only by having a strong church rooted in the truth of God will you have an original

Christian contribution to society. Weak churches will produce communities that instead of transforming society will adapt themselves easily to a pagan pattern.

Many young people in Latin America, who were motivated by the Gospel to love their neighbor and be concerned for justice and freedom in their society, have often become Marxists simply because their churches did not provide biblical instruction about Christian discipleship, or because they were blind to clear demands from the Bible and opportunities and challenges provided by new social situations.

For Christians living in the second situation, the call is a call to faithfulness to the Gospel and to the Lord. The evangelical community in the Anglo-Saxon countries has money, influence, and numbers that could really make it a decisive force for the reform of their society. By creating a false and anti-biblical dichotomy between evangelism and social action, by closing their eyes to the example of evangelicals in England in the nineteenth century, and by spiritualizing the Gospel to heretical extremes, they have let secularism take the initiative in education, politics, the media, and international relations. Christians in the Third World who contemplate the so-called West, expect from their brethren a word of identification with demands for justice in international trade, for a modification of the patterns of affuence and waste that arc made possible because of unjust and exploitative trade systems, for a criticism of corruption in the arms race and in the almost omnipotent maneuverings of international intelligence agencies. There are many channels to express this concern for justice, like active involvement in lobbying, revision of investments, and working through international control organizations. Christians in the West can do all that without in any way decreasing in their missionary and evangelistic fervor. It is only a matter of taking seriously the Gospel that we proclaim we believe and that we are so prone to defend against heresy. It is a matter of recognizing that Satan is alive and at work, not only in some parts of the world, but everywhere, and that some Western leaders who are eager to proclaim allegiance to Christ, arc leading their nation by the route of abuse, injustice, and evil that has only brought destruction and judgment from God in history. Many, many hearts have been opened to the Gospel in the Third World by the firm stand of men like Martin Luther King or Alan Paton. The message of Christ does not need the help of a spectacular "show" in order to attract the attention of the people. Where it is proclaimed in a relevant way, where it calls men to repentance and conversion pointing to the real personal and social evils, where it demonstrates the power of the resurrection against the power of Satan, it has in itself all the dramatic realism that it had in the lips of Christ. This is the message that has to be proclaimed in the West by every available means.

Christians in the West, especially evangelicals, have justified their inaction, conformism, and silence on the basis that the New Testament believers were not involved in the political and social life of their day. But tax exemption or prayer in the schools are privileges that New Testament Christians did not have, and modern Western Christians accept. These privileges show that Western Christians are involved socially and politically in their society in a different way than New Testament Christians, and they should consequently accept the responsibilities of this new type of involvement when it comes to changing structures for the better. If as evangelicals we rejected the liberal adaptation of the Gospel to the rationalism of the nineteenth century, we should also reject the adaptation of the Gospel to the social conformism or conservatism of the middle class citizen in the powerful West.

For Christians living in the third situation, that is, in a society that has become hostile to the Gospel, the call is also to faithfulness to the Lord. The Word is there, it cannot be modified. The cost of obedience can be death, and those who enjoy the so-called freedom of the West should not think that disobedience to Caesar is a duty only if Caesar is not a capitalist.

When society becomes utterly totalitarian, sometimes the Christian community with its refusal to render unto Caesar what belongs to God becomes the only place where freedom is possible, and it is maintained even at the cost of second-class citizenship. The church has lived in very different regimes and situations and has survived at the cost of martyrdom.

The hope of evangelization of the world does not lie in the fact that some nation will impose some political or economic regime favorable to the Gospel. It rather rests in the hands of Jesus Christ the Lord who has used in the past, emperors and tyrants as well as humble slaves and poor itinerant preachers to take his Word to the uttermost parts of the earth, in unexpected, surprising, divine ways indeed!

FOOTNOTES

[1] Clifford Christians, Earl J. Schipper, Wesley Smedes, *Who in the World,* ed. by Eerdmans, 1972, p. 125.

[2] Tibor Mende, "The Development Crisis: the Real Questions" in *Cooperation Canada,* N.6, CIDA, Ottawa, Jan-Feb. 1973, pp. 3-9.

[3] *Who in the World,* p. 125.

[4] Acts 24:17; I Cor. 16:1-3; II Cor. 8:1-7, 9:1-15.

[5] *A World to Win,* InterVarsity Press, London, 1972, pp. 27-28.

[6] C.F.H. Henry and W.S. Mooneyham (eds.) *One Race, One Gospel, One Task* (World Congress on Evangelism), World Wide Publications, Minneapolis, 1967, Vol. II, sections III and IV.

[7] Ibid. p. 177.

[8] Ibid. pp. 197-200.

[9] Ibid. p. 252.

[10] Ibid. "Nationalism and the Gospel," pp. 305-308, and "The Ethics of Political Nationalism," pp. 312-316.

[11] Ibid. Samuel Escobar, "The Totalitarian Climate," pp. 288-290.

[12] B.E. Fernando, "The Evangel and Social Upheaval" (Part II), in *Christ Seeks Asia,* Asia South Pacific Congress on Evangelism, W.S. Mooneyham (ed.), Rock House publications, Hong Kong, 1969, pp. 118 ff.

[13] Paavo Kortekangas, "Social Implications of Evangelism," in *Evangelism Alert* (ed. G.W. Kirby), World Wide Publications, pp. 131 ff.

[14] Leighton Ford, "The Church and Evangelism in a Day of Revolution," in *Evangelism Now* (U.S. Congress on Evangelism), World Wide Publications, 1969, 1970, p. 62.

[15] Samuel Escobar in "The Social Impact of the Gospel," in *Is Revolution Change?* (ed. Brian Griffiths), InterVarsity Press, 1972, pp. 100 and 98. This chapter is the English text of the message on the subject presented at the Bogotá Congress on Evangelism and published with the other papers of the Congress under the title *Accion en Cristo para un Continente en Crisis* (ed. Caribe), 1970.

[16] G.B. Duncan, *ibid.,* pp. 60, 62.

[17] John R.W. Stott in *One Race, One Gospel, One Task,* vol. I, pp. 39-40.

[18] C.R. Erdman, "The Church and Socialism," in *The Fundamentals* Vol. XII, 1911, pp. 116, 118.

[19] C.F.H. Henry, *Evangelical Responsibility in Contemporary Theology,* Eerdmans, 1957, pp. 46-47.

[20] Documents of the Interamerican Congress of Catholic Action, quoted by Stanley Rycroft, *A Factual Study of Latin America,* 1963, p. 207.

EVANGELIZATION AND MAN'S SEARCH FOR FREEDOM, JUSTICE AND AND FULFILLMENT

Samuel Escobar

In the first place, I want to thank God for the hundreds of brethren whose encouraging words have come from around the world in relation to my paper. This fact shows that the evangelical community is grappling with these issues and that there is a ferment of renewal that, in my opinion, comes from the Holy Spirit. He is moving his people to look to the world around with the compassion of Jesus Christ, and to be obedient to the clear teaching of the Bible in relation to human needs and the total liberation that the Gospel brings for man. I think that the organizers of the Congress were not mistaken when they chose as a motto, the words of Jesus Christ in the synagogue of Nazareth, defining his mission and ours:

"To preach the Gospel to the poor;
To heal the brokenhearted,
To preach deliverance to the captives
and recovering of sight to the blind,
To set at liberty them that are bruised."

These are words that cannot be spiritualized in a world like ours, where there are millions of persons who are poor, brokenhearted, captive, blind and bruised.

It has been pointed out in different responses that evangelicals *are* doing many things in different parts of the world in order to meet with the whole Gospel the men who are searching for freedom, justice, and fulfillment. I praise the Lord for that fact, and I only wish that instead of my standing here this morning, we could have some of those who are deeply involved in service to the needs of men. I am thinking of men like Justo Gonzalez, Sr., and Arturo Parajon, who have been traveling and living sacrificially, opening the eyes of Latin American churches and mobilizing them to serve the needs of the people in literacy and medical work. I think of men like William Bentley, a pastor working among the black minority in Chicago, one of the toughest cities of the world. I think of Ted MacDougall working out of his farm in Prince Edward Island in Canada, dealing with drug addicts and drug pushers, inmates in jail and kids in trouble by the hundreds, winning them to Christ and helping them to readjust in society. I think of Michael Patterson, an Anglican medical doctor in the north of Argentina, serving forgotten Indian minorities, a specialist in tropical diseases who spends his life in a remote area where no other doctor wants to go.

I think of Walter Hearn, an outstanding chemist and university professor, who has decided to live in a simple way and to identify with students in their way of dressing, their needs, and their fights in the University of California at Berkeley. I think of the brethren in the People's Coalition group in Chicago and their brave radical evangelical paper *The Post American*. I think of Mark Hatfield, an evangelical voice, sometimes lonely but always clear in the Senate of the most powerful Western nation.

I think of hundreds and hundreds of anonymous servants of God who are creatively working to alleviate the needs of people around them and help them in their efforts in search of better social structures. I also think of men like Solzhenitsyn and other Christians in different parts of the world who are refusing to accept passively and in silence the impositions of unjust authorities. And I think of a good friend who is a prisoner for the cause of the Gospel in Cuba and who in prison not only has given a verbal testimony of his faith but has done his best to alleviate the needs around him, turning sheets into shorts, for instance, so that his fellow prisoners would not go completely naked.

And as I know that some people like these are here in this audience, I would like to say to all of them a word of thanks and encouragement, praying that they will keep faithful in what they are doing. Some of them have been criticized and told that they should abandon their efforts for the pursuit only of numerical growth of congregations. I hope they will not believe that such is the official position of the Congress.

Many of the questions I have received can be answered by pursuing a point that Howard Snyder has clearly stressed in his paper "The Church as God's Agent for Evangelism" (II. B. 1-4). I especially would like to call your attention to his eloquent quotation from John Howard Yoder: "Pragmatically, it is self-evident that there can be no procedure of proclamation without a community, distinct from the rest of society, to do the proclaiming. Pragmatically, it is just as clear that there can be no evangelistic call addressed to a person inviting him to enter into a new kind of fellowship and learning if there is not such a body of persons, again distinct from the totality of society, to whom he can come and with whom he can learn."

I think that the first and powerful answer to the social and political needs of men, to the search for freedom, justice, and fulfillment, is given by Jesus in his own work and in the church. Jesus takes seriously the problems of property, power, relationships, which are essentially the problems that cause social and political maladjustment and injustice. As Yoder himself has emphasized, Jesus creates a new people, a new community where these problems are dealt with under the Lordship of Christ. This is the community, *distinct from the rest of society,* that we find around Jesus first, then growing in Jerusalem and then expanding into the world. In this community there is a new attitude to money and property (Luke 6:29-31,35; Acts 2:43-45, 4:34, 20:35; Jas. 2:14-16; I John 3:16-17). In this community there is a new attitude to power and its exercise (Luke 22:23-27 and parallels in Matthew and Mark; II Cor. 10:8, 12:10-15; I Pet. 5:1-3). It is a community where human barriers and prejudices have been overcome under Christ's rule (Gal. 3:28; Col. 3:11; Philem. 15-17). It is a community ready to suffer for justice and good (Matt. 5:10-12; Acts 7:51-60, 16:16-24; I Pet. 3:13-18).

This is the biblical model of evangelism, the radically different community that calls men to faith in the crucified and resurrected Christ that has transformed their lives, and the new life in the Spirit that enables them to follow the example of Christ. Such a community has a revolutionary effect in changing a society.

Let us take a specific example. It is false, as some have written, that

Paul did not do anything about the evil of slavery. He did at least three things. *First*, he announced the Gospel equally to masters and slaves. His own life-style and training added credibility to his message in both social classes. *Second*, as part of his message he taught basic truths about the nature of man (Acts 17:26, a common origin for all men) and the new type of relationship that human beings had under Christ (Gal. 3:28). These truths were contrary to the basic tenets of the then prevalent philosophy, in which slavery was based. *Third*, he asked specifically for an application of his teaching in the context of the Christian community (Philemon). It has been demonstrated that by addressing himself to the slaves as moral agents (Col. 3:22-25; Eph. 6:5-8), he was doing something completely new in his day, treating them like responsible persons, not like things or animals, which was the way in those days. Moreover, Paul asked from masters in the same passage what not even the most advanced moralists or philosophers would have asked at that point.

Thus Paul, in his teaching and practice in the primitive church, was attacking slavery in its very base. The example and influence of the church in the first century and later the active involvement of Christians in civil life brought eventually the abolition of the system.

When the south of Africa was discovered by the Portuguese in the fifteen century, slavery soon appeared again, and in a matter of decades Christendom had accepted it. However, in 1774, in the wake of a spiritual revival, a great evangelist, John Wesley, published his short treatise *Thoughts upon Slavery*. After an historical and a restrained though ghastly portrayal of the inhumanity of slavery, he pierces prophetically to the moral issues involved. Countering the argument that the slave traffic was a legitimate business, he asks: "Can human law turn darkness into light or evil into good? Notwithstanding ten thousand laws, right is right and wrong is wrong still . . . I absolutely deny all slave holding to be consistent with any degree of even natural justice". . . Proceeding he dealt a timely blow at such "loyalty" as conceives Empire and patriotism in terms only of mercantile or geographic expansion, for concerning the British West Indies he urged: "It is better that all these islands should remain uncultivated forever; yea, it were more desirable that they were altogether sunk in the depth of the sea than they should be cultivated at so high a price as the violation of justice, mercy and truth."

In today's language, we could say that for Wesley, development without social justice was unacceptable. I pray that God will raise in this Congress evangelists like Wesley, who also care about social evils enough as to do research and write about them and throw the weight of their moral and spiritual authority on the side of the correction of injustices. Wesley, however, did *more than writing*. He encouraged the political action that eventually was going to abolish slavery in England. Six days before his death, Wesley wrote to the famous evangelical politician William Wilberforce, encouraging him in the name of God to fight against slavery.

More than sixty years ago, a group called Peniel Hall Society bought some land in Bolivia, in order to help Aymara peasants with a school and a hospital. As was the practice until recently in Latin America, the land was sold to them with 250 Aymara serfs who belonged to the estate. After a long period of failures and hesitations, the project in 1920 was handed to the Canadian Baptist Mission Board who eventually brought an agricultural missionary. After the fruitless efforts of several years, "it finally dawned on the missionaries that their position as land owners and serf masters was overriding every benevolent attempt to uplift the people."

Finally, in 1942 economic serfdom was abolished, the land was parceled and the Indians were given title of property to their plots. Norman Dabbs, the missionary martyr, comments: "Both missionaries and peons felt that a crushing weight had been lifted from their lives."

When ten years later a nationalist revolutionary government passed the desperately needed law of land reform, the pioneer experiment of the Baptists in Huatajata was recognized as a valid antecedent. The amazing fact is that the freedom of Indians and the distribution of land was immediately followed by church growth in the area; and also after the revolution of 1952 a wave of church growth started in Bolivia.

These examples are illustrations of how Christians in what I have called first and second situations can be obedient to God's Word. We need a revival of life in our churches around the world, so that they again will be communities "distinct from the rest of society." We need evangelists that are also prophets like John Wesley. Where possible, we need Christian politicians like Wilberforce. We need imaginative missionaries, ready to pioneer in areas of social justice and evangelism.

Please notice that the simple liberation from human masters is not the freedom of which the Gospel speaks. Freedom in Christian terms means subjection to Jesus Christ as Lord, deliverance from bondage to sin and Satan (John 8:31-38) and consequently the beginning of new life under the Law of Christ (I Cor. 9:19), life in the family of the faith where the old human master becomes also the new brother in Christ. However, the heart which has been made free with the freedom of Christ cannot be indifferent to the human longings for deliverance from economic, political, or social oppression. And that is what many expect from the one who evangelizes. Not that he says: "I come to announce to you a spiritual freedom and because of that I do not care about your social, economic, or political oppression." But rather that he says: "I care for your oppression. I am with you in your search for a way out, and I can show you a deeper and most decisive deliverance that may help you to find a better way out of your social and political oppression."

That is what Christ did. He identified with the oppressed. For instance, he became poor both in taking upon himself the human limitations and in the social strata that he chose to live in when he came. When Jesus, who made himself poor, tells me, "You always have the poor with you," I listen to him. He added to that, let us remember, "And whenever you will, you can do good to them" (Mark 14:7). But when a rich man tells me the same sentence, I have the suspicion that he really means, "You always have the rich with you . . . . and that should not change."

What is the image that our missionary and evangelistic work projects? Do we stand with the rich or with the poor? Do we stand usually with oppressors or with the oppressed? What a contradiction it would be, says James, if not being rich we would be forgetting the poor and favoring the rich (Jas. 2:5-9). Please consider that in my opinion the tough question is not, "Are you rich?" The question is, "Where do you stand when you preach the Gospel?" "Where did your master stand?"

A dramatic example of the dilemma was recently presented to me by a missionary friend who works among a tribe in Latin America. He was torn apart by the dilemma of standing with his poor unknown tribe of "savages" or rather with the oil company that wanted to use him to move the Indians out of the area, getting them away in order to continue with exploration, thus eliminating "the Indian problem." This may become a difficult area for decisions, especially for those willing to reach parts of the so-called "fourth world," remote areas, where the desperate search for raw materials and oil also is going to center now.

If this is not taken seriously by the evangelists, in both their style and their message, the credibility of the Gospel is at stake. I do not think we can measure the effects that were registered in the conscience of evangelicals and of the hearers of the Gospel by the firm stand that evangelist Billy Graham took on racial issues from the very beginning of his career. His refusal to preach to segregated audiences closed some doors and provoked disaffection. I think that it stems from his biblical convictions about the nature of man and God's design for him. I praise the Lord for it! He did not downgrade the demands of the Gospel in order to have access to a greater number of hearers or in order to have the blessing of racists that would consider themselves "fundamental Christians." A stance like this is already communicating something about the nature of the Gospel that gives credibility to the Gospel itself when it is announced. This is especially so for those who are the victims of injustice and are conscious of it.

In some societies and nations, there is desperate need for healing in the area of interracial relationships. In those cases, the Christian church might be the only place where the miracle of encounter, acceptance, and coexistence can happen because the redemptive power of Christ acts. To perpetuate segregation for the sake of numerical growth, arguing that segregated churches grow faster, is for me yielding to the sinfulness of society, refusing to show a new and unique way of life. This would be an example of reducing the Gospel to make it more palatable. Such "numerical growth" might not be the numerical growth of the church of Jesus Christ. I wonder sometimes if — taking into account the demonic forces at work behind racism, prejudice, oppression, corruption, and exploitation of the weak and the poor everywhere, and taking also into account evangelistic and missionary efforts which are totally unaware of those facts — the Lord would not tell us: "Woe to you zealous evangelists, hypocrites, for you traverse sea and land to make a single proselyte, and when he becomes a proselyte, you make him twice as much a child of hell as yourselves" (Matt. 23:15).

Thus, in some parts of the world there is this kind of subtle opposition to the Gospel when it is seen as a threat to entrenched prejudices and privileges. But I also recognize that there are other societies where hostility to the Gospel goes to the point of forbidding its proclamation in public and even persecuting the believers. In the face of this type of open opposition in what I have called the "third situation," concerned prayer and expectancy are very important. The initiative in missions and evangelism comes from the Holy Spirit and he might be preparing the way for the Gospel in unexpected ways. Leslie T. Lyall, a veteran missionary from Asia, says, "The Christian world has become familiar in recent years with the dangerous talk of 'closed doors.' Such talk however, may betray an old-fashioned 'colonial viewpoint.' Closed to whom? Presumably to the unwelcome emissaries, the 'neo-colonialists' of the West. But if 'closed doors' in Burma have shut out the Western missionary, they have also shut in the Christian church which remains as a witness to the living Christ behind those doors. Since missionaries were asked to leave by the government, the number of baptisms annually has been maintained and even increased, while there are more students in the theological colleges than ever."

There are places where hostility is even greater. New strategies have to be developed. *First,* it will be necessary to support and encourage the Christians in those areas without embarrassing or endangering them. *Second,* to build a new system of promotion of missions that is not based on glamorous pictures and statistics of success. *Third,* to mobilize laymen of different nationalities into areas of life where their presence could be accepted. These steps demand a change of political attitudes, the recognition of what is good in other systems and regimes, and the disposition to work humbly under the limitations that they create.

Another area that has been pointed out in responses is the danger that if we concentrate on working out the social implications of the Gospel, we will forget evangelism, and that history proves that fact. I would like to affirm that *I do not believe in that statement.* I think that the social gospel, for instance, deteriorated because of poor theology. The sad thing is that those who have the right theology have not applied it to social issues. The practical answer must be seen in a different area. We have to rediscover the ministry of teaching in the church, the close link between evangelism and church life, and the role of the layman in the world. Let me explain.

In the life of our Lord, and in the life of the Apostles, there was no separation or gap between preaching and teaching. Both were important and essential to their ministry. I think that the idea that you can "evangelize" and leave teaching for ten years later is anti-biblical. Teaching is an indispensable part of the life of the body and if it is not provided, a group called church can degenerate into nothing but a social club or a sect. Part of the teaching is *how to live in the world as a Christian:* the ethics of the Kingdom. Laymen then penetrate society by a *way of life* that is new in family relations, business, citizenship, and every area of daily life. Consequently, to mobilize the laymen is not only to teach them short summaries of the Gospel, mini-sermons, and to send them to repeat these to their neighbors. It is also to teach them how to apply the teaching and example of Christ in their family life, in their business activities, in their social relationships, in their studies, etc. Those who teach need to be solidly rooted in the Word of God but also very aware of the world around them, so that they can help in the application. In societies that are increasingly hostile to Christianity, this task is more crucial and necessary, because you cannot take for granted that the value system and the social uses are "Christian." We desperately need this ministry in the Third World! We desperately need this ministry in the Western nations!

I agree with the comments of some responses that oppression and injustice is not only something that comes from powerful nations, but that within every country, including especially the Third World, there are local oppressors, privileged elites, and conservative middle classes that oppose any change that may disturb their privileged position, even if that change is going to benefit the majority. I know that in some Latin American countries, while there are foreign missionaries spending their lives among the poor or the Indian minorities, for instance, there are hundreds of national graduates who attend "fundamental" churches but show no concern for their own fellow countrymen. They have no concern for their material or spiritual welfare. This is the result of an evangelism that has not presented Christ as Lord and has not been followed immediately by training in discipleship. Moreover, I think that many of those second-generation evangelicals are pagans in need of conversion and if we do not realize that, we are only mobilizing them to reproduce pagans like them under "evangelical" disguise. It is a fact that this type of church is not able to communicate the Gospel to either the rising masses or the restless youth at the university.

I agree that heads of governments are wrongly blamed for decisions and policies that simply reflect the general trend of their societies or the interests of powerful groups in them. It has also been pointed out to me that evangelicals in North America or England are not as influential or powerful as I had thought in my naive Third World view. But, on the one hand, I still believe that one man empowered by the Holy Spirit can be used by God to turn the tide of life in a nation or shock its conscience. Preachers and evangelists we need, and we should pray for men of the stature of Daniel, John the Baptist, Peter Waldo, Savonarola, Calvin, Luther, Knox, Wesley, Niemöller, and so on. There is almost general agreement in the responses about the pagan and anti-Christian forces that are shaping the life and policies of nations in the West. If that is recognized, why should we defend those policies, legitimize them, and become defensive when they are attacked?

Because of my specific reference to aspects of the international situation, I must say, of course, that I do not believe that the so-called West has the monopoly of abuse, exploitation, and oppression of the poor and small nations. The energy crisis in the world has demonstrated how even nations that are "not developed" can exploit the less developed ones, not to mention the dependency created in other areas, and also exploited by the so-called socialist blocs of nations.

But please remember that precisely the freedom that Christians have in the Western nations, and the possibility of intelligent participation at decision-making levels, is a talent that has to be used, unless the day comes when it will be taken from us. But if we take refuge in a non-biblical, unethical eschatology, to use the expression written by some of the respondents to my paper, we are simply refusing to use our hands for fear, trying to keep them clean, not realizing that they are already dirty. It is commonly a forgotten lesson that in the very land where Marx studied the conditions of the working class and forged the notion of revolution as the only way to change, his doctrine could not be applied. A spiritual revival brought also an alignment of the Christians with the poor and the oppressed, not only a sentimental alignment but a definite political and social alignment for change. Contrariwise, it was in those countries where Christians as a majority aligned themselves with the powerful or else refused to let their influence be felt in a transforming way upon the masses, where violent revolution finally became the only political alternative. This is not a rule without exception, of course.

Moreover, for the time being, Christian resources are concentrated in the Western nations and if they are going to be mobilized for the missionary task, the need for Christians to become aware of the complex issues and the ambiguities by which the missionary task is surrounded has to be taken seriously. I hope that the same eagerness and use of technology which is used to give us figures of populations in need could be used to clarify, as far as possible, the unique character of the Christian message as different from what we call today Western culture. I have found the younger generation of North American evangelical students far more aware of world issues and problems than some of the leaders who forge the policies of mission boards. May the Spirit give us ears to hear what he is saying through the impatience and critical attitude of youth. May our structures not crush missionaries before the end of their first term but be flexible to change as New Testament structures were.

We live in a fallen world which is trapped in injustice and sin, and what happens at the political and financial level is what also happens in our own personal daily life. I see sin in East and West, corruption in North and South. We have come to a point in history in which it could be said that if a world war comes, none of the parties will be "defending Christianity." The idea of a "holy war" is absurd and untenable for me in 1974. Because of this, I think that in this Congress we should come as *brothers and sisters* from among all nations, who live in a hostile world where we have been called to be salt and light. We come here to encourage one another in the task of evangelization. We come here to encourage one another in the difficult task of living as sheep among the wolves everywhere, and not to defend our governments or our social and political way of life. There is very little that can be defended in this world today! As part of this mutual encouragement, we reaffirm our hope that the Kingdom may come soon in fullness. But as an evidence of that hope we should also reaffirm our willingness to be the community of disciples of Christ which tries to demonstrate in the context of development or underdevelopment, affluence or poverty, democracy or dictatorship, that *there is a different way* for men to live together dealing with passions, power, relations, inequality, and privilege; that we are not only able to proclaim that "the end is at hand" but also to encourage one another in the search to make this world a bit less unjust and cruel, as an evidence of our expectation of a new creation.

THE CHURCH AS GOD'S AGENT IN EVANGELISM

Howard A. Snyder

*Rev. Snyder, Sao Paulo, Brazil, is
Dean of the Free Methodist
Theological Seminary.*

The Church *is* God's agent of evangelism. To speak of the evangelistic task without relating this to the Church is to lose the biblical perspective and develop an incomplete evangelism.

But the statement, "The Church is God's agent of evangelism" can be either a meaningless cliché or a profound insight — depending on how the words "church" and "evangelism" are understood. The aim of this paper is to ask how the Bible presents the Church, and what it means biblically to say the Church is God's agent of evangelism.

The Church is the *only* divinely-appointed means for spreading the the Gospel[1]. As Melvin Hodges has written, "The Church is God's agent in the earth — the medium through which he expresses himself to the world. God has no other redeeming agency in the earth."[2] Further, evangelism makes little sense divorced from the fact of the Christian community. The evangelistic call is a call *to something,* and that "something" is more than a doctrine or an experience or the exercise of faith or even, narrowly, Jesus Christ. The evangelistic call intends to call persons *to the Body of Christ* — the community of believers, with Jesus Christ as its essential and sovereign head[3].

I shall attempt to show how the Church is God's agent of evangelism by responding to three questions: first, what is the Church, biblically understood? second, how does the biblical Church grow? and finally, what insights for church structure emerge from this understanding of Church and evangelism?

PART ONE: THE CHURCH BIBLICALLY UNDERSTOOD

The Bible says the Church is nothing less than the Body of Christ. It is the bride of Christ (Rev. 21:9); the flock of God (I Pet. 5:2); the living temple of the Holy Spirit (Eph. 2:21-22). Virtually all biblical figures for the Church emphasize an *essential, living love relationship* between Christ and his body. This underscores the overwhelming importance of the Church in God's plan and reminds us that "Christ loved the Church and gave himself up for her" (Eph. 5:25). If the Church is the *body* of Christ — the means of the Head's action in the world — then it is an essential part of the Gospel, and ecclesiology is inseparable from soteriology.

1. Traditional views of the Church

The biblical view of the Church may be contrasted with two traditional views which correspond roughly to the "visible church" — "invisible church" distinction[4].

a. *The institutional view* identifies the "visible" institutional structure with the essence of the Church and makes no significant distinction between the two. Thus most denominations are called churches, and in practice "church" and "denomination" mean the same thing.

There may be nothing wrong with calling denominations or institutional structures "churches" — but *this is not what the Bible means by "church."* When Paul or Peter or Jesus Christ say "church," they clearly do not refer to an institution or organization[5].

b. In contrast, *the mystical view* puts the Church far above space, time, and sin as an ethereal reality comprising all true believers in Christ and known only to God. This view is a little like Plato's theory of ideas — what we see may be imperfect, but a perfect Church exists invisibly.

There is, of course, an invisible church — or rather, the true Church of Christ surpasses visible reality. But *this is not what the Bible normally means by "church"*[6]. There may be an invisible church, but this mystical conception is not very helpful in understanding the life and growth of the Church on earth and in history.

Both these views have one thing in common: *they fail to take culture seriously.* In the institutional view the Church becomes so wedded to its particular culture that the culturally-determined nature of much of its life and structure is unperceived. Thus the Church becomes culture-bound. This creates problems especially when cultures change or when cross-cultural evangelism is attempted.

In the mystical view, however, the Church floats nebulously *above culture* and never becomes involved in the limiting dimensions of space, time, and history. Cultural factors — which affect theology, structures, and evangelism — are not taken into account.

Thus both the institutional view and the mystical view are inadequate. Both cloud the clear biblical meaning of the Church — one by too close an identification with culture, the other by removing itself from culture. In both cases it is really culture which becomes "invisible."

To understand the Church biblically we must move beyond the traditional visible-invisible conception and move back to the prior and more fundamental biblical view. We must take the Church seriously in such a way that space, time, and history (the dimensions of culture) are also taken seriously.

2. The biblical view of the Church

In contrast to traditional views, the Bible describes the Church in the midst of culture, struggling to maintain its fidelity while tainted by the corrosive oils of paganism and Jewish legalism. This view of the Church is sharply relevant for the modern age.

a. *The Bible sees the Church in historical-cosmic perspective.* Scripture places the Church at the very center of God's cosmic purpose. This is seen most clearly in Paul's writings, and particularly in the book of Ephesians. Paul was concerned to speak of the Church as the result of, and within the context of, the plan of God for his whole creation (Eph. 1:9-10, 1:20-23, 3:10, 6:12)[7].

What is this cosmic plan? According to Ephesians, it is *that God may glorify himself by uniting all things in Christ through the Church*[8]. The key idea here is clearly *reconciliation* — not only the reconciliation of men to God, but the reconciliation of all things, "things in heaven and things on earth" (Eph. 1:10). Central to this plan is the reconciliation of man to God through the blood of Jesus Christ. But the reconciliation Christ brings extends to all the alienations that resulted from the Fall — between man and himself, between man and man, and between man and his physical environment. As mind-boggling as the thought is, Scripture teaches that this reconciliation even includes the redemption of the physical universe from the effects of sin as everything is brought under proper headship in Jesus Christ[9].

Paul emphasizes *individual and corporate personal salvation* through Christ, and then goes on to place personal salvation in cosmic perspective (Eph. 1:3-23; Col. 1:3-20). The redemption of man is the center of God's plan, but it is not the *circumference* of that plan. Paul alternates between a close-up view and a long-distance view, for the most part focusing on the close-up of personal redemption, but periodically changing to a long-distance, wide-angle view that takes in "all things" — things visible and invisible; things past, present, and future; things in heaven and things on earth; all the principalities and powers — the whole historical-cosmic scene[10].

According to Ephesians 3:10, the Church is the earthly *agent* of the cosmic reconciliation God wills[11]. This means the Church's mission is broader than evangelism. Evangelism is the *center* of the Church's role as agent of reconciliation, and therefore is the *first priority* of the Church's ministry in the world. But the mission of the Church extends to reconciliation and "substantial healing" in other areas as well[12]. To the extent the coming of the Kingdom of God takes place in space-time history before the return of Christ, God's plan is to be accomplished through the Church.

b. The Bible sees the Church in charismatic, rather than institutional, terms. According to the New Testament, the Church is a charismatic organism, not an institutional organization. The Church is the result of the grace (Greek, *charis*) of God. It is through grace that the Church is saved (Eph. 2:8), and through the exercise of spiritual gifts of grace (*charismata*) that the Church is edified (Rom. 12:6-8; Eph. 4:7-16; I Cor. 12:4-8, 14:1-5; I Pet. 4:10-11). "According to Scripture, the Church *is* a charismatic community"[13].

God gives his gracious gift of salvation on the basis of Christ's work and through the agency of the Holy Spirit. This provides the basis of the Church's community life. The pure light of God's "manifold grace"[14] is then refracted as it shines through the Church, as light through a prism, producing the varied, many-colored *charismata,* or gifts of the Spirit. This provides the basis for the Church's diversity within unity. The Church is edified through the exercise of spiritual gifts as "the whole body, joined and knit together by every joint with which it is supplied . . . makes bodily growth and upbuilds itself in love" (Eph. 4:16).

This is important for evangelism, because the New Testament relates evangelism to spiritual gifts (Eph. 4:11-12). In order for the Church to be alive and growing, it must be based on a *charismatic model,* not an *institutional model.*

The question of a charismatic or institutional model for church life and structure is becoming urgent in contemporary society. Technological development, the population explosion, and other factors are speeding up the pace of change and squeezing humanity into a potential global ghetto. This acceleration puts new strains on all institutional structures. Alvin Toffler analyzes these trends in his book *Future Shock* and argues that "the acceleration of change has reached so rapid a pace that even bureaucracy can no longer keep up." This means that "newer . . . more instantly responsive forms of organization must characterize the future." We are seeing the "collapse of hierarchy" as "shortcuts that by-pass the hierarchy are increasingly employed" in all kinds of organizations. "The cumulative result of such small changes is a massive shift from vertical to lateral communications systems"[15].

Whether this is good or bad for the Church depends on whether the Church is structured according to a charismatic or an institutional model. Biblically, it is clear that the Church *should* be structured charismatically, and any church so structured is already largely prepared to withstand "future shock." But churches which are encased in rigid, bureaucratic, institutional structures may soon find themselves trapped in culturally-bound forms which are fast becoming obsolete[16].

c. The Bible sees the Church as the community of God's people. The essential biblical figures of body and bride of Christ, household, temple, or vineyard of God, and so forth, give us the basic idea of the Church. But these are metaphors and not a definition. I believe the most biblical definition is to say *the Church is the community of God's people*[17]. The two key elements here are the Church as a *people,* a new race or humanity, and as a *community* or fellowship.

"People" and "community" are two poles which together make up the biblical reality of the Church (Figure 1). On the one hand, the Church is the people of God — a concept with rich Old Testament roots which underlines the objective fact of God's acting throughout history to call and prepare "a chosen race, a royal priesthood, a holy nation, God's own people" (I Pet. 2:9; cf. Exod. 19:5-6). The Greek word for "people" is *laos,* from which come the Latin *laicus* and the English "laity"[18]. This reminds us that the *whole* church is a "laity," a people. Here the emphasis is on the *universality* of the Church — God's people scattered throughout the world in hundreds of specific denominations, movements, and other structures. *Seen in cosmic-historical perspective, the Church is the people of God.*

Figure 1. THE CHURCH AS THE COMMUNITY OF GOD'S PEOPLE

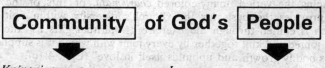

| Community | of God's | People |

Koinonia	*Laos*
Charismatic organism	Cosmic-historical reality
Locality of Church	Universality of Church
Fellowship	Mission
Small group	"Great congregation"
Spiritual gifts	Kingdom of priests
New moral nature	New humanity

On the other hand, the Church is a community of fellowship, a *koinonia.* This more-New-Testament emphasis grows directly out of the experience of Pentecost. If peoplehood underlines the continuity of God's plan from Old to New Testament, community calls attention to the "new covenant," the "new wine," the "new thing" God did in the resurrection of Jesus Christ and the Spirit's baptism at Pentecost. The emphasis here is on the *locality* of the Church in its intense, interactive common life. *Seen as a charismatic organism, the Church is the community of the Holy Spirit.*

The Church, then, is the community of God's people. It is a charismatic organism established by God as the agent of his cosmic plan for human history. It was to this Church in its inconspicuous, unpromising beginnings that Jesus Christ entrusted the Great Commission.

PART TWO: CHURCH-CENTERED EVANGELISM

Just as all biblical figures for the Church imply life, so do they suggest growth and reproduction. It is of the nature of the Church to grow and reproduce just as God's plan has always involved the charge, "Be fruitful and multiply" (Gen. 1:28). So when we discuss evangelism, we are really asking: how does the biblical Church grow? Normal (that is, biblical) church life will normally produce church growth.

1. What is Church-centered evangelism?

Church-centered evangelism is evangelism which builds the Church. It springs from the life and witness of the Christian community and results in the reproduction of the community in an ongoing process.

C. Peter Wagner and others have rightly criticized views of evangelism which do not go far enough in the direction of church growth. Speaking of "presence" and "proclamation" evangelism, Wagner insists that neither is adequate, for the goal of evangelism must be persuasion. Christian *presence* must be the basis for Christian *proclamation,* which in turn must reach the goal of *persuading* men and women to come to Christ. In this view, the ultimate aim of evangelism is to make disciples[19]. The line of reasoning is as follows:

PRESENCE ▶ PROCLAMATION ▶ PERSUASION

But is it enough even to say the ultimate goal of evangelism is to make disciples? While making disciples certainly implies the formation and edification of the Christian community, this is only implicit, not explicit. To do justice to the biblical understanding of the Church, we must go one step further and say that *the goal of evangelism is the formation of the Christian community.*[20] It is making disciples and, further, forming these disciples into living cells of the Body of Christ — new expressions of the community of God's people. Church-centered evangelism is concerned, then, with propagation (in the fundamental sense of reproduction or multiplication) as well as with persuasion:

PRESENCE ▶   PROCLAMATION ▶

PERSUASION ▶   PROPAGATION

In this process, propagation or reproduction feeds into a continuous

cycle which, empowered by the Holy Spirit, makes the Church a dynamic,
living organism. The goal of evangelism therefore is the formation of
the Christian community, the *koinonia* of the Holy Spirit. This is not a
total definition of evangelism, because it does not include the many
possible motives and means involved. There may be various legitimate
motives for evangelism, but the *goal* must always be the formation of
the biblical Church. This is necessary in order to reach the really
ultimate goal of evangelism: the glorification of God.

2. How the biblical Church grows

What are the dynamics of such evangelism?

The dynamic is the Holy Spirit. Looking at the New Testament
and church history, we can perceive some of the ways the Spirit works
in producing church growth. I wish to emphasize particularly four
factors which are essential components of growth and which are grounded in the basic biblical nature of the Church[21]. They are:

a. *Direct evangelistic proclamation.* The mandate for proclamation
is central in God's cosmic plan, for this plan centers in what God is
doing *for man* — the redemption that brings eternal salvation and builds
the Church.

The Church after Pentecost evangelized irrepressibly. The great
concern and dynamic of the early church was to tell the Good News
about Jesus and the resurrection; to bear witness to what they had
seen, heard, and experienced[22].

The evangelistic task of the Church is to proclaim the good news
of salvation in Jesus Christ throughout the world, making disciples and
building the Church (Matt. 28:19-20; Mark 16:15). Evangelism is the
first priority of the Church's ministry in the world for several reasons:
the clear biblical mandate for evangelism; the centrality and necessity
of personal conversion in God's plan; the reality of judgment; the fact
that changed men are necessary to change society; the fact that the
Christian community exists and expands only as evangelism is carried
out. The church that fails to evangelize is both biblically unfaithful
and strategically shortsighted.

b. *Multiplying Christian congregations.* Evangelistic proclamation
is not an end in itself, however, but must lead beyond itself to making
disciples. Not mere numerical growth but the multiplication of local
churches is the test of a healthy, growing church. The biblical ideal is
neither to produce a host of new Christians who live unattached, separated lives, nor to expand existing local churches until their membership bulges into the thousands. The biblical pattern is to form new converts into local congregations and to multiply the number of congregations as new converts are added[23].

The ministry of Paul and other New Testament evangelists was a
church-multiplying ministry. We know that converts in many cities
quickly ran into the thousands; yet for nearly two hundred years no
church buildings were erected[24]. Such growth under such conditions
can be explained only as the multiplication of small congregations. It
is not surprising, therefore, that the New Testament often refers to "the
church in your (or their) house"[25].

Normal growth comes by the division of cells, not by the unlimited expansion of existing cells. The growth of individual cells beyond a certain point without division is pathological. Church growth studies verify that "only as the number of churches is multiplied does the Christian part of the overall population increase" in a given society[26].

Growth comes by the multiplication of *congregations of believers,* not necessarily by the multiplication of church buildings or institutional structures. If the Church can grow only as fast as buildings are built, or pastors academically trained, or budgets expanded, then growth is limited to the resources available for these purposes. Church growth is not limited by such factors when based on biblical principles.

c. Building the Christian community. Even the multiplication of Christian congregations is not the final goal, however. Multiplication must lead to the edification of the Christian community in each particular case, for God's will is that "all attain to the unity of the faith and of the knowledge of the Son of God" (Eph. 4:13).

Evangelism requires the existence of a witnessing community if church growth is to become a continuing process. As John Howard Yoder has written, "Pragmatically it is self-evident that there can be no procedure of proclamation without a community, distinct from the rest of society, to do the proclaiming. Pragmatically it is just as clear that there can be no evangelistic call addressed to a person inviting him to enter into a new kind of fellowship and learning if there is not such a body of persons, again distinct from the totality of society, to whom he can come and with whom he can learn"[27].

This is true even in the most pagan society where no organized church yet exists. For even there, as soon as Christian witnesses enter the society the Church is present (Matt. 18:20), and hearers are called to join the incipient community. While one can, of course, point to some exceptions, this seems to be the normal biblical pattern[28].

Protestantism in general has emphasized the individual over the community. Too often the Church has been seen more as a collection of saved souls than as a community of interacting personalities. But the model of Christ with his disciples, the example of the Early Church, and the explicit teachings of Jesus and Paul should call us back to the importance of community. Authentic Christian living is life in Christian community. Individual and corporate edification go together and should not be separated[29].

Fellowship and community life are necessary in order to prepare Christians for witness and service. Every Christian is a witness in the world, but his effectiveness depends largely on his sharing the enabling common life of the Church. And this common life becomes truly enabling only as the community becomes, through the indwelling of Christ and the exercise of spiritual gifts, the *koinonia* of the Spirit[30].

d. Exercising spiritual gifts. A primary function of Christian community is the awakening and disciplining of the gifts of the Spirit. The important discussions of spiritual gifts in Romans 12, I Corinthians 12-14, and Ephesians 4 all place gifts in the context of the community life of the Church[31].

The somewhat parallel lists of spiritual gifts in I Corinthians 12:28 and Ephesians 4:11 are particularly important here[32]. Placing these two passages side by side gives us a composite picture of church order according to biblical and charismatic principles, and suggests a functional distinction between two kinds of spiritual gifts:

I Corinthians 12:28	Ephesians 4:11
Apostles, prophets Teachers	Apostles, Prophets, Evangelists, Pastors, Teachers
then	for
Workers of miracles, healers, helpers, etc.	the equipment of the saints for their work of ministry

There are, first of all, the leadership gifts: Apostle, prophet, evangelist, pastor, and teacher (assuming the addition of "evangelist" and "pastor" in Ephesians be considered the further subdividing of those designated "apostles, prophets and teachers" in I Cor. 12:28). The Spirit gives these *basic leadership gifts* primarily for instruction, order, and equipping.

But these are not the only gifts. An undetermined number of other gifts are bestowed by the Spirit. These gifts are given "for the saints' work of ministry" and include "workers of miracles, healers, helpers, administrators," tongues-speakers, and many others. The purpose of the basic leadership gifts is clearly "the equipment of the saints for the work of ministry" through the exercise of *their* gifts.

We have here merely a *functional distinction* between leadership gifts and the remaining gifts of ministry. We must be careful not to read the modern clergy/laity dichotomy into these passages. Prophet, teacher, evangelist, and pastor were non-technical and non-professional terms in the New Testament. There is no basis here (or elsewhere in the New Testament) for any division of the Christian community into "clergy" and "laity," since all Christians are the *laos* (people) of God and all have some "work of ministry"[33].

The contemporary church needs the spiritual gifts of apostle, prophet, evangelist, pastor, and teacher — and God has promised to give them. These gifts are necessary in order for the Church to function biblically as the community of God's people[34].

As to the gift of evangelist, it is significant that the word "evangelist" occurs only three times in the New Testament. The apparent reason for so few references is that the New Testament church did not see evangelism as primarily the work of specialists. Evangelism was the natural expression of the life of the Church. There was no need either to exhort believers to evangelize or to raise up a special class of evangelists to insure that evangelism occurred.

Why, then, does Paul even mention "evangelists" as a spiritual gift? Simply because men who were strictly evangelists, and recognized as such (as distinct from apostles and prophets, with whom they presumably had much in common) had arisen in the Church — for example, Philip. Paul recognized these men as being within "God's ecclesiology." The normal life of the Christian community will produce growth, but God especially calls and raises up men with a particular evangelistic gift, sometimes for evangelism within the same culture and sometimes for cross-cultural evangelism. These are God's special gifts in order that new frontiers may be crossed and the Great Commission be fulfilled[35].

Not only the gift of evangelist, however, but *all* spiritual gifts are relevant for evangelism in one way or another. Although not all Christians are called or gifted to be evangelists, spiritual gifts contribute to evangelism in at least five ways. First, several of the God-appointed leaders — particularly apostles, prophets, and evangelists — do essential evangelistic work in the world. Second, many individual believers use their gifts for evangelism as they are equipped spiritually to do so by the equipping ministers. Third, those who exercise the more "inward" gifts of teaching, encouragement, contributions, etc., provide the continuing spiritual support (and sometimes even economic support) for those who carry on evangelism in the world. Fourth, those who exercise their gifts within the community to sustain its inward life contribute to evangelism through the training and integration of new converts into the Church. Finally, this harmonious overall functioning of the Christian community is itself a demonstration of the truth of the Gospel and thus a witness in and to the world, preparing the way for evangelism.

Figure 2. HOW THE BIBLICAL CHURCH GROWS

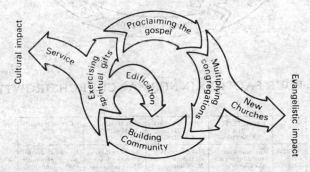

In summary, the biblical Church grows through *proclaiming the Gospel, multiplying congregations, building the Christian community,* and *exercising spiritual gifts.* Examining these four components of growth, we see they are not isolated factors, but each contributes to the other in an ongoing cycle of edification and expansion (Figure 2). When the Church is growing biblically, Gospel proclamation leads to the multiplying of congregations. This provides the Church's major evangelistic impact in the world as new churches are formed. Within each congregation, however, true Christian community must be built. As the community "upbuilds itself in love," a kaleidoscope of spiritual gifts is awakened and begins to function. Through their gifts, believers minister outwardly to the world and inwardly to the Christian community. One result is "substantial healing" in the various areas of society; this produces a significant cultural impact. Some gifts are more directly evangelistic and thus strengthen and continue the Church's evangelistic thrust — and so the dynamic cycle of normal church growth is completed.

This cycle is what happens on the horizontal plane, as it were. Such growth is truly biblical, however, only as the Church maintains a living and vital relationship vertically with God. Thus a more complete conception of the Church's life is suggested by Figure 3. A careful evaluation of each of the elements in this diagram should reveal the weak links in the evangelistic work of any church or evangelistic organization. (Some further aspects of this fourfold analysis of church growth are suggested by the accompanying chart, Figure 4).

Figure 3. **NORMAL CHURCH LIFE**

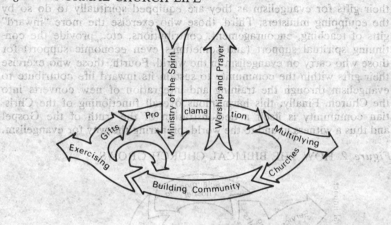

Figure 4. **FOUR FACTORS IN NORMAL CHURCH GROWTH**

	EVANGELISTIC PROCLAMATIONS	MULTIPLYING CONGREGATIONS	BUILDING COMMUNITY	EXERCISING GIFTS
WORDS OF CHRIST	Go into all the world and preach the Gospel — Matt. 16:15. You shall be my witnesses — Acts 1:8	Make disciples of all nations — Matt. 28:19. Jerusalem . . . Judea and Samaria and to the end of the earth — Acts 1:8	Teaching them to observe all that I have commanded — Matt. 28:19. That they may be one as we are one — John 17:22	He who abides in me . . . bears much fruit — John 15:5. Greater works than these will he do — John 14:12
EXAMPLE OF CHRIST	Proclamation of the Good News	Preparation of disciples for this ministry	Community life with disciples	Jesus' preaching, healing, counseling, teaching, etc.
LIFE PRINCIPLE	Seed planting	Reproduction, cell division	Metabolism, "body life"	Vine and branch, diversity within unity
FUNCTION	Communication, gaining converts	Establishing new churches, conserving fruit, follow-up	Spiritual maturation, equipping, "perfecting" discipline	Ministry inward and outward, evangelism, fulfillment, self-expression
RELATED MOVEMENTS	Mass evangelism and personal evangelism movements	"Church Growth," some missionary movements	Renewal Movement small-group movements	Charismatic Movement, Pentecostalism
DANGERS OF PARTIAL EMPHASIS	Lost fruit, spiritual starvation, "evangelistic technology"	Exaggerated denominationalism, "success mentality," accommodation to the world	Exaggerated subjectivism, self-centeredness, withdrawal from world	Exaggerated individualism, neglect of doctrine, factiousness

This is how the biblical Church grows, and this is the meaning of church-centered evangelism. To complete our analysis, however, we must now turn to the crucial question of how the biblical Church structures itself in order to grow normally.

PART THREE: STRUCTURES FOR AN EVANGELISTIC CHURCH

The Bible gives very little specific guidance regarding church structure. It presents a clear picture of what the Church is intended to be and gives the early history of the Church in two cultural contexts: Palestinian Jewish society and first-century Graeco-Roman society[36]. On the basis of this biblical witness, the Church in each epoch forms those wineskins which seem most compatible with its nature and mission within the particular culture.

There can be no question of finding a biblical pattern for denominational structures or even for the detailed organization of the local church, for the Bible is silent here[37]. What we must do, therefore, is look for general principles or insights which seem to be implied by the biblical description of the Church. A church structured in harmony with the biblical understanding of the Church will, by definition, be an evangelistic church.

1. Church structure and para-church structures

Here we face a crucial problem. We see that biblically the Church is the community of God's people, not an organizational institution. But when we look at the contemporary church, we see not only the community of God's people; we find also a proliferation of denominations, institutions, agencies, associations, and so forth. Such structures obviously have no explicit biblical basis. How should we view them?

The two most common tendencies have been to say these structures are actually a part of the essence of the Church, and thus "sacralize" them[38], or else to take an anti-institutional stance and say all such structures are invalid and must be abandoned. A more helpful option, however, is to view all such structures as *para-church structures* which exist alongside of and parallel to the community of God's people, but are not themselves the Church. They are useful to the extent they aid the Church in its mission, but are man-made and culturally determined. Whereas the Church itself is part of the new wine of the Gospel, all para-church structures are wineskins — useful, at times indispensable, but also subject to wear and decay.

In dealing with the whole question of church structure, then, we should make a very clear distinction between *the Church* as the community of God's people and all *para-church structures,* whether denominations, mission agencies, evangelistic organizations, educational institutions, or other ecclesiastical forms (Figure 5). It is critically important — especially when we are dealing with a worldwide, multi-cultural situation — to emphasize that the Church is a *people,* not an organization; it is a *community,* not an institution.

Figure 5. THE CHURCH AND PARA-CHURCH STRUCTURES

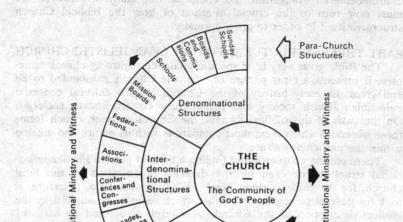

Distinguishing Between the Wine and Wineskins

Several benefits come from this distinction between the Church and para-church structures. (i) That which is always cross-culturally relevant (the biblically-understood Church) is separated from that which is culturally bound and determined (para-church structures). Thus one is free to see the Church as *culturally relevant and involved* and yet not as *culturally bound.* (ii) One is free also to modify para-church structures as culture changes, for these are not themselves the Church and therefore are largely culturally rather than biblically determined. (iii) Finally, this distinction makes it possible to see a *wide range of legitimacy* in denominational confessions and structures. If such structures are not themselves the Church and are culturally determined, then whole volumes of controversy and polemics lose their urgency and become merely secondary. Widely varying confessions are freed (at least potentially) to concentrate on that which unites them — being the people of God and carrying out the evangelistic task — while relegating structural differences to the plane of cultural and historical relativity. Thus the crucial consideration for structure becomes not *biblical legitimacy* but *functional relevancy.*

The accompanying chart (Figure 6) suggests further implications of this distinction between the biblical Church and para-church structures.

Figure 6. DIFFERENCES BETWEEN THE CHURCH AND PARA-CHURCH STRUCTURES

The Church	Para-Church Structures
1. God's creation	1. Man's creation
2. Spiritual fact	2. Sociological fact
3. Cross-culturally valid	3. Culturally bound
4. Biblically understood and evaluated	4. Sociologically understood and evaluated
5. Validity determined by spiritual qualities and fidelity to Scriptures	5. Validity determined by function in relation to mission of the Church
6. God's agent of evangelism and reconciliation	6. Man's agents for evangelism and service
7. Essential	7. Expendable
8. Eternal	8. Temporal and temporary
9. Divine revelation	9. Human tradition
10. Purpose to glorify God	10. Purpose to serve the Church

2. Guidelines for church structure

From the biblical picture of the Church we can now distill three fundamental principles for structure. I believe these principles provide a basic biblical foundation for church structure in any cultural context and help lead to effective evangelism and church growth.

a. Leadership should be based on the exercise of spiritual gifts. Hierarchical or organizational patterns must not be permitted to obscure or overwhelm the basic biblical pattern of charismatic (that is, Spirit-appointed and endowed) leadership.

In the New Testament, leadership was at first provided by the original eleven Apostles, and later by Paul and an expanding group of other apostles, prophets, evangelists, pastors, teachers, bishops, deacons, and elders[39]. As we have seen, the New Testament considers these spiritual gifts[40]. It is clear therefore that in the New Testament leadership was based on the exercise of spiritual leadership gifts which were recognized (either formally or informally) by the Church[41].

All spiritual gifts should be emphasized, not just the leadership gifts. But these gifts are especially crucial, for their function biblically is precisely to awaken and prepare the other gifts (Eph. 4:11). Thus not only leadership, but the entire life of the Church is based on spiritual gifts.

b. Secondly, *the life and ministry of the Church should be built on viable large-group and small-group structures.* The early church's common life of worship, fellowship, nurture, and witness reveals a dual emphasis: "in the temple and at home" (Acts 5:42). While the community life of the Church centered primarily in the home, worship and nurture took place both in the temple and in small house gatherings (Acts 2:42, 2:46-47, 4:34-35, 5:25, 5:42)[42]. Although worship in the Jewish temple eventually ceased, both large- and small-group gatherings seem to have characterized the life of the early church throughout the Mediterranean world[43].

These were the two foci of early church life: the large congregation and the small group[44]. This was also the pattern the disciples had followed with Jesus. For two or three years Christ's disciples spent much of their time either among outdoor crowds, in the temple, or in private small-group conferences with the Master[45]. There was always this small-group — large-group rhythm, the small-group providing the intense community life which gave depth to the large-group gatherings.

Theologically, large- and small-group gatherings are the structural implications of the Church as the people of God and the fellowship of the Holy Spirit. As I have elsewhere suggested[46], peoplehood implies the necessity of large-group gatherings while fellowship or community requires small-group structures.

Church history reveals a recurrent tendency to absolutize and institutionalize the large group, wedding it to a specific building and form, while at the same time neglecting or even condemning the small group. Virtually every major movement of spiritual renewal in the Christian Church has been accompanied by a return to the small group and the proliferation of such groups of some kind in private homes for Bible study, prayer, and the discussion of the faith[47].

Whatever other structures may be found useful, therefore, large-group and small-group structures should be fundamental. Although the specific form of such structures may vary according to culture and circumstances, both are necessary to sustain community and witness. No other structure or form should be allowed to subvert or replace either the large corporate group or the small fellowship group[48].

c. As previously suggested, *a clear distinction should be made between the Church and para-church structures.* Christians must see themselves as the community of God's people, not in the first place as members of an organization. In many a contemporary church this would be revolutionary.

Each church should be helped to understand that institutional structures are *legitimate* (provided they really aid the Church in its life and witness), but not *sacred.* The important thing, therefore, is not to prescribe which para-church structures should or should not exist in the Church, but to understand the relativity and limitations of such structures.

In summary, the Church as the community of God's people should be structured on spiritual gifts of leadership and on some form of large-group and small-group gatherings. Beyond this, the Church should take care to distinguish between its essential self and all para-church structures so that it does not become culture-bound — and so that, conversely, in periods of upheaval the wine is not thrown out with the wine-skins. These three principles are illustrated in Figure 7.

Figure 7. A MODEL FOR CHURCH STRUCTURE

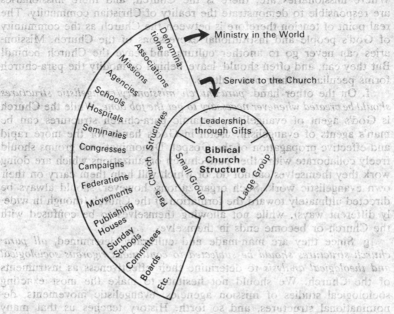

3. Implications for Cross-cultural Evangelism

Several conclusions for cross-cultural evangelism follow from the foregoing discussion.

a. *The Church as biblically presented is always cross-culturally relevant.* This is true because the Church is a cosmic-historical, charismatic organism that proceeds from divine action and transcends any particular cultural form.

b. Similarly, *the basic structures of charismatic leadership and small-group — large-group gatherings are always cross-culturally viable.* This follows from the foregoing analysis; it has also been abundantly demonstrated throughout church history and in the modern missionary age.

c. On the other hand, *para-church structures are not necessarily cross-culturally valid.* Since these are culturally determined, particular para-church structures will be transferable from one culture to another only to the extent that the two cultures are compatible. Basic adaptations will often have to be made.

d. *The exercise of spiritual gifts will result in cross-cultural evangelism.* Since the book of Acts and through the ages, God has been calling and sending out his charismatically equipped missionaries. The Antiochian pattern (Acts 13:1ff) has been repeated countless times, and will continue to be repeated until Christ returns (Matt. 24:14). It is God who calls and who gives gifts, and the gift and the call go together.

e. *The Church is itself a missionary structure, and any group of missionaries may be a legitimate embodiment of the Church.* This means there can be no question of the Church versus "missionary structures."

Where missionaries are, there is the Church, and there missionaries are responsible to demonstrate the reality of Christian community. The real point of tension therefore is between the Church as the community of God's people and institutional expressions of the Church. Missionaries can never go to another culture and leave the Church behind! But they can, and often should, leave behind or modify the para-church forms peculiar to their own culture.

f. On the other hand, *para-church missionary/evangelistic structures should be created whenever necessary to get the job done.* While the Church is God's agent of evangelism, dynamic para-church structures can be man's agents of evangelism, useful in God's hands for the more rapid and effective propagation of the Gospel. Denominational groups should freely collaborate with other para-church organizations which are doing work they themselves cannot do, or which will help them carry on their own evangelistic work. Such organizations, however, should always be directed ultimately toward the formation of the Church (though in widely different ways), while not allowing themselves to be confused with the Church or become ends in themselves.

,g. Since they are man-made and culturally determined, *all para-church structures should be subjected to continuous rigorous sociological and theological analysis* to determine their effectiveness as instruments of the Church. We should not hesitate to make the most exacting sociological studies of mission agencies, evangelistic movements, denominational structures, and so forth. History teaches us that many such structures will eventually succumb to institutionalism and become hindrances rather than helps to the Church. The fact that God has raised up a movement is no warranty against eventual infidelity or self-centeredness. Having clearly distinguished such structures from the essence of the Church, we can freely ask to what extent these forms are actually functional.

PART FOUR: SIX PRACTICAL STEPS TOWARD EVANGELISTIC RENEWAL

a. *Undertake a study of the biblical nature of the Church.* Many local churches could be revolutionized through a year-long study of the Church. Preaching and teaching could be coordinated with small-group Bible studies in which the Church is the main topic. The focus would be on such books as Acts, I Corinthians, Ephesians, and Colossians, with adequate attention also being given to the Old Testament development of God's plan (particularly the concepts of the Covenant and the People of God). The reading of significant books on the Church should be a part of this process. In English, such popularly-written books as *Fire in Coventry, A New Face for the Church, Full Circle, Body Life, The Congregation in Mission,* and *Brethren, Hang Loose* (representing a wide range of denominational traditions) are particularly helpful[49].

My own mission in Brazil has benefited immeasurably from a series of sixteen Bible studies on the Church, using a simple study guide which we prepared.

b. *Evaluate the quality of the community life of the church.* Some form of self-study — again using small groups — can be undertaken. The task of evaluation provides the objective focus, while small-group interaction deepens the subjective experience of community. Lawrence Richards in *A New Face for the Church* gives solid guidelines for such evaluation together with examples and illustrations. Here again, reading and Bible study should be mixed in.

c. *Attempt to think through what the Bible teaches about the gifts of the Spirit.* More heat than light radiates from this subject, but the biblical teachings are clear. Both pastoral and small-group emphasis on gifts (the two should go together) would focus on such passages as Romans 12, I Corinthians 12-14, Ephesians 4, I Peter 4, with accompanying study of the related doctrine of the priesthood of believers. The aim would be to create a "gift consciousness" and help each believer identify and use his gift(s). The books *Full Circle* and *Body Life* are especially helpful here, and C. Peter Wagner has excellent material on gifts in *Frontiers in Missionary Strategy* and *Look Out! The Pentecostals are Coming.*

d. *Attempt consciously to transcend the clergy/laity dichotomy, both in thought and speech.* As a starter, a pastor might stop using the word "layman" for a period of time and see how this forces him to rethink his understanding of the Church. (Personal experience has shown this to be a rewarding discipline!) Small groups could study the biblical concepts of "ministry" and "people" and begin to build their discoveries into their thought and speech. The goal is to remove any unbiblical dualism here and create the awareness that all believers have some "work of ministry."

e. *Consider the possibility of forming one or more new congregations by the division of the church.* Some churches will never begin to grow until they divide. Churches of several hundred members should seriously consider gathering together several families who live in the same area and using them as the nucleus of a new congregation. This is often more effective than preaching missions, "revival" campaigns, or other intensive short-term efforts, because it creates a second *center of growth* and deepens the involvement of all who participate.

This process of multiplication could be the natural outgrowth of the previous suggestions given above. The new group formed does not immediately sever its connection with the mother church, but begins to carry on its own evangelism and community life through small groups, personal evangelism, and worship services. With sufficient growth, the group will have to move to a large basement or garage or other structure, or rent a school or small hall. By concentrating on people rather than programs or buildings, the group will soon be able to support one or more full-time workers. As normal church growth occurs, further division' can take place.

f. *Identify segments of the surrounding population especially open to the Gospel where new churches could be planted.* Going one step beyond the previous suggestion, a local church might actually seek out "receptive populations" within easy reach of the Church and attempt to minister there. In urban centers, particularly, some church members will probably live near specific groups which may be highly receptive to the Gospel. Such groups might include inner-city or outer-city poor, ethnic or occupational groups, or those institutionalized in hospitals or prisons. Two or three families with the active support of the entire church could initiate an evangelistic ministry with the specific goal of planting a new self-supporting congregation.

With regard to both these last two suggestions, Melvin Hodges' little book *A Guide to Church Planting* provides excellent counsel for the church wishing to begin a church-planting ministry.

Conclusion

There is no salvation outside the Church unless the Body of Christ be decapitated, separated from the Head. The Church is the body of Christ; the community of the Holy Spirit; the people of God. As such, it is the agent of God's plan for the reconciliation of all things.

It is in the perspective of cosmic reconciliation that we may understand the evangelistic task of the Church. The Church is God's agent of evangelism because evangelism is at the very heart of God's cosmic plan.

If the Church has not been sufficiently recognized as God's agent of evangelism, it is because it has too generally been confused with its various culturally-bound institutional expressions. The need of the hour is to understand the Church as a Spirit-endowed charismatic organism which is cross-culturally valid, not as an institutional organization molded by the world. Once this distinction is made, the normal growth of the Church can be understood and planned for, and the various para-church structures, including denominations, can be dealt with and used effectively.

Let us not devalue the Body of Christ! Let us not relegate God's agent of evangelism to a secondary role of simply one means among many. For from the Cross to eternity it remains true that "Christ loved the church and gave himself up for her, that he might sanctify her . . . that he might present the church to himself in splendor, without spot or wrinkle or any such thing" (Eph. 5:25-27).

FOOTNOTES

[1]. God's activity in the world is not confined to evangelical redemption; it also includes preservation and judgment. Thus God also acts outside the Church and even in judgment on the Church. But when it comes to redemption, the Church is the only agent God has chosen.

[2]. Melvin L. Hodges, *A Guide to Church Planting,* 1973, p. 15.

[3]. The doctrine of the Church has not received sufficient attention in contemporary evangelicalism. This seems to be a general lack among evangelical churches worldwide, but one which is now coming to be recognized.

[4]. K.L. Schmidt comments that in the attempt "to try to understand the antithesis between an empirical Church and an ideal" in the Post-Apostolic Church, "there arises an awareness of the twofold nature of the Church as the Church militant and the Church triumphant. Such

speculations introduce a distinctive ambiguity into statements concerning the Church. This is equally true of both the Greek and the Latin fathers. The greatest of them, Augustine, whose comprehensive thinking set the Church in the center of Roman Catholic life and thought, is the very one in whom the relation between the empirical and the ideal Church is not made clear. If genuinely Gnostic speculation was held at bay, speculation still established itself in the form of Platonism . . . Protestantism, with its distinction between the invisible and the visible Church, has its own share in this unrealistic Platonism."

Schmidt says further that the Church "as the assembly of God in Christ is not invisible on the one side and visible on the other. The Christian community, which as the individual congregation represents the whole body, is just as visible and corporeal as the individual man . . . If Luther distinguished between the invisible and the visible Church . . . he did so without accepting the Platonism of his successors." Gerhard Kittel, (ed.), *Theological Dictionary of the New Testament,* G. W. Bromiley, 1965, III, 533-534.

[5]. I recognize there is a problem with the word "institution," for any "established practice, law, or custom" may be considered an institution *(Webster's New Practical Dictionary)*. In this sense baptism and the Lord's Supper, for instance, may be thought of as institutions, and it is difficult to make a distinction between "institution" and "church." But I am here using "institution" in the more restricted (and more popular) sense of "an established society or corporation" — in other words, as a formally structured organization, whether this structuring has come about by law, a constituting assembly, or merely accumulated tradition. I am aware that some prefer to use the phrase "institutional church" to describe what I here refer to as "community," but this is not the sense in which I am using the phrase.

[6]. See Kittel, op. cit.

[7]. This same cosmic-historical perspective is evident throughout Scripture. All the promises of cosmic restoration in the Old Testament prophets apply here, reaching their climax in Isaiah. In the New Testament the essential message of the Revelation is the uniting of all things under the lordship of Christ. And Isaiah, Peter, and John speak of a new heaven and a new earth (Isa. 65:17, 66:22; II Peter 3:13; Rev. 21:1).

[8]. "God's plan is to unite and reconcile all things in Christ so that men can again serve their maker," (Bernard Zylstra, quoted in *Perspective,* Newsletter of the Association for the Advancement of Christian Scholarship, VII:2, March/April, 1973, p. 14).

[9]. Eph. 1:10, II Cor. 5:17-21, Rom. 8:21. The Greek word "to unite" or "to gather together" in Ephesians 1:10 comes from the word for "head." The idea of Christ as the head of the Church and of all things (e.g., in Eph. 1:22) naturally suggests the thought of uniting all things under the headship of Christ, and this accounts for Paul's using the rather uncommon word "to unite, to bring under proper headship" in Eph. 1:10. See Kittel, op. cit., pp. 681-682.

¹⁰. I Cor. 8:6, 15:28; Eph. 1:22, 3:9, 4:10; Col. 1:17-20; cf. Heb. 1:2-3, 2:8-10.

¹¹. Eph. 3:10 — "that through the church the manifold wisdom of God might now be made known to the principalities and powers in the heavenly places." The phrase is ambiguously translated "by the church" in the English KJV, thus masking the force of the fact of the Church as the *agent* of God's plan.

¹². Historically the people of God have disagreed not so much over what God is doing as to when he will do it. Most Christians admit that, in one sense or another, God is bringing history to a cosmic climax. But one branch has said, "Not now; then!" And, in reaction, another group has said, "Not then; now!" Those who postpone any real presence of the Kingdom until after Christ's return ("Not now; then") do not expect any substantial renewal now except in the realm of individual human experience — not in politics, art, education, culture in general, and not even, really, in the Church. On the other side are those who so emphasize present renewal in society in general that both personal conversion and the space-time future return of Christ are denied or over-shadowed, and man's deep sinfulness is not taken seriously. Hopefully, Christians today throughout the world are coming to see that the Kingdom of God is neither entirely present nor entirely future. The Kingdom of God (the uniting of all things in Jesus Christ) is now here, is coming, and will come. Francis Schaeffer well expresses this balanced view when he speaks of a "substantial healing" now in all the areas of sin-caused aliena-tion. What God promises is a substantial healing now and a total healing after Christ's return. F. A. Schaeffer, *The God Who Is There,* 1968, p. 152; *Pollution and the Death of Man,* 1970, pp. 66-69.

¹³. C. H. Pinnock, "The New Pentecostalism: Reflections by a Well-Wisher," *Christianity Today,* XXVII:24 (September 14, 1973), p. 6.

¹⁴. I Pet. 4:10; cf. Eph. 3:10. In the Greek the word "manifold" (poikilos) often has the sense of "many-colored," in the sense of the variety of colors in flowers or clothing. W.R. Nicoll (ed.), *The Expositor's Greek Testament,* 1961, III, p: 309.

¹⁵. Alvin Toffler, *Future Shock,* 1970, pp. 143, 139.

¹⁶ Toffler (citing Max.Weber) reminds us that bureaucracy, as an organi-zational form, appeared with the rise of industrialism, and suggests that it is passing away as many societies move into a post-industrial phase (p. 126). If this is true, it may be highly significant for denominational and other ecclesiastical organizations.

¹⁷. Hans Küng similarly defines the Church as "the People of God . . . the community of the faithful"; the Church is "the community of the new people of God called out and called together" *Structures of the Church,* tr. Salvator Attanasio, 1964, pp. X, 11.

¹⁸. Technically, the Latin *laicus* comes from the Greek *laikos,* "pertaining to the people," which in turn derives from *laos.* Whereas laos occurs frequently in the New Testament, *laikos* is not found at all.

¹⁹. C. P. Wagner, *Frontiers in Missionary Strategy,* 1971, pp. 124-134. Cf. Donald McGavran, (ed.), *Eye of the Storm,* 1972, pp. 205-218.

²⁰. Some will perhaps say that anything which goes beyond producing conversions is no longer evangelism but becomes follow-up or nurture. The point is, however, that the evangelistic task is not really complete until it becomes self-perpetuating. Wagner comments, "Some regard follow-up as a separate step which comes after evangelism itself, but this is a fallacy all too common in evangelistic strategy." "Jesus did not separate follow up from evangelism. He included them all in the same package of 'making disciples,'" *Look Out! The Pentecostals Are Coming,* 1973, pp. 45, 46.

²¹. These are internal factors inherent in the biblical nature of the Church. McGavran and others have rightly pointed out the importance of external factors which determine the receptivity of a people and are conditioned by political, religious, ideological, socio-economic, and other influences. These also need to be taken into consideration, but do not relate directly to the nature of the church itself.

²². Michael Green, *Evangelism in the Early Church,* 1970, p. 48.

²³. The optimum size of local congregations will vary according to cultural factors, and no arbitrary limit can be set. Church growth research would seem to suggest, however, that once a congregation has grown to a few hundred members the rate of growth will slow down unless new branch congregations are formed through growth-by-division. Where notable exceptions to this pattern are found, closer examination will usually reveal that the local "congregation" running into the thousands is in reality a whole congeries of smaller "sub-congregations" in which growth-by-division is taking place as the normal pattern.

²⁴. W. W. Oetting, *The Church of the Catacombs,* 1964, p. 26.

²⁵. Rom 16:2; I Cor. 16:19; Col. 4:15; Philemon 2. Cf. G. W. Peters, *Saturation Evangelism,* 1970, pp. 147ff.

²⁶. Neil Braun, *Laity Mobilized: Reflections on Church Growth in Japan and Other Lands,* 1971, p. 21.

²⁷. J. L. Garrett, Jr., (ed.), *The Concept of the Believers' Church,* 1969, p. 259.

²⁸. Neither Jesus nor Paul normally evangelized alone. Almost immediately after his baptism, Jesus had disciples around him — an incipient Christian community (John 1:29-42). Jesus sent his disciples out two-by-two, not one-by-one. Peter took others with him to Samaria and to Cornelius' house in Caesarea (Acts 8:14, 10:23). Paul was nearly always accompanied by one or more companions. Although there are exceptions to this pattern (Philip in Acts 8:4-8 and 8:26-40, Paul in Athens), they do seem to be exceptions, not the rule. Normally, where the missionaries went, the Church went with them (in the sense of at least one companion), so that the evangelistic call was a call, in part, to an already-existing and demonstrated communal fellowship. This gives new

meaning to Christ's statement about being present in the midst of two or three gathered believers (Matt. 18:20), as well as to the concept of "household evangelism."

²⁹. "The New Testament speaks always of the upbuilding of the community. I can edify myself only as I edify the community," Karl Barth, *Church Dogmatics,* tr. G. W. Bromiley, 1958, IV, 2, p. 627.

³⁰. One of the important functions of community life is the maintenance of discipline. Here community and doctrine come together and "orthodoxy of belief" is joined to "orthodoxy of community" (to use Francis Schaeffer's terms).

³¹. Cf. H. A. Snyder, "Misunderstanding Spiritual Gifts," *Christianity Today,* XVIII:1 (October 12, 1973), pp. 15-18.

³². The most important passages on gifts in Paul's writings are, of course, Rom. 12:6-8, I Cor. 12:8-10, I Cor. 12:28, and Eph. 4:11. In these passages we find four different listings of the gifts of the Spirit. While the lists are essentially similar, it appears that Paul had something different in mind, in terms of the functions of these gifts, in I Cor. 12:28 and Eph. 4:11 than he did in Rom. 12:6-8 and I Cor. 12:8-10. In the latter two passages the emphasis is on the fact of the gifts themselves; of the diversity within the unity in the body of Christ. This is seen in the fact that Paul here speaks of prophecy, teaching, healing, etc., rather than of prophets, teachers, healers, etc. In the former two passages the emphasis is on the gifts as they relate to the functioning of the Church.

³³. The flexibility and fluidity of New Testament terminology is important to bear in mind. In general, "pastors and teachers" (Eph. 4:11) are probably synonymous with the deacons and elders Paul elsewhere speaks of, and which he himself appointed in the churches he founded. Paul specifically mentions on one occasion "elders . . . who labor in preaching and teaching" (I Tim. 5:17). Likewise "bishops" seem to designate those with the general oversight of more than one congregation within a city; they can be considered as exercising the gifts of pastor, teacher, and perhaps apostle.

This same terminological fluidity appears in the *Didache* (c. A.D. 120), where "apostle" and "prophet" are used almost interchangeably and "bishops and deacons" are associated with the prophetic and teaching ministry.

³⁴. For evidence that the term "apostle" was used in the early church for more than the original Twelve, see Michael Green, *Evangelism in the Early Church,* p. 167.

³⁵. In this connection, C. P. Wagner has suggested the possibility of a specific "missionary gift" bestowed by the Holy Spirit to enable certain people to exercise other gifts they may possess in a cross-cultural situation. Although the New Testament does not mention such a gift, there is no reason on this account to rule it out. Legitimate gifts of the Spirit may be many and varied, and no biblical list appears to be complete. Further, those whom God calls to serve in a particular way he also

capacitates for this service. The value of Wagner's suggestion is that it emphasizes that missionary ministry is charismatically determined; that effective cross-cultural communication depends upon the exercise of spiritual gifts. While one cannot dogmatically affirm the existence of a missionary gift, the elasticity of the New Testament conception of spiritual gifts permits this possibility, and the concept is pragmatically useful. (*Frontiers in Missionary Strategy,* p. 79).

[36]. Neither of these cultures was homogeneous; both contained identifiable subcultures, as the New Testament itself reveals.

[37]. Francis Schaeffer suggests eight biblical norms for church structure in *The Church at the End of the Twentieth Century,* 1970, pp. 59-67. Although these suggestions go somewhat beyond what I have presented here and put less emphasis on spiritual gifts, they are not in conflict with the position of this paper.

[38]. This is the traditional Roman Catholic view, but many Protestant groups also tend in this direction.

[39]. It seems to me that we have no biblical authority for arguing that the charismatic leadership gifts ceased after the New Testament period. Such gifts have often existed throughout church history, but have not always been recognized as such.

[40]. That the functions of deacon, elder, and bishop were associated with spiritual gifts is suggested by such passages as Acts 20:28, 21:8; I Tim. 4:14; I Pet. 5:1; II John 1.

[41]. The ministry of the first deacons (Acts 8) and of Paul and Barnabas as missionary apostles (Acts 13:1-3) was recognized formally by the Church; the evangelistic ministry of Philip and the apostolic ministry of Apollos seem to have become recognized informally as a result of their effectiveness.

[42]. Peters, *Saturation Evangelism,* p. 33.

[43]. Green, *Evangelism in the Early Church,* pp. 194-222 and passim.

[44]. G. W. Webber discusses the importance of these two foci in *The Congregation in Mission,* 1964, pp. 121-131, and *God's Colony in Man's World,* 1960, pp. 58-59.

[45]. Robert Coleman emphasizes the importance of Christ's life together with his disciples in *The Master Plan of Evangelism,* 1964. According to Coleman, Jesus "spent more time with his disciples than with everybody else in the world put together" (p. 43). This is strong support for the priority of community and the importance of structures which nourish community.

[46]. "The Fellowship of the Holy Spirit," *Christianity Today,* XV:3 (November 6, 1970), pp. 4-7; "The People of God — Implications for Church Structure," *Christianity Today,* XVII:2 (October 27, 1972), pp. 6-11.

[47]. The years immediately preceding the Reformation witnessed a pro-liferation of small home Bible study groups (W. S. Reid, "The Grass-Roots Reformation," *Christianity Today,* XV:2, October 23, 1970, pp. 62-64). The Anabaptist Movement from the start strongly emphasized community life, and this was nourished by in-home worship. The *collegio pietatis* of the Pietist Movement was essentially a small-group structure (Donald Bloesch, *The Evangelical Renaissance,* 1973, p. 118). The Wes-leyan Revival in eighteenth-century England was largely sustained by the "class meeting," a carefully structured form of the small group (H. A. Snyder, "Church Renewal Through Small Groups," *United Evan-gelical Action,* XXX:2 Summer, 1971, pp. 29-31). In the American Holi-ness Movement of the 1880s and 1890s, literally hundreds of small-group prayer and Bible study meetings sprang up (Vinson Synan, *The Holiness-Pentecostal Movement,* 1971, p. 42). Histories of revivals often emphasize the great amount of prayer that preceded them; is it more than coincidence that such prayer was usually the result of small-group prayer meetings? Church history shows that the modern-day emphasis on small groups is merely a revival of what has always been characteris-tic, of the Church at its best. See also D. M. Kelley, *Why Conservative Churches Are Growing,* 1972, pp. 126-127.

[48]. Dean Kelley in *Why Conservative Churches Are Growing* rightly emphasizes that discipline or "strictness" is a characteristic of virtually all significant and society-transforming religious movements. Such disci-pline is best maintained by the community itself, and this in the con-text of the small group. Not only is this sociologically valid; it squares with what Jesus and Paul teach (Matt. 18:15-20; I Cor. 5:3-13).

[49]. See bibliography.

BIBLIOGRAPHY:

I know of no book which deals specifically with the topic of this paper, and few books on related subjects really reflect the biblical view of the Church. The following books are particularly helpful for recover-ing the biblical meaning and dynamic of the church.

R. E. Coleman, *The Master Plan of Evangelism,* 1963.

R. C. Girard, *Brethren, Hang Loose,* 1972. A popularly-written case study of church renewal.

M. L. Hodges, *A Guide to Church Planting,* 1973.

David Mains, *Full Circle,* 1971. One of the best books on rediscovering the Church in an urban setting.

G. W. Peters, *Saturation Evangelism,* 1970. Contains an excellent section on "household evangelism"; the treatment of "saturation evangelism" does not give adequate attention to the Church.

Robert Raines, *New Life in the Church,* 1961. Experiences of renewal, particularly through small groups, in a Methodist church in the U.S.

Lawrence Richards, *A New Face For the Church,* 1970. The best and most definitive book by an evangelical to date on the Church and church structure. Creative and practical.

F. A. Schaeffer, *The Church at the End of the Twentieth Century,* 1970.

R. C. Stedman, *Body Life,* 1972. Excellent material on normal church life.

Stephen Verney, *Fire in Coventry,* 1964. Renewal in an Anglican church in England.

C. P. Wagner, *Frontiers in Missionary Strategy,* 1971. One of the few books on missions which does justice to the biblical view of the Church.

G. W. Webber, *The Congregation in Mission,* 1964. Discoveries in congregational life growing out of the experience of New York's East Harlem Protestant Parish.

THE CHURCH AS GOD'S AGENT IN EVANGELISM

Howard A. Snyder

Participants in this Congress have already had opportunity to study my paper on "The Church as God's Agent in Evangelism." In that paper I attempted to show that the affirmation, "The Church is God's agent in evangelism" makes sense only if we understand what the Bible means by "the church."

By way of summary, let me review the main points of my original paper.

1. The Church biblically understood

Traditionally we have thought of the Church as both a visible institution on earth and as an invisible mystical communion which transcends both space and time. The second reality was considered more basic and more important and helped counterbalance the imperfections and flaws of the visible reality.

This dualistic way of seeing the Church is not necessarily incorrect, but it has led us at times to undervalue the importance of the Christian community on earth and to depreciate cultural considerations. In the bibical view, the earthly and cosmic perspectives fit together in one whole and do not leave us with two incompatible churches or with a split-level view of the Church.

a. *The Bible sees the Church in cosmic-historical perspective.* The Church is the people of God which God has been forming and through which he has been acting down through history. Our space-time world is part of a larger spiritual universe in which God reigns. God has chosen to place the Church with Christ at the very center of his plan to reconcile the world to himself as the body given to the conquering Savior (Eph. 1:20-23).

b. *The Bible sees the Church in charismatic, rather than institutional, terms.* While the Church is in a broad sense an institution, it is more fundamentally a charismatic community. That is, it exists by the grace (Greek, *charis*) of God and is built up by the gifts of grace (*charismata*) bestowed by the Spirit. As seen biblically, it is structured the way the human body is structured, on the basis of *life*. At its most basic level, it is a *community*, not a hierarchy; an *organism*, not an organization.

c. *The Bible sees the Church as the community of God's people.* Here the cosmic and the charismatic are united, and we see the Church as both within the world and transcending the world.

Since the Church is the people of God, it includes all God's people in all times and in all places, as well as those who have now crossed the space-time boundary and live in the more immediate presence of God.

But the people of God must have a visible, local expression, and at the local level the Church is the community of the Holy Spirit. As Samuel Escobar has well said in his paper for this Congress, "God calls those who become his people to be part of a community. So, the new humanity that Christ is creating becomes visible in communities that have a quality of life that reflects Christ's example."

2. *Church-based evangelism*

From the biblical perspective, evangelism can best be understood as the outgrowth of the normal body life of the Church. Evangelism must therefore be Church-centered. Or, perhaps better, evangelism must be *Church based.* It centers in Christ and is based in the life of the witnessing community.

Among other factors which could be noted, I have emphasized that the biblical church normally grows through (i) direct evangelistic proclamation, (ii) the multiplication of local congregations, (iii) the building of Christ-centered community, and (iv) the exercise of spiritual gifts. Each of these four factors contributes to the others in an ongoing cycle of edification and expansion.

Structures for an evangelistic Church

Neither denominational structures nor para-denominational structures such as Christian schools, evangelistic associations, and missionary societies existed in New Testament days. It should be self-evident that such structures have no explicit biblical basis. Therefore, *such structures are not themselves the Church,* although they may bear some important relationship to Christ's body.

It is for this reason that I have chosen to call *all* institutional and organizational structures, including denominations, "para-church structures." Such structures exist alongside of and parallel to the community of God's people, but are not themselves the Church. They are useful to the extent they aid the Church in its mission, but are man-made and culturally influenced.

The Bible gives us three basic structures for the Church: leadership through spiritual gifts, the large-group gathering, and the small group. All biblical material concerning apostles, prophets, pastors, deacons, bishops, and so on, should be seen as part of the New Testament pattern of leadership through gifts of the Spirit. Large-and small-group gatherings were also normative in the Early Church and still have validity today.

The Church is God's agent of evangelism, then, as it truly becomes the community of God's people.

Delegates' reactions to my paper have centered around four basic questions with which I shall attempt to deal during the remainder of my time this morning:

a. Precisely what is meant by "para-church structures," and how do these relate to the Church?

b. In what sense is the Church charismatic and in what sense institutional?

c. Is the principle of the multiplication of congregations biblically based and applicable in all situations?

d. Precisely what is the role of spiritual gifts in the evangelistic ministry of the Church?

The first two of these questions relate to the problem of *the visible reality of the Church.* I shall address myself first to this problem, and then to the questions of growth-by-division and the exercise of spiritual gifts.

PART ONE: *The visible reality of the Church*

I have emphasized that the Bible presents the Church primarily as a charismatic community, rather than as an organizational institution. It is necessary, however, to define more precisely what we mean by "institutional" and "charismatic."

1. *Is the Church an institution?* The Church as the people of God is definitely *not* an institution in the same sense that General Motors, Oxford University, or the United Nations are institutions. On the other hand, the Church does have an institutional side in the same way the family does, and the Church has given rise to literally thousands of institutional structures which, sociologically, are markedly similar to other human organizations, corporations, and bureaucracies.

It is sociologically naive to say the Church is in no sense an institution. *Any pattern of collective behavior which becomes habitual or customary is an institution.* In this broad sense the Lord's Supper is an institution, and even a small-group Bible study, if it meets continually over a period of time, becomes an institution.

A certain degree of institutionalization is therefore inevitable and even desirable. It is, in fact, one result of the fact that man lives in space and time. Institutionalization would be unimaginable in eternity!

David O. Moberg, one of the few qualified sociologists of religion within evangelicalism, has written,

"Every religious organization has some degree of formalism or institutionalization. This is true of groups that claim to be 'merely a fellowship, not a denomination,' and of those so informally and loosely organized that they claim to lack organization altogether."

In this sense, some institutionalization of the Church is already evident in the New Testament. The striking thing, however, is that the institutional elements were decidedly *secondary* in the Holy Church, and were highly *functional* No officially structured, formalized organizations in the sense of modern-day denominations or societies are to be found in the New Testament. Institutionalization of this more rigid, hierarchical, and organizational type grew up only in the third century, in part as a reaction to the charismatic excesses of the Montanists.

These considerations lead to the following conclusion: *The Church will inevitably manifest some institutional patterns, but no institution can ever be the Church.* The Church can never be *essentially* an institution, even though it will necessarily be institutional in some aspects of its life.

In many areas, the Church today is encased in rigid institutional structures which impede growth. Perhaps 80 per cent of such structures are not formal and official, but are simply traditional and cultural. In the United States, for instance, few if any denominations have adopted an article of faith stating that worship services must be held between ten and twelve o'clock on Sunday morning — and yet this is one of the most rigid institutional *patterns of American Christianity.* In many areas, the same thing applies to liturgy, the decision-making process, ideas about the "clergy," and even methods of evangelism. Much of this is simply tradition; only a small percentage is a part of official church polity. And yet it is precisely this traditional, only half-perceived part of church structure which is most rigid, most resistant to change, and often most deadening to the Church's life. I am reminded here of John Wesley's initial reaction to "field preaching" in England, two centuries ago: "I should have thought the saving of souls a sin if it had not been done in church."

Is there hope for churches whose spiritual spontaneity and community life are stifled by rigid institutional forms? This is a question of *institutional renewal.* In such churches, individual spiritual renewal among the believers is not enough, and by itself may provoke divisions and factions, just as new wine bursts old wineskins. A general principle for highly institutional churches is that *institutional renewal must accompany personal renewal.* Where this is not possible, the old institution may have to be abandoned and new structures formed. There are times when old wineskins must be replaced by new ones.

Is the Church, then, an institution? In the broadest sociological sense, we may say it is — but even in this sense the institutional element is strictly secondary and derivative and must be functional. In the more restricted sense of a formally constituted, hierarchical organization, the Church is not and never can be an institution, for the Church is the community of God's people.

2. *What does it mean to say the Church is "charismatic"?*

As the community of God's people, the Church is essentially a *charismatic community* rather than an institution. The New Testament and the writings of the first church fathers show that the Early Church saw itself as a charismatic community. With the gradual institutionalization of the Church, however, the idea of the Church as an organization became more prominent and largely crowded out the charismatic-organic view. Thus "in the history of theology the Church as assembled community of the faithful has been too often neglected in favor of the Church as institution," notes Roman Catholic theologian Hans Kung.

I use "charismatic" here in the precise biblical sense of pertaining to the working and empowering of the grace (*charis*) of God. In this sense "charismatic" has no specific reference to glossolalia except in the general sense that tongues-speaking is one of the charisms mentioned in the New Testament.

The charismatic emphasis — and particularly the doctrine of spiritual gifts — is too important to be abandoned because of controversy over a word. "Charismatic" is a good and highly biblical term that needs to be restored to the Church in all its biblical significance. As Geoffrey Bromiley has commented, Reformation Protestantism today must come to "a fresh realization that Christian ministry always is, and has to be, a charismatic movement."

As Bromiley suggests, the charismatic emphasis relates particularly to the *ministry* of the Church — and thus is important for evangelism. Too often the churches I know are *not* charismatic communities in which each person ministers according to the gift he has received. Rather they are simply organizations not fundamentally different from other organizations in the same culture. Such institutionalized churches attempt vainly to minister through ever improved programs, training, and techniques. Under unusually talented leadership such churches succeed, and everyone praises that success and uses it as a model. But in the majority of cases such "spiritual technology" fails and leaves local churches frustrated and starving for real spiritual fellowship.

I suggest, therefore, that the contemporary church should self-consciously seek a *charismatic model* for its life to take the place of the prevailing *institutional model.*

A *charismatic* or *organic model* is one characterized by community, inter-personal relationships, mutuality, and interdependence. It is flexible and leaves room for a high degree of spontaneity. The Bible gives us such a model for the Church: the human body. The human body itself is charismatic, and the Body of Christ is charismatic.

As I have already suggested, basic components of a charismatic, organic structure for the Church include leadership and ministry through spiritual gifts, community life through the use of small groups, and worship, teaching, and public witness through large groups. I propose that there be further study to develop more fully a charismatic-organic understanding of church structure, particularly at the national and worldwide levels.

3. *The Church and para-Church structures*

It is precisely here that the distinction between the Church and para-church structures is useful. This distinction is definitely *not* merely a restatement of the visible-invisible view of the Church. The Church is both visible and invisible, and so are para-church structures; even a secular organization has its invisible dimensions, as Jacques Ellul reminds us — I am distinguishing, rather, between the Church as biblically understood, and auxiliary ecclesiastical structures which did not exist in New Testament days but which have grown up through church history.

In my invitation to present a paper at this Congress, I was specifically asked to deal with the question of para-church structures in relation to evangelism. I was aware that "para-church structures" was understood to mean non-denominational and interdenominational organizations such as Intervarsity, Campus Crusade for Christ, and the Billy Graham Evangelistic Association. But in attempting to make a biblical (rather than merely pragmatic) analysis, I encountered a basic difficulty. I could find no *biblical* basis for a fundamental distinction between denominational structures and para-denominational structures. The more basic distinction seems to be between *the Church* as the body of Christ and the community of God's people, and *all institutional structures,* including denominations. Thus I would make a basic distinction between the Church and all para-church structures, and then sub-divide such institutional structures into *denominational* and *non-denominational* structures.

There is a fundamental difference here between Protestant and Roman Catholic views of the Church, although the implications of the Reformation in this area have never been carried through to their logical conclusion. Protestants who distinguish between biblical revelation and church tradition should have no difficulty making a distinction between the biblical Church and institutional church structures. The categories are parallel. The biblical Church is grounded in biblical revelation; all para-church structures are based in post-biblical church tradition.

In regard to evangelism, I would particularly stress the following two points:

a. Biblically speaking, it is irrelevant whether evangelism is carried out by a denomination or some non-denominational structure, for in both cases the sponsoring structure is in reality a para-church institution. It is not fundamentally important whether foreign missions, for example, are carried out by denominational mission boards or by independent missionary agencies. Both forms of evangelism may be equally *valid or invalid*, depending on their relationship to the biblical Church.

b. All evangelism, regardless of the agency which sponsors it, is legitimate only as it plants and edifies the Church or extends its witness. Evangelistic and missionary efforts which form new Christian communities or add to those already formed are legitimate if they are really building the Church as biblically understood. If they are not, they are a waste of effort, regardless of how they are structured or of the biblical legitimacy they may claim. Of course, it is fundamentally important that all evangelistic and church-planting efforts take care to contribute to the visible and spiritual unity, rather than disunity, of the Body of Christ.

This means that the important thing for evangelism is that *the biblical Church be built* — that is, that local Christian communities or fellowships be multiplied, that such communities truly demonstrate the quality of life seen in Jesus Christ, and that the Church live in the world as the redeemed people of God. From a biblical point of view, questions of denominational or non-denominational affiliation or structure are strictly secondary.

PART TWO: THE PRINCIPLE OF GROWTH-BY-DIVISION

I will limit myself here to a few of the more fundamental questions which relate specifically to the biblical view of the Church.

1. *Is growth-by-division a biblical principle?*

Growth-by-division (the multiplication of local congregations) is not a biblical principle in the same sense that Christian community life or the exercise of spiritual gifts are biblical principles. It is rather a conclusion reached through studying the New Testament Church and church growth throughout history. Its biblical basis is twofold: The analogy from physical life and the example of the Early Church.

We know that the Early Church grew rapidly, that its life centered largely in small home gatherings, and that it experienced an intense corporate or community life which strongly attracted non-believers. The faith quickly spread from town to town and from one province to another. This growth can be explained only as a process of multiplying local cells of believers.

This conclusion is reinforced by the analogy from biological life. The Bible specifically uses natural reproduction and growth as an analogy for spiritual things and for the Church. The principle by which life extends itself is the principle of reproduction and cell division.

2. *Is growth-by-division possible in all situations?*

The multiplication of local cells of believers is more difficult in some cultures than in others, but is totally impossible only under the most repressive totalitarian regimes. Where the vigilance of the state is practically complete, this principle will be difficult to follow. This is something we must leave in the hands of God.

It is important to point out, however, that I am not speaking here either of the multiplication of *buildings* nor the multiplication of *official government-sanctioned church organizations*. I am speaking of the proliferation of local, perhaps highly informal, cells of Christian believers. In totalitarian regimes, these may not be able to grow into large churches. But even in such situations the multiplication of small fellowships is often possible, even if risky.

In some cases the Church must simply continue to live as the suffering Church, its community life restricted almost totally to individual families, awaiting either the day of harvest or the day of deliverance. In the majority of cases, however, growth-by-division *can* take place if there is the vision for it.

3. *Is growth-by-division wise in areas where many Christian churches already exist?*

Let me state once again that I am not speaking of multiplying buildings or organizations. In many Western cities, the last thing the Church needs is more buildings! What it often *does* need, however, is to rediscover true Christian community. The small group is helpful here. And as small groups are formed, they will tend to multiply. The number of official organized churches may remain the same, while the number of real *biblical* churches is actually multiplying rapidly as more and more individuals discover new life in Christ and a new life-style in Christian community. Rather than discouraging such a movement, the organized churches should encourage and stimulate it, seeking to guide it in biblical channels.

4. *Does not division usually occur for carnal, rather than spiritual, reasons?*

Too often this is the case. Many churches have multiplied and grown, not because they had a vision for growth, but because the brethren couldn't get along with each other! This is clearly wrong, and yet God has miraculously used such divisions for the growth of the Church.

But unholy splits develop often precisely for the *lack* of a healthy vision for church multiplication. If new churches are formed with the vision for eventual growth-by-division, if this is the focus, then growth will occur naturally for the right, rather than the wrong, reasons. Church division for inferior motives does not cancel out the principle of growth-by-division, any more than cancer invalidates the principle of normal cell division. It is a question of planning for growth-by-division for the right reasons, rather than letting it occur for the wrong reasons.

5. *Where does the Church find sufficient leadership for new congregations?*

The answer to this question is found in the fact of spiritual gifts and in the community life of the Church. If we live with our brethren in true Christian community and if we expect the Spirit to provide the necessary spiritual gifts, the right gifts of leadership will appear at the right time to take care of the demands of growth.

The multiplication of congregations should result from the growth of small-group fellowships. Such groups offer the ideal structure to awaken, discipline, and train spiritual gifts. When the Church is truly the community of God's people, it is God the Spirit who provides the necessary leadership. This is his promise to us.

PART THREE: EVANGELISM AND SPIRITUAL GIFTS

Finally, I would make the following affirmations concerning the importance of spiritual gifts for Church-based evangelism.

1. *The doctrine of spiritual gifts is a necessary and valid emphasis*

The basic question is not whether specific spiritual gifts, such as apostle, prophet, or tongues-speaking, are valid today. The question is whether the Spirit still "gives gifts to men," and the answer is *yes*. Precisely which gifts he gives in any particular age is God's prerogative, and we are justified in making no *a priori* judgments about this. We have no biblical warrant to restrict the *charismata* to the Early Church, nor to outlaw any specific gift today.

2. *Spiritual gifts play a fundamental role in evangelism*

All Christians are called to some "work of ministry," but this ministry is not the same for each person. The ministry of each believer is largely determined by the spiritual gifts which he has received. We will impede church growth and create frustrated Christians if we try to force believers into ministries — even in evangelism — for which they are not spiritually gifted.

Paul clearly states that his "gift of God's grace" as an apostle was "to preach to the Gentiles the unsearchable riches of Christ and to make all men see what is the plan of the mystery" of the Gospel (Eph. 3:7-9).

Philip was an evangelist. Agabus was a prophet; we have no evidence he was an evangelist. Dorcas was "full of good works and acts of charity" (Acts 9:36); it was thus that she exercised her spiritual gifts. Lydia of Philippi led a prayer group and practised the gift of hospitality (Acts 16:13-15). Silas was a prophet (Acts 15:32), and Phoebe was a deaconness (Romans 16:1). And so on throughout the Early Church. Not all of these were evangelists, but all were witnesses to the grace of God. And each one, in his own way, was useful in the evangelistic witness of the Church.

The way to biblical evangelism today is to bring each believer to discover and use his spiritual gift. When this happens, not only does evangelism occur, but there is also *a valid Christian community* to welcome new converts and *a valid Christian life-style* of faith and good works that creates no credibility gap with the world.

3. *The Church's leadership ministries are based on spiritual gifts*

One of the most ubiquitous institutional structures which has grown up in the Church through centuries of tradition is the professional clergy, with the resultant clergy-laity dichotomy. The very basis of this dichotomy is undercut by the biblical teaching that the entire Church is a people or laity (*laos*) and all Christians are ministers. Biblically, everyone here today is a *layman*. And every one of us is a *minister*. And we are all called to the *ministry*.

A professional, distinct priesthood did exist in Old Testament days. But in the New Testament this priesthood is replaced by two truths: Jesus Christ as our great High Priest, and the Church as a Kingdom of Priests (Heb. 4:14, 8:1; I Pet. 2:9; Rev. 1:6).

The New Testament doctrine of ministry, therefore, rests not on the clergy-laity distinction but on the twin pillars of *the priesthood of all believers* and *the gifts of the Spirit*. Today, four centuries after the Reformation, the full implications of this Protestant affirmation have yet to be worked out.

The New Testament view of ministry relates directly to evangelism. For one thing, it is no longer a question of "getting laymen involved in evangelism"; rather it is a question of helping the Church to live as a priestly community of interdependent gifts. God himself will gift some men and women for specifically evangelistic ministries, and he will gift others to minister in other ways which are supportive for evangelism (prayer, social work, hospitality, healing, counseling, administration, and many, many others).

CONCLUSION

In conclusion, I would like to offer two simple suggestions which may be helpful in aiding this Congress to formulate a biblical strategy for worldwide evangelism in these days.

The first suggestion is that *local churches throughout the world be encouraged to make use of small-group meetings as a basic structure for the Church's community life.* If this principle could be self-consciously endorsed, and if millions of small-group fellowships could be formed around the world to seriously pray, study the Bible, and share the joy of life in Christ, a revolutionary outbreak of New Testament Christianity could shake this whole groaning world.

Second, I would suggest that wherever possible in cities around the world, *large public rallies be held regularly, uniting in the city all the people of God who will cooperate.* If in major cities around the world all true Christians could unite *regularly* in a monthly "great congregation" to praise God, hear the Scriptures, and bear witness, the impact would be incalculable. Such rallies would give public, visible testimony to the unity of the Body of Christ and put the Faith in the center of the public arena once again. They would also help individual believers and local congregations to identify with the larger body of Christ. I suggest that "The City" is the primary context in which Christian unity needs to be demonstrated today.

Evangelism and the growth of the Church are not a matter of *bringing to* the Church that which is needed for success in the way of methods, techniques, or strategies. *Evangelism is rather a matter of removing the hindrances to growth.* Once these hindrances are removed — not only individual sin but also human traditions, worn-out structures, and fundamental misconceptions about the nature of the Church — then the Church will grow through the power of God within it.

When Lazarus was raised from death, he was "bound with bandages, and his face wrapped with a cloth." Jesus said, "Unbind him, and let him go!" (John 11:44).

This is a lesson for the Church today. The Church has resurrection life within it; it has been called to life by Jesus Christ. The body of Christ does not need a new suit of clothes. It does not need to have something added. It needs only to be unbound and let go.

Jesus Christ is life! The Church, his body and bride, is life! Our need today is to return to the Word of God and let it speak to us concerning the Church and its place in God's cosmic plan.

Let both the Spirit *and* the Bride say, "Come!"

FORM AND FREEDOM IN THE CHURCH
Francis A. Schaeffer

Dr. Schaeffer, Huemoz, Switzerland,
is the leader of L'Abri Fellowship.

My original paper presented four points which are needed if we are to meet the need of our generation. These four points are: two contents and two realities. If you have not read my original paper I would say, please do so.

The first content of my original paper is the need of a clear doctrinal content concerning the central elements of Christianity. There must be no compromise with liberal theology, including neo-orthodox existential theology. There will be borderline things in which we will have differences, but on the central issues there must be no compromise.

With this goes the need to emphasize content in our messages. We are not to fall into the cheap solution (which seems so fascinating at first) of just moving people to make decisions without a sufficient content, nor after they are Christians not giving them sufficient content for their comprehension and for their lives.

Another element of the way in which we must be careful of the content which we present is that we on our part must not destroy the absolutes of the Word of God in the opposite way than the liberal destroys the absolutes of the Word of God. The liberal destroys the absolutes concerning the Word of God by philosophically not believing that such a thing as absolutes exist and religiously specifically not believing that the Bible gives absolutes. We can destroy the absolutes of the Word of God in the opposite way. We can add other things to the absolutes of the Word of God and in this way destroy the absolutes also. We can take the middle class norms, we can take our culturally related things, and we can elevate them to become equal with the absolutes of the Word of God. And when we do, in our own way we destroy the absolutes of the Word of God almost as badly as the liberal destroys them in his way.

The first point of the original paper is the need of a clear doctrinal content concerning the central elements of Christianity. A corollary of this is that we must *practice the truth* we say we maintain. We must practice this truth in the area of religious cooperation. We must practice this truth in the area of religious cooperation where it is costly. We must practice this truth in the area of religious cooperation where it may be observed. If we say that Christianity is truth yet for any reason, including evangelism, we blur the line between liberal theology and biblical Christianity in the area of religious cooperation, we lose credibility with the world today which does not believe that truth exists in any form. The hallmark of our generation, in contrast to the previous generations, is that this generation does not believe that truth exists. All is relativistic. There is no such thing as "truth as truth." And this is why it is not a tautology to use the expression "true truth" to make this plain.

The first reason we should not have religious cooperation with liberalism is because of the teaching of the Word of God on this subject. But the second reason, which all too many evangelicals have forgotten, is that we lose credibility with the watching world when we say that we believe that biblical Christianity is truth and then have such unclear religious cooperation.

Thus the first point of the original paper is the need of a clear doctrinal content concerning the central elements of Christianity and the corollary of that is the need to practice this truth in the area of religious cooperation.

The second content given in the original paper is that we must give honest answers to honest questions. Christianity is truth and as such it touches all of life, including the intellectual and the cultural. There is no dichotomy between the spiritual and the intellectual and the cultural. No part of life including science and art is autonomous from the norms of Scripture. God made the whole man and the whole man is redeemed in Christ, and the Lordship of Christ covers the whole of life. The Lordship of Christ includes man's so-called spiritual things. It also includes his intellectual and creative things, his cultural things. It includes his law, his sociology, and his psychology. It includes every part and portion of man and his being.

This second point in the original paper, namely the giving of honest answers to honest questions, also carries with it a corollary: we must in compassion for the lost be willing to do the hard work necessary to be able to answer the questions of this generation. We must be ready to answer the questions of this generation and not only the generation which now is past. We are not to say either in attitude or in words, "Don't ask your questions, just believe." We are to follow the example of Christ and Paul who in their ministry constantly answered the questions of those who surrounded them.

Mind you, answers, even the right answers, are not all that are needed for salvation. Salvation is something else. As I would express it for the twentiety-century man, salvation is bowing twice — first metaphysically and then morally. First of all we must bow metaphysically and acknowledge that we are not autonomous, we are not a product of chance. Rather than being autonomous, God is the Creator and he has created us and we are the creature. Thus in the area of being we must bow and acknowledge that we are not autonomous. Not all men analyze it so. Perhaps with the people you are talking to they would not understand the words I am using. But the thoughts must be there if a man is really going to be saved. We have seen people come to L'Abri who have "made a profession of faith" who have never once considered whether God exists. First of all, to be saved we must bow metaphysically and acknowledge that the infinite-personal God is there and that we are creatures. Then we must bow morally because now we stand before the flaming holiness of the God who is there and who has revealed himself through Scripture. And as we do stand before him we see that we are sinners. So we now must bow morally and raise the empty hands of faith and accept the finished work of Christ plus nothing as he died in substitution, in propitiation upon Calvary's cross in space and time. In doing this we have bowed metaphysically and morally, and this is necessary for salvation.

But while mere answers are not to be confused with salvation yet nevertheless, on our part we must have the compassion to answer the honest questions which men and women have. And this answering the honest questions is also a part of evangelism, not to be separated from it.

Thus the first two points are two contents. The first content that we need is a clear doctrinal content concerning the essential elements of Christianity, with the corollary that in this area we must practice this truth we say we believe in the area of religious cooperation. The second content, we must give honest answers to honest questions with the corollary that we must have compassion enough for a lost world to be willing to do the hard work that is necessary in order to answer their honest questions.

This brings us to *the first reality* of the original paper. There must be some true spirituality in our personal and in our corporate lives. Christian truth may indeed be stated in propositions. But Christianity is more than mere propositions, even the right propositions. Upon the basis of the truth and reality of these propositions, we are to be in a living relationship with the God who is there. The heart of the matter is to love God with all our hearts, with all our souls and all our minds. Without a true individual and corporate spirituality, orthodoxy is less than orthodoxy. There must be something real of the work of Christ in our moment-by-moment lives. There must be something real of the forgiveness of specific sins brought under the blood of Christ, something real in Christ bearing his fruit through us in the work of the Holy Spirit. There is nothing more ugly in the world and which turns people aside, than a dead orthodoxy. It will not be perfect in this world until Jesus comes but nevertheless there must be the reality of the spiritual if we're to meet the needs of our generation.

The second reality given in the original paper is that of the reality of the beauty of human relationships. First, there must be a beauty of human relationships on our part with the non-Christian man. The second commandment of Jesus is to love our neighbor as ourselves, not just the Christians as ourselves. We are to show a beauty of human relationships on every level we touch with the men in the unsaved world. But if this is true concerning the need of a beauty of human relationships toward the unsaved man, it is then especially true that there must be an observable community among the true Christians. And that community must cover the whole scope of life.

This covers the points of the original paper.

In regard to the replies I received from my paper (I received about 1,400), I want to say, "Thank you." The first thing concerning these replies is that I was really very deeply touched by the fact that so many of you wrote so warmly saying that the paper indeed delineated the needs of the church of our generation.

Then secondly, on the basis of the minority of replies, I was impressed with the need of responding in two directions simultaneously. Actually, I would say this is not only the case in regard to the minority of the answers I received, but it seems to me that wherever we go in the evangelical world today we must speak in these two directions simultaneously.

First, we must say if evangelicals are to be evangelicals, we must not compromise our view of Scripture. There is no use of evangelicalism seeming to get larger and larger, if at the same time appreciable parts of evangelicalism are getting soft at that which is the central core, namely the Scriptures. I would like to repeat that. There is no use of evangelicalism seeming to get larger and larger if at the same time appreciable parts of evangelicalism are getting soft at that which is the central core, namely the Scriptures.

We must say with sadness that in some places, seminaries, institutions, and individuals who are known as evangelical no longer hold to a full view of Scripture. The issue is clear: is the Bible true truth and infallible wherever it speaks, including where it touches history and the cosmos, or is it only in some sense revelational where it touches religious subjects? That is the issue and I would like to repeat it. The issue is clear: is the Bible true truth and infallible wherever it speaks, including where it touches history and the cosmos, or is it only in some sense revelational where it touches religous subjects?

The heart of neo-orthodox existential theology is that the Bible gives us a quarry out of which to hew religous experience but that the Bible contains mistakes where it touches that which is verifiable — namely history and science. But unhappily we must say that in some circles this concept now has come into some of that which is called evangelicalism. In short, in these circles, the neo-orthodox existential theology is being taught under the name of evangelicalism.

The issue is whether the Bible gives propositional truth (that is, truth that may be stated in propositions) where it touches history and the cosmos, and this all the way back to pre-Abrahamic history, all the way back to the first 11 chapters of Genesis, or whether instead of that it is only meaningful where it touches that which is considered religious. T. H. Huxley, the biologist, the friend of Darwin, the grandfather of Aldous and Julian Huxley, wrote in 1890 that he visualized the day not far hence in which faith would be separated from all fact, and especially all pre-Abrahamic history, and that faith would then go on triumphant forever. This is an amazing quote for 1890 before the birth of existential philosophy or existential theology. He indeed foresaw something clearly. I am sure that he and his friends considered this some kind of a joke, because they would have understood well that if faith is separated from fact and specifically pre-Abrahamic space-time history, it is only another form of what we today call "a trip."

But unhappily, it is not only the avowedly neo-orthodox existential theologians who now hold that which T. H. Huxley foresaw, but some who call themselves evangelicals as well. This may come from the theological side in saying that not all the Bible is revelational, or it may come from the scientific side in saying that the Bible teaches little or nothing when it speaks of the cosmos.

Martin Luther said: "If I profess with the loudest voice and clearest exposition every portion of the truth of God except precisely that little point which the world and the devil are at that moment attacking, I am not confessing Christ, however boldly I may be professing Christ. Where the battle rages there the loyalty of the soldier is proved, and to be steady on all the battle front besides, is mere flight and disgrace if he flinches at that point."

In our day that point is the question of Scripture. Holding to a strong view of Scripture or not holding to it is the watershed of the evangelical world.

The first direction in which we must face is to say most lovingly but clearly: evangelicalism is not consistantly evangelical unless there is a line drawn between those who take a full view of Scripture and those who do not.

Now having said this however, we must not stop there but immediately turn to the second consideration. We must quickly turn around and say to those who constitute the real evangelicalism that just as there needs to be an orthodoxy of doctrine there needs to be an orthodoxy of community. We should exhibit to a watching world that the blood of Christ does solve differences among men, including the sociological differences among men. In practice as well as in theory, this should be observed in the way true Christians care for each other. In the early church, the church practiced community all the way to the care of each other materially.

As I said in a recent *Christianity Today* article: if I were writing my early books over again, for example *The God Who Is There* and *The Church at the End of The 20th Century*, I would make just one change. I would spell out in the books that which I have always stressed in my discussions. That is, that in our western world when the Christians held the consensus from the Reformation until the recent days, in certain things there were those things that were less than Christian. Two of these were the areas of race and the area of the use of accumulated wealth. When Christianity held the consensus these areas were not stressed as they should have been, and by identification with the evangelicalism which preceded us we must tell the Lord that we are sorry. The proper emphases on questions of race, and on the compassionate use of accumulated wealth simply were not dealt with as they should have been dealt with in the day when we held the consensus in the western world. If the church had been faithful to these biblical concepts when we held the consensus, it would not now be alienated from large blocks of people from whom the church is now alienated. The real reason, however, for stressing the proper attitude toward race and stressing the compassionate use of our accumulated wealth is not to evangelize these large blocks that we are now alienated from. The real reason for stressing these things is because these are right upon the basis of the teaching of the Word of God.

There has been a platonic element in some evangelicalism, and one aspect of this is that we have acted as if giving to missions is spiritual but using our accumulated wealth for man's needs, including the needs of our brothers in Christ, is not as spiritual. There is nothing like that in the New Testament. Christians did give to Paul so that he did not always have to make tents, but most New Testament giving was to care for the material needs of other Christians. Both kinds of giving are needed and both kinds are equally biblical and both kinds are equally spiritual.

The orthodox evangelical church with its proper base of the fully inspired Scripture should exhibit to a watching world that we care for each other's material needs — not only in the local church but over long distances. In the early church the Gentile Christians of Macedonia sent their gifts to help the Jewish Christians in Palestine. This, in those days, was a larger distance than circling the earth in our present day. There is no communism in the Bible as we know the word communism today. This does not exist in either the Old or the New Testament. But we do find when we look at the practice of the early church that there was a loving compassionate use of their wealth. We should add that we cannot hope to speak to the young people who have a Marxist Lenin ideology until we show by our teaching and our practice that we take seriously the question of that which is set forth in the Scripture, the compassionate use of accumulated wealth. There is to be a compassionate use of our accumulated wealth whether that wealth is great or small, towards men as men and especially toward our brothers in Christ.

The evangelical church must not be as it has all too often been, only a series of preaching points and activity generators. It should exhibit a true beauty of community over the whole spectrum of life in a way that may be observed by the world. Have our young people gone naturally to the church as a sure place of community when they had their creative problems, their psychological problems, their intellectual problems and so on? Too often we must sadly say that they have not expected a practicing community to be found there.

We have many young people come every year to L'Abri who have come from evangelical backgrounds, orthodox backgrounds and many of them say, "You are our last hope." What do they mean? Well, they mean that either of one or two things, or a combination of the two, have turned them aside. Those two things are either they have not received honest answers to their honest intellectual questions, or they have not seen the beauty of community in the church. In contrast to this, the church should have a true beauty of community — not only in theory but in practice over the whole sum of life among the Christians. This too is a part of the Good News.

My favorite church is the church of Antioch in the book of Acts. There Jewish Christians were no longer held back by racial thought and they told the Good News to their Gentile neighbors. And the Gentiles began to be Christians. Beautiful. Wonderful — Gentiles began to become Christians. But let us not miss the point that at the same time something else occurred. And that is, that at that time racial prejudice was destroyed.

There was a man there named Niger — in all probability he was a black. And the church included the whole spectrum of the social scale — from Herod's foster brother to the slaves. We should teach and practice the beauty of community in our churches, missions, schools and institutions covering no less a spectrum. Less than this is less than the New Testament standard. This is the ideal and we must keep that ideal before us and do what we can to meet that ideal in the place of our responsibilities.

The devil never gives us the luxury of fighting on one front — this is something that is learned when one studies church history. And in our day we must struggle simultaneously with the two things of which I have spoken. That is, a clear and high view of Scripture as infallible and the practice of community among us.

For many years I have thought visually concerning this. I see the first danger point as a great dragon with fire and smoke coming out of his mouth and nose. To escape I tend to back up to be as far away from this terrible beast as I can. But I am apt not to notice that there is another beast, equally fearsome behind me, and if I am not careful I will back into his mouth and be destroyed.

In front of us as evangelicals is the danger of the compromise of Scripture. We must turn away from this. But beware, behind us is a sterile orthodoxy without the practice of the beauty of community which reaches across all languages, all colors of skin, and all social strata.

Or it may be reversed and may come in the opposite direction. You have looked and you have seen no beauty of community in the area of race and color of skin and social strata and these other things. And as you have seen this as sub-Christian you have seen this beast, and then you turn to back up away from this beast. But beware. For you now there stands the other beast of thinking you can let down on the Scripture and make Scripture less than the full Word of God. You back up into the mouth of the second beast and you are destroyed. It can come equally in either direction. The emphasis on the orthodoxy, the backing into the dead orthodoxy, or the emphasis on community and the backing into the loss of the orthodoxy and especially a full view of Scripture. We must equally beware of both beasts and fall into the mouths of neither.

It is easy to be touched by one of these dangers or the other. It is even possible to be touched by both of them simultaneously. We must say *no* to both and stand for a clear view of Scripture and simultaneously exhibit among us the true beauty of community — a community which touches the intellectual, the cultural, the creative, and the material needs. A community which touches the whole spectrum of men and the whole spectrum of life.

As I think of this Congress my own personal opinion is that the place this Congress will have in history will depend upon the way these things are dealt with. First of all, in the Covenant, but even more important than dealing with them clearly in the Covenant, they must be dealt with clearly as we scatter from this Congress and go back to our places over the whole world.

FORM AND FREEDOM IN THE CHURCH
Francis A. Schaeffer

There are four things which I think are absolutely necessary if we are going to meet the need of our age and the overwhelming pressure we are increasingly facing. They are two contents and two realities.

THE FIRST CONTENT: SOUND DOCTRINE

The first content is clear doctrinal content concerning the central elements of Christianity. There is no use talking about meeting the threat of the coming time or fulfilling our calling in the midst of the last quarter of the twentieth century unless we consciously help each other to have clear doctrinal position. We must have the courage to make no compromise with liberal theology and especially neo-orthodox existential theology.

Christianity is a specific body of truth; it is a system and we must not be ashamed of the word *system*. There is truth and we must hold that truth. There will be borderline things in which we have differences among ourselves, but on the central issues there must be no compromise.

Evangelicals can fall into something which really is not very far from existential theology without knowing. One form of such "evangelical existentialism" is the attitude, if not the words, "Don't ask questions, just believe." This sort of attitude was always wrong, but it is doubly wrong today when we are surrounded with a monolithic consensus which divides reason from non-reason, and always puts religious things in the area of non-reason. This conference is a failure if we do not call each other away from this idea. It is not more spiritual to believe without asking questions. It is not more biblical. It is less biblical and eventually it will be less spiritual because the whole man will not be involved. And so consequently, in our evangelism, in our personal work, in our young people's work, in our ministry wherever we are, those of us who are preachers and are preaching, those of us who are teachers and are teaching and those of us who are evangelists must be absolutely determined not to fall into the trap of saying or implying, "Don't ask questions, just believe." It must be the whole man who comes to understand that the Gospel is truth and believes because he is convinced on that which is good and sufficient reasons that it is truth.

Moreover, we must be very careful to emphasize content in our messages. How much content will depend upon the people with whom we are working. In a university setting, the content will be slightly different than in a situation where people are not as educated. Nevertheless, whether we work with a man or woman who is not as educated or whether we work with an intellectual, in all instances, the Gospel we preach must be rich in content. Certainly, we must be very careful not to fall into the cheap solution (which seems so fascinating at first) of just moving people to make decisions without a sufficient content, without their really knowing what they are making a decision about. We in L'Abri have had people come to us who have "accepted Christ as Savior" but are not even sure that God exists. They have never been confronted with the question of the existence of God. The acceptance of Christ as Savior was a thing abstracted. It had an insufficient content. In reality it was just another kind of trip.

Likewise, in a Christian school or college we can try just to religiously move the students on the basis of something apart from the intellect, separated from the disciplines and the whole study. We must say "no" to this.

What we need to do is to understand our age to be an age of very subtle religious and political manipulation, manipulation by cool communication, communication without content. And as we see all these things, we must lean against them. We have a message of content; there is a system to Christianity. It is not *only* a system, true enough; it is not a dead scholasticism, true enough; but it *is* a system in that the person who accepts Christ as his Savior must do so in the midst of the understanding that prior to the creation of the world a personal God on the high level of trinity existed. And if they "accept Christ as their Savior" and do not understand that God exists as an infinite-personal God and do not understand that man has been made in the image of God and has value, and do not understand that man's dilemma is not metaphysical because he is small but moral because man revolted against God in a space-time fall, in all probability they are not saved. If we "evangelize" by asking for such "acceptance of Christ as Savior," all we have done is to guarantee they will soon drift away and become harder to reach than ever. Not everybody must know everything — nobody knows everything; if we waited to be saved until we knew everything, nobody would ever be saved — but that is a very different thing from deliberately or thoughtlessly diminishing the content.

Another way to fall into an "evangelical existentialism" is to treat the first half of Genesis the way the existential theologian tends to treat the whole Bible. The first half of Genesis is history, space-time history, the fall is a space-time fall, or we have no knowledge of what Jesus came to die for and we have no way to understand that God is really a good God. Our whole answer to evil rests upon the historic, space-time fall. There was a time before man revolted against God. The internal evidence of the whole book of Genesis and the external evidences (given in the New Testament in the way the New Testament speaks of the first half of Genesis) show that the first half of Genesis is really meant to be space-time history. We must understand that here we are dealing with history — that is, space and time, the warp and woof of history.

In relationship to this is the danger of diminishing the content of the Gospel in a reverse fashion. Bible-believing Christians who stand against the liberal theologian when he would say there are no absolutes in the Bible can make the opposite mistake by adding other elements as though they were equally absolute. In other words, the absolutes of the Word of God can be destroyed in both directions. That is, the liberal theologian can say, "After all, there is no such thing as an absolute, and specifically the Bible does not give absolutes," or the evangelical can reach over into the middle-class standards and say, "These standards are equal to the absolutes of the Word of God."

The obvious illustration is how the church treats the hippie or a person dressed in this different way. Young people come to us at L'Abri from the ends of the earth, become Christian, and go home and then try to find a church that will accept them without all the change of life-style. I do not mean they try to retain a promiscuous sex life which would be against the Word of God or a drug life. I mean, for example, the way they dress or talk. It is one of my greatest sorrows. The evangelical church often will not accept the person with his life-style unless it fits into the middle-class norm in that particular geographical location. And unhappily, we often do not realize what we have done when we do this. It is not only a lack of love. We have destroyed the absolutes of the Word of God by making something else equal to God's absolutes.

If you ask me why the evangelical church has been so often weak in the question of race in the past, I think it was the same. We were surrounded by a culture that had racial prejudices and did not look at all men as equal, and we allowed this to infiltrate the church. We made taboos apart from, and even against the Word of God, and we held them to be equal with the absolutes of the Bible. But to exalt a cultural norm to an absolute is even more destructive today because we are surrounded by a totally relativistic society. As we make other things equal to the absolutes of the Word of God, it may not be more sinful in the sight of God than it was in the past, but it is more destructive. Consequently, when we talk about content, we are talking about something very practical indeed. We must have a strong, strong doctrinal content.

And as we have a strong doctrinal content, we must *practice* the content, *practice* the truth we say we believe. We must exhibit to our own children and to the watching world that we take truth seriously. It will not do in a relativistic age to say that we believe in truth and fail to *practice that truth* in places where it may be observed and where it is costly. We, as Christians, say we believe that truth exists. We say we have truth from the Bible. And we say we can give that truth to other men in propositional, verbalized form and they may have that truth. This is exactly what the Gospel claims and this is what we claim. But then we are surrounded by a relativistic age. Do you think for a moment we will have credibility if we say we believe the truth and yet *do not practice the truth in religious matters?* If we do not do this, we cannot expect for a moment that the tough-minded, twentieth-century young person, including our own young people, will take us seriously when we say, "Here is truth" when they are surrounded by a totally monolithic consensus that truth does not exist.

Consider an example in the academic world. One girl who was teaching in one of the major universities of Britain was a real Christian and very bright. She was teaching in a sociology department whose head was a behaviorist, and he told her she had to teach in the framework of behaviorism or lose her post. Suddenly she was confronted with the question of the practice of truth. She said no, she could not teach behaviorism, and she lost her post. This is what I mean by practicing truth when it is costly. And this will come in many, many places and in many, many ways. It will come in the area of sexual life form, being surrounded by permissive sexualists and asexuality. We must be careful by the grace of God to practice what we say the Bible teaches, the one-man, one-woman relationship, or we are destroying the truth that we say we believe.

But nowhere is practicing the truth more important than in the area of religious cooperation. If I say that Christianity is really eternal truth, and the liberal theologian is wrong — so wrong that he is teaching that which is contrary to the Word of God — and then on any basis (including for the sake of evangelism) I am unwilling publicly to act as though that man's religious position is not the same as my own, I have destroyed the practice of truth which my generation can *expect* from me and which it will *demand* of me if I am to have credibility. How will we have a *credibility* in a relativistic age if we practice religious cooperation with men who in their books and lectures make very plain that they believe nothing or practically nothing of the content set forth in Scripture?

Incidentally, almost certainly if we have a latitudinarianism in religious cooperation, the next generation will have a latitudinarianism in doctrine, and specifically a weakness toward the Bible. We are seeing this happen in parts of evangelicalism today. We must have the courage to take a clear position.

But let us beware. We certainly must not take every one of our secondary distinctives and elevate them to be the point where we refuse to have fellowship on any level with those who do not hold them. It is the central things of the Word of God which make Christianity Christianity. These we must hold tenaciously, and, even when it is costly for us and even when we must cry, we must maintain that there is not only an antithesis of truth but an antithesis that is observable in practice. Out of a loyalty to the infinite-personal God who is there and who has spoken in Scripture and out of compassion for our own young people and others, we who are evangelicals dare not take a halfway position concerning truth or the practice of truth.

Thus, with regard to the first content there are three things to recognise: first, there must be a strong emphasis on content; second, there must be a strong emphasis on the propositional nature of the Bible, especially the early chapters of Genesis; and third, there must be a strong emphasis on the practice of truth. We can talk about methods, we can stir each other up, we can call each other to all kinds of action, but unless it is rooted in a strong Christian base in the area of content and the practice of truth, we build on sand and add to the confusion of our day.

THE SECOND CONTENT: HONEST ANSWERS
TO HONEST QUESTIONS

The second content is that Christianity is truth, and we must give honest answers to honest questions. Christianity is truth, truth that God has told us, and if it is truth it can answer questions.

There is no dichotomy in the Bible between the intellectual and cultural on the one hand and the spiritual on the other. But often there has been a strong platonic emphasis in evangelicalism, a strong tendency to divide man into two parts — his spiritual nature and everything else. We must take that conception like a piece of baked clay, break it in our hands and throw it away, and consciously reject the platonic element which has been added to Christianity. God made the whole man; the whole man is redeemed in Christ, and after we are Christians the lordship of Christ covers the whole man. That includes his so-called spiritual things and his intellectual, creative and cultural things; it includes his law, his sociology and psychology; it includes every single part and portion of a man and his being.

The Bible does not suggest that there is something in man which is spiritual and that the rest of man is unrelated to the commands and norms of God. There is nothing in the Bible which would say, "Never mind the intellectual, never mind the cultural. We will follow the Bible in the spiritual realm, but we will take the intellectual and the creative and put them aside. They are not important."

If Christianity is truth as the Bible claims, it must touch every aspect of life. If I draw a pie and that pie composes the whole of life, Christianity will touch every slice. At every sphere of our lives Christ will be our Lord and the Bible will be our norm. We will stand under the Scripture. It is not that the "spiritual" is under Scripture but that the intellectual and creative are free from it. Consider the ministry of Paul. Paul went to the Jews, and what happened as he talked to them? They asked Paul questions, and he answered. He went to the non-Jews, the Gentiles, and they asked him questions, and he answered. He went into the marketplace, and there his ministry was a ministry of discussion, of giving honest answers to honest questions. There are three places in the Bible where Paul was speaking to the man without the Bible (that is, to the Gentiles), without the man with the Bible (the Jew) being present. The first was at Lystra and his discussion there was cut short. Then we find him on Mars Hill where they asked questions and Paul answered; this too was cut short. But one place, happily, where he was not cut short is in the first two chapters of the book of Romans. And there we find carried out exactly the same kind of "argumentation" that he began at Lystra and on Mars Hill.

Many Christians think that I Corinthians speaks against the use of the intellect. But it does not. What I Corinthians speaks against is for a man to pretend to be autonomous, to draw from his own wisdom and his own knowledge without recourse to the revelation of the Word of God. It is a humanistic, rationalistic intellectualism — a wisdom that is generated from man himself as opposed to the teaching of the Scripture — that we must stand against with all our hearts. Paul was against the early gnosticism, wherein a man could be saved on the basis merely of such knowledge. Paul did answer questions. He answered questions whenever they arose.

Consider the ministry of our Lord Jesus himself. What was his ministry like? He was constantly answering questions. Of course they were different kinds of questions than those which arose in the Greek and Roman world, and therefore his discussion was different. But as far as his practice was concerned, he was a man who answered questions, this Jesus Christ, this Son of God, this second person of the Trinity, our Savior and our Lord. But someone will say, "Didn't he say that to be saved you have to be as a little child?" Of course he did. But did you ever see a little child who didn't ask questions? People who use this argument must never have listened to a little child or been one! My four children gave me a harder time with their endless flow of questions than university people ever have. Jesus did not mean that coming as a little child simply meant making an upper-story leap. What Jesus was talking about is that the little child, when he has an adequate answer, accepts the answer. He has the simplicity of not having a built-in grid whereby, regardless of the validity of the answer, he rejects it. And that is what rationalistic man, humanistic man, does.

Christianity demands that we have enough compassion to learn the questions of our generation. The trouble with too many of us is that we want to be able to answer these questions instantly, as though we could take a funnel, put it in one ear and pour in the facts and then go out and regurgitate them and win all the discussions. It cannot be. Answering questions is hard work. Can you answer all the questions? No, but you must try. Begin to listen with compassion, ask what this man's questions really are and try to answer. And if you don't know the answer try to go some place or read and study to find some answers.

Not everybody is called to answer the questions of the intellectual, but when you go down to the shipyard worker you have a similar task. My second pastorate was with shipyard workers, and I tell you they have the same questions as the university man. They just do not articulate them the same way.

Answers are not salvation. Salvation is bowing and accepting God as Creator and Christ as Savior. I must bow twice to become a Christian. I must bow and acknowledge that I am not autonomous; I am a creature created by the Creator. And I must bow and acknowledge that I am a guilty sinner who needs the finished work of Christ for my salvation. And there must be a work of the Holy Spirit. Nonetheless, what I am talking about is our responsibility to have enough compassion to pray and do the hard work which is necessary to answer the honest questions. Of course, we are not to study only cultural and intellectual issues. We ought to study them and the Bible and in both ask for the help of the Holy Spirit.

It is not true that every intellectual question is a moral dodge. There are honest intellectual questions and somebody must be able to answer them. Maybe not everybody in your church or your young people's society can answer them, but the church should be training men and women who can. Our theological seminaries should be committed to this, too. It is part of what Christian education ought to be all about.

The Bible puts a tremendous emphasis on content with which the mind can deal. In I John we are told what we should do if a spirit or a prophet knocks on our door tonight. If a prophet or spirit knocks on your door, how do you know whether or not he is from God? I have a great respect for the occult, especially after the things we have seen and fought and wrestled against in L'Abri. If a spirit comes, how do you judge him? Or if a prophet comes, how do you judge him? John says, "Beloved, believe not every spirit, but test the spirits whether they are of God: because many false prophets are gone out into the world. Hereby know ye the Spirit of God: every spirit that confesses that Jesus

Christ has come in the flesh is of God" (I John 4:1-2). Now that is a
very nice answer; it has two halves. First, it means Jesus had an eternal
pre-existence as the second person of the Trinity, and then it means he
came in the flesh. When a prophet or a spirit comes to you, the test of
whether he should be accepted or rejected is not the experience that
the spirit or the prophet gives you. Nor is it the strength of the emotion
which the spirit, the prophet, gives you. Nor is it any special outward
manifestations that the spirit or the prophet may give you. The basis
of accepting the spirit or prophet — *and the basis of Christian fellowship* — is Christian doctrine. There is no other final test. Satan can counterfeit, and he will. I am not speaking against emotion in itself. Of
course there should be emotion. I am saying that you cannot trust your
emotions or the strength of your emotions or the boost your emotions
give you when you stand in the presence of the spirit or the prophet.
This does not prove for one moment whether he is from God or the
devil or simply from himself. And the same is true with Christian fellowship. These are to be tested, says the Word of God, at the point at which
the mind can work and that is on the basis of Christian doctrine.

So, therefore, there are two contents, the content of a clear doctrinal
position and the content of honest answers to honest questions. I now
want to talk about two realities.

THE FIRST REALITY: TRUE SPIRITUALITY

The first reality is spirtual reality. Let us emphasize again as we have
before, we believe with all our hearts that Christian truth can be presented in propositions, and that anybody who diminishes the concept
of the propositionalness of the Word of God is playing into twentieth-
century, non-Christian hands. But, and it is a great and strong *but*, the
end of Christianity is not the repetition of mere propositions. Without
the proper propositions you cannot have that which should follow. But
after having the correct propositions the end of the matter is to love
God with all our hearts and souls and minds. The end of the matter,
after we know about God in the revelation he has given in verbalized,
propositional terms in the Scripture, is to be in relationship to him. A
dead, ugly orthodoxy, with no real spiritual reality must be rejected as
sub-Christian.

Back in 1951-52 I went through a very deep time in my own life.
I had been a pastor for ten years, and a missionary for another five,
and I was connected with a group who stood very strongly for the truth
of the Scriptures. But as I watched, it became clear to me that I saw
very little spiritual reality. I had to ask why. I looked at myself and
realized that my own spiritual reality was not as great as it had been
immediately after my conversion. We were in Switzerland at that time
and I said to my wife, "I must really think this through."

I took about two months, and I walked in the mountains whenever
it was clear. And when it was rainy, I walked back and forth in the hay-
loft over our chalet. I thought and wrestled and prayed, and I went all
the way back to my agnosticism. I asked myself whether I had been right
to stop being an agnostic and to become a Christian. I told my wife, if
it didn't turn out right, I was to be honest and go back to America and

put it all aside and do some other work.

I came to realize that indeed I had been right in becoming a Christian. But then I went on further and wrestled deeper and asked, "But then, where is the spiritual reality, Lord, among most of that which calls itself orthodoxy?" And gradually I found something. I found something that I had not been taught, a simple thing, but profound. I discovered the meaning of the work of Christ, the meaning of the blood of Christ, moment by moment in our lives after we are Christians — the moment by moment work of the whole Trinity in our lives, because as Christians we are indwelt by the Holy Spirit. This is true spirituality.

We went out to Dakota, and I spoke at a Bible conference. And the Lord used it and there was a real moving of God in that place. I preached it back in Switzerland. And gradually it became the book, *True Spirituality;* and I want to tell you with all my heart that I think we could have all the intellectual answers in the world at L'Abri, but if it had not been for those battles in which God gave me some knowledge of some spiritual reality in those days, not just theoretically, poor as it was, of a relationship with God moment by moment on the basis of the blood of Jesus Christ, I don't believe there ever would have been a L'Abri.

Do we minimize the intellectual? I have just pled for the intellectual. I have pled for the propositional. I have pled against doctrinal compromises, specifically at the point of the Word of God being less than propositional truth all the way back to the first verse of Genesis. But at the same time there must be spiritual reality.

Will it be perfect? No, I do not believe the Bible ever holds out to us that anybody is perfect in this life. But it can be real, and it must be shown in some poor way. I say *poor* because I am sure when we get to heaven and look back, we will all see how poor it has been. And yet there must be some reality. There must be something real of the work of Christ in the moment by moment life, something real of the forgiveness of specific sin brought under the blood of Christ, something real in Christ bearing his fruit through me through the indwelling of the Holy Spirit. These things must be there. There is nothing more ugly in all the world, and which turns people aside, than a dead orthodoxy.

This, then, is the first reality, real spiritual reality.

THE SECOND REALITY:
THE BEAUTY OF HUMAN RELATIONSHIPS

The second reality is the beauty of human relationships. True Christianity produces beauty as well as truth, especially in the specific areas of human relationships. Read the New Testament carefully with this in mind; notice how often Jesus returns us to this theme, how often Paul speaks of it. We are to show something to the watching world on the basis of the human relationships we have with other men, not just other Christians.

Christians today are the people who understand who man is. Modern man is in a dilemma because he does not know that man is qualitatively different from non-man. We say man is different because he is made in the image of God. But we must not say man is made in the image of God unless we look to God and by God's grace treat every man with dignity. We stand against B. F. Skinner in his book, *Beyond Freedom and Dignity,* but I dare not argue against Skinner's determinism if I then

treat the men I meet day by day as less than really made in the image
of God.

I am talking first of all about non-Christians. The first commandment
is to love the Lord our God with all our heart and soul and mind, and
the second is to love our neighbor as ourselves. After Jesus commanded
this, someone said, "Who is our neighbor?" and Jesus then told the story
of the good Samaritan. He was not just talking about treating Christians
well; he was talking about treating every man we meet well, every man
whether he is in our social status or not, every man whether he speaks
our language, or not, every man whether he has the color of our skin
or not. Every man is to be treated on the level of truly being made in
the image of God, and thus there is to be a beauty of human relationships.

This attitude is to operate on all levels. I meet a man in a revolving
door. How much time do I have with him? Maybe ten seconds. I am to
treat him well. We look at him. We do not think consciously in every
case that this man is made in the image of God, but, having ground into
our bones and into our consciousness (as well as our doctrinal statement) that he is made in the image of God, we will treat him well in
those ten seconds that we have.

We approach a red light. We have the same problem. Perhaps we
will never see these other people at the intersection again, but we are
to remember that they have dignity.

And when we come to the longer relationships, for example, the
employer-employee relationship, we are to treat each person with
dignity. The husband-and-wife relationship, the parent-and-child relationship, the political relationship, the economic relationship — in every
single relationship of life to the extent to which I am in contact with a
man or woman, sometimes shorter and sometimes longer, he or she is
to be treated in such a way that — man or woman — if they are thinking
at all, will say, "Didn't he treat me well?"

What about the liberal theologian? Yes, we are to stand against his
theology. We are to practice truth, and we are not to compromise. We
are to stand in antithesis to his theology. But even though we cannot
cooperate with him in religious things, we are to treat the liberal theologian in such a way that we try from our side to bring our discussion
into the circle of truly human relationships. Can we do these two things
together in our own strength? No, but in the strength of the power of
the Holy Spirit it can be done. We can have the beauty of human relationships even when we must say no.

Now, if we are called upon to love our neighbor as ourselves when
he is not a Christian, how much more — ten thousand times ten thousand times more — should there be beauty in the relationships between
true Bible-believing Christians, something so beautiful that the world
would be brought up short! We must hold our distinctives. Some of us
are Baptists; some of us hold to infant baptism; some of us are Lutheran
and so on. But to *true* Bible-believing Christians across all the lines, in
all the camps, I emphasize: if we do not show beauty in the way we
treat each other, then in the eyes of the world and in the eyes of our
own children, we are destroying the truth we proclaim.

Every big company, if it is going to make a huge plant, first makes a pilot plant in order to show that its plan will work. Every church, every mission, every Christian school, every Christian group, regardless of what sphere it is in, should be a pilot plant that the world can look at and see there a beauty of human relationships which stands in exact contrast to the awful ugliness of what modern men paint in their art, what they make with their sculpture, what they show in their cinema, and the way they treat each other. Men should see in the church a bold alternative to the way modern men treat people as animals and machines today. There should be something so different that they will listen, something so different it will commend the Gospel to them.

Every group ought to be like that, and our relationships between our groups ought to be like that. Have they been? The answer all too often is no. We have something to ask the Lord to forgive us for. Evangelicals, we who are true Bible-believing Christians, must ask God to forgive us for the ugliness with which we have often treated each other when we are in different camps.

I am talking now about *beauty* and I have chosen this word with care. I could call it *love*, but we have so demoted the word that it is often meaningless. So I use the word *beauty*. There should be beauty, observable beauty, for the world to see in the way all true Christians treat each other.

We need two orthodoxies; first, an orthodoxy of doctrine and, second, an orthodoxy of community. Why was the Early Church able, within one century, to spread from the Indus River to Spain? Think of that: one century, India to Spain. When we read in Acts and in the Epistles, we find a church that *had* and *practiced* both orthodoxies (doctrine and community), and this would be observed by the world. Thus they commended the Gospel to the world of that day and the Holy Spirit was not grieved.

There is a tradition (it is not in the Bible) that the world said about the Christians in the Early Church, "Behold, how they love each other." As we read Acts and the Epistles we realize that these early Christians were really struggling for a practicing community. We realize that one of the marks of the Early Church was a real community, a community that reached down all the way to their care for each other in their material needs.

Have we exhibited this community in our evangelical churches? I want to say no, by and large, no. Our churches have often been two things — preaching points and activity generators. When a person really has desperate needs in the area of race, or economic matters, or psychological matters, does he naturally expect to find a supporting community in our evangelical churches? We must say with tears, many times, no!

My favorite church in Acts and, I guess, in all of history, is the church at Antioch. I love the church at Antioch. I commend to you to read again about it. It was a place where something new happened: the great, proud Jews who despised the Gentiles (there was an anti-Gentilism among the Jews, just as so often, unhappily, there has been anti-semitism among Gentiles) came to a breakthrough. They could not be silent. They told their Gentile neighbors about the Gospel, and suddenly, on the basis of the blood of Christ and the truth of the Word of God, the racial thing was solved. There were Jewish Christians and there were Gentile Christians and they were one!

More than that, there was a total span of the social spectrum. We are not told specifically that there were slaves in the church of Antioch, but we know there were in other places and there is no reason to think they were not in Antioch. We know by the record in Acts that there was no less a person in that church than Herod's foster brother. The man at the very peak of the social pile and the man at the bottom met together in the church of the Lord Jesus Christ and they were one in a beauty of human relationships.

And I love it for another reason. There was a man called Niger in that church and that means black. More than likely he was a black man. The church at Antioch on the basis of the blood of Christ encompassed the whole. There was a beauty that the Greek and the Roman world did not know — and the world looked. And then there was the preaching of the Gospel. In one generation the church spread from the Indus River to Spain. If we want to touch our generation, we must be no less than this.

I would emphasize again that community reached all the way down into the realm of material possessions. There is no *communism*, as we today know the word *communism*, in the book of Acts. Peter made very plain to Ananias and Sapphira that their land was their own and when they sold their land they were masters of what they did with their money. No state or church law, no legalism, bound them. What there was was a love in the Early Church that was so overwhelming that they could not imagine in the church of the Lord Jesus having one man hungry and one man rich. When the Corinthian church fell into this, Paul was very scathing in I Corinthians in writing against it.

Note, too, that deacons were appointed. Why? Because the church had found difficulty in caring for one another's material needs. Read James 1. James asks, "What are you doing preaching the Gospel to a man and trying to have good relationship to him spiritually if he needs shoes and you do not give him shoes?" Here is another place where this awful platonic element in the evangelical church has been so dominant and so deadly. It has been considered spiritual to give for missions but not equally spiritual to give when my brother needs shoes. That is never found in the Word of God. Of course the Early Church gave to missions; at times they gave money so that Paul did not have to make tents. But Paul makes no distinction between collections for missions and collections for material needs, as if one were spiritual and the other not. For the most part when Paul speaks of financial matters, he does so because there was a group of Christians somewhere who had a material need and Paul then calls upon other churches to help.

Moreover, it was not only in the local church that Christians cared for each other's needs; they did so at great distances. The church of Macedonia, which was made up of Gentile Christians, when they heard that the Jewish Christians, the Jews whom they would have previously despised, had material need, took an offering and sent it with care hundreds of miles in order that the Jewish Christians might eat.

So, there must be two orthodoxies, the orthodoxy of doctrine and the orthodoxy of community. And both orthodoxies must be practiced down into the warp and the woof of life where the Lordship of the Lord Jesus touches every area of our life.

Thus there are four requirements if we are to meet the needs of our generation. They are the two contents and then the two realities. And when there are the two contents and the two realities, we will begin to see something profound happen in our generation.

THE NATURE OF BIBLICAL UNITY
Henri Blocher

Rev. Blocher, Rosny-sous-Bois,
France, is Professor at the Faculte de
Theologie Evangelique of Vaux-sur-Seine.

If faith is on the decline in the world today, if unbelief is spreading it is because of the divisions in Christendom! Who in the twentieth century has not heard this refrain? But, to many people the evangelization of the world appears as the other side of the ecumenical undertaking; they are not far from believing that the coming together of once separated churches is nowadays the privileged form of testimony.

This way of considering things should be received with much reserve. The rejection of the Gospel by the world has many other roots than rivalry between "Christian labels." In the places where ecclesiastical fusions have occurred, within the past twenty or thirty years, evangelism does not seem to have profited much from it[1]. One can wonder, according to Professor Carl Wisloff's delightful illustration, whether the big Atlantic liners are really so superior to small boats when the purpose is to go out fishing![2]

Watch out, however, because when we set excess and deformation aside, we can also lose a true idea. The Bible also establishes a link between the unity of the church and its growth through the addition of new members. The first summing up of the book of Acts suggests a relation between the outstanding unity among the first believers and the adding by the Lord to their community of all those who came to salvation (Acts 2:44-47). (The same distinctive expression comes back, in the original, at the beginning and at the end of this passage, and it evokes unity.) Several of the following passages emit the same sound: Acts 4:32-33; 5:12, 14; 9:31. In the prayer usually quoted about Christian unity, Jesus asks his disciples to be one so that the world may believe that the Father sent him (John 17:21, 23). In the powerful synthesis brought to us by the epistle to the Ephesians on the same subject, the unity of the tightly bound body is accomplished through a constant edification, inseparable from evangelism (Eph. 4:1-16).

If we are truly concerned about evangelizing the world, we must understand the nature of the conditions and the consequences of Christian unity according to the New Testament. This is what we want to do, defining principles in order to apply them better to the contemporary situation. To prevent an arbitrary choice in the matter of texts, we shall let ourselves be guided by the Apostle Paul's so wonderfully complete and condensed passage previously pointed out (Eph. 4:3-6), without, however, being compelled to undertake a detailed exegesis of it, or depriving ourselves of the help of other passages.

One Spirit

Very roughly outlined, caricature-like, today's two main conceptions of Christian unity are in opposition to each other, and are likely to attract our attention.

As for the first, unity is *lost,* and it must be found or built again. It will take the shape of a *visible* unity, institutionalized, administrative. We are revealing no secrets whatsoever. Those who seem indwelt by the keenest "ecumenical" passion have often deplored the wish in the high-priestly prayer (of Jesus) is not being fulfilled among us. The loss of unity seemed to be obvious to them when they saw for themselves the confessional separations, the doctrinal condemnations, and the refusal to acknowledge the validity of the sacraments and ministries of other churches. They greeted as steps toward unity the unions that gathered varied communities into the same organization. Of course, the official documents of Amsterdam (1948), Evanston (1954), etc., are careful to assert the unity given "in Christ." Some use a dialectical language: unity is lost as concerns us, but subsists within Christ. The division is at the same time a shameful reality and an "ontological impossibility." The formula would normally mean that it cannot be.[3] According to common opinion, however, the dominant feeling is that absence of unity is sought for. Likewise, in order to avoid producing the specter of the super-church, specter or scarecrow, others do not insist so much on the administrative unity but leave the image of the desired unity more fuzzy. As a general fact, however, the emphasis remains on the unity of the visible institutions as a goal proposed for our efforts.

Most evangelical Christians are turning toward a very different vision. They believe unity is given, and they stress it; it is *invisible* and "spiritual." No one can destroy the link which joins all the true believers, the answer to Jesus' request, a request the Father could do nothing but fulfill, because he always grants his Son's requests. The existence of varied denominations has nothing to do with this certain unity, definitely obtained in the "Spirit."[4]

"Spiritual" Unity

The scriptural presentation very strongly shows that we are one in the Spirit. Christian unity is seen as the gift of God rather than the fruit of our works. It also shows that it is essentially different from the administration centralization brought about in the economic and political realms. Paul is not afraid of repetition to emphasize it (Eph. 4:3, 4): the unification of all believers belongs to the real mission of the Holy Spirit. "One body" first depends on "one Spirit." The prayer of Jesus (John 17) goes in the same direction. It crowns the revelation of the Upper Room which above all announces the coming of the Comforter (or Advocate) when the mission of the Son will be fulfilled (John 14-16). This order of events invites us to understand that the unification which will follow the fulfillment of the work of Christ and the coming of the Spirit are one single event. Paul proclaims to the Corinthians, "For by one Spirit are we all baptized into one body." Earlier he showed them, in the enveloping of the Israelites by the cloud when they left Egypt, the type of their baptism in the Holy Spirit (I Cor. 10:2). As the cloud, a symbol of the mysterious (spiritual) presence of God, separated the children of Israel from the Egyptians and sealed their unity as people of God, so too does the Spirit work out the unity of the New Covenant people. At Pentecost, to which these verses refer, the sign of the speaking in tongues showed that God wanted, in his grace, to recreate that which had been destroyed at Babel, to gather together the dispersed members of a torn humanity. I will add to this point that in the development of the theme in Ephesians, Paul sees the parts of the body serving the unity, in the ministries which he elsewhere calls the gifts of the Holy Spirit (Eph. 4:11ff.; I Cor. 12:4, 5). Unity is most certainly, of the Spirit. And Christian experience echoes in witness. We know our unity when we feel the presence in the other believer of the same Spirit that lives in us. We thrill to the words of the Chinese martyr, Shu Yi, who named the "secret organization" tying all Christians together, "The Holy Spirit."[5]

The Trinitarian Pattern

It is in the Spirit that the Father and the Son from all eternity are one. Jesus explicitly considers the unity of the believers as the reflection, the analogy, of the trinitarian unity (John 17:11, 21, 22). Paul supports, in speaking of unity, one of the strongest trinitarian affirmations of the New Testament (Eph. 4:4-6).

It is possible to draw some consequences. If the pattern is trinitarian, the unity is not obtained to the detriment of the diversity, as though there were a tension between the two. The two themes closely intertwine without difficulty in the text, and even the repetition seven times (Eph. 4:4-6) of the word "one" can have a symbolic sense: a unity "harmoniously differentiated." The divine trinity is not only a pattern, but a foundation of that marriage of unity and diversity which holds under suspicion all enterprise of bureaucratic uniformity. Only the Trinity makes it possible to keep the One and the Multiple from struggling as two opposite principles. Many Christian thinkers have understood this point, from Tatian, apologist of the Syrian School of the second century, to Cornelius Van Til (of the Reformed School of Philadelphia). It establishes this paradoxical law which we observe in creation: the higher the position of a being in the existing hierarchy (from dust to man), the more its internal unity grows, as well as its differentiation.[6]

Yes, but...

The fact of unity in the Spirit, according to the pattern of and based on the trinitarian foundation, seems to favor the second conception of Christian unity. Should we adopt this concept without discussion? Let us not forget what it leaves somewhat in darkness: that the gift of God is to be kept, that is, cultivated (Eph. 4:3), that the invisible unity must be expressed in a visible way. Alas, a very evident contradiction can show up: some believers who are one, and will always be so, betray in their conduct that spiritual reality which sustains them. God is faithful, but the unfaithfulness of the Christians hinders "the effect of the fact," the action of the grace of God.

When Paul warns against the danger of divisions, he not only asks for a soft and patient attitude, he also brings up the official ministries in the church (Eph. 4:11) and the completeness of the doctrinal agreement (Eph. 4:13-14). "Evangelicals," haven't we fallen into an easy self-satisfaction when we have acclaimed our spiritual unity? The subtle temptation of any vast evangelical gathering is to conceal the sharp edges of the difficulties which have not been smoothed out, these elements of disunity which persist — and the problem of expression comes up again in a different way. How can we recognize the unique Spirit which should unite us? We have to try the spirits, and we must, by all means, avoid falling into confusion under the cover of unity; it would be like falling again into Babel under the cover of Pentecost! It could also be dangerous for a man to have confidence in his spontaneous feeling about this. The risk of a tragically false refusal exists. We all feel badly about Luther at Marburg when he judged that other remarkable man of God, the reformer Zwingli, as being prompted by another spirit.

One Hope

The association of the Spirit to Hope, leads us to the same thoughts (Eph. 4:4). It is constant in the New Testament. The gift of the Spirit was the promise for the "last days" (Acts 2:17). The Spirit is a Spirit of adoption, which makes us co-heirs with Christ, the seal upon us for the Day of Redemption, the down-payment or the first fruits of the inheritance to come (Romans 8:15ff, 23; II Cor. 1:22, 5:5; Eph. 1:13ff., 4:30, etc.) The miracles he accomplishes are "powers of the world to come" (Heb. 6:5), signs of redemption, yet to come, of the body.

This association delivers us from the temptation of a satisfied passivity. Our unity also is "in hope," the unity of walking together, the unity of the pilgrim people moving toward a unity at last perfectly expressed and which would take in everything. We are united to struggle and pray so that "the total unity will some day be restored." We know the biblical expression the "shalom" of the Kingdom! The earth will be filled with the knowledge of God like the bottom of the sea by the waters, and the gathering together of all things under the same Lord, Jesus Christ, when he is gloriously revealed.

But this association of the Spirit to our active hope of the end also brings us to the crucial question. "One hope" excludes all other hopes, solely human, that is, the various secularized messianisms, the despairs more or less made known, the courage of the absurdity, the mystical escape, or the anarchist fury. Should we not beware that some monstrous mixtures will arise under the cover of a language taken from the Scriptures? The rapidity with which the "theology of hope," preached so brilliantly by the German theologian Jurgen Moltmann, was transformed into a "theology of the revolution" (favorable to Marxism) should be a warning to us. On the other hand, what may be said of the differences of evangelicals on eschatological questions (on the doctrine of the Last Days)? Do not they break the unity of hope?

The crucial question concerns in fact the hope in its ties to *faith*. It concerns the Spirit in its fundamental relation to Christ and to his Word (I John 4:1-6). We can hope to answer it by considering the second part of Paul's summary, "one Lord, one faith, one baptism."

One Lord

The Spirit leads to Jesus Christ. He does not speak about himself, but glorifies the Son (John 16:13, 14). The second divine mission is dependent upon the first: the Spirit has only to apply the effects of the work of Christ. He unites us to the Head so that all his grace flows over the members of the body. His instrument, his "sword," is the Word, the intelligible discourse of Jesus and of his witnesses. (The Holy Spirit works *by* and *with* the Word, as Lutherans and Presbyterians, respectively, like to point out.) Thus the subjective experience of salvation is always founded, anchored, in objective truth. There is an idea abroad today which must be received with the utmost reserve. It holds that the Holy Spirit represents the alogical or paralogical aspect or pole of spiritual reality. This idea has its place in the theology of Emil Brunner, for example who, after having been attracted by the irrational thinking of Bergson, hooked his wagon to a moderate existentialism[7]. But such an idea does not appear in the biblical revelation concerning the Spirit, who is perfectly one with the Logos. The Apostle Paul contrasts the Holy Spirit's mode of action with that of the spirits of paganism, to the paralogical dynamic which carried the Corinthians away, out of control and without reflection, toward *dumb idols* (I Cor. 12:2). The Spirit is the Spirit of the Lord, he manifests himself by the sober, clear, intelligent confession: "Jesus is Lord."

Paul designates with equal sobriety the two great pillars of objectivity: "One faith, one baptism" (Eph. 4:5).

One faith

Most commentators understand clearly that Paul speaks of faith in the objective sense (that which one must believe: as according to the recent French ecumenical translation of the Bible). "One faith" evokes the great structure of truth which the apostles, evangelists, pastors, and doctors must communicate in order to assure unity in the teaching as against doctrinal instability (Eph. 4:11-14). It is "the model of doctrine" to which the believers had been committed (Rom. 6:17, literal translation), "the form of sound words" to be held faithfully (II Tim. 1:13) "the faith which was once delivered to the saints" (Jude 3), the truth which should "sanctify" the believers, setting them apart so that they may be one according to Jesus' prayer (John 17:17-19)[8]. No experience of unity, no matter how dynamic or exciting, can replace the unity of the faith. For the New Testament, all communion in the Spirit which lacks the dimension of beliefs (I have used this unpopular word on purpose!) absolutely must be examined with great care. It could turn out to be an illusion or false, perhaps even the work of other "spirits." With these biblical principles thus laid, without ambiguity, we face the most burning questions.

From the leaders of most of the churches, an almost unanimous chorus glorifies *doctrinal pluralism*. "It is the only one adapted to a pluralistic culture," we are told. Many claim a New Testament basis for this. They are following E. Kasemann and find irreconcilable traditions on every page. Pastor Louis Simon expressed it in typical fashion. "The diversity of convictions, of Christologies, of ecclesiologies, is in the very make-up of the Word of God[9]." When he says "diversity," the context shows that he means *opposition* and he exalts this opposition as the condition of life and liberty. At the same time, it is suggested that to demand a clear-cut statement of faith is almost pharisaical blasphemy: *blasphemy* because the mystery of God cannot be expressed in man's language; *pharisaical* because the orthodox judges the others from a dominating position and makes salvation dependent on an intellectual "accomplishment." One more step and chaos itself is in turn invited to sing the hymn to the liberty of God. Of God? More accurately of man!

To the pluralist discourse, we can only answer in the manner of Luther: we cannot, *non possumus*.

Diversity without conflict

All of this is contraband goods which they want to hide by flying the New Testament flag. Only a criticism subject to an apostate *a priori* finds contradictions in the apostolic testimony. It creates these contradictions by refusing to approach the text with a sympathetic outlook, and completely overlooks the obedience of faith. We certainly do recognize the diversity of the New Testament, and with joy! The language, the point of view, the key concepts change from one sacred author to another. But the striking thing to us is an unartificial harmony of teachings given so diversely. Its miraculous character leads us to confess: this is not the work of man. Thus, for example, we recognize the same truth when the synoptic Gospels speak about participation in the coming Kingdom, the Johannine writings about the new birth and receiving eternal life, and Paul about the resurrection with Christ and the new creation. This multiplicity of presentations helps us to a higher appreciation of the unique, same message.

To describe the concern for a clear-cut statement of faith as pharisaical shows both the lack of understanding of the pharisees' error and the lack of joy of being freed from the darkness of error, of being freely enlightened by the truth of the Word of God. The clear statement of faith is not a human accomplishment, but rather the effect of sanctification by truth, a work of God. Invoking the sublime mystery of God in order to refuse orthodoxy is to pronounce words filled with the authority of wisdom and godliness, but used, in fact, only to satisfy theological carnality (Col. 2:23). It is a pagan dualism between God and the language he created. But we proclaim that God has the power to reveal himself in the language of the man he created in his image. It is so easy to blame the incapacity of language. But, be careful, the Bible denounces lying as the basis of deformation. Thinking that liberty is real only in incoherence is to hold an entirely anti-Christian notion of liberty. This is going back to the old belief of pagan mythologies: out of chaos comes newness of life.

Facing error

If the biblical authors agree on one point, it is on their warnings against false teachers. Micah, Jeremiah, and Ezekiel fought false prophets. Paul, Peter, and John are agreed on this. Paul complains that believers too easily receive another gospel, another Jesus, an-

other spirit (Gal. 1:6; II Cor. 11:4). He demands that the faithful separate themselves from those who leave the teaching they have received
(Rom. 16:17). Peter is no more indulgent (II Peter 2). John seems the
most severe on this matter: you must not even greet those who deny
the doctrine of Christ (II John 9-11; I John; Rev. 2-3). No unity is
possible outside the one faith. Jesus himself said, "He that is not with
me is against me; and he that gathereth not with me scattereth abroad."

But he also said, "He that is not against us is for us" (Mark 9:40).
What do you say when two brothers who serve the same Lord in the
same spirit, differ in doctrinal questions which at least one qualifies
as a matter of faith?

Paul makes a clear difference between the fundamental agreement
necessary for two brothers to walk together, and the divergencies,
even among adult Christians, which should not restrain the expression
of Christian unity (Phil. 3:15). But this is not a complete solution. Was
Paul thinking of insignificant subjects, small details, or more important points?

The famous and well-balanced saying of Rupertus Meldenius, "On
the necessary points, unity; on the questionable points, liberty; in everything, love"[10], leaves no answer to the difficult question: what is included in the first category and what is included in the second? Among
those who quote the saying, we find the entire spread from strict
separatism to total laxity.

Our situation is not that of the early church. That is where the
difficulty arises. The New Testament does not provide many indications corresponding to our present problem. The physical presence of
the apostles, who were able to give a fully authoritative answer on the
doctrinal and practical questions which came up, left little room between obedient faith and open rebellion. The errors have also become
more and more subtle. In some situations even true Christians are
easily turned aside by erroneous words.

We should not disregard the work of the sixteenth and seventeenth
century theologians. Luther had already classified his article at Smal-
kalden (1537-38) in three categories, and Calvin speaks of two classes
(*Institutes* IV 1, 12).

The Lutherans have defined the fundamental articles of faith. These
are classified as primary and secondary (these may be ignored, but
cannot be denied without overturning faith). They also defined less
important articles, such as the anti-Christ.[11] The modern evangelicals,
however, often feel that the famous "theological fervor," typical of
those times, made them less tolerant than the Apostle Paul.

We will formulate some guidelines as a suggestion:

*The possibilities of expressing Christian unity are proportional to
the doctrinal agreement reached.* The fellowship and cooperation which
express unity have various stages and forms. They can be institutional,
permanent, frequent, occasional, exceptional; in worship, evangelism,
teaching, social work. Two ministers can feed the same flock, or join
on the same platform to protest against pornography. I suggest that we
draw several concentric circles on a paper. The inside circle could be
the one where Paul met the Philippians (Phil. 3:15); others would cor-

respond to a less complete agreement that would permit only looser associations.

We do not, therefore, follow those who only see the subject of unity as *everything* or *nothing*. We propose a "little by little" relationship, the strategy of the "flexible defense" rather than the massive retaliation-like atomic reprisals.

And we stand on the exhortation of Paul to the Thessalonians (II Thess. 3:14, 15). Without making differences between moral questions and dogmatic questions, the apostle prescribes discipline for any brother who disobeys the teaching while still considering him a brother. The decisive point is this: a brotherly attitude softens the blow of separation. In this way we define a situation of intermediary discipline, at some point between the judaisers on whom Paul pronounces a curse, and that of the Philippians with whom Paul walks in the same spirit. Paul measures the hardness of the separation to match the importance of the differences.

The revealed truth (always singular in the Bible) unfolds like an organism. Jesus himself teaches us this by stating the "heart" of the Old Testament, the two interdependent commandments on which stand all of the Law and the Prophets (Matt. 22:40) and also by vigorously emphasizing the differences in accusing the Pharisees (Matt. 23:23f). The way Paul reasons and discusses shows there are articles of faith with differing degrees of importance. Surely, since the truth is organically one, if it is denied on even a small point, it is by implication, denied. But since it is organically diversified, it is not permissible to emphasize to the extreme this logic of implication in order to separate from the brothers. Since it is the secondary nature of the differences that permit cooperation, and since this secondary nature is flexible, our rule of proportion stands.

Five criteria make it possible to evaluate the relative importance of a doctrinal question under discussion. Each person gives instinctively a factor of importance to the various doctrines he professes. But other factors, like the tendencies of personalities or the circumstances of education, are likely to deflect toward error such a spontaneous evaluation. It is necessary to utilize principles which are independent from the individual or denominational tendencies.

a. *The biblical criteria.* The place given to a subject in the Bible, especially in the New Testament, is an indication of the importance Jesus and the apostles attributed to it. Naturally, the importance of a doctrine cannot be measured by the number of verses which present it, but even that factor can be of help. The doctrine of the atonement is found throughout the Scriptures, as the blood is in the body — according to Vinet's image. It surely is of an altogether different importance than the prescription of a veil for the women, whatever interpretation is given to it since it is found only in one passage (I Cor. 11).

b. *The theological criteria.* The clearer the consequences, and the more they relate to the very center of evangelical truth, the more this point is of importance. There are strategic doctrines. If you touch one of them, everything falls. Others are on the periphery and one difference will leave the rest of the building standing. The factor of theological analysis was the favorite factor of orthodox theologians of the seventeenth century. It is that factor that Paul was using at the time of the Galatian crisis. Whosoever demands more than faith in order to be accepted by God, makes the death of Jesus Christ logically unnecessary (Gal. 2:21). The doctrine of circumcision was strategic. But on the other hand, it should be noted that Reformed people like Hodge and Baptists like Spurgeon had, basically, the same theology, except for the doctrine of the visible church and infant baptism[12]. This doctrine is thus less central.

c. *The practical criteria.* It is also necessary to analyze the consequences on a practical as well as a theological basis. What are the implications for the organization of the church, spiritual life, the methods, and the message of evangelism? Some practical differences seem tied to a doctrinal point, while, in reality, other hidden factors (sociological, personal, etc.) produce them. The matter of infant baptism, which is not central from the theological standpoint, has important practical consequences. On the other hand, the Monothelite controversy, which puts Christology in the balance, may not create a lot of upsets in the practical life of a church.

d. *The historical criteria.* In order to deliver us from the narrowness of our personal horizons, there are no better and more precious helpers than our brothers and fathers in the faith. They have not been infallible, but we must respect and appreciate the wisdom God gave them and profit from it. We always run the risk of using the irony of Paul: "What? came the word of God out from you? or came it unto you only?" (I Cor. 14:36). Thus we can discover that throughout the history of the church, until the nineteenth century, Christians have decided against division in connection with the millennium. The oldest pre-millenialist declaration, after the apostolic period, is the one of Justin Martyr around A.D. 150. It underlines the fact that many Christians, having a pure and pious faith, had another opinion.[13] Would it be wise to be more intolerant than he was? He has been followed in his brotherly attitude by most of the Christian generations. It is quite different with the doctrine of Holy Communion, about which division arose. Rightly or wrongly, the question carried much weight.

e. *The contemporary criteria.* God has given such clarity to his Word that the essentials of the message cannot be hidden to the respectful and wise reader. Where men of God, scientifically capable and professing to be obedient to the Scriptures, find themselves heavily numbered on both sides of a discussion, we can conclude that the object of the discussion does not belong to the vital heart of Christianity. For example, the view of the intermediary state we see as biblical is opposed by some evangelical theologians. We judge by this that it is of a secondary nature.

With the help of these criteria, we could trace a big circle, of first importance, corresponding to the dogma of the divinity of Christ and the incarnation. There would be no fellowship with those who would be outside, with those who break down the doctrine of Christ. Another very important circle, inside the first, would be the authority of the Scriptures, the written Word of God, without fault or contradiction.

This doctrine is strategic. With those true brethren who do deny this position of Christian orthodoxy we can only envisage an occasional or exceptional cooperation. Total ecclesiastic fellowship, an even smaller circle, requires a minimum of agreement in ecclesiology. Two other examples may be given. The great discussion of Calvinism and of Arminianism does not stir up an unimportant question. Its importance may in fact justify a few regroupings. On the contrary, differences in eschatological matters, among those who firmly believe in the personal return of the Lord "to judge the quick and dead," should not hinder a full expression of Christian unity.

Christians ought to consider as abnormal their differences in matters of faith, even secondary ones. The weight of history often makes us fall from sheer discouragement. We then comfort ourselves with a "spiritual" notion of unity which is a far cry from the New Testament pattern. With a high degree of determination and the help of all ministries we must move with all our energies toward unity of faith and of knowledge, to the maturity of the full stature of Jesus Christ (Eph. 4:13).

Let us not confuse customs, language, or style of presentation with faith. The Bible sometimes demands separation, more or less severe, for doctrinal reasons. It forbids it for any other. But we too often let these other reasons deprive us of the expression of unity. We all tend to give to the expression of faith the value of faith itself. The Bible is very little concerned — so little we are amazed to realize it — with the external form of prayer, to the atmosphere and to the emotional flavor of Christian experience. It does not seem interested in the rigidity or the freedom of liturgical order (even though it condemns disorder) (I Cor. 14) or of the number of "oh's" and "ah's." The preferences in this realm are not illegitimate. Our sensitivity is us. It is only "natural" that they play a role in the liberty of expressions of Christian unity. But true unity will be supernatural! It is evident that we all need to learn the price of diversity.

However, the liberty we enjoy as to the forms does not mean that all external signs are left to our little individual or collective ideas. The Christianity of the New Testament is built upon a second pillar of objectivity: the unity of order, after the one of truth. To use Paul's expression, after "one faith, one baptism."

One Baptism

Without doubt, the apostle is referring here to the Christian water baptism, a public witness joined to a confession of faith (Rom. 10:9, 10). "In Jesus' name" is an expression with a commercial touch, implying that the baptized is brought to the Lord's accounting, as one of his personal properties (cf. I Peter 3:21). We can stand in wonder at the fact that baptism appears in the list of the seven realities through or in which Christians are one. Doesn't this lead us to exalt it beyond what is just? Isn't Paul giving a warning against such an exaltation when he points out the fact that Christ did not send him to baptize but to preach the Gospel, which message alone God used for the salvation of believers (I Cor. 1:17). As for me — and I am Baptist — the application of the very five factors cited above leads to the following conclusion, regarding the differences of opinion evangelicals have about the method, the subject, and the meaning of the baptism of water. We are to give medium importance to this complicated problem, neither fundamental nor marginal; second without being secondary. How can we explain the place of baptism in Ephesians 4:5?

Would water baptism establish Christian unity? Many, through the influence of the great Catholic tradition, would like to relate the unity of "all the baptized" (an expression not found in the New Testament!) with the causative efficacy of the rite, which is supposed to *confer* the Spirit, at least when it finds faith. This interpretation, for me, is excluded: it confuses water baptism with baptism of the Spirit. We shall leave to one side the theological arguments that Reformed theologians like Auguste Lecerf masterfully developed[14]. It will be enough to notice that the confusion of both baptisms neglects the clear distinction of both in the story of Cornelius (Acts 10, 11). It is the Lord who baptizes in the Spirit. His disciples baptize in water. No confusion is permitted between the two; there is no dependence of the first on the second[15].

When Paul outlines "one baptism," he is using, we believe, a figure of speech close to synecdoche: baptism is *the part for the whole*. The doorway to the visible church, the first institution of Jesus Christ for his community, baptism represents the whole of the ecclesiastical order.

In the economy of grace, "faith" is not the only objective structure; our subjective experience of the Spirit is linked to the life of a definite "society," a society with its rules and rites, its discipline and leaders, in charge of exercising discipline. "One baptism" means that the true, entire expression of our unity cannot leave aside the ecclesiastical order no matter how painful this reminder might be for us.

Paul's epistles and the rest of the New Testament forbid the neglect of this part of Christianity. The main official ministries are presented to the Ephesians (4:11). They play the role of the joints of the body (verse 16). The little tableau in the book of Acts describing the life of the primitive church, often mentions the activity of the apostles and of their assistants in this realm (Acts 2, 6, 15, etc.) As long as the evangelical Christians do not reach a common comprehension about the ministries, something will be lacking in the expression of their unity. And the same must be said of baptism, this time considered for itself, and about the Lord's Supper. Without speaking about inter-communion in the manner of certain people, we cannot deny that brothers who are not able to sit down openly at the same table, are not living the fullness of their brotherhood. As evangelical Christians, we do not have these problems of orders, the great divisions that have torn Christendom apart, but we do not have the right to feel satisfied with mere partial agreement, "forgetting" the various elements the New Testament wants us to experience together!

Among the ministries, there are some in which more than one local community is interested. In addition to the apostles, without successors, one can quote the case of Apollos. It reminds us that the unity of all churches, according to the biblical concept, should also become strong — by a public witness, appearing in an *ordered* manner. The Scripture imposes no form to this presence, but we do see Paul very concerned about obtaining the hand of fellowship from the apostles of Jerusalem so that his "course" as an evangelist might not be in vain (Gal. 2), and his collection for the poor in Jerusalem (II Cor. 8, 9) might be a demonstration of solidarity for all members of the body of Christ. In the interests of world evangelism, which involves all of us *together,* should we be thinking of other ordered expressions of our unity beyond this very meeting in Lausanne? Some permanent expression?

One God and Father

The Apostle Paul in his letter to the Ephesians did not conclude his summary with the two expressions that so strongly push us into progress toward unity: "One faith, one baptism." And we should do well to follow him. Here, as elsewhere, (I Cor. 3:23, 11:3) his theocentric emphasis is: "One God and Father" (Eph. 4:6). Unpleasant as it could be to some modern theologians who hate the "metaphysical" which contrasts with the eclipse of the Father in today's thinking, the New Testament is theocentric.

It protects us from a subtle temptation, that of re-establishing *man* in the center under the pretext of Christo-centrism or Spirito-centrism, that of falling back again in anthropo-centrism while we pretend to be concerned with spiritual experience, healthy doctrine, or correct order. In the unity of God, all unity gets its roots. From the sovereign grace of God proceed all the positives of salvation, objective and subjective. For the glory of God, the Spirit's working operates in us, as the Lord Christ's work avails for us.

In Eph. 4:6, the clause that concerns the Father is of trinitarian structure: *"above all"* corresponds to the Father; *"among all"* to the Son, who lives with us until the end of the world; *"in all"* to the Spirit who makes us temples of God by living in us. Here the Trinity is summed up from the standpoint of the Father who sends the Son and the Spirit. This way we more clearly see the unity and plurality without tension in the divinity. So we see how the two main lines of objectivity and of subjectivity must stay distinct and wholly joined — under the predominant thought of the Trinity and to the praise of the Fatherly purpose of grace.

The consequence is eminently practical. Most of us are heirs of the Reformation, which found again the objective economy of the revelation and of the redemption, and heirs of the pietist and revivalist traditions, which emphasized the subjective work of the Spirit. If we are ready to complement each other and to correct each other, it is while fighting for a total trinitarian Christianity that we will learn to express better our unity in the Spirit of Christ, to draw closer to each other on all questions of faith and ecclesiastical order, to walk more freely together to propagate the Gospel. To the glory alone of God, the Father, Son, and Holy Spirit.

[1] Cf. Vernon Mortenson of Wheaton (1966). "Missions and Evangelical Unity," *The Mission of the Church in the World,* (Harold Lindsell, ed.; French translation, 1968), pp. 189 ff; Rene de Visme Williamson, "Negative thoughts about Ecumenism," *Christianity Today* XX (August 30, 1968) p. 1131.

[2] Amsterdam Congress (1971). See the official volume, *Evangelism Alert*, 1972, p. 163.

[3] This is Barthian. Cf. K. Barth, Dogmatics IV, IXXX, pp. 36-38.

[4] Cf..Goran Janzon, *Les Evangeliques anglais devant le Conseil (Ecumenique des Eglises: Essai d'analyse des attitudes et des arguments*, (thesis presented at the Indpendent, Evangelical Seminary, Vaux sur Seine, France, 1973).

[5] Cited by Y. Congar, "Unite, Diversite et Divisions," *Sainte Eglise*, 1963, p. 111.

[6] Ff. H. de Lubac, *Catholicisme, les aspects sociaux du dogme*, 1947, p. 285.

[7] Brunner ties the Spirit to the "paralogical" in *Das Missvertandnis des Kirche*, 1951, pp. 47 ff; cf. p. 165; with force in his *Dogmatique*, vol. III, 1967, pp. 29 ff.

[8] Klass Runia, Reformation Today, 1968, pp. 56 ff., shows clearly that the question here is doctrinal truth as well as personal truth. His entire book treats thoroughly the subject of this expose. Its reading is strongly recommended.

[9] "Le scandale de l'Unité" in *Parole et Dogmatique, hommage à Jean Bosc*, 1971, p. 230.

[10] Cf. Philip Schaff, *History of the Christian Church*, Vol. VII, 1910; reprinted 1965, pp. 650 ff, and Y. Congar op. cit. p. 118.

[11] R. D. Preus, *The Theology of Post-Reformation Lutherianism*, 1970, pp. 148 ff.

[12] Heinrich Heppe, *Die Dogmatik der evangelish-reformierten Kirche*, 1935, pp. 34-36.

[13] *Dialogue avec Tryphon*, 80.

[14] A. Lecerf, "Le Soli Deo Gloria et L'efficacite des sacrement," Bulletin de la Societe Calviniste No. 44 (December 1940); "Des moyens de la Grace, Notes dogmatiques II," *Revue Reformee*, No. 22 (1955/2).

[15] When Paul says "one baptism," of course he does not exclude this distinction. For the Spirit, the New Testament does not use the substantive "baptism" but only the verb "to baptize," and this is from a stylistic point of view, a metaphor. Against a causative conception of baptism, we refer to two powerful demonstrations, Karl Barth's Testament, Dogmatique IV/4, 1961, and to this exegetic masterpiece: J.D.G. Dunn's thesis *Baptism in the Holy Spirit*, 1970.

THE NATURE OF BIBLICAL UNITY
Henri Blocher

Your criticisms were valuable beyond even my anticipations! Never before have I had such an experience; I have found it enriching — and, in several instances, quite moving. Many thanks in the Lord! And now, I feel perturbed, for I am about to disappoint you who have encouraged me. Time permits me to touch only on a small number of the points which you raised.

I will not attempt to deliver to you a shortened version of this exposition, for it already needs to be condensed. I would simply remind you, that its theme is *biblical foundations* rather than the *means of application*, and that its correct title is: "Our Christian unity according to the Bible." Without neglecting the central issues of this Congress, the exposition deals with the theme of *Christian unity as expounded in the New Testament.* This is but one stone in the edifice of this Congress. I believe that it is preferable to place one stone carefully rather than to try to construct a whole wall too quickly.

In fact, I believe that we must come to grips with the difficulties of the subject and with elements that might generate discussion amongst us. It is for this that the exposition does not develop the theme of love, which is the cement of our unity, nor the clause "one Lord." As to the principle in these cases, I am sure that we all agree. It is in coming to the practical aspects that we all confess our insufficiency.

1. *Ephesians 4 and the trinitarian model*

The Apostle Paul's passage on Christian unity, in the fourth chapter of the letter to the Ephesians, enables one to consider the difficulties from a viewpoint that is in itself biblical. This text, which is more structured, more concise, and at times more precise than the high priestly prayer of Jesus, is less often a subject of meditation. I have thus proposed that we examine it. I must, however, make one confession: I hesitated in my choice because of the formula "only one baptism," since I foresaw the possibility of a controversy as a result of its commentary. But I was convicted: I was not to be any more cautious than Paul, any more cautious than the Holy Spirit!

Too often, as evangelical Christians, we cover the shame of our differences with Noah's coat. We sing, "We are one in the Spirit" — and it's sincere, it's true, and it's necessary. But we forget the equally necessary biblical emphasis on the *expression* of unity and on agreement in thought and deed. We prudently leave a number of tabooed questions to the side; such prudence is not of the Holy Spirit!

We will return to the question of baptism, but first I would like to comment on the first of the seven affirmations of unity (or unicity) in Paul's summary: "only one body," the body of Christ (Ephesians 4:4). My exposition does not treat it in any particular paragraph; for essentially the exposition is, in its entirety, but a development of the clause "only one body." These words signify Christian unity; and the following six affirmations remind one of its bases and aspects. I will, however, add three remarks on the choice of these words and of the image of the body. These remarks will support the content of the whole passage.

First, the body is the prime example of *unity within diversity* or of *diversity within unity*. Paul emphasizes it to the Corinthians in his remarks on spiritual gifts (I Corinthians 12). Second, the notion of "body" entails that of *visibility* — a body can be seen. If our unity is that of a single body, it will not be able to remain invisible. Finally, the church is a body, the body of Christ — and specifically in the sense of a bride, just as the woman is the body of her husband.

Paul uses the image of this thought, as can be seen in the next chapter of the epistle to the Ephesians (5:25 and following); and, as a Dutch Benedictine monk, Dom Paul Andriessen, has demonstrated throughout all the epistles, the church is not the body of Christ as if she were the extension or prolongation of the Christ in a sort of mystical fusion, but rather in the clear relationship of *alliance*. The church is the body of Christ as the community of those who believe in him, who obey him, who love him because he first loved them, and who purify themselves in the hope of his return. If such is the union of the body of the church to her Head, then the union of Christians in the unity of the body, which is dependent upon it, will manifest similar characteristics: faith, obedience, hope, and love.

The model of alliance is not the only one which helps us to understand the nature of Christian unity. By its trinitarian construction, Paul's condensed formula, "only one Spirit, only one Lord, only one God and Father," invites us to consider a yet higher model — that of the Divine Being himself: only one God, but in an eternal differentiation of Father, Son, and Holy Spirit. The high priestly prayer clearly expresses this. Jesus asks: "That they be one as we are one." Notice the adverb "as"! There is an analogy to the trinitarian unity and — more specifically in John 17 — to the unity of the Father and the Son.

In what way are the Father and the Son one? Saint Augustine demonstrated that the Father and the Son are eternally one in the Spirit. He called it the knot of love of the Father and the love of the Son. This thought has a sound biblical foundation. The Holy Spirit is both the Spirit of the Father and the Spirit of the Son. He, the third Person, bears a name that designates the Trinity as a whole. God is Spirit. The final vision in Revelation symbolically represents it as a river of living water running out from the throne of God the Father *and of* the Lamb; this underscores their unity. It is the very same Spirit that unites us, thus reflecting through the work of grace the union of the Father and the Son.

The union of the Father and the Son in the Spirit does not alter their distinctiveness. They are not merged: being one, they remain several. This is the second point that must be emphasized and which man's natural thinking has no small difficulty in understanding! Indeed, in creation itself, the more one ascends the ladder of beings, the more one finds unity and distinctiveness. A horse, for example, is characterized by more unity than a mass of rock, and, *at the same time,* has a far richer internal differentiation or diversity. This is an invitation to conceive of the highest unity as also the most differential.

But natural human thinking remains deaf to this message. Man's thinking introduces an opposition between unity on the one hand and diversity on the other — and thus makes them incompatible. One can see this in many religions and philosophies of the East and the West. Whence does this fatal tendency arise? The natural thinking of man — of fallen man — does not listen to the Word of the living God, of God the Creator of the world. Man's thinking begins with the world; and, in order to make its gods, it absolutizes elements or aspects of the world. However, *in the world*, even if unity and diversity increase together on the ladder of beings, they can never be found to the absolute degree — thus absolutely linked. Unity and diversity are often disassociated in the world. The kind of unity that meets the eye (poor unity) excludes diversity. Natural thinking, which absolutizes these aspects of the world, fatally turns unity and diversity into two opposed principles. Biblical thinking alone — liberated by the living God from the bondage of "world elements" — invites us to conceive of a unity which comprises in itself the richest diversity.

The question is not of interest to philosophers and speculative theologians alone. The choice of the model of unity influences the whole of cultural life! As for myself, I understood the scope of application of the trinitarian model about fifteen years ago after reading an article in a military publication on Islamic society. Torn between unity and diversity, natural man appears to be condemned to vacillate incessantly between individualistic monarchism and oppressive dictatorship, between monolithic totalitarianism and disintegration.

The modernist theologians of our day preach doctrinal *pluralism* and contend that they find it in the New Testament. Their idea is that diversity destroys unity. In their view, James contradicts Paul, John contradicts Mark. This is the total disintegration of biblical witness. We affirm, on the contrary, a diversity within unity, differences of approach of viewpoints of language, of procedure — but without conflict. Compare Paul and the author of Hebrews: their example is to the point. They speak of the Old Testament in significantly different but perfectly complementary ways. So the unity that we must maintain is of the same kind as the internal unity of the New Testament, which seeks to let the same truth spread, taking in the diversity of our temperament, of our gifts, and of our situations.

The trinitarian model enables us to notice another complementary fundamental. The exposition will deal with it in its conclusion. In the diversity of trinitarian roles, the *objective* work was the *Son's:* revelation and redemption, the teaching of truth, the expiation in our place. The *subjective* work is the mission of the *Spirit:* regeneration and sanctification, opening of the heart to the truth of the Son, and transformation unto likeness. The emphasis of the Reformation was on the *objectivity of grace;* and this emphasis remains in larger churches that came out of the Reformation to the degree in which they did not forsake their heritage. On the other hand, the *subjective* work has been of more interest to the pietistic, revivalistic, and — dare I add — "charismatic" tradition. A unilateral and exclusive emphasis, as we know, leads to heresy. We can now see that it upsets the equilibrium of the "trinitarian model," and we understand perhaps how this model can help if we keep it constantly before us.

2. *Only one baptism*

Perhaps it is because the question of baptism is related to the great duality of the evangelical heritage that it was so frequently mentioned in your remarks. I must therefore deal with this question, although I am about to walk on eggs. The Lord, I hope, will enable me to do so — he who allowed Peter to walk on water!

I made clear that "only one baptism" signified here "the baptism of water." Many of you wrote to me suggesting rather the baptism of the Holy Spirit! Unfortunately, I cannot agree with this. I have consulted all the knowledgeable commentaries on the epistle to the Ephesians in the library of our department — and not one chose that interpretation. I do not believe that the fact is to be explained only on the basis of the poverty of our library. Indeed, I do not bow down before the specialists as before an infallible arbiter! But there is a fundamental reason for their choice in this case, and it seems to me to be decisive. It is only the *verb* "to baptize" that is used at times in a metaphorical sense for the effusion of the Spirit; the *noun* "baptism," is never used in this way. It designates baptism by water. Even Dr. James Dunn, who exceeds all others in including "in the Holy Spirit," recognizes this when finding the verb "to baptize."

Others of you said: "There is but one baptism, both of water and of Spirit." Without using a demonstration that others use very well, I will say that it is a strong conviction on my part that Scripture distinguishes and teaches us to distinguish. Even if we argue that the clear separation in the case of Cornelius is an exception, Scripture proves at least *two* realities: the ritual of water given by men, and the work of the Lord who pours out the Spirit. These two do not constitute a pure and simple identity. On this, I believe we can all agree. The real problem is the relationship *between the two.* I do not wish to upset my Lutheran brethren or those who think as they. I do not wish to convey the feeling that I am capitalizing on my privilege as a speaker to engage in baptistic propaganda. I will leave for some other time the exposition of concepts I hold as true. Luther would give assent to a proposition which satisfies me and which will express the common core of our baptismal doctrines: the work of salvation and the communication of the Spirit — within or without baptism — is only operated through the agency of the Word of God accepted in faith.

I must comment a little more on the place of the baptism of water, "only one baptism" in the epistle to the Ephesians. The Apostle Paul, who said, "It is not to baptize that the Christ sent me" (I Cor. 1:17), certainly did not make the ritual of water in and of itself a fundamental principle of Christian unity. The commentators are themselves at times perplexed. I do not deny that "only one faith" and "only one baptism" can be taken to apply to the subjective aspect of salvation. After having mentioned the "one Lord," Paul could refer to the adhesion to the Lord in *only one faith,* the common trust that ties us to him; *only one baptism,* the confession and the committal of this faith. In this case, the word "baptism" would refer to the spiritual reality that the ritual signifies — such as it does in a most clear fashion in the first letter of Peter (3:21).

This interpretation does not seem to me to be the best in this case. The comments of the Apostle himself in verses 13 and following show that he is thinking of faith in the objective sense — faith transmitted once and for all, faith as the structure of truth and model of doctrine. In its subjective sense, faith often varies; and even if one does not take one's weaknesses into account, how many differences can be seen both synchronically and diachronically! It is more straightforward to say "only one faith" when referring to the faith: those-things-which-we-believe.

"Only one baptism" must then likewise refer to the objective side of Christian unity. I suggest that we see in this a stylistic phrase which is not contrived or far-fetched; a stylistic phrase which designates a part for the whole. Paul says "only one baptism," but he is thinking of the whole of the *ecclesiastical order* of which baptism is the first institution. If a political leader, in order to promote national unity, proclaims, "Only one head, only one justice, only one school, only one sword," it can be readily understood that "sword" represents the whole of the national defense, both as symbol and as element. Likewise, "school" means more than a school; "school" here encompasses all forms of education and of cultural molding. The function of the word "baptism" in Paul's language is analogous to that of the word "school" or "sword" in the political oration. The reign of the one and only Lord upon his church is carried out through the existence of an order, of rules and rituals for our life in common, of disciplines and official ministries. That this is, in fact, the Apostle's thought is confirmed to us through his comments, since he deals with ministries in the church — distributed in the harmonious measure of Christ's gifts and purposed to allow the orderly growth of the whole body.

If this order, represented by baptism, is of such importance to Paul, what are we to say of our divergencies, in view of what he says? Or in view of such-and-such a paragraph of the Confession of Faith? "Only one baptism" — is it not painfully ironic in the situation that made my previous remarks necessary? Must I deny any unity between my Lutheran brethren and myself if I hold that their baptism is not that of Scripture? Must they do the same? The problem of baptism could synecdochically be to us the totality of that which separates us as Lutherans, Anglicans, Reformed, Baptists, Mennonites, Pentecostals, Plymouth Brethren, Quakers.

3. *The rule of proportion*

The answer that I recommend begins by the refusal of all-or-nothing type solutions. Indeed, our differences concerning baptism, for example, are not *"nothing."* These differences reduce the possibilities that we have to express our Christian unity. But they do not destroy *everything.* They do not oblige me to treat my brothers of another persuasion as if they were antichrists or as if they were false teachers not to be greeted. The rule of proportion must be observed.

To justify this rule — and especially to apply it — is no easy task. Our present situation is no longer that of the early church, where most divergencies required an all-or-nothing discussion.

Indeed, we still experience and know all too well the kind of divisions found in the church at Corinth, engendered by carnal motives —

born of pride and jealousy, of fear and foolishness — often aggravated by misunderstandings.

In these cases, the division is sin; repentance must restore the *whole* communion. Of course, it is still true nowadays that certain scandalous sins demand, on the contrary, a rigorous separation — as the separation from the incestuous (I Cor. 5:11). But I speak not of such examples of division: they are clear, too clear! One has to simply obey.

Our delicate problem is that of divergencies of a doctrinal or ecclesiastical order between true brothers. Two sincere Christians, who have a mutual esteem, come to incompatible convictions as a result of reading the Bible. Such a situation was rarely found in New Testament times, yet such a situation is the central problem in the existence of several Christian confessions or denominations. The diversity of administrative structures, the variety of labels, is not that which bothers me; even carnal motives, which historically played a role, can be placed before God in repentance. But the lack of agreement in matters of faith and obedience is another matter. It is because of my conscience that I cannot be a Lutheran and that a Lutheran brother can not be a Baptist; and the New Testament does not give me any very explicit instructions as to what has to be done.

Before the Lord, a certain separation appears to me both as an evil reality and as an inevitable obligation. I am unable to comfort myself hastily in saying, "I am in the Spirit with my Lutheran brethren," for this unity is only expressed in a multilated form — for it is not quite "an only faith" and "an only baptism." I cannot say, "Let's forget all this; what is important are our actions, our lives — not theology." For we are sanctified through truth (Jesus said "truth" before saying "life"), and Paul calls us to the unity of full knowledge *(epignosis)* and not that of ignorance (verse 13)! I may not claim that the questions which divide us are unimportant, but neither may I treat my brother as a pagan or a publican: he is my brother!

Each of us must witness to and live the truth of Scripture as he or she sees it; and yet we cannot be infinitely divided!

Paul comes to help in two passages. He shows clearly to the Philippians that secondary divergencies must not keep us from walking together. We must continue to fight and to pray for a better understanding. But division is not necessary; and, hence, is not permissible. But what when the questions — although not primary ones — are neither secondary ones? The second epistle to the Thessalonians lays down the principles of a *moderate and mitigated* separation. This deviation from the apostolic tradition is sanctified, but brotherhood must not be forgotten.

This principle is our rule of proportion. It applies, of course, in many different ways according to the instance. The greatest discussion will bear on the *scale* we are to use. Who is to decide if a question is an essential one, a secondary one, or a major or minor one? Who will assess its degree of importance?

I have proposed five criteria and would like to make two fundamental remarks on their use. First, they are not a recipe which automatically gives the answer to the problem; nothing replaces loyalty, humility, and prayer. How are these criteria to help us? The object is less to *determine* the importance of a point than to *discipline* our groping research. The criteria are there mainly to protect us against the snares of subjectivity; to keep us from taking our personal inclinations and intuitions for the voice of the Holy Spirit — and that we might escape the narrowness of our tradition, of the culture of our age.

It is through the combination of criteria that we will approach exactitude with a margin of possible error. Implicit in the proposition I am making, particularly in the first and in the last two criteria, there is the conviction in the *clarity* of Scripture, which is amply manifest and which will keep us not too far from the truth.

It is perhaps not a bad thing that time fails me to comment on each criterion and on the results at which it enables one to arrive. Our common work must begin in the construction of a common scale, through careful thought of our agreements and differences.

Conclusion

The suggestion I wished to make in developing the question of my exposition — over a possible lengthening of this Congress — has been integrated into a project that we will all discuss, which is now submitted for your consideration. This also applies to the outline of a bold and wise proclamation.

Together, we could also define a code of good manners — a framework of obligation for evangelical collaboration. There should be some simple rules that all would respect and automatically conform to. This could help us to avoid irritations and would soothe many wounds.

I hope I have conformed to such a framework in the way in which I have spoken to you. Otherwise, please forgive me.

In the practical application of biblical principles of unity, the emphasis should also be upon biblical teaching and theology. In this respect, I should like to recommend the manifesto of a group of international students from Trinity Theological Seminary, near Chicago. One must also encourage such movements as the International Fellowship of Evangelical Students, who are pioneers in biblical unity in evangelization.

Let us remember that the essential thing, which is the most effective in the long run, is the *changing of mentality*. First we must be deeply convinced of the truth of these verses in Ephesians. God desires us to express more perfectly the unity already given to us by the Son in the Spirit without in any way lessening our love of the truth. We must will as he wills, in spite of our differences — and, at the same time, specifically acknowledge these differences. This is an urgent matter.

Too often, as evangelical Christians, we have majored on minor differences — at the same time confusing the truly essential with the secondary. Others, however, in order to be involved with the world, have abondoned our one and only foundation.

Today our witness must be one of discernment, immovably grounded on the basic affirmations of the faith — in a wise and sober appreciation of other questions, together with brotherly assistance, with respect and esteem one of the other, and with a sincere desire to make progress. May the Lord help us to do this. Then our task will not appear as sectarian proselytization; our working together will not run the risk of falling into modern confusion. But the unity of our witness will be for the spread of the Gospel throughout the world.

THE CROSS AND WORLD EVANGELIZATION

Festo Kivengere

"Man," the upward-looking one, became a creature in dilemma when he lost his bearings (his compass direction). This tragic experience happened when the upward-looking one turned away from the direction of life and became the downward-looking one, or the "inward-looking one." Away from the "life-direction" he turned to "death-direction." Away from light he turned to darkness. Away from the center he became eccentric. No wonder the inspired record described man in this state as "lost"!

Life fell apart — the world became *strange and hostile,* man's fellowman became *a threatening stranger.* Circumstances went out of his control. He lost the ability to cope with himself, his circumstances and his neighbor. An uncomfortable awareness of emptiness — sometimes less felt, sometimes more acutely felt, but increasingly crippling — dogged his life.

His life has, since this experience commonly called "The Fall," always been lived in the midst of conflicting pulls:

1) The upward pull towards the original ideal;
2) The downward pull towards deterioration into the base kind of living of slavery to violent appetites and passions;
3) The outward pull towards things and people against him;
4) The inward pull towards his own likes, feelings and ambitions.

The cry of his heart seems always to have been, "Oh, for a balanced existence in the midst of these great pulls!" It is into these life-breaking contradictions that *God, in Christ,* came. For man in such conflicts was destroying himself. Therefore, God took up the rescue in his self-sacrificing love! "God was personally present in Christ, bringing this hostile world of men back into friendship with himself," says St. Paul (II Cor. 5:19). Thus as he was baptized in the river Jordan among sinners — sinless as he was — refusing to be counted apart from those he came to rescue, so God's Good News, which is Jesus Christ, with out-stretched arms in a mighty embrace, lay hold of our broken lives on *the cross* and its almighty act of love, condemned the hostility to death, releasing the captives.

So the Cross of Christ became God's almighty salvation for us sinners:

a) *In its divine origin* — ending our despair of ever reaching God through our futile man-made endeavors to goodness and providing the fresh and life-giving way to fellowship with God (Gal. 4:4, 5);

b) *In its downward reach* — getting beyond the very roots of our depravity and helplessness, thus dealing with our deepest need of moral dilapidation and releasing the cripples;

c) *In its inward penetration* — replacing our wrong center which made us *self-centered* — by the new and right center — Christ, who makes us "Christ-centered," and so rescues *us from our inner fragmentation. The Cross brings inner wholeness.*

d) *In its outward outreach* — removing the conflicting elements in our relationship with our fellowmen as well as our world as a whole.

Here, then, is the centrality, the all-roundness, the cruciality of the Cross (the self-sacrificing love of God in Christ) — in the sharing of God's Good News with his world (in evangelism).

Let us now look at the Cross in its practical aspect in evangelism:

1. *The Cross is the message of evangelism.* There is no Christian faith without the Cross. Christianity was born *on the Cross.* It was the love on the Cross of Calvary that broke down all the barriers of *cultural, national, racial* and *intellectual pride;* which stifled religious aspirations with their (anthropocentric) *humanistic* polarizations.

a) The Cross spells out the desperate moral need of man. Nothing less than the love that God demonstrated in Christ on the Cross could have come anywhere near to meeting our deep-seated *guilt.* And any so-called "good news" which does not reach this shuddering need of our moral insolvency is not worthy of the name. Nor is any evangelism which does not deal with this universal human malady worthy of the name. The Cross primarily deals with human moral guilt, and divine judgment over it and his forgiveness. The Cross is, therefore, the message of *Good News* to all men everywhere.

b) The Cross spells out how seriously God dealt with our sin. It is the price love paid to remove the tragic estrangement our sin had brought between us and God and between us and our fellow

2. *The Cross is the motivating power of evangelism.* It is the light shed from the Cross that scales fall from our eyes and we begin to see the wonder of his incredible redeeming love and the utter wretchedness of our sinfulness. In the Cross, for the first time, we see the reality of the wholeness of Jesus Christ for undone humanity, we see in this "whole Christ" on our behalf, for our well-being, as P.T. Forsyth puts it, "full judgment, indeed, there, but the grace uppermost, as he bears in himself his own judgment on us." (Person and Place of Christ, page 74).

As the Holy Spirit illumines this great act of divine love "for us," the dawn of the glorious hope rises upon the whole human race with healing in its wings! In the rays of this redeeming love we see as never before that God has removed the once impenetrable barrier in our way of approach to him, and now he forgives us upon what he has borne for our sins on the Cross! Through the Cross we have free entry into an open presence of God! Thus the Cross becomes *the motivating power in evangelism.* All are welcome. There is no too-far-gone case in the light of this tremendous love! In the midst of *chaos, tumult,* and *philosophies of despair,* and sad divisions among professing Christians, we can lift our voices still, and point to the only place of healing — to the Cross. God was present in Christ removing the polarizing barriers between us and him and bringing us into friendship with himself (and with each other).

3. *The Cross is the inspiration of evangelism.* The Cross is the flesh and bones, the heart-beat of evangelism; divert from this vital pulse and, inevitably what remains of evangelism is a dry exercise in neatly-put, but lifeless, statements of faith; devoid of power to heal broken lives and broken relationships. We may be as morally upright as the elder

brother who never "disobeyed a single order" from his father and yet was completely out of tune with his father's attitude towards his returning brother! Here, I would like to pause and plead with you all as well as myself to re-examine our attitude towards our brothers and sisters whom we regard as being outside the pale of the evangelical camp. Are you in tune with the Father's attitude towards those outside your own conviction? Are we as uncompromising in love as we are in criticism of those "for whom Christ died"; outside our own circle of conviction? St. Paul makes a penetrating statement under the inspiring power of the Cross in his second letter to the Corinthians, chapter 5:21, "God (in his incredible love for us) treated Christ as sin, who knew no sin, for us sinners that we may be brought into right relationship with God through him." If this is what God went through to bring us into right relationship with himself, then we are left no room, no choice for any aloof attitude towards any of his children! There is no justification whatsoever for any other attitude than that of the love he demonstrated on Calvary's Cross for the world. Evangelism flowed direct from the Cross towards those who were in the very act of crucifying the Lord, to desperate criminals crucified with him! The Cross inspires evangelism and there is no other inspiration for evangelism besides.

4. *The Cross — the price of evangelism.* According to biblical record, the Good News became a living, practical reality for us men when he who was equal with God "emptied himself" of all glory in order to come and share our humanness. It cost him his life to reach us in our misery. According to the prophet of evangelism, Isaiah, "He has poured out his soul unto death . . . He was counted as a sinner among sinners." And as James Denney clearly puts it in his book, *The Death of Christ,* "The regenerating power of forgiveness depends upon its cost." The Cross spells out in shining letters that there was no limit to which God could not go in his redeeming love. The challenge that grips the whole life as one sees the extent of what God was willing to undergo on our behalf on Calvary, is so penetrating that all values are evaluated, the whole outlook is changed and most of all, what we regarded as sacrifice becomes humbling privilege. This is what filled Isaac Watts' heart with wonder and praise as he sang:

> "Were the whole realm of nature mine
> That were an offering far too small
> Love so amazing so divine
> Demands my soul, my life, my all."

This is what St. Paul meant when in the light of impending danger to his life, he burst out, "But life is worth nothing unless I use it for doing the work of telling others the Good News about God's mighty kindness and love" (Acts 20:24).

St. Paul's words echo those of the Lord who actually hung on the Cross, before he was crucified, "I have a terrible baptism ahead of me, and how I am pent up until it is accomplished" (Luke 12:50).

This is the only way we can look at our lives . . . our possessions, our gifts, our status and abilities in the light of the Cross in evangelism. Any witness who evades this price is out of focus with the Cross, and falls short of the target of evangelism. We must re-examine our priorities in evangelism in the light of the Cross. May the Lord spare us the deadening tendency of resting in neat, evangelical clichés, in sheltering in secure fences round our lovely cliques, by the power of his liberating Cross. Then we, as his disciples shall stand where the Master stood and then all we are and have will flow in gratitude to him, and in service to the world he died to save.

Can we still withhold anything in the light of the Cross, and still claim to follow him?

"Love so amazing, so divine,
Demands my soul, my life, my all!"

5. *The Cross is the uniting power of evangelism.* Only through the constraining vision of Christ and him crucified can the Christian church repent of its unfortunate weakening divisions and dividedness in its ranks, the wastage of its man-power, and the corroding hoarding of its material means. We need to catch a fresh vision of our Lord's words: "He who spares — loses" but "He who lets go — gains" and the commentary of these words seems to me to come from St. Paul's words in Rom. 8:32, "He did not spare even his own Son but instead of sparing him he gave him up on our behalf." This is the right attitude of those of us who have looked at the Cross, towards the material means available for us in this ministry. The Cross is where there can never be any justification for the *"hoarding attitude,"* the *"sparing attitude,"* the *"withholding attitude."* This sparing attitude does not apply to money and buildings only, but it covers persons as well. It is our physical lives which are to be offered as a living sacrifice to God. There is a tragic practice among those of us who desire to further the cause of evangelism to hoard gifts in our denominational ghettos, while open fields go on starving for good teaching and preaching. There are wealthy pockets of the Christian community who are unaware of needy areas where good men have no facilities for training for preaching the good news. May the Holy Spirit so inspire our spirits with the consuming vision of "He did not spare even his own Son," during this Congress that we shall leave here under the compelling vision of God's love in Christ for the world as we see it *in the Cross.*

6. *The Cross is the drawing power of evangelism.* It is the Lord Jesus himself who drew the attention of his bewildered disciples at the end of his physical ministry — as it is recorded in John's Gospel (12:32), ". . . When I am lifted up (on the cross) above the earth, I will draw all men to me." No matter what methods we may use in sharing the Good News with men, still the drawing power is the Cross of Christ. It is Christ, the one crucified, who wins rebellious lives, melts stony hearts, brings life to the dead, and inspires stagnant lives into unsparing activity. It is the crucified who makes us see the world *alive with need for forgiveness.* It is the crucified who crosses out our fancies and introduces us to the inestimable value of people. It is the crucified Christ who destroys our prejudiced evaluations of our fellowmen as racial cases, tribal specimens, social outcasts or aristocrats, sinful characters, and religious misfits, by giving us the fresh evaluation of all men as redeemable persons "on whose behalf Christ died." Evangelism fails miserably when its purpose becomes to draw men to its programs of preaching or social

concern. Men are to be drawn by the power of the self-sacrificing love of God in Christ into new life in him. The Cross gives flesh and bones to evangelism. It is in the Cross that the truth becomes incarnate and reaches us where we are and as we are. It is the Cross which encourages us to cross over the barriers of our particular camps to meet God's world. The Cross of Christ is the panacea for the deep troubles of the human race. It is the hope for my beloved country of Africa with all its conflicting problems. It is the panacea for the so-called richer nations of the West, with their disturbing disintegrations of lives in the midst of material plenty.

Christ, the one crucified, is the power and the wisdom of God in evangelism. The Holy Spirit uses the Cross to remove not only sin and guilt, but also the crippling effects of fear and suspicion. The Cross is God's liberating power in evangelism.

We can never speak about the Cross and remain immune! The revelation through the Cross brings all sorts of men into the focus of the soul! It is under such exposure that you may have to leave your religious exercise (sacrifice) on the altar and go first and be reconciled to your brother; and then come and continue your worship!

The Cross in evangelism forces us to go and wash our Judah's feet in ministering love. In conclusion, I plead that as we receive the bread and the cup we will open our hearts to the estranged brothers and sisters. That we will allow the Cross to lead us out of the spiritual ghettos of our security — to him — and as we go out to him we shall meet many who come to him from other camps and shall have fellowship with them round the Cross. Then the communion with him and with each other will be a life-liberating and satisfying experience, sparking off the fire of evangelism for which our churches are in desperate need. And our age is waiting for the redemption of God's children from the corroding influences of this world's powers of evil into the glorious liberty of the fullness of life in the New Kingdom of our Lord. Let us approach with boldness, and enter the presence of God through the Cross and enjoy fellowship with God and with each other; and by the power of the Holy Spirit proclaim God's good news to our age. "As for me — God forbid that I should boast about anything except the cross of our Lord Jesus Christ" (Gal. 6:14).

Section IV:
Public Meeting at Laustade

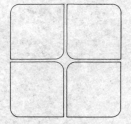

LAUSTADE '74 MESSAGE

Billy Graham

Greetings in the name of our Lord, Jesus Christ. I'm delighted to be back in Lausanne when the sun is shining. The last time I came to visit in this stadium and to preach in this stadium, it was pouring rain. The weather changes faster in Lausanne than any place I've ever been, I think. I left my room this morning and it was very cold, like wintertime. I have three suits with me; one is for warm weather, one is for cold weather, one is for medium. I decided to take the cold weather suit and here it is, summertime again. But it is wonderful to be in this city. As you've already heard, there are nearly 4,000 people behind us here from 150 countries of the world. Switzerland has a long history of interest in evangelism and missions. In the sixteenth century alone, there was one year when you sent 143 missionaries to other countries.

Lausanne is a wonderful city. I have been here now two weeks and it is one of the most hospitable, friendly cities I've ever been to. I've been riding back and forth on the metro. I have seen something you don't see very often anymore in the United States. I've seen men getting up and giving ladies seats. I notice that you say "please" and you say "thank you" in ordinary conversation. And you still have time to talk with friends in a sidewalk cafe. We in America are too busy.

I had an interesting experience the other day. I stopped to get some English newspapers at a newsstand. My wife and friend were in the car waiting for me outside. I got back in the car after my purchase. The lady from the newsstand came running out to the car and grabbed me by the arm. She said, "Are you an American or are you an Englishman?" I said, "I'm an American." She said, "Oh, I'm very happy. I've just won a bottle of whiskey. I was talking to my friend in the store. She said you were English. I said you were American. We had a bet."

There's another thing about this city that makes us from America stand in awe. It's called the "city of kings." So many royal people have chosen to live here. I noted yesterday downtown that you had cleared the streets and there were the markets. Thank you on behalf of all of us in this Congress for your hospitality and your friendship.

Now the Psalm that was just read a moment ago. I was going to preach a sermon on it, but we've already had three great sermons and I don't think you want to hear a fourth. So I'll only mention what I meant to say, but I want to explain how you today can make this same commitment to Jesus Christ. We have heard how a man from a Hindu background came to Christ. We've heard a former Buddhist who came to Christ. We've heard a man from Africa tell how he came out of paganism. How can you, in intellectual, sophisticated Switzerland come to the same Christ?

In the twenty-third Psalm there are three things that David, the Psalmist, touches on. He was a ruler in war and in peace. At this moment there's fighting in Southern Europe, in Cyprus. We do not know where it is going to lead. The armies of the world are beginning to marshal. Bombs are being put in airplanes. This is how the first world war started, how the second world war started. It is our prayer today that this will not be the third world war. I'm going to ask that we all stand and have a moment of prayer for peace. Let us have a moment of silence. Pray for the people of Cyprus; pray for the people of Turkey and Greece; pray for the people who are the diplomats of the world, that God will move upon them to have peace instead of war. Amen.

David was the great king of ancient Israel. He had been a great warrior. He was also a great king in peace. One night he was sitting out under the stars thinking and he mentioned in this Psalm the three greatest problems the world has ever faced. He wrote this thousands of years ago but it applies to you and me today.

First, he said, "He restores my soul." The Bible teaches that you have a soul. You have a body, but living inside your body is your soul, or your spirit. That is the part of you that is made in the image of God. It is the part of you that has the ability to contact God. We have in America what we call "soul music." I asked a black American friend one day, "What do you mean by 'soul'?" He said, "Everything that is worthwhile in a man is soul." Now you have a soul. Every person in this stadium has a soul. Now the Bible teaches something has happened to your soul or your spirit that affects every phase of your life. It teaches that we were made in the image of God and we were made perfect. Man lived in a perfect world, in utopia. There was no suffering, no starvation, no war, no hatred, no death; a perfect world. But something happened. Man rebelled against the Creator and that rebellion is called "sin" in the Bible. Sin infected the entire human race. It affected your soul, it affected your body, it affected the way your intellect works, and it caused death to come upon the whole human race. So that's why we find men all over the world groping for God.

Sin has caused alienation from God. And we are under judgment. The Bible says, "It is appointed unto men once to die and after that the judgment." So in India, in Africa, in China, the Soviet Union, in America, in Switzerland, there are millions and millions of people searching for God and there are thousands of students today that are searching for purpose and meaning in life. This is why the suicide rate in most of the world is climbing dramatically. Young people are not finding the peace, assurance, joy satisfaction, and fulfillment that they are searching for. They need their souls restored. David said, "He restores my soul."

How does God restore your soul? God looked down upon the human race. From the moon, we saw the earth when the men walking on the moon took pictures. The earth looked no bigger than my thumb, taken from the moon. The Bible says, "God so loved the world." That's what makes this world in the universe so important. That's what makes you as an individual so important. God loves you! God loves you so much that he decided to save you. You were alienated from God, separated from God, in the bondage of sin, filled with guilt, searching for a way out. Jean-Paul Sarte says there is no way out. Many of the modern philosophers say there's no way out. God says, "There is a way out. I have provided a way." What is that way? "God so loved the world that he gave his son, Jesus Christ." It is incredible, almost unbelievable, that the mighty God of creation would himself, in the person of his Son, come to this earth, and that is exactly what he did. Jesus Christ came to this earth. He made the blind see, he made the deaf to hear, he had compassion upon the poor, but that is not why he came. He came not only to serve, but he came to die.

Look at the Catholic churches of Switzerland. Look at the Protestant churches. They all have a cross. Why? Because the Cross is the heart of Christianity. On the Cross the Lord, Jesus Christ died for you. You see, because of sin there is judgment. God says, "You have broken the law. You deserve death. You deserve judgment. You are under condemnation." On the Cross Jesus Christ took the death, the judgment and the condemnation. The Bible says that God laid on him the sins of us all. You're a sinner under judgment. You're a lawbreaker under judgment.

Right here in Lausanne, we parked too long the other day in our car. We came back and there was a ticket on the windshield. That's happened three times. We're under condemnation. We have to pay the price. Whatever they say to pay, we pay. We broke the law. Now one time we only broke the law by just a few minutes, but it was enough to bring a fine. So we're learning that you can't break the law in Switzerland. You cannot break God's law. But you have! I have! I'm a sinner, a lawbreaker. What is the fine that I have to pay? Death, judgment, hell. We've broken God's law. But Jesus Christ went to prison for us; he went to judgment for us; he paid the fine for us. They put nails in his hands, they put a crown of thorns on his brow, they put spikes in his feet. He hung on the Cross. He could have come down from the Cross. He refused. He stayed there because he loved you and he loved me. He took my sins. Now God says, "Because he died, because he paid the price, I will forgive you. But more than that, I will justify you." Justification means far more than forgiveness. Suppose you offend me. I may forgive you but I cannot forget. God forgives but he also forgets. God has the ability to forget your sins, and God can justify you just as though you'd never committed a sin. That's what the Cross is all about; Jesus Christ did not stay on the Cross; he was raised from the dead and today he is a living Christ and a coming Christ. There is a kingdom yet to come. Peace is going to come to the world. The kingdom of God shall some day prevail. Christ will come back. He will set up his kingdom and you and I that have believed and trusted in him will be members of that kingdom.

Has your soul been restored? Do you know Christ in your heart? Mao Tse-tung, the ruler of China, said, "My greatest concern for China is that the souls, not just the minds or the bodies or the emotions or the wills, but the souls of people be possessed by commitment." In America and in Europe we are putting a great deal of emphasis on the mind, the body, and the emotions by our materialism and all the other things. But what about our souls? Alexander Solzhenitsyn left the Soviet Union and came to Switzerland. He was protesting against the fact that Russia was caring more for the bodies and minds of her people than for their souls. This is the same problem in America. It's also the problem of Western Europe. We are too materialistic. We need our souls restored and that can only come through a personal commitment to Jesus Christ. Why can it only come through Christ? Why not through Buddha? At the end of his life, Buddha said, "I am still searching for truth." Jesus said, "I am the truth; I am the life. No man comes to the Father but by me." One time he said, "I am that I am." When he said that, he set himself apart from every other man that ever lived. Was he th Son of God? If he was not the Son of God, then he was the greatest liar in history or he was a mental case. And you have to decide. You have to decide by faith. You cannot understand it all intellectually. Now the Gospel *is* intellectual. It appeals to the mind. It has great logic but in that first step when you come to Christ, you may be a professor at the university or you may be just a simple worker, you have to become as a child and come in simple faith to Jesus Christ. The man from India, the man from Japan, the man from Africa all had to come by simple childlike faith and say, "I believe." When they did that, their lives were changed. Their sins were forgiven. A new life came to them and that same Gospel is available to you today, free. David said, "He restores my soul." Has your soul been restored?

The second thing David said was, "I shall not want." We live in a world filled with problems of poverty, race, and pollution. But your personal problems concern you even more. Boredom — one of the great psychologists in Switzerland recently said that boredom is the greatest problem in Europe. Another problem, guilt. One of your great psychiatrists wrote a book entitled *Guilt and Grace.* He stresses the terrible and tormenting thing that guilt is and he says only God can get rid of the guilt. Loneliness — you can be in a crowd, at a party, everybody laughing and talking. All of a sudden there is a bit of loneliness that sweeps over you. Psychologists are calling it "cosmic loneliness." What are you lonely for? Lonely for God. You were made for God and without God you cannot find fulfillment. Are you lonely that way? Many people turn to alcohol, drugs, sex, anything to escape. They say, "I want to get away. I want to run." So man is on the run, trying to escape these lonely feelings. You no longer need to run. You can come to Christ this afternoon.

The emptiness in life today is reflected in modern art, literature, philosophy, everywhere. There was a student at one of our great universities in America and she was crying for three days. They sent her to the university psychiatrist. He couldn't find out what was wrong. Finally her father came and she finally told her father. She said, "Father, I want something but I don't know what it is." God. She was searching for God. And that's why so many thousands of young people today are committing suicide all over the world. In America, in Europe, in Japan, the final escape seems to be suicide. But that is no escape. You can take a gun and blow into your head but you don't kill yourself. You only kill the body. Your soul goes out into eternity, still separated from God, still lonely, but it's too late. The Bible says, "There is a time to come to Christ." Have you come to Christ? Have you put your faith and your confidence in Him?

And then the last thing David said, "Yea, though I walk through the valley of the shadow of death, I will fear no evil." The greatest crisis that you will ever have to face is the day that you die. And you're going to die. Now all of us hate war but I'm going to say something that will shock you. An English professor at Oxford University, C.S. Lewis, said this, "War does not increase death. Death is total in every generation and death is the result of sin." Some day, the Bible teaches, God will give us a new body. But when you face that greatest crisis and you have to walk through that valley alone (no one else can go with you), if you are in Christ, he's there. He is your shepherd. He is the good shepherd leading the sheep. When General Eisenhower was dying, he sent for a clergy friend of his and he said to the pastor, "Would you tell me once again how I can be sure?" The pastor took out his Testament, showed him exactly how it came to be that Christ died for our sins, held the hand of the great American and had a prayer. When he left, the former president of the United States had a big smile on his face and he said, "I'm sure." Are you sure? Are you certain? It could happen to you.

There is a girl here this afternoon. She is a nurse in Niger, Africa. She was born and until she was fourteen years of age she lived in the German part of Switzerland. She came to the French part of Switzerland when she was fourteen. She felt lonely. She also had a disease of the lungs. She cried herself to sleep at night. One night in the middle of the night she called upon Christ. She said, "Oh, Christ, come into my heart." Christ came into her heart. He took the tears and the loneliness away. Later she saw a map of Africa. She said, "I will give my life to Christ in Africa." She's there giving out bread and also the bread of life.

Do you know Christ? You can today. You say, "Well, what do I have to do?" Three things. Listen! First, you must repent of your sins. You say, "Well, what is that?" That means that you change, change your thinking, change your attitude toward God, determine to make Christ first in your life as Lord and Savior, be willing to change your whole life-style, your whole way of living. That's repentance. Have you repented? You say, "But I'm a member of the church." There are thousands of people that are in the church today that have never truly repented. I was in a Reformed church when I came to Christ. I was head of the young people's society. The clergyman thought that I was the finest Christian among the young people, but he didn't know me very well. He didn't know the hunger of my heart. He did not know the sins of my life. When I was seventeen years of age I gave my life to Christ and he changed me as he did these three men. Most of you that are here today are more like me than you are like them. Many of you are in the church but you don't know Christ.

The second thing; by faith you must receive Christ. By faith! "But as many as received him, to them gave he power to become the sons of God, even to them that believe on his name." You say, "Well, intellectually I would say I suppose I believe." But faith means more than that. It means your total commitment, your total life, everything given over to Jesus Christ.

The third thing; you must be willing to obey Christ and follow Christ, even though when you go home and tell your parents and friends that you came to Christ, they may kick you and beat you. You must be willing. "Oh but my friends or my parents would never treat me the way they did Dr. Hatori. They may think that I'm a little strange or a little different, but they would treat me with great kindness." But many of your friends would look at you very strangely. They see you carrying a Bible, reading the Bible, studying the Bible, praying, going with Christian groups. They'd see a great change beginning to take place in your life. Then there would be a certain type of psychological persecution. Jesus said, "You have to be willing to deny self and take up the cross and follow me." Then after you come to Christ, you serve Christ by doing all the good deeds you can and getting involved in all the social things that you can to help your fellowman. But first there must be that step and Jesus said you must do it publicly. He said, "If you're not willing to confess me before men, I'll not confess you before my Father which is in heaven." That's one of the reasons I ask people to come forward and make a public commitment of their faith in Jesus Christ. If you really mean business, you don't mind who knows or who sees. That is what I'm going to ask you to do this afternoon.

Now let me warn you about one thing. Don't put it off. Do it now. When will we ever see another moment like this in Lausanne? Right now God is speaking to your heart. There's a little voice inside you that says, "You need this Christ." That's the voice of God. Come and receive him today, now. The Swiss are the watchmakers of the world. You are called the timekeepers of the world, and this is your time with God. What a tragedy if you help make or sell a watch but you miss God's time. This is God's moment and God's time. The Bible says, "He that hardeneth his heart being often reproved, shall suddenly be cut off and there will be no remedy."

I'm going to ask hundreds of you to get up out of your seats, come on the track right in front of where you're sitting and say, "I want Christ in my heart today." A simple act, but very important. It could mean a new change in your life. I'm going to ask everyone to bow in prayer as people come. Just stand on the track around. People are already on the way. You come and join them.

TESTIMONY

K. N. Nambudripad

Good afternoon, friends. I wish to tell how the Lord Jesus saved me from sin and misery and gave me his peace and joy.

In 1959, I was a resident in neurosurgery in Bristol, England. I was lonely and shy. My wife and four children were far away in India. One evening in a cocktail party I was sipping orange juice. A Christian nurse who was also drinking orange juice came to me. In the conversation that ensued, she told me of Jesus Christ, her Savior. I argued with her and told her my Hindu religion was good enough for me. However, when I went back to my room I began to think about Jesus. As a twelve-year-old boy I had heard of Jesus; I had read about him, and I had been greatly attracted to Jesus as a man.

I began to read the Bible which was placed in my room by the Gideons. I was greatly affected by the new reading of this book. I was affected by its authority. I said to myself, "This is not at all like the Hindu books which I am used to. This sounds true. The writers have a real experience of God." I said, "John, who was a fisherman, had an experience of God which I, a Brahmin philosopher, did not have." I said, "I must too have this experience."

It is now fifteen years since that encounter and surrender happened. Many trials and tribulations and difficulties have been my lot. I was put in a psychiatric clinic by my people. I was given electric shock, but the Lord was constantly with me. The Bible became my living friend and reality. I praise his name!

Now my wife and children, who had left me, are back with me and they are Christians. Now depression has left me. I don't get depressed any longer. Jesus keeps me away from depression. I'm never lonely. Jesus is with me. When I operate, he helps me with wisdom and humility. When patients consult me with their tremendous problems, Jesus gives me compassion. Jesus has forgiven my sins; I have no guilt feelings; I can tell it to Jesus.

All the Hindu philosophy that I have learned is worthless when compared to the love of Jesus. I now get great joy in serving Jesus in Christian Medical College and Hospital, Ludhiana. And when I have free time, I witness in open air meetings to the blessed love of Jesus Christ. He has delivered me. He has saved me.

Thank you very much.

TESTIMONY

Akira Hatori

Can you see me? When I interpreted for Dr. Billy Graham in Tokyo in 1967, they elevated me one foot-and-a-half. This time, only eight inches.

Forty-some years ago I was a Buddhist. Being the firstborn of the family it was my duty to worship at the Buddhist altar every morning. I offered a bowl of freshly cooked rice and a glass of water and chanted before the altar. There was also a Shintu god shelf in my house. There were many paper gods there. There were many, many gods in my household but no joy, no happiness, no laughing, no communication because there wasn't Jesus in my house. We used to eat around the table, but there was no communication between the man and his wife or the parents and their children. No communication!

Some years back I had a telephone call after midnight. It was from Boston, U.S.A. "Are you Mr. Hatori?" the party said. "Please speak anything about Japan for five minutes. We are ready to broadcast you all over the United States." I had been in radio evangelism for twenty-three years. That was the first time for me to preach in pajamas.

This is the day of communication but we didn't have any communication of love between the parents and children in the family because there was no love, no Jesus. My father and mother used to fight against each other day and night, every day. As a young boy, I wondered, "What is life's purpose? What is life for? We are born alone, hate each other, fight against each other, discouraged and frustrated, and die alone. What is life's purpose?" I didn't know. As a sixteen-year-old boy, I was a boy with an empty heart. I hated God. I hated my parents. I was empty myself.

At that time, I was going to high school. There was a teacher who hated Christianity there. He used to say that Christianity is the enemy of Japan and the emperor. One morning he came to our classroom and said, "Are there any Christians in this classroom? Raise your hand. I'll fix you." I didn't expect anyone to raise his hand, of course. But one gentle, quiet boy stood up and said, "Teacher, I'm a Christian. I believe in the Lord, Jesus Christ who died for my sins and rose again for my righteousness." That short, but great testimony struck my heart very deep. We became very close friends because I wanted to know his heart's secret. Then he invited me to a country church. It was a rainy day, the first time for me to get into the Christian church. There I met a very large, old missionary lady. She was not too beautiful, but her love was as large as her body. She loved me and she communicated Jesus Christ to me so lovingly and kindly. She said to me, "Akira, murder, stealing, fornication — these are nothing but your sin. Inside you is a darkness which shuts out the God of creation, the God of salvation." She said, "Nothing can chase away the darkness but the light. Akira, open your heart and receive Jesus Christ as the light of the world. That light will chase your sins away and you will be a new creature today." By the grace of God I opened up my heart that night and received Jesus Christ as my own personal Savior.

And then this meek Miss Bennett, the lady missionary, said to me, "Akira, you go home tonight and you say to your father that you became a Christian tonight." I said, "Yes."

I went home, and all of a sudden, fear came upon me. My father was a stubborn man. He used to kick and beat his wife. He also hated Christianity, so before I entered the house I knelt down and I offered, for the first time, my own prayer, "God, help me." I went into the house to my father and said, "Daddy, I became a Christian tonight." He got angry and threw me down harshly on the floor because he knew judo. He took me by the neck and led me in front of the Buddhist altar and pushed me down and said, "Worship, worship." That was the first night that I became a Christian.

It wasn't easy. I went into the Japanese army and I was the only Christian there. Because I professed that I was a Christian, I was beaten, I was kicked, and I had a great many persecutions there. But I've never regretted that I became a Christian and received Jesus Christ as my Lord, because after I became a Christian, my mother, my sister, my father, and even my Communist brother became Christians. They all have the assurance of eternal life and I have a happy home; loving, singing together, reading the Bible together, praying together, and laughing together.

Also, I have a burning heart! I know what I am living for now. To live is Christ! To die is gain! I'm happy with Jesus Christ. I invite you to open your heart and receive the wonderful, loving Jesus, your Lord. Let me say I love you all here.

Thank you.

TESTIMONY

Festo Kivengere

I come from the land of the great sunshine of Africa, the land which historians gave the name, rather wrongly, of the dark continent. We have plenty of sunshine, but we have not received the "sonshine" of Jesus Christ.

I want to give the glory to him because he acted graciously in my life. I was born in a traditional non-Christian African home. My parents had never heard about Jesus Christ but my father was a very religious man. He worshiped God through the agents of the spirits of our dead ancestors. He was seeking after God like most Africans do. He was groping after him because we believe that the security of everything depends on him. Oh, but what a terrible thing when a seeker fails to find that which he is seeking for. I was raised under that atmosphere. Being the firstborn, my father introduced me into this worship very early. He taught me by example. He took me to the worship. We sacrificed together. And yet we never found that god. He remained a distant god — someone too far to help you when you need him. That is where I grew; seeking, never finding; thirsty, but without water; afraid, but without the truth.

Then light came through missionaries, and I want to praise God this afternoon for sending missionaries to Africa. I am not afraid to say that I am the product of missionaries. Bless them! They were compelled by the love of God from Germany, from Switzerland, from Britain, from all over, from America and they wanted to share the message with those for whom Christ died. The missionary who introduced me to the light of the Gospel was a black man so I came in contact with Christianity through a black face. I entered knowing but without actually finding. I knew about Jesus; I read about him; I appreciated his ethics, but I never met him. The living Christ of the New Testament I had not yet found. My knowledge increased my guilt. After eighteen years in Christianity, I became tired of Christianity, I became tired of missionaries, I became tired of church tradition because there was an area which needed to believe in Jesus Christ and it had not yet been touched.

Then there was an afternoon I shall never forget. You see, I came from the land of groping and I entered the land of knowing without finding. And it was during that time that I nearly committed suicide because of frustration. I had a good job, I was a young teacher, politically minded. But on this particular Sunday afternoon (and during that time, I was an agnostic) I was coming from a drinking party on a bicycle and I met a young African, a friend of mine, and he confronted me with a fresh experience of meeting Jesus Christ and it shook me. This young African was real; there was joy in his eyes. I felt he was alive and he told me why. "Jesus has come my way. My sins are forgiven," he said. Then he said, "I love you." We were on the road, not in a church because I no longer went to church those days. I went to my house after I visited him. I exposed my poor life to the love of God in Jesus Christ. I spoke from suffering. I presented my emptiness to the love which took Jesus to Calvary and in his amazing grace, I don't know how, he entered into the heart of that ene- my. He was not afraid of confusion. He entered in, realistically. He spoke and I understood. He touched my wounds. He lifted my burdens. He forgave my sins. He liberated me. I got off my knees. I ran, I jumped, I got excited! And I want to tell every African about it. I am an Anglican Bishop and we Anglican Bishops don't usually get excited. We are as careful as the Swiss people.

But now since he met me, I become excited because Jesus is wonder- ful and when he had liberated me, he sent me to an African whom I hated so that we might be reconciled. He was not a Christian but when I asked him to forgive me, he put his arms around me, and he who was my enemy became my friend. Then I went to another man, this time it was an English man. I had hated him. He was fifty miles away and the Lord said, "You hated that man, but I love him, and he's your brother." I protested, "How can he be my brother? He's white (or rather, he's pink) and I am black (if you like, I'm chocolate). How can he be my brother? He speaks English and I speak my mother tongue." Jesus said, "He's your brother. I died for him. I died for you. You hated your brother. Go to him. Cycle the fifty miles. Go to that man. Ask him to forgive you and tell him you love him." I went to his house. I found him there. I put my arms around him. I said, "I'm sorry. I hated you but now I'm free and I'm no longer suffering from the disease of hate. I love you. You're my brother." My, I was liberated! I left his house as if I had wings to fly.

Do you want to fly this evening? Welcome Jesus into your heart and life can never be the same.

Section V:
Evening Presentations

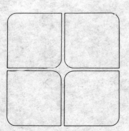

THE SUICIDE OF MAN

Harold Lindsell

*Dr. Lindsell, Washington, D.C., USA, is
Editor of Christianity Today.*

I will talk to you today about the death wish of mankind. To put it in another way, I think the world is in the process of committing suicide. I realize there are some people who are totally optimistic and others who are totally pessimistic. I must say that if you look at the world from one perspective you have reason to be optimistic. God is at work and great things are happening. Many people are being saved. But if you look at the world from the other perspective, the perspective of the world itself, you will quickly discover that the world is in the process of committing suicide.

You and I know that the world did commit suicide once before. It happened in the days of Noah. God judged the civilization of that day and all people on the earth died apart from eight souls who were rescued in the Ark. Civilization came to an end; mankind committed suicide.

I have here an excerpt from the *Saturday Review of Literature,* a well known American magazine. The editor, Norman Cousins, wrote about the Nigerian-Biafra war. He said: "No problem need any longer be considered insoluble. No one is going to believe any longer that we can sustain life on the moon but are unable to do it on earth." Henry Pitney Van Dusen, former president of Union Seminary in New York, a theological liberal of the optimistic variety, wrote a letter to the editor in response to Norman Cousins' observations. He said: "I know no one who faces the facts and has taken accurate measure of the manifold symptoms of profound, perhaps mortal, sickness in American society that still clings to such illusions. Denial of or blindness to the harsh reality merely aggravates the illness." Here is a former optimistic liberal who has become a pessimist. He no longer is optimistic. He no longer expects Utopia. Rather, he asks: Do we not have a mortal illness that will bring culture or civilization to an end?

Bertrand Russell, the atheist, said in his book *A Free Man's Worship:* "All the labor of the ages,...all the noonday brightness of human genius are destined to extinction in the vast death of the solar system, and the whole temple of man's achievement must inevitably be buried beneath the debris of a universe in ruins."

Listen to Ruben Alves from Latin America. For two years he was an associate professor at Union Seminary in New York. In the Spring 1974 *Union Seminary Quarterly Review* he wrote: "What is given, in our historical situation, does not make room for any sort of optimism. But I know, also, that without hope, man cannot survive...So I am stretched between the anthropological need for hope and the historical impossibility of hope...One thing I know for sure. In the business of living, one must not live by certainties..." So speaks a man who once was a Fundamentalist; who once believed in absolutes and entertained hope; who still yearns for love and justice but who says he does "not see grounds for justice and love to triumph in the world." This is his thinly-veiled invitation to universal despair and racial suicide.

I remind you that man can commit suicide in one of two ways. One way is to be in revolt against the creation itself. God the Creator is a moral being who has ordained that civilizations shall move according to the principles or laws which come to us from natural revelation. You can trace the rise of empires through history whether it be that of Egypt or Rome or some other nation. These cultures or civilizations flowered because they more or less obediently followed the revelation of God given in nature. But the time came when these cultures stubbornly revolted against the laws of God in natural revelation, and these cultures disappeared.

There is a second way man can commit suicide. He can cut himself off not simply from God's creation, but from God the Creator. It is my opinion that the unregenerate people of the world who are far more numerous than the saints of God, and the nations of the world, are committing suicide both ways. They are cutting themselves off from God's creation as it relates to his natural law. They are cutting themselves off from God the Creator as revealed in Jesus Christ his Son. You may well ask the question: "Why do you think the world is committing suicide?" Let me suggest some of the forms which this suicide or death wish of civilization takes.

First, man is committing ecological suicide. Every great city of the world has had its atmosphere contaminated. Tokyo, London, New York, and Moscow do not have pure air for their people to breathe. The overpopulating of the planet by human beings will soon leave us with standing room only. The effects of radiation through atomic explosions have been serious. The balance of nature has been destroyed, sometimes without intention, by the use of pesticides and other pollutants. Scientists have discovered that the South Pole has been contaminated from gasoline fumes in California and the use of DDT on American farms. Rachel Carson wrote a book called *The Silent Spring*. In it she forecast many of the unfortunate consequences of ecological imbalance which we are now seeing before our own eyes. The lakes of Switzerland, the rivers of India, even the oceans of all the world, have been raped and exploited. Death and decimation have come to marine life. The whale life in the oceans will shortly become extinct. Bird and animal life in many places around the globe faces devastation and eradication. The air we breathe, the water we drink, the food we eat, all attest man's unceasing quest for ecological suicide.

We are also committing scientific suicide. In the last thirty-five years we have more than doubled the knowledge that the world possessed in all of the preceding generations of man's history. At the rate we're going we will more than double or triple the knowledge of mankind by the end of this century. Learning and advancement, however, have not brought peace and security but peril and fear. The net effect of scientific advance has produced overkill. The nations of the world have a potential destructive capacity in nuclear energy so terrifying that if these weapons were to be delivered by intercontinental ballistic missiles or by air power, virtually all life on this planet would be destroyed. Indeed, we have chemicals, liquid and gaseous, some so noxious that a single drop on any part of a human body is fatal. Only a few years ago in the western part of the United States hundreds of sheep died accidentally when shifting winds spread gases that decimated all the sheep of the area. Many nations have a vast array of chemical and biological agents called germs. If the great powers ever decided to release this kind of destructive potential in warfare, the world as we know it could indeed come to an end. We're also unraveling the genetic code. Scientists tell us that the possibility exists for the creation, perhaps through cloning, of the true superman, a scientific monster with great brain power, with physical strength and powers, with great physical beauty, but with the moral stature of an idiot.

In the field of medicine, what the physicians have done almost defies description. Some of this knowledge has been very beneficial. We have reached the place where we have pain pills, sleeping pills, birth control pills, energy pills, pills to stunt growth, pills to produce growth, hormones for sexual potency as well as pills to control conduct. Ours is a world of pill therapy. We are in the age of curative medicine with heart transplants, kidney transplants, and the use of artificial organs. We have powerful drugs that knock out and cure pneumonia, stop syphilis, and get rid of gonorrhea. We have hallucinogenic drugs that are supposed to give meaning to life. We have pep pills and marijuana and acid so that we can take trips into outer mental space. We've extended life in a medical sense but we've offered nothing worth living for.

Sweden is regarded as the showcase for the welfare state, a paradise in which all men's earthly needs are cared for and guaranteed by the state. Instead of a paradise they have an alarming increase in juvenile crime, wide-spread alcoholism, increased drug addiction, a high suicide rate, and sexual aberrations, all at a time when church attendance flags and God has become less real. The welfare state neither there nor anywhere else has brought in the Kingdom.

See what science has done for war. Remember that the latest conflict between Arabs and Israelis provided an opportunity for the great powers of the world to test the efficiency of their most modern military hardware. The world *is* preparing, if you please, whether it knows it or not, for Armageddon. In Vietnam there is a very temporary truce. They are gathering their forces again to engage in another round of that conflict.

War between North and South Korea is likely to erupt in the not-too-distant future. On the borders that separate China from the Soviet Union great hosts of armed forces are balanced one against the other. In Latin America dictatorship after dictatorship has arisen, whether it be in Bolivia or in Chile, whether it be a dictatorship to the left or to the right. In South Africa black and white are poised one against the other. In the United Kingdom the Catholics and the Protestants in Ulster are at each other's throats.

Yes indeed, the nations are loading their guns, their knives are being sharpened, the planes are gathering on the runways, the bombs are poised waiting to be released. Make no mistake about it. All we need is one match to start the conflagration. All we need is one mistake of human judgment and a great military catastrophe will overtake the world.

Man is committing moral suicide. Within two-and-a-half blocks of my office in Washington there are more pornographic outlets than you are likely to find in any other major city around the world. Yes indeed we have pornography. We have sexual freedom. We have fornication, adultery, homosexuality, wife-swapping, rape, sodomy, incest, pandering, prostitution, voyeurism. You name it. We've got it. The movies and legitimate theater are sex-oriented. They concentrate on the abnormal and the illegitimate under the guise of freedom of expression. A new morality that is immorality under an undefined and contentless concept of love abounds around the world. Every man, every woman, is doing what is right in his own eyes.

We are also committing sociological suicide. In the United States one marriage in four will break up, or twenty-five percent of all marriages end in divorce. It used to be that the Roman Catholic Church was 'way behind the statistical averages because they have consistently taught that there is no divorce for any reason including adultery. But the turn of the tide, the trend of the times, is catching up with the Roman Catholic Church and even among this part of our population they have almost reached the national rate of one out of four divorces. In Italy divorce is now possible. Yes indeed, there has been a breakdown of the home. Young people no longer respect their parents. Our colleges and universities have been hotbeds of revolution. Whether it be Japan, Thailand, Brazil, Germany, Ireland, or Portugal, youth is on the march, flaunting their disrespect, disobedient to parents, denying the values that have traditionally undergirded family, community, and national life. Respect for law and peace is being destroyed; morality has been abandoned; crime has increased; drug addiction and alcoholism abound everywhere; the major cities around the world are in a state of decay; the rich nations are getting richer and the poor nations poorer. Society is becoming unglued.

The world is committing intellectual suicide. In our day the dialectic has overtaken Aristotelian logic. Aristotelian logic is based upon the law of antithesis. Francis Schaeffer has done a good piece of work at this point. He tells us that if A and B are opposites they are irreconcilable; they cannot be brought together. But the dialectic, as put forth by Hegel, picked up by Marx, and used in current society, argues that you can have a thesis and then you have an antithesis or the opposite of it. When the two opposites come together a new synthesis emerges. And this is logically irrational. It is biblically untrue.

We are committing intellectual suicide by creating nonpropositional versions of truth. At a time when science has stressed reason, religion and philosophy have abandoned it. All over the world men are saying that life itself is really meaningless. It is irrational. It doesn't make sense. Read the writings of Jean-Paul Sartre or Camus. Hear them say over and over and over again that there is no God and reason is folly. Thus atheistic existentialism does whatever it pleases because it doesn't make any difference. For them life is meaningless. One young college student speaking to this issue said: "When you are on the Titanic you might just as well go first class. The ship's going to sink anyway."

Men everywhere are committing theistic suicide too. Not many years ago the death of God theology swept through American universities and theological seminaries. For many, God is dead or irrelevant. God is denigrated by a homocentrism which places man at the center of life. Life for so many has become humanistic, and religion including Christianity has been relativized. Some say all men are religious by nature and all we need to do is synthesize the good elements in each religion to form a new and universal faith. This view undercuts the notion, traditional in Christianity, of special revelation. Many people have not accepted the Calvinistic doctrine of predestination, which teaches that God has sovereignly saved some people and passed by others. But today there are those who believe that all men will be saved and thus they embrace a far more rigid dogma of predestination since even those who don't want to be saved will be saved. Thus a noted theologian and philosopher in the liberal tradition, Paul Tillich, could make this statement. He said: "Even those who deny God are by that fact affirming God and are justified."

At the heart of theistic suicide lies the autonomy of man, man who thinks he is subject to no power outside of himself; who thinks he is a law unto himself; man who is the creator of his own absolutes, the judge and the jury of his own life.

Men and nations are committing suicide. This is a dark picture that I have painted.

In the midst of man's race with death, the tool he now uses is revolution. In one place it may be economic revolution; in another it may be social revolution; in another it may be political revolution; in another it may be religious revolution. Men by revolution think they will shatter the bonds that bind them. They hope for a better life with freedom and dignity. But they miss the true message that is to be found in revolution. The struggle is not a struggle between man and man or nation and nation. The real revolution is the warfare between God and Satan. It is the revolt of darkness against light. It is a warfare that is being fought in the whole cosmos, even in the unseen world far out beyond the sight of men or the hearing of their ears. The fallen angels of Satan are engaged in a titanic struggle against God and his holy angels.

The Word of God assures us of the doom of this present world and of sin and Satan. In II Peter, chapter 3, it says: "The heavens *shall* pass away. The elements *shall* melt with fervent heat. The earth *shall* be burned up." Yes, the seal of death is upon this earth. Nothing can save it. It must die before it can live again. The judgment has already been pronounced.

Thank God that the new is even to be found within the old. God's Kingdom is emerging in the midst of man's quest toward suicide. God has a people, and he is calling out this people for his name from among all the nations of the earth. His body the Church is being completed. The final holocaust is delayed until his purpose is fulfilled, his Gospel preached, and all nations reached with the Good News.

The door of the Ark still remains open. The hour is late but it is not too late. The restraining power of the Holy Spirit is being lifted and men when left to themselves become what men when left to themselves always become. It is only the Holy Spirit in common grace who holds things together. When his restraining power is lifted then all things will fall apart. In the Book of Hebrews, chapter 12, the Scripture says: "Indeed, so terrifying was the sight that Moses said, 'I tremble with fear.' But you have come to Mount Zion and to the city of the living God...See that you do not refuse him who is speaking. For if they did not escape when they refused him who warned them on earth, much less shall we escape if we reject him who warns us from heaven. His voice then shook the earth, but now he has promised, 'Yet once more I will shake not only the earth but also the heaven.' This phrase, 'Yet once more,' indicates the removal of what is shaken, as what has been made in order that what cannot be shaken may remain. Therefore let us be thankful for receiving a kingdom that cannot be shaken."

In the midst of a world that is committing suicide and of God's Kingdom that cannot be shaken, the Apostle Paul describes the characteristics of unregenerate men who move irresistibly toward suicide. He says that "in the last days there shall come times of stress, for men will be lovers of self, lovers of money, proud, arrogant, abusive, disobedient to their parents, ungrateful, unholy, inhuman, implacable, slanderers, profligates, fierce, haters of good, treacherous, reckless, swollen with conceit, lovers of pleasure rather than the love of God, holding the form of religion but denying the power of it. They will listen to anybody and can never arrive at the knowledge of the truth. These men oppose the truth, men of corrupt minds and counterfeit faith" (from II Timothy, chapter 3).

In the book of the Revelation there is the description of the Laodicean church which is an apostate church. As John writes of it he says, "For you say, I am rich, I have prospered, I need nothing." But the tragedy of this church was that it thought it was what it was not, and it is what it doesn't think it is. John concludes by saying: "You do not know that you are wretched and pitiable and poor and blind and naked."

In the Gospel according to Matthew, Jesus tells us that when unregenerate men come toward the end of their great desire to commit suicide, in that hour when multiplied wickedness has overtaken the earth, then the love of many believers shall wax cold. You cannot become cold unless first you have been hot. You cannot lose a love that you never had. Here then is the description of people who had love and heat, yet Jesus says that because wickedness is multiplied, most men's love will grow cold.

God still has a message for his people in the midst of this world that is proceeding apace toward suicide. You and I who love him are to occupy till he comes. We are his army and his disciples. We are expendable, for the world is on fire and we ourselves may be consumed in the burning. The night is coming when all of us who know Christ can work no more.

There is the sound of music in the air and two bands are playing. One is the music of death unto death and the other the music of life unto life. And the great cosmic question is, "To which music do you march? Which piper do you follow?" You know, I can hear the sound of music. I hear the marching feet. I see the glory light. I see a Cross on which is lifted up the Son of man. I hear a multitude singing from every tribe and nation and kindred and people and tongue. And they sing, oh how they sing; and this is the song that they sing: "Unto him that loved us, and washed us from our sins in his own blood and hath made us kings and priests unto God and his Father; to him be glory and dominion for ever and ever. Behold, he cometh with clouds, and every eye shall see him, and they also who pierced him, and all the kindreds of the earth shall wail because of him. Even so Amen." They sing, yea, they sing. How great is the music of their song as they sing. They say, "Mine eyes have seen the glory of the coming of the Lord. He is trampling out the vintage where the grapes of wrath are stored. He hath loosed the fateful lightning of his terrible swift sword. His truth is marching on. He has sounded forth the trumpet that shall never sound retreat. He is sifting out the hearts of men before his judgment seat. O, be swift my soul to answer him be jubilant my feet. Our God is marching on." We march with him in the hope of victory. We march with him for the salvation of men. We march with him because he calls to service. We march with him so long as one man still needs to hear the Gospel. We march because men must be saved from their suicide.

ACTS OF THE HOLY SPIRIT '74
W. Stanley Mooneyham

Dr. Mooneyham, Monrovia, California, is
President of World Vision International.

Narration (with slides): Since the beginning of time the earth has been a symbol of God's creative power. But for us here tonight in Lausanne, the earth symbolizes more than that initial creative act of an omnipotent God — it represents the circle of Christian faith as by the power of God men and women from every tongue, from every tribe, from every nation, have become one in the Spirit.

Introduction
Good evening, and welcome to the "Acts of the Holy Spirit '74." When closing his account of the life of Jesus, the Apostle John said the whole world could not contain the volumes if all the events in that miraculous life should be recorded.

The same could be said of the Acts of the Holy Spirit. While the book of Acts in our New Testament closes after chapter 28 with Paul in Rome, thousands of faithful servants of Jesus Christ have been writing church history with their lives, their witness, and their deaths. 1974 is no different except in one respect. Right now — as Jesus anticipated in Acts 1:8 when he said, "Ye shall be witnesses unto me, both in Jerusalem and in Judea, in Samaria, and unto the uttermost parts of the earth" — we *have* gone beyond Jerusalem, Judea, and Samaria. Tonight Christ has his witnesses at the ends of the earth. And their witness and their work bear the mark of supernatural power, for people are being confronted with the claims of the Gospel and many are being converted to Jesus Christ.

Tonight we want to share with you some of the things the Holy Spirit is doing. Without him, evangelism languishes and dies. It is he who is the great evangelist. It is *he* who lifts up Christ. It is *he* who empowers and blesses the witness of believers.

We will travel to some big cities and to some out-of-the way villages. We will meet a variety of people — some on the screen and some in person — each illustrating in his own way something of what the Holy Spirit is doing today. They do not think of themselves as being unusually talented or specially gifted. But through their lives they are having an extraordinary impact on the lives of others. Many of these people are here tonight. In fact, every single one of you, as you serve others in the name of Christ, is a part of the Acts of the Holy Spirit '74.

The world of youth
Narration (live): Within our world, there is another world. It is the world of young people. In some societies they make up as much as 65 per cent of the population. Young people are certainly important for the church tomorrow, but their talents, their strengths, their lives, are equally vital for the church today. To ignore our youth or overlook them simply because they are young is both foolish and dangerous.

In Asia alone there are more children than the combined populations of Europe and Africa. The church had better come up with a strategy and a commitment to accept, love, and evangelize these young people. Youth today are more free and more mobile than at any time in history. They are challenging established, long-cherished traditions in every area of life. We adults are sometimes frustrated and distressed by this, but it also means that youth around the world are more open to truth and eternal realities than ever before.

Everywhere I go in the world I see young lives being dramatically transformed. In some parts of the world the most dynamic segment of church life is found among the youth. The energy and commitment which these young people bring to the task of evangelism continues to remind the Church that God will not be frustrated by traditions which exclude them. God will have a witness.

For the next few minutes let's take a global look at God at work in the world of youth.

Narration (film): Music and young people are almost synonymous, and the Christian youth of Latin America are no exception. Whether in small performing groups or in large church choirs these youthful followers of Jesus Christ express their faith through song and instruments. They even take their music to the streets and challenge the cities and villages with the Good News.

But it is devotion to the Scriptures that ultimately guides the life and testimony of Latin American youth. These young Christians meet in small Bible study groups. Many invite their friends, and through these sessions the numbers confessing Christ increase more than ever before.

Narration (slides): In Africa, the Holy Spirit continues to stir the hearts of young people. More and more of Africa's most talented youth are accepting vocational opportunities within the church. Many are rejecting the more lucrative benefits of secular employment to place their talents in direct service to the church. Their youthful enthusiasm and dedication will become the legacy of tomorrow's leadership within the Church of Africa.

In some churches the young people prepare dramas and compose songs for the worship services. They lead in prayer and testify of their faith in Jesus Christ. Other young people observe their dedication and place of responsibility, and as a result are challenged to follow the way of Jesus. The Rev. Gottfried Osei-Mensah, pastor of the Nairobi Baptist Church, comments on the renewed interest in Christianity expressed by youth.

G. Osei-Mensah: I think as far as Africa is concerned, during the days when the national spirit was high we thought as soon independence was obtained from the colonial powers, everything would be smooth. I think the young people have seen over the last decade or so that this is in fact not so, and so they cannot find reality in nationalism. I think they are looking desperately elsewhere for reality and many in tropical Africa are looking to Christianity to find it.

Narration (slides and film): Last December in North America, 14,000 students attended the triennial Inter-Varsity Missions Convention. Five thousand of these young people expressed a desire to serve God in a missionary capacity. This response was five times greater than ever before. It reflects the growing commitment to world evangelism evident throughout the student population. Many authorities see the resurgence of evangelism among youth as a result of the Jesus Movement. The Rev. Chuck Smith is a pastor in California whose ministry has touched on the lives of thousands of young people. He reports on the continued growth of the Jesus Movement.

C. Smith: The Jesus Movement is really the wide acceptance by young people of Jesus Christ as their Lord and Savior and complete, total commitment to him. I believe this is a growing factor. They were seeing that materialism wasn't happiness. So they were saying that the answer must lie someplace else and they began searching for the answer. Apostles and evangelists of the drug culture came along and said, "Look, kids, here's where it is." But many began to see the discrepancies in the drug culture itself and found that drugs weren't really it. Then, of course, they were in a greater void than ever before. Jesus Christ and his teachings of where you can find love and a relationship with him were what they were looking for, and after finding him many became fantastic evangelists and began to share their faith openly. For instance, I anticipate that our next baptismal service will be the largest baptismal service we have ever had.

Narration (slides): A convention of Asian Christian students held a short time ago in the Philippines, indicates that students in Asia are accepting the evangelism mandate in a new and exciting way. Dr. Isabelo Magalit, Asian director of the International Fellowship of Evangelical Students, reports.

Dr. Magalit: We are seeing the beginnings of an Asian missionary movement and the clearest evidence of this has been the recent first Asian missionary convention in Baguio, held last December, when almost 800 young people from all over Asia came together. The majority were Filipinos, but almost 200 people were from a dozen other Asian countries. It is a very thrilling prospect and I believe that the convention has been used greatly by God, and all the feedback that we have received since the convention has been that there is a continuing work of the Holy Spirit in the lives of many young people.

Narration (film): All of us here this evening have a deep concern for the life of the Church in those nations which openly oppose the Gospel message. Yet we are convinced that the Spirit of God continues his work in spite of the most formidable obstacles. Even the censorship and rigid control maintained by a political ideology cannot restrain the growth of Christ's Church. Observe how the Jesus Movement has penetrated the borders of Eastern European countries, so that hundreds of young people under Communism are expressing their faith in public rallies. Even the great cultural revolution of China cannot stop the testimony of the Holy Spirit. David Wong interviews in Hong Kong a Chinese youth who found Christ in the Peoples' Republic of China.

D. Wong: This is Ah Kim. Just a few months ago Ah Kim and four of his friends risked their lives and swam across the deadly ocean between China and Hong Kong. Ah Kim was born in 1949, the same year the "new" China was born. Ah Kim experienced Communism and found his life empty. He found Communism could not satisfy him. Ah Kim found the Lord as his own personal Savior through an old, faithful Christian lady when he was sent to a commune. Ah Kim typifies many, many young people in China today. They are searching, they are longing, and they are seeking the truth that can satisfy them. Ah Kim found Christ as his own Savior in Mao's China. We praise God, for he himself has preserved his witnesses inside the mainland of China.

Narration (live): Ah Kim, like thousands of other young people around the world, reminds us that the search for truth can be fulfilled only in Jesus Christ. As the Holy Spirit invades these searching hearts, the growth of the Church continues.

What an exciting opportunity faces us as we follow the Holy Spirit out into the world of youth today.

Evangelism-in-depth

Narration (live): In the early 1960s, a new concept in evangelism was introduced in Latin America and it brought great blessing to the churches. The concept was called "evangelism-in-depth." It was an attempt to organize an entire country for evangelism and outreach. Churches cooperated in the training of laymen, in house-to-house visitation, in public marches and demonstrations for the Gospel, and in evangelistic crusades.

So important was this concept of in-depth evangelism in Latin America that it wasn't long until similar programs were launched in many places — New Life for All in Africa, City Penetration Plan in India, Sodoim Dendo in Japan, Evangelism Deep-and-Wide in South Vietnam, and Christ the Only Way Movement in the Philippines are but a few of these efforts.

Now, a decade later, Evangelism-in-Depth is pioneering again. The leadership of this movement evaluated both the successes and mistakes of the past. As a result, a new experiment has begun in Santiago, Chile. The original concept of evangelism-in-depth was for a one-year, pre-packaged program which was then applied to a local situation. It was often evident that a pre-packaged program not sufficiently anchored in the culture would fail to take root and grow.

At the heart of the new experimental program is a series of community studies which make it possible for the Christian leadership to develop a program based on a thorough understanding of all the local spiritual, social, and cultural factors. In other words, the evangelism program arises out of the social situation rather than being imposed on it.

After the community study is finished, the Christians come together in small "reflection groups" for serious study of the demands of Scripture in the light of their actual living situation. This confrontation of the Word of God with everyday realities forces each Christian to consider his own responsibility for personal spiritual renewal.

The third step is the formation and beginning of a program of evangelism which is truly relevant. It is a program the Christian community itself has helped to design, and therefore Christians are motivated to action.

The fourth phase of the experiment is consolidation. The purpose of this last phase is to make the program continuous and cyclical with the prayer and expectation that two things will happen: (i) The churches will experience continual renewal, and (ii) a life-changing experience will be produced in every believer.

Let me give you the four steps again: (i) community studies, to define the actual situation; (ii) reflection groups, to confront community and personal needs with the Word of God; (iii) action programs, to implement an evangelistic strategy defined by social situation, and (iv) consolidation, to make the program cyclical with continual revival in the churches and a definite life-changing experience for every believer being the result.

Now let's go to Santiago, Chile, for an on-the-scene report.

Narration (film): Santiago, capital of the Republic of Chile, is a city of great culture and sophistication. It is a city of workers, students, merchants.

In recent days, the winds of political change and unrest have swept through the country. At the same time, the non-violent breezes of a spiritual awakening have been stirring in the hearts of many Chileans to respond to the Christian message. A new experiment in in-depth evangelism has been initiated. The past year-and-a-half has been a time of building relationships, of training key Christian leaders, of community research to form a knowledge base on which to build a multi-faceted strategy and the beginning of "reflection" groups where people are confronted with the demands of the Scriptures.

Alberto Mottesi is director of Evangelism-in-Depth in Chile, and Jeff Myers talks to him about his ministry.

J. Myers: Brother Alberto, I am very much interested in evangelism-in-depth. Can you tell me, what is evangelism-in-depth?

A. Mottesi: Many have tried to define evangelism-in-depth, but synthesizing, we can say that it is a serious intent to mobilize all Christians to become witnesses for Jesus Christ.

J. Myers: Good. What are the goals of evangelism-in-depth?

A. Mottesi: We have three overall goals. The first has to do with the mobilization of the church. And when we speak of mobilization, we are not referring simply to activism. Rather, we refer to that which the Holy Spirit does in the heart of the pastor; the mobilization that the Spirit and the Word perform in the heart of the servant of Jesus Christ, amplifying his vision and placing in his ministry a more missionary dynamic. I refer also to the mobilization that the Word and the Spirit perform in the homes of Christians, and to the church a new missionary attitude within the community.

The second goal has to do with total evangelization. We believe that it is possible to bring together all methods, all men, and all talents in order that, before the second coming of Jesus Christ, the present generation shall have been confronted with the demands of the Gospel.

And the third goal that we have is visible unity of the Body of Christ in evangelization.

We are commencing here a new epoch in the ministry of Evangelism-in-Depth. The year 1974 is the year of renewal and reconciliation.

1975 is the year of evangelistic saturation and discipling. 1976 is directed toward a total development of the church.

J. Myers: Brother Alberto, can you explain to me something of this which is called "reflection group"?

A. Mottesi: We believe that Christians can experience a new evangelistic challenge, a new dimension for a new style of evangelizing life in this day according to the evangelistic demands of the Word of God. To that end, we are organizing hundreds of small groups where believers unite to study the Word of God.

Renewal of the church

Narration (live): On the continent of Latin America, there is another exciting dimension of the Holy Spirit's work. It is the renewing of the inner life of the church and nowhere is it better illustrated than in the life of one church and one man. The church is Faith Tabernacle in Buenos Aires, one of the largest churches in Argentina, and the man is pastor of that church, the Rev. Juan Carlos Ortiz.

S. Mooneyham (live interview): Brother Juan, I would like to ask you some questions about the renewal experience through which your church has been going. Now obviously, renewal is not just an accidental happening to a church, but I also doubt that we can say that renewal can be programmed or structured to begin at a given time or moment, since it is obviously a work of the Holy Spirit. From your own experience at Faith Tabernacle, how did renewal begin in your church?

J. Ortiz: We were a very successful church, speaking in terms of numbers, but even when we continued to increase numerically, something was lacking and I noticed it. I was not satisfied with the work we had been doing. We worked hard sixteen hours a day and the church attendance was up, but when we relaxed a bit the church went down, so I seemed to be depending upon my effort. We decided to stop all the activities and I went out of town to pray and fast and ask the Lord about the problem. We had numbers, but we did not have satisfaction.

The Spirit told me three things. First, he told me that our church was not growing, it was just getting fatter. He said that we only had more people of the same quality. While we used to have 200 members without love, the number had grown to 600 without love. That is not growing; just getting fatter.

The second thing the Lord told me was that we had a business company, not his church. He reminded me of our sophisticated follow-up system in which we were faithfully applying to our church all the knowledge we had gained at various congresses. We had a telephone follow-up system, letters for every age group, and so forth, but the Lord told me I was applying human promotion to his church and asked me where his involvement entered into these activities.

The third thing he told me was that ours was not a church — his family — but an orphanage and I was the director. He said that the people came to church, sat down, and we fed them all milk. In order to have a family church, he said, we should have everyone personally cared for, with each individual being fed for his own needs. Those three things completely changed our point of view on renewal in the church.

S. Mooneyham: So renewal started with you and your own experience with God?

J. Ortiz: Yes, and when I got back I found there were other pastors who had the same problems and questions and confusions. We met together and there were more pastors praying and fasting until the Lord started to give us some answers. This was not an experience for just our church, but there were churches of many different denominations that became involved in this renewal of the life of the church.

S. Mooneyham: What is the basis of the fellowship that you have with these other churches and pastors?

J. Ortiz: In the beginning we were wrong, for we felt that our common experience of the baptism of the Holy Spirit would be the basis for unity, but as we saw in the Pentecostal churches a sense of disunity even though they had experienced this baptism, we realized this was not the proper basis of fellowship. The basis of fellowship, we believe, is the Lordship of Jesus Christ and love. We should not feel that the charismatic group is the body of Christ. We should live together — the charismatic and the noncharismatic — in the same Body.

S. Mooneyham: I know that sometimes the talk of renewal can be very threatening to the people of a congregation because it seems that you are questioning their previous spirituality. How did you handle this with your congregation?

J. Ortiz: The first step was to call together the elders of my church and we went out to the country for two or three days. I posed to them my problems and my burdens and they accepted the challenge — we were pastor and deacons together. Before I had been like the employee of the church, but after our meetings together I became like a biblical teacher and they became like biblical disciples. The authority changed from the board to the pastor.

I was at the same time relating to other pastors in the city, because when you are alone or by yourself you can lead the people into mistakes.

After six months, each one of the board members did the same thing with two or three other persons — going out to the country, spending time in fellowship, and making disciples of them. It took two years to change the whole church into disciples. We were 600 when we started. After the renewal began, we were 400— so we lost 200 for the demands of the Gospel. As soon as we had the whole church under discipleship, we multiplied so that we are now 1,200.

S. Mooneyham: You did a very interesting thing in that you dropped the word "member," substituted something else for it, then went back to "member." Tell us about that.

J. Ortiz: Yes, in order to get things done, you have to take complete steps. If you do not take specific steps, it is the same as sewing without making a knot at the end of the thread — you make holes in the cloth, but you do not sew anything.

When we started this program, we told the people we would not use the word "member" any more because it brought to our minds a society or club-type membership — you go to class, pay your dues, and so forth and you can be a member of the club. In reading the book of Acts, we did not find the word "member" anywhere, but we did find the word "disciple" so we started using that term. Before, you could have asked my people if they were members of the church and they would have said yes, but if you had asked them if they were disciples, they would often have to say, "No, but I want to be one." So we started discipling people and teaching them, not through messages, but through commandments to do concrete things.

Then after one-and-a-half to two years of discipling, we re-discovered the word "member." It was in the Bible, but it was in the epistles with an entirely different meaning. It was not the club-type member, but the body-type member. We saw that membership in the church is a body-type of membership and we discovered four things about a member.

The first is that a member is someone who unites two other members together, as the forearm unites the arm with the hand. So a member of our congregation must have one person whom he is teaching and one from whom he receives teaching.

The second meaning of "member" for us is a person who passes nourishment. The nourishment he receives from the rest of the body, he passes on to his disciple.

The third thing about a member is that he passes orders — the orders he receives from the head.

The fourth meaning is that the member sustains the other members. As the joints sustain each other, so in our congregation we sustain each other. We are like a bunch of grapes. If you take the pastor, you take the whole bunch because we are all related to each other. It is very difficult to lose members — you cannot just lose a member of your body because it is sustained by all the other members. So it is with the church. When a person is baptized, he is a member of the Body in the truest sense of that word.

S. Mooneyham: That is really a marvelous concept. I understand that in anticipation of possible political problems you closed down the church for one month. You thought that sometime perhaps the church would have to go through persecution and you wanted to give the people a chance to test themselves and their renewal experience under a persecution-type situation. For some churches that would be like committing suicide! What happened at Faith Tabernacle during that month and after?

J. Ortiz: The political situation was very uncertain in our country and we wanted to be prepared in the event that a radical group might at some point take over the government and close the churches. So we started cells in the homes. We had more than 200 cells meeting all over the city — in homes, beaches, restaurants, in Catholic churches, and so forth. We closed down the church building completely because in the event of an enemy take-over, that would probably be done. We passed the word about this to the disciples, and those people who were not disciples went to the building and wondered why it was closed. The enemies of the church said that the police had closed it.

By meeting this way we had to change a number of things, including our financial arrangements. Because we met in cells, we decided to have the tithes and offerings come through the leaders of the cells. Each leader knew who was tithing and who was not, and at the same time in such a small group each one knew what the others earned, so the tithes had to be right. That month we more than doubled the income of the church.

Now we meet every Sunday in the church, but I prefer to have the offerings taken in the cells!

S. Mooneyham: I wish we could talk longer about your experiences at Faith Tabernacle, but we must now move on to other parts of the world.

Culturally-related evangelism

Narration (live): One of the things the Holy Spirit is teaching us today is that there need be no fixed pattern of evangelism. The Holy Spirit will not be locked into any one method, and it is wrong for us to try. He who was sent to lead the Church in evangelism must be allowed his sovereign right to choose the method for each time and each place.

If there were no diversities of people in the world, then we might with some justification insist upon one method of evangelism as being the "best" method. But the very ethnic and individual differences represented in the Palais here tonight point out clearly why Paul felt it necessary to become different things to different people — why he refused to stereotype his witness.

Thank God that in the growing light of cultural realities some of the rigidity and inflexibility which characterized evangelical witness in the past are giving way to new and varied patterns of proclamation and church planting. Hopefully, all of us are learning some new lessons. One thing has become abundantly clear — evangelism that is truly related to a man's culture is far more effective than methods which are imposed without regard for ethnic and cultural considerations.

Much comment and a tremendous volume of literature which speaks to this important issue is now emerging from Christian leadership around the world. We can sum it up with this statement: If we want to reach the world for Christ in our generation, we must become increasingly sensitive to the forms of each culture as channels for the Christian message.

I want you to see three different illustrations of how cultural realities are being made use of in evangelism. First, we are going to India and meet Dr. Subbamma, one of God's great women in the world. She is constantly on the move in her state of Andhra Pradesh where she has set up many study communities called *ashrams*. An *ashram* is a form indigenous to the culture of India which she has adapted for evangelism among Hindus. In her work alone, there are some five to six thousand Hindus involved in *ashrams* — people who are constantly being exposed to the Gospel of Jesus Christ.

S. Mooneyham (film interview): Dr. Subbamma, why do you have such an interest in working with Hindus?

Dr. Subbamma: Oh, I am so glad you asked me that question in that way. I was born in a Hindu family myself, and God in a wonderful way sought me, found me, and filled me. From the time I became a Christian, I really felt the burden to disciple the Hindus. This is why I am so interested in the Hindus.

S. Mooneyham: People around here tell me that one way you carry out your ministry is through an ashram. What is an ashram?

Dr. Subbamma: Well, I could give you a hundred definitions. Right now, I would simply say that it's a place of worship, fellowship, and service.

S. Mooneyham: Why is it so effective here in India among the Hindus?

Dr. Subbamma: We do some things in ashram — meditation, study of the Word of God, study of other religions, studying the different cultural aspects, and so forth. We do not have any rigid formula for ashrams because we want to give freedom to people, as this is one thing that appeals to Hindus and Indians in general.

S. Mooneyham: Once a person has been a part of an ashram for a period of time, do you push for a decision for Jesus Christ?

Dr. Subbamma: No, not at all, we won't push them. They come and we just welcome them in any way they want to come — and they go as far as they can go. But it is amazing in such a short time that they are coming to Christ.

S. Mooneyham: Do you see this as a continuing work of God among the Hindus?

Dr. Subbamma: I feel that the Lord is really at work among these caste Hindus, and these people are coming forward to accept him. They never wanted this kind of Christianity because we called it a religion. Now we must present them with Christ, more than with all of our religiosity.

S. Mooneyham (live interview): After having seen her on film in the midst of an ashram in her country of India, I would now like you to meet Dr. Subbamma in person.

Dr. Subbamma, I wanted to ask you a couple more questions about the ashram because I am intrigued by this method of evangelistic outreach which you are using in India. Obviously, most of the people who come to the ashram are unbelievers. In what ways do they get involved with the Word of God so that they may be exposed to the claims of Jesus Christ?

Dr. Subbamma: First of all, I would like to tell you that there are many kinds of ashrams in India, but these ashrams we started in 1968 are Christian ashrams although they are mainly intended to reach non-Christians and Hindus. When these people come to the ashram, they often come with some knowledge of Christianity. We want to make the ashram a worship service in which they can get involved, and above all we give them Christian fellowship. We welcome them as one of us, give them the Gospel message in a manner they understand such as pageants and indigenous ways they are used to.

We also have service projects in which they can be involved. One Hindu family is helping with an agricultural project. We pay them a bit of money and they have become very much a part of the program. One Brahmin woman came to help us with the cooking and she is now a beautiful Christian. We also have an educational program and we welcome non-Christians into each of these programs because we want them to be involved and are happy when that happens. The Holy Spirit is at work and the people are coming to know Christ through this method of evangelism.

S. Mooneyham: I know that many high-caste Hindus from Andhra Pradesh are coming to know Christ, and one of the primary means of these people — who up to now have been very resistant to the Gospel —

making this change is the ashram program. Tell us about one person who has come to know Christ through this means.

Dr. Subbamma: One woman came to an ashram and became a Christian, and through her influence she brought about fifty people to Christ from her village. They are all baptized and even more than that have come to the ashram and heard about Christ. She has been the inspiration for many women — and a number of men — coming to Christ. She goes to all her relatives in different villages and talks to them without giving a lecture or preaching to them. She tells them that for so long she had worshipped lifeless idols and that now she knows and believes in the Lord Jesus Christ.

Everyone can see that she is very happy and has the joy of Jesus in her life. More than twenty of her relatives have become Christians, and among them one of her sisters has accepted the Lord. Her husband, who is still a Hindu, has nonetheless provided the funds to build a church.

S. Mooneyham: We are all very excited about what God is doing through you and this work in India. It is just one more evidence that the Holy Spirit is choosing a variety of methods for the proclamation of the Gospel.

Narration (live): Now we go to a great Asian metropolis where we see another example of the importance of an evangelism that is sensitive to cultural realities. Rapid urbanization is a worldwide phenomenon and one of the challenges facing the church is to design a strategy which will meet the needs of those who live in the great high-rise apartment buildings of our modern cities.

Narration (film): Singapore...City of the Lions...thriving, bustling, prosperous city of two-and-a-half million people. Multi-racial Singapore with its citizens of Chinese, Malay, and Indian stock.

Everywhere the people of the world are gravitating to the large cities, whether Asia, Europe, or the Americas. Because of land limitations in these urban areas, in most places the only way to build is up...whether you live in Hong Kong or New York.

And this is what is happening in Singapore. Here twenty-story homes in the sky are the rule, not the exception, and for Christians in Singapore this new style of living presents tremendous challenges for the church. How will the modern people of affluent Singapore be reached with the Gospel? James Wong, an Anglican minister, shares some thoughts about this issue in his rapidly changing city-state of Singapore.

J. Wong: We are standing on the twentieth floor of a huge high-rise apartment in the satellite town of Toa Payoh in Singapore. In fact, what we see here, all these high-rise apartments coming up rapidly at the rate of nearly one new apartment every thirty minutes, was not imaginable ten years ago. This whole place was a big swamp and this housing estate itself typifies the whole dynamic progress and development of modern Singapore. By 1980 almost 70 per cent of the more than three million people will be living in these high-rise apartments.

I believe the government here in its modern, far-sighted, and long-term planning system has a wonderful lesson to teach the church with respect to our evangelistic efforts and strategy in reaching the world for Christ. This has not come about by accident, but it is the result of much planning, effort, thinking, coordination, skills, and vision. I believe, too, that if Singapore — like other modern cities in the world — is to be reached for Jesus Christ, then we must think through very, very seriously and creatively new patterns of high-rise or urban evangelism.

At present only five per cent of Singapore is evangelized and I believe if the other 95 per cent are going to hear the Gospel, we have to think through a way of planting a church or a household group in each of these blocks where we have more than a thousand people in huge apartment buildings. I believe that our real strategy will depend not so much on building the traditional western edifice, but rather will concentrate on household evangelism where the Christian family in this apartment block will invite the neighboring non-Christian people to visit and share with them the Gospel of Jesus Christ. Insofar as we can think of a scheme to train our lay leaders and mobilize them and encourage them to be aggressive, open, and attentive to the opportunities, this will be one way of reaching Singapore for Jesus Christ and saturating the whole city with a knowledge of him.

Narration (live): Out in the lobby of the Palais de Beaulieu there is a population clock which is a dramatic reminder of the rapid growth of world population. But there is another statistic connected with that clock that has equally great significance for evangelization. The world is actually becoming more illiterate than literate because of the rapid population increase. How shall we reach these masses of people who can neither read nor write?

Something is happening 200 miles into the interior of the West African country of Liberia that should give encouragement to us all. What is happening there shows that illiteracy is not necessarily a hindrance to belief or proclamation. An evangelistic explosion has taken place among the people of the Gbazon tribe during the past eight years. Immediately after conversion the people begin to memorize Scripture. God has given the Gbazon people the amazing gift of committing entire books of the Bible to memory.

God's messenger to these people has been Augustus Marwieh, whom some of you will remember from the Berlin Congress in 1966.

S. Mooneyham (live interview): Gus, you were the messenger of God that brought the Gospel to the Gbazon people. I note that this happened in 1966 and I remember that the World Congress on Evangelism was held in 1966. I am wondering if there is any kind of relationship between these two events.

A. Marwieh: At the Berlin Congress, Dr. Billy Graham spoke on the topic, "What Is Evangelism?" As he spoke, he wound up my soul like a clock with inspiration to such an extent that ideas, compassion, burdens, and everything just jammed me up until I didn't know what to do with myself. When I returned to my hotel room, I was literally sick. I had never, never in my life had such a burden. I felt that Billy Graham should change his type of evangelism and start preaching to Christians instead of unbelievers. I thought if he could give Christians a burden like the one he gave to me, he could evangelize the whole world.

That burden did something to me and to my people, and the result of that is the work that is being done now in the eastern part of Liberia.

S. Mooneyham: So it was after that experience at the Berlin Congress that you went to the Gbazon people. You know, one of the things I remember most about you from Berlin is the way you play the drums. Let's bring out your drums and let you show us how you praise God in Liberia with your own music.

Now by means of film we are going with Gus Marwieh and Bob Larson of the World Vision staff to visit the Gbazon people. You will meet Nancy Blatty, a delightful woman who, though illiterate, has been gifted by God with the ability to put the stories of the Bible into native song and dance. Thus she communicates the Gospel in this beautifully natural cultural form without benefit of any written words.

But Gus, there is a scene with which this film opens that looks to me like a kind of war dance. Would you explain the significance of that to us?

A. Marwieh: It isn't a war dance, but a victory dance. However, it is not to celebrate a victory over an enemy, but to celebrate the completion of a certain job like harvesting the crops.

S. Mooneyham: A victory dance! Let's go to Liberia and see what victories the Holy Spirit is bringing to pass for Christ.

R. Larson (film interview): Gus, were you born in this jungle?

A. Marwieh: Literally, I was born in this jungle. My mother was digging casaba, and while digging this vegetable she found herself in childbirth and there in the casaba farm by herself she gave birth to me. I grew up in the village, a naked boy, never wearing clothes until I was 14 years old. That was when I started school, beginning with a book borrowed from the wife of one of my cousins.

R. Larson: As I have walked around these last few days, it seems that there is very little literacy here. Is it possible to have a program of evangelism without literacy?

A. Marwieh: God has done such a wonderful thing, Bob. He has given our people a tremendous memory and they can literally memorize whole books of the Bible. So literacy is completely nil. We are starting schools here, but still that doesn't stop the progress of the Gospel. We are translating the Bible in the language of the people on tapes, so the people are hearing the Gospel and many of them are memorizing the Scriptures from the tapes.

Also we have schools in the various villages teaching the people how to read and write. We have about twelve schools in the various villages. But we wanted to use what we had while the people were hungry for the Word of God. We didn't want to wait one minute.

R. Larson: About ten years ago there were no Christians in this village. What has made the difference?

A. Marwieh: God had prepared the hearts of the people. I don't know what means God used, but when we came here God really had the people hungry and prepared for the Word of God so that when they heard the news of our coming, there were thousands ready to meet us. When we preached the Word of God, there was a great movement that swept across the whole tribe.

R. Larson: And what about Nancy?

A. Marwieh: Nancy Blatty? She is a marvelous person. She has created so many songs — she is a creative genius. She has adapted many Bible stories and verses of Scripture to music. She is doing a marvelous job.

The film shows the women of the village singing in the background while Nancy Blatty dances and quotes passages of Scripture almost from Genesis to Revelation.

R. *Larson:* Would you call what has happened in this tribe a "people's movement"?

A. *Marwieh:* That's right — a people's movement in which tribes and villages turned to the Lord.

R. *Larson:* What do you see for the future?

A. *Marwieh:* God sometimes chooses one person to do a great work and sometimes he chooses a nation as he chose Israel. I believe God has chosen the Gbazon tribe for a great work in Africa, because there are so many great talents that could be used of God to set a movement going throughout West Africa.

People movements

Narration (live): And so by all means — not one method or two or three, but a variety of ways — the Holy Spirit makes sure that Christ is lifted up so that men will turn to him.

As Gus Marwieh pointed out, what has happened among the Gbazon tribe in Liberia may well be called a "people movement." It is an expression, heard more and more today. It represents church growth, not by addition, but by multiplication as entire villages turn to serve the living God and whole family units or clans are converted to Jesus Christ.

People movements have occurred or are presently happening in such diverse places as Nigeria, Thailand, the New Hebrides Islands, among the Nagas of India, among the Dyaks of Indonesia, the Montagnards of SouthVietnam, and the Aymaras of Bolivia, to name only a few. In 1973-74, some 4,000 members of a Dyak tribe in Borneo, which heretofore had been unreached, were converted to Christ in less than two years.

The phenomenon of people movements is not always understood, but it is a valid, increasingly common expression of church growth. For instance, when a village in Nagaland converts from animism to Christ, it does not mean that salvation is any less a personal and individualistic experience. What it does mean is that God is dealing with individuals, but within the communal environment of an entire class, caste or tribe.

In your Congress registration envelope you received a staggering compilation called an "Unreached People Survey." Many believe that if these ethnic and tribal groups are going to be reached in time, it cannot be done on a one-by-one individual basis, but only by a dramatic movement of the Holy Spirit working among them as a group. Let's take a look now at how the Holy Spirit is presently working in some of these people movements.

Narration (slides): Missionaries and national leaders serving the Aymara-speaking peoples of Bolivia report an increasing receptivity to the Gospel. In the past year churches like the Friends, the Methodists, the Seventh Day Adventists, the Assemblies of God, and others have experienced a rapid growth rate ranging from 15 to 100 per cent. In one year's time, the number of Adventist churches was increased from 90 to 200 congregations. Obviously there are no simple human explanations for this. But as the living conditions of the Aymaras have slowly improved over the past twenty years, the people become more mobile and they are breaking with old traditions and patterns of life. Thus they are becoming receptive to new things, including the evangelical witness.

But their responsiveness to Christ is due to more than just methods of evangelism employed by missionaries and churches. God's Spirit is moving in this community and nearly ten per cent of the one-and-a-half million Aymaras are now believers in Christ.

In nearby Ecuador, missionaries have worked among the Quichua Indians for over 70 years with very discouraging success. Then suddenly in 1967, 131 people were baptized. By the next year the believers totalled 315 in eleven congregations, and in 1973 there were 8,000 baptized believers in over 100 congregations.

The growth of the church among the Quichuas was originally centered in Chimborazo Province. Several Quichua pastors and missionaries have been badly beaten and the Quichua believers themselves, by the hundreds, have been assaulted and had their homes attacked.

But whenever persecution strikes, the establishment and growth of the church seems to follow closely. And Christ's believers among the Quichuas are growing by at least 16 per cent annually.

Narration (film): In April of 1972, the peaceful life of some 11,000 Stieng tribespeople in South Vietnam was interrupted. An enemy attack near their home in An Loc resulted in many deaths and their evacuation to a refugee camp near the capital city of Saigon. A year later they were again evacuated, this time to Bao Loc.

When their troubles began in 1972, the Stieng tribe had about 1,300 Christians — and that was the sum total of ten years of hard missionary witness. But God clearly used their suffering in the war to lead them to Christ. In 1973, there were over 3,600 new converts. And today, more than 55 per cent of the Stieng tribe — some 6,000 people — are baptized believers.

We asked Pastor Dieu Huynh how it all happened.

Dieu Huynh (film interview): When we think the whole thing over, we realize God has blessed our people in an amazing way. Part of it was because of some of the miracles that were performed among the people. Some of them were sick and were then saved, and are still alive. Two of the witches have turned to believe in Christ. There is such a rapid growth because the Stieng people did not have anybody to believe in. They now know about God and they believe in Christ.

Narration (film): Yes, God is indeed building his Church in some amazing ways. One of the most unusual outpourings of his Spirit has been evidenced among soldiers in the Army of the Republic of Korea.

In early 1970 there were only twenty-five chaplains serving fewer than 65,000 Christian soldiers. Then suddenly that year, there was an explosion of spiritual interest and nearly 25,000 soldiers were baptized in 1970. In 1971, 30,000 more men were converted and the following year, 43,000. In April, 1972, and again in October, 1973, mass baptisms took place for more than 3,200 men.

In the past four years, more than 125,000 military men have come to know Jesus Christ as their personal Savior, and the number of chaplains serving them has grown from twenty-five to nearly 300. While Christians in Korea now represent nearly 12 per cent of the population, within the Korean army their numbers account for 30 per cent.

Narration (live): Much of the focus of this Congress has already been on Asia, both as an area of tremendous need and opportunity. We are going to talk with two men who have been involved in places in Asia where the Holy Spirit has done a spectacular thing. The Rev. Longri Ao is head of the Nagaland Missionary Movement in India, and the Rev. Petrus Octavianus is president of the Indonesian Missionary Fellowship.

Gentlemen, let me ask you, first of all, to say a word about the people movements which you have witnessed in your own countries. What do you think, Brother Longri, are some of the factors which have produced this movement in Nagaland?

Longri Ao: The people in Nagaland have been through a series of political turmoils during the last 20 years creating unrest, uncertainty and anxieties in their minds. This has driven them to Jesus Christ. The people in our churches have been very active in witnessing for Jesus, and thousands of people— not less than 10,000 every year — accept Jesus Christ as their Lord and Savior. When you were with us in the interior, Dr. Mooneyham, you saw how thousands of people walked for days, carrying their food and their children, to hear you speak. After they had been there a few days, many were different men and women.

S. Mooneyham: It was one of the most moving experiences of my life. I have seen tribes in Nagaland that are 80 per cent Christian — your own Ao tribe, for example — where a century ago there were no Christians.

Longri Ao: That is right. A century ago we were head-hunters! One man was converted two years ago, but before he had taken about forty-five heads. Now he is a great soul winner! Another man had decorated his house with the forty-five heads he had taken, and he is now treasurer of the church and a soul-winner as well.

S. Mooneyham: From head-hunter to soul-hunter, and now he is decorating heaven with souls!

Brother Octavianus, what do you consider to be the contributing factors to the people movement in Indonesia?

P. Octavianus: First, I want to say that revival is going on in Indonesia, but I have never before accepted an interview regarding it because I do not want to sensationalize the news of it. But after our praying about it together, I have decided that I want to make it known here that the world can be reached with the Gospel of Jesus Christ.

There are three important factors regarding revival in Indonesia. One, it is God's time. God is ready now to reach nations that have never been reached with the Gospel. Two, I believe there has also been preparation from man's side. In 1957, several prayer groups began to gather together for prayer at five o'clock in the morning at a time when our country was under the power and influence of the Communists. We prayed expecting great things from God, and he is willing to answer those prayers. Three, the country of Indonesia has five principles which the people are encouraged to practice. One of them is to believe in God. The revival broke out in 1964, a year before the attempted Communist coup. Because the coup failed, most of the people lost their faith in Communism and were looking for something in which to believe. That was an open door for the Gospel of Jesus Christ.

S. Mooneyham: Each of you has described some of the elements that have produced a people movement in your culture. There have been questions as to whether the people are really changed. Do you think the people are genuinely converted to Christ, and is there evidence of this conversion, or is it just mass hysteria?

Longri Ao: Oh, no; they are truly converted. After these revival meetings drunkards are changed and become sober, responsible people; broken homes are united; the head-hunters become soul-winners. So many of these changes are taking place in our country. This ministry is not limited to pastors, but it is a lay movement as well. All the people are involved, going out in groups to the various villages to tell people about the love they have found in Jesus. The people do become changed, and the change is permanent. It is the work of the Spirit of God.

S. Mooneyham: Have you seen the same things happening in Indonesia, Brother Octavianus?

P. Octavianus: Yes, I have. The people who turn to Jesus Christ burn their charms and fetishes. I have seen the repentance and confession of sin, and the joy of repentance in their lives. There is definite evidence that these conversions are real.

S. Mooneyham: For a moment let's take a look at the big continent of Asia which is less that 2 per cent Christian. Humanly speaking, that doesn't leave much room for optimism. Yet, the Anglican Bishop of Singapore, Bishop Chiu Ban-It, says he confidently expects a new movement of the Spirit within Asia which will make Christ the chief cornerstone of the continent. Do you share his optimism and, if so, why?

Longri Ao: Oh, definitely! India as a whole, and particularly the tribesmen living in the high mountains, are emerging to be a missionary people. We are sending out missionaries. I am head of a missionary movement and we believe that in spite of great difficulties we shall very soon be sending out missionaries beyond our borders. Now we have many missionaries to the unreached tribes within our borders.

S. Mooneyham: How do you view this, Brother Octavianus?

P. Octavianus: We cannot say that everyone will be saved before the second coming of Jesus Christ, but when I first went to my village there was not one single Christian. You came to visit us shortly after that, Dr. Mooneyham. Then in 1967 I was speaking at a Christmas meeting attended by a group of non-Christians. I suddenly felt the Holy Spirit moving and changed my message from a Christmas message to an evangelistic sermon. In this meeting thirty-seven people of this village accepted Christ. Now in just this one village there are more than 250 Christians. We also have congregations around my village — some are small and some are large.

S. Mooneyham: You mean that when I visited you seven years ago there were no Christians in your village and now there are congregations? Praise God!

I believe that what you gentlemen have reported gives all of us encouragement to pray that the Spirit of God may move on this vast continent in a way that has never been seen before, so that millions may be won to Christ. On that continent, of course, is China with one-fifth of all the world's people. Some who have gone into China recently tell stories of how many of their relatives are hungry for the Gospel. Who can dare say what God is now doing in the People's Republic of China? Might he be creating a spiritual vacuum among one-fifth of the world's people which only Jesus Christ can fill?

We know the Spirit of God blows over all boundaries made by man and he will see that Christ is lifted up. We are encouraged to believe and pray with you that God will continue to do this great work in Asia.

Evangelism and social action

Narration (live): A great deal has already been said in this Congress about the relationship of evangelism and social concern. The Holy Spirit seems to be showing us that the debate which has gone on for nearly a century is really a non-issue. We thank God for that! As Dr. Graham reminded us on the opening night, faith and good works are handmaidens of the Gospel which cannot be divorced.

There are two mandates in the New Testament. One is witness; the other is service. To ignore or deny either of them is to seriously cripple the church. Social action is certainly not Christian evangelism, but to engage in evangelism of souls without recognition that those souls also have bodies is foolish and unreal.

Neither is the changing of social structures to be equated with evangelizing a country, but to ignore political injustice and economic abuse while we talk about the transforming power of Jesus Christ is to weaken and discredit our message.

In preparing for this presentation tonight, we surveyed some 150 evangelical leaders around the world and asked them to point out significant trends in their areas. From every part of the world came reports that evangelicals are ministering to human needs, as well as spiritual needs, in the name of Christ. Concern about medical care, sub-standard housing, food shortages, illiteracy, political injustice and economic inequality is being translated into Christian action.

It is my deep conviction that love which is just talked about can be easily turned aside, but love which is demonstrated in tangible acts of Christian caring is irresistible. I believe this is what our next film segment is trying to say.

Narration (film): In any country of the world, poverty knows no boundaries not even in the beautiful city of San José, Costa Rica. On the outskirts of San José, there is a squatter village called Pueblo Nuevo, or "new community." It is a not a very nice place in which to live, but for the moment it's about all the people have.

Ernesto Rodriguez cares about these people, and his concern is not just temporary relief — or, as he says, a "band-aid" operation — because there are some real changes taking place. Ernesto is a follower of Jesus Christ, and his work here in Pueblo Nuevo is a demonstration of God's love in action. He knows where the people hurt. As a new Christian three-and-a-half years ago, Ernesto didn't know much about theology.

He just knew that as a follower of Jesus, he had to respond in love to those in need.

Orlando Costas from Evangelism-in-Depth talks with Ernesto about evangelism and social action.

O. Costas (film interview): What really struck me, Ernesto, is how you have been able to engage in evangelism which was relevant to the context of the situation in which these people were living, as well as being inter-related with their problems — the lack of housing, the lack of land, the lack of know-how.

E. Rodriguez: It began with the principle from which I started, for the Lord moved me with compassion to go to Quantifilo and serve. I went there and I loved these people. To me, all these people are still my family. When I saw their condition, I wanted to help them in all the ways I could. Out of that love, I not only gave them the Good News, but I tried to identify myself with them. The principle we use to teach these people is our love for them, and not to bring them to be part of a certain religion. They are human beings...I love them because the Lord loved me first. The next step is to teach them to help each other because of love, and slowly the whole community begins to talk with each other and help each other.

O. Costas: I understand the whole community was transformed because you got new land and housing. In other words, there were some structural changes that took place in the life of that community.

E. Rodriguez: Primarily, I organized the resources that were available in the country. I did not get any help from the outside, but tried to help the people learn to do things for themselves.

O. Costas: You know, Ernesto, I think this is the message. Evangelism and social action are not two separate things. The social service that we do with evangelism doesn't have to be mere "band-aids," but it is possible for the church to be involved in bringing about deep, profound structural changes in a given community.

E. Rodriguez: This is definitely true. If you have a child, you love him and get him the things he needs. So it is with the people to whom you take the Word of God. You must help them along as you can. It's love in action.

Conclusion

Narration (live): And so the Acts of the Holy Spirit go on. His work will not stop until our Lord returns. Jesus said, "When he, the Spirit of truth is come...he shall not speak of himself...he shall glorify me." The task of the Holy Spirit is to lift Christ up to the world by all means. Jesus said, "And I, if I be lifted up from the earth, will draw all men unto me." Wicked hands lifted him up on a cross to die the death for sinners. Now loving hands, strengthened by the Holy Spirit, lift him again as the crucified, risen, triumphant and coming Lord!

"It is not by might, nor by power, but by my Spirit, saith the Lord."

One of the most dramatic moments in the Old Testament occurred shortly after Elijah was taken to heaven in a chariot of fire. Elisha watched the chariot disappear, then turned around and picked up the cloak of Elijah. On that very same day he had seen the great prophet strike the Jordan River with it and they had walked across on dry ground. Now

Elijah is gone. Elisha, who has asked for a double portion of the spirit of the prophet, walks back to the Jordan. He takes the cloak and smites the water with the cry, "Where is the Lord God of Elijah?" Again the water parts and Elisha walks back on dry ground. In response to faith, God showed his power!

The cry arises today from barren and fruitless havest fields — "Where is the Lord God of Elijah?" It comes from sterile and lifeless churches — "Where is the Lord God of Elijah?" It ascends from the depths of a persecuted and suffering church, from the inner souls of weary and struggling servants, from the agonized spirits of those who yearn for revival and renewal — "Where is the Lord God of Elijah?"

Without appearing flippant, I would like to answer that question. Elijah's God is where he has always been. He is where Elisha found him. He is here...now...present...powerful. He has never been away.

I want to ask a question that to me is more relevant for our time. *Where are the Elijahs of the Lord God?* Where are the men and women of faith for whom God will open and close heaven? Where are the prophets who with boldness will challenge the tyranny and injustice of rulers who govern without God? Where are the confident and courageous witnesses who will stand — alone, if necessary — before the twentieth century prophets of Baal and discredit their false claims with fire from heaven?

When we have more Elijahs, we will have more of Elijah's God. Oh, that God may give such men to the Church of our time! Men like John Knox who, pressed in his spirit with a burden for his land, cried out to God, "Give me Scotland or I die!" Men like Francis Xavier who stood knocking at the door of China, groaning out his plea, "O rock, rock, when wilt thou open to my Lord?" Men like John Sung of China who was willing to count everything but loss that the masses of Asia might hear the name of Jesus. Men like Sadhu Sundar Singh who renounced all to be one of God's true holy men of India. Men like Dwight L. Moody who heard someone say, "The world is waiting to see what can be done through one life fully surrendered to God" — and determined to be that man.

Men like General William Booth, who undaunted by persecution and ridicule, helped shape the course of church history as founder of the Salvation Army. Among the many wonderful stories told about him, there is one which always stirs me deeply. It is said that as he would read the Book of Acts — reliving the victories of the early church, sensing again the power that transformed the apostles from timid men into bold witnesses, feeling once more the impact of the Gospel upon pagan cultures — as he read of the Acts of the Holy Spirit in the early church, he would drop his head onto the pages of his Bible and wet them with his tears as he sobbed out this prayer over and over and over: "Do it again, Lord, do it again!"

May this be the prayer of Lausanne: "Do it again, Lord, do it again!" As you revealed your power through Elijah and turned the hearts of the people back to you, "Do it again, Lord, do it again!" As your power exploded through the first-century church to turn the world upside down, "Do it again, Lord, do it again!"

We live in a time of tremendous need. It is a time of political upheaval, of military posturing with weapons which could destroy mankind, of economic uncertainty which could bring social collapse — "Do it again, Lord, do it again!" We confess that our churches are lukewarm and many of your people are absorbed in materialism and pleasure, but in spite of our sin and faithlessness — "Do it again, Lord, do it again!"

It is a time when it seems that the four horsemen of the Apocalypse — famine, disease, war and death — are ready to ride and ravage the earth. Let your church be ready for apocalyptic days — "Do it again, Lord, do it again!"

With nearly three thousand million yet to believe in the Lamb of God that takes away the sin of the world, "Do it again, Lord, do it again!" Before the last trumpet sounds and Jesus Christ returns in power and glory, "Do it again, Lord, do it again!"

In a few days we will leave Lausanne, Lord, and go back to our people and our work as your men and women. We will be writing another chapter in the Acts of the Holy Spirit. As you have helped your people in every age write chapters of victory, of conquests, of praise to your Son — "Do it again, Lord, do it again!"

Amen.

LIVING THROUGH AN APOCALYPSE

Malcolm Muggeridge

*Mr. Muggeridge, Sussex, England, is an
internationally-known journalist and
commentator.*

Whenever I come to the town of Lausanne I always think of a corpulent Englishman named Edward Gibbon, who some two centuries ago was settled here to complete his majestic *History of the Decline and Fall of the Roman Empire,* a great masterpiece written with elegance and detachment which characterized the eighteenth-century mind. It is only fair to add that his detachment, if not his elegance, deserted him when he was confronted, not with the breakdown of an ancient civilization, but with actual disorders near at hand consequent upon the revolutionary situation which had arisen in France — what might, perhaps, be regarded as the first shots in a process fated to submerge the civilization Gibbon so rejoiced in and regarded as the acme of all human achievement. We are all, I think, a little like this, and easily endure the troubles of the past while beating our breasts lustily over those of our own time.

Even so, let me boldly and plainly say that it has long seemed to me clear beyond any shadow of doubt that what is still called Western Civilization is in an advanced stage of decomposition, and that another Dark Age will soon be upon us, if, indeed, it has not already begun. With the Media, especially television, governing all our lives, as they indubitably do, it is easily imaginable that this might happen without our noticing. I was reading the other day about a distasteful but significant experiment conducted in some laboratory or other. A number of frogs were put into a bowl of water, and the water very gradually raised to the boiling point, with the result that they all expired without making any serious effort to jump out of the bowl. The frogs are us, the water is our habitat, and the media, by accustoming us to the gradual deterioration of our values and our circumstances, ensure that the boiling point comes upon us unawares. It is my own emphatic opinion that the boiling point is upon us *now,* and that as a matter of urgency Christians must decide how they should conduct themselves in the face of so apocalyptic a situation.

To talk in this strain, to draw attention to the fact that the temperature of the water is rising alarmingly, is, as I well know, to invite accusations of pessimism. In my opinion, the boot is on the other foot. If I ridicule a prospectus for a housing estate to be built on the slopes of Mount Etna, I am not being a pessimist. On the contrary, it is the advocates of so ruinous and ridiculous a project who are the true pessimists. To warn against it and denounce it is optimistic in the sense that it presupposes the possibility of building a house on secure foundations — as it is put in the New Testament, on a rock, so that when floods arise and streams beat violently against it, it stands firm.

In other words, the most pessimistic attitude anyone could possibly take today would be to suggest that a way of life based on materialist values, on laying up treasure on earth in the shape of an ever-expanding

Gross National Product, and a corresponding ever-increasing consumption stimulated and fostered by the fathomless imbecilities of advertising, could possibly provide human beings made in the image of their Creator, sojourners in Time but belonging to Eternity, with a meaningful basis for existence. So each symptom of breakdown, however immediately painful and menacing in its future consequences, is also an occasion for hope and optimism, reminding us that truly God is not mocked, and that men can no more live without reference to him now than could the Children of Israel find their way to the Promised Land without his guidance and support.

A scene that has stayed in my memory bears on the point. I was in a New York television studio with Mother Teresa for one of those morning interviews which help Americans to munch their breakfast cereal and swallow their coffee. It was the first time she had ever been in an American television studio, so she was unprepared for the constant interruptions for commercials. This particular morning, as it happened, the commercials all had to do with different sorts of packaged food, commended to viewers as being non-fattening and non-nourishing. Mother Teresa's own constant preoccupation is, of course, to find the wherewithal to nourish the starving and put some flesh on human skeletons. It took some little while for the irony of the situation to strike her, but when it did she remarked in a quiet but perfectly audible voice: "I see that Christ is needed in television studios." A total silence descended on the studio, and I fully expected the lights to go out and the floor-manager to be struck dumb. A word of truth had been spoken in one of the mills of fantasy where the great twentieth-century myth of happiness successfully pursued is fabricated — an unprecedented occurrence. Actually, since the commercial was running we were not on the air, and the impact of Mother Teresa's interruption was soon spent. All the same, I felt that in the Book of Life, if not in the *New York Times,* it would rate a mention.

In many respects, then, crack-up conditions are more conducive to the understanding and practice of the Christian religion than ostensible stability and prosperity. The Apostle Paul's amazingly successful evangelism, remember, took place during the reign of the Emperor Nero, a ruler who makes even some of ours seem positively enlightened and far-seeing. Moreover, the early Christians had the inestimable advantage of believing that the world would shortly come to an end — a belief that, as Dr. Johnson said of a man about to be hanged, wonderfully concentrates the mind. The ill consequences of the opposite proposition — today's dogma — that the world will go on indefinitely, in the process getting better and better, have become all too clearly apparent. Sooner or later the world must end, anyway; whereas the utopias men persuade themselves are just round the corner, whether realized through the final installation in power of the triumphant proletariat, or through the fulfillment of an American Dream of eternally burgeoning health, wealth, and happiness, or whatever, never even begin.

Think of the advantages the early Christians derived from their conviction that the Last Days would soon be upon them! For one thing, they were spared the illusory hopes in revolution and counter-revolution, in insurrections and liberations and conspiracies, which then, as now, abounded. With thoughts of an imminent Apocalypse, who today would bother his head unduly about such alluring future developments as supersonic flight, computerized literature, birth pills for tiny tots, or transplant surgery with a view to changing our spare parts as they wear out and so keeping us on the road indefinitely like vintage cars? What a blissful relief for the early Christians to turn aside from the capers of an Emperor Nero and the turgid rhetoric of his critics and joyously await the promised Second Coming of their Lord and Savior! It almost looks as though the best hope of revivifying institutional Christianity would be to convince the Pope, the Archbishop of Canterbury, the Metropolitan Nikodim, and other dignitaries that the world would shortly be coming to an end. Or — maybe better — to get the World Council of Churches to pass a resolution in this sense at its next meeting.

It is in the breakdown of power that we may discern its true nature, the skull beneath the skin, and realize that what the Devil offered Jesus in the wilderness — the Kingdoms of the Earth, to do what he liked with — was, like all his propositions, a fraudulent one. On the other hand, it is when power seems strong and speaks with a firm voice that we are most liable to be taken in, and to suppose it really can be used to advance human freedom and well-being. We forget that Jesus is the prophet of the loser's, not the victor's camp, proclaiming as he did that the first will be last, that the weak are the strong and the fools the wise, and that the poor and lowly, not the rich and proud, possess the Kingdom of Heaven.

the decay of the institutions and instruments of power. On every hand intimations of empires falling to pieces, money in total disarray, dictators and parliamentarians alike nonplussed by the confusion and conflicts which encompass them, and the very weaponry at their disposal so monstrous in its destructiveness as to be unusable except to blow our very earth and all its creatures to smithereens. Confronting this scene it is sometimes difficult to resist the conclusion that Western man has decided to abolish himself, creating his own boredom out of his own affluence, his own vulnerability out of his own strength, his own impotence out of his own erotomania; blowing the trumpet that brings the walls of his own city tumbling down; and, having convinced himself that he is too numerous, laboring with pill and scalpel and syringe to make himself fewer. Finally, having educated himself into imbecility, and polluted and drugged himself into stupefaction, he keels over, a weary, battered old brontosaurus, and becomes extinct.

Here I speak with some feeling, since it is through a realization of the fantasies of power that I have come to recognize the irresistible truth of the Gospel of love that Jesus came into the world to expound. The trade of journalism which I have followed for something like half a century is calculated to induce this awareness. Who can be engaged in the quest for news without realizing that what he purveys bears as little relation to what is happening in the world as *Muzak* does to music? Indeed,

the two — *Muzak* and what might be called *Newzak* — are decidedly
similar, the one being a drooling melange of tunes and the other of ostensible events, both calculated to keep the mind of a motorist in a suitable
condition of somnolent vacancy as he cruises along mile after mile of
motorway. How many liberations celebrated that only led to new ser-
vitudes! How many reigns of peace ushered in that only generated new
wars! How many liberators installed in power only to become even more
ferocious tyrants than those they replaced! The splendid words of the
Magnificat go on being fulfilled; the mighty are put down from their seats
and the humble and meek exalted, the hungry are filled with good things
and the rich sent empty away. Yes, but how soon, how very soon, the
humble and meek who have been exalted become mighty, and in their
turn fit to be put down! How quickly the poor who have been filled with
good things become rich, thereby likewise qualifying to be sent away!

My earliest memory of the public scene is of the First World War. I
was given to understand that it was a war to end war and make a world fit
for heroes to live in. God, I gathered, was on our side, and when victory
was achieved his spokesman turned out to be Woodrow Wilson, who in
Princetonian accents delivered to us Fourteen Points as Moses had Ten
Commandments. Later, in the columns of the old *Manchester Guardian* I
thundered away about how the League of Nations would ensure peace for
evermore if only everyone would disarm, and institute free education for
all and universal-suffrage democracy. As the events of the interwar years
unfolded, it was borne in upon me that the governments of the world
were failing to follow this enlightened advice.

Jesus, I was brought up to believe, was a most high-minded and
altogether estimable man, who, if not actually a paid-up member of the
Labour party, would have been if a Labour party had existed in Palestine
in his time. By setting up a welfare state, in accordance with Labour party policy, dismantling the British Empire, and otherwise reforming our
capitalist-imperialist ways, we should effectively bring his Kingdom to
pass, whereas, through the centuries of Christendom, it had been relegated to celestial regions, thereby inducing the downtrodden and oppressed to be content with their lot. Alas, the Labour party in due course
was in a position to form governments, but Jesus' Kingdom seemed as far
off as ever, if not farther. As for the dismantled British Empire, its liberated components tended to become mirror images of the authoritarian
regimes which had been dispossessed.

Feeling thoroughly disheartened and disillusioned, I directed my
hopes for a better world towards the U.S.S.R., where, the then Dean of
Canterbury, Dr. Hewlett Johnson, regularly proclaimed from the
cathedral pulpit, Stalin was busily constructing the Kingdom of Christ.
At the time, the dean was commonly regarded as a buffoon; on the contrary, he has proved to be something of a pace-setter, and would today
find himself very much at home among large numbers of his fellow clergy. Managing to get myself posted to Moscow as a newspaper correspon-
dent, I soon realized that, far from giving a new validity to liberty,
equality, and fraternity, the Soviet regime was rapidly turning into one of
the most absolutist tyrannies of history, presided over, in the person of
Stalin, by one of its most cruel and obscurantist tyrants. The only origi-

nal feature, as compared with other tyrannous regimes in the past, was that for some bizarre reason it met with the unstinted approval of the flower of our Western liberal intelligentsia, who, as long as it was humanly possible, went on applauding each restriction of liberty, each brutal suppression of dissidence, which at home their lives were dedicated to opposing.

Thenceforth I had no expectation whatsoever that man could perfect his own circumstance and shape his own destiny. As Pascal put it: "It is in vain, O men, that you seek within yourselves the cure for your miseries. Your principal maladies are pride, which cuts you off from God, and sensuality which binds you to the earth. Either you imagine you are Gods yourselves, or, if you grasp the vanity of such a pretension, you are cast into the other abyss, and suppose yourselves to be like the beasts of the field and seek your good in carnality."

So, without God, we were left with a choice of megalomania or erotomania; the clenched fist or the phallus, Nietzsche or Sade, Hitler or D.H. Lawrence.

Meanwhile, I managed to sleep-walk my way through the Second World War and its aftermath, increasingly conscious that the weird human scene which I had to go through the motions of reporting and commenting upon and interpreting, and its cast of men seeking power with a view, as they all insisted, to promoting the public good, belonged rather to fantasy than reality. In a way it was easier to cope with it as editor of *Punch* than as what passed for being "serious" journalism, except that, in trying to ridicule those, as the Book of Common Prayer puts it, set in authority over us, one was constantly frustrated because, as it turned out, they were themselves infinitely more absurd in what they did and said than one's wildest inventions.

This applied particularly to the clerical echelons, whose strange gyrations were the envy and despair of the professional humorist. What satirical invention could hope to equal a bishop in gaiters appearing in a court of law to testify that *Lady Chatterley's Lover* was a representation of Christian marriage at its best? Or a dialoguing Jesuit looking for common ground between the Sermon on the Mount and the Communist Manifesto — like an ardent vegetarian exploring the possibility of teaming up with the Worshipful Company of Butchers. Or a priestly dispenser of gelignite to freedom-fighters as representing the readiest means of manifesting how they love their enemies and seek the good of those who persecute them.

The fact is that the quest for power itself is a deadly serious one. Dictators, like brother-keepers, abominate laughter, which the saints have all loved, hearing it ringing out from heaven itself, louder sounding when heaven's gates swing open, abating and dying away as they swing to. Shakespeare makes his King John refer to "that idiot laughter, a passion hateful to my purposes," therein speaking on behalf of all power-maniacs at all times. In this sense, power is a sort of pornography of the will, corresponding to the other sort — equally humorless — of the flesh. When the Roman soldiers played their sick joke on Jesus, dressing him up in a scarlet robe, putting a crown of thorns on his head, bowing low before him in mock reverence as King of the Jews, they were not, as they supposed, just ridiculing a poor deluded man about to die; they were holding up to ridicule all kings, all rulers, all exercisers of authority who ever had been or were to be. They were making power itself derisory, ensuring that henceforth we should see thorns beneath every crown, and beneath every scarlet robe, stricken flesh.

The only alternative I could discover to the ultra-solemn quest for power was Jesus' ultra-joyous quest for love, but I confess I did everything in my power to evade it. Contrary to what is often suggested, a hedonistic way of life, if you have the temperament for it and can earn a living at it, is perfectly feasible. The earth's sounds and smells and colors are very sweet; human love brings golden hours; the mind at work gives great delight. Unfortunately, however, I was driven to the conclusion that something was lacking in the hedonistic set-up, some essential ingredient, something I had vaguely glimpsed, and whose lack made everything else seem somehow savorless. The words that most often sounded in my ears were Peter's reply on behalf of the twelve when Jesus asked them whether they, too, proposed to desert him: "Lord, to whom shall we go? Thou hast the words of eternal life." If only there had been someone else, some other words, some other way!

This is how I came to see my situation, in a sort of dream or vision, something more vivid and actual than most happenings and experiences. I am confined in the tiny dark dungeon of my ego, manacled with the appetites of the flesh, shackled with the inordinate demands of the will — a prisoner serving a life sentence with no hope of deliverance. Then I notice that high above me there is a window through which a faint glow of light comes filtering in — seemingly far away, remote and inaccessible; yet, I realize, a window looking out onto Eternity. Inside, darkness, a place of fantasies and furies; outside, the white radiance of God's love shining through the universe, what the Apostle Paul called the glorious liberty of the children of God.

And the window? I know what that is, too — the Incarnation. Time and eternity intersecting in a cross; Now becoming Always. God revealing himself as a man, and reaching down to us, in order that we, reaching up, may relate ourselves to him. Now I observe that the window is not, after all, far away, but near at hand, and that seen through it everything makes sense, so that, like the blind man whose sight Jesus restored, I can say: "One thing I know, that whereas I was blind, now I see." Thenceforth, whenever I am looking through the window I see life as being full of joy and hope and brotherliness, whereas the moment I turn away the darkness encompasses me again. The ego once more lifts up its cobra-head, the servitude to the appetites and the will resumes. I am back in prison.

Through the window I look out on reality; within, there is only fantasy. Oh, the glory of reality, the horror of fantasy! The one, Heaven; the other, Hell — two states as clearly differentiated as are light and darkness, joy and wretchedness, life and death. As Simone Weil writes:

"Nothing is so beautiful and wonderful, nothing is so full of sweet and perpetual ecstasy, as the good; no desert is so dreary, monotonous and boring as evil. But with fantasy it is the other way round. Fictional good is boring and flat, while fictional evil is varied and intriguing, attractive, profound and full of charm."

Blake was making the same point when he wrote:
This life's dim window of the Soul
Distorts the Heavens from Pole to Pole
And leads you to believe a Lie
When you see with, not thru, the eye.

He might have been predicting the coming of television, which pre-eminently requires us to see with, rather than through, the eye. And what a multitude and variety of lies it has induced belief in!

Let me conclude by recounting briefly two recent experiences which seem to me significant in relation to what I have been talking about. Both occurred while I was preparing the commentaries for a series of religious documentary films. In the first case, I found myself standing amidst the ruins which are all that now remain of Carthage, and trying to reconstruct the scene there when, in the year 410, the Bishop of Hippo, better known as Saint Augustine, heard the news that Rome had been sacked. For him, it was the end of civilization and to the world as he had known it — a world in many respects uncannily like ours, with a similar obsessive interest in public spectacles of violence and eroticism. Augustine compared Rome's destruction with Sodom's, and told his flock not to lose heart, since "there will be an end to every earthly kingdom."

You are surprised that the world is losing its grip and full of pressing tribulations. Do not hold onto the old man, the world: do not refuse to regain your youth in Christ who says to you: "The world is passing away, the world is short of breath. Do not fear, thy youth shall be renewed as an eagle."

Then Augustine devoted the remaining seventeen years of his life to the deeper question of the relation between earthly cities like Rome which men build and destroy, and the City of God, which is everlasting, embodying his conclusions in his great work *The City of God,* which defined for successive generations of Christians what they owed to God and what to Caesar.

Now I move on through fifteen centuries, and stand beside Tolstoy's grave at Yasnaya Polyana, in Russia, where he lived. As Augustine held the secret of what would follow the fall of Rome, so I had somehow the feeling that what lay ahead for us might be sought here where Tolstoy was buried, at the edge of a ravine and looking over a forest, with no monument or memorial, just as he wished it to be; simply a mound of earth, as usual piled high with flowers. Speaking about him in that place, about his beautifully lucid exposition of the Gospels, about his incomparable short stories — parables, like Jesus', about his distrust of all governments, all systems of power, as instruments for ameliorating our human condition — was one of the most enchanting experiences of my life. The words were addressed only to a camera and a camera crew, along with one or two Russian helpers, but they seemed to fly into the clear September air and lose themselves among the silver birches like joyous birds. I thought of Russia's fifty years and more of ruthlessly authoritarian rule, reaching into every aspect of the lives of those subjected to it, into their work and play and education, into their innermost thoughts and hopes, of how this immense apparatus of power, probably the greatest concentration ever to exist in the world, had been dedicated to the extirpation of the Christian religion and all its works; and of how nonetheless, thanks to the genius of Tolstoy, Jesus' message, the enchantment of his words and presence, what he came into the world to do and say and suffer, had remained accessible.

For confirmation we have Solzhenitsyn, the Soviet regime's foremost rebel, who so brilliantly and forcefully challenges its pretensions, in the name not of freedom or democracy, or of any of the twentieth century's counterfeit hopes, but of his Christian faith, with its insistence on the absolutes of love rather than the relativities of justice, on the universality of brotherhood rather than the particularity of equality, on the perfect freedom which is service rather than the perfect service which is freedom. The odds against its happening were astronomical, but it has happened. If, when I was a journalist in Moscow, someone had said to me that the most distinguished Russian writer and the product of the Soviet regime would write as Solzhenitsyn has, and I quote, "I myself see Christianity today as the only living spiritual force capable of undertaking the spiritual healing of Russia" — if anyone had predicted that which was said by such a one as Solzhenitsyn, I would have given a million to one against it. Yet it happened. Surely, a miracle, and one of the greatest.

For me now the experience of living in this world is nearly over. My lines, such as they are, have been spoken, my entrances and exits all made. It is a prospect, I am thankful to say, that I can face without panic, fear, or undue remorse, confident that, as an infinitesimal part of God's creation, I am a participant in his purposes, which are loving, not malign, creative, not destructive, orderly, not chaotic; and that, however somberly at times the darkness may lower, and however men may seem at times to prefer the darkness, the light that first came to Galilee 2,000 years ago, and through the succeeding centuries has illuminated all that was greatest in the work and lives of men, can never be put out. The other day there were published in English the last words Tolstoy wrote. They, too, were about his light, and he concluded: "That, my dear brother, is what I have been trying to say." I echo his words.

A LAYMAN LOOKS AT WORLD EVANGELIZATION

Ford Madison

Let me ask you, who are Christian leaders, what do you want from us? What do you want from common, ordinary believers?

Does the non-professional layman fit anywhere into your planning for world evangelism? Much of what I've heard here has emphasized systems and methods and materials and the sending of thousands of professional missionaries, but what about the millions of ordinary Christians? God's Word says in II Cor. 5:17, "Therefore if any man be in Christ he is a new creature: old things are passed away; behold, all things are become new." Vs. 18, "And hath given to *us* the ministry of reconciliation." Vs. 19, "Hath committed unto *us* the word of reconciliation." Vs. 20, "Now then *we* are ambassadors for Christ."

What do you want from us? In the last five months I asked many, many laymen — and several pastors — What is a good layman? What do you think most pastors want? The consensus is:

1. our attendance at all meetings
2. our money
3. our support of "their" programs
4. "Do not try to change anything."

Is that *all* you *really* want? My attendance and my money?

Laymen want to be involved in what counts. I believe the church's real program of evangelism should start when the building is closed and empty. Jesus said, "I don't pray that the Father take you out of the world but that he be with you in the world." The world is between Sundays. Monday, Tuesday, Wednesday, Thursday, Friday, and Saturday. That's where the people are ... that God so loves.

The most exciting, greatest enterprise I have found is to be involved with God in the life-changing business. He is calling out a people and then building them up together. E.M. Bounds has written, "We are constantly looking for better methods but God is looking for better men. Men *are* God's methods." The Gospel is changeless, and I believe God's basic method of communication is changeless. God — the Holy Spirit — in people. The Word made flesh.

Why say, "Go here or go there," when, behold, the power to evangelize is within us?

Waldron Scott, who prepared an audio/visual presentation "The Task Before Us," helped me with some numbers: If each nominal Christian in the world (and there are about one billion) were motivated and trained to win only one person to Christ in a year and would train that person to repeat the process, the world could be reached in less time than it took to prepare for this Congress. Less than two years. If only 10% of these professing Christians would be faithfully winning and training it would take 5 1/2 years.

Of course, everyone won't win someone. But let's not close our minds and hearts to the tremendous potential of winning and training. As Paul wrote in II Tim. 2:2, "The things thou hast heard of me among many witnesses, the same commit thou to faithful men who are able to teach others also."

If each of us in this room, without any outside help, would in addition to our other duties, win and train just *one* person yearly and then they'd do the same thing repeating the process yearly, we could evangelize our world before the end of this century.

I can't win thousands but I can win and train one just like the man won and trained me. Just like I can't swallow a whole elephant but I can take one bite at a time. And remember, there are thousands like me...it wouldn't take 1,000 long to eat an elephant.

What do laymen want? We want to be involved in what really counts. And we need you to show us how to study the Bible, how to pray, how to live in love, how to witness, how to have Christ formed in us.

We need you. We want to be one with you. Let's withstand Satan by closing the gap between the clergy and laity. *This is not a biblical division!*

We need your leadership, your challenge. What do you want from us? I hope you'll want more than nominal commitment to use the common believers. I hope you'll want laymen so much that you'll challenge us in commitment, train us to win and train others so that we, too, might be personally involved in world evangelization.

A LAYMAN LOOKS AT WORLD EVANGELIZATION

Jan Nickolaas Huwae

The 20th century is the layman century. Church leaders and ministers around the world are in agreement that the mission of the church is to evangelize and propagate the Gospel of our Lord Jesus Christ.

To insure that the church will not die but flourish, evangelism done by laymen is fast becoming a part of the regular church program. To carry on an active, effective program of evangelism, the church *must* have the full support of its laity. Every believer can and should be a witness. In effect, they are either good or bad, for the Scripture points out very clearly that we are "epistles of Christ" known and read of all men (II Cor. 3:2,3). More than that, we are in the world the holy priests and ambassadors of our heavenly Father to witness and to glorify Him (II Cor. 5:20; I Peter 2:5).

The layman in this twentieth century is a potential witness. He need not be a super-salesman nor a super-human being to be used of God. In fact, God has called the foolish things of the world to confound the wise, and the weak things to confound the mighty (I Cor. 1:27). We need but to turn our life and our personality over to God and we can say like Paul, "I can do all things through Christ which strengtheneth me." There is no excuse for not serving God daily as a witness. Not that we should leave our business to serve Christ, but make it our business to serve Christ in and through our business.

In order to do that, first of all we must have:

1. *Personal assurance* of sins forgiven, of life eternal, of positive relationship and of positive present possession.

2. *Awareness of responsibility* to glorify God, to bear witness and have fellowship one with another, to read and obey God's Word, to spend time in prayer, to obey God's will and the Holy Spirit.

3. *The disicipline of devotions* — through daily devotions we get a knowledge of the Bible and keep close to the Lord to maintain a victorious, spirit-filled, dynamic Christian life. With Christ in control life is balanced and effective.

We have already pointed out that the mission of the church is to evangelize and propagate the faith. Every believer then as a member of the body of Christ becomes responsible to bear witness.

Witness means: To give facts or evidence, to testify to one with a personal knowledge of anything.

Let us briefly find out and answer the following questions.

1. *Who should witness?* To consider reverends, pastors, and bishops, as the only group specially called to serve the Lord is irrelevant to God's standpoint. "Ye shall be my witness or ambassador ..." (Acts 1:8; II Cor. 5:18-20) means everyone — every believer, every born-again person. It can be a doctor, a lawyer, a teacher, a clerk, or a policeman like me. We have only to obey the Great Commission as a good Christian soldier.

We thank God that since the beginning of the twentieth century there are many spiritual fighters without using any church title who witness to the great salvation and proclaim the Word of God.

2. *When shall we witness?* There is no set time of day, week, or month. The early-century Christians were busy daily. Our life is a witness and will be until we die. Maybe we are very busy with our business earning money and have no time at all to witness for Christ. But the Bible says, "For what shall it profit a man if he shall gain the whole world and lose his own soul?" Businessmen might well learn the art of making a living, but not many of them have learned *"how to live."*

3. *Where shall we witness?* Acts 8:4, "Therefore they that were scattered abroad went everywhere preaching the word." Our Jerusalem is the office, shop, school, neighborhood. Each of us as laymen have our sphere of influence. We are called to be "the fishers of men." The ponds are everywhere.

4. *What shall we witness?* You don't need to be a good speaker but you can give facts and personal testimony. Who were you before you met Christ and accepted him as your personal Savior? You can give facts or testify what happened during the conversion and then what Christ has done for you. Once you were blind, namely spiritual blindness, walking in the darkness and going to hell, but once you accepted Christ Jesus as your personal Savior by faith and grace, your soul awakened, your mind enlightened and your will converted. The result is your conscience is purified and your affections renewed.

5. *How shall we witness?* We work not on our own, but we are workers together with God. God provides the Holy Spirit for witness as the power and the guide to witness. God provides his Word for faith and practice and God promises to bless it. We must faithfully sow the seed, his Word. Our part is to be willing to witness by our life. Our lives should be attractive for the Savior.

Before I close my presentation, let me ask you, "What is your occupation? A doctor? A merchant?" Do not run away from these callings. Who you are and what you are God will use as a tool in his hand to proclaim the Gospel, to bear witness in your position in the community.

A LAYMAN LOOKS AT WORLD EVANGELIZATION

Luis Santiago Botero

Since I was touched by the Gospel in the university fifteen years ago, I have been disturbed by several features of the contemporary church that it seems to me do not adjust to the instrument proposed by God to take the light to the world. I wanted from the beginning to be just a plain Christian. Denominational differences have been for me, as they are for many who seek the Gospel, a burden. The lack of unity between brethren belonging to different organizations and their insistence on emphasizing whatever separates them, has always disturbed me very much. You cannot find in the body of Christ the unity required so "that the world may believe" (John 17:21).

One of the most relevant distortions that I find in the contemporary church is institutionalization, understood as the organic conformation of the church to a business enterprise model or to a social club. To this you must add the professionalism of the ministry, once clergy and laymen are distinguished, with the consequent dependence of the members of the congregation with respect to the ministers in order to function as church. The communication of the Gospel has thus become the task of specialists, with the risk that it may no longer be the normal task and the privilege of every believer. On the other hand, isolation of the redeemed in church buildings, does not allow them to effectively be the salt of the earth. The buildings for the assembly of the faithful have become a substitute of the very notion of church.

Within such a frame, the Holy Ghost finds very little freedom to move. The Word of Life does not reach those to whom it is addressed, and the life of fellowship between the brethren is very limited. We do not see nowadays many Christian communities of which they can say they persevere unanimous every day as in the example of Acts 2:43-47, communities where the fellowship in Jesus Christ reflects itself in inter-family relations, in mutual help, in secular work, in service and in all realms that give practical expression of our faith.

I find another hindrance to the extension of the kingdom of God in the marginalization of the church from the contemporary world, caused by institutionalization, by the absurd dichotomy between the material and the spiritual, and by a wrong interpretation of what separation from the world means, which we have adopted as an excuse not to give a permanent witness in our work, in our social and family relations, in our responsibilities as citizens, in the arts, and in sport. This other worldly position, qualified by a conservative ethic that we stress too much in our message, has made us lose our contact with reality. We do not go to the world to seek those for whom Jesus died, expecting that somehow they will become interested in attending our evangelization meetings. Our message sounds very strange to the ears of the man without Christ, or there is no response at all because the message is not relevant to his problems. The proclamation of the Gospel fails in being an existential witness. We do not take advantage of our situation in the world where the

Lord has inserted us to be his witnesses. We are then no longer sensitive to the opportunities of infiltrating in all sectors of contemporary society, as a living testimony, giving freedom to the Holy Spirit so that our mouth brings forth the abundance that should overflow our hearts (Luke 6:45).

I am quite worried about the emphasis given to evangelistic methods by the contemporary church that this Congress reflects. It seems as if we would insist in refining the model given by God for the extension of his kingdom with means that do not produce the same impact nor the same result as the simple existential proclamation through personal and collective witnessing of those that recognize that Jesus is Lord. I believe that technological innovations, efficient organization, the psychology of communication and other contemporary ingredients have a lot to contribute to a wider and more effective spreading of the Gospel. However, I believe that those are accessory means that eventually may reinforce or complement, but that in no case should be a substitute for the methods of the Holy Spirit, spreading his gifts through men and women transformed by his power in the context of daily life, and operating in multiple ways in the church, the life of fellowship being the evidence offered by Jesus when He said, "By this shall all men know that you are my disciples, if ye have love one to another" (John 13:35).

We need nowadays to depend more on God and on the power of the Holy Spirit. The main motivation for our effort in evangelization must be the compassion for those for whom Christ died, not the satisfaction in statistics or in spectacular and multitudinous meetings. If we are not able to make disciples through our witnessing, to integrate them to fellowship in our communities and to support them so that they will be witnesses there where the Lord wants them, we will not be collecting the harvest but spreading it.

But thank God that in spite of our imperfections, the people of God are growing. While traditional churches burdened by institutionalization are mainly concerned with their doctrinal or methodological distinctions, in building impressive temples, and in preparing literature mostly for internal consumption, the Holy Spirit is moving powerfully among the youth, among the marginal groups of society, within the traditional churches and even in Bible-centered groups of Catholics, renewing the body of Christ and extending the message of God spontaneously to the thousands that were not attracted by our meetings.

The human categories that we have introduced in the church reflect also in missionary effort. We find discrimination between servants of the Lord of different nationalities. The professionalization of the ministry has turned many disciples that should be proclaiming the Word into spectators. The distinction we make between foreign missionary and native witness, as well as the distinction between clergy and laymen, has no biblical foundation. We are all sent by Jesus Christ to the world and we have the responsibility to be witnesses in Jerusalem, in Judaea, in Samaria, and in the uttermost parts of the earth.

On the other hand, I think that missions before they send a worker abroad where he will probably have to struggle against cultural and linguistic barriers, should make sure that national workers are not available, because often nationals are willing to serve but they lack financial and logistical backing in their country. There are probably many other unexplored ways that could contribute to improve our missionary strategy. For example, in those countries that are closed to the Gospel because of idealogical, nationalistic, or religious reasons, I think there must be tremendous possibilities of sending disciples of missions. We must inform Christians with a missionary vision about the opportunities of study or work in their secular field of activity, and provide the necessary support so they may be inserted in places that cannot be reached by the conventional missionary.

Finally, I would like to make a remark that is pertinent to the countries of the Third World and particularly to Latin America. Our churches are constituted essentially by the proletariat and in a lesser but rapidly increasing degree, by the lower middle class. There is practically no witness among the higher class, the one which has the political and economic power, because the members of our churches rarely have access to college education. They abstain from political participation and their presence in the cultural life of the country is not significant. There is an urgent need for a strong witness among the people of the leading class. Our brethren coming from the lower classes must be encouraged to go to the universities and to become witnesses in influential positions, and those professionals or businessmen that are already there must have our earnest support so they may faithfully declare their faith in Jesus Christ in such a difficult environment.

It is true that Jesus sent us to preach the Gospel to the poor in the first place. For God the professional, the politician, the high official is not more valuable than the illiterate city worker, the peasant or the most primitive Indian. But it is noble that those who are located in the top of the pyramid of society, those who have leadership in the country, and have many eyes upon them should have priority in our evangelistic effort. The impact of the conversion of VIPs from government or private sectors may have repercussion in our countries as important as the conversion of Saul of Tarsus, Nicodemus, Joseph of Arimathea, or Cornelius the centurion. Thus, in the strategy of evangelization of all the sectors of contemporary society in our generation, it is vital to multiply our prayers and our efforts in order to reach those located in key positions.

EVANGELISM IN THE HARD PLACES OF THE WORLD

Dr. Chua Wee Hian
Dr. Frank Saphir Khair-Ullah
Dr. Subodh Sahu

C. Wee Hian:

At this Congress, we have heard exciting reports of God at work around the world. In many countries of Africa and Asia, we have seen thousands and thousands of men and women turning from idols to serve the living God. Churches are growing; congregations have multiplied. Christians in the Third World have banded together to establish missionary agencies and fellowships and are now engaged in cross-cultural evangelism. Today we realize is a day of opportunity and we have seen the Gospel spreading and making tremendous advances. This note of triumph and expectation has been struck repeatedly at this Congress. What is our response? Surely our response is to rejoice and to praise the Lord.

The Apostle Paul bids us to rejoice with those who rejoice, but he doesn't stop there. He also bids us to weep with those who weep. Too often in our Christian circles, particularly in evangelical circles, we tend to glamorize the spectacular. We live, as it were, continually in Palm Sunday when we think of the triumphal entry of Jesus into Jerusalem. In our ministries, we forget that there was Gethsemane, there was Golgotha. Sometimes we forget that Jesus was also the suffering Messiah; he was also known as a man of sorrow, acquainted with grief.

Let me give you a personal testimony. When I was asked to preside at this gathering, I turned down the invitation twice. This is all in writing so it is in the Congress records. Later on I discovered that the planning committee, the program committee refused to accept "no" for an answer. When I was wrestling with this whole problem, God rebuked me. I said to him, "Lord, I'm involved in areas where there is tremendous response. Thousands of students have been discipled and won for Jesus, and are having a tremendous ministry in their churches. I can speak of God at work in a mighty way, but not the hard places."

As I read my Bible, I began to see God speaking to me very clearly. Paul, in Phil. 3:10 prayed, "That I may know him, the power of his resurrection and the fellowship of his suffering." And the Lord was saying to me, "You don't know me in the fellowship of my suffering because you don't care enough for people who are persecuted, for my people who work in hard places." And then again, he seemed to be saying to me, "Wee Hian, you have no concept of the church as the Body of Christ." The Word of God tells us that if one member suffers, all suffer together. When one member is honored, all rejoice together. All of us must identify ourselves with those who are suffering for the sake of the Gospel. We must also come together as a solid front of men and women who are willing to stand behind our brothers and sisters who are working in resistant cultures.

Tonight's meeting is a call to prayer. It's not a meeting for publicity.

I must warn you — we are going to show you different data. These might be very dramatic but I want us to take these things in the right context. It's a call to prayer and not to publicity. At the end of our meeting together we shall break up into small groups to pray for the things that we have seen with our eyes and heard with our ears.

The hard places of the world. What are these areas? These are areas where the Gospel has not taken root; these are areas where messengers of the Gospel are continually buffeted; these are cultures that resist the unique claims of Jesus Christ and its adherents are members of different religions and are unwilling to turn to him, to believe in him. We think of the world, of over 600 million Muslims, of nearly 500 million Hindus, of over 600 million Buddhists and Confucianists. These appear to be impregnable strongholds.

Let me cite you some examples. A few months ago a missionary in a Muslim country heard a knock at his door. The police went in; they served a summons on him, "You are to leave this country within twenty-four hours." There was no appeal; there was no argument. Again, I know a Muslim student who was converted some years ago. He went back to his family and tried to tell them that he had become a follower of the Lord Jesus Christ. A few days later, the local Christians found him, dead. He was poisoned. I can tell you too of many cases of Hindu students and of other Muslim students who have been thrown out of their homes, of their communities, and they have become outcasts. These are *hard* places.

Hard areas also refer to countries where the political regimes are hostile to biblical Christianity. Immediately, our mind turns to China, the world's largest nation with over 800 million people where today there is very little freedom of religion. Some years ago, the Red Flag, which is the theoretical journal of the Chinese Communist party, said, "Christianity and Communism are like oil and water. They do not mix and we want to get rid of Christianity."

But tonight let's begin by turning our thoughts to cultures which are resistant to the Gospel. Let's begin first of all with the world of Islam. It's my pleasure to ask Dr. Frank Saphir Khair-Ullah of Pakistan to report on the world of Islam to all of us. He is an Islamic scholar; he has written and presented a paper here at this Congress entitled "Evangelism Among Muslims." He is also the director of the creative writing school in Lahore, Pakistan. Dr. Khair-Ullah comes from the background of a former Muslim family and his heart beats with those who are concerned to bring the Gospel to Muslim communities.

Dr. Khair-Ullah:

I think if I succeed in giving you an impression, a human impression of the difficulty that one faces in the world of Islam, I would feel quite satisfied. It is not only the minister who brings the Gospel to the Muslims who finds it difficult in the area in which he is working, but we have to look sympathetically in a human way at the world of Islam, at the individuals that Islam constitutes, in order to realize and feel something of their difficulty.

A Muslim, before he can come to our Lord Jesus Christ, has to cross many barriers. In a Muslim country, it is so difficult to detach oneself from the nationality and culture. People who become Christians are sometimes accused of losing their nationality or being de-cultured. The important thing is that we should pray that those people who come to the Lord Jesus Christ in the world of Islam may retain their place in society and in the family. The Muslim society is a very close-knit society. Everything that a member of the society does is known to the other person and in that society you have a close-knit family. The family is not like the Western family where each individual is free to go his own way. Every action of the person is noted and we find that if you make a decision for Jesus Christ, you have to leave that family and you have to give up so much. That cannot be done without certain difficulties.

Then, you have the difficulty of the barrier of will. A Muslim is brought up in a religious way in which he leads a very good devotional life. We should not condemn all Muslims as people who have no deep feeling of religion. A true Muslim, a serious Muslim, says his prayers regularly five times a day. He believes in his five pillars of the religion; he believes in keeping fast in the month of Ramadan; he desires that he will visit and pay homage to Mecca once in life or more, if possible; he believes in giving tithes. In these ways he leads a very religious life. His mind is so conditioned that he believes, like us evangelicals, that his holy book is truth and comes from God. To break away from there and to be liberated and to be able to hear what God is speaking to him through his book and through the Bible is not an easy matter. And we find that the Christians who approach Muslims must approach them in a sympathetic, human way, trying to understand their problems. There were in the past other methods — preaching in public, in the streets — but we have found now that the only methods left to us are personal evangelism and, what we have recently discovered as a most successful method, Bible correspondence schools. I noticed that in Africa, Asia and Pakistan the Bible correspondence schools have a very good response. In my country the response was so good that the people took notice of it and on the 23rd of December, 1973, one of our leading papers had a front-page article entitled, "Beware of the Poison in Closed Envelopes." He wrote a whole article on Bible correspondence schools, gave some of the lessons, and even reproduced the application form and warned people that the Christians are trying to poison the youth of the country by giving these free courses. And we can praise God. Seventeen of the people took that form that was shown as a sample, filled it in and sent it to the Bible correspondence school. As a result of that article which was telling not to do it, one of the students of the Bible correspondence school wrote an article and sent it to the principal of the school, saying, "I have sent a copy of it to the magazine that published the article and I am sure that they are not going to print that article, so will you please take it and print it in your own bulletin." It was a wonderful witness of one of the young people who was a Muslim who had read this article and was fully with us in seeing what work has been done.

Then we find that very often radio ministry is very effective. From Radio Sri Lanka, from Addis Ababa, programs come. People listen to them very intently. You see, I was talking of these barriers. A Muslim would not come to a Christian in Pakistan, but when he is by himself, he can take the correspondence course, he can hear the radio, and we should pray that this work will be especially blessed. Then we have some people working entirely among Muslims. In my country there is a St. Andrews' Brotherhood where Rev. Aslum Kahn, who is a convert himself, from Islam is working among the Muslims. And during this last six months, I have been at three of these baptisms, public baptisms. In each of them, we found that the young man who had been baptized suffered persecution from the home. He was threatened that he should not go back home, and it's not an easy thing. For us, I feel, it's a luxury to be a Christian in the Western world. You are free. You can do whatever you like. But when you accept the Lord Jesus Christ in a country like mine, you may be forced to be a secret disciple, and when you are a secret disciple, a group like St. Andrews' Brotherhood — or there are groups in other countries — take them and speak to them, encourage them, train them. After all, in the Bible we read of many people who were secret disciples. There was Nicodemus; there was Joseph of Arimathea. These were the secret disciples and so we have many secret disciples in Islam. Recently, about a few years ago, a Muslim doctor was put in charge of a Christian hospital. A great many of the Christians said, "Why is a Muslim doctor in charge of a Christian hospital?" When we saw the life of this Muslim doctor, we said, "How good his life is. He is just as good as any Christian." And you know, during the last six months, we discovered that this doctor, whom we took to be a Muslim, had been baptized in Bristol about seven or eight years ago. A secret disciple all that time. Only recently he has confessed that he is a disciple of Jesus. Now, do we condemn such people? We remember that Naaman was a secret disciple too and he appealed to the prophet and he said, "When I go with my master into the temple of Rimmon and if I bow, would I be forgiven?" In these hard places, we should praise God that there are so many people who are coming to our Lord Jesus Christ. We do not see the fruit openly, but we should not slow up, we should not slacken up. What has happened is that the church is finding that so few are converted from Islam (in fact, during the last three years, so many Christians have backslidden). You know that when our schools and colleges were under our own control, we saw so many Christians, but when our schools and colleges were nationalized, we found some of the people losing that zeal that they possessed before.

A year ago, I was asked to write a paper on the future of Muslims in Pakistan. And I read the papers daily and I had a number of cuttings where I read that, "So and so Christian has now embraced Islam," "So and so, with his family, has become a Muslim." So our difficulty in these hard places is not only that we have to reach them, but that we have to strengthen the church, make them consolidated in their place and pray for these Muslims that in various ways they may come to the feet of our Lord Jesus Christ. We should pray hard for these people because the Lord has put that burden on us that we should not be self-satisfied but we should go out and win them over for our Lord and Savior.

Dr. Wee Hian:

Our next speaker is a personal friend of mine, the Reverend Subodh Sahu from India. He works in the state of Orissa and his main ministry is to train Christians to be effective disciple-makers. Together, Rev. Subodh Sahu and his colleagues would go out to evangelize Hindus and Muslims. He will tell us something about the hard and difficult world of Hinduism.

Rev. Subodh Sahu:

The hard places of the world — the world of Hinduism. 83 per cent of the people of India are Hindus or adherents of Hinduism. They number nearly 453 million. The hardness is as follows.

They claim, historically, Hinduism is an ancient religion, rather *the* ancient religion. They consider all other religions as upstarts in the field. Therefore, their attitude is one of pride which makes it hard.

Secondly, the intolerance of the philosophy of syncretism. It seems contradictory but actually this is the true condition — intolerance of the philosophy of syncretism. As a weapon, they want to wield it against the Gospel. Their desire is to block the Gospel. They want to assimilate the Christians and the Gospel into the Hindu fold and into their philosophy. They even say, "Believe whatever you want to, but remain within the Hindu fold."

Thirdly, Hinduism is, by nature, pseudo-political. The common concept of the Hindus is as I narrate here. Hinduism and India nationalism are inseparable. They mean that one who is not a Hindu cannot be a patriot. They commonly look at Christianity as the religion of the Western people — people, who, until the recent past, indulged in colonialism. Moreover, the Western culture has almost nothing to offer to the average Indian and, on the contrary, it has some things which are not admittable to the Indians. Therefore, as they associate religion with culture in their own thinking, they become prejudiced against the Gospel and it seems to be repulsive to them.

Fourthly, the reality of any faith and its true expression is attractive to anybody who seeks reality, but the nominality of the Indian Christians' faith and life is repulsive to the Hindus. The Lord said in his day, "Unless your righteousness exceeds the righteousness of the Pharisees and the Sadducees. . . ." Can it be also said, unless our righteousness exceeds the righteousness of the Hindus, unless we excel in loving them, we cannot bring them into the Kingdom of God? Also the "Christ-plus" of the so-called Christian presentation — let me explain — Christ plus tradition, Christ plus ritualism of the so-called Christian presentation offends the Hindu. They want and need only Christ and Christ of the Bible.

Lastly, Hindu intellectuals who are not reached for Christ while they are doing post-graduate studies in Western universities see and often fall a victim to the scum of the Western way of materialistic life and return hardened against the Gospel and harden others also against the Gospel.

But nothing is too hard for our Lord. In the face of this hardness, we who are disciples of Christ in India (I don't mean only Indians), we who are disciples *in* India need to give our testimony to the resurrection of the Lord Jesus in the great power of the Holy Spirit and make disciples so that our fellow Indians will repent and will learn the secret to live by faith, not by works. They will surely have their eyes opened and they will be drawn away from darkness into light and from under the power of Satan to God. And may we exercise our throne rights in being united with the Lord himself to bind the powers of darkness who control the minds of those who are within the fold of Hinduism so that when we bind the strong man of the house, we can plunder the goods. Our living Lord who revealed himself to Sundar Singh, to Bakht Singh, to Naaram Nambudripad and to many others — our living Lord will continue to reveal himself and will add to his true Church daily those who are being saved. And surely, our Indians will hear the voice of the Lord.

THE HARD PLACES: CHRISTIAN WITNESS IN COMMUNIST COUNTRIES

*An interview between Rev. Michael
Bourdeaux and Chua Wee Hian*

C. Wee Hian: One-third of the world's population live and march under the red flag. Its citizens occupy one-quarter of the land area of our earth. Thousands of Communist cadres and agents actively seek to propagate the "gospel" of Marx and Mao. They brook no opposition. They demand that their people render everything to the Party and to the state, even the things that belong to God. In most Communist countries the Church is still being persecuted; restrictions are engineered and enforced to prevent the active and dedicated propagation of the Christian faith.

Tonight we are delighted to have Rev. Michael Bourdeaux with us. He is the director of Keston College, a center devoted to the study of Communism and religion. He has agreed to be interviewed and to share with us some of his deep concerns for God's people and God's work in Eastern Europe.

Michael, could you please tell us something about yourself and your involvement with Christian work in Eastern Europe?

M. Bourdeaux: My involvement began as a student at the University of Moscow, devoting my life to the study of communism, speaking on behalf of Christians in communist lands, and writing books to provide accurate information.

C. Wee Hian: Have you visited all the countries in Eastern Europe?

M. Bourdeaux: All except Albania. I was able to worship with Christians in these countries.

C. Wee Hian: How much freedom is there today to worship God and to witness to Him in Eastern Europe? One hears stories of persecutions and tortures - how true are these accounts?

M. Bourdeaux: Eastern Europe is not a monolithic bloc — it must be studied country by country. There are different degrees of freedom. In countries like Poland, Yugoslavia, Romania and East Germany, there are possibilities of teaching religious knowledge to children, Bible study groups and classes.

C. Wee Hian:	In what countries then are Christians harassed and persecuted?
M. Bourdeaux:	Albania and the Soviet Union. In Albania, religion is completely outlawed. In the Soviet Union, laws controlling religion are very strict. Often Christians are not allowed to meet for worship and fellowship, so they have to break the law to meet in the *open air*.
C. Wee Hian:	Michael, what about Bibles? Can these be obtained easily, e.g., in Poland or the Soviet Union?
M. Bourdeaux:	It is easy to purchase Bibles in Poland. There's even a Christian *bookstore* operated by the Bible Society that sells Bibles openly. Since the Revolution of 1917, only a few thousand Russian Bibles were printed and distributed in the Soviet Union. Bibles are precious and literally are worth their weight in gold! Russian believers have to *hand-copy portions* of Scripture.
C. Wee Hian:	Earlier on, you referred to Christians in the Soviet Union as those who had to break the law to preserve and propagate their faith. Could you cite one or two cases of Christian "lawbreakers"?
M. Bourdeaux:	One of the best known cases is *Aida Skripnikova*, who was imprisoned twice for her faith. She was arrested as a young girl for distributing Christian literature in the streets of Leningrad. As a sequel to imprisonment she is gathering young people and testifying to her experience of suffering.
C. Wee Hian:	I presume that Christians are tried in a public court before they are sent to prison. Could you give us an inside picture of a trial?
M. Bourdeaux:	It's a hostile court-room — people booing and jeering. *Transcripts* of proceedings are recorded by Christian friends and written on cloth. Aida used the dock as her pulpit! Publicly she witnessed to her Lord. By her example and encouragement she persuaded many to stand firm for the Master.
C. Wee Hian:	When was Aida actually imprisoned? Is she still in gaol?
M. Bourdeaux:	1969. Released in 1972.
C. Wee Hian:	That was a few years ago. What about recent months? Have you had any evidence of fresh persecution?

M. Bourdeaux:	Yes, a case of brutality on May 2. A policeman shot at a crowd that had gathered for a meeting in Magilyov. A *17-year-old boy* was wounded. The Christians surrounded the policeman and confiscated his identity photograph. However, this incident is not a daily occurrence.
C. Wee Hian:	How many Christians would you say are now imprisoned in Soviet Union?
M. Bourdeaux:	Between 2,000 to 3,000. I know that there are at least 200 Baptists who are imprisoned for their faith.
C. Wee Hian:	I am sure that most of us in this Congress would like to know where and how you obtain information from the Soviet Union Christians. What about some of the vivid pictures that you have showed us?
M. Bourdeaux:	Members of the Baptist Council of Prisoners' relatives assembled information and sent them through every means possible.
C. Wee Hian:	So far, you have spoken about the Baptists as the objects of persecution. What about those from other Church traditions?
M. Bourdeaux:	There's also *Father Dimitri Dudko,* a bold witness, successful in youth work. Recently he was removed from the Moscow church.
C. Wee Hian:	I don't think we'll need to stretch our imagination to grasp the plight of families caused by the imprisonments of their breadwinners? What happens to these deprived families?
M. Bourdeaux:	Humanly speaking these families would starve but relief is supplied by the Council of Prisoners' relatives and Christian friends. *Mrs. Rytivoka and her children* were helped through this scheme. She is now organizing relief for others in similar situations.
C. Wee Hian:	Michael, what responsibilities do we Christians in the so-called "free world" have to our brothers and sisters in Christ in Eastern Europe?
M. Bourdeaux:	First we must re-affirm our status as members of Christ's body. *St Paul has stated,* "When one member suffers, all suffer...."
C. Wee Hian:	In practical terms how could we express our solidarity and unity?
M. Bourdeaux:	Our first responsibility is to pray with intelligent prayer based on facts and information. *Keston College* exists to research and gather accurate facts, to publish relevant in-

C. Wee Hian:
M. Bourdeaux:

C. Wee Hian:

M. Bourdeaux:

C. Wee Hian:

formation on the state of the church in Eastern Europe. We also invite students to help us *assemble and gather information.*

What about more direct help and aid?

Sending gift parcels and greeting cards helps, as does strengthening radio broadcasts into communist lands.

Wee Hian, you are wearing an England badge. I know that you live and work in London. But as a Chinese Christian, could you tell us something about the situation in China?

A veteran China watcher in Hong Kong used to say, "China is a big country." By this he meant that various regions, cities and villages adopt different legislative policies as to matters like local government, religious, and social behavior. In a few towns, we learn of Christians meeting publicly for worship services. In other areas, they meet in small groups, secretly and unobtrusively. Most are still afraid of the suspicious neighbor. No one knows who is the friend or the foe. With the clamor of radical youth sections to apply the pure principle of Leninism and Maoism - religion is branded as something feudal and backward, to be rid of permanently.

In spite of severe restrictions, the Gospel is still transmitted through individual Christians. They firmly believe that it is still the power of God unto salvation for those who have faith in Christ.

Is there any news seeping through Hong Kong?

Very little. The Christians in China are wary of Christians in Hong Kong and the USA who present sensational and often exaggerated accounts of the actual happenings. They certainly do not find it easy to live under the red flag especially when there are so many restrictions for them to gather to worship as Christian communities and to proclaim the living Christ to their contemporaries. It's interesting that one of the last messages of Nee To-sheng, known to many here as "Watchman Nee," to Chinese Christians in Hong Kong was to encourage Chinese Christians to continue faithful to their Master and to prepare Bible study materials and guides for suffering Christians in mainland China.

THE POWER OF GOD

Edward Hill

*Rev. Hill, Los Angeles, California, USA, is
the Pastor of Mt. Zion Missionary Baptist
Church.*

This has been a foretaste of heaven.

I tell you — if your bell is not ringing, your clapper is broken.

Having lived in a two-room log cabin just twenty-three years ago, in the sandy hills of Texas, I never dreamed in all of my log cabin days that I would see you, before kneeling with you at Jesus' feet.

I have no excellence, education, nor theological training to commend me to you.

My major was not theology; and in America, the more I hear some theologians talk, I am more and more grateful that my major was agriculture.

Approximately seven centuries or more before the birth of Christ, there was a prophet who tried to tell the people of God what he saw concerning their future. Over and over again — yea, more than any other — he spoke of God's love, judgment, mercy, and the coming signs of not only Israel but the nations of the earth.

It is in the 52nd chapter that I hear Isaiah roaring with both a sound of optimism and yet warning. He says to a nation who seemingly was determining to leave God and his laws: "Awake! Awake! Shake thyself. Arise, put on thy strength. It is I."

Up and down these halls, in every room and from this podium his voice has been saying, "Wake Up! Wake Up! Put on thy strength."

Let me review where I have heard him say, "Awake!" and the instructions he has given.

Wake Up! Wake up to the authority of God's Word!

There can be no uncertain sound regarding the Bible's being truth without error; and the preacher who departs from the Scripture is not liberal — he is lost.

This Congress has declared, "Awake to the knowledge of the consequence of a lost soul."

A lost soul is not a second-class passenger on the same train with the saints. My Bible says that a lost soul is damned already.

A lost soul is separated, dead, miserable, no life, no eternal life, no joy in the Lord, no forgiveness of sin. He is headed to a real hell with real fire to live forever.

Wake Up! Wake Up! Wake up to the destiny of your lost children and of your lost neighbors.

Not only have we been awakened to the consequence of a lost soul, but we have been awakened to the numerical extent of man's lostness.

In spite of thousands upon thousands of missionaries and millions upon millions of dollars spent, the statistics chill us regarding the lostness of man: church membership dwindling in America, churches closing in Europe, churches staggering in Australia, crawling in Asia.

Of the approximately 450 major known groups in the world, 60 of them have 0% Christians; 195 or more groups have less than 5% Christians. *Wake Up! Wake Up!*

In those countries where we have greater percentages, we have less than 40% active in worship, less than 10% in prayer, and less than 2% who have won a soul to Christ.

This Congress has awakened me — and I trust you — to the great need we have as evangelicals to demonstrate our love and show forth evidence of our conversion through appropriately meeting the social and physical needs of people throughout the world.

The social concern, or what has been called the social gospel, gives great problems to many, but not to me. For I have never seen it as an "either/or" choice. The following analogy may help.

In my country baseball is a favorite sport. The game requires that one hit the ball that the pitcher pitches and then tries to run to first base before the ball can be picked up and thrown by the opposing team. If the person makes it to first base safely, he or she is then expected to run from first base to second, then to third from second base and then to home plate. It is only when they reach home plate that they have scored.

Now there are some things that you cannot do in baseball: You cannot score on first base. You cannot get to second base across the pitcher's mound. You cannot take a trip to third base and score.

You must touch first base first, then second base, then third base, *and then home.*

In the Gospel, there is a first base. First base is "reconciliation to God through Jesus Christ." The Bible says, "Verily, verily, I say unto you, you must be born again."

"Seek ye first the kingdom of heaven and its righteousness."

To this we will all agree. But many evangelicals have said in deeds that when you touch first base, you should then quit the game, go to the bench and wait on the rapture. But you cannot score that way! For there is a second base in the Gospel.

Second base is where, "men reconciled to God, formed a visible brotherhood." Second base is where no east, nor west, nor north, nor south is seen. Second base is where the unbelieving world ought to look at our behavior and call us Christians.

There are those who suggest that this, really, is the only essential base. Thus, many try to get to second without going to first. But in the words of Dr. Martin Luther King, you will not have strength to form a brotherhood on second until you have touched first.

It is at first base that we gain the love, forgiveness, compassion, and understanding. It is at first base that the desire to love others is generated.

For a little while men may, out of political expediency or social courtesies, hold hands on second base; but if they have not been to first their fellowship will soon tear with the least pull.

Our Gospel also has a third base. Brothers must not hold hands on second until Jesus comes. They must proceed to third where, "motivated by Jesus' love — filled with agapē, the hungry are fed, the naked are clothed, the wounded are bound, the untouched are touched, the broken-hearted are healed, the captives of unjust circumstances and discrimination are set free, the far-off are brought close, and those without shelter are sheltered."

But do not stumble at this point as many have. For many have said that it is at third, and third alone, that we should concentrate all of our efforts. Thus, many churches and many preachers have recently emphasized the need of community improvement — and community improvement alone. "This, and this alone, should be our objective as a church," has been recently stated by many church leaders. They tell us to ignore the Gospel, which requires personal repentance and personal acceptance of Jesus as Lord, and proceed to third and build for man a "Utopia" here on earth. They say if this is done revolutions will cease and world peace will come.

If this were true, then the city of Beverly Hills, California, would be the new heaven on earth; for in this city, there are fabulous homes, streets of granite, flowers of beauty, skyscrapers, fabulous restaurants, excellent schools, golf courses and country clubs, no unemployment to amount to anything — and the average income in Beverly Hills is $50,000 a year. But yet, this city has a psychiatrist on every other corner, and produced more hippies than any other community.

Don't ignore first, nor second base. For if you do, man will not have the moral stamina nor the spiritual capacity to stand on third without forgetting God.

If you preach to me, tell me first of the need for salvation. Persuade me, second, concerning the need of a brotherhood; and for God's sake join hands with me to build a better community. But, please, don't leave me in your message on third base.

For a little while houses and lands will suffice; but like Abraham, my soul looks for a city "whose Builder and Maker is God." In your message, don't leave me at third. *Take me home.* For no matter what you build on earth, no matter how firm your foundation, God has written on it, *"Temporary."*

Therefore, the Gospel must have a home base. The Gospel must tell all men that by and by they have got to move, and there are only two places to go: heaven or hell — and heaven requires reservations.

Wake Up! Wake up to the dangerous satanic-inspired polarization of cultures and graces.

For a long time in my country the cry to unite was largely ignored by white evangelicals; and, tragically long after integration was settled in sports, politics, and public schools, the ears of evangelicals began to open. But by then, Satan had successfully turned the hearts of many Negro people from the call of integration to the call of "Blackism" and separatism.

This call pleased many whites for it gave them the opportunity to be comfortable with their bigoted and prejudiced concepts of other people.

It also gave many so-called "Black leaders" platforms and news coverage that they neither deserved nor could obtain other than through violent, militant acts. So today racial polarization in the United States is as much of a problem as it was twenty years ago — particularly in the hearts and souls of Black young people.

Call it what you want — "nationalist spirit, cultural recognition, intra-development of a people," — but the very thought of separation of races on the basis of color or language will continue to be a poor witness to the unbelieving world and the bulwark for those in whom racial prejudice dwells.

There is no biblical explanation for the man who testifies of his first-base conversion but is hostile to a second-base interracial fellowship.

Awake! Awake! Wake Up! Wake up to the reality of a real, living devil, who is in our world and at work. Believe it or not, we live in a world increasingly being filled with cults, witches, and "isms" that ought to be "was'ms."

Too long the reality of the devil has been told as a fairy tale.

The reality of Satan's work can be seen abundantly destroying the minds of young people, creating faulty theology, cold churches, blasphemous babblers on university campuses, and frustrated preachers. *Wake Up! Wake Up!* We have a devil on our hands!

Wake Up! Wake up to the hostility towards the Gospel! Unfortunately, the welcome mat is not spread to Gospel preachers in many parts of our world. Many of our brethren will face persecution and suspicion even for their presence here. In my own country, among my own people, the Gospel preacher faces danger and death.

Three years ago the Black Panther Party meeting in Berkeley, California, declared that unless the Negro preacher was taken out of the pulpit, Negroes would not become Communist nor anti-American. Therefore, at that meeting, they labeled Christianity as "the enemy of the black man," and the Negro preacher as "the chief agent of the enemy"; and a mandate was given that they should be assassinated.

Three years ago a list of more than one hundred preachers was made. Unfortunately, the despicable act which killed Mrs. King — which was intended for Dr. King — may be only the beginning of a great bloodshed. And if they succeed in taking the leadership of Negroes from Christian leaders, then Belfast will be a Sunday picnic, compared to the bloody confrontation in America. *Wake up! Wake up!*

Wake up! Wake up to the prayer needs; awake! awake! to our educational needs; awake! awake! to our need of all resources; *awake! awake to the urgency of our task.*

At midnight one night the clock mechanically made a mistake and struck thirteen times. A little boy frightened by it ran into his grandmother's room screaming, "Grandmother, Grandmother, it is later than it has ever been before!"

My brothers and sisters, we need to do some screaming; for it is later than it has ever been before — *it is late.* Thus, know, "In the last days, perilious times will come. Men shall be lovers of themselves more than lovers of God . . . . In the last days, fathers shall destroy sons, and sons, fathers . . . ."

It is late!
"Wickedness in high places . . . ."
It is late!
"The love of many shall wax cold . . . ."
It is late!
"The minds of men will be carnal . . . ."

It is late!

Confusion, chaos, wars, turbulence: *It is late!*

But not *too* late! For God has reserved the last chapter for himself. John said he saw it.

As a follow up of Lausanne '74, there must be the Lausanne call of '75.

If while we have been here, we have seen the need of one million missionaries, then we must call for them in 1975.

If while here, we have seen the need for ten billion dollars, then we must call for it in 1975.

If while here, we have seen the need for every pastor to take a leave of absence from his church and go into the unreached areas of our world and preach the Gospel, then we must do that.

It is late; and yet not too late. If we have seen these needs and do nothing or make no call, then we make mockery of our very presence and we dishonor our God and his Christ.

Our future must not be business as usual, but rather unusual business. We must be fishers of men rather than keepers of the aquarium.

Now, with all of these calls to "Wake Up!" — calls sounded up and down the halls of this great Congress — I am sure that you are heavy-laden. I am sure that you are weary.

I preached this text at our church; and one of the sisters said, "With the pastor hollering, 'Wake Up' so many times, how can anyone get any sleep!"

I am sure that you — along with me — are overwhelmed. We feel our own inadequacies. We know that within us there is neither strength nor resources, power nor knowledge to match these mountains. Indeed, our task makes our efforts look like grasshoppers. But we need not limit our plans to our strength.

So as I close I must tell you that there is a power available to us. There is a power that can change the minds of men.

There is a power that can make enemies, footstools and stumbling blocks, stepping stones.

There is a power that can make a straight line with a crooked stick.

There is a power that turns harlots into missionaries.

There is a power that can turn cursing and swearing men into Gospel preachers.

There is a power that can open red seas, furnish manna from on high, cause walls to fall by marches, and confound enemies.

There is power available to us.

He who has called us and sent us has not, and will not, leave us; but rather, he is ready to empower us.

For this power, we need not wait.

We can move now for the power of God seldom descends upon those whose feet have not touched the water.

Let's go — for he promises that he will not forsake us nor leave us. He promises that as we go there will be strength for the day and courage for the battle.

It was in the thick of the fight that the sun stood still.

It was in the thick of the fight that the fire fell on Mount Carmel.

It was in the thick of the fight that the Red Sea divided.

It was in the thick of the fight that the prophet saw horses and chariots surrounding the enemy.

Wait no longer!

Look for no other signs!

Put out the fleece no more!

Awake!

Move!

Make plans equal to his strength, not yours!

Let our vision be a challenge to God's resources, not ours.

If we do, the world will begin to see that in our God there is no match to his power.

"Hast thou not known? Hast thou not heard that the Everlasting God, the Lord, the Creator of the ends of the earth, fainteth not, neither is weary? There is no searching of His understanding."

"He giveth power to the faint; and to them that have no might, He increaseth strength."

"Even the youths shall faint and be weary, and the young men shall utterly fall; but they that wait upon the Lord shall renew their strength; they shall mount up with wings as eagles: they shall run and not be weary: and they shall walk and not faint" (Isaiah 40:28-31).

It was in the thick of the fight that the prophet saw horses and
chariots surrounding the enemy.

Look for no other signal!

Make plans equal to his strength, not yours!

Let our vision be a challenge to God's resources, not ours.

If we do, the world will begin to see that if our God there is no
match to his power.

"Hast thou not known? Hast thou not heard that the Everlasting
God, the Creator of the ends of the earth, fainteth not, neither
is weary? There is no searching of His understanding."

"He giveth power to the faint; and to them that have no might He increaseth strength."

"Even the youths shall faint and be weary, and the young men shall
utterly fall: but they that wait upon the Lord shall renew their strength;
they shall mount up with wings as eagles; they shall run and not be weary;
and they shall walk and not faint." (Isaiah 40:28-31)

Section VI:
Evangelistic Strategy Papers and Reports

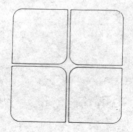

THE GREAT COMMISSION

R. Keith Parks

Dr. Parks, Richmond, Virginia, USA, is
Secretary for Southeast Asia for the
Southern Baptist Foreign Mission Board.

The first impression regarding a paper on this subject was that it was unnecessary for the select group gathering for this Congress. After long and serious deliberation there was a reversal of this initial impression. The need for a careful evaluation of the Great Commission is found in the fact that many Christians misunderstand what it meant when it was given, and how it relates to each individual and to each group of Christians. There is in the Christian community today a tendency to misinterpret or disregard the intention of Christ when he expressed the Great Commission.

This paper will deal with the Great Commission as found in Matt. 28:18-20; Mark 16:15-16; Luke 24:44-49; John 20:21-23 and Acts 1:8. All of these are seen as statements of the Lord Jesus Christ describing his intentions for his disciples in his world.

The basis of the Great Commission

The content of the Great Commission is not an extra that is added as an afterthought at the conclusion of the life and teaching of Jesus. Rather its origin is in the nature of God himself. Since God is the one true God, all created things are his possession and under his dominion. Thus the worldwide scope included in the Great Commission is consistent with his essential nature. Also the essence of his being is love. That love is defined in simple grandeur in John 3:16 where its object is the world. And in John 1:29 Jesus is heralded as "the Lamb of God which taketh away the sins of the world." Countless other references, such as II Cor. 5:19, I John 2:2, Eph. 1:8-11, 3:5-13; Col. 1:27-29; Acts 17:26, reveal that the one true God encompasses the entire universe through creation and through loving recreation in the death and resurrection of his only begotten Son, Jesus Christ.

Closely related to this concept, yet uniquely distinct from it, we find the Great Commission based on the authority of Jesus Christ. In one sense this is a repetition of the above emphasis, in that just as Jesus is one with God, everything that was said about the universal nature of God and his love for a world would be applicable to Jesus Christ. However, in a unique sense Jesus has the authority to commission his people to disciple all peoples.

This authority is based on his human experience in which as fully God and fully man he himself went forth to make disciples. Then through his sacrificial death with its resurrection quality, he demonstrated his eligibility for full authority. He carried out his divinely appointed mission as God's sacrifice for human sin, and by his own volition handed his soul back to God. In this divinely shrouded mystery he moved into the throne room of death, hell and Satan. He destroyed Satan's power, removed death's frightening hold on humanity, and robbed hell of all who would believe on him as Savior. It was this Jesus who in quiet, supreme confidence could stand on the mount in Galilee and say to those who gathered there and to all who would gather to him throughout human history, "All authority is given unto me." This is the basis for the Great Commission.

The Great Commission is, however, rooted also in the condition of mankind. There are many things taught about man by those who rely on some form of human reasoning or religious ritual or scientific knowledge or psychological experimentation. But, according to the revelation of God, every human being is in a condition of separation from God. He is cut off from the only source of life. He is in the grip of death, being contaminated by sin, being hopelessly, helplessly dominated by Satan. This condition of humanity is another basis for the Great Commission.

The significance of the Great Commission

It is important to recognize that the specific statements of the Great Commission were given during the forty days between the resurrection and the ascension of Jesus Christ. Yet the various accounts do not add a new or unique truth to other teachings in the Scripture. In fact, as early as Gen. 12:3, we find the first specific indication that God's choosing of an individual from whom he would raise up a family, and ultimately a nation, was for the specific purpose of blessing all humanity. The truth is repeated throughout Scripture that God gives spiritual blessing in order that those blessed may be channels through which God can bless the maximum number of people.

It is clear that the concept of God's desire to reach all people and of his intention of using individuals whom he has chosen to reach these peoples is an early truth in Scripture. It is equally apparent that from the early time of God's sharing his purpose, man was given freedom to obey or disobey since he is a spiritual being created in the image of God himself. The fact of man needing forgiveness and the assurance of Christ's abiding presence is taught long before the giving of the Great Commission. Therefore, Jesus' repeated statement of this concept was not to teach new truth or communicate a new command or to describe a task that had not been defined previously. Rather it was a concise summary that would crystallize and make practical what the early disciples had experienced, learned, and felt. The fact that it was stated to the ten disciples who had gathered on the night of his resurrection is of importance. Both Luke's description (Luke 24:44-49) and John's statement (John 20:21) were taken from Jesus' first post-resurrection meeting with the ten apostles. Although undoubtedly he said many things that night, the Spirit of God laid on both of these a sense of divine importance that this must be recorded for Christ's people. Perhaps Mark's reference (16:15-16) is to that same night, although it may be referring to the following Sunday evening when Thomas was present. Matt. 28:18-20, which is commonly regarded as the classic expression of the Great Commission, was not stated on either of these meetings. This was said on the Mount in Galilee. Jesus referred to this prearranged meeting when he saw the women just after his resurrection. Perhaps this was the same gathering referred to in

I Cor. 15 where five hundred were in attendance. All we know that was recorded about this meeting was the commissioning of these who had gathered there to disciple the nations. It seems that the reference in Acts 1:8 was on the Mount of Olives on the day of the Lord's ascension, a full forty days after the resurrection.

In other words, the emphasis most frequently recorded of the teaching of Jesus immediately prior to his ascension was dealing with the Great Commission. It obviously was considered by our Lord and Master to be one of the most urgent emphases that he needed to leave with his disciples. He evidently felt that it was important to underscore this teaching through repetition. It is, so far as we know, the last thing he said before disappearing into heaven. If in his economy of words and careful use of time he placed this kind of significance on that teaching, then we should make every effort to fully understand and consistently practice that which he taught.

From a pragmatic viewpoint, there are other elements of significance. This sharply focused summation of what this group of followers was to do gave them an understandable and workable plan of action to translate to the world what Christ had done and taught. These words undoubtedly echoed in their hearts to focus their attention beyond the Jewish limitations that had attempted to contain the teachings of Christ. This clearly stated worldwide objective would be used of the Holy Spirit to break down their prejudices and to avoid their tendency to settle down in Jerusalem. It was the appropriate climactic note to the life and teachings of Jesus and the opening trumpet blast launching the newborn Christian fellowship toward the ends of the earth.

The meaning of the Great Commission

Considerable emphasis has been given to the fact that in Matthew's statement the word "go" is in fact a participle. Difference of opinion comes as to whether this is a participle that has an imperative inherent in it, or whether it was simply a statement that as Christians were going they were to disciple the nations. Some have used this participle to insist that Jesus did not command his disciples to go. He did, they continue, command them to disciple the nations as they went. Whereas linguistically a case could be made for this viewpoint, it has some inherent dangers for the Christian community. Some would conclude that Jesus has never commanded us to go to all the world. He has simply said, if you happen to be going for some other reason, you ought to disciple the nations wherever you go. They thus have deleted from the teaching of Jesus a vital element and have diluted the Christian experience. Without arguing the particular verse in question, it would be wise to analyze the total biblical teaching and the experience of the Early Church.

An analysis of John 20:21 reveals Jesus sending each of us on the same mission on which his Father sent him. In Mark's Gospel the final statement given immediately prior to his ascension, the empowering of the Holy Spirit, is for the purpose of sending Christians to the ends of the earth. The very fact that the early followers were called the "sent forth ones" (from *apostello*) indicates that Jesus was committing his followers to a worldwide task. The whole experience in the book of Acts describes without any question the fact that the early gathered community of Christians was a going-forth, discipling community rather than a community that just happened to go somewhere and disciple the nations. The early experience at Antioch indicated that under the leadership of the Holy Spirit, Paul and Barnabas were set apart and sent forth. Although it may seem to be laboring the point, it does appear to be urgent that the Christian community never lose sight of the fact that the command to go to the ends of the earth is essential in the Christian experience and in the teachings of Jesus Christ. Some are sent forth under the command of Christ on a specific mission to disciple the nations.

It is also true, however, that the various versions of the Great Commission emphasize that every Christian is under this mandate. An error equally dangerous to that of not believing that anyone is commanded to go forth as detailed above, is that which says only a specified few who are called missionaries are sent to the ends of the earth. It is clear in the statements of the Great Commission that every Christian, wherever he is, is commanded to disciple others. The fact that out of the original eleven perhaps no more than one was really "at home" in Jerusalem, could suggest that the emphasis Jesus is making is not that we are to go to our homes to start, but that we are to be involved in discipling wherever we are when we commit ourselves to Christ. We are to continue discipling at every place he leads us. This is the privilege and obligation of every Christian and every gathered body of Christians who desire to be obedient to Jesus Christ. There is error built into the concept which suggests that this is a specialized instruction to those who would be involved in communicating Jesus Christ in cross-cultural boundaries which are popularly known as foreign missions. Nor is this a special restricted kind of order given to the ordained pastor or deacon or the one sent forth within the boundary of his own nation or his own community. This is the expression of Christ's will for every Christian and every group of Christians.

The meaning of this Commission also needs to be clarified at the point of whether it has within it a developmental or progressive concept. Was Jesus teaching that the Christians should fully meet the spiritual needs and fully disciple those in Jerusalem before they moved to Samaria, and culminate that task before they moved to Judaea, and finish that work before they moved to the ends of the earth?

Probably none in attendance at this conference is troubled with these misconceptions. However, it is remarkable that a number of Christians justify their involvement locally and their neglect of the rest of the world on the basis that "Jerusalem" has great need and they cannot spare personnel or resources for the rest of the world until they do a better job at home. It is instructive to note the experience of these first-generation Christians. Peter, who was called to work primarily among his own people, the Jews, was sent early in the Christian experience to Cornelius, a Gentile. Further affirmation is found in the fact that, whereas Paul became known as the apostle to the Gentiles, inevitably and invariably he communicated in the synagogue, to the Jewish people wherever he went before moving on into a Gentile community. By precept and example those who were nearest Christ demonstrated that all of the elements regarding location or kinds of people to be discipled were to be carried out simultaneously rather than sequentially. The Great Commission means that every Christian and every group of Christians is to be engaged simultaneously, discipling every kind of person living in every area of the world in each generation.

Further meaning is found in this command of Christ as he describes clearly the purpose of sending Christians. Either implied or stated in each of the expressions of his commissioning is an emphasis on the salvation of the lost world. In Matthew's Gospel, when he talks of discipling the nations and then baptizing them, there is implicit in that statement that they are first to turn from sin, become followers of Jesus, and then publicly identify themselves as Christians. In Mark's statement about going forth into all of the world and preaching the Gospel to every creature, the purpose is that they might believe and be saved. The sobering counterpart is that to disbelieve is to be condemned. In Luke's Gospel again the emphasis is given that repentance and remission of sin should be preached in Jesus' name beginning at Jerusalem and going out among all other nations. It was the witness to this truth that was laid upon the new Christian community. John's Gospel has an even more disturbing note. He states that as they went out to remit sin, the sins of these people would be remitted, but as they retained sins, the sins of those hearers would be retained. There are, of course, various viewpoints as to the meaning of these words.

The above reference could mean that as Christians are sent forth (in the manner and for the purpose Christ was sent), failure to bear witness will mean that the world has no witness and will retain their sins. But to bear a witness would mean that those believing would find their sins remitted. A variation of this interpretation is that those receiving the witness retain the freedom of choice. Upon hearing, those who refuse, retain their own sins; and those who believe find their sins remitted. The essential meaning is the same, although the emphasis shifts slightly between these two interpretations. Nevertheless, it is clear that the purpose of the sending forth was to save men from their sins.

It appears to be obvious, however, that a simple proclamation of the Gospel and an initial yes or no to Jesus Christ was not all that was included in the Great Commission. There is mention in both Matthew and Mark of the command to baptize. Although it does raise questions to read too much into terminology like this, it does have some implications. In the subsequent practice of the New Testament believers, the common experience was that baptism was related to a public acknowledgment of Jesus in the context of a Christian community. It seems that Jesus was emphasizing that his sending forth was not just to announce the Gospel in passing, but was also to minister to the new converts in such a way as to identify them with other Christians in their locality. This appears to mean that the charge of Jesus Christ is more inclusive than simply bearing a brief witness and moving on. However, there are some who feel committed to this type of ministry particularly in the light of a possible interpretation of Matt. 24:14. Yet it appears that the command to the whole body of Christians requires more than a seed-sowing ministry to fulfill the intention of the Lord's command.

Of course, the further emphasis in Matthew 28 urging the teaching of those discipled to observe all things whatsoever Jesus had commanded certainly lays upon the followers of Christ a significant and heavy responsibility that will never be fully completed before the Lord does return.

Another meaning that seems to be an indispensable ingredient of the orginal Great Commission, but is implied rather than specifically stated, is the fact that this Commission was given to the gathered community of Christians as well as being incumbent on each individual believer. This is suggested by the fact that it was stated to the Christian community each time it was uttered. It is also evidenced in the succeeding practice of the newly-born Christian gatherings. To mention only one example would be to call attention to Acts 13 when the ecclesia at Antioch was instructed by the Holy Spirit and subsequently sent forth Paul and Barnabas on what has been referred to as their first missionary journey. Throughout the New Testament this appears to be the practice where the group felt the responsibility of sending forth and of supporting prayerfully and financially those who were sent.

The ecclesia gathered at Antioch, at Ephesus and Philippi are representative of others who participated in the sending forth of called-out ones as the Holy Spirit moved among them. This reveals first of all that when the Gospel is preached and individuals are won, they will be drawn by the Holy Spirit into a fellowship which we call the ecclesia of Jesus Christ. It appears clear also that these original fellowships felt there was a responsibility laid on them to be involved in the carrying out of the Commission of Jesus Christ. Not only by example, but by teaching as reflected in Ephesians 3, we draw these conclusions. In Eph. 3:5-12 we see Paul indicating that the mystery of God had revealed that by the proclamation of the Gospel the Gentiles (the peoples) would be brought into union and fellowship with the original chosen people of God. He goes on to explain that Paul was made a minister of this Gospel, but clarifies it in verse 10 that it is through the ecclesia of God that this mysterious working will be demonstrated not only to the world but to the principalities and powers in the heavenly places. It seems evident, therefore, that the Great Commission lays a command and responsibility on the gathered Christian community as well as the individual believer.

This leads to another strong and clear teaching of the New Testament that may have been lost in modern times. There is error in the minds of many regarding the mission privilege of the newly gathered ecclesia. There are many who mistakenly believe that a Christian community that is still young and without many material resources should not be expected to be involved in witness to the uttermost parts of the earth. This is a contemporary distortion of the Gospel. The clear teaching of the New Testament is that from the initial gathering of a group into a fellowship which we call the ecclesia of Jesus Christ, that group was reaching out into its own Jerusalem, further to its own Samaria, past its own Judaea to the uttermost parts of the earth. Through the prayers recorded in the New Testament, through the going forth of the early Christians, through the setting apart of those to go out and the support in prayer and finances, it is without question a fact that from the first the

New Testament ecclesia felt a divine obligation to be obedient to the Great Commission of our Lord Jesus Christ. For anyone today to imply, to suggest, or to teach that Christian communities of recent birth should not be faced with the clear privilege and responsibility of a worldwide ministry is to rob them of a part of their inheritance in Jesus Christ. Every Christian community is at its inception to be involved in obedience to the Great Commission.

On the opposite end of the spectrum are those Christian groups who are saying that since there are growing bands of Christians in countries that have been historically the place to which they have sent missionaries, their responsibility has now been removed, and that they are only to respond to the invitation of the Christians in a given locality. This is also contrary to the teaching of the New Testament. The Great Commission of our Lord Jesus Christ has not been revoked or withdrawn. Even if one percent or five and ten percent of the population becomes Christian, there is no scriptural base for a Christian community to withdraw from that arena, waiting for an invitation by this emerging Christian body. Certainly Christian courtesy and spiritual wisdom must be exercised. Naturally, cooperation and joint planning have great advantage, but the command to disciple the nations is still incumbent on every existing community. The total Christian community must continue to be aggressively involved in worldwide mission endeavor until the Lord returns.

The assurance in the Great Commission

As best we can read the early record, the largest number who heard Jesus give the Great Commission was 500 people. In the light of all of the powers and forces in the world today, it seems almost ludicrous that he would have the audacity to say to that handful of people, "Disciple every creature throughout all the earth." Yet other than the specific command, there are two elements that changed the total atmosphere in the proclaiming of the Great Commission. As was mentioned earlier, the basis for it was declared to be the authority of God in Jesus Christ and all of the power in heaven and on earth. But in four of the five statements referred to in the introduction (Mark being the exception), there is another specific element. In each of these, reference is made to the Holy Spirit as being inbreathed into the followers of Jesus Christ in order to provide the personal, immediate power of the Godhead as the active agent in accomplishing the plan and purpose of God in this world. Whereas this could be pursued in each of the accounts, John will be our focus. He describes the sending forth of Christians as being on the same basis that Jesus Christ was sent forth from God. His was a unique incarnation, a mystery that still defies clear understanding. Yet Jesus seems to be saying: Just as I had resident within my human body the presence and power of God, so you, as you go forth into this world, have the responsibility of wrapping your bodies around the divine presence and power of God. Implied in this and clarified in other teaching is the fact that just as Jesus was crucified, so the individual believer must deny himself and get up on his cross daily and die in order that the Holy Spirit may live fully and freely in controlling power in his life. It is only through the indwelling of the living God that the Great Commission becomes reasonable.

It may well be that the failure of the Christian community to go to the ends of the earth and disciple the nations has been more at this point than at any other. Perhaps it has not been that the Christian community has failed to understand the command. Perhaps it has not been that the Christian community deliberately ignored or neglected or disobeyed the command that they understood. It may be that the lack of fulfillment of the Great Commission has been at the point of a blurred understanding of how it was to be done. Some have tried diligently and earnestly through careful planning and promotion and publicity to carry on extensive evangelistic crusades and witnessing programs. Some have given themselves and considerable resources to mass media either in terms of radio and television or of printed material in various forms. Some have grasped education, either of the masses in secular education or of the leadership of the Christian community through theological education, and have attempted to comply with the Great Commission in these terms. Others have sought through various service ministries of healing or of feeding the hungry or of housing the homeless to communicate the Gospel to the world. None of these things is bad. Neither is any of them the full and complete intention of the Great Commission.

The biblical teaching is that the intention of Jesus Christ as stated in this command only becomes a possibility through the power and indwelling presence of his Holy Spirit. It is probably accurate to affirm that if the Holy Spirit controls and fully indwells and empowers the life of Christians who have the restraining teaching of God's Word as their guideline, the Christian community will without question fulfill this imperative of our Lord and Savior Jesus Christ. It may be equally accurate to say that when this command is not fulfilled, there is a lack of the full empowering of the Holy Spirit.

It needs to be kept in sharp focus that what is being discussed is not some scheme flowing out of the creative intellect of humanity. What is being discussed is something that flowed from the heart of God from all eternity. The Great Commission describes a work that is based on the very nature and authority of the living God. It describes his work. It involves his called-out and sent-forth people. It is effected through his indwelling personal presence. It has as its objective his world and his created peoples made in his own image.

As Jesus closed the Great Commission in Matthew, he promised his immediate personal presence until the consummation of human history. He did not use the term "until the end of the age" as though time was going to dribble away. Not as if the spring of the universe would become weak and wind down, and power would finally be no more. He used the term rather in an ascending concept. He indicated that his power working fully and freely in this world would bring humanity to the culmination and consummation of its history in the fullness and presence of the power of Jesus Christ. He promised his abiding presence. Yet it could be affirmed that his abiding presence was promised on the basis of obedience to his Great Commission. It just might be true that those of his people who are not obedient to his command have forfeited at least the awareness and perhaps the fullness of the abiding presence of Jesus Christ which he promised. But there are many who are clear in their understanding, and faithful in their obedience. They have died to self and know the power of the indwelling Christ. Through them the nations will be discipled. Christ is with them until the consummation of this age.

MISSIONS STRATEGY

Ernest W. Oliver

*Mr. Oliver, London, England, is Secretary
of the Evangelical Missionary Alliance of
Britain and also Secretary of the Regions
Beyond Missionary Union.*

Strategy is defined as "the art of conducting a military campaign." While determining a strategy for the achievement of a goal will depend upon logistics and tactics, we must not confuse the choice of a strategy with the choice of methods to be employed. Speaking of the victories of the Chinese Red Army, Mao Tse-tung said, "This army, which entered the arena of civil war as a small and weak force, has since repeatedly defeated its powerful antagonist and won victories that have astonished the world; and it has done so by relying largely on the employment of concentrated strength.... Our strategy is 'pit one against ten,' and our tactics are 'pit ten against one': these contrary and yet complementary propositions constitute one of our principles for gaining mastery over the enemy."

Our Lord's Commission was given initially to a very small minority. The band of faithful men around him was commanded to "go therefore and make disciples of all nations, baptizing them in the name of the Father and of the Son and of the Holy Spirit, teaching them to observe all that I have commanded you; and lo, I am with you always to the close of the age" (Matt. 28:19-20). Never was such a small weak force given such a mighty task. So effectively did they carry out their commission that the numbers of disciples grew daily, and when the persecution over Stephen flared up, these disciples went all over Judea and Samaria preaching the Word. The strategy to be employed was of personal witness to Christ, a strategy to continue right through to the ends of the earth (Acts 1:8). The manner of their witness was dynamic and persuasive, disturbing the Jews and the pagans as probably nothing had done for centuries. "These men who have turned the world upside down have come here also" (Acts 17:6). The campaign of personal witness to Christ and of discipling the nations was being successful and continued to be so. Eusebius of Caesarea (266-340 A.D.) said, "Many successors of the apostles reared the edifice on the foundation which they laid, continuing the work of preaching the Gospel and scattering abundantly over the whole earth the wholesome seed of the heavenly kingdom."

The continuing strategy of the church of Jesus Christ today must be that of the minority incessantly launching and sustaining its mission of making disciples of all nations. The church must see the world as a world to win for Christ, through witness to Christ. To quote the Frankfurt Declaration, "The surrender of the Bible as our primary frame of reference leads to the shapelessness of mission and a confusion of the task of mission with a general idea of responsibility for the world." Wrong strategy must lead to "the shapelessness of mission," to isolated groups fighting their own little battles and running their own campaigns for objectives completely unrelated to the great strategy of making disciples of Jesus Christ.

We must confess that, with few exceptions, the general rate of church growth, i.e., the discipling of the people of the world, is either static or slow in the face of world population growth. If we accept that the growth of the church is in direct ratio to the degree of total involvement of the church in evangelism, then a strategy must be planned to facilitate that total involvement. Latourette rightly said, "Increasingly the determining question of all mission programs must be, 'What will most contribute to an ongoing Christian community?' " Ongoing in the sense of witnessing and expanding in number and influence.

1. The divine strategy

Let us be clear that the creation and sustaining of the motivation for such a strategy remains the prerogative of the Holy Spirit. Lesslie Newbigin writes, "The secret of the recovery of missionary advance lies in taking more seriously the New Testament understanding of the work of the Holy Spirit." A mission begun with the declaration, "You shall receive power when the Holy Spirit has come upon you: and you shall be my witnesses in Jerusalem and in all Judea and Samaria and to the end of the earth" (Acts 1:8), and continuing with such assurances as "being sent out by the Holy Spirit...they proclaimed the Word of God" (Acts 13:4-5) can only be sustained by the divine strategy of the Holy Spirit.

It is the Spirit of God who alone is able to make the witness fruitful. Methods and means must be justified by their availability to the Spirit to fulfill the divine purpose.

We set up a large hospital in Kathmandu, the capital of Nepal, a country long resistant to the entrance of Christian witness. The establishment of the hospital and its maintenance is a very costly business. True, at all times it seeks to demonstrate the love and compassion of Christ, but that alone cannot be the purpose. One day I sat at the bedside of a brilliant Nepali scholar dying from cancer, and through the Word of God led him to put his trust in Christ. The Spirit of God led him to call, "Lord," so that when his relatives took his frail body down to the banks of the sacred river to await death, almost with his last breath he proclaimed to those around him his faith in Jesus Christ.

We have just returned from a visit to the mountains of Irian Jaya. Missionary Aviation Fellowship planes, at great expense and at much danger to its pilots, carried us as they have carried the missionaries over the past fifteen years, into communities of Christian believers who less than twenty years ago were cannibals. We sat down amongst these people, now learning to be disciples of Jesus Christ, and many of them now in turn discipling neighboring and adjacent tribes.

The methods of institutional work and of modern transportation are justified, because they have been available to the Holy Spirit to carry on this strategy of discipling men and women for Jesus Christ. In his book *Missionary Principles,* Roland Allen wrote, "Refusal to study the best methods, refusal to regard organization as of any importance, is really not the denial of matter, but the denial of the Spirit. It is sloth, not faith."

The Eternal Spirit of God is the Holy Spirit of today, fully aware of and more than equal to the contemporary issues affecting the lives of men in any given country; aware of the needs of the intellectual in Nepal, of the cannibal communities in Irian Jaya. If the Holy Spirit is recognized as the motivator and the sustainer of the mission of the church, then he will give the wisdom for planning the methods and means to meet those needs in a way that witnesses to the power of Christ.

2. The current strategy

The strategy remains basically the same, to witness and make disciples in a world that is estranged from God. This is God's continuing ministry to his world, this is his strategy to bring home his elect from every nation. It is not a strategy that the Christian Church, as a minority in the world, has devised in order to win converts to itself, but it is a strategy that the Church worldwide must sustain in fulfilling the purpose of the Head of the Church.

Bishop Stephen Neill described the existence of the Church throughout the world as "the greatest significant fact of our era." Its significance really lies in relation to the mission of the church throughout the world. Mission is no longer an issue for which an isolated Christian like William Carey instigated an inquiry into "the obligation of Christians to use means for the conversion of the heathen" of 1792, when it was assumed that "the heathen" lived in countries of Asia and Africa. There is certainly some justification for an inquiry into the racist assumptions of the missionary movement from Western countries in the nineteenth century, but there can be no doubt that it was "the great century" for the expansion of the Church. Largely because of the efforts of the so-called "imperialistic" missionaries of the late eighteenth and the nineteenth centuries, we can think of and plan for missionary strategy in a manner which is almost staggering in its potential. In fact any mission's strategy which does not take into account the existence of the Church worldwide is a century out-of-date. Following the Edinburgh Missionary Conference in 1910, when the realization of the potential partnership of the churches in Asia and Africa slowly dawned upon the churches of the West, there has been an increasing recognition of the fact that "mission" is no longer for the Western churches a matter of "from us to you" but rather of "from all of us together to the whole world," as well as "from you to us."

There is absolutely no doubt in my mind that a truly contemporary and successful missions strategy must pay more than lip service to the existence of the Church worldwide — it must actively enter into positive and practical demonstration of that existence for the sake of the evangelization of the world.

The West recognizes that the churches of the so-called Third World, in spite of being small minorities, are being much more successful in evangelizing their own people than they are in the West.

If this International Congress is to achieve anything, it must be in the creation of facilities whereby the evangelical churches throughout the world can truly become partners in making disciples. This must begin with an appreciation of our unity in the Body of Christ and an acceptance of the fact that we all, from whichever country we may come, live in the midst of a needy people: that in our witness we all need the support and the fellowship of each other. The British Evangelical Alliance's Commission on World Mission in 1971 called its report "One World, One Task," and our strategy must recognize practically that this is the situation facing us.

Church unity as sponsored by the World Council of Churches finds little support from the evangelical missionary societies, because the International Missionary Council's integration into the W.C.C. in 1961 identified the missionary movement with a single concept of unity and a rigid ecclesiasticism. Is it possible to recognize "One World, One Church" without subscribing to the organizational unity of the various denominational churches? When we decline to join in the church unity movement are we in fact denying the very strategy of the worldwide church's united role in mission, which we would strongly support? We clearly must recognize the importance of organization as demonstrated by the plight of small churches which die in isolation in all countries. The evangelical fellowships which are steadily growing in many countries, offer the most promising means of maintaining unity of encouragement and action both nationally and internationally, without seeking to impose any one form of ecclesiasticism upon their members. The structures of churches and of missionary societies will necessarily and inevitably change to meet the current situations and opportunities arising in pursuit of our strategy, and I believe that the development of national evangelical fellowships is the Spirit's provision of a channel to make those necessary changes possible and effective. Without imposing ecclesiastical limitations they make cooperation possible.

3. The carrying out of the strategy

Instead of reverting to Mao Tse-tung's example of the success of "the employment of concentrated strength," we should look at the Gospel illustration of the great shoal of fishes threatening to break Peter's net, when "they beckoned to their partners in the other boat to come and help them" (Luke 5:7). This principle was followed when the church in Jerusalem, hearing of the Lord's blessing in many conversions in Antioch, sent Barnabas down to teach them, and when it was too large a movement to handle alone, Barnabas went to Tarsus to bring Paul for a year's vital ministry of teaching the church (Acts 11:19-26).

There are more evangelists, church planters and Bible teachers in the world today than at any time in the history of the church. Obviously this is consonant with the growth of world population, but in terms of present strategy it has more significance than that, a significance which surely cannot be lost upon those in churches in all lands who are concerned with the task of world evangelization. These facts must also be related to the potential mobility in terms of easy travel, to the great advances in linguistic facility, and the mass media. The men are available, and there are many more who could be available if adequately trained; the money is available in the hands of Christians; and the channels of communication are available in a diversity and to an extent never known before. The stage is set for the greatest missionary movement in all directions from hundreds of centers all over the world; and it is set at a time when there is evidence of a deep hunger to discover the true meaning of life in the hearts of young people everywhere.

But the strategy of the involvement of the Church worldwide must be taken seriously even at the expense of our long-established traditions and organizations. It is the work of God that must move forward, the building up of the Lord's Church and its continuing evangelistic outreach and influence in the world, and not our own organizations.

The carrying out of this strategy involves a number of different areas and aspects of the work of the churches all over the world. I have tried to write this paper to be applicable to the Church in any part of the world because while the bulk of overseas missionary endeavor still emanates from the churches of North America, Europe, and Australasia, the numbers of African, Asian and Latin American churches becoming involved in overseas work is increasing. It is therefore time for us to think and act together.

a. Cooperation. There is a separate paper on mission structures, but in the area of strategy, thought must be given to the kind of structures that cooperation demands. Is it possible to carry out the kind of strategy which calls for a polling of all available resources to accomplish certain objectives, with the separate missionary society structures which exist at present? We might even go further and ask if it is possible to carry out the strategy from any missionary society structure which keeps itself separate from the church or churches it has brought into being. Is there, in fact, any more room for the separate existence of a missionary society if there is to be this kind of cooperation? How can we better ensure the building and sustaining of closer relationships between the evangelical churches in one country with those of another? I want to make a plea for the setting up of missionary fellowships by those societies working in given areas of the world. In this way they could pool their information and resources and meet more directly needs presented to them by the evangelical fellowships or other structures in those areas. This would help in a number of ways: (i) in presenting a more cohesive picture of the situation and needs in the particular area of concern; (ii) in channeling back into the "homeland" help in personnel and methods to assist in the work of the churches in that "homeland"; (iii) in assessing the priorities for the fellowship of service; and (iv) overcoming the present confusion of a multiplicity of societies.

Surely we all now accept that there is no further room for the maintenance of proprietary rights by a missionary society over an area or over a church. At least we know that the churches in such an area no longer accept such exclusive rights by a missionary society.

There are, of course, pioneer areas where societies have recently started work and where the churches have only just been formed, but for the most part societies are working in areas where churches have existed for many years. In some cases small churches have been formed and in other cases there are large growing churches, but it is recognized that the original purposes of the societies' operations have been fulfilled. Let societies stand back and face the possibility that another twenty years' service by them may not produce any large increase in the size of those churches. Of course, a society can continue to serve a group of churches, maintain institutions, but surely the time must come when it is recognized that the church or group of churches is adult and is the center of witness in the place. Is it not then time for individual missionaries who feel so led of the Spirit to integrate into the life of the church or churches, while the society combines with others having similar interest in selective ministries to all the evangelical churches of that country?

In Britain there are signs of the birth of this kind of cooperation. Some societies are beginning to say to each other either, "We all serve one ethnic or religious group, let us do our praying, thinking and planning together," or "We have all served separately for many years in this same area; let us now combine to see what God has for us to do together for the whole area. Perhaps we can undertake together some of the tasks and ministries that have been missed by us all, and which the evangelical fellowship in that area would like to see done by somebody."

There are obviously particular areas in which the type of cooperation I have mentioned could be most fruitful. One of these is that of theological education. During the last few years national evangelical bodies have set up some kind of commission or fellowship for the study of methods of theological education, e.g., the Association of Theologians and Theological Schools in Asia (TAP-ASIA); the Theological Fraternity of Latin America; and the Theological Commission of the Association of Evangelicals of Africa and Madagascar. These represent the concern and purpose of the leaders of the churches in those areas so to educate the ministry and laity in the biblical foundation of their faith, that they can stand up against all the cultural and other contemporary influences that would wean them away from Christ. The strengthening of the theological and Bible colleges should be the concern of all evangelical Christians and certainly presents an area of fruitful cooperation. Similarly, courses in discipleship and lay evangelism are areas calling for cross-cultural cooperation.

b. Specialist societies. The Bible Societies have for long been recognized by all missionary societies and churches as the servant of all. While individual societies have done a great deal of translation work, the specialist task of finalizing, checking, printing, and publishing of the Bible has been left to the Bible Societies. The Leprosy Mission was recognized as the authority on the care of these sufferers in the context of the Gospel. Now we have other specialist societies in the realms of Christian literature, linguistics, radio, and aviation. Generally this recognition of the specialist societies has been universal and they demonstrate the great value of concentration upon a particular avenue of service for the good of all. Missionary societies have shown their recognition by the seconding of personnel and the channeling of funds to these societies. The strategy of pooling our resources should be reflected in an increasing recognition of their place and the use of their services. It may well be that they have a great deal to teach missionary societies working in the same geographical area concerning the value of pooling resources.

c. Institutions. The mission institution, school, or hospital has been one of the great media for communicating the Gospel. The primary school in Central Africa might be regarded as the main instrument in the evangelization of that area. The mission hospital in India held a very secure place in almost any community, and in many cases societies can say that the majority of their converts came through the hospital. There are those who cry, "Down with Institutions!" for they believe hospitals and schools have had a voracious appetite for personnel and funds entirely out of all proportion of their fruitfulness in conversions. What is to be their future in the strategy of mission? In some cases the question may simply be, "What is their future?"

We will look at them under two sets of conditions. First, where they are essential to witness; second, where witness is possible without them. Under the first must be included, primarily, witness in those countries which will only allow Christian witness when it is accompanied by medical and educational institutions. As executive secretary of the United Mission to Napal from its inception in 1954 to 1961, I appreciate only too well such a situation. Five hospitals, three high schools, a technical institute, and a number of primary schools were the bases from which over 100 missionaries from twelve countries have worked. Churches have been established under an entirely evangelical Nepali and Indian leadership, and the missionaries for the most part have contributed to the life of those churches. I have just been back to Nepal, to join in their twentieth anniversary meetings, and it is now the time to look back and see what God has done through this united effort and to praise him for the privilege of being his messengers in that land. The government of Nepal has just taken over the schools and is in the process of taking over the hospitals, as we had expected them to do. The missionary personnel are for the present permitted to stay in their posts and it is likely that the process of taking over the hospitals could extend over ten years. These institutions have provided the opportunity we sought, and we do not have to decide on their future.

But what of the institutions which we struggle to maintain in other lands, where there is no such government restriction? The churches cannot run them, they cannot afford to, nor do they want to tie up ministerial personnel in administration. How do they fit into the strategy of discipling the nations? It may be that some Christians would want to run them on purely humanitarian grounds, seeing service for its own sake as an integral part of witness. But is there really a place for this or that institution in the strategy of the minority discipling the majority? Institutions are usually very highly regarded by those who run them, and it is often very difficult to submit to an objective assessment of their value in the strategy of the mission of the church. But we believe that such an assessment has to be made. Few individual missionary societies today are able to staff adequately their hospitals and keep them up to date with modern equipment. In India this difficulty was accentuated by the policy of the Indian government against the entry of new expatriate missionary medical staff. Yet it was seen that a number of these hospitals were strategic to the life and witness of the church in areas of extreme resistance. Should they be handed over to government or should they be abandoned because of lack of staff? Better that than let them deteriorate. The answer has been found in the setting up of the Emmanuel Hospital Association, an Indian-based evangelical body which has taken over the direction of the hospitals. The E.H.A. has been able to attract Indian doctors to the staffs of these hospitals in the belief that their maintenance of a positive Christian witness is vital to the area.

   d. Groupings of men. In the world today there are new and growing communities which should greatly influence mission strategy and the use of personnel and funds. This is not a situation which faces one agency but all the churches wherever they are.

(i) Youth and particularly the student world. In most cases half the population falls into this category, and while they present an immediate need, the decisions they make today influence not only their own destiny but also that of their country. We believe there is an unprecedented receptiveness because of the rapid secularization of their outlook, and also there is an urgency because of the influences of humanism as well as Communism and Marxism, sowing the seeds of political rebellion. Missionary societies have not yet realized the significance of this huge segment of the population; and all support must be given to the work of the International Fellowship of Evangelical Students and similar bodies in their attempts to reach the student world.

(ii) Urban attraction. The growth of cities continues and they therefore have great significance for any strategy of mission. Peru's capital, Lima, for instance, holds fifteen per cent of the total population of the country. Kinshasa has 1,300,000 compared with about 250,000 in 1960. The Evangelical Fellowship of India has for some years now encouraged penetration plans in a number of Indian cities, when the local churches have worked together for twelve months' concentrated evangelistic effort among different sections of the urban community.

(iii) Traveling students and immigrant communities. For different reasons, these two groups are strategic sections for evangelistic effort today. The first because of their potential for the church on their return home, and the second because of their need to find Christ in the new environment away from the old religious ties.

Can we look at our programs in the light of these strategic groupings? Where are our churches' outreach or our missionary societies' endeavors chiefly concentrated? Half the population of the world is questioning, venturing youth. Is our hand stretched out to them, or are we still reaching over their heads or evading them in our journey to less significant groups? Without forgetting the unreached inaccessible tribes who need Christ, are we really involved in evangelism among the great sea of city dwellers?

e. Training for this strategy. There is need for a review of training methods in all theological and missionary training colleges. We call for church planters. Where is training for church planting available in our institutions of training for the ministry? The strategy is to make disciples to the ends of the earth — God's strategy for the saving of men in his world. Where can we really learn to disciple men? The missionary for today, wherever he comes from and wherever he goes, must be trained for this task. Are we training men for a task that does not exist, in a world that no longer exists? These men and women must be prepared for mobility of operation, be flexible in outlook, and highly skilled in their particular gifts. In pursuit of their missionary vocation many of them will have to win a place for themselves alongside professional men of other faiths or no faith, and their opportunities for witness will not be many if the quality of their work is poor. They have to be men prepared to assess their work honestly and regularly, to move purposefully toward the goals they set for themselves in witness and teaching. Missionary work can no longer be sealed within the inviolable evangelical vacuum. It is the manner in which a man acts and reacts amid a host of varying situations and influences that stamps him as a Spirit-filled man fulfilling the Spirit's unswerving purpose of witnessing to Christ.

MISSIONS STRUCTURES

David J. Cho

Is it right that mission structure for world evangelization should remain unchanged in an age which has seen drastic developments in politics, economics, and the military situation during the century-and-a-half after William Carey?

Is it acceptable that the need of world missionary cooperation should still be unheeded during these fourteen years after the merger between the International Missionary Council and the World Council of Churches?

Is it still not too late for one-way mission traffic from West to East to be replaced by a two-way system?

What is the best and most effective financial policy for world missions in our generation?

What should be the national and cross-territorial cooperative structure for the newly growing Third World mission agencies?

What are the immediate problems of non-Western mission bodies in mutual, cooperative, and effective structure in connection with a Western counterpart which has a history of 150 years?

The purpose of this paper is to call for decisive action to shift from a hemispheric mission structure to a global one, from a one-way to a two-way traffic system.

1. Organizational structure

a. *Structural inversion and functional discord* — Any organization for mission must be a working organization. The principle of the organizational structure of mission should be one that emphasizes workable structure. The mission structure, therefore, is a constant process of innovation according to the degree of church growth and spiritual maturity on mission fields.

Planting structure in embryo is inadequate for cultivating time. Cultivating structure has to be renovated to fit in growing time as a third stage. And growing structure toward its maturity has to be reshaped to become reciprocal in the face of emerging missionary successors.

Eurican mission seems to have no choice but to engage itself in the formation of a fourth stage in cooperation with Latfricasian mission which has now reached its full-grown stage, passing through that of planting, cultivating, and growing. The first reason was that the organizational structure of Eurican mission has long endangered itself on the field because of its own structural inversion and functional discord. The structural inversion is called for when national personnel resources — not only in numbers but in educational level, expertise, and spiritual ability — over a period come to outweigh missionary resources, thus causing a dynamic imbalance. Functional discord, on the other hand, arises when Eurican missionaries and national leaders think very differently on matters of policy.

The intention of mission is that an established national church is to be not only self-governing, self-supporting, and self-propagating, but also out-reaching across national barriers as soon as it receives the Gospel, in an attempt to share it with other nationals.

Another reason was that whereas the tremendous man and materialistic power which has been developed by Eurican missions for these past 150 years has so far been left largely intact, this potential power has not yet been mobilized for the benefit of the unreached world.

Here we see that structural inversion and functional discord between mission agencies and national churches could well be solved through united efforts to develop national churches into sending structures.

b. *There is no subordinate relationship* between sender and receiver in the Acts of the Apostles. Paul who himself had been sent by another also immediately made the very churches that received the Gospel from him sending ones. Thus was his own missionary machine expanded into multi-national organizations within a decade — and in this way avoided the potentially harmful effects of any subordinate pattern and possible domination by mission bodies.

The denominational missions of modern Protestant Christianity have made transplantation of their own missions their prime goal and method; this resulted in a sender-receiver, or paternalistic-subordinate, relationship. The biblical pattern is reflected rather in the example of a relay race in which each runner can be a relayer as well as a receiver of a baton, each intent on running until he finishes his allotted course. Their common responsibilities, therefore, are constantly to attain the unattained or to reach the unreached.

c. *Free floating structure* — Third World Christians are often bound to their own ecclesiastical, bureaucratic structure mainly because of denominational policies. The Jewish hierarchy in Acts 4 prevented the Apostles from preaching the Gospel, demanding, "By what power, or by what name, have ye done this?" By the same token, modern Protestant counterparts try not only to deter spontaneous mission movement from expanding, but also to limit it within the denominational structure.

Just as missionary zeal has faded away after the I.M.C.-W.C.C. amalgamation, so would the missionary fire in the Third World quickly be extinguished if the latter were to be controlled or limited by ecclesiastical bureaucrats.

The striking feature of the Third World is its variety of culture, which multiplicity is applicable also to organizational and dynamic features. Every nation, organization, or region needs to have its own free floating structure according to requirements and available resources. However, to the eyes of Western brethren who have been accustomed to see solid, concrete structure, this might appear fragile, uneasy, even dangerous. In contrast, people of the Third World who used to accommodate themselves to "sampans," adobe houses, or bamboo shelters, generation after generation, tend to think nothing of such varieties. If, however, the monolithic aspirations of the Western brethren were to interfere inadvertently in Third World mission affairs, the growth of the latter will doubtless be withered.

2. *Personnel structure*

a. *Cross-fertilization structure* — For the free-floating structure of Third World mission to develop, and for the purpose of eventual East-

West missionary cooperation, cross-fertilization structure should be formed to build up the foundations. Sometimes an element of goodwill rivalry between East and West will be needed in missionary advocacy and enterprise. It will take some time to harmonize and understand the difference of culture between East and West. Thus the dissociation in the early stage will in fact prove that the organization of Third World mission is neither exotic nor made up of external inhibition. In this connection, Western mission organizations may be requested not only to eliminate self-assertiveness so as not to bring down Third World missionary personnel as the controlled agents of the West, but to depend upon each other through genuine cross-fertilization structure, of which the following chart shows a basic concept.

Usually there will be activists and prime movers in each Third World country; in order that they should not, as it were, monopolize the movement, there should be frequent meetings and consultations with Western colleagues to highlight respective opportunities and resources, surplus and needs.

b. Third World competitive elite and controlled liaison — The bureaucratic and charismatic Latfricasian church leadership, dominant until recently, is gradually being replaced by a group of innovating, enterprising leaders who are neither administrative liaison officers nor controlled agents. Their attitude toward the changing world is clear-cut; they are afraid of no unknown future, nor of untried projects, and are men of action who will carry through their divine calling, men full of vision, challenging thought, and a sense of responsibility combined with vigorous activities.

It is by this uprising new leadership that Eurican mission personnel and leadership are challenged. The former, in many instances, excel in knowledge, experience, and ability. They can be described as innovative leaders, technical experts, unifiers, and superb organizers. In a sense they are strong competitors against existing personnel structure, distrustful of controlled agents or ecclesiastical bureaucrats.

To bring to the fore and to train these potential innovators in the Latfricasian church, missionary statesmen of Eurican mission must know how to distinguish true from false, genuine from make-believe — for once the latter is in control monolithic aspiration may be achieved, but creative and autonomous leadership will soon disappear.

3. Financial structure

Organization, personnel, and finance are the three pillars of missionary structure. These three always interact. If, however, harmony and effective adjustment among these three are not successfully worked out, the innovating tendency will wither away and a regression role show itself. The mutual relationship between Eurican's financial assistance and Latfricasian mission should not be in the form of so-called "assistance" but "East-West joint investment" in a third mission field or project, as in the case of the Apostolic church in which both Macedonian and Corinthian churches shared in contributions to the impoverished Jerusalem church. Whatever the case, receivers have no choice but to look up to givers and, like it or not, to become West-controlled agents — thus the regression role reappears.

Multi-nationalization of missionary funds is a natural result of cross-fertilization structure. By that we mean that Western missions no longer should take sole responsibility for providing missionary resources, but with their own plus those of Third World mission, both on an equal level can invest in a new project in any unevangelized zone of the earth. Some suggestions for this new venture follow.

a. Task force approach — (i) East-West common investment in joint projects for missionary task force's cross-cultural research and training. (ii) Assistance program for task force's various research and investigation trips on the field. (iii) Financial assistance to task force's various meetings and seminars.

b. Pilot project approach — (i) Provision of needed equipment and technical assistance in order to encourage the pilot project of Third World mission in unevangelized areas. (ii) Strategic financial assistance to newly developed missionary projects by task force's research and investigation. (iii) Special assistance program for Third World mission's participation in Eurican mission's special projects in a place such as the Middle East.

c. Functional approach — (i) Mutual supply and technical cooperation on the part of East-West specialists and technicians in their respective fields. (ii) Mutual exchange program of information on new situations and experimental results as well as of specialists on planning, scholars, and trainers. (iii) Training for functional workmanship on specific mission fields.

d. Indigenous approach — This is made not in terms of finance, but of ideas, mobilizing those who received theoretical training in the West and practical training in their own lands. Eurican mission inspires and encourages them to go the unevangelized areas. While stimulated by outside elements, the attempt in practice is made for and within their own countries.

e. The "Cross-Border" approach — This is made possible only when Third World missions have grown into maturity in terms of personnel and finance, and come on an equal footing with their Western counterpart in all ways, and when personnel, financial, and technical exchange can be made on a completely equal basis.

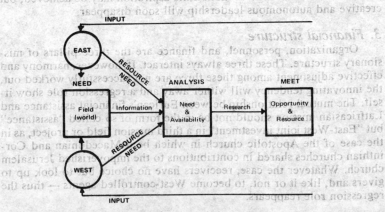

4. *Necessity of geographical structures*

The constitutional nature according to geographical and cultural classification based on national or regional units can be divided into operational structure and associative structure.

a. *Operational* — This structure signifies a direct and mutual relationship in missionary operation in the one nation or same region. This is a link between activities and agent, between the identical activities done by different agents, and between similar agents carrying out different activities. This may be further divided into reciprocal and cooperative structures.

(i) Reciprocal structures can be divided into two phases. The first relates itself to what is called "home" church by Latfricasian missions, "field" church by Eurican missions. What has to be corrected in this connection is a conventional thought-pattern: Eurican home churches — sending societies — missionaries — churches on the fields. A corrected pattern is: Eurican home churches — Eurican sending societies — Eurican missionaries — Latfricasian churches — Latfricasian sending societies. This is a problem of Latfricasian missions in their own countries while that of Eurican missions on their fields to Latfricasian sending societies. Phase two is in direct opposition to phase one. A large number of Latfricasian churches and missionaries exist both in America and in Europe. Some of these are working for Euricans and for aborigines, and sometimes even for Third World nationals. Not a few Korean missionaries have established Japanese churches in the United States, and another Korean missionary residing there founded a Thai church in two years. Still another Korean missionary started a Chinese church. Phase two, therefore, presents an entirely different case from the former.

In the case of phase one, local or national churches are planted by Eurican missionaries, and missionary sending agencies are also recognized as the fruits of Eurican missionary efforts. In the latter case, even though Latfricasian missions are working in America or Europe, there is no direct relationship with Eurican churches or missions, and the work is being carried out independently. The question is: in phase one, how to establish a mutually beneficial relationship with each other without undermining each other's integrity; in phase two, how to maintain a good relationship with the host church without being isolated.

(ii) Cooperative structures also can be divided into two phases. Phase one is both a cooperative structure between Eurican mission which has pioneered a field in a Latfricasian country and a "third" Latfricasian mission which has come to the same field, and a further relationship between the latter and its predecessor, namely, Eurican mission or field force. Phase two, which is at present rarely seen but which will increase in years to come, concerns a cooperative structure between the churches that are established by Latfricasian mission and the missions themselves.

b. *Associative* — This structure can be built up by mission organizations in one nation or region through smooth and mutual relationship and interest, and from a conviction that associative structure can do better than single agents.

The structure in any one nation should include a variety of organizational, personnel, and financial structure of mission organizations, and different features of each denomination within the evangelical faith;

moreover, different and flexible characteristics of the structure (geographical, cultural, political, economical, and ecclesiastical peculiarities) should be preserved. The need can be summarized into three principles: (i) Segregational — This is applied only to the common problem and concern of the structure, since each mission body is independent in terms of its organizational structure and of its financial policy.

(ii) Decentralization — There is no need of strong, controlling, or centralizing establishment for the structure, for each association has its own right and independence. Thus only for the common purpose and project can it be united on a horizontal level.

(iii) Liaison — Associative structure requires an administrative method on the basis of complete mutual agreement as well as administrative personnel of liaison type. This type of coordinator must not supervise or command, but be a man of fairness, virtue, passion, accuracy, experience, and positiveness.

Why, then, do we need such a loose, decentralized, and separative organization without a single leadership? Can we really carry through our great tasks with such a loose and seemingly weak organization? The weak yet strong point of evangelical church and mission is its variety, independence, and minuteness. The vertical relationship with God is independent, but no matter how varied and independent our missionary projects, we are still bound with one common denominator — the horizontal relationship which is called the binding of the Holy Spirit. One single, easily tearable weak sheet of paper cannot hold anything, but if folded can demonstrate real toughness and can sustain several hundred times its weight. This is why we demand an associative structure. A biblical example can be found in the mutual relationship among Paul, Cephas (Peter), and Apollos in the Corinthian church (I Cor. 1:10-17, 3:4-9). As Paul says, moreover, "According to the grace of God which is given unto me, as a wise masterbuilder, I have laid the foundation, and another buildeth thereon. But let every man take heed how he buildeth thereupon" (I Cor. 3:10).

Epilogue

Effective and solidified structure can accomplish a hundredfold or even a thousandfold of tasks. No matter how many resources we may have, unless these are exploited and utilized to the full extent they are nothing but weeds on the roadside, or gravel on the dry riverbeds.

If the tremendous heavenly resources, which so far have been left untouched in the wilderness of the Third World were to be exploited, only then will East and West be fully and unreservedly united to achieve a great missionary purpose in this generation.

One of the basic elements of this united missionary task force is mutual confidence, and the first step to that end is an effective and continued communication, for only this can produce mutual respect, understanding, trust, and cooperation. An effective communication is made possible through a continued fellowship. If genuine fellowship and dialogue are repeated, and if there is no self-assertion or egotism, we shall truly share burden, pain, destitution together, and present a common front to our unfinished tasks.

The second element is organic relation. With this we can activate ourselves on the basis of mutual trust. An organism is alive. Whatever living organism can reproduce ... "be fruitful and multiply, and replenish the earth, and subdue it" (Gen. 1:28) — this is the first and prime mission which God has given to men, and His most fundamental commission.

FORMULA FOR CHURCH/MISSION RELATIONSHIPS

J. Allen Thompson

*Dr. Thompson, Miami, Florida, U.S.A., is
General Director of the West Indies Mission.*

"Effective partnership between Christians of the West and the Christians of Asia and Africa is one of the vital needs of the Christian mission of our time." Since Canon Max Warren wrote those words in 1961, broad and intense discussion on church/mission relations has dominated world mission thinking. Books and articles have been written, congresses convened, surveys taken. The end is not yet.

In all, the debate has been helpful. Volunteer mission societies with superficial ecclesiastical roots have been forced to restudy the doctrine of the church and discover principles for their relationships. Denominational boards with a settled ecclesiology and fixed church/mission outlooks have been challenged to reexamine their structures as possible causes of apathy in fulfilling the Great Commission. As a result, relationships between churches and missions that appeared fixed are giving way to new forms that give evidence of the dynamic of God in life and service.

Basically, two types of relationships built on distinct truths form the spectrum of current patterns.

Integration. Based on the view that the church of Jesus Christ is enduring and the agent of evangelism, most denominational societies follow the policy of amalgamation so that their missionaries from abroad become part of the structure of the emerging church overseas. Paul Rees, an exponent of this view, writes:

> Some form of parallelism may serve as a temporary measure but it is not the wave of the future. It is the gurgle of the past. Neither continuing parallelism nor planned withdrawal is what the Asian and African Christians want from the missionaries. They want integration, membership, the kind of mutual commitment that makes of twain one.

In a more recent editorial, Dr. Rees contends that confusion in church/mission relationships arises from the unresolved question of the "comparative validity of the church on the one hand and, on the other, the separate missionary society."

Separation. The opposing view, built on the premise that mission societies are not churches but "friends of the church" commissioned to proclaim the Gospel, holds that missions should retain their identity and work alongside the emerging church. C. Darby Fulton of the Presbyterian U.S. church wrote in *Evangelical Missions Quarterly:*

> The key word is cooperation — a mutual recognition of the autonomy of each, and a resolute mind to work in harmony of purpose and program. The functions of the two bodies are different. The mission is not a church. It does not engage in ecclesiastical control. It therefore offers its services to the national church ... by presenting

itself as a task force.

A similar stand was taken by the delegates of the mission congress held in Wheaton, Illinois, in April, 1966:

The proper relationship between churches and missions can only be realized in a cooperative partnership in order to fulfill the mission of the Church to evangelize the world in this generation .... The missionary society exists to evangelize, to multiply churches and to strengthen the existing churches. Therefore we recognize a continuing distinction between the church established on the field and the missionary agency.

It is too simplistic a view, however, to presume that the question of church/mission structures is resolved by this dichotomy. In fact it borders on distortion. Far too many actual relationships have elements of both concepts. This either-or dichotomizing methodology commits us to a rigidity incapable of adjusting to the rapid march of history, incapable of creative "experimentation and response" to the tremendous opportunities of our day. Form must remain fluid if it is to be effective.

How can this be done? In this paper I propose an *approach* to church/mission relationships, not a structure; a methodology, not a specific pattern. The formula I submit includes three elements: biblical principles as foundational, a strategy that is dynamic, and a "mentality" that is open and sacrificial.

Isolate biblical principles

The Bible provides broad and basic principles, not detailed organizational patterns. Therefore it is very difficult to isolate specific guidelines that defend a particular church/mission structure. Granted this problem, I contend that the discovery of related principles provides the *modus operandi* which will bring release, freedom, and answers to the dilemma we face in given situations. The principles once isolated are applied according to the needs of culture, stage of church growth, effectiveness, and possibility. The following principles enunciated by leaders of the old China Inland Mission as they faced transition in the mid-60s illustrate my point:

1. *The missionary* — The validity of the role of the missionary arises from the continuing function of the New Testament apostle. He proclaims the Gospel to the unbelieving world (Romans 1:5; Galatians 2:7-9) and organizes converts into local congregations (Acts 14:21-23; Titus 1:5). This role is distinct from the prophetic and pastor-teacher roles (Ephesians 4:11). Furthermore, the missionary is as permanent an expression of the life and witness of the church as the pastor-teacher. From this, we conclude that missionaries are to be part of God's work until Christ returns.

2. *The mission* — The New Testament distinguishes between structured local congregations (churches) and the structured apostolic band called by God to evangelize the heathen and plant new churches. Whereas the apostles were of the Church, their corporate ministry of missionary outreach necessitated among themselves patterns of leadership and organization, recruitment and finance, training and discipline, distinct from comparable patterns within local congregations. This significant distinction gives biblical

sanction to today's structured missionary fellowship.

3. *Church and mission* — Because of the absence of biblical precedent, it seems questionable for any missionary society to allow itself to become fully assimilated into any local ecclesiastical structure. Its functions cannot be successfully duplicated by any one congregation or by several congregations working together. If attempted, this eventually reduces the missionary task of God's people to mere church-to-church interchange, something that would soon eventuate in no one "coveting earnestly" the apostolic gift (I Cor. 12:28-31). Hence, if God intends both church and mission to retain their separateness there must be some solution to the tension that currently exists between national church and western mission.

4. *Cooperation in mission* — The Apostle Paul in his missionary activity never sought to commence a new work in any locale without first seeking to relate himself to that which God had begun in the area prior to his arriving on the scene (Acts 19:1-7; Romans 15:23, 24). A parochial outlook was foreign to his spirit and practice. Today's missionary must likewise be concerned to strengthen the life and witness of each congregation he touches, while not losing his sense of priority for "the regions beyond."

5. *Flexibility in mission* — Missionaries are not to regard themselves individually or corporately as either central or enduring when compared with the local Christians and churches that have resulted from their ministry. In the final analysis national Christians and local congregations, by their permanence of existence and possibilities for continuous outreach, are God's tools for preaching the Gospel to every creature (Acts 19:10). On the other hand the permanence of the apostolic calling implies the inevitability of its constant change and adaptation.

These principles suggest the following implications:

1. God has ordained that world evangelism should be the responsibility of his church. Churches are therefore responsible and accountable to God to carry out his missionary purpose.

2. Historically, God has raised up organizations to assist and serve the church in fulfilling God's missionary purpose. Christian organizations that remain unrelated to the church must justify the reason for their existence. "Missionary agencies that administer their affairs without authority *from,* consultation *with,* or accountability *to* the churches must find their models elsewhere than in the New Testament."

3. While retaining its identity, the mission should increasingly surrender its functions as the church is able to assume them. The church may mature to such a stage that the presence of the mission is no longer needed even in a secondary role. In such a case the mission may consider its objectives completed and rechannel its resources to other unevangelized areas, alone, or preferably in conjunction with the national church.

4. Missionaries are to identify with the church on their field, worship and serve through it, and be under its authority in this relationship.

Develop a dynamic strategy

Step two in our formula is the structuring of a strategy that incorporates the principles agreed upon. Most of us in missions are activists, not theologians. For that reason we are not enamored of biblical presuppositions. Beyond that we are "talkers," not strategists, and react rather negatively to action plans.

Ralph Winter in reviewing Max Warren's edition of Henry Venn's writing makes an apt observation. Whereas Venn gives insights that today would be regarded of the "latest" variety, they were written well over a hundred years ago! "If these ideas are not really recent," Winter asks, "do they not work or are they too difficult to apply?" His conclusion: "I would rather believe that then, as now, relatively few missionaries study and reflect upon the strategy they are following." This fact among others is one of the contributory causes of friction and tension in church/mission relationships. The lack of tomorrow-mindedness, the failure to design a course of action that takes into account the many variables in world evangelism and church planting, is one of our besetting weaknesses. When tensions in church/mission relations arise they catch us off guard. This shortcoming is tragic, but correctable.

My objective in this section is not to go into a detailed exploration of strategy planning but rather to give an overview and thereby demonstrate areas vital to church/mission relations. Keep in mind that we are using the word "strategy" to refer to the overall boundaries within which plans are to be carried out.

Viewing Lower Zax as an unevangelized area, let us project a 10-year plan of evangelistic action. The strategy could contain elements as suggested in the following diagram.

Notice first, the goal. It is not limited to the evangelization of Lower Zax, but from the beginning accepts responsibility for world evangelism. This means that the pioneer evangelist has a long-range view of reaching areas beyond Lower Zax. This motivates him to keep abreast of happenings in other areas, to pray for the work of God worldwide, and to communicate world awareness from the beginning to his converts and young churches.

Objectives narrow the goal. They move from the individual, to the group, to the world. Always a new dimension is added as a former one has gained momentum. Of course, to be measurable, the objectives are assigned specific numerical and qualitative expectations.

Next, consider the four important variables, each of which affects greatly the type of relationship established and mood set in each phase: key person, principal activity, assistance, and structure. The pioneer evangelism phase is the easiest in terms of relationships because of the excitement of the work, the absence of friction among comparatively few leaders, the good spirit that assistance and cooperation bring, and the informality of structure.

Tension appears or accelerates in Phase II as transition in roles begins. The temptation to hold back leadership is strong. The role of the evangelistic missionary (whether national or foreign) is often threatened. Here the seed of future church/mission relationships is planted. If emerging leaders are taken into confidence, treated as equals, trained in an atmosphere of self-respect, and involved in the work, then the basis for true partnership is set.

The process by which roles are exchanged is also a critical factor in determining whether relationships remain wholesome. The basic cri-

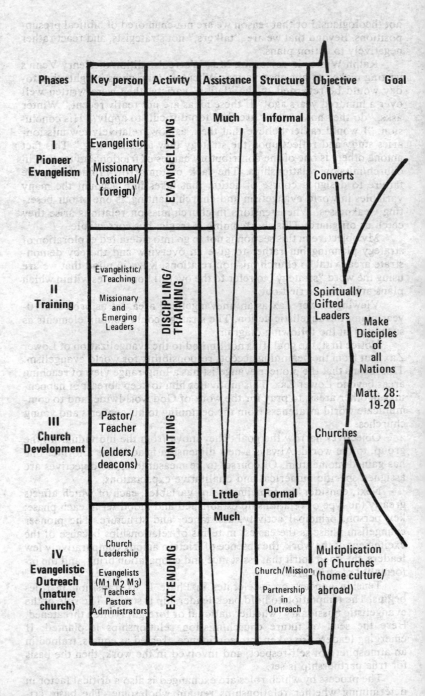

Phases	Key person	Activity	Assistance	Structure	Objective	Goal
I Pioneer Evangelism	Evangelistic Missionary (national/ foreign)	EVANGELIZING	Much	Informal	Converts	
II Training	Evangelistic/ Teaching Missionary and Emerging Leaders	DISCIPLING/ TRAINING			Spiritually Gifted Leaders	Make Disciples of all Nations Matt. 28: 19-20
III Church Development	Pastor/ Teacher (elders/ deacons)	UNITING			Churches	
IV Evangelistic Outreach (mature church)	Church Leadership Evangelists (M_1 M_2 M_3) Teachers Pastors Administrators	EXTENDING	Little Much	Formal Church/Mission Partnership in Outreach	Multiplication of Churches (home culture/ abroad)	

terion for assigning tasks should be the presence of spiritual gifts validated by the church, not race, rank, or tenure. Foreign missionaries as well as national workers should submit to the judgment of the church regarding their gifts and be assigned to tasks accordingly.

A second source of tension is methodology or the principal activity. At times missionaries have innovated, not being fully aware of what they were doing. At other times they have digressed and initiated ministries that appeal to their interests, or that are applauded in the sending country, or provide quick sources of funds. A great deal of discipline and heart-searching is needed at this point. Objective interaction with fellow workers about approaches, determination to be governed by objectives, and a passion to put method under critical judgment are necessary qualities.

A third area of tension involves assistance — finances as well as personnel. My view is that at the beginning of any evangelistic church-planting cycle much assistance is needed, preferably from national churches but also from abroad. Churches must send and support workers as they pioneer these areas. As the work grows, however, leaders from the outside must be curbed. Local leadership is now emerging. Offerings and participation are rising. A continual flow of imported leaders or too much outside money can quickly kill initiative in a growing work.

Most of the tensions in finance, as I have observed or been a part of, are due to lack of open communication between church and mission. A frank exchange of views and careful decisions regarding the use of funds and the deployment of personnel can do much to influence the spiritual vitality of the church. Outside money when needed should go to the church, not individuals, to be used to assist the work primarily in opening new areas, and given on a decreasing scale. Never should money be given in a way that curbs the autonomy of the church.

The fourth delicate area is that of formal structures. Better to build strong interpersonal relations of trust than to expect that written agreements will resolve conflicts. Most confidence breakdowns result from lack of communication, not from lack of documents. This is why I suggest postponing written agreements until Phase IV of the strategy plan. Perhaps the most critical area here is not one of assigning responsibilities to church and mission, but that of joint decision-making.

Suggestions:

1. Agree mutually on *objectives.*

2. Confer together (national church and mission) regarding plans to move into a new area and try, if at all possible, to undertake the project as a joint endeavor.

3. Establish a procedure for continued decision-making that assures open and full discussion between church and mission leaders.

4. Formalize working relationships in writing, not to avoid responsibility or place blame, but to facilitate review and evaluate progress.

5. Share administrative insights and establish management training programs.

6. Design an evaluation system that requires realistic appraisals at specified intervals.

A final word regarding "dynamic" strategy. Peter Wagner has rightly been critical of short-sighted missions caught in the "church planting syndrome." Once the church is planted in a given place, those missions believe their work is over and withdrawal begins. It is better to move on to Phase IV in your work and prepare for the most exciting and dramatic period of evangelistic outreach. As the mission joins hands with the national church reaching new people either in the same geographical area or in a cross-cultural situation, God's blessing begins to flow. In response to missionary vision, introspection gives way to selfless involvement in others. Resources of men and money begin to appear, and the church and mission in partnership reap a harvest. A hidden dividend soon is evident. The church and mission deeply involved in evangelistic action forget to squabble. In addition, a new cycle of strategy has been initiated that has the inner resources for continual recycling as illustrated in the second diagram.

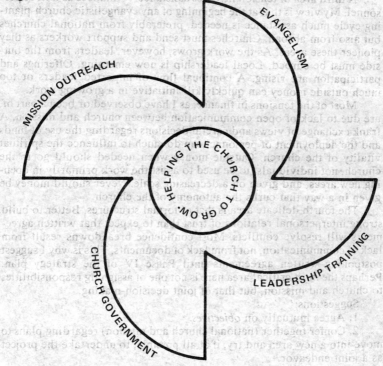

EVANGELISM

MISSION OUTREACH

HELPING THE CHURCH TO GROW.

CHURCH GOVERNMENT

LEADERSHIP TRAINING

Dynamic Strategy

Cultivate a servant mentality

A final ingredient in our formula for achieving effective church/mission relations is a self-emptying, open disposition. Principles and strategies are devoid of life until implemented. Then people touch people. And this is an important clarification to keep in mind, that a church and a mission cannot relate apart from the activity of persons.

Breakdowns in relationships most often are due to the inability of persons to relate to each other instead of inappropriate working agreements.

Pointers:

1. Maintain a high degree of personal identification with people you serve. This requires deep motivation, complete understanding, and mutual acceptance.

2. Take the road of service. Max Warren, calling for a new initiative in church/mission relations, says, "Essentially the newness of this approach will be found in the humility which will be demanded, the self-emptying of much pride of possession which will be involved, and the readiness to take the form of a servant. Recently Eduardo Velasco, a Brazilian student at Reformed Theological Seminary in Jackson, Mississippi, made a similar plea:

> Missions should work through national churches, be they strong or weak. This would be accomplished through responsibility in partnership. This is not a new solution. It is avoided because it costs. It costs not dollars but lives. It involves the setting aside of bias and prejudices in each partner in such a way that the Holy Spirit and his calling on each other be the only realities in their partnership. This is the beginning and the end of any fruitful and lasting mission.

3. Recognize and respect equality and mutuality. Even the closest of identification does not mean the loss of identity. It means the sympathetic entering into the life of another. "Partnership in missions is a sacred and comprehensive concept of equals bound together in mutual confidence, unified purpose, and unified effort, accepting equal responsibilities, authority, praise, and blame; sharing burdens, joys, sorrows, victories, and defeats. It means joint planning, joint legislation, joint programming, and involves the sending and receiving churches on an equal basis."

4. Embrace an attitude of partnership. George Peters makes a strong case for church/mission relations as an *"attitude,* a spiritual, social and theological relationship, a philosophy of ministry, a way of life and missions."

This attitude is built on a deep recognition of a Christian's identification with the body of Christ and a response to the fellowship of the Spirit of God.

Conclusion

Two truths, interrelated and basic, undergird church/mission relations: (1) God greatly desires that the world be evangelized; (2) God loves the church and has ordained that it be his agency for evangelism.

In applying the formula suggested in this paper, these truths must be maintained in proper balance. The emphasis on one to the exclusion or negligence of the other will produce serious aberrations. Careful and constant application of both will result in growth and effectiveness.

Perhaps a graph transferred from the management world will serve to crystallize this point.

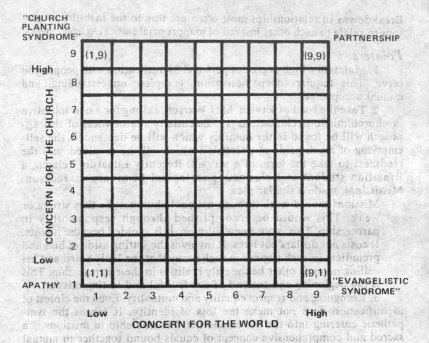

Concern for the world

The church/mission grid depicts concern for the church on the vertical axis and concern for the world on the horizontal with increasing degrees of interest. Numbers in parentheses correspond to the major *styles* of relationships. The 1,1 pattern, devoid of interest in world evangelism or the church, is an IMPOVERISHED, APATHETIC approach. The 1,9, emphasizing solely ecclesiology, is caught in the "Church Planting Syndrome." The opposite extreme, 9,1, with a high concern for the world but no concern for the church, is the "Evangelistic Syndrome." The balanced approach, of course, is represented by the 9,9 PARTNERSHIP position, equally committed to the church *and* world evangelism.

Hopefully, under God, *partnership* of church and mission can become the style of our relationships. It will go a long way to remove the unbiblical pattern of a "churchless mission" or a "missionless church,"

INTER-MISSION RELATIONSHIPS

S.O. Odunaike

*Mr. Odunaike, Yaba, Nigeria, is Personnel
Manager of the British Petroleum Nigeria
Ltd. He is also General Supervisor of the
Foursquare Gospel Church in Nigeria and
Chairman of the Nigeria Evangelical
Fellowship.*

" 'Master,' said John, 'we saw a man casting out devils in your name, but as he is not one of us we tried to stop him.' Jesus said to him, 'Do not stop him, for he who is not against you is on your side' " (Luke 9:49-50).

"Some of course, are preaching the Good News because they are jealous of the way God has used me. They want reputations as fearless preachers! But others have purer motives, preaching because they love me, for they know that the Lord has brought me here to use me to defend the truth. And some preach to make me jealous, thinking that their success will add to my sorrows here in jail. But whatever their motive for doing it, the fact remains that the Good News about Christ is being preached and I am glad" (Phil. 1:15-18).

"Let God's curses fall on anyone, including myself, who preaches any other way to be saved than the one we told you about; yes, if an angel comes from heaven and preaches any other message, let him be forever cursed" (Gal. 1:8).

1. The biblical ground for inter-mission relationships

I hope the above Scriptures sufficiently lay the groundwork for our treatment of this vital subject. Two of the Gospels, Mark and Luke, record the incident in which our Lord strongly rebuked sectarianism. The context was the same in both records. Jesus was in Capernaum and while on his way to a house, the disciples had engaged in some private discussion among themselves. The topic was of great interest to all of them, for it majored on position, influence, and authority. "Who should be the greatest?" This seems to be the one thing that bugs most religious circles today. The plague is still with us. Everyone wants to be a leader. So it was with the disciples. Jesus had been talking about his forthcoming death in Jerusalem. "The son of man shall be delivered unto the hands of men." But this sublime truth they did not understand. I doubt if they even tried to understand it. There was something else that engaged their thoughts and which they understood perfectly. Jesus was speaking about a new order. They all wanted to be part of the new order — whatever it meant. More important to them, the new order must have some leadership — and each one wanted to be that leader. This resulted in a dispute among them. Is it not true today that the "leadership plague" is crucial to the barrier to relationships which ought to exist among Christians?

Our Lord's answer was simple. He allowed them all to have their little talks. Then on getting into the house, he asked them for a confession:

"What was it that ye disputed among yourselves by the way?" Of course, they were too ashamed to say. They held their peace. He then called for a child whom he set before them as an object lesson in the humility they lacked and so desperately needed. "Whosoever shall receive one of such children in my name receiveth me." The message did not really sink in, for John asked his question about the one who cast out devils. Were they wrong in forbidding him to do so? You were wrong, said Jesus in effect, "Although he is not part of our group, his mission being essentially similar to ours, he is ipso facto one of us."

Jesus dealt with the *task*. Paul in his letter to the Philippians deals with the *motive*. Paul says he knows of some who preach Christ out of an insincere motive. They are jealous of Paul's success. And how true this is today! We hear of one group doing particularly well in an area of Christain service — and we perhaps rush there from ill motives. Paul says they want reputation as fearless preachers—that is, they must have said or done things deliberately to hurt or cause offence. Paul adds that they wrongly think that they can excite similar feelings within him by making him jealous of their success. I am not entering into judgment of people's motives, says Paul, neither am I taking a stand against them because they may or may not be sincere in their motives. Rather, and contrary to all their expectations, I rejoice, in that whatever their motive for doing it, the fact remains that the Good News about Christ is being preached and I am glad.

If these were all the revelations concerning this matter, the Lord's people would be put into much confusion of thought. But writing to the Galatians, Paul pours out hot imprecations on some preachers of the "Gospel." At first sight this might appear contradictory to the above. Here Paul does not rejoice, he curses. Why? Is it because they do not belong to the Pauline party? What does he mean by "preaching any other gospel than that which we have preached unto you"? Is this not being unduly narrow and dogmatic?

Now some have used this Scripture as the basis of "no relationship" with any group that does not sign the dotted line on every tenet of faith embraced by their group. Frankly, I cannot endorse such a stand because it would give the stamp of "infallibility" and "exclusiveness" to some "form of words" which men have put together from the Holy Scriptures in the light of their own particular understanding of the Word. One thing we need to note here is that Paul is not talking about someone whom he regards as a "brother."

He is talking about some whom he categorically denounces on a ground which is relatively simple and clear. Let us note the difference — the individual in Philippi preaches Christ, albeit from a wrong motive. *The one in Galatians does not preach Christ.*

2. The right balance in inter-mission relationships

Here Paul strikes an important balance which we should note in considering "across-the-border" relationships with other Christians. Some ecumenists teach that all division is sin, even division between the Christian and the world. We cannot go along with such fallacy. Of course, we know that there is the world which is the object of God's love, but there is also the world-system, opposed to God, masterminded by Satan, which is the object of God's wrath. To the former, we are to bring the proclamation of glad tidings of reconciliation; we are to announce the Messiah; we are to bring them to "kiss the Son whilst he is yet in the way." But with the latter, we are to "come out from among them and be separate" (II Cor. 6:17). We are to "love not" for "whosoever therefore will be a friend of the world is the enemy of God" (James 4:4).

I think this question of maintaining a right balance in our relationships is very important, because if we don't get it right we are likely to cast away many of God's children or confuse others in such a way that they will recoil from any attempts at fostering meaningful relations between Christians. The question is, when should we say, "He that is not against us, is for us"? When do we *rejoice* in the act, regardless of the motive? And when do we *reject* relationship with the "brother" in spite of the act? I believe that the marks of false teachers are so numerous in Scripture that no mistake should be made in detecting them. To highlight some of the basic ones, *false teachers will deny:*

— a personal God
— the incarnation of God in human flesh
— the person of the Holy Spirit
— the virgin birth
— the sinless life of Jesus Christ
— the divine miracles performed by Jesus Christ
— his physical death, burial and bodily resurrection
— his ascension to the right hand of the Father
— his Headship of the Church
— his personal and imminent return for his saints

I do not speak as a theologian but as a churchman. But I am convinced that where there is a true and hearty desire for relationships based on the Word of God, his directives are so plain that "he may run that readeth." Even "the wayfaring men, though fools, shall not err" (Isa. 35:8).

3. The need for inter-mission relationships

From this sketchy treatment of the general framework for "relationships" I turn my mind specifically to "inter-mission relationships." I thank God for the numerous agencies it has pleased him to raise up over the years as light shining in dark places to reach the habitations of cruelty and publish glad tidings to the poor. As a churchman from the Third World, whose privilege it has been to serve the Body of Christ in Africa and elsewhere for more than two decades in various capacities, I think I may comment on the manner in which "the sending church" has been a blessing to "the receiving church" in the matter of missions.

a. *An antidote to Sectarianism* — These have indeed been numerous but this is not the place to recount them. Rather, what we are considering is the question of "inter-mission relationships." In their book *Nigeria under the Cross,* Michael Marioghae and John Ferguson, commenting specifically about the Church of Jesus Christ in Nigeria, said: "Europe has imposed its sectarianism upon Nigeria and Nigerians have very properly revolted against this." What is said of Nigeria here can be said of

Africa, Asia, and Latin America in varying degrees. Perhaps the word "revolt" is rather strong but when one considers the stance of the proponents of "authenticity" in Zaire, one really wonders if "revolt" is indeed inappropriate. Too often traditional jealousies and rivalries that have stood for centuries and bear no relevance to the heartbeat of the "evangel" are transported across the seas only to leave "the receiving church" bewildered. As chairman of the Nigeria Evangelical Fellowship and president of the Association of Evangelicals of Africa and Madagascar (AEAM), I have witnessed scenes where genuine efforts at fostering relationships on the "Foreign Mission field" are frustrated as a result of pressures from "Home Mission Boards" who happen to pitch in different camps at "home."

b. *An incentive to promotion of evangelical fellowship* — This is not always understood by nationals who sincerely wonder why there cannot be more meaningful relationships for Christ's sake and the Gospel's. We have now held three major evangelical conferences in Africa — 1966, 1969, and 1973. On each occasion, invitations went out to over forty countries in Africa to evangelical churches/missions both within and without structured evangelical groups. No fewer than an average of thirty African countries have been represented at our conferences. The Africans, talking to us feel they need to go back home and draw the line in favor of an evangelical fellowship. But what happens? As an example, we find that in one country, there are four or five evangelical denominations that are offshoots of various missions.

The field supervisors of two or three have directives from their home boards that they are not to have too much to do with works established by a certain mission. The field supervisor, therefore, applies all types of pressures to dissuade the Africans from going into a fellowship with the other groups. It is unnecessary for me to list country after country where we have known this to happen. My question is, on what ground does the home mission board take such a stand?

I hope I have said enough to indicate that I do not believe the Scriptures teach us to embrace all and sundry so long as they name the name of Christ. But the Scriptures definitely tell us when to reject a "brother." My submission is that the grounds on which most missions "reject" other missions' agencies do not always conform to what the Scriptures lay down. With false teachers we should not and cannot compromise. But what do we say about divisions based on differences of revelation on things like:

— infant baptism versus adult baptism?
— mode of baptism, immersion or sprinkling?
— charismatic operation of the Holy Spirit?
— ministerial dress?
— antepost millennialism?

Are these related to that for which Paul said we should "curse" anyone who teaches or embraces that which is contrary to what we hold? I do not wish to throw stones but we would have had only a grand picnic at great cost and much grief to our Lord if we do not take this opportunity to search our conscience in this matter of inter-mission relationships.

A missionary is necessarily a leader. Thus it matters very much which way he leads. It is not therefore surprising to find that there are only about fifteen countries in Africa with evangelical fellowships. Of these, there are at least three known countries that are reluctant to relate to a continent-wide association of evangelicals as a result of missionary action. If ecumenists go too far left, does that make evangelicals correct for going too far right? What is more, to what extent is it right to transport attitudes and prejudices which are probably relevant in one land, within the context of a particular historical setting, into another land which bears little or no sympathy to the case in point? If "the Jews have no dealings with the Samaritans" is that why the Jewish missionary society and the Samaritan missionary society should foster similar divisions and near hostilities among converts in Hongkong, Bangui, Basutoland, and Nepal? Is there no "common ground" in the "everlasting Gospel"? I am not asking that this conference try to undo centuries of history. Rather, what I plead for is a realignment of thoughts and attitudes towards one another right from the base — which in this case is at the missionary society/association level. We thank God for what is already being done in this direction, but I am sure a lot more can be achieved.

c. *More effective utilization of resources* — The Lord's people have not always been the richest on earth, but the material resources which it has pleased the Lord to bestow on his Church could surely be better utilized with greater coordination among missions and missions' agencies. There are projects like graduate schools of theology, trans-national communication of the Gospel, research, and several other projects that are better handled on a joint basis than for everyone going his own little way. Much dissipation of energy, unnecessary duplication of effort and scarce resources can be avoided in the field of literature, if this line of thought and action is vigorously pursued. What about a joint onslaught on an unevangelized area? Why concentrate missionary endeavor in one particular area? We must of necessity solidify our frontal attack somehow, somewhere, if the unreached two billion of the world are to be effectively evangelized.

d. *Government representation* — Furthermore, the image of missions before the world and government functionaries is always better enhanced with a greater representation of cohesion among missions and missions' agencies.

e. *The maintenance of a proper evangelical identity* — I have little doubt that some of the thoughts outlined above were part of the motivation for the First All Africa Church Conference held at Ibadan, Nigeria, in 1958. Unfortunately, many who have watched that movement since then cannot but be struck by its rapidly changing face. If today many evangelicals in Africa do not properly consider themselves as belonging within the movement, let it be said for the sake of history that that which repels them today has not always been there. To illustrate the point, we recall that the Second All Africa Church Conference was preceded by an All Africa Christian Youth Assembly at Nairobi. The theme of the assembly was "Freedom under the Cross." By the time that conference was over, these "young Christians" were declaring that they had come "to see that political action is not enough." A report of the conference recorded this conclusion: "If we are to understand the relationship between freedom and authority, or the meaning of our lives here on earth, we do not begin with the idea of freedom as a philosophical concept. We begin with the Cross as a historical reality, and with Jesus, whose life, death and resurrection have given meaning and content to the idea of freedom. . . . It is important that we keep this order straight, for to reverse the order and begin with the idea of freedom and only ultimately refer the idea back to the Cross might produce a wonderful religious ideal, but it is to miss the astonishing truth that there is no true freedom except under the Cross." That was in 1963. But the situation today is vastly different. Bangkok 1973, with its concept of "Salvation Today" shocks the conscience of millions of evangelicals.

Where do we turn? These trends surely greatly emphasize the need for intensive and cohesive cooperation among missions and missions' agencies the world over. I would like to stress the need today for a world missions body arising from this Congress. There appears to be an urgent need today, in the light of the objectives of ICOWE, to consider the formation of an international association of evangelical missionary agencies.

What is the biblical basis for missions? I was invited to Western Germany in January, 1974, to participate in a series of meetings preparatory to the synod of churches. Some of the burning questions raised included: What is the role of missions today? What causes should missionary funds support? What do the "unevangelized" of the world need — reconciliation with God or economic emancipation? What is the place of Black Theology in missions? Is the "lostness of man" as crucial in missions today as it was in the days of Hudson Taylor? Someone must speak to these issues. If truth is not diffused, error will be. We cannot afford to deal with these matters in isolation or we shall be swamped under the avalanche that is swiftly sweeping under our feet. Many of these problems are common to all of us. That was my pleasant surprise in Germany. I spoke from my heart the same truths that it had been my privilege to share in the backwoods, cities, colleges, seminaries, and institutions of Africa, Asia, and the United States. I found that the same questions were being asked. The same answers met the need, perhaps in a different way. This is why I am more than convinced of the place for a platform to plan together a common strategy to deal with common problems relating to missions.

If I may summarize, the call for the type of association suggested above is based upon the performance of very useful tasks, some of which are: To present an evangelical identity and present it to the Christian public and to government; to affirm the biblical basis of missions; to exchange information and promote research; to coordinate the use of resources (personnel, finance, training etc.); to plan together common strategy to deal with common problems.

Furthermore our experience in Africa has highlighted the need for close liaison between churches and missions. I would suggest the encouragement of associations of missions' associations and individual missions with national evangelical fellowships or alliances of churches. I hope from what has been said that we clearly have in mind what relationships to "rejoice" in and what to "reject." My plea is that this "rejoicing" should be in a concrete, organic form to give meaning and content to the relationships. If we are to complete the task of world evangelization by the turn of this century, if this Congress is given to finding, under God, how this supreme task is to be speedily accomplished, then I hope that evangelical missionary agencies, missions' associations, national evangelical fellowships, and all areas of churches seek the mind of the Lord for one common worldwide platform whereby this desire of the Lord can prosper in our hands.

CROSS CULTURAL EVANGELIZATION FOREIGN MISSIONS REPORT

Secretary Wilfred A. Bellamy

The church in the Third World assumed high priority in all papers and the responses to them. The group was concerned for the primacy of the church and for another look at the relationship between church and mission. This latter point became by far the most significant issue to emerge during the six days of meetings scheduled.

The group grappled realistically with structures and strategy but came to no hard-and-fast conclusions. On the contrary it was clearly recognized that the initiative for evangelization in the Third World is being transferred to the church and that mission must now serve in a subordinate role, always providing that such a role does not usurp the sense of call and obedience of the missionary to his Lord.

It was noted that Western structures, rather than enhancing the church, tend to frustrate and stultify church activity. Missions must therefore take care, lest the structures which they employ be either knowingly or inadvertently passed along to the national church, thus creating an inappropriate structure for the indigneous body. The church was also recognized as having the right to express its own needs, assume the authority in decision making which affects it, and to take or leave the assistance offered by the mission.

On the other hand, however, the group firmly confirmed the need for two specific bodies (church and mission) to be maintained in a relationship mutually acceptable to both parties. There was some disagreement at this point especially from Third World delegates who apparently desire a closer relationship than dichotomy offers. Much was heard concerning a preference for "merger," "marriage," or "integration."

The Congress note on the "equality of man" was not absent from the group. It was pointed out by several speakers that there is no real difference between missionary and national believer in terms of status and therefore no difference in status should exist. Rather missionary and national believer should work in close harmony with a determination and dedication to accomplish the task which our Lord gave to the church.

This naturally led to discussion concerning resources and their use. The group strongly expressed the view that church and mission should become involved in a pooling and distributive relationship which would centralize both funds and personnel, applying them to the task.

Concern was frequently expressed both from the platform and the floor that communication be improved between church and mission and vice versa. Again and again it becomes all too apparent that the church seldom understands the problems of the mission nor its resources. Nor does the church have a say in the deployment of missionaries in the ministry. On the other hand the mission seldom understands the inner dynamics of church government, seldom joins in membership in the church, and mistakes for slackness and inefficiency the patience and caution of national colleagues. There is a need for greater cooperation, openness and fellowship at a deeper level between missionary and national believer. This will build mutual confidence and trust, a much needed dimension in church-mission relationships.

Some practical ideas which came from the group include the formation of an Information Service which would make worldwide missionary news available, especially as it relates to Third World Missions. Their encouragement and stimulus received high priority from the group and it was felt that such a service would facilitate greater understanding between such agencies and also assist in sharing ideas and strategy.

In summary, therefore, the group concluded that before structures and stategy can assume a true significance for cross cultural evangelization, important though they are in themselves, deeper issues must first be dealt with — namely the question of church-mission relationships and a re-examination of their own scene by every mission and related churches. Thus it was felt that the task of evangelization would surge forward as differences which have militated against this are dealt with by both organizations, and a better expression of love and fellowship emerge within the total Body of Christ. When this is seen in tangible demonstration we believe that the earth will truly hear the voice of our Lord.

EVANGELISM AND THE MEDIA: A THEOLOGICAL BASIS FOR ACTION

Philip Butler

*Mr. Butler, Seattle, Washington, USA,
heads Intercristo, an international Christian
communications group.*

A bewildering number of cultural patterns, methods of operation, personal opinions, and theological traditions come sharply into conflict as we review the world of Christian mass communications — particularly as it relates to evangelism.

The church, faced with a staggering rate of technological and methodological change, is hard pressed to "keep up." Combine this change with the shaking of the cultural/moral foundations in most parts of the world, and the church has found itself on a sea of controversy with largely no compass.

Much of this controversy is born out of the fact that the church has very few professionally trained media personnel aggressively working in evangelistic use of the media. Possibly more significant, however, the church has not established a *theological basis* for use of the media. It has been "every man for himself."

We have been victims of a myopic view of Scripture. It is consistently said, "One does not find television or cinema in the Bible." This is true. The unstated conclusion, however, is the most dangerous part of this observation. Because television is not in the Bible, it is inferred that "we cannot look to the Bible for guidance as to how to make, distribute, or use our television program." This kind of thinking has had a devastating impact. It has left us with fragmented, often ineffective, use of the media. Most unfortunate, this lack of biblical basis for our use of the media has emasculated our confrontation of the lost. Indeed, one must say that the church's use of media for evangelism today is largely out of touch with those in greatest need.

This paper seeks therefore to outline basic concepts consistent with proven communications theory, providing a correlation with the Word of God.

Scripture calls for use of media

First, Scripture gives a clear mandate for use of the media. From the outset of Genesis, God has given man responsibility for dominion over the natural fruit of this world's element. The question is not, is it right to use high-speed presses or television (or radio, audio-visual aids, cinema, etc.). Rather, it is a question whether or not the specific medium is the right one for the situation under consideration. In Gen. 1:26-31, God placed responsibility for the media in our hands. And the media are vehicles either for redemption or condemnation.

But other scriptural references point more specifically toward a mandate for use of mass media. Review passages like Eph. 5:16-17 and Col. 4:5 where Paul instructs us to "buy up the time." Efficiency of the media in reaching such large numbers at low cost is a most practical response to our Lord's command for wise stewardship found in Matt. 25:14-30 — the parable of the talents. Such passages should give the church cause to think about the consequences of not aggressively using the media for evangelism. What will God require of *us*?

The first chapter of Hebrews is one of the clearest statements in Scripture regarding God's *own* use of media. God, after many types of communications through the centuries, at last chose the incarnation itself as the ultimate statement in his use of media. He chose to put his message in the form of a living soul. John 1 states, "The Word became flesh and dwelt among us ...." God used countless other media throughout the Scripture to communicate with men, such as plagues, pillars (of salt, fire, cloud), animals (remember the ass that spoke?), rainbows, and manna. His message of concern, love, judgment, and desire for reconciliation always came through.

The Scripture points to goals

There is an ancient saying: "How will one know when he has arrived if he does not know where he is going?" So it is with mass communications. There must be precisely defined goals — plans for what is expected in audience response and what, ultimately, we want to have happen as a result of this response. The Lord himself spoke to this issue repeatedly in the New Testament. The matter of setting goals or knowing what is expected is covered in such passages as Luke 14:28-30 and Phil. 3:13-14. In these sections we see the clear necessity of goals — defined and visible on a day-to-day basis. The Lord had his face "set like a flint" for the Cross. He knew where he was going. And in John 17 we find him saying, "I have finished the work you sent me to do." Job complete.

Too often our goals are nebulous and ill-defined, leading to hazy thinking and, finally, great frustration and conflict. Setting general and specific goals is essential both for our entire communications program and for specific evangelism segments. If we do not know what we want the audience to do, it is certain the audience will not know!

Media form and audience should "match"

The Bible and communications professionals agree — the message is best transmitted when medium, style of content, and audience are carefully matched. The Apostle Paul makes a strong case for understanding that the audience is remarkably varied from location to location, culture to culture. He points out that the form for the message may have to be modified to meet different audiences, even within a single geographic location. Note what he suggests in I Cor. 9:22: "I have become all things to all men that by all means I might save some." Also, contrast Paul's speech to the Athenians in Acts 17 with his appeal before Agrippa in Acts 26. This is a plea for us to break down the audience into its natural segments — by language, education, ethnic or religious patterns — whatever is necessary for effective communication.

One observer commented, "How do you climb on a moving train? Do you approach it from a right angle? Certainly not! If you do you will most likely be killed. The only way to climb on a moving train is to come alongside, approximate its speed and step on."

Evangelism — speaking to everyone

I Tim. 2:4 indicates that it is God's will that all men should be saved. II Peter 3:9 indicates the same thing. John 3:16 points to "whosoever." Why is it, then, that so much of our media content is directed only to those who are already predisposed to listen to, read, or view our message? Whether it is a great daily newspaper in New Delhi, a television station in Frankfurt, or a specialized magazine for businessmen in Argentina, the same elements are always present: an audience composed of antagonists at one end of the spectrum, the spiritually seeking at the other, and the great mass of the indifferent in the middle. While specific research is lacking, those at the "seeking" end of the spectrum are certainly in the minority. Unfortunately, most so-called evangelism in the media addresses itself to this latter small group. From the above Scripture passages and others, however, we see that God desires that *all elements* of this spectrum should consider Christ.

We in the media have no excuse for not engaging the mind of the totally antagonistic or indifferent. The problem is that it is so much easier to speak to the seeker or the believer who is already convinced. For biblical evangelism to be effective in mass communications we must engage the total range of unbelievers, but, it is a natural function of this type of strategy that there will be less visible results. Of course, the spectrum of individuals and their spiritual condition is very fluid — ever-changing. The individual planning a film, working on a radio program, or writing a book must realize that *he does not control* where people are in the spectrum. Yet it is our responsibility to share the Good News with *everyone.*

Natural guidelines flow from looking at this scriptural imperative of speaking to all men; it is likely that specific content must be prepared for the various portions of the spectrum. Individuals who are antagonistic or indifferent will only "tolerate" certain kinds of media content. At the same time, those who are genuinely seeking answers are usually willing to consider a much more specific, more pointed spiritual message.

Evangelism — it is a process not a one-time event

Men and women who come to Christ in a moment of faith are born anew. Yet the series of factors that have brought them to this point of decision must be carefully considered if we are to make proper use of the media. Every individual who has in faith claimed Christ as Savior has done so *because of a composite of events* or influences in his or her life. No single incident ever ushered a person into the kingdom.

The Scripture makes clear that there is the three-fold nature of evangelism — sowing, watering, and reaping. In I Cor. 3:6 we hear Paul outline this sequence with distinct clarity as he speaks about his own role in contrast to that of Apollos and the Lord himself. In Matt. 9:38 Christ suggests the disciples pray for harvesters to go into the field to reap. The implication clearly is that there had been sowing and watering to bring the harvest to the stage where it was ripe — ready for reaping.

What is the importance of this scriptural principle for those of us using mass communications media? First, our content must be *specifically* targeted for these tasks. As suggested in the previous section, one single message can rarely bear the full responsibility. With antagonists and the indifferent, we must sow and water. With those who acknowledge spiritual need, we must focus on the task of reaping.

The worldwide problem with Christian use of the media, however, is that we tend to focus on the reaping portion of the task, for it is the message that brings the visible results. Few are willing to assume responsibility, take the risks required for sowing and watering through the media. This is the tough business. Usually this task takes the form of Christian content or Christian viewpoint in a setting that has broad, general appeal. As C.S. Lewis has suggested, we do not need more Christian books. What we do need is more books by Christians about everything else. A man whose life has been transformed by Christ cannot help but have his world view show through.

Look at what Christ himself says in sections of Scripture like John 4:35-38. If your message is one of reaping, you must realize that there have always been those that have gone before in the hard places, sowing and watering with a message to the mind that was not yet ready to accept. And, in reaping, you have only joined in their labors.

Our task, then, is to speak to all men, not a select few. And, when we do so, our strategy must include the total task of sowing, watering, and reaping for it to be true evangelism.

Evangelism and the media: what form for what function?

Let us assume that we have agreed that we must confront the lostness of man where the lost man is presently congregating: television program, magazine, radio program, or newspaper. Further, assume that we have agreed that we are going to provide a message that genuinely speaks to the man or woman in terms he or she understands — the cultural environment and spiritual condition considered. Now, what will you say? How will you present truth?

Turn to the remarkable passage in Matt. 11:2-19 as we hear Christ speak to the issue of form versus function. As in Luke 7:18-35, he outlines in this section the sharp contract between the life-style of himself and that of John the Baptist. One was an aesthetic, cut off from society. The other was immersed in men's affairs. Christ said to the bystanders, you have rejected both life-styles — and in doing so have missed the truth. You would not tolerate either form in which the message (function) of truth was resident. Neither form conformed to your preconceived ideas of the "package" in which truth could be carried.

Christ concludes this section by crying, "Wisdom will be justified of herself!" Truth is truth and does not need man's endorsement of the package to confirm its own reality.

Grasping this truth could be absolutely revolutionary to the cause of evangelism through the mass communications media, worldwide. If we understood this principle, we would be set free from the curse of traditional forms which we impose on media usage. Particularly, the approaches developed in the West for media would be abandoned when they did not work in other cultures. Better yet, we would be free at the outset to say, "What method will best suit communication of the truth in this given cultural situation?"

With this scriptural liberty the mass communications staff is then faced with the question of knowing the nature of his audience, where the unreached audience is presently congregated and what media form will best suit his message (function) as he seeks to share the life-changing Word of Christ.

Media versus the Holy Spirit's influence

It is a generally held view in communications theory that media do not *change* attitudes but, rather, tend to reinforce pre-existing ones. This then means that we must be aware of man's sinful nature as outlined in Jer. 17:9, Psa. 51:5 and Rom. 3:23.

Man's *nature* is outside the control of media. Only the washing and regeneration of the Holy Spirit will change the heart of man as mentioned in Titus 3:5. Again in John 6:44 there is a clear statement regarding the limitations of the media to effect any permanent change unless *God* draws those who are to be saved.

While the Scripture points to positive principles for use of mass communications, there are nonetheless some solemn warnings. Take, for example, the passages of Luke 8:4-15 or Mark 4:3-20. Christ here shows that it is possible for the truth to lodge in a mind and, under certain circumstances, dislodge later — not having had a basic change take place. So, it appears that media can inspire a "conscious only" conversion — an intellectual commitment without the washing and regeneration of the Spirit. The medium may be a convincing radio program, or the highly persuasive rhetoric of an evangelist. A clear warning to the counting of numbers — especially before discipleship has taken place!

Evangelism and our credibility

In communications theory there is a basic section of research that deals with credibility or believability of the message. The higher the credibility of the messenger, the more weight or faith will be placed in the message. This is often closely related to your knowledge of the messenger — his proximity. You tend to trust the word of a neighbor before you trust the word of a stranger. You transfer the image of your neighbor's reliability to the content of his message — even though the message may be something foreign to you. This is why, for example, short-wave radio is rarely as believable as medium wave or local radio. Many other factors besides proximity influence credibility. But the audience must have reason for believing what we say!

Christ knew the importance of credibility being linked to his message. Read over passages like John 10:38 and John 21:24. Christ said, "You may not believe what I say, but you cannot deny what you see going on before your eyes."

In a fascinating passage in I Sam. 3:19, "...the Lord was with him (Samuel), and did let none of his words fall to the ground." Samuel's words were known to be valuable — they were not cheap but considered important by those around him. Because of this we read later in Chapter 9 that Samuel is characterized as "...an honorable man; all that he saith surely cometh to pass; peradventure he can show us our way that we should go." What more eloquent testimony could be given to credibility of the message!

The quality and authenticity of our media content must be of such nature that individuals unfamiliar with the message of the Gospel will consider the authority of the Gospel because of the other things about our presentation that are familiar.

Mass media and the Church — integration for evangelism

Now we come to the most critical issue of all — the relationship of the mass media to the church.

Scripture points to the fact that it is the *Church* that constitutes Christ's bride. It is the *Church* that is prayed for by Christ himself. It is the *Church* that is given the role of completing the task of reaching all men everywhere with the Good News of reconciliation with the Father through Christ. The mass media, in themselves, have no significance in evangelism — *until they are linked back into a complete circle of strategy with the Church.*

How do we fare when this issue is evaluated in the light of present practices? Largely, we are a failure; functionally, there is little or no link between mass communications strategy and the church.

By church we must understand that I speak of the local, visible body of believers — the group the audience can identify and locate.

Media personnel are principally committed to a form of evangelism that carries with it little responsibility. We "preach for decisions," then leave the collection of the saints, their upbuilding and integration into a cohesive body to a hazy, ill-defined role of the Holy Spirit. Functionally, we seem to trust the Spirit will collect the bits and pieces (the results of our evangelistic effort) into some group that can have fellowship, communion, and the vital roles given the Body in the total task of evangelism. Our Lord in the Great Commission said that evangelism is not complete until we "teach them whatsoever I have commanded you..." (Matt. 28:20). That is conversion *and* discipleship.

An honest look at sections of Scripture like Romans 12, Ephesians 4 and I Corinthians 12 gives good cause for us to ask, "Where do the mass communications media fit into God's media plan for his body?" Does our strategy call for integration with the other media outlined in such biblical passages?

Communications programs that do not specifically tie back into the local, visible church are incomplete and unscriptural.

A framework within which to work

We are, then, brought to conclusions about a biblical basis for evangelistic use of the media.

First, the Scripture gives a mandate for use of the media — woe be to us if the church does not use these resources placed in our hands by God. God himself has used all media that were expedient to the cultural situation — all forms to accomplish his purpose.

There must be clearly defined goals for our use of the media. If we do not know precisely why we are using mass communications — the audience certainly never will.

Our form or style of message must carefully correlate with the audience we are trying to reach — taking into consideration the full range of cultural factors present.

Our media strategy must acknowledge that we do not start from a "zero" as far as audience God-awareness. This should profoundly influence our content.

True evangelism is not just speaking to those *evidently* interested in the Gospel. God wills that all men come to know him. Antagonists, indifferent and seekers alike, have equal right to the Good News.

It will, however, be a process for all. There is sowing, watering, and reaping that must go on in every heart and must be considered in all our media and communications planning.

We cannot be bound by traditional form for the message. Our preconceived ideas about how to package the message may seriously deter effective communication, if not destroy it altogether.

But mass communications media have limitations. No medium other than the Holy Spirit of God has ever produced true conversion. And media personnel must be aware of the distinct possibility of methodically saving men — "conscious only" conversions.

Finally, mass communication is only as valuable in evangelism as it effectively comes to grips with an integrated plan for relationship with the local, visible church.

While countless other communications principles are touched on in Scripture, these concepts, placed into practice in every Christian communications program, will have a singular effect. It is the only hope, if the world is truly to "hear his voice."

THE AUDIENCE FOR CHRISTIAN COMMUNICATION

James F. Engel

*Dr. James F. Engel, Wheaton, Illinois, USA,
is Professor of Communications and
Director of the Billy Graham program in
communications at the Wheaton College
Graduate School.*

The world of today represents a rapidly changing environment characterized by burgeoning population growth, teeming cities, young people
breaking free from tradition, and dramatic growth of materialism as a
motivating philosophy. More than ever before, successful communication strategy requires a sophisticated analysis and understanding of the
audience, if the church is to succeed in penetrating societies with the
message of Jesus Christ. This paper explores the important questions of
why an understanding of the audience is crucial, the types of information
needed for Christian communication, and some implications for overall
strategy.

The communication process

Assume that an African tribesman turns on his transistor radio and
hears the sounds of a hymn followed by the beginnings of an evangelistic
sermon. What will his response be? In large part, the answer given by the
reader will reflect an underlying theory of communication.

According to one theory which is widespread among some Christian
leaders, the primary task of the communicator is to expose the audience
to the message and God will do the rest to bring the reader or listener to
himself. *Exposure,* in other words, is the basic consideration and the
message itself is secondary so long as it contains biblical truth.

In one sense this point of view has merit, because it is undeniable
that the Holy Spirit is the agent responsible for human response to the
Christian message. More fundamentally, however, it errs by overlooking
that a perceptual filter is part of the God-given psychological equipment
of every human being. Psychologists have demonstrated conclusively
that exposure is only the the first stage in communication. The message
input then must be processed through a filter which contains the accumulated experience, information, values, attitudes, and other dispositions of
the individual. Furthermore, it is now known that this filter can function
to prevent the entry of unwanted messages into the central nervous
system and, conversely, to enhance the probability that compatible information will be processed and acted upon.

Returning now to the African tribesman, the second theory of communication recognizes the very real possibility that the radio may be
turned off through disinterest, or that the message will be completely
misunderstood, or that it will not be retained in memory. The key lies in
whether or not the filter is open to begin with, and whether or not the

message is phrased in such a way that it is compatible with his felt needs, interests, and background. To disregard the functioning of the percep-tual filter is to raise the very real possibility that communication will never occur and the word will thereby return void!

Is such a communication theory biblical? While the Bible obviously is not a textbook in psychology, it is interesting to learn from the example of Jesus. He invariably approached people in terms of felt need and based his messages on an awareness of his audiences. For example, it would have been absurd for him to tell the woman at the well that she should sell all she owned and give it to the poor, while telling the rich young ruler that he needed living water. On the contrary, Jesus recogniz-ed that filters are open at the point of felt need and the individual is receptive to messages which speak to these issues.

Notice, however, that Jesus did not only contend with the need of the moment. Rather, he took occasion to capture the attention and in-terest of his audience and to move from that point to present necessary spiritual truth.

The basic principle, then, is that people process communication messages in such a way that they see and hear what they want to see and hear. This has profound implications for communication strategy. First, the communicator who bases message and media on his own ideas of what the audience should hear is pursuing an approach which is fraught with peril. The audience, in effect, is disregarded and it may well be that the message is avoided, miscomprehended, not retained, or not acted upon. An *adaptive orientation,* on the other hand, begins with an under-standing of the audience and utilizes both messages and media which are appropriate. It is recognized that those in the audience are sovereign and, in the final analysis, have full ability to screen out unwanted or in-appropriate messages.

While the adaptive orientation takes full cognizance of human infor-mation processing, a careful distinction must be drawn between *constants* and *variables* in strategy. All biblical content, especially the commands, should be viewed as a constant which never changes. The church is com-manded to worship, for example, and this is a constant. The program or strategy of implementation of a constant, however, is a variable which changes as circumstances change. In one sense, therefore, the Christian message never changes when it is expressing basic biblical truth, but there is ample latitude to adapt that message to unique individual cir-cumstances in terms of its phrasing, emphasis, and practical application. The danger enters when outmoded communication methods are main-tained with scant attention paid to effectiveness.

Understanding the spiritual status of target audiences

Evangelism is communication of biblical content. Granting the prin-ciple that messages and media must be adapted to the audience, what does this mean in terms of the historic role of the church? The answers are contained in the Great Commission passage in Matt. 28:18-20. The role of the Great Commission is to "make disciples in all nations" by bringing people from no real awareness of Christ to some level of spiritual maturity as illustrated by the following diagram:

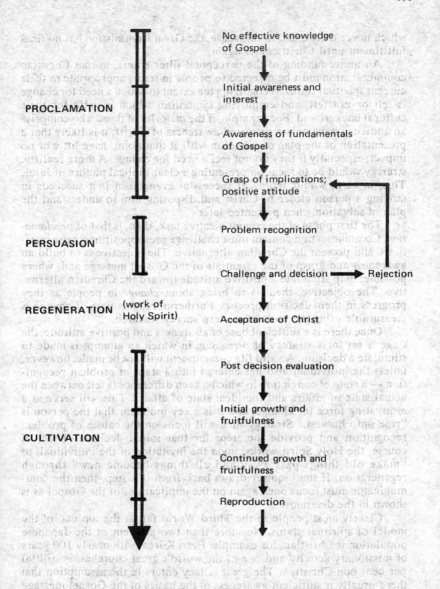

PROCLAMATION

PERSUASION

REGENERATION (work of Holy Spirit)

CULTIVATION

No effective knowledge of Gospel

↓

Initial awareness and interest

↓

Awareness of fundamentals of Gospel

↓

Grasp of implications; positive attitude

↓

Problem recognition

↓

Challenge and decision → Rejection

↓

Acceptance of Christ

↓

Post decision evaluation

↓

Initial growth and fruitfulness

↓

Continued growth and fruitfulness

↓

Reproduction

↓

SPIRITUAL DECISION PROCESS

Everyone falls somewhere on this continuum. It is the task of communication to utilize an appropriate combination of message and media so that the Holy Spirit can function to draw the individual to Christ for an initial conversion experience and then to conform him to the image of Christ over a lifetime. Becoming a disciple is thus a decision process which never truly ends. In this sense, the Great Commission has no final fulfillment until Christ comes again.

An understanding of the perceptual filter enters, in that Christian communication must be directed to people in terms appropriate to their current spiritual status, recognizing the extent to which a need for change is felt or not felt, and employing symbolism which is valid for their cultural background. For example, if the majority of those who comprise an audience have only a distorted awareness of Christ, it is likely that a presentation of the plan of salvation will, at that point, have little or no impact, especially if they do not feel a need for change. A more realistic strategy would be to focus on presenting a clear biblical picture of Jesus. This, in turn, would represent successful evangelism if it succeeds in moving a person closer to Christ and disposing him to understand the plan of salvation when presented later.

The first phase of the communicative task, then, is that of *proclamation*. Communication content must challenge presuppositions, raise questions, and present the Christian alternative. The objective is to build an awareness and grasp of the essentials of the Gospel message and, where possible, help stimulate a positive attitude toward the Christian alternative. The objective, then, is to bring about *change* in people as they progress in their decision process. Furthermore, this type of change is measurable using the tools of modern survey research.

Once there is a sufficient base of awareness and positive attitude, the stage is set for a strategy of *persuasion* in which an attempt is made to stimulate a decision. A valid life commitment will not be made, however, unless the individual also has entered into a stage of problem recognition — a state of conviction in which a keen difference is felt between the actual state of affairs and the ideal state of affairs. This will serve as a motivating force for change, and it is a key indicator that the person is "ripe unto harvest." Strategy then will focus on the causes of problem recognition and provide the steps for that initial decision. Then, of course, the Holy Spirit works, upon the invitation of the individual, to "make old things pass away and all things become new" through regeneration. If the inquirer draws back from this step, then the communicator must focus once again on the implications of the Gospel as is shown in the diagram.

Clearly most people in the Third World fall at the top end of the model of spiritual status. No more than two per cent of the Japanese population is Christian, for example. Even Korea, with nearly 100 years of missionary activity and one of the world's great churches, is still 90 per cent non-Christian. The great fallacy enters in the assumption that there usually is sufficient awareness of the basics of the Gospel message to permit large scale results from a strategy of persuasion based on Western-style models of evangelism. More frequently, the communication task is one of proclamation through messages designed to speak to audience understanding in culturally relevant terms.

We only compound the error when we assume without evidence that communication, to be effective, must result in large numbers of converts and consequent church growth. This will happen *only* when there are large numbers who have progressed to the point that persuasion is the appropriate strategy. The fundamental purpose always is to bring spiritual growth in people as they progress in decision processes, not just numerical growth in the church. In this sense, church growth objectives are just a special case of a much broader task:

Biblical and culturally relevant principles are equally necessary to bring the convert to maturity in Christ. Some need initial follow-up to help allay the inevitable doubts which seem to accompany a decision of such magnitude. Others are beginning to grow and need more solid food. Still others are beginning to reproduce their lives in others through evangelism and through teaching "faithful men" (II Tim. 2:2). All will require help in terms of both understanding Christian doctrine and applying it to life. Without a knowledge of the spiritual status of believers, how can communicators even hope to perform their necessary role?

Communication strategy, therefore, cannot be undertaken without an understanding of the spiritual status of the audience. The result otherwise will be to utilize messages and media which are inappropriate and thereby result in little or no movement from one level of spiritual status to the next.

Proclamation and persuasion

What audience information is necessary to achieve success in bringing people to an initial conversion experience? It seems, at the very minimum, that it is necessary to know the extent to which members of the audience have a proper biblical understanding of God, the nature of man, the uniqueness of Jesus, and the steps necessary to make a life commitment. Without proper awareness on these dimensions, it is doubtful that a commitment can be made which will remain and show true fruit.

In addition, the communicator must understand the life-styles of his audience. What are their basic goals in life? What activities are important? What opinions are held on those issues which are central to lifestyle? Particular attention should be directed to those points of felt need and dissatisfaction which signify problem recognition. Of special significance is ascertainment of whether or not there is erosion of basic religious or philosophical values. If so, this is a clear signal that human filters are open and receptive to messages which put forth a logical and realistic avenue for change.

Finally, it is necessary to understand something of basic decision processes. What cultural norms or values are operative? Are decisions made individually or is it necessary to focus on the family, or even on a whole tribe, as a decision-making unit? And what sources of information are efficacious in the decision — i.e., what is the relative influence of the various mass media versus word-of-mouth at the stages in the decision?

Cultivation of the Christian

The Christian communicator also must accept the responsibility of building the Christian to maturity if we take the Great Commission mandate seriously. The starting point once again is the relative stage of spiritual maturity of given audiences. Typically a pastor chooses sermon topics on the basis of what he thinks his congregation should hear. To a certain extent this is consistent with his exhortative role, but it will be totally ineffective in building the flock spiritually if it ignores the difficulties congregation members are having in applying faith to life. The pastor, and any communicator for that matter, must begin with the people where they are, ministering to felt needs, bringing relevant scriptural truth to bear in practical and understandable ways.

What should the communicator know about the Christian audience? A definitive answer is beyond the scope of this paper, because the answer must, of necessity, reflect a concept of the properties of a mature Christian. Nevertheless, at least three characteristics will be evident in a Christian who has reached the stage where he or she can reproduce life in others: (1) an adequate doctrinal understanding; (2) a grasp of the manner in which doctrine is applied, under the empowering of the Holy Spirit, to meet the recurring needs and problems of life; and (3) a willingness to yield to Christ on a moment-by-moment basis.

Taking this as a guide, it is apparent that the communicator must begin with an understanding of the doctrinal awareness of the audience. Where there are deficiencies, clues are provided for needed message content. Doctrinal knowledge, however, is an insufficient measure of maturity. Doctrinal knowledge, in itself, is of little value if it cannot be applied realistically to the problems of life. Surveys of Christians in the Western world and elsewhere repeatedly indicate the existence of vast areas of unmet problems and resulting spiritual need. It is small wonder that the evangelical church is becoming impotent, without spiritual muscle. Much significant evidence can be gained by focusing on life-style. What are the motivating goals in secular life? What basic values are held? What activities are important? What are the areas of felt need in all phases of life — in the home, at school, on the job, at play? The church must speak to these issues unequivocally if we are serious about building Christians to sufficient maturity that they can reproduce the life of Christ in others. Finally, the communicator must understand those areas where the Christian may be resisting his duty. The social needs of the community, for example, may be unmet and there is little demonstrated desire to take affirmative action. This can serve as a signal for needed exhortation from the pulpit or through the various media. Can this understanding be gained simply by observation and intuition? This is perhaps possible if the audience is very small, but there is the ever-present problem of the "Christian mask." People often are reluctant to reveal needs and shortcomings, and the result is that the body of Christ is inhibited in its functioning. One useful remedy is to utilize properly-designed questionnaires, and this approach is proving to be useful in churches in many countries of the world. Research technique, however, is the subject of another paper in this section of the World Congress.

Some implications for strategy

While many implications for communication strategy have been mentioned throughout, it is worthwhile to stress three essential points: (1) recognize the existence of audience segments; (2) utilize appropriate combinations of media; and (3) measure communication effectiveness.

Audience segmentation

It should be apparent upon careful reflection that there is no such thing as the audience for Christian communication. In reality, there are many audience segments, each of which presents a different communication challenge. Analysis will reveal, for example, groups whose lifestyles, needs, backgrounds, and spiritual status differ from others. The communicator then must design messages and utilize media which will be effective for each group. If this principle is not grasped, it will mean that some are receiving totally inappropriate combinations of message and media.

Segmentation may require that the sermon, that evangelical mainstay, be augmented in a variety of ways to meet the needs of different groups. Within a congregation, only by accident can one sermon suffice for all, especially when a congregation is large. Use also might be made of audio-tapes, Bible classes, small-group discussions, literature programs, and other means to adapt to needs of segments within the church.

Combinations of media

It is necessary to experiment with the communication media to discover the relative effectiveness of each in terms of the model of spiritual status discussed earlier. Radio, for example, often proves to be an effective tool for proclamation, whereas it generally plays a smaller role in cultivating the Christian, especially when compared with other means such as books and audio-tapes. The same can be said for other media, and the principle here is that each should be used in combination with others, including the spoken word, to help people advance in their decision processes. This implies, of course, that there must be a *cooperative strategy*, designed to facilitate the spiritual decision-making process for various audience segments. The days of one medium functioning in isolation from others hopefully are drawing to a close.

Measurements of effectiveness.

It was stressed previously that Christian communication is successful only if it can be demonstrated that it has been influential in moving people from one stage of maturity to another. Statistics on church growth are only one indicator of success in winning and building men.

Conclusion

Throughout this paper it has been stressed that communication undertaken without adapting message and media to an understanding of the audience can and often does return void. Why? Because it is a mere caricature of "the Word." Nowhere does the Bible say that man is without responsibility in the communicative process. God is demanding in a new way that we show ourselves as "workmen worthy of our hire."

COORDINATION OF CHRISTIAN MEDIA FORCES: WINNING THE GLOBAL BATTLE OF EVANGELIZATION

Timothy Yu

*Dr. Yu, Hong Kong, is Dean of the Faculty
of Social Sciences and head of the
Communication Department of Hong Kong
Baptist College.*

Putting our whole body into the task

Communication is a total cultural phenomenon; the solution of communication problems therefore lies in the coexistence and cooperation of all the modern mass media. When we communicate we put our total organism into the task. We seldom can talk to somebody on one thing while thinking of another.

In mass communication which enables the Christian Church to communicate collectively with its target audience, it should also enter the relationship of communication with its whole body, the combination of all its media forces, including individual Christians.

The mass media are but instruments placed in the hands of the media people. They can perform only the functions each of them can perform in accordance with the specifics of the particular medium. The experienced advertising planners know this. They devote much of their time and effort to the complex business of formulating the best possible "media mix."

Regarding the indispensability of media coordination, here are a few lines from a book with which you are all familiar: "Our bodies have many parts, but the many parts make only one body when they are all put together .... Suppose the whole body were an eye, then how would you hear? Or if your whole body were just one big ear, how could you smell anything? .... So he has made many parts, but still there is only one body." Source: I Cor. 12:12-20. Date: A.D. 59.

So the issue of coordination is not a new one, but it has taken on a significant new dimension which poses serious problems for all Christian communication media, now and in the future, if we do not find an answer. What Paul wrote to the Corinthians concerning the diversities of spiritual gifts to men applies comfortably to the mass media, which are nothing but extensions of the human body, of our abilities and senses. The rule that "the body is one and one in Christ" has already given us the keynote to which the Christian media orchestration should be tuned.

Mass media are interrelated

There are many things you can do with a screwdriver; you may tighten screws or loosen them, pierce a hole, even stab someone in the back. But there are things you cannot do with it: pull a nail, cut a piece of glass, spoon-feed a child.

A mass medium is like the screwdriver. It has a function, a range of uses. The limits of that range are not always very clear. A skillful user may achieve wonders with the most "frail" medium. But there is a line where he has to stop because the medium is totally inadequate to do what has to be done. With a pen and paper a good writer can write for hours, but he will need a camera to take pictures that help illustrate what he says in the article. "A good picture is worth a thousand words."

Much of the available experimental knowledge in the field of media effects study indicates that there are some built-in differences among mass media. Some media are space-organized, such as printed materials, still pictures, and art objects. Space-organized media offer more favorable conditions for difficult concepts, for criticism, and selectivity on the part of the audience. Some are time-organized, such as a radio broadcast, having advantages for learning of simple material, and for encouraging suggestibility in an audience. Others are space-and-time organized, sharing the strengths and weaknesses of space media and time media. These include sound films and television.

These functional differences, or "gift diversity," of the mass media not only demonstrate themselves in time and space organization, but are also discernible in the degree of audience participation, speed of communication, and sense of permanence.

High audience participation tends to create a sense of involvement, a group influence. A medium of high-participation such as television seems particularly fitted for the work of exchanging and sharpening opinion; whereas a medium of low-participation such as a book is good in transmitting condensed information on the culture to new members of the society.

Speed of communication is maximum in television and radio; some in magazines; less in films; least in books. Yet books give the greatest sense of permanence. Next come films and magazines. Least permanent are radio and television.

Media of low participation, low speed, and greater permanence lend themselves to teaching, to the process of forming public opinion; while media of high participation, high speed, and less permanence would seem to commend themselves to swift and widespread communication, to report or persuade.

Two Stanford communication experts after a thorough study of the mass media as sources of public affairs, science, and health knowledge, had the following to say:

"Tentatively, we can say that the public affairs, science, and health information to be learned from television is more closely related to events, more likely to capitalize on the present moment, than is the information to be obtained from newspapers and magazines, which can afford to offer more perspective.

"...From the parade of events through television, which is the most vivid and dramatic carrier of events, we tend to fill in facts and findings, but to add concepts and understanding we are likely to turn to the slower print media which can somewhat more easily offer perspective and interpretation.

"This is one reason why the print media are more likely to serve as a source of long-term science and health knowledge, and the broadcast media as a source of political facts which are useful in an election campaign that calls them forth, and may be forgotten thereafter."

Here again we have research evidence that even in the function of dissemination of information on a particular subject these differences of mass media exist.

Media are but extensions of the human body. No medium is all-purpose. If you adopt a space-organized medium such as magazines, or time-organized such as radio, it increases and limits your capacity at the same time. Mass media are interrelated and intercomplementary. "Those organs of the body which seem more frail than others are indispensable" (I Cor. 12:22).

Different forms to reach different audiences

Each message takes a form for the medium to carry to its destination. Language is the basic ingredient of all mass communication forms, but not the only one. "There are many forms of work" (I Cor. 12:6).

Words, spoken and written; pictures, printed or on a screen; other symbols, verbal or non-verbal; all are important components of the structure of a message. A message is the lengthened shadow of its author, providing the skeleton of the form he sees fitted to the medium.

A writer who has an idea and intends to get this across to his readers will first decide which form he should use that will most effectively and almost fully express this idea. He may write it into a poem, prose, a novel, or a drama. Each form has certain unique requirements and holds certain distinctive appeals. To reach this uniqueness or to achieve this distinctiveness, the process of an adoption becomes necessary if we want to change from one form to another, and keep more or less the same theme.

In a broad sense, each medium is an unique form which is good for certain types of message. A news event reported by newspapers differs in many ways from a television one. A fleeting emotional expression of a man which requires a few hundred words to describe takes only a fraction of a second on the small screen; yet television will find its time too precious and its capacity too limited to depict in details, to disclose in depth, the psychological factor or the cultural root of this emotional facial movement. These differences are so patently valid as to be beyond the need of objective demonstration.

Marshall McLuhan's "The Medium is the Message," it seems to me, is but the same old message expressed in his typical semi-logical, fascinatingly provocative form. What he actually was saying is that the different media present different sensory stimuli; that one is perceived visually, another aurally, and the like; that different media require different treatment of the material; that there are eye-men and ear-men who are especially skillful in receiving space-or time-organized communication. But these were all things said before by many others.

McLuhan is right at least in one point. We are in a new world, and our techniques are such that we have given ourselves a new form of communication, but we have not figured out yet the right way to use it. We use television, but without knowing what we do. I believe this is why we are here to find out the right and effective ways to use all the different forms of communication for one task: world evangelization.

So now it is clear that a message may take different forms to reach effectively its target audiences. This is especially important where socio-economic factors make a difference in media distribution, usage and habit.

Under normal circumstances no medium can claim to have the full attention of people in all walks of life, nor of audiences of the whole spectrum of faith. It is not omnipresent or omnipotent in terms of audience participation and involvement. All media must work together with different forms of message to have an above-average coverage of the population of a certain area.

A radio message may be less effective in reaching a busy white-collar worker or a non-set-owner than a printed message. A message in the form of a daytime serial may be as persuasive to housewives as a prominent evangelist's 15-minute TV talk. Sermons are not the only way to preach, and, in order to meet the particular requirement and appeal of different media, require adaptation by skillful writers or producers.

We all know that language is the basic ingredient of all mass communication forms. The word "language" used here means both the written and spoken. Many a man has raised the question whether the written language is still as important as it was even ten years ago in effective evangelization.

For many years, Christians have regarded illiteracy as the major obstacle to social progress as well as to world evangelism. Therefore the first and foremost task was usually to remove that obstacle and teach the people to read. But now we know it is no longer the obstacle it once was. In fact, preschool children in Hong Kong or in Tokyo learn quite a bit from television, which has replaced reading to a great extent. The "Sesame Street" series in America is proving this point quite dramatically.

To bring across the simple truth of God's salvation to the minds of people in areas where the literacy rate is low, it may no longer be necessary to require them to learn to read first, if and only if the ear-organized and ear-and-eye organized media such as radio, television, and film can be effectively developed and widely used.

I am not making a bid to write off the importance of the printed media. What I am saying is that we Christians have a variety of evangelizing tools and combinations from which to choose with considerable confidence and that they can be used effectively, for certain specific purposes.

Media at the receiving end are also interdependent

At the receiving end of a mass communication process is the audience, relatively large, heterogeneous and anonymous. A pastor who speaks to a gathering of 500 from a platform can feel more comfortable and confident than a radio evangelist in that he can see his audience and receive immediate feedback, and interact with its members on a face-to-face basis. The audience needs no other receiver than the natural organs, such as eye and ear. Yet when it comes to the reception of mass media communication, the audience needs a "dock" to receive the "vehicle" that carries the message. This receiving instrument or device is an extension of his seeing-hearing mechanism. The printed media provide both the message and the receiver, the paper, in the form of books, magazines, and newspapers; and in ordinary situations, the reader pays wholly or partially the cost of both. We have Christmas "gift subscription" of a magazine, but we have not heard of a Christmas "gift radio program."

We sometimes buy a TV set as a New Year's gift to a friend for him to receive television programs. Radio and television require the audience themselves to provide the receiver, the set; while movies require a reel of film provided by the sender and projection equipment provided by the audience, to complete the process of communication.

The audience exposure to a message disseminated through various media closely correlates with the availability of these receivers. Televised programs, though powerful in persuasion, cannot reach homes without a television set. Radio waves can penetrate the Bamboo Curtain and reach far beyond, but only to those who happen to own a short-wave set, and have the courage to listen in.

Not only the availability of the receivers should be considered when Christian media strategists decide when and whether to use certain media. Two other considerations need also to be taken into account on the receiving end: cost and specific need. Not only the language barrier has prevented the majority of the Indian people from enjoying television, the cost of obtaining a set is beyond the reach of their purchase power. As to the third matter, it should be pointed out again that the different media do not meet precisely the same needs. For instance, television and films are good teaching means, because they both carry sound and sight. Comparing the two, it is clear that films have one advantage and one disadvantage vis-a-vis television. A film can be stopped for comment, or repeated to clear up a point. Television, on the other hand, is a much more efficient system of delivery than films; it can be changed and kept up-to-date.

For certain purposes certain combinations of media are necessary. Beside every TV set there is almost always a "TV Guide," and newspapers ordinarily carry radio/TV program schedules. TV is asked to advertise magazines and newspapers. This again proves the interdependence of media. Wider and longer exposure on the side of the audience can be accomplished through close media cooperation to make known to the public where and when they can receive the message they need through the receivers available or accessible to them. "God appointed each limb to its own place in the body" (I Corinthians 12).

Stage of media development differs from country to country

The development of mass media goes forward with economic development, and differs with political centralization, geographical barriers, and cultural heterogeneity. Based on existing statistics in approximately one hundred countries, two communication researchers have found that modern communication grows along with the other elements of society that one would expect to be related to communication — urbanization, literacy, per capita income, school attendance, and so forth.

At any given time when we find a country where income, urbanization, industrialization, school attendance, and other such social factors are relatively high, we can be quite confident that the number of radio receivers, the circulation of newspapers, and the flow of information throughout the country will also be relatively high.

The stage of national development therefore makes a difference in the stage of communication development and both together make for differences in the uses of mass media for various purposes.

The advent of modern mass media to developing countries does not necessarily follow the same order as it did in more advanced countries: magazines may be first, then newspapers and radio and television. Nor do the media develop at the same speed and with the same dimension. In general, we can only say that the more the economic growth, the more likely a country is to give the mass media a major role in its development program. Political centralization, or to be more accurate, political ideology makes a difference in the mass media development which varies with the degree to which power and control are centralized.

R.R. Fagen, by comparing media growth in "modernizing autocracies" with that in "modernizing democracies," has found that strongly centralized countries seem to be more likely to put above-average resources behind the mass media, so as to develop the media system somewhat out of phase with the general social and economic growth. He has demonstrated that even though the two groups had about the same average national per capita income, the rate of radio growth was much greater in the autocracies than the democracies. On the other hand, a politically centralized state is more likely to own and control the media, and therefore is more likely than other countries to use those media single-mindedly to further economic development.

As an example of the effect of geographical barriers, let us think of Indonesia, which, because its islands are so many, has to give radio a fuller development than the printed media. As an example of the effect of cultural heterogeneity, we can think of India with its horrendous language problem. As a result of this problem, India can hardly have a national newspaper, and has to think about using communication satellite for a nation-wide educational television broadcast program. Yet a national leader in a small country like Cuba, which has no important geographical barriers and uses one common language, is in a position to talk to all her people at one time through the small screen.

What is the implication of these findings? Is it not clear enough that strategy of media evangelism should be phased in accordance with the media development in each country? Well-designed and thoroughly-researched coordination is necessary to achieve this.

"God has combined the various parts of the body...." (I Corinthians 12).

All media can be used to teach and report

Why should we discuss media coordination? Is it not because the Christian media lack the necessary coordination at a time when the tradition-bound demarcation of media has already begun to fade out?

Historically, Christianity was an individually-directed and orally-organized religion. "Tongues like flames of fire".... "They began to talk in other tongues."

Traditionally, Christians were pulpit-centered, and to them the printed medium was a natural extension of the man who preached from the pulpit. Many of the books published after the arrival of the printing presses were collections of sermons.

To these Christians, Gospel tracts represent the orthodox means to reach men in the street. They could see the men and women to whom they hand the tracts. The audience is within their reach in the same sense that the congregation is within the sight of the preacher. Gospel tracts are therefore an extension of the pulpit.

As for periodicals, a weekly is as far as they could go. Newspapers? No! Not only could they not see who was receiving the message, but to a Sunday-oriented mind they are too frequently published.

To those Christians who have accepted the use of radio at all, it is but another form of the pulpit. This might explain why in the early stage of our Christian radio development, and even now in some areas, radio was crowded with amateurish sermon-type programs.

To them, television was mainly for entertainment, too far away from the teaching function of the pulpit. Television was once described as a devil's instrument of degeneration on and corruption of the human mind. Therefore, it was regarded as taboo in Christian homes.

The eye-men of the Gutenberg Age should turn their ears to the voice that the ear-men have heard and listened to: "Much is given, much is required." All the modern mass media God has given to us are capable to inform, to reach consensus, to teach, and to entertain. The role the Christian mass media is asked to play is more of a reporter and a teacher than an entertainer, yet personnel in entertainment programs, where programs are properly projected can become top class teachers and reporters.

The rapid arrival of the Communication Revolution Era is already forcing a drastic change in the tradition-rooted attitude toward modern mass media. Ours is an age in which we shall soon see a world newspaper, a direct-to-set-owner television broadcast, all to be made possible by the high-power satellites hovering above the equator.

The *British Economist* in its booklet, "The Communications Revolution," has the following to say concerning this age, "The changes that are coming...should end the sense of isolation that parts of the world have felt for centuries."

Isolation is already a luxury few Christian media can afford to have. The age-old concept, "to be my own boss," the individualism born from human egoism, should give way to Christ-centered international-minded coordination and co-operation. All mass media, old and new, must be adequately used to teach and report the Good News for modern man; at the same time, we remember also the demonic possibilities latent in media.

How media coordination can be implemented

Proclamation of the Good News to all nations is a cross-cultural communication process. If the Christian church could have systematically collected and analyzed data based on studies of the missions she has sent out for centuries, then the specific characteristics of this process could have been isolated and evaluated, and would have been of tremendous help in the planning of the much needed media coordination.

MARC, the Missions Advanced Research and Communication Center located at Monrovia, California, has initiated a series of studies on this and other subjects. This effort should be encouraged and supported to bring more light to the problems with which we are now confronted.

Judging from what we have said concerning the nature and functions of mass communications, we perhaps know why well-designed and well-researched coordination is imperative. When we come to the question of how this can be implemented, thorough discussions and exploration of all the possibilities by people who are working with Christian media are required.

In some cases we may need mergers and affiliations such as have taken place in the United States between publishing houses and electronics firms. In other areas partnership may be in order. But everywhere there is the need for coordination among all Christian media to meet this challenge unprecedented in the history of human communication.

There are four kinds of coordination. First, coordination within one medium. For instance, the publishing houses should find out by themselves what kind of audience each of them, either individually or jointly, wishes to reach. One publisher may choose youth as its audience, another may be aimed at an urban readership.

Second, coordination within all Christian media. For instance, the publishing houses may do the follow-up work for a radio station or a TV program through a Bible correspondence course or other printed projects; radio may be asked to "fight" in rural areas where illiteracy is high; the printed media can do in-depth teaching in the urban district.

Third, coordination through the secular media. This includes coordinated sponsorship of programs, supply of syndicated material, and provision of trained personnel.

Fourth, coordination between the Christian mass media and the interpersonal communication among individual Christians and the non-Christian world.

An effective implementation of this coordination may take the following steps:

    a. A coordinating office or a communication center on each of the continents — the command tower, under collective leadership.

    b. A communication foundation or a Christian World Bank to finance worthwhile projects.

    c. A research center with scholars from a variety of academic disciplines, responsible for investigating cultural patterns, national and tribal mores, linguistics, music, system analysis, mass persuasion techniques, etc.

    d. A post-graduate-level school of communication with Christian professionals from the mass media teaching men

and women for careers in communication research, teaching, and as professional specialists in radio/TV, journalism, film, and other connected fields.

A country goes to war with its complete armed services, a combination of military, naval, and air forces. We Christians should enter into
the global battle of evangelization with united, accorded, and well-coor-
dinated media forces if we are to win.

We have no objection to the diversification of Christian media. Yet
media coordination has today become a necessity. It not only makes
media diversity meaningful; it makes a global communication of the
message of Christ possible.

COMMUNICATIONS RESEARCH

Menkir Esayas

*Mr. Esayas, Addis Ababa, Ethiopia, is
Director of the Department of Audience
Research and Planning for the Gospel in
Ethiopia.*

In his book, *Man's Need and God's Action,* Reuel L. Howe, who is recognized by many as a practical theologian, expresses compelling ideas as to the basic concepts of communications as they relate to the Christian faith. He writes:

"We have the gift of the new relationship from God in Christ into which baptism is the door. He gave us this gift not for ourselves only, but for all men. The Christian Church exists primarily for those who are not in it, which is to say that our chief aim is missionary. The first meaning of baptism for us is that we are cared for, but its second meaning is that we are called to care for others; first we are ministered unto; but finally we must minister. How easy it is, however, for us to think of the church as existing primarily for those who are already in; how easy it is for us to be concerned for our parish's success, prestige, and adornment and to forget those to whom we are sent. We may be so forgetful of our mission as to resent any reminders of our responsibility to those outside and to resent, also, their intrusion into our "fellowship" when they appear as a result of others' invitations. On the contrary, the Christian's mark of maturity is his readiness to seek out and care for, or minister. All of us having been baptized are ministers of Christ, both laity and clergy."

As part of the concept of baptism defined in the preceding quote, it would seem that Christian communication has an essential function to fulfill in the broadcast sense of the mission of the church. The key essence here is one of "seeking out" and then ministering. The process of seeking-out is a complicated procedure in all areas of scientific involvement, not least within the area of communications. However, while difficult, this "searching" is also the most necessary if there is to be any element of effectiveness and any consolation in knowing that a job is being done well.

The church is beginning to realize the significance of the use of mass media as a cogent force of propagation. However, what is still needed is the knowledge of how to disseminate its message to receptive audiences.

The realized need of audience analysis is not limited to our age. The phenomenon can be traced back as far as to Plato, Aristotle, and other Greek philosophers who took great pains to understand their audiences in order to communicate with them. Shakespeare was obviously well aware of his audience, as he drew upon it for many characters in his plays. Christ exemplified in the Gospels the art of knowing to whom one is speaking so as to communicate in the most meaningful manner. In any communication endeavor the question of *whom are we talking to* is perhaps the most crucial one if our communication is to bear fruit. Christ makes this point clear as we see him speak with absolute precision to a variety of different types of audiences, individuals and masses alike. His discussion with Nicodemus certainly is not in the same fashion as to the Samaritan woman. He spoke to the men on the road to Emmaus in a different way than he spoke to the Roman commander whose child was dying. His address to the elders and scholars in the temple was not in the same manner as his address to a crowd of 5,000 hungry and helpless people.

So we, whether starting outreach or re-thinking on existing outreach, must know who our audiences are and what they are made of. We have demographic information, information which gives us indications of people, who they are, what their age groups are, their backgrounds, social situations, their aspirations, their education, their sentiments, and in what ways they live and perceive the world around them. The *type of audience* is a phrase which may remind communicators of segments of audiences which characterize our present day. It is said that there is no one monolithic audience "out there" for any communication medium. Instead one can think of tens, hundreds, and even thousands of different *sub-audiences*. And it is, therefore, essential for the communicator to think in terms of a specific segment of a given population as his audience. In evangelism as well as in any other communication undertaking, one has to say here that there is a time where the Bible has to be put aside and life in the target audience area studied in detail and the total needs determined. It is said that "the fisherman must think like the fish if he expects to catch any of them."

In a writing, I once came across the correlation of the communicator to a lover:

"The missionary broadcaster is wooing the world for Christ. Research is required to find out the best hour to call or to visit in order that courting may be conducted under the most favorable conditions. It involves finding out what the interests are of the person we are courting, so our conversation may be directed to this. What problems has she had today? What are her tastes in music and in people that will cause her to smile upon us, to accept us, and to listen while we tell about the Risen Lord, the fierceness of his power, the depth of his love?"

A study of the cross-section of a society within any one country of a geographical giant is enough to convince one that there can be no complacency in the evaluation of the communication of words for effectiveness and for anticipated and desired responses. To compound the study with the complexities of all the countries in a given geographical area, each with its own distinctive mark, may leave one astounded. The so-called mass audience if taken as a whole, could become a cause of frustration, but it need not be completely bewildering.

In a sense, with communication, Paul's philosophy of being "all things to all men" is not a pragmatic philosophy. One has to understand that when the average person, if there is such, listens to any communication medium he is expecting entertainment. In most Christian communications undertakings we are not in the business primarily to entertain, although programs in this sphere are certainly to be desired from the standpoint of strategy and psychological necessity. The theme, as I have experienced in the last ten years, in Christian communication, seems to be *to persuade the listener that in Christ there is a measure of communication to which he can relate with significant meaning, no matter what his status and philosophy of life.* To communicate this theme effectively it seems that one must be discerning in one's choice of an audience and in one's choice of a medium so that one can be at least "something to some men." To put this in communication language, the Christian communicator must be concerned with what's known in communication as *"the potential audience," "the available audience," "the actual audience."* But more specifically, with the *"most valuable audience."* These breakdowns are not necessarily the absolute determining factors in Christian communications. For the Christian Gospel is for all men, in all places, at all times, with the power of the Holy Spirit at work reconciling men to God. However, in any communications undertaking the determination of certain groups of people to be exposed to a given medium is extremely essential. Speaking, for example, of what may be termed the "valuable audience" for any communication may cause us to pose questions before producing a certain message, questions such as: "What is the audience made of? Women, men, children? In what age groups are the ones who are most available for a given medium and at what time, in what sex, what background?" And consider also the availability of listeners, or a given audience to the times during the day or the night when they are either at home, at work, or at whatever circumstance they may be.

It is often said that the Christian message is irrelevant to the needs and problems of today. I maintain that it is not the message which is irrelevant, but the thoughtless way in which it is often presented. Changing the content of the message is an exercise in futility. Reconciliation to God through Jesus Christ has, through the ages, satisfied the deepest hunger of men's hearts. But changing the presentation to suit the audience is absolutely essential, and it is the failure to change the presentation that makes the message seem irrelevant. It is at this point that the Christian communicator has to be disciplined or commit himself or herself to the principles of communications to effect the desired message, thereby making it relevant to the intended receiver of the message.

The rationale for communications research

The first question that one is confronted with here is a basic one. *Why is communication research necessary?*

The first consideration may be *to understand the audience delineation.* It cannot be emphasized enough that for a message to achieve the purpose for which it is designed, it must reach a certain type or types of audiences, and must also reach a sufficiently large number of them to warrant the expenditure of time and money required to put a particular program on a given medium or point. Both the size of the audience reached by a given program and the type of people making up the audience are matters of considerable importance.

In communications research the main categories of audience delineation are as follows. In effect, these are audiences rather than audience. In some areas, they are characterized as sub-audience.

a. *The potential audience* of a given communication undertaking will include all those (men, women, boys, girls, and young children) who live in a given area equipped with the necessary communications medium or are able to relate to that medium and which can be reached by the medium conceived satisfactorily.

b. The second classification of audiences for our consideration in the discussion of communications research would be the audience included in what is called *the available audience.* This includes, of course, all (men, women, boys, girls) included in the potential audience and who, at the particular time that a message is relayed, are in a position to participate (this would mean listening, reading, etc.), if they wish to participate. In most cases, this would mean that those in the available audience must at the time of the program broadcast, or at the time the communication is made available, be at home, be awake, and be able to relate to the communications.

In the cases of radio and television, the available audience is influenced strongly by *the exact time of the day.* The number of possible listeners who are at home and awake would be substantially different, for example, in the case of electronic media at six o'clock in the morning and at eight o'clock or nine o'clock in that same morning. In considering "available audience," time becomes vitally important. The size and composition of the available audience naturally vary at different hours during the day. It has been calculated that enough people are always out of their homes, or at night asleep, that the available audience never at its peak includes more than 75 percent or 80 percent of the individuals who make up the potential audience.

Any grouping is somewhat, of course, artificial and the dichotomy of sub-audiences within the available audience is very difficult. Some easily researched things that often correctly divide the audience in significant sub-groups, as has been indicated earlier, are developing categories such as age, sex, language, education, residence, religion, status, occupation, etc. Any group is somewhat artificial in its characteristic ascertainment, because every individual within a group or a sub-group is different. But if a Christian communicator is to use communication media, some sort of grouping must be done. The factors mentioned often are useful as indicators of individuals who may have a "world view" which is similar — they may share, more or less, similar experiences, and they may understand the same kind of exposition or participate in the same kind of discussion.

c. The next category of audiences, or sub-audiences, is one which is termed as the *actual audience.* This is the one comprised of, in the electronic media, the listener, viewer, or in print media, the reader who is actually participating in a given communications at a specific time. Say that the percentage of *actual* audience in terms of the *available* audience can only be calculated in terms of particular program or programs at a given time. Naturally, the actual audience will consist of a percentage of the available audience. The actual audience is the most important for two primary reasons: (i) it helps the communicator to understand his effectiveness in reaching a percentage of people who are tuned to a given station and therefore gives him some figures with which to work as the cost and time estimate; and (ii) it helps the communicator to be more specific in his choice of message which will enable him to reach the most valuable audience.

    d. *The most valuable audience* has already been discussed but it is important to note that it seems that this factor should be the most important factor in determining communication policy. Without some careful consideration of the nature of the "right" audience in terms of the projection of effective communication of ideas, the Christian communicator will be continually "shooting in the dark."

    The second consideration under the rationale for communications research is the *determination of the composition of message receivers.* The main consideration in determining such a composition is to try and have information available which will help in understanding the receiver in terms of the variety of habits, and the variety of division of the population which is further classified in various social groups. You will understand what I am talking about more clearly if you have some knowledge of the social structures of some of the African cultures and particularly in the country where I come from. Where, for example, social classes go much deeper than a superficial division of upper class, middle class, lower class, and the different shades of upper, middle, lower classes. It gets deeper into the hereditary birth tradition, which is embedded in the personality make-up of individuals. And so it is that when one is to address one's self to any of the sub-groups, within a very deeply integrated and clearly identified sub-group, one has to be discerning in the preparation of any message.

    These classifications which are deeply sociological and psychological in nature, sometimes can automatically dismiss Western concepts and social class, group identification, and group dynamics. In countries of Africa and Asia, one finds one's self staggered with the complexity of group dynamics to be carefully assessed and analyzed. It is not merely a question of population density and ideological identity. It is density in the deepest sense of a personality structure of which to a great extent modern scientific endeavor has not given adequate explanation.

    The third consideration is *being informed as to who is on the receiving end of the communications.* There are, of course, three basic pieces of information vital to effective communications involved in this category, and in the case of Christian communication, it would be necessary to add a fourth. For example, age, sex, and educational status are simple and necessary breakdowns of *available, actual* and *most valuable* message receivers. It is not necessary here to further elaborate on these categories except to reemphasize that these factors can be instrumental in determining a more effective communications strategy. If, for instance, it were found that the percentage basis of listeners at a given broadcast time, out of a hundred homes for a 60-minute listening period was:

		MALE	FEMALE	YOUTH	CHILD
SEX		25%	50%	20%	5%
AGE		40-50	30-41	17-21	8-15
EDUCATION	COLLEGE	2	1	0	0
	HIGH SCHOOL	10	15	8	0

the type of program in that case, in order to be effective, should concentrate for that hour in terms of numbers, on the women in the 30-41 range and having no high school education, so that out of one hundred available listeners one could possibly get an effective program to thirty-five women if the consideration were numbers. Many other equations can be deduced from this simple equation, depending upon strategy and, of course, the medium involved. Another significant factor in the preceding analysis would be the added information concerning the ideological breakdown. If, for example, these women were all Muslims, the method of communicating Christian philosophy would have to be different than if the women were Christians. The question would then arise: to whom should you, a Christian communicator, disseminate the message in terms of preference at that given hour — to the Christian or to the Muslim?

The fourth consideration is the understanding of the inherent strength of acceptability for the recipient of the given message. There is considerable variation in broadcasting between listeners who fall between different sex or age or educational or cultural groups in their degree of *liking* for the different types of broadcast programs. Here we can say that the attractiveness that any program has for listeners depends on the kinds of appeals offered and the strength of these appeals. It is not the purpose of this paper to develop the use of these presentations, ways, or appeals, but only to acquaint ourselves with some concrete material which can be harnessed for use by the Christian communicator. What can be said further is that, by and large, most message receivers within a given group will behave in a predicted fashion, or will respond in a presumed manner to a given appeal within a program. Allowances must always be given for individual variations, of course.

The degree to which communications recipients within any particular groups will have a sense of involvement may depend in part on the nature of the "appeal" of a given program, in part on the characteristic of the individuals within the group, and in part on those experiences which are common to all or to most members of the group. All of the various things which make for differences between groups are in considerable degree based on differences in past experiences or on differences in present interests which may not find their foundations in past experiences.

The fifth aspect to consider is the need for communications research in order to organize programming in terms of defined audience needs.

It is obvious to those who have some knowledge of psychology and sociology and particularly in the light of our previous discussion that the knowledge of the make-up of an audience is important in trying to relate to the various segments of that given group or audience. Some of the factors that need consideration along this area are:

a. What sort of audiences are available to receive your message? In the area of electronic communication media, one has to take into consideration certain information that needs to be ascertained before sending the message. For example, (i) interference, (ii) television, (iii) medium wave stations, (iv) number of shortwave receivers in use? If, for example, there is only a small or perhaps no audience available for broadcasting on shortwave, or if your programs are on medium wave and the bulk of your audience is not within the reach of the medium wave target, then perhaps concentration has to be in the areas where these factors are operative. The question of the composition of your audience whether literate or illiterate, rural or cosmopolitan, has to be answered.

Having determined the composition of this audience, one has to look into the breakdown of that audience. That information must be put in analytical form so that it can be used in strategic planning. One rural group I came across had been invited by the gentle persuasion of a given leader to listen to a radio program. I underline the term *rural* in this case. The group sat down obediently as the leader turned his set on, and over the air came the strains of the Elizabethan era of classical music. A silence that was ominous settled over this group. The leader, overcome by regret and embarrassment, looked at his group apologetically, turned off the set, and of course continued with his group activity as was his normal custom. This incident, though very simple, rings a bell in many a Christian communicator who has prepared a message and used a medium without any consideration as to who is to benefit from that message, using that particular medium. This indeed is the sad picture of many communicators, particularly in Africa today.

b. What is the Christian communicator able to deduce of the persuasive elements to be used in reaching the actual audience? For example, the Christian communicator should try to collect information as to:

(i) Its own credibility as a communicator, attempting to determine just what image is being reflected by the message, in terms of the *average* listener. If the Christian communicator is considered to be a high credibility source, its programming, its message will be more readily acceptable to the receiver. If it is of a low credibility, then ways must be found of boosting the image. After all, communications have rules and principles and no message has the guarantee to be readily acceptable particularly because it is a "Christian message." Those who have been in the communications business for a decade or two should expect some kind of image which ought to be conveyed to a given communication recipient.

(ii) The influence of the communication with respect of various programs which should be evaluated in terms of purpose of such programs.

(iii) The personality and susceptibility of the audience to persuasion. This takes on special importance when we consider that the effects of a communication are partly dependent upon the characteristics of the individual members of the audience. The need is to try to find out, for instance, how much social pressure affects the auditors when exposed to ideas which may cause them to make value judgments.

The sixth and final rationale for our consideration in the need for communications research is the idea of analyzing of the purpose of the message in terms of the needs and responses from the communications recipient.

Certain Christian communications have specific objectives and a purpose for being engaged in communications. In some cases it would be *direct proclamation,* in other cases it may be only educational programs. In still other cases it may be a combination of proclamation, culture and information. Be that as it may, the need for evaluation and assessment of our intended purpose and the content of the message in view of the communications recipient and the expected response need to be investigated in the most honest and meaningful manner. For example, in terms of pragmatic involvement, how would the Christian communicator expect his message to affect a broad audience? Also in terms of the audience make-up in general, how can the *widest possible audience* be reconciled with the need to be truly honest and effect communication to an *actual audience*? Further, how does that relate to the *most valuable audience*?

Some Christian communicators see the need of the communication of the message as one being a *Nurture program* of the life and ministry of the Christian churches. The question I would like to pose here is twofold:

a. How is the Christian communication agency to be used as a strengthening medium in the work of the church?

b. Are believers or members of a given church being nurtured by the programs broadcast? We need to know how if they are. We need to ask why if they are not.

Still others in Christian communication have the aim of assisting churches in their *Witness and Outreach*. How is this being done and how effective is the result? It is the responsibility of the Christian communicator to realize that he is dealing with man, not in a vacuum. He is dealing with man who is, partially (significantly) a product of his social setup, of his culture and aspirations.

Others communicate to help education and culture flourish. This is done in many cases without giving any thought to *what sort* of "education" and *whose* culture is being flourished.

Marshall McLuhan has at least convinced us of one thing: that the media can have a dynamic far in excess of the message they contain. A given area's social pattern, emotions, behaviors, are to a large extent molded by the dominating medium. People also tend to think and perceive in patterns related to the media used in their conditioning. There is some truth in this understanding. The Christian broadcaster should constantly investigate these possibilities. This must be done by a constant study to investigate particularly the electronic media with other media. Constantly searching and planning, producing, using and evaluating, the Christian communicator should leave no *means* — or no channel — in his efforts to reach the listener, the viewer, the reader, etc., and to introduce him to the one who is himself both message and medium.

The steps indicated above when seen in a *system* for a communication projection may be diagrammed thus:

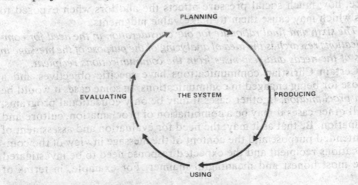

A projected program of communication research

The particular categories of involvements in communications research are many, and it would be presumptuous of me to give one model or one approach to communications research. It seems as if any given model does not present us with a permanent solution as to how we should go about doing communications research. It varies with experience, with areas, with the kind of communications involvement. The method to be used in communication research, therefore, should take into consideration primarily the need for a truly honest and a systematic assessment of the situation — and as far as possible scientific in its operation. Several approaches could be taken into consideration as far as communication research is concerned, and this would be dependent upon the need of the kind of the survey in mind. Approaches like "in depth" interviewing, "participant observation" on a restricted scale, would be one way. The other may be using a broader basis for which the number of variables are taken into consideration for investigation. The point here is that it is highly advisable, unless for specific purposes the approach on a limited scale, on an in depth interviewing basis, is called for. Particularly is this true in areas where the instruments, of scientific research, as we know them in the West today, are not one hundred percent reliable, particularly in areas where such scientific exercises are still in their infancy and the society is still free from the bondage of "opinion poll, colonialism." Particular categories of the involvement in communications research that I would like to discuss briefly in this section, and which need our attention when researching, may be divided into the following steps:

a. *Investigation:* This involves the encompassing of agencies which are conducting or have conducted research in the particular area. This should be followed up by inquiring about the availability of the information that has been gathered.

b. *Analysis:* After the investigation of the possibility of, or existence of, research materials, the next step would be the analysis of that particular information received. This can also be part of the basis for further communication research.

c. *Preparation:* Once the analysis is compiled from existing research, the information catalogue, the time schedule arranged, etc., the next phase of operation would be the preparation — and includes planning of the survey, (selecting and training of personnel, designing the questionnaire, the pre-testing of the questionnaire, the sampling to be used).

d. *Pursuance or conducting the research:* The next phase is that of the actual pursuance of audience research. This procedure is a pragmatical and technical involvement which need not be outlined in detail here but which needs to be mentioned in order to present, for the layman's understanding, a comprehension of a few ideas which might be helpful. This phase includes actual visitation of the area to be surveyed; and the programmed working arrangement and schedules previously organized are to be put in operation. The important aspect of audience sampling is carried out.

The following diagram shows the steps involved in the above briefly identified sequence of research.

PROCEDURAL STEPS IN THE PLANNING RESEARCH

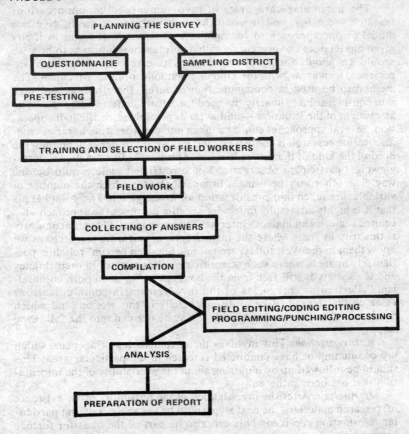

e. *Application:* This term is perhaps the most vaguely understood and one which, particularly in Christian communication, fails to be adhered to. After having conducted all the scientific research necessary, great laxity is characteristic when it comes to the application for the findings of the research. It must be understood and expected that not all the results that we obtained after an expensive research exercise will positively impress us about our work. Some of the findings, in fact, are surely indicative of our weakness in communications endeavor, and it is at this point that communicators and policy makers find it most difficult to accept the bare facts represented by plain figures. On the other hand, figures should be taken as "indicative" rather than determinants of Christian communication. However, the results would be samples of the various types of pertinent information which could accrue from such research.

Second, the results of the research should present definite patterns of audience-availability and this information should be used in, if necessary, redefining the overall strategy of the communicator. The thrust of communication should be emphasized in the areas — whether rural, urban, or both — where there is a substantial, and more precisely, an actual audience.

Third, the results of the research should present either a basis upon which to build further research, or a justification for not continuing such a program. In either case it is important that an evaluation of a research program be completed at the close of the designated period without postponement, as a healthy sign of a desire for improvement and above all for effective service.

The next diagram will indicate a sort of timetable which may be used as a sample for a timetable for a research program. The table indicates an eighteen-week program of a survey presently under operation by Radio Voice of the Gospel. The programmed communications research under this timetable involves a questionnaire designed for a multimedia investigation, and may serve as a possible sample of devising a timetable which is extremely essential for any communications research undertaking. The table is by no means all-inclusive, but I hope it will give you an idea of what I mean by the need to plan communications research *within a given period*.

PROPOSED AUDIENCE RESEARCH TIME TABLE

TOTAL 7.5 WEEKS — AREA TO BE SURVEYED
TOTAL 11 WEEKS — CENTER

	1	2	3	4	5	6	7	8	9	10	11	12	13	14	15	16	17	18
1 PLANNING	▨																	
2 QUESTIONNAIRE DESIGN		▨	▨															
3 PRE-TESTING OF QUESTIONNAIRE					■													
4 SAMPLE DESIGN					■													
5 SELECTION AND TRAINING OF INTERVIEWER							■											
6 FIELD WORK																		
7 FIELD EDIT																		
8 CODING EDITING												▨						
9 PROGRAMMING												▨	▨					
10 MACHINE PUNCHING													▨	▨				
11 MACHINE PROCESSING														▨				
12 FINAL REPORT															▨	▨	▨	▨

Conclusion

The Christian communicator, today more than at any other time, is confronted by the challenge of being irrelevant to a people (audience) characterized by *change* — changes that are rapidly occurring not only from generation to generation, but from one given week to the next. People today are better educated and much more sophisticated than ever before, with more varied appetites, more cultivated tastes. They now have longer weekends and wider interests. They are becoming hard to satisfy, hard to fool, and above all, easier to bore!

This is the human situation in which the Christian communicator finds himself today. His task is to make the Gospel relevant to this rapidly changing situation. To do this on a day-to-day operation basis is not the answer. The effective communicator must constantly know his audience and must constantly be searching for the most appropriate means for effective communications.

RADIO AND EVANGELISM
DAVID CHAO AND PHILLIP BUTLER

Rev. David Chao, Hong Kong, is Professor
of Communications at Hong Kong Baptist
College.

Radio has been given us by God as one of the most remarkable tools available in this modern age. Radio brings a number of unique characteristics to the challenge of the Great Commission — characteristics that should give radio a major role in our strategy to "let the earth hear his voice."

The first thing that sets radio apart from most other media is that it deals exclusively with the "theater of the mind" — the individual listener's imagination. Because there is no visual side to radio waves, the visual is constructed in the listeners' minds. This characteristic brings a range of creative opportunities to the radio broadcaster that are short-circuited by other media.

Further, radio, lacking the demanding visual treatment of television or films, is much less expensive when it comes to program production. A diversity of ideas can be treated in radio that are simply impossible in other media. Radio's lower cost, in production and technical expense, is a major reason recommending it to our use in evangelism. A natural corollary with the lower production cost of radio is that it is possible to reach individuals with the Gospel at a much lower cost per thousand.

Wide geographical coverage is one of the unique properties of radio— "omnipresence" in the range of its single coverage. Local medium-wave, and UHF (FM) stations typically have less coverage than do superpower medium wave or short wave stations. However, it is quite typical for an entire nation, in some cases, entire continents, to be covered by a single transmitter.

Unique features of radio

The wide coverage of radio brings certain unique properties with regard to audience penetration. For example, radio knows no geographical, social, political, or ideological boundaries. Radio leaps mountains, national borders, and quite often the barriers men have erected in their minds. The only constraints are signal strength and program content — attractiveness to the potential audience. Muslims, for example, might be unwilling to attend a Christian church. However, they might be curious enough to keep their radio tuned, in the privacy of their home or business, when a Christian program comes on — particularly if that program speaks to the individual's interest and/or need. The same certainly holds true for "closed" countries, places where the Gospel cannot be preached "openly," where missionaries or Christian workers are not allowed. In these circumstances, radio becomes a cornerstone of any contemporary strategy — because of its singular ability to transcend national borders and ideological barriers. This massive coverage carries certain drawbacks. The believability of the message tends to decrease the farther the listener is from the source of the signal. (You trust your neighbor's word before you do that of a stranger from the other side of town.) For this reason, shortwave stations beaming from great distances are often less credible than a local station known to the entire population in the area.

Despite the problems just mentioned, almost universally radio has become an authoritative voice — for governments and the private sector as well. Because of this, there is an implied authority whenever *anything* is heard on the radio. While this transfer of credibility is severely limited by the type of program, the source of the signal and other considerations, the strength of radio's built-in reputation for authority is another reason it must be considered in our strategy for evangelism.

Hand in hand with the universal nature of radio's signal is the mobility afforded the listener as he or she tunes in. When you sit in a quiet room or atop a silent mountain peak, the air is still filled with the signals of radio — all you need is the right kind of set to tune in or "decode" the signals. Combine this great signal coverage and mobility with the sharply decreasing cost of radio sets and you come as close as the world has ever seen to having the one truly universal medium.

Compare cost with media like television and films, and radio is particularly attractive — especially in areas where education and literacy are low. It takes no education to understand one's own language when it comes from the radio "box." And, while many more things could be pointed out regarding radio's special nature related to the church's strategy for evangelism, these points will suffice to show clearly how radio should be an essential element in our planning.

Determining the goal

However, before plunging ahead with the radio, the most critical issue to be considered is our goal. Time spent in carefully reviewing what we want to accomplish with radio is essential — *the* essential to any strategy.

As I write this paper there is a program of classical music coming from my radio. It is classical music familiar in the West. Listeners to this type of music are quite specific in their interests and background. They listen for specific reasons. This program would be quite out of place in many parts of the world. And, while such a program might be an ideal carrier for an evangelistic message in some places, it would be totally inappropriate in others. Knowing the nature of your goals regarding the use of radio is the foundation for any good use of the medium.

Here are some of the questions we must ask if we are to use the medium of radio properly: What is the audience I am trying to reach? What are the characteristics of this audience — age, education, vocation, religious background and customs? Where is the audience located and can I reach them with my signal? What is the audience's habit regarding the use of radio — when do they typically listen, how often and to what kind of programs? What other media do they use and how — magazines, films, etc.? What is the spiritual purpose of this program? What kind of response do I expect from the programming I produce? (We must realize that if we do not know what we want the listener to do, he most certainly will not know!)

We are considering radio and its relationship to evangelism. This immediately narrows the possibilities for our goals. But even here we too often think in traditional terms — that evangelism means the listener "makes a decision for Christ" as a direct result of the program while listening, or later as he/she refers back to the program content. However, this type of goal for the evangelistic use of radio is far too narrow — too restrictive for effective use of the medium in a strategy of evangelism.

It is possible for us to develop a strategy in which radio is simply a means to establish contact with an otherwise unreachable listener. Our plan may be to carry little "evangelistic" content (i.e., Scripture, preaching, etc.) on our program but, rather, use the program to make contact with the listener — allowing literature, personal follow-up, or other media to carry the process of evangelism to its conclusion. Is this a lesser evangelistic use of radio? Of course not!

Too long the church has seen radio as an "end" in our evangelistic enterprises rather than seeing it as a "means" to the end. Once this idea is sorted out in our minds, we are then open to a whole new range of possibilities regarding use of radio. One group using radio saw the programming as a tool for building up the local church in its listening area — giving them instruction in evangelism, prayer, and other essentials. In turn, the radio producers worked closely with church leaders to insure wide listenership — seeing the local, individual believer as the main element in personal communication of the Gospel to the unreached in that area. In this case, radio was clearly seen as a means to the end of evangelism. Well-defined goals and a plan for execution of these goals are essential.

When considering radio and the total task of evangelism, especially in the light of the local church's role, we must carefully consider if we are going to sow, water, or reap on the air. Reaping is by far the most often found program content when one thinks of evangelistic programs. But is sowing or watering any less evangelistic? If sowing or watering is our prime goal in the use of radio, we must have a careful plan for how radio fits into a complete picture which, ultimately, will allow for the reaping. Sowing and watering are much less "popular" ways to use radio; produce less specific, visible evangelistic results; and are often more controversial than the more traditional forms of radio. Further, such efforts are often hard to finance — it being difficult to explain to the supporting constituency what the results of such programming have been — particularly when the constituency has been used to the more traditional forms of Christian radio.

An ongoing process

The listener is not a tape recorder. He/she does not retain everything heard. And, if the listener could retain everything, it might not be a time when they could act on the information. This brings us to the issue of time required for spiritual change. While conversion takes place in a moment, the process of coming to that moment may require a great deal of time. We only have to read New Testament passages like Luke 2:52, I Peter 2:1-5, or John 14:9 to realize that the Lord spent great periods of time with his disciples explaining to them the way of life. Even then, they often misunderstood his message. We too, then, should be prepared to use the medium of radio over extensive periods of time — particularly if we are involved in a sowing and watering ministry. For, fortunately, we do not know who in the audience is ready to accept Christ as Lord. That knowledge is the sole privilege of the Holy Spirit. Our task is to be faithful and consistent.

Three elements make up our ability to deal with this issue: when the listener listens, how often he/she listens, and how long they listen when they *do* listen. Combine these elements and we have a clue to our ability to affect the listener over a long period of time. Multiply the frequency of listenership by how long the listener tunes in and you have a good idea of the potential period of time you might have access to the listener. (Example: a listener listens one hour per day, five days per week. The "exposure span" for this listener would be five hours per week or twenty hours per month!) Such a simple revelation should have drastic effect on our use of radio for reaping. For typically, radio listeners are "repeat customers." If the programming is attractive, they will return time after time often for years.

Control of radio

Around the world radio has developed typical styles. Radio may be either in the hands of government control or the private sector. Usually, programming is either commercially supported (advertising, etc.) or it is non-commerical (quite typical of state broadcasting systems). Finally, those using radio generally fall into two categories — those producing programs, or those actually operating complete stations.

We must carefully weigh the circumstances in our geographical area with regard to radio. If all broadcasting is government controlled, our ability to use radio may be limited to certain types of program content and, therefore, very specific audience and response goals. If, on the other hand, radio in the area is controlled by the private sector, there may be a wider possibility for programming — providing materials the stations badly need. Or, in some cases, it may be possible to buy time for religious programs. In Latin America and certain places in Asia this is particularly true.

Christian radio programming has generally taken two forms: the ownership and operation of actual broadcasting stations or the production of programs for release on stations owned by others (Christian or non-Christian).

Station ownership and operation particularly suits itself to control of the complete schedule. If you control the entire station and its policy, you can generally control the purpose and content heard on the air. This approach to Christian use of radio, however, has severe limitations. One of the problems is that such an approach demands a high volume of program production — the day's schedule "must be filled." And typically, there is compromise in quality of content to meet the necessary demand of quantity. Additionally, there is the issue of costs. Providing equipment, creative staff and maintenance for a full radio station is an enormous task — even in local coverage. The complexity of the task and the financial responsibilities when considering super-power, wide-coverage facilities become formidable. Despite these problems, such stations have often been the only source of the "Good News" to large sections of the world who, otherwise, would be cut off. So, we must be thankful for the vision and faith of those who have mounted such operations!

Program production inherently has certain aspects that recommend this approach. First, of course, reduced cost and complexity of operations in contrast to station operations. But, beyond this, there is another factor that is often overlooked. If radio program producers are to get on the facilities owned by others (particularly non-Christians), their programs must be of sufficient quality and interest as to attract a wide audience. Unfortunately, too often Christian program producers prepare programs for stations where the standards are low, or by simply buying the time they are able to get on the air — the station operator being more interested in the revenue per quarter hour than he is in total penetration of the audience! This latter situation has most frequently been exported from the West and, lamentably, has been carried on in other areas of the world.

Radio and the local church

Flowing naturally out of these considerations regarding radio is the issue of integration of radio with other media, with the local, visible church. We must ask ourselves, how does our use of radio for evanglism tie in with personal witness, prayer, the "community" of the local church, Christian literature, films, etc.?

Radio faces certain characteristics that make it difficult to firmly identify answers to this question of integration — particularly with the local church and its witness. First, radio is a medium of wide coverage; the local church is — local. Second, radio tends to appeal to individuals — not to communities — and the local church is a community of believers. Third, radio typically in its large coverage will have many local churches within its coverage area — with no specific responsibility to any one of them.

No one has ever made a "decision for Christ" as a result of listening to a single radio program. Rather, such decisions are the composite of many media influencing the individual's life. Paul states in Romans that man is without excuse for God has revealed himself in the world around us. In other words, God has already used the medium of natural things to communicate. Radio, even in the most isolated circumstances, builds on what God has already done in communicating to man. Typically there is prayer, personal witness, and sometimes a host of other factors that have brought the individual to the place where the message on the radio brings that decision. This points up the essential element of consistency in our Christian communication. If one message is heard in personal witness, another heard on the radio, and still another heard when the person is invited to a Christian home for hospitality, there is a great problem in communication.

To insure integration with the church in our listening area, those involved in radio programming should consider: (i) The possibility of establishing advisory people, laymen and church leaders, who can make recommendations or suggestions regarding need in their area; (ii)

Whenever consistent with our goals, aid the churches in communication between themselves — often an important service in remote or rural areas; (iii) Deal with the local church's problems realistically — know them first-hand through personal contact and feedback from the church; (iv) Consider making the local church part of the follow-up plan in your strategy of evangelism; (v) Consider making the local church a distribution center for literature or other materials offered by radio; (This is particularly difficult in areas like Muslim countries and Latin America, where the Roman Catholic church membership finds entering a Protestant church offensive; however, it must at least be considered.) (vi) Consider making radio the central, coordinating element in a national or regional strategy for evangelism. Radio's efficiency of cost, speed of communication, universal coverage, and flexibility for last-minute change in content make it ideal for such a role.

Combining resources

One of the major problems confronting Christian use of radio is the "bits and pieces" approach to program production. There are literally hundreds of agencies producing programs varying in length from one minute to one hour. In turn, these programs are aired on Christian or secular stations — typically with little thought as to how they relate to each other. So quite often there are a few minutes of this, a few minutes of that, and a few minutes of somthing else. Nothing could be less attractive to the non-Christian — an issue of prime importance if we want to attract, hold, and convince the unreached.

Seemingly the only course for action in this case is for program producers to form cooperatives. Some producers have fine talent, others exceptional strategies and planners, still others have financial resources. Combine these elements and it would be possible to produce programs of greater length and more frequent schedule — both essential for evangelism. We have seen how in countries like Nepal and Afghanistan Christian agencies have been forced to band together, combining the best of their individual resources into a cooperative in order to work in the country. Certainly broadcasters must consider the same approach in order to get maximum benefit from the massive resources required for optimum use of the few available frequencies!

So, then, radio brings unique properties to the challenge of evangelism. However, there must be carefully defined goals and a plan for implementation if these unique capabilities of radio are to be captured for maximum effectiveness. Finally, there must be more careful integration of radio's efforts — with other broadcasters, with other Christian media, and with the local church.

FILMS AND EVANGELISM ... "COMMUNICATING THE GOSPEL BY MEANS OF THE FILM"

Peter Church

*Mr. W. Peter Church, Johannesburg,
Transvaal, South Africa, is Director of Go-
Tell Communications.*

This is our world

What makes our generation different from those which have gone before? Many things; but among the phenomena which have shaped the twentieth century is communication — the media. We can scarcely imagine a world without radio, television, film, the telephone, the press. The destinies of men and nations are swayed by the rapid transmission of news and ideas. Fashions and life-styles are transmitted from country to country and from continent to continent with bewildering speed.

These changes often leave us groping and confused. Old landmarks of morality and standards of behavior often crumble and vanish before we can discover where the cult or change began.

Another important factor in understanding the media and the role which they can play in world evangelization is the staggering increase in the population of the world.

This then is our world

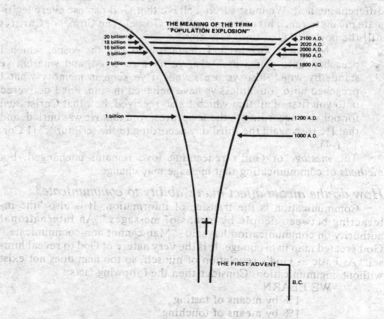

THE MEANING OF THE TERM "POPULATION EXPLOSION"

20 billion — 2100 A.D.
18 billion — 2020 A.D.
16 billion — 2000 A.D.
5 billion — 1950 A.D.
2 billion — 1800 A.D.
1 billion — 1200 A.D.
— 1000 A.D.

THE FIRST ADVENT

B.C.

From the time of creation it took till the year 1200 after Christ for the world's population to reach the figure of one billion. The second billion came 600 years later; THEN — the explosion.

And this is the challenge we face

Certain nations have made enormous strides in curbing the population growth, but the situation facing the Christian Church today is clearly stated by Leslie Lyall in his book *A World to Win.*

> "In 1900 - 38% of the world's population was Christian
> In 1950 - 30% of the world's population was Christian
> In 1970 - 26% of the world's population was Christian
> If this trend continues, by the year 2000 the Christian population of the world will be less than 10%"

Is there an answer? Yes, ...but!

One of the most serious problems in facing the task of world evangelism is the tendency to over-react. By nature we seem to be "either-or" in our assessment of the methods with which we may reach the world with the Gospel of Christ. Through different convictions we believe that we must use either one method of evangelism, or another. We seem to feel that the task can be accomplished either by the simplicity of personal proclamation, or by media. It is my firm conviction that we need to adopt an attitude of "both - and." This would allow for an acceptance of what the Apostle Paul describes as "all means." But it is in this area of Christian activity that we have seen so much injury to the Body of Christ. Personal jealousies, prejudices, and animosities have blinded even men of spiritual stature and caused them to embark on campaigns of assassination against another brother who dared to use some new or different method. We must surely believe that God can use every legitimate means to reach his creation with the Gospel. The Gospel of Christ is still the power of God unto salvation.

> "Moreover, brethren, I declare unto you the gospel which I preached unto you, which also ye have received, and wherein ye stand; By which also ye are saved, if ye keep in memory what I preached unto you, unless ye have believed in vain. For I delivered unto you first of all that which I also received, how that Christ died for our sins according to the scriptures; And that He was buried, and that He rose again the third day according to the scriptures" (I Cor. 15:1-4).

The *message* of God's redeeming love remains unchanged, but *methods* of communicating that message may change.

How do the media affect man's ability to communicate?

Communication is the transfer of information. It is also "the interacting between people by means of messages." An international authority on communication has said, "Man cannot non-communicate." God created man in his image. It is the very nature of God to reveal himself. As basic as God's revelation of himself, so too man does not exist without communication. Consider then the following facts:

WE LEARN
    1% by means of tasting
    1% by means of touching

3% by means of smelling
11% by means of hearing
83% by means of *seeing*

WE REMEMBER
10% of what we read
20% of what we hear
30% of what we see
50% of what we *hear and see*

(Survey conducted by the Secony Mobil Oil Co.)

With these statistics before us it is not presumptuous to say that the most effective means of communication available to the church today is the sound motion picture — "The Film."

As early as 1893, Thomas Alva Edison was conducting the first "peep shows" in the United States. By means of moving pictures he was putting to work the inventions and discoveries of the pioneers of the moving picture. In 1896, Joseph Jefferson produced a moving picture story, "Rip van Winkle." By the year 1910, the film industry in the United States of America was well on its way to becoming the premier form, not only of *communicating information* but of *entertainment*. Through the early years of this twentieth century, dramatic development took place throughout Europe, and the film industry established itself as the principal means of communicating with the masses.

Why these dates? Simply to convey the fact that it took the Christian community, or more accurately, the Christian Church more than half a century to grasp the significance of this particular form of communication. The reasons for this are dealt with by other speakers. I refer more specifically to the paper "Evangelism and the Media: A Theological Basis for Action," by Phillip Butler.

The traditional attitude of the church is summed up in the fact that many individual churches, and sometimes entire denominations, have written into the by-laws and constitutions of the church that "The Film" is evil and may not be exhibited on the church premises. Some do not go that far, but certainly will not allow a motion picture to be exhibited in "the sanctuary."

An unchanging commission

The Master commanded us to "go into all the world and preach the Gospel" (Mark 16:15). What does this mean? For many years my interpretation of this commission was based on a geographical concept. It seems to convey to many that the Gospel is to be carried into every inhabited part of the earth. This is true! But there is another consideration. It is my firm conviction that this commission includes not only geographical boundaries, but also social and behavioral dimensions. A man's "world" is where he "lives." It includes the place where he works, where he finds his recreation, where he goes for entertainment — every sphere of his daily activity. This is where we need to take the Gospel. It is at this point that the media and particularly the film have such significance in our times.

Even in many of the developing countries of the world, the film is the major form of entertainment. This would be true in the context of the cinema, television, and the rapidly rising home movie industry. This then is the background to the consideration of communicating the Gospel by means of the film.

Understanding the film

These are the processes and people responsible for a film.

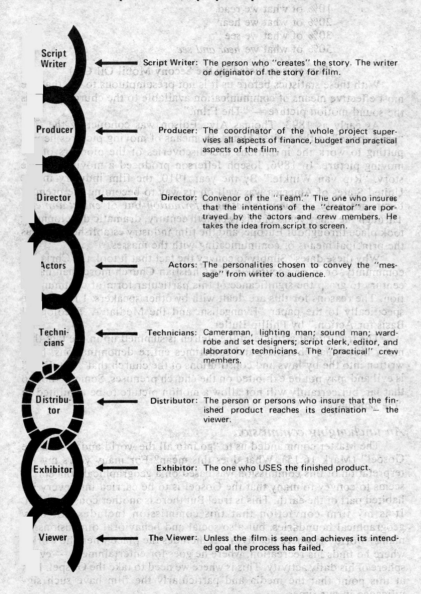

Script Writer: The person who "creates" the story. The writer or originator of the story for film.

Producer: The coordinator of the whole project supervises all aspects of finance, budget and practical aspects of the film.

Director: Convenor of the "Team." The one who insures that the intentions of the "creator" are portrayed by the actors and crew members. He takes the idea from script to screen.

Actors: The personalities chosen to convey the "message" from writer to audience.

Technicians: Cameraman, lighting man; sound man; wardrobe and set designers; script clerk, editor, and laboratory technicians. The "practical" crew members.

Distributor: The person or persons who insure that the finished product reaches its destination — the viewer.

Exhibitor: The one who USES the finished product.

The Viewer: Unless the film is seen and achieves its intended goal the process has failed.

Note: The link in broken lines indicating THE DISTRIBUTOR is intentional. It is my observation that this is the weakest link in our present use of the film for evangelism.

Using the film

The use of media is not presenting an alternative to the power of God's Spirit. Hear the words of Jesus: "And when He (The Holy Spirit) has come he will convince the world of its sin, and of the availability of God's goodness, and of deliverance from judgment" (John 16:8). It is the prerogative of the Holy Spirit to convict men of sin, righteousness, and judgment. It is our duty to convince men concerning the truth of the Gospel. It is our responsibility to convince the mind of men; it is God's work to convict the heart and turn man to himself. Neither can we abdicate our responsibility by declaring that the whole work and prerogative is God's. We have to say with Paul, "Woe is me if I preach not the Gospel." "Now then we are ambassadors for God. We beseech you in Christ's stead, be ye reconciled to God" (II Cor. 5:20). As we face the challenge to reach and teach mankind the Gospel of Christ, there is available to us today an array of tools and aids previously unknown in the history of man. There is hardly a corner of the globe today where we cannot reach our generation with dedicated use of the media. In highly industrialized countries man is subject to the influence of multimedia. His whole life is shaped by the media: radio, film, television, the press.

All these have profound influence upon the manners and morals of society. Even in developing countries we have available to us the use of one or several of these means of communication. For example, in 1955 there were an estimated 55,000 transistor radios in Africa. By 1965 this figure had risen to five million!

The film and the local church

A noted Christian leader involved in the use of media in proclaiming the Gospel has used the following illustration: The church can be likened to a highway construction company. Imagine this construction company given the task of constructing one of our modern freeways. With all its technical and scientific knowledge it is no easy task to lay the impressive network of highways and expressways which have made their appearance in all the developed countries of the world. With this in mind this author has said that the church is like one of these construction companies, but *it is trying to do the job with a teaspoon.* The analogy may sound strange, even ridiculous, but in the face of the staggering challenges which face us today the church must rethink its total program of world evangelization.

What part can the film play in this task?

Once prejudice against the film as a medium of communication has been overcome, there are limitless possibilities in its use.

Any local church wanting to attract the members of the community surrounding the local assembly needs only to take a local cinema or theater, screen a good Christian film, and with adequate publicity and advertising they are certain to draw people. This is not generally true of the normal preaching or sermon-orientated type of program which the church has become so tied to. *The Gagging of God,* by Gavin Reid is a must for any person wanting to research this point further. Not that we advocate the supplanting of the traditional preaching of God's Word. It is a mistaken notion to think that if a message is on film it is no longer the proclamation of God's Word. The task of the church is detailed by Paul in Col. 1:27,28, "We warn every man we meet ..." that is *Evangelism* ... "and we teach every man we can ..." That is *Follow-up.*

Someone has described much of our church program today as being "keepers of the aquarium — rather than fishers of men." In the total program of the local church, the use of films can be of untold value. The film can help the church to communicate with a media-oriented society. It can also make use of the film to gain maximum advantage in its teaching and training role.

The strength of the film as a tool for evangelism

1. This form of communication combines all the elements of communication which insure greatest possible effectiveness. More than any other single means, the human senses respond to the stimulus presented by the film.

2. Once a film has been produced, its message is constant. Depending on the quality of the film, the message which it contains will always be the same. If the correct film has been selected for the correct audience, then one is sure of the message having its desired effect.

3. Through the means of films a single message can be communicated to unlimited numbers of people. Correctly produced, distributed and exhibited to the correct audience, a film can touch untold multitudes. Through television and by means of sub-titling and dubbing in foreign languages, a film is a unique messenger.

4. The film provides unique opportunity for using gifts within the body of Christ. Consider diagram No.2 which gives the production of the film in detail. You will immediately realize that within this framework there is opportunity for creativeness which rarely exists apart from the use of media. From the most talented technician right down to the ordinary man in the pew there is a new world of opportunity. Not everyone can *make* a film, but even the least talented can learn to use a projector or organize a film show.

The weaknesses of the film as a tool for evangelism

1. There can be a reliance upon the film as a novelty which replaces true strategic planning and a faithful personal presentation of the Gospel. It can be argued that by the use of the film we could replace personal responsibility within the life of the church. This need not be so. A well-equipped evangelist armed with projector and film does not necessarily have to be unspiritual or ill-prepared in prayer. Conversely, even if an "evangelist" (i.e., the ordinary Christian) is ill-equipped or not endowed with physical abilities and natural gifts, he could still use a film to evangelize because the message is contained in the medium — the film.

2. I now want to concentrate on weaknesses not in the use of the film in evangelism but in the production of the film for evangelism. I refer again to diagram No.2 (production of the film). The two main areas of weakness in this all-important consideration are: a) Research.

Someone has aptly said the problem with the pulpit today is we are answering questions people are not asking. To avoid this pitfall not only in our preaching but also in the use of media, and more specifically in the production of films, we need adequate research. It would appear that this is one of the main problems in the production of the film today. People of creative ability are often turning out films which they themselves have a compulsion to create. Because of this, many films are unsuited and as a result lie unused by the church and its workers.

b) Distribution.

Every successful commercial enterprise is based on the principle of marketing. No matter how good a product, unless it is properly distributed, marketed, or sold — whichever word one wishes to use — that product will never see the light of day, or it may have only a poor or very limited circulation. At this point we touch upon the all-important question of distribution of Christian films. If one were to take any Christian publication dealing with the media, I would be bold enough to say that you would rarely, if ever, find any reference to the question of marketing and distribution. One's remarks could be very specific at this point, but I would rather leave the point made to be grasped and considered.

3. One of the major weaknesses in the use of the film is often the lack of "feed-back." "Feed-back" is the reaction of the one who received the message. This could be a decision registered by the person viewing the film or a response to some specific stimulus received through viewing the film. This problem can be overcome if the local church would rise to the challenge of using the film in communication. If a local church uses films, then that church should be responsible for the recording of attendances and decisions. That church should then, just as in every other presentation of the Gospel, assume the responsibility of following up and nurturing those who indicate a desire to follow Christ.

Conclusions

There are two suggestions which I wish to make.

1. (Rationalization) We must learn to pool our resources and coordinate our activities. Vast sums of money are being spent in sometimes disastrous ventures. Through united research, production, and distribution we can utilize the media and more specifically the film to communicate the Gospel to our generation. Yes, it will cost money, and large sums of money. But God requires of us that we be good stewards. Let us rethink our priorities and, after honest evaluation, move forward in a program of evangelization which will reach the billions who have never heard.

2. (An international Christian film festival) My colleague, the Rev. Tony Louch and I attended the International Film Festival, in Cannes from May 9 to 24. The purpose of our visit was to observe the functioning of the secular film industry. Let me say immediately that not every secular film produced is necessarily a success. There *are* failures. But at this annual event every facet of the secular film industry is benefited. Buyers and sellers meet in the marketplace; distributors acquire the latest product; producers and directors mingle; technicians see the latest developments in techniques. The entire industry takes a momentous step forward.

Can we do something similar? Can we have a common meeting ground where the newest Christian films can be screened, where Christian workers can view all that is available to them in their task of proclaiming Christ? We need this kind of interchange to help us in the challenging and exciting task of using all the means that God has placed at our disposal to make Christ known, *NOW*.

NURTURING AND DISCIPLING NEW CONVERTS

Theodore Williams

*Rev. Williams, Bangalore, India,
is General Secretary of the Indian
Evangelical Mission, a pastor and
evangelist-at-large of the Methodist Church.*

Someone may ask, "Why should a congress on world evangelization devote time to considering the nurture of believers?" We must remember that our consideration of strategy, methods, and priorities relating to world evangelization will be incomplete if we do not give some attention to the question of discipling converts and establishing churches.

Discovering the basis

In the *biblical pattern of evangelism,* bringing people to a decision for Christ is not the end. When our Lord called the twelve disciples,"He appointed twelve, to be with him, and to be sent out to preach and have authority to cast out demons" (Mark 3:14-15). He did not stop with the proclamation of the kingdom of God or with leading people to choose the kingdom. He made disciples. In his Great Commission, Jesus said, "Go therefore and *make disciples* of all nations, baptizing them in the name of the Father and of the Son and of the Holy Spirit" (Matt. 28:19). He did not say, "Go and preach" but "Go and disciple." In the following verse he points out how they have to do it, "teaching them to observe all that I have commanded you" (Matt. 28:20).

Paul did not stop with mere proclamation of the Gospel or with leading people to faith in Christ. Wherever he went, he established local churches which became nerve centers of evangelism. His method is summarized in Acts 14:21-23. He and Barnabas preached the Gospel, made many disciples, visited them again, strengthened them and exhorted them, gave them the right leaders for the church, and left them in the hands of the Lord. In Ephesus, Paul preached in the synagogue for three months regularly, then gathered the disciples and taught them daily in the school hall of Tyrannus for two years. As a result, the Gospel spread all over the province of Asia (Acts 19:8-10).

In I John 1:3, John writes about the proclamation of Christ, "That which we have seen and heard we proclaim also to you, so that you may have fellowship with us; and our fellowship is with the Father and with his Son Jesus Christ." The purpose of the proclamation is that they may have fellowship. Individual conversion is not the ultimate goal of New Testament evangelism. It is the bringing of the converted ones into fellowship with each other and with God. It was in this fellowship that nurturing and discipling of new converts took place. This biblical pattern is contrary to the excessive individualism that is often seen in our evangelism today.

Discerning the need

First, we note that nurturing and discipling are needed *to conserve the fruits of evangelism*. The Achilles heel of modern mass evangelism is the follow-up. Often hundreds of people respond to the invitation and make a personal decision in a mass evangelistic meeting. There are very few of these who really follow on to become disciples and effective witnesses. There are many drop-outs in spite of our best follow-up methods and literature. The reason is often because the church shares no responsibility in the follow-up program. Nurturing and discipling of new converts is the work of the church, and should not be pushed on to any other agency.

A new believer is often very alert and eager to learn new spiritual truths and take fresh steps of obedience. He is eager to listen to any teaching that supposedly comes from the Bible. This is what makes him a target for false teachings and false cults. If he is not nurtured in the truth and if his soul is not satisfied with the right kind of spiritual food, his hunger may be misdirected.

Second, nurturing is very essential in order *to make strong, balanced witnessing Christians* out of new believers. A promising new convert is sometimes tragically led into some by-path by the devil, and he becomes lopsided in his Christian life and witness. He emphasizes that which should be peripheral and neglects that which should be central. The reason is a lack of balanced Bible teaching. Or, he may go on living a fruitless, self-complacent life which lacks warmth and involvement. This is because as a Christian he is not taught what his privileges, responsibilities, and resources are. What a tragedy to see a number of Christians who meet week after week in some wonderful fellowship sing choruses, listen to sermons, and go about totally indifferent to the needs of their fellowmen around them, and never making any impact on them!

Defining the goals

What is our goal in nurturing new converts? Paul writes, "His gifts were that some should be apostles, some prophets, some evangelists, some pastors and teachers, for the equipment of the saints, for the work of ministry, for building up the body of Christ" (Eph. 4:11-12). The aim of nurturing is not to go on endlessly teaching the new convert so that he is always at the receiving end. He must take his place along with other believers in building the body of Christ. He must become a mature Christian, mature in love, taking his part in the corporate growth of the body of Christ. He also becomes stable in his faith, not carried away by every "wind of doctrine" (Eph. 4:13-16).

There is a threefold growth which we look for in those whom we nurture and disciple. First, there must be *maturity in love*. Second, there must be *soundness of doctrine*. Third, they must be *involved in building up the church*. Christian behavior, Christian belief, and Christian service must go together. Growth must be manifested in all these three realms.

In a world that is so mixed up in its standards and values, the new believer must stand true to the standards and values of the kingdom of God. True, the miracle of new birth alters his basic attitudes and changes the direction of his life. But the constant teaching of the Word of God is necessary to establish him in the kingdom's way of life. A young Christian mentioned in a conference how he was tempted constantly in his work to accept the gifts that people forced upon him when he helped them in the normal course of his duty. All around him everyone including his co-workers and superiors accepted such gifts without any disturbance of conscience. But as he became grounded in God's Word he clearly saw that this was wrong. Christian behavior is the product of Christian nurture and discipleship.

The Christians in Asia are often caught between the crosscurrents of non-Christian philosophies and ideologies. Most of the resurgent non-Christian religions have a political appeal. To be a Christian is considered to be anti-national and unpatriotic. Subtle pulls for compromise have silenced many a witnessing voice. The increasing number of godmen with their numerous followers from the West have much popular appeal in India. Their teachings are very subtle, counterfeiting Christian teachings on many points. Added to this is the theological confusion within Christendom. In such a situation Christian belief must be clearly defined and established. The new convert must know where to turn for the authority of his faith, and he must know how to submit to that authority.

It is not enough to have the correct Christian behavior and be established in the right Christian doctrine. The new believers must also be involved in Christian service as a member of the body of Christ. In churches where there is a faithful teaching of Scripture, the believers are faithful in their stewardship of money, in their witnessing, and in their service. Sometimes we withhold the whole counsel of God, fearing lest we lay unnecessary burdens on new believers. But let us not forget the command of our Lord to "teach them to observe *all*" that he has commanded us.

Even after many years of their existence, there are still many churches in Asia which are not financially self-supporting. The reason is that the believers in the early days had not been taught to give according to the biblical pattern. In the same way, missionary vision and concern is very much lacking in many of the churches. The biblical understanding of missions has not been given to the believers and they are not aware of their responsibility for world evangelization. This vital failure in the nurture of the early converts has led to years and years of stagnant, nominal Christianity in many parts of Asia.

Determining the methods

The question now is, "How to nurture and disciple the new converts so as to meet the need we have outlined and fulfill the goal we have laid down?" In any local church, the first means one can think of for nurture is the *pulpit ministry*. In the listing of the various gifts for the building up of the church, Paul mentions the pastor and the teacher together in Eph. 4:11. The pastoral ministry and the teaching ministry are two sides of the same coin. The pastor is also the teacher. No faithful shepherd of his flock can abdicate his responsibility to feed them. What a privilege it is to stand Sunday after Sunday before his congregation and to teach them the riches of God's Word! There is no substitute for this. This task must have the top priority in the ministry of a pastor.

Such a systematic teaching of his congregation through the pulpit will demand the best of his gifts and time and effort. He who is willing to invest these freely will reap his reward with great joy. The sermons must be planned so that there is order and continuity. They must be biblical, practical, and relevant. As far as possible, the pastor must occupy his own pulpit every Sunday. Informal discussion times can be planned to clarify or discuss the issues raised by the sermon.

Weekly adult Bible classes can also be used for systematic teaching. These can be held in the church. Younger adults can be in one group and the older ones in another group so that there is more freedom in sharing and discussion. These groups should not be very large. Interaction and give-and-take in personal relationships are important in this teaching situation. New converts feel neglected in the impersonal atmosphere of a large church. So it is necessary that they get the care and personal attention they need in these small groups.

These Bible study groups must be informal. Open, frank discussions must be encouraged. Any honest question must be allowed and the answer found in the group. There must be intimate, transparent fellowship between the one who teaches and those who are taught. Not all the teaching is done by words alone. The responses and the reactions of the one who is the teacher to various situations make a deep impression on the new believer. The teacher must be willing to expose himself and his responses to the scrutiny of those whom he is discipling. Discipling cannot be done from a distance. If we build a *wall* around ourselves, we cannot effectively make disciples. There is a costly self-giving in disciple-making. Paul wrote, "We were ready to share with you not only the gospel of God but also our own selves" (I Thess. 2:8). Writing to the Corinthians, he said, "I will most gladly spend and be spent for your souls" (II Cor. 12:15).

There are two other situations besides the church where discipling can take place. Small *Bible study groups in homes* can be greatly used to nurture the new believers. The advantage in this is that the whole family can sit together with the Word of God and study it. This is bound to affect their life in the home and their family relationships. Several families in an area can join together and meet regularly to study the Word of God. Such home Bible study groups should be linked with the local church. The local church can provide trained lay men and women to lead these groups. Home Bible study groups are often recommended as very effective means of evangelism. They can also be used for nurturing and discipling new believers.

The *place of business* can also be used to nurture and disciple new believers. A Christian in industry or in business will have several people working with him. That becomes *his* sphere of witnessing and disciple making. Not only are his words important but even his attitudes, his reactions and his actions speak aloud. What a wonderful opportunity to lead men into the faith and then to build them up in the faith! When a new believer sees discipleship demonstrated to him right in front of his eyes in his factory or in his business, the impact is strong. Moreover, this impact does not come from the pulpit from a paid teacher, but from one who like himself is in industry or in business to earn his bread.

A believing teacher with a passion to obey the Lord's Great Commission may make disciples in a few years among his pupils and his fellow-teachers. A believing factory worker or office worker may do the same among his colleagues. These believers are then linked to the local church so that they grow together with the rest of the body of Christ.

Distributing the responsibility

The best place for nurturing and discipling the new convert is the local church. It is often thought that if a new believer is sent to a Bible school or seminary where the Scriptures and doctrine are taught, he will become strong in the faith and grow in his Christian life. This is a mistaken notion. The Bible school is not the place to nurture a new convert. I have known a young man, a convert from a non-Christian faith, who came into a Bible school immediately after his conversion and ended up as a miserable failure in his Christian life. He was made much of and regarded as a showcase sample. Very soon he became the favorite of a few teachers in the school and instead of learning to walk in the light, he fell a prey to deception and sin.

It is also wrong to isolate the new convert in an artificial environment such as that of a mission compound. Well-meaning and undiscerning missionaries have taken converts fron non-Christian faiths under their wings, pampered them with a paternal attitude, and spoiled them for Christ and his church. The place of nurture is not the mission compound, it is the local church. It is in fellowship that the new convert is discipled, not in isolation.

Personal attention to each individual is important. About his own ministry of teaching and nurturing, Paul says that he was "warning *every man* and teaching *every man* in all wisdom" (Col. 1:28). To the Thessalonian believers, he writes, "Like a father with his children, we exhorted each one of you and encouraged you and charged you" (I Thess. 2:11). However, care must be taken that the new believers do not depend completely on the one who disciples them. Oswald Chambers points out that when a man becomes a necessity to a soul, he has got out of God's order.

In every church there must be *many disciple-makers*. The *pastor* alone cannot nurture and disciple the new converts. There must be *trained men and women* who can take the responsibility for the small Bible study groups or "discipling groups," and the *entire congregation* must be trained to share responsibility and to give Christian fellowship. Even *new converts* who have had some training and experience in their Christian life and faith can be put to work in this way. They can be made responsible to nurture others. In nurturing others, they themselves will learn to take their problems to the Lord and look for the answers. In this way they will also grow. In one church the pastor has organized a small group known as "The Great Commission Corps" — a few hand-picked lay people who have given themselves to the ministry of teaching and nurturing others. Their usual program is study of the Word, prayer, and sharing of experiences, problems, and encouragements. To this select group the pastor imparts the very best of his knowledge and experience, and they in turn go out to disciple others.

What a high calling is ours — the call to disciple men and women to love and serve our Lord! God's Word says, "Since you are eager for manifestations of the Spirit, strive to excel in building up the church" (I Cor. 14:12).

TRAINING BELIEVERS TO EVANGELIZE THEIR COMMUNITY

John Peters

*Rev. Peters, Manitoba, Canada, has been
teaching Evangelism and Christian
Education with the Janz Team in
Switzerland and Germany.*

Constant change characterizes the world about us today. Revolution rides rampant over one continent after another. Affluence and starvation are co-existent on earth. Technology is widely worshiped. Political corruption has shaken most governments. Confusion and despair are evident. Suicide rates cöntinue to climb. Crime and enslavement to self and Satan are on the increase. Meaninglessness and lack of purpose portray man as lacking a cause to live for. Moral degeneration and divorce are increasing. Dr. Carl Gustav Jung wrote, "The central neurosis of our time is emptiness." Existentialist theology and philosophy have brought widespread frustration, delusion and heartache. People are hurt, wounded, and lonely. Millions are looking for reality, meaning, and purpose for life. This is the condition of our world, the community that has no one but the Christian Church to communicate to it the life-bringing message of the Gospel of Jesus Christ. This was and is the task that our Master has entrusted to us.

Biblical basis for evangelism

God's Word clearly teaches us the privileges and the duties of his church in fulfilling the task he has left it:

As his flock the Church must *hear* and *follow* its Shepherd (John 10).

As Christ's bride she must *love* and *wait* for her bridegroom (John 21; Rev. 22).

As his servant she must *obey* and *watch* for her Master (Matt. 25).

As his wife she must *submit* to and *reverence* her Husband (Eph. 5).

As his family it must *fellowship* and *live* for him (I Thess. 1; II Cor. 5).

As God's temple it must be *holy* and *edifying* (I Peter 2; Eph. 4).

As Christ's body it must *work the will* of its Head and *witness* for him (I Cor. 12; Luke 24).

We live in the age of the Church. It holds the key to world evangelization, the task that her Master began (Acts 1:1) and then committed unto her for completion (Acts 1:8). Evangelism must be the Church's passion. Paul expresses that great manifesto of evangelistic motivation in II Cor. 5:10-21. With holy compulsion he cried, "Woe is to me if I preach not the gospel" (I Cor. 9:16). In *The Inescapable Calling*, Dr. E. Kenneth Strachan states that

"...the essential mission of the church of Christ for which it has been equipped by the Holy Spirit is to proclaim the good news of salvation to every creature in all the world, and to attest the reality and power of the Gospel through the holy lives and genuine love of its members, their devoted service to mankind everywhere, and their patient endurance of suffering. The church fulfills this mission so that men may be led to acknowledge Jesus Christ as Lord and Savior and thus be incorporated into the fellowship and service of his church, while it gives faithful warning of coming judgment to the nations in the sure expectancy of his return to reign."

Evangelism must be the order of the day in the church's ministry. D.T. Niles beautifully defines evangelism as, "one beggar telling another beggar where to find bread" — the Bread of Life. In *The Christian Persuader* Leighton Ford writes,

"Evangelism is a cross in the heart of God. Urgency comes as we share the mind of Christ and His apostles, who plainly saw man as lost or found, as blind and perishing, or enlightened and saved, as dead in sin or alive in Christ. These phrases of Paul also tell us something about God: that God is light, and that God is love. The man who is not deeply convinced of the holy and righteous wrath of God, the inevitability of judgment — that it is 'appointed unto men once to die and after this the judgment' (Heb. 9:27) — is not likely to make an effective evangelist.

"We find evangelistic compulsion in the knowledge that God 'so loved the world.' His love was not a vague and sentimental benevolence. It was a costly and holy love in action. 'God commended his love toward us, in that, while we were yet sinners, Christ died for us' (Rom. 5:8). There is an historical exclusiveness about Jesus Christ. God has spoken a loving Word, but a unique and final Word, in Him. This is the 'once-for-all-ness' of the Gospel, the 'offence of the cross,' the 'hard particulars' of the kerygma. God sent His Son into the world not to condemn, but to save. But there is a condemnation if men love darkness and reject the light.

"When the Christ of the judgment seat and the Christ of the Cross becomes the Christ of the heart, we cannot help looking at others through new eyes — the eyes of Christ — and sharing with them the one who means so much to us.

"This then is the source of our urgency — not merely a cold, theological deduction; not frothy, unstable experience; not grim, stoic obedience; but the ready response of our entire personality to the grace of the Lord Jesus Christ. For He is the Great Evangelist. And it is Christ in my mind, Christ in my heart, and Christ in my will who makes me an evangelist."

Total evangelism is the strategy to which the Church of Jesus Christ must be committed today. Each member of the Body of Christ has been called to be a witness (Acts 1:8). The seed is the Word and field is the world, beginning with our own community. Only as Christians penetrate the world about them with the Gospel are they true to their calling.

Philosophy of the Church's Program

In order that this mandate can be fulfilled the church must carry on an effective Christian education program. In *An Introduction to Evangelical Christian Education,* J. Edward Hakes writes, "True Christian education is education that centers in God, not in man. It is education that begins with God and is carried on under the direction of God." True Christian education is therefore deeply involved with God's program of evangelism, and must base its aims and program upon the basic truths, meanings and values of God's Word.

Hakes also says: "It is in God and in His Son that the life of man has meaning; it is interpretation of facts in the light of the revelation of God that gives man a sense of true values. This necessitates the relating of all of life to God so that it may be lived in fellowship with Him to His glory. True education keeps paramount this relationship, seeking to bring all of man's experience under the control of God.

"Since God is the source of all truth and reality and since education therefore is inescapably Christian, its purpose must be Christian. That is, its purpose is inherent in Christianity, God's revelation of His will given man in the Bible. God gave man this revelation that each individual to whom it is made known may live as he was created to live and become what his Creator intended him to be. The sole purpose of true Christian education is one with the sole purpose of man's life, namely, that man may become like God."

Pertinent purposes defined

Inspired by the Holy Spirit of God, the Apostle Paul clearly and concisely states the aims of Christian education in the Church in II Tim. 3:15-17. The comprehensive aim,"That the man of God may be perfect, throughly furnished unto all good works," is given in verse 17, but the specific aims which are prerequisites to its attainment are also outlined. As the Church faithfully teaches and proclaims God's holy Word we can expect:

(i)   to see individuals being brought to Christ for salvation (v. 15)

(ii)   doctrinal truths and standards being understood and accepted (v. 16)

(iii)   wrong attitudes and practices in the lives of believers being revealed and reproved (v. 16)

(iv)   the putting off of sin and unspiritual living (v.16)

(v)   growth in righteous living and holiness (v. 16)

(vi)   attainment of Christian maturity (v. 17)

(vii)   equipping and thorough preparation and training for service (v. 17)

(viii) dedicated involvement in the work of the ministry (v. 17), (Eph. 4:12).

This is what God's Word claims it is capable of accomplishing. The responsibility for the establishment of a climate in which this can happen rests with the Church and its leadership.

Preparing our personnel

In Eph. 4:11-12 we see that God gave to the Church men with special gifts, in order that "Christians might be properly equipped for their service" (Phillips), through which the body of Christ would be built up. In churches around the world this principle has been tried and proven.

That great Christian leader of Asia, Bishop Azariah of Dornakal; vigorously promoted the slogan "Every Christian a Witness." He believed that the Church is "the divinely appointed instrument of evangelism in the world." He depended on prayer, teaching of God's Word, systematic training of believers for right living, service, and evangelism; he used music and drama to implant truth and to evangelize, he inaugurated annual weeks of witness in which thousands of believers went out to the villages of their area to witness for Christ. Numbering 8,000 believers in 1912, the diocese of Dornakal came, by the time of his death in 1945, to have the greatest number of Christians in any diocese of his church in India, with over 220,000 believers.

Melvin Hodges, speaking of the rapid growth of churches in South America says, "Basically their growth is the result of lay witness, not clerical activity."

Eileen Lager in her thrilling accounts of In-Depth Evangelism in Nigeria, in the book *New Life for All*, reports how "with every Christian telling" a lay movement of personal evangelism was born that touched much of the African continent.

W.A. Criswell says that the secret of the unbroken stream of converts during the past fifteen years in the First Baptist Church in Dallas, Texas, is the involvement of his lay people in witnessing and personal evangelism from day to day.

James Kennedy, known through the Coral Ridge Program for Lay Witness, states that 95 per cent of those converted in his church are led to Christ by his members.

Principles for programming training

Each member of the church is a potential evangelist. Pastors and leaders must become trainers and coaches who expect their members to make the goals (Eph. 4:11-12; II Tim. 2:2). Training programs to equip Christians for the ministry of evangelizing their community and the world must be instituted. The programs used will vary with the country, the nationality, the denomination, and the social structure of the culture, but should answer to basic principles of true Christian education. All programs of the church should be:

   (i)   Bible-based — II Tim. 3:14-17
   (ii)   Christ-centered — Col. 1:18
   (iii)   Spirit-empowered — Acts 1:8
   (iv)   Leader-guided — Acts 8:31
   (v)   Learner-geared — Ezek. 3:15; Luke 10:23
   (vi)   Church-edifying — Eph. 4:12, 16
   (vii)   God-honoring — Eph. 3:20-21 — Highest Aim!

Robert E. Coleman has written a stirring book, *The Master Plan of Evangelism,* which graphically portrays Jesus' basic strategy of world conquest. He lists eight guiding principles of the master plan "not to be understood as invariably coming in this sequence....since actually all were implied in each and in some degree they all began with the first."

   (i)   Men were Christ's method,"He chose twelve" (Luke 6:13): *Selection.*
   (ii)   He stayed with them, "I am with you always" (Matt. 28:20): *Association.*
   (iii)   He required obedience, "Take my yoke upon you" (Matt. 11:29) :*Consecration.*
   (iv)   He gave himself away, "Receive ye..." (John 20:22) : *Impartation.*
   (v)   He showed them how to live, "I have given you an example" (John 3:15) : *Demonstration.*
   (vi)   He assigned them work, "I will make you fishers of men" (Matt. 4:19) : *Delegation.*

(vii)   He kept check on them, "Do ye not yet perceive" (Mark 8:17) : *Supervision.*

(viii)   He expected them to reproduce, "Go and bring forth fruit" (John 15:16) : *Reproduction.*

Before Jesus ascended to heaven he said, "As my Father hath sent me, so send I you," (John 20:21). In training believers to share in the task of world evangelization we do well therefore to apply the principles Christ used!

Proposed procedures in training

How can the Church train believers to evangelize? Various procedures have been used effectively by Christian churches and denominations around the world. Let us briefly look at a number of them:

a. *Bible teaching for all age groups in the church.* There will be variations in forms and manner of work but without thorough instruction in God's Word, the task of world evangelization will never be realized. (II Tim. 3:15-17; II Tim. 2:2; Rom. 1:16). The best known way is the church school or the departmentalized Sunday School. Family devotions, Bible clubs, home Bible classes, Bible memory programs, Bible camps, and correspondence Bible courses are further tried and tested means of Bible teaching. Workers are trained for teaching and leadership.

b. *Training in personal evangelism and soul winning.* All Christian parents, church workers, yes, even all church members, should be taught and helped to communicate the Gospel to others (I Peter 3:15). Courses can be prepared by pastors or leaders but there are excellent courses available such as:

   How to work for Christ, by R.A. Torrey
   How to win Souls by Eugene Harrison and Walter Wilson
   During the week witnessing by Kaufmann
   Evangelism Explosion by D. James Kennedy
   How to Give away your Faith by Paul Little
   Transferable Concepts by Bill Bright
   Ten Basic Steps toward Christian Maturity by Bill Bright
   Personal evangelism by Macaulay and Belton.

c. *A good literature program and library stressing evangelism.* Books and magazines that stress evangelism are a must. A few books in addition to those already named are:

   Born to Reproduce by Dawson Trotman
   Don't Sleep through the Revolution by Paul S. Rees
   The Romance of Winning Children by F.G. Coleman
   The Art of Fishing for Men by Percy B. Crawford
   The Inescapable Calling by R.K. Strachan

d. *On-the-job training in evangelism.* This is a very effective means of training patterned after Jesus' method. Classes in counselor training for church evangelism or joint evangelistic crusades are a wonderful means of training for soul-winning. In the worldwide ministry in crusade evangelism the counselor training program of the Billy Graham Evangelistic Association has helped thousands of lay people to become soul-winners. Dr. Parr used the house-to-house visitation plan, in which inexperienced members accompanied and were trained by experienced

Christians, to build up the great Gilead Baptist Church in Detroit. Campus Crusade takes participants in their seminars out for personal witnessing as part of the course. As in New Testament times, the Church today must move believers out to reach their neighbors, their community, the whole world, for Jesus Christ.

e. *Bible schools, institutes on soul-winning, special conferences, etc.* The church must encourage lay people to take time to attend training possibilities outside the church such as:

Bible Schools — long and short term
Campus Crusade Institutes
Navigator Conferences
Sunday School Conventions
Basic Youth Conflicts Seminars
Child Evangelism Classes
Youth for Christ Retreats
InterVarsity Training
Gideon Conventions
Christian Leadership Conferences
Christian Businessmen's Organizations

f. *Well-prepared and suitable helps for witnessing.* Believers must be equipped with good tracts and booklets that will be effective in witnessing and in pointing seekers to Christ. Among others, the excellent booklet *The Four Spiritual Laws* (Campus Crusade), has been an effective tool in sharing their faith for thousands of Christians around the world.

g. *Music, radio and television.* Believers should be encouraged and trained where possible to use these wonderful means of communication to present the claims of Christ.

Practical programs and possibilities of evangelizing in the community

The church that wishes to become involved in evangelizing its community has a great potential both in its membership and in its use of different agencies and programs of outreach. Some means that have been successfully used in many areas are listed here:

Systematic Bible teaching for all
    Sunday School
    Cottage Bible Study Groups
    Vacation Bible Schools
    Deeper Life Seminars
Visitation programs
    Surveys
    "Christ for Everyone"
    Literature Distribution
    Invitation Distribution
    Cradle Roll
    Home Department
    Absentee Follow-up
Prayer meetings
    Prayer Breakfasts, etc.
Camping and retreats

Children's Camps
Youth retreats
Family camps, etc.
Good News Clubs
Club work
  "Boys' Brigades"
  "Pioneer Girls"
  "Awana Clubs"
Film ministry
  Evangelistic Films
  Moody Science Films
  Filmstrips
Coffee House Ministry
Missions
  Foreign Missions
  Rescue Missions
Street Meetings
Telephone Ministry
  Dial-a-Message, etc.
Reception
Transportation
Hospitality
  Teas
  Luncheons
Ministry in institutions
  Jails
  Senior Citizens' Homes
  Homes for the Retarded
  Children's Homes
Travel
  Guided Tours
  Study Tours
Music
  Bands
  Choirs
  Orchestras
Recordings
  Records
  Cassettes
Family education
  Seminars
  Counseling
  Training for family devotions

Conclusion

The urgent task of evangelizing the world's millions is the Church's inescapable calling. As we realize our indebtedness to God and man as Paul the Apostle did (Rom 1:14), and dedicate ourselves to the teaching and training of believers so that they too will be prepared and ready to communicate (Rom. 1:15) the powerful life-saving and transforming

Gospel of Christ (Rom. 1:16) in their community and throughout the world, we can expect God to move in a wonderful way in revival evangelism in our time.

CHRISTIAN EDUCATION FOR EVANGELIZATION IN THE LOCAL CHURCH

Marge Alcala Isidro

Mrs. Isidro, Manila, Philippines, is Chairman of the Christian Education Department of the FEBIAS College of the Bible in Manila.

1. Introduction

a. *The mandate of family witness in the seventies.* **Significant** trends and strides are emerging in the seventies both in the local and international scene, of which Christian educators are acutely aware. The family is caught in this maelstrom of change. These changes have dislocated family relationships. Some of the factors which left a shattering dent in the family and community relationships are industrialization, increase in technology, mobility, urbanization, and decline of religious influence. These warrant innovations and new shapes in teaching families to witness in the community.

(i) *Industrialization* — With the advent of industrialization, more families are employed. With it came bigger incomes and more material things. Industrialization means affluence and leisure. It also means disintegration of family life. The younger children are left in the care of a maid or a *yaya* while mothers go to work. In the mad rush for acquisition of things, especially in Asia where people had so little for so long, children are given secondary attention, but religious values and practices have been relegated a second place in the lives of families.

(ii) *Mobility* — This is characterized by geographical movements from place to place so that family members can no longer determine where their real home is. The social mobility is movement from one stratum in society to another. Whether going up or coming down the ladder, this change creates loneliness and bewilderment. There is also a chronological mobility especially traumatic for an older person because it may mean loss of job due to early retirement, loss of money and better living conditions, loss of home, or even loss of a loved one. The problems triggered by mobility are rootlessness, alienation, and loneliness.

(iii) *Technology* — Advanced technology brought explosion of knowledge. Along with this is an assumption that man is supposed to know more and therefore act more maturely. This is more myth than truth. Educational principles repudiate this assumption, because maturity does not come by mere acquisition of knowledge but is a process of nurture and growth. Advanced technology inevitably brought on problems of anonymity and depersonalization with its emphasis on automation. Man has been reduced to a series of slots on an IBM card. Children now have more free time because chores have been taken over by gadgets or by maids in more affluent homes. Living has been so modernized, but not without attendant hazzards to family life.

(iv) *Urbanization* — This has contributed to "immunization against contacts with people." The urbanites are characterized by "indifference, reserve and a blasé outlook." Louis Wirth explains this as "devices for immunizing themselves against personal claims and expectations of others." Urbanization hurt both the rural areas and the cities by creating an imbalance in population distribution as a result of the exodus into the urban areas. The more fortunate city migrants may rent an apartment or live with relatives; but the poor and jobless, with no relatives to live with, settle in slum or squatter areas — a phenomenon flourishing in most Asian cities. Here they achieve some kind of community life reminiscent of their rural life. Urban life is fragmented and segmental, it is referred to as a society *(or Gesellschaft)* by Ferdinand Tönnies, while the community *(or Gemeinschaft)* is characterized by cohesiveness, inclusiveness, and organic togetherness. The Gesellschaft is a product of urbanization. People have become anonymous to each other, even if they carry on transactions regularly, but the contacts remain "unifaceted and segmental."

(v) *Energy crisis and run-away inflation* — These twin stark realities confront every family in the seventies. Is there hope of survival? What can evangelical Christian families do to help alleviate these fears? There is hope in Christ, and this hope must be communicated through the Gospel witness by families. This paper is addressed to the subject of "Teaching Families to Witness in the Community," the Gemeinschaft, where people are known as people, not just faceless ciphers. The Lord Jesus said, "Ye shall be witnesses unto me ..." (Acts 1:8); this is the mandate for family witness in the changing seventies.

b. *The meaning of the word "witness."* The term "witness" comes from the Greek word *martureo,* which means "to bear witness" and from which the English term "martyr" is derived. A martyr is one who is convinced that his testimony is true and therefore would give his life to defend it. Acts 1:8 is a standing order for the witness to give evidence or substantiation of the truth that the message of Christ is authentic. In the context of Luke 24:36-48, it is implied that what was seen, heard, or experienced must be told. The first-hand testimony must be substantiated by personal experience and by God's Word. A witness does not give his opinion. A witness appears in person. There is no witness by proxy. No Christian is exempt from witnessing. In fact the New Testament roster of witnesses to our Lord includes God the Father (John 5:37), the disciples, the early Christians, and us today.

c. *The ministry of the Lord Jesus Christ to families.* A rather cursory study of the ministry of the Lord would reveal that he did not limit himself to the ministry of crowds or individuals, but included also homes and families.

(i) *Ministry of healing* — We find Jesus in the home of Peter rebuking the fever from the mother-in-law of Peter (Matt. 8:14); the healing of the blind man was in a house (Matt. 9:27-29); the nobleman's dying son was restored to health (John 4:46-54). Even if Jesus did not step into the house, the ministry was within the context of a family. The miracle resulted in the conversion of that entire household.

(ii) *Private instruction and conversation* — He made the home the setting for further explanation regarding tribute (Matt. 17;25); for elucidation of the problem of marriage and divorce (Mark 10:10-12); and to teach humility he used a child, probably a child of the host (Mark 9:36-37).

(iii) *To get in touch with people* — Jesus took time to be with the Pharisees and sinners in the home of Levi (Matt. 9:10; Mark 2:14ff.). He visited in the home of Zacchaeus and the private conversation with his family resulted in the salvation of the whole household.

(iv) *To comfort in time of sorrow* — Matt. 9:18-26 and Luke 8:49-55 recorded the raising to life of Jairus' daughter. Another well-known account of the comforting presence of Jesus in a home was the raising of Lazarus back from the grave (John 11). Jesus availed himself of the opportunity to help in time of sorrow.

(v) *To enjoy a family fellowship* — Perhaps there is no other household in Judea where Jesus was more at home than in the closely knit family of Lazarus, Martha and Mary. The Lord stayed in their home to instruct, to comfort, and in fact to rebuke at one time (Luke 10:38-42; John 12:1-8). This was the house in Bethany where Jesus was at home.

(vi) *To bless a new couple* — The first miracle of the Lord was performed at a wedding. He not only graced the occasion with his personal presence, but blessed the home by providing for its need. The new couple started their life with the Lord in their midst. Even if the Scripture is silent as to the sequel of that story, we can surmise that they must have made a dynamic witness about the Lord's being their wedding guest. (John 2:1-11).

What are the implications of the ministry of Jesus in the home for family witness today? Heb. 13:8 reminds us that "Jesus Christ is the same yesterday, today, and forever." In this context, it implies that Jesus is just as interested to minister to the varied needs of families in our communities today as he was in the past, but that he would like for us to do the honors of presenting him to others.

2. Community witness of families in the New Testament

a. *The witness to families as recorded in Acts.* Luke sketched the witness made to families in a very interesting manner. It must be noted first of all that the disciples witnessed from house to house (Acts 5:42), and without doubt families must have been saved through this witness. Acts, chapter 10, gives an account of Cornelius and his family being prepared to receive the witness while at the same time God was dealing with the witness. This seems to be the first account where a family invited its neighbors to listen to the Gospel (vv.27,33). The result was conversion of the whole family as well as those who listened to Peter. In Acts 16:11-15, God prepared hearts in Thyatira to receive the witness of Paul. There Lydia and her whole household believed and were baptized. In Acts 16:25, for the first time, prayer and songs were recorded as a form of witness heard by prisoners. The more glorious note in this account is the conversion of the Philippian jailor and his family (vv.30-34).

Throughout the New Testament it is noticed that the witnesses took their message to people, except for a few "Come and See" invitations to meet the Lord Jesus (e.g., John 1:39 and 4:29). It is said of D.L. Moody that "he never waited for open doors, he went instead to closed doors and threw them open." He went after souls. If our faith is worth having, it is worth sharing. Acts 8:1-4 attests this truth. The story of the dispersion of the early Christians was in the eyes of unbelievers a tragic event. But this was a blessed dislocation — for men, women, children, most probably entire households — for the Christians testified wherever they went. One can imagine that people were curious to find out what kind of faith this was that would warrant such persecutions. They must have asked, "Why do you adhere to your faith if all it brings is persecution?" To this they gave dynamic witness for they went everywhere preaching the Word. They put legs to their faith. They verbalized their witness. What they believe mattered. Christianity is not mere credence but also conviction and knowledge of what we believe and why we believe. In the words of a noted physicist, "To be a Christian is to be personally and individually involved in one's belief, an involvement that orientates the life in accord with one's beliefs." This necessitates sharing of one's beliefs in the daily round of activities as opportunity presents itself.

b. The witness of families during the time of Paul — Paul started his witnessing ministry right after his conversion. The first record of a household conversion as a result of his witness is found in Acts 16:14-15. This is the family of Lydia, the seller of purple in Thyatira. Aquila and Priscilla, an Italian couple from Rome, were converted through the witness of Paul (Acts 18:1-3). This family shared with Paul the ministry of witness (Rom. 16:3-5). Their house was used as a church (I Cor. 16:19). In Acts 18:7-8, Paul used the house of Justus who was saved at an earlier date, as a base to reach Crispus, a ruler of the synagogue. The family of Crispus came to know the Lord and many other Corinthians believed and were baptized. The household of Aristobulus, and the household of Narcissus (Rom.16:10-11) imply families who were won to the Lord. I Cor. 16 gives a list of Christian households, e.g., of Stephanas, first believers in Achaia. The home of Nymphas was a church in Laodicea (Col. 4:15). The household of Onesiphorus was included in the greetings of Paul in II Tim. 4:19. Once more, we see in Philemon 1:2 a church in the house of Apphia and Archippus. Evidently, Archippus was the leader of this church in his house because in Col. 4:17 we read this reminder from Paul, "And say to Archippus, take heed to the ministry which thou hast received in the Lord, that thou fulfill it."

Though this is but a brief perusal, a few implications may be gathered from these passages reminding us that Christian households saved through the ministry of Paul offered their homes for church services. This was a bold form of witness in communities where Christianity was suspect among its pagan neighbors. God used one man to begin the work but God also used families to do a continuing witness. It is not presumptuous to say that God reached Asia Minor through Paul and these Christian families. The Pauline Epistles are a commentary to this outreach.

The privilege and responsibility of witnessing

In the early sixties the spotlight was focused on laymen and the responsibility to witness. The seventies should rise up to another challenge and must begin to tap the potential of families and to mobilize them for the work of witnessing. According to the 1970 survey of MARC and COFAE the whole family ranks number two in influence and in leading respondents to the knowledge of the Lord Jesus Christ. This is significant as coming from Asia and the South Pacific countries, because central in the value orientation of individuals is the family and its authority.

The family is strategic in witness. The family is here to stay. Institutions come and go, people come and go, ideas come and go, but the family remains basic in the midst of change. The family is strategic because it provides church leadership through its adults, it is the source of financial support in the church, and also supplies the constituency of the church for all its agencies and programs.

Oscar Feucht makes the cogent observation that the home is "the school of Christian living, the most fundamental institution in the world, the nursery of every generation, the college of life, and the training ground of the child." In this same vein, he further states,

> The families are launching pads for their children...parents are not all authors of books, but they are all writing the lives of their children...parents can enrich life or they can mar or scar a life depending on the type of nurture they give or the lack of it.

Incidentally, many families today are destitute of good relationships. When they reach out for help even from Christians, they are electrified and hear only the noisy static of our harried busy lives. It is the responsibility of Christian families to reach out. In an era of supermarkets, superstars, superjets, and super-everything, it seems as if man has succeeded in "super-ing" everything to cover the emptiness within. Man is almost afraid to be left alone lest he be confronted with the impoverished state of his own life. So super-fences have been built around the homes and personalities. Psychologically, the more elite, moneyed and sophisticated families have built walls of complacence, nonchalance, and smugness. The poor level also built walls of "bahalana" and "I couldn't care less" attitudes. Walls of anger, apathy, resignation, even shirking of responsibility, have been put up. The emerging middle class has built walls of competition, drudgery, and busyness, hence there is no time for the family, no time for God, no time for the church. These are formidable phalanxes that need to be broken down or penetrated by family witness. It is to families like these that we have been commissioned to communicate the Gospel.

On the other hand, criticism has been hurled at the Christian community because they have organized walls around them also by creating Christian ghettoes. Bible classes have degenerated into a comfortable fellowship of the same Christian people. These activities are good but often sap the vitality of Christians because they spend so much time together for a long time thus robbing themselves of the opportunities to make aggressive witness. Some Christians in walled compounds hardly reach out to people outside their fences. This unity is more like "glued-togetherness." We have not been called to a cloister or to build a city of the redeemed here on earth. Would to God that Christians in the Christian Gemeinschaft would take the initiative to reach out to other families.

a. *The goal of family witnessing* is to interest another family in Christ through a Christian testimony; to represent Christ before other families; to contact families in the community needing witness; and to win families for Christ.

b. *The qualifications for family as a witness* include the following: (i) a conversion experience, a definite point in time and in history when one can say, "I have accepted the Lord Jesus Christ as personal Savior and Lord." (ii) A conviction that souls are lost and going to hell if Christ is not accepted. (iii) A compassion for or sensitivity to the needs of the lost and a sense of urgency (Rom. 9:2). (iv) A concern which follows rules of courtesy and consideration in witnessing to others. "The right to talk intimately to another person about the Lord Jesus Christ has to be earned, and you earn it by convincing him that you are his friend, and really care about him " — this is sound advice. It will help us to be careful that we do not nag people into heaven.

c. *The message of the witness* — I Cor. 15:3-8 is the Gospel message in a nutshell. Paul Little expresses it this way, "The Gospel, then, is Jesus Christ Himself, who He is, and what He has done, and how He can be known in personal experience." Or it can also be expressed in the Roman Road of Salvation (i) Rom. 3:23 — man's need of salvation; (ii) Rom. 6:23 — the penalty of sin; (iii) Rom. 5:8 — God's provision for salvation; (iv) Rom. 10:9-10 — man's response to God.

d. *The methods of witnessing* — The pastor is the key to family witnessing. He is the main teacher and the rallying point. So he must personally challenge families in his church through his pulpit messages, through personal counseling and personal approaches, to sell the idea of witnessing.

The writer has delineated four kinds of witness to aid in the teaching of families in order to witness in the community:

(i) *Silent witness* — Some people are suspicious of words but an eloquent silence proven in the Christian family living together, playing, working, or serving the Lord together in loving harmony will be used of God to draw others to himself. Not shouting out but shining out the transforming power of God in the family life. To help families shine out for the Lord is to deepen their spiritual foundations by strengthening the family altars. The pastor then should provide guidelines for establishing the family altars. Many families do not have family altars because they simply do not know how to go about having one. It would be a good idea to demonstrate through skits or dramatizations actual family devotions in church. Or the pastor might invite one family at a time throughout the year to join his family during family devotions. Or the pastor may go to the homes and help families conduct devotions. When the family altars are strong, the blessings do not stop within the four walls of that home. They will naturally live out their religion. The family altar is the first base in witnessing. This kind of witness is witness by life. This is not the "tongue-tied" kind of silence pointed out by John Stott in his book. Tongue-tied silence has been used as a cloak for timidity and unconcern for the lost. This silent witness is really a transformed life wrapped up in a person or family and that person or family is sent walking and living in the community for the Lord Jesus Christ. The home is the showcase of

God's grace and, as such, a godly family is a silent witness to God's goodness, more eloquent than a torrent of words.

(ii) *Verbal witness* — Teach families to verbalize their witness. This is the other side of the coin of witness. While there is place for silence, it can never fill the hunger for spiritual things any more than a horse can live on shade. So verbalized witness is also called for. A meaning that cannot be verbalized remains a private meaning. So teach families how to give a surefire three-minute testimony. The following are borrowed ideas and have been adapted for teaching families how to testify: (1) what we were before we became Christians; (2) how we became Christians; (3) what Jesus Christ means to us now. Another is a suggestion by C. S. Lovett: (1) why we call ourselves Christians; (2) what is our authority for this?; (3) how do we know that we are really saved? Finally, this last one is recommended as a way to help make the testimony coherent and clear. First, write a friend about your experience, and then invite a non-believer to read the letter and find out whether he understands the message. Then practice verbalizing it to your family, and after you have gained some confidence, share it with an unchurched family. Perhaps these ideas have been taught to individuals but have we tried to teach them to families?

Teach families to memorize Scriptures. The Roman Road to Salvation cited previously is a good set to begin with. Families must be taught some witnessing phrases to memorize as well. Also they must be encouraged to underline some witnessing verses. When a family knows some of these functional things, fear for verbal witness would be alleviated.

Challenge newly baptized Christians to witness. Bishop Azariah of Dornakal, South India, has a unique way of inviting newly baptized members to witness. He asks them to place their hands on their head and say after him, "I am a baptized Christian, woe is unto me if I preach not the Gospel." There is no need to copy the practice, but surely the pastor can impress this urgency upon new believers to witness verbally.

(iii) *Active witness* — This implies putting legs to our witnessing. The pastor can teach active witness by his personal example. He can also take families along with him during his visitation. He should teach them how to make a community survey. He should teach them how to visit first among their own friends and then visit the folks who are friendly with the people in the church. These are low-threat levels of witness. Then teach them how to go prospecting.

Of course the pastor should find those families who have natural talent for public relations, especially for the active witnessing ministry. The shy family may be given less threatening assignments than those suggested above. One word of caution is in order at this juncture: extra care and skillful diplomacy must be applied so that a family which possesses "tongues loose on both ends," as one writer picturesquely puts it, should not be assigned to go out doing verbal witness. Appeal to them about doing work on the home base, such as preparing snacks, recording, filing, etc.

Teach families to make friends with their neighbors by a vase of freshly cut flowers, a crocheted doily, a book, a hot dish, or any small gift items taken personally to the family for which it is intended. Watch the

"For Sale" or "For Rent" signs and be the first to welcome the family to the community. New couples and new babies are opportunities for friendship and witness. Assign a family for each of those to be visited. Teach them to sponsor newcomers to the community. Assign families to be on the lookout for guests in the worship service and to follow them up at home. "Some 'families' would never be reached without a warm handclasp, an earnest searching gaze, a quiet word and occasionally a tear and a prayer." Assign families to visit before the special services of the church, to interest guests in the activities of the church. When families go calling it would be a nice idea if they could bring along a church activity handbook with pictures of the activities in the church. Pictures usually will catch attention. Teach families to find out avenues to people's *hearts and then to show care* and concern in practical and visible means. This is active witness.

(iv) *Creative witness* — This does not mean the spectacular but the innovative or unique approaches to family witnessing, like sharing a cassette tape of music and messages, loaned out or listened to together. Also capitalize on the relevance of cultural values to Christian life, for instance, the Filipino value called *utang na loob,* — a positive human experience which can be the basis of the Christian value of gratitude and loyalty. For *utang na loob* speaks of a deep sense of gratitude to a person, for example, who saved another from drowning. It speaks of a commitment in return for a debt that cannot be paid. The implication of this value in witnessing is to appeal to a family's debt of gratitude to the Lord Jesus for what he is and what he has done for them on the Cross. It would be a part of wisdom to understand the cultural values of a people and to capitalize their relevance for the ministry of witnessing.

Encourage a family to adopt an unchurched family. Then sponsor a "Come Double Sunday" when this adopted family comes to church with the foster family during a special service.

With the present energy crisis, more families stay home. They are forced by circumstances to be together. Take advantage of this opportunity of non-activity. Share hobbies and other wholesome activities together — like gardening, fixing a fence, painting for men and crocheting, knitting, or sewing for women, and take this opportunity to "gossip the Gospel." View slides or filmstrips together and draw some lessons from them. Read the Bible together, underline words or phrases that are significant, and give some explanations.

Again, in the Philippines, families put a premium on special days and thanksgiving occasions for graduations, promotions, a new house, a successful venture, healing, or a family "balikbayan" (back-to-country). Christian families who have built bridges of friendships with unchurched families have a natural entree into these homes, and what a tremendous opportunity for witness. Families have a unique constellation of influence within the community; they must be taught to look for and recognize opportunities for witness, or encouraged to create openings for witness.

The more affluent Christian family may take advantage of vacations, weekends, or other holidays, and plan to go off with an unchurched family. The close association during the few days together will provide avenues of witness. The privacy of the occasion will contribute to greater openness to the Gospel. A creative family may also use a one-day or a few hours trek, ride, walk, or cycling and picnicking with another family. In the course of this fellowship, try to get in a word for the Lord.

These are only a few ideas which a pastor or a Christian educator may use to challenge Christian families to witness in the community. It would be a good idea to highlight the completion of this training by a commissioning service dedicating the families for the task of witnessing. Below is an example of a certificate that might be awarded to the candidates.

"We the *Isidro Family* will be responsible for the *Herrera family*, to pray for them, to make a regular visit in their home, to fetch and bring them to church when opportunity affords it, and we are responsible to introduce them to the Pastor and to the church family."

_____   __   _____
Signature of Family   The Pastor

_____   _____
Date   Church

4. Contemporary Filipino families who witnessed

From the upper middle class suburb of Manila comes this example of a family whose Christian life was strengthened through a personal visit of a family, which eventually led to a home Bible study in the house and to the conversion of the husband. This family began eagerly and earnestly to share their faith. They witnessed to another family who were their close friends and invited them to the home Bible class. After a few months of classes this family also found the Lord. Both men are retired commodores of the Philippine Navy. The excitement about families reaching their own community, is that they minister to the families on their level.

A Bureau of Internal Revenue official was converted in a home Bible class in his own house. One Sunday morning he heard the dynamic preaching of the Word in a church. He decided to bring along his wife. She came, although reluctantly, but enjoyed the message and the warm fellowship extended to her. They kept coming. During a Holy Week family camp the family attended, and in one of the evangelistic meetings the wife came under deep conviction and accepted the Lord. Later the children came to know the Lord. Mr. Isidro had the privilege of baptizing the entire family. The man started a Bible class in his home for his neighbors. At the end of the first set of lessons he conducted a graduation ceremony for about twenty-six people who completed the course. These folks had never been in a Protestant church, so he personally chauffeured two carloads of them to observe the service. They were introduced to the pastor and to the church family. They liked the friendly atmosphere. They just started coming of their own accord. It is exciting to note that these folks witnessed to their families first, and entire households have come to know the Lord. This is the story of a family who was used to bringing to the Lord some ten households which built the Tagalog congregation in Caloocan City.

5. Conclusion

Families are like "God's stock market" to borrow the phrase of G. Christian Weiss. The more Christian families invest in it the more the dividends are reaped in terms of families won to the Lord. Therefore it is imperative that families be encouraged and taught to reflect upon the possibilities of multiplying their lives by witnessing in the community. There is a need to teach families to claim unsaved families in the community as their personal responsibility or liability on their account to God — families who will resolve with Joshua, "As for me and my house, we will serve the Lord," (Jos. 24:15). We need families who will say with Charles Wesley, "Let me commend my Savior to you." We need families who will sustain faithfully the three-dimensional relationship of witness in the community as very succinctly pointed out by Dr. Gangel: "...first of all, very presence and behavior in the community is an example of Christ and his Church and a demonstration of the grace of God to all of those who know them and can observe their life. Secondly, the family actively witnesses together through the program of its church, through personal sharing of faith on the part of the family members, and perhaps through collective witness of one kind or another. Finally, the extension of family witness finds fruition as young people go out from the home, and like the displaced children of the Bible, carry their witness with them into various forms of Christian service or a multitude of other occupations and geographical locations.

Any dedicated Christian family can be a 3-D (three-demensional) witness for the Lord. The following chorus is a pertinent reminder of the nobility of the task of witnessing:

"Lord, lay some soul upon my heart, And love that soul through me;

And may I nobly do my part, To win that soul for Thee."

This paper does not pretend to offer a panacea for all the implications of teaching families to witness in the community, but it has tried to stir our imagination to do creative thinking regarding ways and means of tapping the potential of Christian families for witness in the seventies.

STRATEGY REPORT MASS MEDIA

John Fear

A census of the 300 participants who attended the six sessions revealed that two-thirds were actively engaged in evangelism through the media. The numbers were as follows: radio (65); literature (45); cassettes (40); films (30) and television (20). However, fewer than five percent had worked for five years outside the parochial field.

Objectives

a. To discover a blend of clearly defined goals, supported by a scriptural mandate, academic training, and professional expertise.

b. To devise a means of coordination, so that an interlocking relationship is established between the diversity of media engaged in the global battle of evangelism.

c. To recognize that if biblical evangelism is to be effective in mass communications, the content must be specifically preared for the total range of unbelievers and not only for the small minority of "seekers."

d. To encourage the proliferation of Christian publishing, broadcasting, and film production units throughout the world.

Radio

It is technically possible to cover an entire nation or continent by a single transmitter. Further, radio knows no geographical, social, political, or ideological boundries. However, no one makes a "decision for Christ" as a result of listening to a single radio program. Such a decision is a process resulting from the many media influences to which the individual has been exposed. Therefore if radio is to succeed in penetrating societies with the message of Jesus Christ, a thorough analysis and understanding of the target audience is essential. It was agreed that the most effective role of radio is the sowing and watering of the seed — leaving direct proclamation to personal confrontation. It was pointed out that advertising does not of itself sell the commodity. That occurs only when the interested party comes face to face with the salesman. The basic problem in programming cultural, educational, or informational material is the risk of losing Christian sponsorship, i.e., the "saints" won't pay for the message which the "sinner" needs to hear. The message must be both heard and comprehended by the listener.

Christian communicators should not be afraid to expose their work to evaluation by secular researchers. There is a need for careful audience research and the training of national Christians in engineering, script writing, program production, and station management.

At a time when commercial radio and television are resorting to manipulation techniques, there is a danger of manipulation in gospel broadcasting. However, the thin line between persuasion and manipulation is determined by integrity of motive and issues in short or long term results. Manipulation occurs when the listener is unaware of the true message being transmitted to him. The media which the Holy Spirit uses are the media which open men's hearts.

Because Christian media are subsidized there is a tendency for substandard performances to be tolerated.

It is anticipated that in two years' time SONY will be marketing a radio set, within the purchasing powers of the masses, which will be able to receive a signal from the high-power communication satellites orbiting the Equator. This opens up a whole new dimension in radio evangelism because signal reception is not dependent on surface transmitter facilities.

Future goals

a. There is a need for a genuinely biblical, theological basis for our use of mass communications media. Writing on the subject is needed as well as teaching in Christian schools and training centers throughout the world.

b. There is a need for truly professional training and experience in Christian use of the media.

c. Christian use of all media is essential — secular as well as church-related. This will require our realization of the strategic role of Christians in commercial and state media. It necessitates our bringing these men and women into fellowship and planning for evangelism through all levels of media.

d. There should be a local-church centeredness to our use of mass media. Coordinated integration of the media is a priority. The local church must be seen as a part of that integrated plan — playing its unique and vital role in the total task of evangelism and discipleship.

e. Communication groups should be developed in each country. These fellowships of communicators could provide encouragement and practical assistance for evangelism through the media.

f. Evangelicals must make energetic efforts to discover what media are already available in their countries — opportunities are often lost due to lack of awareness and action on our part.

g. An international communication resource center is needed which will provide for the exchange of information and ideas and provide for directories of people, materials, literature, and films.

h. The church must grasp *new* media — satellites, data transmission, and other remarkable media forms which are already reshaping world commerce and political structures. They should be considered and used for evangelism.

i. Communication congresses, on a regional basis, to be convened as quickly as possible. These congresses to provide for full display of current hardware; the exhibition of Christian communication output from around the world, including the field of films, audio-visuals, literature, television, radio, and other media.

j. The coordination of audience research projects was considered to be a priority.

Conclusion

We need a radical change in the church's view of mass communications media. There must be a totally new awareness of how completely the media presently dominate our lives and the awesome potential for evangelism. Whereas, earlier generations eagerly grasped the emerging media opportunities, e.g., morality plays and the printing press, the contemporary church needs to exploit urgently the vast communication networks available today. Power, communications, and action are available if the church, under God's Spirit, takes hold of this remarkable field, with vision and an aggressive spirit.

CITYWIDE CRUSADE EVANGELIZATION

Luis Palau

*Mr. Palau, Portland, Oregon, is an
Argentine associated with Overseas
Crusades. He has conducted evangelistic
crusades all over Latin America.*

John Wesley, George Whitefield, Jonathan Edwards, Charles G. Finney, Dwight L. Moody, Elias Schrenk, R.A. Torrey, Billy Sunday, John Sung, Billy Graham — what a sense of vibrating excitement grips the imagination at the very reading of the names of such great men! They are more than individuals; they symbolize potent movements of God. God used them to write history — nation-changing history. Their lives touched millions and brought hundreds of thousands into the kingdom of God by faith in Jesus Christ. Their powerful influence touches our own lives, even to this day. They are some of God's choicest servants in the last three centuries of the history of the Christian Church.

Moreover, all the above-named had one thing in common: each practiced citywide crusade evangelization. And the power of those crusades — by the continuing action of the Holy Spirit through their anointed writings, life-stories, and still-standing institutions — continues to inspire young men to serve Christ in every land.

1. Basic definitions

By *citywide* we mean the concerted effort by a group of local churches, preferably on a transdenominational basis, to thoroughly evangelize a city and its surrounding population centers. In some cases it may even involve a series of "satellite crusades." These are a grouping of cities that simultaneously hold citywide crusades. The purpose is to make a deep-seated, lasting impact on a whole vast region in a nation.

By *crusade* is meant:

a. The harnessing of the spiritual gifts of all the believers in the Body of Christ in the city, to make a united Gospel impact on the non-Christian population.

b. The ideal objective is that every individual in that city ... clearly hear the call of God and the claims of Jesus Christ ... experience the new birth (John 3:3,5), and begin a walk with God in the fellowship of other believers, either in previously established local congregations or by the formation of new house-churches.

c. The expected result is that many hundreds, or thousands, of those who hear the Gospel and the claims of Christ will receive Jesus Christ into their heart and begin to walk with God in the fellowship as previously mentioned.

The desired and expected results of citywide crusade evangelization are many. But *the basic and somewhat immediate* expectancy is:

(i) That all those called of God in that city, who have not yet done so, and for whom "the fulness of time" has arrived, will respond by repentance and faith, receiving Jesus Christ as Savior and Lord.

(ii) That those who thus respond to the sovereign call of God and "believe on the Lord Jesus Christ" will begin to grow spiritually with a goal of maturity through a love and study of Holy Scripture, through allowing the indwelling Jesus Christ to control them by the Holy Spirit and through prayer; will be baptized in water; will become active and ever more effective members in the fellowship of the Body of Christ in a local congregation of believers (a local church); will understand and utilize the "gifts of the Holy Spirit"; will begin quickly to spread the Gospel of Christ that saved them, to their relatives, friends, and out to the whole world as God directs their lives.

By *evangelization* is meant:

a. The preaching of Jesus Christ to the non-Christian, utilizing the authority of Holy Scripture under the anointing of the Holy Spirit.

b. Preaching the basic facts of the Gospel to every person in the cultural and social situation in which he finds himself.

c. *Communicating* the eternal truth of God clearly and understandably to all age groups.

Certainly citywide crusade evangelization is *only one* method of fulfilling the Great Commission left to the Church by its Head, our Lord and Savior Jesus Christ. But a most valid method it is! Otherwise Christ would not have given "evangelists" to his church. (Eph. 4:11-12). And it is more valid than ever in this day of massive metropolitan and cosmopolitan cities, exploding population growth, and a mass-media-oriented new generation.

Effective crusade evangelization actually incorporates into its organization practically all other known methods and Holy Spirit-given gifts. Every Christian in the area who wishes to can actively and thoroughly share in a citywide crusade with all of his God-given gifts, abilities, and possessions to "take their city for God."

2. The historical precedents for citywide evangelization

a. *Biblical precedents.* The Scripture recognizes the basic methods for reaching people with the Gospel to be:

(i) The evangelization of individuals

(ii) Evangelization of groups

(iii) The example of our Lord Jesus Christ. In the New Testament, nearly 150 times we read that the Lord Jesus spoke to "the multitudes." It tells us that "the multitudes pressed him," and because they pressed him, he had to get into a boat to be able to speak to them. So many surrounded him that on some occasions he had no time to eat. The Lord often addressed himself to cities as a whole in his declarations ("Oh Jerusalem, Jerusalem!"), ("Woe unto you, Bethsaida!") (Matt. 9:35-38; Luke 4:14-22; Matt. 5:1).

(iv) The example of the Apostolic Church. St. Paul practiced evangelization to the masses. He first of all went to the marketplace. Why? That's where the masses gathered! When the angry crowd gathered in Ephesus (Acts 19), enraged by the turning away from idolatry which the Gospel produced, Paul could hardly be held back from going out to preach to the crowd in the theater. (I am personally convinced he could not bear the sight of a theater filled with people and no one to preach Christ to them.) See Acts 28.

b. *The precedent set by the post-Apostolic Church.* Kenneth Scott Latourette's *A History of The Expansion of Christianity* mentions many great servants of God who were engaged in mass evangelism.

3. The rationale for citywide crusade evangelism.

a. *Citywide crusade evangelization, done in the power of the Holy Spirit is the communication of the truth of God to multiplied thousands of people.* And certainly this is God's deepest desire even if the listeners refuse to hear or believe (II Cor. 2:14-16; Mark 13:10; Matt. 9:36-38).

b. *A city becomes "God-conscious."* When it is done properly and in God's time, a citywide crusade can extend its influence even beyond its borders, to a whole nation. The result is that the harvest of souls coming to Jesus Christ is often multiplied. The conscience of thousands becomes sensitive. The fact that the Bible has real-life, day-to-day answers for modern man's inner dilemmas makes thousands upon thousands ask the right questions: questions about eternal life, forgiveness of sins, victory over selfishness and temptation, happiness and harmony in the home, honesty in all of life.

This "God-consciousness" provoked by a citywide crusade becomes an amazing bridge to the souls of men. Christian believers find themselves — if they walk sensitively in the Holy Spirit — crossing that bridge of witness at all times and in almost all places daily to witness with authority of their Savior.

c. *Government and national leaders are practically forced to hear the Gospel during citywide crusades.* As did governors (Acts 13) and kings (Acts 26) in giving Paul a hearing, so today the leaders of nations ought to hear the Word of God. In most countries of the world, they do not pay attention to our message ordinarily. But when they see a mass movement of people, or an impact on television and the mass media in general, leadership usually listens!

d. *Citywide crusades have enormous validity, also, because there are spiritually hungry people lost within the vastness of a city who for years, like Cornelius in Acts 10, have been searching and, so to speak, waiting for the Good News of God.* Historically, these searchers have become awakened and alerted by the mass movement of the crusade. Then they are drawn to the message of the living, resurrected, powerful Jesus Christ. Thousands of these searchers that have lived in the shadows of big cities have responded eagerly to the Gospel and have been transformed into "new creatures in Christ," (II Cor. 5:17).

e. *The population explosion around the world calls for citywide crusade evangelization.* A new generation is constantly "coming of age." In other words, even if a given city can be said to have been evangelized previously, a new set of children grows up and must be fully evangelized. Constantly the modern move from the rural to the urban cities brings in thousands of new individuals to the cities that can and ought to be evangelized.

"Preach the Gospel to every creature" was not a suggestion, but a command of our Lord. The Body of Christ in any given city cannot quietly rest in simply functioning to build itself up and have moments of worship without a specific effort to reach out to the vast sea of human beings around them that are not related at all to the family of God. This never-ending desire and passion of the Body of Christ to reach out to the lost can be, in a great measure, fulfilled from time to time by citywide crusades. These do not, in any way — as we shall see in the next section — nullify the on-going, daily witness by life and lip of every member of the Body. On the contrary, it is both a complement to that daily witness, a stimulus to it, and a door-opener to future continuing sharing of the Good News for years to come.

f. *Some 145,000 people around the world die daily and go to eternity (every 24 hours) according to statisticians.* Research shows that a vast proportion of those eternal souls pass into eternity having *never heard* that there is hope and eternal life and a resurrection to come and the forgiveness of sins.

Thus, millions upon countless millions keep passing on to face a Christless eternity and the judgment of God without the knowledge of God's plan of salvation. It means that God, our loving God, has not been glorified before their eyes by the proclamation of the Gospel.

This is an intolerable situation! I, personally — and I am sure that every thinking, intellectual Christian joins me — cannot tolerate the thought of so many millions going to eternity without Christ and without hearing of our Savior, and still remain static and indifferent.

Naturally, panic is not the answer. Certainly the Body of Christ must continue to function and life is to be lived normally. However, a citywide crusade gives the Body an opportunity — I would say at least three times in every "generation" — to confront their neighbors, known and unknown, and the whole city in which God has placed them, with the marvelous, saving grace of God.

g. *A neglected duty calls for extraordinary measures, thus citywide crusade evangelization has unusual validity.* Let us not deceive ourselves. Even though *ideally* the whole Body of Christ ought to be witnessing continually, and *ideally* this witnessing should cover the earth with the Good News, this has not been done over the 2,000 year history since Christ came to earth. Nor is it being practiced by all those who claim to be "Christian" in our day. There is no indication that every true believer is actively propagating the faith, even in this generation, in free countries.

Therefore, citywide crusade evangelization is a necessary instrument for the "stepping into the gap" of a segment of the church that has been negligent in its responsibility.

h. *Youth — which are usually otherwise indifferent to Christianity and its message — are attracted by the mass crusade approach.* There is a drawing power to the movement of masses of people. And today, according to statistics, around 50 per cent of the world's population is young. Thus, citywide crusade evangelization must be used if we are to communicate Christ to the young generations.

i. *Citywide crusades have a soil-testing function. Crusades reveal responsive and non-responsive populations. This facilitates local church planting and/or strategic decision-making by denominational and mission executives.* Sometimes crusades are organized *because* a city or area is known to be responsive. At other times, however, crusades should be carried out *to discover* if a particular area is or is not especially responsive to the Word of God.

Recent worldwide statistical information demonstrates that in the decade of the 70s, across the free world, with minor exceptions, citywide crusades are having a positive response and much of the desired effect. This is harvest time around the world and therefore we ought to practice it with urgency.

j. *A citywide crusade makes true believers present a strong, a united face as the Body of Christ to a watching world.* When directed by the Holy Spirit, in fact, citywide crusades break down barriers within the Body of Christ. Members of the church who had either never met, or who previously had animosities born of non-relationships between each other begin to experience "the love of God that is shed abroad in our hearts by the Holy Spirit" (Rom. 5:5). It is true that some argue that since the Body of Christ is not as united as the Savior wished, the unity of a crusade is not deeply real. However, in God's sight, the unity *is real.* Any step which tends to bring believers together as one and which tends to foster love for one another must be welcomed and stimulated.

This uniting factor of citywide crusades, well documented historically and experienced even in our generation, ought to be, among others, a strong argument in favor of citywide crusade evangelization. The members of the Body of Jesus Christ thus tell the world that though they do have differences — which no one is trying to hide during a crusade — nevertheless, we have a core of biblical faith that binds us both to Jesus Christ and to one another despite those real differences on secondary matters.

"By this shall all men know that you are my disciples," said the Lord Jesus in John 13:35, "if you have love for one another." The love that the believers display in a citywide united crusade leaves a strong imprint on the minds of the non-believing population.

k. *Citywide crusades make it possible to touch "The Untouchables" with the Word of God.* Today's great, massive cities in their geographical and architectural structure and design make it, in many cases, impossible to evangelize by the ordinary means employed by a single local church. Many high-rise apartment buildings are impossible to enter for a personal witness or the placing of a piece of literature — much less a face-to-face, clear, prolonged presentation of the Gospel of Jesus Christ.

Modern, citywide evangelistic crusades employ (as shall be shown in the next section) all mass communications media available. The use of this media, *coupled with* the mass movement in the city, which is played up and made common knowledge by newspapers, radio, and television news, makes even the most "untouchable" citizens read, listen, and have a chance to be affected by the Holy Scripture.

By the "untouchables" I mean also the upper classes, the very wealthy, the professionals that in many countries of the world have not yet been truly evangelized. In our generation — particularly in the decades of the 1960s and 1970s — these "untouchables" are raising their eyebrows when they are being obviously confronted with the saving word from heaven by all media that reaches them. This is a new situation for many areas of the world. Particularly, I can speak for the Latin American nations, and I believe many in Africa and Asia too. There is no question in the mind of most thinking Latin Americans that citywide crusades have been God's instrument to "open up" our society as never before in history to the Gospel of Jesus Christ.

l. *A citywide evangelization crusade is the prophetic voice of the people of God to a nation.* When carried out in the power of the Holy Spirit, in our generation which has so many mass media tools available, it is a historical moment in which the authoritative, prophetic Word of God can shake a city, even a city numbering millions, with a confrontation with the living, Almighty God. This public proclamation of the Cross, the resurrection, and the life of Jesus Christ in us, on the part of the whole Body of Christ to the whole city and sometimes the nation, is a visible, massive, public manifestation of the great power of the Gospel of Jesus Christ preached to the multitudes.

It is this prophetic, public, massive preaching of Jesus Christ that so often opens up a city. And that city can never again be the same because its population has heard the voice of the Living God! The message has been preached by the Body of Christ, in unison, through the voice of an evangelist who is backed up by hundreds and thousands of fellow believers. Thus confronted, even stout opponents of the Gospel of Jesus Christ must reflect and consider, and some will be converted.

For we "believe in the Holy Ghost" and it is the Holy Ghost that "convicts men of sin and of righteousness and of judgment" (John 16:8). And when the Holy Ghost, speaking through the voice of one messenger — and many hundreds of other messengers anointed by the same Holy Spirit — presents the message of the Gospel, it is bound to leave an imprint on the whole city and each individual that cannot be forgotten in a lifetime.

m. *A citywide crusade is the joy and the happiness of all the people of God together, singing, praising, witnessing, praying, and listening to the Word of God proclaimed.* By their presence and by their participation they are saying, "Amen! We are one with the preacher. What he is proclaiming is what I would proclaim if I were in his place. What you're hearing is what I would say, if I had his gift. This is our message to our city."

This makes the people of God happy. There is no more exciting picture in the book of Revelation, besides our bowing before the throne of God himself, than to see time and again the multitudes described as, "I heard around the throne and the living creatures and the elders the voice of many angels, numbering myriads of myriads and thousands of thousands, saying Worthy is the Lamb who was slain..." (Rev. 5:11-12).

No wonder in some circles citywide crusades were mistakenly called "revivals." What they were trying to say, in my opinion, was that though the crusades were aimed at the unbelievers, and the goal was their salvation, they themselves had been so thoroughly transformed and revived spiritually that they fell into using the confusing term, "Let's have a revival." And although the term is a misnomer, it is a great revelation of what happens to the people of God in many a citywide crusade that is carried out in the fullness and anointing of the Holy Spirit.

n. *For many, a united crusade is the end of their inferiority complexes.* In nations where the Gospel has not thoroughly permeated the society to the point where there are thousands upon thousands of believers, the coming together of several thousand in a public stadium brings to the heart of the lonely Christian from some small chapel in some hidden corner of the city, or to the group of believers in a small town outside of the city, a sense of belonging and of oneness with the larger company that is the whole Body of Christ universal. The positive effect of this factor alone cannot be measured in the life of lonely believers in many parts of the world. It is therefore a source of ministry to the Body of Christ.

o. *Citywide crusades are the occasion when for the first time many a Christian leads another person to accept Christ as Savior and Lord.* For many reasons that cannot be analyzed in this paper, thousands upon thousands of Christian brethren have never had the experience of personally leading another soul to believe upon and receive by faith Jesus Christ. In fact, I have met Christian ministers in this situation. During a crusade, however, due to the training, the sense of spiritual power, the excitement, the harvest of souls that is going on around them, they launch out and get a taste of this perhaps the most exciting, stimulating, experience in the Christian life.

In a crusade, we practice an evangelism of decision. And this creates a consciousness and a sense of responsibility. The crusade also shows indecisive or timid believers how a person is led to Christ. And when they see the simplicity and the beauty of it, they want to have a part! And so many do, that consequently they become continuing witnesses for the rest of their days.

p. *A citywide crusade is the moment of spiritual renovation and a new dedication to Christ on the part of many Christians.*

q. *It is placing mass communication media at the service of a sovereign Creator and at the service of the kingdom of God.* Television, radio, the press, the films, and theater, even the telephone system, deserve to be the instruments of the divine sovereign Creator communicating to his creatures. Certainly God allowed the discovery of these fantastic means of communicating God's truth, not to corrupt, but to redeem, to mature, and to bless humanity. Citywide crusades, in this last third of the twentieth century, have at their disposal, for the glory of God, these amazing modern tools. And souls are saved when they are used!

r. *Local churches grow numerically (as well as spiritually) and new congregations and new preaching points are opened up as a result of citywide evangelistic crusades.* If there is room for the new "babes in Christ" within the buildings and the facilities of already existing local churches, these grow during and after a citywide crusade. When there is vision on the part of denominational, mission, and local church leaders, and the plans are laid for initiating new local congregations, these are planted time and again, consequent upon a crusade. In fact, sometimes new local congregations are born as a result of a crusade, without any plans having been laid in anticipation. The sheer volume of converts, plus the sovereign action of the Holy Spirit, produces this most desirable result. Citywide crusades, therefore, create a new sense of responsibility within the existing churches regarding the planting of new local congregations when the geographical and population configuration calls for it.

s. *Christian young people are stimulated to form their own evangelistic groups as a result of citywide crusades handled in the Holy Spirit.* "Teaching by example" becomes a functional and fruitful parallel side-effect of the crusades. The passion to reach out to the lost displayed by the leaders and older Christians awakens in the younger generation a vision for the lost and a passion within themselves to reach out within their lifetime. The thrill of a citywide evangelistic crusade, from a theological standpoint, is that it combines the impact to the masses with the intimate personal touch to the individual. When practiced wisely, in the Holy Spirit, the public proclamation of the person and the message of God becomes very personalized in the person-to-person encounter between members of the Body of Christ and those who are responding to the call of God. Even those who are rejecting the message proclaimed often come face-to-face with an individual Christian who confirms the Word preached and reinforces it through personal conversation. It is the Holy Spirit, who in His sovereign action, "personalizes" the message to the individual's conscience, heart, and spirit.

t. *The public confession of faith in Christ tends to reinforce the decision in the individual's mind, in our day, in the same manner that baptism was considered by the person being baptized, in the beginnings of Christianity.* In many parts of the world today, baptism still has an enormous impact. However, particularly in Protestant and Catholic lands, the public impact and the personal impact on the individual of baptism seems to have been reduced to a minimum. (It still remains strong in nations where "Christendom" has not had a strong showing. The public confession before a crowd of fellow citizens leaves an inner mark, strengthening the inward conviction and determination of the heart by an outward demonstration to those hundreds of watching neighbors, friends, relatives, and townspeople.)

u. *Historically, God has honored evangelization to the masses and has used it as an instrument to introduce revivals.* We speak of the "Evangelical Revival" of the eighteenth century, which took place under the leadership of John and Charles Wesley and George Whitefield. These men were evangelists who practiced massive evangelization across the British Isles and in North America. God honored their strenuous evangelistic campaigning. Thousands upon thousands were converted and there was an effect on the land. Fifty years later, historians looking back, called it "a revival."

The same can be documented for what is popularly called "Second Worldwide Evangelical Awakening." If, historically, we honor these men who were used of God to introduce revivals as a direct consequence of massive evangelization, what a privilege to follow in their steps!

v. *In these last three decades of the closing twentieth century, citywide crusades glorify God and please the heart of God.* When all is said and done, this should be the ultimate motivating factor for all Christian activity. A citywide crusade, conducted in the power of the Holy Spirit, glorifies God because: it proclaims the glory of his name; it exalts the person and the work of Jesus Christ; it presents his substitutionary death on the Cross and his powerful resurrection from among the dead; it proclaims his power to transform and change men, families, and even nations. It glorifies God because it demonstrates his love and power in the unity displayed by the believers, and the love and affection that they display in their work together in evangelism.

4. What constitutes a citywide crusade?

a. *What it is not.*

(i) A citywide crusade is not merely a series of evening evangelistic meetings where songs are sung and the message is proclaimed.

(ii) It is not proclamation only. It involves a varied ministry within the Body of Christ and to the non-Christian world.

(iii) It is not a "one-man show." It involves all or most of the Body in a given city.

(iv) It is not merely the mobilization of a thousand or ten thousand Christians within the churches, for a show of numbers.

(v) It is not merely a mechanical organization that, on a purely humanistic basis, gets a movement going.

b. *When is a citywide crusade truly effective?*

(i) When it is conducted in the power of the indwelling Christ and under the anointing of the Holy Spirit. This is particularly crucial on the part of the leadership and the men whom God has indicated to lead the crusade.

(ii) Only when the message is the clear and true biblical Gospel, especially emphasizing the death on the Cross and the living, resurrected, almighty Jesus Christ, present to save and transform the individual and his home.

(iii) It is effective when done in union with all or most of the Body of Christ.

(iv) It is particularly effective when a "touch from God" first cleanses, revitalizes, and renews the old believers in the city.

(v) A crusade is truly effective when the multi-faceted gifts of the Holy Spirit are functioning and being practiced by most of the Body of Christ in that city.

(vi) A crusade is effective when the Christians, in particular the spiritual leadership of the local congregations, are maturely responsible and truly alerted to the vital need of immediate spiritual care, discipling, and building up of the new babes in Christ.

c. *Potential dangers of citywide crusades.*

(i) There is the danger that Christians will expect more from a crusade than it can deliver. We counteract this by presenting true, realistic goals and objectives for the crusade.

(ii) There is the danger that Christians will want to turn the crusade into exclusively a "happy time" for the believers. Holy Spirit-led preparation, reviving, and training in the pre-crusade phase should cancel out this danger.

(iii) There is the danger that Christians will think a crusade is a substitute for continuous, ever-expanding personal witness and normal local church outreach. Again, this danger is dispelled by the leadership's example, the objective teaching of Scripture before, during, and after the crusade.

(iv) There is the danger that even church leaders, missionaries, and ministers will "leave it all to the Team." This is perhaps the greatest danger. It evidences itself in the criticism that is leveled at visiting crusade teams by so-called "objective studies of crusade results." The way to counteract this danger is: to make sure that leaders, missionaries, and ministers *fully comprehend* that all the Body of Christ in the city is responsible for the crusade, that it is not a "Team" crusade, but a crusade by the Body of Christ and with the Body of Christ in the city.

    d. *What a citywide evangelization crusade is in action.* A citywide evangelization crusade is the whole Body of Christ working together and using its spiritual gifts to accomplish the great commission of Jesus Christ in its generation within the border of its "Jerusalem" (Acts 1:8). It is a wise investment of the time, gifts, money, and love of the Church of Jesus Christ for the accomplishment of its God-given objectives.

    Dr. Leighton Ford indicates that a crusade can be subdivided into three major phases: Preparation, Penetration, and Preservation. *Preparation* would include giving a vision to the Body of Christ; awakening believers; revival and renewal within the Body; edification through Scripture teaching and sharing; equipping the saints (Eph. 4:11-16); and a minimum organization for maximizing effectiveness and results. *Penetration* involves the obvious personal and massive evangelization of the whole city, as well as the initial discipling and building up of those who were converted during the crusade. The *preservation and continuation* phase seeks to edify, disciple, incorporate, and see spiritual reproduction in those who come to Christ during and immediately following the crusade.

    (i) The *preparation* is basically oriented towards the Body of Christ in the city. The biblical bases are such passages as Eph. 4; I Cor. 12-14; Col. 1:24-2:7.

    There should be *pastors' congresses and conferences* to stimulate the awareness and reality of the oneness of the Body of Christ, to enlarge the vision for worldwide mission, to renew their personal relationship with God, and to emphasize the "priesthood of all believers" and how to lead all members of the Body to use their spiritual gifts.

    The *awakening and reviving of believers* will be concerned with teaching on the indwelling life of Christ, how to walk in holiness through the Holy Spirit, and imparting a vision of the lost without Christ and their present and eternal state.

    Another vital feature of preparation is *intercession and particular prayer emphasis* for the city and the salvation of the lost.

    Finally there is *equipping,* that is training and discipling, according to Eph. 4. This will include: how to be a "big brother or sister" to new converts in Christ and disciple them; how to hold home Bible studies with new believers or seekers; how to start a new congregation as a result of the crusade; personal witnessing and sharing of our faith in Christ, including Scripture memorization; how to conduct effective evangelism of children; how to reach out to youth; preparation for the ministry of music in the penetration phase of the crusade; and equipping for special outreach to jails, door-to-door visitation evangelism, Scripture distribution, and other means.

    (ii) The *penetration,* or the evangelistic phase of the crusade, will be concerned with the following:

Massive public rallies or meetings in an attractive public stadium or auditorium, usually in the evening. These are the massive meetings which capture the attention of the city and the news media, and draw many to hear the Gospel.

Aggressive personal visitation and personal witnessing by all believers, utilizing literature and their personal conversion stories everywhere.

Daily television evangelism and counseling "live" on the air.

Counseling centers in various zones of the city, to supplement the television ministry. In these centers Bible teaching is conducted daily, and problem-solving counseling is freely given to all who seek it.

Daily radio evangelism through the press and magazines.

Evangelism in parks and street meetings, both children's and general evangelism.

Breakfasts and luncheons for witness to politicians, business people, professionals, and the wealthy who otherwise do not attend crusades.

Film evangelism wherever doors open. Morning Bible classes with ministers, elders, missionaries, and Christian workers.

Schools of evangelism that run simultaneously with the crusade, during the day. These will include practical Bible teaching; basic training in evangelism; and the organizing of students to help denominations or missions that wish to start new local churches in virgin territories within or around the city.

(iii) The *preservation and continuation* phase of the crusade begins during the evangelism penetration phase with the cultivating of open doors produced by the crusade's impact, and the edifying and discipling of new babes in Christ. This phase will involve the following:

"Big brother or sister" ministry in the homes.

"Bible Teaching Week" in all local churches the week after the crusade closes.

Daily radio Bible teaching for continuity in simple truths.

Records, tapes, and literature for edification in the hands of converts.

"Welcome Day" at each local church for new converts.

Doctrinal "Baptism-Day-Oriented" Sunday School class for new Christians in local churches.

5. When a citywide evangelization crusade should be considered

a. When responsive people are found in any given city. One way to discover a responsive population is by a probing ministry through mass media seed-sowing, as well as a measure of harvesting through the media.

b. When a group of spiritual, concerned individuals sense that "the time is right."

c. In my opinion, every major city should consider a well-organized, deeply-prepared crusade every five to ten years.

d. In times of social unrest and moral disorientation in a nation, a well-organized citywide crusade should be considered.

6. Conclusion

"Let the earth hear His voice" is the theme of the International Congress on World Evangelization. If we are to accomplish that goal in our generation, as is the will of our Lord and Savior, Jesus Christ, then citywide evangelization crusades must figure prominently in our worldwide strategy.

I believe that, as Dr. Billy Graham said at the end of the World Congress in Berlin in 1966, "It is possible; it is probable; it is imperative!" The whole earth *must* hear His voice!

CITYWIDE CRUSADE EVANGELIZATION REPORT

Secretary: Peter Thompson

Mr. Moses Ariye, from Nigeria, opened the session and introduced Luis Palau, from the Argentine, who has conducted evangelistic crusades all over Latin America. Mr. Palau spoke on citywide crusade evangelization, and made the following definitions. "By citywide we mean a concerted effort by a group of local churches, preferably on an interdenominational basis, to thoroughly evangelize a city and its surrounding population centers." Turning to the definition of evangelization, Palau said there were three points: First, the preaching of Jesus Christ to the non-christian, utilizing the authority of the Holy Scripture under the anointing of the Holy Spirit; second, preaching the basic facts of the Gospel to every person in the cultural and social situation in which he finds himself; third, communicating the eternal truth of God clearly and understandably to all age groups.

Palau conceded that citywide evangelism was only one means of fulfilling the Great Commission left to the church, however, he added that citywide evangelism was "a most valid method."

Describing what a citywide crusade was *not,* Palau underlined that crusades are not hymn sings and Gospel sessions nor are they an attempt to show strength for the local church or an organization which on purely humanistic grounds gets a movement going. "A crusade," added Palau, "is most effective when done in union with all or most of the Body of Christ. It is particularly effective when a 'touch from God' first cleanses, revitalizes and renews the old believers in the city."

Palau warned that there is a danger that Christians will expect more from a crusade than it can deliver. "We counteract this by presenting true, realistic goals and objectives for the crusade."

Concluding, Palau said a citywide crusade should be considered when a responsive people is found in any given city. He ended by saying what Dr. Billy Graham said at the conclusion of the World Congress in Berlin in 1966, "It is possible; it is probable; it is imperative; the whole earth must hear his voice!"

FOLLOW-UP IN CRUSADE AND CHURCH EVANGELISM

Charles Riggs

Dr. Riggs, Nashville, Tennessee, USA, is Director of Counselor Training and Follow-Up for the Billy Graham Evangelistic Association.

Follow-up has been defined as the process of giving continued attention to a new Christian (new babe) until he is integrated into the church, discovering his place of service, developing his full potential for Jesus Christ, and helping to build Christ's church. This may sound a bit idealistic, but it is a pattern set forth in Ephesians for reaching the lost and building the church. "Some of us have been given special ability as apostles; to others he has given the gift of being able to preach well; some have special ability in winning people to Christ, helping them to trust him as their Savior; still others have a gift for caring for God's people as a shepherd does his sheep, leading and teaching them in the ways of God. Why is it that he gives us these special abilities to do certain things best? It is that God's people will be equipped to do better work for him, building up the church, the body of Christ, to a position of strength and maturity; until finally we all believe alike about our salvation and about our Savior, God's Son, and all become full-grown in the Lord — yes, to the point of being filled full with Christ" (Eph. 4:11-13). Many books have been written on follow-up. No book is, however, quite as clear or as pointed on the subject of follow-up as the New Testament. The Apostle Paul is the pace-setter. His strategy and methods were fruitful and effective in his time and should work today.

Of utmost importance was his love and concern for new Christians. He was willing to become involved in their lives, in spite of the cost. "Because we were yearning for you so tenderly, we were willing, not only to share with you God's good news, but to lay down our very lives too for you, all because you were so dearly loved by us" (I Thess. 2:8). This may be one of the greatest obstacles to follow-up today, the unwillingness to give of ourselves and of our time to become vitally involved with a new Christian.

The Apostle Paul was deeply concerned for the new Christian because he knew the power of the evil one to spoil his work. "For I am jealous over you with godly jealousy: for I have espoused you to one husband, that I may present you as a chaste virgin to Christ. But I fear, lest by any means, as the serpent beguiled Eve through his subtlety, so your minds should be corrupted from the simplicity that is in Christ" (II Cor. 11:2-3).

His chief concern obviously was for their growth and development. His goal was their maturity. "Oh my dear children, I am suffering a mother's birth pangs for you again, until Christ is formed in you " (Gal. 4:19). "And we proclaim him, admonishing every man with all wisdom, that we may present every man complete in Christ" (Col. 1:28).

With this aim in mind, the maturity of the individual, the Apostle Paul by his *letters* kept in constant touch with churches and individuals, pouring out his great heart of love. "For to this end also did I write, that I might know the proof of you, whether ye be obedient in all things" (II Cor. 2:9). His *prayers* revealed the desire in his heart and his longing to be with people, ministering to them in their deepest needs. He prayed specifically, long and often for their growth. "Night and day praying exceedingly that we might see your face, and might perfect that which is lacking in your faith" (I Thess: 3:10).

When he could not go personally, *he sent on follow-up missions men that he had trained.* "So when I could not bear it any longer, I decided to be left behind in Athens alone, and so I sent my brother Timothy, God's minister in the preaching of the good news of Christ, to strengthen and encourage you in your faith, so that none of you might be deceived amid these difficulties" (I Thess. 3:1-3).

No doubt the greatest secret of his success, he returned *personally* to individuals and church groups to meet with them face to face to teach them. His first mission was launched from Antioch with Barnabas. "While th ¬hristians were worshiping the Lord and fasting, the Holy Spirit sai Set Barnabas and Saul apart for Me to do the work I called them for.' Then they fasted and prayed, laid their hands on them, and let them go" (Acts 13:2-3). They visited many cities, preaching with great power and authority before returning to Antioch. They then took a second major trip and the prime objective appeared to be follow-up. "And some days after, Paul said unto Barnabas, Let us go again and visit our brethren in *every city* where we have preached the word of the Lord, and *see how they do*" (Acts 15:36). On this trip they further evangelized but also ministered in depth. "Now while they were passing through the cities, they were delivering decrees, which had been decided upon by the apostles and elders who were in Jerusalem, for them to observe. So the churches were being strengthened in the faith, and were increasing in number daily" (Acts 16:4-5). "And he settled there (Corinth) a year and six months, teaching the word of God among them" (Acts 18:11) The Apostle Paul again returned to Antioch and after some time departed on another trip for the purpose of follow-up. "After spending some time there (Antioch), he started out again, and by a definite schedule traveled all over Galatia and Phrygia, imparting new strength to *all the disciples*" (Acts 18:23).

A precedent is clearly set. New Christians do need care for various reasons and the care should be administered by someone. True, the Holy Spirit is able to minister to individuals — but the Scriptures provide the food necessary for growth and the new Christian must be fed. The one who wins a person to Christ is logically the one who should help work with the new Christian since there is a natural affinity. By "work with" I mean being available for further help and counsel, encouraging the inquirer to get started in good devotional habits, making certain that he is regularly attending a church where he will be nurtured and become active for Christ. The "Evangelism Explosion" program is an excellent example of the church at work today, reaching people for Christ, nurturing them and helping them become active Christians. Workers are trained not only to witness and win people to Christ but also help them become active in the life and outreach of the church.

Crusade evangelism follow-up

There will always be evangelistic meetings where numbers of people will respond to an invitation to receive Christ. Some measures need to be taken to give immediate and individual care to these people and help them continue in the faith. The following suggestions come out of our crusade experiences of many years.

Personal counseling. A clear commitment is the first step in good follow-up. Unfortunately, in many evangelistic efforts, issues are not made clear and people respond to an invitation for various reasons without having their real needs met. This becomes evident in the follow-up. The inquirer often becomes a "drop-out."

Effective follow-up can only begin in the life of one who has been born again by the Spirit of God. When the Holy Spirit is at work in the life of the individual, drawing, convicting and regenerating, then one can say with assurance, "Being confident of this very thing, that he which hath begun a good work in you will perform it until the day of Jesus Christ" (Phil. 1:6).

Personal counseling, although not a "cure-all," can be of immeasurable help in any meeting where people are invited to receive Christ. Mature counselors, able to diagnose and rightly use the Scriptures, can be used of the Holy Spirit to make the issues clear. They can introduce material and follow up those they have counseled.

In our crusades, we train counselors to give personal counsel and to follow up crusade inquirers. The help they give will, of course, depend somewhat on the maturity and the burden of the counselor. Some years ago we were in South America and a missionary, helping as a counselor, told us that he had committed his life to Christ five years earlier in Scotland. His counselor was still praying for him and helping with his support. This was an unusual situation but we have found through the years that counselors have been very faithful and helpful in counseling and following up inquirers in our crusades. We ask counselors to telephone, write, or visit each inquirer they counsel and send us a report.

Bible study correspondence. As an important part of the counseling program, each inquirer is given a "Knowing Christ" booklet to help clarify his commitment. This booklet is the first in the "Living in Christ" series and contains the Gospel of John plus Scripture memory verses, devotional reading, and two question-and-answer Bible studies. The material in this booklet is aimed at answering questions the inquirer might have immediately after his commitment, and to help give him a simple but firm anchor for his faith. The three other booklets in the series contain additional studies, Scripture verses and devotional aids. Many churches in the United States are now using this material for follow-up.

Church follow-up. New Christians need to be brought into a meaningful fellowship with other Christians in the church. For this reason, on the same night of the commitment, through the efforts of scores of volunteer workers, the name of each inquirer is sent to a local pastor. This makes it possible for the pastor or a church representative to follow up crusade referrals, day by day. Immediate follow-up is most important, even if it is only a telephone call. It does show a concern and gives the inquirer an opportunity to ask questions and get further help.

Through the seminars and schools of evangelism we encourage a pastor on two levels:

(i) Nurture activities to feed and develop those who have responded as crusade inquirers.

(ii) Ongoing evangelization which harnesses the keen interest and enthusiasm of "turned on" believers who have been active in the crusade.

Specific suggestions are made to integrate the new inquirer into the mainstream of church life:

(i) A reception for all crusade inquirers. A social setting in which the membership may be introduced to inquirers and help establish new friendships in the church family.

(ii) A review of church programs is recommended. Scheduling a new-member-orientation class, finding places of service and activity, etc.

(iii) A spiritual adoption plan, providing a spiritually mature friend to act as a "parent" or sponsor for each inquirer. Parents are specially trained by the pastor to guide inquirers in Christian growth and development.

Specific suggestions are made to continue the outreach of evangelization — utilizing the gifts of the membership to meet the needs of the community where the church congregation meets.

(i) An evangelistic visitation plan, designed to provide a perpetual calling effort to systematically visit each church prospect and present the Gospel story in the home.

(ii) Try some new methods, such as film crusades, beach invasions, shopping center outreach, et cetera.

(iii) Local church campaigns to mobilize the energies of crusade workers in prayer groups, choir, ushers, visitation, "Andrews," and focus on opportunities open to the local church.

Three principles of follow-through are identified:

First, the pace-setting leadership of the pastors and church leaders. This follows the example of Jesus who said, "Follow me" and follow through came in the context of his dynamic life-style.

Second, the learn-to-do-by-doing. This means on-the-job training with emphasis on practical demonstration.

Third, matching resources with opportunities.

Discovering the talents, gifts and skills of the congregation and applying them to the practical situations of need that confront the congregation in its setting.

Literature follow-up — A few days after his commitment, each inquirer receives a letter of encouragement from Dr. Graham with further helps. Then on a monthly basis the inquirer receives DECISION magazine containing several pages of helpful material, i.e., Bible studies, inspirational testimonies, sermons and other articles to strengthen his faith. At times, the inquirer receives Dr. Graham's book *Peace with God* which contains the "Rules for the Christian Life."

Bible study follow-up — A small-group prayer and Bible study fellowship provides a good environment for the new Christian. An opportunity to come together on a regular basis to share what God is doing in the life can be enriching. We have developed "Studies in Disciple-

ship," a seven-lesson study to be used by the churches in follow-up. Each member of the group covenants to pray daily for other members of the group, prepares a written Bible study and shares with other group members.in a discussion-type study. The leader does not teach, he leads the discussion. We call them "Nurture Groups." The lessons in this study deal with Christian assurance, the Lordship of Christ, the authority of the Bible, effectual prayer, walking in the Spirit, and witnessing for Christ.
weekly assigned projects are aimed at helping each individual establish a daily time of fellowship with Jesus Christ and become involved in ministering to the needs of others.

A discussion-type series for teens, "New Scene," has also been developed and it covers the same general area of concern as the Discipleship studies. However, a different approach is taken, allowing the teen a great deal more versatility in doing his lesson. Hopefully, this makes the study more attractive and interesting, yet biblical and basic to the Christian life.

Prior to the crusade, hundreds of church representatives are trained to lead "Nurture Groups." They learn-to-do-by-doing. Over a four-week period, they meet once a week in groups of ten, to become familiar with the lesson material and techniques in leading a discussion. Having had this experience, they have a greater confidence in leading follow-up nurture groups after the crusade is over.

Post-crusade follow-up survey — To make absolutely certain that every inquirer has been contacted and given further help as necessary, we have developed a post-crusade survey. About three weeks after the crusade ends, giving opportunity for the normal channels of follow-up to function, every inquirer is called by a trained worker. Questions are asked and if the inquirer is doing well the interview takes no more than a few minutes. This interview helps reveal weaknesses in our follow-up. It also provides opportunity for further counseling, which is often necessary.

We are able to enlist many more people in the Bible study nurture program and give the inquirer additonal help, where necessary, in getting established in a church. This may seem like a duplication of effort since we have asked both the pastor and counselor to contact the inquirer. Our experience indicates that not only is the survey necessary, but the call is most appreciated by the inquirer.

Special follow-up — The preceding facets of follow-up are routine in most of our major crusades. We have adopted the "shot-gun" approach to follow-up, trying a lot of different things, trusting one method will take hold.

Additional programs of follow-up may be used from crusade to crusade if and when they seem appropriate.

Radio follow-up — A series of fifteen-minute messages on the new life in Christ has been developed through the efforts of several Team members. At times, we broadcast a daily program in the evening for several weeks. This gives a good continuity to the follow-up program and reaches hundreds of individuals at one time.

Special student follow-up — In crusades where there is a large student population, especially college-age, we organize follow-up on campus. The name of each student inquirer is sent to a student leader on campus, where prayer and Bible study groups have been scheduled to follow up the crusade.

Special teas and coffees — In some cities we have had special meetings for groups by occupation, such as nurses, people in the entertainment profession, and business executives. Having them mingle with fellow Christians and listen to someone respected in their own profession either give a testimony or a message, is a good way to reach busy "hard-to-reach" people. This meeting can provide a springboard to further opportunities of ministering to them.

Conclusion

God is faithfully calling out and building his church, using a variety of people and methods. No doubt, more important than the material or method is the man. E.M. Bounds said, "The world is looking for better methods, but God is looking for better men." Should we not ask ourselves, "Are we in perfect union with Jesus Christ, with no unconfessed sin to hinder his working effectively in and through our lives?" Are we totally surrendered to God's will? Are we using fully the God-given abilities to help build his Church? Are we completely yielded to the Holy Spirit and trusting in his enabling power to do the work of the ministry? Are we completely open-minded, willing to learn from others, willing to accept new ideas, and willing to adopt new methods and materials, even if they do not originate from within our group? Are we setting a good example in prayer and Bible study, so that we can say with the Apostle Paul, "The things you have learned and received and heard and *seen in me*, practice these things, and the God of peace shall be with you" (Phil. 4:9).

How we as individuals answer these questions may well determine how deeply we become involved in God's work of calling and building his church.

FOLLOW-UP STRATEGY GROUP REPORT

Charles Riggs, head of the Billy Graham follow-up team, introduced each session with a short talk on follow-up. He showed us the Billy Graham material that is used in follow-up. On the night the person is counseled he receives the first in a series of booklets (or "bottles of milk" as Mr. Riggs called them). These were designed to tell the new believer about the Christian life and introduce him to the basics of it, i.e., Bible reading, regular praying, etc. Contained in the first book was a copy of the Gospel of John. After the person had read through it, there was a lesson to be completed and returned to the Billy Graham office. Once this was received in the office, the second bottle of milk was sent to the believer.

They had also developed a booklet that was good to use in home Bible study groups. It was entitled *Studies in Discipleship*. But as Mr. Riggs put it, telling is not teaching and listening is not learning, as we learn by doing. So this book was designed to do just that. As the new believer studies, there are questions that are asked to promote discussion.

After the name of the person was received by the office, it was sent to a local minister in the area for follow-up. In addition to that, the person who counseled then is asked to follow them up within 24 hours. The office also contacts the person three weeks after the crusade and finally, in some areas, radio time is bought and talks are given for a period of a week. All of this is done in order to keep in contact with the new believer. It is hoped that if one method failed the others would succeed.

With all of this said, Mr. Riggs then stressed the most important side of follow-up and that was men. All of our methods and means can never replace the men God uses. If the people involved are not led by the Spirit of God our methods would fail. He stressed the fact that follow-up begins with the pacesetter — one who is walking with God daily in prayer and Bible study. Godly men (Psalm 12:1). The person needs not only to be filled with the Spirit but also walking in the Spirit (Eph. 5:18; Gal. 5:16).

As people involved in follow-up we need to feed-protect-train people. We need to see reproduction coming from the new converts themselves. In order to do all of this we need men and women who are able to say with Paul, "I am willing to spend and be spent" (II Cor. 12:15). Follow-up takes time and demands a sacrifice. It is a time of helping new converts over rough patches and we need to be available when they need us. The only place that we are to take the new converts for an answer to their problems is to the Book. For it is only as they look at the Bible and go to it that it becomes a mirror reflecting the things that are wrong in their lives. God is able to speak to them from the Bible and we need to get the convert to learn to have a regular quiet time. Not only that, but Mr. Riggs encouraged us to get the new convert to memorize the Word of God, so that it can be used by the Spirit as a sword. God's Word needs to become the direction and control of their lives.

We then faced some problems people encounter in follow-up.

Question: Do we have any statistics to show the percentage of people who went on for God, under the above follow-up method?

Answer: There was much debate as to what was the most effective method of follow-up. Some people felt that the Billy Graham method was not successful, in their area. Dr. Bob Ferm has interviewed many thousands of inquirers and has found that over a period of years, forty-five to ninety percent of all the people that had been followed up were active in church life.

It was also pointed out that in Oak Hill Bible College in England 50 per cent of all its students had been converted at a Billy Graham rally. Similar figures were available for Australia.

Question: A question was put to Mr. Riggs. How do you keep from becoming slick and mechanical in your work? After so many crusades don't you find the methods push the spiritual life out?

Answer: He replied that every crusade he does, he goes into it as though it were his first. This way we can always be open to the leading of God, should he Want to develop new ideas and methods. Our reliance was not on the methods that we used, but it needed to be constantly on his Word. If we could look at our follow-up process as living and growing then we can never say we have arrived at the perfect method.

Question: How does one prepare churches to accept the new converts?

Answer: One method that was suggested: to have Bible studies in homes so that the new convert is not only coming to Sunday meetings. This would mean that members of the church open their homes to new converts from their area for Bible studies and discussion groups.

This would not only give the converts a sense of belonging, but it would also give the church members a chance to get to know the converts on an informal level.

The emphasis from all over the world was on lay Bible study groups. Mr. Ben Siaki from the Philippines shared with us something of what the Lord was doing in his country. They had developed what was called the C.O.W. program.

CHRIST THE
ONLY
WAY.

But a cow has to have legs to stand on and this is where the strength of the program lies.

LAY
EVANGELISTIC
GROUP
STUDIES

This was a method where new converts were brought into small groups to study God's Word. In a recent survey done, out of 900 people that gave their lives to Christ, 276 had become active church members and another 142 had joined L.E.G.S. groups and were growing in the Lord.

Another way of getting churches involved would be to send a complete set of follow-up material to a particular minister. Then ask him to appoint someone who would act as a parent to the new convert. This would be a very effective way of having the personal interest. It would also introduce the new convert to church life.

The converts need to be brought into a church where they could grow in God.

Question: What does one do when you hold a crusade in an area where there are no evangelical churches? Where do you send the new converts?

Answer: A person from Africa provided a very good answer to this. What they had done in their follow-up work where they have faced the same problem was to train the new converts (sometimes for up to ten hours a week) in the Christian life. They then send their converts back to the churches not to be fed but to feed. This resulted in a few things:

a) The new convert had an ideal opportunity to share his faith.

b) If he did come into any difficulties there was someone to help him.

c) The Gospel was being shared in a group or church that did not normally hear it.

Question: How do you do follow-up in a small group or pastorate and not in a big organized crusade?

Answer: A gentleman from Uganda faced this problem as well as the fact that there was no follow-up material in his own language.

He found that the only answer was to mobilize the church members to do the follow-up work verbally. Again it was brought out that the most effective follow-up tool is people.

Question: All the methods and materials are good, but how do you follow-up illiterate people?

Answer: We found that most of our follow-up material was very western-oriented. In some places of Africa and Asia you could not ever get an address, for many of the people did not have a street or box number as we know it in the west. Therefore, it would be impossible to post follow-up material to them. Again the answer rests in the man involved in follow-up.

It was suggested that these be a type of teacher who could travel around among groups of new converts giving them Bible studies.

Something very important was brought up and that was that the new converts should be taught to memorize the Bible. Even though our follow-up is western-orientated the Bible is not. Every culture group can do this without any fear of being influenced by another culture. For the Word of God is totally relevant to every culture, tribe or group of people.

One participant from Africa started an extra class in his church just to cater for the new believer, where they were taught the basics.

Someone suggested a local broadcasting company be approached with the view of giving time on the radio. An isolated village could then be given or loaned a radio and they could hear the Word of God that way. This was done very effectively in Australia, where portions of "Good News for Modern Man" were read daily on the radio.

At this point a plea was put out to the Bible societies. It was asked whether all the English translations were necessary when there were tribes without Bibles. It was suggested that some of the money be redirected to help these other groups get the Bible in their own language.

We then dealt with a very interesting aspect of dealing with the illiterate. This was through the medium of cassettes.

Someone suggested that Bible studies be put on cassette in the mother tongue of the country, then be distributed to outlying villages. In the village would be a recorder and the whole village could hear the Bible study. With this idea it was suggested that the tape be returned after a week or two, wiped clean and a new Bible study put on it. This would save money.

Another method was suggested whereby a church or local minister could secure a set of tapes on Christian maturity. Then he would lend them out, one at a time, to the people concerned. When they returned the tapes he would ask them a few questions and have a discussion with them. This would save the time of teaching them the lesson. The new believer could listen to the lesson in his own home.

A challenge was put forth to the great Bible teachers of the world to send copies of their sermons (on loan) to some struggling countries. It was also suggested that those who had the resources to provide equipment should do so as unto the Lord.

Follow-up films could also be used, but these would have to be restricted to English as most of the films are in that language.

List of people currently involved in follow-up and where information may be obtained.

For the Whole World
Billy Graham Organization
c/o C.A. Riggs
2512 Deerpath Drive
Nashville, Tennessee 37217
U.S.A.

Campus Crusade for Christ
Arrowhead Springs
San Bernardino, CA 92403

For Malaysia
Goh Keat Peng
Scripture Union
386 Jalan 5/59
Petaling Jaya,
Western Malaysia

It was asked whether someone could not be appointed to do research into follow-up in different countries. A group of men have agreed to pray for one another and write to one another in order to keep abreast with new ideas.

RURAL EVANGELISM IN ASIA

Ki-Sun Joseph Cho

Dr. Cho, Tokyo, Japan, is Professor at
Tokyo Christian College

Politically, economically, and religiously, Asia is the focus of the world's attention today. Militarily, the East and West power blocs are in a dangerous confrontation everywhere, and we are in the situation of not knowing when the confrontation will begin. The oil problem is making economic sparks fly which are endangering the whole world economy. Religiously, in Asia the pagan power of Buddhism, Hinduism, and Islam are strong. But in 1973 in Seoul, Korea, for the first time in its history, occurred the amazing explosion of Holy Spirit power through the Billy Graham Crusade. And this happened in Asia.

But we must not overlook the fact that in the midst of all of this movement the farming villages of Asia both politically and economically, and especially evangelistically, were forgotten and passed by. Through the report of the Food and Agriculture Organization of the United Nations (FAO) we know that the population of Asia in 1971 was 2.1 billion — and 1.4 billion (67 per cent) of them were farmers. We must pay attention to these 1.4 billion who live in a cultural valley, and without ever hearing the Gospel pass from this earth like a wide river of lost souls.

1. The present condition of Asian farm villages

In Asia there are twenty countries having a farm population of 60 per cent or above. And in most of those countries the farming people still do not have any modern cultural benefits. Also, the farming technique is low, and the farming income is so poor that it is very difficult to compile statistics relating to it. Not only this, but the differential between city and farming village in culture and economics is growing greater year by year. In one country of Asia the farming population is 70 per cent. In that country the city dwellers' yearly expenditure will average $90 per person, but the farmers' only averages $20 per person. The city dweller spends 53 per cent of his money on food, but the farmer spends 85 per cent of his meager funds on food. This means that the farmer just barely manages to eat. But this figure does not mean that their stomachs are full. The percentage of illiterates is 30 per cent in the cities, 60 per cent in farming villages. This shows us how far from the civilized world they are.

If we take an illustration from Japan, where the differential between city dweller and farmer is smaller than other countries: among the wage earners in the chief industries, the farmer ranks lowest, receiving only half of the average wage for all industries. The production index of the farming family in Japan comes to less than thirty per cent of that of the city laborer. Yet the birth rate in the city is 2.9 children per married woman, whereas in the farming villages it is four children per mother. In other Asian countries the average for city mothers is 3.5 children, and for farm mothers six children.

2. The present condition of Gospel evangelism

In the countries of Asia the farm villages not only are given the cold shoulder politically and economically, but are neglected in evangelism. Christian evangelism in farming villages is confronted by many obstacles. Even in Korea where there have been many effective results of Gospel evangelism, the farmers are still hungry for the Gospel. Most of the pastors are in the cities, and although several hundred students graduate from theological seminaries every year, there is still only one pastor for every two to three farming village churches. This is one of the better rural situations, because most of the villages of Southeast Asia still have not even heard the Gospel. In 1971 I took fourteen students from my college and did research on conditions in the farming villages of Japan. This was in a farming area that could be reached within two hours by train from Tokyo. In five days we researched 700 farm houses. We were very surprised to discover that 97 per cent of those farmers had never heard the Gospel. The other three per cent had heard through radio or by receiving a tract when they had been in the city. The nearest church to that farming village was about a one-hour walk, and it was a weak church of about twenty members. Hardly any of those village children had heard the familiar song "Jesus Loves Me." Sitting down in the garden of one of those farm homes, and thinking of the billion-and-a-half farmers in Asia, I couldn't help but pray.

3. The social organization of the Asian farm villages

There are many differences according to the country, but let us think in general about the social organization of Asia's farm villages. In most countries the farm villages consist of a group of thirty to forty homes formed into a community centered on the land being farmed. The village is occupied mainly in private production, but the community is organized in the same way we find in primitive societies. In addition to the privately owned farm land, there is community or collectively owned mountain, woodland, and water resources. Therefore there must be some collective labor and production, so it is natural for the farming village to have a very tightly knit community character. In the nations where agrarian reform has not been achieved, the character of the collective community is connected with the system of the absentee landlord. In other words the vertical relations between landowner and tenants, and the horizontal relations of common ownership and collective labor make up the basic structure of the farming community. One other element of the social organization of the Asian farm village is the family system. In America and Europe the family most commonly comprises husband and wife and unmarried children. But the Asian farm family consists of all members and the position regarding relatives is very complicated. In Asia the idea is not that a man and woman get married and start a new family, but that the woman marries into a family that already exists. In principle, the newly married couple live in with the husband's parents and grandparents. Thus in the farming family the vertical household concept (a line of descent from the husband's ancestors) is widespread, and the more important relationship is not husband and wife, but parent and child. The absolute power of the head of the family and the importance of lineal descent is the basis of the farming community structure.

We must understand the importance of "the home" which is ruled by the strong authority of the head of the family as the center of everything. "The home" does not include only the members of the immediate family, but also the house, furniture, family land, domestic animals, and even the tools. And it includes all the past ancestors as well as the present living members. Therefore "the home" is more important than the human rights of the individual, and sometimes for the sake of "the home" an individual's personality is ignored, and it is considered natural that a person be willing to sacrifice himself for the sake of the family. The lineage and social standing of the home means that the family members are expected to honor the family name and conform to the family customs.

And even if the home starts a branch family, the head home is still the center, and a "same family society" is constructed. Added to this is the family connection on the wife's side — so the circle gradually becomes wider. As outlined above, the farming village is a complicated social structure made up of the land-relationship connected with production and the blood-relationship connected with the home.

4. Difficulties of farm village evangelism

Every Asian country recognizes that evangelism in farming villages is more difficult than in the cities; indeed, many feel it is impossible. Apart from countries where for reasons of ideology or national policy Christian evangelism is not permitted, I want to list the problems of evangelism in Asia generally.

a. Each village has its own peculiar and historical tutelary deity, or local god. For example, according to the survey of the Agriculture Ministry of Japan in 1970, 63 per cent of all farming villages had their own village god. And 27 per cent of the villages had a god in cooperation with an adjacent village. And only ten per cent of villages did not have a local deity. Religiously speaking, the villagers are the parishioners of the local god, and the chief home of the village serves as the chief priest. In addition to this traditional faith group, each home is a member of some Buddhist temple because of the order given by the Tokugawa government in A.D. 1600, when the ban against Christians was given. They feel no contradiction in believing both Shintoism and Buddhism. To people in this kind of religious grouping, it becomes very difficult to receive a different religion like Christianity.

b. As explained above, the farm village is a strongly-bound community formed by land and blood relationships. They have been fused into this closed society for a long time, and this makes them very obstinate and exclusive, and they have a negative reaction to strangers: they do not wish the latter to come into the collective community that has functioned well since the time of the ancestors. It is very difficult for a Christian or a pastor to enter into this closed group.

The following survey will show how important their community life is to them and how they will suppress the autonomy of the individual for the sake of the community. In the 1963 survey by Professor Fukutake of Tokyo University into the consciousness of farmers in Okayama Prefecture, 62.5 per cent of the people felt they should suppress their individual opinion for the sake of the peace of the community; 15.7 per cent felt that it was better to ignore any personal opinion; 6.6 per cent remained silent and would express no opinion; 13.2 per cent felt that a person should express his opinion, if he felt it was correct; and 2 per cent had various other views. This means that 86.8 per cent of all the village people felt that for the sake of the community peace an individual should not express his opinion. This is village society in Japan. To become a heretic (a Christian, for instance) in such a social structure would mean an immediate threat to a person's position in that society. In such a context, it is very difficult for a person to become a Christian.

c. The feudalistic idea and family system that says it is natural that an individual and his opinion should be ignored for the sake of the "home" is generally held to in all farming villages of Asia. In this system the power of the head of the family is very strong. The income from the family industry (farm) is not considered as an individual's income. The income from the labor of the entire family goes into the hands of the head of the home. And no expenditure can be made without his permission. He has not only complete authority over production and consumption, but also over the social life of the family members — concerning such things as entering school, marriage, and friendships.

Against such a system, to convert from the ancestral faith of the family to another one is the same as deserting the "home." The offender becomes a sinner who blackens the family name, brings sadness and shame to the whole family, and makes them feel humiliated and embarrassed.

It is anticipated that a new generation with new education will gradually bring in a new system to the farming villages. But at the present time the farming villages are very difficult compared to the cities.

d. In every Asian country the economic difference between city and farming village is enormous. Not only is there a difference, but it is very difficult for the farmers to escape from poverty. One of the great obstacles to rural evangelism is that the farmers are all poor. When the Gospel seed is sown it does not grow, but not only that: the local village church never seems able to attain self-supporting status. This keeps evangelism from taking root. The young evangelist tries very hard for a few years, but disappointed at the lack of results, or for the sake of his children's education, he moves to the city where conditions are at least a little better. Thus the fact that the Lord's church is unable to support itself but depends on outside help, even after many years of work, is not a good testimony, and becomes an obstacle to evangelism.

e. Finally, a perennial problem in farm village evangelism is the fact that the young people always move away to the city. They always leave the village when they finish middle or high school to get additonal education, or to find work. For them, there is no charm or vision in the farming village which has many disadvantages and lacks cultural benefits, therefore they leave the village when opportunity offers. Every time I go to survey the farming villages I hear the older farmers complain about losing the young productive power. The problem is really, however, losing succession to the "home." This is the same problem for the village church. Even if English classes are used as a means of getting middle and high school young people to come to church, within two or three years all of them move away to the city — and cannot therefore be brought up to become pillars of the church.

5. Needed: a special kind of worker

For the farm villages where the harvest is great, the Lord is seeking and needs specialized workers. The farming village is certainly not good soil for sowing the Gospel seed, establishing churches, and training believers. Until now missionaries, pastors, denominations, and theological seminaries have not been interested in this unproductive field of farm village evangelism. But we cannot forget the salvation of 1.4 billion farm people in Asia. Someone must take the Gospel to them. Someone must carry God's Word — that gives joy, hope, and eternal life into these dark valleys. These 1.4 billion are waiting for and really need God's love and salvation.

The farm village evangelist must be a Gospel worker and at the same time a leader of the farm people in many ways. First, evangelistically he must know the Lord's pain of heart for these souls. Then he must be a true friend of the farm people, and pray for them. Then he must be qualified to be a leader of the farmers in many ways. In other words, a leader of the farmers in technique, socially, and evangelistically.

More than ten years ago, a young Japanese evangelist got a vision of rural evangelism and decided to go into a farm village. First, he learned the technique of growing strawberries on hillsides. During the winter, on the south side of a hill he would make stair-type rock walls and plant strawberries in between them. The strawberries that were planted in the fall would bear fruit just about Christmas and New Year. Since this method did not need a hothouse or fuel for heating it was a very economical method. And since the strawberries were sold in a cold season when there was a high demand for them, the profit likewise was very high.

After learning this technique he purposely went to a poor farm village far from the city. This village was very poor, so in the winter all the men went to the city to work in construction projects. These were people who could not get enough to eat without this seasonal labor. The evangelist chose this village because land was cheap, and in order to obtain good results in a place everyone thought impossible. Thus would glory be brought to the Lord, and it would be a good example of effective Gospel presentation.

At first he did not say he was an evangelist or even that he was a Christian. But silently he made a new strawberry patch, and grew his berries. The farm people noticed this peculiar stranger and watched him curiously. At Christmas he harvested many fine strawberries, and made a greater profit than any of the farmers could have imagined. They gathered at his house and begged him to teach them how to grow strawberries in this way. For the first time, he told them that he was a Christian. He arranged that if they would come to his house every Sunday and hear what he had to say, he would teach them how to grow strawberries.

Now that entire village is Christian, and he is not only the pastor of the church, but head of the village. Not only has evangelism had good results, but that village has become famous for strawberry-production.

When I have gone into the various villages of Japan on survey, the farmers do not open their hearts and talk to me at first. But when I start talking about cows and chickens, and when they know that I am a specialist on these subjects, their attitude quickly changes and they ask me to teach them various things, and come to me to talk about this and that. And in the end they open their hearts and listen to the Gospel. They say that if someone like me who is a pastor as well as a specialist on agricultural matters comes to live among them they would gladly receive him. And they say that with such a leader they would be willing to build a new village structure with the church as the center.

I think that the ideal evangelistic worker for the farming villages should be able to increase the income of the farmers, build up their cultural life, and actually become one with them in their community life. He should plough and live and suffer and cooperate with the farmers, and love their souls and lead them to the Cross. The farm villages need workers who will touch them skin to skin and communicate to their hearts.

6. The need for special training institutes

As long as human life continues on earth, farmers will be needed. Farming is a very fascinating and hopeful industry from the viewpoint of enterprise and continuance, according to how it is managed. The farm is neither physically nor spiritually a barren land, but a place where with hope and vision you can have much success. Especially spiritually, it is a golden and fruitful field.

Workers suitable for farming villages are needed, as are educational institutions to produce such specialists. Of course we need workers for evangelism, not just consultants and advisers or pioneers who are simply farming village leaders. We need people who are first saved, and who dedicate their lives for the Lord's glory and the salvation of souls. Then in order to enter into the farming villages they receive the technical education so that they are armored on both sides. For instance, they can lead in the techniques of farming, and when the animals get sick they can treat them along with the farmers, and at that time evangelize.

In some Asian countries there are already institutes for rural evangelism for this purpose. For these I have several suggestions. First, let us form a mobile international staff. This staff should consist of a Christian specialist in each of the main departments of farming — horticulture, animal husbandry, veterinary medicine, management, etc., and also a specialist in evangelism, and pastor of rich experience. This staff would move around Asia, cooperating with national evangelistic institutes, teaching high-level techniques and training in practical ways. The graduates of these institutes would go into the farming villages and become local leaders and evangelists. These people, with the church as the center, would form a new farmers' movement, and make an organization in a central location to lead systematically in jointly purchasing productive materials and selling agricultural products.

Second, in one of the Asian countries an international institute should be founded and from the various countries selected young farm village evangelists would study theology and advanced agricultural technology; and then go back to their own countries and become leaders in their own training school. Farm village evangelism will not succeed without a native leader; he can do much more than a missionary from a foreign land.

Third, I would like to propose something like an international rural evangelism alliance. We should call conferences of specialists in rural evangelism from various countries so that rural evangelism might be done more effectively. This international organization would carry out specialized study and plan for permanent evangelism. Such a project should be supported internationally. Again and again I say that for the 1.4 billion farmers in Asia we need organization, funds, and workers. From now on is not too late. We must study and then carry out this work.

RURAL EVANGELIZATION STRATEGY REPORT

Secretary: Alistair Kennedy

The small, but geographically representative group, which met to discuss Rural Evangelization and to hear Prof. Cho's paper relating to rural Asia was staggered at the immensity of the need.

Cho stated that 60% of the world's population is unevangelized. In many cases due to social structures these people are very resistant to the Gospel, though often the degree of resistance is not known since the Gospel just has not been preached to them. One participant suggested that what we need is a congress on rural evangelization alone!

There was much appreciation of Dr. Cho's excellent paper and time was given to discussing the problems it highlighted and the suggestions it made regarding evangelism through agriculture.

The usefulness of the institutions which Prof. Cho suggested be established was questioned by some. It was suggested that their effectiveness would depend on whether they developed from grass roots and were run by people with direct experience of church planting in rural areas.

It was pointed out also that married family men already acceptable for leadership in our area would carry more weight if trained than an outsider. Training should not be at university level for the people.

Another speaker referred to the difficulty in many subsistence farming areas of people leaving their land for more than a few days at a time for training. From experience in Sri Lanka one participant emphasized that evangelists should know agriculture, but others felt there was a danger in approaching evangelism through agricultural development where government was already heavily involved in this field. There was a danger of competition and confusion especially if government was doing the job better.

Dr. Cho said that there was this difference that whereas the government people were doing it with cold minds the Christians were doing it with warm minds and hearts. The scope for trained Christians working in government agricultural programs was noted.

Since the group comprised people from five continents it was felt improper to confine the discussion to Asia alone. In broadening the discussion there was much useful interchange of ideas which are proving fruitful in various situations. A participant from Malawi, where many workers migrate seasonally to South Africa or Rhodesia, noted that a very effective work of evangelization is done among these men while they are away from their villages. Men from Mozambique where missionaries have little access are reached as migrant laborers and then return home to spread the Gospel. This contribution drew attention to the fact that individuals from areas which are resistant due to family structures or other problems can be evangelized when modern life uproots them even temporarily.

This is seen also in Ghana where 80,000 people uprooted in the construction of the Volta Dam are being reached by evangelists who are teaching them to become fishermen as a new way of life.

From Pakistan it was emphasized that village people can be reached through their hunger for entertainment. By taking a singing team into a village, or by showing a film, a crowd can be gathered.

Rev. Tom Kumi from Ghana highlighted the use of a people's own cultural practices in a positive way and also the advantages of getting down alongside them. In Ghana the cocoa industry seasonally draws large crowds together. Evangelists go to the farms and work with the people at the harvesting. Then at meal breaks, etc. they take the opportunity of telling about Christ. They are accepted and trusted because they have worked with the people. A missionary to Haiti still feels his cultural distance from the people even after nearly thirty years. His strategy is based on the fact that a farmer will talk to his neighboring farmer so he trains the Christian farmers to witness. Alongside this is a local church program of community help. Rev. Augustus Marwieh (Liberia) told how from a personal experience of leading a team for one month into the back country to evangelize, a plan was developing to make every pastor spend one month evangelizing in a new area.

In Liberia also great use is made of our radio station, radio receivers and casette recordings. However it was pointed out that though mass media equipment is tremendously effective, many churches such as that of the Nagas cannot raise the money required. A request was made that some central agency be established to supply such equipment.

Mr. Alex Smith (Thailand) outlined the approach which has proven effective in establishing many rural churches. After evangelization great emphasis is placed on immediately gathering believers into churches which from the start are self-supporting and pastored by part-time leaders who receive in-service training. One evangelistic approach is to adapt the method of traveling merchants who visit the villages to sell wares and draw a crowd by showing films.

The goals defined by the group for forward movement in world rural evangelization are as follows:

1) That the church in every country, with its own situation in view, should set goals for itself in rural evangelism. A necessary preliminary to this would be a national survey to pinpoint the areas of need and to discover responsive areas.

The overall aim is the establishment of churches in all unreached rural areas.

2) There must be a burden of concern for rural evangelization that will issue in prayer. We must seek to communicate the vision for the unreached rural areas of the world and to motivate ourselves and others to earnest prayer that God will do mighty things in this situation.

3) There must be a full exploration of all the various effective means for reaching unevangelized rural areas and a study of how these can be implemented in new areas.

4) In the light of the widespread problem of full-time evangelists and pastors tending to gravitate away from rural areas to urban areas we should aim to emphasize:

    a) the raising up of part-time evangelists and pastors in the areas where they live and giving them in-service training.

    b) those involved in theological education of full-time workers should seek to impart to students the vision of the rural areas and to attempt under God to motivate them to the costly sacrifice of life involved in this work.

The proposed strategy that emerged from our group has the following recommendations:

1) That the church in every country should carefully examine and survey the needs of rural evangelization in their own land.

2) As part of any post-congress association there should be an international research center on world evangelization. This would comprise various departments of which rural evangelization would be one of the most important.

The task of such a rural evangelism unit would be to coordinate the results of national surveys and to circulate resource needs for the various areas of opportunity which emerge.

It would also circulate news of techniques found to be effective in the form of case studies.

3) Following on from an adequate survey of needs and resources at local levels and as implementation gets under way, the groups felt that Dr. Cho's suggestion of a movable international team of experts in the various branches of agriculture might prove useful.

If this specific type of training is found necessary local workshops are more desirable than Prof. Cho's other suggestion of an international institute in one place.

The staff of a movable institute should also be available to help train Christian communities in ways to raise their economic level so that churches can become self-sufficient at an adequate level.

4) We would recommend the establishment of an international rural evangelism alliance as Prof. Cho suggests. This should be composed primarily of people actively involved in rural evangelization.

5) Because of the centrality of this issue to the whole task of world evangelization, our group recommends that at an early date national conferences on rural evangelization should be convened. These should lead on to regional conferences to pool experiences to stimulate rural evangelization in unreached areas, and to challenge all countries in the region to consider rural areas as one of their key targets for evangelization.

THEOLOGICAL EDUCATION AND EVANGELIZATION

Bruce J. Nicholls

Mr. Nicholls, Yeotmal, India, is Professor of
Theology at Union Theological Seminary.
He is the International Coordinator of the
Theological Assistance Program of the
World Evangelical Fellowship.

Thirty-six years ago, the International Missionary Conference at Tambaram, Madras, stated, "It is our conviction that the present condition of theological education is one of the greatest weaknesses in the whole Christian enterprise." Here at Lausanne we must confess that this statement is still true as far as evangelicals are concerned. We believe that sustained evangelism depends on our depth of commitment to the truth of the uniqueness and finality of the Gospel, and on our capacity to mobilize the whole church in continuous evangelism. This involves both theology and education. Evangelism, church growth, and missions depend on faith that is reformed according to the Scriptures and on experience that is constantly renewed in the Lordship of Christ and in the power of the Holy Spirit. We may posit the equation: Reformation plus Revival equals Evangelization. Theological education is the handmaid of this process.

PART ONE: THE THEOLOGY OF WORLD EVANGELIZATION

In order to develop an effective strategy for the role of theological education in world evangelization, we must first verbalize our theology of evangelism in the context of the people to whom we proclaim the Gospel.

1. The importance of a theology of world evangelization

We live in a world of rapid social and ideological change. The absolutes of Christian beliefs and practice are fast disappearing. In a relativistic age marked by human alienation and social disintegration and at the same time rising humanistic optimism, ecumenical Christianity searches for "a comprehensive notion of salvation" in which a reforming biblical theology seems uncomfortably out of place. Emilio Castro reflects on the Salvation Today Conference: "Bangkok is pleading not for less salvation but for more salvation." The secularizing of theology which dominates current theological activity shifts authority from a theology of the Word to a theology of experience. Action reports become more influential than biblical exegesis. Liberation from political, economic, and social oppression is given more emphasis than personal and spiritual conversion. The mood is anti-supernatural and non-theological. Secular means of participating in revolution are justified by the rightness of the projected ends.

At the same time evangelicals are also in danger of being anti-theological by giving an unbalanced emphasis to experience. We believe that biblical piety in terms of worship and the manifesting of the fruits of the Spirit in holy living are fundamental to vital Christianity and vigorous evangelism. But when experience is divorced from conviction and theological understanding, zeal in witnessing withers under the pressure of opposition or becomes heretical under the pressure of personality or ideological cultism. With the rise of liberal theology many evangelicals retreated into a non-theological pietism. Today in the flush of the charismatic movement there is a danger of experience in the Spirit blurring conviction in the Word. Theological education must insure that truth and grace are held together.

God's instrument for world evangelization is the Church. As the Body of Christ, it is a divine fellowship of believers called out for the purpose of worship, witness, and service in the world. In the New Testament the ministry of teaching is given prominence in the life and witness of the Church. Jesus Christ is portrayed as one who taught in the synagogues, and who gave specialized training to his twelve disciples. He used a variety of teaching methods including exposition of Scripture, debate, object lessons, and parables. Paul taught regularly in the synagogues. In Ephesus he taught daily in the hall of Tyrannus for two years (Acts 19:8-10). His letters indicate his skill as a teacher.

2. The Gospel is given of God

The theology of world evangelization begins with the "givenness" of divine revelation. Without God's self-disclosure we would have no Good News to proclaim. Non-revelatory religions such as those of ancient Greece and of the East are essentially man's knowledge of himself and his search for God. Biblical revelation is personal, Jesus Christ being the final Word of God. It is historical, God revealing himself in acts of saving history. It is verbal and propositional, God speaking through his prophets and apostles. Historic evangelical Christianity has always believed the Bible to be God's inspired and infallible Word, a unique and entirely trustworthy record of God's revelation. It is therefore our objective authority in all matters of faith and conduct.

The Bible as revelation defines the limits of the content of the Gospel, and as inspired of God its form is given to us. We cannot accept the content of the Gospel and change its form without modifying the content. The present-day attempts to take the Gospel out of its essentially Hebraic form and indigenize it into a secular or African or Aryan cultural form results in changing its message, for in each case there are religious presuppositions in these cultures which conflict with the biblical Gospel. Thus biblical revelation and inspiration guarantee the unity and uniqueness of this one Gospel.

A systematic understanding of the Gospel is possible because revelation is rational, reflecting the personal and rational character of God. Divine law is an expression of the non-contradictory nature of God. Man created in the image of God has the capacity to "think God's thoughts after Him." The cry of the Psalmist is for the knowledge and understanding of God's law (Ps. 119:33f.); and the prayer of Paul for the churches is that they may grow in the knowledge and understanding of God (Eph. 1: 17-19; Phil. 1:9-11; Col. 1:9-10). While the Gospel is final, our understanding of it is not. We depend on the Holy Spirit to renew our minds and to illuminate the truth of the inspired Word.

3. The Gospel judges and renews culture

The Gospel is never proclaimed to men living in a vacuum. All men are conditioned by their cultures and hear the Gospel through their conditioned minds. All have a philosophy of life even if they have never consciously articulated it. All have grown to accept some assumptions about the nature and existence of God, his relationship to the world and to man, the nature of suffering and evil, and about life after death and how to achieve it. All have adopted a personal and social ethic.

All men, being made in the image of God, seek after God and therefore all religions and ideologies contain some truths of general revelation (Rom. 1-2). But all men as sinners are in rebellion against God and his law, and as systems all religions and ideologies suppress the truth and create God in their own image, projecting their own form of idolatrous worship. Man's religion and culture have developed through interaction. The Gospel judges all culture and fulfills only those elements that are consistent with biblical revelation.

The Gospel, therefore, cannot be equated with any one culture, for all cultures transmit human sinfulness. Where the Gospel has taken root, some elements of culture will be rejected, others renewed, and new patterns of culture will emerge. John F. Robinson writes, "The Christian in Africa should be in his particular culture the embodiment of those African values which are consonant with the will of God, and he should express them in a distinctively Christian way. Only then will the Body of Christ in Africa have become the incarnation of the Gospel that God intended it to be."

4. The proclamation and defense of the Gospel

God's desire is that all men be saved and therefore all are capable of understanding the Gospel. In its essence, the Gospel is very simple so that even a child may understand and believe. We are commissioned to preach the Gospel to all the world, trusting the Holy Spirit to convict, convince, and convert the hearer. From the youngest to the oldest we are called to be witnesses. The dictum of Anselm, "Credo ut intelligum" ("I believe so that I may understand"), still stands as the divine order.

Apologetics as the defense of the Gospel is an essential element in the evangelistic task. The philosophies of men have to be evaluated, presuppositions which are contrary to the Gospel laid bare, and false doctrine and practice condemned. This will involve careful study and reflection. Our own understanding of the Gospel must first be subjected to the light of the Word of God. The younger churches of the Third World may be just as guilty of cultural accretions as the older churches of the West. Paul was astonished how quickly the churches of Galatia turned to a different Gospel (Gal. 1:6-9).

There is a natural tendency towards the synthesis of biblical thought with human philosophy. The theological issues delineated in the Frankfurt and Wheaton Declarations point to some of these syntheses. Catholic sacramentalism harmonizes Aristotle and biblical theology;

Protestant universalism reflects the influence of Kant and Hegel; syncretistic theology in India points to the influence of neo-platonism and Vedanta philosophy, and so forth.

We are called with Paul to both the proclamation of the Gospel and the defense of the Gospel. Few evangelical missionaries are engaged in this task of "pre-evangelism" and Christian apologetics. There is virtually no appropriate literature being produced, with the consequence that few from the educated or upper classes and few orthodox religionists are being won for Christ. These are the leaders and policy makers of modern society and such are needed in the churches.

5. The contextualization and communication of the Gospel

The current ecumenical catchword is the "contextualization" of the Gospel. This term includes all that is implied in indigenization but also takes into account "the process of secularity, technology, and the struggle for human justice, which characterize the historical movement of nations in the Third World." Some educators mean by this that the cultural and religious context, the social and political struggles, determine the form and to some extent the content of the Gospel. This "situation" theology relativizes the Gospel to each cultural milieu and leads to theological syncretism. The advocates of this view assume a plurality of Gospels in the New Testament (after Kasemann). They believe that God is anonymously at work in all human structures and interprets salvation in terms of humanization.

Evangelicals affirm that the structures of theological interpretation can be indigenized but that the Gospel itself cannot be. Our task is one of communication. In this sense Gadiel Isidro of Manila defines contextualization as "the attempt to analyze the situation and then from an absolute perspective of the Gospel make this absolute unchanging Gospel speak with revelance to the needs of Asia." Communication includes research into the problem of language and translation, analyzing the changing patterns of culture and religion, and entering into the pain of human suffering caused by political, social, and economic oppression. Communication means personal involvement, discerning areas of spiritual need as points of contact, areas of agreement as bridges of communication and clarifying biblical thought forms to insure transference of meaning. It recognizes that the Holy Spirit is the real agent of communication.

In order to construct a theology of evangelism we must systematize doctrine around the goal of mission and evangelism. Each element of the biblical Gospel must be given its full emphasis but special attention will be given to those doctrines that are rejected or misunderstood by particular religious cultures. For example, in a theology of evangelism in the context of Hinduism, the doctrine of God is ultimately personal, moral, and, as Creator, is crucial to the communication of the Gospel. Western systematic theologies developed out of controversy with Rome and European philosophy are still revelant today in some cultural contexts but not in others.

The biblical concept of the kingdom of God is central to our understanding of world evangelization as the papers of Dr. Beyerhaus and others have shown. The Gospel of the kingdom is Good News concerning salvation in Christ. Salvation begins now through God's reconciling and justifying act and will be completed with the resurrection of the body, and with the renewal of creation. In the person and work of Christ the kingdom has come; in the Church as the messianic community, it is being visibly continued; and in the triumphal return of Christ it will be fully realized. In the Cross, the power of Satan was broken and at the Final Day it will be destroyed. The Church is the messenger of this Good News to all the world, and is the agent of social renewal preparing for the coming of Christ as Judge and King. Thus, in this Gospel age, the Church's primary task is world evangelization to bring back the King. God is even now preparing the nations and creation for that Final Day of Judgment and Hope.

PART TWO: STRATEGY IN THEOLOGICAL EDUCATION AND WORLD EVANGELIZATION

1. Objectives in theological education

The basic objectives of theological education need to be constantly re-evaluated.

Theological education must be *person-centered*.

First and foremost it must be centered in Jesus Christ. Priority must be given to private and corporate worship, the devotional study and meditation on the Word, and the practice of the presence of Christ in daily life. Secondly, it must be centered in the student for whom the training program exists. The student should have a voice in the structuring of courses and in the planning of the total program, for unless the student is convinced of the relevance of materials studied, motivation in learning will be weak, and the learning process is likely to stop with the final examination. Inter-active study materials such as the programmed instruction materials used in theological education by extension courses, insure a more effective student-centered learning process. Thirdly, theological education must be centered in inter-personal relations including fellowship within the group and witness and dialogue with those outside it. Discipleship training is training men and women for others. To this end, care must be given to the student-faculty ratio, and to their joint participation in the church's worship, fellowship, witnessing, and service in the community. The depth of personal relationships established will determine the quality of the training received. Theological education by private study is a poor substitute for the fellowship of the group.

Theological education must be *content-centered*.

The biblical doctrine of the "givenness" of revelation suggests that a knowledge of the content of the Gospel is all-important to our ministry. The study of the Bible as the Word of God must be the center of our curriculum. However, biblical knowledge in abstract is of limited value. The devil could pass an examination in Bible content. "Knowing" in Scripture is never just conceptual knowledge, it is always experiencing the truth. The knowledge of God is spiritual wisdom and understanding. The relational knowledge of the truth also involves the use of the mind.

Thus a content-centered theological education emphasizes the study of theology — biblical, historical, systematic, apologetic, and culminating in a theology of evangelism. Few training centers have major courses on the theology of evangelism. The development of such courses is urgently needed today.

Theological education must be *communication-centered*.

The population explosion, the escalation of knowledge, the discovery of new communication technology mean that unless new skills in communication are acquired and used those who have never heard the Gospel will multiply faster than those who have. Theological education must not only give attention to pulpit homiletics and pastoral counseling, but also to training in effective teaching methods, the use of traditional media of communication (drama, art, music and literary forms), and also the skills of modern technology (radio, films, TV, cassette tapes). The student must be taught to penetrate the secular media with the Gospel. Further, more emphasis needs to be given to the place of worship, dialogue and debate, and "presence" in the effective communication of the Gospel.

2. The integration of academic, spiritual and practical in theological education

Theological education is in crisis. The function of the Church in the world is being questioned and the roles of the clergy and the laity are being reevaluated. The complexity of modern society is a sign of both the maturity and confusion of our age. Some theological schools emphasize the academic, others emphasize piety and devotional life, and others the practice of evangelism or social involvement. All three areas of training are pressing for new courses and more time. We are faced with the question of how to maintain a balance between "knowing," "being," and "doing": and how to integrate these into an effective training program. The following points are suggested for discussion.

a. *Training in community* — Theological education is education of the whole person in relation to God and in service of other persons. This can only be achieved in community. Such communities should be microcosms of the Church as the messianic community of the kingdom. Worshiping, studying, living, eating, and witnessing together will reveal areas of maturity and weakness in the lives of each student. Every student should live in the dormitory or on campus in the case of families for at least one academic term, as a requirement for graduation. This must not be lost sight of in extension education programs, though the period of community living may be much shorter. Every facility should be given to students to create their own fellowship and community life.

Every theological teacher should have had pastoral and evangelistic experience as a qualification for faculty service. Both teachers and local pastors should share in the planning of the practical field assignments of the students. The teacher is usually the student's model for the integration of the academic, spiritual, and practical. Most of us were more influenced by the lives of our teachers than by their classroom notes!

b. *Controlling the standards of theological excellence* — Theological education is a ministry of the Church, and its objectives and standards must be controlled by it. To allow the professional theological experts to determine their own goals and the increasingly secular universities to determine curricula and academic standards is to endanger the doctrinal purity, spiritual vitality, and practical relevance of the training program. All of us know of theological schools of which this is sadly true. While a university-controlled degree program may still be important in some cultures and church situations, the system of accreditation has much to commend it, especially to those in the Third World. The dangers of lowering standards and of inbred thinking can be avoided through schools forming "clusters" or in the development of strong associations of schools, and by close interacting with the universities through joint participation in seminars, lecture series, and in some cases joint hostels. The system of accreditation of schools by an accrediting association as distinct from university affiliation has the potential for greater integration of the academic, spiritual, and the practical.

In an examination-controlled system, the spiritual and practical become of secondary importance, at least in the minds of the student. More effective use of seminars and assignments, essays and term papers involving tutorial guidance, can insure greater inter-disciplinary reflection and the relating of theology to evangelism, church life, and to society. Regular self-evaluation questionnaires can stimulate motivation for integration, and if carefully prepared can give a high degree of objectivity in evaluating spiritual growth and the degree of achievement of communication skills. Regular reports from teachers and pastors on the student as a maturing person and on his field work, together with regular counseling and discussion sessions, can also give an objective evaluation of the areas of training other than those purely academic. Each cultural region must develop its own model for accreditation. This is also true for theological education by extension programs.

c. *Flexibility of field education* — In order to integrate the three areas, a more flexible approach to field education is necessary. The lengthening of the traditional three-year course to four or more years is desirable but not always possible. Most schools provide for practical training concurrent with academic studies, through week-end ministry, during long vacations, and through student pastorships. Further training is possible through internships for a year prior to the final year of training or through a postgraduate "curacy" following training. Some schools devote one term a year to training in specialized subjects such as industrial evangelism, sex and marriage counseling, youth work, and drug addiction. While every student should receive a basic core training in evangelism and pastoral care, both the classroom and field training should provide for specialized vocational training such as chaplaincy ministries in hospitals, factories and schools, teaching ministry in Christian schools and theological institutions, Christian educational ministries and social welfare work. Insufficient attention has been given to helping students discern the gifts of the Spirit in their own lives. Opportunity for specialized training in the functional ministries represented by these gifts must be encouraged.

3. Restructuring the curriculum design

The restructuring of the curriculum is a continual process. The design must correspond to the objectives. Theological institutions generally give little attention to verbalizing their behavioral objectives, hence the curriculum grows like a patchwork quilt. We suggest for discussion four behavioral objectives:

(i) The student will become a mature person in Christ and in inter-personal relationships.

(ii) The student will become an effective communicator of the Gospel in the context of world evangelization.

(iii) The student will become skilled in church planting, pastoral care, and in training others.

(iv) The student will become a sensitive and responsible participant in the various structures of society.

The curriculum should be designed to maintain a balance between the training of the mind to enable the student to cope in any situation, and vocational training; between "formation" and "information"; between the reflective theologian and the active evangelist.

Four areas of study are suggested:

(i) Exegetical studies, including biblical languages and introduction, book studies and exegesis, biblical theology and hermeneutics.

(ii) Culture and society, including cultural anthropology, literature and the arts, philosophy, cultural religions and ideologies, man in community.

(iii) Applied theology, history and ethics, including the history of the expansion of the Church, missions and ecumenics, the theology of the Church, apologetics, the theology of evangelism, personal and social ethics.

(iv) Communication, including evangelism and church growth, education and administration in the church, pastoral counseling, communication media, pedagogical training.

4. New patterns of theological training

If evangelism is the mobilization of the whole Church in continuous witness, then theological education is the training of all "the people of God" in the task of fulfilling the Great Commission. This is inherent in the doctrine of "the priesthood of all believers."

We must continue to emphasize the importance of *residential training*. The traditional pattern of three-four years full-time training for the evangelistic, parish, and mission ministries of the Church needs constant renewal and is crucial to the Church as an institution. The use of vacational and one-year residential courses for laymen is proving successful and needs further experimentation. Short refresher courses for ministers and missionaries are also valuable. Residential training offers the advantage of training in community with better staffing and library facilities.

New patterns of *non-residential training* are proving increasingly necessary and effective. Theological Education by Extension, pioneered in Latin America and now spreading rapidly through Asia, Africa, and to some degree in the West, is a significant break-through in non-residential training. TEE offers a decentralized form of theological education in which the teachers conduct weekly or bi-weekly tutorial classes in sub-centers for students continuing in their regular employment. Through the use of inter-active study materials, audio-visual as well as written, students are enabled to learn through self-study, normally one hour a day for each course, followed by the regular tutorial class for discussion. The adequate preparation of work books and "programmed instruction" texts for each course and the training of faculty to use them is proving crucial to the growth and success of the movement. In some countries TEE is an extension of the seminary and in others of the mission or the church, or it stands as an autonomous movement with its own structure.

TEE is being used for a wide range of training programs including continuing education for pastors with little or no formal training, for newly literate pastors in rural areas, for laymen ranging from the newly literate to university graduates, as lay leaders in local churches and in the establishing of new churches through house movements and cell groups. TEE promises new dynamic in training many new leaders in evangelism. Correspondence course schools have also a valid place in non-residential training and in direct evangelism, provided there is adequate follow-up of the students taking courses.

Another form of non-residential theological training is leadership training for evangelism through *cell groups*. These evangelistic groups normally grow out of the local church and feed back into it. They should be kept small with a balance between committed Christians and unconverted neighbors, friends or work associates. These groups meet in neutral places such as homes, restaurants, offices, or in factories. They are kept low-keyed and are based on the discussion of the issues of modern living with the aid of prepared materials or Bible studies. The training of the committed Christians leading these groups is proving crucial to the success of the movement. This must be done through special classes or study groups. The Christ the Only Way Movement in the Philippines now has over 6,000 such training groups witnessing through 10,000 Lay Evangelistic Group Studies. The training of the cell group leaders is a valid form of theological education requiring specialist staff, teaching materials, and church-related promotion.

5. Articulation of the theology of evangelization

The articulation of the theology of evangelization is an important aspect of theological education. There is a serious dearth of in-depth literature prepared for evangelism among specific groups and cultures, and also literature giving an evangelical response to apologetic, ethical, and socio-political issues confronting the churches today. Such literature is needed at all educational levels using the media of articles for the press, magazines and journals, monographs and pamphlets, books, and also scripts for radio, TV, and tape ministries.

Two areas of theological education that are catalysts for articulating the Gospel are:

(i) Evangelical theological societies — as a forum for the interchange of ideas and views between evangelicals on current theological issues and as fellowships to articulate the biblical faith in the context of mission and evangelism, Evangelical Theological Societies have a significant role in theological training. The potential for ETS at the local and national level is far greater than is being realized at present. Existing societies function through local and national study groups and annual conferences, and through lectureship series and tape services. A newsletter or journal is essential to the cohesion of the society. In some countries the society is open to all clergy and laymen with a genuine theological concern, in others it is limited to those with a specified theological degree. It is essential that the ETS has a prepared publishing program.

(ii) Centers for advanced theological studies — the need for a worldwide chain of evangelical research centers for advanced theological studies, each with a particular functional or socio-cultural emphasis, is now being recognized as important to the task of world evangelization. The goals of these centers are similar to those of the more functional ETS except that they offer a deeper level of theological involvement through full-time research, residential, library, and tutorial facilities. Some centers offer a postgraduate degree program, others a non-degree research program with a view to a publishing ministry, while others offer both. The basic orientation of these centers is to articulate a biblical theology of evangelization and an evangelical apology to contemporary theological and cultural issues, and to undertake research in missions and communications. The Tyndale House Library, Cambridge, England, has for several years provided excellent facilities in biblical research. The Asian Centre for Theological Studies and Missions in Seoul, Korea; the Theological Research and Communication Institute in New Delhi and Yeotmal, India; the proposed Theological Community in Buenos Aires, Argentina, all point to the fulfillment of this need. Other centers in Africa, Australasia, Europe, and North America are needed.

6. Cooperation through a network of relationships

Evangelical leaders worldwide are in agreement that we do not want a pyramid-type power structure controlling evangelical activities. The genius of our evangelical heritage is cooperation at grass-roots local and national levels, principally along functional lines especially in evangelism. In terms of geographic cooperation, "Fellowships" rather than "Councils" characterize the pattern of evangelical cooperation. However, congresses on evangelism such as those held at Berlin, Bogota, Singapore, Amsterdam, and here at Lausanne point to the need for cooperation at the cultural level of regions or continents. Evangelism, missions, mass media, theological education, and relief are functional areas where cooperation is proving necessary. Here as elsewhere the coordination structure must be kept small and low-keyed. This is felt to be particularly true in developments at the international level. Levels of cooperation in the area of theological education include:

(i) The national level — Cooperation at the national level has already been discussed in terms of associations of theological schools, accreditation associations, evangelical theological societies, associations for theological education by extension, and cell group movements. These function either as autonomous structures or as the theological members of national Evangelical Alliances or Fellowships. In some countries, particularly in the Third World, there is serious overlap in theological training and unnecessary wastage in the duplication of plant, staff, and uneconomic programs. The merging of schools with like objectives is to be strongly encouraged.

(ii) The regional level — The development of regional theological associations is an encouraging evidence of evangelical cooperation. These associations provide a service, catalystic and coordinating ministry, in areas of mutual concern. In the Third World, the Asia Theological Association (formerly known as TAP-Asia), the Latin American Theological Fraternity, the Theological Commission of the Association of Evangelicals of Africa and Madagascar are effectively fulfilling this role. Their goals are similar but there is considerable diversity in their structures and programs. Affirmation of the biblical faith is the basis of cooperation. Normally, membership in these associations does not preclude membership in other regional or international structures. These associations share information through newsletters, publish bulletins, sponsor consultations, new seminaries, and centers for advanced theological research. They encourage extension education, cell group movements, and Bible teaching ministries. The development of accreditation agencies for Bible schools and colleges is likely to become a significant aspect of their ministry in some regions. There is need for further cooperation in the training of faculty both within their region and overseas and exchange of faculty between colleges and in the sponsoring of pedagogical courses for faculty. The improvement of libraries, the preparation and publishing of textbooks for residential and non-residential programs are also urgently needed. The development of similar associations in other areas of the world is to be encouraged.

(iii) The international level — An international theological service agency is needed to share information between continents and to provide such ministries as are requested by the regional associations. Such an agency must be kept small so that the autonomy and the effective functioning of the national and regional associations are not threatened. At present the Theological Assistance Program of the World Evangelical Fellowship is endeavoring to fill this role. *Theological News* and *Programming* are its official organs. One of the functions of the international agency should be to establish an Evangelical Theological Assistance Fund to give financial assistance through the regional associations to theological projects such as scholarships for faculty training, grants for study conferences, textbook production, research programs and centers, and the administration of the regional association. The Biblical Library Fund is already functioning in one of these areas. The international fund should seek to give assistance to those needs which are not at present being met by other funding agencies but which evangelicals view as crucial to the task of theological education and world evangelization.

Questionnaire.
NB: If necessary, answer only those questions which are relevant to your situation.

1. What place should courses on the theology of world evangelization have in any theological training program? Suggest goals, content, and structure.

2. List and discuss the current theological issues that you consider to be serious obstacles to world evangelization. How should they be met?

3. What are the theological and practical issues in communicating the Gospel to men of other cultures and faiths? How would you interpret the concepts of "indigenization" and "contextualization"?

4. What are the priorities in strengthening evangelical Bible schools and seminaries?

5. Discuss areas of cooperation in theological training (union schools, training and exchange of faculty, accreditation, library and textbooks, seminars and conferences, etc.).

6. Discuss strategies for the training of the laity in world evangelization.

7. Evaluate the future of Theological Education by Extension. Discuss the success and difficulties of schemes with which you have had contact.

8. Evaluate the future for Evangelical Theological Societies or Commissions. Discuss the success and difficulties of such societies with which you have had contact.

9. Discuss the need for centers for advanced theological studies, including objectives, management and finance, and geographic spread. Is there also the need for one advanced international center and, if so, what would be its distinctive function?

10. Suggest priorities in theological publishing in order to strengthen theological education in the context of world evangelization. Discuss the training of writers and the subsidizing of publication.

11. How should theological education be financed? To what extent can it be indigenized? Is there a need for a new world theological fund, and how should it be financed and managed?

12. What patterns of cooperation in theological associations are needed at the local, regional and international levels? What is the future of TAP? Is there a need for a new world organization, or can the World Evangelical Fellowship be strengthened or revitalized?

THEOLOGICAL EDUCATION AND EVANGELIZATION REPORT

Theological training programs intended to equip pastoral and evangelistic ministry in many cases are outmoded and antiquated. Any advance in this crucial area must begin with a reconsideration of the basic objectives of theological education. Irrespective of the level sought, attention must be given to the integrated development of the student's total person in his *being, knowing* and *doing,* to the end that the man of God be equipped:

1. To lead others to commitment to Jesus Christ as Savior and Lord.
2. To sustain in commitment those who have believed.
3. To mobilize the church to effective evangelistic activity.

Theological educators should pay greater regard to the spiritual gifts of the seminary candidate, his teachability in the intellectual sphere (e.g., Paul's concept of being "taught by the Spirit"), and emotional and spiritual maturity capable of embodying the fruit of the Spirit (love, peace, patience, etc.).

The training of leaders for evangelization must be pursued under the Spirit in an atmosphere of excellence both in the academic and practical spheres. Quality must not be sacrificed for quantity. In practice, the pressures of academic concerns frequently undermine the spiritual development of the student. The division of a student's curriculum into alternating or concurrent periods of formal instruction and field service should contribute towards the development of both mind and spirit. Lack of objective criteria for the evaluation of ministerial and evangelistic skills is a conspicuous deficiency demanding careful research. Whatever the pattern of theological education, the art of evangelization is frequently best communicated through the example of a seasoned evangelist or pastor. Principals and professors of theological training institutions should themselves be theologians with a passion for evangelism, since the art is "caught" as well as "taught." Perhaps the cell concept, wherein the mature student guides a core of inexperienced students, could be employed with profit both in formal instruction and in field service.

Theological education for evangelization in the traditional residential pattern must come to grips with the following obstacles. The typical residential program tends: 1. to decontextualize the student by isolating him from his cultural milieu; 2. to generate an unhealthy dependence of the third world student upon the sponsoring institution; 3. to lead to stagnation through lack of input from the external world. It is recognized, however, that the obstacles of the residential institution are by no means insurmountable. Indeed, the residential pattern offers the distinct advantage of providing an ideal laboratory in which the New Testament ideal of community can be experienced. Further study should be given to the ways and means of deepening the sense of community in theological education between the student, the professor, and the church in the world. It is urged that the student-professor relationship be extended in field service and internship experience. The TEF publication "Learning in Context" has some helpful comments on new patterns of theological education.

The strategy of theological education for evangelization ought to pay due regard to new patterns of non-residential education such as theological education by extension. Extension education is a potentially effective tool for advancing evangelism because of the greater flexibility of its curriculum and its ready application to the people at the local level. Perhaps the time is coming when Third World leaders trained in TEE techniques can be enlisted to promote extension education in the service of evangelism in given areas in the Western world.

The biblical principle of the priesthood of all believers (I Pet. 2:1-10) where each member of the church is endowed with gifts of the Spirit, underscores the fact that laymen in the local church likewise must be trained and equipped for evangelism. Attitudes of paternalism and professionalism on the part of some clergy, which hinder involvement in local evangelism, must be squarely faced and forsaken. Valuable training programs which equip lay people for a ministry of evangelization are being developed through specialized training centers and functional institutes in many parts of the world. Such lay training programs for evangelization supplement the theological schools and also the teaching ministry of the local church, and ought to be done in cooperation with the local fellowship.

The task of educating a force for evangelism on a global scale necessitates careful consideration of the issue of the "contextualization" of the Gospel. In the face of confusion arising from fluidity of usage, particularly in some ecumenical circles, the following definition of contextualization is proposed: "Contextualization means the translation of the unchanging content of the Gospel of the kingdom into verbal form meaningful to peoples in their separate cultures and within their particular existential situations." In this regard it is reaffirmed that this Gospel of the kingdom as defined in Holy Scripture is *totally relevant* to man in the totality of his need. This follows because the Gospel was designed and provided by the same God who made the human heart and who knows the depths of man's alienation from Him and from his fellows. All who do the work of the evangelist are under solemn obligation to *guard* this relevant, revealed Gospel. The task in evangelism is to communicate the Gospel to all men in terms meaningful to their cultural identity and existential condition. The *problem* in contextualizatin as popularly understood is that one can all too easily drift into an unwarranted and God-displeasing syncretism. By this is meant the sort of accomodation to the cultural values of a people that results in a mixture of biblical truth and ethnic religion. Syncretism invariably and inevitably dilutes and distorts the fact that Jesus Christ alone is Lord and Savior. Furthermore, when one attempts to translate biblical truth into the language and culture of a people, one is under solemn obligation to produce what will be no more and no less than the normative Word of God. The more one reflects on the task of contextualization; the more conscious one becomes of the larger task, of seeking to structure theological thought within each separate culture in such a way that the total corpus of biblical truth is more faithfully communicated to every man in his own culture.

A strategy of theological education for evangelization must come to grips with the dearth of classical reference works, textbooks and monographs on the biblical foundation of the faith and on issues of contemporary theological concern in the Third World. Little creative theological writing by spokesmen of the younger churches has been produced. The following recommendations are put forward to stimulate the production of relevant theological literature in the Third World: 1. theological institutions should offer writing sabbaticals to promising professors; 2. a collective approach needs to be made to theological funding agencies for assistance in this area of theological literature; 3. extensive bibliographies need to be developed.

Centers for theological research can be a vital stimulus to effective communication of the Gospel. Clearly, the structure and content of such research facilities will differ from continent to continent and culture to culture. Thus it is recommended that each major geographical region develop its own theological research center which reflects the uniqueness of its own cultural situation. The proposed research centers ought to pursue study in the following areas: 1. theological research translating basic biblical concepts such as "God," "man," "salvation," etc., into cultural contexts; 2. an analysis of contemporary competing ideologies which tend to discredit the authenticity and relevance of the Gospel, e.g., Neo-Marxism, religious syncretism, etc.; 3. area studies from a cultural, historical and socio-political perspective, so as to better understand the structures and problems of countries resistant or closed to the Gospel; 4. methods of evangelism and the production of suitable evangelistic materials. In relation to the above goals, it is recommended that coordination at the international level implement a system of exchange of ideas and personnel between the various theological research centers. On a level of international coordination, an evangelistic research committee could take responsibility for the development of evangelistic research tools in a resource pool of available materials, and for the establishment of an evangelistic research lending library to serve as the central deposit for evangelistic and missionary publications and archives.

Optimum effectiveness in the task of training communicators of the Gospel demands new patterns of cooperation in theological education. Such regional and international relationships would facilitate the sharing of new educational methods, curriculum planning, etc., and advise concerning the availability of new publications in the various theological disciplines. To implement these objectives, it is recommended that in addition to cooperation in existing theological associations, evangelical associations of theological schools, theological societies and professional theological journals of modest proportions be created on the regional level, where desirable. The calling of conferences to study specific problems in the area of theological education would be of further help. Finally, the older churches could demonstrate their concern for world evangelization by assisting their brethren in the younger churches to establish theological training institutions in strategic centers of the world. The goal to which the entire church must press with urgency is the equipping of gifted national educators to bear the responsibility of training their own peoples for the effective evangelization of the world.

CHRISTIAN HIGHER EDUCATION AND WORLD EVANGELIZATION:

A Strategy for the Future

David L. McKenna

*Dr. McKenna, Seattle, Washington, USA, is
President of Seattle Pacific College, and is
also President of the Christian College
Consortium.*

If only we had listened to God! In his earliest conversations with the man he created, God talked about the oneness of the earth and the steward-ship of its resources. The ideas of a "Global Village" and "Spaceship Earth" are nothing new. But, as a symptom of our sin, we split the world into pieces of self-interest and blazed a trail toward extinction with our polluting wastes.

Mercifully, God is speaking again. Our fantasies of selfish growth and unlimited resources have been exposed by ecological prophets wear-ing the mantle of Malthus. God must laugh as he hears us talking today about the oneness of the world and the management of resources as if we had just invented the first survival kit for the human race.

World evangelization also depends upon a global view and steward-ship of resources, but like the earth it has been victimized by selfish in-terests and wasted resources. Our sin is not always conscious. Selfishness frequently comes in the form of competitive ministries, and waste is justified by doctrinal differences. Behind the veil of these attitudes is the same thinking that has taken us to the brink of extinction in the secular world — self-interest in viewpoint and self-indulgence in resources. We can no longer afford these luxuries. If we are as serious about world evanglization as the human race is about survival, we, too, will let God speak again.

The relationship between Christian higher education and evange-lism illustrates our shortcoming. Each claims the redemptive purpose and the global scope of Christ's continuing mission. Like C. P. Snow's "two cultures" of art and culture in the academic world, however, Chris-tian higher education and evangelism tip their hats but they do not speak. Communication between the two ministries is limited. They tend to divide into narrow, competing specialties rather than complementary tasks in the Kingdom of God. Worst of all they seek to multiply by using duplicated resources of men, money, space, and time. To me, the two cultures of Christian higher education and evangelism point out the ma-jor issue in world evangelism to which this Congress should address it-self. Berlin and Minneapolis gave us solid position papers and strong resolutions. Our need now is a plan of action. Therefore, my purpose is to reassemble Christ's great commission as a whole-world view in order to rediscover the principles of stewardship and reinforce the perspective of size as the strategy for the future of Christian higher education in world evangelization.

The Great Commission: a world system

Christ gave us a "world" view in the final charge to his disciples. He talked about the size of our task and the stewardship of our resources. For our motivation he gave us a *purpose*. To measure our results he gave us an *objective*. Then in keeping with his promise, Christ gave us the *power,* the *method,* and the map to carry out his command. The result is an integrated system, flawless in design, worldwide in scope, and timeless in application.

Purpose. Jesus said, "...you will bear witness for me...away to the ends of the earth" (Acts 1:8). He gave us the definitive *purpose* of being his witnesses and the measurable *objective* of the "ends of the earth." Consequently, when we set our priorities, define our roles and make our decisions, each choice must be pre-tested by the purpose of making Christ known. Then, after our choices have been implemented, we must measure our effectiveness by the extent to which Christ has been introduced to those who do not know him. *Evaluation* will show whether our work fulfills the Great Commission, or if our priorities and our plans are self-condemned by the very purpose for which we exist as Christians. As shown in Diagram "A," Christ's purpose, objective, and evaluation make the Great Commission a complete system in itself.

DIAGRAM "A"
PURPOSE AND OBJECTIVE

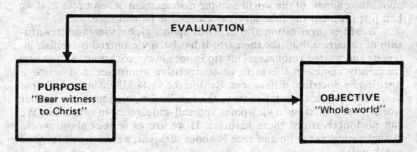

Power. A "system" is not complete without power to achieve the objective. Power is different from authority. By definition, *authority* is the formal ability to control behavior, while *power* is the more informal ability to change behavior. Jesus made this distinction when he responded to the question of the anxious disciples, "Lord, is this the time when you are to establish once again the sovereignty of Israel?" (Acts 1:6). His answer was, "It is not for you to know about dates or times, which the Father has set within his own control. But you will receive power when the Holy Spirit comes upon you..." (Acts 1:7-8).

Human desire is for control — the power that corrupts. Jesus himself was denied that authority. Yet, he did say, "Full authority (power) in heaven and on earth has been committed to me" (Matt. 28:18). No contradiction was spoken. Through his death and resurrection, Jesus had won full and uncontested power to change men, but not the authority to control them. God's power to control men and events could not be delegated from Father to Son or from Son to disciples. Resurrection power could be. So Christ legitimately claimed all power and then promised it to his disciples through the Holy Spirit. Power to change the behavior of men was delegated to the disciples as the primary resource which would enable them to bear witness to Christ to the ends of the earth.

Method and strategy. As witnesses for Christ, the disciples were called to follow a developmental *method* with people. Jesus said, "...*make* all nations my disciples; *baptize* men everywhere in the name of the Father and the Son and the Holy Spirit, and *teach* them to observe all that I have commanded you. And *remember,* I am with you always, to the end of time" (Matt. 28:19,20). Developmental tasks for the Christian witness include a personal *commitment* ("make"), a public *symbol* ("baptize"), sound *doctrine* ("teach"), and a continuing *sacrament* ("remember"). As a mini-system within itself, Jesus' developmental method of witnessing is designed to produce the "whole man of God."

Jesus had in mind the whole world as well as whole men. So he added a developmental *strategy* in the form of a spatial and societal network as the arena for the witness. He told his disciples that they would bear witness, "...in *Jerusalem,* and all over *Judaea* and *Samaria,* and *away to the ends of the earth"* (Acts 1:8). A "Global Village" for the Gospel must have been mind-boggling for the disciples in the first century.

They needed a manageable mission. So Jesus explained the strategy for the Great Commission as a network of interrelated parts. Variations by space and culture were included in the plan that Jesus gave to them. *Jerusalem* represented an advanced, urban civilization; *Judea,* its rural, developing counterpart; *Samaria,* a third world of ethnic variations, and ancient religious hostility; and the *"ends of the earth,"* unknown nations — primitive or advanced — with ethnic, linguistic, and cultural barriers. This developmental strategy now becomes part of the larger system of the Great Commission that includes resources, method and strategy as the means to implement Christ's purpose and achieve his objective. Diagram "B" shows the *plan,* its parts, the "feedback loop" or evaluation process which now tests every phase of the system against its primary objective.

DIAGRAM "B"
THE PLAN AND ITS PARTS

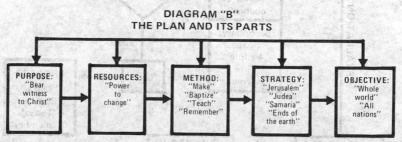

| PURGOSE: "Bear witness to Christ" | RESOURCES: "Power to change" | METHOD: "Make" "Baptize" "Teach" "Remember" | STRATEGY: "Jerusalem" "Judea" "Samaria" "Ends of the earth" | OBJECTIVE: "Whole world" "All nations" |

Ignition by decision. Integrated systems, even perfectly conceived, are sterile until they are "turned on" by decisions. To avoid having the Great Commission known just as a theoretical model for world evangelization, Jesus called for two decisions. One was for *preparation* when he told the disciples, "You must wait for the promise made by my Father, about which you have heard me speak: John, as you know, baptized with water, but you will be baptized with the Holy Spirit, and within the next few days (Acts 1:4-5). After they had received the primary power resource of the Holy Spirit, he then commanded them to take the initiative, *Go* and...bear witness for me..." (Acts 1:8).

"Wait" and "Go" decisions make the Great Commission run or stall. Having given an integrated model for world evangelization, Jesus left the choices in the disciples' hands. They could say, "Yes" and world evangelization would begin. They could say, "No" or, "Maybe" and the mission would fail. Each generation has the same decisions. An International Congress on World Evangelization can reassemble the model of the Great Commission by words, papers, votes, or consensus. But, unless the "Wait" and "Go" decisions are made, a magnificent vehicle will remain on the launching pad.

When "Wait" and "Go" decisions are put into the integrated system of the Great Commission, they are like the "breath of life" into the lump of clay. The system comes alive with the reverberating flow of action in which disciples are involved. Diagram "C" shows how complete and dynamic our Commission is.

DIAGRAM "C"
THE GREAT COMMISSION:
AN INTEGRATED WORLD SYSTEM

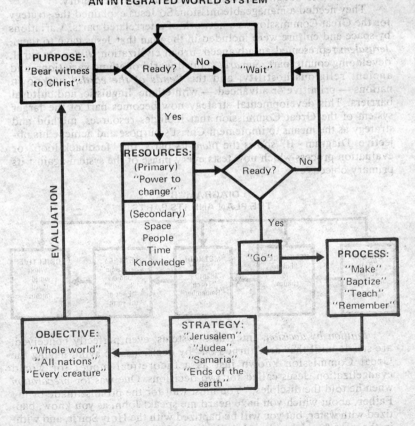

As we noted earlier, the system has no defects in design. If peopled and activated, world evangelization would become a reality. Therefore all of our ministries must meet the standard of being working and contributing parts of the Great Commission.

Christian higher education and evangelism

What is the relationship between Christian higher education and evangelism in the world system of the Great Commission? As two working parts of the same system, they have both common and complementary relationships:

Common Relationships. To achieve the objective of the Great Commission, Christian higher education and evangelization have a common *purpose, power,* and *objective.* Motivation for both these ministries springs from the primary *purpose* to "Bear witness to Christ." This does not mean that higher education and evangelization are indistinguishable. Each has its specialized role. For instance, recent inquiries about the purpose of colleges and universities in changing times have focused on the question, "What motto is on the flag that flies from the masthead of higher education?" Secular institutions may fly the single flag, "Knowledge Is Important," while the banner over Christian colleges and universities may read, "Faith and Knowledge Are Important." But at the tip of their masthead, Christian institutions must hold the standard that reads, "Bear Witness to Christ." No other watchword can justify the existence of Christian higher education. Evangelism, whether individual or institutional, must fly the same flag.

Power is the common resource for education and evangelism. Each must ignite its purpose by waiting for the baptism of the Holy Spirit in order to receive the ability to change men. As education and evangelism become more specialized, temptations increase to substitute formal authority, money, or secondary resources for the power of the Holy Spirit. No alternative resources are specified in the Great Commission. Either there is the power of the Holy Spirit energizing the whole system, or the objective will never be reached. "Waiting" must characterize the spiritual life of education and evangelism if the primary power source is to be tapped.

Christian higher education tends to count brains while evangelism counts noses as the products of their process. Both must be measured by the *objective* of the Great Commission. What are we doing to extend the witness for Christ to the whole world? If our plans were pre-tested and our products post-tested by this objective, we would probably have to change some of our priorities and decisions. The adage, "A fanatic is one who redoubles his efforts after he has lost sight of his goal," should not apply to either Christian higher education or evangelism.

Complementary relationships. Christian higher education and evangelism have different but supportive relationships in the *method* and *strategy* of the Great Commission. In the developmental *method* of "Make...Baptize...Teach...Remember," education and evangelism have differentiated tasks. Christian colleges and universities have shied away from the image of being "soul-saving stations" and evangelistic efforts have been accused of breeding anti-intellectualism among Christians. According to the system of the Great Commission, however, each has a responsibility for the integrated process of producing whole men in

Christ. Yet they are different and bring complementary strengths to the process of making whole men. This relationship can be understood from the analogy of the individual gifts that the Holy Spirit gives to the members of the Body of Christ. "There are varieties of gifts, but the same Spirit. There are varieties of service, but the same Lord. There are many forms of work, but all of them, in all men, are the work of the same God. In each of us the Spirit is manifested in one particular way, for some useful purpose" (I Cor. 12:4-7).

Varieties of gifts, varieties of service, and many forms of work apply to organizations as well as to individuals. Education and evangelism need each other. Their complementary gifts need to be mutually developed in the process of making whole men and with the objective of reaching a whole world. Furthermore, they need each other as a check-and-balance against over-specialization which aborts the Great Commission by making conversion, baptism, teaching, or the sacrament an end in itself.

Interdependence between higher education and evangelism also characterizes their relationship in the *strategy* for the Great Commission. In the network from Jerusalem to the ends of the earth, evangelism is the vanguard for bearing witness to Christ. Although there have been many starts and stops along the line, evangelistic efforts are reaching out to Jerusalem, Judea, Samaria, and the "uttermost parts of the earth." Much of the effort is lost, however, because converts are not cycled through Christ's developmental process for the whole man and then cycled out into his strategy for a whole world.

Christian higher education should touch each piece of the world evangelization network. At Jerusalem, it becomes a stabilizing force for the moral values which Christianity brings to a culture. In Judea, it is a moral tracking system as the culture grows and changes. In Samaria, it has the openness to explore new options across cultures. For the ends of the earth, Christian higher education had the institutions spotted around the globe like stepping-stones to the uttermost parts. Also, their institutions house the flesh and the fire of the young, upon whom world evangelization ultimately depends.

In common, then, education and evangelism share the *purpose* of bearing witness for Christ, the *power* of the Holy Spirit, and the *objective* for making the witness known to the ends of the earth. As distinct ministries, they are responsible for developing complementary relationships in the *process* of making whole men and in the *strategy* of reaching the whole world. Together, they must conserve the limited resources of space, time, men and money by reducing duplication and waste. Together, they must ignite the world system of the Great Commission by being willing to "Wait" and ready to "Go."

A plan of action

By 1984, Orwell predicted that a powerful world system would control our lives. As a counter-system to an Orwellian world, Jesus gave us the design for world evangelization with the power to change, not control, the lives of men. Even now, these two systems are on a collision course. While the final outcome of the inevitable clash was settled on the Resurrection morning, the battle is ours for this generation. Feedback, current and prophetic, tells us that our most important task in this International Congress on World Evangelization should be to reassemble and reactivate the Great Commission as the world system for the Christian mission in the struggles for a balance-of-power that are just ahead. For Christian higher education and evangelism, at least four action steps are needed.

First, Christian ministries of the world need a pledge for *organic cooperation*. It is time for a Lausanne Declaration of commitment to the Christian world system. The Declaration should be an affirmation of the integrity of the Great Commission — its *purpose, process, strategy,* and *objective*. Individually and collectively, we should agree to:

Pre-test our priorities and our plans by the purpose of bearing witness for Christ.

Develop our complementary strengths in the process of making whole men in Christ.

Rework the strategy lines for world evangelization to utilize the spatial and cultural relationships between education and evangelism.

Measure our results by the objective of bearing witness for Christ to the whole world, all nations, and every creature.

Renewal for the relationship between Christian higher education and evangelism will begin when the leaders of both ministries have signed the Lausanne Declaration as their common commitment.

Second, Christian higher education and evangelism need a plan for *operational collaboration*. Jesus' process for developing whole men will never be fulfilled worldwide if we each assume that we have to "do it all by ourselves." Strategy teams of educators and evangelists need to sit down, review the process in the Great Commission, propose an operational network of the "Make...Baptize...Teach...Remember" ministries of a city, a culture, or a continent, and then ask for collaboration in an operating referral system. Christian churches, colleges, crusades, and committees would find new strength and meaning as they proved that "whole" men are made through "whole" systems.

Third, the potential for *resource coordination* between Christian higher education and evangelism should be explored. An integrated system of the Great Commission does not need organic or operational coordination. It does need the coordination of limited secondary resources of space, time, men, and money. Christian higher education may be the place to start. Following the pattern of the Christian College Consortium in the United States, it is feasible to envision a worldwide network of educational institutions pledged to the Christian world system. The resources that they would bring to the system could be traced by a computerized directory — listing location, programs, people, and facilities. This could save some of the duplicated costs that are incurred when we assume that we must build new facilities at strategic spots across the world either to extend the Gospel or to protect the developmental process with our converts. The stewardship of limited resources is not only wise, it may well gauge the quality of our witness to the world.

In a similar vein, we need on a worldwide basis resource coordination of Christian scholars who can give invaluable support to evangelization. One of the surprising outcomes of the Congress on Evangelism in Amsterdam in 1971 was to bring together Christian scholars from universities across the Continent. Many of them met for the first time and were encouraged to learn that they were not alone in the academic community. A worldwide talent bank of Christian scholars could be developed by a computerized directory that would make it possible to identify some of the most powerful minds in the academic world. As members of an "invisible Christian university," they might correspond or meet for fellowship, speak together on Christian ethics, teach the doctrines of Christ and supportive disciplines, break down the artificial barriers between education and evangelism, and challenge secular scholarship. World evangelization implies the full and effective utilization of all of the resources in the Body of Christ.

Fourth, educators and evangelists must come together in *spiritual unity* around the "Wait" and "Go" decisions of Christ's world system. We are apt to forget that many of the great spiritual awakenings in the world have been ignited by youth on the campus. Perhaps we also forget that unless their awakenings fired youth and the campus, the impact is limited. Therefore, rather than educators assuming that evangelism is not their "bag" or taking the stance that "if it comes, it comes," they should be leaders in making "Wait" and "Go" decisions a part of living and learning on the campus. Evangelists, rather than assuming that they are wilderness voices for "Wait" and "Go" decisions or that their task is limited to "making disciples," should consider the campus as an ignition system for the Great Commission.

Having seen Christ's final charge to his disciples in its wholeness, the results are fresh and frightening. As a world system of the Christian mission, it has the integrity of purpose which fills every part with meaning. Christ promised the resources that would be needed, outlined the process to be followed, and set out the strategy to achieve the objective. Then he activated the system by calling for decisions that move all the parts into a powerful and expanding flow toward world evangelization. Put together as beautifully as the Body of Christ itself, a systems view of the Great Commission shows no deficiencies of design that would sabotage its fulfillment. At the same time it is frightening to contemplate the impact of the Great Commission as a world system upon evangelization. Internally, competitive ministries and wasted resources can no longer be justified. Externally, a concerted effort would lead us to an early and inevitable confrontation with the pagan world system. Are we ready for worlds in collision? Those of us who have heard the call of Christ will have to answer the question.

CHRISTIAN HIGHER EDUCATION AND THE EVANGELIZATION OF THE THIRD WORLD

Okgill Kim

Dr. Kim, Seoul, Korea, is President of
EWHA, Women's University.

As early as 1886, when Mrs. Mary F. Scranton opened the first school for girls in Korea, she had this to say about the relationship between Christian higher education and the evangelization of Korea:

"I emphasize the fact that they are not being made over again after our foreign ways of living, dress and surroundings, because it occasionally appears from home and even in the field that we are thought to make such big changes. This is not so. We take pleasure in making Koreans better Koreans only. We want Korea to be proud of Korean things, and more, to know it is a perfect Korea through Christ and His teachings. In the short time we have been at work here we see that we are slowly doing what is in our hearts to do and are showing Korea Korean possibilities..." (*The Gospel in All Lands*, 1888, p. 373.)

With this clear understanding of the mission of education for women in the spirit of the Christian Gospel, the present Ewha Women's University in Seoul, Korea, was founded. Mrs. Mary Scranton, an American missionary, mother of the first American Methodist medical missionary to Korea, found her mission to make Koreans better Koreans and to make perfect Koreans through Christ and his teachings. And even today we believe that our mission is to perfect our traditions in and through the life and teachings of Jesus Christ our Lord.

We Korean women, as so many other Asian people, dress and live and talk like Westerners these days. But it was not the conscious and deliberate effort of the missionaries to impose Western ways of life upon Asians. At least the American lady who made women's higher education possible in Korea believed the mission of Western education and Christian evangelization was to "show Korea Korean possibilities..." Mrs. Scranton believed that only through Christ and his teachings would Koreans be able to discover themselves and to perfect themselves as Koreans. It was not to force Koreans to give up their own ways, but to show them new ways of being Koreans. It was the purpose neither of evangelization nor of the educational mission to make Koreans American but rather to allow them to become truly Koreans. In doing this and only this, our founder Mrs. Scranton showed us the true meaning of Christ and evangelization in the name of our Lord.

"The Third World"

To our first missionaries to Korea, it appears to me, the question was not so much about the relationship between educational or medical work *and* evangelization. They were questioning the relationship between the Christian mission and the world to which they brought the Gospel. I was

asked today to speak on the question of the evangelization of the Third
World through Christian higher education. But what is the third world?
And who named it? No missionaries to the East called us the third
world, though they have called us heathens.

"The Third World" is a name used in international politics, the
force that was formed in the United Nations forum to stand over against
the power blocs of Communists and the free nations. Now it seems to
mean all those nations in Asia and Africa which have been variously called "underdeveloped" or "developing" nations or the "have nots" of the
world. But it is not a religious name.

Those countries which have received the Christian Gospel in the last
two centuries are not, as far as I am concerned, the religious third world.
We are not religiously underdeveloped or have nots. We have religious
traditions, perhaps heathen, but deep and precious. Therefore, our topic
today has to be formulated as the evangelization of the Third World in
its international and political as well as its economic and cultural milieu,
especially through our effort in Christian higher education.

Actually we do not know exactly what the Third World is. One thing
seems to be clear, that is, the peoples in the Third World want to get out
of the category "third world." Another thing is that the peoples in the
Third World are in the process of discovering the identity of the third
world. As far as I know, we as Koreans want to get out of the state of economic underdevelopment, and at the same time we do not want to identify ourselves with either Americans or Chinese. We want to know exactly
what Korean means when we say that we try to make Koreans more
Korean and not Western. We call these efforts "nationalism." The Third
World you are talking about is striving to achieve economic national
growth and development, and to discover their nationhood culturally.
The ideology of the Third World in general is neither democracy nor
Communism but nationalism. The peoples in the Third World are all
alert to discover national identity which has been lost through the
Western economic, political, and cultural invasions. The governments of
the Third World are all set for building up powers which they have lost
by the invasions of the first and the second world wars in the twentieth
century. They are trying to regain their power which Western nationalism of the nineteenth century destroyed. They want to gain their national
identity through gaining power, just as the Western countries gained
their national power in the nineteenth century. In order to maintain the
newly gained independence, the peoples of the Third World have to
follow the nineteenth century models of Western nationalism.

This upsurge of nationalism in the Third World has been able to
mobilize its peoples to work hard for the betterment of their economic
condition. The ideology was able to mobilize intellectuals to work on the
discoveries of their respective cultures through the development of national language, arts, and religions. But at the same time the ideology of
nationalism was able to set the people over against the Western powers
and cultures. With harsh words in the English language they learned
from their former masters, they sometimes reject and condemn anything
that is Western. With this trend we must recognize at the same time, the
peoples of the Third World were suppressed under the name of national-

tradition and in the context of his society. Hence, when we say that we try to save a person in and through Jesus Christ, we have to consider him as a Korean or a Kenyan, or a Frenchman concretely. I think, in this sense, our missionary friend was right to think that the mission of education is to make a Korean more Korean in and through the life and teachings of Jesus Christ. If we translate this into our own language, this is to say that the Christian Gospel is to make the individual person grow into his historical tradition and into his own society. Our task of education through the teachings of Jesus is to make a person anew in his historical and social situation. Evangelization is not to take a person away from his historical tradition or his social roots; it is to give a new awareness of person in his own historical and social context.

This is not to say that Christian evangelism is to let a person become an old man, let him go back to his old way of doing things. The task of Christian evangelism is to make the old new. This is to transform the old culture and traditions into the new ones. It is to make everything new in Christ. This is to be able to see things in different ways, new ways, and the true ways in Christ.

The peoples in the Third World have no way of seeing the world in Christ. We have old and deep traditions of Confucianism, Buddhism, Hinduism, Shamanism, or Mohammedanism. Christian evangelism has to work among these different religions, cultures, and traditions. Is Christian evangelism a denial of all these religions and traditions? If this is the case, Christian evangelism is a denial of a person in his social and historical context. We cannot do this. Christian evangelism is to make human beings better human beings, who are able to appreciate and understand their own nature historically and socially. Christian evangelism is to help a person to discover his own identity and to help transform and change himself in the new light of the Christian Gospel, which has this tremendous power to change people and their society and their history as a whole.

Now Christian higher education must be supportive of this notion of Christian evangelism. Christian higher education is in the spirit of Christian evangelism to make a person a better person. In this sense, and only in this sense, has Christian higher education its relevance and its connection with the Christian Gospel and mission of Christian evangelism. In this way we can say that Christian higher education is a kind of service department, as the medical mission belongs to the service department of the total evangelism of the Church. In the sense that Christian evangelism has to do with individual persons as sons and daughters of God, and in that it tries to make a person in the true image of God, Christian higher education has to do with making persons truly God's children; in that sense it is truly Christian evangelism.

In our part of the world, we have daily chapel services in our universities and colleges and even in high schools as a part of the regular curricula. I understand that this is possible only in Christian schools in the Third World. It is important to have daily chapel services and revival meetings on the college campuses as a part of evangelism in the world where only a few percent of the population have ever heard of the Bible and Jesus. But we cannot have the illusion that this is the whole of Christian evangelism on the university campuses in the Third World.

We must learn how to make the total curriculum of Christian higher education a type of Christian evangelism. Especially in the Third World where the slogan of economic and technological development is loud and clear, the question of the connection between Christian evangelism and higher education is an urgent and critical issue. Also in the Third World where Christians are in the minority, the total influence of the Christian spirit seems to have been in the minority or non-existent. If Christian higher education will dedicate itself to the task of true Christian evangelism — that is, to make a person truly a person — then the total experience of higher education in the Third World has to be related with the persons in the Third World within their social and historical context.

Some Constructive Suggestions

In the light of these ideas I would like to suggest the following implementations:

First, we must learn how to organize the curricula of the Christian higher education in the Third World. And when we consider the reformulation of our university curricula, we must concentrate on the question of the person as a child of God living in the particular society and historical setting. I have been proposing to our faculty back home to make our curricula centered around the process of self-identity of a person in the traditional cultural contexts of being Korean. So our history department and language and other humanities departments have been working to open up courses that will help our students to realize the true picture of their cultural makeup.

Second, our social studies curricula will be formulated in such a direction as to help our students to see the world community, not in terms of the relationship between the haves and the have nots, but the relationship among those nations in the Third World. It is sad to find that our students know more about America and Europe than about their immediate neighbors in Asia.

Third, in the field of fine arts and music, we have been trying to encourage our faculty and students to cultivate the educational forms of our own cultural heritage in the arts. This is not to reject the Western traditions in the arts, but it is intended to discover new forms of art which may come out of continuous work in combining the arts of West and East.

Fourth, in the field of natural science and technology, our effort is directed not only toward catching up with Western technology, but toward searching for new patterns of development unique to the people in the Third World.

Fifth, I would like to propose to those leaders of Christian higher education in the Third World to have a cooperative relationship among ourselves. We may be able to open up many areas of work together. But we may begin with opening an academic course on better understanding ism early in the twentieth century. And nationalism of the Third World is now affected by another ideology, Communism, especially in Asia.

Our first woman missionary and one of the founders of Christian higher education in Asia foresaw future problems and the direction of Christian evangelism in the Third World. It was the Christian mission to help the people of the Third World to discover themselves and improve. Christian mission has to do with the national identity. But this is not to say that Christian evangelism has to do with the ideology of nationalism or any other ideologies. This is to say that the first and the foremost job for Christians in the Third World is to assist those desperate searches for identity and to solve problems of survival.

Poverty and Population

We have the problems of poverty and population. The problems of poverty and population go hand in hand. Where there is the problem of poverty, there is also the problem of population. Where there is the problem of population, this becomes a problem because it is the cause of poverty. Where there is the problem of poverty, there is also the problem of economic growth; and when the economic growth is a problem there is the problem of political system and ideology. When population grows, poverty sets in, and when poverty spreads, the sense of insecurity among the people opens up all kinds of possibilities: wars, dictatorship, communism, and the total crisis of the world. We must here underline the fact that poverty and over-population create insecurity which leads to new religious movements among the desperate poor. To put it simply, the new religious movement is nothing but superstition, a heathen movement in the twentieth century.

Evangelization of the Third World in the twentieth century cannot be something that may lead our people to other-worldly business and neglect of what is going on in the world. This is no better than those new religions which attract so many of our poor people. One task of evangelization in the Third World is to exorcise twentieth century ghosts. The contemporary ghosts in the Third World take up two forms: (1) religious or superstitious escape from this world, and (2) modern scientific solution to all problems. Religious solution cannot defeat the technological problems of poverty and population; and at the same time the technological solution cannot take care of the religious and spiritual problems of contemporary man.

We are hearing more often and more loudly that the problems of poverty and population of the Third World can be solved by making the Third World the bases of economic development of the more powerful countries of the first and the second worlds. The Third World cannot grow economically, politically, and at the same time spiritually when it only remains as another kind of economic empire of the West. Nor can the Third World solve its vast problems by just following the patterns of the European countries in the nineteenth century. We cannot exploit other poor countries in the Third World. Nor can we solve our problems if we are poor and miserable. This is the dilemma we are all caught in and we just cannot escape from it.

We as evangelicals have thought in the past and think even now that evangelism will somehow solve the problems of poverty in the world; it is not our direct problem to tackle. By taking this line of thinking we become quite removed from the concrete and desperate problems of the world. We have been accused of being incapable and incompetent in vast areas of our endeavors — in medical and educational fields especially.

Social Gospel

The so-called liberal Christians have brought the Third World version of the social gospel in recent years. Economic development and growth have been associated with Christian mission. This gives us the impression that Christians have taken up all the problems in the world. And the effort was nothing but an imposing of a Western way of growth and modernization upon the peoples of the Third World. Now they do not seem to be able to solve various difficult problems that have come out of the rapid and all-out effort of gross national economic development. Revolution of any kind cannot be accepted any longer; for the peoples of the Third World have been sick and weary of revolutions in their lifetime.

The best and simple answer would be to say that we need both kinds of evangelization to the Third World. But I think this is too easy an answer, but it is simply too difficult to follow in action. Yes, we need both kinds of emphasis, but at the same time neither will solve our problems in the Third World today. We have to go back to our first proposal. The question has to be tackled from the point of view of the people of the Third World. We have to find our own problems and we have to find our own solutions to the problems in and through the true spirit of the Christian Gospel. We must learn in our own way how to become truly Korean, truly Japanese, and truly Brazilian in our respective ways.

I believe that the true spirit of Christian Gospel which can be powerful and meaningful to the people of the Third World is that Jesus is to make human beings more truly human. Therefore, evangelism that has nothing to do with human growth and development, and economic growth that is forgetful of human beings in the system, are meaningless. And when we say that we need both kinds of emphasis in the evangelism of the Third World, we are saying that we must commit ourselves to human beings and their growth toward Jesus Christ. Any kind of nationalism that is to sacrifice individual human beings has to be rejected by Christians. Any kind of solution to the problems of the desperate Third World that has nothing to do with the true concerns of humanity cannot be followed by Christians in the Third World today. For we believe that Christ came to the world to save individual human beings, and not to save the authority of a human ideology, and not to maintain the human economic and political systems. He has not come to the world to save the laws of one government or the doctrines and decrees of the Christian world.

Christian Education

Man is not only a social animal. He is also a historical being. To save an individual human being, one has to think about him with his historical our own cultural area. This would lead to exchanging of information and professors and students among Christian institutions of higher learning in the Third World. And through this kind of cooperative endeavor in Christian higher education, we may be able to organize ourselves regionally in order to improve the conditions of Christian higher education for excellence in academic work. And perhaps through these organizations we may request financial as well as technical assistance from friends in the first world.

In closing, I would like to introduce to you the spirit of our work in Korea which was set by our first Korean president of Ewha Women's University, Dr. Helen Kim. She writes her experience of her school day as follows:

"I fell upon the floor and asked God to forgive all my sins committed against Him. I immediately felt His forgiveness. This was followed by a remarkable vision. I seemed to see Him take the three bags of my sins away, showing me what to do the rest of my life. He pointed out to me a big dug-out moat where a mass of Korean women were crying out for help with their hands outstretched from the haze and confusion that covered them... From that time on, my life has been directed by God's hand toward the one course of humble service to the womanhood of my country and the emancipation of the women of the world..." (From *Grace Sufficient,* pp. 29-30.)

Dr. Helen Kim's vision was people's hands streched out to her for help. It came to her through her prayers. Our evangelical mission can take no other way than to go to the world to serve for them and to emancipate them for a better life.

CHRISTIAN HIGHER EDUCATION AND WORLD EVANGELIZATION

Myron S. Augsburger

Dr. Augsburger, Harrisonburg, Virginia,
USA, is President of the Eastern Mennonite
College and Seminary.

How does the new humanity being created by the risen Christ break in with meaning upon the contemporary world? This issue confronts the "community of Christ" on every front as we seek to live under the direction of our Lord. Education is not an auxiliary to the life and mission of the Christian community in this age; it is rather an essential part of the Church in that mission. World evangelism means the crossing of linguistic and cultural boundaries, and such involvement calls for education. With the cross-cultural interchange, the philosophical framework of our time, the impact of secularism, Marxism, Islam, and Buddhism, it may well be that Christian education now becomes a frontal aspect of the mission of the Church.

Christian faith is most authentically expressed by the lives of people transformed by the Holy Spirit into a covenant community in Christ. Proper articulation is important, but not apart from the evidence of the new humanity Jesus is creating in the fellowship of faith. For this new age it is new people that are important in authenticating the evangelizing Word. Christian education will promote both the quality of the new community Jesus purposes to create and a clear expression of the New Testament kerygma of Christ the Lord.

The relation of Christian education and evangelism

By education is meant, of course, the transmission of cultural, social, and spiritual values from one generation to another, with stimulus of analysis and interpretation. Christian education is education which happens from the stance of a Christian world view, from the mind and heart of one who answers to the Lordship of the risen Christ, and who as a disciple lives and thinks under the direction of the Spirit of Christ. Such a person in education will be true to the Heilsgeschichte, to the saving acts of God in history, to God's revelation of himself ultimately in Christ, and to the heritage of the spiritual and ethical dimensions which we know as the Christian faith.

Christian education is the communication of a perspective and spirit by one who teaches; it is a stimulus which creates within his students an interest in understanding the Christian world view and the claims of the risen Christ. Christian education takes seriously the mission to which Christ calls us, "As the Father hath sent me, even so send I you." With this calling we live with a unique responsibility to the three billion people today who do not know Christ. The Christian educator in many countries of the world may serve in state-operated schools or in university settings. He may serve in special training programs designed by the Church for discipling of people in commitment to Jesus Christ, providing specific training for the representation of Christian faith in Bible institutes, seminaries, etc. Or, for others, Christian education will happen in the context of that unique type of school in North America known as the "private" Christian college. But wherever it takes place, Christian education is not so much the structure of the institution nor of the curriculum in itself as it is the perspective which is guiding that education, and the purpose which it is fulfilling in introducing students to an adequate understanding of the work of God in history and the claims of the risen Christ in a contemporary world. Nothing stimulates world evangelism more than the conviction of God's will for men, as it is known in Jesus Christ.

Education and evangelism are by their very nature directly related. Both are essential aspects of the life and existence of the Church. Emil Brunner is quoted as having said, "The church exists by mission as fire exists by burning." The Bible says, "Faith comes by hearing and hearing by the Word of God" (Rom. 10:17). Faith is response to evidence. Christianity with its historicism rather than mysticism needs to be understood to be adequately experienced. Education, if it is Christian, shows the relationship of the perspective of faith in Jesus Christ to all of the disciplines studied, sciences, arts, humanities, etc., because the total world stands in relationship to the Creator and to the purpose of that creation. "All truth is God's truth," and when truth is properly understood it will be seen in consistency with the One who is the personification of Truth itself, Jesus Christ our Lord. Of him, Paul writes, "The truth is in Jesus" (Eph. 4:21), and, "All things are by Him and through Him and unto Him, and in Him all things cohere" (Col. 1:16-17). When this is understood in the context of the normal education experience rather than only in special courses of indoctrination in the Christian creed, the student discovers the relevance and universality of the Christian faith. Christian education, like evangelism, is making faith in Christ an option for thinking men. In fact, education may appear to be a more tolerant aspect of Christian mission than evangelism, as the latter is usually conceived.

This does not mean, however, that Christian education can be primarily theoretical and less concerned about evangelism. Professor Jan M. Lochmann has said regarding his book, *The Church in a Marxist Society,* "Tolerance is to be differentiated from indifference, hence the ideological struggle." Education is called to engage in the dialectical approach by its very nature. Reinhold Niebuhr has interpreted dialectic as meaning that there is always an "ideological taint" in our interchange. The recognition of this is Christian realism. The tolerant man is aware of this taint, but his tolerance means that he takes his fellowman seriously! Tolerance will seek to interact with others in the struggle for truth.

Christian education must prepare people for honest interaction with persons of differing ideologies. Tolerance recognizes that truth is something for which you stand, and that it can only be corrupted when persons seek to settle an issue by force. Christian disciples will seek for interaction in the world, which interchange itself attests freedom and calls all men to pursue the quest for truth. We must recognize especially in the interaction between East and West that ideology is the function of man, man is not the function of ideology. In this connection Professor Lochmann expresses a word of caution, "It is better to speak of the ideology of a Christian, than of a Christian ideology, as though all Christians must agree." This is especially relevant for missions as we think of cross-cultural dimensions.

If our faith is an authentic, New Testament faith, it will be concerned for its articulation. We are not authentic if we only enjoy a "private" spiritual piety, if we only pursue our career in education for personal advantage, but we are authentic when we relate deed and word in expressing the character and articulating the meaning of our faith. We do not express faith in a "solid" form, rather we express the action of faith, rooted in the sovereign promise of God in his faithfulness as he continues to act in history.

The responsibility of Christian education in global perspective

Living in the last half of the twentieth century, in a day in which the world has become as interrelated as one neighborhood, it is imperative that we think of education for the whole world. Christian education serves with full awareness that Jesus Christ introduced the kingdom of God and in doing so announced a kingdom that is *global*. This kingdom is among us, but does not come by observation, it is made up of people whose lives are transformed by the Spirit of God, who confess Jesus Christ as Lord. It is a global, or universal, Kingdom, for God's purpose is to bring to all men the knowledge of Christ. It is the new humanity in Jesus Christ, a new people of God in whose lives the *Imago Dei* is being restored. The church is a new community, a covenant fellowship. As such, we reach out hands to persons unlike ourselves, affirming that greater than our differences is our oneness in the fellowship and purpose of Jesus Christ. To be a part of this kingdom means to be a disciple of the risen Lord. In education we are disciples, and we seek to develop around the globe a chain of disciples who will be disciplers of others.

This new humanity in Jesus Christ is to be a model which speaks to society. There is no Christian culture as such, and no Christian nation as such; the field is the world. Jesus taught that the kingdom is as a field in which good seed had been sown, but in which, also, the enemy has sown tares. The Christians, or the disciples, Jesus said, are the good seed. The tares are the children of the age who are not servants of Christ. The field is the world and in the world the two grow side by side until the judgment. As disciples of Christ, as the new humanity, we are in the world but not of the world. But in the world we are an exhibit of a new people of God, and this exhibit serves to make faith an option of those who do not know the life of Christ.

But we must beware of absolutizing the nature of the act of faith in our interpretations. God is the Personal Being who became clear in Jesus Christ, therefore we do not use the Incarnation or the Cross as something with which to "crush" others. With our Trinitarian understanding of God, the ultimate expression of mutual love, it is incumbent upon us as Christians to extend love to all men as a means of communication. Christian education is thus directly related to the evangelistic mission of the church, for the dissemination of Christian insight is being true to the dialectic of truth, and makes possible believing faith on the part of the inquiring mind.

Christian education has about it the possibility of becoming the cutting edge of the church for "this one world." As a Christian I am a man in Christ, and in the humanity of Christ I am a man in context with other men in society as a Christian. I can thus relate in the freedom and character of the humanity of Christ. Now, from the global nature of the Christian community, from the primary nature and meaning of the kingdom of Christ and of my membership in that kingdom, I must share in the development of a worldwide fellowship of the redeemed. This calls for a clear sense of evangelical mission. As Christians, we, more than anyone else, need to develop world understanding, respect, and appreciation for the variety and values of other cultures. The love of Christ will enable us to accept and esteem one another in our various cultures as children of God, the values of those cultural practices standing or falling in relationship to the Lordship of Christ and not in relationship to the judgments of one culture upon another. The charge that missions are a form of imperialism can be answered by the trans-cultural nature of the kingdom of Christ. The global Christian community needs to rediscover the New Testament meaning of fellowship. In the Acts of the Apostles, when the three thousand people converted to Jesus Christ from a variety of cultural orientations, they committed themselves to the covenant of the redeemed in a fellowship which transcended every other commitment (Acts 2:42). Education for such a fellowship will deal with the total life in relationship, not simply with the mind and its intellectual criteria.

The relevance of Christian education for the Third World

Christian education has as its goal the development of informed disciples who in turn will disciple others. This perspective calls for an authentic awareness of compassion, the ability to identify with the needy, and the willingness to suffer in service. The meaning of Jesus' own calling breaks in upon us, "The Spirit of the Lord is upon me because He has anointed me to preach good news to the poor. He has sent me to proclaim release to the captives, and recovering of sight to the blind, to set at liberty those who are oppressed, to proclaim the acceptable year of the Lord" (Luke 4:18-19). To understand compassion is as valid in the educational enterprise as any other aspect of the studies of sociology and psychology. To experience this we must understand authentically the culture of our neighbors lest we misinterpret and fail to read the true character of human need. The need is not primarily in cultural differences, and we must avoid seeking to impose our culture upon another or to transform that culture into something that reflects our own.

In the Third World, today the frontal area for the growth of the church and the spread of the kingdom of Christ, it is imperative that those of us from the Western world respect what God is doing among our brothers. Last year in Africa alone, some eight million people were baptized. In the Far East in countries like Indonesia, Taiwan, Thailand, India, and Pakistan, thousands of persons have been baptized into the Kingdom of Jesus Christ. The education of these new disciples must be with the understanding of Christian faith in terms of their own culture and their own history.

In most of our educational programs history, for example, is taught from the perspective of "colonial" history. This one illustration alone points up the challenge for Christian educators to be fair to our brethren and honest with history in educational transmission. In the review of African history, the Western world teaches from the perspective of colonial history. While attention should be given to David Livingstone and to H.M. Stanley, we should consider hundreds of dedicated Africans who worked with Livingstone, giving their lives in Christ to his work and cause. Are they not also martyrs in building the kingdom of Christ in Africa? Do they not belong in the annals of history even with far greater prominence than Stanley?

Or how do we educate for understanding by Africans whose question has not been, "Is there a God?", but rather, "How can one know and walk with this God?" How does one bridge from an African pattern which often is quite Old Testament, to a New Testament pattern where the God who revealed himself to Abraham, Isaac, and Jacob and who revealed himself to the African fathers is now fully known in Jesus Christ? Who better than the African in education can show his brethren the knowledge of God in Christ which supersedes the sometimes valid but preliminary insights of the past?

Education is the transmission of the great heritage of history in which man stands, but there is selectivity in that transmission. What we select is determined by our perspective. Christian education will select the best in humanness, for Jesus Christ demonstrated in his person the greatest expression of humanness that the world has ever seen. Even in his resurrection, as Carl F.H. Henry has put it, He expresses "the character of humanity God approves in the eternal order, He is the moral image to which all the people of God will ultimately be conformed." In the Incarnation it became clear that humanness and sinfulness are not synonymous, otherwise Jesus Christ as the Son of God could not have become man. Thus in his Incarnation we have the greatest affirmation of humanness the universe has ever seen. This is also the evidence that Christian truth deals with the whole person. This provides perspective for the church in evangelism. We, like Jesus, must relate to men where they are.

In many nations of the Third World, when independence came and the peoples were freed from the colonial powers there were some major changes. Two of these strike us now as quite significant. First, banished was the old colonial propaganda that permitted a people to be a people for themselves with their own self-image. Second, the Christians were now seen to be helping with social problems, the building of schools, construction of water dams, the building of hospitals, etc. This is Christian concern for the total need of man. A third change which followed, but was not immediately seen, became effective in the next years, for as the older missionaries retired, the leadership in the church became national. Such leadership meant that now the people who were preaching Christ were people who were among their own people, they were people who had to live what they preached.

These three basic changes have followed independence in country after country of the Third World. There is now a new thrust of people reaching others for Christ in their own cultural or ethnic group. These new communities of disciples are reaching their neighbors and calling them to be disciples. The role of the common man is elevated and as he lives the Christian life and studies the Bible his society is affected, and principles of love, righteousness, and equality come to the fore.

A further dimension that has already dawned is the preparation and sending of missionaries from the Third World to the rest of the world. This appears to be the current program of the Holy Spirit in missions. The rise of missionary societies in Third World countries is God's answer to the charge that evangelism is the Western world spreading its religion. While it is true, as Donald McGavran has so effectively pointed out, that the evangelizing power of the church is most effective in its own cultural or ethnic group, there is a dimension of power in the confirmation of witnesses to Christ who come from various cultures. The witness from the Third World may be the very confrontation the secular world needs to call it to look seriously at Christ. An example in this regard outside the Christian faith is the impact of the Indian guru in the United States. This is the age of the international man, and missions must use this international interest to communicate the Gospel. What better way for persons from the Third World with a New Testament faith who are sent to the West in missions than for them to serve in centers of education and reach secularized youth?

The role of Christian education in "This One World"

Dr. Lesslie Newbigin has written effectively about "a Faith for This One World." With similar perspective I am emphasizing education in faith and in missions for this *One World*. Since the Church of Christ is global, and the kingdom of Christ transcends nationalism, it would follow that what belongs to the church in one setting belongs to the total Church in the total world. In countries where the Church has resources in persons and in things, we have a direct responsibility to share, as did the church in Acts, with the church in other countries that have so little.

Our greatest resource will continue to be people, disciples. There will be a continuing place for specialists who can serve as agents of reconciliation through relief work, through agricultural work, and through educational work in a variety of countries. But such must recognize that they are their brother's brother, and they must work under his direction, as partners in the kingdom of Christ. The Western man must give up his ambition to administer programs. He must be willing to work in the Spirit of Christ with the towel and basin, washing his brother's feet. His ministry in another culture must have an altogether different image than that of being an administrator of others. This means that education for this One World must teach us to understand, to respect, and to esteem our brethren in their culture — to benefit from their faith and experience.

Another factor in education for this One World is prophetic discernment as to where God is working. It is his work, therefore we must ask, "What is God doing in his time? What is the cutting edge of the church?" It is easy on the one hand to say that God is working most evidently in the Third World context today, that this is the frontal area of growth in the church. We must be cautioned, however, that we do not abandon the more difficult area of evangelism — the Western secularized world with its philosophies of either secularism or Marxism. Significantly, several analyses of Church growth in the last several years point up that the Christian Church has grown during the last decade in every country except Europe. Regardless of whether this can be demonstrated other than numerically, the Western world is not seeing the impact for conversion to the Christian faith as has been recently a characteristic of the Third World.

This is a challenge especially for Christian education. It is basically the intellectual or philosophical aspects of life which appear to have undercut the impact of the Christian faith in the Western world. The issue of atheism is at the forefront again in the challenges confronting theology, whether in Marxism or in secularism. This is the issue to which Joseph Hromadka addresses himself in *Evangelium fur Atheister*. Western man has taken the Christian values from the Christian Gospel and by claiming to give these respect in his philosophy of life has insulated himself against the claims of the risen Christ as Lord. Secularism has become the new religion for Western man. With this stance, he claims to have found in ethics the essential values of the Christian faith and sees faith as primarily self-actualization. Secular man has sought to free himself from what he calls the "myths" of the resurrection of Christ, the reconciliation of man with God and the regenerating transformation of the Holy Spirit. This atheism must be met with the "Good News" of the Gospel, that God can be known in Jesus Christ.

Secular man can be confronted with the awareness that the secular cannot claim wholeness for itself. The Christian educator must interpret the dimension of the Spirit, as known and understood in Jesus Christ, as the only dimension which offers man meaning and the fulfillment of his own essential personhood. The understanding of reconciliation has a central place in Christian education, both in the experience of faith by which man is reconciled to God and in the related aspect of reconciliation to God being the ground for reconciliation between men.

This also has about it an eschatological dimension, for education must take seriously man's relation to the future. Concern for the future is no longer thought of as "pie in the sky" for tomorrow. Christian awareness, that relation with Jesus Christ as Lord, which has in it our anticipation of his return and ultimate purpose, has also an understanding of meaning for the future in the way we relate to his created world and expedite its care for the sake of posterity. The ecological concerns of our time, the increase of the human population, the need for food production and sharing on a worldwide scale, the care and stewardship of the natural energies and resources, all serve to focus our attention on the importance of our brother. These are also basic dimensions of Christian mission. Education for this One World must give priority to the needs of our fellowman, recognizing his place in the Kingdom of Jesus Christ.

The renewal of missions in Christian education

Christian education must grapple with the newest dimensions in missions. The word "missionary" is not a bad word. We must, however, remove the expatriate image from the word "missionary." We can then reinstate the term missionary as an important concept, even as a better term than "fraternal worker." The missionary must no longer be thought of as the foreigner but as the national, as the Christian worker who fulfills the calling of Christ in his life by being a person with a redemptive mission among his fellows. We need a renewed emphasis on the "vocational missionary" as a person who gives his life to this cause of evangelism, to sharing the Christian message in every way possible.

There is a unique value in Christian mission when the preaching-leadership comes from people who live their Gospel at home among their own people. Those who are expatriates, serving, teaching, or preaching in a culture other than their own, need to discover how to accept what Bernard Joinet calls being "a stranger in my Father's house." To serve with this perspective if I am a missionary, he says, "I must 1) accept myself as a stranger, 2) accept to serve the others as they want to be served and not as I would like to serve them, 3) accept to receive and become interdependent in the same way Christ struck up a dialogue with the Samaritan woman by asking her, 'Give me a drink.' Only then can I give."

The missionary must respect the fact that the dynamic for the new period of missions is not in his articulation but in the community of believers. In this new community, worshiping and discipling one another, loving and learning from one another in Christ, a new people of God breaks in upon society. The message is one of reconciliation to God in Christ, a reconciliation expressed in the agapaic relation of the community of disciples. As Marshall McLuhan has said, "The medium is the message," so our method of evangelism, of education must be an extension of the fellowship aspect of the new people of God. This fellowship can include the expatriate as a "brother" in the local "anywhere congregation" of disciples.

For Christian education to fulfill its mission of discipling people, it will need to accept the challenges before us. First, we need some of the greatest minds of the Christian Church involved in the mission of evangelism. Second, we need a responsible scholarship with respect to the intellectual or philosophical framework of our own time, the development of understanding which enables us to interact with the thought patterns of the age without surrendering to their structure in a compromise of Christian faith. Third, we need the humility which does not have to have the right answer on every occasion but can stand alongside to learn from others while sharing the love and joy of Jesus Christ. Fourth, we need to maximize the value of the human personality, that our first calling is to love as Christ loved and thereby enhance the fellowship of the new people of God which the risen Christ is creating. Fifth, we need an obedience to the Holy Spirit which will permit him to express compassion through us.

Education should not surrender the calling to confront people with the knowledge of Jesus Christ, but should confront persons in a manner that will make faith an option through intellectual awareness. But neither should education yield to the temptation to assert itself as more credible than direct evangelistic preaching. To do so, would be to intimidate persons who with less intellectual sophistication still may communicate most effectively by love and human understanding. Christian education must prepare whole persons to minister in the Spirit of Christ. At best, education must always confess that it is a tool, seeking to understand and represent the Christ who is far greater than its own understanding.

We acknowledge with joy that we are able to experience the love of Christ which passes intellectualizing! The experience of the Lordship of Christ goes beyond the articulation of the mind — this is our strength, and our corrective.

CHRISTIAN HIGHER EDUCATION AND WORLD EVANGELIZATION

Secretary: J. Houston

This was a small group, indicative of the low profile that higher education has in education. And yet it was clearly seen that some of the greatest minds of the Christian Church today are needed in the tasks of evangelism. For we need a responsible scholarship that equals the intellectual and philosophical framework of our time. This was the theme of the first paper presented by Dr. Myron S. Augsburger, "Education and Evangelism for This One World." "Education," he argued, "is not an auxiliary to the life and mission of the church community in this age; it is rather an essential for the church in that mission." For education and evangelism are by their very nature related. Education, if it is Christian, will show the relationship of the perspective of faith in Jesus Christ to all the disciplines of the campus. It will show that all the world stands in relationship to the Creator and to the purpose of that Creation (Col. 1:16-17).

This is desired in secular education, so Christian education must prepare people for heart interaction with people of differing ideologies, living in this *one* world. But we must realize too that ideology is the function of man, and that man is not the function of ideology. Faith, however, cannot be authoritative if we enjoy only a "private" faith, pursuing our careers for personal advantage. We need to articulate its relevance in all aspects of our lives.

Considerable emphasis was made on the relevance of Christian education for the Third World as the frontal area of church growth. In addition to its emphasis by Dr. Augsburger's paper, Dr. Okgill Kim made this her theme in "Christian Education and the Evangelization of the Third World." She saw "that the first and foremost job for Christians in the Third World is to avoid those desperate searches for identity and to solve problems of survival."

Curricula must center, therefore, around the cultural identity of the people or nation concerned, eliminating the colonial biases that the Western educators have imparted. Students need to see the true picture of their cultural makeup. They need also to see their relationship to the world community in ways deeper than the jealousies and arrogance of the "have-nots" and the "haves."

After her paper much of the discussion centered on the need to have more interchange of personnel between the West and the Third World, so that educators on sabbatical leave, as part of their integral teaching experience, could volunteer to serve in Third World educational needs.

Dr. David L. McKenna stressed in his paper, "Christian Higher Education and World Evangelization: A Strategy for the Future," the need to economize resources by avoiding duplication and waste. Reference was made to the need to promote a worldwide talent bank of Christian scholars that could be developed by a computerized directory. This already exists in the United States resource coordination in the Christian College Consortium. The open university system pioneered in Britain might also be a pattern Christian educators could imitate.

As theological education is particularly fragmented by denominational interests, much could be done to formulate coordination and cooperation in this field of education. It was also felt that too many students from the Third World tend to become deculturalized overseas, so that more emphasis should be given to promote the educational needs of colleges within the Third World.

In summary, the group emphasized the crucial importance of the campus in today's society. Past evangelical revivals began on university and college campuses, and evangelical scholarship has also laid the foundation of many universities. Today, however, Christian higher education is often a euphemism for poor scholarship. We have to earn again the right to be heard so that scholarship goes hand in hand with evangelism. The Christian educator has a much broader mandate than to "witness" evangelically; he has responsibility, too, to train students in all the professional skills required in contemporary society. The recognition that we live in God's world is a cultural mandate that needs a deeper reflection than is customarily given.

DEPTH IN EVANGELISM — An Interpretation of "In-Depth Evangelism" Around the World

Orlando E. Costas

The generic term *In-Depth Evangelism* stands for a worldwide evangelistic movement which had its *formal* inception in an experiment carried out in the Republic of Nicaragua in 1960. It can be succinctly described as an effort to *mobilize the church of Jesus Christ with all of her resources for a comprehensive witness in the world*. It represents, at once, a dynamic evangelistic concept, a comprehensive strategic methodology and a coordinated, functional program which in the last decade-and-a-half has become one of the most formidable challenges before the contemporary church around the world.

Since it is a movement, however, it can neither claim to be the possession of a single entity, individual person, or institution, nor to have a definitive, authoritative interpretation. Therefore, this paper should not be construed as the official word of the movement. It is simply the interpretative analysis of a participant-observer who is, naturally, conditioned by his own vital situation, theological categories and tactical approach.

Nevertheless, there is a conceptual framework grounded on a serious analysis of the theological roots of evangelism, which characterizes the style of In-Depth Evangelism. Such an analysis has led, in my opinion, to the development of several conceptual pillars which shape its strategic methodological structure.

PART ONE: A COMPREHENSIVE VIEW OF THE WORLD

One of these pillars is its comprehensive view of the world. The seriousness with which the Great Commission has been taken plus the principle of global objectives have given to the movement a holistic world view. The world is thus conceived in its complexity — a complicated mosaic which dramatizes how much there is yet to be done for the evangelization of the world. Let us outline three of the most important pieces of this mosaic.

1. The geographical dimension

A look at a world map reminds us much too quickly of the many lands where the Christian faith has not yet penetrated. Studies keep popping up which show large geographical blocks that remain beyond the frontiers of the faith or where it is spreading disproportionately. Asia, for example, which comprises two-thirds of the inhabitable earth, is overwhelmingly non-Christian. In Africa there are many regions that are practically closed to the Gospel or remain largely unevangelized. In the Americas and Europe entire regions are undergoing a rapid process of dechristianization. Today, more than ever, the Church needs to take seriously the geographical dimension of the Great Commission.

2. *The human dimension*

Clusters of men and women are brought together by family, linguistic, ideological, educational, and professional ties and make the mosaic more interesting and complicated. They challenge geographical and political boundaries. They shape the course of history. They work for or against the Gospel and thus constitute a constant challenge to the evangelistic enterprise. They force the latter to evaluate its performance and be on the lookout for new approaches. They further dramatize how far the Christian Church has to go to reach the fulfillment of its evangelistic goal; the discipling of *all* the peoples of the earth (cf. Matt. 28:19).

3. *The structural dimension*

The world of places and people gives way to the world of *structures*. Since man is a creature of time-and space, he is not only bound to a specific locality and cultural ties, but by social, economic, and political structures that shape his existence. His behavior is governed by a set of values, which are at first biological and psychological in nature (they respond to man's struggle for survival). As man cultivates his relations with his fellowman, however, these values take social dimensions which are slowly structured into organized bodies. In time, these structures develop corporate "personalities" and exercise a tremendous influence (in some cases an almost absolute control) over personal behavior.

The geographic regions, the cultural ties that bring together the peoples of the earth, and the different structures that shape their existence form the stage of human life. They are the world that God so loved that he sent his only Son to redeem it from sin and death. It is to this world that the church has been sent to witness to the Gospel.

To evangelize "in-depth" is, therefore, to take seriously the totality of this mosaic. To see the world not as the sum total of individuals, but as a dynamic interaction between the different groups of peoples that inhabit the earth. It is to be concerned not only about the geographical penetration of the Gospel, but also about its cultural and sociological impact. It is to see the Great Commission not only in terms of going to all the regions where there is human life, but to all areas of life where people dwell — from the family cluster to the sophisticated socio-economic structures of our age.

This conception of the world lays as much emphasis on the skyscraper as on the bush, on the solitary individual as on groups of people. It also complicates the evangelistic enterprise, for it places a tremendous burden on the witnessing community. If the world to which the church is sent is a conglomerate of peoples, places, and relationships, its evangelization must involve a matching comprehensiveness in resources, methods, and strategic action. To awaken the church to this reality is one of the goals of the In-Depth Evangelism movement.

PART TWO: A COMPREHENSIVE MESSAGE

In addition to a comprehensive vision of the world, in-depth evangelism is a comprehensive interpretation of the Gospel. Its quest into the theological roots of evangelism has led to the rediscovery of the Gospel of the kingdom of God as the central thrust of the evangelistic message. This in turn has led to an analysis of the kingdom in relation to the evangelistic enterprise.

1. A message about the kingdom of God

The kingdom is a new order of life characterized by the sovereign rule of God in the person of his Son, Jesus Christ. In him God has made himself present in human history. He is the fullest expression of God's love for man and the embodiment of his will. He thus calls unto himself a community of men and women who respond by faith to his love and pledge an unconditional commitment to him.

While God's kingdom is particularly present in this community, it extends across all principalities, dominions and powers. No sphere is outside Christ's domain. Before him all other authorities — earthly and otherwise — are made relative. Little wonder that he is referred to as the King of kings and the Lord of lords, the beginning and the end!

What makes Christ's rule unique is not the absoluteness of his authority. It is rather the astonishing fact that he is crowned king by becoming a servant!

...though he was in the form of God, (he) did not count equality with God a thing to grasp, but emptied himself, taking the form of a servant, being born in the likeness of men. And being found in human form he humbled himself and became obedient unto death, even death on a cross (Phil. 2:5-7).

This kingdom is highlighted by its orientation to the destitute and downtrodden. It is a place for the weak and the sick and not for the noble and the strong. Anyone who wishes to enter therein must become, therefore, poor in spirit and sensitive like a little child.

For this reason, the world does not acknowledge the authority of Christ nor is it able to sense the signs of his sovereign rule. Only the redeemed Christian can see the kingdom at work and understand its mystery, for she has been miraculously transformed by the regenerating power of the Holy Spirit in her calling out of the darkness of this world into the marvelous light of the kingdom of God. She has thus been commissioned to bear witness, in the power of the Spirit, to the reality of God's kingdom in the world, to call those who remain in darkness, and unmask and rebuke the rulers of darkness for their opposition to the liberating work of the kingdom.

The kingdom is a paradoxical reality. This is accentuated by the fact that while it is already present it has yet to be revealed in its fullness. This accounts for its apparent hiddenness in the world. Even the redeemed community is not always able to decipher the signs of the kingdom. She too reflects her transitional situation by the inconsistencies of her work. Thus she must be constantly reminded of her mission and be called to the renewal of her vows.

The kingdom also reflects its paradox in the fact that it is a sign of liberation and of judgment. At the same time that it opens a new future, it announces the end of the kingdoms of this world. This makes the Gospel an announcement and a denouncement. What on the one hand is good news, on the other becomes bad news.

The kingdom is, in consequence, a comprehensive reality. It affects not only the personal present and future of the peoples of the earth but their collective present and future as well. For it liberates and judges people in their context. In making relative the powers of this world, it also makes relative the absolute pretensions of each person: his self-centeredness and egolatry. In calling men and women to submit their lives to the King, the Gospel also addresses itself to their cultural ties and structural realities and calls them to repentance and obedience. The kingdom can thus take form in the personal life of those who enter therein, through the regenerating power of the Spirit, and also in the structures of society and the dynamics of culture, through the leavening function of the Gospel. No aspect of human life is outside its realm, but neither can the kingdom be possessed or manipulated by any of the components of human history. For the kingdom is sovereign and transcendent. Its presence in history is dynamic and not static, mysterious and eschatological. We can proclaim it, anticipate it in our lives, demonstrate it, seek it, celebrate it, pray for it. But we cannot bring it about by our wisdom and power. It stands outside our control, because it is *God's* kingdom.

2. A message that demands integrity

Such a message demands integrity. It must be fully interpreted. Its meaning must be clearly expounded. The mystery of the kingdom must be unveiled. Its contrast to the existing order must be clearly shown. The character of the salvation that it brings and the judgment that it proclaims must be explained. Otherwise the mission is cut short and the message diluted.

But this is precisely one of the fundamental crises in contemporary evangelism: a truncated mission and a diluted gospel. We need desperately to recover its *comprehensiveness* and the depth of its proclamation.

PART THREE: A COMPREHENSIVE VIEW OF THE CHURCH

Equally comprehensive is the concept of the church that is implicit in the In-Depth movement. In a sense, this is a corollary of the aforementioned concepts. For the church is a consequence of the Gospel and reflects the complicated nature of the world.

1. A dynamic organism

The church is viewed, first of all, as *an organism*. It is a living body of interacting parts. As a consequence of the Gospel and first fruits of the kingdom of God, the church carries on the life process generated by the action of the Holy Spirit. Consequently, she is *a growing* body, for growth is essential to life, and an organism which becomes stagnant eventually dies.

The growth of this organism is, however, multidimensional. This is so because growth is in itself a complex phenomenon. It takes place at different levels and in many different ways. Moreover, as a dynamic organism, the church must experience growth at the various dimensions of her life-process and at all levels of her interacting parts in order to avoid stagnation and decay.

This means that the church must experience *numerical growth*. That is, there must be a continuous ingathering of new believers — people who are directly confronted with the Gospel and invited to enter the kingdom of God by faith in Jesus Christ as Lord and Savior. Those who respond must be incorporated into the church by baptism. They must be led to become active components of the church's fellowship by worshiping God, serving their neighbor in Christ's name and witnessing, personally and collectively, to God's redemptive action in Jesus Christ and his liberating power.

As a dynamic organism, the church must also experience internal, *organic growth*. That is, its parts must ever mature in their interaction with one another. This has to do specifically with the various systems of relationships which are uniquely present in every concrete expression of the church — its form of government, financial structure, leadership, types of activities in which the time and resources of believers are invested, etc. These structured relations, which are indispensable characteristics of the church, must experience continuous expansion and renewal.

Beyond this, the church must grow in the understanding of the Word of God — until she attains "the unity of the faith and of the knowledge of the Son of God, to mature manhood, to the measure of the fullness of Christ" (Eph. 4:13). The church must constantly reflect upon the meaning of her faith in Christ in the light of society's multiple situations. In this life we will never know all there is to know about Christ and his Word, but we need to work toward a greater and unifying understanding of our Lord. A church which does not reflect on the Word (with all of its implications) will eventually die, because she will stop the growth process at the level of *the conceptual* and cognitive.

As an organism which must spread and affect her environment, the church must grow further *incarnationally*. That is, her involvement in the life and problems of society must become ever more intensive and committed. She must intensify and expand her participation in the afflictions of the world. Her prophetic, intercessory and liberating action on behalf of the weak and destitute must be more and more efficacious. Her preaching to the poor, the brokenhearted, the captives, the blind and the oppressed must constantly experience greater depth. Otherwise she will not be able to effectively enlighten the path of life, nor adequately give flavor to the earth nor leaven the structures of society. In this case, she will become practically and functionally a walking corpse.

2. A community

In the second place, the In-Depth movement views the church as *a community*. It sees the church as a people with a common origin and a common destiny. The practical outworking of this concept may best be described in three familiar imageries.

The church is like *a family*. It is a fellowship of persons brought together by the reconciling experience of the Gospel. They have a common calling and hope in the Spirit, a common faith in the Lord Jesus

Christ and a common God and Father of all, "who is above and through all, and in all" (Eph. 4:6). The church is the place where each believer puts into practice his experience of reconciliation through fellowship with other believers. It is the place where everyday experiences are shared with others, where the common calling to the praise of God's glory (Eph. 1:6) is exercised, where the common faith is celebrated, and in the midst of which the common hope is kept alive.

The church is also like *a school*. A place to reflect on the meaning of the faith in the light of the multiple challenges of contemporary society. A place for mutual edification — a teaching-learning setting. A training center for participation in God's mission in the world.

And the church is also like *a team*. A group of people with a common task. Their mutual roles and efforts must be coordinated in order to reach their common goal. It is thus the body through which each believer can fulfill his witnessing vocation.

3. A social institution

To these conceptions must be added that of the church as *a social institution*. That is, the church as a complex system of relations and values. This is another way of saying that the church is not only a miraculous community, but also a human phenomenon. Therefore, it is bound to reflect human qualities. These are not bad in themselves, for after all man is a creature of God, made after his own image. They have been affected, nevertheless, by sin and have accordingly an ambiguous character and stand under the judgment of God.

To say, then, that the church is a complex social institution is to affirm its historical diversity, pluralistic style of life and multiple structural manifestations. Thus the history of the church, while having unquestionable common threads, is a multiphase history. To understand it one must study the history of each of the church's historical expressions. This makes of the history of Christianity a compilation of the histories of Christian churches.

Because of its historical diversity, the church has developed a pluralistic style of life. This is why in one context the Christian life can be practiced in one way and be different in another. This does not mean that there aren't historical, ethical, missiological and liturgical imperatives. What it does mean is that the actualization (fulfillment) of these imperatives may vary according to specific situations and circumstances.

This leads to the multiple forms which the church may take internally and externally. Traditionally, it has been said that the church takes three forms in human society: (i) the local congregation, (ii) the denomination, and (iii) the total community of believers active in a united effort. However, there have been in history, and there are in our days, multiple informal structures which cannot fit into a traditional theological definition of the church as a social institution and which are most definitely engaged in tasks which correspond to the church's mission. I am referring to the so-called para-ecclesiastical structures: Christian institutions such as seminaries, hospitals, schools, social service agencies, bookstores; special interest groups, such as missionary societies, student groups, lay associations; and what has come to be known as the "underground church" — regular inter-confessional gatherings of

Christians for worship, sharing and witness. Surely these too should be considered legitimate expressions of the church in the measure that they gather believers for fellowship, worship and study, and constitute points of reference for witness and service.

However, even when we follow a more traditional approach to the historical manifestation of the church, we discover formal and informal structures that must be taken into account for the dynamic fulfillment of the church's task. For it is in and through these structures that believers are to be found. A local congregation, for instance, is not found, functionally and practically, in the membership roll. Rather it is found in the Sunday worship service, in the church school, in the officers' meeting, in the Women's Fellowship, etc. These are the areas to consider for a strategic advance at the level of a local congregation, for they are the places where the people are to be found and where the functions of the church are carried out.

Because the church is conceived of as a dynamic organism, a community with a multiphase mission and a complicated social institution, In-Depth Evangelism calls attention to the imperative of a comprehensive approach to the involvement of the church in the fulfillment of her witnessing vocation. The issue, in the perspective of this interpreter of the In-Depth movement, is this; it is not how many Christians can be enlisted for action nor how the church can "saturate" society with the Gospel. Rather it is how we can get this dynamic organism to *grow integrally*, how we can get this community to be *at the same time* a living-worshiping-fellowship, a dynamic training center, and an effective team in a complicated world; and how we can put all of her structures at the service of the Gospel of the kingdom so that evangelism — the proclamation of the Gospel, and the subsequent invitation to confess Jesus Christ as Lord and Savior and be incorporated into the life of his kingdom — will no longer be a superficial, commercial, manipulative whitewash, but a comprehensive enterprise where the Gospel is shared in depth, and out of the depth of man's needs and multiple life situations.

PART FOUR: A COMPREHENSIVE METHODOLOGY

This is precisely the challenge to which the In-Depth movement tries to address itself through its comprehensive strategic methodology. The key to this methodology is the mobilization of believers for witness.

1. The meaning of mobilization

To mobilize is, first of all, to motivate — to induce someone to do something; to set him in motion; to spark the necessary fire to lead him to take some kind of action. In evangelism, to motivate a person or a church is to get them going in the direction of the fulfillment of their witnessing vocation, get them to share their faith with others. To accomplish this, one needs *at least* three indispensable resources: (i) the dynamic action of the Holy Spirit, (ii) the active ministry of the Word of God and (iii) a contagious evangelistic setting. These resources, however, operate interconnectively. There is no evangelistic setting (atmosphere) without the action of the Holy Spirit and the Word. There is no action of the Spirit in which the Word is not actively present and does not create an evangelistic consciousness. Nor is there a serious confrontation with the Word in which the Spirit is not active and does not turn the face of the community to its witnessing vocation.

To mobilize is, secondly, to recruit. In this case, to recruit believers and their resources (personal and collective) for witness in the world. This involves the task of making believers aware of the importance and nature of witness-bearing. While every believer is called upon to be a witness, not all believers can, ought or should witness in the same way. For everyone is given different gifts and is placed in different life situations. Just as not all team members participate in a game in the same way, so in evangelism not all believers play the same role. All, however, can, should and must be prepared to explain personally the meaning of the faith when the circumstance so requires it, and all should know where each fits in the total witnessing responsibility of the church.

Third, evangelistic mobilization involves organization. Believers must be led not only to understand the nature of witness-bearing and their own contribution to the witnessing task of the church; they must not only be led to become aware of the imperative of evangelism and be enthusiastic about the advance of the Gospel in the world. They must be involved in that aspect of the church's witnessing task to which God has called them. This calls for a coordinated program into which each can fit and have a part.

Without a program, the mobilization of believers becomes a truncated effort and a frustrating experience. It is like a team that spends all of its time training and receiving pep talks from the coach without ever engaging in a formal game.

A program is a necessary corollary to motivation and recruitment (information and training). And in so far as it is the practical outworking of a reflective process, it becomes itself a training effort — because it provides the context in which Christians can put to action that which they have received from God's Word and where the dynamic of the Holy Spirit in the believers becomes operative in concrete situations.

And, finally, to mobilize is to supervise. That is, to be on the lookout for trouble areas in the practical outworking of the program; to be ready to adjust and adapt the program to new situations; to spend time with believers, particularly, helping them to do their task effectively; to be consistent in the implementation of the program. But to do all of this with imagination, always looking for new ways to help God's people to fulfill their calling.

2. The process of mobilization

The foregoing premises point in the direction of a dynamic process. To fully understand it, one needs to see *how* it works. How, then, does it operate in the on-going life of the Christian community?

a. *Conscientization* — This is a Brazilian-originated word. It means literally "conscience awakening." It is applied here to the first step of the mobilization process: bringing believers to a *conscious awareness* of their witnessing responsibility to the Gospel in every situation of life.

The mobilization of believers for evangelism requires that they be made aware of the fact that evangelism is not a "take it or leave it" affair but a *must* in the life of every Christian. Christians must be made aware of the fact that evangelism is not the franchise nor the sole responsibility of pastors, evangelists and missionaries, that it is rather the responsibility of the whole church. To be honest to Scripture, evangelism is the business of the LAITY — the ordinary people of God. The professional church-man participates only as an ordinary member of the body of Christ. This is what the Apostle Paul says so emphatically in Eph. 4:8,11. When Christ

"...ascended on high he led a host of captives, and he gave gifts to men. ...And his gifts were that some should be apostles, some prophets, some evangelists, some pastors and teachers, for the equip-ment of the saints, for the work of ministry, for building up the body of Christ..."

In other words, the pastor, the evangelist, the teacher, the apostle (missionary!) is called to be at the service of the church, to train it for the ministry (witness-bearing) that will bring about the growth of the Body of Christ. This training involves the task of making believers not only aware of their own responsibility, but also of the comprehensiveness of the Gospel *and the evangelistic task*. They thus must be brought to an under-standing of evangelism as a total process of disciple-making. This process involves words and deeds, testimonies of one's experience with Christ, and the interpretation of his Lordship and Saviorhood in the light of the everyday problems of people.

In order to bring a group of believers into a conscious awareness of the imperative and comprehensiveness of the evangelistic task, there needs to be a contagious evangelistic atmosphere. How? Through wor-ship, prayer, Church school, Bible study, preaching, fellowship, personal visitation, retreats, encounter groups, etc. The entire program of a group of believers (a local church, a student group, etc.) must emphasize the imperative, comprehensiveness, privilege, and opportunities for evange-lism today.

b. *Analysis* — A second stage in the process of mobilization is the discovery of the concrete reality in which believers find themselves. In a local congregation this involves an analysis of its own *needs* and *resources* and those of the community in which it is located.

In relation to the needs of the congregation, there needs to be an analysis of its major deficiencies. The criteria to be used for this analysis are three-fold: (i) the biblical model of the church; (ii) the believers' own examination of their performance; and (iii) concrete facts gathered from the church's records: numerical growth rate, financial and leadership situation, community involvement, church attendance, missionary pro-gram, etc. Churches tend to grow lopsidedly. They tend to move like a pendulum — at times they put all of their emphasis on a given aspect of their ministry, at others they tackle something else. Many times they do this unconsciously. Other times they think they are doing what they should — until they are confronted with the hard facts of the Word of God and their objective behavior. This is precisely the value of the analysis stage — it permits believers to take a hard look at where they are.

In relation to the larger community, there needs also to be an analysis of all its needs. Too often believers try to do evangelism without an adequate understanding of the needs of the people that they want to evangelize. The consequence of this approach has proved much too costly for the advance of the Gospel. In the analysis of a community, one can discover key points that can help him structure more effectively both the message and the evangelistic approach.

The analysis of the needs of the believers and of the target area must be accompanied by an analysis of their personal and collective resources. This calls for the development of a profile of the body of believers and the secular community. That is, the gathering of key information which can succinctly describe the "personality" (main characteristics) of each.

Accordingly, there needs to be intelligent observation. At the congregational level, there needs to be careful observation of the effectiveness of people, talents and methods. This will avoid a much too common error — putting people to work in the wrong place. At the community level, there needs to be a careful identification of the key social institutions (schools, service agencies, churches, clubs, etc.), the social and religious values of people, their style of life and their major interests (personal and collective). This will permit the building of bridges for a more effective communication.

c. Planning — Effective mobilization involves planning for action on the basis of that which has been observed and analyzed. Too often we learn a lot about people — their needs, characteristics, etc. — but fail to relate it to what we are aiming to do. In evangelistic mobilization, we need to bear in mind that an analysis is useless unless it leads to hard, bold evangelistic planning.

Effective planning involves, among other things: (i) goal setting; (ii) selection of materials, personnel and methods; and (iii) tactical preparation (what comes first, second, third, simultaneous, etc.).

Goal setting is important because it permits people to think about where they ought to go and to check themselves on the way, to see whether or not they are going in the right direction, and if not, to find out why not. In evangelism, Christians need to differentiate between ultimate and penultimate goals. The former are the comprehensive objectives implicit in God's mission to the world — *discipling the whole world with the whole Gospel through the integral growth of the whole church.* Penultimate goals, however, have to do with those things which a body of believers feels it must do to work systematically toward the accomplishment of their ultimate goals.

For example, if in the stage of analysis a congregation discovers that its rate of numerical growth is very good but that its organic, conceptual, and incarnational growth is not comparable, in the planning stage the satisfaction of these needs would become penultimate goals. That is, they would become program priorities, without, of course, reducing that which is already being done. Supposing, on the other hand, that a given congregation has been using an evangelistic approach which in the stage of analysis proves to be unproductive. In the planning stage, the development of more effective methods would become a programmatic goal.

The selection of materials, personnel and methods is contingent on the setting of the program goals. The idea here is to prepare the materials, to recruit the specific personnel for the different tasks that will need to be done, and to select the methods that will best serve to accomplish the set goals. In all of this, however, the mobilizing of as many believers as possible must be kept in mind. Otherwise one can fall into the "professional rut" of developing a very professional program with few actors and many spectators. This will kill any mobilization effort because it will limit participation to an elite. To avoid this, there needs to be the involvement of local human resources in the selection and preparation of materials, the distribution of program responsibilities, and the elaboration of adequate methods.

Tactical preparation is important for effective communication. Too often goals are not reached because the way to reach them has been rough and rugged. People have to be brought to do things *a step at a time*. Accordingly, in planning for evangelistic mobilization, one needs to think about all possible obstacles that might hinder the next step. This will permit the anticipation of problems and will smooth the communication process.

For such planning to serve effectively as a mobilization instrument, it must be done in community. Participation in the planning stage is an indispensable evidence of being mobilized for witness. No outside specialist can do the planning for a group of people and expect them to be adequately mobilized. People need to do their own goal setting if the goals are to be accomplished by them. They need to be involved in the decision-making process if they are to carry out the decisions that are made.

d. *Coordination* — Effective mobilization involves putting into action what has been planned in a coordinated effort. This requires a functional, flexible, and adaptable program. If the program is too rigid, it must be loosened up; if it is too loose, it must be tightened; if it does not appeal to autochthonous cultural symbols, if it does not respond to the questions people are raising, if it does not "scratch where it itches," it must be made more adaptable and relevant.

e. *Evaluation* — To guarantee the latter, there needs to be a continuous, endless effort of evaluation. Unless the mechanism of evaluation is inserted from the very beginning, a mobilization effort is headed for failure and ineffectiveness — for it will suffer from inadequate supervision, goal-checking, and continuation (follow-up). This, in turn, is likely to bring about frustration and a setback in the advances of the Gospel.

3. Conditions for effective mobilization

Three basic conditions must be met to guarantee an effective process of mobilization:

a. *Mental transformation* — An effective mobilization effort is bound to clash with several traditional concepts. The idea of a pastor-oriented church is challenged by the lay-oriented character of the mobilization methodology. The tendency toward program-centeredness, where a given program is, functionally if not theoretically, seen as an end and not as a means, is challenged by a goal-oriented approach, where the program varies according to the specific objectives. There is furthermore a necessary reevaluation of the specific contribution of outside leaders. Whereas in traditional evangelistic efforts (campaign or crusade evangelism), for instance, a great deal of the emphasis is place on outside leadership (an evangelist, a coordinator, Christian artists, etc.), in mobilization evangelism the emphasis is on *local leadership.* Outside leaders are viewed only as *resource persons.* The stars of the show, however, are the local people.

To all of this must be added the emphasis on centripetal-centrifugal action on the part of the body of believers. This challenges either the idea that the church is to be found only in the gathered congregation or the notion that the church is only to be found in the *diaspora* — dispersed in mission throughout the world. But in a true and effective mobilization effort the church is seen in a double action: (1) being *brought together* by the Holy Spirit and the Word for empowering, instruction, analysis and planning; and (2) being *sent* into the world *to learn* how to best serve the world, to *bear witness* for Christ by word and deed, *to be redemptively present* in the struggles of the world and *to call* the peoples of the earth to enter the kingdom of God.

Some believers are so traditional in their thinking that they reject the In-Depth approach. There are many, however, that have opened themselves to the idea of a lay-oriented church, goal-oriented strategy and a coming-going body, and in so doing have experienced something of what Paul had in mind in Rom. 12:2: "Do not be conformed to this world but be transformed by the renewal of your mind, that you may prove what is the will of God, what is good and acceptable and perfect."

b. *Sacrificial action* — A second demand of a mobilization effort is a lot of sacrificial action. That is, being willing to spend time — lots of it — in preparation, in ministry, in evaluation. Also, being willing to put the necessary resources — financial and others — at the service of the integral growth of the church. Too many people say they want results, but are not willing to pay the price. They say they want growth, but are not willing to work to achieve it. They say they want to live meaningful lives for the kingdom, but are not willing *to rearrange their priorities.* An evangelistic mobilization effort is not a pastime, a hobby, or a programmatic appendix to be carried out once a month, or one or two weeks of the year. It demands the *total time* of a given congregation because it presupposes that the church exists for that. It is contingent on the comprehensive view of the church outlined above, which, in turn, is grounded on the outlined comprehensive interpretation of the Gospel and sees the church's mission field — the world — comprehensively, as a complicated, time-consuming, talent-and-money-demanding field.

c. *Think BIG* — No evangelistic mobilization effort is possible without a comprehensive faith. That is, the capacity to believe in the God who raised our Lord Jesus Christ from the dead and made him Lord over all things; the God who from "of old is working salvation in the midst of the earth" (Psa. 74:12) and who has called the church to "disciple all nations, baptizing them in the name of the Father and of the Son and of the Holy Spirit, teaching them to observe" whatsoever he has commanded; and who has promised, accordingly, to be with the church always to the end of the world (Matt. 28:19-21).

It is on this basis that the In-Depth Evangelism movement calls the church to lay aside its inferiority, minority and defeatist complex, and move ahead with the Gospel. For a consecrated minority can make a powerful impact in a complicated world. Indeed, it can become a real prototype of a new world.

4. Program pattern

The In-Depth approach can take many different programmatic forms. In the early stages of the movement, the first experimental program (held in Nicaragua in 1960) was adopted as the model for Latin America. As the movement began to spread in other parts of the world, other patterns were developed to suit cultural and socio-ecclesiastical situations. By the end of the '60s, Latin Americans also began to revamp their program pattern. Today there are literally dozens of In-Depth evangelistic programs around the world. Let us consider four different types, from four different continents, developed to suit the needs of four different situations.

1. Situation one: a nationwide interdenominational effort (Cameroun)

"New Life for All" is a continuous nationwide in-depth evangelism program carried out by the National Evangelism Office of the Republic of Cameroun. The latter is an agency of the National Federation of Protestant Churches.

The aim of this continuous campaign is to organize all Protestant Christians to work together "for the proclamation of salvation in Jesus Christ to all the people of Cameroun before 1980." The means to achieve this goal is a mobilization program which has the following characteristics:

(i) *Prayer* — This is the "hub" on which the effort turns. Prayer cells have been organized and continue to be organized throughout the country, especially in the homes of believers.

(ii) *Instruction* — The idea here is to motivate believers for evangelism and to help the church experience growth through confrontation with the Word. This is done by the following activities:

Evangelistic institutes. These are held in every province at least once a year. They are geared for pastors, church officers, and catechists. They are usually five days in length and are divided into three parts: Bible studies, stressing the importance of right living; a practical seminar to show how to teach from the manuals and other materials that have been prepared by the National Committee; a practical witnessing experience in the neighborhood where the institute is held.

Bible study groups. Those who participate in the evangelistic institutes go back to their parishes and teach the handbook and other materials that have been studied. Every year new materials are developed so that the groups may be able to continue to grow and multiply their effectiveness by forming new groups in which the material learned can be shared with others. These groups spend additional time in fellowship and sharing. They have become strategic evangelistic outposts in the heavily Muslim northern region.

(iii) *Visitation* — Natural visitation efforts to neighbors and friends are encouraged. New contacts are stimulated — to help people in their needs and difficulties, especially the old, the poor and the sick; to become their personal friends; and to pray for them. These contacts may open up opportunities to share a personal word about Jesus Christ. Groups are also organized for systematic visitation, and once a year — on the Day of Pentecost — a National Day of Visitation is held where the entire Protestant Christian community is encouraged to go out in evangelistic visitation.

(iv) *Meetings* — Pastors are encouraged to frequently preach evangelistic sermons. Special evangelistic meetings are held at local congregations and occasionally city-wide crusades are held. But believers are advised "not to make the mistake of thinking that evangelization consists in big meetings and rallies. The evangelistic meetings must be carefully prepared in prayer, by Bible study, and home visitation."

(v) *Special efforts* — Every year there are special "Heli-Missions" that go on for a period of three months. These consist of special evangelistic and "diakonite" teams which are transported by helicopter into remote areas for periods of four to five days. The teams are mostly made up of lay leaders and specialized missionaries (medical doctors, rural development and literacy specialists, etc.). In addition, there are special school efforts geared toward the evangelization of students and the strengthening of Bible groups operating in the schools. There are also radio programs, mostly for believers, which are basically promotional and teaching efforts. They transmit news about the program and have been used on occasion to teach some of the manuals. To all of this must be added the bi-lingual (French and English) magazine, *Onward* (French *En Marche),* which is the largest Protestant magazine in the country and serves as a promotional literary arm of the effort.

(vi) *Evaluation and planning* — Once a year, the Executive Committee, made up of representatives of the various denominations represented in the Federation of Churches, comes together to evaluate the work done and to plan for the strengthening of the program on the basis of the evaluation. The seriousness with which this task is taken is one reason which accounts for the fruitfulness of the National Campaign of Evangelism.

2. Situation two: a denominational effort (South Vietnam)

Evangelism Deep and Wide (EDW) is an adaptable, continuous and progressive evangelistic program of the Evangelical Church of Vietnam (Christian and Missionary Alliance). Its purpose is to train the church "to effectively obey the Lord's command to go into all the world and preach the Gospel to every creature — winning them, discipling them, and baptizing them in the name of the Father, Son and Holy Spirit." There are two parts to this purpose which are implicit in the name of the program: (i) to deepen the church in its understanding of the Lord and the Scriptures, to the end that evangelism can become an ongoing activity. And (ii) to spread the Gospel over the entire country aiming at the (solid) evangelization of at least ten million Vietnamese in the next decade and their establishment into local congregations. The program is thus divided into a six-stage continuous cycle of activities to be carried out by each local congregation.

a. *Preparation* — Although EDW is an approved denominational program, each local congregation must decide for itself whether or not it wants to participate. Accordingly, the program begins with a stage of preparation. This involves an initial explanation by the National Committee to the pastor, his church board, and congregation. This may be explained at first to the pastor at a district meeting, but eventually all the available material must be studied carefully by the congregation.

Once the latter decides to participate in the program, a local five-member EDW committee is appointed. Each member is given a responsibility — the pastor is in charge of preparation, and each of the other members takes over one of the following responsibilities: prayer cells, training, outreach, and establishment.

The appointment of the committee is followed by a study of the church. This is done by the pastor with the help of the church executive committee, the EDW committee, and as many other laymen as desired. In this study the church's responsibility and strength are determined. The geographical area, population density and characteristics plus the religious situation are carefully considered through the aid of a questionnaire prepared by the National EDW Committee. Attention is also paid to "the different occupations represented in the church family, how many are active in present church affairs, and how many are interested in becoming active in the EDW program." This is followed by the setting of long-and-short-range goals. In the former, the church visualizes "the number of churches there should actually be within the area of their responsibility, in order to have the area fully evangelized." In the latter, the church sets a number of shorter goals "that eventually will bring it to its desired goal."

b. *Cells* — These are the key to the whole program. They are small clusters of believers in every local church that meet on a regular basis in homes under the leadership of laymen who have been trained and appointed by the local EDW committee. According to EDW leaders, these cells are the core of the mobilization thrust of the program. They serve as centers for prayer, biblical and practical evangelistic training, evangelistic outreach, and the establishment in the faith of new believers. These cells meet regularly at least twice a week — once for prayer, another time for training. During the year cycle, however, there is a specific period (two months) in which most of the time is spent in prayer, although with evangelistic overtones, since the specific purpose of the prayer meetings is to intercede for non-believers. As time advances and the program enters into new stages, the prayer cells become also training, evangelistic and follow-up centers.

c. *Training* — This too overlaps somewhat with other stages. In the Preparation phase there is training. Pastors, for example, are trained to lead the program. Every year they are brought together for further training. Key laymen are trained by the pastor and are further brought together for more training at zone schools. They, in turn, teach the rest of the church under the leadership of the pastor. The latter also uses the pulpit to instruct the congregation as a whole. Then there is the constant training of new believers — plus the family altars.

There is, however, a specific training stage where believers are trained by key laymen for evangelism and spiritual growth. These sessions take place at the level of the cells and are oriented around a reflection-action axis. That is, *they are not* all theory and no practice. Rather they seek to involve laymen in practical experience of evangelism at the same time that they are studying about it.

The whole program is dependent on a continuous educational thrust. It seeks to build up the spiritual life of believers, motivate and prepare them to share their faith with others personally, spontaneously and collectively, through their participation in house-to-house visitation, their contribution to special evangelistic meetings, and the establishment of new believers.

d. *Outreach* — After the training stage, the cells take a third specific function: they become the nucleus for evangelistic action. Witness bands are organized for the mobilization of every believer in the church and the execution of a clear plan of action. The bands map out the area of responsibility, dividing it into neighborhoods (or zones). They carry out a seed-sowing program using as a point of reference the areas where there are cells in existence but extending the outreach into new areas. The idea is not only to share the Gospel personally but to follow up the homes and individuals to whom the Gospel has been proclaimed, leading to the Lord those who so desire and channeling the new converts into the nearest cell.

In addition, specialized outreach groups are formed to reach businessmen, students, the military, etc., or to express God's love through social service. These groups are complemented by other supportive activities such as evangelistic meetings at the level of local congregations or city-wide, special radio and TV programs, correspondence courses, and newspaper evangelism.

But the key to the evangelistic outreach is the cells and the action of the Witness Band. Everything else, *including the large mass meetings,* are seen as supportive activities.

e. *Establishment* — An essential part of the program is the emphasis given to the establishment of new believers in the faith. This begins by the personal follow-up of the new convert, is followed by his incorporation into the nearest cell, is continued by the pastor in his baptismal class and the eventual involvement of the believer into the life of the church. In those areas where there are no churches, a nucleus of believers is formed and a new congregation is established.

3. Situation three: a program strategy for a local congregation (North America)

Goal-oriented Evangelism in Depth (GED) is a program strategy developed by In-Depth Evangelism Associates (IDEA) of Miami, Florida, for the implementation of a goal-oriented in-depth evangelism strategy for local congregations in the USA and Canada. Its objective is to involve local congregations in the process of total mobilization for the total evangelization of their communities with visible expressions of the unity of the body of Christ. They seek to accomplish this objective through the following steps.

a. *Where the church is headed — commitment.* Once a local church has had a chance to discuss the biblical goals of the GED strategy, they commit themselves to follow through with it for a minimum of one year. They are then counseled by a member of the staff of IDEA.

b. *Where the church is — research.* This is followed by the gathering of pertinent information to help the church find out where it is now. "For the initial year of GED, the information covers three areas": (i) Data about the community (" census statistics and other information describing the people living within the service area of the church — how many, their backgrounds, attitudes, and problems"). (ii) The past performance of the church (numerical growth rate, evangelistic activities, etc.) (iii) A congregational survey on a typical Sunday morning to get an idea on the congregation's level of personal witness, personal relationship with Christ, their brethren and neighbors.

c. *Where the church is — analysis.* Following the gathering of this information, a group of church leaders and other interested persons meet for a weekend retreat. They analyze together the meaning of the collected data. "As a result of this analysis process, there will be a sizable list of weaknesses and opportunities." From this list the "... group selects the priority concerns needing urgent attention related to both the community and church."

d. *How the church moves ahead — one year possibility goals.* At the same retreat, the group discusses each priority need identified and asks, "Where does the Lord Jesus want us to be one year from now?" "The answer becomes a one-year Possibility Goal for each area of need toward which the congregation will pray, plan and work."

e. *How the church moves ahead — program determination.* Task forces are then formed at the church with representation from the group that was present at the retreat. The latter is constituted as a core group with responsibility for the oversight of the program. Each is assigned a Possibility Goal and is responsible for the development of a set of activities that will achieve that goal, bearing in mind the principles of total mobilization and total evangelization with visible unity. The combined activities of the task forces become, then, the GED program for that year.

f. *How the church moves ahead — short-term goals.* Each activity will have both a date and a specific goal. This provides for periodic checkups and progress.

g. *How the church moves ahead — immediate action.* Each task force then determines who will do what, by when, where and how. Once this is approved by the core groups, it is launched.

h. *How the church continues to move ahead — evaluation.* From the moment the program is launched, evaluation starts with frequent checkups. Careful figures, statistics, and graphs permit the measurement of the Possibility Goals. At the end of the year, the congregations face up to the question: "How did we do?" This implies a thorough assessment of the program, the gathering of additional information and the setting of new goals.

i. *How the church continues to move ahead — recycling.* Before the end of the first year of GED, the church decides whether it wants to renew its commitment to the goals and strategy for another year. If it does, it re-cycles the steps of the program strategy but with its feet more firmly on the ground.

4. Situation four: a city-wide interdenominational effort (Santiago, Chile)

This is a program sponsored by the evangelical churches of Santiago in cooperation with the Institute of In-depth Evangelism of San José, Costa Rica. It is aimed at the integral growth of the church as defined above. It has four basic components which can be succinctly summarized in the code: PR²AC.

a. *Program components* — *P* stands for *preparation.* Time is dedicated to the creation of an enthusiastic, optimistic, and a spiritually renewed atmosphere conducive to the communication of the principles of in-depth evangelism. In addition, churches and leaders are recruited, committees are organized and materials selected.

R² stands for *renovating reflection.* An attempt is made to involve as many believers as possible in study and prayer, thereby setting the ground stage for a deep *spiritual* renewal that will equip them for a broader and deeper evangelistic action in their own neighborhoods. There are retreats for pastors, study and prayer cells, special youth congresses and deeper life meetings. In addition, information regarding the state of the church and the overall religious and social situation is gathered, analyzed and interpreted, at a popular level, to the participating groups. By means of the studies, the information gathered plus the dynamic input of the Holy Spirit gives believers fresh insights that permit them to set realistic penultimate evangelistic goals and formulate hard, bold plans to reach them. At the same time, it drives them to informal, personal evangelistic experiences.

A stands for *action.* Time is specifically set for the implementation of the evangelistic plan of action and the achievement of the established goals. It involves multiple evangelistic efforts — from house-to-house visitation to the formation of new congregations and the celebration of evangelistic crusades.

C stands for *consolidation.* That is, the strengthening of that which has been done. It involves, among other things, integration of new believers into the church, program evaluation and the possible re-cycling of certain activities with the goal of making evangelistic outreach and church growth a continuous process.

b. *Program implementation* — In Santiago, Chile, a highly industrialized metropolitan center which is politically, economically, and socially troubled, the program is being currently carried out for a period of four years. The program components are being implemented as follows:

(i) 1973, "Year of Preparation and Experimentation." Two districts of Santiago were selected for experimentation before tackling larger areas of the city. In spite of some difficulties, due to the socio-political conflicts in the country, there were churches that started the program cycle during that year. This trial experience proved invaluable because it not only brought into the open some practical difficulties, but also revealed important needs in the larger Santiago community and paved the way for the full implementation of the program.

(ii) 1974, "Year of Reconciliation and Renewal." The city as a whole is now the arena for the *Preparation* and *Renovating-Reflection* stages. Given the recent events that have taken place in Chile in the last several months, the emphasis on reconciliation and renewal has been identified as a felt need. The idea, then, is to lead believers in Santiago to live a reconciled life among one another, setting thereby a model of reconciliation for the secular community, and to experience a spiritual renewal that will lead to the revitalization of their witnessing vocation. Five pastoral retreats have been planned by geographical sectors. Study and prayer groups have been formed and will continue to be formed throughout the city. For the latter, a discipleship course that was prepared and used in the two experimental districts is currently being revised and will be published shortly. Continuous research is providing more detailed information regarding population sub-groups. Toward the middle of May, an evangelistic crusade geared toward reconciliation and renewal will be held with the participation of one of Latin America's leading evangelists. And given the openess for the Gospel discovered among the residents of the four eastern districts, and the limited number of congregations in their respective neighborhoods, a special emphasis is being made on the organization of home Bible studies that may lead, in due time, to the formation of new congregations. Some were already organized in 1973 on an experimental basis and have proven to be very effective.

(iii) 1975, "Year of Evangelistic Penetration and Discipling." This corresponds roughly to the *Action* and *Consolidation* phases of the program. Theoretically, the fuller development of these phases will need to await the results and evaluation of this year's activities. Nevertheless, the following activities are already anticipated: unlimited evangelistic efforts, organization of churches from the study groups, and special efforts to reach social groupings — such as university students, labor unions, women, youth, professionals and businessmen, etc.

(iv) 1976, "Year of Total Church Development." This will involve work with denominations in helping them set goals for recycling efforts on their own. It will also involve special activities with key congregations to help them expand further their range of ministry, if possible, to the regions beyond. Finally, there will be a comprehensive evaluation of the program and a study of the feasibility of carrying it out in a nearby city such as Valparaiso.

What do these four different situations show? First, that In-Depth evangelistic programs are relative to the needs, cultural characteristics, historical circumstances, and resources of the church everywhere. *There are no fixed program patterns.*

Second, that the In-Depth *strategy* is applicable on any continent, to any historical and ecclesiastical situation. It can be applied in a local congregation as well as in an entire denomination, in a city-wide setting as well as in a national interdenominational context, in Africa and North America as well as in Asia and Latin America.

Third, that even the principles of the In-Depth strategy vary in emphasis from place to place. Thus, multiple structural action may be emphasized in one place, while in another the emphasis may be on local congregations; some may put more emphasis on planning and research, others on action and outreach. They all strike a common chord: the mobilization of the church with all of her resources for the continuous propagation of the Gospel at all levels of society.

Fourth, that as a movement, In-Depth Evangelism is, theoretically and practically, a project in the making. No one can claim to live up to its high vision nor to fully comprehend all of its implications nor to successfully fulfill all he has understood.

Even so, In-Depth Evangelism remains a formidable prophetic movement in the midst of a divided, evangelistically troubled church. Firmly rooted in solid biblical principles, the witness and example of the early primitive Christian community, and the urgency of our time, it challenges the church around the world:

To be what God meant her to be — a dynamic organism with an imperative worldwide, comprehensive witnessing vocation.

To re-orient her priorities in order to fulfill her calling.

To analyze and evaluate her past and present performance.

To reflect seriously on God's Word, the complicated nature and state of the world and the best way to use the gifts that he has given each and every believer in the expansion of his kingdom.

To take seriously the imperative of manifesting visibly and concretely the unity of the Christian faith so that the world may believe.

Above all, to stop talking about evangelism and start acting evangelistically in every sphere of her life, so that the knowledge of Christ may truly cover the earth as the waters cover the sea.

IN DEPTH EVANGELIZATION PROGRAMS REPORT

Secretary: H. Payne

The group was quite representative with participants from a dozen different countries scattered from the Americas to India with widely differing cultures and problems. Thus it was impossible to establish an "average" profile of the group though there were many points of similarity between countries.

Much time was given to discussing the foundational elements of In Depth Evangelization Programs:

1. What the church should be as an evangelizing force. (a family for fellowship, a school for instruction, a team for action.)
2. The need for a complete and authentic message, e.g., Gospel.
3. A knowledge of, and contact with, the world of our day.
4. Mobilization: what it means and requires of the church, i.e., motivation, recruiting, organization, supervision, sacrificial action, thinking big.

The ultimate goal was defined as a change of the churches' life-style. This is to be accomplished through a mental transformation of Christians in their attitude and concepts regarding evangelism, the world and the church.

Intermediate goals were:

1. To place evangelism at the center of the churches' life.
2. That social concern be the natural and necessary fruit of a holy life instead of an artificial appendage.
3. Revitalization of the pulpit.
4. Reestablishment of genuine unity in the church.

Eventual action steps proposed in planning and implementing of this new strategy:

1. Research and analysis of the situation and the church.
2. Information, inspiration and motivation of churches and leaders.
3. Recruiting of helpers and staff.
4. Organization, training and action in local churches.
5. Efforts of evangelism on a regional or national level.
6. Follow-up evaluation, recycling, continuation.

Resources required:

1. A definite plan of action.
2. Convinced, effective leadership in proportion to size of project.
3. Reasonable unity among cooperating missions, churches and denominations.
4. Adequate literature for: publicity, communication, training, evangelism and follow-up adapted to the situation.
5. Finances.

Vital questions and answers that were discussed.

1.   Can Christian work maintain its integrity if it accepts the cooperation of non-christians?

Answer: Yes, if the whole Christian message is constantly coming through and being demonstrated in a vital way through all its activities.

2.   Must all that the Church does be aimed at evangelism?

Answer: No, but evangelism is the chief task of the church and should influence and leaven all it does.

3.   Is evangelism a testimony of personal experience or an obedience to Scripture?

Answer: It is both, but it is more, as shown in the opening paragraphs on foundational elements of in depth-evangelism.

4.   How does one bring about the transformation in church mentality, necessary to successful in-depth evangelism?

Answer: Change the classic Bible study hour into a discipleship class and develop a theology of evangelism.

5.   What constitutes "mobilization"? When can we say a church is really mobilized?

Answer: Jesus had 12 Apostles. When we have a sufficient number of key people to move the whole church we can consider that group as mobilized. We must win key people, mobilizing the "structures of the church, revitalizing the pulpit, making it contagious.

6.   Is salvation only individual or can it be corporate and "cosmic"?

Answer: Romans 8:22 seems to indicate that the whole creation has been touched by sin and will partake in the redemption or "restoration of all things" cf. Job 15:15; Isa. 65:17; Rev. 21:1. Tribal, clan and corporate conversion were not fully discussed.

7.   What about social concern?

Answer: It must be an integral, vital part of witness, not an "additive," nor an afterthought. The Gospel is for the whole man. We should be careful that our "passion for souls" does not lead us to forget the whole personality. Love that does not see and feel physical need is not love at all. Jesus said, "I was sick, hungry, thirsty, naked and in prison and you visited me and ministered to me." Matt. 25:35-45.

This is a many-sided matter. Prosperous and literate Europeans have their needs as much as third world aboriginal tribes and nations. We must learn to love to the point that we can discern the human needs of those to whom we have been sent, and minister to them.

8.   Will in-depth evangelization work in conservative, sceptical Christianized Europe or America?

Answer: It is a basic premise of in-depth evangelization strategy that all principles must be adapted to local and different situations. Obviously God has his times and his ways. We cannot say, in any situation, "Do this and you are sure to succeed." Yet Jesus said to his brothers (John 7:6) "Your time is always ready." The Christians must decide, and when God has spoken to them, they will feel responsibility for carrying through. Often it is the leaders who stand in the way. Sometimes it may take longer and we may have to begin with smaller "pilot projects" to demonstrate the sense of this strategy. People learn by "seeing" and doing. It has proven effective to start with weekly lay contact meetings for information and motivation.

The question of a continuing association or communication network was raised with a view to mutual encouragement and in formation, but it was felt that the office of in-depth evangelization in San Jose, Costa Rica, was functioning and would best serve as an agent for inspiration and interchange of materials and methods.

THE SOCIAL RESPONSIBILITIES OF EVANGELIZATION

George Hoffman

Jesus said, "I came that they may have life, and have it more abundantly" (John 10:10), or, as the New English Bible translates it, "life in all its fulness." If we are concerned to follow in the steps of our Lord Jesus Christ, we too must come to people prepared to share this life "in *all* its fulness."

As Christians for whom the Bible is authoritative, we have just as much (if not more) right to be concerned for man's total development as anyone. Unfortunately, in the debate on development, the evangelical voice has seldom been heard, largely through our own default, and once again we have retreated from, if not wholly evacuated, yet another area where we have let other Christian and non-Christian voices and programs dominate the scene, preoccupied with man's "horizontal" development at the expense of being concerned for man's *total* welfare — yet another casualty perpetuated by the false dichotomy between the so-called "social" and "spiritual" gospels. Dr. Visser't Hooft, in his retiring speech as general secretary of the World Council of Churches, put it succinctly at the Uppsala Assembly, "A Christianity which has lost its vertical dimension has lost its salt, and is not only insipid in itself, but useless to the world. But a Christianity which would use the vertical dimension as a means to escape from responsibility for and in the common life of men is a denial of the incarnation of God's life for the world manifested in Christ."

Trevor Beeson, a left-wing radical Christian writer in England, has drawn attention to this unresolved tension between those who emphasize the "horizontal" ministry and those who emphasize the "vertical" ministry. And he laid the blame on "the absence of an adequate theology to undergird the great program of social action." As evangelicals, surely we believe that we have such a theology. The question is, have we the compassion? And have we the concern to match such a theology?

Good citizens

One of our shortcomings lies in the fact that because we do not agree with *all* that some men say, we tend therefore not to listen to anything that they have to say. Take, for instance, that avant-garde theologian of Cambridge, Dr. John Robinson, former bishop of Woolwich. Although, for instance we could not see eye to eye with him in his book *Honest to God,* we cannot but recognize some of the biblical truths he expounds in a later work *On Being the Church in the World.* In it he focuses attention on God's rule throughout society, and our role within that society. He draws particular attention to Paul's use of the world *"politeia"* (citizenship) in his Epistle to the Philippians, and he sees significance in the fact that although a Christian's ultimate "citizenship" is in heaven, Paul recognizes the importance of our citizenship here on earth. For in Phil. 1:27, the Apostle uses the same word when he refers to our "manner of life" within society. A more suitable translation could in fact read "behave worthily as citizens." Consequently, John Robinson argues that there is no department of the world's life into which we as Christians are not commissioned to go. "They find themselves concerned with evangelization and with civilization." In other words, "being worthy of the Gospel of Christ" means not only a concern for evangelization, it also involves a concern for civilization. It was no doubt with this understanding in mind, together with his breadth of vision for the whole of God's world, that Dr. Billy Graham wrote in his book *World Aflame,* "We as Christian citizens have no right to be content with our social order until the principles of Christ are applied to all men."

Bringing deliverance

This Congress has taken for its mandate the words recorded in Luke's Gospel, chapter 4, where Jesus states that he is commissioned to preach the good news to the poor, to proclaim release to the captives, and recovering of sight to the blind, and to set at liberty those who are oppressed. If we are to make this mandate meaningful we must of necessity meet people as Jesus did, at their point of need. For if we consider each of these specific injunctions and see how Jesus expounded and explained them, both in his teaching and ministry to people in their need, the social implications of the Gospel will drive us to social involvement for the sake of the Gospel.

In *"One World - One Task,"* the report of the British Evangelical Alliance Commission on World Mission, there is an appendix on Christian Mission and Christian Service. There Andrew Walls draws attention to God's creation mandate to subdue the earth and care for its inhabitants. "The proper use of the planet is therefore the direct concern of the Christian as a man in Christ: it is part of his obedience as man." Mr. Walls goes on to say, "Questions of world poverty, of world food supply, of all the vast infra-structure of health, medicine, education, and government which undergird it, are his direct concern because God has so instructed man, and because they are duties of man as man. He can work wholeheartedly with other men, even if they do not know his Lord, in fulfillment of the mandate. These things cannot be treated either as a distraction from the Gospel, or as a sort of bribe to make it more palatable: they are part of man's response to the first command God gave him."

If, then, we are going to take seriously the words of our Lord Jesus Christ and bring deliverance to the captives, it will embrace deliverance from the constant threat of exploitation; deliverance from the indignity of a lifetime of servitude and unemployment; deliverance from the menace of death by starvation and malnutrition; deliverance from the threat of disease and chronic ill-health through insanitary living conditions and the degrading squalor of some of our urban ghettos. These must all be seen as part and parcel of bringing deliverance to the captives of poverty, injustice, exploitation, and neglect. To talk and speak of just a "spiritual deliverance" is to truncate and devalue the glorious Gospel of our Lord Jesus Christ. And, argues Canon Michael Green in *Runaway World,* "Unless Christians share his love for people, his hatred of poverty and disease and ignorance no less than sin, then their religion is not the religion of Jesus, whatever they may claim."

Remember the poor

In his book, *The Social Conscience of the Evangelical,* Sherwood Eliot Wirt declares that the whole Bible could be considered from the sociological viewpoint as a defense of the poor. A casual glance at a concordance makes it abundantly clear that God has a continuing concern for the poor, a concern which he discharges through his people. It was a concern that became incarnate in Christ. The very fact that the poor had a share in the Gospel was one of the Messianic signs that he told the disciples to share with John the Baptist. When the church sent out Barnabas and Paul on their mission to the Gentiles, the one and only obligation they laid upon them was to "remember the poor," "which very thing," said Paul, "I was eager to do." Echoing the words of Deut. 15:11, Jesus reminded us that we shall always have the poor with us, and "whenever you will, you can do good to them" (Mark 14:7). "By implication," says Hendriksen commenting on the parallel passage in John 12:8, "Jesus is saying to the Church of all ages that the care of the poor is its responsibility and privilege." And along with the responsibility and privilege there is the threatened judgment and reward recorded in Matthew 25. And it is no good looking for an escape clause in confining the words of our Lord either to a previous dispensation or to a narrowly circumscribed Christian community. As John Calvin says in his commentary on Matt. 25:45, "Christ is either neglected or honored in the persons of those who need our assistance. So then, when we are reluctant to assist the poor, may the Son of God come before our eyes, to whom to refuse anything is a monstrous sacrilege."

The economic equation that threatens mankind

It used to be said that the greatest threat to mankind was the Einstein equation which split the atom. This threat has now been replaced by an economic equation which divides the world: 25 per cent of the world's population enjoy 75 per cent of the world's wealth, whilst 75 per cent of the world's population are left to eke out an existence on the remaining 25 per cent that is left. In Colin Morris' eloquent plea *Include Me Out,* he forecasts a revolution that will convulse the planet and "expose our present ferment in the church as the gentle eccentricity of those who pick the flowers on the slopes of a rumbling volcano." You see, the developing countries have now become convinced that continuation of suffering from hunger, ignorance, disease, and injustice is *not* inevitable. At the Third World Medical Conference on Medical Education it was stated that "they no longer believe it is a rule of nature, or a law of God that they should be born to misery and hasten to an early grave." This is the spirit that won political independence for over 700 million people in Asia and Africa in the last three decades. They want freedom, but they also want food and homes and health and work and play. They no longer want the world to be divided, as an Indian writer has said, "between people whose vocabulary includes the word 'holiday,' and the rest."

Now I, for one, don't believe that in Psalm 146 God's roles as Provider *for* the poor and Defender *of* the poor are put in juxtaposition by accident. "Happy is he whose help is the God of Jacob, who executes justice for the oppressed, who gives food to the hungry" (verse 7). And there are many who argue that throughout the emerging nations, the hungry will never be given adequate food until justice for the oppressed has been executed in their land.

Take South America, for example: the economic sickness of Latin America is aggravated by the fact that 10 per cent of the population controls 90 per cent of the land. In Brazil, for instance, two thousand people own land enough to make collectively a territory larger than the combined area of Italy, Holland, Belgium, and Denmark. In Chile, before President Allende came into power, 2 per cent of the population owned 52 per cent of the land. The root of the trouble in many of these Latin American republics is the fact that the aristocracy constitutes an "establishment" power pattern which, often reinforced by the Roman Catholic Church, is tied in with government. The effect is that in many countries society stagnates rather than develops and human life is degraded by hunger and disease. Millions of people are denied the opportunity of realizing their potential as human beings (i.e., the quest for the "Humanum" to use the words of the secular theologian) and of participating fully and genuinely in the life of society.

To deal with the root of this problem, many would argue that the socio-economic system *must* be changed. The imbalance *must* be rectified. New and more *just* relationships between rich and poor *must* be created. To change the system, to put right the imbalance between rich and poor is the responsibility of those who hold power and those who can influence that power, to insure that the system be changed. To bring pressure to bear on those who wield power is then the responsibility of all who believe in justice and human right. In his book *Don't Sleep Through the Revolution,* Dr. Paul Rees quotes Ruben Lores, formerly of the Latin American Mission and one of the pioneers of Evangelism-in-Depth. "Today all over Latin America there is turmoil for a change not only of the *conditions* but of the *patterns.* We must have either accelerated political evolution or a chaotic revolution."

Of course, there are those who read about the Maoist infiltration into East Africa and the Marxist insurgents in South America, and dismiss these particular problems of the developing countries as an exaggerated Communist plot. But it is both irresponsible and dangerously naive to dismiss the social and political unrest of the so-called "Third World" as simply the work of the Communists. "If our social insights go no deeper than that," says Paul Rees, "we are re-enacting Rip Van Winkle — sleeping through a revolution." Therefore, I believe we need to state, along with Samuel Escobar, that although evangelicals respect the state and the structures in which they live, we are not afraid of change, nor do we link the destiny of the church to the subsistence of particular forms of social and political organization. Dr. John Stott reminds us in *Christ the Controversialist* that it has "not been characteristic of evangelicals in the past to be shy of social action or even, when necessary, of political action."

The quest for justice

We need to recognize what the Old Testament teaches, namely that one of the characteristics of a society which has rejected God's law is injustice. And one of the roles of the prophets speaking in God's name and on behalf of God's people was to condemn injustice, exploitation, and the abuse of power. In the face of the present situation, is this role any less reduced today? You see, it is no good just loving a man condemned to a life sentence of poverty and oppression, while at the same time we remain silent regarding these factors which are responsible for them. "Love is not a substitute for justice," said Leighton Ford speaking at the U.S. Congress of Evangelism in Minneapolis, "and since not all men are or will be converted to Christ, and since even we Christians have imperfect love, we have a responsibility to seek justice in society."

The Foreign Minister of Tanzania said the future of Christian churches in Africa would be determined by the way they defended justice, freedom, and human rights, and so created conditions for peace. Opening a conference of senior Anglican clergy in Africa earlier this year he questioned why the church had not condemned outright apartheid, colonialism, and exploitation in Africa. And he asked, "Is it simply that the church is blind to injustice?"

But in our quest for justice one of our distinguishing marks as Christians must be a concern for people and not particular political theories. Archbishop William Temple pointed out in his introduction to *Christian Social Reformers of the 19th Century* that Shaftesbury, like Wilberforce, was stirred by sympathy for individuals. "He had no theories about the Rights of Labour or any such abstractions. He was no democrat, and he actively disliked Trade Unions. But his conscience protested at the conditions under which men, women, and, above all, children were working in the factories. So he became the pioneer of factory legislation, deliberately invading the sphere of industrial and economic organization in the name of humanity and at the dictation of Christian faith." The world cries out for such Christ-like invaders today.

If we really are concerned, then, to extend "the abundant life" as Jesus expounded it, we shall have to grapple far more seriously and strenuously with those factors in society which prevent men from enjoying life in all its fullness. We shall have to give far more attention to causes instead of being preoccupied with effects — with the disease more than with the symptoms. Although we shall always be called, as Jesus was, to render "first aid" to the casualties of a sick society, we must be more prepared to speak out and to influence those things which cause corruption, prejudice, and victimization within our societies. Jesus did. And so must we if we are to follow in his footsteps.

"You give them something to eat"

Over 250 years ago, Jonathan Swift, the Irish writer and journalist, stated, "Whoever could make two ears of corn or two blades of grass to grow upon a spot of ground where only one grew before, would deserve better of mankind and do more essential service to his country than the whole race of politicians put together." An overstatement? Maybe in the comparison. But surely not in the sentiments expressed — especially when one regards the conditions prevalent in our modern world.

The magazine *The New Internationalist* reports that "the world's food is so precariously balanced that one more season of shortage could lead to global disaster." Already seventeen countries of the world face serious or perennial food shortages, and another thirteen are in danger of shortages. And it is estimated the total number of people affected is 950 million, about one-third of the world's total population.

Jesus still says to his followers through his Word, "You give them something to eat" (Matt. 14:16). If we are to redress the imbalance in the world and meet the basic need of man, as well as obeying the teaching of our Master, we shall have to divert our energies and potential resources to developing and preserving our neglected agricultural potential throughout the world. As René Padilla states in his paper, "There is no place for statistics on how many souls die without Christ every minute, if they do not take into account how many of those who thus die, die victims of hunger."

According to A.H. Boerma, the Director General of Food and Agricultural Organization, the world food situation is more difficult than at any time since the years immediately following the devastation of the second world war. In a period when the world's population increased by 75 million mouths, world food production has actually declined. This is the startling and disturbing conclusion that the F.A.O. comes to in its annual report, "The State of Food and Agriculture 1973." And if up until now it has been easy for the developed countries to dismiss food shortage as not their problem, the F.A.O. points out that for the first time in years the developed countries are going short as well.

In Psalm 65 the psalmist praises God for visiting the earth and watering it. He is acknowledged as the God of the whole world, "who greatly enriches it." But, the riches that God intends to be shared by everyone, have been hoarded and squandered, devastated and destroyed by a minority. While God on the one hand enriches the earth, it is man who through his selfishness has impoverished it and limited its resources. Nearly 70 per cent of the people living throughout the developing countries depend upon agriculture for their livelihood and by 1985 this number is expected to increase to nearly 90 per cent. And yet between one-third and one-half of the world's population suffers from malnutrition while only 10 per cent of the world's arable land is actually cultivated.

In our socio-economic programs a much higher priority must be given to the rural developments with the utilization of intermediate technology at local level. In these programs people must be helped to help themselves recognizing that the success of any program is directly proportional to the amount of local input in the way of planning, indigenous materials, assumed responsibility, and willingness to work.

Take the "Faith and Farm" project in Nigeria, for example. It is geared primarily for the farmer and his household who make up 95 per cent of the population of Nigeria. The aim of this highly succesful project is to train African Christians to teach other farmers and their families to recognize that Jesus Christ is Lord of every part of their lives. As a result, starchy, low-yielding crops have been replaced by nutritional foods with reinforced proteins. Inefficient hand-tools have been replaced by more practical instruments. Harvested crops have been properly stored and protected from the ravages of white ants and other termites. But more. Children sick and dying from disease and malnutrition have been given a new lease of life by a regular reinforced diet, and thousands of unemployed school-leavers have been given not only useful occupations but a new-found dignity and a fulfillment in a rewarding enterprise.

Interest in everyday problems

In the northeast area of Nigeria, where the work has been extended, one incident took place which is not in isolation, and serves to illustrate the evangelistic by-product of this kind of program. One of the Faith and Farm agents saved the grain store of a Muslim and his family and protected his valuable millet and guinea corn against destruction by white ants. This was all the food that the family had for the year. Quietly the African Christian farmer shared his skill and knowledge as he worked alongside the Muslim farmer in preserving his crops. Later the Muslim inquired, "What makes you give up your time and come to help me?" The farmer replied, "Because we want to be like our Master, Jesus Christ, who fed the people when they were hungry." And that day the Muslim farmer listened with sympathy to the Gospel message for the first time, and he began to understand it. Another Faith and Farm worker explained that the better yields on his own farm were due to the powder he mixed with the seed before sowing in order to keep the insects away. His pagan neighbor agreed to try it for himself. It worked. And a venture developed because the pagan neighbor began to learn that the Christian God, through his servants, is interested in his everyday problems.

In another area of Africa a group of Christians in Western Dahomey realized that to stay on their over-populated, worn-out land was not honoring to God; furthermore, as one leader expressed it, to continue working hard and getting practically nothing for it brought you to the point where you began doubting your own ability. Next to go, he added, was your self-respect. They moved therefore to an area about a hundred kilometers away and soon found themselves welcoming non-Christians to the settlements. Within a short time, nearly all the strangers had become Christians. So began a movement that has proved to be as much an evangelistic enterprise as an agricultural one, with some school-leavers seeing for the first time a future in the type of farming the settlements offered. Before long there were nine of these settlements, each started by a small group of Christians which grew as more people joined them.

Our development programs, then, must be more comprehensive and inter-related, crossing the traditional lines of demarcation. For instance, we can help a man to grow more food, but that is of little value if we do not teach him how to store that food without much of it being eaten by insects. We can teach a man how to grow food of better nutritional value, but there is little point to it if we neglect to show him how to make sure that the water he drinks is free from disease.

Development with dignity

It has been said that when a man has lost his dignity he has lost everything. And that is the first thing he loses when he becomes unemployed. He loses the respect of his neighbors. He loses the respect of his family. But worse. He loses respect for himself. This is one of the major sociological problems in the aftermath of disaster or national upheaval. But here, as in so many other areas, "man's extremity becomes God's opportunity."

In one of our rehabilitation programs in Bangladesh, we had the privilege of supporting a dynamic young New Zealand missionary, Peter McNee. In the course of eighteen months he built over 1,200 houses in the Chandpur district that had been devastated by the civil war. But not only has he rehoused whole communities — he has helped to restore their dignity by helping them to help themselves. The houses we built together cost no more than 50 pounds each, because the local people rebuilt their own houses with timber and corrugated sheeting purchased by TEAR Fund under the supervision and direction of Peter McNee who taught more than twenty local Bengali carpenters with his "on-the-job-training" techniques. Recently, the Bengali foreman who was Peter McNee's right-hand man was soundly converted to Christ through what he saw in the life as well as through what he heard from the lips of this dedicated young Baptist missionary.

"Give a man a fish and you feed him for a day," says the Chinese proverb, "Teach him how to fish and you feed him for life." We have been able to prove the wisdom of this philosophy in this same area of Bangladesh with this same remarkable young man. Utilizing the local jute products, we have again helped to restore the dignity of whole communities of unemployed Bengalis by teaching them how to make jute handicrafts. In one village the program was introduced with seven pence worth of jute: now the village is self-supporting with a turnover of 250 pounds worth of goods per month.

Across the border in India, TEAR Fund has been able to assist EFICOR (The Evangelical Fellowship of India's Committee on Relief) which has a similar vision of restoring the dignity of men and women who are being mercilessly exploited by unscrupulous businessmen making colossal profits at the workers' expense. In Bombay, for instance, we have located women who are slaving (that seems the only appropriate word) for 75 paise per day (approximately 3 1/2 pence) cutting watch-straps for plastic toy watches. Others put clips on elastic bands for which they get 6 paise per gross!

Now, in case corrugated sheeting, jute handicrafts, and plastic watch-straps sound a little out of place in a paper of this kind, and at a conference of this nature, may I remind you of what the Apostle Paul wrote to Titus, "Those who have come to belive in God should see that they engage in honourable occupations, which are not only honourable in themselves, but also useful to their fellowmen" (3:8). And again, "Our own people must be taught to engage in employment to produce the necessities of life; they must not be unproductive" (3:14).

An overriding concern, then, for the dignity of man gives motivation to our involvement in the working conditions of men and the provision for the unemployed who are often the victims of a corrupt society or the unfair distribution of wealth within that society. Referring to the situation in India, P.T. Chandapilla, General Secretary of the Union of

Evangelical Students of India said, "Evangelicals must do something more than they have ever done to affect the political and economic progress of national development. In the area of national commitment evangelicals are quite backward. Either they live in India as citizens of heaven, or with loose feet longing for citizenship in some western country." Sad to say, those words are not confined to India: they are universal.

Functional literacy

One of the major factors retarding the growth and development of large communities in developing countries is the widespread illiteracy. But in tackling this particular problem, one recognizes a basic mistake that we have made in the past and which must not be repeated in the future. Literacy must be seen as a means to an end, and not an end in itself. Ultimately it can do far more harm than good to impart, or at times impose, our more sophisticated patterns of academic education per se. All we succeed in doing is making dissatisfied people into educated people but still dissatisfied, because we have failed to relate their education to life. One still hears humorous (or horrifying?) stories of rural schools in Africa where they are taught the history of the Tudor times in England and unmeaningful geographical facts about a world outside they will never see or meet, and at the same time are left ignorant of how to develop their own land, raise their animals, tend their crops, and care for their family. Functional literacy, or work-oriented literacy, is one of the greatest needs we must be prepared to give time to, if we really are concerned to make men whole and are going to tackle the cause of the problem and not just treat the symptoms. "In the Philippines," points out Dennis E. Clark in his lively book *Mission in the Seventies*, "educators now realize that the thousands of unemployable college graduates in India or Pakistan would have been better equipped with a technical school preparation, a business course, or agricultural training."

Functional literacy not only serves to meet the needs of the community, it gives motivation which is often lacking through disenchantment of seeing the effects — or lack of lasting effects — from the old academic literacy system which has been responsible for creating ghettos of educated but unemployed dissidents. Functional literacy very simply seeks to identify the local and immediate problems of a community, and gear its visual aids, vocabularies, and primers to solving those problems.

As the people outline their difficulties and begin to discuss the possible answers, they will then see their need for a certain amount of literacy work. They will see the need to understand diagrams, to count, and to work out simple calculations for the area of their land — for instance, the number of plants required, and how much feed is required to keep their cattle or poultry healthy. These very practical and down-to-earth matters help them to recognize the value of becoming literate and to put into practice what they are learning.

Joseph Jibi, the leader of a Faith and Farm project in Nigeria, wrote, "People have to be taught not only how to grow their vegetables, but also how to use them. Only when they understand the importance of fruit and vegetables in their diet will people come to use them in everyday life." This is functional education par excellence.

In different parts of Africa this simple system is being worked out most effectively in areas that are cultivating bananas and other nutritional crops. More widely, the system is being employed to good effect in the field of what is known as "home economics" — again a very simple but very effective, down-to-earth, relevant, and meaningful improvement not only in educating people, but in raising their living standards and hopes for becoming self-sufficient and self-supporting, and at the same time improving the general health, hygiene, and welfare of their own families.

No wealth without health

The renowned British Prime Minister, Benjamin Disraeli, once said that the wealth of a nation lay in the health of her people. Now although the subject of medicine is being covered in a separate session, I am sure that our medical colleagues would want us to recognize the contribution of medicine toward "fulness of life." In a day when the World Health Organization informs us that 100 million people die or are disabled every year in developing countries because of a shortage of people with even the most elementary medical training, we cannot look upon medical ministry merely as an avenue for evangelism — a means to an end. It is part and parcel of the church's total mission, that is, if we are to be true to the commission and example of our Master, "who went about doing good and healing all that were oppressed by the devil" (Acts 10:38). It was part of his tripartite ministry that is clearly spelled out in Matt. 9:35, where we are told that "Jesus went about all their cities and villages, teaching in their synagogues and preaching the gospel of the kingdom, and healing every disease and infirmity. As Dr. Kenneth Scott argues in *The New Era in Medical Missions,* medical missions are not a superfluous or even an accessory responsibility of the organized Christian world. They are fundamental, along with preaching and teaching.

A missionary doctor, writing from West Africa, believes that the first thing he has to offer that will be seen and accepted is his professional ability and integrity, "That is what we are expected to have," he writes, "and, to begin with, that is the only thing that is wanted. From that point slowly we may hope to proceed. When there is respect, one can expect liking to come in, and then, the Lord willing, fellowship and Christian love." At another conference I had the privilege of sharing in, a young missionary doctor who is also a first-class surgeon shared with the conference some of the questions he had been forced to ask himself in his medical work in East Africa relating to public health programs and the setting up of a "kwashiorkor" clinic. At first he had been plagued by the question, "Am I being a missionary? How many people am I winning for Christ?" This, he argued, was leading him up a back alley, until the Lord spoke to him and gave him peace in his own heart, helping him to see "that I was doing it because the Lord had commanded me to be compassionate, and I knew he wanted me to be a doctor. I am not just doing medical missionary work," he said, "in order to win people for Christ, but to care for people for the sake of Christ." And I thought later of something that Samuel Escobar wrote in his *Social Responsibility and the Church in Latin America,* when he took some Christians to task for having a guilty conscience over their schools and hospitals and health centers. "If in them we evangelize, splendid; but let us not use them," he argued, "as a medium of coercion to force upon others the Gospel. It is not necessary. In themselves, they are the expression of Christian maturity." Life in all its fullness, then, cannot be proclaimed *in vacuo* — neglecting the command and the example of our Lord Jesus Christ, who brought "wholeness" to people who were in need of healing. But let us not fall into the trap of looking upon this ministry as a disguised form of evangelism, for as John Taylor rightly concludes in his book *For all the World,* "There is nothing in the Gospel that suggests either that Jesus healed men, or that he gave his healing powers to others, in order to make disciples." His healing ministry was an extension of his total mission and an expression of his love. Love without strings, "Not just in word or in speech, but in deed and truth."

The whole Gospel to the whole man

In this sketchy and all too inadequate glance at some of the social implications of the Gospel, I have tried, by way of illustration, to underline what Senator Mark Hatfield states in his collection of addresses, *Conflict and Conscience,* where he argues very clearly that we must find viable means to relate the Good News to the turmoil of our era. We must see, with him, that there is no point in wasting time and energy answering questions that nobody is asking. There is no purpose in harnessing our talents today to fight the theological battles of yesterday at the expense of the *real* socio-theological problems that will confront us tomorrow. "As we have addressed ourselves to the theological problems of organic evolution in the past," says Senator Hatfield, "let us turn to the theological problems of social revolution in the present. To do less is to concern ourselves with only half of the Gospel."

I wonder, then, if we are being recalled to reconsider our whole strategy of Christian service and evangelism and to recognize that the time is limited when we can embark on evangelistic enterprises per se at the expense of the total welfare of the people we are seeking to save. Is this not the unscriptural luxury of a bygone era? And, by force of circumstances, e.g., the restriction being enforced upon missionary activities concerned solely with evangelism, are we not being driven back to the example of our Lord Jesus Christ who was concerned to take the whole Gospel to the whole man? Is it fair to conclude that many of our Christian campaigns are unreal and unbiblical because of their sole preoccupation with man's spiritual welfare? These are questions we are being forced to ask.

Furthermore, as Marshall McLuhan has reminded us, "The medium *is* the message." So too is the messenger, and the manner in which he communicates his message. Form cannot be divorced from content, nor vice versa.

Moreover, living in our "global village" with its increasingly interlocking cultures and network of communications, our societies themselves are becoming increasingly interdependent. So too must our ministry. Again, as Senator Hatfield puts it, "We as evangelicals must regain sensitivity to the corporateness of human life. We must become sensitive to issues of social morality as well as to issues of private morality. We must learn to repent of and respond to collective guilt as well as individual guilt. This becomes increasingly important as the structures of life become more interdependent and interrelated. An ethic which deals solely with personal morals is singularly inadequate if it fails to deal with war, poverty, and racial antagonism as well."

If as Christians we believe that we are called to "bear one another's burdens," we must know what it means to share one another's burdens. I recall that someone once asked Solon the great Greek lawmaker, how justice could be achieved in Athens. "It can be achieved," he replied, "if those people who are not directly affected by wrong are just as indignant about it as those who are personally hurt." May such indignation drive us to a more real fulfillment of our task in bringing fullness of life to those we seek to serve.

THE SOCIAL RESPONSIBILITIES OF EVANGELIZATION REPORT

Secretary: J. Raymond Knighton

*Several strategy groups were arranged
spontaneously by participants at the
Congress. This report is from one of those
groups*

We believe that the meeting of human need in whatever form it confronts us is simply obedience to the command of God and a "faithful confession of the Gospel of Christ" (II Cor. 9:13).

We rediscovered the interrelation of privilege and responsibility. For instance, when we enjoy the privilege of proclaiming Jesus Christ as Lord, we have the consequent responsibility to express this servant relationship in service to others (II Cor. 4:5). Proclamation then can never be divorced from service. Again, as St. Paul stated, "I have completed the Gospel of Christ" (Rom. 15:19).

We believe that it is not coincidental that this interrelation has been a recurring theme throughout this Congress. "It is in our service," said John Stott, "that we can find the right synthesis between evangelism and social action." René Padilla reminded us that "together with the kerygma and the didache went the diaconia." Michael Green warned us that "we cannot isolate these constituents of mission without destroying them and devaluing the Gospel." As a result of this emphasis we recognize "that which God has joined together," we as evangelicals should not put assunder.

We affirm, therefore, that our social action and compassionate service are not to be considered as a form of bribe to make the evangel more palatable. Not only is it unnecessary, it is unbiblical as our compassionate service and social action are essential constituents of our total Christian mission. We do not believe, therefore, in evangelization through social service but recognize that social service must be part of our evangelization, being in itself an essential expression of the love of God for his world.

We deplored the disparities and the uneven distribution of the resources in God's world. And we wish to repent of our corporate and individual identification with a status quo which has exploited, perpetuated, or at best ignored the factors which have led to the conditions that are responsible for dehumanizing our fellowmen and degrading the image of God in which they were made.

We recognize that much of the relative poverty in our respective societies is poverty of opportunity and not just poverty per se. Moreover, believing that prevention is better than cure, we acknowledge the need to devote more thought and action to helping those who are the victims of the unjust structures and the unequal distribution of the resources within our society. Recognizing that "it is God's gift to man that everyone should eat and drink," (Eccles. 3:13), we stand rebuked by the Bible for failing to fulfill our duty "to share your bread with the hungry," (Isa. 58:7).

As a result of study we saw the need to "open our mouths for the dumb, for the rights of all who are desolate" and to "maintain the rights of the poor and needy" (Prov. 31:8-9). Or, as the Living Bible puts it "speak up for the poor and the needy and see they get justice." We agreed that the ways in which this duty should be fulfilled differed throughout the world. Unless we were to act like ostriches in the face of the overwhelming teaching of Scripture, we must fulfill our rights and responsibilities on behalf of those whose rights and responsibilities were proscribed or denied. We believe what Colin Morris writes in *Include Me Out,* "If the church turns a blind eye to the injustices around it, the world will turn a deaf ear to everything else the church tries to say."

Acknowledging that our concerns must be as wide as God the Creator who became incarnate for the sake of his creation, we saw afresh the necessity to make a greater measure of sacrificial involvement in God's world for Christ's sake; that is, care for people as Christ cared, to bear one another's burdens more effectively by caring for one another more meaningfully, and by sharing with one another more realistically. In this ministry of caring and sharing there must be a mutual recognition and respect for each other by both the donors and the recipients if we are to be truly "workers together with Christ."

In the face of these responsibilities that we considered, we call upon evangelical churches and agencies to cooperate more effectively and to coordinate more efficiently in assisting those we seek to serve and thereby prevent the scandal of unnecessary duplication and wasted effort.

This can be achieved by:

1. An ongoing consultation between the organizations involved in relief and development.
2. The dissemination of information relating to the help available through the various evangelical agencies.
3. Matching the offers for service with the opportunities for service and investigating more effective ways of training, preparing, and mobilizing people for social service in every sphere.

We recognize only too well that the heart of all our societies' problems is the problem of the human heart and that there is no overall panacea for the ills that abound. Nevertheless, we urge evangelicals to think through the basic biblical principles that relate to our social responsibilities and face up to the demands and the commands of Scripture in meeting human need and tackling the social problems that confront us at local, national, and international levels.

In conclusion, we recall the words of Dr. Josip Horak of Yugoslavia speaking at the Berlin Congress on Evangelism, "The most important thing for Christians today is not simply to talk about their opportunities but to use them properly."

And we remembered what Leighton Ford said at the Minneapolis Congress on Evangelism, "God will judge us and this Congress by whether we let our convictions be translated into revolutionary action."

Social action is simply obedience to the command of God. We should not evangelize *through* social service, but rather see social action as *part* of evangelization. We repent from the disparity of wealth we have caused or permitted, and stand condemned by the Bible for our lack of concern for the needy. Our concern and sacrifice must be as wide as God's, and we must all cooperate to fulfill the needs. We recommend ongoing consultation between relief organizations, dissemination of help available through evangelical agencies, and the matching of opportunities of service with offers for service.

EVANGELISM AMONG THINKING PEOPLE

Os Guinness

Mr. Guinness, Huemoz, Switzerland,
formerly with L'Abri Fellowship, is now a
freelance writer.

"Man is obviously made for thinking." "Thought constitutes man's greatness." "Man's greatness comes from knowing he is wretched. A tree does not know it is wretched." These sayings of Blaise Pascal, the French genius and apologist, remind us that when we approach man as a thinking being we see him simultaneously at the point of his greatness and at the point of his wretchedness — great because made in the image of God, wretched because given over to the futility of his darkened mind in rebellion against God. So to consider and practice evangelism among thinking people is to know God as Creator, to confront the uniqueness and dilemma of man and face the deepest questions and challenges of our generation.

In introduction let me briefly say three things. First, in speaking of "thinking people" rather than "intellectuals" I am deliberately putting the stress on whole people in real-life situations — those whose faculty of understanding is a dynamic and integral part of their lives. For too many people, "intellectual" is a term of description which is unhelpful and misleading, supporting the myth of a neutral rationality and suggesting a rarefied world of the mind, detached from practical issues and everyday living.

Second, I presuppose without apology that the Christian who knows God through Jesus Christ as the Truth is a man who thinks in believing, and believes in thinking. To require a negation of the mind as part of knowing "the foolishness of God" is to miss the irony and meaning of Paul's point. It also opens up a dangerous shortcut to the foolish and disqualifies the Gospel unnecessarily from being the good news that it is.

Third, the confines of a short paper militate more against an adequate treatment of this subject than most. Much is omitted, much merely presupposed, and much touched on with only regrettable inadequacy.

1. A unique opportunity

It would be difficult to express adequately the excitement of the present moment for anyone who loves God's truth and seeks to relate it to our time. Five hundred years of virtual European dominance in the world have ended, and with it is disappearing a whole complex of accepted ideas and traditions. It is the challenge of a new, emerging civilization, as yet only sensed, which makes this a unique moment. New value, new principles, new patterns of thought are in demand. Our generation is in a shopping mood for answers.

The vital role of thinking people at such a time should be obvious. Already the private and public importance of creative thinkers is exaggerated. This will increase. From the establishment viewpoint a nation's knowledge and know-how will be its basic resource, education will be a major industry, and all will be directed by an elite. From the standpoint of liberal or radical dissent, independent thought and critical judgment are needed controls against unthinking mass movements or totalitarianism. For the average man searching for diversion and entertainment in a crowded market of personal philosophies and life-styles, the thinker is the often unacknowledged source of his pre-packaged beliefs and fashions.

The present is also important because many of the former obstacles to Christian faith are disappearing. Much of the opposition to Christian truth is in evident disarray and unbelief has rarely been so unsure of itself.

A selective example of this, and in some ways the most significant from a purely intellectual viewpoint, is the current transformation of Western consciousness. For centuries secular humanism has been the open rival of Christianity and the only real candidate for replacing Christian truth as the foundation for a modern culture. Suddenly it has overreached itself. What we have witnessed in the 1960s is the self-confessed "Striptease of Humanism" (Jean Paul Sartre). The notions of humanist man's autonomy, self-sufficiency, and a high value for individuality and freedom, have been exposed and found groundless. With astonishing speed a new consciousness is emerging. The optimism of liberal humanism and the promise of dialectical materialism are still powerful politically but intellectually they are discredited.

In the ensuing clash of epistemologies (the "mechanist" versus the "mystic") the various structures of intellectual thought are becoming shaken to the foundation. Long maintained subjections to Christian belief are suddenly devoid of force. Long-cherished certainties of unbelief have proved insubstantial, even dangerous. Reason and faith are coming to be seen as blood-brothers rather than arch-enemies. In a surprising about-turn the case for unbelief is at its weakest for centuries, while the philosophical, moral, and historical justifications for Christianity have rarely been stronger.

This is our opportunity. God's truth alone provides the key to the many dilemmas confronting man at the close of this turbulent century.

2. The general eclipse of a Christian mind

To understand this unique opportunity is not to say that Christianity is therefore recognized by contemporary thinkers as the answer to the modern dilemma. Sadly, the reverse is true; and we must not move out to speak unless we know something of the practical causes of this situation. At few periods in Christian history has the faith of the believer appeared so deficient and intellectually disreputable — and this is not because of the offence of the Cross, but because of an eclipse of the Christian mind.

It is all the more striking when one remembers the debt owed, under God, to thinking men in the early church (from the Apostles John and Paul down to Origen and Augustine) or to the young intellectuals with minds on fire who formed the spearhead of the Protestant Reformation (such as Martin Luther and John Calvin). The eclipse of a Christian mind can be noted at any of three places.

a. *Lack of a clear, Christian voice* — Thinking people today, outside Christian circles, are almost universally unaware of a credible Christian voice. Ignorance, misconceptions, and prejudice have combined to create an abysmal caricature. Many are repelled by what they have known at first hand (Nietzsche, Carl Gustav Jung, and Ingmar Bergman, for example, are non-Christian thinkers who are all sons of Christian ministers) and most have never heard enough to respect, let alone consider seriously.

Jean-Jacques Rousseau's eighteenth-century assessment is frequently echoed today. ("One of the palliatives modern Christianity has to offer is that it has managed to create a verbal jargon without meaning which is supposed to satisfy everything except reason.") Gordon Rattray Taylor predicts that soon "Christianity will only provide a solution for tender-minded conservatives." Theodore Roszak, a historian surveying the present scene, describes modern Christianity as "socially irrelevant if privately engaging." Professor R.C. Zaehner says, "Few intelligent young men have ever turned to the churches since the eighteenth century."

b. *The dissipating effect of a misguided liberalism* — One question Christians have always faced is: How far can Christian truth be translated into the thought-patterns of other philosophies or religions? Acclimatization to non-Christian thought can lead to assimilation of non-Christian premises, and so to compromise, if not capitulation. In the so-called practice of "spoiling the Egyptians" the motive of the Early Church was never that the pagan thinker might merely *respect* the Christian, the motive was always that the Christian thinker might *reach* the pagan to win him to Christ.

The shame of much modern theology is that it has no such excuse. Along with the uniqueness of Christian truth, evangelism itself is being discredited. For almost 200 years a defining feature of much theology has been its compromise with the presupposition of naturalistic philosophy. Such theology has been called a "New Theology" but really it is the product of secular premises baptized in Christian terminology. These theologies are short-lived because they have no life beyond the life-span of their parent philosophy. They are the lingering echo of the Hegelian, existentialist, positivist, or idealist premises behind them. Being themselves the product of secular thought, they can never be considered as answers to secular dilemmas.

Christian theology thus becomes merely the Christian's way of looking at things. Evangelistic and missionary endeavor is toned down to being open-ended dialogue. What passes for a defense of the faith is what previous ages would have seen as a denial of the faith. Such liberalism dissipates the power of the Gospel, and the end of this road is the loss of truth and the decay of witness.

c. *The stifling effect of a misguided conservatism* — If a part of the Church has progressively surrendered to the premises of modern thought, another large part has made the equally unfortunate, though opposite, error of withdrawing into isolation. Failing to analyze the currents of secular thought but instinctively realizing the threat they represented, many churches have saved themselves from compromise only by a reflex movement of retreat.

But the cost of withdrawal into high-cultural isolation has produced a brand of faith marked by social and intellectual insecurity. This in turn creates many problems, only one of which is the withering of effective witness among thinking people. The Lordship of Christ is strictly confined within a narrowing spirituality. Questions are not encouraged. Wider implications of faith are ignored. Culture is not taken seriously. Christian thinking is limited to thinking on Christian topics. There is almost no field of Christian discourse and discussion. And the cutting-edge into the social, political, and intellectual world beyond is minimal. Such misguided conservatism stifles the power of the Gospel, and the end of this road is social and spiritual containment.

Thus at the very moment when twentieth-century man is most aware of his dilemma and is most in need of answers and truth, historic Christianity has been effectively shorn of its greatest strength — its claim to be true. Is Christianity true? The rehabilitation of this claim, and the pursuit of its implications for a powerful Christian mind, must be the consuming passion of the Christian thinker today. No other single question could be so explosive in the contemporary situation. Politically, for example, a conviction of what is absolutely true or ultimately real is a most subversive idea in a day of false totalitarian truth or mass image-making. For our purposes too, it is the pursuit and practice of truth which is the key to evangelism among thinking people.

3. Evangelism and the practice of truth

If the issue of truth is central to our challenge to modern thought, then a demonstration of truth must go hand in hand with our declaration of truth. Truth is to be proclaimed and it is also to be practiced. God's work must be done in God's way; God's truth must be shared on God's terms. This sense of integrity (of being "true to truth") is especially vital in a day like ours with its relativistic values. "Means" have become "ends." The question, "Is it true?" has been replaced by, "Will it work?" or, "How will it sell?"

But if Christianity is true, it works only because it is true; it is not true because it works. This is far more than a play on words. The entire uniqueness of Christianity lies in this difference. The Living God is there or he is not there. Either he has spoken or he has not spoken. These things are either true or false. They are not merely *true for us.* If this titanic claim is to be taken seriously, its implications must be reflected in all we say and are. Absolute integrity is the only fitting vehicle for absolute truth. To fail in this accidentally or deliberately, in smaller or greater ways, in our message or in our methods, is to risk placing ourselves under the charge of Paul's question, "Will you never stop falsifying the straight ways of the Lord?" (Acts 13:10).

Not only do we dishonor God and falsify his truth, we also hinder those we seek to reach. Thinking people are not generally more honest (or less honest) than most other people, but they are often more perceptive and critical. Many of them are marked by a deep-rooted mistrust of professional evangelism. Much of this arises from our careless disregard for the practice of truth.

This might be considered in two areas.

a. *The practice of truth and the question of balance* — Truth is one, but it is often expressed to us in terms of polar truths (e.g., God's sovereignty and man's significance). Here the practice of truth involves the balance of practicing both aspects of truth at once. Our most common errors are not usually those of deliberate misrepresentation or manipulation, but rather of accidental imbalance, or unconscious omissions or extremes. To examine ourselves periodically might be helpful.

For example, there are certain poles of balance especially important for the apologist-evangelist, beyond each of which is a disastrous extreme on either side. Notice that in most cases an occupational hazard or a character trait will pull us towards one extreme or the other. Have we thought these through? Are we maintaining them? Are we practicing a balance between ...

(i) Reason and faith in our own understanding and our appeal? (avoiding the extremes of dry rationalism or emotional irrationalism which vitiate much apologetics or evangelism).

(ii) Presuppositions and evidences in our handling of truth? (avoiding the extremes of appealing to either unsubstantiated premises or question-begging evidences which are a sad feature of much apologetics or evangelism).

(iii) Involvement and separation in grappling with non-Christian thinking? (avoiding either compromise or remoteness and irrelevance).

(iv) Stressing the divine and stressing the human side of responsibility? (avoiding the perils of a theological determinism or a virtual Christian humanism).

(v) Careful thought and warm feeling in our approach? (avoiding arid intellectualism or emotional manipulation).

(vi) Clarity for the truth and compassion for the man? (avoiding a polemic spirit or a deferential vagueness).

(vii) Intelligibility and freshness in our expression? (avoiding a complicated, sterile precision, or "emotional connotation words" and private jargon).

(viii) Spontaneity and structure in method? (avoiding the extremes of being spiritually haphazard or tiresomely and self-consciously methodological).

(ix) Personal involvement and wise detachment in dealing with people? (avoiding the extremes of being emotionally bound up with or impersonally remote from them).

These nine areas, if followed through, pick up many of the basic questions with which today's apologist-evangelist must grapple.

b. *The practice of truth and the question of inconsistency, error, or wrong* — My aim here is not to level criticisms, but to plead for a spirit of humble self-examination before God, that in the light of his searching standards we may review what we say and the way we say it. Together we can then go forward, mutually encouraged, corrected, and challenged, to demonstrate still more clearly the truths we declare. By God's grace we must put behind us much of the image of salesmanship and anti-intellectualism, even manipulation and fraudulence which is attached to the public understanding, or misunderstanding, of what we are about.

Without this, can we expect people to take us seriously? How are thinking people really to believe what we say? Can we have integrity in our own eyes, let alone before God? Perhaps the sting of this can best be felt by raising the questions which are typical reactions to the evidence for truth which we present in practice. Behind them all is the haunting query, "If Christianity is true, why . . .?"

For example:

(i) *After visiting a local church* ... Why the fear of questions? Why is the faith of the church unable to answer the questions of the university? Why do Christians have such a schizophrenic mind, keeping a compartment for faith and a compartment for life? Why does so much witnessing seem to be motivated by anything but truth? By subconscious guilt ("how many people have you witnessed to this week?"), or by unbiblical appeals ("win the world by . . .")? Why have Christians confused their social mores with God's absolutes and made so many of them into taboos? Why such a general denial of the arts and the particular misuse of the arts for the sake of evangelism? Why the polarization between the "simple Gospel" and the "social gospel"? Why such concentration on minor points (such as smoking and drinking) to the virtual ignoring of major principles and issues (such as justice, mercy, violence, race, poverty)?

(ii) *After listening to individual Christians* . . .

Why are intellectual questions dismissed as evasions of moral problems? Why are doubts so often suppressed? Why are truth and love, truth and experience, truth and beauty usually posed as opposites? Why are so many Christian opinions so parallel to secular opinions, but wrapped in religious language (e.g., current apocalypticism, or the unhealthy fascination with the supernatural)? How can I know Christianity is true if it requires such a leap of faith? What difference is this from a drug experience or from make-believe? Or,

(iii) *On encountering professional evangelism* . . .

Why such constant disparagement of the mind? Why so much appeal to the emotions? Why so little content presupposed on which to decide? Why all the talk of "souls" and so little of whole people? Why the obvious exploitation of the testimony of the famous? Why is it so often a case of the more simplistic the message the more sophisticated the techniques? Why the need for always being bigger and more successful? Why the creation of Christian "celebrities" and "one man denominations"? Why the unconscious manipulations or the open fraudulence in public appeals for money, or in prayer letters?

A host of other questions spring to mind, which we must ask ourselves. For example, why have so few intelligent people seriously considered Christ today? (Can it partly be because our apologetics are too academic, too polemic, and almost completely confined to an inter-seminary debate among Christians?) Why do non-Christians generally raise questions and see errors before Christians do? (e.g., the rising disquiet over the grave dangers of confusion and commercialism as Bible sales become "big business" was raised by secular voices first; and they are not slow to notice the blatant materialism and sometimes open lies which characterize much advertising in certain Christian magazines.)

Part of our failure to get thinking people to take the Gospel seriously is born of a credibility gap. We claim Christianity is true — a claim which is awesome by contemporary standards, but then we whittle down our claims by the patent incongruity of our practices of the truth. The way we operate speaks louder than what we say. Without the practice of truth, evangelism is in danger of becoming a giant institutional mouth, or as E.M. Forster dismissed it scornfully, "Poor talkative little Christianity!"

4. Approaching the thinking person

a. *Approach him personally.* The thinking person is not approached best in a crowd, precisely because his thinking puts a high premium on independent thought and private judgment. A public, professional approach is therefore least effective, or effective mostly in the opening stages of stimulating the search, or in the closing stage of making a conclusion. Lectures, sermons, seminars, group discussions, lending books, all have their special place, but there is no substitute for talking man to man. In doing this, sensitive, spiritual, and intellectual discernment involves at least three things.

(i) *Understanding a general anatomy of the unbelieving mind* — Just as a medical doctor sees each particular patient against the background of his general studies and his knowledge of previous cases, so the apologist-evangelist approaches each person as an individual but understands him against the background of the biblical picture of the unbelieving mind.

Passages such as Genesis 3, 4, 11; Romans 1, 2; II Thessalonians 2 should be studied carefully, especially with an eye to such key concepts as why each man has his own worldview, what is the purpose and place of natural revelation, how the rebellious mind refuses to bow to God's truth, in what sense judgment is the consequence or the logic of a man's settled choice, and what is the point of contact with those who recognize neither God nor the Bible.

The heart of this understanding centers around man's *inversion of truth* (man's "grasping the truth in unrighteousness," Rom. 1:18). This is the process whereby man turns God's truth on its head and uses it for his own purposes, against God. Yet he is still unable to deny the reality of the created universe around him and the image of God within him. So sinful man is inescapably caught in a tension between what he is and what he seeks, between the pull of the truth of God's world and the pull of the pseudo-truth of his own worldview (his world within God's world).

We therefore have a frame for helpful discernment. The more consistent a man is to his own worldview the less close he is to God's world, and therefore the more uncomfortable he is and the more he is forced to *face his dilemma.* On the other hand, the less consistent a man is to his own worldview the closer he is to God's world, and the more he must *find a diversion* (to save himself from recognizing the truth and having to bow to God). Every man is somewhere between the pole of dilemma and the pole of diversion, though the great majority of men are obviously nearer the pole of diversion. Few have either the consistency or the courage to approach the logic of their presuppositions and face the dilemma of a world without God.

(ii) *Learning the language of our contemporaries* — With history as our example and with the incarnation as our ideal, we evangelicals, who spare no effort to train a missionary to speak a foreign language, must be as concerned to learn the intellectual, cultural, and artistic language of those around us in our own countries. This cultural language-learning must not be confused with the style of the "trendy evangelist" whose stock-in-trade includes handy references to current trends, films, books, and popular songs. The latter is a cheap relevance. What is needed is persistent prayerful grappling with the premises, images, expressions, patterns, and traditions of those around us. Only as we really understand them will we effectively relate to them.

(iii) *Listening to the individual as a person* — Listening is the opening practice of compassion and courtesy in evangelism. The Christian is a man committed to taking truth seriously and taking people seriously. This distinguishes true evangelism from a sales technique, from proselytizing, and from simplistic methodologies which approach all men in the same way. (All of which thinking people are quick to detect.)

Listening is not a means to an end. It is a value in itself. The good listener is like an expert and appreciative wine-taster, who savors the wine and knows at once the soil, the year, and the quality of the vintage. As we listen, we should carefully discern: Does he have other needs which must be met first (food, medicine, comfort, a place to stay)? What is his worldview and philosophy of life? (Is it implicit or explicit?) Where is the treasure of his heart guarded? What is his deepest longing, aspiration, or hope? (With some thinkers, thought is a diversion or a profession; with others it is a serious commitment and a consuming passion.)

God's care for the individual is at the heart of Christianity. By contrast, indifference is the most common way that man denies his fellow-man today. Thus our aim is not to exploit his views, but to get to know him. So the moment of listening, the active giving of ourselves to another man made in the image of God, is often the first opportunity to show this care.

b. *Push him to the point of conviction.* The conviction of truth and the conviction of sin should not be separated. So when one has found where a man is in his heart and mind (seen, biblically, as one) our task, with God's help, is to push him towards conviction. This we do by a deep challenge (not necessarily verbal) to be true to the logic of his presuppositions and his worldview. We know that this will increase the tension between who he is and what he seeks until a breaking point is reached. The man is then faced with the bankruptcy of his own worldview and the challenge of God's truth as his only solution and salvation. In praying towards this end, it is helpful to remember three things.

(i) *The "logic of a man's presuppositions" is more often found in life than in words.* Mere verbal arguments, even if "successful," can too easily be seen as sophistry ("Isn't it, after all, your business to know the answers and arguments?" — they say.), and many critiques knock down only a caricature of a man's idea. This leaves the man himself untouched. True personal knowledge is not detached from life anyway, so "logic" must be brought to bear on "life" and "life" brought to bear on "logic." If we forget this we assume more responsibility than we should.

(ii) *Don't always answer questions, ask them!* It is sobering to reflect that the great bulk of Christian apologetics is aimed only at the tiny proportion of people who think and care deeply enough to consider the questions we attempt to answer. Books, lectures, discussions, seminars reach only those who think in the way catered for by books, lectures, discussions, seminars. The vast majority of people are untouched and indifferent.

Thus the problem of the Christians's failing to answer questions is a real one, but limited in effect. The larger problem is that few questions are being asked at all. Most of our contemporaries have little interest in answers of any kind. Unless we learn to raise questions, as well as resolve them, we only hope to foster the monolithic indifference which is our greatest problem anyway. This would involve two things.

First, the use of questions to raise further questions. Questions must be asked of people where they are. If only a minority read serious books, then serious books raise questions only for a minority. If more are affected by mass communication and the audio-visual arts (such as television, music, drama, poetry, cartoons, etc.) then we must use mass communications and audio-visual arts to raise questions. (incidentally, this does not mean that the media best for asking questions are also the best media for answering them. Often the reason they are so good for raising questions is the very reason why they are no good at answering them!)

This calls for an imaginative, sensitive cooperation of Christians in the various arts. If we were to practice the Lordship of Christ over culture we would be producing naturally a flow of plays, films, novels, poems, and songs, all dealing with universal human questions, treating modern issues and raising a thousand questions on every side. These would have no integrity and little appeal if evangelism were their only motivation (the trouble with so much "Christian art" already) but as one side of their total purpose their value to evangelists would be enormous.

For example, we have seen Sir Kenneth Clark's brilliant television series "Civilization" and Dr. J. Bronowski's only slightly less subtle humanist television tract "The Ascent of Man." Who will plan and produce a cultured overview of civilization from a wise, balanced Christian point of view? Of course, it goes without saying that having raised questions we must in honesty prepare ourselves to answer them.

Second, the use of questions to push towards conviction. Questions are vital here for various reasons. Because a thinker may go on to follow the logic of the question into areas beyond our knowledge and into problems beyond our understanding — areas of logical implication which we have, perhaps, neither the wisdom nor experience to enter. Moreover, it is imperative that a man sees and feels the logic of his presuppositions for himself. Merely stating his dilemma to him will not impress a man. He must know it by his own wrestling and struggling (a complete study of Christ's use of questions is very instructive at this point).

(iii) *Use his prophets.* Paul quoted the Old Testament Scriptures to Jews when he was in the synagogue, and quoted Cretan poets to Athenian philosophers on Mars Hill (and not vice versa). In the same way, when speaking to a man who rejects or ignores the Bible's authority, it is useful to make a point which he can hardly ignore by citing one of his own prophets in a telling way. If used rightly (i.e., not lifting the quote out of context, etc.) nothing speaks to modern man so tellingly as the searching novels, plays, and films of sensitive men. For many people, it was this warning from "their own side" which forced them to begin the search which led to faith in Christ.

As one pushes a man towards the point of conviction, relying on the convicting and convincing ministry of the Holy Spirit, two things should be borne in mind.

First, search for the appropriate pressure point in a man's thinking. Conviction has nothing to do with trapping a man in countless logical inconsistencies. The pressure point is that place of deep inconsistency or unfulfilled aspiration where the cherished purpose of a man's life is guarded, and where in consequence God's revelation cuts across him most forcefully. Two men could easily have the same deep logical inconsistency, but maybe for only one of them does it matter sufficiently to be a pressure point.

Second, gently apply pressure until it becomes a point of true conviction. As a man approaches the danger point (the moment when he perceives the logic of his presuppositions) he can go only one of two ways — evasion or conviction. He will either turn on his heel, or fall on his knees. It is when the bankruptcy of his own position is smartingly understood that he is ready for the last step. In all this approach there must be no appeal that is not in tune with truth.

c. *Point him to faith in Jesus Christ.* At first sight this third step is the most obvious and should require the least elaboration. Yet today it deserves perhaps the most. Exactly here — in the step of becoming a Christian — a remarkable deficiency of understanding is apparent today. This is behind the appalling numbers of young "converts" falling away. It is producing a weakened Christian mind and is drastically blunting our witness to intelligent people.

New Testament faith is spoken of as a "persuasion" of the truth (Acts 17:4) and it is important to appreciate something of the levels of understanding pre-supposed in this persuasion. To miss one of these levels is not to make conversion invalid, but it does critically weaken a man's understanding of his faith — sometimes disastrously. Four particular levels are discernible, each a level in the sense that the higher builds on the lower and includes it as it moves on. (Thus a level is *not* a stage.)

(i) *First level presupposed: understanding one's critical dilemma* — The Gospel is not felt to be good news to the man who does not feel his bad situation. Without this awareness, man's autonomy means he will not bow to God, so to speak "neutrally" to him is to invite him to set himself up as judge and "play god" with God's truth. His needs are stressed first, not because the Christian *believes* in God because of his need, but because he *dis* believes in his previous worldview because of his need. If this deficiency in understanding is carried over into the Christian life it breeds an attitude of indifference and self-sufficiency — the opposite of "There, but for the grace of God, go I."

(ii) *Second level presupposed: understanding God's truth as the answer* — This level entails an adequate understanding of the difference made because of who God is and what he has done. Christian presuppositions are explained and expounded, first to meet the specific needs which the individual's worldview hadn't and couldn't answer, and then to go on to inform all of life and its questions with Christian answers, values, and principles. That Christianity gives these answers and sheds this light does not in itself prove that Christianity is true, but it does fuel the fires of the urgency of this question.

(iii) *Third level presupposed: understanding God's answer as the truth* — This is logically different, though not always practically different from the second level. Today it strongly needs emphasis. This level of understanding entails a serious examination of Christian claims and evidences and their appropriate verification (only tackled, please note, when levels one and two are presupposed, i.e., man's autonomy is shattered — level one — and he is seeing things from a Christian framework — level two). The questions of this level are satisfied only when a man can believe in God, knowing he has sure and sufficient reasons, and therefore he can know *why* he believes *what* he believes. In fact, what many Christians mean by their "leap of faith" is that they have missed out on this level altogether.

(iv) *Fourth level presupposed: the understanding regenerated and renewed* — This level alone overlaps with the experience of becoming a Christian, but it is not in a vacuum. It is the logical outcome of the other three levels, all gathered up within it, so that a man bows before God in repentance and faith, and receives not only the forgiveness for his sins and the gift of the Holy Spirit but a renewing of his mind. (To follow this on to the development of a Christian mind leads us beyond our purpose.)

In conclusion, we must never forget that in attempting to reach thinking people for Christ, there are no shortcuts, no gimmicks, no ready-made formulas. No evangelist or Christian can have thinking people as his "specialty." Only men of God's truth will win men to God's truth. Normally, there will be no substitute for sheer hard work, studying, praying, thinking, and outthinking our contemporaries to the glory of God.

EVANGELIZATION AMONG INTELLECTUALS REPORT

Secretary: Chen Ai Yen

Evangelicals are challenged to think through their faith and their methodology of proclaiming Christ in a balanced and credible way this afternoon. In leading a very lively discussion, Mr. Oswald Guinness said that thinking people present a unique opportunity for Gospel presentation because of their vital role in society at a time of "bankruptcy of secular thoughts."

Mr. Guinness believes the world is now looking for alternative answers to the Renaissance idea of the complete supremacy of man as an individual. Democracy is at stake, and thinking men around the world are searching for an answer which would relate men more to the state, to society, to the universe. Is the evangelical prepared to meet this need? Is he ready to think, to raise questions, and to bring thinking men to a point of conviction about the claims and promises of Jesus Christ?

Mr. Guinness deliberately avoided the use of the word "intellectual" which seems to concentrate only on the mind of man rather than on the "whole" man. Instead he used the more extensive term of "thinking men" to include the majority of modern opinion-makers, and in fact all sincere and honest seekers of truth with whom Christians have to come into contact in real-life situations. How are they to be approached?

According to Mr. Guinness, the best approach is "person to person." Even though there is still a place for other methods, thinking man has to be approached alone because he puts a high premium on independent thought and private judgment. The principle is to maintain a balance between polar truths such as God's sovereignty and man's significance and to practice truth with consistency and honesty. Evangelicals should remember that witnessing to the "whole" man rather than being concerned only with his soul is essential. They should also carefully omit using secular sales or psychological tactics in their presentation of the Gospel.

EVANGELIZATION OF CHILDREN

Herman H. ter Welle

*Dr. H. H. Ter Welle, Soest, The
Netherlands, is the Founder of the In de
Ruimte Fellowship, which has a national
children's ministry and a three-year Bible
training college.*

What a fantastic experience! Fourteen hundred workers from thirty-five
European countries came together in Amsterdam in August, 1971, for
the European Congress on Evangelism. Billy Graham's opening message,
"The Biblical Mandate to Evangelize" was like the marching orders of a
general. When the address closed with William Carey's motto, "Expect
great things from God, attempt great things for God," my heart fairly
shouted, "Amen." That is what we long for in all the various countries of
the continent of Europe, and indeed of the world. Children's evangelism
is not incidental. It is not without engagement. It is a must for the whole
church!

a. *Disillusion* — In Amsterdam three years ago, Cliff Richard and his
team presented a program to a capacity audience. It was a highly professional demonstration of how modern youth can be reached. Yet at the
end of that day I was not very happy. My thoughts went back to the afternoon workshop for the evangelism of children under the leadership of
Miss Claire-Lise de Benoit from Switzerland. It was a very small group,
mostly ladies. The program had been carefully prepared, but out of the
discussion came forth one unanimous heartfelt cry about the loneliness of
the children's worker in the total program of the evangelization of the
church today.

That congress had been an inspiration to evangelism in general, but
produced also a deep disillusion about the field of children's evangelism.
On the whole, we are not really convinced of the desperate need of that
third of mankind that is most open for the Gospel, and out of whom the
world leaders and the authorities of the future will arise. What if the
Communist leaders of today had been converted when they were still
children? At the end of the workshop a few of us met for prayer. "Lord,
let a worldwide emphasis be placed on the evangelization of the child in
your church."

b. *A new vision.* Something was born. Our desire quite naturally expanded into a plan of action. On September 1, 1972, more than 150 leading children's workers from sixteen European countries assembled in
Lausanne. Their theme: "Launch out into the deep and let down your
nets for a draught" (Luke 5:1-11). Three points stood out:

(i) The Lord's order to Peter, "Launch out." It was not so much new
techniques for the lowering of nets, but the fact of being present and
ready for a general mobilization at the great *command,* the overwhelming task of the actual lowering of nets to draw in the huge shoals of little
fish. The enemy is deceitfully lowering his nets, but the Lord is still there
with his command to all of his disciples today.

(ii) The disciples called for help. We have been doing children's work perhaps with a feeling of distress ("nobody is interested in my little work"). We need to rediscover fellowship in the service of children, learning how to draw the net *together*. It is the Lord's business. He wants the little fish in the net of the Gospel. So we must work together and many barriers will fall and we will really be one.

(iii) The results. The two boats were full to the point of sinking because they worked together. And Peter had a new vision of Jesus. He saw his greatness, his holiness, his wisdom. He said, "I am only a sinner." So am I. So are we all. The Lord Jesus must be magnified in our work. We should not just talk to children, but win them. When Jesus Christ is the center and we Christians are revived by a new vision of him, then the children are drawn to him through us.

This Congress offers wonderful opportunities for workers from all over the world to join hands in that Great Commission. Our aim is always threefold: to pass on to the whole church as a matter of priority the vision to evangelize children *now;* to create an international fellowship among leaders in the field of evangelization of children; and to pool ideas and materials in such a way as to unite inter-country projects like the dissemination of information and exchange of talents.

c. *A general mobilization* — With three billion people on earth, the world's population is growing at an alarming rate of some eighty million children annually. The great burden of our hearts is: how will this newest generation be effectively reached with the saving Gospel of the Lord Jesus Christ in greater measure than ever before?

In this closing period of our age before the return of our Lord, we need a worldwide awakening of responsibility for spiritual education such as is stressed in the Bible in order to prepare the newest generation to stand in the difficult times ahead.

In this specialized evangelistic strategy paper for advanced study in the field of the evangelization of children, the two major subjects involve the role of the family and the mandate of the Church.

PART ONE: THE ROLE OF THE FAMILY

1. The ministry in the Christian home

The motto of Israel in Deut. 6:4 ("our God is one") is immediately followed by a summary of the law, "Thou shalt love the Lord thy God with all thy heart, and with all thy soul, and with all thy might and these words ... shall be in thy heart *and thou shalt teach them diligently unto thy children.*"

Parents are the first representatives of God to their children. The fifth commandment is significant for the family, "Honour thy father and thy mother, that thy days may be long upon the land which the Lord thy God giveth thee" (Ex. 20:12). The Hebrew word for honor *(kabed)* has more of a sense of "esteeming important" than it is a demand of obedience. Father and mother should make such an impact upon their children by their godly example that the children see them as the leaders in whose footsteps they long to follow.

This is essential in the great task of rearing children in the Christian faith. Except by honoring the God-given authority in the family, there is no future for the next generation. Lewis Mumford said, "It is a very responsible thing to be a grown-up for we become part of the causation of life." The parents are the ones who are called to arouse the children's appetite for the Bread of Life. It pays to win the honor of your children. The promise is, "That your days may be long upon the land which the Lord your God gives you." The future existence of our homes and our nations are at stake! Even Socrates warned against scraping every stone to pile up wealth while taking such little care of the children to whom some day it must all be relinquished.

The first step in religious education is to dedicate the children to the Lord. In I Samuel we find successively the story of Hannah and her son, and of Eli and his sons (1-2). The contrast is immense. Eli spared his sons and lost them altogether. Eli was condemned by a man of God because of his failure in his children's religious education, "Thus saith the Lord ... why honourest thou thy sons above Me? .... But now the Lord saith .... For them that honour Me I will honour and they that despise Me shall be lightly esteemed" (2:29-30). Hannah, on the other hand, had received the child out of God's hand *and gave Samuel back to God.*

A key verse is found in I Cor. 7:14, "For the unbelieving husband is sanctified by the wife, and the unbelieving wife is sanctified by the husband: else were your children unclean, but now are they holy." Here a secret is being revealed about the powerful ministry of the Christian home. If a man accepts Christ as his Savior, then the Lord not only enters into his life, but also makes His abode in the family. When a mother becomes a Christian, then immediately God is there to act as a Father to the whole family. The Bible calls God's people "sanctified," and this affects also the children. They are either "holy" or "unclean."

Let us study this for a moment. There is a vast difference between a Christian home and a non-Christian home, and between children of believers and those of unbelievers. In Gal. 1:15-16, Paul said about himself, "But it pleased God, who separated me from my mother's womb, and called me by His grace, to reveal His Son to me." What did he mean about having been separated from his mother's womb? In II Tim. 1:3 we find the following, "I thank God, whom I serve from my forefathers, who loved God with a pure conscience." His forefathers, who loved God in the light they had. Paul's father and mother prayed for him even before he was born. The first thing they did when he was born was to bring him to the temple. He was separated unto God from his mother's womb.

In II Tim. 1:2, Paul calls Timothy "my beloved son." Why? He was the natural son of Eunice and raised with God's Word. However, he was the spiritual child of Paul's ministry (I Tim. 1:2). This is what we have experienced as children's workers over and over again: boys and girls accepting the Lord Jesus Christ in our ministry, and the greatest influence on them has been the faith of the home. In verse 5 of II Tim. 1, Paul writes to his friend, "When I call to remembrance the unfeigned faith that is in thee, which dwelt first in thy grandmother Lois, and thy mother Eunice and I am persuaded in thee also."

How sadly Psa. 58:3 gives the contrast, "The wicked are estranged from the womb; they go astray as soon as they are born, speaking lies."

What a blessing it is to be born in a Christian family and dedicated to God from your earliest moments on earth. Catherine Marshall in one of her books tells that her minister father's eyes filled with tears when she as a child made her decision for the Lord. I love Acts 2:39, "For the promise is unto you, *and to your children,* and to all that are afar off, as many as the Lord our God shall call."

What are we to do with our children when they become adults and are on their own? The answer can be found in Job 1: His sons were mature. When they had their parties Job was not sure that everything was right. What did he do? He sanctified them. "He rose up early in the morning and offered burnt offerings according to the number of them all: for Job said: It may be that my sons have sinned and cursed God in their hearts. Thus did Job continually." The burnt offering is the total dedication. It is entirely presenting them into the hands of God. Job sanctified his children, even after they were grown up and responsible for themselves.

We want to plead for a new kind of family-consciousness in the Christian Church at large, being aware of the glories, responsibilities, and blessings of forming a family.

2. The ministry, through the Christian home

In the Early Church, they daily were of one accord in the temple and broke bread from house to house: they ate their meat with gladness and singleness of heart (Acts 2:46). There was a happy harmony between ministry in and through the home and the public testimony and teaching through the church as a body of believers together. Today we have on one hand the church as an instituiton without the real ministry of the home, and on the other hand there are small home-groups scattered all over the world, often without a strong and clear public testimony.

We plead for a restoration of the home-ministry, especially among children (and their relatives) without the danger of little groups that split off from the local church as a whole. It is a truth that small boats are more suitable for fishing than big Atlantic liners (Carl Wisloff's observation).

One of the main conclusions of the first European Congress on Evangelism of Children was that the best way of evangelizing the multitudes of unreached children is through the Christian family, in close fellowship with the local church. A general mobilization of Christians is called for to undertake this great task of family reconstruction, comments Miss Claire-Lise de Benoit, who took the initiative in our first congress.

This plan is open to all believers. They may become a substitute spiritual mother or father for children in their neighborhood who do not come from Christian families, thus creating little cells or units of children in homes where they feel at ease in learning to pray, love the Bible, and know and trust the Savior.

If all Christians conscientiously put themselves to this task so that our world is permeated with children's "cells," what a breakthrough we will see in the ranks of the enemy, and what progress in the reconstruction of the family!

(i) What is the aim of such a children's "cell"? To win children to Jesus Christ by offering them instruction in the things of God, and a dialogue around an open Bible in the atmosphere of a Christian home.

(ii) Who can create such a cell? All those who personally know the Lord revealed in the Scriptures, who have a heart wide open for children, who are married or single, young or old, whose occupation does not matter, and who can offer their own home, or help in the home of another.

(iii) Which children should be invited? Those who live near your house, flat, or studio, in your neighborhood.

(iv) How many children ought to be invited? At least one! No rule can be laid down, but the idea is to set up small groups of five or six children. Today, families with more than six children are rare, but congratulations to those who can cope with a large group!

(v) When should a children's cell be created? Do not wait for a favorable opportunity. After you have prayed and received your marching orders from the Lord, take the initiative. Invite the ones and twos who are living around you for an informal time of sharing the life of Jesus.

Let us deal more fully with how one goes about starting a children's cell.

(i) Invite the children at the most convenient time for them. The actual meeting need only be a short one, thus not encroaching too much into a free afternoon or time set aside for homework. It is better to meet for a short time once a week than for a long time every three or four weeks.

(ii) Welcome them as you would your own children. Refreshments can help in making them feel at home.

(iii) Take time to get to know them, to listen to them, and to take an interest in their news.

(iv) Pray with them, and teach them to pray. Bring to the Lord the things which have been shared together and so let them discover that God is alive, that he loves us and is interested in each one of us, and that He intervenes in our lives in response to prayer.

(v) Read some verses from the Bible with them, and let them discover that the Bible is a living book in which God himself speaks. Avoid reading the same passages over and over; use a plan of your own, or one of an existing Bible reading program. Think over the passage with them and ask them questions about what has been read. Make a simple and practical application.

(vi) Transform into prayer what God has said in his Word and so show how he speaks through his Word and we answer in prayer.

(vii) Let the leader of your church know about your initiative and the existence of a children's cell in your home.

(viii) Contact the parents of children you have invited and explain clearly your objective. Ask how the children enjoy the little group.

(ix) Know that God has promised in Matt. 18:20, "Where two or three are gathered together in My name, there am I in the midst of them."

(x) Pray, pray, and pray again. Pray daily for each child personally, that God will give an increase (I Cor. 3:7). Prayer can also open gates of steel.

What advantages are offered by these children's cells?

(i) The possibility, as they multiply, of reaching a maximum number of children.

(ii) An opportunity to serve God offered to all, even to the Christians who have little experience or training and who would hesitate at the thought of talking to a group of children in a Sunday School. An elderly person is not afraid in the presence of two or three children, and he or she can cope with them in the home.

(iii) The almost entire suppression of the discipline problem. In your home you are the master of the situation, endowed with a natural authority.

(iv) The establishment of a more direct, natural, authentic contact with each individual child, because of the restricted number.

Of course, it is necessary to point out the need of harmony between lip and life testimony, due to the fact that our reputation is being made daily by our own neighborhood. The children benefit as much from the welcoming atmosphere of a home, its quiet joy and its tidiness, the warm affection and interest which is shown to them, as they do from the words they hear.

It follows that there are dangers to be avoided: an attempt to steal the affection of children from their parents; a sectarian spirit; a desire to win the children's popularity; competition with existing activities; an incomplete or false teaching; pressure on the children (Jesus said, "Let the children come to me," he did not say, "Force them to come").

At the close of this section we appeal to all participants who are involved in a ministry for children to complete this strategy with their own remarks.

a. How would it work in your area of the world?
b. How could we promote this in the church worldwide?

PART TWO: THE MANDATE OF THE CHURCH

1. Teaching the children within the church is a must

Although the first task to teach the children belongs to the parents, the second agent in evangelizing the children is the church, which has the commission to teach all nations (Matt. 28:19) and to teach all believers (Matt. 28:20).

One-third of the world population are children, and they should be taught how to know Christ. The task of the church to educate the people of God means men, women, and also children (Deut. 31:12).

On the whole, one can notice within the church a sense of inferiority when it comes to the evangelization of children. There are very few theological colleges and seminaries which have an appropriate place in their curriculum to train the future church leaders in the field of children's evangelism. It is impossible to overestimate the importance of spiritual education for children, and difficult to get through to the church at large how shamefully it neglects the vast field of passing on the great heritage of Christ to the younger generation.

In the past years there has been a revival in youth evangelism in many parts of the world. We are thrilled to see how young people arise and take their place in the testimony of Jesus. It is our great desire that those leaders from all over the world who read these pages and who do come to Lausanne, will unite in prayer and receive God's marching orders to accept the great challenge to emphasize the worldwide ministry among boys and girls.

2. The infant period: God's appointed time to learn

Animals are mature shortly after birth. Children have a long period of dependence and preparation. God has purposely created humanity in this way because man has the high calling of being created in the image of God and having dominion over all the earth (Gen. 1:26).

If we believe that knowing God is indispensable for an adult to live in a responsible way, then religious education should have priority in the family and in the church. In Muslim and Communist countries, children are taught first their ideologies and second their future education. How much more do we have to listen to God's book of wisdom, where is laid down the eternal principle of the greatest pedagogue of time and eternity, "Train up a child in the way he should go and when he is old he will not depart from it" (Prov. 22:6).

Dr. Elmer Homrighausen of Princeton Seminary has stressed this truth, "No one inherits Christianity biologically, nor does one become a Christian by proxy." It has to be taught to every new generation or it will die. The newborn infant has not an iota of Christian faith or character. Whatever he attains he will acquire from the surroundings and experiences; where he lands will depend entirely on where adults guide him.

Dr. Clarence H. Benson gave some important remarks on the same verse. In *An Introduction to Child Study* he writes, "Men who have questioned the infallible certainty of this law have not realized what is meant by the word 'train.' Many children have been *told;* some have been *taught;* few have been *trained.* Education is not merely a telling process. It is not even a teaching process. It involves training. What is the difference? Telling is helping to know, teaching is helping to know and to grow; training is helping to know and grow and do. Education is not merely the acquisition, but *use* of knowledge. In fact, the educational program like the digestive process, involves the four steps of acquisition, assimilation, appropriation, and application."

Children are born with the curiosity to learn. They want to know. Paul Harrison in his excellent little book *What makes 'em tick? How Children learn,* warns against killing their curiosity and losing the most powerful ally to children. Let us satisfy their curiosity by telling them about God's creation, just as the Bible tells it. It is a unique and wonderful story that the world did not come into existence by chance, but the worlds were framed by the Word of God, so that the things which are seen were not made of things which do appear (Heb. 11:3).

We should tell the children about man's being created in God's image (Gen. 1:26) and magnify the Lord's creation at length. Let them be amazed about the grandeur of a man's being crowned with "glory and

honour" (Psa. 8:5). Immediately explain to them the Fall, to give them
the answer for evil. The truth according to observation in nature leads to
the exclamation of Baudelaire, "If there is a God, then he is the Devil."

Dr. Francis A. Schaeffer spoke about the need for teaching children
the truth. "Did God make the world as it is? The great teaching of Scripture is that He did *not* make it as it is. It is abnormal! We must drive this
home to our children from the earliest age; they should learn it almost
with their mother's milk. We live in an abnormal world, a world in which
nature is abnormal; a world in which men are alienated from each other;
a world in which the great alienation is that man is alienated from God."

Next, we must tell about Jesus not only as Savior but even more as
Lord. I am disturbed by the sweet stories that have no content, and
would like to emphasize in their teaching his supernatural birth by a
virgin; his divinity, his miracles, his teaching, his substitutionary death,
his physical resurrection body, his personal second coming, his reign on
earth, his judgment, heaven, and hell. This prevents children from having a conversion of faith in faith, and helps them to a real knowledge of
the Lord Jesus Christ as the Way, the Truth, and the Life. There is no
relativity in the Gospel. We have and we present the absolute and only
truth. What a stimulation to go out and to teach all nations!

3. The conversion of children: necessary and possible?

We have underlined already that the crucial question is not how we
see children, but that we see them at all. The great tragedy in the church
is that we do not see the children at all. In most services they are not considered as a part of the congregation, but as difficult outside elements to
be kept separate. The reason so many youngsters criticize the church is
that they were not taken seriously as part of the church when they were
small.

The full salvation of Jesus Christ is for the children. They are heirs
of salvation. But Paul says in Rom. 10:14, "How shall they believe in
Him of whom they have not heard?" II Peter 1:3 says, "His divine power
has given us all things through the knowledge of Him, who called us to
glory and virtue."

So it is our responsibility to make sure that *all* children hear the
message and receive knowledge of him who gives them glory and virtue.
It is a joy and reality that even if the children are too small or are lacking
common sense to understand the word "conversion," we may often see
that in their hearts the six-and-seven-year-olds experience a wonderful
and real fellowship with Jesus, a spirit of prayer, and natural concern for
little brothers and sisters who reject Jesus. The Holy Spirit works in the
heart of the children in a mighty manner. Thus although they naturally
are heirs of salvation, they really become partakers of salvation through
their acceptance of Jesus Christ as Savior although they may misunderstand some of our terms. The more our words are in the power of the
Holy Spirit, the easier do they grasp the reality beneath our words. So let
no one think children's work needs less devotion or less prayer;
children's work is the work above all other works that must be done
under the full anointing of the Holy Spirit.

To children we may proclaim the power of the Blood of Jesus to
cleanse from all sin; to separate from the powers of darkness; and to sep-

arate them from the hereditary taint laid upon us by our ancestors (a mostly forgotten and highly important side of the precious Blood). I Pet. 1:18-19 is a wonderful message for thousands of desperate youth who are wandering astray, burdened by a bad family, a bad ancestry.

In these days when children ten years old are taking drugs, and seven-year-olds are already emotionally ill, we should preach the whole Gospel to young people of all ages, telling them the three sides of the Gospel:

    (i) Christ *for* us paying our guilt on the Cross.

    (ii) Christ *in* us, living his life and so overcoming our old self.

    (iii) Christ *through* us, filling us with life and power to be a blessing to others through the Holy Spirit.

Thus, making them feel the necessity of turning to Christ and handing over their lives to him (which means conversion), we can go on to point out to them the way and blessing of full surrender and full victory.

Regarding the ability of children to grasp the Christian faith, we hear professional educationalists object that the Bible is not a book for children. During the first European Congress, Dr. Francis Schaeffer stressed that there is only one Gospel for both adults and children. Children's evangelism is not a different Gospel but is a translation problem, in which we must proclaim the great truths of the Christian faith in a very simplistic manner. The most decisive period for the development of man's intelligence is said to be between two and six years of age. One of the main points in education is that if the child does not understand the subject it is not his fault, but the teacher's. How then can we wait to teach children the fundamental facts of a God-given revelation?

These psychological views are not the decisive factor in the evangelization of children. The greatest reason for my belief that little children can really understand the vital truths of the Gospel is that I believe in the Holy Spirit's ministry to communicate the message of salvation and sanctification to their hearts. There is no adult, no matter how intelligent, who can understand the Gospel without the enlightenment of the Holy Spirit (cf. John 16:7-8, 13-14).

My great burden concerning Christian education in the Church of Jesus Christ is the lack of recognition of the essentiality of the Holy Spirit's ministry. Corrie ten Boom wrote a booklet called *Common Sense Not Needed,* in which she explained her Gospel ministry to mentally retarded children. What a perspective, that the Holy Spirit can illuminate the hearts of even these children! God can communicate his truth to them because man is created in God's image as a spiritual being who is receptive to the teaching of the Spirit of God regardless of the mental capability of the individual (I Cor. 1:2).

Let us go ahead in teaching all nations, starting in their younger years. Then we will hear again and again testimonies like that of Solzhenitsyn who accepted Christ in his younger days, deviated as an adult, but came back to Him when he was in Siberia, when he saw the folly of the abnormal world. Praise the Lord! Proverbs 22:6 is true!

EVANGELIZATION AMONG CHILDREN REPORT

Secretary: Anthony C. Capon

A. The vastness of the need and opportunity among children

We reminded ourselves afresh of the extremely high (and ever increasing) proportion of the world's population which is under the age of fifteen years. According to the UNESCO report, in 1970 312 million people were under the age of fifteen in the developed countries of the world, and *1.1 billion* in the less-developed world: a total of about 1,420,000,-000, or almost half of the total world population at that time. What a vast mission field — a whole new generation to be introduced to Jesus Christ!

B. Insensitivity of the church at large to this need and opportunity

We noted the lack of any sense of urgency for reaching the children of the world with the Gospel by pastors or church leaders. It seems hardly realized that the main lines of a person's character and life-style are already laid down by the time he enters the teen years, and that vast opportunities are missed if we wait until young folk reach their teens before attempting to bring them to commitment to Christ.

C. Reasons for this comparative lack of concern

We endeavored to analyze this apparent blindness to the challenge of children's evangelization:

a. A lack of understanding on the part of church leaders of the nature and psychology of children, their spiritual and mental capabilities, and the way their minds and personalities work.

b. A failure to realize that children, at a remarkably early age, can experience Christ's salvation and be used in God's service, in spite of the fact that many of the leaders themselves were introduced to Christ in their childhood. It seems generally accepted that the most one can do is teach children the Bible in the hope that they will make a decision for Christ in their later teens.

c. The complete absence of an evangelical theology of children and children's evangelization. This has resulted in theological confusion and has led to great uncertainty about the theological validity of children's evangelism.

d. Inadequate training in children's evangelism by theological colleges and Bible seminaries.

e. Lack of literature at a high academic level dealing with the objections of educationalists to the teaching of the Bible to children. A shortage of other well-reasoned literature on the principles of children's evangelization.

f. The fact that converted children cannot for some years make a significant contribution to the church in terms of financial contributions or service on committees.

g. The great problems of follow-up, leading to the conclusion for some that if we cannot adequately follow up those who profess faith in Christ, we ought not to be evangelizing.

h. Disillusionment with children's evangelism because of the shallow, high-pressure type of work in which some engage.

i. Arising out of this, the fact that young people and adults spuriously "converted" as children are among the most difficult people to reach with the Gospel.

We did not feel that any of these causes need present an ultimate obstacle to the instatement of children's evangelization as a high-priority item in the church's concerns. We resolved to tackle each of them with great seriousness.

D. The opportunities in many countries for evangelical work in the schools

In a number of countries it is still possible to teach the Christian religion in the state schools. Where these possibilities exist, we have access to almost all children in the country.

a. We must not fail to seize opportunities when they exist. At the same time, we must use them with due respect for the limitations imposed on us because we usually operate within a pluralistic state system.

b. We should encourage Christians to enter the teaching profession, and aim to have Christians on school boards, where they can influence syllabus development.

c. A need exists for training teachers in Bible teaching and in the evangelization of children.

d. We should explore the possibilities of setting up Christian groups in primary schools as well as in secondary schools, meeting during lunch hours and after school.

e. The need was stressed for Christian educators to maintain an evangelical position in the world of educational and social study.

f. Where religious teaching would be undertaken predominantly by unbelievers, it would be better to have none at all.

E. The opportunities for children's evangelization in families and homes

Often the schools are closed to Christian witness. But even when they remain open to us we should remember that the family is the basic God-given unit. Throughout the Bible the normal setting for the instruction of children in the faith is the home.

a. God has laid the primary responsibility for introducing their own children to Jesus Christ on the parents. To this end we need much more training of parents in the Christian upbringing of children than we see at present in our churches.

b. We should encourage the production of suitable literature which parents can use in the home as a means of introducing their children to the Bible and to the Christian faith. Contemporary stories of God at work, in children's language and style, would also be of great value. There should be more pooling of resources, and cooperation in publishing between various language groups.

c. We commended the use of the home as a base for Christian outreach to other children in the community. Besides the well-known "Bible club" approach, we noted the possibilities of informal gatherings of four or five children, including perhaps friends of the children in the family.

d. In such informal home situations, the presentation of the Bible message must be simple and amply illustrated, and we appreciated examples given by Miss Annie Valloton about Bible story-telling accompanied by simple sketching.

F. The opportunities for children's evangelization in the church at large

The church has a twofold responsibility so far as children are concerned: a responsibility toward the children of its own people and toward the children of non-Christians in its community. We call attention to the following needs and opportunities.

a. The need for effective and consistent training of Sunday School teachers in the evangelistic aspect of their work with children. There is a responsibility to acquaint the children with personal faith and commitment to Christ Jesus.

b. The need for earnest prayer on the part of the church for children all over the world. We commended the idea of an annual day of prayer for children.

c. The opportunities presented in many cultures (but not all) for evangelistic campaigns among children, either in the church building itself or on neutral ground.

d. The proposal that public evangelists should include in their teams specialists in work among children, who would supervise the counseling and follow-up of children. In certain cases it might be possible to undertake parallel evangelistic meetings among children during the period of evangelistic campaigns.

e. The need for training children's evangelists in theological seminaries and Bible schools, and for better training in children's work to all students in such schools.

f. Increasing opportunities for reaching children through camps and other vacation activities in many countries. Use made of such opportunities should always be geared to the local cultural situation.

g. The urgent need for more and better evangelistic literature to use among children. Such literature must be imaginative, simple, clear, and colorful. Combined editions in various languages could substantially reduce costs.

G. Conclusions

a. We call for new awareness by all Christians of the challenge to reach for Jesus Christ that half of the human race who are children.

b. We call upon the church to devote its best brains to an urgent study of the theology, principles and practice of children's evangelization, relating these studies also to the subject of child development and educational theory.

c. We call for new emphasis at every level on training for children's evangelism, so that multitudes of children throughout the world may be faithfully and lovingly reached with the Gospel.

d. We call upon God's people everywhere to pray earnestly for these ends.

H. Summary:

The problem: Over one billion children, but the church is apathetic.

Reasons for apathy: Lack of understanding of spiritual and psychological aspects of children. Practical problems of follow-up, spurious conversions.

Opportunities: Increase number and efficiency of Christian teachers in schools so as to take full advantage of existing opportunities. Christian influence throughout the teaching profession. Supreme responsibility of the parents. Need for good literature. Use of home as center for child evangelism. Consistent training of Sunday School teachers. Campaigns either specifically for children or with special children's section. Specific training in seminaries. Evangelistic literature for children.

Conclusions:

1. New awareness of challenge to reach children.
2. Study of theology, principles, and practice of child evangelism.
3. Training for child evangelism.
4. Prayer.

EVANGELIZATION AMONG SECONDARY SCHOOL STUDENTS

J. V. Managarom

Mr. Managarom, Madras, India, is Area Director for Youth for Christ in Central Asia.

I deeply appreciate the organizers of the Congress setting apart some time in the program to consider the subject of evangelization among secondary school students. No one can deny the fact that laying a spiritual foundation in the lives of young people while they are going through secondary education is of utmost importance. To a large extent, many of the problems we are facing among university students would be solved if proper and effective evangelization was being carried out at the secondary schools. The future leaders of our world would be better leaders if they could be reached for Jesus Christ during their secondary education.

We are living in an age when evangelization among secondary schools is greatly diminished, due to the secularization of governments which eventually prohibit religious teaching and activities in the schools as part of the curriculum. This has partly resulted in a generation of teens who have become a problem to society. While enormous strides have been taken to strengthen the physical, mental and social needs of the students, the spiritual need has been greatly and — in the majority of cases — totally neglected. But in the midst of this situation there has never been a generation of young people more open to first-century Christianity than this present questioning generation.

True their minds have been denuded of heroes by the all-prying press, "But, the rugged Christ of the first century who says, 'Follow me,' is more attractive to youth than he has ever been," said Rev. Jay Kesier, President, Youth for Christ International, U.S.A. If this had not been true, many of us who have been working among them would have been wiped off the scene by the overwhelming changes that are occurring today.

Today's generation of teens

Today's teens constitute a large proportion of the world's population. They are not only an increasing generation but also a changing generation. They are becoming taller in height, bigger in size and even faster in movement. Besides this, they learn more, buy more, travel more, and see more than we did twenty to twenty-five years ago.

The teens of today get into more sex problems, break the laws of the country and educational situations so much that one can hardly skim through a daily newspaper without reading about some disturbances and chaos created by teenagers.

What are these students before the eyes of the world, and in our eyes? "Just children" to the parents; "a menace" to the police; "weapons to be used to an end" to the Communist; "a market" to the businessman; "the unreachable" to the church; but to themselves they are "adults."

Dr. Billy Graham says, "The young person is one who is in the most difficult period of his entire life, living in a world of his own and making decisions that will determine his life in twenty years...."

The situation of the teenagers in the U.S.A. is a good example of today's generation.

"There are now 30 million teenagers more than in 1947. Since 1955, over a million teenagers have been added to the U.S. population each year. *Look* magazine reported in 1967, "The tape measure and the scales prove that they are bigger and a stop watch will show they are faster. Any parent can tell you that they are smarter or at least savvier. The F.B.I. can prove they are more lawless; most churchmen will agree they are more sceptical. This year some 29 million teenagers will spend up to 20 billion dollars on products ranging from surf-boards to false eyelashes. Teen boys will purchase 40 per cent of all men's slacks, and one-third of all men's sweaters. Fourteen-year-old girls will buy cosmetics their mothers could not have afforded even if they had been on the counters in 1944. Fellows and girls will jet at youth fares further in one year than their grandfathers traveled in their lifetime. Via TV they will watch courses in seduction in full color in their living rooms that could not have been seen in theaters twenty-five years ago. Unmarried girls will have twice as many illegitimate babies as those of twenty years ago. In school they will yell words and phrases across the lunchroom tables that their parents did not understand until after marriage. Almost half of the graduating class will go on to college compared with one-fourth that went on twenty years ago...." *James Hefley.*

This is becoming more and more prevalent not only in the affluent modern Western world but also in the fast-developing Eastern world.

In India, right now, 79 million students study in secondary schools. Writing about the situation of education in India, one author said, "What India is trying today, is to harmonize her old values with the values of the modern world. The old values are spirituality, toleration, and universalism under vague concepts like 'Dharma,' under more specific concepts like the family, marriage, religious and caste practices. And when they try to harmonize these old values with the values of the modern world they have created a great confusion in the minds of the young people. The average teenager today in the East, is terribly confused between the old values of their own cultures and traditions and the values of the modern world that are sweeping all over the world."

At one of the large youth congresses held in India, during the Question Hour, one of the students sent in the following question, "Is it right to go steady with a girl while in high school?" The note was anonymous and the writer had spelled the word "right" as "wright." So, I had to say, the person who wrote this question should first know how to spell "right" right before he begins to start going steady, and concluded by explaining that it was necessary for him to become a mature person before involving himself in making a mature decision of this nature. This is an illustration of the young person's confusion which he faces in the East, because of the Western influence relating to sex.

Describing the confusion of the young person on the American Continent, Barry Moore wrote, "61 per cent of America's young people experiment in drinking, sex and drugs, because of natural inbred curiosity, the continuous brainwashing of the advertising media, and the absolute lack of parental guidance." They experience severe social and academic pressures. The Director of Psychiatry of the University of Wisconsin wrote a book entitled, *The Roots of Student Despair* and said that as many as 800 students a year look for psychiatric help because of intense frustrations. Shaky world conditions, unstable family foundations, stringent educational demands, pressure to conform to teenage society, and the failure in "living it up" do anything but deeply satisfy, have left them with strain and anxiety. Dropping out from society is a form of "escapism." Some have disengaged in this way, because they have felt that there were better things in life. "But," says *Weekend* magazine, "when you ask what they intend to do to obtain these better things they retort with empty phrases, and no concrete suggestions." Others used this drop-out idea to run away from discipline, propriety, purity, and as a means of having one's own way. "When our society has so much to offer, why are they missing the chance to seize their opportunities? Why are they experimenting, becoming frustrated, and seeking escape? The answer is, our American young people all over are overwhelmingly confused."

The answer to this confused generation

The answer to the search of this confused generation is Jesus Christ. Let me make it clear that it is not tradition-bound Christianity but it is Jesus Christ. Dr. Kenneth Keniston, Associate Professor of Psychiatry at the Yale University School of Medicine said in a report, "Many of the traditional avenues to meaning and significance have dried up." Traditional religious faith is not for most sophisticated undergraduates. "As a means of ascertaining the meaning of life traditional religions often seem to the students to be worn out, insincere or superficial. Similarly, the great classic, political, liberalism, conservatism, Marxism or Fascism, arouse relatively little interest among most undergraduates. One by one, then, many of the traditional sources of meaning have disappeared, at the very same time that academic life itself, because of its intense pressure and professional specialization, seems to many students increasingly irrelevant to their major existential concerns." Very often we find teenagers raising the banner: "CHRISTIANITY — NO! JESUS CHRIST — YES!" This shows that young people in the schools are looking for a personal relationship with Jesus Christ, which alone can satisfy their spiritual need. A young drug addict said this in his testimony, "I do know this. I'm through with drugs for several reasons, the most important of which is, I have found more lasting satisfaction in a relationship with the Lord than any drug has ever offered."

In the early adolescent years, a high school student has a genuine need for a settled belief about nature and God, and this is why some psychologists say a religious conversion is distinctly an adolescent phenomenon. When Christ is presented as the Savior, as the Lord of his life, with all his demands of discipleship, the young high school student responds to it and accepts Christ as his own Savior and decides to follow him. So, our message is clear. It is the fact that the Gospel is the power of God unto salvation to every one who believes.

The understanding of youth

Any effort to evangelize a high school student should start with an effort to, first of all, understand him. We must understand his cultural, religious, social and mental background to the present time. The background changes from country to country and varies even within a country from state to state. This is one of the problems we have in a country like India with so many different religious practices and languages. One has also to remember that the religious interpretations of today are very different from those of thirty years ago. The needs are similar in other Asian countries too. We must project ourselves into adolescent life and understand some of the pressures that are molding his attitudes and responses today. Many of the students have feelings of distress, despondency, anxiety, and a sense of incompleteness, a fear of eternal punishment, morbid conscientiousness, and struggles against sex interest. Adolescents often suffer over the problem of death. A sixteen-year-old girl wrote, "The more I read about the splendor of life, the more I see its tragedy, the fleetingness of time, the ugliness of age, the certainty of death; the inevitable is always on my mind. Time is my slow executioner. When I see a large crowd on the beach, or at a ball game, I think to myself, who among them is going to die first? And who last? How many of them will be here next year? Five years from now? Ten years from now? I feel like crying out, 'How can you enjoy life when you know death is around the corner?' "

Such thoughts often tend to produce depression, brooding, and constant introspection. Doubts begin to increase as they see the conflict due to the opposing factors in the school and the world and probably in the churches. Very often doubts tend to end in painful mental conflicts. As they go through these conflicts, we find that they do make some adjustments. Some place implicit belief in the traditional religion. They find security in the community that believes the same things. But there are many others who gradually work out a personal religion; and there is a small minority who are able to adopt as a permanent adjustment the attitude of suspended judgment, resting in the conclusion that they do not know the explanation of the universe or the meaning of life or God. But the unknowable is, however, likely to be extremely painful, especially for the intelligent but emotionally immature youth.

While the basic spiritual nature of a secondary schooler is unchanged, his way of thinking and his emotional responses have changed. Hence the evangelist, concerned in order to show the student the way through to repentance and faith in Christ Jesus, should know him — not merely be acquainted with him. The student's needs, concerns, ideals, etc., should be known. Then the confidence of the student will be won and a genuine relationship in a relevant way can be built.

In our approach to the secondary school students, we need to keep in mind the fact that needs vary from person to person and the secondary schooler has his load of needs, such as the need to be loved, accepted, secure, honest, spiritual, and successful.

The need to be accepted

In a world that is rapidly advancing materially, scientifically, and technologically, the danger of reducing people to mere numbers is great. Hence the need for acceptance. One of the secondary schooler's greatest fears is to be rejected by his friends and associates. Because of this, he is willing to go with the crowd and do what the crowd does even when he knows that what the crowd is doing is not right. He finds his greatest self-esteem and stability not in what he is doing, but with whom he is doing it. He feels he is needed and accepted within the group, and this results in many strong gangs or cliques being formed, usually of the same sex.

The need to be secure

Our world is insecure. We live under the shadow of the atom and hydrogen bomb, as well as more sophisticated weapons of war that have made the total annihilation of our world an uncomfortable possibility. Furthermore, the rapid progress of many developing countries in Asia, with the coming of industrialization has demanded mobility, and mobility prevents the establishment of permanent roots in society. Parents are all too often busy, and in order to keep the home fires burning have resorted to both husband and wife seeking employment. In today's progressive India, the traditional Indian woman who was always home-bound is now fully occupied with jobs outside the home in both private and governmental concerns thus having little or no time to spend at home with the growing secondary schooler. They fail to help him as he makes the most major decisions in his life.

The need to be honest

Because of insecurity and the contradictions of the adult world that he sees, saying one thing and doing another, he demands logical reasons for his expected behavior, and rebels against any hypocrisy. He wants answers that are frank — the "straight from the shoulder" variety, and would rather you would not answer his many questions than to give him an evasive or vague answer.

The need to be loved

This is a basic need that remains from birth, and the fulfilling of it largely depends upon the home background. When a secondary schooler has been starved of parental love, he soon begins to confuse sex gratification with love, and love with sex. Thus many a maladjusted young person's problems can be traced back to his home.

The need to be successful

Our world in its eagerness for progress has confused material affluence, fame, and success with happiness. This is so much so that in Asian countries, parents often determine the vocation of their children, telling them to become a doctor or an engineer and that failure to do so would mean disaster. All this confuses a young person about what he wants out of life. In a recent survey it was estimated that forty percent of teens feel that they will be "failures." They are thus in need of guidance and help to see realistic goals for their lives.

The need to be spiritual

This is the age in life when the secondary schooler wants a flag to follow, a creed to believe in, and a cause to serve. An age when he is in need of a faith that can stand the test of life. These are some of the most fertile years for spiritual growth, though he would rarely show it outwardly. He is not interested in a faith for himself alone, but in his boundless enthusiasm he is looking for something that can remake his world and be applicable to his generation. Many of the educationists in East and West were very quick to realize that the lack of morality was appalling when religious instruction was left out of the school curriculum. So they substituted moral instruction. While many students may believe in the moral standards, they realize the lack of power to achieve that standard by themselves.

Ultimately he wants a freedom that comes from within, a freedom that delivers him from the bondage and tyranny of sin, and a freedom made possible on the Cross that brings him the knowledge of sins forgiven and peace between him and God.

Communication

a. *The message.* One of the continual problems we face in our ministry is, "What shall I communicate to the teenager?" One should keep in mind that there are basically two things to be presented in relation to evangelism:

(i) The plan of salvation in such a simple way that any teenager without Christ might find him.

(ii) A message that will challenge, inspire and motivate the Christian teen to live a Christ-like life. I do not wish to spend much time arguing that the presentation of Jesus Christ is the message. I firmly believe that the unchanging Christ is the need of the teenager in a changing world.

b. *The method.* It is very important to consider the way the message is to be proclaimed. Young people are not satisfied with "pat answers" any more. They want something that will meet the need that they have. Many of the phrases and terms that are used in sermons are strange words to the teens. We must present a message that makes sense to the teen who is not familiar with theology. So we need to work on sermons, Bible study notes and literature for the secondary schooler so that the way they are presented makes sense. This involves a study of the terms that they understand. A specialized research in communicating to the young person is involved. If the presentation of the message is too intellectual, and they do not have enough knowledge to understand all that is said, it goes above their heads. I have never forgotten a statement which Dr. Billy Graham made when he visited India in 1956. He said, "Men know a lot about science, psychology, etc., but very little about religion. The average religious knowledge of a man is that of a 13-year-old boy. Therefore, I preach as if I am preaching to a 13-year-old boy..." If he made this statement referring to the adults, one realizes how important it is for us to be clear in our communication to teenagers.

On the other hand, if it is too simple, they begin to think that it is not practical or relevant. Hence we need to find a balance of presentation that meets the intellectual needs of the young person and at the same time appeals to his emotions and to his world, so that he is convinced of the truth of the message. May I at this point caution the Western evangelist, who thinks the Asian teenager readily says, "Yes" to the claims of Christ. The Asian teenager has no difficulty in accepting Jesus Christ as one of the Saviors of the world, but it is a different thing when he has to believe on him as the Savior.

c. *The messenger.* Let us consider the person who communicates the Gospel. A few years ago, young people used to run after the popular preachers. But the trend is changing. Now they listen to the man who is available to talk to them. So the person who communicates should be a person who is available to them to answer their questions and to help them in their practical needs. Therefore we must be physically, emotionally, and spiritually available to the teenagers if we hope to communicate with them.

Whenever we think of the qualified messenger we often have in mind adults such as the pastor, evangelist, Christian school teacher or layman who is interested in the work among teens, but we often forget a group that could be a real key in communicating to the teens. This group I wish to present to you are the Christian teenagers themselves who are readily available to them on the campus. I do not want in the least to undermine the thousands and thousands of those dedicated men and women, all over the world, who are doing their best in ministering to the teens through their churches and youth organizations. But we would be failing to tap a legion of resource personnel for communicating to teenagers if we did not give serious consideration to the Christian teenagers.

The church, therefore, must get involved in equipping and training the Christian teenagers which will enable them to attain spiritual maturity and also learn the many things that are involved in leadership, and in communicating their faith.

The responsibility of the church in training Christian teenagers

The church therefore, must get involved in equipping and training the Christian teenagers which will enable them to attain spiritual maturity and also learn the many things that are involved in leadership, and in communicating their faith.

There are many Christian organizations involved in evangelism in the secondary schools which have their specialities and unique contributions to make. However, only the Church of Jesus Christ can meet the total needs of the modern teens. This applies both to the nominal teen and the delinquent teen. While the banner, "CHRISTIANITY — NO! JESUS CHRIST — YES!" raised by the teenagers is a challenge to the Church to wake up, this should not in any way give room for us to think that they should not be brought into the fellowship of the Church. Every worker whether he belongs to interdenominational, non-denominational organizations, or a church, should remember that the teenagers who are reached for Jesus Christ should be channeled into Bible believing and Christ-exalting churches. Therefore, the pastors have to play a vital role in developing the Christian teens. While it is not easy for pastors to have the kind of relations they would like to have with the teenagers who come to their churches, there are many things that they can still do.

For example, the pastor should personally get acquainted with them by showing up at their functions, scheduling an instruction program in which they can get involved, taking a teen Sunday School class for one quarter per year, schedule a personal interview at least once a year with each teenager.

The pastor should make arrangements for young people to be used in the churches. Those who can sing or play musical instruments should be used in the church choir, in their own teen choir, and also opportunities must be given in the church programs to use their own special musical abilities, whether singing or playing an instrument. Pianists could be used in different parts of the Sunday School for the opening exercise.

May I suggest some ways of winning the non-Christian teens and using the Christian teenagers to communicate to other teenagers?

a. *Challenge teenagers.* To make his school campus his mission field but give him guidance. Very often young people get frustrated because they attempt to reach everybody and not reach any one. They will eliminate the frustrations if they concentrate their efforts on one person.

b. *Organize teen musical teams.* I have never known any better strategy that can be used to overcome the various barriers in reaching teenagers with the Gospel than that of using teen musical teams. Musical teams are able to gain entry into countries ruled by Hindus — like Nepal and Burma, which have totally closed the doors to foreign missionary activities, and share the Gospel without much difficulty. They are often warmly welcomed by Roman Catholic and Hindu heads of institutions.

c. *Conduct youth congresses.* These congresses give opportunity for young people to participate in musical talent contests, preaching contests, quiz contests, etc. Also, by conducting youth festivals and youth music festivals wherever we go, we find that when young people know that other young people will be present, they are there.

d. *Conduct youth camps.* Camps play a vital role in evangelizing teens, encouraging the Christian teens to witness to non-Christian teenagers.

e. *Conduct clubs in homes.* This has become more and more a necessity as government regulations in many countries do not permit religious activities in school campuses. Conducting clubs in homes has become more effective for evangelism among secondary schoolers. This makes it easier for teenagers of other faiths to come more freely than going into a church or a Christian religious instruction class in a school.

f. *Conduct evangelistic missions.* In many countries the door is still open for conducting missions in schools. The Scripture Union and Inter-School Christian Fellowship have experienced great blessings through such missions for many, many years. These missions could make use of the Christian teenagers to invite their non-Christian friends and be an influence and help to them.

g. *Conduct vacation Bible schools.* Conducting of vacation Bible schools during the days when the schools are on holiday is another program that has been greatly used to bring teens to Christ. Here again, the Christian teenagers can help a lot in this program.

There are two international evangelical youth organizations that are actively engaged in the ministry of evangelism among secondary schools. In addition to this there are several other organizations and church groups that do an effective ministry among them in different parts of the world.

In closing, may I urge the leaders of all these organizations to learn from one another so that our strategy may become more effective. We desperately need to learn from one another's experiences and knowledge.

Conclusion

The true test of our ministry of evangelism among secondary school students is the ability of the young person to say to us, "I understand what it is that you are saying." It is then up to him to make an evaluation of the message. His response will then be based upon his evaluation. Positive response will mean that the young people to whom we minister will have a faith of their own, created by our Lord Jesus, the Author and Finisher of our faith, rather than one imposed upon them.

EVANGELISM AMONG SECONDARY SCHOOLS STRATEGY GROUP REPORT

The paper prepared by J. Victor Managarom was presented to the group and briefly discussed. The spirit of the paper was accepted and the burden for this work was found to be the same for all regions represented. The specific needs, however, varied in the different countries.

There was, unfortunately, some confusion over consecutive attendance at this strategy session which meant that few delegates attended all three sessions, thus hindering a progressive discussion of the problems tackled.

During the second and third sessions the members divided into groups representing Africa, Asia, South America and North America, Europe, and Australia. The following problems and observations emerged regarding school work.

1. The importance of biblical teaching was stressed. This should appear regularly in the program of voluntary Christian societies and in the formal teaching of religion in school curriculum. Major doctrines should be taught but matters that could lead to division and were of secondary or of denominational significance should be avoided. If questioned on these issues, there should be a balanced and scriptural reply. Personal counseling would be preferable at this stage.

2. There is a widespread need for materials to be used in school evangelism. Books and other aids are needed by the teachers in presenting a true biblically-oriented program.

3. The Christian teacher is the key person in high school evangelism. Worldwide prayer ought to be devoted to raising up more dedicated Christian teachers. Young people must be challenged with the opportunities existing in education today.

4. Leadership training is a constant necessity. Teachers and student leaders want regular training to aid them in running high school Christian meetings. Bible study aids, program suggestions, etc., must be available to encourage Christian growth and maturity. Suitable staff (S.U., YFC, and other organizations) are needed to improve and lead meetings.

5. There is a need to communicate in the language of the high schoolers. The approach should not be so stereotyped and inflexible as to be ineffective and not speak to the real needs of youth. It was stressed that we should always speak of Christ and not merely of church. The established church is often a barrier to reaching youth and after Christ has been accepted there is sometimes a need to work out integrating youth into a church.

6. Problems do vary from region to region. In the east, for example, students are very interested and involved with politics whereas sex is the prevailing obsession in the west. Every effort must be made to answer their needs as they exist and not be content with telling simple Bible stories. The students must be made to think through their position with the Christian faith presented as a challenge for genuine understanding.

7. Many ideas were mentioned as to how this work could be improved but the overall feeling of "youth reaching youth" was thought to be

most effective. Students must be encouraged to witness to their fellows and not to rely on the organized meetings alone.

8. Follow-up was recognized as being a problem. It was stressed that this should always be as personal as possible and genuine friendship, integration in a Bible study or teaching group and personal letters were most important. Materials which stressed Bible reading (Navigators, Scripture Union, etc.) are available and every effort must be made to teach Christians the *whole* counsel of God — and not the "milk" alone.

EVANGELIZATION AMONG COLLEGE AND UNIVERSITY STUDENTS

Michael Cassidy

It is my hope in this paper not simply to make some observations, but to raise some of the questions and problems for student work as I see them.

1. The challenge, opportunity, and needs

a. *The challenge* — Few need persuading about the challenge, opportunity, and needs on the modern campus, but it is well to remind ourselves of these. With over half the world's population under the age of twenty-one, the high school and university campus becomes an increasingly critical focus of Christian concern. In 1957 there were ten million students in the world, of which the U.S.A. had three million. Now in the U.S.A. alone there are over seven million and 3,000 campuses. Asia, which previously lagged in its university facilities, suddenly has over four million students. Tokyo alone has over 500,000. Numerous Third World countries did not even have a university twenty years ago. Now no country is without one. Twenty years ago no one had heard of Student Power. Now it is a cliché.

b. *The opportunity and need* — This phenomenon represents not only an incredible opportunity for strategic evangelism, but an immense area of human need. As such, it is important that those who would evangelize the student should not simply think of him strategically — as a key person, a potential leader, a future opinion-maker — but as a young human being, often with deep if not desperate needs, for whom Christ died. The Christian therefore has a special incarnational responsibility to be *on* the campus. This is particularly true when the local church is failing to make the desired impact. Carl Henry writes of one campus he visited, "The local churches of *whatever* persuasion were reaching less than 10% of the entire student body of 6,500."

2. The Christian origin of the university

The Christian has a unique right to be on the campus, not simply as an agent of evangelism, but as an agent of reminder that the university as we know it is really a uniquely Christian creation. It was born out of the medieval synthesis with its unified Christian worldview. The original scholastic guild or *universitas magistrorum et scholarium* was based on the Christian presupposition that man lived in a "universe" — a reality which cohered as unity, and was turned *(versus)* into one *(unus)*. Such a presupposition was theological through and through. Reality was all of a piece, a single coherent whole, regular and predictable. It could therefore be systematically studied and would yield itself intelligibly to man's intelligence, being the creation of an Ultimate Intelligence.

Not only that — the earliest universities like Oxford, Paris, Bologna, and Salerno were avowedly "vocational." They came into existence not primarily to train people for a job or to earn a living, but to supply persons "fit to serve God in church or State." Underlying all academic pursuits was the notion *Dominus Illuminatio Mea* (God My Illumination.) Theology, as the Queen of the Sciences, controlled and coordinated the whole academic enterprise. Jesus, as heart of the universe, was the key to everything.

This basic view, and its relation to academic studies, was later articulated by Edward Pusey, the famous nineteenth-century spokesman for the Oxford Movement, "History without God is a chaos without design or end or aim. Political economy without God would be a selfish teaching about the acquisition of wealth. Physics without God would be a dull inquiry into certain meaningless phenomena. Ethics without God would be a varying rule, without principle or substance or center or regulating hand. Metaphysics without God would make man his own temporary God, to be resolved after his brief hour into the nothingness out of which he proceeded."

In fact, what we are on to here is the *logos* doctrine of John's prologue. Theologically put, the university is in a sense the offspring of the *logos* doctrine, "for in Him are hid all the treasures of Wisdom and Knowledge" (Col. 2:3). Truth is personal before propositional. Small wonder that, centuries before, Justin Martyr (Second Apology XIII) could say of Plato and the Stoics that "whatever things were rightly said among (them) are the property of us Christians." They shared in the *logos*.

And the same is true today. Whatever real truth is found on the modern university campus belongs to us and to our God and to his Christ. It is this which enables us to step onto the campus with our heads held high. Indeed, the Christian has not only the special right, but the deep obligation so to speak the Gospel into the modern university as to help restore that structure of inner meaning which has collapsed in secular society. It is only as the modern anthropocentric university rediscovers its theocentric origins in the *logos* that it has any hope of achieving its true destiny and purpose. F.R. Barry observes that "we must not forget the warning of what happened when Roman education became 'rhetoric,' teaching people how to be clever and get on in a careerist society, while it gave up teaching them how to be good."

The Christian therefore can and must approach the modern university, erected as a shrine "To An Unknown God," and declare, "What therefore you worship as unknown, this I proclaim to you" (Acts 17:23). We then proclaim Jesus not just to lost individuals, but to the university as a lost institution.

3. The complexity of the modern campus

a. *The nature of the modern university* — Modern students of communication consistently stress that communication involves not simply the sender, and his message, but the medium of communication and above all the *receiver*. What is heard by the receiver is "a mix" of transmitted message, medium influence, atmospherics, and the receiver's own social, cultural, and intellectual input. It is therefore probable that the mechanics and processes of "reception" should occupy us equally or more than the processes of "transmission." Newman used to stress that those who deal with doctrine should listen to "how the faithful breathe."

The fact is that everyone brings a "pre-understanding" (what the Germans call *vorverstandnis)* to their reception of new ideas. In other words, no one hears a statement or reads a text "as it is." No one comes *tabula rasa* (as a clean slate) to the experience of receiving new data. Each person in a measure is a prisoner of his history.

The fact that everyone, perhaps the student particularly, has his own hermeneutical processes is of tremendous importance for student evangelism. It forces us to face seriously the nature of the modern university as receiver and target of our student evangelism, and to ask who and what we are dealing with. While our message is kerygmatic, our approach must be situational and contextual. Francis Schaeffer puts it this way, "If a man goes overseas for any length of time we would expect him to learn the language of the country to which he is going. More than this is needed, however, if he is really to communicate with the people among whom he is living. He must learn another language — that of the thought-forms of the people to whom he speaks. Only so will he have real communication with them and to them. So it is with the Christian Church. Its responsibility is not only to hold to the basic, scriptural principles of the Christian faith, but to communicate these unchanging truths 'into' the generation in which it is living."

This raises my first key question for Congress discussion: *"What is the nature of the modern university as receiver of our message, and how should its nature affect us in our approach and presentation?"*

b. *Some observations:*

(i) The university as heterogeneous rather than homogeneous — The challenge of the university is that of the world in microcosm. Each campus has not one, but many cultures — and certainly numerous subcultures. Each group (sportsmen, musicians, scientists, philosophers, radicals, women, lecturers, administration, ground staff, hostel staff etc.) has its peculiar presuppositions, interests, life-style and "pre-understanding" apparatus. The student worker, as a professor friend of mine says, must "get used to multiple logics." In other words we are doomed to frustration, if not failure, if we treat as a corporate whole an institution whose constituent parts may have much less in common than they think. One strategy will not do. Multiple strategies (and Christian groups?) are necessary.

(ii) The university as unique — It should also be noted that each university *as a whole* is different and "unique." To understand campus A is no key to campus B. While "standard-reading" books like Francis Schaeffer's *Escape From Reason, The God Who Is There,* and Os Guiness' *Dust of Death,* may illumine some broad underlying presuppositions and patterns in today's student world, nevertheless each campus demands its own homework from the student worker. Transference of patterns of witness, no matter how successful, from one situation to another, is asking for trouble.

(iii) The university as extended society — Complicating things further is the fact that the university and its students are not an island. Charles Troutman observes that "as individuals, students are closely related to neighborhoods, extended families, churches, clubs and any number of other sociological groupings. This complex inter-relatedness makes it plain that if students are to be reached for Christ, more is required than adapting evangelism to their sub-culture."

Related to this is the problem of permanents (the local urban community in which the university is placed) and transients (the students). Town-gown dynamics cannot be ignored by the student-worker.

(iv) The university as intellectual help or hindrance to evangelism — In a special way the university in any locale is an intellectual pace-setter, and its intellectual ethos and stance either help or hinder student evangelism.

In the Western and First World countries the university atmosphere is generally antithetic to the Gospel. If the campus in microcosm reflects the world in macrocosm, then the Western campus like Western culture, is marked in the words of Os Guiness, "by a distinct slowing of momentum or perhaps more accurately, by a decline in purposefulness and an increase in cultural introspection. This temporary lull, this vacuum in thought and effective action, has been created by the convergence of three cultural trends, each emphasizing a loss of direction. The first is the erosion of the Christian basis of Western culture, an erosion with deep historical causes and clearly visible results. The second is the failure of optimistic humanism to provide an effective alternative in the leadership of the post-Christian culture. And the third is the failure of our generation's counter-culture to demonstrate a credible alternative to either of the other two-Western Christianity and humanism. He adds, "Today the cultural memory of traditional values hangs precariously like late autumn leaves; and, in the new wintry bleakness, optimism itself is greying."

It is into this kind of basic ethos that the Christian is called to step. It is within this strange amalgam of vacuum, lostness, inquiry, and indifference that he has to try to find the points of contact for meaningful ministry. The student worker here has to work in an atmosphere that is not fundamentally helpful to his cause.

On Third World Campuses, however, in Africa at any rate, the situation is notably different and Christian strategy must vary accordingly.

While in some British universities the humanist societies are larger than the combined religious societies, in Nigeria, for example, a sociological survey indicated that nearly 93 per cent of the students at three Nigerian universities described themselves as Christians, and only 2.6 percent said "No Religion." Not only that, but the same survey in one university showed that 62 percent of those who called themselves Christians went to church weekly and a further 20 percent monthly. Nearly 75 percent said they prayed daily.

In 1972, Bishop Don Jacobs, formerly of the University of Nairobi, polled some 500 secondary school and college students which included Muslims and traditionalists as well as Christians. To the question, "Do you believe the Bible?" about 80 percent said Yes; 15 percent were not sure; and only 5 percent replied No. All of this would appear to be a help to the Gospel.

A second major question thus presents itself for discussion: *"What do First and Third World Campuses have in common? How do they vary? And how do the differences affect our approach and strategy as Christians?"*

4. Some issues on the modern campus

Anyone who would aspire to Christian service on a campus must not only research the nature and spirit of the campus, but the questions and issues. These will vary from campus to campus. A carefully planned, processed, and analyzed questionnaire might well be illuminating for any aspirant to a relevant student ministry.

This brings us to another major question for Congress consideration: *What are the Issues on the modern university campus?*

Herewith some guesses, without any attempt to elaborate on possible Christian answers. These will hopefully emerge in discussion.

a. *The non-issue* — On several campuses where we have been no one could really say what the intellectual issues were. Everyone seemed personally preoccupied with their own lives, studies and pleasures. The biggest issue became the non-issue. How far this is prevalent elsewhere is hard to say. And how does one deal with it?

b. *Hedonism* — A pleasure-oriented society will inevitably spawn pleasure-oriented offspring in its institutions. How do you pry a man loose from his toys? One warden of a university residence noted that in one British university the main student issues seemed to focus on residence and living structures, cafeteria costs, etc., and how these affected the students' own needs and comfort. It was all inward-looking and physical. Faith and knowledge were not key words, but experience. The senses were all in all. This introduces the next issue.

c. *Sex* — I recently asked a university graduate what he considered the major issue for the modern student. "I don't care what anyone says," he replied, "the bed-rock issue is sex. Students are gripped with man as a natural being, a biological creature with biological needs which are aggravated by social stimuli. The present, existential satisfaction of these is all that matters. What's nice is good for you. The basic issue thus becomes personal moral freedom, along with the nature and the responsibility of man." Sexual repression and puritan discipline are to be outlawed. The issues of behaviorism and moral relativism are also concealed within the sex issue.

d. *The quest for the personal and human* — The sex issue, I suspect, is more profoundly related to the quest for the personal and intimate. Another student I questioned said, "There is a search for identity. This is the product of modern life where many individuals are isolated and alienated from the world in which they live. Through education and the structures of society the individual is subjected to a whole mass of herd instincts, herd programming, and corporate decisions. The individual is thus lost in an overwhelming sea of public opinion and demands." Not only that, but the individual is increasingly forced to participate in collective sin. Thus technocracy, bureaucracy, "the System" (that complex interlock of political, economic, and social relationship), and a world where "thousands pass and no one meets" all combine so to depersonalize and isolate the individual that his whole life-style becomes a process of protest against dehumanization and manipulation. What modern student would not agree with Martin Buber's analysis: "The ills of the contemporary world spring from the injury done to the essentially personal nature of man."

e. *Meaninglessness* — Perhaps this is the key issue, at least on First World campuses. Life has lost its structure of inner meaning. The fabric of life seems disordered and out of joint. We are caught in what Graham Greene calls an "aboriginal calamity." Alienated from himself, man is alienated from other existents and from the whole scheme of things. There is a loss of center. Aldous Huxley put it this way, "I was born wandering between two worlds, one dead and the other powerless to be born, and have made in a curious way the worst of both." The self-sufficiency of man will no longer do. Being master of his fate and captain of his soul has proven intolerable. It is not lost on the student that the most acute atheistic philosophers are consciously philosophers of despair. To quote John Macquarrie, "There are philosophers who would say bluntly that man's existence, as finite possibility thrown into the world, is self-contradictory. Man in Sartre's famous phrase is a 'a useless passion,' for his very existence is such as to make nonsense of his aspirations and potentialities. And indeed, we have still to add the final touch to the picture — death. This existence of man ... will terminate in any case in death, and this looks like the triumph of finitude and negativity over whatever sparks of positive and affirmative being show themselves in man. An existence of contradictions, coming finally to nothing in death — this is an absurdity." Nor does there seem any place for hope if the universe is a closed system, empty, impersonal, and godless.

The student feels all this acutely, and is often driven to despair — witness the fact that in 1966 (which is the only year for which I have figures) more than 100,000 college students in the U.S.A. alone threatened suicide, more than 10,000 attempted it, and over 1,000 succeeded.

f. *Death* — Perhaps some of the above explains why death, even to youthful people, is a real issue on the campus. In almost every university mission we have done in the last seven years, we have held a symposium on death, with different viewpoints presented. Significantly, these have been packed out.

g. *Agnosticism* — The agnostic considers issues "head first," heart second. Belief must be supported by demonstrable facts. Christianity would appear to many to be low on such facts. The focus of authority is in a sense the issue. If the enthroned reason of autonomous man is held to be the final authority, faith would appear to be disqualified on the basis of an imagined incompatibility between faith and reason. The biblical view of truth constitutes a profound and powerful challenge to such a man.

The issue of *history* also arises here. The agnostic, who is sceptical of the historical base of Christianity, must be forced to face the full implications of the Christian claim that real history is the focus and center of Christian revelation. In biblical faith, everything depends on whether the central events really occurred. This kind of claim the agnostic must face in academic integrity.

Yet in fact it is probably so that most modern student agnostics have not thought themselves into their agnosticism, but drifted into it on the tide of secularism. Not having thought themselves into the position, they do not have to be reasoned out of it by appeals to the mind, but challenged out of it by appeals to the heart and will, or loved out of it by caring Christians.

h. *Other issues* — These might be listed as follows: comparative religion and the nature of truth, science and faith, the future, violence and suffering, affluence and leisure, crowd conformity, ecology, the occult, the heathen, miscellaneous political causes, public morality (e.g., Watergate), the irrelevance of "the church," etc.

With the modern university's complex nature and wide range of student issues before him, how is the Christian to proceed?

5. Christian strategy for the modern campus

Over all our attempts to reach the modern university, we must write the word THINK in letters of fire. We cannot be haphazard. We must THINK. We must know where we are going. We must PLAN. The following procedure is humbly suggested as a point of departure for discussion.

a. *A fellowship must be built* — New Testament evangelism and growth was an outflow and overflow of fellowship (see Acts 2:42-47). As they continued in the Apostles' doctrine, fellowship, breaking of bread, and prayer, people were added to the Church daily. Evangelism is born not just out of "me and God" but "us and God." There is therefore in student evangelism no greater priority than building a strong, local body of student believers who will incarnate the Gospel and give it credibility in the eyes of the whole campus. Jesus prayed, "That they may be one ... so that the world may believe ...." (John 17:21). A quality *koinonia* of believers not only authenticates the Gospel, it proclaims it. The fellowship is both medium and message. The Body of Christ on campus must be so built and trained that Christians within each group (e.g., Inter Varsity Fellowship, Campus Crusade, Navigators, Student Christian Movement, denominational societies, etc.) will exhibit towards each other the kind of love, trust and acceptance which demonstrates the Church of Jesus Christ as the truly alternative society. The Christians, in a loving web of relationships, should be experiencing the community they are offering. The campus will need to see not simply how deeply they agree, but, more significantly perhaps, how lovingly they disagree. Christian groups, remembering the need for "multiple logics," will make room for each other and not impose uniform standards and styles on one another. Sometimes groups dress up their uncooperative attitudes in the rather self-righteous guise of "an unwillingness to compromise the truth," when the real problem is an unwillingness to acknowledge the work of the Spirit in the other group or to face what membership of the catholic church involves.

Through charitable and open communication, the plans and purposes of different groups should intersect smoothly and not contradict or clash. It is when "every joint," and "each part" is working properly that there is "bodily growth" and an "upbuilding in love" (Eph. 4:16).

The building of fellowship in the Christian groups would seem to involve a balanced program of worship, prayer and teaching (particularly through biblical exposition), training, (through classes, retreats, camps), recreation (through which people discover each other in their common humanity), and practical service. Coventry Cathedral's plan of renewal was: *Pray* together, *Play* together, *Work* together. In that order.

Of critical importance in the building of the university fellowship is a clear and thorough coordination with those involved in the high school ministries (e.g., Scripture Union, Young Life, Youth for Christ, Schools and Varsities camps, etc.). Young believers coming up from the high schools should be systematically referred to those involved in the student ministries.

Another key question therefore: *"How best can the fellowship of student believers be deepened and strengthened?"*

b. *A vision must be conveyed* — The vision, I believe, which must be caught is that of the Total Body of believers (students and staff) reaching the total campus with comprehensive penetration at every level of the institution. Christians should not be a ghetto group, but a militant band of infiltrators, witnesses, and caring agents. Not only will they remind the campus of the true and full purpose of education as a search for truth, but they will seek both to evangelize individuals and to convert the structures of the university.

The vision of full Christian involvement in sport, student politics, student government, residence life, the campus newspaper, the cultural activities of the university should be held high. Jim Johnston of the Students' Christian Association (South Africa) writes, "The breakthrough into different segments of university life can come as Christians out-think, out-feel and out-live the non-Christian in the area of non-Christian strength." The aim is not simply what Gavin Reid calls "indrag," but *outreach,* through every member's involvement, to every person on the campus, where they are.

c. *A strategy must be planned, worked, and evaluated* — Looking at the total campus, the fellowship of believers will need to analyze the task, break it down into manageable units, brainstorm on relevant strategies, mobilize the forces, and assign the tasks. The overall strategy should be diversified, comprehensive, and inclusive. Being willing to run the risks of relevance, those responsible for planning will also see to it that their strategies remain flexible and subject to constant evaluation. "What are we trying to produce?" — and — "Are we producing it?" will be two key and ever-recurring questions. We must beware of the successes of yesterday surviving beyond their usefulness or relevance.

d. *Outreach must be undertaken* — All the fellowship, analyzing, and planning is of no avail until or unless evangelism actually happens. Herewith some tried and tested means of outreach:

(i) Individual and personal student witness — (ii) The witness in private and in class of the Christian professor or lecturer, particularly in disciplines like science and psychology where so often non-Christian views are vigorously and disturbingly propagated.

(iii) The special thrust aimed at *freshers* — At Oxford and Cambridge, for example, O.I.C.C.U. and C.I.C.C.U. members will often return several days before the beginning of term to help new students get settled and adjusted. The processes of my own conversion were thus initiated. The "Freshers' Sermon," to which the Christians seek to get all the freshers, then becomes a powerful evangelistic follow-up on the practical kindness previously demonstrated.

(iv) The pre-evangelistic tool of *psychedelic light shows* and multimedia presentations (e.g., I.V.C.F.'s "Twenty One Hundred" developed by Eric Miller; and Clear Light Productions, "Cry Three").

(v) Visitation evangelism — Room-to-room visits of students by Christians is best used in conjunction with a printed invitation to a special meeting. Opportunities of personal witness will often arise in such situations.

(vi) The straight lecture: e.g., on a theme of apologetic interest — the Resurrection; the New Testament documents; science and faith; freedom and meaning, etc.

(vii) Symposia — in all our recent university missions we have used symposia extensively and invariably had them packed out. With a real campus issue plus three or four articulate protagonists, the symposium often has a drawing power far in excess of the monologue lecture. Giving a voice as it were, to the "opposition" is appreciated by dialogue-oriented and anti-doctrinaire students. The Christian view, as truth, will also authenticate itself impressively when juxtaposed with alternatives.

(viii) Local church proclamation and teaching — Blessed indeed is the campus located close to a downtown church with a vigorous preaching and teaching (preferably expository) ministry. Christian students can take inquiring student friends into such contexts with impressive results following.

(ix) The Christian home — Committed Christians in a university town can use their homes in effective outreach, not just through discussion evenings, but in friendly caring. This ministry can be particularly meaningful to international Third World students studying in First World countries.

(x) Literature — Every group of Christian students in every university hall or residence should have a book ministry. At every meeting for outreach or discussion a book table should operate. A strategically located book table outside a varsity dining hall produces surprising interest and significant sales. The excellent range of I.V.F. and I.V.C.F. books and booklets, plus the fine Campus Crusade tools (e.g., Four Spiritual Laws, Ten Basic Steps to Christian Maturity, etc.) should be in constant use. *His* magazine, *Collegiate Challenge,* and other student magazines have further usefulness. At Cape Town University the Christian students started their own campus newspaper, *Comment,* which has had a vital impact on the entire university. Christians should also submit articles regularly to the secular campus newspapers.

(xi) The university chaplain and denominational group — On some campuses, student chaplains and denominational groups have significant ministries as ecclesiastical agents and groups in contradistinction to the para-ecclesiastical agencies (e.g., I.V.F., C.C.C., etc.) already referred to. However, in my own experience the university chaplaincy appears to be a laboring and not often effective phenomenon. How to improve it or whether to dispense with it is a matter probably overdue for debate. Whether the denominational group (e.g., the Anglican, Methodist, or Catholic Society) belongs on campus, or downtown in the local church is also a matter worthy of Congress discussion and suggestions.

(xii) Music and drama — The folk singer or folk group, and the dramatist or dramatic group again can make an impact, particularly in pre-evangelism, where more conventional approaches will often fail.

(xiii) The student center — "In great cities, where students are often upset and dissatisfied with the dismal atmosphere of the overcrowded campus and cramped student lodging houses, a well-equipped student center can be very attractive." The student Y.M.C.A. has proven this in many places.

(xiv) The university mission — Most universities have a tradition of a mission every three years, so that each generation of undergraduates should have the opportunity of facing the claims of Christ in a special way. This is a useful tradition, although one should add that there are times when a university is not ready for a mission, the Christian groups on the campus being too weak and divided. A mission can never be a substitute for the work of the local body, nor can it do what the local body cannot or will not do. Our experience is that the "success" or otherwise of a university mission is directly related to the quality and vitality of the student fellowship(s) out of which it flows.

The basic aim of the missioners, I believe, should be to come as a catalyst to activate the local body of Christ and to harness in assistance the resources of the wider Body of Christ. The mission team should therefore seek to:

Build the local fellowship — Several training camps or retreats for the involved Christians are accordingly planned. The vexing problem of cooperation between groups normally surfaces at this point. On really large campuses, where the evangelical groups are very strong, they can probably go it alone. On small campuses the widest Christian cooperation, in my judgment, is necessary. Otherwise more problems of Christian alienation are left in the post-mission situation than "going-it-alone" is worth.

Build the assisting team — The days of the solo student missioner are over. A team effort with three or four main missioners is necessary, and the more variety on the team the better. There should be enough assistant missioners to place one in each student residence.

Plan a diversified program — The program based on researching the local campus issues, should have three phases — preparation, proclamation, preservation. The proclamation phase is aimed not just at the students, but at the total campus community. In our most recent university mission there was a missioner to the teaching faculty and administration, two to the generally forgotten cleaning, grounds, and kitchen staff, plus other missioners for the students themselves.

Secure prayer — The indispensable importance of this goes without saying, both from the local body and beyond.

Secure the support of the university authorities — Support from the top, from the chancellor or vice-chancellor, who can be invited to serve as patron of the mission, makes the mission officially a truly university affair, and not a Christian sidekick.

Mount a first-rate publicity program — Such is the amount of publicity competing for the students' attention, that unless the mission publicity is really first-rate, containing not only originality and challenge, but also humor, it is doomed to burial and suffocation. Hans Burki of Switzerland writes, "We must emphasize that only the best in terms of layout is good enough for posters and leaflets." Combined with personal invitations from Christian students to their friends, and only then, will such publicity work and work effectively.

Do effective pre-evangelism — Pre-evangelism light shows, music festivals, religious art-exhibitions, symposia, comparative religion lectures, etc., can all be used effectively in the softening-up process to prepare the campus for the more direct proclamation. There is also value in securing openings for the missioners, where their qualifications permit, into different university faculties and societies — e.g., English, Drama, Music, Engineering, Personnel Management, Politics, etc. This way students hear the missioners in the classroom or society situation, which is real student ground, and not just on the religious ground of the mission meeting.

Proclaim the Gospel clearly — It should be noted that this can be done using more than one speaker. In a recent student mission I shared the platform and the message each evening with an African colleague.

Meet and counsel students personally — The availability of the assistant missioners for counseling in the student residences is always of vital importance and usefulness.

Follow-up thoroughly — This has to be done primarily by the campus Christians themselves. Hopefully, their residence cells and study groups, which have often been operating before the mission, are ready to receive and nurture the new inquirers. Such inquirers need both fellowship and teaching. An entirely doctrine-oriented body (where people simply get "sorted out" theologically) will not hold such inquirers. An entirely friendship-oriented body, with no clear theological teaching, will draw the inquirers, initially, but not ground them adequately, or hold them permanently. "The Apostles' doctrine, fellowship, breaking of bread, and prayer" must all be present within the receiving groups if follow-up is to be effective.

This leads to my last observation regarding university work generally.

e. *Follow-up must be sustained* — The follow-up ingredient must be integral to the overall strategy of campus evangelism all the time. To catch fish and let them go is the height of folly. The C.I.C.C.U. man who led me to Christ insisted not only on my going to two corporate Bible studies a week, but also on a personal study with me once a week for a year after he had led me to Christ. This was of incalculable help. Campus Crusade summarizes their philosophy — Win, Build, Send. One cannot really better that.

6. Conclusion

Bill Bright has said, "Students represent the major source of manpower to help change the course of history. They need to be reached for Christ." The challenge is that simple, that difficult, and that glorious. May this Congress accelerate the fulfilling of the Great Commission in this generation, particularly as it affects the student world.

EVANGELIZATION AMONG COLLEGE AND UNIVERSITY STUDENTS REPORT

Catalyst
The paper given by Michael Cassidy raised seven basic questions which were discussed in small groups the following day. These comments are not necessarily the consensus of the whole group, but rather represent the report given by each study group. It should be noted that some comments will only be appropriate in certain cultural or geographical situations.

1. What is the nature of the modern university as receiver of our message and how should its nature affect us in our approach and presentation?

Modern universities continue to be in the process of questioning their goals, and priorities to achieve these goals. These questions are answered in different ways and at different times in various parts of the world.

a. *North American and parts of Western Europe:*
   1) Faculty have a different emphasis than the students, *primarily* adding to the knowledge of their academic discipline through research; *secondarily* teaching; *thirdly* service to the university as a whole, a society.
   2) Concern to help students find meaning in life and come to know and understand themselves would be considered important only by a minority. Many faculty members outside the area of their specialized work have no sense of overriding purpose either for their university as a whole, or for the society in which they live.
   3) In contrast, such concerns would be of vital importance to most students. But other than knowledge in one or more academic disciplines, students are often not sure what they want from the university. Many feel lost and rootless in an impersonal technological society that has no concern for human needs. Their concern is primarily with their own future. The needs of society, though not ignored, are secondary.

b. *Universities where Marxism is dominant* — Less emphasis is placed on the preferences of the traditional student and more concern for him to find a place in which to serve society within the framework and presuppositions of that philosophy.

c. *Universities in the Third World* — There is often a sense of nationalism and of nation building among both faculty and students which gives purpose to much of student and faculty activities.

In our approach to university students, faculty, and staff, in all three of these situations, we can appeal to their concern for a sense of coherent meaning in their lives. Also, from a Christian perspective we can question the priorities given at universities in the selection of topics for research and the content of curricula.

2. Chaplaincy: Should evangelicals participate or opt out?

a. Evangelicals should not opt out of university chaplaincies. Rather they sould seek for openings where possible.
b. Chaplains should be always available for staff and students.
c. Encourage interdenominational chaplains (seems to be working well in Africa).
d. Chaplains could give leadership and unity to the smaller Christian groups on campus.

3. How can we prepare high school students for university?

a. Referral and follow up from Christian organizations working in high schools.
b. Special effort to contact first year students immediately on their arrival on campus.
c. Camps, conferences, seminars, etc., especially designed to prepare high school students for the university experience and to interact with Christian faculty and students.
d. Books that can help students anticipate the intellectual and moral problems they may face; to be read and discussed with more mature Christians.
e. Important equipment for the new student is an ability to discern and analyze the anti-Christian presuppositions of many systems and professors. The student should have a maturing apologetic and doctrinal understanding.
f. The Christian home and home church can be a vital source of support, stability and encouragement.
g. Concern to show high school students the relevance of Scripture to hard twentieth century questions.
h. Training in personal discipline in terms of Bible study, prayer, etc.

4. University evangelism is a hostile situation

a. In some geographic areas (i.e., Moslem and Hindu societies) the university students are the most responsive group to the Gospel.
b. *Problems:*
   1) government restrictions on Christians;
   2) university policies against Christian meetings;
   3) student political organizations put pressure on Christian students.
c. *Christian responsibility to:*
   1) make clear to the individual the costly implications of becoming a Christian;
   2) to minister to all the difficulties which a new Christian will face as a result of conversion; to provide family care and support for the new believer.

    d.   *Principle:* No rigid strategy for evangelism can be superimposed by persons or agencies outside the situation. Strategy must arise indigenously to be sensitive to the particular problems in each situation and the leadership of the Holy Spirit.

    e.   *Method:* primarily cell groups and friendship evangelism.

5. How best can the fellowship of student believers be deepened and strengthened?

    a.   The quality of our fellowship with one another is a reflection of the quality of our individual relationships with God.

    b.   Need to clarify meaning of "koinonia" and to differentiate between fellowship and friendship. Fellowship is a sharing of the common life in Christ, which may be experienced in a variety of situations and activities.

    c.   *Some practical suggestions:*

        1)   strategic prayer groups as a specific evangelistic arm

        2)   action groups — cell group principle with a variety of emphasis, ie., service, or special project, etc.

        3)   social activities to get to know one another, see others' gifts, enjoy one another in the Christian "open home"

        4)   evangelistic teams — medical/social/etc., for example, Philippines and Indonesia

6. Marxism, Social Revolution and Student Evangelism

    a.   The Marxist opposes faith in Christ, because he thinks he is dealing with "Christianity" which he may:

        1)   identify with capitalism;

        2)   recognize as a Western missionary, and therefore Western capitalist import;

        3)   misunderstand as an offer of words, but not an offer of social justice and social change;

        4)   identify as conservatism.

    b.   The solution to evangelism is associated with three factors:

        1)   Evangelism is to be carried out in the context of a demonstration of meaningful life for individuals who know Christ;

        2)   Evangelism ought to involve debate, but to be conducted in a context of demonstrating the unifying power of Christ among believers;

        3)   Evangelism should show that Christianity is not tied to any political system.

7. How to motivate students for evangelism

    a.   The starting point is the quality of the spiritual life of individuals and the group. Motivation is primarily internal and spiritual and is not a product of a program.

    b.   Therefore, encourage personal discipleship of believers and have mature Christians who give leadership in these qualities, as well as evangelism.

c. From Zaire was a concerted effort to contact "less dedicated"
   Christians:
   1) ask the committed Christians to pray specifically for the in-
      different Christians.
   2) ask the committed Christians to visit the indifferent Chris-
      tians.
   3) make sure the core group live what they believe.
d. Training in apologetics, biblical content, etc.
e. Immersion-principle
   "Take them, don't send them." Link Christians up with non-
   Christians; expose them to non-Christian ideas, etc., so they can
   understand the emptiness experienced by those who do not
   know God, and also see in a fresh perspective the strength and
   beauty of the Christian alternative.
   1) *Germany* — Navigators take a disciple to learn by observ-
      ing a one-to-one conversation. *Canada* — take several stu-
      dents to a rap session, etc., for them to see more mature
      Christians in action and also to gain confidence in the
      biblical answers.

It only takes a few converts to begin to inspire confidence. Involve
new converts in witnessing.

Recommended book: *Starting As A Christian Student* by David Jack-
man, InterVarsity Fellowship.

I. *Goals and objectives of campus evangelism in the next decade*
   1. Reach every student, faculty and staff with the Gospel.
   2. Responsibly disciple the students — win, build, train.
   3. Aim at penetrating campuses which have no existing
      groups.
   4. University missions for every student generation, but there
      is a danger of students living for missions or counting on
      them to do the evangelizing.
   5. Aim at building up a mature, alive, consistent fellowship
      on our campuses which will genuinely reflect the Body of
      Christ.
   6. Need to help students see God's call to ministry *within* the
      academic structure.
   7. Aim to have a strong evangelical church with an expository
      teaching ministry near to each university campus.
   8. To encourage students who come to Jesus Christ to prove
      his Lordship in their thinking, their studies, their campus
      involvement — in fact in all of life!

II. *Obstacles and hindrances*
   1. The apathetic attitude in Christians
   2. Lack of serious, persistent prayer
   3. Lack of responsibly involved and committed faculty
   4. An unclear understanding of the Gospel
   5. Pressure of school work and other commitments
   6. Lack of consistent leadership in student groups
   7. Train students in a variety of evangelistic methods, i.e.,
      ties

8.   Antagonistic attitudes of some churches
9.   Failure of Christians to be truly involved in life of the campus
10. Pressure from non-Christian families
11. Often if a student has become a Christian on campus, when he leaves, if he has no church tie he has a very difficult time.

III. *Resources necessary*
1.   Holy Spirit — his guidance, leadership, and strategy is vital
2.   Faculty, staff, and pastors who love, care, and have time for students
3.   Local church with a strong, expository ministry
3.   Use of Christian homes near campus
5.   Christians who are obedient to God, effective witnesses and/or trainers of others
6.   Meaningfully involved graduates
7.   Literature
8.   Trained teachers to build up the groups in solid biblical content

IV. *Steps in implementation*
1.   Encourage communication among various Christian groups and plan concerted strategy.
2.   Strategically place Christians in university residences and other places of influence.
3.   Provide framework and opportunities for students to get to know other Christian students and faculty.
4.   Encourage bright Christian students to think of university teaching, and train them now for student involvement.
5.   Plan a variety of evangelistic approaches to meet the various groups that make up the university.
6.   Hold special evangelistic camps and conferences, lecture series, etc.
7.   Train students in a variety of evangelistic methods, i.e., evangelistic Bible studies, etc.
8.   Develop and strengthen graduate fellowships.
9.   Keep an eye open for students who would mature to be traveling secretaries, etc.

Specialized comments

Africa — organize writers' course and workshops.

EVANGELIZATION AMONG WOMEN

B.V. Subbamma

Dr. Subbamma, East Godavara, South India, is a member of the Lutheran Church and has developed a unique ashram program in India. She has authored New Patterns for Discipling Hindus.

In this issue strategy paper I would mention the tremendous task of evangelizing women in the world, but I concentrate on evangelization among Hindu women in India. While dealing with Hindu women, it becomes necessary to include Hindu community at various points.

To fulfill the Great Commission of our Lord in this generation, we need new strategies for helping to accomplish that goal in every country of the world. As you know, about half of the world's population are women. It is evident that in the life and teachings of Jesus Christ, he gave equal importance to women. In the life of the church, women play a very important part. In the great task of evangelizing the nations, Christian women have equal responsibility with men to bear witness to the redeeming love of our Lord. In countries like India where women are more responsive to the Gospel, special effort should be made to disciple such groups of women, using the patterns that are practical in their situation. I am involved in the Ashram Evangelism among Hindus in India. In general, the Hindu community is more receptive to the Gospel than ever before, but Hindu women are even more responsive to the Good News. In this paper, I would present the tremendous opportunities that we have to proclaim Christ to Hindu women. I also would like to bring to your notice the various problems that one has to face in discipling Hindus and especially Hindu women from caste background.

Social structure

Before we take up the issue of evangelizing Hindu women as well as the Hindu community, it is necessary to understand the social structure of the Hindu community. Indian society has been divided into four big groups or castes. The Brahmins, Kshatriyas, Vaisyas, and the Sudras. In addition to the above are the untouchables or schedule classes, who are now being called Harijans. The division of the village into a number of castes constitutes one of the most fundamental features of its social structure. The individual's position in the caste structure is fixed by birth. The caste system gives to Hindu society a segmentary character. In such a community Christianity has taken roots among the two communities of the Harijans, (Malas and Madigas) in South India and other lowest-stratum people in other areas. In most cases the church is located in the palem which lies some distance away from the village proper.

The Rev. S.W. Schmitthenner, president of our Andhra Evangelical Lutheran Church, made a survey of evangelism among Hindus and presented a paper in 1968 on "The Structure and Outreach of the A.E.L. Church in Rural Andhra." He pointed out three reasons for the lack of evangelization among Hindus. First, the present congregational structure imposes limitations on the outreach of the rural church. The very location of most rural congregations hinders the outreach. Second, even good congregations failed to witness to the caste people in the village. The segmented nature of society in an Indian village makes it difficult for even a successful method or idea to spread from the palem to the Sudhra part of the village. "For the most part, the Hindu looks upon the Christian palem as a Harijan palem," says Paul Wiebe. The idea of Christ appeals to him, but not the idea of patterning his style of life and worship after that of the Harijans. Among attitudes of Christians that are detrimental to the spread of the Gospel, the most critical failure on the part of the congregation is lack of evangelical motivation. Most Christians do not feel the responsibility of discipling Hindus. The third reason he suggests is that most of the pastors do not consider outreach as part of their work. The present theological education does not train the candidates to disciple non-Christians. Bishop Lesslie Newbigin of Madras says that the training of the ministry is not for a mission to the world, but almost exclusively for the pastoral care of established Christian congregations.

Mr. Schmitthenner believes that the widespread influence of the Reddys, Kammas, and Kapus throughout the other castes of the village as well as their capacity to absorb and introduce new ideas, has great implications for those who seek to permeate all of society with the Gospel of Christ. He added, "Never before have the caste people showed such an interest in the Gospel." Through his survey Mr. Schmitthenner found that the number of women converts from Hindu background is far greater than the men. This outreach has been done mainly by about two hundred Bible women and lady missionaries in our A.E.L. church. On the basis of sociological study he points out that religious change can be brought through women in Andhra. The same situation prevails in many parts of India.

Obstacles for evangelism

The women converts might have been more effective witnesses among their own people, if they were allowed to become disciples of Christ in their own culture and worship in their localities. Unfortunately what happened in the past was, in most cases that these convert women were left to themselves without much Christian fellowship. Because of the many social obstacles they cannot become a part of the Harijan Christian community. For some it became almost impossible to live with their families, and they were given shelter in mission compounds. Either way, their widespread Christian influence has been cut down. Despite this unfortunate situation, in some places the convert women started to have prayer cells in their houses, the Bible women helped to conduct Sunday worship service and have prayers with them on weekdays also. Such prayer cells in the midst of caste communities attracted several non-Christian friends. For example, Bhagyamma in Nidubrolu had prayers in her house for about fifteen years, then it became a congregation of nearly a hundred women and a few men. Recently, they started to construct a church in their locality. Another woman, Chittamma of Veeravasaram, conducts prayers in her own house. Because of her influence, seventeen women and her brother-in-law became Christians.

There are several women converts like this who became the main source of influence to bring the Gospel to many caste women and to some families.

To Hindus, for the individual and for groups to have spiritual experience is not objectionable but joining another community is difficult. Christianization by asking converts to join other social and ethnic groups not only causes much loss to the individuals, the family, and the community, but is also bad for the resulting church and prevents further spread of the Christian faith. Because of the work of the women evangelists, there are many caste women who believe in the Lord Jesus Christ. But they are not able to be baptized since baptism is understood to entail leaving one community and joining another. This means not merely the rite of baptism but the abandonment of one's own culture and kindred. Ways must be found by which people may become Christians in each Indian culture and community.

Personal experience

I take this opportunity to add my personal experience. I was born in a Hindu family and in a miraculous way Christ entered into my life. I accepted Christ and decided to be baptized at the age of eighteen, while studying in Andhra Christian College, Guntur. At the time of my baptism the burden to evangelize non-Christians came to me. Having such a call, I tried to present Christ to my non-Christian friends, in the patterns that are customary in our Lutheran church. I began to understand that many are willing to accept Christ, but are very hesitant to join the church for social reasons. I have long felt the desire to work out a solution for the many seemingly unnecessary problems which prevent non-Christians from becoming disciples of Christ. Today Hindus are more responsive than ever before, but the growth of the church among them is nevertheless regrettably small. The problem is complex. Among other things, Hindus want to become Christians in their own culture and to worship in their own localities. There is a great urgency to start new patterns of evangelism among Hindus. The doors are opened for communicating the Gospel, and churches must be planted among these receptive homogeneous groups before the doors are closed again.

Christian Ashram

Knowing the urgency of evangelism, I started a Christian Ashram in June 1968, at Rajahmundry, believing that an alternative structure of this type might help to promote the Gospel. I am convinced that the crucial question which faces us in the form of this problem of diversity and of ineffective structures is the problem of strategy. One can, of course, mount a direct attack against practices and organizations one finds ineffective. This is a dramatic way to proceed; it is certain to attract attention. It is even more certain to generate considerable heat and hostility and to bear the fruits of bitterness. Under such circumstances, wisdom suggests that it is better to concentrate one's energies in the creation of alternative structures to serve newly emerging needs than to dissipate one's energies in combat. Build new structures alongside of old ones. This is a simple but effective strategy for situations of diversity and change. Wherever new needs have developed, or one notices groups of people not served through existing structures, the appropriate course of action is to develop ways and means of meeting these situations. The result may be a plurality of forms. This can be a sign of strength, not of weakness. A consequence may be that some practices both old and new will disappear, so long as other forms are available to meet needs. This development is a healthy one. The church is not bound to one set of forms — it can use variety. Building alternative structures to extend the ministry of the church is not a new strategy in the life of the church, but it is one that has not been consciously employed. Perhaps the time is now ripe to accept this strategy consciously and deliberately.

The Christian Ashram can play a very important part in India. The Ashram is an ancient religious institution of India, but it is not an institution in the ordinary sense of the term. It is an organism rather than an organization, and it is very well suited to the religious conditions of India. Ashrams have demonstrated that Christ can unite people of different creeds, castes, and colors into brotherhood. There are many kinds of Ashrams, but one that I have envisaged is "Patana Paricharya Dhyana Ashram" (study, service, and meditation). It is a place of worship, fellowship, and work. When we started the Ashram in 1968, 183 women, a few men and twenty-eight children came to the Ashram during the first month. These were all Hindus and caste converts. The program is most informal. Indigenous worship with Bhajana, and Burrakathas are popular (story telling by Indian dance). Sharing experience is very beneficial for the strengthening of each others faith. Fellowship has been greatly appreciated. The women who attended the first session kept bringing their friends and relatives. Another pleasant experience was that the women that came enjoyed hearing the Gospel so much that they were inspired to share it with their friends and neighbors. So they invited us to conduct Gospel meetings in the midst of non-Christians in their villages. Large crowds of men and women heard the Gospel. It is amazing how a single woman or a few women newly introduced to the Christian faith can influence the whole community. To cite a couple of examples; Addala Surayamma came to the Ashram in 1968 and stayed only for two days. After two weeks she brought her husband and bought a Bible. From then on she kept bringing people to the Ashram from her village and also from the neighboring places. Surayamma and some of her relatives were baptized, Surayamma's house is their place of worship. Another woman, Subbayamma a recent convert, has great enthusiasm to share the Gospel with her friends and relatives. About fifty of them became Christians. They worship in Subbayamma's house. Subbayamma's sister also helps to promote the Gospel. On February 12, 1974, she brought two women for baptism to our Ashram. She and her friends meet for prayer and fellowship in her house. Her husband is still a Hindu, but bought a site to build a church.

Despite many good results, we have experienced much tension at the Ashram. The amazing responsiveness of the Kammas and Kapus and others amazed me. Dozens of women indicated a desire to be baptized but hesitated because they would have had to be baptized in the Harijan Christian church building which is at a distance from their residence. I started to wonder whether there was not some way for the tremendous task to be accomplished. While I was pondering this issue, four members from the Lutheran Church in America visited the Ashram program. They recommended that I do further research regarding this project. Accordingly I spent two years in the United States and completed research which enabled me to devise an effective Christian approach to Hindus. Soon after I returned to India, I started to establish Ashrams in several parts of Andhra Pradesh and in different denomination areas. We have twelve Ashrams: Rajahmundry, Guntur, Peddapuram, Kakinada, Chirala, Bhimavaram, Vadali, Mandapeta, Eluru, Narasaraopeta, Nuzvidu, and Vijayawada. The common goal of these Ashrams is to reach the unreached non-Christians with the Gospel, but each Ashram has freedom to develop methods to communicate the Gospel according to the cultural background of the people. I wrote two books: *New Patterns for Discipling Hindus*, and *Christ Confronts India*, making suggestions how the evangelization could be carried out among millions of Hindus in our generation. However much I am ambitious to emphasize the importance and the practicality of my suggestions, I am also conscious of the fact that it should not be a blueprint. It is my intention that the program should grow with the people that participate in it.

House churches

We are thankful that Ashrams are attracting great numbers of women and some men to Christ, but the enthusiastic and committed new converts and inquirers have no place to meet and no one to lead them in spiritual matters. I am convinced that house churches are most practical in this situation. Floyd V. Filson has written about "The significance of the Early House Churches." As the Christians grew in number, they met in different houses. A study of the Acts and Epistles reveals that the chief place where believers are said to have held their meetings in their homes. About twenty times, we read of Christians carrying out their united worship in the home of a believer. Four times "the church in the house" is specifically mentioned, (Rom. 16:5; I Cor. 16:19; Col. 4:15; and Philemon 2).

Existing churches are places for the nurture of Christians only. In other words, they are "shut in churches," whereas house churches have doors open to non-Christians to worship. On January 6,1974, two rich Hindu women were baptized at our Ashram in Rajahmundry. We went to visit them on February 10 (Sunday), and were thrilled to see them in worship service in their own house. The place was filled with many non-Christian friends. They meet not only on Sunday but for different periods almost everyday. This is how house churches can help to have daily worship to which the Hindus are accustomed.

Can Hindus become Christians in their own culture?

Please note that Hindus often do not object to a person's believing in the Lord Jesus and praying to him. The great obstacle is joining a church of a Harijan community. I know this is a wrong attitude, but merely to say this is not helpful. The question is how to change this attitude. The best thing is to smooth the path by leading them to accept the Bible as their rule of faith and practice. After they accept Christ they will naturally understand that they are one with the Christians of any background. Let me say that I have no desire to perpetuate caste exclusiveness and a caste pride. The separation which I propose must be understood as temporary and provisional. It is merely a stage in a long journey. In the beginning, a certain amount of freedom and flexibility are needed to try out and explore various ways and means to disciple Hindus. After enough of them are converted, the stigma of Christianity being an "outcaste religion" will disappear, then there will be greater possibility for Christian unity. I am a firm believer in the Universal Church and the brotherhood of man. The long-range goal must be full brotherhood with full equality of opportunity. As congregations multiply, thousands of converts will do many things with the existing church which will build up the unity of the church. Common theological training will help all church leaders to have the same faith and the same doctrine of foundation. Common communion services can be arranged occasionally. Christian festivals can be celebrated together.

Indigenous churches

The kind of congregations I am proposing must be indigenous churches from the beginning. First, let us come to a clear understanding of the term "indigenous." In much missions-thinking, a church which is self-governing, self-supporting, and self-propagating is an "indigenous church." I agree with William A. Smalley that this is a false diagnosis. He says, "An indigenous church is a group of believers who live out their life, including their socialized Christian activity, in the patterns of the local society, and for whom any transformation of that society comes out of their felt needs under the guidance of the Holy Spirit and the Scriptures." The church in every land must be a church of that land and that culture. But what I am suggesting goes further than that elementary truth. The church must be a church of each sub-culture. There should be freedom for each ethnic unit in each land to follow its own culture. Our present concern is with establishing churches among caste Hindus. So it is necessary to constitute the congregation in the pattern familiar to them. Churches which are really indigenous to the ethnic units will have s structure different from that of the existing churches. Indigenous churches "spring up in the soil from the very first seeds planted," says Roland Allen. They create their own structures and polity which evolve naturally from the patterns already common to the local culture and society.

Leadership training

The success of the Ashram program depends on its personnel to disciple the great number of Hindu women and men. We certainly need hundreds and thousands of women and men leaders. New structures demand new patterns of leadership. To start congregations in the caste sections, Christians with zeal in evangelizing non-Christians must be trained. As the converts from different caste backgrounds are available they should be trained for this ministry. After having adequate training, each pastor can be placed in charge of several house churches, depending on the ability of the person. Each of the house churches can be led by an unpaid local man or woman. The pastor is like a spiritual father.

To train a sufficient number of leaders at the local level to adopt theological education by extension is good. It is not possible for many of the middle class men and women to leave their homes and work, and to go to some distant centers for long periods of time for training. It would fit in well, if the layleaders of the congregation were trained by teachers from among themselves, working in their midst by extension. Dr. Wilfred Scope, with his many years of experience in India, thinks very highly of Ashrams and informal training. In the Ashram movement, which has combined study and meditation with fellowship and dialogue among non-Christian friends, it would be possible to arrange for short courses to train natural leaders.

Ordination for women

Going back to my specific subject of evangelization among women, especially in India, because of the cultural background, there must be women leaders on different levels, lay as well as ordained. If some women can be ordained for the special ministry among Hindus, we can hope to reach many women, and through them many families also. Thus churches can be multiplied. With the help of ordained women, house churches can easily be established. In Indian culture it is easier for a woman to approach families also. In present-day India particularly, women are given important places in social and political affairs. When a woman can be accepted as a prime minister, I see no reason why an Indian woman cannot be a pastor. More than in Western countries, women ministers like lady doctors are needed in India.

In the past, Indian churches did not entertain the thought of ordaining women, holding that their sponsoring churches in the West would not ordain women. But now things have changed with Western churches; women are being ordained. In Denmark, ordination of women has been practiced since 1948; in Czechoslovakia, since 1959; in Norway, since 1961; in Sweden, since 1960; in Germany, twenty of the twenty-seven member churches of the Evangelical church of Germany permit the ordination of the women. Japan Lutherans ordained a woman pastor in 1970. The Lutheran Church in America in its 1970 convention voted that women be permitted to be ordained with all the privileges pertaining to the pastoral office.

The traditional view that only men should be ordained is being challenged because of the change in the position of women in society. And the development of biblical interpretation permits such basic considerations. There must be equal opportunity for all persons to share their gifts in their chosen vocations. The church should be a community of people, men and women, rich and poor, black, yellow, and white. Moreover, it is essential for women to be ordained to promote the evangelization of Hindu women who are responsive to the Gospel.

Ashram evangelism

We have seen that through Ashram evangelism we are able to reach Hindu women with the Gospel. It is evident that Christ can enter into families through women. We are convinced that house churches are most practicable to attract non-Christians and that eventually they develop

772 LET THE EARTH HEAR HIS VOICE

into large churches. This has happened in a number of places. For example, Chandramma in Govada accepted Christ and started prayers in a house. Gradually her family and many other Hindus became Christians. They have built a church in the village. Seetharavamma in Amruthlur became a convert and through her influence, a big congregation arose, and their house church has been developed into a large church. In Mirzapur, Savithramma proclaimed the Good News to Hindu women and families, using her house for worship. In the last few years about one hundred families became Christians and have built a beautiful church. There are several women like this who are the main cause of the wide spread of Christianity. Through Ashrams following the above pattern the whole nation can be evangelized.

Who runs the Ashrams

For many reasons, the existing churches cannot take the initiative for this task, but if any outside organization sponsors the program, at least for some years, the different denominational churches cooperate. The Division for World Missions and Ecumenism of the Lutheran Church in America granted funds for three years for this program. In India our Lutheran Church, the Canadian Baptist Church, the Church of South India gave buildings to establish Ashrams. They are also providing leaders whom we are training and using at the Ashrams for evangelization. The Division for World Missions and Ecumenism asks us to find ways and means to support this work; their three-year period will end by 1974, when again they may decide what financial help to give to the Ashrams. It would be very helpful if Lausanne would take an interest in the possibilities of promoting Ashram evangelism. Along with the Divison for World Missions and Ecumenism and various denominational churches in India, many other world organizations, churches, and individuals may cooperate in this program. This is too big a task for any one agency. This program provides a wonderful opportunity to participate in the evangelization of non-Christians in India.

Conclusion

As Director of Christian Ashrams, I see a great future for this work. But if the world church does not cooperate, the churches in India will not be able to handle the situation. I would like to make a few suggestions for Lausanne to consider regarding Ashram work. An interdenominational committee on an international basis may be formed to discuss this matter and report to the body which does the follow-up work of the International Congress on World Evangelization. For better understanding of the Ashram movement, a team of friends might be sent to India for a period of time to participate in this program. Another possibility is that a few of us can be invited by other countries to demonstrate Ashram activities. Since we are especially talking about evangelization among women, the women representatives at the congress may be interested to support Ashram evangelism through the women's organizations of their respective churches. I ask you to pray that our Lord may use all of us to make this program and other evangelism programs in the world a great success. Nothing is more pleasing to Jesus Christ than presenting him to the nations of the world. Let me conclude this paper by quoting Acts 1:8, "But ye shall receive power, after that the Holy Ghost is come upon you: and ye shall be witnesses unto me both in Jerusalem and in all Judaea, and in Samaria, and unto the uttermost part of the earth."

EVANGELISM AMONG WOMEN REPORT

Chairman: Mrs. Gien Karssen

Summary three sessions:

Dr. Subbamma shared Ashram evangelism as an example of how women can be reached with the Gospel in her country, but how the same basic and biblical principle can be used in other cultures. The last session was set apart for interaction with each other and sharing of ideas, problems, and possible solutions.

After these discussions we all closed in prayer, knowing we as women need God's guidance and wisdom to do the work he gave us to do in our sphere of influence.

Session 1 and 2:

Background — Dr. Subbamma is from a Hindu background. When she became a Christian she received from God a burden to evangelize Hindus. However, she saw that Hindus want to become Christian in their own culture and worship, and in their own localities. She has written two books about this subject.

New patterns for discipling Hindus and Christ confront India

Ashrams — This is a community of people belonging to various castes and religions, living together for a short or long period of time. There is time to hear and study the Word of God, to meditate, to share, to sing and clap hands, all in a very relaxed and informal way. The Gospel is presented in various ways, among them the use of narrative stories, all designed to help the people understand how they can identify with the biblical truth being presented. They start where the people are.

Where was the first ashram started? From June, 1968, to June, 1974, the ashram movement started twelve ashrams for women and families on an interdenominational basis in Andhra. These ashrams are Christ-centered and people-oriented. The use of indigenous methods attracts large crowds of Hindus to the ashrams to hear the Gospel of Christ. After they become Christians they are trained how to pass on the Gospel to others in the places where they live and work. Through Mobile Ashram Evangelism the Gospel is taken to the people in villages and towns.

What is the relation to the churches? The ashrams want to be a cultural bridge between the people and the churches. Pastors are invited to come in order that they might see what the program is all about. Between most churches and the ashrams there is good communication.

Why are women important? Through the ashrams many Hindu women are reached. Because of them whole families and Hindu communities can be reached and are being reached. In India every woman may go to a man and talk to him. This is not possible the other way around.

Session 3:

Discussion questions:
How can we learn from each other and use the biblical principle in our situation? What individuals and organizations are active in your part of the world? What can we do to improve situations?

Input was gathered from Laos, Spain, Norway, Zaire, the Netherlands, and the U.S.A.

Problems:
1) Churches in most cases have no outreach programs;
2) Lack of motivated, faithful people;
3) Lack of discipled people who in turn can train other faithful people (II Tim. 2:2);
4) Lack of training, both spiritually as well as practically.

Steps to undertake and possibilities to evangelize

1) Reach people where they are. Try to identify with them, which involves our total commitment to God and our fellowman.

2) Look for programs that will help people discover how practical the Christian life is, and how it influences our total life.

3) Look for a place where people can meet together, to learn to understand Christianity in a new way. This can be a step-by-step development (as in the Ashrams).

4) The program must be oriented to the audience and its needs (as is done in the Ashrams).

5) A loving atmosphere, and a place where people will experience peace, joy and love, the fruit of the Spirit of God. This will attract people, through the work of the Holy Spirit.

6) Training:

a) How women daily can experience the Christian life and can live in the power of God's Holy Spirit.

b) How they can study the Word of God and have an effective prayer life.

c) Why they should evangelize and how they can share Christ with others.

d) How they can train other women and disciple people who also will know how to share Christ in life and words with others.

e) Practical outreach programs.

f) The role of a woman and how the Lord can use her in her sphere of influence.

Offered possibilities by such organizations as Navigators and Campus Crusade:

1) Training in how to start Bible study groups.
2) How to start prayer groups.
3) How to share Christ with others.
4) Conferences and literature.

EVANGELISM AMONG THE BLIND, DEAF, AND HANDICAPPED

David J.C. Judson

*Mr. Judson, Beirut, Lebanon, teaches in a
school for the blind connected with the
Lebanon Evangelical Mission in Beirut.*

Jesus said, "Preach the Gospel to every creature." This command is all-inclusive, and means that *every* person, even those in the minority groups, which we call "handicapped," has the right to hear the Gospel — although the world's thirty million blind are scarcely a minority!

We must start with two basic definitions, to set the limits of this paper.

a. *Definition of evangelism* — We shall consider evangelism simply as "Reaching people with the basic message of the Bible, and presenting the facts of sin and personal salvation through the risen Lord Jesus, in such a way that the Holy Spirit can lead them to repentance and faith."

b. *Definition of "blind, deaf and handicapped"* — Degrees of handicap vary immensely; the problems of the partially-hearing or partially-sighted, solved by a deaf-aid or low-vision aid, are totally different from those whose handicap or sense-loss is more complete. This article will consider "handicapped" to mean *those who are prevented, specifically because of their handicap, from hearing and responding to the Gospel through the normal channels.* Included in this category would be those unable to mix freely with others or get out to church services or public evangelistic meetings, and also those suffering from a sense-loss which means that a special mode of communication is necessary, such as Braille for the blind person, and the manual alphabet for the deaf-blind. For sake of completeness we shall also refer briefly to the mentally handicapped, but really a separate study is needed to cover evangelism in this specialized area.

My definition is concerned with primarily the younger age-groups, i.e., those born handicapped, or those who become handicapped in earlier life. While it is true that statistically the majority of handicapped people in a country are in the eventide of life, their handicap is usually a direct result of old age; we could call them the "age-handicapped." During the earlier portion of their life they probably had opportunity to hear the Gospel. Special methods often are not applicable to them — e.g., they are too old to learn Braille, but the church nevertheless should have a caring ministry that rescues such people from spending their latter years in solitude and loneliness.

1. Attitudes in the Bible towards the handicapped

a. *Caring* — The Old Testament reveals the *care* of the people of God for those who were physically handicapped. "Don't curse the deaf or put a stumbling-block before the blind" (Lev. 19:14). "I was eyes to the blind, and feet to the lame," says Job (29:15). As well as physical help, material help is stressed, "Open thine hand wide unto thy brother, to thy poor and to thy needy in thy land" (Deut. 15:11). Such was the effect of this concern that "it is significant that in the Old Testament scarcely a trace of beggars and begging in the street can be found."

While the handicapped, not being able to earn a living, were provided for adequately, there seems the possibility that they were regarded as second-class citizens. Lev. 21:16-23 states that no person with a "blemish" could be a priest, and a list of physical handicaps follows. I feel this is no reflection on the handicapped person, but rather a wonderful reminder of the holiness and whole-ness of God. The sacrificial lamb, too, had to be "without blemish," and both priest and lamb point forward to the Lord Jesus Christ, our passover Lamb and great high priest. So we can understand the reason for the prohibition.

By the time of Jesus, the commendable concern of the people of God in the Old Testament for the handicapped (e.g., II Sam. 9:13) seems to have broken down, and under the Roman occupation we meet many beggars in the streets as we travel around with Jesus, and so Jesus restresses the importance of almsgiving (Matt. 6:1-4), and of concern for the "poor, the maimed, the lame and the blind" (Luke 14:13). Paul, too, exhorts the Ephesian church to "support the weak," and remember the words of the Lord Jesus, "It is more blessed to give than to receive" (Acts 20:35). In the epistles, churches are urged to remember the needy, and these would naturally include those unable to work because of physical disability e.g., Heb. 13:1-2; Rom. 15:25-27. James re-echoes the strong warning of the Lord Jesus ("Lord, when saw we Thee an hungred and fed Thee?..." Matt. 25:33-39) with his equally strong "If a brother or sister be naked ... and ye give them not ..." (Jas. 2:14-17).

b. *Healing* — The few healing miracles of the Old Testament seem to concern those with diseases such as leprosy, or raising from the dead. The writers of the Gospels, however, include many instances of the blind, deaf, and lame being healed by Jesus. Indeed, part of the proof offered to John the Baptist that Jesus was indeed the Messiah was the fact that "the blind receive their sight, and the lame walk, the lepers are cleansed, and the deaf hear ..." (Matt. 11:5). It is not clear from the Gospels how widespread the healing ministry of Jesus was. About twenty healing miracles are recorded, but presumably there were many more. Luke 4:40 states that at sunset any sick were brought to Jesus, "and He laid hands on every one of them and healed them." Therefore the emphasis of the ministry of Jesus is more than merely care and compassion for the handicapped, or even the exercise of faith, and the administration of forgiveness; it is primarily physical restoration.

Moving into the Apostolic era, a number of cases of miraculous healing are recorded in the book of Acts. While the basis of Mark 16:18 for this ministry is disputed, the Lord's commissioning of the twelve (Matt. 10:1) and the seventy (Luke 10:9) included the command to heal the sick, and this ministry was presumably to be continued after the ascension. Acts 5:12-16 shows the remarkable extent of this ministry.

The giving of the Holy Spirit at Pentecost marked the beginning of the Church era, and Paul records that included amongst the gifts of the Spirit to the Church are the gifts of healing and miracles (I Cor. 12:9,

10). That Paul himself possessed the gifts of healing and miracles is evident from the raising to life of Eutychus, and the "special miracles" which God performed through the pieces of clothing taken from him (Acts 19:11,12). However, there are no specific cases recorded of Paul's healing those with a physical handicap, and it is clear that his ministry of healing was insignificant compared with his ministry of teaching and preaching.

2. Attitudes in the church to-day

Following the biblical example, both *healing* and *caring* should be found in the church of today.

a. *Healing* is a difficult and controversial subject. If all the handicapped were healed, there would be no need for special societies. It seems that in many places today God is raising up those with a gift of healing. But reports of the totally blind or totally deaf being healed are almost negligible. "We personally have never known blind people who have regained physical sight through spiritual healing. God can do this, we are sure, but he has not chosen to in our experience," says Stella Heath of Torch Trust in England. Kathryn Kuhlman quotes many examples of healing, including that of a partially-sighted man, but none of restoration of sight or hearing to those totally impaired. Indeed, the foreword of one of her books mentions the financial help given by her organization to a school for blind children for whom Miss Kuhlman wanted to do "everything humanly possible." T. L. Osborn, however, quotes many examples of the blind and deaf being healed. During his thirteen-week campaign in Jamaica in 1949, "over a hundred deaf-mutes and over 90 totally blind people were healed." Up-to-date cases from, for example, churches involved in the charismatic movement, would be interesting. My personal conclusion is that there is a difference between *healing* and *miracles* (I Cor. 12:9, 10), and that the restoration of major sense losses or physical limbs requires a miracle rather than the more usual spiritual healing.

While both *healing* and *caring* must have their place in the full-orbed ministry of the church today towards the handicapped, the primary emphasis must be upon *evangelism*. We follow Jesus' example of "preaching the gospel to the poor" (Luke 4:18), and his command to "go into all the world, and preach ... to *every* creature." We follow Paul's emphasis on preaching rather than healing or caring, and his example of "travailing until Christ be formed in his hearers" (Gal. 4:19), rather than securing better social conditions for the oppressed. But obviously the Gospel cannot be presented in a vacuum; account must be taken of physical conditions of the handicapped, and practical help given in the name of Christ. Often, particularly in the less-developed countries, *caring* and *evangelism* must go hand in hand.

3. Why treat the handicapped in a special way?

a. *They are special people* — A Christian wishes to show the love of Christ to all men, therefore he is sensitive to the needs of the handicapped. It is no coincidence that it was the committed Christians who pioneered the cause of the deaf and the blind in England in the nineteenth century, with true Gospel aims as well as welfare activities.

The handicapped person has suffered certain "losses" which make him different, psychologically and physically, from a "whole" person. T.J. Carroll, referring to the blind in his chapter, "The Sighted Man Dies," cites the losses of psychological security, basic living skills, communication, appreciation, occupational and financial status, and concludes with a section on "losses to the whole personality." The Christian's help in getting to know the handicapped person as a friend, and in relating to him as man to man where physical differences are ignored, can be vital in restoring a measure of integrity. Genuine friendship has immense value in itself, as well as being a necessary prerequisite to effective evangelism.

b. ... *but they don't want to be different!* There is a real danger of insulting the handicapped by putting them in a special category to which there is a definite stigma attached, (cf. "leper" in the Old Testament). This leads to various complexes and wrong attitudes in the handicapped themselves, and resentment at being treated as "different," "the objects of charity," etc. Many handicapped people are fiercely independent! Unfortunately, much of the assistance they receive is in the form of "charity" from well-meaning people who are trying to "help" the less fortunate, from a superior position, possibly to ease their consciences, rather than from a position of equality and as an expression of Christian love. Even Christians and Christian societies working among the handicapped can be guilty of wrong motives. What if some of the blind could see some of the deliberately pathetic pictures of them published in Christian magazines, in order to attract funds? In order to produce lasting results, all Christian work among the handicapped must be based on the treatment of the handicapped person primarily *as a person,* not an "object" to be pitied, evangelized, or exploited.

c. *Special methods are needed* — There are two problems here — *reaching* the handicapped person in a physical sense; and *communicating* the Gospel to him.

(i) *Reaching* — In many countries a child who is blind, deaf, or physically handicapped is considered to be worthless, and a disgrace to the family. Many probably never live more than a few years; many remain shut in their homes, totally cut off from the outside world. While this happens primarily in less-developed areas, there are cases in Western countries where parents hide away their handicapped child and refuse to take advantage of the welfare services offered.

If the handicapped person is an adult, his life is often very restricted; possibly much of his time is spent at home. Therefore the problem of actually *finding* the handicapped people, both children and adults, is a very real one. The normal methods of reaching the non-handicapped are church services and activities; special evangelistic meetings; personal contact through friendship, e.g., at work, through social contacts; systematic visits to homes; Gospel literature, radio, and TV. The average handicapped person is unlikely to go to church or special meetings, and has a very limited social life, and therefore correspondingly little chance of having a Christian among his friends. Gospel radio is inapplicable to the deaf, though potentially a great blessing to the "shut-ins" with other handicaps. This leaves home visits as the only "normal" method of evangelism that is likely to be effective in reaching the handicapped. Obviously this is a very slow, inadequate method, and therefore special methods are needed to seek and find the handicapped person where he is.

(ii) *Communicating* — Having found a handicapped person, there is the problem of communicating the Gospel to him. Barriers of bitterness and prejudice first have to be broken down. Physical needs may have to be attended to. Only then have we an adequate platform for the presentation of the Gospel. Here the deaf present a special challenge, as even the initial contact must be made by a specialist, and the message must be suited to the limited vocabulary that the average person born deaf possesses. In the case of the blind, verbal communication presents no problem, but follow-up literature and portions of Scripture must be in suitable medium; in Braille or Moon for those able to read, or on the cassette-tapes that are becoming universally available. The deaf-blind can only be reached by communication through touch, by those familiar with the manual alphabet. For those who do receive Christ, there are differing problems within each handicap-group with regard to Bible study materials, Christian literature, and integration into, and worship, fellowship, and service within a local church.

4. Methods of evangelism

To try to categorize and summarize all that is being done in outreach to each of the handicap groups is a vast and difficult task, requiring factual information on a worldwide scale. All I have been able to do since being asked to write this paper is to send letters and questionnaires to a selection of individuals and societies concerned with the handicapped, to pastors of churches, and to handicapped people themselves. Their replies have been most interesting and helpful, but I recognize that the picture given is far from comprehensive; further information is welcomed!

I shall summarize the main methods of outreach, and then consider their applicability within each handicap group.

Method 1: Through individuals and churches.

Method 2: Through Christian institutions, such as schools, workshops, etc. (this is the traditional approach of missionary societies).

Method 3: Through special societies organized for evangelism within a handicap group, (e.g., The Deaf Christian Fellowship (G.B.); Torch Trust for the Blind (G.B.); Christian Foundation for the Blind (Australia); Gospel Association for the Blind (U.S.A.); The Disabled Christians' Fellowship (G.B.).

Method 4: Through suitable literature, cassettes and tapes, records, etc. (This is part of the ministry of the above societies, and also of specialist societies such as Christian Literature for the Blind (England), and The John Milton Society for the Blind (U.S.A.). The major denominations in the U.S.A. also have departments for the production of literature in Braille.)

a. *The physically handicapped* — Method 1 should be the main method of outreach. There are usually no peculiar communication problems, and the task of reaching them where they are should be the responsibility of the local church. They do not want to be treated as "special cases," but churches should recognize that special provision may be necessary in the following areas:

(i) *Transport* — Many churches organize transport for handicapped members; in other churches it is left for individuals to bring their friends. One church reported that "more would be able to attend if transport was laid on in an organized way." For handicapped people with their own cars, special parking facilities near the church door are necessary.

(ii) *Easy access* — Modern churches today are often designed with specially wide doors and no steps to give easy access for those in wheelchairs.

(iii) *A special room* — double-glazed, facing the pulpit, and with an amplification system, is provided by some churches. It can be used by those with distressing ailments that cause embarrassment, so that they can see and hear without disturbing others. Such a room can also be used by mothers with small children.

(iv) *Care for the "shut-ins"* — Many handicapped people, especially the "age-handicapped," are house-bound, and often very lonely. If they cannot come to church, the church should come to them. "Time to be friendly and kindly is an irreplaceable necessity in evangelism amongst the handicapped," said one minister. Regular visits and help in physical matters (shopping, etc.) provide a basis for sharing the Gospel. Tapes of Bible studies and church services can help the house-bound person to feel part of the church fellowship, and household communion services should be used much more than they are.

However, it must be recognized that not all churches are able to reach the physically handicapped in their area; that many handicapped people are conscious of being "different," and therefore avoid public gatherings; and that they do tend to enjoy the company of those similarly handicapped. Therefore there is a place for special societies, like the Disabled Christians' Fellowship (G.B.), using Methods 3 and 4, who have found a "vast field for evangelism amongst the disabled who have had little or no contact with Christian teaching." Their monthly magazine has a wide circulation, and many have been converted through their rallies and holidays. Other services such as a tape and cassette library are also available.

b. *The mentally handicapped* — Those who are severely handicapped mentally are usually in institutions. An individual approach is necessary (Method 1), with the truths of the Bible explained in very simple terms. Valuable work is done by individual Christians who visit such institutions, and also by hospital chaplains. Each local church should be aware of the mental institutions in its area, and alert its members to their need for voluntary helpers. However, I feel there is also a great need for "specialist evangelists" in this area, who are gifted and trained in methods of communication with the mentally handicapped.

c. *The blind* — Each of the four methods is being used in reaching the blind. In a survey of twenty-one blind Christians in England and Lebanon, eight were converted through a church, five through personal witness, (i.e., thirteen through Method 1); four through the influence of Christian schools (Method 2); one through a house party for the blind (Method 3). Three were already Christians before the onset of blindness.

Though this survey was very limited, it can be a pointer to the effectiveness of the different methods — 1 and 2 being used more to bring blind people to the point of conversion, whereas 3 and especially 4 are used more to help blind Christians in areas of fellowship and Bible teaching.

Method 1: The fact that a person is blind does not stop him from listening to a sermon, or to the personal witness of a friend. Therefore most blind people can be reached with the Gospel through an active local church. Problems encountered will include (i) actually finding the blind person, since often they live sheltered lives; (ii) overcoming suspicion and a "chip-on-the-shoulder" attitude, by friendliness and helpfulness; (iii) persuading the person to come to church or to a rally, where problems of transport, mobility, and mixing with people may have to be overcome; (iv) leaving suitable literature or portions of the Bible — the Christian worker must be conversant with what is available in large print, Braille, Moon, or on cassettes or records (see Method 4).

Method 2: Christian institutions. In the last century, the development of schools and workshops for the blind in countries such as England was often in the hands of Christians, who founded such institutions with evangelical aims. Now in most developed countries the welfare of handicapped groups such as the blind is in the hands of the state, hence institutions have become secular. Christian missions, however, have used schools for the blind to good effect as part of their evangelistic outreach in less-developed countries. In one place, work among the blind was in fact the spearhead used to open up a "closed" land. But as governments assume more responsibility for the handicapped, the Christian institution may find itself redundant, and new avenues of service sought, e.g., in areas of blind welfare not covered by the state, or in concentrating on a spiritual ministry on the lines of Methods 3 and 4. Well-established institutions must be prepared for such changes.

Christian institutions such as schools and workshops should be seen as a service to the community and to the individual blind person, as well as a means of spreading the Gospel. There will always be a tension between the educational and welfare aims of the institutions, and their evangelistic aims, but there need be no conflict between these aims if those responsible determine that their institution be run as effectively as possible, in service both to the Lord and to the community. There can be excesses on either side. The School for the Blind in Beirut used to teach Braille solely so that pupils could read their only textbook, the Bible, and become Christians. Fortunately we have progressed from that position! Perhaps the other extreme is more common today — some Christian institutions have regrettably departed from being actively evangelistic, and are secular in all but name.

Methods of evangelism within an institution vary greatly, from formal Bible teaching to the personal witness of dedicated staff members. Many schools for the blind are residential, and take children from an early age, therefore there may be ten or more years of Christian influence; this is a wonderful opportunity, and many respond to the claims of Christ. But the dangers inherent in any institutional work are often accentuated in schools for the handicapped, viz., (i) advantage must not be taken of a "captive" audience, and "decisions" pressed for, especially among younger pupils; (ii) advantage must not be taken of the psychological dependence of many younger blind people, especially girls, who make "decisions" in order to please, or to be accepted; (iii) "hardness" to the Gospel can develop among older pupils, through constant exposure to the same messsge, or bitterness at being handicapped; (iv) those converted must be adequately prepared for living the Christian life outside the shelter of the institution, and linked up with an active local church wherever possible.

*Method 3: Special societies.*Reaching the blind through the local church (Method 1) assumes an ideal situation; in fact, most churches do not live up to this ideal! Therefore in recent years, societies have been formed to cater in a special way for the spiritual needs of the blind, usually in developed countries where their material welfare is cared for by the state. As well as providing literature, etc., (Method 4), these societies aim to supplement the outreach of the local church, by: (i) holding regular meetings specially for the blind in an area or town (e.g., the monthly "Torch" fellowship groups in Great Britain); (ii) holding outings, camps, and house parties for the blind; (iii) employing full-time traveling evangelists (often blind themselves); (iv) encouraging Christian unions within schools for the blind; (v) having a residential center where counseling and guidance can be given.

The fact that Torch groups in Great Britain have multiplied rapidly, from one group to thirty-five over the past five years, and seen much blessing, shows the effectiveness of such a method. Many blind people are gregarious and come to special meetings when they would not come to church. Others are determined to be independent, and avoid such groups! Most groups have a varied program, some meetings being evangelistic and others more for fellowship. Meetings are usually held in an easily-accessible central building, and other features are a willing band of sighted "helpers," and refreshments after the meeting. Such groups should be careful to maintain an evangelistic outlook, as their existence is difficult to justify merely as a "fellowship club for the blind." The monthly groups should not be regarded by members as a substitute for regular church attendance, and those converted should always be linked up with a local church.

Camps and house parties in suitable locations give an opportunity for a longer, more systematic presentation of the Gospel. Advertisements through secular channels insure that non-Christians are invited. If the speaking and the counseling are done by those experienced in evangelism among the blind, much good can result. Some societies have a residential center which is available for blind people to come to and stay for a limited period, to obtain help with emotional or spiritual problems; many have been converted, built up in the faith, and helped through times of adjustment, bewilderment, and crisis through these visits.

The use of an evangelist who travels to visit local groups, encourages school Christian unions, and brings the work of such societies before the Christian public, is an important development. The ministry of a man who is himself blind is especially relevant here, and God is using such men in effective evangelism among not only the blind but the sighted as well. From Ethiopia it is reported that "many people will listen to the blind evangelist who will not listen to a sighted preacher. His joy in the Lord makes a deep impression..."

Method 4: Literature, tapes, etc. All Christian societies for the blind, many denominations in U.S.A., and a number of missionary institutions are involved in the production of literature, cassettes, tapes, and records. Most of the output is devotional rather than evangelistic, and the vast majority of it is in English.

(i) *Literature* — Not all blind people are Braille readers, therefore literature in Moon type, and in large print, is necessary as well. The Bible Societies have been responsible for the production of the Bible, or portions of it, in Braille in many foreign languages; however, much remains to be done. Secular societies such as the Royal National Institute for the Blind (G.B.) produce a selection of religious books and hymn books, but these need to be supplemented by evangelical productions from the Christian societies. Current productions are mainly of a "lighter" variety, and there would appear to be a need for more commentaries and books on Bible teaching. While the English-speaking world is well-served (our school for the blind in Beirut receives Christian magazines in Braille from at least seven sources!), the need for production in foreign languages is urgent.

(ii) *Cassettes, tapes, and records* —Many blind people cannot read Braille or Moon, or may be illiterate. The cassette revolution has, over the past few years, been utilized by Christian societies; many of the books brailled are also put on cassette or tape, and the Christian message carried into many more homes. One advantage is that the blind person can share this message with sighted friends. In less-developed countries where Braille literacy is low and little or nothing is available in Braille in the local language anyhow, tapes or records provide an immediate means of reaching the blind. The Bible on tape or records is of use to the Braille reader too who has storage problems with the bulky Braille volumes; in countries where whole families live in small houses, space is very important.

Libraries of cassettes and tapes, and also of Braille books for which there is a limited demand, are being effectively used in some countries, mainly by those already converted.

Christian societies are only just beginning to realize the tremendous potential of literature and tape in evangelism. Many blind people are voracious readers and ardent listeners. Material must be relevant, attractive, and well-produced, so that their thirst is met with the Water of Life.

d. *The deaf* — As with the blind, the degrees of handicap vary immensely, from the hard of hearing and partially-deaf, to the deaf-mute and deaf-blind. The effectiveness of the methods of outreach used varies accordingly. The problems of the hard-of-hearing and partially-deaf should be solved in developed countries by personal deaf-aids, and by amplification systems in churches. However, a survey of seventeen churches in Great Britain revealed that only eight were equipped with an amplification system. One minister commented, "One of the greatest failures in Gospel communication occurs when people with defective hearing fail to hear the preacher. If more preachers would pay attention to voice production, the Gospel would be heard by more people who already come to our churches." Bearing in mind the large numbers of older people in the churches who are hard-of-hearing, preachers should speak loudly and clearly, and churches should cooperate by installing effective amplification systems.

For those born deaf or who lose their hearing in early years, the eye replaces the ear. In developed countries, these children pass through state schools for the deaf, and learn to lip-read, to speak as well as possible, or to use manual signs or finger-spelling. Their speech is usually limited, and their vocabulary small. Therefore, among all the handicapped groups, communicating the Gospel to the deaf presents most problems.

Method 1: Churches and individuals. Outreach to the deaf is a difficult task for the local church; if there is no one trained in communicating to the deaf, then the best that can be done is to show care and concern, and leave literature, such as *Joy,* the quarterly gospel magazine produced by the Deaf Christian Fellowship in G.B. For those converted, integration into the local church presents many problems too. In the U.S.A., many of the larger churches have a special section for the deaf, with an interpreter standing next to the pastor. The deaf group meets separately for Sunday School, and in midweek, and in some cases has a representative on the diaconate. This method may be satisfactory in a city church of large membership, but essentially it is not "integration," as the deaf really are acting as a "church within a church." Many feel that total integration into local churches is not practical for deaf people, because of the communication problem; their limited vocabulary and limited awareness of abstract concepts; and the proportion of music and singing in most services.

Therefore *Method 3, Special societies and churches,* seems to be the answer. In England the Anglican church has been foremost in Christian work amongst the deaf for over 130 years; they work through about 70 local voluntary associations throughout the country, with the object of "promoting the social, general and spiritual welfare of deaf people." The emphasis given to social or spiritual welfare varies from area to area. In some places the government welfare provision is far from adequate, so more time is spent on social problems, but "If we had more staff, we could and should do far more in the way of direct evangelistic and spiritual work," said one association. The general pattern for these Anglican associations is for pastoral work to be in the hands of an area chaplain, who also conducts services for the deaf, either in borrowed churches or in a special center for the deaf. It seems that they place little stress on direct evangelism.

More recently in England the Deaf Christian Fellowship, an interdenominational, evangelical faith mission, has come into existence. Its aims are primarily spiritual, and through trained regional workers individuals have been converted and small fellowship groups, and "Churches of the Deaf" formed, which have their own elders and deacons, and function as a local church. Ideally, preaching is by those trained in communicating with the deaf, rather than by interpretation. The D.C.F. also organizes holiday conferences, groups for Bible study, and a short annual Bible School course, as well as producing literature.

In less-developed countries, a wholly "spiritual" approach is not practical, as basic social needs must first be met. For example, in Africa only one-third of the countries have special schools for the deaf, and hence countless deaf people are illiterate and lack any means of communication. Therefore, an evangelical society such as the "Christian Mission for Deaf Africans" combines an educational ministry with other forms of more direct evangelism through Christian centers, Sunday Schools, camps, and Bible correspondence courses.

The pattern for reaching the deaf, then, involves special societies leading on to special churches; in fact, the deaf are the only handicapped group who need something special when it comes to worship. The form of worship in deaf services needs to be carefully thought out. With the exception of "symbolic" services such as baptism and communion, most ordinary church services depend entirely upon hearing. For the deaf, other senses must be used, physical expression, such as a deaf choir singing with their hands; as much congregational participation as possible; visual aids for sermons; and ideas from the Anglican side include the use of vestments and incense as aids to worship.

The *deaf-blind* are a special category, for whom touch, either through Braille or the manual alphabet, is the means of communication. Although their numbers are small (about 3 percent of the blind in the U.S.A. are deaf too), they must not be neglected. In England there are a few services (monthly or bi-monthly) arranged in certain centers, but the most effective method of evangelism is through a dedicated friend learning the manual alphabet and communicating the Gospel individually.

Method 2: Institutions. As with the blind, missionary societies have pioneered work among the deaf in many lands, opening schools and engaging in welfare work. The points made about institutions for the blind apply equally to work among the deaf, except that most institutions will run their own chapel services rather than encourage their pupils to go to local churches. Reports of youth clubs for the deaf have come from England and Lebanon, where activities are pursued, and personal work done among the members.

Method 4: Literature. Many deaf people with limited vocabularies and knowledge of sentence construction find general literature incomprehensible. Therefore many societies for the deaf produce special literature; e.g., the Anglican church has produced a book of simple prayers; the D.C.F. produces its quarterly magazine *Joy,* aiming to present the Gospel message and Christian teaching in a way the deaf can understand. In Africa, Bible correspondence courses have been distributed. But much work yet remains to be done if the deaf are to be built up in their faith through literature; where church services or fellowship groups are few and far between, literature seems to be the key.

I have had no information about what versions of the Bible deaf Christians use; presumably the modern English versions are most helpful. One school reported that Bibles with good illustrations were greatly appreciated.

It seems to me that Christian work among the deaf is less dveloped than that among the blind, perhaps because of the peculiar difficulties involved, or perhaps because deafness does not evoke as much public sympathy, or stir Christian hearts as much as blindness. This situation must be remedied, and the needs of the world's deaf publicized among the churches. Many countries lack any evangelistic work among the deaf. All societies feel that many more deaf could be reached if they had more workers. The need for suitable literature for the deaf is urgent, and two people separately have voiced the need for a Bible college for the deaf in England or Europe. Now is the time for prayer and action.

5. The challenge of the future

a. *Reaching the handicapped* — Developing technology has made the world's handicapped more accessible, and has improved communication methods. Governments are increasingly catering for welfare needs. The Christian church, through specialized societies, must provide for their spiritual needs, harnessing technical advances for the spread of the Gospel. At present, the approach throughout the world is fragmented. There is a need for a greater awareness of, and cooperation between, the agencies at work. Within each handicap group there appears to be a need for: (i) a world survey of evangelical work; (ii) the formation of a world-wide, or area-wide fellowship to share news, ideas, and prayer requests in an occasional magazine; and (iii) a directory of evangelical agencies, listing the services they provide.

b. *Alerting the churches* — Many churches are unaware of the needs of the handicapped in their own area, and of the evangelical agencies that could help. A simple booklet, such as "A guide to reaching the handicapped," could be produced and widely distributed in each country, giving hints on possible approaches, and names and addresses of relevant sources of help. Stemming from a greater interaction with the handicapped in their own area, the vision of the local church will be lifted to become a missionary concern for the handicapped in the world.

c. *Channeling the results* — Lessons from the past must be learnt; there is the danger of over-response by the emotionally sensitive, or by those who hope for material gain if they profess conversion. Then there is the danger, once some are really converted, of putting them in a showcase and spoiling them. Our aim should be so to present Christ that a real, intelligent decision can be made, and then so to strengthen the young Christian that he becomes active in his own right. Perhaps the key to evangelism among the handicapped in the future is for handicapped Christians themselves to be channeled back into the task of reaching their own group with the glorious Gospel which transcends physical barriers and makes each believer "a new creature in Christ Jesus."

EVANGELISM AMONG THE DEAF, BLIND, AND HANDICAPPED REPORT

1. A lack of awareness of a vast need

The group meeting to discuss this paper was small and consisted almost solely of those interested in evangelism among the blind; three participants themselves were blind. It was regretted (a) that there was not more representation in so large a Congress of workers among the deaf or other handicapped groups, and (b) that so few of the participants in the Congress showed interest in this strategy group. Admittedly, other groups were meeting concurrently, and work among the handicapped is only of peripheral interest to most church and mission leaders, since the handicapped are a minority in their countries. But minorities must not be neglected. The 30 million blind people in the world, countless numbers of deaf and physically handicapped, and increasing numbers with mental or multiple handicaps, demand the attention and concern of the Christian church. The Lord Jesus spent much time with the "handicapped" of his day!

2. Major points of discussion

It was felt unfortunate that work among all handicaps had been grouped together, since the needs of each group are so specialized, and require different approaches. Most of the discussion centered on the needs of the blind.

The basic ideas of the paper were endorsed and the following additional points were raised:

a. *Service with welfare authorities* in England provided Christians with a great opportunity of reaching the handicapped and sharing the Gospel. Too often this field of humanitarian concern has been left to the sociologists with no Christian convictions.

b. *Fellowship groups for the blind* should always attempt to be integrated with the sighted to avoid a sense of patronizing and to allow blind people a meaningful place in a world increasingly oriented toward the sighted.

c. The value of the *cassette recorder* was stressed in reaching the blind and physically handicapped, especially as it is being used increasingly in the education of the blind. Cassette production could well be considered as important as braille production for Christian societies.

d. *Work among epileptics* was also considered. As with the mentally handicapped, epileptics often have an acute awareness of God. The need for Christian institutions to care for and provide sheltered workshops for this often-neglected group was stressed. Specialists in this field need to be aware of the possibilities of demon possession.

3. Agencies at work among the blind, deaf, and handicapped.

In addition to those societies mentioned at the end of the paper, informal conversations with Congress participants revealed many countries where effective work is being carried on. Unfortunately, it was also apparent that there are many countries where little or nothing is being attempted.

Further information has been provided by:

The John Milton Society for the Blind, 366 Fifth Ave., New York, New York, 10001, USA;

Lutheran Braille Workers, Inc., 11735 Peachtree Circle, Yucaipa, Calif., 92399, USA;

Southern Baptist Convention (Sunday School Board) 127 Ninth Ave.N., Nashville, Tenn., 37203, USA.

4. Suggestions for future action

a. The need for a *worldwide survey* of work within each handicap group was stressed, in order to provide information about what is being done, to prevent duplication and to pinpoint the gaps. Torch Trust for the Blind of England is already undertaking such a survey for the blind preparatory to an international conference in 1976.

b. This survey could lead to the production of a *directory of evangelical agencies,* and this in turn could lead to area-wide fellowships for the sharing of news and views.

c. The need for churches to become aware of the vast needs of the handicapped world both on their doorstep and overseas was considered essential. *A manual* listing the evangelical agencies within a country and giving suggestions about reaching the different handicapped groups should be prepared and distributed widely to churches so that local Christians can play their part in reaching the handicapped.

EVANGELISM OF THE HINDUS

Dr. K.N. Nambudripad

This is an essay on evangelization of the Hindus in India. Being a retrospective study, it may lack in scientific methodology, and prepared in a hurry, it may lack depth and thoroughness.

One can do no better than begin this paper by praising God for his grace to us in India in sending large numbers of his servants with the good news of Jesus Christ. In grateful memory of these innumerable company, this paper is thankfully dedicated to them.

This paper begins with the assumption that God is always the author of all evangelistic activity; that God has no partiality, wishing that all may be saved and that none may perish; and that he loves all mankind. It is also assumed that the finest among human agents are but unworthy servants, when all is said and done. As such, any glory or credit that accrues, goes only and solely to God.

First, we shall look at the history of evangelism of the Hindus. Then we shall try to see if we can draw some lessons from this. We shall then enter into a discussion on men, message, and methods in evangelism of the Hindus based on our lessons from history. At the end we shall briefly look at some modern concepts on this subject.

The history of evangelization of the Hindus is shrouded in obscurity. There is a general tradition that Thomas, the apostle of our Lord, brought the Gospel to India, and a particular tradition strongly held by the Kerala Syrian Christians that Thomas came to Kerala, preached the Gospel both to the Jews and the Hindus in 52 AD, and that he established seven churches. Having appointed elders from four Brahmin families, he left Kerala, later to be martyred in Mylapore near Madras.

This is not the place to enter into the merits or otherwise of this tradition. Suffice it to say that the lack of inscriptions, monuments, or records does not have the same validity in a land where records are scarce even for Indian history, where Brahmins never wrote down their scriptures, but always passed it on by oral tradition. If this tradition is reliable, it proves several things. Firstly, that even in the first century the good Lord remembered the poor Hindus and even sent one of his twelve chosen ones. Secondly, that if divine methods are used, Brahmins could easily be converted, and that in much less than two decades, seven churches could be established in a pagan land stretching from Kotungallur to Kollam even in the first century, in most unsettled times.

If the period of the Thomas visitation and the tradition itself is covered in obscurity, the next two or three centuries are even more obscure. One knows almost nothing about how this church fared, whether it evangelized the neighboring Hindus, or how it grew. We are up against almost a total blank.

The next event in history seems to be the visit or visits of some Syrian Christian families to Kerala between the fourth and eighth centuries. There is more evidence for this than the Thomas tradition. Perhaps they were traders who were facing persecutions in their own land of Syria, which we know did occur at various times. Did the Syrians evangelize? If they did, we have no record of their success or otherwise. There is a tradition that some of these Syrians intermarried and others did not. Does this mean that Hindus of the neighborhood married these visitors, or did the neighbors get converted before marriage? We have no means of knowing now. It seems doubtful that these merchants, so fond of the pepper trade, could be great evangelists, particularly when one remembers that for centuries the Bible was hidden from the common man (as the Bible was in Syriac and only a few knew the Syriac language). These Syrians were well known in those eventful times for their trade and for their martial qualities. They were respected by the Hindu chieftains and princes. However, one sees in these influxes the Divine Grace to the end that there should be a nucleus of Christians in India always.

One must sadly admit that although it is likely that there were Christian communities in other areas also, we know nothing of their whereabouts or doings, since nothing has survived of these groups.

The next important event in the history of the Indian Church was the coming of the Portuguese in 1498, under Vasco da Gama, mainly as adventurers and traders. But it must be said that these Portuguese had been sent by their kings to spread Christianity also. The pope had gaily divided the world into two halves and given the eastern half to the Portuguese. It must be said to the credit of these Portuguese settlers, that for the next two and a half centuries they tried with great zeal to spread Christianity in the land under their control, their headquarters being Goa. Some of the methods they employed, like encouraging Portuguese men to marry Kerala belles (after baptizing the latter), destroying temples and mosques in the area under their occupation, and assuring the poorer sections of the Hindus Portuguese protection as incentives to conversion, were highly irregular, to say the least. But it must be said to their credit that at least they were very zealous in their Christianization program. Thousands of low caste Hindus were converted.

Among the Portuguese two names stand out for their zeal, Francis Xavier and de Nobili. The first was a Spaniard who had rejected the teachings of the reformers while studying in France, and had come under the influence of the zealot and fanatic Ignatius Loyola, another Spaniard. Xavier did marathon service in teaching and preaching, baptizing many and instructing more. He travelled widely in south India, but finally left India for other eastern lands. One gets the impression that even he was disgusted at the quality of the converts the Portuguese had made. He was, perhaps, even more disgusted with the life the Portuguese led, full of greed and avarice for earthly gain. The other person, de Nobili, who came to Madura, South India, was a pioneer among the Jesuits in his method of approach to the Hindus. He believed that to convert the high caste Hindus he must himself become like one, and so he donned the Hindu saffron robe of the mendicant or Sanyasi. He called himself a Kshatriya and engaged a Brahmin cook, studied sanskrit, and the vedas, and gave infrequent but long discourses to inquirers on the lines of Hindu students of philosophy. He further declared that a Hindu need not leave his social or economic background, but could continue to use the same caste marks, wear tufts of hair like any other Hindu, could wear the sacred thread and could continue to live in the same family background as long as he did not worship idols. This he called the theory of accommodation. At first the whole thing must have seemed a novel thing to many Hindus and a few Brahmins were "converted," but as the novelty wore off, only low caste Hindus were converted later. It must be said to his credit that he at least saw a problem in the high caste Hindus' hardness to the Gospel and also saw the need to divest western forms from the Gospel of Jesus Christ. In this he was indeed a pioneer.

However, he made the mistake of going too far and made Christianity look the same as Hinduism. One gathers from Abbe Dubois that even after 200 years there remained many Hindu customs like caste among these Christians of South India. There is even now a greater tendency among the south Indian Christians to casteism than the north Indians. One would just like to point out that there is nothing new in the methods now being advocated by many churches, whereby Hindu forms are given to Christianity. It is at least as old as de Nobili himself.

The next period one may call the time of Protestant missions, although the Roman church also made tremendous advances in this period. Before we do so, we must pause to state how good God always has been to send repeated streams of his people so that those Indians and Hindus who wish to come to Jesus may do so. One also suspects that when one generation becomes weak in teaching and Christian leadership, he brings his others to replenish and reinforce.

Only an omnipotent and gracious God could have arranged all the factors that led to the modern missionary movement, now associated with the coming of the Protestant missionaries. Men in important positions, like the king of Denmark, were moved by God to send missionaries to India to evangelize the Hindus.

Thus came the first German pair, Ziegenbalg and Pluetschau, to Tranquebar in South India. These products of the pietist movement in Halle laid the pattern for most of the later Protestant missions. First establishing something like the much-maligned but necessary mission compound; then translating the Scriptures into local languages which had never been done before in all the centuries of Christianity in India; teaching and instructing from the Bible and exhorting to live good godly lives. As pioneers they did very well. They were accused of paternalism, which was perhaps inevitable and pardonable in those early days, and anyway it is far easier to criticize them than to find an alternative.

Towards the end of the eighteenth century there came William Carey to Bengal with the avowed object of converting the Hindus, and trusting in the promises of God (Isaiah 54:2,3), with his motto, "Attempt great things for God, and expect great things from God." Elements in his work which were new were that the work should support itself financially and that Christian education was essential for growth. For this he started Serampore College, emphasizing translating the Bible in various Indian languages. He also made the Western churches aware of their great responsibilities to evangelize the Hindus of India.

God's hand in these decades is also seen in raising up Christian members of the British public like Wilber Force, who fought a prolonged battle for the cause of evangelization of the Hindus. But the East India Company would not allow missionaries to come to India.

This period is also remarkable for the number of Christian institutions like hospitals and colleges which sprang up all over the country. At one time it looked almost as if India might turn to Christ in a big way but it never happened. This era of Protestant expansion was also characterized by a new sense of responsibility which the Indian church felt for evangelizing their own countrymen. Indian church leaders grew in number and stature. Christian knowledge, education, and literature has multiplied at an astonishing rate.

This period is also noteworthy for great expansion of the Gospel to the tribal areas, and great mass movements. To these missionaries must go the credit for giving at least one phrase to the Indian people, the so-called "missionary spirit," but to them must also go the discredit that centuries passed and they were not able to evangelize the Indians.

What lessons can we learn from this history of evangelization of Hindus? First, there is much more than accident in these repeated influxes of Christians to the land of the Hindus, some more, some less concerned with the salvation of the Hindus. Surely there is the hand of the Almighty in all of this, and it is consistent with the kind of God the Bible speaks about.

Except for the Apostle Thomas, whose arrival is not beyond dispute, there seems some kind of progression in the evangelistic fervor of our visitors. God has thus prepared our generation for the great leap forward. God is preparing us for this.

What is equally obvious is that in spite of all these centuries of evangelism, in 1971 only 2.67 per cent of the population were Christian, and that they live in only a few states of the union. Other states are virtually without Christians. Moreover, even these are mostly urban, so that villages remain practically untouched. The conclusions are obvious.

Then perhaps, we can learn something about missionary methods from history. There seems no mathematical relationship between method and results, although this is only an impression. One missionary goes to a tribal area and wins thousands to Christ while others sweat and labor for decades and nothing seems to happen. In some institutions, like hospitals, no one is converted, while in others many are converted. A man like de Nobili, who sacrificed much, gained no more than many missionaries who worked among some other groups.

There is no recognizable pattern between methods and magnitude of converts. Unfortunately, we do not know enough about the prayer life of all these missionaries so that we can't try to equate their "production" of converts with their prayer life. The life of men like Praying Hyde, however, shows that there may well be a relationship between prayer and conversions.

Perhaps we can draw one conclusion safely, that no evangelist can reproduce better Christians than himself. The Portuguese reproduced unsatisfactory Christians of whom even one of their own felt so disgusted. De Nobili did the same. Syrians did the same. Perhaps the Protestant missionaries have done the same. It seems a fairly valid conclusion, because one tends to copy the example given. This is human weakness. Great is the responsibility of the evangelists to live holy lives before God and men. History also teaches, lest we should forget it, that Christianity is no more a foreign religion than Islam or Hinduism, for it also came from outside India. In apologetic preaching in India, this should be hammered home much more often than is ever done.

Can we learn anything about the message and its relevance to India and Hindus from history? Although the evidences are few, it would seem that the great interest in Christian education evidenced by the Hindus from the time of Duff in Bengal, the great appreciation that Christian service in Christian institutions have drawn from Hindus generally, and the fact that the spirit of service is not only widely recognized but called "missionary spirit" would go to show to some extent that the message of Christ as proclaimed in India, has some relevance to the Hindu mind.

Further, the impetus that the wide Christian teaching has given to neo-Hinduism and Hindu reformers like Raja Ram Mohan Roy, Keshab Chander Sen, Vivekananda, and Sri Aurobindo seem to indicate that the message of the Bible in India in these latter times has produced some lasting changes in Hindu thinking. The formation of many groups like the Prarthana Samaj, in the west of India and the Arva Samaj in the north, and the Brahmo Samaj in the east seem to indicate that a new spirit did arise in Hinduism. From these, it would seem that the message has gone home in some measure at least, to provoke the thinking Hindu to action, however perverted. It seems safe to assume that the Gospel which has been preached in India may have not dealt a mortal blow to Hinduism, but certainly has seriously injured it.

In a sketchy appraisal of the history of Hindu evangelization, one did not have the occasion to point out how institutions started with very good intentions and soon lost their essential original Christian character and thrust. This seems the inevitable conclusion one draws from a careful survey of educational and medical institutions at least. Even the orphanages in the south are facing serious problems. Can we say that the phase of Christian institutions in evangelism is finished or nearly so? The only alternative seems to be to enter areas of Christian service like leprosy work, care of the mentally retarded and epileptic, village medical work, and perhaps public health work also, where others are unwilling to serve. One recognizes great possibilities in the first three categories. Unfortunately, the Indian Christian medical doctors and their mentors don't seem to realize this. For a long, long time to come, these areas are likely to be open.

One did not have time to review in this short historical survey, the effect of church unions and indigenization of Hindu evangelization. It will be remembered that both these projects were started to make evangelization of Hindus easier and it is fair, therefore, to ask if more Hindus have been converted in these last twenty-seven years when these measures were taken. It is almost certain that those groups who have formed such unions have had very little conversions. It seems paradoxical that those groups which refused to unite just for the sake of unity, have had more Hindu conversions than the others. As far as one can make out from available data, there seems no basis for thinking that the Hindus resist conversion because Christians are divided. Church unions, therefore, seem to have forgotten to lay the golden egg. From all accounts, they have done very little in Hindu evangelization. With regard to indigenization, one has to be more cautious. Perhaps it depends on what one means by this word. If by this is meant divesting the Christian message from its European garb, and Christian worship from Western forms, then perhaps there has been some useful results. There is some reason to think that the Western apparel and accompaniments may hinder the effectiveness of the message to the Hindus. However, the evidence is not altogether unequivocal.

Time did not permit us to survey the history of such movements as ashrams, and the use of Hindu thought forms to Christian message in India. There may be some substance to the statement that Sadhu Sunder Singh is supposed to have made that for Hindus the Christian message must be given in Indian glass tumblers or containers or something to that effect. One feels that something like this was done by the apostles in the West when they went from the Jews to the Greeks. One is reminded that John used the Logos concept and Paul may well have used the words, flesh and spirit, from the Greek gnostics; but it cannot be doubted that they did use Greek thought forms to convey the typically Hebrew message to non-Hebrews. Once it is realized that there is a real danger in such an exercise, one feels there is real scope for such messages.

There is little doubt that none of the historical Christian movements we studied laid emphasis on this, and those pioneers like de Nobili, who did, went too far.

This takes us to what is today called Indian Christian theology. This is such a huge subject that one cannot adequately deal with it in a paper like this. Yet, one must say that there is a real need to express the message of Christ in thought forms understandable to the Indian mind, if this is possible without damaging the content of the message. As Sunder Singh tried to say, but what no one at the time heeded, there is a real need to give the Gospel wrapped or contained in Indian dress or Indian containers. It is interesting that this process does go on involuntarily almost among the poorly-taught Hindu converts; and it is fascinating to see how they use Hindu thought forms and expressions in their explanations for fellow Hindus. Some conservatives are likely to think that the wrappings and trappings do not matter and all that matters is the message. This is an over-simplification. These thought forms and phrases are very much part of the message, just as language is a means of communication.

It should also be remembered that just as one does not use Greek, the original language of the Gospel, so also one may have to discard Western phraseology and thought forms and adopt Indian thought forms and expressions to the Hindus so that the message may make some sense. One wonders how many evangelists have the courage to ask Hindu listeners what they thought about the message, whether they understood it. Often they will be told that most of it was incoherent to him. "We did not understand a thing," is a common criticism by Hindus of the ordinary evangelist's message. One wonders how separated evangelists can become from the common people of this land. One can only call it ludicrous in the extreme when some American returned evangelists use Americanisms which mean nothing to the Easterner, let alone the Hindu.

There is much truth in the idea that anything foreign is rejected immediately by the human being. Just as he rejects a kidney or a heart, man rejects the Gospel also, if it is made to appear foreign to him. One has learned from one's sad experience how one's highly developed Western ideas go like water off a duck's back when given to the average Indian. The tragedy is that so few of the evangelists deal with ordinary men and women. They are always travelling and meeting the same kind of nominal Christian crowd and inquirers that they have ceased to think about the common man at all.

It is an essential step in human tissue transplantation to expose the recipient to immunosuppressor drugs. Something analogous to this may well have to be done in preaching the Gospel to Hindus also. Like tissue transplants the original qualities of course should not be sacrificed in this process wherein lies the beauty and challenge of transplant surgery. One would think that there is immense beauty and joy in trying to communicate to Hindus the Gospel in forms he can understand. Nobody should think that this is possible only to great theologians. Any Tom, Dick, and Harry can carry on a long conversation with a Hindu and learn his thought forms. Each Hindu is different. There is immense scope for great originality which the blessed Holy Spirit can give to illumined minds.

This is a strategy paper. What is the best strategy for the Hindu? One should at once say that we should recognize the enemy, his strength and his weakness. One should also in the same breath say that the enemy is Satan who has deceived the poor Hindu and not the Hindu himself. "We wrestle against powers and...not against flesh and blood," says the apostle. This is important to recall lest we hate the Hindu and treat him as our enemy. One must also remember that the only weapons which prevail against this foe are spiritual weapons. In worldly methods, Satan and the world are task masters, and we don't have a chance against these.

The evangelist's method against Satanic deception of the Hindu is therefore not weapons of argument, reasoning, logic, nor even Indian Christian theology, but truth, righteousness, faith, and so on, as seen in Ephesians 6. If there is one thing that sounds foolish, it is this. One would think that Joshua must have at first thought it was silly to walk round and round the well-fortified city of Jericho. What a silly spectacle that must have been. Yet there is a lesson there for us which we in India have not yet learned fully: that the author of saving faith is God Almighty alone and that without his help and cooperation, all preaching is plain drivel, useless gibberish. One cannot over-emphasize this aspect. One thinks of the many occasions in one's experience when a poorly-attended Gospel meeting was due to lack of prayer.

Spiritual weapons alone can produce spiritual victory and conquests. How does one react with the Hindus? Logically he is the victim of a great fraud and deception and, therefore, is behooves us to treat him with the compassion he deserves, provided he understands that one is not agreeing with his religion nor his philosophy. This subtle ability to hate the sin and love the sinner is rather a difficult art and needs much practice. Nothing is communicated if not conveyed with love. To communicate to the Hindu, one must love the Hindu. This is easier said than done, as anyone knows who has tried. It is like walking on a razor's edge. His behavior patterns are based on his worship of monkeys, cows, snakes, rats, and even genitalia, and such behavior does not endear one to a civilized Christian. Only the Spirit of Jesus Christ can give one the power to love such unlovely beings. But basically, it must be emphasized that he won't be saved unless someone loves him.

It is sad that we have no material with us to do some research on the part love from a Christian played in Hindu conversions. But one has a hunch that this is considerable. One fears that converts fight shy of this point and are not utterly honest, fearing that their testimonies may be spoiled by the public avowal of human love as an inducement for conversion. One has no doubt at all that nothing can be truly communicated without love, not even science. Fear and suspicion bar learning and communication. One has no hesitation in saying that the Hindu is weakest here. His loneliness, his lack of a love experience, his desire for love. Here he is very vulnerable. Should not one attack here?

The Hindu is strongest in philosophical and argumentative discussions. Here one should give him a wide berth. Dialogues with him on the whole are quite useless. It is more likely that he will make you a Hindu rather than vice versa. He is in his element in debate of any kind.

To conclude then, evangelization of the Hindu is urgent business because there are so many unconverted Hindus (about 540 million). Moreover, they may convert Europe and America to Hinduism if one is not careful. They have been known to do this with Buddhism in history. Further, there is every chance they may become a very important people in this geographical area. And surely Hindus are more vulnerable today than at any other time in history perhaps. They are fast losing faith in almost everything Indian. There is a vacuum in their experience of life and they are hungering for reality. Only Christ can fill it. There is the ominous possibility also that they may turn to communism or other ways. And above all, Christian compassion demands that we help them in their hour of spiritual need.

Our enemy is Satan, not the Hindus. Our weapons are spiritual, not carnal. Our hope is not in clever methodology, but the power of the Spirit, and love and prayer. The most important thing is to stop talking about it and start doing something about it. After all, this is God's work. He is committed to bless us.

Note: The question is often asked, "Is there a Christ of Hinduism, the hidden Christ, etc.?" This is a controversial subject. One does not wish to enter into any controversy. But one feels that there is no more Christ in Hindu scriptures than many other great religion or mystic poetry. Various claims have been made. All one can say honestly is that one has not seen any Christ in Hinduism.

EVANGELIZATION OF HINDUS REPORT

Chairman: Mr. Paul Sudhakar
Secretary: Mr. S. K. Bose

While not containing a sequential strategy, this report deals with seven strategic areas of outreach to Hindus. The report begins by enumerating these seven areas, hence a further summary is not needed here. The following main points were discussed:

1. Caste system among the converts and churches;
2. Indigenization in the Indian church;
3. Evangelization of Hindus with love, prayer and use of Hindu thought-forms;
4. Evangelization with minimum social dislocation;
5. Special and careful awareness of our common enemy — Satan;
6. Overcoming denominational barriers towards their ultimate elimination;
7. Specialized para-church institutions for evangelization; e.g., Ashrams, literature, and hospitals, supported by churches.

The group had enthusiastic discussions and participation. All recognized the vicious and wicked presence of caste among the Christians, mainly in South India. All agreed that every caste element should be discouraged and should not be compromised in any way.

All felt that as soon as possible the Indian church should be indigenized. The Western influence and foreignness should be removed from our churches without compromising with Hinduistic (religious) ways. We would welcome missionaries but only as colleagues and workers, not as leaders or controllers.

It was emphasized that while evangelizing among Hindus we should use Hindu thought-forms and words to communicate effectively. Western methods, phrases, and ways should be avoided. Hindus are disillusioned and are searching. They should be approached with love, compassion and prayer. Care should be taken that there is a minimum of dislocation from their social ties. This does not mean compromising with Hindu religious doctrines, e.g., caste, etc. We must be relevant to Hindus and meet them where they are spiritually, economically and socially. No material helps or promises should be given where evangelization is concerned; such helps can be given after, if necessary, and at the discretion of the church or according to the merit of the case.

We must be aware of Satanic deceptive activities and therefore use Power-encountering ministries according to the gifts of the Spirit. The Word of God should be used carefully and prayerfully.

While we should be aware of Hindu social systems and culture, it should not be over-emphasized, realizing that all are one in Christ and in Christ we are new creatures. There is no fear in love and there is freedom and liberty in Christ.

Historically, it was pointed out that various evangelistic methods have been used but gradually the form, traditions and rituals took over and thus God used other means. Now under the Protestant era, institutional evangelism is carried on. Care should be taken that again traditions may not overtake the real spiritual fervor.

We ought to encourage establishment of small local churches and house churches with a minimum of formalities and outward form. Indian Christian theology should be avoided when it contradicts the Word of God.

EVANGELISM AMONG HIPPIES AND OTHER SUB-CULTURAL GROUPS

Ron Munstra

*Mr. Munstra, the Hague, Netherlands, has
worked extensively with drug addicts,
hippies, and Jesus People for several years.*

Writing about evangelizing hippies is not so easy since the words hippie, sub-culture, etc., have different meanings in different countries. The hippie-culture in the U.S.A. differs widely from the culture in Europe, and furthermore in our country (the Netherlands) today's youth-culture greatly differs from that of a few years ago. This is why it is hardly possible to compile an instruction booklet for evangelizing among hippies in all circumstances. However, we will give you our own experiences in this paper. Our group has worked amongst young people in the Netherlands, Belgium, and the Ruhr area in Germany.

Anyone beginning with evangelizing work should not be disheartened too soon. In the beginning we had one disappointment after another. We knew nothing about hippies or drugs, we only had a compassionate heart. The youngsters we took in our home at first seemed to be more interested in a warm bed and a good meal, than in the Gospel. It was not until a few really converted people from that sub-culture came to us, fully prepared to serve the Lord, that we saw positive results in this kind of work.

Initial needs

One of the first requisites when a hippie accepts the Gospel is to move him out of his environment, otherwise he will never be able to break the bonds of his former life. A reception center, therefore, must be available. If the hippie is an addict he will have to be freed from his addiction in the first place. It sometimes happens that a person is freed as a result of a single prayer, but more often than not the person will have to go through a weaning period. We believe that, for a person who has accepted Christ, the best way to get rid of drugs is by way of the "cold turkey" cure. This is the only way to get absolutely free from medicine, since in many instances the medicines (drugs) given to drug addicts to free them of their addiction have an enslaving effect themselves (e.g., methadon), or make the patient drowsy (valium, librium). A quiet room is required for giving a person the "cold turkey" cure, as this cure often brings with it paranoidal symptoms. Very often the patient is in great pain. Someone has to watch by the patient constantly, for the "cold turkey" can be dangerous. It has happened that an addict has died in prison when his supply of drugs was suddenly stopped. In such a critical stage a Christian can pray to the Lord, but if he has not enough faith he should see to it that he can always call a doctor.

Keeping watch over a patient is also necessary since the patient's body, during this "kicking-off" period, occasionally yearns for drugs so much that he cannot but run away to satisfy this strong desire. This does not mean that the addict does not "want" to get freed, and so for his own sake he should be stopped at all costs. We have often experienced that we could not hold him — at this stage an addict often has the strength of 10 men — and so we went down on our knees to ask the Lord to do it for us. And soon the runaway would come back very quietly. It is then that we see how mighty the Lord is. It is of great importance to tell and addict from the very beginning that it is Jesus who can help him, and to teach him how to pray. Very often such a desperate prayer is answered by the Lord in a wonderful way and the addict knows that Jesus lives and that praying really helps.

The "cold turkey" is only the beginning. The former addict will have to begin a new way of life. This is not at all easy for though he has been taken away from his old circle, very often his old life exerts an extremely strong pull. His old friends will do everything in their power to get him back to the "scene." Moreover it will not be at all easy for him to resist the temptation to take drugs.

Joining a group

The best surroundings for receiving an ex-addict is a group of young people of his age who positively serve the Lord. Here he meets conviviality, real friendship, love, a kind of a home. This is very important, for the background of many addicts is a lack of love. The former addict will feel happiest if there is a person in the group or among its leaders with whom he can get a special relation of trust. In the beginning this trusted friend will be most important to him, but it is the main task of this friend to point to Jesus, so that He will take the friend's place more and more.

Further, the ex-addict will have to learn that he forms a member of the group. At first, one is inclined to view the addict as a patient. This, of course, is wrong. If you treat him as a normal person and a full member of the group he will not behave like a patient, but do his best to live up to expectations.

Anyone asking for help to get rid of his addiction is taken into our center. We give him a probationary period of three weeks. In those three weeks he can "kick-off" and recuperate if necessary, and prove that he really wants to start a new life. Then he will have to start working, unless his health is poor. If he cannot work he has to be kept busy with all kinds of odd jobs in the home. Those who have been addicted to amphetamine (called "speed"), cocaine, etc., can best "kick-off" while at work, since they have to get rid of an enormous quantity of unnatural energy. To be busy at work is most important for all ex-addicts as it takes their thoughts away from their former life; and because they now can provide for themselves they need not be dependent on others.

The best way to help a newly converted person is to make him share his experiences of the Lord with others. More and more, it has been our aim to bring young people to discipleship, for discipleship is the only way to save a person permanently. The sooner a convert has learned to do something with his newly found faith and finds that his faith is confirmed — e.g., when he sees that former friends to whom he has born a witness, have accepted the Lord or when his prayers have been answered —

the more his longing grows to experience the working of the Lord and to give up all the things that stand between the Lord and himself. Each member of the group must learn to build up a personal relation to the Lord and should not be afraid to bring his faith into practice. By this the group has become most important for this work. If an ex-addict is having a difficult time he can turn either to the leader or to his friends in the group for a talk or for prayer.

It is essential for a group that there are a number of positive young people who act as a foundation to the group. They have to set an example of living with the Lord, they must be able to help when someone in the group has problems, and they must have a good relationship with the staff. These positive people have to keep their eyes on everything that happens in the group. It can happen, for instance, that there are a number of negative persons (e.g., some ex-addicts who are not yet very strong spiritually) in the group who always stick together, which clique will easily pull down other "weak brethren." Too much association among such brethren should be discouraged. It is better when strong persons take care of them and help them to grow in the Lord.

Bible reading, Bible studies, preaching, and prayer are the bases on which the group is built. It may seem strange to them, but many young people find the answer to all the questions, which often have brought them deep into trouble, in this old Book. To play up to a person, "acting popular" and gentle preaching have no effect at all. But the straight Gospel appears to be a two-edged sword that cuts deep into the souls of young people. Young converts, coming out of deep distressing circumstances, often have a great hunger for the Word. By hearing and reading the Word, the mind of young people is renewed, and their thoughts turn more and more to the Lord and less to the world. Other things the group is doing for the Lord are edifying for all concerned. When we started witnessing in the streets as a group, suddenly everyone experienced that when you hand out something of the Lord you receive much more in return. There was a new need to read the Bible, since it proved that knowledge of the Bible is most necessary when talking to strangers in the street.

Origin of the group

Up to now we have talked about "the group" and taken it for granted that the group is so important. Now we will relate how the group was born. Originally our aim was to work among the "hippies" — whatever that may be! There are no real hippies in this country however: we could call them drug addicts, scene-people, or the like. We did contact them and took them to our home, but results were poor. It was not until a number of young people gave their full time and attention to the job that things started moving. We then contacted "hippies" and also an entirely different kind of young people. These were boys and girls with leanings to the "hippies," but who hadn't sunk so deep. Some of them had taken drugs, most of them were still at school or had taken a job. They gladly accepted the Gospel and felt it to be much better than the life they had hitherto led. They did not need the kind of help drug addicts needed.

They lived at home, but attended the services, joined the group for witnessing in the streets, and frequented the center whenever they could.

Gradually more and more people of different backgrounds came, many of them from the schools, older and younger working-class youths, even parents and grandparents. Since the group combined so many different people, almost everyone felt at home. The boarders ("interns") are those who are in trouble (drugs or otherwise) and those who want to work for the Lord and to receive practical training. This training entails that one learns in daily life to put into practice all that the Bible teaches. You are incorporated in the daily work and learning all its facets, e.g., preaching, giving Bible readings, praying for one another, helping addicts, coaching the newcomers and the weaker members of the group, visiting parents, etc.

During the period of internship, the individual's character is molded, because he has to live together with many people and has to take account of every one of them. In daytime everybody has to work, but in the evening attention is paid to spiritual things. There is a program for every night of the week, two normal services, Bible studies, witnessing, pastoral care and prayer.

The people who are not interns belong to the group, too, of course. They can come as often as they like and take part in all activities.

We have seen that God does not give his plan to one person only (the leader), but wants to give to the whole group. It often happens that God makes his will known to the staff, but at the same time makes it known to some members of the group too, and this causes a unity between staff and group.

Conducting a "post"

When the interns have improved enough spiritually, they can be sent to a post (a settlement of our own "organization" in another city). Naturally not everyone is fit to lead a post. In the first place he has to be called, and he has to be a person who wants to know more and more about the Lord. This has to be so because he has to preach, give Bible studies, take pastoral care, etc. In all this he can't rely on anything but his Bible and his contact with the Lord.

We start a post by renting a house that fits our purpose. It has to have room for services (a large living room will do) and it should be built in a way that we cannot cause too much nuisance to the neighbors because of singing during the services. A house in the center of the city is ideal. We send a few people to the post who find ordinary jobs and together pay the rent and the other living costs.

In the beginning there sometimes is a full-timer who is occupied daily with evangelizing and prayer; after a while everybody is working and the spiritual work is done in the evenings and at the weekends. If there are converts at the posts who are fully prepared to serve the Lord, they are sent to the center to be trained. People in need of help often are sent to the center too. On the other hand, ex-addicts or people with other problems at the center, who need change or some rest, are sent to one of the posts for a while.

At the center as well as at the posts we found that a group needs a father and a mother. The people we are dealing with often have much trouble and need someone with whom they can talk. Therefore every post needs a girl who can do this part of the work and do also the other domestic work.

To found new posts is not only necessary to reach as many people as possible, but also to keep the home-group alive. The home-group gets new things to pray for every time a new post is founded. The strongest people are sent away every time, and this will force the people who stay behind to be more spiritual and take a greater part in the work. Movement and flexibility is necessary. For this reason we do not have too many written rules. Of course, there are some domestic rules, and we forbid the use of drugs and smoking in the house. We also forbid interns to listen to music from their old life, for this can be propaganda for the use of drugs. Sometimes music has left impressions during the use of drugs that are evoked again when they hear the music. Other rules, as the Bible teaches us, are not obligatory in the group. In Bible studies and sermons the importance of these things is pointed out. If it strikes home to someone he will live by it.

One of the things we have not talked about is that the young people, who often come from a lawless, "democratized" atmosphere, must learn to submit to leadership. There is no spirit of dictatorship in the group, but everyone has to learn to accept the guidance of a leader. One of the young men is in charge of every post and also of the main center. He leads the group when they go out, organizes the work around the house, and is responsible for all that happens. He can only be a good leader when he himself has learned to listen to what the group has to tell him.

To return to the posts-center relationship: the ties between the posts and the center remain strong, because there is a fairly regular contact, as well in the human level as in the organizational level. Several times a year, meetings are held in the center. Everyone from the posts can come on such an occasion, and all the leaders will be there. During such weekend gatherings, specialized Bible studies are held. There are ordinary services, often baptismal services are held, and there will be a communion service. The whole group will go out in the street together to witness and sing there. Between all this there is a lot of time for recreation. During the weekends everybody gets to know each other a bit, old friends meet again, and the converts from the posts feel that the center is their center too. Apart from these weekend gatherings, which often are held during great feast days (like Christmas, Easter, Pentecost) or during the school holidays, the leaders of the posts often come to the center to talk things over or just to relax.

Every month the posts have to send their accounts to the center, where the bookkeeping of the whole work is done. During the holidays it is possible for those who are not yet interns, to stay a while at a post or in the center to learn more about the work. While there they are expected to assist generally. The leaders usually never stay longer than seven months at one post; after that they switch to another post or come back to the center for a while. Once in a while, the founder of the work comes to every post to preach.

Evangelizing hippies

To reach the people, one has to evangelize of course, but there are many ways to do that. You have to adapt the way of evangelization to the people you want to reach. To reach hippies you have to go the places where they are to be found. Most of the time we go there with some tracts, and start talking to a boy or a girl. We have learned that in Europe it is no use to approach "hippies" with would-be hip slang. It will be just ridiculous to them, because you are pretending to be someone you are not. If a well-dressed shorthaired, middle-aged person tells a hippie that "Jesus is the best trip," it will not be accepted. If there is no such pretence, one stands a better chance of a good talk.

A former addict or drug-user who has been converted and is spiritually strong enough will be the best witness to his old friends. The changes in his life, the happiness he has from the Lord, etc., will show them that Jesus can help them too.

A method of evangelization which reaches a great number of people is for a large group to take guitars and other musical instruments and sit down to sing. Sitting down is very important because we are more visible than when we stand and there is no distance between the people who stand and listen and the group that sits and sings. The singing attracts the attention.

When there are enough people standing around the group, one of the group gets up and tells them about Jesus or gives his testimony, then he invites everybody to drop by our center or to come to a service. During the singing, some of the group hand out tracts and sometimes start a talk with people in the audience.

When we cannot go with a group big enough to sing we usually take some tracts and hand them out to the people in the street and try to start a conversation.

Apart from these methods of evangelization we often get invitations from schools, youth clubs, children's homes and even the youth prison to tell them about our work and our faith, and to sing.

The singing is very important to us, not only as a part of the service, but also because we get a lot of invitations by it. Naturally, everyone's testimony must be affirmed by his personal attitude, and the fact that we always have to bear testimony of our Christianity in word and deed makes us feel how much we need the Lord.

These are our experiences in the work with young people. Though we started that way we would never advise to aim at hippies only. We believe that it is best to have a group of people with all kinds of different backgrounds and ages in which everybody feels happy — a kind of very large family. But this is only our opinion, and our experience. The Lord will do new things even in work that is started. The only good way to do a work for the Lord is to do it his way.

EVANGELISM TO HIPPIES AND OTHER SUB-CULTURE GROUPS REPORT

In discussing ministry to "hippies" and other subcultures, we must first consider the definitions of these groups. A subculture could be those involved in a "trip" of some sort, whether it be drugs, surfing, or any other thing which possesses much of their time and interest. The groups which we discussed dealt specifically with ministry to both the drug addict and the so-called "freaks." In this report we wish to share discussion about one specific ministry which has been quite effective, to look at both positive and negative methods in this type of evangelism and to make specific recommendations to further enhance our resources in this field of ministry.

We were privileged to have present the author of the paper, Mr. Ron Munstra from the Netherlands, and he was able to provide tremendous enlightenment on the subject because of his vast experience. Ministry to these types of people requires a person with real commitment, love, and a call from God to give all that he has so that these people may be won to Christ. Mr. Munstra's ministry began with a deep conviction and desire to communicate the Gospel to the "freaks" in a park near his home. He would go to the park and begin sharing with these young people and inviting them to his home. As he invited them to his home, they saw in Ron a person who was concerned for them, who would listen to them, and was willing to get involved with them. As young people came to know Jesus as Lord, he found it necessary to begin a house-ministry which could take these young people who really wanted help from Jesus, and were willing to submit to Christ. They would rent a house for approximately ten people and would staff it with people called to this ministry. Through personal contact in the parks and on the streets, they would share with people that Jesus could set them free. Mr. Munstra has stressed the importance of accepting them as they are and personally ministering to their specific needs. When asked about the change from the old life to the new life in Christ, and if there were hassles in giving up bad habits, Mr. Munstra replied, "A person is a patient in a sense. When he comes into the program he is treated until he is better and after that he must decide personally what he must keep and what he must give up."

Mr. Munstra brought with him a young man who was converted through this ministry. The young man said that if they had told him that he couldn't smoke and couldn't drink or other things which he was into at the time of contact, he would have told them to forget it.

He was accepted and was led to Christ, and sometime afterward he was sitting with a cigarette in his hands, thinking to himself, "If Jesus were here, would he smoke this?" In his heart he knew the answer would be "no" and immediately asked Jesus to help him quit. There was a definite emphasis on providing a proper atmosphere that functioned as a real family. One member suggested that what they really desired was acceptance, security, success, love, spiritual answers for their needs, and honesty. Ultimately, as they accepted Christ, they became members of the family of God and received help for all six of these needs.

Some of the things which really enhanced the ministry was their open and honest approach to these young people and the willingness to "get their hands dirty:" As the young people came into the house, they found a sense of belonging and realized how much they needed Jesus and their brothers and sisters in Christ. There is real koinonia and body ministry in that they work together and minister to each other. In this particular ministry, the young people work and share in all the expenses.

Some of the problems they have to work with come about because many young people want to kick their drugs only with the motive of coming off and getting new thrills when they start again. Therefore, Mr. Munstra will accept only those who really mean business with God and are willing to have Jesus become Lord of their lives. Another very real problem is their acceptance into the traditional church structure. It seems that one thing must take place if we truly are going to evangelize the world. We must pray that each of us can begin to see mankind through the eyes of God. Another area which needs to be understood is that of cross subcultures, that within the subculture groups there may be the same basic root causes; but individualized ministry to each group is different and necessary.

Some ministries that are in existence today are:

1. "The Family," run by the Reverend Dr. Arthrol Gill of Australia.
2. Mr. Vic Ramsey of England.
3. "Youth with a Mission," which has ministries in Morocco, Nepal, and other places in the East.
4. "Love Liberation," under Floyd McClung in Amsterdam, Holland.
5. Hamburg, West Germany, with "The Salvation Army."

There are many other ministries like this and we would like to recommend that this Congress through its research committees seek out other ministries like Mr. Munstra's. We would suggest that they contact their leaders and ask them to write about their work, including how they began, what it has developed into, some of the methods and a record of their work, any problems which they may have, and how they are dealing with them. We believe that this would be most helpful. After these papers were compiled they could be edited by the Congress and made available as a resource for this field of ministry.

It appears from our group discussion that the priority for the worker is to be called of God, to be filled with the love and compassion of Jesus, and to have the willingness to be totally involved in this ministry. It was also apparent that the most effective way of reaching out to these young people was through providing a facility which could give them the warmth and love of belonging to a family and attempting to meet their needs spiritually, physically, and culturally. As there are many variations in a ministry like this, we believe that obedience to the Holy Spirit and his specific direction would be the most important priority in effectively accomplishing this ministry to "hippies," "freaks," and members of other subculture groups.

EVANGELIZATION AMONG JEWS

Victor Smadja

Mr. Smadja, Jerusalem, Israel, is an elder of
the Messianic Assembly in Jerusalem and a
leader of youth work in Israel.

Living in 1974 almost twenty-six years after the founding of the state of
Israel it would be difficult, if not impossible, to talk about sharing the
good tidings of the Gospel with our kinsmen the Jewish people without
declaring publicly:

    a. That the state of Israel is God's work through men even though
those men did not necessarily understand that they were instruments in
God's hands;

    b. That the state of Israel is a fulfillment of the Old Testament
prophecies concerning the founding of a Jewish state in the latter days,
and not merely the result of force of arms as has been claimed by some;

    c. That the mistakes of Jewish leaders and people will never alter the
purposes and promises of the Living God to the Jewish people. God
works in accordance with his plan and his faithfulness.

    I want to further limit this study to the situation since 1948. Not only
do we choose this date because it marks the inception of the state of
Israel as an independent nation, but there is also, tragically, a break in
the Jewish believer's presence in the land of Israel. Unfortunately,
because of the War of Independence in 1948 and 1949, almost all Jewish
believers left the country for a number of reasons, never to return; and
work among Jewish people had to begin anew and afresh in Israel. So
there is the phenomenon of a new work in Israel since 1948, particularly
among the immigration of a return home by Jewish people from a worldwide dispersion.

    Although our basic approach to the subject of reaching our brethren
will be from our own national viewpoint, we believe that it will still be
valid on a worldwide basis barring some specific problems peculiar to
the present state of Israel.

    The heritage which the Christian Church has bequeathed through
the centuries has been so frequently negative about the Jewish people,
and the difference between "Christianity" and true faith in Jesus Christ
has often been so great, that it is necessary to rethink the whole subject of
evangelism concerning the Jewish people in general and Israel in particular. Evangelism among the Jewish people calls for different methods
than those used among other peoples.

    Why is it so hard to reach the Jewish person for Christ in the first
place? There are many reasons. The tragedy of behavior of the "Christian" Church in the past is historical fact which cannot be erased, along
with the hundreds of years of persecution and anti-semitism, and also
partly because most Jews look upon any person who is not a Jew or
Muslim as being "Christians." Thus to become a "Christian" is to lose
one's identity as a Jew. When the claims of the Messiah are made by missions and churches, the Jew is asked, from his Jewish point of view, to

become a non-Jew and to join one unit of a group which is classified as Christian.

The Jew who thus accepts this concept is therefore outside the mainstream of the Jewish context and virtually denies his identity as a Jew. Unfortunately in the so-called Christian countries of the world the Jews who have accepted Jesus as their Savior have often made the attempt to forego their Jewish identity, and this places a further stumbling block before their fellow Jews who might otherwise be open to the Gospel of our Messiah. We cannot emphasize enough the tragedy of this phenomenon, and earnestly urge our believing Jewish brothers to rediscover their identity in Christ. On the other hand, it is necessary to remember that God entered into a covenant with Abraham and his seed *forever*, and that this covenant is the basis of his dealings with Israel. God's covenant with Abraham was and is an unconditional covenant emanating purely from his love, and resting firmly upon his faithfulness for its fulfillment. As such, God's covenant cannot be broken.

We who are Jewish people and believe in Jesus Christ recognize in him our own Messiah who came to seek the "lost sheep of Israel." Having believed in Jesus, we remain Jews. We have not become "Christian" (the name given to the Gentile idol worshipers in Antioch who embraced faith in Jesus as their Savior). Instead we belong to the root of the olive tree while the Gentile believers have been grafted into the tree which is Israel. Unless we understand and declare that we do not introduce something foreign to the faith of Moses and the prophets of the Old Testament we become destroyers of the Jewish nation who are worse than Hitler who murdered our fathers and mothers, our husbands and wives, our sons and daughters. It is necessary to restore the Jewishness of Jesus and to put him back into a Jewish framework.

Our faith is in the Messiah of the New Testament. It is not in the fathers of the Church who each in his own way stood against the first Jewish church in Jerusalem. It is not the faith of the leaders of the Protestant Reformation as, for example, Luther who became an anti-semite in his latter days. Nor is it the faith of the manifold denominations of the present-day Protestant Church. Our unity with Gentile believers is in Jesus Christ — the body consisting of both Jews and Gentiles. It is not in a theology which is so often Hellenistic in nature. Of course, we all readily recognize the spiritual bond among all believers in the body of the Messiah. There is a oneness of all believers regardless of who they are. But does it stop there? Do we overlook the ethnic identity of believers to say that ethnic identity is not necessary? On the contrary, missions and evangelism to other cultures generally pay careful attention to the cultures in which they have to operate. But what happens when evangelism or missions preach to Jewish people? We have a curious phenomenon of evangelism that if Jewish people believe in Christ, then they are no longer called Jews but Christians! I do not want to become too involved with the doctrine of the church, but I am raising an urgent plea that we once again come back to our New Testament to see if we have overlooked some basic considerations regarding the believer in Christ. When we look to the Scriptures and the brief report of the first group of Jewish believers in Jerusalem, we find men who retained their

Jewish identity and from that point of reference declared the Messiahship of Jesus to their fellow Jews. With the passing of time the number of
Gentile believers far outstripped the number of Jewish believers. Subsequently the Gentile leaders of the church took offense at the Jewish traditions of our forefathers. Changes took place because they desired to separate the church from the Jewish people. Why, for example, do we
celebrate the crucifixion of our Lord on the Friday before Easter instead
of on Passover eve? Is there any place in the New Testament where a Jew,
though a believer in Jesus as Savior, should give up his ethnic identity?
No. Instead, I find that every one of the New Testament writers, with the
possible exception of Luke, were Jewish. Even Paul, though suspect by
Jewish scholars today, affirmed again and again as to who were his kinsmen. Paul also makes the profound statement, as a believer in Jesus the
Messiah," ...for I am an Israelite, a descendant of Abraham, of the tribe
of Benjamin" (Rom. 11:1). Therefore, for the sake of evangelism among
Jewish people and especially in Israel, we must reassess again this matter
of the role of ethnic ties of the Jewish believer to his people.

The national fellowship of Israeli believers

Now, alongside the missions, etc., we are also seeing the growing
presence of a national fellowship of Jewish believers and Arab Christians
in the land of Israel. We are organized in groups called assemblies but
we have no organic tie with any denomination. These assemblies are
found in Jerusalem, Haifa, Tel Aviv, and Beer Sheva. We also have one
group of Arab Christians in Nazareth in fellowship with us, recognizing
us as being Jewish believers.

As Jewish believers, we are called Messianic Jews. One of Israel's
most popular dictionaries, *Even Shoshan,* defines Messianic Jews as "a
sect of Jews who have declared themselves as Jews in their nationality
and for their faithfulness to the State of Israel, and as Christians in their
religious expression." By "Christian" we mean an expression of our particular Messianic faith in Jesus as Redeemer and his atonement for sin, as
well as our hope for oneness with God some day because of our faith and
trust in him. The Messianic Jews are a dwelling presence, witnessing in
the land of Israel today.

The assemblies of Jewish believers provide the nucleus for fellowship. There is a growing consciousness for a worship pattern that will fit
into the Jewish context. Since we live in Israel, and since the seventh day
(Shabbat) is the day Israel sets apart for worship, the Messianic Jews also
worship on this day. While our hymnal contains the standard hymns sung
in the Christian West among evangelicals, we are including a new hymnal
reflecting more Jewish life. We sing the Psalms in a Jewish idiom. In addition, since Israel follows the Jewish year calendar, we also seek to fit
into it, but at the same time we try to provide the redemptive fulfillment
in each of the feasts and holidays. These feasts that we observe become a
testimony to the nation that we certainly are Jews and that we also
remember our history. But at the same time there is also a witness of the
fulfillment that Yeshua is the Messiah of the nation of Israel.

Therefore, we see immediately the distinctive problem of the work
of the missions and the denominational churches in trying to bring
Jewish people into worship patterns that reflect the Gentile Christian

West. At the same time, one can also recognize that it is much easier to bring an interested Jewish person into the assembly of Jewish believers. There will be a natural bridge for the Jewish person to cross over to find his redemption. Accordingly, one can raise a very serious question as to whether missions, each as a unilateral force, have any longer a place in the land of Israel. This does *not* mean that there is no place for Gentile Christians with distinctive talents who come and work with the national fellowship of believers under its leadership and guidance. We welcome those who come and help in this way.

We insist that we are *not* raising any barriers between Gentile Christians and Jewish believers; we are merely emphasizing the best possible method of trying to reach our people in Israel. We are aware of the problems that have arisen between the missions and national churches in other areas. Israel presents an even greater problem because of all that has gone on in the past between the church and the Jewish people. Now that there is a national fellowship of believers, a greater credence can be given to the force that can be unleashed through the providential work of God in the land of Israel, so that there can be the riches of fulfillment for Israelis who will believe.

Possibilities of evangelism

Traditionally, Jews are not open to the Gospel, for the reasons given above. There are, though, increasing numbers of Jews who are or would be open to the Gospel, both in Israel and in the rest of the world. For instance, many immigrants from Russia have strong messianic convictions, yet they know very little of Scripture. Many of these persons have come to Israel seeking because they feel that there is still something missing in their lives. We know what that missing something is!

Before we explore the positive side of Jewish evangelization, there are a number of negative aspects which should be considered, both in Israeli and in world Jewish evangelization. The usual conception of passing out tracts on street corners and conducting street corner meetings is resented, and in many cases is forbidden by law in Israel. This does not mean that evangelism is too cramped or restricted. It just means that we need to be familiar with the ways that will work. We need to be open to the Lord's guidance to other ways that will become possible. Evangelism is never a static procedure, and the Spirit of God both creates new situations and shows us new opportunities.

As mentioned before, the antagonism which exists between Israel and the church is a hard fact of history. Theological differences between various groups of Christians are not understood by most Jewish people. Most Jews do not understand the question of the Trinity, and this is a stumbling stone for them. It also does no good for the so-called evangelical church to try to explain the difference between the different churches and then wash their hands of the whole matter. The Jews must see a truly repentant and believing life in Jesus in the life of the believer.

The state of Israel has a sentimental appeal to denominations and sects of every description. Israel has become to them a dumping place. This condition is all very confusing to the Jews in Israel and also to the many thousands of Jews who come just to visit in Israel.

Foreigners generally take one of these positions in Israel. There are those who do not represent any officially recognized missionary society (i.e., officially recognized by the state of Israel). Such people are often aggressive in their approach and work without responsibility and without seeking to establish a local church, but rather seek followers for their particular sect. Then there are the officially recognized missionary societies which take part in the local assembly, seeking to help out wherever possible. Then there are those groups who compromise by being silent even to the extent of actively seeking not to evangelize, basing their approach on the premise of just being a "Christian presence" among the Jews.

A number of problems with missions and foreign Christian organizations are:

a. Worrying about their visas and permission to remain in Israel, which often causes them to shift the focus of their efforts from the Jewish population to the Arab population, because they do not want to pass over their property to the local church — not because they receive suddenly a "call from heaven" to the Arabs.

b. Compromising their mission in Israel by remaining silent concerning the Gospel, even to the extent to signing an agreement with the government not to evangelize among the Jews.

c. Seeking by any means possible to produce "Hebrew Christians" who then serve as propaganda agents concerning what they are doing in Israel. In such instances there is seldom any discernment as to whether the individuals involved are novices in the faith or whether there is any movement in their lives towards genuine spiritual maturity. Such individuals are often pressured into writing reports which are more often than not the fruit of their imaginations rather than true accounts of what really is happening.

d. There are mission groups which seek to be involved in work for the purpose of raising money to support their own Jewish worker in Israel. There are groups which tell about their work in European and American publications when very often no one in Israel has ever heard of these people. There are also mission groups which send to Israel couples who go about their witness without responsibility and then when the trouble starts they leave the country, making it that much harder for the local believer in Israel afterwards.

e. There are also the "Supro Pro Israel" Christian Gentiles who even evangelize in Europe, declaring that "we don't have to evangelize Jews," and that "God will deal with his people himself and someday...all Israel shall be saved." In Europe they speak about Israel and pour out money for it, but this money is given to the state, not to the church. Where is the spirit of Paul who was concerned only with the brethren?

f. What about the evangelical Christians who are touring Israel — visiting the country and the places of the early churches of the past — do they ask themselves whether there is a body of Christ in Israel today? It is compromise when all that the church is doing today is intended not to upset Israel! To the latter this seems an answer or a subsidy for the six million Jews who were killed in Germany of whom my father was one.

On the positive side I want to present an aspect that has come about as we have searched our souls in this matter of communicating our faith. It has become very evident to all of us that if we wanted our people to be interested in the claims of Jesus the Messiah, a biblical repentance would not come merely by arguing the relative merits of Judaism *vis-a-vis* the beliefs of Jewish believers in Jesus in a general way; neither would a repentance come merely by discussing the identity of Jesus as the Messiah, etc. The dominant note in our studies seemed to be the necessity of calling our people to the *consciousness of sins,* and the conviction that without the emphasis on this need, one will not be able to help our people to see Jesus as the atonement for sin. Frankly, we feel that we need to work on the common ground with which our people are familiar, namely, the Law.

Let us earnestly seek to get this common ground when we present Christ to the Jewish people. Otherwise they cannot hear what we are saying, and our efforts to reach them are wasted. We need to stop declaring that the Jews crucified Jesus, and instead declare with Peter that your sin and mine caused Jesus to be crucified. We need to declare that what Jesus says is not new, but that he spoke to the lost sheep of Israel. Jesus is coming to reign in Jerusalem over a Jewish nation which will gladly receive him. Let us use the necessity of repentance as our jumping-off place. Let us bring the Jew under the influence of the Law (which is a schoolmaster whose purpose is to bring us to Christ). There they can see the holiness of God and their personal sinfulness. Only then will they be in a position to realize the necessity of a way of forgiveness and thus the necessity of the Messiah and Savior. If the Church of Christ does not discover its proper relationship to Israel and change its attitude, it will continue to lose opportunity to witness to Israel. God has a very specific message for Israel in these days — a message which will prepare Israel for the revelation of her Messiah. The Lord wants us to proclaim this message. He wants to work through us if we are ready and willing to be used. Brokenness is the way of usefulness in the sight of our Lord.

Opportunities for evangelism

I would like to point out what is being done here in Israel and how we hope to implement new approaches which God makes possible.

a. *Literature* — We plan for the translation and printing of appropriate Christian books in which we feel our people will be interested. As recently as ten years ago, we had practically no books or Bible study helps available to our people in Hebrew as compared to the many thousands of books available to believers in the Western countries. We have therefore translated and printed books on biblical subjects in Modern Hebrew. We now have approximately thirty titles completed such as Billy Graham's *Peace With God;* David Wilkerson's *The Cross and Switchblade;* Francis Schaeffer's *The God Who Is There;* Corrie ten Boom's *A Prisoner and Yet;* as well as a number of books from the *Living Bible.*

Although some bookstores are willing to carry some of our titles, we have found that the best way for us to accomplish our distribution is through teams of young people. They are given minimal training in approach to Jewish people, with the main emphasis on selling these books on a door-to-door basis. Many thousands of books have been sold in this way. Many times these young people have opportunity to share their faith and testimonies.

We are interested also in other phases of literature as well. We are planning a first printing of the *Voice of Messianic Judaism:* aimed at reaching the intellectual Jew. We are choosing or writing appropriate articles which are to appeal to and challenge Jewish thinking people regarding biblical truths and the claims of Jesus the Messiah.

b. *Radio evangelism* — We have been using the shortwave facilities of Trans World Radio, advertising these programs through distribution of leaflets with an offer of correspondence courses for the past five years. The shortwave signal was narrowed to cover only a portion of the Middle East, and our coverage was also limited since very few persons listen to shortwave, even though we advertised the programs widely. We came to the conclusion that we have to make all of our efforts to beam the Gospel on medium wave transmission, since we have so few believers who are able to prepare the radio programs. Our vision is enlarged now as we see the new waves of immigration from Russia and seek to prepare messages in the Russian language. It will not be superfluous to use the new facilities of Trans World Radio from Cyprus in English to develop and expand the possibilities in this language also, since a large segment of the population in the Middle East speaks this language in addition to its own.

c. *Youth work and young couples' meetings* — About every six weeks we have a general fellowship meeting for young people in Israel. The meetings are located in different places so as to insure that all the country's youth can come at one time or another. At these fellowship meetings the young Jewish and Arab believers can come together, and unsaved Jews and Arabs can be invited to hear the Gospel and to make a profession of faith. At least once a year the youth meeting is planned with young couples in mind. During the young couples' meetings problems of being a family of believers in Israel can be dealt with.

Usually in July or August, we try to rent a camp site at the Sea of Galilee or at the Mediterranean for a week of camping in connection with the youth meetings. We find that such camps are an excellent time of opportunity to help our young people. But this is also a good time to reach unsaved youth. Decisions for the Lord have been made in these camp meetings in both salvation and the dedication of lives. But our big problem from year to year is to find camp sites that are willing to receive us or accept us because of our large numbers of seventy to ninety persons.

We are planning for the future, God willing, a center for camps and conferences so that we may continue the above activities on a more permanent basis. In this connection we are praying for a believing Jewish couple from either Europe or North America who are trained specifically in camp and youth work and would be willing to immigrate to Israel as Jews, making this project their life's work.

The local assembly of Jerusalem holds a day camp for one month in July for the children of believers, when we endeavor to reach our own children with the message of the Gospel. By having them for at least one month's well-planned program, it gives us ample time for ministering to them on their level.

d. *Correspondence work* — Emmaus Bible correspondence studies have been translated into Hebrew, and tracts are distributed to offer Israelis this correspondence course. People are invited to send in the cards so that they may take advantage of this offer for Bible study by mail. Some response has been received through this approach, and some Israeli Jews are now studying the Scriptures in their homes. This is a good evangelistic approach and we hope to develop it further.

e. *Miscellaneous* — We are looking to a return of Jewish believers from abroad so as to aid the growth of the assemblies in Israel. We are aware of the great strides of evangelism in the United States among Jewish youth, and we hope that some thoughts from this paper may be of help in this matter. It is our desire that a good number of these young Jewish believers will be able to come to Israel and become a part of our nation in every way. This will add to our assemblies and give new life and inspiration to us. In addition, as an increasing number of Jewish believers immigrate and become Israelis, the government will begin to recognize that Jewish believers can be a part of the country and people of Israel. Government leaders will realize that Messianic Jews are not trying to deny their identity but rather to seek it. At the same time government leaders will be confronted by the fact that through this witness many respectable and responsible Jewish believers in many walks of life are coming from good backgrounds and seeking to work in the great adventure of Israel.

We also encourage Gentile postgraduate believers to come either to teach or study at the different universities, to stay for a year or two, to learn the language, to get to know Israelis better, etc. Many a Gentile believer in an *Ulpan* (language study center) or on a kibbutz has been instrumental in witnessing to Israelis. We have then seen these Gentile believers bringing their Jewish contacts to the assemblies where they can be exposed to the preaching of the Word of God from within the Jewish context. Some of these contacts have found the Lord.

Conclusion

Israel is passing through a time of crisis after the last war of Yom Kippur, and a time of spiritual despair. The Israelis have lost the confidence which they put in the Israeli army. The political situation is unstable and the division between the Labor Party and the Religious centers on the question of "Who is a Jew?" The military situation is not easy - the price is high. So many of our young people are falling as a sacrifice to our willingness to live.

From where will come hope and salvation? From the evangelical church, the silent church which did not open its mouth in the last war? Yes, it is true today as in the past; from where cometh my help? My help cometh from the Lord....the Lord Jesus Messiah of Israel. Amen!

EVANGELISM AMONG MUSLIMS

F.S. Khair-Ullah

*Dr. Khair-Ullah, Lahore, Pakistan, is
Director of the Creative Writing Project of
the Christian Publishing House of Lahore.*

The intention of this paper is not to provide ready made answers to any of the problems discussed but to raise certain issues to stimulate thought and discussion. The paper also does not claim to present a well-thought-out strategy among the Muslims — an evangelist must keep his tactics in a fluid state and act according to the situation under the guidance of the Holy Spirit.

I have leaned heavily on the rich experiences of many past and present writers who devoted the best of their lives as evangelists among the Muslims. I would strongly recommend all those who are interested in the subject to study their works diligently.

First, we must realize that Islam is not merely a religion: but a complete code of life. We who live in Pakistan know this very well and we become all the more conscious of it when we try to separate our religion and nationality. This fact may not be fully appreciated by others than the nationals themselves and therefore it needs to be stressed at some length.

In February, 1974, an Islamic Summit Conference of all the Muslim states was held in the historic city of Lahore — where in 1940 a resolution was passed by the Muslim League demanding a separate homeland for the Muslims of India where they would be free to practice their religion without hindrance. The aim of the Summit Conference was to stress the unity of all Muslim countries. It was a wonderful experience for one to have gone through. Radio, television, newspapers, and magazines all were harnessed to emphasize the Islamic spirit of the occasion. No sensitive heart could be unaware of the thrill of the religious fervor displayed by the common people. To watch the live televised transmission of the Jumma prayers from the Badshahi Mosque, was to feel the sense of brotherhood, the pride of belonging to a fellowship of all believers in One God from Algiers to Indonesia.

We as Pakistani Christians had a divided feeling. We could feel what our compatriots were feeling and yet we were not fully with them. It was only when the Lebanese delegation arrived and their foreign minister, who is a Christian, made a statement that some of us partly associated ourselves with what was going on. Our depressed spirits further recovered a bit on the arrival of the patriarch of Antioch along with a group of Arab Christians who threw their weight on the Muslim side on the question of Jerusalem. Our sense of inferiority in belonging to a "rootless minority" was to some extent overcome. This peculiar problem of the Christians was further limelighted by two letters that appeared one after another in *The Pakistan Times,* an English daily, on February 26. The first one was by Mrs. Khanna, a Christian lady, who has from time to time written articles and letters on the subject of problems of

Pakistani Christians. She advocated that we Pakistani Christians should fully associate ourselves with our countrymen and consider ourselves as Pakistanis first and Christians afterwards. She even went to the extent of blaming the "British-sent" missionaries for making us Christians foreigners in our own country. Mr. Joshua Fazal Din — a Christian leader and a former deputy minister in one of the former governments — in his rejoinder in the same paper (March 4) rightly stressed the fact that we are Christians first and Pakistani afterwards. He further paid tribute to the missionaries for the wonderful contribution they had made to the various languages and literature, and who had served our country by their humanitarian institutions at the grass roots. Mr. Fazal Din pointed out that Mrs. Khanna's confusion was due to her ignorance of the fundamental difference between Christianity and Islam. Christianity gives precedence to religion, while in Islam the state and religion tend to merge into one another. He went on to say, "It is because of this clear teaching of Christianity that over the ages many people have been leaving their homelands as pilgrims whenever they have felt that their own state was refusing to 'accept' them as full citizens 'in the name of Christ.' "

If this is how the Christian leaders feel, how much more must a Muslim feel on this question of religion and nationality. The Gospel is not preached in a vacuum — it is to be preached to men and women who have feelings and an intellect and a will. Unless we appreciate the social and cultural complex within which they exist, we cannot effectively communicate the Gospel to them. A Muslim is not simply an individual — he is a member of a close-knit society and within it a member of an even closer-knit family — an idea that the people from the West may not be able to imagine. A Muslim on hearing the call of our Lord is subjected to many conflicting loyalties — those of family, of society, and the state, besides the personal inner conflicts. How true what our Lord said regarding this matter: "Do not think I have come to bring peace on earth. I have come to set a man against his father, and a daughter against her mother..., and a man's foes will be those of his own household."

This is the price that a follower of Christ has to pay, but can we help him to resolve some of his difficulties?

Kenneth Cragg raises this question, "Is it possible to familiarize the Muslim with the truth that to become a Christian is not merely a shift of communities, that it does not rob Muslim society, as such, of a potential servant and the local community, as such, of a loving son? How can we demonstrate that to become a Christian is to remain responsible in some sense for 'Muslim' citizenship?"

Cragg has raised this question in regard to that of baptism. He earlier stated, "In the first place Muslim society is not individualistic but communal. Therefore, is the individual the appropriate unit of baptism? Perhaps forms of the new allegiance might be more meaningfully fulfilled in community. Official baptism may have in Muslim eyes an appearance of treason, because of strong communal and national ties to Islam. In the New Testament days and in the modern West, baptism does not mean a rejection of particular citizenship. In the modern East it seems to mean that. The Muslim in the Arab world thinks of the Christian Church as a separate *millet* perhaps with different language, cer-

tainly with a different 'ethos' and different cohesion. What is a renunciation of sin looks to one's kin as denunciation of all that makes one
'belong.' "

The problem for which Cragg is seeking a solution is that of the new
convert finding himself being cut off from his old society and of his not
being accepted in the local Christian church. He writes a little further,
"The newer churches of Western planting, especially in the Arab world"
(and I would include Pakistan in this too although for other reasons!) are
not spontaneously hospitable to the Muslim seeker. His good faith may
be doubted, his presence mistrusted and his interest questioned."

J.T. Addison gives reasons why the work among the Muslims of India was neglected. One reason he gives is that very few are adequately
equipped for such work. "The chief reason, of course, is that since
Muslims...are...a peculiarly exclusive and unresponsive minority, it has
always been easy to turn from them to more readily exploited opportunities. And of such opportunities India has long had many to offer, with its
mass movements, for many years past, among the depressed classes and
the lower castes. It is only natural that the attention of most missions
should have been chiefly absorbed in meeting the demands of those who
have been eager to accept Christianity rather than in laboring to change
the hearts of those who despise and reject it. But, however plain the
reasons may be, the more difficult case has suffered in consequence. Few
missionaries have been set apart for this special task; there is a deplora-
ble lack of Indian evangelists capable of dealing with Muslims effectively; and there is extremely little Christian literature."

What was true in 1942 in pre-partition India is even more true in
Pakistan in 1974. Among the nationals, except for the Rev. Aslam Khan,
himself a Muslim convert, of St. Andrew's Brotherhood, Lahore, I cannot recall any minister whose work is exclusively among the Muslims.

Some of the earlier missionaries succeeded because they made themselves one with the people. They mastered their language, they learned
their way of living and adopted their dress, and identified themselves
with them completely. You have only to read the thrilling account of Dr.
Pennell's experiences as he moved about in Pathan dress, even mistaken
by the British and not allowed to travel in a railway compartment reserved for "Europeans only." If you wish to reach the heart of the people,
you have to be one with them to win their trust and confidence. If we are
the agents of "reconciliation" can less be expected from us than what our
Lord did for us by being born among us and living as one of us?

To get to the heart of a Muslim, there are at least four barriers to be
crossed — or he has to cross some of these barriers to arrive at a point
where he can accept the discipleship of our Lord.

There is the barrier of *culture and nationality,* and then the *intellectual* and the *emotional* barrier, and finally the barrier of *"will"* which
must be surrendered before Christ can come into our hearts.

I think the best way to learn something of the strategy required to
break down these barriers is to study some of the methods successfully
employed in the past. It is obvious that they would vary from place to
place and from time to time. We should not rely too much on these skills

for it is, after all, the Spirit that bloweth where it listeth, but still our Lord told his disciples, "Follow me and I will make you fishers of men." Fishing is a game of skill and patience and we too must acquire these two qualities.

The first of the evangelical missionaries who had a special burden for the Muslims was Henry Martyn (1781-1812). His initial effort was to make the New Testament available to Muslims in their languages, so he set out to make translations in Urdu, Persian, and Arabic. Combined with this he used the older method of street preaching. It was during one of these street sermons that an influential Muslim, a keeper of the jewels of the court of Oudh, Sheikh Salih, while standing on the fringe of that group, heard Henry Martyn preach in his language. Curiosity led him to seek the place of this Englishman. He was able to persuade Sabat, who was assisting Martyn with the translation, to make him the calligrapher. As he copied out the Gospel in a fair hand for lithoprinting he was converted and was baptized in 1810 by the Rev. David Brown, taking the name of Abdul Masih ("the slave of Christ"). Bishop Heber ordained him as the first native priest of the Anglican church. "He understood the implication of the Gospel and years before medical missions were known in India (indeed any organized missions, since Martyn and his successors were East India Company chaplains), Abdul Masih established a dispensary for which he qualified himself and on which he spent his own personal resources. It was his pioneer example that stimulated English medical ministry in the sub-continent."

Sometimes God gives to one person the gift of winning many souls — "those who turn many to rightcousness shall shine like the stars for ever and ever." One of these stars was Pfander (1803-1865). In 1820 he was at Basle Missionary college. He was a brilliant linguist and the college decided that he should translate the Scriptures in the Asiatic languages; for this purpose he went to Armenia in 1825. Here he realized that preaching the Gospel among the Muslims could not be done in the same way as it is done in the West. The Muslims possessed a Holy Book which they regarded as heaven-sent and they considered the Christian Scriptures as abrogated. So he set himself to study the Quran and the Hadith. His study convinced him that millions of Muslims who believe on Allah and the Quran and the Prophet of Arabia could be easily won for Christ, the Lord of the Universe, if only they were guided aright. He further realized that the Christians of that area had been dominated by Muslims and their theology, and many had embraced Islam. Pfander wanted to win back these lost sheep and to show to the Muslims the right path, so he wrote his famous book *The Balance of Truth* (Mizan-ul-Haq) in 1829. In 1835 he came to India and learnt Urdu and completed his *Mizan-ul-Haq*. Pfander carried on his bazaar preaching and public debates.

In 1845 one of the government servants wrote a reply to *The Balance of Truth*. Then followed a series of books by Muslim scholars refuting Christianity. Pfander made an appeal to his European friends to send him the latest theological books which would help him to reply to the Muslim scholars. The interesting background is that it was the Roman Catholic bishop and his priests who used to supply to the Muslim scholars books by Strauss, Feuerbach, and others, so that the Protestants be put to shame. They also supplied them the books of the early heresiarchs like Marcion, the Ebionites, Arius, and others.

The enemy's favorite weapon is to divide the ranks of God's people and thereby neutralize and make of no effect God's "Good News." Even today this is happening in Pakistan. One of the separated groups of the church by attacking another group in its magazine, supplies enough material to the Muslims to accuse us of changing the Scriptures. Every attempt to make a new translation meets with this objection from this body, encouraging various Muslim groups to attack the Christians.

"Pfander possessed three requisites for public controversy — absolute command of the subject; absolute command of the language-idiom, the thought-idiom and the manner-idiom of the people with whom he spoke; and absolute command of himself."

One of the most memorable public controversies was held at Agra. Pfander was assisted by the Rev. Thomas Valpy French, later bishop of Lahore. "Both sides claimed the victory of course, but two of the ablest of the Sheikhs on the Muslim side afterwards came out for Christ — names ever memorable in Muslim-missionary annals, Imad-ud-din and Safdar Ali."

Maulvi Imad-ud-din wrote many books on Islam. He was a learned person and used his knowledge most profitably in the service of his Lord. Unfortunately, most of his books are now out of print. He was the first of the nationals who produced a great deal of literature for the Muslims. He was very fortunate that his patron was Bishop French, himself a keen worker among the Muslims and participant in public debates. It was Bishop French's idea to have a divinity college in Lahore, primarily for the converts from Islam, so that they could be given full training and go and work among the Muslims. The old method of public debate may be out, but the debate continues in a different form. Sometimes it still takes place in the correspondence columns of a newspaper. Recently a lively controversy took place in *The Pakistan Times* over the Gospel of Barnabas. Dr. Jan Slomp of the Christian Study Centre, Rawalpindi, took up the cudgels on behalf of the Christians. But the fight was neither equal nor just. Jan Slomp's rejoinder was never given in full, and his replies were allowed to be scrutinized by his adversary before they were printed so that a counter-reply appeared almost immediately after his letter, thereby giving the impression that the Muslims had an answer ready with no loss of time.

A great deal of anti-Christian material is being produced in the country. It is the duty of Christians to see that suitable answers are available for those who are honestly interested in the truth. Bishop Lefroy long ago realized that an evangelist among the Muslims needed to possess these qualities: "He must have a complete mastery of the Quran in Arabic and must have a thorough knowledge of the commentaries, enriched by an acquaintance with theological classics of Islam. But training will be of little use unless he displays in argument entire fairness and complete good temper and patience. To these must be added a large-hearted sympathy that will prompt him to lead his opponent on from truth he already knows to Christ, the TRUTH. And never for an instant must he lose hope."

Public debate and controversy may break down the intellectual barrier, but this alone rarely wins a person's heart. Lefroy realized this: "Most of the older controversial literature on the Christian side," he commented, "is ... very *hard* indeed, as though intended rather to confute the enemy than to win the disguised friend. Similarly, much of our preaching seems to me rather as though we were hoping to convert men by throwing brickbats at them, in the form of truth."

The first great error that the Christians made was to wage the Crusades — the effects of which are felt even to this day in Muslim-Christian relationships. Even around the 1530s Erasmus wrote, "The best way and most effectual to overcome and win Turks would be if they shall perceive that thing which Christ taught and expressed in His life to shine in us ... in my mind it were best before we should try with them in battle to attack them with epistles and some little books."

In the twentieth century we have moved much further than the strategy of conflict. The idea of dialogue is another way of saying that we together should seek to find the truth. If we want others to know about our faith, it is as much our duty to study honestly *their* faith as well. Most of the writers of the present century advise us to avoid the attitude of antagonism — an attitude that has been bedeviling our relationships down the centuries since the Crusades. We must be honest in recognizing the best that is in Islam. David Brown in his book *The Way of the Prophet*, (1962) writes:

"Thus to decry Muhammad for his failings is to forget his heroism and essential truth of his prophetic message; to concentrate on Qur'anic contradictions and errors is to miss its teaching about God's activity in nature, or the duties of mankind; to attack Islam because of what it failed to do is to forget the Ages of Splendour and the contributions which Islam has made to the culture of Western Europe. Thus the desire to refute and to destroy all too easily blinds the Christian to those evidences of God's mercy which he may be able to discern within Islam...But...this is a wrong way to witness because it confirms the Muslim in his Islam, and therefore, in his prejudice against Christ and his Cross. The natural reaction of any man when his beliefs are attacked is to maintain them the more resolutely and even to discover better reasons for doing so....The results of missionary preaching during the past century and half demonstrate with tragic clearness how unproductive such method really is."

Of late there has been recognition among Muslims of how honestly Christian scholars have studied Islam. Here is the view of Dr. Sadeg Razazadeh Shafaq, Head of the Department of Philosophy, Tehran University, Iran. He was addressing the International Islamic Colloquium held in Lahore in 1958. It was given under the title "Christianity and Islam," in the section on Islam's attitude towards and relations with other faiths. "As I have already indicated in one of the sessions of the Continuing Committee of the Muslim-Christian Co-operation, the universities of both faiths should create special institutions studying Islam and Christianity under modern light. Such institutions will help gradually to do away with the traditional misunderstandings, misrepresentations, and misinterpretations. In this respect, Christendom is already far ahead of the Islamic world, for many centers of study of comparative religion have been set to work in Europe and America, with good results."

Here is another view of a younger man, Muhammad Daud Rahbar, taken from his review of Cragg's book, *The Call of the Minaret,* "With justification he (Cragg) deplores the ignorance among the Muslims about what Christianity is and means (pp.246-247). How impatient the Christian scholar could feel when a Muslim scholar talks polemically without knowledge of the elements of Christianity, just as a similar ignorance about Islam on the part of Christians vexes the Muslim. But the position is one of unbalance. Christians have studied Islam with more depth than might have been expected from any non-Muslim community. Muslims often remark that such study is perverted and wrongly motivated. But at least it is a study and it is "motivated." Do we not have among Muslims, as a kind of counterpart, a "motivated" ignorance of Christianity?

"Can any Muslim scholar in the whole Islamic world claim with conviction that he knows more about Christianity than the average Christian Islamicist in a Western University knows about Islam? Do not we Muslims rather talk about Christianity from ignorance than from adequate knowledge?"

To help our Muslim brother to cross the intellectual barrier, we must supply him with the best possible literature on the subject. Unfortunately, there is an utter lack of new and up-to-date literature for this purpose in our language. Even our apologetic literature is old material rehashed. We need scholars who would keep in touch with all that is being written by Muslims about Islam. There are movements within Islam which are questioning some of the old orthodox dogmas and practices, on which traditional Islam has been built. In their struggle we should be able to help them to find the truth. The scholars should also keep track of all that is being written about Christianity by Muslims and to give suitable reply where it is needed. Muslim scholars have not been sitting idle, they have been building up a great offensive and defensive bulwark in their books to forestall any Christian incursions into Islam. It is our duty to provide both the Muslim and the Christian with material which would help him to see the truth, and make up his own mind. Anyone reading the cleverly written article in the Urdu Encyclopaedia of Islam on Injil (Gospels) would need to know the correct Christian point of view to avoid falling victim to a scholarly misrepresentation of truth. There is a spate of anti-Christian literature produced by the Ahmadiyas and the Jam'at-i-Islami and it is our responsibility to provide correct guidance to the people. It is not only the "apologetic" literature that is needed. People are hungry for devotional material (compare some of the Sufi and other Muslim devotional material) and the material connected with the life of Jesus Christ, for whom they have great admiration. And even though the Muslims do not believe that Jesus Christ was crucified, some of them cannot resist being attracted by the beauty of the whole situation.

A young Pakistani Muslim poet, Hassan Bakht, published his collection of Urdu poems under the title *Har Shakh-i-gul Salib* ("Every Branch of the Flower — a Cross"). Most of the poems are woven around the idea of the cross as a symbol of suffering and sacrifice. Let me translate one of the typical verses, "Bakht, have you felt the power of the Cross? It spreads out its arms inviting you to an embrace."

Christian reading rooms and bookshops have played an important part in winning people to Christ. My own father was converted by a series of visits to a reading room set up by Mr. Hughes, an Islamic scholar, and Dr. Jukes in Peshawar. My father had bought a few books and taken them home, but was not allowed to study them. If it had not been for Said Shah, the national attendant of the bookshop who discovered my father's difficulty and invited him to his house for a meal and provided opportunity to read to his heart's content, he would never have come to follow Jesus.

A wonderful piece of work in teaching the pure Word of God to people is being carried on by the Bible Correspondence School in Pakistan. Thousands of Muslims are taking these courses. In spite of opposition from various quarters, the work is progressing wonderfully. May we be able to devise ways of following up those whom the Word of God has touched and who wish to take the next step.

We should praise God that in an Islamic country like Pakistan the doors are still open to preach the Gospel. Only recently, the Central Minister of Religious Affairs and Information, while addressing a group of Christians claimed, "The minorities in Pakistan were enjoying the same religious rights and privileges which could be favorably compared with any country. There was full freedom of propagation of any faith in Pakistan. What we only want is that the sentiments of the followers of other religions must be respected."

Are we fully using these opportunities? Are we also prepared for such a time when our expatriate friends will have to leave the country? Eric W. Bethmann, in an excellent book, *Bridge to Islam,* says, "It might happen that some countries will close their doors completely to all foreigners. That would be regrettable. Yet it does not matter by whom Christ is proclaimed, whether by foreigners or nationals of the country. The witness of the latter will be more valuable and eventually the work will be done by them. These national workers often become more effective by the withdrawal of the foreign political influence, because horrible accusations that they are fifth columnists, tools in the hands of a foreign power, traitors to their own country, cannot be hurled against them any more. If they now proclaim the message of Christ, then they witness for Christ and for him alone."

But has the national church been prepared for this work? I think this is the weakest part of our program. The Greeks who wanted to see Jesus came to Philip, because he apparently had a Greek name. Will our Pakistani brothers come to us to inquire about Jesus? Unhappily the Pakistani church is not prepared for it. There are so many factions and there is such disunity among us that our witness among our Muslim brothers is a cause of offense. We display no love among ourselves, fight tooth and nail, run to the non-Christian courts, and drag the name of our Lord into the dust — "Let not those who hope in thee be put to shame through me, O Lord God of hosts; let not those who seek thee be brought to dishonor through me, O God of Israel" (Psa. 69:6).

Our preaching will be of no effect until there is a real repentance and revival in the church. Only then we can go out and proclaim Christ as our Lord, and witness to him through our life, through our love and concern for our Muslim brothers.

The intellectual, the social, the emotional barriers may be overcome, but unless by the grace of God we touch another heart with love, it may never really come to know the much greater and wonderful love of God for him. A recent convert who was struggling with the social and intellectual barriers, while still a Muslim wrote these words, "It is stimulating to think that cases of conversion through sheer *reasoning* between dogmas of two religions are very rare, perhaps non-existent. In cases of conversion where prosperity, social status, security, vengeance against native society, emotional experimentation and the like, are not the motives, the change of faith is motivated perhaps infinitely more frequently by love for charming virtues, of a magnetic person, or love for a group of lovable associates, than by cold religious arithmetic."

It was this loving friendship of some people that won Dr. Muhammad Daud Rahbar finally to Christ. I think the message for the twentieth-century evangelist among the Muslims is perhaps best given in these words:

"In place of a frontal attack launched on the intellectual level, the best of modern missionaries to Islam pursue a mode of approach which was seldom neglected by their predecessors but which was never quite trusted to bear full fruit — the method of intimate personal fellowship, of loving service, of sympathetic testimony, and of united prayer. Believing that the essence of conversion is direct experience of the saving power of Christ, they seek to lead the Muslim to that experience by helping him to sense his deepest needs, by appealing to what he has already known of God in his inner life, and by sharing with him what Christ has done for them. In counting upon Christ himself, and not theories about him, to exert the drawing power, they are aided by the fact that 'the character of Christ does attract the Mohammedan and is doing so more and more....The most hopeful note in the Islamic world today is the, to many, irresistible attraction of the Person of Jesus Christ.' To make the Muslim feel that attraction through deepening friendship, through a guided study of the New Testament, through leisurely conference, and through that prayer together which confesses God's Spirit alone can convert — this is the primary aim on which all else depends."

EVANGELIZATION AMONG MUSLIMS STRATEGY GROUP REPORT

Chairman: Dennis Clark
Secretary: Phil Parshall

Preamble:

In a packed room with over 75 nationals and missionaries in attendance, the great and crucial issues of Muslim evangelism were discussed. The input of Christian ministers from countries as geographically diverse as Indonesia and Morocco added significantly to the cross-pollenization of views regarding the various methodological options open to the servant of Jesus Christ. An informed Christian leader challenged the group by stating that "never in recent history have so many Muslims been coming to Christ." Yet the reality of the over 600 million adherents of Islam yet to be evangelized left a sobering impression on the gathered participants.

Methodology:

A number of tradional means of Muslim evangelism were suggested such as visitation, films, radio, institutional outreach, studied ministry, open air meetings, literary programs, reading rooms, and tract distribution. However, several more creative postulations evolved as the delegates interacted with each other. In various areas indigenous drama and musical programs have been successfully presented as a means of communicating the Gospel. Particularly, it was felt, Christmas and Easter provide ready-made opportunities for this form of sharing Christ.

Recently a healing campaign took place in a major city of the Islamic world. Over 20,000 people stood in rapt attention in a littered brick field to hear the message of a visiting evangelist. The response was so great that on the fourth night the police moved in and arrested the five members of the preaching-healing team. All were declared persona non grata and expelled from the country. Perhaps such a ministry on a discreet church-related basis could be used of the Lord as have the similar great campaigns of Latin America.

Correspondence schools such as those found in Lebanon and Bangladesh continue to prove useful in seed sowing. It was agreed that more emphasis must be placed on follow-up through rallies and camps in order to obtain maximum results from these efforts.

Several experiments are under way with the use of "Fraternities of New Believers" as a type of halfway house for the purpose of winning and discipling Muslims. A culturally attractive form of worship is adopted with the view of minimizing societal dislocation for the inferior.

The use of cross-cultural national missionaries from within the area now under review was a proposal accepted by all present. In the past teams of Indonesians have visited several Asian countries, the most notable of which was Pakistan. Their ministry was well received. It is hoped that in the near future a team of Asian or Middle East converted Muslims can minister on a much broader basis.

Cultural Consideration:

The cultural disorientation of the convert was discussed at length. The following areas should be fully explored:

1. The need of acceptance on the part of the Christian Church. Most converts are greeted with suspicion if not outright hostility by the established Christian community. The believers suspect the convert of impure motivation. Rejection rather than warm, loving acceptance is the norm. The Church should recognize this unchristian attitude and seek to open their doors and their hearts to the honest seeker of truth.

2. Worship forms should be modified to be more familiar and compatible for the convert. Western church liturgy is not an essential for the small struggling church which is surrounded by Muslim masses. It was postulated that prayer five times a day could be retained. Fasting as taught in Scripture could be emphasized. Scripture memorization and recital of great church creeds would act as substitutes for Koranic readings. Removal of one's shoes and bowing for prayer could act as a further point of non-compromising identification with the converts' traditional religious background.

3. The possibility of establishing a homogenous convert church should be explored. This may take the form of a worshiping group meeting on Friday at 1 p.m. in various homes of converts. Societal and cultural dislocation would thus be minimized. Also this type of service would be very attractive to the inquirer. The few "Fraternities of New Believers" operative in the Muslim world, such as the one in Pakistan, are the closest counterparts to the "convert church" that we have today. This is due to the fact that Muslims come to Christ usually as isolated individuals and not in any type of mass movement.

4. Muslim-oriented language should be used when possible. There has been the suggestion that two translations of the Bible be made, one for Muslims using Islamic thought forms and the other in the more traditional Christian vocabulary. Often the Muslim is totally bewildered by the language found in the local vernacular translation of the Scriptures. Effective communication is dependent on the proper choice of words. In Islamic outreach the Christian community has often been insensitive to this vital area.

5. Deferred baptism should be considered. Kenneth Craig and others have recognized the stigma baptism carries in a Muslim society. It is usually regarded as an outward sign not only of conversion but also of family and national betrayal. The convert immediately becomes an outcast from his own society and thus almost inevitably becomes a mission dependent. Could not the young Christian retain his firm faith, defer baptism, and at the same time have a visible witness among his own family and friends?

There are areas where it was felt no compromise could be effected. Biblical absolutes must not be compromised though cultural relativism should be prayerfully encouraged. Items within the Islamic religion which would be forbidden for the convert include: prayers for the dead, fasting and almsgiving for merit, vain repetition of prayers, obligatory circumcision, and attendance at the prayers in the Mosque.

Resource Assistance:

Instruction for the convert is a necessity. This can be provided for preferably by another Muslim convert. Other options include the local pastor, a dedicated layman, correspondence courses, extension seminary, or even a short time in a Bible school.

The work of the "Fellowship of Faith for Muslims," 205 Yonge St., Toronto, Canada, was noted with appreciation. This group edits a monthly bulletin of news and prayer requests relating to the Muslim world. Also they seek to co-ordinate a listing of available books on the subject of Islamics. The Congress participants felt such a service would be best located within the context of the Islamic world, perhaps in Beirut, Lebanon. A traveling secretary working out of such an office could be a valuable asset in the coordination of Christian ministry among the Muslims.

Conclusion:

Prayer was emphasized as an absolute prerequisite for the servants of God who have been entrusted with the responsibility of propagating the Gospel among the one-seventh of the world's population which owes allegiance to the religion of Islam. Importunate seeking of God was seen as the key to an effective ministry among Muslims. "Not by might, nor by power, but by my Spirit saith the Lord of hosts," (Zech. 4:6). (Note: It was recognized that some of our brothers and sisters in certain nations suffer the possibility of government action against them. In correspondence with these Christians, sensitivity to the circumstances in which they live should be emphasized.)

Summary: Evangelism among Moslems:

Methods of:

1. Indigenous drama and musical programs
2. Preaching-healing ministry
3. Correspondence schools
4. Fraternities of new believers, halfway houses
5. Cross-cultural missionaries from other Moslem areas

Ways of overcoming the cultural barrier:

1. A loving, accepting Christian church (cf. present situation)
2. Worship *forms* taken from Moslem worshiping practice
3. A homogenous convert church
4. Moslem-oriented language. New translation of Scripture
5. Deferred baptism

Resource Assistance:

1. Instruction for the convert (person, written, etc.)
2. A traveling coordinator and a monthly news and prayer bulletin

EVANGELIZATION AMONG BUDDHISTS AND CONFUCIANISTS

Lit-sen Chang

PART ONE: GENERAL SURVEY

1. Our formidable rivals

Buddhism and Confucianism are two major world religions. It is generally estimated that there are more than 400 million Buddhists and about 300 million Confucianists (a figure drastically reduced after the Communists took over mainland China). Geographically speaking, they occupy the vast continent of the world, and have about one-fourth of the entire world population. Ideologically speaking, they have manifested for over twenty-five centuries their toughness and arrogance in their way of thinking. Spiritually speaking, they are strongholds erected by Satan to impede the spread of the light of the glorious Gospel of Christ. Strategically speaking, they are formidable rivals which should not be ignored by any missionary strategist in approaching the tremendous task of world evangelization.

With the great upheaval resulting from World War II there has been a great resurgence of Buddhism. Buddhism was usually considered as a hobby of elderly retired people, but now it has caught the hearts and minds of young people. Buddhism has a systematic conception of philosophy and is taking the initiative of outreach. It even looks down upon Christianity and considers its supernaturalism as unscientific and as a naive religion for the child of superstition. It is no longer a quiet and secluded religion in a monastery; it has turned out to be very aggressive and has even made an impact on the West.

Since the Communists have taken over mainland China, Hong Kong has become a center of activities of Chinese intellectuals as well as a center of resurgent Confucianism. A New Asia College was founded as its headquarters, and a "Manifesto to the world on behalf of Chinese culture" was issued as another significant evidence of its resurgence. Over against the "cultural revolution" in Red China, a "renaissance of Chinese Culture" movement was promoted under the leadership of President Chiang Kai-shek. This movement is in fact another form of the resurgence of Confucianism.

2. The right approach

The author of this paper was not only an ardent follower of these two religions, but was the founder-president of Kiangnan University which was intended to be the headquarters of the resurgent movement of Oriental religion and civilization. In 1950, while he was on his way to India (in a sense, as his road to "Damascus"), with a plan to unite religious leaders in India to start this movement, he was mysteriously intercepted by God and, by his Providence, led to Java where he was later gloriously converted. So this paper is not merely a piece of academic work, but rather a personal witness of his conversion.

In order to win Buddhists and Confucianists to the Lord, we must first be identified with them and thoroughly understand them (of course, without compromising). This author could have been converted in his teens when he was in a Christian university, but instead he remained in pagan darkness for fifty long years. After his conversion he came to know that those years were not altogether wasted, but rather had a divine purpose in preparing him to know the aspirations and problems of Buddhists and Confucianists so that he could be used by God to win them to the Lord. As Dr. Philip Schaff pointed out in defense of Christianity against paganism, "The only formidable rivals are Brahmanism, Buddhism and Confucianism. These must be met by learned missionaries." An ancient Chinese strategist has said, "The surest way to victory is to know our adversaries." One of the causes of our failure of missions is our lack of such understanding and knowledge.

In formulating our missions strategy, we should avoid the mistakes of the "eclectic" and the "expulsive" approaches — the former will lead to the "suicide of missions," the latter will result in the "suffocation of missions." Our strategy must be "creative" in order to win Buddhists and Confucianists to the kingdom of love and light of Jesus Christ. We are not to be hostile or belligerent to them; nor to oppose them or destroy them; nor even to impose a religion on them. We are just to stretch out our arms to embrace them, to share with them the saving knowledge of Jesus Christ, who is the only Savior — the Way, the Truth, and the Life. We are to help them to know this Savior so that they might be delivered from bondage to freedom, from darkness to light, from death to life, and from the power of Satan unto God.

Paul's strategy was neither "eclectic" nor "expulsive." He started from a point of contact in view of the relationship between general revelation and special revelation, but went on by warning the Gentiles to repent, and pointed out the absolute difference between general revelation and special revelation, emphasizing also the supreme uniqueness and finality of Christianity.

3. The danger of theological confusion

The root cause of the "suicide of missions" lies in theological confusion without differentiating general revelation from special revelation. As Augustine pointed out from his experience of conversion, the apologists of the first century only stressed the similarities of some fundamental principles in Greek philosophy and Christianity; their eyes were closed to the more striking dissimilarities. They overemphasized general revelation and twisted the Bible by quoting Acts 14:17 and especially John 1:5,9, and falsely argued that since the light lights every man that comes into the world, therefore, all religions — including Buddhism and Confucianism — must be good for they all come from the same light, the general revelation of God.

It is true that God does reveal himself to all creatures — to natural men; but the Bible also teaches us that "the natural man receives not the things of the Spirit of God" (I. Cor. 2:14), for general revelation is absolutely insufficient to enlighten man to know the way of salvation and the only Savior of mankind.

There is a group of religious philosophers and liberal theologians who quote the Bible out of context by stressing the point that "Light shines in darkness and lights every man that comes to the world" (John 1:5,9). William Temple, for example, remarked, "All that is noble in the non-Christian systems of thought...is the work of Christ upon them and within them...By the Word of God...Buddha, Confucius, Jesus Christ conceived and uttered such truths as they declared...there is only one divine light and every man in his measure is enlightened by it." Such view might well approve Buddha's claim that he is the "Enlightened One," and also support the self-righteous Confucianists who claim "to illustrious virtue to renovate the people and to press on to the highest excellence," and are "able to make illustrious his lofty virtue." But they are not aware of the great truth as set forth in the Bible, "I was shapen in iniquity; and in sin did my mother conceive me" (Psa. 51:5); "The heart is deceitful above all things, and desperately wicked" (Jer. 17:9); "Light is come to the world, but men loved darkness rather than light, because their deeds are evil" (John 3:19); "For I know that in me (that is, in my flesh,) dwells no good thing" (Rom. 7:18); "The god of this world has blinded the minds of them which believe not" (II Cor. 4:4).

4. The vanity of pagan religions

From these quotations we can readily see the vain deceit of the claims of Buddhists and Confucianists. For instance, Buddha claimed to be the "Enlightened One," but in fact, he was an atheist. The "Bo Tree" under which he was said to have been "enlightened" might well be interpreted as a sort of "tree of knowledge" which was the root cause of the death of all men (cf. Gen: 2:17; Rom. 15:12). While "Nirvana" is the "raison d'etre" of Buddhism and the eternal destiny of Buddhists, yet Buddha's answer to this life and death issue was very evasive. When a young mother asked Buddha to give a cure for her dead baby, Buddha, instead of raising her baby from death as Jesus did to the only son of a widow of Nain, retorted with sarcastic words, "You thought that you alone had lost a son? The law of death is that among all living creatures, there is no permanence!" Thus, according to Buddha's own words, Buddhism is a "law of death" rather than "the way of life."

Confucius earnestly sought after the way to heaven, as he once proclaimed, "If a man in the morning hear the way, he may die in the evening without regret." But he confessed that he even does not know the mystery of death and life; and his disciples were disappointed because their master never talked with them about the way to heaven; nor did he talk about "the extraordinary things and spiritual beings." Confucius had never claimed himself to be a prophet, but rather confessed, "Learn as if you could not reach your object, and were always fearing lest you should lose it." He also lamentably confessed, "The leaving virtue without cultivation; the not thoroughly discussing what is learned; not being able to move towards righteousness...; and not being able to change what is not good: these are the things which occasion me solicitude." Confucius only teaches "attainment" but provides no "atonement." As he himself confessed, his own attainment was a tragic failure. He was not enlightened about the "Truth" and "Life"; nor does he know about "the Way to heaven."

From the above discussions and from the words and confessions of Buddha and Confucius it is clear enough beyond doubt that Buddha is not the "Enlightened One" as he so claimed; and Confucius is not a prophet even though he was respected as the "Great Perfection, Ultimate Sage and Foremost Teacher" by his followers. Their religions are indeed vain deceit. The teeming millions of Buddhists and Confucianists are in fact blinded by "the god of this world" and shut up in the shadow of death. So it is our solemn task to send "the light of the glorious Gospel of Christ" and "to open their eyes, and to turn them from darkness to light, and from the power of Satan unto God..." (Acts 26:18).

5. The need of theological penetration

To accomplish this task demands an honest evaluation of our strategy of missions and a thorough examination of the causes of our failure. We do not deny the significant achievements made in the past by evangelical missionaries; but we also need the insight to discover and the courage to confess our shortcomings and recognize the hard fact that the evangelization of the Orient is still an unfinished task. The program of Christian missions has shown our insufficient knowledge of the non-Christian religions and culture in the Orient. There has been a lack of profoundness in our understanding and a lack of theological penetration into the hearts and minds of their people — especially the intellectual.

We have an urgent task to infuse a new spiritual life into this dying world by a "theological penetration" to the system of philosophy and religion which have spoiled millions of souls. We should realize that the religious heritage in the Orient is so deeply rooted that we cannot brush it aside with a casual sweep of the hand, but it demands profound theological penetration. We must know that one of the chief causes of the success of Buddhism was its cultural and doctrinal penetration. It reached the most thoughtful intellect and penetrated into the deeper layers of the hearts and minds of the people. Confucianism too has exerted a tremendous influence on Chinese life. It has dominated Chinese thought for twenty-five centuries. It molded the national character, touched every corner of human activity, and permeated into all departments of life whether moral, social, or political. Without theological penetration — mighty through God to the pulling down of strongholds, casting down imaginations, and every high thing that exalts itself against the knowledge of God and faith in Christ — evangelization among Buddhists and Confucianists would never be a reality.

This author, an ardent follower of Buddhism and Confucianism for nearly fifty years, after his conversion has weighed them in the balances and found them wanting (Daniel 5:27) as "vain deceit." (Col. 2:8). It is his hope and prayer that this paper, although brief as limited by space, will be used by God to help us to understand the fallacy and futility of these two religions through a penetrating theological analysis, so that we might be able to find a creative approach and formulate an effective strategy for evangelization among Buddhists and Confucianists.

PART TWO: THEOLOGICAL ANALYSIS OF BUDDHISM

1. *Its teachings on God*

Many world-known scholars of religion agree that Buddha denies the existence not only of a Creator but any absolute being. According to the Buddhist world view, "Where there is no being but all is a coming to pass, there can be recognized not a substance." They not only deny the existence of God or the Creator, but even transmute the universe into a void and illusion.

Although there are references to the "gods" in their literature, there is no reference to "God." These gods are the old deities of the Hindus. They are finite beings; they are also subject to impermanence and death, and to sin and moral infirmity. So to the Buddhists the gods were not needed and worship was useless.

Some scholars argue, however, that they do use the terms "the Supreme" and "the Perfect," etc. In his conversation with Upasaka, Buddha did claim that he was the "Supreme Master," "the Perfect Buddha." But, as has been said, the only god in Buddhism is what man himself may become, for self-deification is one of the chief characteristics of heathenism.

Again, some scholars argue that Buddha did not categorically deny the existence of God, so that his position might be better called "agnostic." But, as Kellogg said in this respect, "Whether we call it atheism or agnosticism, from a moral point of view, it is virtual atheism."

As a matter of fact, millions of Buddhists in the Orient do worship Amida and Adhi-Buddha as their "Supreme God." For man cannot live without God; if there is no God, he must invent a God. But this is not the authentic teaching of Buddha; it was the new doctrine of Mahayana Buddhism which was transformed in some measure as a result of its contact with Christianity. Moreover, it is the manifestation of "His eternal power and Godhead" (Rom. 1:20) and the spontaneous cry of human beings. So in practice, these Buddhists do not believe according to Buddha's teachings. This is a strong proof that Buddha was not able to satisfy the aspiration of his followers and that his teaching is not the truth. Buddhism is a subtle form of atheism.

2. *Its teachings on man*

a. *On the meaning of life* — According to the "Four Noble Truths," to live is evil in itself because it involves suffering. The origin of suffering is our desire. In order to be delivered from suffering, one must be delivered from existence; in order to be delivered from existence, one must know the true existence is the Nothing. The Nothing alone is certain; Being, which originated in and from Nothing, must again go to Nothing, for it is essentially Nothing.

To such teaching we must answer that the origin of suffering is not desire, but sin. Desire is not evil in itself; only desire which is against the will of God is evil. The extinction of suffering is not accomplished by annihilating desire, but by repentance and surrendering to the will of God and by the purging of sin by the precious blood of our Savior shed on the Cross.

The "Four Noble Truths" only inform us about the disease but they give no medicine; they only abhor suffering but provide no remedy. We also know the suffering of mankind (Rom. 8:22), but we know too that "the creature itself shall be delivered from the bondage of corruption into the glorious liberty of the children of God" (Rom. 8:21) by virtue of the "suffering" for us on the Cross by our Savior, who shall "bring many sons unto glory" (Heb. 2:10), to eternal bliss; not to "nothing," not to "eternal extinction." Only those unrepentant sinners, including those misled by Buddha, are going to "Nothing" and eternal perdition! Thus we can see the so-called "Four Noble Truths" are not truth, but horrible fallacy and radical nihilism!

b. *On the nature of man* — Besides the "Four Noble Truths," Buddhists believe the doctrine of "five Skhandas." Man consists of an assemblage of these five qualities: Rupa (form or body), Vedana (feeling), Sanna (perception), Sankhara (reaction), Vinnana (cognition), but none of these corresponds to the notion of soul. The body is constantly changing. Man is never the same for two consecutive moments, just like a candle which is dying by burning. Man is no more than a Nama-Rupa (name and form), just like a "chariot," an illustration they often used, it is a "name" given according to its "form." Such a life-view is quite similar to De Mettrie's "L'homme Machine." Thus Buddhism is in fact materialism. According to the authentic teachings of Buddha, there is no God nor soul. But millions of Buddhists in the Far East, constrained by the witness of their own conscience, believe in the existence of the soul and hope to live in a "Western Heaven" after death. Thus, again they do not believe according to Buddha's teachings, but in opposition to his teachings. This is another evidence of his fallacy.

c. *On the destiny of man* — According to the "law of Karma," the Karma of the previous set of skhandhas of sentient being determines the locality, nature, and future of the new set of skhandhas of each new sentient being. All that you see and feel bodily or mentally of yourself, will pass away. There will remain only the accumulated result of all your actions, words, and thoughts. The question naturally arises about how the record of man can survive since they teach that the soul itself never existed. Buddhism acknowledges a mystery here; no real explanation can be given. Besides, since Buddha denied the existence of God, this so-called "law of Karma" is nothing but a vain imagination, because it has no "lawgiver."

Another doctrine regarding the destiny of man that must be discussed is that of Nirvana. It is the *raison d'etre* of Buddhism; yet no doctrine of Buddhism has been so much in dispute as this. It has been widely maintained that it means "extinction"; but others held the view that it does not mean the extinction of being, but only the extinction of the three fires of passion, and therefore it really means "the highest bliss." Unfortunately, Buddha's answer regarding Nirvana was very evasive. When his most intimate disciple, Ananda, asked him why he had not given a definite answer to this question, Buddha said, "If I had answered 'the ego is,' then that would have confirmed the doctrine of those who believed in permanence; if I had answered 'the ego is not,' then that would have confirmed the doctrine of those who believed in annihilation." But if no definite answer to such a fundamental doctrine has been given, then what is the foundation of their faith?

In China, where Mahayana Buddhism prevails, Nirvana has been interpreted as a return to the original and all pervading "Buddha essence" (Tao). This is a Chinese anomaly. Here is more evidence that what Buddhists believed is in opposition to, rather than in accordance with Buddha's original teaching.

3. *Its teaching on salvation*

a. *The nature of salvation* — The entire doctrine about the nature of salvation is summed up in the "Four Noble Truths"; it is simply deliverance from suffering through the destruction of desire and existence. Its basic doctrine is presented in Vinaya Pitaka, where we read:

> "By the destruction of thirst, attachment is destroyed;
> by the destruction of attachment, existence is destroyed;
> by destruction of existence, birth is destroyed;
> by destruction of birth, old age, grief, lamentation,
> suffering, dejection, despair are destroyed."

This simply means the eternal extinction of the personal self-consciousness, and to attain this is the supreme object of Buddhism. While Jesus Christ promises eternal life, Buddha holds to eternal extinction of individual conscious life as the highest good. Since to live is suffering and therefore evil, the nature of salvation is the destruction of existence which is, in fact, committing "spiritual suicide."

b. *The ground of salvation* — In Dhammapada V. 165, we read, "By one's self, the evil is done; by one's self, one suffers; by one's self, evil is left undone; by one's self, one is purified. Lo, no one can purify another." This teaches that personal merit is the sole ground of salvation. It is not by grace, but by work and one's own merit that one is saved. But the tragic fact is that it also teaches that when one's merit is exhausted, he will again fall into "samsara." Thus, merit is not the reliable ground of salvation. To accumulate merits is as futile as for one to hew "broken cisterns that can hold no water" (Jer. 2:13).

c. *The means of salvation* — According to Buddhist teaching, "The true existence is nothing; the nothing alone is certain. Being, originated from nothing, must go to nothing." To know this is the destruction of delusion, and then of thirst and then of attachment and existence and then of suffering. This is their way of salvation. So the basic means of salvation is knowledge. It is not by "faith" that we are saved, but by knowledge —seeking one's own enlightenment; not by the power of God, but by the wisdom of man (cf. I Cor. 2:5). We are told that Buddha was "enlightened" under the Bo Tree, and came to the knowledge of salvation, as he claimed:

> "The all-subduing, the all-knowing, am I, in everything that I
> am, without a spot. I am a delivered one. By my own power, I
> possess knowledge...In the world, including the heavens, there is no
> one like unto me. I am the holy one in the world. I am the Supreme
> Master. I alone am the Perfect Buddha.

Thus we see that Buddhism is a most radical form of self-deification and auto-soterism. If Confucianism can be called Pelagianism, then Buddhism is Pelagianism run mad!

They believe that every sentient being is a "potential Buddha." If a man could only come to this knowledge, he would be instantly saved, but as it is recorded in the Bible, this is the satanic scheme (cf. Gen. 3:5, 2:17).

Dr. P.A. Sorokin, great authority on sociology, warned mankind that "at the dawn of human history the misused tree of knowledge cost humanity its Garden of Eden. A similar misuse now threatens to destroy the very tree of human life." We should surely be aware of misusing the Bo Tree of knowledge, lest we "shall surely die"!

d. *The effect of salvation* — We are told that a saved Buddhist is a man who not only ceases to hate, but also ceases to love; not only ceases to desire evil, but also to desire good; is not only delivered from the desire of long life in this world, but also from the desire to live in heaven. In a word, a Buddhist should have no attachment whatsoever. The secret of salvation is the detachment from all things.

We do not deny the negative value of Buddhist teaching. It is not wrong to urge mankind to die to self, to die to the flesh, to die to the world. But if there is no positive answer and glorious hope, it would only lead the world to pessimism and nihilism.

From the Bible, we see a striking contrast between Christianity and Buddhism. We do not only die to self; we have Christ live in us (Matt. 16:24-25; Rom. 6:3; Gal. 2:20). We do not only die to the flesh (those who belong to Christ have crucified the flesh with its passion) but we are at the same time born again in the Spirit and renewed by the Spirit (Rom. 6:4-11; Gal. 5:24; Eph. 4:22-24). We do not only die to the world ("by Christ, the world is crucified unto me, and I unto the world," Gal. 6:14); but at the same time, God has "delivered us from the power of darkness and has translated us into the kingdom of his dear Son" (Col. 1:13). While "the earth and the works that are therein shall be burned up...nevertheless we, according to his promise look for new heavens and a new earth, wherein dwelleth righteousness" (II Pet. 3:10,13).

While Hinayana's teaching cannot satisfy the aspiration of Buddha's followers, many Mahayana Buddhists in China believe in putting their faith in Bodhisattva, who by his infinite compassion and stock of countless merits may deliver them from Samsara, and thus they hope to be received into a heaven of eternal bliss. However this is not Buddha's authentic teaching, but a Chinese anomaly. And according to K.S. Latourette, this resemblance between Mahayana Buddhism and the Christian faith was the result of the Christian preaching at a very early date in the northwestern part of India. Here again we find evidence that there is a strong contradiction between the teaching of Buddha and the practice of his followers.

4. Its teaching on the Last Things

a. *Individual eschatology* — According to the Buddhist teaching, man is nothing but "Nama-Rupa," there is nothing substantial remaining after death, so death is the end of man. As Max Muller puts it, "Buddhism is only a gospel of helplessness and universal doom!" What a striking contrast between Buddha and Jesus who raised the son of the widow of Nain as recorded in Luke 7:11-17! Buddha only knew "the law of death" and he himself was under the law and died miserably after an attack of dysentery. And before his death he helplessly uttered these sad words, "Decay is inherent in all component things!" While Jesus said, "I am the resurrection and the life; he that believes in me though he were dead, yet shall he live. And whosoever lives and believes in me, shall never die" (John 11:25-26).

   b. *General eschatology* — Regarding the future of the world, Buddha holds no brighter prospect. Buddhism teaches a future destruction of the world by fire, by water, and by wind. Some scholars have imagined that this is a point of resemblance with Christianity. But such view can hardly stand after careful examination.

   In the first place, while the Bible only reveals one such world catastrophe in the future, Buddhist scriptures falsely predict a cycle of destruction and renovation. This presents a pessimistic philosophy of history with no hope of the glory and triumph of the righteousness of God.

   In the second place, Buddhist eschatology is nothing more than speculation or vain deceit, because there is no historical fact or sign to prove it. But Christianity is a historical reality. From Genesis to Revelation, from time to eternity, it is all centered in Jesus Christ. Biblical prophecies have been fulfilled and proved by historical facts; and now his second coming is also being fulfilled and proved by the signs of this troubled world. All systems that have not arisen from the revelation of God will then pass away. The hundreds of millions of Buddha worshipers will not have a single votary. Where is the wise? Where is the disputer of the world? He has perished by the power of death and by "the law of death" as Buddha said. But our Lord Jesus Christ, who is over all, God be blessed forever, will be the life, the blessedness and the glory forever and ever.

PART THREE: THEOLOGICAL ANALYSIS OF CONFUCIANISM

1. Its teachings on God

   In ancient China, God was acknowledged as a Supreme Being, a Ruler in heaven (Shangti); but Confucius was a humanist, and, though he did not deny the existence of a Supreme Being, he only recognized him as a mere abstract concept of nature, but not as a Person. Confucius was a "liberal," very much like the modern "higher critics." He refused to talk about "extraordinary things and spiritual beings." When he edited the ancient Chinese canonical classics, he must have deleted much material of high spiritual value which was supernatural and beyond his understanding. As the Bible says, though he "knew God" he "glorified him not as God." As a result there came a spiritual degeneration. For most people, God became an impersonal Tien (Heaven) and they became "vain in their imaginations, and their foolish heart was darkened"; and still worse, "they changed the glory of the incorruptible God into an image made like to corruptible man" (Rom. 1:21-23). They worship dead men instead of the living God. And thus the tide of ancestor worship began to grow into an overpowering swell.

After the Han dynasty and through the influence of the Neo-Confucianism of the Sung and Ming dynasties, the traditional conceptions of the so-called "Tien-Jen-Hah-Yih" (unity between heaven and man) were developed and culminated into a system of Pantheism. They believed in "Tai-Chih" (the Supreme Ultimate) and "Wu-Chih" (the Supreme Ultimateless), having no shape, body or person whatsoever. Every man possesses the Supreme Ultimate. "One is All, All is One." They deify themselves and in fact, deny the personal God; and became naturalists or "practical atheists."

2. Its teachings on Creation

Since Confucius did not believe in a personal God the Creator, the origin of life and of the universe remained as a great mystery and only left his disciples in perplexity. It was recorded in the Confucian *Analects* that Confucius was not able to give an answer regarding these problems, except by raising an interrogation, "While you do not know life, how can you know about death?" And his disciples expressed their disappointment by saying that "the Master's discourses about man's nature and the way of Heaven, cannot be heard." Therefore, this problem of Creation only left his followers to speculate.

During the twelfth century, Chu Hsi, the greatest scholar of Neo-Confucianism, advanced the view that the universe and all things were composed of two principles, "Li" and "Chi." These two are co-eternal, infinite, distinct, and formed the groundwork of Creation. According to Chu Hsi, "Li" was conceived as the psychic principle — an *élan vital* of dynamic energy, and "Chi" was represented as the material form or the "flesh" of all things. According to such a doctrine there was no room for a Creator. As a result, Chu Hsi led many Confucianists into naturalism, materialism, or agnosticism, and the living and almighty God was expelled and had no relation with the lives of the Chinese people.

3. Its teachings on man

a. *On the nature of man* — Confucianism exhibits a keen interest in man. It taught that man's nature was originally good and that its degeneracy was the outcome of ignorance and of a clouded mind. But it failed to explain that this so-called clouded mind is the consequence of the fall of man. Since "sin entered into the world" (Rom. 5:12), man's heart has been polluted. It has been a futile attempt to clean the clouded mind by self-righteousness without the "remission of sins" (Luke 24:47). Only the blood of Christ who through the eternal Spirit offered himself without blemish to God, can purify our conscience from dead works (cf. Heb. 9:14).

b. *On true manhood* — The central idea of Confucianism is to develope true manhood. Their chief aim is "to illuminate the illustrious virtue, to renovate man, to press on to the *summum bonum.*" Confucianists are taught to establish and develop one's own character as a starting point to develop true manhood. They strive for self-perfection aiming at "the unity between heaven and man." But they are ignorant of the tragic situation of mankind in his "total depravity" and that true manhood can only be restored by turning back to God and becoming "partakers of the divine nature" (II Peter 1:4) through regeneration.

4. Its teachings on sin and salvation

Like all other non-Christian religion, Confucianism teaches nothing about original sin, redemption, forgiveness, atonement, and sanctification.

The three Chinese terms "Tsui," "O," "Kuo," mean respectively "sin," "evil," and "transgression"; but none of them carries anything like the connotation of the word "sin" according to the Bible, even though Confucius did point out that "sin against Heaven leaves man in a state of utter helplessness, and with nowhere to pray."

Confucianists thought that human degeneracy was the outcome of ignorance and a clouded mind, and that sin was simply something incidental not original, external not intrinsic, so that it could be wiped away by one's own effort. They believe that man causes his own downfall, and therefore he can work out his own salvation. As in Pelagianism, regeneration simply consists in one's moral reformation and development.

In the history of China, from Confucianism to Neo-Confucianism, from Confucius and Mencius down through the ages to Chu Hsi and Wang Yan-Ming (1473-1529), those great "sages" taught the Chinese people that there is no original sin and that only acts of conscious volition are considered to be sin. Man is as able to desist from sin as to commit sin. So it was urged that man can stamp it out by sincerity (Ch'eng) or devotion to doing good.

The present author was an ardent Confucianist and a strong advocate of the doctrine of Wang Yan-Ming who stressed the importance of the "unity of knowledge and practice of righteousness," so he has no prejudice against those Confucianists who are really earnest to do good with all "sincerity." But the tragic fact is that "we were dead in trespasses and sins." It is utterly futile to urge a dead man to do good works. We are saved by grace through our faith. One great problem which has vexed all Confucianists in China for several thousands of years is that no man can attain the "unity of knowledge and practice of righteousness." One noted Confucian scholar recognized this fact and said that this is the "tragedy of saints." This argues for us that it is not by "attainment" but by "atonement" whereby we must be saved.

5. Its teachings on ancestor worship

Confucianism has been considered by many scholars of the world as a religion of ancestor worship which has been practiced and regarded as a proper manifestation of filial piety. Such false notions have hindered countless numbers of Chinese from accepting Jesus Christ and at the same time posed a dilemma for many missionaries, because the Bible teaches filial piety but condemns idol worship — including ancestor worship.

But the true meaning of filial piety is not ancestor worship. This is a misinterpretation and distortion. According to the first chapter of "Hsaoking" (Canon of Filial Piety), "Filial Piety is the root of all virtues and the stem out of which grows all moral teachings.

"It commences with the service of parents;

"It proceeds to the service of the Ruler;

"It culminates by the establishment of the character."

Again, OuYang Shieu, a noted scholar and statesman in the Sung dynasty, in one of his famous essays wrote, "It is more important to provide respectfully and affectionately for the needs of the parents when they are alive; rather than worship them by burning paper money and spreading a feast before ancestral tablets which are mere superstitious practices."

These classical sources suggest that there is no necessary logical relation between filial piety and ancestor worship. Filial piety is the root of all virtues. It only commences with the respect of parents, it should be culminated in the fear of the Lord, our Father in heaven. Therefore, faith in God is not in contradiction with, but is rather the ultimate fulfillment of, true filial piety in its fullest sense. Strictly speaking, only a Christian can really know and practice filial piety.

6. Its teachings on the Last Things

a. *Individual eschatology* — Knowing nothing like the Christian doctrine of immortality, Confucius was concerned primarily with man's earthly career here and now. He avoided answering questions about the life hereafter. Before his death, he lamentably said, "The wise man withers like a plant." He was a naturalist and considered death as a mere natural law of all organic matter, not as the judgment of God (Gen. 3:17) or "the wages of sin" (Rom. 6:23).

b. *General eschatology* — Confucius was a confirmed humanist; the whole system of his teachings was centered in the realm of the things temporal and not of the things eternal (cf. II Cor. 4:18). His disciples were disappointed for they never heard his teaching concerning the way to heaven. His final state is a golden age of so-called "Great Harmony," a kingdom of the righteousness of man, not the Kingdom of God. He promises no hope "for new heavens and a new earth wherein dwelleth righteousness" (II Pet. 3:13).

All humanistic systems, no matter how beautiful and glorious they seem to be, are only "cut flowers." A great sociologist, after his exhaustive search, found no cure whatsoever in any human systems. "In the course of human history, several thousand revolutions have been launched with a view toward establishing a paradise on earth," but "none of them has ever achieved its purpose....The best way out of crisis was marvellously formulated a long time ago by Jesus Christ in Matthew 6:31-36. Without the kingdom of God, we are doomed to a weary and torturing pilgrimage from calamity to calamity, from crisis to crisis."

But the day of the Lord will come like a thief, and then the heavens will pass away with a loud noise, and the elements will be dissolved with fire, and the earth and the works that are upon it will be burned up....But according to His promise we wait for new heavens and a new earth in which righteousness dwells" (II Pet. 3:10-13).

"And God shall wipe away all tears...and there shall be no more death, neither sorrow, nor crying, neither shall there be any more pain: for the former things are passed away. And He that sat upon the throne said: Behold, I make all things new...." (Rev. 21:4-5). This is the hope of glory which is in Jesus Christ, and has been hid from ages and from generations (Col. 1:26-27). This is the hidden wisdom which God ordained before the world unto our glory: which none of the princes of this world knew...but God has revealed them unto us by his Spirit (I Cor. 2:7-10). We must be ready to tell Confucianists the reason of this hope that is in us (I Pet. 3:15).

EVANGELIZATION AMONG THE BUDDHIST AND CONFUCIANIST

Secretary: Wayland Wong

This study group had several problems that caused limitations to the effectiveness of our discussions. First, the group was small, averaging four or five persons each time, and most of the participants attended only one session. This made it difficult to have continuity and depth. Second, no one had access to the paper before the first session and the writer was not able to be present as a resource. After reading the fine paper, which presented the theology of Buddhism and Confucianism, it was felt that the scope of the paper was beyond our particular need in trying to reach the masses of people in Asia who were mostly nominal Buddhists. This paper would be more helpful for those trying to reach the intellectual Buddhist, and those who are very serious about Buddhist teachings. Certainly, this paper would be helpful for anyone trying to do evangelism in Asia.

Because of the composition of our group, we concentrated upon evangelization amoung Buddhists. It is believed that the majority of Confucianists are also nominal Buddhists in practice.

First a brief report was given from each country represented: Thailand, Laos, Vietnam, Cambodia, Hong Kong, Tibet, Japan, and Sri Lanka. Over 90 percent of the people of these countries are normally Buddhist. Thailand has over 50,000 temples and 400,000 monks. Although there are two major branches of Buddhism and there are differences in the practices of each country, the similarities are great.

In some countries like Cambodia, Buddhism is the state religion and is being promoted by the government. In Thailand nearly every government office has a Buddhist image. Some countries have a strong resistance to Christianity. In Sri Lanka the monks try to ridicule it. In Tibet the lamas have warned the people against accepting Christian tracts.

Buddhism is very syncretistic in each country. In Japan the people have Buddhist shrines and Shinto shrines together in the same room. Animism and ancestral worship are all part of Buddhist worship in most countries. (It is reported that Sri Lanka doesn't have ancestral worship).

In many countries the young people are restless and disillusioned with much of what they see. They are searching for something. Many have rejected Buddhism because it has not satisifed them. In fact, many young people now feel it is a foreign religion.

With so much poverty and suffering in many Asian countries it was repeatedly mentioned that the Christian Church must show genuine love and concern for the masses of people through organized efforts to help relieve the people. The church must manifest the love of Jesus Christ for the people.

In trying to evangelize the Buddhist, probably the greatest hurdle is the "foreignness" of Christianity that has been presented and the identity of Buddhism with Asian culture and society.

Specifically we dealt with several areas:

1. In presenting Christianity, the person of Jesus Christ from the Gospels must be the main message. Gospel stories about Jesus, his life, his attitudes, his love, his relationship to people, are attractive to people. A Sri Lanka pastor has had much success doing this. He warned that comparison and contrasting Jesus Christ with Buddha only creates a barrier to the listeners because they would automatically want to defend Buddha. So let the person of Jesus Christ make its own impact.

2. Literature and translation work must be improved. Translation of Christian terms and the use of certain words have had some tragic errors which have proven to be a real hindrance. Often it has proven foreignness. Better translations and more agreement in terminology are needed. Attractive tracts on the person of Jesus Christ and geared to each particular country are desperately needed. Attractive and easier-to-read Bibles must be more available. Many young people are willing to read about Jesus Christ and have requested correspondence courses. We must capitalize on this hunger while there is still opportunity.

3. The national churches must experiment more with indigenous forms of expressions of their living faith. Forms of worship, hymnology, structures, have all given evidence of foreignness. National pastors have been guilty of unconsciously taking on the western habits of western missionaries and have become foreign to their own people. A Thai pastor has returned to the custom of greeting people rather than shaking hands with the people, especially with women. This was much more acceptable by the people.

4. Christians must keep their social contact with their non-Christian relatives and friends and know how to be a Christian in their midst. Their love and concern for them must be deeper than before. If any activity or ritual is rejected because of compromising of faith, it must be done with the least amount of offense and it must be substituted by other means to prove greater love and loyalty.

5. Family-related conversions must be taken more seriously when trying to evangelize in Asian countries. Too often individual conversion outside of the family has been the norm. This has proven to be a major stumbling block for the rest of the family to become Christian. In fact, it has caused many reversions. The social ties are so strong that many young Japanese Christians have returned to nominal Buddhism because they couldn't face the social barriers. Wherever family conversions have occurred, relatives are often converted also. If heads of households can be won to the Lord, then whole families can be brought into the church. Greater efforts must be used to try to reach the parents of children from the Christian schools and Sunday Schools with the Gospel first, before the children are given a chance for a commitment to Jesus Christ. There may be danger in this, but it also has greater opportunities.

In conclusion, we must say that the real barrier to Christianity among the nominal Buddhist population in Asian countries has really been a social and cultural one. But as the national churches mature and wake up to this problem, there is real hope that each country will know how to break down many of the barriers that have kept the majority of people from really considering Jesus Christ.

The church also needs to understand that the Gospel will affect culture in four different ways. First, there are many things that are good and will not be touched by the Gospel. Second, there are some things that will be rejected because they go contrary to the Word of God. Third, there are some things that will be changed to a higher level because of the influence of the Gospel. And fourth, the Gospel will add new dimensions to a culture which will make it even a better culture to live in. All this can only happen as the Christian community grows and takes up its full responsibility to its own country and culture.

THE EVANGELIZATION OF ANIMISTS

Alan R. Tippett

*Dr. Tippett, Los Angeles, California, USA,
is Professor of Anthropology and Oceanic
Studies in the School of World Mission at
Fuller Theological Seminary.*

The title given to me seems to imply the existence of a concrete religious system, called *Animism* — something which might be set over against, say, Hinduism or Buddhism, not only for purposes of description and study, but also as a subject requiring a strategy for evangelistic approach. Because the greatest number of currently open doors for the Gospel are among animist people, the inclusion of the topic is certainly appropriate, in spite of any intellectual problems the title may raise. Therefore, to avoid the loss of time in debating semantics in our sessions, this preamble seems desirable.

1. Animism

Some scholars prefer to subdivide Animism and to deal with the sub-units — Shamanism, Fetishism, Ancestor Worship, and so on — treating each as a religion in its own right, thus avoiding the term Animism altogether. This may have some descriptive advantages, until one discovers that the sub-units are not discrete: several may be found interwoven together, and their practitioners may have multi-functional roles. These "religious systems" are thus found to be merely functional distinctions within what certainly looks like a general religious system, with no more diversity than Hinduism or Buddhism; and now we are back again to the notion of Animism.

The term Animism is certainly to be preferred to *Tribal Religion(s),* because Animism is active in great cities like Los Angeles, New Orleans, or São Paulo, and has many non-tribal aspects. It is preferable also to *Primitive Religion(s),* as it is neither chronologically nor conceptually primitive; indeed, it is currently much alive, and frequently quite sophisticated. Nevertheless, we should recognize that we are using the word as a term of convenience to provide a frame of reference for our discussions, presupposing that Animism is a discrete enough philosophical "system" among the religions to warrant our consideration of an evangelistic strategy for winning its followers to Christ. This is precisely the same position the members of our other groups will find themselves in, for Hinduism, Islam and Buddhism may also be manifested in a great diversity of systematic forms.

The popular use of the term Animism comes down to us from E.B. Tylor (1871). He did not give it the technical meaning it acquired from the comparative religionists, of a "kind of religion," but used it to signify "the deep-lying doctrine of Spiritual Beings, which embodies the very essence of Spiritualistic as opposed to Materialistic philosophy." It was, for him, a "minimum definition of religion" which saw the animistic way of life as accepting the reality of spiritual force(s) and beings, over against the materialist outlook on life. "In its full development," Tylor agreed, it formulated concrete beliefs in such notions as the soul(s), the future state, controlling deities and subordinate spirits, especially when these beliefs result in "some kind of active worship."

I believe this is a realistic approach, because it permits us to talk about animism and biblical religion in the same philosophical or conceptual structure, and to weigh one over against the other; and therefore to understand the meaning of commitment when a present-day animist comes to his "moment of truth" and makes his decision for Christ. Thus the very term "evangelizing animists" puts us into an identifiable category of communication and response. We are not dealing with secularists or scientific agnostics, whom we would need to approach by means of a different path in order to witness. But Animists and Christians have one thing in common — they accept the spiritual view of life. They do not need to be convinced of the existence of the supernatural. This opens many ways for dialogue; even though, at the same time, it exposes us to many problems and dangers, which we shall examine in a moment.

In spite of the wide range of categories, forms, and functions that may be identified in the study of animistic communities, and which compel us to admit that perhaps every animist community is different from every other one, I firmly believe that Animism can be examined as a cohesive thing, and that enough universals can be identified to permit us to discuss the evangelization of this kind of community in general terms. I believe we should be able to deal with tribes in the forests of Africa, in the highlands of New Guinea, or in the hogans on the mesas of New Mexico under this head — and to a large extent also the drug cults of Hollywood. My purpose, therefore, is to generalize as far as I can, and to delineate some common problem areas for discussion, rather than diversify one form of Animism as over against another. But I hope the diversity will be apparent in our discussions.

Whether the evangelist be from an old or a young church, if he is witnessing cross-culturally he will be hoping to leave some kind of an indigenous church behind him. The fellowship group will have to be the Body of Christ ministering the mind, touch and heart of Christ in its cultural and animist world; for evangelism is not merely the winning of individuals, but also their incorporation into relevant local fellowship groups. Therefore, before I enumerate my common problem areas, I must examine the biblical data base from which I operate.

2. The biblical theology of Animism

From the biblical point of view there is really no such thing as a taxonomy of religions for comparative study. Not even Hinduism or Buddhism has any biblical standing as a religion. For the people of God there is only one God, and all those who do not serve him are grouped together in a single category. Although there is sufficient data in the biblical narrative for a whole textbook on Animism, the common practice of classifying religions, with Animism at one end and Christianity at the other, as if in an evolutionary scale of development, is not in tune either with Scripture or with the anthropological data.

Of course, I may turn to the Scriptures and read about the deities with whom the people of God came into contact from time to time on their pilgrimage — of Dagon, of Chemosh, of Molech, of Tammuz, and of Bel. I also learn of their confrontations with fertility cults, of heathen sacrifices and libations, of ceremonial inhumanity like infanticide, of making cakes to the Queen of Heaven, and of worshiping the smooth round stones of the valley. We have everything — from individual and domestic ritual acts to national assemblies and the worship of national war gods — rites performed in the fields, by the wayside, in groves and high places, and in great temples. We have divination, necromancy, and sorcery, and numerous other ideas covered by the biblical word "idolatry." We could break down the whole animistic system of the biblical world into categories for study, but in the last analysis the Bible disposes of them *as a single category* in the first two commandments (Exod. 20:2-6) — anything that would usurp the Lord's place in the life of his people and set itself in God's place is grouped together as "over against Him" and idolatrous.

Nevertheless, when we consider the world of biblical times — the first two millennia before Christ and the first Christian century afterwards — we find it very similar to that of our own. The people of God stood over against all the forms we meet in Christian mission today, on all the various levels — private individual, domestic, peasant, and national. The characteristics of each of these levels recur through history with the kind of lives people live on those respective levels, and do not fit into a chronological evolutionary scale from the simple to the sophisticated. The Bible deals with both tribal and great religions, with both simple and complex, with both oral and written religious traditions — and it treats them all under one rubric both in the Old and New Testaments (Exod. 20:2-6; Rom. 1:19-25).

In the same way Walter Freytag had argued for the notion of the *people of God*, a biblical concept, as set over against the biblical counter-concept of the *Gentiles* — the "not-people-of-God" — because they are nations serving other gods, and have not yet come to the life of faith that makes people new creations and permits them to belong to the community of faith. This lines up with the concept coming from the Old Testament where "Gentiles" or "heathen" is *goyim* (the plural), for which the Septuagint adopted ethnos in many places — ethnos being the original root of the word "heathen" (again "ta ethnē," plural). Canaan was occupied by heathen nations, but was to become the possession of the seed of Abraham, through whom all the *goyim* of the earth would be blessed. The heathen would come to seek the Messiah (Isa. 11:10), who would minister judgment to them (Isa. 42:1), and offer light and salvation to the ends of the earth (Isa. 49:6). In the New Testament also, "ta ethnē" is used of the nations who are over against the Lord (Matt. 24:9; 25:32, etc.) and as the object of evangelization (Matt. 28:19; Luke 24:47; Rom. 16:26; Rev. 18:3; etc.).

The people of God are the Chosen Ones. But they always have a *responsibility* to the Gentiles. The latter were not excluded from Israel. Even in the Old Testament times they had their rights as resident strangers under the Law. The doctrine of the rights of the resident stranger in Israel is expressed in the Deuteronomic source and in the narrative of the book of Ruth, which is a practical demonstration of the

Deuteronomic Laws — Deut. 1:16; 10:9; 14:21; 24:17, etc., and Ruth 2:2f; 2:8-10, etc. But in the New Testament, when the notion of the people of God is separated from the historical people, and we meet the new Israel, we also see the universal purpose of God for the whole human race. The possibility of incorporation into the New Humanity is there, but the Gentiles, or heathen, are still not yet incorporated (Eph. 2:11-22), because they are still living in opposition to God, worshiping "not-gods" (Gal. 4:8), deifying themselves, and they are classified as under the realm of the prince of this world (Eph. 2:1-3; I Cor. 10:19-21). This is why the Christian mission must continue "until the end of the age" as the Great Commission indicates.

In this paper I wish to speak of evangelization in a somewhat wider sense than just bringing individuals to an act of "decision for Christ." It is this, of course — but more. It involves both a step of commitment and an experience of consummation, in which the Spirit witnesses with the convert's spirit that he is now a son of the Father, and if a son, then an heir through Christ (Gal. 4:6-7) — that the blessing of Abraham might come to the Gentiles, or heathen through Christ, receiving the promise of the Spirit through faith (Gal. 3:14). This is a process, bringing folk out of heathenism — here defined by Paul as "worshiping not-gods" (Gal. 4:8). The picture we have here of conversion from heathenism is that of a *process* — an *on-going experience.*

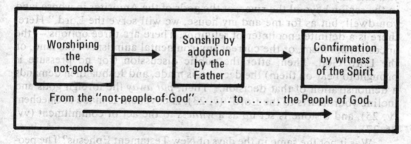

Adoption into the household of God brings the convert into a *group experience.* Some kind of incorporation into the fellowship group is always part of the evangelization process. This comes out clearly in the opening verses of I John, where witness (vv. 1-2) leads up to joining in the fellowship (v. 3), and from that verse on, John is dealing not with an individual in isolation, but one in context, i.e., in a state of fellowship (vv. 6-7).

Now, as we consider the evangelization of animists, it should be remembered that we are not dealing with individuals in isolation, but with men brought from death unto life — life *within a fellowship group.* We cannot escape the truth, that to give a man the Gospel of personal salvation demands incorporation into a fellowship group as a concomitant. Evangelization implies the existence of, or planting of, a church.

3. The evangelization of Animists
The conversion of animists and their incorporation into fellowship

groups involves us in each of the following problems, which I have conceptualized anthropologically because I think that such a treatment best opens up the subject for our discussions. I am reminded of the question of Henri Maurier, "Does not every theology have to be accompanied, in counterpoint, by as concrete an anthropology as possible? It is not enough for the apostle to learn what God has said; he also has to understand the men to whom he is bringing the Word."

a. *Pay attention to the problem of encounter.* Animists cannot just *drift* into the Christian faith. True, they may attach themselves to the fringe of some congregation as interested spectators, and maybe even become what we sometimes call "sympathizers," and it may well be that by so doing they will fall under the influence of the Spirit of God and be brought to vigorous commitment; but the passage from heathenism to the Christian faith is a definite and clear-cut act, a specific change of life, a "coming out of something" and an "entry into something quite different," a change of loyalty — or in the biblical analogy, a change of citizenship (Eph. 2:12-13).

The notion of making a definite act of commitment to the Lord is a biblical concept in both the Old and New Testaments, and was normally accompanied by some kind of ocular demonstration of the commitment. The book of Joshua ends with such an episode (24:14-15) — "Choose you this day whom you will serve; whether the gods your fathers served in the region beyond the river, or the gods of the Amorites in whose land you dwell; but as for me and my house, we will serve the Lord." Here, there is a definite encounter of religions. There are three options — the ancestral animism, or the current environmental animism of the land, or the Lord God. Then, after the public discussion (for no pressure is brought to bear on them) the decision is made, and Joshua then demands a demonstration of that decision. "Then, *put away* the foreign gods and incline your hearts to the Lord" (v. 23). A covenant is made at Shechem (v. 25), and a stone is set up as a *witness* to the act of commitment (vv. 26-27).

Was it not the same in the days of New Testament Ephesus? The people movement among the workers of magic led to the public burning of their magical literature — and so large a bonfire it was that the value of the books burned was recorded as 50,000 pieces of silver (Acts 19:18-19). Be it noted that this demonstration was both an *act of commitment* and an *act of rejection,* a spiritual encounter. Indeed, the anthropologist, Van Gennep, would have called it a *rite of separation,* because it marked a precise cutoff from an old life and status, before entering into a new one. Was it not to these same Ephesians that Paul so articulated it? Put off the old man (4:22), and put on the new man (4:24) — "put-off" and "put on," as one changing clothes.

The biblical evidence of this demand for commitment to Christ in some form of dramatic encounter shows the convert(s) demonstrating that the old way no longer has power over him (them), and henceforth he is "God's man" (the collective, "people of God"). Thus Paul, seeking to encourage the young man Timothy, addresses him, "O man of God," committed now to fight the good fight of faith, and to strive for Christian perfection (I Tim. 6: 11; II Tim. 3:17).

In the animist world today the public demonstration, or *rite of separation,* varies with the cultural climate — fetish-burning, burial of ancestral skulls, casting the sacred paraphernalia into the sea or river, eating the forbidden totem fish or animal, according to the pattern of their animism. These are cultural equivalents of Joshua setting up the stone of witness, and the Ephesian magicians burning their books. This is symbolism, but more than symbolism. Psychologically men are strengthened to keep their covenant by having made a public confession and having done it as a *company of converts.* "Let the redeemed of the Lord say so!" said the Psalmist (107:2).

The symbolic rejection of the old way not only involves a religious encounter, but thereafter it serves as a continual reminder of the act of rejection that alone can save the convert from syncretism or polytheism. It was just at this point that Paul had trouble with the Corinthian Christians, who found it easier to incorporate Christ into their heathen pantheon, than reject that pantheon for Christ. "No way!" says Paul, "Ye cannot drink the cup of the Lord and the cup of devils" (I Cor. 10:21). And it is precisely at this same point that the modern mission among animists is really Christian or just another kind of Animism.

b. *Pay attention to the problem of motivation.* Animists may be interested in Christianity for many and varied reasons — some good, others bad. Many factors may bring a field to ripen unto harvest. Of course, we are interested in all enquirers, but problems are bound to arise if the evangelist accepts all such inquiry at its face value without really evaluating the basic motivation; which may be for as materialistic a reason, for example, as the fact that the power of western armies and navies in war surely makes the religion of these powerful foreigners better to have on your side than against you.

Many supposed converts misunderstand both Christianity itself and the salvation it proclaims. They misunderstand their own needs also. The book of Acts (Ch. 8) supplies us with a good example of the problem. On the surface, the conversion of Simon, the sorcerer, at Samaria was quite genuine when he came to Philip (vv. 9-13) and believed. However, shortly afterwards, when confronted with Peter's ministry and the gift of the Spirit, it is immediately apparent that Simon had a complete misunderstanding of the nature of the Gospel, due to his wrong motivation: he thought he could buy the gift of God with money (vv. 18-24).

Animists sometimes respond because the Christian mission offers a ministry of healing which seems to be more effective than that of their own shamans and medicine-men. Animist chiefs have even invited missionaries to live in their midst in order to have a trade store in their community — this meaning a regular supply of steel knives, fishhooks, nails, and axe-heads, all of which are not only utilitarian, but are also symbols of wealth and status for both this chief among other chiefs, and this tribe among other tribes.

The motivation for accepting Christianity naturally affects their view of Christianity, the character of the Gospel, the nature of their Christian ethics, and their concept of Christian responsibility.

Let me give you an example of the problem as I met it repeatedly in Papua, New Guinea. One of the real problems there is that of the Cargo Cult. It even occurs where there have been prolonged pre-baptismal training programs. Indeed, perhaps the unduly long period of training has itself made baptism appear as a goal rather than an entry into an experience of nurture and growth. It gives the impression that converts "have arrived," as it were. They came enthusiastically in the first place, but now they want to "back out" in syncretistic cults which deny much that they have been taught. I met a young New Guinean who put it this way to me, "A few years ago I became a Christian because I wanted to achieve the white man's status and wealth. I wanted a good job, with a good wage and a house like the white men have. I worked hard in mission educational institutions, and I was baptized. But now it is all empty and worth nothing." The young man was thoroughly disillusioned with Christianity because his motivation had been wrong in the first place. His spiritual advisers had not detected this. They had interpreted his industry as a behavior-change due to conversion, and now he is a potential trouble-maker.

I also picked up a report from a missionary who had shared his all with a New Guinea colleague — a national pastor — whom he trusted implicitly. After many years, the pastor, recognizing this missionary's openness, asked, "Now we have shared everything, won't you tell me the secrets Jesus gave you?" The missionary was staggered to discover that even his pastoral colleague had what they call "the cargo mentality," which must have been there in his mind from the very motivation of his first attraction to Christianity. One major cause of Cargo Cults is the wrong expectation converts have had of Christianity.

I do not want to give the impression that all conversions from Animism are like this — that would not be true. There are thousands and thousands of wonderful warm-hearted Christians who really know Jesus as Lord. But, nevertheless, it remains quite true that we have never really faced up to the problem of motivation when the convert first comes for instruction. We ought to be asking the question — what is the role of the pastoral counselor when the would-be convert first moves forward to respond to the Gospel?

   c. Pay attention to the problem of meaning. Paul and Barnabas cured the cripple at Lystra in the name of the Gospel after proclaiming the Word, thinking thereby that the name of God would be praised. The people took the incident to mean that the two evangelists were the Greek gods, Mercury and Jupiter, anthropomorphized; and they brought forth their approved religious paraphernalia and the sacrifice, to worship them — the very last thing Paul and Barnabas wanted (Acts 14:8-13) — and, indeed, the people could hardly be restrained from this intention (v. 18). Here we are confronted with the problem of meaning. The proclamation, no doubt, was faithfully given, but alas, quite misunderstood.

Anthropology has a number of suggestions to offer the evangelist in this area of communication — at least to indicate why this kind of thing can happen. Let me enumerate a few, for purposes of discussion.

The biblical case I have just cited represented a confusion which arose from the *world view of the listeners.* Seeing the miracle, which was beyond the normal powers of science as they knew it, and therefore had to be due to supernatural factors, they interpreted it in terms of their own mythology. Every cross-cultural missionary runs into this problem sooner or later. It is the problem of translation and of Scripture interpretation. Every word selected — the word for God, for the Spirit, for the Son of God, for sin, for love, for pray, for forgive — comes from a non-biblical world view, and is a potential for misunderstood meaning. If it is a problem for the evangelist who speaks in the language of his listeners it is doubly so for the evangelist who does not learn the language, but uses a third party to come between him and his audience.

The meaning of the message can be distorted also by *the image of the evangelist* in the eyes of his audience. It was for this reason that western missionaries to China before the Communist days, were often heard as imperialists and capitalists, even though they did not think of themselves in that way. As one scholar put it, they became essential to the Revolution, so that Christianity could be rejected. I know the documents of one place where missionaries worked for sixteen years without a convert, living devout, industrious lives, and by their very industry giving the impression that salvation was merely a Gospel of hard work and trade — the very last thing they desired to do.

Then again the *evangelist's conceptualization of his message* can condition the meaning ascribed to it. Is he proclaiming a faith prophetically, or a teaching philosophically? Does the teaching of Scripture come through in a foreign or denominational garment? Is it presented as a moral, legal code, or oriented to the joy of the Lord and the glory of God? Is it directed to the problems of the evangelist, or to the felt needs of the listeners? The animists have come from a world of power encounter and presumably they therefore need a God who speaks and demonstrates with power. The preaching of a purely ethical Gospel is hardly likely to inspire such a people; but a life transformed by a God of power will lead to a new ethic. Why do the charismatic figures of so many nativistic movements retain the use of the Bible in their cultic practices? Several prophets have spoken on the point. Recognizing the power of the Word, they have pointed out that the missionaries of each denomination interpret the Word in their own way, and asked, "Why cannot we do it in our way?" And this they then do — in terms of their mythology.

Thus there are three points where the message of the Word may be blurred in communication: (i) *at the "advocate end"* (evangelist), *(ii) at the "accepter end"* (convert), and (iii) *in the message itself* (the theological emphasis of the evangelist). We can no longer run the risk of sending out missionaries (westerners or nationals) without some cross-cultural training, and, of course, it follows also that they should be competent interpreters of the Word.

d. *Pay attention to the problem of social structure.* At first thought we may wonder what social structure has to do with evangelization. This is because many of us are individualists, and we assume that everyone should do things the way we do. But the peoples of the world do not have identical social behavior patterns, and this creates problems when evangelization is cross-cultural. The people to whom the evangelist goes may organize their daily life very differently from him, and he should remember that the process of evangelization should lead to the formation of fellowship groups, and that these should be indigenous and not foreign in structure. At least, the evangelist ought to be aware of social structure, and reckon on the Holy Spirit being able to use ways of life different from his own. Let me cite two examples of the importance of social structure for evangelization.

(i) Most animist societies are communally orientated: i.e., they tend to operate in homogeneous groups. These groups, of course, do not ignore the individual; but he is always an individual within a group context. Groups are multi-individual. Discussions of important issues for decision go on and on until a *consensus* is reached. This may take a long time but it eliminates the problem created by "majority decision" which denies some of the rights of the minority that is out-voted. These communal societies have a high degree of social responsibility, and often the individualistic foreign evangelist has trouble with group decision-making. Groups exist at different levels of social organization, and authority for decision may lie at different levels — e.g., decision-making in domestic affairs, agriculture, religion, politics, and war may be the responsibility of household, extended-family, village, or clan. It is important for the evangelist to identify these because the manifest behavior of the multi-individual group in turning from heathenism to Christ will have the appearance of *group movements* — households, villages, age-grades, extended-families or clans, according to their normal social organization. Unless it is so, it will not be meaningful to the people.

There is nothing strange or unbiblical about this. The apostles found that the rural villages and townships of Palestine often "turned to the Lord" as whole communities, like Saron and Lydda (Acts 9:35), whereas in other cases, like that of the centurion at Philippi (Acts 16:30-34) and Crispus, the chief of the synagogue at Corinth (Acts 18:8), the groups became Christian as households. They were acting within the regular operative social mechanisms of daily life.

(ii) In the same way, those who respond in these group movements have to be formed into fellowship groups or churches; and the operating character of these should either reflect or, at least, be compatible with their familiar structures. This applies especially to any leadership patterns introduced. For example, a common blunder in church-planting across cultures has been to appoint a young Christian leader (on the grounds that he can read and has had some education) over a new Christian community in a gerontocratic society, normally led by a council of elders, where the basic values are maturity, experience, and grey hairs. In this way the evangelization of these people brings an unfortunate and unnecessary bone of contention.

These two illustrations, at the levels of decision-making and leadership, will serve to make the point that effective evangelization requires a church indigenous from the beginning; and the more foreign organizational structures imposed on a church-planting situation the more problems will be created for the subsequent generation which has to find the passage "from mission to church," which can be a painful experience.

e. *Pay attention to the problem of incorporation.* One of the tests of valid biblical evangelism is the provision of a way for incorporating converts into the fellowship of believers. The Bible demonstrates this in several ways. First, there are passages, like the introduction of John's first letter, wherein the notion of *witness* (vv. 1-2) is associated with that of fellowship (v. 3); and the Great Commission itself, which does not end with "Go and make disciples," but continues "baptize and teach." For the purpose of study, we take these texts separately, but in reality they are wholes. The analysis must be adjusted by synthesis, or our evangelization is only partial.

Second, the notion of the fellowship is crucial in biblical argument. True, we can speak of evangelism as bringing individual men face to face with Christ, but we cannot leave it there, because the New Testament did not leave it there. Christ is, of course, the Ultimate, and in that sense we need no more than to be with him. But for this present point of time in which he has been born, the convert has to be incorporated into some precise fellowship group, the Church, which is Christ's Body. In the records of the early Church (Acts) and the letters which tell us so much of its inner life, the configuration which holds it all together structurally is the church — be it theologically the Church Universal, or practically the local church. Remove that concept from the New Testament and look for a disembodied collection of isolated people who had met Christ, and you will soon be disillusioned. Christian activity and theology are always spoken of in collective figures — Christians are "fellow citizens," "members of the household of God," a "priesthood," a "nation," a "flock," a "fellowship," the "members of the Body," or "the church which is at..."

Fellowship-forming or church-planting is thus part of evangelization. Right at the beginning of Acts (1:13-14), we have a fellowship group in prayer, and immediately a worshiping, witnessing, growing body (Acts 2:46-47), meeting for instruction, fellowship, breaking of bread and prayer (v. 42). Thus is the Church his Body, fulfilling his ministry in this world in this day, and if evangelization does not mean that, it is defective.

To pass from this biblical base to the situation in the animist world, where men are being won to Christ in communities completely different in both social life and values perhaps from that to which the evangelist belongs, the latter has to consider what a convert from animism needs to find in the fellowship group into which he is incorporated. How does he get his new experience of Christian *belonging,* so that he becomes a participating, worshiping, witnessing, and serving member of the Body of Christ *in his own kind of world?* I hope for a profitable discussion of this issue, not only to provide us with some worthwhile directions for ministry in such situations, but also to help cross-cultural evangelists at large to appreciate a problem which many of them have never thought about at all.

f. Pay attention to the problem of the cultural void. Over the last ten years I have been able to visit a great many young churches whose members have come to Christ out of animist backgrounds. Apart from their wide range of cultural differences, there are also manifest spiritual differences. Some of them, though quite strange to me culturally and linguistically, have nevertheless been obviously vibrant with life, creative in their worship, using their own indigenous forms of music and art with enthusiasm, and performing significant service ministries in the animist world about them. On the other hand, others have been the very opposite. They have tried to worship according to patterns more familiar in the West, and sing hymns in Western music and to have many quite obvious accouterments of European denominationalism. These churches have been misfits in their own worlds. They limp along as if almost ready to die; as if trying to be what they really are not. In some cases they are even led entirely by a foreigner, and there is little, if any, congregational participation; and financially their work is possible only with the aid of foreign funds. If they have a national pastor, he is a little replica of the foreign missionary. How is this church ever going to see itself as the Body of Christ, ministering the mind and heart and Word of Christ to the animist world outside? In a hundred years of history it has no more than a hundred members, and is currently static. The truth remains that the Christian programs of evangelization used over the last century of Christian missions produced these two kinds of churches. And I believe that in each case their characters were, more often than not, formed in the early periods when the first fellowship groups were being formulated. I believe that the majority (I did not say all) of our second generation problems have their roots in faulty follow-up of the original religious awakenings. In church growth parlance we say, "The people movement has to be effectively consummated."

One of the problems of following up a great movement of the Spirit of God in bringing many persons to Christ, is not just to incorporate them into a Christian group, but to be sure that it is an indigenously structured and meaningful group, in which they can participate in their own way. Thus, for example, a New Guinea convert should not have to become American or Australian to be a Christian: linguistically and culturally he should be a *New Guinea* Christian. Likewise the fellowship group should be New Guinean. The members' participation, praying, worship, and service ministry should be New Guinean. A gifted New Guinean animist musician, on becoming Christian, should be a *New Guinean* Christian musician — and so on.

If we get into this kind of a situation where evangelists dispose of all cultural values and creative arts on the presupposition that they are all incompatible with Christianity because they have been used previously for heathen purposes (as many evangelists do argue), we find ourselves with creative people who can no longer create, and would-be participators who become non-participant, and before long the cultural voids we have created begin to be felt. Cargo Cults are only partly due to foreign domination; they are also due to cultural voids. Those who believe they are called to evangelism should remember that evangelization does not take place in a vacuum.

The problem of *maintenance* (as the anthropologist, F.E. Williams, called the preservation of traditional techniques and values in a situation of changing culture), of course, involves a value judgment — can this or that element be preserved and be made truly Christian? Or will its maintenance involve the church in syncretism? The New Testament warns us that we are bound to meet this problem and that it must be faced squarely. This is why I began this statement with "The Problem of Encounter." But, even so, when the basic commitment to Christ has been effectively faced, there will yet remain an indigenous way of life which is also worth winning for Christ. It should be possible for a tribal man from, say, Africa or New Guinea, to be a Christian without having to reject his tribe. It must be so or we could hardly hope for the "great multitude which no man can number of all nations, and kindreds, and peoples and tongues (standing) before the throne and before the Lamb" in that day.

I asked a tribal man whose people had come into Christianity from animism, but whose Christian life was largely innocuous and foreign, making little impact on its surrounding world, "What happened to your tribal skills?" He told me sadly that they had "melted away" and that life was empty because of it. He was feeling the cultural void. Something within him was crying out to be creative. He had discovered another Christian church in his country which utilized the indigenous arts and crafts to the glory of God, and he felt his own tribe had been robbed of something precious. A basic question recurs: What does it mean to a Christian convert from animism to be a Christian in an animist world, and to be a participating member in a fellowship group of converted animists? This applies to more than arts and crafts. How does the converted animist meet the physical and spiritual needs that spring from the tribal way of life — problems of danger, of death, of sickness, or sorcery — and how does one discover the will of God for him?

Evangelization does not end with an offer of the Gospel, or with the conversion of an individual, but with the coming into being of an ongoing fellowship, which is the Body of Christ in that kind of world.

EVANGELIZATION AMONG ANIMISTS REPORT

Introduction: It should be stated from the outset that this study group represented a wide spectrum of participants with conflicting experience. Therefore the success of this study group will be measured in terms of the problems and burdens shared rather than solutions found or strategy formulated.

In his paper Dr. Tippett structured his comments on six problem areas which those seeking to evangelize among animists must constantly keep in mind. They were: the problem of encounter, the problem of motivation, the problem of meaning, the problem of social structure, the problem of incorporation, the problem of culture void.

From the study group point of view the lines were less definitive but it was the matter of encounter which occupied more time than any other factor. In his paper Dr. Tippett states: "Animists cannot just drift into the Christian faith...the passage from heathenism to the Christian faith is a definite and clear-cut act, a specific change of life, a 'coming out of something,' and an 'entry into something quite different'..." While all agreed heartily with this, the question of how much of the "old" could be brought into the "new" produced a very wide variety of opinion.

Converts from ancestor veneration in Africa spoke of having been led even as young children — led by the Holy Spirit — to cut all ties with the whole system. From India the heart rending suffering of new believers, many of them children, was causing their advisers to question whether a more gradual break with the social-religious customs that tie the family so closely would lessen the conflict between new converts often isolated among large numbers of heathen. Over against this position of a clear cut severance of all ties with the "old" came first hand accounts from the Pacific area and South America of old functions being given new meaning. Old crafts and art once used to convey evil connotation are now dedicated to Christ and made a vehicle of Christian concepts. So there remained the two stances. The problems of the first could easily be seen in providing meaningful functional substitutes to fill cultural and religious voids. The problems of the second school of thought, as expressed by some participants was the impossibility to truly disassociate the past meaning in the carried over form.

With regard to the problem of motivation a number of examples were put forward. In the northeastern part of India conversion often resulted from a "power encounter" — through a vision, a dramatic healing, etc. The danger resulting from such conversions was felt to be the probable lack of any deep inner transformation resulting in a short lived experience. Yet it must be recognized that God is using this means in many people movements. This must wherever possible be followed by a love and truth encounter so the new convert can quickly be brought from what may be a simple "conversion" — turning from...to an inner transformation through acceptance of the truth in Christ.

As the group moved to the area of meaning, we again saw many problems raised but few concrete solutions agreed upon. How are we to ensure that the meaning we give to words will be translated to the hearer when the whole religious vocabulary in his language has an evil or perhaps immoral connotation? Or even more difficult — how to convey truth for which no suitable words exist in the hearer's language? Some vivid examples were terms for a Holy, loving God; the Holy Spirit...Some examples from the translation of the Scriptures into Eskimo dialects of Canada told of introducing entirely new words taken from English but given an Eskimo form. Others advocated the use of an indigenous term with a qualifying clause or adjective. All agreed that this problem was a continuing one for which the evangelist must continually seek the help of the Holy Spirit.

As time had overtaken us the last session was primarily given to the essentiality of providing definite forms of incorporation into a fellowship body. This was seen in its scriptural content from I John 1:1-4. Specific examples were also given of the loss of new converts when not immediately structured into the body of the Church. Often because of race or class difference they were welcomed to the church but not incorporated into a relevant group and soon drifted away again.

Two solutions were suggested supported by experiences participants were currently undergoing in their own lands. One recommendation was to commence separate ethnic or class churches where participants feel at home. Others disagreed affirming that converts be incorporated into multi-ethnic or multi-class churches. A good compromise was suggested in allowing separate ethnic groups to form their own churches but be incorporated into a larger fellowship coming together often enough to maintain a unity within the body.

In summarizing the discussion Dr. Tippett suggested a most useful set of points aimed at assisting the evangelist to adjust his method and approach. All peoples fall into one of the following positions suggested Dr. Tippett.

a. The period of awareness. This initial contact period leads one to
b. The period of realization. The hearer realizes this message has relevance to him and he must decide to accept it or reject it. This in turn gives way to c. Encounter or the *demonstration* of his decision.
d. From encounter the next step, to be taken as quickly as possible, is that of incorporation — the fitting of the new "member" into the "body." The process however continues and the new body-member now begins the process of maturation.

To keep such a grid before us should enable us to make our contact and message most effective whatever the present position of those to whom we minister.

EVANGELISM TOWARD ATHEISTS

Junji Hatori

*Rev. Hatori, Nagoya, Japan, is the Pastor of
the Jiyugaoka Church.*

1. Introduction: atheists in Japan

When I was given this subject my first thought was of the virtual non-existence of real atheists in Japan. It is, of course, true that many Japanese do not believe in either God or gods. The fact that they do not believe in them however, is not the same as denying the existence of a deity. For instance, they participate in Shintoistic rights. They feel it is good and necessary to take part. Failure to participate is regarded as a socially despicable attitude.

Their attitude toward Buddhism is almost the same. To an average Japanese, religion is a matter of ethos, i.e., it is a matter of the customs and ethics of the society. Japanese "atheists" do not have a god whom they *have* to deny or whom they *have* to rebel against. The nation of Japan possesses so many gods and religions that probably the number is so large that it is difficult to find a similar phenomenon in any other developed country. Truly Japanese are a "religious people" (Acts 17:22-23). Here, I cite Paul's words concerning the Greeks because I feel Japanese are similar to the Greeks of those days in that the thinking of Japanese is realistic, worldly, and optimistic.

The religious attitude of many Japanese is that they recognize a god or gods only when it is necessary to do so. They do not relate their actual daily lives to their god's blessings. They ignore god or gods entirely. They are totally indifferent. I would call Japanese indifferent atheists.

There are two types of indifference. One type regards all religions the same. Another type is the simple indifferent attitude toward any god. The usual Japanese "atheists" belong to the second type. Theoretically, if we analyze them according to categories of thought they are simply agnostics. Probably what I have been describing can be applied to almost all cultures and nations of the world, but it is perhaps most evident in Japan.

Evangelism toward atheists in Japan is, therefore, virtually the same as evangelism among the youth in today's world. Today's youth evangelism is directed to the kind of young people whose characteristics are that of anti-establishment and anti-conventionalism. Today's youth in Japan are very anti-traditional. Because of that, we might judge them and say that they have gone away from old Japanese thinking. They themselves might use borrowed atheistic terms, but these are only "borrowed capital." When they reach middle-age, we see them fast turning back to liking things "Japanese." They start wearing a kimono and live with god-shelves in their homes.

It is my desire to set up guidelines for evangelism among atheists in Japan considering the above mentioned factors. Twenty years ago I was a card-carrying member of the Japan Communist Party. At that time I was a belligerent atheist. Nobody can speak away from one's own background, and I will have to give these proposed guidelines with my own background in mind.

2. Problems facing Japanese youth

It is impossible to treat all the problems in this small treatise. I will deal with some of the most important aspects.

a. *Estrangement* — Youth is suffering from estrangement. The word estrangement is used in various meanings. Here, we will use it in its comprehensive sense.

According to the investigation of one leading medical school in Japan (Jikei Medical School) it is reported that 24.5 percent of 7, 8, and 9th graders have thought of suicide at least once. They also report 34.1 percent of 10, 11 and 12th graders and 40.6 percent of college students in Japan have pondered suicide. *Mainichi Shimbun* in its February 8, 1974, editorial reports that 65 percent of Kyoto University students have desired to commit suicide at least once, and that every year five or six actually do so. Kyoto University is one of the best schools in Japan. Recently its president in his inaugural message appealed to all the freshmen not to try suicide. Estrangement is a real problem. What are the causes of this estrangement into which so many people are driven?

(i) There is estrangement in urban society — Roughly 10 percent of the whole population of Japan is living in Tokyo. The 350 miles between Tokyo and Osaka is a long chain of big cities. This strip city called "Tokaido Megalopolis" contains more than 30 percent of the whole population of Japan. We can say that most all Japanese are forced to live in big cities. Hence it is no longer possible for Japanese to enjoy community life. A small village-like-community around the paddy field has disappeared. The "tonari-gumi" (neighborhood group) community unit of 6-10 households in village life is gone for good. In the modern urban society of Japan, nothing substitutes for these historical community units of society. People have left community gods back in their village. These protector gods and goddesses were the Baal of Japan. The old Japanese life was strongly knit together by an imposed "gonin-gumi" (obligation) group. This was a powerful weapon for feudalistic Japan. Now, as these have disappeared, Japanese are not able to maintain a sense of solidarity, because they lack faith in the "creator God." When modern Japan began, and the people started to live as individuals, each one lived an uncontrolled and highly individualistic existence without any regard for other individuals as well as society. This style of living is harmful; therefore, in the Japanese language, the word "individualism" has taken on a very undesirable flavor.

Thus, in Japan, urban society is a conglomeration of individuals without any sense of solidarity, and the size is just enormous. In these days we witness various sorts of citizens' movements, and almost all of them are protest movements, negative in character. We can call them corporate egotism and they have failed to produce or create a new community life. (Common among people in urban life is the "victim" complex. With this complex in their mentality, estrangement is further strengthened. In a society like this, the youth feel they are the worst of the victims.)

(ii) There is estrangement in technological society — The cause of estrangement in Japan is found right in these conglomerates of godless individuals. This estrangement is further enhanced by the characteristic features of modern society. Although modern technological developments with the aid of computers have produced great results, they have also produced a kind of society that tends to ignore the human individual and his value, and this immeasureably enhances estrangement of human individuals. Discontentment among the workers in highly automated factories has already been portrayed thirty years ago in Charlie Chaplin's *Modern Times*. The present technological society is much worse than that of Chaplin's day.

The concept of systems engineering was given birth by wartime necessities. Together with PART technique, this concept regards a human being as a mere factor, the most fragile in the whole system, and bound to make errors. The main concept is that the laying out of the master plan would be taken up by computers. Then this highly calculated and well-analyzed master plan is executed through human individuals. These people are not required to possess any creativity. The only creativity necessary is at the top level. Thus most human individuals are not playing a vital role. In fact, it is one factor which could be detrimental to the whole system. This is typical of the principle underlying the modern concept of systems and technology.

In the computer-controlled society, each individual is regarded as a mere sheet of punch card or a code number, and no more than that. The well-known play on words "computopia" is rather nothing more than the society of estranged people. It seems that our modern society is moving toward this destiny, and there is a strong reaction against this tendency from the young people.

(iii) There is estrangement in work — This, according to Karl Marx, is the situation in which the labor of one individual is sold to others completely, and the said worker has no claim on or share in his own product. If we ask the same question of a blue collar or white collar worker of today's society he will give us the same answer, though with a slightly different nuance. He feels that neither his labor nor his product is creating the bond which unites human individuals. In times past, artisans and manufacturers had pride and contentment as they saw other people using their products. Can we see this today? Look at a woman worker in a Sony color TV factory assembling TV sets. During any given day she has to solder the same part to a TV set over and over again. Can she be proud of the fact that her color TV will go to the US and that a certain family will watch the set? Various research reveals that when Japanese are asked about the value and purpose of life, most of them answer that it is to have a "meaningful" life. Also, according to United Nations research, of all nationalities the Japanese are known to express their dissatisfaction with the present condition of their lives to the greatest degree. This made Japanese politicians quite embarrassed at one time. In the present Japanese society, the only thing people can claim as a result of labor is "yen." We see people working just for money. It is clearly evident that "ugly Japanese" are being born this way, and that an "economic animal" also is being born. We may be able to interpret the "workaholic" condition of the Japanese as a screaming cry of a nation which does not possess the knowledge of God. Because of this lack of knowledge of God it has no way of rescue from this horrible estrangement.

(iv) There is estrangement from self — This most horrible fate is exactly the condition of the Japanese youth now. Among them "sommu-shugi" is found. This might be translated as "three-nothingism" or the style of living which continues to lack three things. It is a purpose-less, interest-less, and vigor-less living. They do not find purpose in their lives, they do not have interest in what is happening around them, and their lives lack vigor. They live just by inertia. It seems that though they are living in society, in fact they are not. They are estranged from themselves.

The problem is that this is seen among not only part but almost all of the youth in Japanese society. The problem of suicide and the desire for suicide indicate this fact. Frustration is the password among them. Though this might be said of all youth throughout the world, many people point out that the infamous Japanese school system, especially its examination system, aggravates these facts. I agree with this. However, the true reason for this tendency is that they do not know God and they never think about God. Even the Delphic oracle "Know Thyself" is not a concern or interest to these young people. It is much more so with the true Word of God. It is a matter of course that they have been estranged from themselves and that they do not know themselves. They have completely lost sight of themselves.

b. *They have lost logic or certainty* — Another problem they face is that they have lost the principle of logic or the criteria of judgment. This also can be seen throughout the world. However, again I feel this is most evident in Japan.

(i) They have lost logic because of a dualistic world view — Francis A. Schaeffer has pointed out this factor sharply in his books, especially, *Escape from Reason*. When we deny God and when we hold the dualistic world view that this world is divided into two spheres, spiritual and natural, we find at once that we cannot understand this world logically. As Schaeffer rightly points out, immediately young people find that there are "boundaries of despair." They desperately find that they cannot understand the world, human life, and themselves. And they discontinue the effort to understand these, either by reason or by logic.

It is easily understood that this loss of ability to understand will take place much easier in Japanese society where people did not know God from the beginning. In such a society things are not judged according to truthfulness, but according to merit or demerit.

(ii) There is disbelief of tradition in adult society — Each one has his own world. They have to keep that world. The world in which today's youth have been reared is one of confusion and disorder. Adults did not act with authority because the establishment lost their confidence altogether after World War II. Youths of any age would disbelieve adults, and this disbelief and reaction became deep-rooted in Japanese society because of the postwar disorder and confusion. Doubts and disbelief were thrown at everything old, everything established, and every-

thing outside themselves. What had been highly regarded and believed in
was rejected without first being examined. Everything that tended to
bind youth was rejected. In connection with this refusal of tradition and
established society there arose the disbelief and refusal of logic and
reasonableness itself. Finally the youths started to believe only in themselves. To them recognition of the possibility of logic is to recognize what
is surely outside themselves. Therefore they refused logic too. What was
left, then, was to make their feelings and sentiments absolute, and to
recognize nothing else. Present youth is called a "feeling generation."
Their motto is "feeling" and they live exclusively according to that "feeling."

It is utterly difficult to reach them from the outside world. They
ought to be reached from within themselves. This is what we face when
we want to approach them. By vetoing logic they lost the way to reach all
that is sure.

c. *Distortions found in society* — Young people have lost sight of
themselves in their solitariness. They do not know what to depend on and
in that condition they are injected into society. What shape is the society
they are thrown into? The society they are thrown into is filled with contradictions and dishonesty. It is a distorted society, one in which they feel
they are estranged. Their "victim-consciousness" reacts sharply to the
dishonesty and the distortion in the society. The infamous pollution
problem, profiteering by big business and oil companies, and very detrimental social welfare policies in Japan all make them more irritated and
more militant toward the established society.

We also have to recognize the "*criminal*-consciousness" among
university students. Japan has become rich. It became rich by exploiting
Southeast Asian countries, they say. These are the countries Japan once
trod down during the war. They say we are treading them down again,
this time in the form of economic invasion. Students feel they are a part
of this criminal Japan which is threatening Southeast Asia for a second
time. Their guilt consciousness is multiplied when they see that, as elite,
they themselves might be sent out of the country to exploit or become involved in such exploitation in one form or another. Because of this guilt
complex, they feel they are criminal, and they feel they have to do something in order to atone for these past and future sins. The duplex of victim complex and crime complex overwhelms them and they crazily look
for an atoning part which they feel they ought to play in the present society.

3. Marxism a proposed solution

To these hordes of frustrated students, Marxism appears as the only
system of thought which offers solution. When these students touch
Marxism, they feel that for the first time they have grasped a perfect
world view. Here for the first time in their lives is certainty. Let us discuss what kind of role Marxism is playing for them.

According to Arnold J. Toynbee, Marxism to them is "a mere ersatz
Christianity." In his book *A Study of History*, Toynbee says that "Com-
munism is a secular ideology which aims to substitute for Christianity."
He says Russia adopted this because it was regarded as a formidable

heresy by Western Europe. The situation is very similar in Japan. Japan tried to import everything from the Western world except Christianity. In the past 100 years Japan covetously imported and digested all the thoughts, knowledge, technology, and systems of operations from Western culture, but because Japan has carefully avoided importing Christianity, all these thoughts and technology came to Japan without the roots which upheld them when they were in the Western world. In the Western world, I feel, that whenever there is a system of thought or organization, it is always existing or functioning in relation to the existence of God and his revelation either positively or negatively. When Japan imported those ideas it was like a vase full of cut flowers without roots. But I had to have roots. In Japan, Marxism was accepted as the root.

Thus in Japanese society people choose Marxism not in contrast to the Gospel of God, but rather as its substitute. Sometimes an earnest young man in this country will say it like this, "I am now trying to choose either Marxism or Christianity. I have been thinking carefully about their pros and cons." When he says this, his consciousness is not that he is making a lifetime decision, but rather that to him the two are very similar good things and he is trying to evaluate the two and choose the better one. This sounds very incongruous to the Western mind.

Why does something like this happen? Beside the Gospel, only Marxism provides Japanese youth with the sureness of logic. Because Japan does not know God and his work, to those godless Japanese youth Marxism appears to be the only answer. Let me quote from Professor Kawai's book, *What is Marxism?* Kawai was a pre-war professor at the Tokyo Imperial University. He was a noted anti-Marxist scholar, an aggressive liberal, and was persecuted by the government because of his liberal views. He says, "Marxism is such a great system of thought. Did Japan have in its culture a corresponding system of thought? No, it never had one." Any thoughts which existed in Japanese society never rivaled itself with even a part of the Marxist system. When Marxism reached Japan, it did not have to fight its own way in, nor did it have to drive out the former inhabitants of the house, because it found the house completely empty. Therefore it just easily walked into the house, sat down there are started to live. Kawai continues, "The average Japanese youth has never thought systematically about the universe, history or ethics." He says that "although in Japanese schools morality and ethics were taught, they were never taught in connection with the present reality. Marxism was the only system of thought that taught people to think in terms of complete reality."

This book was published in 1931 and it does not necessarily give us the up-to-date information about the Japanese situation. However, in essence the situation has not changed during the past four decades. Then, in what aspect does Marxism substitute for Christianity?

Is it in the philosophical and historical phase only? No, Marxism gives people the exact principles of love and righteousness. Once I showed James 5:1-6 to a Marxist student. When I finished reading the passage, he asked me, "Whose word is that? Neither Marx nor Lenin accused the rich that fiercely." Up to that moment this young student thought Marx and Marxists were the only ones who sought social justice, and he was utterly surprised. Young people seek social justice by way of Marxism, but they do not know that the Marxist's concept of social justice was actually stolen from the Bible.

We said that the youth of today is estranged from society and from themselves as well. When these young people are finally tossed into society to take jobs, they find the society full of distortion and injustices. Many of them find Marxism the sure bond which binds young people together. At least this is what they feel. The above statement would be utterly unthinkable and unacceptable to those who do not know Marxism and to those who associate Marxism only with violence and treachery. But to those of us who read the partial truth of the Bible squashed into *Das Kapital* and were enchanted by it, this is a real statement. It is significant that in the history of Japanese society and the Japanese Labor Movement, it was Christians who first became the force to start the labor union. Almost all social work and social movements were begun by Christians. The concept of social justice was introduced into Japan through the church and the Bible.

The same thing can be said of the concept of love. If you look through the Japanese encyclopedia to study the concept of love, you will find the Christian explanation of love. The reason is that the present connotation of the Japanese word "love" was formed by Christian thought. Before Christianity was introduced into Japan, the Japanese word for love meant only the sexual relationship. However, Japanese culture successfully adopted the concept of love without understanding Christianity and the true knowledge of God. Love needs the understructure which supports the concept. What was the underlying concept Japanese culture adopted? It was at first a mere humanism and later Marxism. Japanese people feel they have found true love in Marxism.

Before the churches and Christians found out what the situation really was, Marxism had come into Japanese culture and occupied the place the church, or rather God, should have occupied. Thus Marxism became the ersatz "Christianity" for Japan.

To many youth, Marxism appears to be the answer to social problems. Marxism asserts that it will form and realize the society in which peace and love preside, but it teaches that this society will come only through hatred and struggle. Thus their theme is beset with essential contradiction within itself. In order to overcome this contradiction Marxism employs a unique view of history. However, this unique view of history that utopia will surely come is merely an asset borrowed from the Bible. It is a deformation of the biblical teaching of the millennium.

We can now say that in Japan Marxism was accepted into Japanese culture as a substitute for Christianity. It is a substitute that only resembles the truth, but also it functions somewhat like the truth. Marxism is now functioning like a certain kind of insecticide which has a similar chemical structure to an element which the insect needs for its own body. Therefore the insecticide is accepted into the insect's body and it resides there as an indispensable material. And because the chemical molecular structure is similar to the indispenable material which the bug needs, it stays on and accumulates as more and more insecticide is ingested until the day the metabolism of its life is destroyed and brings the life of the host to the end. Marxism is exactly the same, it has caught and killed so many people and the souls of so many more people.

4. Evangelizing atheists

I have been talking thus far about Japan. This is my country, the country I know best. However, there is another reason why I bring this before you: similar phenomena appear in different degrees in all the Afro-Asian countries. It is my conviction that the following guidelines of evangelism will apply in evangelism of youth throughout the world, and especially for those of Afro-Asian countries.

a. *Faith* — What should be the approach to these young people? I have been stating that most of them have accepted Marxism because Marxism is so similar to the structure of Bible doctrines. Therefore you can almost say that their Marxist beliefs and the evangelical faith can attract each other. By way of example, I will mention one episode. In the early days of the Japan Communist Party, I found that *all* the leaders of the Party had the experience of attending a Christian church at one time or another. Considering the current statistics that the average Sunday morning attendance of Protestant churches in Japan (including the evangelicals and non-evangelicals) is a mere 12.5 persons per church, this is an astonishing fact. I wish somebody had approached them with the real message of the Gospel and they had been led to the Lord at that time.

If my presupposition is right, we can say Marxist sympathizers are the best seekers of the Gospel. Then, how about a dyed-in-the-wool Communist? Looking back on my own experience, I can say that the Party members and convinced Marxists could also be the object of our evangelism. In our witness to them, God is the one who saves. God is unlimited (Mark 10:27).

b. *Love* — The second thing is love and affection to those who have been estranged. With love and affection we have to understand them and become their friends. This love must be true and sincere and it should not be the imposition of our goodwill. This love must be full of long-suffering (I Cor. 13:4). This love might even lead us to study Marxism in order that we can talk with them better.

The study of Marxism is not the same as reading inside stories about Soviet Russia, but rather the study of Marxism itself and what it teaches; its philosophy, its view of history, and its theory of economics. Of course, we do not have to do careful research. All we need to do is read some introductory material written from the critical standpoint and yet academically acceptable. I do not know very many non-Japanese books, but certainly Lester DeKoster's, *Communism and the Christian Faith* would be very suitable.

Let us remember that the purpose of our studying Marxism is not so that we can win an argument. We can never change people's opinions by arguing, nor is it possible to save people's souls through arguing. Argumentation is sterile. To study Marxism is effective and necessary only so that we can point out the problems in their thinking and let them think together with us. For this purpose the right kind of knowledge is effective.

Here I have to refer to one rather important point. I realize that there is a wrong concept of the relationship between Marxism and Christianity. I know also that this wrong concept has a large following. However, I am not proposing that there is harmony between Marxism and Christianity, nor am I proposing the cooperation of Marxists and Christians. Concerning this, Paul says there is no fellowship between light and darkness (II Cor. 6:14). I am only proposing that witnessing ought to be done in love and affection, and that love contain understanding.

c. *Salvation* — We have to remember always that our purpose is the salvation of their souls. We should remember that our purpose is to proclaim Christ in the power of the Holy Spirit, expecting God to do great and mighty things.

The great commandment of our Lord is not an anti-communist movement or a capitalism protection movement. Neither did the Lord call us to fight for private ownership of property. Professor Iijima of Tokyo University says in his book *Christian Concept of Society,* that the concept of private ownership came from Roman law. According to Roman law we can proclaim that a certain thing is mine because I have won it. However, he says, according to the Bible everything is the Lord's. We are just entrusted by God with our present possessions and have administrative power over them. It is well to remember this basic concept.

We are against godless Communism. However, it is not necessary for us to say that God is always with capitalism either. We do not proclaim that God recognizes only capitalism. Our task is higher than protecting any one system of economics. It is our duty to proclaim the Gospel to souls, who are more precious than the whole world itself.

d. *The Gospel* — What we have to preach is the simple Gospel. Professor Kawai argues in his book, "Once a man becomes Marxist, neither parents nor teachers nor state can reconvert him." Kawai had to admit that Japan and he himself never possessed any system of thought which was superior to Marxism. In his book he proposes that in order to find out *the true system* of thought it would be necessary to gather together the best kind of men and the best kind of research organization into one place.

We have, however, already been given that which is superior to Marxism. This is the Gospel with the converting power of the Holy Spirit. Do not forget that every Marxist and every Marxist sympathizer is attracted to love and righteousness. Speak this Gospel to their conscience. Let them realize the big gap between their ideal and their thinking.

Their beloved theme is that they will introduce a world of peace and love, but that it will come only through hatred and class struggle. Let them ponder this, and let them decide if such self-contradiction is really possible or realistic.

The final word is the Gospel of Jesus Christ. The Gospel of the Cross and the Resurrection alone has the power to save souls. Twenty years ago for the first time in my life I heard the message of the Gospel. It was not "persuasive words of wisdom," but the simple preaching of the Gospel, depending on the power of the Holy Spirit. It was the Gospel of "Jesus Christ who was crucified," and that Gospel changed me.

It is my conviction that evangelism among atheists is done only through witnessing to the grace of Jesus Christ by the power of the Holy Spirit.

e. *Prayer* — In closing, I would add one more thing. It is the matter of prayer. I was saved through the preaching of the Gospel to which I was exposed for the first time in my life. Why was that? It was because deep in my heart I already had a kind of conviction of my own sins, and had been suffering from it. Why was that so? It was because my family and the friends of my family were praying specifically for me. There was one person who prayed for me for sixteen years and because of these prayers the Holy Spirit worked within me.

This is my appeal as from the lips of an ex-Marxist, toward the brothers and sisters in the Lord. Pray for those who are under Marxist influence and still are looking for the truth.

EVANGELIZATION OF MATERIALISTIC ATHEISTS REPORT

1. Materialistic atheism may be a useful definition of some people's beliefs; it can also be a misleading one. Many atheists will be materialist in one sense or another; but this should not disguise the fact that atheism takes a number of forms. Our approach to these people requires a sensitive appreciation of their particular situation.

2. Four divisions of materialistic atheism were suggested:

a. *Morality without God.* This will tend to degenerate into either ethical relativism or into hypocrisy. Either the absence of absolute values or their corrupt pretense provides strong reasons for the attraction of Marxism outside communist societies.

b. *Daily labor without God.* The Puritan concept that godly man should receive a just reward for his labor becomes, when God is removed, either practical atheistic capitalism or communist atheism.

c. *Nature without God.* When nature is divorced from its Creator, scientific atheism with its concept of autonomous man leads inevitably to a mechanistic meaningless world.

d. *Society without God.* This produces the materialist in the most evident sense, and also communities that are useless, impersonal, and superficial.

3. Communism, as a major form of atheism, calls for the Christian's special attention. One-third of the world lives under communist regimes. In non-communist societies various types of Marxism attract many more. We are therefore compelled to take communism seriously, both as a system of belief and a revolutionary strategy, in its impact on both individuals and whole groups.

Communism is a world view which consists of philosophical, political, and economic theories welded into a consistent whole. It is materialistic, for it teaches that man is no more than nature consciously reflecting upon itself. It is atheistic, for it teaches that all religion is an inverted freedom on this earth. Its optimistic hope for the future is based on the belief that man is perfectible by man, and on an evolutionary view of the dialectical nature of human history.

In practice it presents a dynamic critique of the inherent evils of capitalist society, sometimes using biblical categories, and a vision of a new world of man's solidarity with man. In this latter sense it often has a special appeal for those societies, like the African, which are built on the notion of a community of goods.

In the non-communist world, at least, there are three basic categories of Marxists: those who are dedicated to working for the party; those who are concerned to eliminate the evils within society, and those who tend to protest against everything. In the first case there is a real commitment to Marxist theory; the second and third may only be based on a petit-bourgeois guilt complex for the injustices of society.

4. a. The Christian response to materialistic atheism must be first a listening response. We need to hear what the atheist or communist is actually saying.

This will mean that some on an academic level should do a profound study of what different forms of atheism and in particular, communism, have to say. Marxism especially is a complex system and will require careful study.

b. The Christian response must also be a perceptive response. The altruist, either in his theory within his group or as an individual, will have his particular objections to Christian faith and also personal problems. It is important to answer the point or thesis he is actually presenting, not the one we may mistakenly assume he is presenting. In some cases the response will be academic; but more often it will be direct and practical — set out in ordinary terms.

c. The Christian response must be above all a biblical response. If it is important to know the atheist's beliefs and attitudes, it is doubly important that the Christian know his Bible and be able to present God's entire revelation to man. The Gospel's full content, which involves an integrated care for man's mind, his well-being, and his fundamental spiritual relationship to God, will be more compelling than a one-sided, other-worldly Christianity.

d. The Christian's response will involve the searching out of common ground with the atheist: this being their common humanity and their deep concern for it.

e. But such a response will not involve an unbiblical accommodation. It will be a Christian responsibility to show the inadequacy of a view of creation without God, to challenge the falsely optimistic views of man which fail to take into account his sinful condition, and declare true redemption offered in Christ to man and the world in which he dwells.

f. As a Christian faces the Marxist system and, more particularly, converses with individual Marxists, he must bear in mind the following facts: (i) the Marxist's materialism built on the premise of a chance universe is no more rational than the Christian view of a personal creation; (ii) history does not bear out the Marxist's evolutionary optimism, ergo, 90 per cent of human living has been the history of war; (iii) the depth of man's alienation, evident in every political and social system, cannot be discovered on the basis of natural revelation; only God's special revelation supplies an adequate cause; (iv) the church has too often shared individualistic bourgeoise attitudes and life styles. It has tacitly supported the vested interests of the rich, instead of being an influential force on the side of the oppressed. Therefore, although the church rejects violence as a shortcut to a new society, it must at the same time demonstrate in concrete ways its nature as a servant - community of caring love, willingness to suffer for righteousness' sake and a personal and corporate holiness of life. (v) The Christian's response will involve the seeking out of common ground with the atheist, this being their common humanity and their deep concern for it. (vi) But such a response will not involve an unbiblical accommodation. It will be Christian responsibility to show the inadequacy of a view of creation without God: to challenge the falsely optimistic mind of man which fails to take into account his sinful condition; and declare the redemption offered in Christ to man and the world in which he resides.

5. Those general principles need to be applied appropriately in different cultural and geographical areas. The group spoke of different needs here:

a. Atheism in the setting of Western culture.

Probably the greatest single cause for Western atheism is that loss of cultural identity which results in an existential rejection of all forms of reality. Escape may be taught in hypocrisy, materialism or a reversion to paganism.

In this situation the Christian must proclaim the creative activity of God in nature and personality, the redemptive activity of Christ in receiving man from his sinful lostness, and the reality of Christian hope.

We would call for a greater use by Christians of some of the available apologetic aids on a simple level. We see the need for evangelicals to engage in much greater research with the aim of producing an appropriate apologetic at a more advanced level. We also see the urgency for a greater awareness of our biblical-theological heritage.

b. Reaching people in Communist Countries.

The state of the church varies greatly in Eastern Europe, with more freedom in some areas than in others. In theory, according to the various laws and constitutions, much freedom is proclaimed but in practice it is quite different.

The concept of the oppressed and the oppressor is expressed only when the party is in the minority.

The general view among people under communism is that they are against religion. The church's reputation and past mistakes have allowed the atheist to prosper.

As knowledge and convictions vary greatly, we must approach people beginning where they are and explain our belief slowly, with real compassion for our listener.

Those who live in the free world should be careful when they comment on the situation in communist societies and not accept every report even when it comes via one who comes from a communist country. Solzhenitsyn, in reply to praise received for his courageous stand against brutality, said, "Why do you praise me? The ones who stay are the real heroes." We strongly affirm that the Gospel is the only solution for oppression in every part of the world. Our responsibility is therefore clear. The question is, how? As far as Eastern Europe is concerned the radio is the only thing that cannot be stopped. This, it was suggested, is possibly the best medium for both spreading the Gospel and encouraging Christians in their present hour of suffering.

c. Roman Catholic Cultures

In Latin America and certain European countries, influenced by the Roman Catholic system, materialistic atheism is usually encountered as some indigenous form of Marxism. Its attraction is due largely to the gross failure of the church to respond to the inequalities in society; the capacity of Marxist analysis to explain the causes of dependence and oppression and the latent moralism inherent in a Roman Catholic up-bringing. Evangelical churches in these countries are also guilty of lack of concern for the desperate poverty of the down-trodden. They need to show, by a complete revision of their life-style and by a message more closely conformed to the whole biblical pattern, that Christian faith is the only really radical answer to man's alienation in society.

d. Present-day Japan

Much has already been said in the original paper concerning our approach to the communists in Japan. It suffices to add only a few more points.

Five years ago, 1969-1970, violent riots took place on many college campuses across Japan. Some pastors were afraid of receiving students into their churches. However, it is clear that the reason why many students were engaged in such violent riots is that they cried out for the dissolution and destruction of their own universities. Their cry reflected their denial not only of the university to which they belong but also of themselves as students. Japanese have been people who accept themselves rather easily. But those riots revealed a situation in which many young people began for the first time in history to radically question their positions.

It is clear that their questioning only goes deep enough to reject being molded into an established social order and not deep enough to accept the fact that they are sinners in the sight of God. It is precisely here that we can build a bridge to cross over to where they are.

Right in the midst of the riots a meeting was held under the auspices of IVF on the campus of Tohishba University. Several hundred students turned up and 50-60 stayed for a second meeting to really seek the Lord. In spite of the violent destruction going on all around and the fact that the Christianity officially represented in the theological department of the university was liberal, many students professed their faith in Jesus Christ.

SOME TRENDS IN THE ROMAN CATHOLIC CHURCH TODAY

Ramez L. Atallah

*Mr. Atallah, Montreal, Canada, is the
Quebec Director of InterVarsity Christian
Fellowship.*

Introduction

The recent changes within the Roman Catholic church have elicited mixed responses from evangelical Protestants. Some are very suspicious of these developments. They dismiss them as public relations techniques which do not reflect genuine internal changes. On the other side of the spectrum are those who welcome the changes believing them to be an unmistakable work of the Holy Spirit leading the Catholic church towards an evangelical awakening. Most of those who have studied the recent situation carefully, however, would be more cautious in their judgment. They know enough to be convinced that Rome is really changing (despite her claim to changelessness), but they are not so naive as to believe that all the changes are in the right direction. That the Holy Spirit is at work within the Roman Catholic church today is unquestioned; but the extent to which he is the Author of a particular trend is still open to question.

The Second Vatican Council (1963-65) gave impetus to many encouraging trends in Roman Catholicism. The documents of that council are considered by many Catholics to be the most up-to-date official position of their church. It is remarkable, therefore, to find, within these documents, statements such as the following:

"Christ summons the Church, as she goes on her pilgrim way, to that continual *reformation* of which she always has need, insofar as she is an institution of men here on earth. Therefore, if the influence of events or of the times has led to deficiencies in conduct, in Church discipline, or *even in the formulation of doctrine* ...these should be appropriately rectified at the proper moment."

For the church that claims it never changes to officially talk about a "continual reformation" and to extend this reformation even to the "formulation of doctrine" seems to reflect a desire for real change. The ambiguities and tensions within the Roman Catholic church today, however, make it difficult to gauge the impact of this and similar encouraging statements. The documents of Vatican II contain some mutually exclusive views of conservative and progressive Catholic theologians. In a recent comment on the current state of the church, John Stott said, "The Roman monolith, which for centuries has appeared inviolable, has at last cracked open. Conservatives and progressives, traditionalists and radicals, are engaged in a fierce power struggle. Because the issues were still open during Vatican II, *the Council endorsed opinions which oppose, contradict and exclude each other.* To many observers the whole church seems to be in unprecedented disarray. Moreover, it is by no means clear whether the final outcome will be the triumph of biblical truth or a disastrous lapse into some kind of existential subjectivism. All Christian people should be praying for those who are caught willy-nilly in this transitional agony."

In view of this complex and ambiguous situation, it becomes impossible to adequately study trends in modern Catholicism within the scope of such a brief paper. The limited purpose of this paper, therefore is to outline and analyze four significant *trends* within the Roman Catholic church today.

Many important areas of change (such as teachings about the Virgin Mary) have not even been mentioned. It has also been impossible, due to limited space, to document every statement which the perceptive reader might question.

The four trends which are presented have been developing for some time. Many observers believe that these trends will continue and eventually radically transform the Catholic church. The writer has not shared all his reservations or criticisms of these trends, rather an attempt has been made to give the reader an insight into what progressive Catholic theologians think is happening to their church. The same situation could be looked at differently by someone else! Thus it is hoped that the reader, rather than being worried that the paper is not critical enough of Rome, would instead investigate the changes seriously.

As evangelical Protestants attempt to understand and evaluate these four trends in the Catholic church, they need to determine how they are to react to them. The last part of the paper presents some challenges to evangelical Protestants arising out of these changes in Rome.

The brief time in which this paper had to be researched and written did not allow the writer to do as much personal verification as he would have liked. Any errors of fact or documentation will, therefore, be gratefully received!

In this paper, references to "church," "Catholic" or "theologian" always refer to the *Roman Catholic context unless otherwise stated.*

PART ONE: TRENDS

1. Reinterpretation of dogma

While most traditional Catholic teaching and dogma remains unchanged, the meaning of these dogmas for today is undergoing radical change. This reinterpretation of dogma is justified by progressive theologians on the basis that it is the *intent* of a particular doctrine which is infallible and unchangeable, rather than its formulation in a particular historical context. This process of reinterpretation allows the modern theologian to emphasize aspects of a doctrine which previously received little or no attention in Catholic teaching.

Thus, for example, the dogma of the "real presence" of Christ in the Eucharist is reaffirmed, but the medieval emphasis upon transubstantiation is dismissed as a scholastic attempt to explain this particular doctrine. Having rejected the philosophical framework of scholasticism, modern theologians are able to place a different emphasis on the church's view of the Eucharist and to present this in language and concepts suited to contemporary thought. This may not make the doctrine more palatable to Protestants. The change of emphasis, however, is often reflected in the worship of modern Catholics. David Wells brings out this fact in his recent book, *Revolution in Rome:*

"Indeed, the Mass is often seen as the occasion when they sacrifice themselves to God rather than, as before, when Christ is resacrificed to God. The new concern is no longer with the automatic transformation of the elements into the actual body and blood of Christ...but with the subjective disposition of the participants in the celebration... *The old teaching is not denied; it has merely been pushed into the background.*

This search for the *intent* of doctrinal formulations is especially fruitful when applied to doctrines which were developed in polemic situations. The emphasis required to defend one facet of a doctrine may have been later misunderstood as a denial of other aspects of the doctrine. For example, the fact that the Council of Trent (1545) condemned what *it* understood as the Reformer's teaching on justification by faith, need not prevent the Catholic church today from viewing the matter differently. Removed from the historical context, and stripped of polemic language, some progressive Catholic positions sound surprisingly similar to that of the Reformers!

While there still are many reactionary and conservative Catholic thinkers, they are becoming a definite minority. A serious study of progressive Catholic writers demonstrates the freedom with which many of them are reinterpreting dogma. To use proof-texts from official Catholic documents in an attempt to affirm that the church has not changed betrays little understanding of what is actually happening. People who do not understand this trend of reinterpretation will continue to challenge Roman Catholics on doctrinal emphases which have lost much of their historical significance.

The question which can be legitimately asked, however, is whether this desire to return to the intent of dogmatic formulations is radical enough! What if the "intent" is still contrary to the progressive theologian's own views? To what extent does doctrine have to be based on Scripture? This crucial question leads into the next trend in modern Catholicism; the new emphasis on Scripture.

2. New emphasis on Scripture

Many have vivid memories of the time, not so long ago, when the Roman Catholic church seemed to be a major opponent of the distribution of the Bible in the free world. Today there is a radical change! The new interest in reading, studying and distributing of Scripture among Roman Catholics the world over has been a significant religious phenomenon during the past decade. It is no longer unusual to hear of official Roman Catholic projects designed to promote greater interest in the Bible. Whereas previously Catholics were often discouraged from reading the Bible, now they are not only encouraged to do so, but are also allowed to use many translations made by Protestant or ecumenical groups. In many parts of the world, Bible study groups are becoming a regular feature of Roman Catholic life.

Official support for this new interest in Scripture can be found in the documents of Vatican II. "Easy access to the Sacred Scriptures should be provided for all the Christian faithful." A Catholic commentator's note following this statement says, "This is perhaps the most novel section of the Constitution. Not since the early centuries of the church has an official document urged the availability of the Scriptures for all." This new emphasis on Scripture was reflected in the discussion and the texts of Vatican II. An attempt was made to use Scripture to support or illustrate much of what was said during the council. An interesting effect of this new emphasis can be noted in article 4 of the *Decree on the Ministry and Life of Priests.* This document affirms that the *primary* responsibility of priests is not the administration of the sacraments but rather the preaching of the Word, "For through the saving Word the spark of faith is struck in the hearts of unbelievers, and fed in the hearts of the faithful."

This new emphasis on Scripture raises the age-long question of the relationship between Scripture and tradition. This question was the occasion of a dramatic debate during the first session of Vatican II. The preliminary draft submitted to the council presented Scripture and tradition as two separate sources of revelation. This draft received such severe criticism that Pope John XXIII personally intervened and set up a new commission to study the matter further. The final document, which was unanimously approved during the fourth session of the council, reflects the thinking of many progressive theologians that tradition is the *authoritative interpreter* of Scripture rather than a *separate source* of revelation. Thus the Revelation of God to man is found in Scripture *as interpreted by tradition.*

The Dogmatic Constitution on Divine Revelation made provision, however, for doctrines such as the assumption of Mary, for which biblical support cannot be found. Article 9 states that "...it is not from sacred Scripture alone that the church draws her certainty about everything which has been revealed." The source of revelation is Scripture, the "certain" interpreter is tradition. A footnote to this text reads, "It does not exclude the opinion that all revelation is in some way, though perhaps obscurely, contained in Scripture. But this may not suffice for certitude, and in fact the church always understands and interprets Scripture in the light of her continuous tradition." Thus tradition can rule that a certain doctrine is "implicit" in Scripture even if this is not obvious from biblical exegesis.

While this loophole obviously limits the authority of Scripture within the church, the change which is taking place must not be minimized. In concluding his evaluation of this new interest in Scripture within the Roman Catholic church John Stott has said:

"Meanwhile, we may and must be thankful for those tentative concessions to the primacy of Scripture, which emerge from the Constitution like the first snowdrops heralding the end of the freeze and the beginning of spring. They at least make it possible for us, in debate with Roman Catholics, to appeal from tradition to Scripture. We can now challenge them to demonstrate that their tradition is in fact a legitimate elucidation of Scripture, and neither an accretion which may be dispensed with nor a contradiction which must be rejected."

Another question raised by the church's new emphasis on Scripture is in regard to its position on the inspiration and reliability of the biblical text.

Article 11 of the Constitution on Revelation states,

"...since everything asserted by the inspired authors or sacred writers must be held to be asserted by the Holy Spirit, it follows that the books of Scripture must be acknowledged as teaching firmly, faithfully, and without error that truth which God wanted put into the sacred writings for the sake of our salvation..."

Some have taken this statement as a clear affirmation of the inerrancy of Scripture. The wording, however, is subject to different interpretations. Most progressive theologians interpret this text as meaning that it is only the truths "related to our salvation" which are without error! This allows them a wide range of liberty in handling the text. They are free to subscribe to many radical and liberal theories about the Bible without jeopardizing their relationship with the church. There seems to be a shift away from viewing Scripture as a source of propositional truth. For them, it is the *encounter* with the Christ of Scripture which is considered infallible, and not the Scriptures themselves. This emphasis on experience in modern Catholic thinking provides a theological background and support for the new awakening of religious experience within the church.

3. *Awakening of religious experience*

There was a time when Catholics left the sterility and formality of their church in search of a more personal and meaningful religious experience. For many Catholics today this seems no longer necessary. Father Edward O'Connor's moving description of those involved in the Catholic Charismatic movement shatters textbook caricatures of Roman Catholics, "These people know God as a person; they have a personal relationship with him. One senses a personal familiarity in the way they speak of him. He is not just an entity about whom they have learned some lessons; nor the ground of being to which they subscribe. In attempting to say what the Spirit has done to them, many have used such expressions as, 'For the first time in my life, I really know God. Previously, I had known *about* him, but that's not the same as knowing him.' "

The Liturgical Renewal, coupled with the Charismatic movement, has revolutionized the nature of religious experience available to Roman Catholics today. They may now participate in worship services conducted in the vernacular, praise God in contemporary folk music, pray in small groups without using a prayer book, experience the gifts of the Holy Spirit, and look for daily help and nourishment from the Scriptures.

From a small beginning at Duquesne University (Pittsburgh) in 1967, the Catholic Charismatic movement has swept through the church at a phenomenal pace! Observers have delineated the following positive effects of the movement on its members:

-intimate knowledge of God
-deepened prayer life
-new love for Scriptures

-deliverance from bad habits and addictions
-physical healing
-experience of peace and joy
-renewed loyalty to the church

The elusive nature of this movement has allowed it to carry the winds of renewal sparked by Vatican II into the most unlikely quarters of the church. It has even at times been able to bridge the gap between progressive and conservative Catholics. The movement's emphasis on *experience* rather than doctrine is in keeping with much of progressive theology. On the other hand, its loyalty to the conservative hierarchy pleases the once-threatened bishops. It must, therefore, be understood as a truly Roman Catholic movement, and not simply an infiltration of Protestant Pentecostalism into the church.

A personal (subjective) relationship with God needs to be balanced by a biblical (objective) knowledge of God. As in all religious awakenings, the danger facing the Catholic Charismatic movement is an overemphasis on experience. Unless the movement becomes grounded in Scripture, it will increasingly be blown about by every new wind of theological opinion.

Will the church be able to contain this movement? Will the Charismatics revolutionize the old structures and lead the church into a personal and intimate knowledge of God? Or will the hierarchy absorb the Charismatic movement to the point of rendering it ineffective? These questions raise one of the most pressing problems facing the church today; the definition of its nature. Is the church a hierarchical organization or is it the people of God?

4. Decentralization of authority

In 1870 the First Vatican Council declared the Pope to be infallible. The next day it was forced to adjourn due to the outbreak of war. In its proclamation of the primacy of the Roman pontiff, the council officially rejected the then-current idea that the papacy should be under the authority of church councils. Because it was so suddenly interrupted, however, the council left undefined the role and authority of the bishops. This factor has since then contributed towards an unbalanced emphasis on the centralized authority of the pope.

The original draft of the *Dogmatic Constitution on the Church,* prepared for the Second Vatican Council, resembled standard Catholic attitudes on this matter. During the course of the council, however, the document was revised and completely re-written. The final draft reflects the tensions in the council surrounding the issue of papal authority.

A superficial reading of texts such as the following gives the impression that the Pope's position of complete supremacy has not changed:

"For in virtue of his office, that is, as Vicar of Christ and pastor of the whole church, the Roman Pontiff has full, supreme, and universal power over the church. And he can always exercise his power freely."

In various ways, however, progressive theologians at Vatican II attempted to neutralize this seemingly unlimited authority of the pope. David Wells outlines four of these: (i) The Constitution of the church was organized and written in a way which emphasized the importance of the people and de-emphasized the centrality of the pope. Only one out of every eight chapters even mentions the pope!

(ii) The declaration that the pope has "full, supreme, and universal powers over the church" was qualified by the sentence immediately following which states that "...he can always exercise his power freely." At first glance this seems to enhance the pope's powers! A closer look at the original Latin text reveals, however, that the words are carefully chosen so as to put in question the validity of a free exercise of power by the pope. The point that this subtle qualification raises is that whereas the pope *can* exercise his powers freely (without consultation with the bishops), such an action is not necessarily *valid!*

(iii) While the progressives could not deny the infallibility of the pope, they tried to neutralize it by the inclusion in the Constitution of two other forms of infallibility: (1) All Catholics can have an infallible perception of the truth through the enlightenment of the Holy Spirit, (2) the bishops have an infallibility which derives from their apostolic office. Theoretically, these three infallibilities of the pope, the bishops, and the people should be in harmony! This sharing of "infallibility" undermines the uniqueness of the pope's authority.

(iv) The concept of "collegiality" was another attempt at preventing unilateral action by the pope. The progressives argued that Jesus first gave authority to *all* the apostles, before singling out Peter as their spokesman. Peter was simply the chairman of the committee. As such, his task was to speak on behalf of the apostles and not to make pronouncements with which they disagreed. By applying this New Testament model to the current situation, progressive theologians insisted that the pope's authority was valid only when he spoke after consultation with the college of bishops!

This attempt by progressive theologians to limit the authority of the pope proved to be a threat to Pope Paul VI. After the council had approved the Constitution of the church, the pope had an "explanatory note" added to it. (Since the council had already adjourned it was not given the opportunity to comment on this note.) In opposition to the whole thrust of the principle of collegiality, the note denied that there was "any equality between the head and the members of the College." It went on to say, "The Roman Pontiff proceeds according to his own discretion and in view of the welfare of the church in structuring, promoting, and endorsing any exercise of collegiality." What this note says, in effect, is that the principle of collegiality is only valid when the position of the college of bishops happens to coincide with that of the pope!

These mutually exclusive understandings of the papacy were brought to the fore in the birth control debate. When Pope Paul made an official pronouncement against birth control, many bishops took him to task. They claimed that he should have consulted them before taking a public stand on the matter. Many of them felt that since he did not consult them his action was not valid. They, therefore, do not feel obligated to abide by his judgment in this case. This feeling is quite widely spread within the Catholic church. Recent surveys have indicated that a large majority of Roman Catholics and their leaders are not abiding by the pope's ruling concerning birth control.

This trend towards the decentralization of authority from the pope to the bishops (and eventually to the people) again raises the troublesome question, "Who speaks for Rome?" It is clear that the pope is still the head of the church. It appears, however, that he no longer always speaks for the majority of Catholics!

With the ambiguities in the church's position on tradition, Scripture, and papal authority, the young parish priests of today have lost many of their traditional moorings. With the new surge of religious experience within the church and with the breaking down of the ancient barriers towards outsiders, everything seems open to question. In this situation of uncertainty and rapid change it is not surprising, therefore, that many Catholic clergy and laymen are turning to the writings of progressive Catholic theologians in search for a sense of direction. These men are looked up to as the new prophets in the church. Even though they often disagree with one another, they still speak with a sense of authority and confidence. It is the views of men like Rahner, Schillebeeckx, Congar, Küng, and others which seem to provide the real authority in the church today. What these men believe about theology, tradition, and the Scriptures is what is being passed on to the Catholic layman by his spiritual leaders.

This dependence on the new Catholic theology makes it imperative for the church to develop a theology which is not only relevant to contemporary culture but also faithful to the historic Christian faith. Will the church let secular society determine and mold its theology? Or will it turn back to the Scriptures in search for the eternal truths of God, and then seek to apply these truths to the needs of modern man?

The future of the Roman Catholic church seems to lie in the hands of its progressive theologians. They are presently molding its theology. Are they also determining its destiny?

PART TWO: CHALLENGES

1. Challenges to action

a. *Encouragement of in-depth study of the Bible among Roman Catholics.* The new interest in the Scriptures among Catholics has made them open to those who are willing to expound the Word to them. Catholic groups are increasingly inviting Protestant lecturers to speak to them on biblical themes. Small group Bible studies, led by laymen, often look to Protestant participants for help.

Evangelical Protestants are especially known for their love for the Scriptures and their ability to study the Bible in depth. They now have a unique opportunity to introduce Catholics to the many excellent Bible study tools and methods which they have developed over the years. Roman Catholics who are interested in studying the Bible need to be helped to "dig" into the text, rather than merely using it as a springboard for religious discussion and meditation.

b. *Dialogue with Roman Catholic theologians.* The influence of liberal Protestant theology on Catholic thinking has, no doubt, been partly due to the ecumenical spirit of liberal theologians who were willing to dialogue with their Catholic counterparts. The present revival in evangelical Protestant scholarship could have an equally powerful impact on Catholic thought!

Protestant evangelical theologians should seek to share their biblical and theological insights with Catholics through all available channels. They need to be especially encouraged to participate in scholarly societies and organizations with Catholic theologians. Because of his many efforts in this direction, Oscar Cullmann's books are now being used in several Catholic seminaries. His strong stand against the Bultmannites must certainly be having its influence on Catholic seminarians and their teachers. There is no reason why such involvement could not be duplicated by many evangelical Protestant theologians!

The present direction of Catholic theology seems to be away from the historical Christian faith. The likelihood of there ever being a solidly evangelical and biblical counter-current within the church depends, in some part, on the extent to which modern Catholic theologians are exposed to evangelical Protestant theology!

c. *Fellowship with believing Roman Catholics* As well as participating with Roman Catholics in small Bible study groups, evangelical Protestants need to be willing to spend time in prayer and meditation with believing Catholics. Fellowship (as distinct from cooperation) should be based upon mutual life in Christ rather than on doctrinal agreement. To refuse to pray with a Roman Catholic because of disagreement with his church may be a rejection of someone whom Christ has accepted.

Fellowship in prayer, Bible study, and personal sharing with true believers within the Catholic church should be encouraged. It should neither be construed as an endorsement of Catholic doctrine, nor should it be confused with organizational cooperation.

d. *Participation of Catholic believers in inter-denominational outreaches* The three above-mentioned challenges of in-depth Bible study, theological dialogue, and fellowship are already being partly accomplished by inter-denominational organizations which involve Roman Catholic believers. These evangelistic organizations invite Catholic believers to participate on the same basis as others. The recent changes in the Catholic church have made many Catholic believers able to honestly subscribe to the doctrinal position of some evangelical inter-denominational groups. As long as they can do this, the organizations are willing to appoint them as helpers, counselors, or even staff members.

In defence of their position, these organizations argue that they do not exclude Presbyterians because of their denomination's views on baptism, or Lutherans because of their peculiar understanding of the Eucharist, or members of the Salvation Army because they do not practice these two ordinances; even Anglicans are not excluded in spite of their emphasis on the episcopacy! On what basis, they ask, should they exclude Catholics who evidence the fruits of the Spirit and are willing to submit to the authority of the organization?

The traditional exclusion of Roman Catholics from such participation needs to be examined in the light of Scripture and the recent changes in the Catholic church. Historical circumstances are not enough to justify such a stance.

2. Challenges to self-examination

a. *Discourage the perpetuation of prejudiced and antiquated caricatures of Roman Catholics* The strong emphasis in the Bible on truth and justice requires evangelical Protestants to be scrupulously honest in their descriptions of Roman Catholics. Personal prejudices and historical antagonism are no excuse for misrepresenting Catholics.

In spite of the rapid change in the Catholic church, some evangelical textbooks still portray Roman Catholics as medieval sacramentalists with all that this caricature entails! This approach makes it very difficult for many evangelical Protestants to grasp the significance of the changes in modern Catholicism.

There is a fear that if it is admitted that Rome has changed there will no longer be the same motivation to evangelize Catholics. Surely this should not be the case! The motive which impels Christians to evangelize unconverted Roman Catholics should be the same as that which impels them to evangelize unconverted Protestants. An accurate and sympathetic understanding of modern Catholicism should not dampen evangelistic zeal towards unbelievers within the Catholic church.

b. *Continuous subjection of Protestant traditions to the scrutiny of Scripture* Since evangelical Protestants accept the Bible as their final authority, they should always be willing to subject all their traditions to its scrutiny. In dialogue with Roman Catholics, the evangelical Protestant must make sure that he is not holding on more firmly to his traditions than to the Word of God.

Many Protestant theological systems were formulated in polemic situations. An aspect of the truth was threatened and it was necessary to defend it. The teaching of the Reformers on justification by faith, for example, was formulated in opposition to the Catholic church's emphasis on justification by works. Some evangelical Protestants misunderstood the Reformers' teaching thinking that their intent was to discourage Christian social action (the futility of "good works"!). The rediscovery of the evangelical social conscience during the past two decades has been an uphill battle against this particular tradition. A return to the Bible clearly demonstrates the important balance between faith and works. Great care should be taken, therefore, to make sure that historical formulations of doctrine are continuously submitted to the scrutiny of Scripture.

In the light of the above, evangelical Protestants should ask themselves whether it is ever legitimate to incorporate a particular theological tradition (be it evangelical or not) in a heavily annotated Bible or a loose biblical paraphrase. The increasing dependence of evangelical Protestants on such "authorized" Bibles should be brought into question. Can these Bibles judge the very traditions which are incorporated in them? If not, then can they be honestly described as "The Scriptures"?

c. *Empathy for evangelical Protestant missionaries in Catholic lands* In their present relationships with Roman Catholics, many Protestant missionaries and pastors are facing an acute dilemma. On the one hand, they are enjoying a new and exciting ministry among Catholics through Bible teaching, discussion, prayer and evangelistic activity. On the other hand, this involvement with Catholics is sometimes strongly questioned by the

Christian workers' churches or mission boards. The latter are afraid that such activity by their missionaries may be a compromise of biblical principles.

Many Christian workers, caught in this dilemma, find it very hard to know what to do. Often, even when they are convinced that their activities do not involve any compromise of biblical principles, they feel forced to either cover up what they do or completely abandon their involvement with Catholics. If they do not do this many of them face the prospect of losing financial and organizational support from their church or mission.

This delicate situation is increasingly becoming the experience of many evangelical Protestants ministering in predominantly Roman Catholic countries. It requires serious, patient, and prayerful consideration by all involved. There should be a real feeling of Christian empathy and understanding for those grappling with these issues. Love must be demonstrated, but not at the expense of truth. Truth must be grappled with, but not to the neglect of love!

d. *Development of a consistent view of Christian experience.* Many believing Catholics are puzzled by the evangelical Protestants' over-emphasis on the *experience* of conversion, and their under-emphasis on the *fruits* of conversion. Some Protestants may need to examine their own view of Christian experience as they increasingly meet Catholic believers who have not had dramatic conversion experiences and yet evidently manifest the fruits of the Spirit.

Evangelical Protestants who are critical of the emphasis on experience in the Catholic Charismatic movement, should consider being also critical of their own emphasis on experience in conversion. The biblical criteria for assessing the spiritual life of a person do not seem to depend on *the way in which* a person was either converted or sanctified, but rather on the results of that "experience."

"By their fruits ye shall know them" is a test which can be equally applied to evangelical Protestants and Roman Catholics. When all is said and done, what the world looks for in Christians is a practical and demonstrable evidence of the inner knowledge of God which they claim to have.

It was a Catholic, Cardinal Suhard, who said that to be a witness is not to engage in propaganda or always to try to convince others that our way is the right one, but rather "to live in such a way, that our lives would not make sense if God did not exist!" AMEN.

EVANGELIZATION AMONG NOMINAL OR SACRAMENTALIST CHRISTIANS REPORT

The subject brought response from a widely divergent group of people. There were those associated with missions primarily among nominal or sacramentalist churches; those whose ministry was entirely within nominal or sacramentalist churches; and those who, by means of a new experience of the Holy Spirit, found fellowship in Christ broke all barriers down.

The group's concern was not primarily with the subject of the paper but was stimulated by the paper in its broader implications.

There was great heaviness of heart expressed for the many people who are culturally bound to churches but not spiritually alive in Christ. Should these people be abandoned to the mercy of God while our whole effort should go to those who have never heard the Gospel? Some members of the group testified to the Lord honoring their work of imposing sacramental disciplines among nominal Christians. Others were encouraged by the simple and honest preaching of the Word in a nominalist situation, and others were greatly encouraged by the apparent work of the Holy Spirit transcending the doctrinal, denominational and cultural differences to bring a new awareness of Christ.

The work among Roman Catholics aroused strong feelings. Those involved in and with Roman Catholic people were suspect. There remains evidence of a Protestant evangelical backlash whenever Roman Catholics are not invited to come out of the Roman church as part of their conversion experience. The group was not able to find one mind on this. Some were prepared to work with people who remained in the Roman church, some insisted on their coming out, some wanted them to come out but would never say so directly, and some were prepared to encourage born-again believers to stay in the Roman church.

In direct response to the paper, a deep sense of thankfulness was expressed for the new openness of the Roman church. The group did, however, *doubt* the proposition that the leadership of the church was in the hands of the progressives. Some felt that the changes were more apparent than real and that the historic mistrust of the Roman church was still justified.

There was *unconditional* approval of meeting with Roman Catholics for Bible study, sharing Christian experience, and praying together.

There was apparent in the group the turmoil that evangelism often creates between those who work in the nominal and sacramental churches, and those whose work is a mission to the nominal and sacramentalist Christians. The group after three days of discussion reached a healthy level of mutual understanding between these two positions.

Nominal Christians were taken to be those whose affiliation to the Christian Church seemed to lack any sense of sharing in the resurrected life of Christ. The state churches of Europe suffer from nominalism, the large free churches of America suffer from nominalism. The problem of evangelism of nominal Christians in a non-Christian culture was stressed.

Sacramental churches suffer from nominalism to a large extent, but the particular problem of many people who by their allegiance to the sacraments suppose themselves to be Christians, is their indifference or hostility to the Gospel that seemingly denies the Lordship of Christ.

One part of the group felt strongly that the Gospel could be preached and Christian fellowship enjoyed without reference to the divisiveness of the historical doctrinal debates that often provide the nominal and sacramental churches with a place to hide from the biblical Gospel.

The consensus of opinion in our strategy group was that evangelism must be thought of in terms of groups.

Participants, numbering about 20, were first asked to think about a particular group that they would like to reach for Jesus Christ, then describe that group.

From there, the group moved to individually thinking about the most important things to consider in reaching their group for Jesus Christ and why these considerations were important.

Based on the participant's understanding of the people he described and on his understanding of the individual's own self, the question was asked, "What action do you believe would be effective in reaching these people?"

In thinking about evangelism, it was pointed out that too often Christians as evangelizers go into an area or town with the idea of evangelizing the whole area and everyone in it, without giving consideration to the various groups in that area. It was noted that there are probably four million groups in the world.

Along this line a Bible study group on every corner of Pasadena, Calif., may not be "the way" to evangelize Pasadena, according to one illustration.

Participants were advised to first, know their selected group, then find the key — as a result of study — that will most quickly, easily unlock the door to reaching that group of people with the Gospel of Jesus Christ.

Each participant was encouraged to think about evangelism, including strategy, to consider and find God's strategy for evangelism; to recognize the authority of God's Word and arrive at a definition of what "evangelism" is; to find the people whom God wants to reach; to determine what they (the selected group) know about the Gospel; to find the change agents in the group; to find and utilize individuals and methods within as a possible force for evangelism; to consider and determine goals; and to plan from possible outcomes to action.

EVANGELIZATION AMONG OCCULTISTS AND SPIRITISTS

Detmar Scheunemann

Rev. Scheunemann, Batu, Malang, Indonesia, is Principal of the Indonesian Bible Institute.

Occultism is "in." Leading magazines give prominent space to the different manifestations of occultism. The film industry has discovered it as the new theme promising flourishing business. What in the past has been a silent powerful undercurrent has become the openly propagated religion of our day. The occult supernatural is fascinating, especially to the younger generation. Wherever a missionary goes today, he is face to face with occult powers and practices. When he counsels young people he will find that many of them have been entangled with spiritism and Asian religions. When he works in a rural area he will discover the occult background of not a few customs and traditions. When we take Christ to the sophisticated and to the masses of the big cities we face an encounter with intellectualism and secularistic thinking on one side, and belief in fortune-telling, astrology, magical healing, and superstition on the other side — a strange paradox!

Working for many years in a Muslim country, I have come to the conclusion that the power of Islam does not lie in its dogma and practices, nor in the antithesis of the Trinity, against the Lordship of Christ and his redeeming death, but in the occult practices of its leaders, thus holding sway over their people. Those working in a Buddhist or Hindu culture also know the direct encounter with occultism, just as do those who proclaim Christ among the old and newly emerging forms of syncretistic Christian spiritism. Paul wrote, "We are not contending against flesh and blood ..." (Eph. 6:12; cf., Rev. 12:9,12).

How do we deal with people who have been engaged in occultism? Is a special deliverance ministry necessary? Does not faith in Christ and the regenerating work of the Holy Spirit set a person entirely free? How do we know that people are bound by occultism or are even demon-possessed? Do we have to rediscover exorcism of old? These are some of the questions this paper tries to answer, not in the way of drawing from a large bibliography, but rather from the range of practical experiences and personal research.

1. The way into bondage: the various forms of occultism

First, we have to uncover the practices of occultism and to understand its various manifestations, thus painting the dark background for the deliverance ministry. We can trace back the different forms of occultism to the essence of the first temptation with which Adam and Eve were confronted, "God knows that when you eat of the fruit of the tree, your eyes will be opened and you will be like God, knowing good and evil" (Gen. 3:5). Thus man's thirst for power and knowledge was stirred, tempted, and finally captured. All forms and manifestations of occultism except for those of an objective character are born out of this desire for power and knowledge. We can therefore divide occultism into two areas.

a. *Occultism relating to man's desire for power.* Bringing into focus the different manifestations of occultism relating to man's desire for power we are speaking first about the occult ways to exercise power over people. In many countries, not only in Asia and Africa, men in leading positions in business, politics, and in the armed forces are regularly advised by modern or old-fashioned sorcerers. They are taught how to defend themselves and how to succeed in their position by using magic sayings (mantera). These might involve casting spells, visiting graves of ancestors and past heroes, fulfilling occult rites at certain days, hours, and nights, requesting power and wealth at certain famous places of nature, and giving over in return to the evil power one member of the family.

In order to carry out *revenge,* a piece of cloth from the enemy, or some hairs, or a photo, or the soil of his footprints is secured and used to attack him from a distance. Men in powerful religious positions often attack the messenger of the Gospel and his family, trying to bring sicknesses and calamities upon them. Here the messenger has to take his position according to Eph. 6:16-17, and place his family under the power of the Blood of Christ, especially if he encounters occult powers.

There is another field where occult powers are exercised: *love and sex.* The means vary from country to country: flowers, special food, the blowing of cigarette smoke into a person's face accompanied by a magical saying, or the awful practice of calling a woman from a distance in an occult way, drawing her against her will into the house and using her for sexual intercourse.

Because they play an important part in the exercising of occult powers we have to explain the use and function of *"fetishes":* objects charged with magical power, used for protection, healing, and occult attack. The words "amulet" and "talisman" are usually used in the context of protection, whereas the word fetish is used for all three purposes. Days, numbers, and signs can also function as fetishes.

Fetishes have been used from early days. They vary in form and quality according to their cultural surroundings and age. Here special studies have to be carried out to uncover the different forms and usages of fetishes in connection with childbirth, bringing up of children, initiation rites, marriage, sickness, death, building and moving of houses, traveling, war, thievery, and other crisis situations in life. The fetishes may take the form of plants, wood, roots, stones, needles, knives, old swords, belts, cloths, jewelry, rings, precious stones, a talisman in the car, the number 12a in the hotel, days of fortune or misfortune, special pieces of one's heritage, etc.

Where does the magic power hide? in the wood? the stone? the belt? The power is not in the fetish but behind it. Fearing, trusting, or using the fetish gives the power of darkness (Eph. 6:12) an opportunity to intervene in human lives and situations. Believing in something outside God opens the door for the principalities and powers of the prince of this world to manifest themselves in giving protection, help, success, and unusual power in a supernatural way. As faith in the living God through

Jesus Christ unlocks the resources of the kingdom of God, so trusting in a primitive or modern fetish invites the intervention of the powers of the satanic kingdom. There is no difference between a Christian fetish like pages of the Bible, crosses, and relics, and Animistic, Hindu, and Muslim fetishes. Many Christians are in occult bondage through using Christian fetishes or Christian mixed with heathen fetishes.

Another field of man's desire to receive or exercise power is that of *occult healing* which takes the form of *black or white magic.* Therefore, there are also some forms of medical treatment that border on the occult which have to be mentioned here. The primitive medicine man and the more advanced and sophisticated healer who use black magic have one thing in common. They use a formula of healing which has to be applied rigidly. Calling on the devil, demons, or evil spirits by using magic sayings, the patient has to undergo a certain treatment, for instance has to swallow strange drinks containing ashes of burned animals, roots, and plants at certain hours in the night, or has to sacrifice certain animals and use old and modern fetishes.

The way white magic operates is not different in essence. It also depends on a formula, but one clothed in Christian clothes. It uses the three persons of the Trinity in a prayer which is actually a magic saying because the prayer has to be said always in the same way to be effective. Often the "Christian" healer goes on whispering old Egyptian or Arabic mantera. Then his strange treatment has to be followed rigidly, too, only it may take on a "Christian"note like burning incense at certain days and hours. It goes without saying that white magic deceives many people. They suffer the same effects as those treated by black magic.

Occult healing often only shifts or transfers the sickness. Some may enjoy healing; psyche may experience detrimental sufferings. One member of the family may be healed at the expense of another member getting sick. This happens often in the family of the occult healer himself. In some parts of the world it is the custom also to transfer the sickness to a corpse or a dying person.

Hypnosis has to be mentioned here because its use needs to be examined carefully. According to Dr. Lechler, a well-respected German Christian psychiatrist, the use of hypnosis can only be justified in diagnosis. But many doctors and psychiatrists are using hypnosis also in therapy. Here should be heard the warning voice of Dr. Paul Tournier who states that every form of hypnosis is an invasion into the personality of man. The negative effects have to be considered seriously as well as the positive. Obviously, the person using hypnosis constitutes the decisive factor. If he is a healer or charmer, hypnosis opens the door for the invasion of occult powers. *Eye diagnosis* is also a case on the borderline between occultism and medical diagnosis. This is not the place to discuss the different systems of eye-diagnosis and to what extent sickness affects the iris, but it has to be stated clearly that eye-diagnosis enters the field of occultism if to the diagnosis of a sickness a word about the future life is added; thus, eye-diagnosis becomes occult fortune-telling where the human eye is not used any longer medically but rather mediumistically.

We should not leave the field of occult healing without marking clearly the characteristics of *divine healing.* First, the prayer of faith does not depend on a formula, its sentences do not carry a magic power, but are an expression of faith touching God on the ground of Jesus' finished work of redemption. Second, the prayer of faith does not depend on a certain manner; I may pray with laying hands on the sick person or without doing so. I may use the anointing with oil, I may kneel at the bedside, or pray from far distance. I may follow the advice of Paul and suggest some medical treatment accompanied by prayer. In every way, I am on scriptural ground (Mark 16:17-18; Jas. 5:16, etc.). Obviously, applying these different ways of praying for the sick needs to be done wisely in the context of the situation and environment of the sick person. Third, the prayer of faith is carried out in the Name of Jesus. Thus it turns the eyes of the sick person from the Lord's servant to the Lord himself. The servant knows he is nothing, the presence of the risen Lord everything. Mark 16:17-18 challenges every believer to become God's instrument in the ministry of divine healing. I Cor. 12: 9 teaches that the Holy Spirit equips certain members of the Body of Christ with the gifts of healing. Thus they are especially set aside for the ministry to the sick. In ministering to the sick it is necessary to understand the background of the sickness: Is it a means to see God's power and glory revealed (John 9:1,3)? Has it to do with sin and judgment (John 9:2)? Is it God's way of dealing with his servants, a hidden way of grace? See II Cor. 12:7-9; Num. 12:10-15; Luke 1:20).

It has become clear that occultism relating to man's desire for power constitutes a large field which has to be explored in its specific forms of cultural environment in order to help the Lord's servant to understand the hidden occult ties often binding Christians and inquirers. In the following we have to survey the different forms of occultism relating to man's desire for knowledge.

b. *Occultism relating to man's desire for knowledge.* Man wants to know if he can communicate with the dead. Spiritism is born. Man wants to know if he can trust his feelings. Hyperaesthesio and telepathy are born. Man wants to know if he can interpret mysterious happenings of the present and understand coming events of the future. Fortune-telling is born.

(i) Spiritism — It is probably not exaggerated to say that the majority of the world's population is engaged in some kind of spiritism, directly or indirectly. Practicing actively different forms of spiritism, like taking part in spiritistic circles or even services, receiving messages from the dead through table-lifting, glass-moving, automatic writings, speaking in trance, materializations, etc. would be termed as direct spiritistic involvement. Whereas observance of cultural, national tribal and family traditions often results in an indirect unconscious involvement, no less dangerous in its effects. In Hinduism, Buddhism, Islam, and Christianity, including Roman Catholicism, spiritistic practices play an important role and cause millions of their followers to suffer the effects of such involvement. Therefore, we have to discover and uncover these many different manifestations of spiritism, explore them in the light of the Bible, and focus them with their key words and practices clearly in our preaching ministry. The following list of manifestations of spiritism is by no means complete but should serve as a stimulus for further research.

Spiritism in the modern world — Many spiritistic circles exist. The spirits of famous dead people are called upon, often in the Christian way of prayer. The spirits manifest themselves through a person who is functioning as a medium and who has often been put into a trance by hypnosis. The spirits may also manifest themselves through moveable things like a drinking glass moving from one letter to another on an alphabet spread upon the table. The same manifestation in a different form is found in Indonesia when students, wanting to know the questions and problems of the coming examination, make a human puppet, form a circle around it, and ask the spirits to answer their questions by the movements of the puppet. Others expect the spirit to answer their questions by automatic writing on the blackboard. And, in fact, the chalk really moves mysteriously. Certain practices of Freemasonry are definitely spiritism. The modern Umbanda and Macumba cults in South America are a rebirth of spiritism in the special cultural environment. The relationship between spiritism and the modern drug culture still needs to be examined. The openness of modern youth to the mystical and supernatural realm gives spiritism another disastrous opportunity. Spiritistic practices often lead to demon possession, from the mild form of taking hold of certain areas of the human personality (like a spirit of hatred, lust, lying, or anger) to the terrible forms of total possession.

Spiritism in cultural and family traditions — The fear of evil spirits and hope of help and protection from ancestors have created many customs, not only in primitive animism but also in the more sophisticated Asian, African, Latin American, and European societies. Here are some examples from Indonesia. The newborn child is given the name of a famous ancestor in the belief that the spirit of the ancestor will protect and help the child all through life. The ancestor may appear later in crisis situations of life. A young couple have to eat a specially prepared meal dedicated to certain spirits the day before marriage. People visit the graves in crisis situations of life to pray to the dead. The graves are visited also at certain days, not to pay respect to the dead or honor them, but to establish contact for help. Or they fellowship with them as in the Chinese family-meal at the graveside. A Muslim family would invite their neighbors for a "Selamatan" (a meal of thanksgiving or in connection with the passing away of a member of the family). The food would be specially dedicated to the spirits before everybody participates.

Spiritism in world religions — Praying for and to the dead is practiced widely by Muslims, Hindus, and often Christians also. The Muslim family holds a special gathering for a dead family member on the third, seventh, fortieth, seventieth, and one hundredth evenings after death. This practice is continued by many Christians in Indonesia, but serving the spirit of the dead in a Christian way. The distinction Catholic theology makes between honoring dead saints and praying to them does not exist in practice. Thus many Catholics enter into spiritism, especially through the Mary cult. Hinduism with its teaching of reincarnation of the soul is also an expression of spiritism. The teaching of Islam differentiates between man, angels, djin (good spirits, also called Islam spirits), and evil spirits. The djin have to hear the Koran and believe it. To foster relationship with the djin in order to receive supernatural power from them constitutes a large field of hidden practices and secrets from which the imam and Muslim leaders execute their powerful influence and are feared. It has been proved again and again that a presentation of the Gospel in power and authority even in confrontation with the secret spiritism of Islam breaks the way into the heart of an orthodox Muslim, whereas an intellectual presentation usually fails. Although the Bible clearly states its position against spiritism, forbidding it (Deut. 18:10-11; Lev. 20:6,27; 19:31), the appearance of the spirit of Samuel in I Sam. 28:12 has been used as Christian warrant to defend spiritism. Whichever exegesis one holds, one thing is clear: Saul died as a direct result of practicing spiritism (I Chron. 10:13-14; cf. Lev. 20:27).

(ii) *Hyperaesthesia and telepathy* — We have to draw a line between the neutral form of telepathy and hyperaesthesia and the occult form. Two people who love each other can understand each other even when separated. They can think the same thoughts, they may feel what happens to the person loved. In the same way a person with the faculty of hyperaesthesia (intense sensibility) may suddenly be confronted by a vision. In the middle of the day he may see clearly what happens many hundreds of kilometers away. However telepathy can become a powerful means of calling and directing people from a distance. Here we pass the borderline and enter the field of occult telepathy. Intense sensibility can also go together with the faculty of clairvoyance. The person sees, for instance, a coffin carried out of a house and in a short while this becomes true. Clairvoyance is often inherited by children whose parents have been actively engaged in occultism. This faculty can also be enlarged and become the means of soothsaying (see Acts 16:16-18).

(iii) *Fortune-telling and soothsaying.* — The Romans of old tried to tell the future by examining the stomachs of certain animals, just as certain tribes in Indonesia still do today. The Egyptian way of telling one's fate out of the coffee grounds in a cup is still practiced in many parts of the world. Not only primitive tribal people know coming events by cries of birds, but educated people in Europe also fear the cry of the nightowl because it brings calamity. But the most popular means to find out about the future in our days is the laying of cards, the reading of a horoscope and the interpretation of handwriting and hand-lines. Not only is much deception practiced by fortune-telling, astrology, and horoscopes, it also has to be emphasized that many people, by believing the soothsaying, get under occult influences. The powers of the darkness are given an opportunity to fulfill the soothsaying which the person believes. Also fear and constant remembrance of the soothsaying can drive a person to fulfill these soothsayings himself. The Bible clearly forbids every form of soothsaying (Deut. 18:10).

In addition to the above we should note also that where occultism has been practiced in the past, or is still being practiced, or where suicide or murder have taken place, objective manifestations of ghosts may take place. "Objective manifestations" means that ghosts are not the subjective experience of certain people but are seen by people not attached to the situation and the place. Many may laugh about these manifestations: doors opening themselves, the noise of footsteps, being gripped at the neck, or being drawn out of bed by unseen hands, seeing horrifying faces, etc. But those who have had such experiences have stopped laughing. Sometimes missionaries are offered cheap houses for sale or rent. They are in most cases ghost houses. The servant of the Lord can enter them in the full armor of God and carry out a good spiritual springcleaning, commanding the spirits in the Name of Jesus to go. However, this should not be done alone, but in the company of believing, praying Christians.

2. The way into liberty: different aspects of the deliverance ministry

On the ground of Christ's finished work at Calvary and his total victory on Easter morning, we are called to lead those who believe in him into the perfect liberty of the children of God. Here are five important aspects of the deliverance ministry.

a. *Analysis: understanding the case.* — Deliverance ministry is personal ministry, which demands time, concern and love. The Lord's servant may during the personal counseling session explain carefully the various forms and manifestations of occultism. Seldom does a person admit when asked that he has been engaged in some form of occultism. However, as he is confronted with the different occult practices, the Holy Spirit sheds light into the past (John 16:8), and instances of occult involvement come to remembrance, even from early childhood. Therefore the counselor needs to have a large understanding of the different forms of occultism and how they apply in the cultural environment in which he is working. Because of this, we have given much space to outlining the various manifestations of occultism. Under the guidance of the Holy Spirit and in a praying attitude, the counselor will pray from this knowledge and help the person in need to understand his occult bondage. The Lord's servant may also observe certain distinct signs and features in the life of the person in bondage which point to occult involvement. In the realm of character, he is hard, egoistic, unsocial and introvert. In the realm of passion there are abnormal sexuality, outbursts (fits) of anger, and kleptomania. In the realm of the soul there is depression, haunted by fear, anxiety, and temptation to commit suicide. Finally, in the spiritual realm there is militant atheism; resisting God's Word or going to sleep when God's Word is proclaimed; hatred towards Christ and especially His atoning blood; inability to concentrate in prayer or mention the name of Jesus in prayer; a negative, cynical attitude towards the Gospel; and inability to believe. Also certain nervous and mental sicknesses may indicate occult involvement. However, here we enter a difficult field. It is not easy to draw the line between mental sickness with a medical background and mental sickness with an occult background. The charisma of the Holy Spirit, the ability to distinguish between spirits (I Cor. 12:10), provides a tremendous help in this delicate task. Christian doctors and psychiatrists anointed by the Holy Spirit with the gift of discerning of spirits are God's special gifts to the church to meet the challenge in the tremendous increase of occult-demonic mental sicknesses in our time.

After the various occult involvements have been brought to light, the counselor has to point out that active or passive occult involvement will bring about a special relationship to the devil which we may call "bondage" or "occult ties." Use of the powers of darkness in a concious or unconscious way gives the devil a right on this person's life. The devil can present the bill as he will surely do, at least when the person dies. Not a few have witnessed the terrible, unpeaceful death of people who have been engaged in occultism. The occult ties and bondages have to be broken and the right of the devil on a person's life has to be renounced and abolished. Why does a person who has accepted the Lord Jesus as his personal Savior and has experienced the forgiveness of his sins and the indwelling of the Holy Spirit still need to be delivered from his occult involvement in the past? Does this not minimize the power of redemption? In Acts 19: 18-19 it is said about the believers in Ephesus, "Many also of those who were now believers came, confessing and exposing their practices. And a number of those who practiced magic arts brought their books together and burnt them in the sight of all." It is not quite clear, if the believers in Ephesus were still secretly practicing occultism — this would be the case as in many churches today — or practiced magic art before they became Christians and were now confessing it and destroying everything attached to it, however valuable. The point is that they made an open break with their occult past and entered consciously into their position in Christ, committing themselves totally. Note that this liberating work of the Holy Spirit took place after Paul had ministered at least two years in Ephesus. Thus, there is a sure scriptural ground for the deliverance ministry among believers. It does not matter how a person enters into the conscious realization of his freedom in Christ including freedom from the futile ways inherited from his fathers (I Pet. 1:18) — the most important thing is that he has entered into his liberty in Christ.

b. *Confession: breaking the power of sin.* — Secrecy is the power of certain sins. Therefore their power can only be broken by bringing them into the light. In principle the Bible does not differentiate between small and big sins, but the list of the sins mentioned in Rev. 22:15 is of special significance. People involved in occultism have entered a direct relationship with the devil. In order to break this relationship it has to be confessed openly. The secret dark practices have to be betrayed. This means that the patient has to confess and name his active and passive involvements in occultism one by one. It is often through the battle of intercession that the secret relationships to the devil are really mentioned by name. Here are other Scripture verses which mention the need of confession: Jas. 5:16; I John 1:9; Acts 19:18; Matt. 3:6. Therefore, we need to prepare and offer ourselves as priests of the church (I Pet. 2:8-9).

c. *Renunciation: setting the prisoner free.* — The early church requested those who had come out of heathen life and worship to renounce openly their relationship to the power of darkness before they were baptized. This prayer of renunciation is not a formula but it must contain the following three points: confession of every occult involvement by name, renunciation of those occult ties in the Name of Jesus, and full surrender to God the Father, the Son, and the Holy Spirit. Thus, this prayer may take the form (spoken by the person in need and led by the counselor sentence by sentence), "I renounce the devil and all his works, every right and relationship he has in my life...now mention the confessed occult practices one by one. In the Name of Jesus I deny them, and I surrender now my life to you — God the Father, the Son and the Holy Spirit, only to follow Thee and to trust in Thee until the end of my life." After the patient has been led in the prayer of renunciation an opportunity should be given to him to offer a free prayer of thanking the Lord. This free prayer will reveal if he has been really delivered from the occult bondage. It is often not without a terrible battle that the person in need follows in the prayer of renunciation. Here the Lord's servant has to bind the powers of darkness on the basis of Matt. 16: 19; 18:18 and set the prisoner free. If the person has not yet received Jesus as his personal Savior, then personal counseling according to normal lines should follow immediately.

d. *Casting out: dealing with demon possession.* — Do not cast out demons where there are none, otherwise the patient really believes that he is demon-possessed. On the one hand we have to act carefully in order to differentiate between demon possession, mental sickness, and emotional fits; on the other hand, we have to act firmly and in authority. Emotional fits can be detected by simply using a needle. Many cases of demon possession can be marked out clearly by observing the following signs: speaking with a different voice; laughing and mocking in a satanic, abnormal way; unnatural physical strength and behavior; and attacks of anger and hatred when the Name of Jesus is mentioned. The person may defend himself against the servant of the Lord by going off into unconsciousness. Other cases similar to mental sickness need the gift of discerning the spirits, prayerful consideration, and the advice of a Christian psychiatrist.

Do not rush into the ministry of exorcism. Jesus teaches to be prepared by prayer, fasting, and faith, (Matt. 17:19-21). We have to wait until a team of believing Christians is ready to support the ministry of exorcism. Jesus' promise given to a small group ministering in faith in Matt. 18: 19-20 is of real importance for the deliverance ministry.

Do not lay hands upon a demon-possessed person, but command the evil spirits in the Name of Jesus to go out! We observe in the Gospels that Jesus commanded the evil spirits when confronted with a possessed person, (Matt. 5:8; 17:18), but He only lays hands upon those who are physically sick (Matt. 8:18; 9:29; Mark 7:33). To his disciples, Jesus gives authority over the evil spirits (Matt. 10:1,8). Paul casts out in the Name of Jesus the spirit of divination from the slave girl in Philippi (Acts 16:18). If we use the mighty Name of Jesus in casting out demons, we need to be in vital personal relationship with him. If we use the Name of Jesus only as a liturgical formula, the experience of the sons of the high priest Sceva may be ours (Acts 19:13-17).

Commanding the evil spirits in the Name of Jesus means that the spirits are confronted with Jesus the risen victorious Savior who has bruised the head of the serpent. Often the spirits try to hide behind the unconsciousness of the patient. Therefore we have to call in Jesus' Name the patient back to consciousness. If the spirits start to agonize the patient bodily, or if they start to speak out of the patient, or if they try to attack God's servant, the victory is very near! Still better if they have to reveal their names, because then certainly they have to go one by one. However, the battle can last for weeks until finally the last most persistent spirit has to leave the person, while the body may be thrown upon the floor, a terrible voice may be heard, or the deliverance may take place in a quiet way. These are the signs that the person is delivered: ability to pray spontaneously, praising and thanking the Lord personally, new shining of the eyes, and deep peaceful sleep.

e. *Follow up: learning to resist the devil.* — Deliverance ministry may be compared with unbinding Lazarus still wrapped in bandages and grave clothes. However, from then on, Lazarus had to walk by himself (John 11:44). The person who has been delivered from occult involvement or evil spirits, has to step out in faith. He or she needs to accept Jesus Christ as personal Savior. Throwing away fetishes and amulets and burning books on spiritism is one step, confessing and renouncing the occult practices another, but then the important third step is receiving Christ and full assurance of salvation. If we fail in the third step a tragedy will take place which Jesus described in Matt. 12:43-45: The evil spirit will reoccupy the empty, swept house with seven other spirits.

The person has to be taught to resist the devil. Therefore he has to understand and enter into his full spiritual inheritance in Christ. He is a child of God, he is redeemed from the sins of his forefathers, he is a new creature, his body is a temple of the Holy Spirit. His old life entangled with occultism has been crucified with Christ. He has been buried and raised with Christ to walk in newness of life, and therefore has to consider himself dead to sin and alive to God. He who is in him is greater then he who is in the world. Putting on the whole armour of God (Eph. 6: 10-20), he has to resist the powers of darkness from this position. He has to be taught to take shelter under the protecting power of the Blood of Christ. And finally he has to be taught to command the devil as Jesus did in Matt. 4:10 using the mighty Name of Jesus. A great help for the newly delivered person is a vital, warm Christian fellowship. He learns to study the Bible and to pray. The sympathetic understanding of fellow Christians and their intercession will help to restore him in body, soul, and spirit. The special fellowship around the Lord's table has been a source of strength and healing, to many former occultists.

Conclusion

The tremendous need for a deliverance ministry is evident. It will still increase as the demonic powers are building up for the reign of the Anti-christ and even try to invade the church. Therefore, deliverance ministry should become an integrated part of endtime-evangelism. It is very dangerous to specialize in deliverance ministry. It is still more dangerous to exploit such a specialized deliverance ministry for sensational reporting, writing, and money making. What our age needs are servants of the Lord, who with deep compassion for those bound by occultism study the various forms of occultism in the different cultural environments, who in simple childlike faith in the authority of Jesus Christ confront and uncover the occult powers, who through preaching and counseling set the prisoners free, who do not allow the devil by unclean lives or motives to have any bridge-head in them, thus, paralyzing their deliverance ministry, but who are totally committed to Christ, filled, anointed, and equipped by the Holy Spirit to lead many occultists into the liberty of the children of God.

EVANGELIZATION AMONG SPIRITISTS AND OCCULTISTS REPORT

"Spiritism is the religion of our day, undergirding all other religion." In these words the Rev. Detmar Scheunemann outlined the dreadful proportions of a problem that can no longer be regarded as the exclusive property of Asia or Africa, but is truly international with its tentacles reaching to every corner of the globe. The very word "occult" means "hidden," and as these works of Satan were brought into the light of open discussion and exposed for what they were, we began to see the true nature of Satan's strategy for these days and how to fight and live in the victory over him that Jesus gained on the Cross.

The alarming rise in interest and participation in occultism, particularly within Western cultures over the last 10 years, was examined and the main motives for each individual evaluated. These were seen as:

a. a desire for knowledge

b. a lust for power

c. a need for comfort, e.g., in the sense of wanting to contact a recently deceased loved one

d. a craving for sex which is often used as a catalyst in occult rituals

e. a need for protection against the occult attacks initiated by others on us

f. the failure of the church to provide spiritual satisfaction has made many turn to occultism. This applies, for example, in the church's lack of answers to some of the problems that the occult poses and the fact that miracles such as healing which used to be part of the regular ministry of the church now appear to be Satan's own province. He is bringing many into bondage while the church of Christ stands in the wings failing to exhibit the faintest flicker of the supernatural power of a living God.

It was seen that occultism was not only rife in the world, but could also touch the church. Christians are not immune from bondage; and part of Satan's strategy was seen to be to so involve Christian leaders and laity that God's work might be hampered, and his churches hindered from rising into heavenly places with her Lord. Some Christians are also inadvertently trapped by the evil one in the use of "Christian" fetishes such as a Bible, or a Cross. An example of this was the way a soldier might take a Bible into war with him in his rucksack, not to read, but for protection! Satan will try anything in his attempts to spoil the Christian's blood-bought heritage of real life in Jesus, but it was stressed that time and again he was being defeated when confronted with the power of the blood of Jesus and the authority of his name.

Much of Satan's mystique and power lies merely in the veil of secrecy behind which he hides. This veil was illustrated by the descriptions of African participants in recalling the dismissal of occult forces by past missionaries as "mere superstition," and the idea that with education the African would soon grow out of them. It was felt that here was a real area with which the Congress was dealing, merely by having these sessions — as many of us were facing for the first time the true reality and implications of demonic activity in this world in which we live. One of the results of these insights, we hoped, would be that after the Congress, attempts could be made to educate ministers and missionaries in preparation for their ministry. Often this has been neglected at great cost! Rev. Bud Elford drew attention to the way many Arctic missionaries from his society came under a demonic activity and apprehension with which they could not cope and so left that particular mission field. This resulted in the beginning of a training and preparation program so that whether the missionaries-to-be accepted the existence of the demonic or not, they were at least prepared when faced with it.

Three main areas were stressed in which all Christians facing these problems need to be personally prepared: (i) To recognize that we are engaged in warfare with Satan and his evil forces; (ii) To be fully equipped by being continually filled with the Holy Spirit; (iii) To be living in purity and holiness, cleansed by the blood of Jesus. Otherwise the evil spirits themselves may well denounce us for what we are.

It was noted that whereas Christian leadership was to be equipped to deal with the problems, at the same time an unhealthy interest in the occult among Christian laity was to be discouraged. It was shown that in some areas of Western Christianity this was becoming the "in thing" even among young Christians. This has led in some cases to an over-interest in either the book or film of "The Exorcist" — to many dangerous practices, such as Christian young people attempting to exorcise those whose problems were psychosomatic, not demonic! Although Satan *is defeated,* that gives us no license to arouse our fleshly curiosity. Satan's activities are illicit and expressly forbidden by God, Lev. 19: 31, 20:6, Deut. 18:9-14, and we should discourage idle interest. A good guideline would be, "Never go looking for demons, but if one appears under your feet, tread on it!"

A strong emphasis was laid in our discussions on the fact that we should not be seeking to produce demonology specialists, but men of God in whose ministries dealing with the demonic was included not as a specialist activity but as an integrated part of a wider field, e.g., evangelism. We need to grow in God and in the authority of the Spirit so that we may discern where Satan is working. Discernment was a gift of the Holy Spirit for this work because Satan so often acts like a monkey, a mere imitator of the things of God, and we need to be able to tell the difference between the reality and the imitation!

We began to gain some understanding of what it means to live in the victory of Jesus. In the realm of the occult our abilities can achieve nothing: it is only in a childlike dependence on Jesus that we find him coming and working through us. That is the reason for the scriptural exhortation to prayer and fasting, not so much in order that we might become more spiritual, but to enable us to concentrate ourselves, without any distraction, on Jesus. We cannot use the name of Jesus as a mere formula, but as the authority in which we live, as we dwell under the Cross receiving daily cleansing and purifying.

Why then is not everyone immediately delivered from Satan as when Jesus expelled demons in the New Testament? We must reject Satan's condemnation of us on this point. If we are pure and honest before God, then he will use us, but only *if* the possessed person is absolutely honest in desiring deliverance. Many of our problems are caused by the changing desires in some people so they try in various areas of their lives to keep the demon and his power while at other times they desire freedom. Confession and repentance on the part of the possessed must be honest and complete.

Scripture foretells that in the last days Satanic activity will increase. How can we in the churches not only educate each other and bring that which is dark into light, but also win the world?

a. We must educate the non-Christian to the dangers of things we too lightly accept like secret societies, hypnosis, Freemasonry, yoga, horoscopes, ouija boards, etc.

b. The film "The Exorcist" should not be seen by curious Christians but exposed for the danger it is. Pre-film literature distributed in the cinema queues and counseling centers open in the immediate vicinity after the film provide evangelistic opportunities for those towns where Christians have not managed to have the film banned.

c. As servants of Christ we need to be culturally aware and need to see how the occult relates to a particular culture and how it may be dealt with in that culture.

d. Our literature and responses must not be immature, sensational or negative, but positive, giving glory to the works of God and not the works of Satan.

Finally, we emphasized the need to move in the fullness of the power of the living God. We need not only to be sealed with the Spirit (Ephesians) but also to be continually filled with him (Ephesians). We need not only the evangelistic, organic, and pedagogic works of the Spirit, but also the charismatic work of the Spirit that he may give us all the gifts we need to be equipped for his service. Satan is defeated and so we look to Jesus. He will give us all we need to deal with the enemy, an anointing of the Holy Spirit, a childlike faith in Jesus, and the authority of the Father. Living thus in lives clean, pure, and totally committed to Jesus makes Satan fear. In the name of Jesus and his victory Satan is utterly overcome but in these days he must be defeated, not merely ignored.

INDUSTRIAL EVANGELISM

Martin Higginbottom

Mr. Higginbottom, Westmoreland,
England, is Director of Outreach to Industry
in Kendal.

At the conclusion of a conference held in Britain some years ago entitled "The Church and Industry," the following statement was issued:
"In the light of the failure of evangelical Christians in this century in the industrial sphere — a failure in which we acknowledge our part — this group of Christians engaged in industry urgently calls upon Christian people and churches to:
1. Adopt a radically different attitude to industry, seeing it as the means whereby God meets our material and social needs today, and an area where God is at work.
2. Become involved in matters of social justice in the industrial sphere, speaking out against unfair practices, exploitation and dishonesty wherever and however they occur, from a knowledge of the facts, and taking action where they have the power to do so.
3. Support in every possible way personal and group evangelism in industry.
4. Support financially the research work of the Christian Teamwork Institute of Education and the evangelistic and teaching work of the Worker's Christian Fellowship and Outreach to Industry.
5. Ask ministers and clergy and other church leaders to consider ways in which their church programs, evangelism and training of young people can forward the cause of Christ in our industrial society.
6. Play their part responsibly in increasing productivity, according to God's purpose."
Now this statement raises a number of important questions. Some concern merely the simple mechanics — the *modus operandi* — of evangelism, but others raise biblical and doctrinal issues — for example, that we as Christians are put "into" the world, but that we are not to be "part of" the world. Social involvement issues were dealt with at the 1971 Amsterdam Conference, at which one of the resolutions was "The Church must earn the right to be heard." Social involvement, as I see it, must not be looked upon as a nettle to grasp but as an inescapable responsibility to be acknowledged, accepted, and used to God's glory.

"Am I my brother's keeper?"

To the above question the resounding answer comes back from heaven, "The blood of your brother cries out to me from the ground." A similar cry is heard again recorded in Jas. 5:4, "Behold the hire of the laborers who have reaped down your fields which is, of you, kept back by fraud, crieth: and the cries of them which have reaped are entered into the ears of the Lord of Sabaoth."

If I eat, wear clothes, live in a house, use the postal services, drive a car — then whether I like it or not I am thereby involved in society. I cannot escape this. Sir Frederick Catherwood in his book *The Christian Citizen* makes the following comments:

"It is no part of my message to minimize the Christian's care for the salvation of men's souls. That is as important as ever. The duty of care for our neighbor is undivided. If we care for his body, we will also find that we care for his soul. If we really care for his soul, we should find that we also care for his body. It is not true Christianity, but false pietism, which divides one from the other.

"Many who accept the full Christian Gospel fail to balance the doctrines of separation, prayer and evangelism, from the very clear statements of our Lord that we are to love our neighbors as ourselves. This commandment is not only just as binding as other doctrines, but is ranked by our Lord second only to the commandment which tells us to love the Lord our God with all our heart.

"The Christian is to be the salt of the earth, he is to be a light to lighten the world, and no one is going to be of any influence or any enlightenment if he seems already to have removed himself from this world to the next."

Enemy-held territory

To have and to hold any true assessment of Christian responsibility, one must recognize God's relationship to the world in which we live. This is God's creation and God has not abdicated — he still rules in the kingdoms of men. His silence is not due to indifference, indolence, or ignorance; he is long-suffering, not willing that any should perish. An enemy has occupied the land, and God's D-Day began nearly 2,000 years ago by the stepping into human history of his Son, Jesus Christ. The Church has ever since been waging war to liberate the people. The command is to go in "to possess the land," or as our great Commander put it, "Go into all the world and make disciples."

In his book *The Christian Persuader,* Dr. Leighton Ford says, "Jesus didn't merely mean the world as the geographical world, i.e., the frontiers of Brazil and the Congo, etc., but he also meant the world of government, education, domestic life, industry and commerce. The world where people live their lives."

Defining industrial evangelism

Industrial evangelism is the whole plan-strategy of carrying the Christian evangel into the workaday world of our nation — an exercise that will of necessity involve "life" as well as "lip." It will have in mind, in the main, a society of people known as the "workers" or "working people" — a term which is easily stated but not as easily defined.

In the Western world the "working class" people could at one time be said to live in certain areas, do certain jobs, and be confined to a certain level of economic existence. This is not so today. Many workers in the Western world earn a larger salary than many at middle and top management; they own their own houses and indeed have a standard of living equal to their supposedly better-off colleagues in the higher executive echelons. Possibly the only area in which they differ is in the sphere of education.

Methods of industrial evangelism

Methods practiced today include:

(i) *Infiltration evangelism*, implemented by groups or cells of Christian workers within an industrial establishment. It appears to be a program aimed at providing Christian fellowship, rather than one of supplying a platform for evangelism. The worker priest is a professional theologian taking up employment in industry.

(ii) *Presence evangelism* — This is initiated by industrial chaplains — men ordained by a denomination, who free-lance among a group of industries. They are not usually in charge of a church. The term "presence evangelism" derives from the fact that industrial chaplains normally do not conduct meetings within industry — they just "presence" themselves.

(iii) *Direct evangelism* — This is programmed by "Outreach to Industry," an organization actually conducting evangelistic meetings within industry.

(iv) *Personal evangelism* — This is implemented by individuals. Outreach to Industry invites individual Christians to attend a course of lectures on witnessing in industry.

The remainder of this paper will be given to discussing direct and personal evangelism.

1. Direct evangelism

a. *The industrial evangelist* — The gift of the evangelist is God's gift through the Holy Spirit to the Church. This was never more true than when it applies to an evangelist to industry, for the whole task of industrial evangelism is extremely delicate and even dangerous. It is a mine-field. Much damage can be done by the wrong person "having a go." Someone who is not called of God or equipped will do more harm than good.

Industrial evangelists, therefore, must be men of faith — miracle-working faith — demonstrating its power through their lives. Such faith will remove the mountains of practical and psychological difficulties which are peculiar to industry. Every time Outreach to Industry conducts a meeting in industry, it is a miracle.

Industrial evangelists must also be men of perseverance. Paul wrote in II Cor. 4:9, "We are knocked down, but we get up again and keep going." The industrial evangelist must have an attitude of mind and spirit that refuses to take "No" for an answer. Acts 16 relates the account of Paul's journey into Macedonia; please note that before this event Paul attempted to go into Asia and Bithynia.

Another essential qualification is wisdom. We are instructed to be " as wise as serpents." We are also instructed to receive wisdom. "He is always ready to give a bountiful supply of wisdom to all who ask Him" (Jas. 1:5). In every phase of industrial evangelism, whether it be in the early days of investigating, or the delicate stages of negotiations with management and unions, or the difficult days of organization, or the thrilling days of implementation, we will be in much need of heaven-sent wisdom.

Finally there must be sincerity — the love of Christ just breaking through us. It is this love that constrains us. Such love is completely disarming; it will always win through. It will never fail (I Cor. 13:8). There is, quite simply, no substitute for love.

b. *Industrial outreach* — This undoubtedly presents a unique opportunity to reach people who do not attend a church and would not be drawn into a major crusade meeting. A qualitative survey would reveal a far higher incidence of unconverted people in an industrial audience than in the audience of a central crusade meeting. The very process of going "out" with the Gospel meets the criticism of "cosy insideness" which is often leveled at the church and which must be regarded with some degree of seriousness. This cosy insideness is a real stumbling block to some non-churchgoers, while the very environment of an industrial meeting, when *used* by the speaker, lends credence to our claim that the Gospel is relevant to the modern industrial situation. Industrial Outreach, when it is carried out on an informal basis, provides unique facilities for real personal contact and the opportunity to relate the Gospel to personal needs expressed in question and answer sessions.

This function of industrial outreach is important enough in itself to merit mature consideration. It could be called *reaching out.* However, when industrial outreach is done within the context of a central crusade, it has another important function: that of *feeding in.* It has been found by Outreach to Industry that invariably an approach to industry results in a willingness to attend the central crusade meetings. The challenge, "We have been your guests, now come and be ours," has produced a response where an ordinary invitation via posters, personal invitations at home, etc., have failed. During the Billy Graham Crusade in the north of England and in London, workers were asked to "name the night," and were then given the appropriate tickets guaranteeing them seats for their families and friends. In many cases these were accepted as a direct result of the initial impact of the Gospel at the factory visit. Thus a properly implemented industrial outreach is not only valid for its own sake of "reaching out" — it is a useful means of "feeding in" unconverted men and women to the main crusade meetings.

(i) *Industry defined* — The term "industry" is a general one covering any establishment where any number of people are employed. The small industries which employ maybe two dozen people are just as important, if not more so, as the larger establishments. In my time I have spoken in banking houses, insurance offices with staffs of twenty to thirty, in department stores — some small, some large — as well as the general run-of-the-mill industries. There are innumerable small industries in town and city, and these afford a wonderful opportunity to reach people with the Gospel. Do not forget the men who stand guard in their district waiting to answer the call to put out a fire, the men who drive the buses, and the policemen.

So great is the scope that the difficulty lies in knowing where to draw the line. We have been invited to speak at social clubs attached to industries, at industrial conferences, management committees and industrial apprentice schools, and we have found it essential to include school-leavers in our program.

(ii) *Size of target* — How much industry can be taken in will be entirely dependent on the availability of speakers capable of handling industrial meetings, and on the number of days scheduled for the industrial outreach. There is no method of determining in advance the likely percentage of "refusals." Outreach to Industry has found that the situation differs so vastly from area to area that it is not possible to say, "Send out X more invitations than you expect to be able to handle." However, as will be shown later, there is good reason to aim at the widest possible field in making the initial invitation.

(iii) *Research* — It is worthwhile spending considerable time in the initial stages in researching information on the companies to be covered. Necessary information would include: correct name and address of company; subsidiary companies, or companies under same control; correct name, title, and position of best contact (normally the managing director); approximate size of company; working hours, "natural breaks," whether shift-work or uninterrupted work-flow; whether Worker's Christian Fellowship operates, and its strength; trades union affiliations.

None of this information is superfluous. Armed with all the facts set out above, you would avoid the possibility of any breach of courtesy, avoid duplication, have a clear picture of how an industrial visit could be "slotted in" with minimum disorganization, and have some idea of what you were "up against" before making any contact. At the same time it would be advisable to discover if there is any Christian influence within the factory, particularly at management or union level.

(iv) *Invitation* — By far the most successful method of getting goodwill, and paving the way towards factory visitation, is to invite selected Top Management to a luncheon as the guest of a Christian who may be a "big name" in the business world, or some local respected person. The name of the host lends stature to the event at a critical time before any persuading can be done. It is vital at this stage that the approach be as "well shod" and as professional as possible; that the luncheon be worthy of the occasion.

(v) *Luncheon* — The purpose here is threefold: to introduce, to inform, and to invite. Working within the goodwill created, and the informal atmosphere of the luncheon, the host should be briefed to introduce and outline the plan to visit industry. He should make use of the fact that many well-known companies have had industrial visits and in many cases requested the evangelist's return. Almost without exception, even where return visits have not been requested, Outreach to Industry has had no difficulty in arranging a second visit on their return to an area, even in those cases where the initial visit was only negotiated with considerable difficulty. Properly handled, industrial outreach is self-perpetuating among those factories which have experienced it.

The host should be briefed to ask for questions from the management present. He should press for company time to be allowed for the factory meetings — and expect to get it! An explanatory booklet should be prepared, outlining the industrial outreach plan, and given to each luncheon guest, and those present should be told that a personal follow-up will be made during the course of the next week or two. The time, energy, and care put into this stage of the approach to industry will pay dividends during the weeks to follow.

(vi) *Follow-up* — Those management who were invited but did not attend the luncheon should be followed up immediately with a letter, a copy of the explanatory booklet, and a request for an interview. If the latter is not acknowledged it should be followed up by telephone. Within a week or two of the luncheon, while the memory of it survives, an approach should be made to the luncheon guests, either by letter or telephone, requesting a personal interview. The purpose of the interview at the factory is to obtain outline approval for a factory meeting and to discover whether "factory time" is likely to be given. If conditions appear favorable, it is usual to discuss facilities and to request an interview with the union leaders or workers' representatives.

(vii) *Meeting the unions* — The purpose of this is to allay suspicion. Outreach to Industry has discovered that if the men suspect that the industrial outreach meeting is management-inspired gimmickry intended to "boost production," etc., few will attend the actual meeting. It is therefore worthwhile to insure that the men's representatives are fully in the picture. If the situation demands it, it could be advantageous to hold a reception for union leaders similar to that for management. It is likely, however, that it will be enough to meet these leaders in their factories.

(viii) *Analyzing the results* — At this stage, the pattern of the industrial visit becomes clear, and the results can be "graded." This involves suiting the factories to the evangelists available. For example, it is by no means true that a capable evangelist is automatically "at home" in the atmosphere of a typical factory meeting. On the other hand, in certain circumstances, where for example management has considerable Christian influence, it is perfectly possible to deliver a normal, three-point sermon. The other reason for grading results is that of giving priority to those factories offering the most advantageous facilities.

(ix) *Organization* — No evangelistic project is greater than its organization. We speak, of course, on a human level. We know that the Holy Spirit will elevate everything on to a new level, but faith in him is no excuse for insufficient organization. If a meeting in industry is to be successful it will require thorough and painstaking attention to detail. We must plan so that the least and lowest in the factory know all about the meeting — its exact time, date, length, and venue. If we are to gain the cooperation and support of the Personnel Management department, we must keep them fully informed of all our plans. We have found, moreover, that publicity can never be overdone, and we need to pray for Holy Spirit initiative in this area.

(x) *Final arrangements* — Only when management and unions have given the green light, and the committee has had an opportunity to make an outline schedule of visits geared to the time available, should dates and times be confirmed with the industries concerned.

(xi) *Implementation* — The great day has arrived, and it is good to remind ourselves that we wrestle not against flesh and blood but against principalities and powers. Anything can go wrong. Arrive in good time at the factory to allow for snags, and also to tie up any last-minute arrangements. Always honor the time allotted. If the company gives forty-five minutes, then conclude the meeting in forty-three minutes. If questions are asked, keep a strict eye on the time so as not to transgress. Should the meeting be held in the workers' lunch-time, then make a brief announcement as people are concluding the meal, and explain what is to happen. Stand down for a few minutes before beginning the actual meeting. At the conclusion of the meeting, have your literature ready. By far the best method, we find, is to ask men to come forward as an open declaration and take the literature from us.

2. Personal evangelism —

Someone has said that the Church has become a "pleasure cruiser," whereas it used to be a "lifeboat." Men were trained to go out on to the stormy seas of life and rescue people. Now we wrap our Christians up in cotton wool, and teach them the fine art of defense. We are even called "defenders of the faith." This was not the way the early church reached the then-known world. We Christians are not interested in survival, we are out to establish a kingdom. Our orders are "ALL the world ... EVERY creature."

We have the potential manpower in the church to impact the world. We need to mobilize the total Church for total involvement and total commitment to communicate the faith. If we can inspire and instruct every Christian to communicate at the point of contact — home, social circle, employment — then it is possible to reach this generation for Christ. Since we spend one-third of our lives at our employment this surely is a major mission-field for most Christians.

Wherever Outreach to Industry carries out its industrial program, it always seeks to set up what is now known as "Workers' Workshops." This is an attempt to inspire and instruct Christians to communicate their faith. Among the many things that are being taught, some are outlined as follows.

a. *Be sure of knowing God's will.* See life as a vocation. Paul has made it clear in his epistles, especially in his epistle to the Colossians, that to be filled with the knowledge of God's will is God's intended pattern for *every* life — whether that life be on some remote mission field or in a factory. This can only be achieved as we read and thoroughly digest Romans 12:1-2. The ramifications of doing God's will will mean (i) working for "THE" Boss, rather than "a" boss. (ii) Read Ezra 7:23, "Whatsoever is commanded by the God of Heaven, let it be *diligently* done ..." If this is God's will for my life, then it demands one hundred per cent obedience and diligence. (iii) "Be ye holy as I am holy." If by standing for truth and justice I lose my job, then this is God's will. I must be prepared for this. My times are in his hands, and if he allows one door to close, he will open another.

b. *Be committed.* Romans 8:14, "For all who are led by the Spirit of God are sons of God." Read Acts 8:26-40. Because Philip was led by the Spirit of God, he made the right decision, met the right person in the right place, and said the right things. Absolute control by the Holy Spirit will mean just this.

c. *Be positive.* Holy ambition is a very desirable Christian attribute, especially if we are seeking God's glory. We need Christian men and women in positions of responsibility at all levels in industry — in management, middle management, unions, etc. Very dangerous, I know, but then as Christians we are called upon to live dangerously. If atheism flourishes in industry today who is to blame — the vocal power-grabbing atheist, or the silent and passive Christian?

d. *Be brave.* "The fear of man bringeth a snare" (Prov. 29:25). One of Satan's greatest weapons is the weapon of fear. We are to triumph over this. There is no sin in fear. It becomes sin when we allow it to paralyze us. We must claim the victory over fear. We are bidden not to fear him who can destroy the body, but to fear him who can destroy both body and soul. Fear must be recognized, challenged, and triumphed over.

e. *Be believing.* If the individual Christian really believes what he professes to believe, we would be moving heaven and earth to make sure that everyone else had the opportunity to believe it also. Are we in danger of giving a mere mental assent to the great truths of the Bible? I think we need to ask ourselves, "Am I living as though I am someone who really believes in life beyond the grave?" General Booth of the Salvation Army is reputed to have said once to his workers that if he could have his way he would send every one of them to hell for five minutes. The man outside our church does not believe that we believe what we profess to believe. Do we give him grounds to think otherwise?

f. *Be prepared.* The *Living Bible* translates II Tim. 2:15 thus, "Work hard so God can say to you, 'Well done.' Be a good workman, one who does not need to be ashamed when God examines your work." I am aware of the dangers of being mechanical in learning the art of soul-winning from books and literature; however, many from experience have proved what a blessing it is to have guidelines. Why should we not learn from men who have great experience as well as being men of God? The Christian is likened to a soldier, an athlete. If he is to be a good soldier and a successful athlete, he must train. This we all recognize. I would urge my colleagues and pastors of flocks to include a regular Workers' Workshop in their church program. Help your people to be effective communicators of the faith.

g. *Be confident.* Jesus said to the woman of Samaria, "If thou knewest the gift of God ..." More than ever before we live in a world which wants truth to be backed home by experience. It is no use saying we have a mighty God and yet living as if he were no bigger than the span of a man's hand. The time must come when we must speak from the stimulus of personal experience. The Christian message is nothing if it is not relevant.

Conclusion

There is no Christian work more thrilling, more gratifying, than that of taking the Gospel to men and women "where they are" in industry. There is no experience more soul-satisfying than that of standing before an audience such as industry presents, where more than eighty or ninety per cent will never have heard the clear presentation of the Christian Gospel.

Industrial evangelism is, in addition, being realistic. Never before in the history of the Church was the need to "go where they are" greater than it is today. It is not my brief to say anything about the cause that has created the great "No-Man's Land" between Church and unconverted.

Sufficient to say that it exists, and few there are from either side who dare go over the top. In the multitude of conferences there wanteth no sin, but he that "doeth" is wiser than he that only "discusseth."

No one would be naive enough to deny the wisdom to learn basic principles, to discuss, and pick brains, but a man will often learn more in one hour of "doing" than in a month of learning "how to do." Therefore, *I appeal to my brethren around the world to launch out into the deeps of evangelism in industry. See how God will open doors for you, and in opening the doors will also give you the definite enabling to go through them.*

May we ... "*go in to possess the land ...*"

"*go into all the world ...*"

"*to every creature ...*"

STUDY GUIDE

1. Where does evangelism begin and where does it end? Realizing, of course, that it does begin and end with the Holy Spirit.

2. Are zeal and knowledge sufficient qualifications to implement the office of industrial evangelist?

3. What part does the Holy Spirit play in communicating the Gospel?

4. Is the Church able to reach the worker with its message? Has it ever reached and is it ever likely to reach the worker?

5. Is the Church adequately training its membership to witness effectively for Christ?

6. Is there precedence for believing that many successful social and industrial reforms have been motivated by the Christian message?

INDUSTRIAL EVANGELIZATION STRATEGY REPORT

For the purposes of our discussion and recommendation we have defined the term "industry" in a general way as follows: any establishment where people are employed.

With this as our guide we record that almost all peoples of the world spend approximately one-third of their lives in the environment of industry.

We believe that a major proportion of these people have not been evangelized and a vision has been given to us and a burden placed upon us for these people. We recognize the task as predominantly a "pioneering ministry" as little appears to our knowledge to have been done with it, except the fine ministry of Mr. Martin Higginbottom through the organization named "Industrial Outreach" and some spasmodic and isolated efforts in a few countries.

We recognize the differing nations and cultures covered within this vast mission field and the consequential varying emphasis and approaches required. Particularly do we mention the differences between an almost wholly Protestant country from those in which other religions predominate and where evangelical Christians are a very small proportion of the population.

There is no doubt in our thinking that the task of industrial evangelization is a huge one, but one that can and must be done. Marx has said, "Workers of the world unite." We believe the time has come for us to say, "Workers of the world — Christ can unite."

We recommend that:

1. An interim international Working Committee be formed to function initially through correspondence:
   A. To prepare, collate, and coordinate literature of an informative and motivating nature for distribution to Christian ministers, leaders, and lay Christians for the purpose of industrial evangelization in every area of the world.
   B. To organize and coordinate such other activities as are desirable and practical.
2. National Committees to be formed in each country:
   A. Where possible, use present participants at this Congress strategy meeting. Where no such delegate for a country is available, then such a national committee be formed on the initiative of interim international council.

For this purpose, names, addresses and present ministries of those persons here present who are prepared to take the initiative in their own country should be recorded for setting up such a national committee.

The interim international council should engage in research and study hindrances to Christian witness in industry, e.g., fear, losing job, other religions, hostility of employers, unions, and how they can be overcome.

A training program should be prepared to assist pastors and lay Christians. Strong efforts should be made to obtain "the acceptance and co-operation of trade union leadership in our approach to their membership." Christian trade union leaders should be approached a) to assist in this matter, b) to encourage them to witness for Jesus Christ within their own membership and the trade union movement in general.

Resources Required

1. We make the following suggestions as to the initial membership of the interim international committee: Mr. Martin Higginbottom, co-ordinator; Mr. L. Cush, Chairman; Mr. Bob Hodel, U.S.A.; Mr. Marpaing, Indonesia; Mr. D. Arputua R.A.J., India; Mr. Sam Dagher, Lebanon; Mr. John Paul, India; Mr. Norman Hudson, South Africa; Mr. S.J. Cabral, Mexico.

2. Professional persons who are Christians can produce suitable literature for motivation and training of both pastors and lay Christians. Mr. Higginbottom has access to such professional people as a result of his research into this matter.

3. Nowhere, to our knowledge is there existing material which specializes in meeting these specific needs. Printed material is needed.

4. We prefer that financial needs be met by the sale of the literature produced, and from donations and income of the national committees. As the need arises finance could be required for:

    a. Travel costs and salary of a key man (as, say, Mr. Higginbottom to travel particularly to the under-developed areas of the third world.)

    b. For salaries and materials for production costs of necessary literature.

        We ask the Congress Planning Committee to consider the ways and means which finances can be provided for the industrial evangelization of the third world in particular.

Conclusion

In all of this we ask for an undergirding of prayer by all concerned that the ministry of industrial evangelization shall be in the power of the Holy Spirit and that all motivational and training literature emphasize the call to prayer by all Christians for this purpose.

URBAN EVANGELISM

Roger S. Greenway

*Dr. Greenway, Grand Rapids, Michigan,
USA, is the Latin American Director of the
Board of Foreign Missions of the Christian
Reformed Church.*

Introduction

Urban evangelism begins in the Bible with Jonah's mission to Nineveh. It is highlighted in the New Testament by the ministry of Paul, the great urban church-planter of the apostolic period. During the first three centuries, Christianity grew best in the urban centers, but that has not been true in the modern period. Protestant churches in general have serious difficulties in the city and their impact on urban life is disappointing.

The purpose of this strategy paper is to focus attention on the city and the task of evangelizing city people. It is written with the conviction that the process of urbanization, which is so frighteningly swift in our day, can prove to be one of God's choicest blessings to Christian missions. But certain things must happen in order for these blessings to be realized, and that is what we intend to talk about.

PART ONE: THE URBAN SCENE

1. Growth and movement of city populations

The astonishing growth of city populations is one of the most awesome characteristics of modern life. Urban populations in the developing countries are doubling every fifteen years and are expected to number more than one billion by the end of this century. The problems generated by such large concentrations of people boggle the mind. Demographers predict that within twenty-five years, five-sixths of the population of the United States will be living on one-sixth of the nation's land, and that half of all Americans will live in two huge megalopolises, one extending from Chicago to Boston and Washington, and the other along the California coast from San Francisco to San Diego.

In the industrialized countries, urbanization began about a century ago and was closely related to industrial development and overall progress. But today, the runaway growth of city populations in non-Western countries is tragically out of pace with economic progress and industrialization. This has produced a kaleidoscope of problems for city governments, residents, and churches.

City populations grow for two principal reasons: internal, human multiplication, and rural-urban migration. People move from the countryside to small towns, and from towns to cities, because urban centers offer more opportunities for social and economic advancement. There are schools in the cities for the children, there are health care facilities, and hopefully a better way of life. Opportunities are few in the country, schools are scarce and inferior, and there is little hope for progress. Ambitious, aggressive families have no choice but to move to the city.

Alongside the mushrooming growth of older metropolitan centers, new towns planned on the drawing boards of urban designers are making their appearance in various parts of the world. New towns are generally created for the purpose of decentralizing existing urban concentrations and redirecting the flow of people to less densely inhabited areas of the country. Brasilia, the new capital of Brazil, is an example of this. Brasilia is one of the largest completely planned capital cities in the world. It was deliberately erected in the heart of Brazil's huge, almost empty interior in order to shift the growth of population from the crowded coastal areas to the underdeveloped middle of the country. Other examples are Canberra in Australia, Islamabad in Pakistan, and Chandigarh, capital of the Punjab. In East Africa, Tanzania intends to abandon its traditional port-capital of Dar-es-Salaam and erect a new capital, Dodoma, in the geographical heart of the country. Some urban planners are predicting that within the next few decades thousands of new cities, even ocean-floating towns, will be created to relieve crowded urban centers and shift the flow of population to new areas.

As one stream of population moves into the city, another tries to move out. Flight to the suburbs has characterized middle class populations in Western countries for several decades. The attitude of middle class people toward the city, and toward residential life in the city, is increasingly negative. Most North Americans, for example, show strong preference for suburban living. During the 1960s, central cities in the U.S.A. registered a 5.3 percent population gain while the suburban areas grew by 28.2 percent. A Gallup Poll conducted in August, 1972, found that only 13 percent of those questioned wanted to live in the city, which was down from 18 percent in 1968 and from 23 percent in 1966.

Protestant Christianity, it seems, prefers the suburbs also. Churches in Western countries have fled the cities along with their members. Old and stately church edifices now stand with broken windows and dreary facades like deserted "white elephants" in the inner city jungles. Around them are the poor, the unchurched, and the masses in turmoil. The congenial neighborhoods which these churches formerly served have changed. The former parishioners now worship God in the new churches they have built in suburbia, where "decent people live."

Public housing complexes, high-rise apartments, and condominiums have already changed the skylines of cities around the world, and the trend is likely to continue in that direction. If rising fuel prices keep people in the central cities and force some suburbanites to return to the cities, the percentage of urbanites living in apartment houses is certain to increase. The reasons why people prefer apartments seem to be universal: cheaper costs, safety, convenience, proximity to jobs, privacy, and freedom. Apartment dwellers develop a life-style of their own, and they are among the world's least approachable people. As the number of multi-residence structures grows, urban life in general will become increasingly conditioned by the peculiar psychology of these vertical villages. Despite their physical proximity, people will become more isolated from one another, and the friendly, open contacts upon which human society has traditionally depended will disappear.

2. Problems of city life

Crime, poverty, congestion, pollution, noise, racial polarity — these are the familiar problems of city life. They make the city so unattractive and hard to bear. Because of these problems, the city for millions is a place to avoid. It is a place to be left to the young and adventuresome, and to the poor and the elderly who cannot get away.

Why is the city plagued with such a disproportionate number of problems? The basic reason is also the most obvious: too many people, with all their needs, sinful inclinations, and diverse characteristics are pressed together in the city. The problems seem endless as the number of babies born each year keeps rising and rural-urban migration increases. Despite all the money that is spent on research and experimental programs, there is no plan in sight which will effectively ease the problems of the city or provide the social services, job opportunities, and adequate housing which the masses require.

Urban problems, like urban sprawl, take somewhat different forms around the world. Yet the overall picture is the same. Rubens Vaz da Costa, president of the National Housing Bank of Brazil, informs us that today over 60 percent of Brazilians live in cities and that in 1980 two out of every three will be a city dweller. While on the one hand he applauds urbanization as a hallmark of development, he says also:

> "Our cities are growing too fast. . .Over 5 million homes are classed as unfit for human inhabitation. . .500,000 units must be built annually just to keep up with present demand. . .only about 26 out of 54 million inhabitants were served in 1970 by water mains. . .only 13 million city dwellers have public sewage disposal. There is no way the 80 million people who live in cities in 1980 can have such service. . . We must learn to slow the rate of population growth so that our cities will not be inundated with people to the point where we can no longer adjust. . .no longer progress. . .no longer survive.

"The Lot of the Poor: A Struggle in Life and Death," was the title of a full-page article in *The Washington Post.* The "poor" referred to were city poor: the widow of a war hero unable to get the help that was owed her because of bureaucratic red tape; a mother of seven facing eviction and unable to find an apartment that would allow children; the body of an apartment dweller discovered after four months, sitting upright in the chair where he had died, alone. About five million people, or one-fourth of all persons over 65 in the United States, have no relatives, says the article. It is no surprise, therefore, that many live alone in bare rooms with little contact with other people. They live alone because they are poor, public transportation is not available or is difficult for them to reach, and the fear of crime prevents them from venturing far from their own residence. Since many of them are without telephones or anyone close by, there are no lifelines between them and the world outside. If they get sick in the night, they cannot call for help. They simply die.

"Urban anguish" is an expression used to describe the mental suffering, emotional insecurity, and utter loneliness of millions of city people around the world. Many of them are new migrants from rural areas, and they do not feel at home in the urban setting. Others are simply the poor, the indigent, and those who are ignorant of the basic services which even crowded, impersonal cities make available. Where but in the city are suicides so numerous and space, even cemetery space, so scarce?

The urban scene is not a pretty picture. But neither was medieval Europe with its crumbling empire, its vast movements of semi-civilized and barbarous peoples, and the external attacks of militant Moslems. Christianity suffered losses then too, and it often responded sluggishly and disappointingly to the challenges of its time. The main current of civilization seemed to be passing Christianity by, and some wondered if its days were numbered.

Nevertheless, from the bosom of the medieval church a continuous flow of missionaries poured out into unevangelized regions. Masses of people entered the Christian fold, and Christianity proved that it could survive the demise of one social order and the rise of a new. In the midst of that dark and uncertain period Christianity took firm root in Western Europe and set the stage for the most unprecedented, global expansion ever seen.

Right now, in almost every part of the world, social orders are changing, vast movements of people are taking place, and problem-filled urban centers are mushrooming. By the end of the twentieth century, ours will be an urban world. Some predict gloomily that Christianity will be lost in the city, and they point to the church's poor urban record as evidence for what they say. Others cling valiantly to the hope that the same Spirit who led the church out of the doldrums in the past will renew her again for urban mission in this hour.

"Arise, go to Nineveh the great city, and proclaim to it the proclamation which I am going to tell you." That is what God said to Jonah, and he is saying it again to churches today.

There lies the city. . .and our mission.

PART TWO: THE CITY CHURCH

1. Christian mission and the poor

The city needs the church and the church needs the city, but how does the one relate to the other? In this section we will look at various ways in which the church can relate to the changing city and fulfill its mission, especially to the poor.

The city needs the church because city life cannot endure, or be endured, without spiritual and moral dimensions. At the same time, the church needs the city because she has been commissioned by her Lord to preach the Gospel to all people, and cities are where people are. Behind every social problem threatening city life there lies a religious issue to which the Word of God speaks. Fundamentally, the crisis of the city is religious. Cities without God are beyond human endurance. Therefore, churches which proclaim the Word of God and the Lordship of Christ over city life hold the key to any real and lasting urban renewal.

Simply stated, the church's urban mission is to proclaim Christ as Savior and Lord, and to call city people to repentance, faith, and discipleship. "What is the city but the people?" To evangelize the city means to bring the Gospel to the people, rich people and poor, powerful and weak. It means to reach all races and social classes, all ethnic communities and tribal communities that live in the city. The city has institutions which are created by city people, and it has laws by which people govern themselves. The city has gods — false gods such as money, power, drugs, and sex — which influence urban life for evil at every stage. In opposition to the demonic forces at work in the city, the church proclaims the Saviorhood and Lordship of Jesus Christ. The result is the moral equivalent of war. Christ's Gospel challenges the vain philosophies of the pseudo-intellectuals and exposes the mass idolatry of men on the street. The church calls men to repent of sin and become new creatures in Christ Jesus.

In order to do this, the church must be present in the city, it must be in contact with city people, and it must proclaim its message in ways which people will understand. Mission to the city forces churches to make hard decisions and to reach out to people to whom they would not ordinarily minister.

Poor people all across the world are clustered in cities. In many ways the evangelization of the city means carrying the Gospel to the poor. This should not discourage anyone, for almost all great movements to Christ have had their base among the poorer classes. The Lord Jesus described his own urban ministry in these words, "The blind receive sight and the lame walk, the lepers are cleansed and the deaf hear, and the dead are raised up, and *the poor have the Gospel preached to them*" (Matt. 11:5). Throughout history, God has given to the poor and the humble an openness to the Gospel that is seldom found among upper classes. It follows from this that churches which fail to preach the Gospel to the poor are missing a great opportunity in the city. "Are the poor hearing the Gospel?" is a useful thumbnail question by which to evaluate an urban strategy.

3. Mission of the neighborhood church

a. *Middle class churches* — (i) *Characteristics:* They are "gathered" congregations located in congenial neighborhoods and ministering primarily to the needs of middle class people. Their membership is generally composed of people of a rural background or of immigrants who retain a certain amount of ethnic identity. The Sunday School is the primary tool to recruit new members and bolster the faith of old ones.

(ii) *Strengths:* Middle class churches minister effectively to people of their own "kind," and they are especially helpful in providing a sense of personal identity and moral religious community to newcomers to the city.

(iii) *Weaknesses:* They have little effect on the urban masses. They serve the needs and reflect the values of middle class people, but they have little appeal to the poorer classes. Today, many of these churches are hard hit by migration to the suburbs and they are unprepared for evangelistic outreach to the new people who have moved into the neighborhood.

b. *Institutional Churches* — (i) *Characteristics:* The Institutional church is a church-centered combination of spiritual and social ministry intended to meet the multiple needs of the urban poor. Included are such features as day nurseries, reading rooms, gymnasiums, counseling services, employment bureaus, and a wide variety of social services.

(ii) *Strengths:* Institutional churches are designed to stay in the inner city and adapt to the needs of changing neighborhoods. They aim to make the church a place where the total needs of persons in the city can be met. They rely heavily on lay men and women working with neighborhood people, and they seek to combine word-and-deed ministry in and through the organized church.

(iii) Weaknesses: Generally, they have been unsuccessful in bringing the urban poor and the working classes into the Protestant church. They have relieved the physical suffering of thousands of people, but they have made little lasting impact on the causes of urban suffering and the systems which keep the poor poor. Historically, Institutional churches gradually lose their spiritual emphasis and give major attention to charitable and social services.

c. Industrial Missions — (i) Characteristics: Industrial Missions aim to make Christianity relevant to modern industry and its problems, and to workers in both labor and management. Industrial missionaries spend long hours talking to working men in factory workshops and to company executives in committee rooms and paneled offices. They aim to apply the Christian faith to the circumstances of industry.

(ii) Strengths: Industrial Missions recognize that a serious communication gap exists between conventional churches and the modern industrial world. The approach of Industrial Missions is to try to bridge that gap by sending religious workers into industry as a mode of Christ's presence. From that base, they intend to communicate Christian teaching in the language of the laboring classes and enlighten established churches concerning the realities of the industrial world.

(iii) Weaknesses: Industrial Missions generally do not produce converts to the Christian faith. Nor do they add members to existing churches or found new ones. While correct in attempting to apply Christian principles to the industrial world, Industrial Missions tend to bypass the question whether laboring men and managers are born-again Christians. Moreover, workers are dealt with almost exclusively in the area of their employment and their families are unreached.

d. The Salvation Army — (i) Characteristics: Product of London's urban anguish and the evangelistic heart of William Booth, the Army was designed to meet the spiritual and material needs of the urban poor. The Army combines evangelistic fervor and social outreach with military-type dress and organization. Its specialized ministries include shelters for homeless men and women, prison work, homes for girls, rehabilitation of ex-convicts; and personal, one-to-one involvement with the city's poor.

(ii) Strengths: The Army has a century-long record of meeting the material and spiritual needs of the urban poor in many countries of the world. It has reached people and met needs with which conventional Protestant churches are not prepared to deal.

(iii) Weaknesses: The Army is neither a church nor a denomination, but a city-oriented missionary organization which has built-in difficulties as far as relating converts to regular Christian congregations.

e. Rescue Missions — (i) Characteristics: City Rescue Missions blend evangelistic fervor of a fundamental, biblical kind with a social concern for every type of human need in depressed areas of the city. Their special ministries include providing food and lodging for the hungry and destitute, homes for wayward girls and unwed mothers, youth programs, and the rehabilitation of alcoholics. Usually, Rescue Missions are independent or interdenominational, though some are sponsored by churches and denominations.

(ii) Strengths: Rescue Missions work directly with poor and destitute people of different races and nationalities in the inner city. They have been responsible for the spiritual and social rehabilitation of millions of people, and have channeled many into established churches. Rescue Missions reach city people that middle class churches are unable or unwilling to reach.

(iii) Weaknesses: Due to no fault of their own, and because of the very nature of their ministry and the people with whom they work, Rescue Missions do not become churches. Because of this, they can never provide the same degree of fellowship, instruction, and moral and religious stability which regular churches offer to families and individuals that enter their membership. Rescue Missions reach out to a floating population, to unstable families and to individuals whose lives have been devastated by sin. Often, their converts are not welcomed by, nor feel comfortable in, conventional churches. Seldom do Rescue Mission converts have what is required for future leadership either in the mission or in a church.

f. Store-front Churches — (i) Characteristics: Store-front churches are generally located on busy streets in poor areas of the city. They have names and characteristics all their own. Their leaders are usually of a charismatic type, and they preach a simple, emotional message that appeals mainly to the uneducated, to women and to children.

(ii) Strengths: They provide emotional release and some religious instruction to people who do not feel at home in conventional churches. Under good leadership, a Store-front church occasionally develops into a strong and stable congregation.

(iii) Weaknesses: Store-front churches are generally unstable and lack adequate leadership. Sermons are superficial and Bible instruction is minimal. Store-front churches have little connection with other Christian congregations and they make little real impact on urban life.

3. Mission of the neighborhood church

Churches perform an indispensable function in the city when they herald the Gospel, teach Christ's Lordship, and motivate their members to promote justice and mercy where they live and work. Churches provide the fellowship which lonely urbanites so desperately need, and the moral support and integration which city families require. Churches in the city can be the most effective instruments for the relief of human suffering and the rehabilitation of individual lives. They can do all this if they know their mission, are committed to it, and are willing to stay in the city and minister to city people.

A Christian church within walking distance in every neighborhood; mission-hearted pastors who will lead their congregations to welcome ragged newcomers and barefoot children into their fellowship; a sense of mission so atmospheric that every child of the church learns to share it — that is what the city needs. And that is the choice which city churches are asked to make. In his book *These Cities Glorious,* Lawrence H. Janssen describes the situation as follows:

> "Every day is a day of decision for some church somewhere. As change sweeps around urban churches they must make decisions affecting the future of their ministry for many years to come. Some will make the decision to remain islands in the midst of a strange sea. Some will remove their place of meeting to the suburbs, and will build a whole new life upon the resources of a community more favorable to the kind of ministry they have projected. Still others will remain where they are, accept the challenge of change and continue to minister as the Body of Christ. Whether or not churches survive as institutions does not matter; whether or not they are true to their mission does."

PART THREE: METROPOLITAN MISSIONS

1. Making disciples and planting churches

The focus of this final section is on the great metropolitan centers of the Third World countries where Christian churches are scarce and large sections of the population have never heard the biblical message of reconciliation.

Unfortunately, Protestants are weak in the area of urban strategy. By and large, Protestants do not know how to evangelize urban masses and multiply churches among them. For too long, cities have been places where Christians get lost and Protestant churches do not grow.

There is urgency about this matter. For while on the one hand city populations are growing and newcomers to the city are more open to the Gospel than ever before in their lives, the opportunity to win urban masses to Christian discipleship does not last forever. Once the new city dwellers have become urbanized beyond a certain point, receptivity changes to resistance and the opportunity to win them to Christ is lost.

For example, the Ramos Millan district of Mexico City was populated by newcomers in the late 1950s and early 1960s. During that time, residents were open to the Gospel and several Pentecostal churches sprang up. Had the denominational churches of Mexico City moved in to evangelize the area, they probably would have planted a number of growing churches among the poor who came to live there. But by the late 1960s, the streets in the Ramos Millan area had been paved, the houses were improved, the poor had moved up to a more stable, laboring class level of society, and when efforts were made at last by some denominational groups to evangelize the area, only a few people showed interest.

The goal of metropolitan mission work should be to plant a Christian church in every new neighborhood. Although this goal may appear to be exclusively spiritual, in reality it is social as well as religious. For churches, composed of the residents of the area, offer more effective remedies for the "hurts" of the city than any other form of association. The loneliness, insecurity, and frustration created by city life are ministered to best through the local assembly of Christians who meet regularly for worship and fellowship and belong to one another as brothers and sisters in Christ. The social impact of the Christian religion through the transformed lives of believers has more influence than any other factor in improving the quality of life in an urban community.

2. Modes of urban church planting

There are various ways to plant city churches and the following five deserve consideration:

a. The chapel to church method — A mission board or committee chooses a promising location, erects a chapel, and appoints a missionary or evangelist to conduct services and develop the chapel into a church. When the group of believers has grown sufficiently, it becomes an organized church. Denominational mission work often follows this method. The high price of land in the city, plus the rising cost of labor and materials, make this method increasingly difficult since it requires a large outlay of money for land and building. Indigenous churches can seldom afford to use this method without large amounts of foreign funds.

b. The mother-daughter method — An established, indigenous church encourages the development of "daughter" churches in growing areas of the city where some of its members have gone to live. Services usually begin in private homes with laymen playing a leading role. The "mother" church helps with some of the expenses and, eventually, when a building must be erected contributes toward the cost. Many older, well-established churches have in this way fostered the growth and development of scores of young churches and the opportunities for this kind of urban church multiplication are unlimited.

c. The Bible school approach — Bible schools train evangelists and future church leaders. A large part of this training consists in practical experience in evangelism. Evangelism is biblically defined and goal-oriented. It goes beyond simply personal evangelism to the planting of churches and community witness. Teachers and students canvass new areas of the city selling Bibles and witnessing to entire families in their homes. When doors are opened, they organize family Bible studies. Neighbors are invited in and Sunday services begin. Eventually, some of these groups become organized churches. The sprawling slums and working-class areas of major cities offer endless possibilities for church-planting by Bible schools. At the same time it is an effective way to train future leaders in the work of evangelism and church growth.

d. Apartment house evangelism — The apartment house has been called the "modern frontier of the church's mission." Unfortunately, no widely successful method has yet been devised for reaching apartment dwellers and planting churches among them. However, in places as scattered and diverse as Singapore and San Juan, Puerto Rico, missionaries and evangelists have established beachheads in large apartment complexes. They have started Sunday schools in private residences within the buildings, and in some cases apartments have been set aside as Christian Day Care Centers. In a few cases, permission has been obtained to conduct Sunday services in the auditoriums which many apartment buildings contain.

One clue to a successful apartment house strategy is to determine the type of apartment which you plan to evangelize. Not all apartment houses are alike. There are low rent apartments which attract poorer families and are the most accessible for evangelization. There are also the middle class apartments designed for better paid office workers and business people. These are less approachable so far as evangelization is concerned. Finally, there are the upper class, high-rise apartments where affluent, single persons or childless couples find the independence, privacy, and personal comfort which they seek. This group is the hardest to reach, and the family orientation of most churches does not appeal to them at all.

  e. The house-church method — Several of the methods already discussed utilize the house-church principle. Simply stated, it is this: the church is not a building but an assembly of believers organized according to biblical patterns and meeting regularly around the Word and sacraments. Any house, apartment, or rented facility, can serve as the meeting place.

  House-churches generally develop out of Bible study groups, which in turn result from house-to-house visiting and personal invitation. Only about one-third of the groups survive to become real house-churches. The success of a house-church depends to a large extent on the number of weekly calls that are made. As a rule of thumb, during the early stages it takes fifteen to twenty calls to get five persons to a meeting. Services begin with six to eight persons. Average attendance for the first year or two may fluctuate between ten and twenty persons, depending on the size of the meeting place and the amount of calling that is done each week. The majority of churches begun in this way do not attain a membership of more than fifty persons for a decade or more.

  It is important that house-churches be related to other groups and to a wider Christian community for fellowship and mutual support. House-churches do not easily fit the rules and structures of traditional denominations, for by their very nature house-churches are highly flexible organizations. Nevertheless, the house-church will probably be the organizational form in which Christianity grows the fastest during the remainder of this century, and therefore church leaders should do everything possible to fit it properly into their ecclesiastical structures.

Conclusion

  In some parts of the world more people can be won to Christian discipleship in rural villages than in large cities. But with the movement of masses of people to the urban centers unique opportunities are created to present the claims of Christ and plant churches. New urbanites are free from the social ties and village pressures which previously kept them from reading the Bible and attending Christian services. In the city they are free to think new thoughts and investigate new religious experiences. During their initial period in the city they are particularly receptive to spiritual truth and the opportunity for personal fellowship. That is the time when they must be reached with the Gospel.

  Concentration of efforts on the teaming masses of urban people in developing countries does not mean that country people are to be neglected. In fact, urban evangelism may be the most effective means of reaching the towns and villages from which the city newcomers have moved. As relatives move back and forth between city and country, the faith which they have heard in the city travels back home. Countless village churches have been started in precisely this way.

The Mayan village of Komchen, not far from Merida, Yucatan, Mexico, was as closed to the Gospel as any village could be until five years ago. Then the local henequen industry failed and the men of Komchen had to commute to Merida to work in the factories. Some of them heard the Gospel in Merida, and they brought Bibles and Christian literature back to their village. Today, there is a thriving Protestant church in Komchen, with local leadership, their own building program, and excellent attendance at their four weekly services.

The church must learn to evangelize the city. The growth of cities is the great fact of our era and it provides the church an opportunity to win great numbers to Christ. No other area in evangelism deserves more urgent attention.

Urban Evangelization Among the Poor

Secretary: Clarence L. Hilliard

Urban evangelization among the poor requires a proclamation of the whole Gospel and a marshaling of the vast abilities and resources of Christ's Church for the purpose of ministry.

Definition of terms

Urban The great metropolitan areas of the world.

Poor People lacking adequate resources to meet essential health, education, and shelter needs.

Powerless People unable to alter the detrimental situation in which they find themselves because they lack both sufficient personal resources and contacts with agents and forces capable of effecting change.

Oppressed People caught in a situation where all forces of authority and power actively or passively, legally or traditionally support individuals and/or agencies that operate to their detriment.

Evangelization The proclamation of the Good News in Christ that does not dichotomize but may distinguish between evangelism" and "social action." In it we declare through word and deed that God has acted through Jesus Christ to reconcile believers both to God and men; to call men to repent of all that denies faith in God, to exercise saving faith in our Lord Jesus Christ; to submit to his reign and seek to establish the righteousness of his kingdom among men.

A number of significant ideas contributing to the subject of the paper were suggested by the group. Firstly, there are many sound biblical reasons evangelicals should have a special concern for the poor, the powerless, and the oppressed. For example, God's great concern for the impoverished is found throughout the Bible. In the Old Testament the burden of the matter is captured by Isaiah,

"Is not this the fast that I choose to loose the bonds of wickedness, to undo the thongs of the yoke, to let the oppressed go free, and to break every yoke? Is it not to share your bread with the hungry, and to bring the homeless poor into your house; when you see the naked to cover him, and not to hide yourself from your own flesh?" (Isa. 58:6,7) (Also see Isa. 61:1,2; Ezek. 16:49.)

In the New Testament the love of Christ further constrains us. Christ cited his holistic ministry of evangelization among the poor as convincing evidence of his Messiahship (see Matt. 11:2-5). In view of the biblical evidence and the great unmet needs, evangelicals must respond to the widespread urban anguish experienced by this vast group around the world.

The general approach of seeking to remedy old individual problems rather than dealing with the causes of injustice and inequality will always create frustration for the thoughtful, sensitive, involved Christian. In order to deal with causes that are fostered and maintained by institutionalized evil, evangelical Christians must develop a technique for (learn) the institutionalization of good. The apostles' teachings on the gifts of the Spirit may be helpful at this point. Scripture teaches that everything we have including all resources and abilities are gifts. "What have you that you did not receive? If then you received it, why do you boast as if it were not a gift?" (I Cor. 4:7).

Believers should employ all they have for ministry to the body of Christ and through the body to the needy world. "As each has received a gift, employ it for one another, as good stewards of God's varied grace...whoever renders service as one who renders it by the strength which God supplies, in order that in everything God may be glorified through Jesus Christ" (I Pet. 4:10,11 c.f. I Cor. 12:7).

Evangelical Christian education must take up the full burden for urban evangelization among the poor, and seriously train believers in a Christian life view. Believers need to understand that not only must we seek to relate the poor to Jesus Christ and get them grounded in the Word, but we must also use our individual professions, skills, and resources in responsible service to the poor of the church local and universal, and through the church to the larger community around us (II Cor. 8:13).

Failure at this level of ministry may go unnoticed in first generation Christians with such deep needs that the most elemental expressions of a caring community are very satisfying. Many second generation youth, however, raised in Christian homes will have appetites for more socially significant roles, including commitments to the cause of the dispossessed on issues of justice and righteousness by God's representative community. At this time in history, a balanced emphasis on the whole Gospel is crucial to meet the fuller challenge to the church to be God's penetrating, full-robed light. The Church must be an unfailing, active influence, and a saving agency within a faithless, selfish, degenerate society.

Christian prophetic preaching must also take its rightful place if the forces of good are to be effectively institutionalized for holistic evangelism among the poor. Evangelicals must clearly proclaim what it means to be Christian on a level that will be fully challenging to every would-be follower of Christ and truly expressive of Christ's establishment of God's new community on earth, that in everything God may be glorified through Jesus Christ our Lord.

In the paper, a number of patterns of urban mission were suggested that one might investigate for help in this area:

Gorbals, Glasgow, Scotland;
  Black churches in America, various denominations;
  Black churches in England, Pentecostal;
  Church of the Redeemer, Houston, Texas;
  Circle Church, Chicago, Illinois, Evangelical Free
  Church of America;
  Evangelical Urban Training Project, England;
  First Presbyterian, Songnam, Satellite City, Seoul, Korea;
  Gorbals, Glasgow, Scotland;
  Inter Link, Wheaton, Illinois, Interdenominational;
  Iona Community, Scotland;
  Pentecostal Methodist "Haven of the Masses," Chile;
  Pontales Interdenominational Church, Mexico City;
  Reba Place, Evanston, Illinois;
  Salvation Army Hough Community Service Center,
  Cleveland, Ohio

In the light of Jesus' explicit priorities, which constitute the biblical theme of this Congress, i.e., "to preach good news to the poor...proclaim release to the captives, and recovering of sight to the blind, to set at liberty those who are oppressed, to proclaim the acceptable year of the Lord" (Luke 4:18,19); in response to the challenge of proclaiming the Gospel to the exploding populations of the urban poor; and in view of our commitment to a biblical understanding of the lordship of Christ, to which we summon men in the obedience of faith, we affirm that evangelicals are required to share God's concern for justice and righteousness, and to commit themselves to strive for their realization in the particular societies within which they are called to live out their faith. Therefore, we suggest the following goals for promoting urban evangelism among the poor:

1.   Evangelicals must make urban communities a priority objective for evangelization.

2.   Seminary education must make training for urban ministry available and meaningful.

3.   Evangelical lay people should seriously consider committing themselves to live in the inner city and other concentrations of urban poor in order to establish effective caring communities whose embodiment and proclamation of the Gospel will thereby be rendered credible and understandable to their neighbors.

4.   Evangelicals should support caring ministries throughout the world, to build up the body of Christ. Ministry in all parts of the world requires support of the body of Christ. Evangelicals, therefore, must be called to commit all their resources and abilities for ministry in and through the body of Christ to the world.

5.   Denominational and cooperative strategies should be devised for the effective evangelization of the urban poor and the establishment of vital, responsible, and growing churches in the many pieces of the mosaic which constitute the urban masses. This concern is particularly urgent in the largely unevangelized, rapidly growing, and often receptive urban populations of the Third World. The forms will vary widely, from large institutional churches to small house churches meeting in apartments or homes. Appropriate forms should be developed for each situation.

A number of other resources were suggested by our group: *An Urban Strategy for Latin America* by Roger Greenway; *Built As a City,* David Sheppard; *Crucial Issues In Missions Tomorrow,* ed. Dr. McGavran; *Missionary Methods, St. Paul's or Ours,* Roland Allen; *A Manual for Social Service,* Salvation Army, U.S.A.; *Mobilizing the Laity,* Jev Braun; *Haven of the Masses.*

For the ongoing work of the strategy group, Urban Evangelization Among the Poor, we propose that a worldwide institute on urban strategy be organized.

EVANGELIZATION AMONG MINORITY RACIAL GROUPS

Patrick Sookhdeo

*Mr. Sookhdeo, London, England, is on the
staff of the Evangelical Alliance working
with those from overseas.*

Minority groups, according to the Rev. In Ha Lee of the National Christian Council of Japan, can be defined thus:

"A group of people generally constituting a homogeneous unit, speaking a common language, claiming a common ancestry, living in a particular geographical area. Within this definition various sub-classifications are possible, such as: ethnic minorities, historical class minorities, aboriginal or tribal minorities, indigenous and non-indigenous minorities. These 'cultural minorities' are peoples who by situation, experience and birth are involved consciously and unconsciously in voluntary and involuntary association separate from, yet part of, a foreign society.

"Such cultural minorities of the world today are where they are culturally, socially, geographically, economically for various reasons. Some left a majority setting (willingly or by force) and have gone to another cultural, geographic, racial setting where they are in the minority. Others are peoples pushed into the backwash of modern movements through immigration of a large number of 'foreigners' who then claimed their own majority rights as landed immigrants. All of these minorities are involved to varying degrees in the phenomena of the age — rapid change, mobility, nationalism, modernization, education, demythologizing, industrialization are the descriptive words that come to mind."

1. Classification of minority groups

Minority groups can therefore be classified into the following categories:

a. *Tribal minorities* — These would include Amerindians in South America, Aborigines in Australia, Konds in India, etc. Because tribal minorities tend to be covered by such missionary societies as Wycliffe Bible Translators, and require specialist handling, for our purposes they will be excluded from this paper, apart from occasional references.

b. *Refugees* — The results of war, political and religious oppression, famine, etc. — these are to be found in most countries of the world and their numbers are increasing. Examples include the Biharis in Bangladesh, Eastern Europeans exiled throughout the world, Asians from Uganda, etc.

c. *Migrant workers* — These have come into being through two causes; the first is the Pull Factor, whereby countries with greater economic, demographic, and social developments in need of manpower have a drawing effect on those outside its borders. The second is the Push

Factor, whereby people living in conditions of high unemployment and poverty leave these areas in search of economic betterment. There are four main areas of migration in the world today.

In Western Europe are an estimated eleven million immigrants, from a wide diversity of races, cultures, and religions. These are made up of three basic categories: Europeans who have moved from one highly developed country to another (e.g., Germans in Britain); migrants from economically backward countries in Europe to more highly developed parts (e.g., Turks in Germany, Southern Italians in Switzerland); and migrants from Third World countries (e.g., South Asians in Britain, Arabs in France, Indonesians in the Netherlands).

In Southeast Asia, many of the countries have communities of Indian and Chinese origin (e.g., Koreans in Japan). In Africa, there are Indian communities, particularly in East Africa, black mine workers in Southern Africa, and other African nationals crossing territorial borders in search of work. In North America are Puerto Ricans, Cubans, Chinese, and others.

d. *Historical racial minority groups* — These would include groups such as Blacks in Brazil, Gypsies in Western Europe, Blacks in the United States, etc.

2. Difficulties encountered by minority groups

Although one is dealing with a wide variety of cultural, social, racial, and religious characteristics, there are a number of points common to most minority groups.

a. *Conflict of cultures* — This occurs in three areas: (i) conflict between newcomers and natives; (ii) conflict between newcomers prepared to accept new values and those who seek to preserve traditional values; (iii) conflict between the children of immigrants who learn to accept the local culture, and their parents who cling to their own culture.

b. *Deprivation* — Here too three areas are involved. (i) Social deprivation: this includes employment, where the people concerned often hold subordinate positions in the labor market; accommodation, where they tend to concentrate in run-down areas with inferior housing conditions; and education, where both they and their children suffer from lack of educational opportunities. (ii) Political deprivation: in some countries, minority groups are restricted in what they can do and where they can go. They may or may not be able to vote, and often have few or no political rights. (iii) Psychological deprivation: members of minority groups who face social and political deprivation often react by withdrawing into themselves. This comes from feelings of insecurity arising from uncertainty about majority attitudes; a sense of loss of identity leading to their becoming unsure about what community, culture, and country they really belong to (which feeling increases with their length of stay); and feelings of inferiority and insignificance which arise when they hear themselves being discussed as a "problem" and when they encounter prejudice and discrimination.

Webster's Dictionary defines prejudice as "an unreasonable or an unjustifiably adverse opinion without any just grounds or sufficient cause." It is basically irrational and because of this it can be easily fed, with any materials which support its views, irrespective of their validity. One example of this is seeing the minority group as the "scapegoat" for all the ills of society, whether they be economic or social. This was illustrated by Nazi Germany's treatment of the Jews in the 1930s, and is seen today in the attitude of the French toward the Arabs, the British toward the Black immigrants, the Dutch toward the Turks, the Japanese toward the Koreans, President Amim of Uganda toward the Asians, etc.

Whereas prejudice can be defined as an attitude, discrimination represents a form of behavior. Segregation of minority groups in education or transportation, restrictions about choice of residence, limitations in economic opportunities, are all examples of discrimination. Christians need to beware that they do not reproduce the attitudes and actions of their majority community in the treatment of minority groups.

The effects of deprivation, both social and political, and that prejudice and discrimination do have a profound impact upon the lives of individual members of minority groups, and also on the groups corporately. Individually a person may become withdrawn, inward looking, insecure, suspicious, ready to treat the least thing as a sign of discrimination. All this leads to loneliness and frustration, lacking the sense of knowing where he belongs, and the questioning of who he is. In Western countries the Black migrant may identify oppression and discrimination with Christianity, and his rejection of it may be on that basis.

Corporately the minority group will build around itself walls which do not allow anyone in or out. They become complete self-contained units, functioning independently of the majority community. Because of this, their culture and religion increase in meaning and fervor, for these become the link with their past, all that they hold most dear, and all that they look forward to. This is illustrated in Britain by Muslims giving cultural and religious instruction to their children of up to twenty hours a week on top of normal schooling. To such a community, conversion to Christ will be seen as presenting a threat to their structure. When the individual is asked to make a decision for Christ, he may interpret this as having to align himself with the majority people and reject his minority group. One of the major problems of evangelizing minority groups in lands with a Christian heritage is that the barrier to accepting Christ is often not theological but cultural and communal. Even if there is no Christian heritage, the group consciousness will still exert tremendous pressure on the individual, and this in part determines the way in which he responds to the Gospel.

3. A biblical understanding of minority groups

Although no specific doctrine, as such, can be built on this subject, there is sufficient teaching in Scripture to warrant a study. This will be done by studying basic biblical doctrines and noting their implications.

a. *The doctrine of Creation* — Scripture teaches that all men are made in the image of God, and that they have a common ancestry in Adam (Gen. 1:27f.). The biblical declaration is that God has made of one blood all nations on the earth (Acts 17:26). This Scripture speaks of one race and one race only, i.e., the human race. Man was not created to exist in a vacuum, but to exist in an interdependent relationship with his brother.

The creation points to the fact that this is God's world, not ours; none of us has a prior claim to it. What have we more than others, that we have not received? Moreover, migration was part of the creation ordinance. God's command to Adam was that he should multiply and fill the earth (Gen. 1:28). The Old Testament contains numerous accounts of both voluntary and forced migrations, of migration of individuals, and migrations of whole peoples. This doctrine of creation cuts across all pride of race, nationality, and culture. It points to man's need of his brother, and his duty to minister to him. He *is* his brother's keeper.

b. *The doctrine of sin* — All men through Adam have sinned (Rom. 5:12). This sin has entered into every part of human life and society. In the Genesis account, after the Fall not only was man's relationship with God affected, but also his relationship with the created world, with his wife, man and his brother man (Cain and Abel), human institutions (Cain built a city), human customs (Lamech started polygamy) (Gen. 3:9,17, 16b; 4:9,17,19). The first point to note is that sin and evil are woven into the very fabric of human society, with the result that injustice and conflict arise. Second, all men are sinners, irrespective of color, culture, class, or nationality. This means that minority groups are no more sinful than majority groups — they are both sinners and so exhibit the traits of sin. Third, anything that separates man from his fellowmen is sin, whether it be pride of race or of culture, prejudice in attitudes, or discrimination in treatment of others.

c. *The doctrine of salvation* — Christ's death on the Cross broke down the middle wall of partition between Jew and Gentile (Eph. 2:11-21). It brought into being a new community comprising men and women of every nation, tribe, and tongue, joined together in mutual love and worship for their Lord (Rev. 5:9,10; 7:9; Gal. 3:28), and characterized by concern for and practical service toward each other. It broke through the racial barrier, the cultural barrier, and the class barrier (Acts 13:1-3 demonstrates this unity in church leadership at Antioch). The invisible unity which bound them together found practical expression in their corporate worship.

d. *The doctrine of God* — Because God is sovereign and in control over nations and their destinies, he has absolute sway over authorities and governments which are a part of his provision for the world. Their authority and role in the maintenance of order and justice come from him (Rom. 13:1-7). This means that they are ultimately responsible to him for their actions. They therefore have a duty to practice justice and to exercise humanity and compassion.

In the Old Testament, the Jews were given specific injunctions on how they were to treat the foreigner and alien in their midst (Exod. 23:9; Lev. 19:34; Deut. 10:19). They were to love the migrant, accept him as an equal, welcome and provide for him, make sure he was not ill-treated, that his rights were safeguarded, and that he obtained justice. To go against these injunctions was to bring the wrath of God upon themselves. One of the reasons Saul was removed as king and the people of Israel afflicted was because of his treatment of a minority group (the Gibeonites, II Sam. 21:1). In Matthew 25, the chapter dealing with the final judgment, Jesus pictures himself as a stranger — an immigrant, an alien — and then bases his judgment on the reception and treatment of this type of person.

From this the following points need to be noted: (i) Discrimination against any ethnic minority group cannot be justified on any grounds. (ii) Political and social expediency can never take the place of moral imperatives. As David Pawson puts it, "When national loyalty becomes an 'ism' and takes priority over moral imperatives, all kinds of evil appear." (iii) Christians because of their calling to be 'salt' must not only be sure that they are not on the side of the oppressor, but that they are positively and actively standing up for rightness, righteousness, and justice, in the treatment of minority groups.

e. *Summary of biblical teaching* — This can best be expressed in the words of Dr. H.D. McDonald of London Bible College, who says:

"The biblical declaration is that God has made of one (blood) all nations that are on the earth; what then is the presence of a minority in the midst of a people, but the God-given opportunity for that people to rise to moral heights, and to test its basic convictions amid the hard realities which such circumstances occasion? Sometimes the existence of a minority, not understood, reacts in judgment upon a nation which fails to meet aright the subsequent moral challenge. The whole drift of Christ's outreach was toward the social and racial outcast while his polemic was directed for the most part toward the religious world. To regard, and to treat another, as a lesser breed without the law, is to undercut the whole biblical doctrine of redemption. For if by one (blood) all are made, is it not also by one blood that all are redeemed? In the teaching of Jesus the neighbor was one of a Samaritan minority; and he bids those who would be followers of his way to have a concern for the outsider on the roadside."

Minority groups should not just be important to the few Christians or churches which may be involved in some ministry towards them, but to the whole church both nationally and internationally. None of us can escape the challenge of the migrant. It was Gandhi who stated, "Civilization is to be judged by its treatment of minorities." So too will the Church.

4. *The Christian's ministry to minority groups*

Before his departure, the Lord Jesus gave to his disciples two commissions, and both of these need to be fulfilled in the evangelizing of minority groups: the commission of compassion and service (Matt. 25:34-36), and the commission of evangelism (Matt. 28:20).

a. *Compassion and service* — The needs of minority groups vary and are dependent on country and conditions. Most of them, however, do have specific needs, and at this basic level a Christian ministry should be exercised. Some suggestions for possible action follow.

(i) Become better informed, not only on the local situation, but also about national issues and personal attitudes.

(ii) Meet and build mutual relationships with individual members of minority groups. An excellent method is by visiting each other's home.

(iii) Discover the specific needs of your minority groups and seek ways of meeting them. In Britain, for example, two areas of need are the large numbers of Asian women who do not speak English, and the problems of children at pre-school age who know only their home culture and language and so find it difficult to relate when they attend a school where English children are present. To meet the latter needs, churches have established home tutorship schemes whereby Christian women go into the homes of Asian women and teach them English. For the children, churches have established play-groups whereby children of the majority and minority groups can meet and play together. In other countries, minority groups may face other problems such as bad housing, unemployment, lack of food and medical care, etc. Christians should seek to discover what these needs are and should actively engage in the meeting of them.

(iv) Remember that the basic needs of minority groups often lie in the emotional and psychological realm. The need is for acceptance, understanding, security, and justice.

The Christian should, therefore, be in the forefront of any movement which would seek the fulfillment of these basic needs. He should also actively stand against injustice, prejudice, discrimination and segregation.

(v) Christians should not dwell on the "so-called" problems, i.e., in the political, sociological and economic realms, that are said to be caused by members of minority groups, but instead see their Christian duty and responsibility to these peoples. God, in his Sovereignty, has allowed such people in their present situations to exist for what purpose but that the church in that land may have the privilege of demonstrating his love and proclaiming his Gospel to those who have never heard.

b. *Evangelism* — It must be borne in mind that often there are language, cultural, and religious barriers involved in the evangelizing of minority groups. This may necessitate the use of specialist workers who can speak their language and are acquainted with their culture and religion. While such a person can be most effective, this must never be allowed to detract from the involvement of the local church. Individual church members are to be involved in this ministry. Members of minority groups often turn to Christ when an ordinary Christian has demonstrated practical love and compassion. This expressed love has the effect of winning their confidence, overcoming their fears, and demonstrating that though culturally or racially different they are equal and wanted. When this takes place and is followed by the proclamation of the Gospel, the heart prepared often responds. This has been the experience of the writer who, as a member of a minority group in Britain, responded to the love that was extended to him by a small group of English Christians, and so turned to Christ.

(i) Materials for evangelism might include the following: Gospel recordings on discs (available in most languages free of charge), cassettes, and tapes; the possible use of radio in the appropriate language; complete Bibles or portions; evangelistic literature and films. The United Bible Societies have started a program of specific literature preparation for migrants in Western Europe. This deals with problems faced by minority groups, and gives a biblical solution. Such material could be produced, as needed, in other parts of the world.

(ii) The planning of an evangelistic outreach. Before this takes place, information must be obtained on background, culture, religion, language, and needs of the minority group. This would help to determine the correct approach and so make the Gospel meaningful and relevant to the people in their situation. Not all minority groups, however, are differentiated by language and culture. Race or even religion may be the characteristic that marks a group as a minority one, e.g., West Indians and Roman Catholics in Britain.

(iii) Special meetings can be arranged. At an "international evening" different cultures and races can be invited to a social gathering with church members, followed by a brief introduction to the Christian faith. Then, too, a debate can be held between Christians and members of another religion; this is a good method of presenting the Gospel. A film evening can offer either evangelistic or educational films in a minority language; this has a drawing effect, bringing people together, and the Gospel can be presented at the end of the evening.

Although initial difficulties may occur during the actual evangelization of the minority group, these do not end with conversion. Some of the continuing difficulties are: treatment of the new convert, for his conversion may be interpreted as a changing of sides and he may meet with rejection from his own people; culture conflict, when he may find difficulty in understanding Christians and in participating in church activities, and which may lead on to loneliness and depression; and relationship of the new convert with the church, particularly if language and culture are involved.

There are three possible solutions to the above problems. (i) Complete integration of new converts into the life and membership of the church from the very start. (ii) Establishing a separate group for the new converts where they can be taught in their own language to worship in a way that is culturally meaningful to them. They can then witness to their own people without seeming to have changed sides. (iii) Establishing a separate group for the new converts where they will be taught in their own language, but will worship and witness with the whole church, hoping in time to achieve full integration.

A point which needs to be noted is that converts often come in a trickle and not in large numbers. They often come also as individuals and not as whole families. It is this that may determine what one does with the new converts. Whatever decision is taken, one needs to be sure that there are no underlying racial presuppositions.

Minority groups are, by and large, a neglected element in our world. As Christians we need to develop a new awareness and concern for those caught in the dilemma of not belonging. They are not a *problem* but our *responsibility*. If the earth is to hear His voice, then the church will have to take seriously these many millions who have never heard the glorious Gospel. If the church fails to evangelize minority groups in her midst, then what right has she to cross the oceans to make disciples of other men far, far, away? How can she claim to love those she has never seen, when she has not loved those whom she has seen?

EVANGELISM AMONG RACIAL MINORITY GROUPS

David Bendor-Samuel

Dr. Bendor-Samuel, Stokenchurch,
Buckingham, England, is Home Director in
the British Isles of Wycliffe Bible
Translators.

The term "racial minority group" can be applied rather widely to any group that is ethnically distinct from, and smaller than, the people or nation within whose territorial bounds it is living. The characteristic which warrants separate consideration for such groups in regard to evangelism is that they are sufficiently different from the majority group(s) as to be very little reached by evangelistic efforts directed to the latter. This is due not only to a difference in race, but also to differences of culture and (generally) language which are also present.

Among the many racial minority groups in today's world, the two following categories constitute a special challenge, and require a distinct strategy of evangelism:

    (i) Immigrant minorities not yet assimilated into the national life.

    (ii) Indigenous minorities with a status which is inferior to that of the national majority.

Groups of the first kind are to be found within many of the developed countries of the world as a result of widely different factors. Examples include groups of Chinese in East Asia, Japanese in Brazil, Pakistanis in England, and Gypsies throughout Europe, to name but a few. Their circumstances, and the strength of their ethnic identity or degree of assimilation into the host nation, differ very widely. In many cases difficulties associated with language do not seem very acute (at least superficially) since members of such groups generally gain a fair command of the national language. There may also be adequate provision for education, which tends to reduce differences of culture over a period of time.

By contrast, many of the groups of the second category are much more isolated from the life of the nation of which they form a part, and barriers of culture and language are more serious. Indigenous minority groups are to be found in almost every part of the world except Europe, the number of minority languages spoken being estimated as upwards of three thousand. It must be noted again that their circumstances and the degree of their isolation differ widely in different parts of the world. Whereas the life of a minority group in the Amazon basis is radically different from the life of Latin American cities in both language and culture, a minority group of sub-Saharan Africa may be close to West African city life in both respects. Generalizations concerning evangelism among minority groups must therefore be understood to allow for exceptions arising from these variations.

How great is the need for evangelism among racial minority groups today? While some indigenous minorities remain which are virtually unreached, some kind of evangelism is being undertaken for many hundreds of indigenous groups, and also among many immigrant groups. Conversions are reported from many areas, but evangelism cannot be regarded as truly successful until an indigenous church is established which is able to carry forward the evangelization of the rest of the minority group. The question is not only, "How much more evangelism remains to be initiated?" but also, "How far is existing evangelism being carried on in a way which will bring the desired results?" and, therefore, "How far is a new approach to this evangelism advisable?"

Special Factors and Problems

The evangelism of racial minorities may involve special factors of location and political sensitivity. More basic problems, however, lie in the area of communication, with differences of language and culture, and in subconscious attitudes resulting from being a minority culture. These will now be discussed briefly. Indigenous minorities will be chiefly in focus, as the more extreme cases, but many of the problems are relevant, though perhaps less acute, for immigrant minorities too.

a. *Difficulties of physical location* — Some indigenous minorities live in places difficult for an outside evangelist to reach, e.g., tribal groups in Papua, New Guinea. Others are easy of access for brief visits, but very difficult for intimate contact over a long period, e.g., Gypsy groups. Even immigrant minorites living in urban centers may present problems of this kind, since it is often hard for an outsider to live among them. The upbringing and education of the evangelist's children may present serious problems in many cases.

b. *Political Sensitivity* — Minority groups frequently constitute volatile material, politically. Governments may seek to prevent work they see as likely to cause disturbance within the minority group, or to foster a spirit of independence. They have often regarded work in the vernacular, and especially the provision of an alphabet and literature, as dangerous, and therefore have forbidden it. They are increasingly sensitive to the activities of foreigners in such situations.

c. *Difficulties of communication* — In a large majority of cases, the people of the minority group normally use their own language for conversation among themselves. In extreme cases hardly anyone in the group speaks another language, and the few that do so only use this for elementary trade purposes. More commonly, many of the menfolk have a fair command of the national or trade language, while women and children, or people living in outlying areas, have only a few words of this, and the vernacular is used for all purposes except talking to outsiders. In other cases there is a good degree of bilingualism, but the vernacular is generally retained for the discussion of personal affairs, including the intimate hopes and fears that are the essence of religious and spiritual matters.

The seriousness of the language problem is generally underestimated. Even with wide bilingualism, it is commonplace for there to be serious misunderstanding of vital aspects of the Gospel when this is presented and discussed other than in the vernacular, while with poor bilingualism, real communication of truth may never really begin. This is not recognized because the misunderstanding that arises is only observable to one who can express the truth both in the trade language and the vernacular. An evangelist using the trade language can only measure the response he gets in terms of the answers he receives in that language, and these answers naturally tend to employ the same words and phrases that he himself has used. He has no means of knowing to what concepts, if any, in the vernacular thought patterns these terms have been related, or how they fit in with other religious conceptions already held. The language problem frequently means that, though the Gospel may be faithfully announced, something else is understood by the hearers.

Communication problems also arise from differences of culture, the most obvious being misunderstandings and prejudices arising from behavior which has an acceptable implication to the evangelist, but another and unacceptable one to the minority group. Such misunderstandings are essentially a failure by the outsider to recognize and use the accepted means of signaling intentions and attitudes. As with linguistic non-communication, the lack of cultural acceptability, or the failure to convey the intended meaning, is not recognizable unless the evangelist understands both culture codes.

d. *Difficulties arising from the minority culture* — These difficulties lie within the mind of the minority group, militating against acceptance of the message as it is perceived. There is often a sense of cultural independence or superiority. The member of the group may feel secure in the assumption that his group is basically different from, or superior to, other groups, so that the religious beliefs of others are not relevant to him. His group has followed other patterns of belief for centuries, and "everyone knows that these are right" and better!

There is also generally a cultural necessity to resist change and maintain solidity. A minority group, if it is to maintain its existence as distinct from other groups, must cling tenaciously to its chosen way of life. It therefore resists all forms of change, and exerts heavy pressure on any of its members that may seem sympathetic to innovations.

The culture of the group may accept and encourage practices which are contrary to the explicit teaching of the Scriptures, and it may discourage or forbid some Christian virtues. Should there be any acceptance of the message by members of the group, this will frequently lead to opposition from the group's leaders, who will regard this development as a threat to their authority and a danger to the continued survival of the group.

Another problem often encountered is the danger of undermining existing culture patterns. Among groups whose way of life is widely different from that of the culture to which the evangelist belongs, acceptance of the Gospel may seem to imply acceptance also of the cultural values with which the evangelist is associated. The evangelist may himself urge the acceptance of new cultural values as necessary to the Gospel, when in fact there is no biblical warrant for doing so. Apart from any urging by the evangelist, materialistic values typical of the "Western World" have commonly been adopted by minority groups along with the presentation of the Gospel, and this has led to cultural breakdown and tragic demoralization as old established patterns of life are undermined. This state of affairs is not compatible with basic Christian values, and it affects adversely the growth of a Christian community.

2. Towards a strategy of evangelism.

a. *Effective communication is essential* — The message must be presented not according to what is most convenient for the messenger, but according to what will most effectively reach the hearers. Elementary though this principle may seem, it is in fact frequently overlooked in practice. Presumably this is because it is a long hard task for most of us to master another language, and because the ability to communicate concerning everyday matters in a national language leads the evangelist to assume that he can communicate spiritual truth in the same medium. But experience has proved this assumption false time and time again. It is not just that key terms will be misunderstood, though this is commonplace. The effects of failure to talk about spiritual things in the hearer's mother tongue — the language of his heart — go very deep, and influence attitudes of mind as well as the capacity to grasp ideas. If the evangelist has not bothered to acquaint himself with the thought world of his hearers, if his activities indicate insensitivity to their culture patterns and values, why should he expect their hearts to be open to his message?

It is essential for the evangelist to have a high regard for the culture and language of the minority group he wishes to reach. His first priority must be to become at home in their vernacular, to understand and where possible conform to their culture, to demonstrate his desire to identify with the people he wishes to help. Time spent among the people in the study of their language is rarely wasted, whereas evangelistic effort before the language has been mastered frequently is, or else it produces superficial results which make the task of discipling all the harder later on. Effective strategy therefore calls for priority to be given to the task of learning how to communicate effectively, i.e., allotting time to studying the language and the people.

It is also desirable to present the Gospel in the way which is most relevant to the life and needs of the group. The evangelist will be accustomed to thinking of certain aspects of the Gospel as crucial, because of the influence of his own background and the established patterns of evangelism within his own culture. But these will not necessarily be the aspects of the Gospel most crucial to another culture. Christ's authority over demon forces may not be of primary importance to a European, but it will certainly be crucial to an animistic minority group whose life is dominated by fear of evil spirits. This underlines the need of the evangelist to sympathetically understand the hopes and fears of those he seeks to reach.

b. *Establish contact with the minority group in some role other than that of "professional evangelist."* This follows from the difficulties outlined above which arise within the mind of the minority group members as they begin to hear the Gospel. The role of the professional evangelist, from the point of view of his hearers, is essentially that of one who is seeking to change them, regardless of whether or not they wish at first to be changed. The potential for provoking resistance to change is inherent in any direct evangelistic approach which challenges men to accept the Gospel as soon as possible after they have first heard it. That essential characteristic of minority groups, their need to resist change so as to retain their own identity, coupled with the fact that they will understand the Gospel so imperfectly at its first presentation, means that an approach which demands a quick response will be favorably received only by a few individuals who are marginal to the group as a whole. The remainder, including the leaders, are likely to adopt a resistant attitude.

Since this kind of result cannot be accepted as adequate evangelization of the group, it is necessary to establish some other role which will allow the Gospel to be made clear in a way which does not demand an immediate response. This avoids triggering a defensive resist-all-change reaction, and leaves the hearer's mind open to evaluate the Gospel in the light of the behavior and character of the man who brings the message. Where the teaching of the Gospel is diametrically opposed to group beliefs at some points, it can only triumph when Gospel truths become self-authenticating. This normally requires time for the new ideas to be reflected on, which also allows for extended practical witness in the life of the messenger.

The role that the Gospel messenger must play, if he is to obtain the privilege of non-pressure personal witness, will be determined by the situation of the group he is seeking to reach. For indigenous groups, that of linguistic investigator or literacy worker may be possible, or there may be opportunities for medical, agricultural, educational, or social work. It is usually important to be meeting a felt need, but the vital thing is to establish personal relationships and a nonthreatening context which allows Gospel truth to be presented and discussed without putting the community on the psychological defensive. If the friendship of group leaders is cultivated and their authority acknowledged, it may be possible to avoid opposition from them, and instead gain them as the first to accept the Gospel, thus making a "people movement" possible.

To adopt a servant role, meeting the felt needs of the minority group in some clear way like literacy or agricultural work, may also be helpful in obtaining government permission to work among minority groups. Such a role is more likely to be viewed as making a positive contribution to the nation than that of the "professional evangelist."

c. *The development of indigenous leadership is crucial to the evangelization of minority groups,* and must be given priority attention from the start. One thing in particular is essential for this. The Gospel must be made available to the group as something distinct from the person of the evangelist, lest too much authority come to center in him. Authority does in fact reside not in the messenger but in the message, the self-revelation of God to men contained in the Holy Scriptures. But if these are not made available to the minority group in a form that they can handle for themselves, and respond to as distinct from the evangelist himself, then authority is bound to come to reside in the latter as the only known expression of the message. Moreover, if the Scriptures are available but are not constantly focused upon as the source of the message; if the believers are not taught to turn to them rather than to the evangelist as their standard and guide; if they are not shown how to use the Scriptures for themselves without the help of the evangelist; then he will inevitably become essential to all the activities of the believing community, and thus be, not a channel for revelation, but a bottleneck inhibiting indigenous development. Hence the translation of the Scriptures, where these do not already exist in the vernacular, accompanied by literacy work where necessary, and teaching concerning the understanding and use of the Bible are items of the highest strategic value.

If strong indigenous leadership is to emerge, the evangelist must also foster from the beginning the recognition that he is not the only person who can present the Gospel or give local leadership. He must learn to refrain from doing some of the things at which he is more capable than the new believers, so as to give to them the opportunity to develop leadership and take responsibility. Planned absence from the area can be very beneficial in this respect, or better yet, the development of a pattern of work in which the evangelist is present only for short-or-medium-term periods of time, and never settles there permanently and allows too much to come to depend on him. Such a pattern may also be an answer to some of the problems of physical location mentioned above.

3. Implementation of strategy

While it is important to consider what is the best strategy for the evangelist to follow, it is equally important to consider how such strategy might be implemented. The formidable list of unmet needs in this area of evangelism today prompts the question, "How can the resources of the whole church be mobilized to meet these needs?"

Who should be expected to undertake this task? No simple answer is possible, since the task is so vast and so varied. For immigrant minorities, surely the responsibility rests on the church in the countries where the immigrant groups are found. This should also be true for indigenous minorities, where a national church exists. In the latter case, however, historical and cultural factors often mean that a national church does not develop much concern for indigenous minorities within the borders of its own land, being more interested in work in other countries. This is regrettable, particularly in view of the advantages that a national evangelist often has over one from abroad, in being able to work without a visa, and not having to adjust to an intermediate language and culture before reaching the minority group. An expatriate evangelist does have certain advantages, however, in that he is able to bring a more objective viewpoint to the study of the minority language and culture. The national evangelist, by comparison, finds it hard not to feel that these are inherently inferior to his own, and therefore exerts unconscious pressure on the minority group to conform to or adopt national ways, and this may well weaken a truly indigenous development. There surely remains an urgent need for both national and expatriate workers in this field.

There is room for personal witness and practical evangelism by non-specialist workers in all minority groups which are accessible to visits by outsiders. But these will be most fruitful when accompanied by the long-term work of specialists who are concentrating their efforts on those strategic points which will make the growth of an indigenous church possible, i.e., Scripture translation, the development of literacy or educational materials, and the training of indigenous leadership. Even for immigrant minorities there will often be a need for someone to study the life of the minority community, and produce specialized materials or services through which the Gospel can be communicated. There is a real and continuing need for full-time specialist workers, supported by the Christian fellowships that have set them apart for such work and adequately trained in the skills that the task demands. This will generally include the study of linguistics, social anthropology, and literacy, in addition to basics like theology, and the principles of evangelism and church planting. Such training is currently provided by Bible colleges, and by such courses as those of the Summer Institute of Linguistics, but it tends to be less accessible to nationals of non-English speaking, or less developed, countries. Strategy therefore calls for specialized training to be more widely available.

A more fundamental problem, however, is the lack of vision and drive on the part of the church to fulfill this aspect of its mission. This may spring from ignorance of the need, or from a false assumption concerning priorities, i.e., that because minority groups contain few persons (compared to majority groups or the growing urban centers) their evangelization is not very imperative — a rather low priority at best. In view of the clear teaching of the Scriptures that God is concerned for every man regardless of the size of the community to which he belongs, and that he is calling to himself a people "from every nation, from all tribes and peoples and tongues" (Rev. 7:9), it is urgent that this assumption be replaced by truth. The task of evangelizing minority racial groups is an essential part of the church's responsibility, not less important or urgent than other forms of work, but of equal importance and urgency, and therefore to be carried forward at the same time. We cannot shrink back from the task because of its extent, as if our resources were adequate for only a part of what the Master has given us to do. Rather we must press forward, trusting in him who has called us to be with us, as he promised.

EVANGELISM OF MINORITY RACIAL GROUPS REPORT

We believe that Christians in all parts of the world should take the following steps toward the evangelization of these groups:

a. Repent of our unbiblical attitudes in regarding them as inferior, and of our failure to show as much concern for them as for groups more numerous or more easily reached.

b. Ascertain the facts about such groups, both in our own countries and in other parts of the world, so as to prayerfully determine our responsibility toward them.

c. Set aside specialist (E-3) personnel to study the language and culture of each group, and by close identification with them communicate the Gospel to them in a way that is relevant to their culture and situation. Personnel sent to cross-cultural situations should, if possible, receive suitable training — including social anthropology and social psychology, with emphasis on the culture of the target group. (The above applies particularly to indigenous minority groups.)

d. Engage in local (E-2) contacts with individuals from such groups, where possible. This could include sharing with and concern for individuals within the home, choice of housing location so as to facilitate contact and involvement, and the provision of evangelistic and worship activities geared to the minority culture as part of the local church program, possibly with specialist staff.

The resources required for the evangelization of all such groups cannot be computed without fuller information. It seems certain however that the number of immigrant groups must be many hundreds, while the number of indigenous groups still needing specialist workers is probably well in excess of two thousand. (The W.B.T. Ethnologue, 1974 edition, lists 568 languages definitely needing Bible translation, plus 3,438 others which may need this.)

Resources currently available include specialist training for workers among indigenous minorities offered by the Summer Institute of Linguistics in Australia, England, Germany, and the U.S.A., with shorter practical courses in a number of other countries.

We recommend that such training and in-service help be made available on a wider basis, to facilitate personnel from many countries engaging in work among these groups. We also call for continued research into the number and circumstances of minority racial groups throughout the world, as a means of stimulating action by the church on their behalf.

EVANGELISM IN HIGH-RISE HOUSING APARTMENTS

James Y.K. Wong

*Rev. Wong, Singapore, is Director of the
Church Growth Study Center.*

It is generally agreed that in Paul's missionary journeys the city presented a special challenge to him. In his strategy he focused the evangelistic thrust on the cities. There were two chief reasons for doing this. First, as centers of commerce and government, cities exercised a vital function — with their concentration of people — to get the Gospel spread out to the surrounding countryside. Second, Paul found that the urban dwellers within the synagogue community were receptive to the Gospel. These two advantageous factors are found also in many of our twentieth-century urban communities — a concentration of people and their spiritual responsiveness.

The future of cities and housing development

The need for planning to evangelize the urban population is seen in the fact that more and more of the world's people will be living in cities. Contemporary population studies indicate that the trend towards a greater concentration of people living in cities will increase rapidly. Note these statistics:

(i) In 1920, the total population in the world was 1.9 billion. By 1970, the population increased to 3.5 billion. Projecting a modest growth rate, it is estimated that by 2000 A.D. the world population will exceed 6.1 billion. But much of this growth will be in the cities!

(ii) In a United Nations population study ("Growth of the World's Urban and Rural Population, 1920-2000"), the facts of the size, composition, and growth of cities from 1920 to 1960 with a further projection of to 1980 are given.

In 1920, approximately 250 million people were classified as urban dwellers. By 1960, this increased three times, to 750 million. During this period, the rate of urban growth was found to be more rapid in the Third World countries than in the developed nations. For example, by 1960 the urban population increased by five times its 1920 size in Latin America and Africa, more than four times in South Asia, and nearly four times in East Asia (by contrast, the overall increase in Europe is only two-thirds of its 1920 size).

Another fact indicated by this U.N. study is that larger cities (population exceeding 2.5 million) were growing at the rate of 4.8 times from 1920 to 1960, whereas the smaller towns (pop. less than 100,000) increased only by 2.3 times over the same period.

As we think through a strategy of evangelism to penetrate the world with the Gospel, we need to give greater attention to urban evangelism — especially in areas where there is a large concentration of people — as in the vast housing estates with high-rise apartments.

Singapore: a case study of modern housing

The home and its environs is man's greatest opportunity for a satisfying life on earth. Yet, a vast portion of the world's population is still housed in sub-standard and over-crowded dwellings. This lack of adequate and decent housing constitutes one of the greatest hindrances to development in many Third World countries and aggravates all other social and economic problems.

Singapore has been recognized internationally as one of the countries with significant achievement in solving its housing needs. This city also provides an example of the kind of social changes resulting from its extensive high-rise housing development and what bearing these changes would have upon evangelism in an urban community.

Historically, the first government attempt to construct low-cost public housing dates back to 1927 when the Singapore Improvement Trust (S.I.T.) was set up. Between 1927 and 1960, the population grew from 500,000 to over 1.5 million, whereas the total number of public housing units constructed by the S.I.T. in this same period was 23,000. Consequently there was an acute shortage of modern housing in this rapidly growing city.

Singapore's housing revolution started after the present government came into office in 1959. In 1960 the state-owned Housing and Development Board (HDB) was formed to replace the S.I.T. Initially, two five-year plans were formulated. The target of 50,000 units in the first phase (1960-1965) and 60,000 units in the second phase (1965-1970) was reached. Presently about 40 percent of the 2.4 million population are living in these high-rise apartments (many of these soar up to 25-30 stories high). Since 1971, the country has embarked on the third 5-year plan, in which presently at least 30,000 units are built each year. In other words, it will take about four years to achieve the same number of units as constructed during the first ten years. By 1975, it is estimated that 60 percent of the population will dwell in these densely populated housing estates. By 1980 it will increase to 75 percent. Thus eventually three-fourths of the people in Singapore will be "high-risers".

Problems created and the church's response

With so many people living in such close proximity (the size of these housing estates ranges from 20,000 to 200,000 residents), a variety of social and community problems are bound to arise. When thousands of urban slum dwellers and rural squatters are uprooted from familiar surroundings and brought together suddenly, tremendous problems of adjustment exist.

This is where the church can play an important role. Alert to the opportunities, responsible Christian witness and service can be directed to help to bring about healthy social change. The church's function in such a situation is to be sensitive to any social-community problems, and in the name of Christ find positive ways of ministering to the social and spiritual needs of the people.

Such a task must be seen in the light of the fact that the church situated in the midst of these housing estates is presented with exciting possibilities of discipling a large section of the urban population for

Christ. It must seek ways and means to serve the needs of the whole man and thus relate its ministry of witness and service together. Without neglecting its cultural mandate, the church's mission must go beyond the meeting of social needs. The primary task of the church is to be alert to the opportunities of communicating the Gospel of Christ and persuade men, women and children — within the family context — to become followers of Christ and be made responsible members of his church.

Opportunities for evangelism

When people experience rapid social change they are also more open to religious change. Several case studies have been carried out in Singapore among the residents of high-rise housing estates. In a community survey of the "religious orientation" of the people living in high-rise apartments (conducted by the author in 1972), he found that the residents were more responsive to the presentation of the Gospel message during the initial period of settling into a new housing estate. His conclusion was that if churches are planted early enough in new housing estates they will have considerable opportunities to exercise an effective service and witness role among the residents. Evangelism and church planting will be more successful when it is being carried out in these spiritually responsive housing apartment blocks if it is initiated right from the beginning as the residents move into the area, rather than waiting until the people have firmly settled themselves in the neighborhood.

A plan for church growth

By their very nature and purpose, high-rise housing estates contain a large number of people living closely together. Since evangelism should always be focused in areas where people are found, these high-rise apartments should be given great attention in church-planting evangelism. It is clear that in all the major cities of the world where there are large quantities of high-rise apartment estates the church should seek to establish new congregations, cell groups, evangelistic centers in their midst. The goal should be to start one active and evangelically oriented Christian center within each of these housing estates and even, if possible, in every block of apartments.

This means that a new style of church structure will need to emerge. These apartment-churches, or cell-groups, should not follow the traditional pattern of church extension — with its "edifice-centered complex." Instead, they will take the form of smaller, more flexible and simple Christian cell units — meeting in homes of Christian families or rented apartments or even in the local community halls.

If such a goal of creative and widespread evangelism leading to rapid church extension is to be adopted, then the churches in these housing estates can expect to increase from a few handfuls to hundreds. Growth will result when more new churches are rapidly multiplied in all responsive segments of the city. Up to now, few places in the world experience rapid church growth in high-rise housing communities because churches have not been able to develop a dynamic ministry among them. Too many of them have perhaps thought in terms of building the traditional type of large church structures (where the shortage of land and its high cost inhibit extensive church planting).

Bold plans for effective evangelism and church multiplication in high-rise housing estates must reckon with creative patterns of the "house-church" ministry. In most modern urban areas, land is both scarce and extremely costly. And yet because these high-rise residential centers have a high concentration of people we need to develop a new structure of church extension which is to be more flexible and simple. It is necessary if the people living in high-rise areas are to be discipled that a greater number of house-churches must be developed.

The advantages and disadvantages of house churches

A number of significant factors favor the rapid extension of smaller and less formal house-churches. Some of these are as follows:

(i) *The New Testament example* — It seems unlikely that the rapid church growth as we read in Acts was contributed to by the building of large assembly places. The gatherings for worship and fellowship, the teaching and nurture of new converts, all took place in an extensive network of house-churches. Abundant references to "oikos" or "the church in thy house" are found in Acts and the Pauline espistles (Acts 18:8; Cor. 1:16). It is also clear from Paul that the regular gatherings of Christians in the homes were no temporary phenomenon (cf. I Cor. 16:19, Col. 4:15, Acts 20:20).

(ii) *The economic factor* — Less capital cost and funding is required to get new churches started. It also allows for more flexibility and mobility of the centers of witness and worship. The house-churches can always be located where people are found to be most responsive.

(iii) *The psychological factor* — Conceivably there will be less prejudice on the part of non-Christians coming to a gathering in the home rather than in a religious sanctuary. Just as Christians are reluctant and resistant to the invitation to attend a non-Christian worship service in a Buddhist or Hindu temple or a muslim mosque, non-Christians have the same feeling when invited to our worship service in a traditional church building.

(iv) *The sociological factor* — Most non-Christians hold the view that churches are for the affluent, the middle-class, and the educated. Conventional church buildings tend to give an image that they are costly structures and meant for those who can afford their upkeep. Apartment house-churches can help to correct this image — that Christianity is meant for the masses and ordinary people living in the same environment.

(v) The strategic factor — House-churches with the apartment blocks would be accessible to all in the community, and their facilities extended until all the resident Christian families living in these apartments are known and identified. Although these house-churches would be small in terms of space, this can be compensated by developing more groups in any given housing area and thereby provide more centers for worship and evangelistic outreach.

However, in proposing this strategy, one needs to be cognizant of a number of obstacles and difficulties. These must be faced and resolved before any workable plan can be executed. A number of factors can hinder a smooth implementation of the above suggestions for church planting in high-rise housing estates. They follow:

(i) *Government restriction* — Many countries have strong zoning regulations regarding the use of properties. Residential apartments are usually meant for residential purposes only. When such restrictive measures prevail in a country they can frustrate any plan for multiplying house-churches in high-rise housing estates.

(ii) *Satanic disruptions* — Evangelistic success is bound to create divisions and conflicts in any society. This is a fact about which the Bible speaks pointedly. Satan has no desire to see people become Christians; he will mobilize all his "powers" to frustrate the Christian cause. For example, in the same location where concerted Christian activity is contemplated, encounter is bound to take place with the adherents of other religions. They cannot be expected to be sympathetic to Christianity. They may object to Christians meeting in their immediate neighborhood for worship, hymn singing, and other forms of Christian activity.

(iii) *Limitation in space* — House-churches are necessarily limited in size. This means the problem of adequate space will become acute for the growing congregation. This limitation will also tend to restrict the variety of activities in which the congregation can engage; so people may be deterred from joining. Another factor might be the environment. People living in the same neighborhood may not find attendance in a house-church within the same block congenial for their religious activities. They may wish for a change in environment. Obviously this can be overcome by the attractive and helpful quality of the worshiping community.

(iv) *Noise and absence of privacy* — Worshiping in a congested area can be a real hindrance in these densely populated housing estates. First, there will be considerable noise surrounding these churches. Second, they will lack the sort of privacy needed for meditation and prayer. Little can be done to ameliorate the noise and provide the privacy. Some people will naturally find these centers distracting and difficult. Others will welcome them. But one should expect that some will use this as an excuse for not going to church.

(v) *Demanding pressures on families* — Meeting in the homes of Christian families demands a large measure of devotion from the whole family, since this will bring no little inconvenience to the family routine. If there are one or two in the family who are not Christians or who are uncommitted, they may resent the regular use of their home for such a purpose. Meeting in homes over an indefinite period may also mean that not too many families will want to offer their homes for such a use. This will then seriously limit the number and permanence of new congregations which can be set up.

(vi) *Attitude towards a holy place* — People tend to associate the worshiping of God with special places. This is an attitude which may take a long time to change. Some may never see how a place can be regarded as holy if it is "unconsecrated." Many people have fixed ideas as to what a religious center of worship ought to be like. A bare hall, no familiar altar, no organ, no stained glass windows — this may not be the kind of place which some people would regard as a church. For example, many would hesitate to come to a house-church for a Christian wedding ceremony.

(vii) *Lack of trained leaders* — If a great number of churches are to be planted then obviously the supply of Christian leaders must be greatly increased. This could be either a problem or a challenge. Obviously if there is a lack of trained leaders it will limit the number of house-churches which can be opened up. Besides, it is possible that these lay leaders will be supporting themselves by a "tent-making" ministry. This will mean a sharp limitation of their time for church service and will inevitably pose the problem of the congregation's receiving inadequate pastoral care. Also, we must expect that the teaching and instruction provided in some of the smaller congregations will doubtless suffer in quality.

Surmounting the problems

It can be said that if there are no obstacles there will be no challenge. If there is no challenge there will not be the incentive to *innovate* and to *accomplish* the extraordinary task. If Christians dare to set their goals and sights high, they can expect, with God's help, the possibility of doing something great for him.

This is a challenge which all urban churches should face in the seventies. The proposal to multiply churches in all receptive segments of the city must be regarded as feasible and that God desires it.

Christians in Singapore are living in days of exciting and unprecedented opportunities. They must see the population's responsiveness as evidence that God himself is at work and that he means to bring in a spiritual harvest.

There are problems, but there are solutions also. The key to effective evangelism leading to rapid church growth has to be seen from different angles. They are:

(i) Develop and train a large number of unpaid leaders to initiate and pastor the new house-churches.

(ii) Develop and create a new pattern of ministry and worship to fit the local situation.

(iii) Out of this impulse towards indigeneity, a dynamic and new style of evangelism (led by dedicated, trained and creative leaders) will emerge.

(iv) When more creative leaders emerge they will find ways and means to overcome the property barrier. Existing church centers as well as new ones, will be fully utilized and a variety of programs will be developed.

(v) Christian impact on the nation — The multiplication of churches inevitably means more people are converted to Christ. With more Christians the impact on society will be greater. There is power in the Gospel. When more people are converted, the potential is present for moral and social reforms in society. Good works, service to humanity, and social concern flow from men's experience of conversion and reconciliation to God. Without neglecting the importance of clear verbal witness, Christians in these high-rise housing estates should be taught and encouraged to take active part in all civic and community activities within their neighborhood.

Conclusion

Here then, is a strategy for achieving the goal — to disciple the whole urban population for Christ. The key factor lies in the church's ability to train sufficient leaders to become "church planters" so that new centers of witness may be rapidly extended to all areas of opportunities.

There should not be tens or hundreds but thousands of new churches. The challenge before the Christians is "not to be limited by the small expectations of our forefathers nor measure tomorrow's advances by yesterday's defeats." In making this proposal for thousands of new house-churches we would not minimize the role and contribution of the larger and older established churches. It calls for a re-evaluation of the role of these older churches. In one respect they can function as the "cathedral church" — in a satellite pattern — with perhaps ten to fifteen smaller house-churches related to them for the purpose of wider support, teaching, and large-scale assemblies. In this way the weaknesses and limitations of the smaller house-churches can be remedied by the larger and more established congregations. Likewise, the lack of vitality and static nature of the older churches will have the stimulation of these fresh and dynamic youthful congregations.

As this plan for growth is implemented, the seemingly static churches in our cities can be transformed into growing and dynamic churches during this decade of the seventies. This then could conceivably become the turning point of Christianity in the world: as it moves rapidly towards the fulfillment of the Great Commission in our generation.

HIGHRISE, FLAT AND APARTMENT EVANGELISM REPORT

Secretary: Waldron Scott

The group consisted of approximately 15 North Americans and 10 Europeans, plus two or three participants from other continents. There were no representatives from Latin America, except on the final day. Africa had no representation except for one white South African. Similarly, Asia was meagerly represented by two from Singapore and two Americans working in Korea and South Vietnam respectively.

Attention is drawn to the composition of the group because this had a clear bearing on some of the conclusions reached by the participants.

Main Conclusion

This study group wishes to call attention, as much as possible, to the fact that the global evangelical community appears to be unaware, or far too inadequately aware, of the significance of urban evangelization in general and of highrise evangelism in particular.

Urban areas represent perhaps the most underestimated evangelistic need in the world today. This especially appears to be the case with respect to Third World countries. Between 1920 and 1960 urban population increased 500% in Latin America and Africa, 400% in South Asia and nearly 400% in East Asia. Most of this urban increase is focused in huge housing complexes which fill the horizons of modern cities everywhere.

In Singapore 60% of the population lives in these highrise complexes. The percentage is even higher in other major metropolitan areas. This is the fastest-growing sector of urban life. Yet most highrise dwellers are unevangelized and unchurched. Unless evangelicals awake to the challenges and opportunities represented by highrise housing, we are likely to fail altogether in our objective of fulfilling the Great Commission.

The conclusion just expressed is the most important statement the group wishes to make known to Congress participants and other readers. In addition to evaluating the need for highrise evangelism, the group discussed the special character of highrise residents and the evangelistic problems presented by them. The group also considered at length the strategy proposed by Rev. James K. Wong of Singapore as well as other alternatives and modifications.

Characteristic Features

Highrise dwellers tend to be suspicious of outsiders (though perhaps no more so than other urbanites). They are frequently lonely and isolated from community life. Many complexes are locked and guarded against outsiders. In some metropolitan areas highrise occupants are transient, in other cities they may be quite permanent.

Highrise dwellers are not confined to a particular economic class. But where a particular complex is primarily composed of residents from lower economic levels, conditions are apt to be crowded. Consequently

residents tend to spend much of their time out on the streets or at entertainment areas away from their flat or apartment. All this presents
special problems to the evangelist.

Problems

The biggest problems identified by the study group are not immediately related to the highrise situation itself. Rather, they are related
to the church: the evangelical community's lack of vision, awareness, and
concern for highrise residents; its unwillingness to allocate personnel to
evangelize this huge sector of urban life; its inability to modify its own
structures to accomodate to this new reality. These appear to be the
greatest obstacles to evangelism and church planting.

As in regard to the highrise complexes themselves, the most difficult
problem evangelistically seems to be that of penetration: actually con-
tacting residents to present the Gospel to them. Reasons for this have
been noted in the paragraphs on characteristic features, above. This is
compounded by lack of privacy, the inability to get along with people.
Still other problems peculiar to highrise evangelism are considered in
James Wong's study paper.

Problems, of course, point to opportunities. And Wong's paper also
lists the special advantages inherent in highrise complexes. The study
group endorsed these and then turned its attention to the consideration
of various strategies.

Strategies

Wong's own strategy for Singapore is impressive. It could well be the
model for church-planting endeavors in many metropolitan areas. In
brief he proposes (a) that evangelists consult beforehand with city planners to eliminate some of the obstacles, (b) that evangelistic teams serve
highrise residents through special ministries, (c) that Christian families
in highrise complexes act as nuclei for the development of "house
churches," and (d) that parish churches become training centers and support facilities for these house churches. Congress participants are urged
to study his paper carefully.

At the same time it was recognized that situations vary and that
alternative approaches must be considered for different cities.

Two participants from Rome reported successful attempts using a
direct visitation approach, as well as a plan which included the presentation of small gifts to residents at Christmas. The Roman evangelists
also urged the military principle of concentration of forces. In one instance they allocated 25 evangelistic church planters to a single sector of
the city, with gratifying results.

Some participants recommended the use of surveys and questionnaires. Others emphasized the value of ministries such as day-care centers for children, dog-walking services, recreational and adult educational facilities, etc. In France and Singapore Navigator materials are
used for initiating evangelistic Bible studies in flats and apartments.
In general, participants emphasized the need to identify the "felt needs"
of highrise residents and then meet those specific needs.

One approach *not* recommended is the widescale distribution of
notices (usually left in mailboxes) or other pamphlets. One participant,

for example, reported zero response from 20,000 tracts distributed throughout a highrise complex. In contrast, a participant from Johannesburg reported a high response from leaving cassette recorders (inexpensive models, of course) with an evangelistic message with residents. Apparently people respond to his expressed trust in them.

A Canadian reported that one church in his area asks newly married couples to establish residence in designated housing complexes with a view of utilizing their flat as an evangelistic base. Other participants pointed out the importance of family "web relationships" as a means of penetrating highrise complexes. Where Jehovah's Witnesses or Mormons have preceded the evangelical witness it may be wise to have material explaining who evangelicals are.

Church Relations

The group seemed to take for granted that the objective of highrise evangelism is church membership, not merely the conversion of isolated individuals. This raised questions about the nature of the church which the participants discussed at some length.

Wong envisioned the multiplying of house-churches in every highrise building. Such churches, however, would be related to a central church outside the housing complex. This seemed to some participants to suggest that these house churches were mere satellites, evangelistic extensions of the mother church, rather than full-fledged churches in their own right. These group members felt it unnecessary to attempt to relate highrise house churches to a central church located outside the complex. They emphasized the legitimacy of house churches as true churches in every respect.

A church capable of sustaining a highrise evangelistic endeavor will be characterized by (a) converted people, (b) sound teaching, (c) inspired leaders with clear vision, and (d) a solid training program for laymen — especially those laymen who already reside in highrise complexes.

EVANGELIZATION WHERE THERE IS GOVERNMENT HOSTILITY

J. Christy Wilson

*Dr. Wilson, Tehran, Iran, has been the
Pastor of the Kabul Community Church in
Afghanistan for a number of years.*

Dr. John Van Ess, a missionary who has since gone to be with the Lord, believed that the Holy Spirit was leading him to go to a place on the coast of Arabia to share the Gospel of Jesus Christ with the people there. He was, however, refused a visa. But because the Lord's guidance was so clear, he went anyway. When he landed, he was asked to show his authorization. He opened his Arabic New Testament to Mark 16:15 and read, "Go into all the world and preach the Gospel to every creature." He asked whether this were a part of the world; to which they answered, "Yes." Pointing to this verse in Arabic, he said that is was not only his permission but also his commission from God to come there and share the good news about Jesus Christ. He then asked if they had any tea. They replied, "Certainly. Sit down, sit down." They gladly welcomed him with a cup of tea, accepted the authorization of the Word of God and listened attentively to the message he had to tell.

Suffering for the sake of the Gospel is nothing new. Our Lord and his apostles lived, preached and ministered under opposition. Christ said, "You will be hated by all nations for My name's sake." Wesley Pippert in his book, *Memo For 1976,* says, "We can make a persuasive case that nowadays no government...is truly Christian. In a real sense, therefore, the Christian in politics always is in a position of dealing with ungodly governments." The situation today is similar to New Testament times when Paul wrote from prison and John from Patmos, as they shared the unsearchable riches of Christ under terrible restrictions. Thus the Bible has much to teach us about evangelization under opposition.

When our Lord was asked a loaded political question, he replied with the wisdom of God as He answered, "Render unto Caesar the things that are Caesar's and unto God the things that are God's." Hereby he established a Christian's dual duty. But the question arises as to how to differentiate and carry out one's responsibility toward God and toward a government. This is where the divine direction of the Scriptures is needed. Let us therefore consider first the Christian's duty to God; secondly, the Christian's duty to a government; thirdly, the Christian's spiritual warfare; fourthly, the Christian's discernment and discretion; and fifthly, the Christian's suffering of persecution.

I. THE CHRISTIAN'S DUTY TO GOD

The Bible clearly teaches that God should have first priority in the life of every individual, family and nation. When our Lord was asked to point out the greatest commandment, without hesitation he stated, "You shall love the Lord your God with all your heart, and with all your soul, and with all your mind." The Scriptures not only reveal God as the

"King of the nations," but also governments that honor him are to be prospered while those who dishonor him are to be cursed, "Righteousness exalts a nation, but sin is a disgrace to any people." On the one hand, the Bible warns, "The wicked shall be turned into hell, even all nations that forget God"; but on the other, there is the promise, "Blessed is the nation whose God is the Lord."

Dr. J.G.S.S. Thompson entitles his exposition of Jeremiah 46-52 as, "The Lord God Omnipotent Reigneth." He summarizes these prophetic messages to the nations with these observations: "1) God is on the throne of the universe and is in absolute control of it. 2) This is a moral world, and the important things in it are not power and riches, but character and morality. 3) This sinful world is under the judgment of God." If God is Sovereign, as the Bible states, his revealed will for the nations must have precedence. Therefore we dare not take lightly his great commission to proclaim the Gospel to every creature, to make disciples from among all nations, to teach them everything that Christ has told us and to baptize converts into God's triune name. But the way this is to be accomplished is directed by the Holy Spirit, as he calls, equips and uses individuals who yield to his leading. At one time, he forbade Paul to preach the Word in the province of Asia, because he knew that he would bring the Apostle back there later on when the whole area would be evangelized. Meanwhile, the Spirit led Luke, Silas and Paul, through the vision of the man of Macedonia, to start the evangelization of Europe. The guidance, places and methods may change, under the direction of the Holy Spirit, but the message remains the same, "the faith which was once for all delivered."

Today the necessity for world evangelization is being challenged by those who proclaim a universalism, supposedly based on the love of God. This is diametrically opposed to the Lord's clear command. Christ, having obtained all power and authority in heaven and in earth by his death and resurrection, orders us to take the good news of his conquest to the whole world. Our Lord clearly linked his victory with our responsibility when He said, "It is written that the Christ should suffer and rise again from the dead the third day, and that repentance for forgiveness of sins should be proclaimed in his name to all the nations."

One often hears the objection of those who oppose missions put in these words, "A loving God could not possibly condemn the ones who have never heard." This is similar to the servant our Lord spoke about who was given one talent. He criticized God as One who reaped where he had not sown. This is what God has determined, that we plant and water, but that he brings the increase. The final efficiency report on that servant was that he was "wicked, lazy" and "unprofitable," and he was cast into outer darkness. What an awesome warning this is to those who do not take Christ's command seriously.

Our Lord affirms, "I am the Way, the Truth and the Life, no man comes unto the Father but by Me." Peter echoes this when he, being filled with the Holy Spirit, states, "There is salvation in no one else, for there is no other name under heaven given among men by which we must be saved." The Apostle Paul expands on this revelation when he says, "Whoever will call upon the name of the Lord will be saved. How then shall they call upon Him in whom they have not believed? And how shall they believe in Him of whom they have not heard? And how shall they hear without a preacher? And how shall they preach unless they are sent?" Earlier in Romans he explains that since all have sinned, they are condemned for their own transgressions, and not because they have not heard the Gospel. However, our responsibility before God is to take the crucial news of Christ's sacrifice for the sins of the world to every person, so that each may have the opportunity to hear, believe, call, and be saved eternally.

Those who hold that people after death will have a second chance also vitiate Christ's command, and go contrary to the clear teaching of the Scriptures which warn, "It is appointed for men to die once and after this comes judgment." Our Lord expands on this truth in his description of what happened to the beggar Lazarus and the rich man after their deaths. This revelation underlines the necessity for carrying out Christ's commission to take the Gospel to every creature in this life.

Recognizing our Lord as our Sovereign God, we know he controls and orders world situations in order to accomplish his purposes. "All things work together for good to them that love God, to them that are the called according to His purpose." Joseph wonderfully realized God's overruling power and providence when he said to his brothers, "As for you, you thought evil against me; but God meant it unto good, to bring to pass as it is this day to save much people alive." Dr. Peter Wagner writes, "God often uses skilled instruments to accomplish his purposes. He used Cyrus and Pharaoh in dealing with his people in Old Testament days. He may also use rulers today, or revolution, or natural disaster, or migrations, or urbanization, to prepare masses of people for the message of Christ."

The Scriptures bring out how history will find its consummation in Christ, in spite of what Satan and all of his forces, including the opposition of man, may attempt. "For God has allowed us to know the secret of His plan, and it is this: He purposes in His sovereign will that all human history shall be consummated in Christ, that everything that exists in heaven or earth shall find its perfection and fulfillment in Him." Thus by knowing and serving Christ we are in a real sense on the winning side. Isaiah also saw this future victory of Christ in history, "And He shall judge among the nations, and shall rebuke many people; and they shall beat their swords into plowshares, and their spears into pruninghooks; nation shall not lift up sword against nation, neither shall they learn war any more."

Our Lord has taught us to pray, "Thy kingdom come, Thy will be done on earth as it is in heaven." This reveals that God wants his wishes carried out here and now in his creation, and his clear commission to us is world evangelization.

II. THE CHRISTIAN'S DUTY TO GOVERNMENT

The Bible acknowledges in a realistic way the faults of government leaders, but at the same time it has much to teach about a Christian's responsibility politically. Some say that since it was politics that crucified Christ, it has been proven that earthly authorities are anathema.

This falls into the error of mistakenly calling something evil "per se," rather than following the scriptural injunction that the use is what makes it good or bad.

The Bible contends that God has established governments for good purposes. Our Lord subscribed to the validity of political institutions when He said, "Render unto Caesar the things that are Caesar's." He also acknowledged the authority of the religious leaders of his day, in spite of recognizing their hypocritical inconsistency in not practicing what they preached. "The scribes and Pharisees sit in Moses' seat: all whatsoever they bid you observe, that observe and do; but do not ye after their works: for they say, and do not."

In Romans 13, the Apostle Paul reveals the Christian's responsibilities toward governmental authority. "Let every person be in subjection to governing authorities. For there is no authority except from God, and those which exist are established by God. Therefore he who resists authority has opposed the ordinance of God; and they who have opposed receive condemnation upon themselves." Just as the Bible presents a chain of command in a family between children and parents, so here God reveals the line of authority between us and our governments. In order that children might honor their father and their mother, as directed in the ten commandments, the Scriptures even dictated the death penalty for those who cursed their parents. In like manner, the Bible warns us against cursing a ruler, and includes this with the prohibition against cursing God.

When the Apostle Paul was struck unjustly as he stood trial before Ananias, the High Priest, he said to him, "God is going to strike you, you white-washed wall! And do you sit to try me according to the law, and in violation of the law order me to be struck?" When bystanders reminded Paul that in saying this he was reviling God's High Priest, he immediately apologized mentioning that he was not aware that Ananias was High Priest that year. He then went on to quote the Old Testament injunction that one was not to speak evil of a ruler of his people. In spite of the fact that Ananias was wrong in ordering Paul to be struck, the Apostle acknowledged that he had spoken out of turn by abusing this ruler for what had happened.

In Romans 13:3, the Apostle goes on to say, "Rulers are not a cause of fear for good behavior, but for evil." In other words, God purposes rulers to encourage good behavior and to discourage evil. Paul continues, "Do what is good, and you will have praise from the same, for he is a minister of God to you for good. But if you do what is evil, be afraid; for he does not bear the sword for nothing; for he is a minister of God, an avenger who brings wrath upon the one who practices evil. Wherefore it is necessary to be in subjection, not only because of wrath, but also for conscience's sake." This passage brings out that a Christian can have a good conscience through fulfilling his governmental responsibilities. "Also pay taxes, for rulers are servants of God, devoting themselves to this very thing. Render to all what is due to them: taxes to whom taxes are due: custom to whom custom: fear to whom fear; honor to whom honor." Our Lord, even though He was Master of the universe, humbled himself to pay the temple tax.

Even though the Bible acknowledges that all men are sinners, and therefore perfection cannot be expected of rulers, nevertheless we are to obey them in the realm over which they have jurisdiction, provided they do not infringe God's higher authority. "Submit yourselves for the Lord's sake to every human institution: whether to a king as to one in authority; or to governors as sent by him for the punishment of evil doers and the praise of those who do right," writes the Apostle Peter. When earthly governments seek to block the carrying out of Christ's commission, the Christian has a prior responsibility toward his Lord. When the apostles were forbidden to speak or teach in the name of Jesus, Peter and John answered, "Whether it is right in the sight of God to give heed to you rather than to God, you be the judge; for we cannot stop speaking what we have seen and heard." Daniel also as a government servant lived and worked so blamelessly that his enemies were unable to find cause for condemnation. When they had a special law passed against praying in order to trap him, Daniel purposely broke this human ordinance in order to carry out his responsibility toward God, even though it meant being thrown to the lions.

John Knox, in an interview with Mary, Queen of Scots, said, "Madam, as right religion took neither original strength nor authority from wordly princes, but from the eternal God alone, subjects are not bound to frame their religion according to the appetites of their princes...The sword of justice, Madam, is God's, and is given to princes and rulers for an end (purpose)." We are to render unto Caesar the things that are Caesar's, but when the government trespasses upon the Lord's jurisdiction, we are to render unto God the things that are God's.

III. THE CHRISTIAN'S SPIRITUAL WARFARE

The Bible clearly brings out that in reality we are not fighting "against flesh and blood, but against principalities, against powers, against the rulers of the darkness of this world, against spiritual wickedness in high places." In other words, our real adversary is the devil and all his forces. These oppose the spread of the Gospel. Along with taking the whole armor of God and attacking the evil one offensively, we are admonished in this battle to pray always with all prayer and supplication in the Spirit. Spiritual opposition delayed the answer of Daniel's prayers by three weeks. Our Lord himself met Satan and overcame him during his forty days of fasting before he started his glorious ministry. With the Bible revealing the power that prayer has in moving the hand of Almighty God, this is the Christian's secret weapon in overcoming forces of darkness.

This points up the importance of praying for political leaders. Paul encourages us to "Pray...for kings and all others who are in authority over us, or are in places of high responsibility, so that we can live in peace and quietness, spending our time in godly living and thinking much about the Lord. This is good and pleases God our Savior, for He longs for all to be saved and to understand this truth." With efficient reporting of world news through the media today, this gives Christians a great opportunity to intercede for leaders who have far-reaching decisions and obligations.

The Scriptures emphasize the necessity of prayer in regard to the evangelization of the world. It was when the church in Antioch fasted and prayed that the Holy Spirit called Paul and Barnabas to start on their missionary outreach for evangelizing the then known world. Wherever they went, Satan raised up opposition. However, through their prayer and witness, they were able "to turn the world upside down" for Christ.

IV. THE CHRISTIAN'S DISCERNMENT AND DISCRETION

"No land is closed to God," said Mildred Cable who evangelized in Central Asia, "and if we look around we shall see that even if the front door be shut, a back door may be open...What we want is a new dimension of the spirit of wisdom to see where there is an opening and how to seize it." Our Lord advised us to be as wise as serpents and as harmless as doves, and where there is no vision on the part of Christians, peoples of the world perish without Christ. Forward-looking believers are beaming the Gospel around the world through radio and TV. However, these ministries need to be expanded.

Scriptures and Christian literature are also being disseminated widely. This, of course, brings up the question whether it is right to distribute such items in countries where governments are hostile. Some Christians differ in their views, but it would seem that God's commission is sufficient sanction. Yet Christ's admonition to be as wise as serpents, makes sensible discretion essential.

Today there is a "diaspora" or scattering of self-supporting Christians all over the world as businessmen, tourists, teachers, students, United Nations workers, and diplomats. Just as the Apostle Paul was a tentmaker, but had evangelism as his primary purpose, so today Christians of many nations have the opportunity of living and witnessing for Christ all over the world.

Along with our Lord's injunction to be wise as serpents, He commands us to be harmless as doves. In other words, He does not want us to offend unnecessarily. The Bible clearly teaches that it is never right to lie, but it also demonstrates that one does not have to tell all. God Himself illustrates this principle of not divulging everything, "The secret things belong unto the Lord our God: but those things which are revealed belong unto us and to our children." Our Lord also told His disciples, "I have many things to say unto you, but ye cannot bear them now."

This ethical principle is further illustrated in the life of Samuel. When Saul sinned and God ordered Samuel to go to Bethlehem to anoint one of Jesse's sons to be the new king, he complained, "How can I go? If Saul hear it he will kill me." And the Lord said, "Take an heifer with thee and say, I am come to sacrifice to the Lord." Here God ordered Samuel to tell part of the truth by his words and acts, but not to reveal all that the Lord had told him to do in the face of a hostile ruler. In the same way, God has commanded us to take the Gospel to every creature, and this often in the face of spiritual and governmental opposition. We therefore are justified in keeping our motives confidential.

This, however, does not sanction the fomenting of armed revolution which Peter Beyerhaus calls "the Mission of Barabbas." This was the tragic mistake of the Crusades. When Peter cut off the ear of Malchus, our Lord healed it, and said, "Put up again thy sword...for all they that take the sword shall perish with the sword." As Christians we are to do all we can to pray for and to influence authorities regarding religious freedom, racial equality and social justice, but in the way of peace.

V. THE CHRISTIAN'S SUFFERING OF PERSECUTION

Our Lord not only warned us but assured us of persecution if we live and witness for Him. "If they have persecuted me," he said, "they will also persecute you." He even prophesied that men would kill us, thinking that they were doing God service. However, he told us to be faithful unto death, and that he would give us a crown of life.

In promising one hundredfold blessing for those who give up their homes, loved ones, and lands for his sake and the Gospel's, our Lord also said that these benefits would be accompanied by persecutions.

When persecution comes, one temptation is to think that we are in the wrong and out of God's will. This is not necessarily so. Shadrach, Meshach and Abednego were condemned for refusing to bow down to Nebuchadnezzar's image, and yet the Lord was not only with them in the fiery furnace but delivered them from it. We are assured that God is "a present help in trouble." In other words, the Lord expects us to endure difficulty but promises to help us in our extremity.

The blood of the martyrs is still the seed of his church. It has been stated with strong support that more Christians have given their lives for Christ in this twentieth century than ever before. This is probably a prime reason for the fact that the Gospel has been taken to more people in this century than ever before. When the Christians in Jerusalem were persecuted, they were scattered and went everywhere preaching the Word. When John Wesley was not allowed to preach in the churches, he proclaimed the Gospel in the open air; and all of Britain was shaken with a great awakening. Persecution, through God's providential overruling, can be a great means of evangelization.

Recently when a young man who had become a Christian in another country was returning home where the punishment for conversion to Christ was death, he was asked whether he was not afraid to go back. He replied, "I have already died with Christ." Absolute dedication to our Lord and his Gospel, with wisdom from the Holy Spirit, is the secret to evangelization under opposition.

EVANGELISM WHERE THERE IS GOVERNMENT HOSTILITY REPORT

Chairman: Dr. David Howard
Secretary: A. C. Emery

Three general discussion periods were held to consider Dr. J. Christy Wilson's paper on *Evangelization Oppositions*. The dialogue fell broadly into four categories:

1. Questions concerning the biblical authority and direction for Christian conduct under these conditions.
2. Individual statements of experiences and attitudes.
3. Description of conditions under which Christians work in different countries.
4. Recommended action to be taken by Christians who are free to worship to support their Christian brothers and sisters. Suggestion that this Congress might take to help the situation.

I. *Questions concerning biblical authority and Christian conduct.*

A. When a convert is made, should he be encouraged to come out openly, through baptism and witnessing, to express his new Christian faith openly? This action in a number of nations exposes the believer to persecution and even death. Those who have had to face this situation felt that biblical example indicated several possible positions for the Christian.

1. To flee. This was the action taken by some believers in both the Old and New Testaments.
2. To hide. This action is being taken by some believers today as it was in Bible accounts.
3. To remain quiet as a secret believer. This also has Scriptural antecedents.
4. To openly confess and accept the risk of torture, imprisonment, or death.

Comment was made that these options were left to the individual in the assurance that wisdom would be given by the Holy Spirit to the converts on the appropriate action they should take.

B. When should a Christian accept the teaching of Rom. 13:1-7 and submit to secular authority and when should he resist and disobey? This question was covered in Dr. Wilson's paper, but discussion expanded upon it. Acts 5:29 "...we ought to obey God rather than man," was quoted as being the proper attitude for Christians to take when secular authority and legislation violates conscience and specific biblical direction. Romans 13 was stated to be quoted by enforcement officials in the USSR when believers are questioned concerning their acts of faith and worship.

C. What should the Christian position be concerning lying when questioned by government authorities? The answer given was, "To tell a lie is always a sin. To say everything is also a sin." Reference was made to the study paper where Wilson mentioned God's command to Samuel to tell King Saul that he was going to sacrifice and not tell the whole truth that he was going to anoint David as king (I Sam. 16:2). Paul in Phil. 4:22 does not give names but writes, "All the saints greet you, chiefly they that are of Caesar's household." The Lord Jesus Christ broke the seal of government when he rose from the dead. Paul was let down the wall of Damascus in a basket. There are times when the believer must resist secular authority to give priority to God's law.

II. *Individual statements of experience and attitudes.* A number of Christians who had personally suffered imprisonment stated that their fellow believers wanted the Christian church to know of their sufferings. They felt the need of the prayers, love, and understanding of Christians throughout the world. God is having the victory in these nations but not without great sacrifice. Fires, arrests, beatings, imprisonments, and death are the fate of many. At times well-meaning journalists print accounts that can be harmful to Christian activity. Subject matter should be cleared with those involved before exposure to the public.

III. *The situation of Christians under national governments that are in opposition to their faith varies from country to country.* Communist opposition is not the same as opposition in some Islamic nations. In the USSR, the Christian church is divided into two groups: the registered Christian and the unregistered or underground Christians. The registered Christians are required to sign a statement accepting restrictions upon themselves concerning teaching children, witnessing, having meetings for young people, prayer meetings outside scheduled church services, and distributing literature. The underground church feels that it must not comply with these restrictions. There is no certain determination of the number of registered Christians and of the underground Christians. Some feel the distribution is about equal. Others feel there are greater numbers of registered Christians. These two groups are beginning to come together. God is working within both ranks.

IV. *What action is recommended to be taken by "free" Christians in helping their brethren?*

A. Prayer. More than anything else, our suffering brethren want and need our continuing prayers for them.

B. Radio. Christian broadcasting is of great encouragement to and a means of growth for the church in these countries.

C. Literature and Bibles are needed.

D. When a tourist is in the USSR, insist on attending a registered church. Ask to see the pastor and ask him to put you in touch with the underground church. He will not do this but it will let him know that you know of the underground church. Smile at your fellow Christians and tell them you are praying for them.

E. A resolution was passed unanimously by this group to recommend to the Congress that it pass a resolution to express its conviction that all nations permit freedom of worship. Believers who are free must give this encouragement to the persecuted.

F. A motion was passed unanimously to refer to the ongoing fellowship or organization concerning the possibility of a continuing effort to secure believers' freedom of worship in all nations of the world. Prayer was given at all meetings for some individuals and for the Christians as a whole in these countries. Love and unity was sensed by those representing many nations.

Addenda: The following statement was subsequently drafted to be included as part of this summary.

Whereas: the participants in the International Congress on World Evangelization gathered in Lausanne, Switzerland in July, 1974, representing 156 countries, have studied together our obligation as Christians to fulfill the great commission given by Jesus Christ to his Church to preach the Good News of salvation to every creature in all nations, and

Whereas: the United Nations, in its universal Declaration of Human Rights adopted in 1948 in Paris, article 13, has declared that "(1) everyone shall have the right to freedom of thought, conscience, and religion. (2) freedom to manifest one's religion or belief,"

We call upon all nations of the world, regardless of their geographical, political, cultural, or religious standing, to guarantee, implement, and protect these stated freedoms for all peoples within their borders.

We also express our deep concern as fellow members of the body of Christ, for our brothers and sisters who are in prison or are suffering persecution for the testimony of Jesus Christ, and we promise to pray and actively work for their rightful freedom as commanded by the Word of God, "Remember the prisoners, as though in prison with them; and those who are ill-treated, since you yourselves also are in the body (Heb. 13:3)."

MOBILIZING YOUNG PEOPLE FOR WORLD EVANGELIZATION

Loren Cunningham

Mr. Cunningham, Lausanne, Switzerland, is the leader of Youth With a Mission.

Mobilizing youth for world evangelization is a challenge that faces not only youth-evangelistic organizations, but a challenge which must be met by every mission, church, and evangelistic movement. Of the countless methods tried over the years, there is one process whose pattern was established by the undisputed leader of all evangelists, our Lord Jesus Christ, and it is this method I would like to set forth in the next several pages. We will trace together the scriptural foundation for this step-by-step development of the building of an evangelical outreach. Let us now follow Jesus himself, our greatest example of leadership.

1. The excitement of vision phase

In Luke 5:5, Simon tells Jesus, "At Your bidding I will let down the nets. And when they had done this, they enclosed a great quantity of fish; and their nets began to break and they signaled to their partners in the other boat, for them to come and help them. And they came, and filled both of the boats, so that they began to sink... And Jesus said... 'Do not fear, from now on you will be catching men.' And...they left everything and followed Him."

When Jesus called Peter, James, and John he challenged them by giving these men a clear demonstration of God's power. The first step to mobilize youth for world evangelism is to challenge them with an exciting God-given vision. Jesus excited his disciples with what they were to do for him. He started by showing them the potential of "God and man" cooperation. There cease to be human limitations when man completely obeys the Lord. Instead of believing the circumstances, they believed him, obeyed him, and had their miracle. They caught so many fish that their nets began to break and their boats began to sink. That's excitement! The Lord told them, in effect, "You saw what I did when you cooperated with me; from now on you will be catching men." They left everything to follow him because he gave them a vision and excited them with the potential of the Holy Spirit working through them to win souls to Christ. In fact they would win so many souls that their nets would break and their boats would sink under the load, IF they would completely obey him and totally believe him. God asks leaders to challenge and lead laborers into the harvest field. We will be successful to the degree that we follow the example of Jesus. Jesus started with the supernatural. We must do the same. How can youth be mobilized for evangelism? Youth are challenged by a vision that comes from God.

The general vision is "Go into all the world and preach the gospel to all creation" (Mark 16:15). The specific vision (or will of God) is doing the right thing, in the right place, with the right people, at the right time, in the right way, with the right attitude of heart! As leaders, we must study the Scriptures to understand his general plan for world evangelism and then wait in the place of prayer for the specific vision. Let us not forget that Jesus "did nothing on His own initiative" (John 8:28). He has set the pattern for us to listen to the voice of the Lord and then to obey him. When you share the vision God gave you with others, the Holy Spirit will excite the vision in their own hearts and it will become their vision.

Every vision that has produced lasting fruit in the youth movement with which I am associated has been one born of God. Independent action on the part of man, however well organized or publicized, always falls short. Youth get excited when they are able to see what God wants them to do and how God can do it through them as they totally depend upon him, cooperating with him in full belief. When the leaders lead, the people will follow (Judges 5:12). We must lead them into the vision of world evangelization.

The leader must receive his specific direction from God, not as the result of a brainstorming session in a committee meeting. How can we teach youth spiritual realities if God is not real enough to us to speak specifically? As my friend Duncan Campbell, the Scottish revivalist, used to say, "Everything is real in evangelism but God." There is a vast difference between the static presentation of a lifeless plan, no matter how smoothly done, and the demonstration of the true power of a risen, living Savior.

It is also important to keep in mind that while youth are frequently open they are almost always sensitive to the genuine and are quickly turned off by the superficial. Never use gimmicks to mobilize youth into such serious work as world evangelism. Many have become permanently alienated from service in the harvest through such practices. By beginning each crusade, outreach project, or training mission with a specific word from the Lord, its leaders can truly expect the blessing of God to be upon it.

Anything is exciting if it is from God, and when you catch a specific vision for world evangelism you will be excited. Youth everywhere get excited when you talk about world evangelism when they know that it is something that God wants done. Your job in mobilizing youth is to tell them what God has shown you and how you know the vision was from God.

2. The experimental phase

Luke tells us, "And He called the twelve together, and gave them power and authority over all the demons, and to heal diseases. And He sent them out to proclaim the kingdom of God, and to perform healing. And He said to them, 'Take nothing for your journey, neither a staff, nor a bag, nor bread, nor money; and do not even have two tunics apiece.' ... And departing, they began going about among the villages, preaching the gospel and healing everywhere" (Luke 9:1-3,6). And in chapter ten, "Now after this the Lord appointed seventy others, and sent them two by two ahead of Him to every city and place where He Himself was going to come. And He was saying to them, The harvest is plentiful, but the laborers are few; therefore beseech the Lord of the harvest to send out laborers into His harvest!" He told them to take no money, no bags, no shoes, greet no one on the way. This was their "short term" experiment. Travel light, travel fast, and get out and do the job.

They had seen the vision. The vision was to catch men. Now they were to experiment. They were not just to observe or hear what someone else had done. Now they were to do it themselves. This is exciting because it means involvement. I have watched this in the lives of hundreds of youth year after year in Youth With A Mission.

We challenge youth to first witness near their home, community or local area in what we call a Domestic Crusade. After a brief training session we send them out two by two. Wherever possible we send an inexperienced youth with an experienced witness. A Domestic Crusade qualifies them to take the next step, which is a "Summer of Service" in their own nation or abroad. Following this two-to-three month experience together with a minimum of three months' training in one of our Schools of Evangelism they may apply for a full-time worker's status for one year's service or more. By not asking for a four-year minimum commitment, or worse yet, a life-commitment to work within a particular mission, we are encouraging them to grow into spiritual maturity and places of responsibility a step at a time. By demanding a major decision prior to the worker's spiritual maturation, Christian organizations tend to lose many potential soul-winners. More on this in topic six.

Whenever God sends young people out for the first time, their motives correct and their heart preparation complete, he always encourages them with miracles — always! By "miracle," I mean a supernatural act which can only be attributed to God. Whether it is financial provision, salvation of a sinner, or a physical healing, God will always encourage these new workers. This is part of the experimental stage of working with God. The disciples that Jesus sent out, the twelve and the seventy, saw signs following. They saw miracles take place through their ministry. They had seen the Lord heal the sick. Now they prayed and the sick were healed. Youth do not want to just sit and learn theory, they want to get involved. They want to see the New Testament principles and promises performed through the power of the Holy Spirit. This is real training! Only when God works through you has true learning taken place. You can study and memorize volumes of theory. You can even get excited over what you should do. But it is only when you step out in faith, when you get out there, become hot, tired, dusty, and hungry, and yet see God at work, only then is it worth the struggle that is involved in world evangelism.

3. The explanation of the cost phase

The third step is the explanation of the cost. In John 6:26, Jesus said, "You seek Me... because you ate of the loaves, and were filled. Do not work for the food which perishes, but for the food which endures to eternal life..." Then his disciples asked, "What shall we do, that we may work the works of God?" Christ began to explain to them what his kingdom was all about. He had just fed these thousands of people with five loaves and two fish. They immediately seized on the idea of making him king. After all, they decided, a king who can feed all of his people by one miracle is the best king a people can have. They wouldn't have to pay taxes.

He could do a miracle and wipe out the Roman army. What a utopia right here on earth! But Jesus, contrary to their imaginations and desires, began to explain to them the cost of what it really meant for them to continue and see the kingdom of God as God envisioned it. The experimental stage is not the culmination of Christian maturity. Miracles are real and for today, but God wants more than miracles. He wants mature men and women who will endure as good soldiers. When the children of Israel went out of Egypt through the Red Sea, they followed the fire by night and the cloud by day. They saw many miracles. Food rained down from heaven. The sick were healed by the masses when the serpent was lifted up. Water came out of the rock. They did not even need new clothes. They saw many miracles, but they had not arrived at spiritual maturity. In fact, they were so far removed from it that they were not even allowed to enter the promised land.

There is a fallacy in Christian circles that miracles take place because of the efforts of a "spiritual giant." Miracles are wrought by God as attestation of his Word. They will accompany his Word as we obey it. And I speak for Christians at all levels of development — yes, even the immature. But it is the one who counts the cost and pays the price of going ahead to spiritual maturity, of going ahead to the point of multiplication, of reaching the place where he can catch so many men that "his nets will break," whom God wants to lead the body of Christ on to this place of spiritual maturity. But Jesus had a screening process and it was simply the price to become fishers of men. And after he outlined it (John 6:41-65), many disciples left him. Yet twelve remained, Peter asking, "Lord, to whom shall we go? You have words of eternal life." Peter was spoiled with the supernatural. He was addicted to the divine; he didn't want to leave because he had seen God in action. Once youth have stepped out, on faith, depending utterly upon God, in obedience to total commitment, they then begin to see God in action. They will never again be satisfied with the product of man's routines and efforts without God. They will be spoiled, and will continually want to see God work in a greater way. But I feel here a need to caution you in your explanation of "cost." Although the cost must be explained to youthful workers, timing is of utmost importance. The full explanation of the ultimate nature of their commitment to God is best delayed until after they have been encouraged by the experimental stage. This is in line with Christ's words, "I have many more things to say to you, but you cannot bear them now" (John 16:12).

4. The exam phase

Every student knows what exam time means. It is the time when he proves to the teacher he has learned the material. We are disciples. Our exam is when we are actually tested, tried, and proven. Moses told the children of Israel, "And you shall remember all the way which the Lord your God has led you in the wilderness these forty years, that He might humble you, testing you, to know what was in your heart, whether you would keep His commandments or not" (Deut. 8:2).

When Jesus died, the disciples had to "die" with him. In order to continue following him, they relinquished all natural rights. The rights of reputation, ownership, family, friends, food, shelter, and even life itself had to be given up. This is the cost that we pay in order to mature. Christ said, "If anyone wishes to come after Me, let him deny himself and take up his cross, and follow Me" (Mark 8:34). "If you try to save something, you will lose it, but if you will lose it for His sake and the sake of the gospel, you will save it." That includes all human rights. The Lord will test every worker in every one of these areas. God will ask us at times to fast or to spend all night in prayer. This is a time of testing but also a time of growth. As God tests us to see if we will relinquish each of our rights, we will actually live through the "cross experience." We will pay the price. God has given us our human rights in order that we may turn them back to him and say, "I love you, God, more than the things you've given me." He will even test us with our ministry. He gives us a ministry and then he asks if we will "give it up." How? He gives us a dilemma. If we don't obey him we lose our authority; and if we do obey him we will lose our ministry in the eyes of others. Then when it looks as if the ministry is gone, God creates something new out of the situation. This has happened to my ministry and to our mission prior to every major advancement. If it is to be a world-wide advancement it is first a world-wide test. God wants his sons, like a grain of wheat to fall to the ground and die. This is that process which precedes a new release, a new authority, a new revelation of Jesus. These principles must be taught to young workers (and old as well) in order that they may have understanding at each step of their growth.

5. *The executive phase*

An executive is someone with *experience, understanding,* and *authority.* John 15:13-16, "Greater love has no one than this, that one lay down his life for his friends. You are My friends, if you do what I command you. No longer do I call you slaves; for the slave does not know what his master is doing; but I have called you friends, for all things that I have heard from My Father I have made known to you. You did not choose Me, but I chose you, and appointed you, that you should go and bear fruit and that your fruit should remain: that whatever you ask of the Father in My name, He may give to you." Our authority actually comes from the Lord. Promotion is not of man. Honor is not from man but from God, the Bible declares. As God releases authority, it brings the disciple to a new level of maturity and authority in his ministry. It happens quite suddenly, almost unexpectedly. He no longer speaks sermons but convictions. Also, God begins exchanging quantity for quality. Please note, these phases of Christian growth are continual processes not just one-time events. Each time God establishes a new ministry or vision for a worker he has to go through these steps again, only at a more sophisticated level. "The refining pot is for silver and the furnace for gold, but the Lord tests hearts" (Prov. 17:3). "The words of the Lord are pure words; as silver tried in a furnace on the earth, refined seven times" (Psalm 12:6).

To the degree that a worker is successful in his exam, to that degree God releases understanding and authority. If at the last he fails part of it, he has released only a partial authority and has to be tested again until he is able to pass the test completely. When he passes it with the right attitude and does all to the satisfaction of God, then God will release the authority. If the Christian has "padded" himself "in case God doesn't come through" and protected himself with extra man-made securities, he will have to take the test again later. When the worker, in a manner of child-like innocence, believes God and passes every test that comes his way, maximum authority is released to him. The young disciple quickly becomes a mature worker.

6. The extensive phase

This phase is concerned with God's plan to reach the whole world. Through Christ we see this ideal. He is building a dynamic growing pyramid of loving stones. Christ is the author and head of the pyramid that grows from the top downward.

Before discussing this ideal let us note what I believe to be one reason for the stunted growth of Christian movements. We all have seen mission organizations that never grow beyond the initial founders. Consider with me a hypothetical organization of several young men, aged twenty to thirty, who get a vision and begin to do what God has told them. Twenty years later they are aged forty to fifty, and yet no one younger has been added. What has happened? They received a vision from God and got excited about it. They stepped out and experimented and found that it was of God, and God's anointing was upon them and their vision. Then they began to understand the price of discipleship. These men went on and passed the test, and a new authority was upon them. They became excellent at winning souls, but it was by the method of a hook and fishing line — winning them one at a time — not "nets full and boat loads." There was no multiplication, just addition. The ratio God wants goes beyond just working with the authority of God on one spiritual generation of workers. He wants our lives to be multipled, leaders begetting leaders, geometrically not just arithmetically. When someone wanted to join this organization the leaders said, "We've very high standards." It is good to have high standards, but the standards they set were not the ones they had when they began. They were standards they developed since they arrived at the Executive phase. Because of these new "high standards," no new people joined their organization. In fact, they themselves could not have joined the organization they founded if they had required the same standard for themselves that they now require of others. So their mission is still winning souls, but it is not growing in staff and workers. Their converts simply go into other movements for service.

A leader must always be willing to take in people who are not as mature as he is. Without this, the Extensive phase will never be reached. I have heard our leaders say, "Some of the eighteen-year-olds are just not mature enough." I look at them and ask, "When did you join?" Most of them joined at eighteen. Our own attitudes change as we grow. Our standards, however, for others should not be as high as for ourselves, especially when they concern beginners. Never lose the excitement of the first phase of ministry, the vision. Always communicate this vision to others and allow them the privilege of making mistakes just as you did when you began. Each year the numbers of workers should increase as the pyramid grows larger. Each year the newest group of workers should also be the greatest in number. Doesn't that mean greater problems? Yes, but you will have leadership with greater experience, understanding, and authority growing up just ahead of the new groups. So as each group is added, years of experience are added to the older groups, and this keeps the work in balance. I always say that in Youth With A Mission we make more mistakes than almost any other Christian organization in the world because we are dealing with thousands of new young workers who make new mistakes. At least we give them the opportunity to make their own mistakes. This is part of growth needed in order to reach the world for Christ. Let us look again at our greatest example — Jesus himself.

He took young men where he found them and led them, a step at a time, into maturity. He first excited them with a vision. You will recall in Luke chapter five, he began with only three students — Peter, James, and John. Then by chapter nine he had a group of twelve, and in chapter ten he had seventy. By the first chapter of Acts his hard core followers had increased to 120. By the second chapter they had reached the Executive phase and ministered with great authority. In Acts 2:41 "... there were *added* ... three thousand souls," and in verse 47, "The Lord *added* to the church daily..." By Acts 4:4 "The number of the men was about five thousand," and in verse 32 they are called "a multitude." In chapter 6, verses 1 and 7 both record that "the number of the disciples *multiplied*," showing they had moved into the Extensive stage of multiplication. Their impact increased so greatly that later, some time after their scattering (chapter 8), they were referred to as "these that have turned the world upside down" (Acts 17:6). The growing church, though young, was on its way to total world evangelization.

It was Jesus, not Paul, that gave us the "Timothy principle." He showed us by his example that we are to have "a John, the beloved." The next circle of influence is Peter, James, and John — the inner circle. They were with Him at the first calling, on the mount of Transfiguration, at the Garden of Gethsemene.

This inner circle of disciples will keep a leader from getting a false "public image" and a public ministry different from his private spiritual growth and life. As we take care of the depth of our ministry, God will take care of the breadth. When we reach a new level of authority in our relationship with God, then God gives us a new authority with men. God will release disciples to us as he sees he can trust us with them. As God releases to us a Timothy or as our ministry grows to two or three followers, we should bring them in close to us and pray, study the Word, and face the decisions of the ministry with them on a day-to-day, detail-by-detail basis. As leaders we must let them see our mistakes as well as our strengths. Let them understand the principles behind each decision. Let them see how we seek to know and apply God's will to our life and ministry.

Our workers must know us both in our reactions to failures as well as successes. We must regularly humble ourselves before them by being open about failures. Then we too grow, especially as we have the humility to learn from our followers. Every leader should look for and expect God to add these disciples to him as he passes his tests as a leader. The

Holy Spirit will recruit them. When he does, the leader's job is to recognize them and receive the responsibility for their discipling. After that will come the twelve, then the seventy, and through them will begin the multiplication. Now, each one that joins the pyramid starts a pyramid of his own. The follower never competes with his spiritual leader. It is unwise to compare ourselves with one another, as we are all to obey our head, Jesus. Many little pyramids make up the big pyramid (Christ) from within, each tracing their leadership and submission to Jesus. Think of the structural strength of the overall pyramid. This is the strength of the body of Christ. Christ is the head over all. When each one of us starts his own pyramid, yet totally submitted to the ones over us that have fed and led us into spiritual maturity, and yet submitted totally to Christ, we will begin this extensive multiplication phase that will culminate in this generation by girdling the globe with the Gospel. At the same time the converts will become workers and the workers will be disciples and become leaders.

Conclusion

Mobilizing youth for evangelism is a process, not a one-time event. The Lord has a unique vision and experience for you as a leader. As you pass your tests, God's authority will come to you. But don't stop there; go on, and allow God to multiply your experience through others. Leaders simply go first, and then lead others through the same phases of growth. Never ask them to do what you yourself have not yet accomplished. This was and is Christ's method to get laborers, to disciple them, and to send them into the harvest field of the world. As this is accomplished in the family atmosphere of fellowship and love, all the spiritual, social, psychological, and personal needs of each worker can be met in the process of world evangelization.

MOBILIZING YOUNG PEOPLE FOR WORLD EVANGELISM REPORT

Young people today, as in every generation, are seeking a challenge to action. They are looking for direction and are open to new ideas and methods. Youth can be excited with a vision. We must put a vision of the task and the means to accomplish the task before them. Young people are full of faith; they have not heard that it can't be done! They believe God and are willing to step out in faith and trust God for miracles. We must put these attributes to work.

Young people must be taught to be disciples and count the cost of being a follower. There is a cross to bear in effective evangelism. Young people will go through trials, difficulties and testings; in many cases they will fail, and we must permit them to fail. They need the experience as well as the authority and guidance of godly men.

Each young person should be encouraged to build his own group so that we don't build superstructures but throw the responsibility back on the young people to lead and develop.

Training is an important factor in mobilizing young people. Short-term training in basics should be followed by training in the field under supervision. Change of location is also vital in mobilizing young people, as it is much easier for them to start in evangelism and get experience away from their home area.

Significant Issues

1. Cooperation with missionaries. Many nationals feel as if they are by-passed and not taken into the planning stages.
2. Cooperation with churches. It seems as though a dichotomy exists between new converts among young people and the older established churches.

It was recognized that bridges should be built as much as possible but also that at some times and in some places new local churches should be established on a different basis where young people will be accepted and allowed to share their life in Christ within a local church body.

Reasons why young people are getting involved:

1. The Holy Spirit's work
2. Leaders beginning to trust young people with work
3. Acts 2:17 (Joel's prophecy)
4. Challenge of discipleship
5. Identification with a cause or challenge
6. Expect results — reproduction (II Tim. 2:2)
7. More coordinated strategy — energy being channeled
8. Obedience to Word of God.
9. Rediscovery of power in prayer and praise
10. Great response — young people can do it
11. Flexibility of youth to be open to new things

Specific Obstacles
1. Denominational barriers
2. Church tradition — extra-biblical
3. Evangelical culture
4. Lack of courage
5. Revivals of religions — Buddhism, Animism
6. Lack of facilities and funds
7. Lack of trust by leaders and missionaries
8. Shallowness of message
9. Strong family ties
10. Materialism
11. Satan's activity through media
12. Peer pressure — loss of face
13. Politics — anti-God
14. Racialism
15. Inconsistency in lives of Christians
16. Corruption

The principle of "go" means a change of location.

Acts 2:7 - Galileans preaching in Jerusalem

Acts 26:4, 20 - Paul in Damascus

Acts 8:1 - all scattered except apostles

Mark 6:5 - Jesus could do no great work in his home town

A change of location will solve many of the problems listed above, e.g., traditionalism, family ties, etc.

Issues and Answers

1. Screening - make sure they understand the cost. Then they rule themselves out.

2. What happens when they get back home? Away from home first gives momentum to come back home. Have them cross denominational lines. It gives them diversity and broadness to see the "body" of Christ as a whole.

3. What do you do if churches are non-receptive? Be submissive. Show an attitude of willingness to help. Yet go on with your work at the same time.

Summary - We must keep our programs on a spiritual level and the problem will be resolved as we submit to the Holy Spirit.

EVANGELIZATION OF WHOLE FAMILIES

Chua Wee Hian

*Dr. Chua, London, England, is General
Secretary of the International Fellowship of
Evangelical Students.*

Year: 1930
Locality: Northwest China
Case studies:
1. The approach and strategy of two single European lady missionaries.
2. The approach and strategy of the Little Flock Assembly of Chefoo, Shantung.

Objectives: Identical — to plant local churches and to engage in extensive village evangelism.

Case study 1. Two gifted and dedicated lady missionaries were sent by their missionary society to Northwest China. Their mandate was to evangelize and plant congregations in a cluster of villages. They spoke fluent Chinese; they labored faithfully and fervently. After a decade, a small congregation emerged. However, most of its members were women. Their children attended the Sunday School regularly. The visitor to this small congregation would easily detect the absence of men.

In their reports and news letters, both missionaries referred to the "hardness of hearts" that was prevalent among the men. References were made also to promising teenagers who were opposed by their parents when they sought permission for baptism.

Case study 2. In 1930 a spiritual awakening swept through the Little Flock Assembly in Shantung. Many members sold their entire possessions in order to send seventy *families* to the Northwest as "instant congregations." Another thirty *families* migrated to the Northeast. By 1944, forty new assemblies had been established, and all these were vitally involved in evangelism.

Now, in terms of dedication and doctrinal orthodoxy, both the Europeans and the Little Flock Assembly shared the same commitment and faith. But why the striking contrasts in results and in their strategies of church-planting?

Consider the case of the two single lady missionaries. Day by day, the Chinese villagers saw them establishing contacts and building the bridges of friendships with the women, usually when their husbands or fathers were out working in the fields or trading in nearby towns. Their foreignness (dubbed "red hair devils") was enough to incite cultural and racial prejudices in the minds of the villagers. But their single status was something that was socially questionable. It was a well-known fact in all Chinese society that the families constitute basic social units. These units insure security. In Confucian teaching, three of the five basic relationships have to do with family ties — father and son, older brother and younger brothers, husband and wife. The fact that these ladies were making contacts with individual women and not having dialogues with the elders would make them appear to be foreign agents seeking to destroy the fabric of the village community. A question that would constantly crop up in the gossip and discussion of the villagers would be the fact of the missionaries' single state. Why aren't they married? Why aren't they visibly related to their parents, brothers and sisters, uncles and aunts and other relatives? So when they persuaded the women or the youth to leave the religion of their forefathers, they were regarded as "family-breakers."

By contrast, the Little Flock Assembly in sending out Chinese Christian families sent out agents that were recognizable socio-cultural entities. Thus the seventy families became an effective missionary task force. It is not difficult to imagine the heads of these families sharing their faith with the elders of the villagers. The grandmothers could informally transmit the joy of following Christ and of their deliverance from demonic powers to the older women in pagan villages. The housewives in the markets could invite their counterparts to attend the services that were held each Sunday by the "instant congregations." No wonder forty new assemblies were established as a result of this approach to church-planting and evangelism.

Evangelizing families in other cultures

The strategy of evangelizing whole families is applicable not only in Chinese communities. It is also effective in other Asian communities, African villages and tribes, Latin American *barrio* and societies. Writing on the rapid spread of the Christian faith in Korea, Roy Shearer observed: "One most important factor governing how the church grew is the structure of Korean society. In Korea, we are dealing with a society based on the family, not the tribe. The family is strong even today .... The soundest way for a man to come to Christ is in the setting of his own family."

He went on to relate repeated situations when heads of families returned to their clan villages and were successful in persuading their relatives and kinsmen to "turn from idols to serve the living God." He concluded: "The Gospel flowed along the web of family relationships. This web is the transmission line for the current of the Holy Spirit that brought men and women into the church."

In her book *New Patterns for Discipling Hindus,* Miss B.V. Subbamma categorically asserted that the Hindu family might be the only social institution through which the Gospel could be transmitted and received. Not all would agree with this assertion, because there are evidences of university students who have professed faith in Christ in the great university centers of India. Some could take this step of faith because they were free from parental pressures. However, as a general rule, Miss Subbamma's observation and deduction are correct.

Evangelizing whole families is the pattern of current missionary outreach in parts of Latin America. There in the Roman Catholic culture of web-relationships, family structures are strong. Exploiting this social pattern the Chilean Pentecostals, like the Little Flock Assembly in Shantung forty years ago, dispatch *families* from among their faithful to be agents and ambassadors of church expansion. Through these evangelizing families, many assemblies and congregations have been planted in different parts of that continent. The phenomenal growth of the Pentecostal movement in Latin America reflects the effectiveness of using families to evangelize families.

At times it is difficult for individualistic Westerners to realize that in many "face to face" societies religious decisions are made corporately. The individual in that particular type of society would be branded as a "traitor" and treated as an outcast if he were to embrace a new religious belief. After the Renaissance, in most Western countries, identity is expressed by the Cartesian dictum *Cogito ergo sum:* I know, therefore I am. Man as a rational individual could think out religious options for himself and is free to choose the faith that he would like to follow. This dictum does not apply in many African tribal communities. For the Africans (and for many others) the unchanging dictum is, *I participate, therefore I am.* Conformity to and participation in traditional religious rites and customs give such people their identity. So if there is to be a radical change in religious allegiance, there must be a corporate or multi-individual decision.

This is particularly true of Muslim families and communities. The one-by-one method of individual evangelism will not work in such a society. A lecturer friend of mine who teaches in the multi-racial university of Singapore once made this significant remark, "I've discovered that for most Malay students (who are nearly all Muslims) Islam consists not of belief in Allah the supreme God — it is *community."* Ambassadors for Christ in Islamic lands should cope not only with theological arguments concerning the unity and nature of God, they should consider the social and cultural associations of Muslims. Where sizable groups of Muslims had been converted their decisions were multi-individual. An excellent illustration would be that of Indonesia. During the past fifteen years, wise missionaries and national pastors had been engaging in dialogues and discussions with the elders and leaders of local Muslim communities. When these decision-makers were convinced that Christ is the only way to God and that he alone is the Savior of the world, they would return to their villages and towns, and urged all members to turn to Christ. So it was not surprising to witness whole communities being catechized and baptized together.

Such movements are termed as "people movements," and many years before the Indonesian happening, Ko Tha Byu, a remarkable Burmese evangelist, was instrumental in discipling whole Karen communities and villages to Jesus Christ. Today the Karen church is one of the strongest Christian communities in Southeast Asia.

The biblical data

When we turn to the biblical records, we shall discover that families feature prominently both as the recipients as well as the agents of salvation blessing.

To begin with, the family is regarded as divinely instituted by God (Eph. 3:15). In fact, all families owe their descent and composition from their Creator. By redemption, the church — God's own people, is described as "the household of God" (Eph. 2:19) and the "household of faith" (Gal. 6:10).

In the Pentateuch, great stress is laid on the sanctity of marriage, the relation between children and parents, masters and slaves. This emphasis is underscored in the New Testament (see Col. 3:18-4:1; Eph. 5: 22-6:9; I Pet. 2:18-3:7).

It is the family or the household that pledges its allegiance to Yahweh. Joshua as head of his own household could declare, "As for me and my house, we will serve the LORD" (Jos. 24:15). Through Joshua's predecessor Moses, Yahweh had taught His people to celebrate his mighty acts by sacred meals and festivals. It is interesting to observe that the feast of the passover (Exod. 12:3-4) was a family meal. The head of the family was to recite and reenact the great drama of Israel's deliverance at this family gathering. Throughout Israel's history, even until New Testament days, family feasts, prayer, and worship were regularly held. Thus the Jewish family became both the objects of God's grace and the visual agents of his redemptive actions. Their monotheistic faith expressed in terms of their family solidarity and religion must have created a tremendous impression on the Gentile communities. One of the results was that large numbers of Gentiles became proselytes, "associate members" of the Jewish synagogues. Jewish families made a sizable contribution to the "missionary" outreach.

by households (*kat' oikon,* Acts 2:46). The apostolic pattern for teaching was in and through family units (Acts 20:20). The first accession of a Gentile grouping to the Christian church was the family of the Roman centurion Cornelius in Caesarea (Acts 10:7,24). At Philippi, Paul led the families of Lydia and the jailer to faith in Christ and incorporation into his Church (Acts 16:15, 31-34). The "first fruits" of the great missionary apostle in Achaia were the families of Stephanas (I Cor. 16:15), Crispus and Gaius (Acts 18:8; I Cor. 1:16; Rom. 16:23). So it was clear that the early church discipled both Jewish and Gentile communities in families.

It was equally clear that households were used as outposts of evangelism. Aquila and Priscilla used their home in Ephesus and Rome as a center for the proclamation of the Gospel (I Cor. 16:19; Rom. 16:5). Congregations met in the homes of Onesiphorus (II Tim. 1:16; 4:19) and Nymphas (Col. 4:15).

Practical recommendations

Having considered the importance of families as both the recipients and agents of the Gospel from the biblical records and from various socio-cultural settings, I would like to propose that we take action on the following recommendations:

(i) The church today needs to review its evangelistic approach to communities where religious decisions are corporate matters and where families function as basic social units. It might need to emulate what leaders and members of the Spirit of Jesus Church in Japan have been doing for some years — developing *sweet potato vine* evangelism. Bishop Murai of this fast-growing Japanese church movement had always encouraged his members to cultivate contacts and relationships with families — "the vine" — as opposed to individuals — "individual fruit."

In the long run, such an approach yields considerable fruit when the whole family turns to Christ and seeks to live as his disciples in the natural framework of the home. Bishop Murai's churches are household churches, and activities are planned by families for families.

Missionaries from the West will do well to heed the words of Dr. Eugene Nida, the gifted missionary statesman and linguist: "We who do not know the meaning of clan life, since we ourselves are not members of such a society, can rarely imagine the pressure upon the individual in such an organization. We take it for granted that anyone can and should make up his own mind about what he believes and what he should do. But this is not true in all cultures, where individuals do not act on their own, but respond as members of families, clans and tribes."

What is urgently needed today is a corps of evangelists and church planters who understand family networks and ties and use these as the transmission lines for the propagation of the Good News.

(ii) Christians should make full use of family occasions for the preaching of the Gospel. Birthdays and weddings are festive events to communicate to relatives and close friends the joy of the Lord. Surprisingly, an occasion that brings relatives near and distant together in many Third World communities is the *funeral service*. Kinsmen and friends would normally turn out in full force to pay their respects to the deceased and to comfort the bereaved. Now if the bereaved were committed Christians, they could turn the funeral service into an occasion of triumph and victory. Christ had conquered death! Their loved one is now with his Lord. The joy and victory of the resurrection could be transmitted effectively at the graveside.

(iii) Christian homes should be encouraged to become outposts for evangelism to the local communities. In an age of impersonal relationships and an artificial atmosphere created by technocracy, many people, especially those living in huge industrial cities, would welcome a change of values. As members of Christian families demonstrate love by sharing and caring, and also by introducing the living Lord to their neighbors and contemporaries, more men and women will be drawn to Christ himself. House-churches and Christian fellowships in the big complexes of high-rise apartments of Buenos Aires, Singapore, Hong Kong, and Johannesburg could be bases for sustained evangelism.

(iv) Families must feature prominently in almost every form of Christian activity and evangelistic outreach. Consider Christian literature. Too much emphasis has been made on individual discipleship. There are very few books which discuss family life and family evangelism. There are many evangelical books which teach young Christians to make a firm stand against their non-Christian family, but very few which teach them to win their entire families for Christ. Christian publishers would do the Church of God invaluable service if they were to produce literature that portrays the Christian family as a corporate force for local evangelism — and when they encourage local Christian writers to instruct young believers to disciple their parents, brothers, sisters, and other relatives. In the case of discipling the older generation, young Christians would need counsel and advice as to how they could invite and involve their church elders in evangelizing their parents and grandparents.

Recently some of my co-workers who are vitally involved in student evangelism have been learning in a fresh way the need to relate student work in a family context. In the past, these workers had seen students wonderfully converted at conferences and also on campuses. However, within a matter of weeks, many of these converts "drop out." In Roman Catholic settings where family ties and traditions are strong, students who profess conversion are branded as those who have been brainwashed by heretical sects. To counter this accusation and, more important, to win the confidence of the elders, our workers would visit the homes of the new believers. A face-to-face encounter with parents had created a bridge of understanding. In the Philippines, there are cases of Christian students who through their consistent lives and through family Bible studies have led their families to a living faith in Christ Jesus.

(v) God may be calling his servants in Asia, Africa, and Latin America to a new strategy in missionary outreach. It is customary in the West to recruit a young man or a young woman and often a young couple for missionary service. Like the Little Flock in Shantung and the Chilean Pentecostals, could it be that God would have Asian families (grandparents, parents, and children) become his special messengers and envoys to communities with strong family networks? Corporate evangelism might well be the distinctive contribution that we could make to the worldwide church.

EVANGELIZATION OF WHOLE FAMILIES REPORT

Chairman: William Thompson
Secretary: Earle E. Fries

The participants in this group coming from some twenty nations, represented the church in all major geographic areas of the world. At the first meeting as participants expressed why they were attending this particular strategy group it became obvious that the Holy Spirit is burdening the church worldwide with the importance of the family and the imperative of reaching the *whole* family for Christ.

This is interesting because in many areas of the non-Christian world, the family continues to disintegrate while in the Christian community the family is coming into clearer focus.

Of course in this group we were dealing with many different cultural backgrounds so the questions, comments and contributions reflected a whole spectrum of orientations. However, this was a cross-cultural fellowship within the body of Christ and brothers and sisters were learning how one another live.

After Dr. Chua briefly reviewed his paper on the subject, there was a brief period of response to its content. A typical example which pointed up the essential nature of this subject to the missionary effort came from a participant from Latin America. It was pointed out that tradition in Latin American countries calls for nine days for prayer and consolation after the death of a family member. Evangelical missionaries have developed a reputation in some areas of going right to the tomb and then on with life without reflection on this life and death. These sensitive family experiences must be reconsidered if the whole family is to play an important part in evangelization within the frame of reference of its culture.

The chairman suggested four questions which were to become the focal points of our discussions. These were:

1. How can the *extended* family be reached for Christ?
2. How can church programs be adapted to meet family needs, instead of merely the needs of various age groups?
3. What methods and programs have been effective in whole family evangelization in your area?
4. How can the *fractured* family be reached and united in Christ?

This report will summarize the discussion in both small groups and the entire group relative to these questions.

Extended family evangelization —

Definition: Extended family means slightly different things in different cultures. However, in general, it means the extension of the family relations from the parent-child relationship (Nuclear Family).

Goal: The goal of Christian evangelization is to unite families *in Christ,* not split them. Splitting was a tactic of the colonialist to weaken and gain control of people.

Procedure: It is essential to identify the head (leader) of the family (the one who makes religious decisions for the family), and reach that one first.

Where a woman is the cultural head of the family, e.g., the Philippines, there is a conflict with the normal biblical position of the male headship (cf., I Cor. 11:3). A possible answer is to deal with the cultural head first. When decisions for Christ are made, deal with the biblical issue as a part of discipleship.

In some cultures decisions are made by consensus, e.g., Ethiopia. This, too, must be respected even though the initial thrust is to the cultural head.

Status in relationships based on age, education, wealth, etc., may determine who will be received as the messenger. For example, those who are parents may listen only to those who are parents.

Bible studies: If one member of a family becomes a Christian, ask to have Bible studies with the entire family. If the husband is not willing, don't go.

Try not to offend, be sensitive to the cultural issues.

Practical ministries of love: Be quick to help the family in need. If the mother is sick, clean the apartment and look after the children.

Literature: Get literature into the family. Use the Bible plus helpful titles. Suggest they be read in family gatherings and offer to give help in understanding.

Church programs and family needs —

Identify needs: It will be necessary to identify *family* needs, e.g., recreational, educational, social, spiritual, etc.

Scheduling: A more flexible time schedule for meetings may be necessary. The church is to serve and in serving it is necessary to consider the needs of those whom it is serving.

Program: Specific family fellowship nights have proven successful. A demonstration of effective family devotions could be presented.

Family church dinners where family units plus "adopted" singles eat together and share and pray together have been successful.

An interesting change in program reported was to dispense with the Sunday evening service once a month and help families work out their own family worship and celebrate it together at home.

Responsibilities: Give *families* responsibilities for church life, e.g., present service as a family, bring flowers, clean church, visit other families, etc.

Pastors or other church leaders could go to new Christian families to teach them how to have family Bible studies.

Methodology in whole family evangelization

Neighborhood evangelism: Several Christian families could move into the same neighborhood to work cooperatively in rearing their own children as a witness to non-Christian neighbors.

Visitation: Christian husbands and wives have gone as teams to visit non-Christian couples. Husbands with husbands, wives with wives.

Home Bible Studies: Look for openings through normal contacts with friends and relatives. In some home Bible studies there are special readings for children from a book such as *Pilgrim's Progress.* Bible studies should be geared to adults. If children are present, they could be included by having them read from a children's edition of the Bible. Family Bible studies should be with one family only.

A limited study of four to six periods was suggested as an initial effort.

Family social events: In some areas, family picnics are popular where non-Christian families are invited for recreation, fellowship and discussion of spiritual issues. Another suggestion was to have family dinners in a Christian home and invite non-Christian families to share a film or family devotions.

Weddings: In some areas a new form of weddings is being used. These involve the Christian bridal party and Christian parents verbalizing their faith and values regarding the marriage relationship with their friends and guests.

Fractured family evangelization

Preventative: Christians should be counseled regarding the biblical teaching concerning marrying only Christians (cf. II Cor. 6:14-18; I Cor. 7:39). In some countries, such as India, a Christian who marries a non-Christian is excommunicated. However, the biblical authority for this was not stated and it was pointed out that this would only drive the believer farther away.

Education: The church has an educational responsibility to teach new Christians how to relate to non-Christian members of their family.

Counseling: Christian husbands or wives who have or have had non-Christian mates can counsel the new Christian regarding the biblical teaching on reaching their mate for Christ (cf. I Peter 3:1-7; I Cor. 7:12-16).

These statements reflect the current practices of various churches around the world. Also included are some yet untried suggested by group participants.

The group did not see a need for an organization for this purpose, but did stress that whole family evangelization should be a high priority item in the total field of evangelization.

REPORT ON WOMEN'S SESSIONS

*Several strategy groups were arranged
spontaneously by participants at the
Congress. This report is from one of those
groups.*

In terms of numbers, women were very much in the minority at the International Congress on World Evangelization, Lausanne '74, but the challenge which was given to them was great. The sessions were organized and chaired by Mrs. Nell Maxwell of Barrie, Ontario, Canada, the Director of Women Alive. The underlying theme of the three consecutive sessions was "Relevancy and Effectiveness in Our Witness Where God Has Placed Us."

The first session was directed primarily to pastors' wives since most of the women at the Congress fit in this category. Mrs. Jill Briscoe, wife of Rev. Stuart Briscoe, of Milwaukee, Wisconsin, addressed herself to some of the basic problems which confront a pastor's wife if she purposes to have an effective ministry.

Mrs. Briscoe presented some startling questions when she asked, "Does God consider women second grade material?" "Has a woman the right to teach or speak?" The answer would seem obvious she said, but "unfortunately, the answer lies greatly in the cultural and denominational background." These factors somehow are often influenced by misguided people and yet are so important in a particular dimension of womens' lives. The fact that they are misguided very often produces a negative situation without any regard to the biblical position. She went on to say that many men firmly state that because a woman must be submissive it is neither her right nor privilege to speak in or on behalf of the church. She further observed that contrary to this concept if a woman is indeed invited by the ruling body of the church or organization to exercise her gift of speaking, under their headship, she is not usurping authority but is rather being submissive and obedient.

A woman must not repress gifts given to her because of someone else's opinion, but must search and find God's will for her life. When a woman finds her true spiritual gift and exercises it, it is charming. She noted that no one can resist a ministry truly expressed in obedience to the Lord.

Mrs. Briscoe challenged the women to examine their lives and see if they had deliberately buried gifts which God had given to them for specific service. She then noted that it is the work of the Holy Spirit to cut us down to size and not build us up. It is at that point that true liberation is found in Jesus Christ and real peace when one is obedient to the will of God for her life.

The importance and relevance of sharing Jesus Christ with people where they are was heavily stressed throughout this presentation with the interspersion of stories from personal experiences.

The diversification of ministries was evident as women from different cultures attempted to interject questions to stimulate discussion on ordination of women, formulation of worldwide women's evangelical organizations and other such topics.

Mrs. Briscoe emphasized that women must never be satisfied with the status quo but rather should open themselves to the will of God that his creativity could work through them.

Organization of time was discussed since it was felt that it was a priority. The importance of this facet of women's lives was stressed as women can be so busy in Christian work that they can develop masks to cover the foulest thoughts and resentments. There is no relevant or significant witness to our peers until we have first learned that the study of the Word of God and meaningful prayer is a prerequisite in order to know the mind of God in these situations.

Honesty in relationships, ability to accept ourselves and hence others were also emphasized as important issues in the whole area of communication. She strongly emphasized the importance of the positive concept in every facet of life. The relationship which we have with the Lord through the study and knowledge of God's Word and prayer will be the determining factor which will decide how we address ourselves to every situation. On pastors' wives she said that many ministries are destroyed because women are not willing to let the Word of God speak to them. However, a pastor's wife would be a freak if she attempted to satisfy the expectation of every person's demands. Hence the necessity to exercise the spiritual gifts bestowed on her by the Lord releasing her to do what the Lord demands and not what the church expects.

In the second session Corrie ten Boom spoke from her vast experiences of the relevancy of a personal and intimate prayer life with Jesus Christ. She told of how the Lord had personally communed with her in times of deep distress. Prayer was meaningful to her in the difficult times, not so much in the area of being delivered from a situation, but rather that the Lord stood with her in the midst of those times.

Ellen de Kroon affirmed what the Lord has taught, and is teaching, in being able to trust the Lord once having committed herself in prayer to him. The relevancy and intimacy of prayer was again emphasized as a very essential factor in the arena of life where one needs new spiritual strength daily.

Millie Dienert, the International Prayer Chairman of the Congress and a member of the Planning Committee, introduced the third session stating that she learned the importance of prayer early in life by the example set by her mother. Methods of ministry may differ worldwide but prayer is common ground. She noted that 1,600,000 people around the world prayed daily for the Congress and that its success would be attributed to the faithfulness of those who prayed.

Mrs. Dienert addressed herself to the factors that affect life's basic relationships and how we cope with problems. It is at this level that our prayer life becomes real. Negative reactions, negative thoughts, criticism and inability to accept others inhibit our spiritual growth unless we experience a meaningful prayer life.

A solid prayer life makes a life truly represent Jesus Christ and not a structure set by man. Prayer falls into three important facets, (i) controlling, (ii) conquering, (iii) cleansing. Mrs. Dienert cautioned that a person's life needs controls and this can only be accomplished by the Holy Spirit. Consequently time spent with the Lord is important but the process of working it out is even more important. The controlling process must begin on our knees, if an honest communication with God is to continue all day.

A strong note was sounded in the area of the ego problem. Women are forever molding the lives of others and have rejected the concept "Not my will but Thine be done." The ever present problem amongst Christians was exposed in that we constantly categorize others in the same way that we make molds. When someone refuses to fit that mold, relationships disintegrate. We cannot accept others mainly because of obstruction caused by our own ego. It is in this stage that the conquering phase of prayer becomes operative, where we are ever reminded that the Lord has the perfect mold. The warning was given with clarity that it is imperative to say genuinely, "Lord, you take over." Prayer of this nature is essentially dangerous because there must, of necessity, be honesty and obedience as God uses others and his Holy Spirit to remove the edges.

The third stage, the cleansing process, was declared to be of utmost importance, for it is at this level that one must honestly ask, "Why am I doing what I am doing in relation to God?" Total commitment demands that we allow the Spirit of God to move in while we move out. There will be no doubt in our minds when God wants us to move.

A prevailing note sounded repeatedly throughout the conference was that the Gospel is not cultural, human needs are not cultural, there are basics, and as Christians we all grapple with the same problems and need.

Mrs. Dienert culminated her remarks with a recurring note, "Prayer is not the hours spent in it, but the continuing process of it through the moments of the day whether sleeping, resting or working — whatever state you find yourself."

Jean Goddard, prayer chairman of South Africa, in expressing her personal experiences in the development of prayer circles for the Congress observed that prayer opens doors and hearts hitherto unopened, drawing together into a fellowship those who were otherwise strangers to each other, yet within the body of Christ.

Jean Reddon, Director of Christian Women's Conventions of Australia, spoke briefly of prayer as a driving force in the personal spiritual growth of the Christian woman, the supportive nature of personal prayer for the ministry of others, the growth experienced as a result of an ongoing prayer relationship with God, and the effectiveness of bridging the gap in the area of relationships within the Christian community.

Miss Reddon expressed strongly that in her opinion God made man and woman to be together. However if it has not been a woman's privilege to be married, she must not drown in the slough of self-pity. She challenged singles to recognize the fact that God does indeed have a plan for their lives; that God has indeed given gifts to all and they must be used.

Bonnie Barrows, Director of Women's Work for Billy Graham Crusades, spoke of the need of creativity in prayer. She exhorted women to plan prayer groups because of the great need for small groups to pray together. She stressed that, "If we fail to plan we most assuredly will plan to fail." A call to learn to pray specifically, to open homes for prayer, to recognize that prayer builds bridges and helps to communicate with others, was sounded to the women.

Joyce Danforth, prayer chairman for Sri Lanka, spoke of what God had done personally through prayer in her life. She declared emphatically that, contrary to women's liberationists, women do not need to take over but rather are to work side by side with men. This can only happen as we learn to sacrificially spend time with the Lord.

In the final analysis it is evident that there is no final limit to what God can do through a woman totally submitted to the will of God. God is on the move and he is most surely using women.

MEDICAL MISSIONS GROUP REPORT

Secretary: Morgan Derham

Several strategy groups were arranged spontaneously by participants at the Congress. This report is from one of those groups.

The group met on Monday and Tuesday afternoons, July 22 and 23. Those who attended included doctors, nurses and paramedical staff from Angola, Bahrein, Berlin, Egypt, Gambia, India, Indonesia, Italy, Kuwait, Nepal, Oman, Pakistan, the Philippines, Sudan, Thailand, USA, and Yugoslavia.

Most of the first session was taken up with participants introducing themselves, describing their work, and stating their special concerns. Topics for further discussion were suggested. At the second session, Mr. Ray Knighton, of M.A.P., introduced the subject chosen for discussion: The role of medical ministries in relation to government health schemes. His impression was that many Christian hospitals had yet to take this matter seriously. He described different patterns of relationship — (a) Total separation; (b) Mission hospitals receiving government support; (c) Mission hospitals recognized by governments; (d) Those taken over by government but retaining staff. He expressed his own beliefs that in general:

    i. Christian institutions should have closer relationships with governments.

    ii. Medical ministries should increasingly develop community and rural health schemes.

Relationships with churches were often unsatisfactory; he commended the Indian Emmanuel Hospitals Association, the Inter-church activities in rural health programs, and the international, inter-agency concept as illustrated by the United Mission to Nepal, and ACROSS.

Subsequent discussion mainly emphasized the same points, and included a report of an evangelical hospital run by a group of churches in Naples, Italy.

The meeting then commissioned its chairman and secretary to detail its findings in the form of a statement as follows: This meeting of participants involved in medical ministries wishes to emphasize the following points:

1. Medical ministries are a legitimate part of the communication of the Gospel of Jesus Christ (Matthew 9:35). They are not to be regarded merely as a means to an end, since they are in their own right a manifestation of the love of God.

2. Not only is there a continuing place for medical ministries, but new areas of opportunity are opening up.

3. Community health schemes, reaching out from existing institutions, are to be encouraged by all means; medical ministries should give a lead in these matters to other authorities, and in training paramedical and similar workers.

4. Medical ministries should cooperate wherever possible
    with government health services, and help to set standards
    of compassionate and fully integrated care.
5. In view of the new opportunities, medical personnel of ev-
    ery kind should be encouraged to offer their services to
    needy areas, long-term or short-term, in general medicine
    or specialized fields.

Section VII:

Theology of Evangelization Papers and Reports

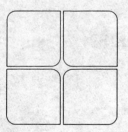

THE AUTHORITY OF THE BIBLE AND THE LORDSHIP OF CHRIST

Eui Whan Kim

Dr. Kim, Seoul, Korea, is editor of the
Presbyterian Journal and a Professor
in the Seminary of the Presbyterian Church.

The issue of biblical authority as the Word of God lies close to the center of Christian theology. Christianity stands or falls with the very question of authority of the Bible as the Word of God. Where we stand on this issue will determine the power of the Gospel we proclaim to the world. The question of biblical authority is, then, not the playing of the theological expert. It is the practical foundation on which the Gospel rests.

Everyone, therefore, who wishes to engage in the proclamation of the Gospel should first confront this question of biblical authority. Preaching is not the act of unfolding our personal convictions, but the act of informing sinners all that God has revealed. Evangelism presupposes submission to the authority of Scripture. In this sense the Lordship of Jesus Christ over every witnessing believer first starts with the question: "How do I accept the authority of the Word of God?"

The source of biblical authority

The acceptance of biblical authority is due to the belief that it is a divine revelation. In other words, what makes the Bible authoritative is that it is a divine Word. The question then arises, "Did God really speak to man?" Some fundamental presuppositions must be considered concerning this point.

First, *divine revelation is possible.* If we believe that God exists and is almighty, of course he can communicate himself to us. The very fact that God is alive proves the possibility of the self-communication of God, because it is the essence of love to reveal itself.

Second, *divine revelation is necessary.* God is bound in Christ to reveal his love toward sinners. In a special sense, revelation is available in the person of his Son, our Lord Jesus Christ. "In many and various ways God spoke of old to our fathers by the prophets; but in these last days he has spoken to us by a Son" (Heb. 1:1-2). About this revelation in Christ, we believe that the Scriptures are the clearest, fullest, and most complete expression and embodiment. And that Christ is the supreme revealer of God. Here we find the source of biblical authority in Christ.

Different views of Scripture

There are four different views of Scripture concerning the authority of the Bible.

First, *there is the Catholic view.* This holds the church to be the seat of authority. Of course the Church of Rome also believes that the Bible has divine authority and that through the Bible God speaks to us. However, that church has actually weakened the authority of the Bible by adding oral tradition to Scripture and by giving the church its *magisterium,* the power of infallible and authentic interpretation. Rome claims to be the true defender of biblical authority. The Bible stands "under" the church.

On this point the noted Catholic theologian Ronald Knox says: "We have argued, first of all, that God is revealed in nature, then that he is revealed in Christ, and finally that Christ is revealed in his church, the Catholic Church. This general outline of certainty is sufficient to make us (if we wish to do God's will) take the church, the revelation of Christ, who is the revelation of God, for our guide on the rest of our journey; to let her teach us, knowing that her teaching must be his."

Knox thus dares to elevate the authority of the church above that of the Bible by insisting on the church's finality. Knox claims also that tradition has equal authority with the Bible. The Bible is thus one of the greatest sources of religious certitude; tradition is the other. By tradition is intended that oral teaching which the Lord gave to his apostles, and which they in turn handed on to subsequent generations.

Against these claims we must ask, "What constitutes the real church? Where is that church to be found?" The church in the fullest sense is best described as "the blessed company of all faithful people," and as such it is the product of divine revelation rather than the source of revelation.

The church is in the narrowest sense the product of Pentecost, and came into being on the Day of Pentecost by accepting divine revelation. Thus as the church began through accepting divine revelation it is difficult to see how it can be the seat of authority. Where does tradition find any support in Scripture for its authority and validity? Says Calvin, "Let us know that the assumption of the name of the church is a false pretense in all who are so carried away by the restraints of the Word of God, as to introduce a torrent of their own invention." As Calvin points out, tradition is no more than an assumption and an invention of the Church of Rome, and the attempt to endow upon tradition the same authority as the Bible has deserves to be condemned in the light of the Lord's own condemnation (Rev. 22:18).

Second, *there is the old liberal view.* The liberal held that man's natural abilities are to be used exclusively in the foundation of religious beliefs. The Bible is not the revelation of the Word of God, but simply an intellectual and philosophical symposium of ancient religious Jews. Only human reason is considered fully competent to discover and to define religious beliefs without any supernatural aid or divine revelation.

This view ignores the fact that man's faculties have been affected by sin. After the Fall, human reason became incapable of finding the truth without any supernatural help. This view ignores that there is such a thing as reality independent of reason. Truth is true whether we accept it or not. A thing must be true before we can accept it as truth. Truth is, first, objective — something presented — and only then is it subjective — something accepted. Thus reason is not originative or authoritative, but only a channel. It creates nothing; it weighs data and settles things as the result of weighing them.

Third, *there is the neo-orthodox view.* According to this also the Bible is a human book. It is not only the record of the religious experiences of men, but also a witness to a revelation of God. Being a product of fallible human beings, it naturally contains errors. Nevertheless, it is a special and holy book in the sense that it is "witness" to the revelation of God, namely, his revelation in Jesus Christ. This "witness" is a human witness and as such it is open to criticism. As a human book, the authority of the Bible is relative, yet at the same time when God encounters us in his free Spirit through this fallible witness, it becomes God's revelation to us and its authority becomes absolute. God's Word in the encounter comes to me, not as information, but as demand, and faith is not mental assent, but the response of obedience.

Revelation is that which happens in the response of faith, rather than any thing that is said to evoke that response. Revelation is an event rather than propositional communication. In this kind of existentialization of revelation the seat of authority still rests on the human side, which makes the revelatory event possible by subjective appropriation.

We see here the essential kinship between the old liberal view and the neo-orthodox view of the Bible. They differ in detail, but both begin from the same starting-point and end up with the same destination. If there is any difference between them, it is only this: while the liberal relativizes the authority of the Bible, the neo-orthodox subjectivizes it and makes Christianity a kind of uncontrollable "Christ-mysticism."

Fourth, *there is the evangelical view.* According to this the Bible is the Word of God in such a sense that whatever it says God himself says. The Bible is not "man's report to us of what God says but (it is) the very Word of God itself, spoken by God himself through human lips and pens." It is "the very Word of God, instinct with divine life from the 'in the beginning' of Genesis to the 'Amen' of the Apocalypse."

The fact, however, that the Bible is the very Word of God does not exclude the divine-human character of Scripture. The Bible was composed by men in human language as they were motivated and guided by the Spirit of God. Because God has used the medium of human language to make his will known and has employed men to put his message into writing, there is variety in the literary form of the Bible. This divine-human character of the Bible makes its appearance like any ordinary book but its content is a message from God. That message is found in the Bible, and the Bible is the Word of God. Because of the fact that the Bible is the very Word of God, the Bible is the seat of authority.

The reformers regarded the Bible as the supreme doctrinal authority in faith and morals, divine in origin and consequently infallible. This position is well presented by the Belgic Confession thus, "We receive all these books, and these only, as holy and canonical, for the regulation, foundation, and confirmation of our faith; believing without any doubt all things contained in them, not so much because the church receives and approves them as such, but more especially because the Holy Spirit witnesses in our hearts that they are from God, and also because they carry the evidence thereof in themselves."

The reformers emphasize the Bible's inherent authority and also its objective authority. They insist the Scripture has authority in and of itself as the inspired Word of God. It is the inspired Word of God which is written and therefore addresses man with divine authority.

The biblical doctrine of inspiration

Down through the ages the church has been convinced that the Bible in its entirety was inspired by God. The word "inspiration" needs to be clearly defined because of various modern uses of it.

Inspiration does not refer to the impression made upon the mind of the person reading the classical work or even the Bible. It refers solely to the impeccable text of the Bible which God breathed. The word "inspired" used in II Tim. 3:16 literally means, according to the Greek dictionary, "God-outbreathed." This term definitely affirms that all Scripture is the product of God's breath. Therefore the biblical meaning of inspiration rises far above the tendency to define inspiration merely as dynamic. Christ did not teach the inspiration of the writers of the Bible but he did teach the inspiration of their entire writings. Christ affirmed the inspiration of the entire Old Testament when he said: "Think not that I am come to destroy the law, or the prophets: I am not come to destroy, but to fulfill. For verily I say unto you, Till heaven and earth pass, one jot or one tittle shall in no wise pass from the law, till all be fulfilled," (Matt. 5:17-18).

That Christ considered the Old Testament inspired is also shown from his repeated question, "Have you not read?" The question is actually equivalent to, "Do you not know that God has said?" (cf. Matt. 19:4, 21:16, 22:31). The same meaning is to be understood by "it was written" (Matt. 26:31, 26:54, Mark 9:12, 14:19, 27). Whoever carefully studies the Gospel narratives in the light of Jesus' attitude toward the Old Testament will agree with Reinhold Seeberg's words: "Jesus himself describes and employs the Old Testament as an infallible authority."

Peter asserts that the Old Testament has a distinct supernatural quality for "holy men of God spake as they were carried along by the Holy Spirit" (II Pet. 1:21). Paul also regarded the entire Old Testament as God-inspired. In Rom. 3:2 he refers to the Old Testament writings as the oracles of God. Thus most of the New Testament assertions about the inspiration of the Scriptures are made about the Old Testament.

Then what of the New Testament? Here Christ's unique position as the center of the Old and New Testaments must come to recognition. He placed his divine approval upon the entire writings of the Old Testament. Likewise he guaranteed the inspiration of the New Testament by his promise of the Holy Spirit. In other words, "He who accredited the Old Testament retrospectively accredited the New Testament prospectively."

This prospective accreditation appears repeatedly in the New Testament. Jesus promised his disciples the Holy Spirit who would guide them into all truth and would bring back to their remembrance the teachings they had heard (John 14:26). Peter asserted that he spoke by the Holy Spirit (I Pet. 1:12). Paul also assured the Corinthians that his message was not of men but from God. Likewise to the Galatians he certified "that the Gospel which was preached by me is not man's gospel. For I did not receive it from men, nor was I taught it, but it came through revelation of Jesus Christ" (Gal. 1:11-12).

In writing to Timothy, Paul quoted Luke along with Deuteronomy as "Scripture" (I Tim. 5:18). Peter designates the writings of Paul "Scripture"

(II Pet. 3:16). Thus even before the close of the canon the Apostles were placing one another's writings in the same category as the Old Testament.

It was the position of the early Christians that the entire Bible was the Word of God. The Church fathers set forth the same testimony. The united testimony of such fathers as Clement of Rome, Justin Martyr, Irenaeus is that the Bible is in its entirety inspired by God himself. Such a high view of inspiration carries with it certain concomitant truths. That is the doctrine of inerrancy and infallibility of the Bible. Infallibility is a necessary inference to be drawn from the doctrine of inspiration. Inspiration is incompatible with errors in the Bible. If the words of Scripture in the original autographs are the very words of God inspired by the Holy Spirit, they must of necessity be inerrant and infallible. This was the attitude toward the Scriptures that was held by the historical evangelical Christians through the ages till the present day.

New voices among the evangelicals on biblical inspiration

On the basis of the above-mentioned view of inspiration, it has been supposed that historically the reformers and the evangelicals of our own day are in common agreement with biblical authority. Now the agreement seems incomplete, however, and we are beginning to hear new voices among the evangelicals which cause us theologically to be on the alert because they seriously question the historic doctrine of verbal inspiration and inerrancy of Scripture.

De Wolf well observed this new change for he writes: "There is a noticeable, though indecisive change in the biblical inspiration and authority. Some of the new evangelicals, unlike most of the fundamentalists, avoid teaching 'verbal' inspiration of the Bible, stressing rather plenary or full inspiration." A survey commissioned by *Christianity Today* clearly shows that hesitancy is now prevailing among evangelicals regarding the infallibility of Scripture.

The survey regarding theological positions among American ministers revealed: twelve per cent liberal, fourteen per cent neo-orthodox and 74 per cent evangelicals, the later comprised of 35 per cent "fundamentalists" and 39 per cent "conservatives." The distinction which was apparent regarding the doctrine of Scripture, showed that fundamentalists subscribed to the doctrine of inerrancy while the conservatives either did not subscribe to total inerrancy or had doubts about the doctrine. Nowadays we are beginning to hear from some evangelicals a cry for a reinvestigation of orthodoxy and a requestioning of biblical inerrancy, thus creating such a new theological climate.

Contemporary orthodoxy, to some evangelical minds, needs to be realigned because it "does very little to sustain the classical dialogue on inspiration. The foundation of new ideas has apparently run dry, for what was once a live issue in the church has now ossified into a theological tradition. As a result a heavy pall of fear hangs over the academic community."[10] Perhaps the basic reason for such a dissatisfaction against contemporary orthodoxy resides in the desire of some evangelical scholars to win a new respectability for orthodoxy in the academic community. To this end they even attempt to reexamine the doctrine of biblical inspiration and infallibility in the light of modern science.

In doing so, a dangerous subservience to science is being signaled. The desire to win intellectual acceptability and to gain a new respectability for orthodoxy has now led into a friendly attitude toward science almost to the point of placing scholarship and science in the seat of authority. The so-called "threshold evolution" of Edward J. Carnell and "the progressive creationism" of Bernard Ramm are chief examples of this new trend.

Lordship of Christ and proclamation

The damage done to the authority of the Bible is not, however, limited to denials of the infallibility and verbal inspiration of the Bible by liberals, neo-orthodox, or others. Damage to the Bible is also done even by those who affirm its fully divine character and inspiration. Some evangelicals consider the Bible as mere communication and statements about God which are directed to man's rational comprehension and demand primarily intellectual acceptance.

Of course, the Bible is communication and should be accepted as statements about God. It is, nevertheless, more than communication and more than statements about God. We should be more than simply "orthodox" about the authority of the Bible. In this respect the Pharisees of Jesus' day were in one way "orthodox," for they rigidly accepted every proposition in the Old Testament.

However, their attitude was severely under Christ's judgment, because they divorced the Scripture from Christ. If we divorce the Lordship of Christ from the Scripture, we become guilty of bibliolatry. We must not see the Bible in isolation from the redemptive act of Christ. If we let the Bible take a place due to Christ alone we are falling into another subtle form of pharisaic intellectual idolatry.

This form of danger is great among those who believe in verbal inspiration and yet fail to see the Bible in living and unbreakable relation with the sovereign Lord Jesus Christ and the message of proclamation that follows. The Lordship of Christ and the authority of Scripture must go hand in hand. The Lord Jesus Christ is the heart of all Scripture. Christ the Word incarnate, crucified, risen, glorified, now lays his total claim upon us in the words of his royal edict, "All authority in heaven and on earth has been given to me" (Matt. 28:18).

Under his Lordship, Scripture presses upon us the Gospel mandate which thrusts us into every corner of our world. Let us go forth then under his unlimited authority to fulfill the unlimited task of world evangelization with unlimited promise: "Lo, I am with you alway, even to the end of the world" (Matt. 28:20).

[1] *The Belief of Catholics,* 1958, p. 129.

[2] *Ibid,* p. 130.

[3] *Calvin's Institutes,* 1949, p. 466.

[4] B. B. Warfield, *The Inspiration and Authority of the Bible,* 1951, p. 125.

[5] Article V.

[6] *Text Book of the History of Doctrines* (tr. E. Baker), I, p. 82.

[7] *Ibid.*

[8] *Present Trends in Christian Thought,* 1960, p. 17.

[9] November 10, 1961.

[10] E. J. Carnell, *The Case for Orthodox Theology,* 1959, p. 110.

AUTHORITY AND UNIQUENESS OF SCRIPTURE REPORT

Chairman: Kenneth S. Kantzer
Secretary: Bruce Fleming

The issues of biblical uniqueness and of biblical authority, along with their corollaries, are matters vital to the Christian Church. Today many questions are being asked that strike at the heart of Christian assurance. These questions reflect the attitude of the age. Inside and outside the church, men are asking: "Can we really expect to find more than relative truth even in the Bible? And if so, just how are we to tell what is *true truth?*"

Claims rivaling those of the Bible are being presented to any who are skeptical of divine revelation. Such claims propose other "sacred writings" and represent attempts either to replace the Bible or to supplement it by offering the Bible *plus* culture, or the Bible *plus* tradition, or the Bible *plus* unique interpretation. These supplementary writings modify and, inevitably, negate the pure Word of the Bible (Mark 7:13; II Pet. 2:1).

For three days during the International Congress on World Evangelization, the Theology of Evangelization Study Group A wrestled with these and related topics. We hope that our conclusions and the following sketchy glimpses into our discussions will help other Christians as well to attain the goal we sought — a pure heart, a good conscience, and sincere faith (I Tim. 1:5).

Our discussion group was to serve not as a replacement for the paper but as a supplement to it. At the start of our discussion not all of us, by any means, were in agreement. After the resumé of the study paper and initial remarks by Dr. Kim, a recognizable minority opinion was still evident. As our discussion progressed, however, and as our facility in cross-cultural and cross-disciplinary communication increased, many apparent conflicts were eliminated. This paper, therefore, reflects the thinking of the vast majority of those present throughout the three sessions.

1. *The uniqueness and authority of Scripture*
    a. Uniqueness. We affirm the uniqueness of the Bible. It is the basic instrument used by the Holy Spirit to reveal the redemptive love of God in Christ Jesus, for it alone adequately transmits the message of the saving work of God (John 20:30, 31; Rom. 2:1 ff.; II Tim. 3:14, 15). All other sacred writings, documents, and books are to be judged in the light of the Bible and are to be given credence only insomuch as they conform to Scripture (Col. 2:8-10).
    b. Authority. We affirm the divine authority of the unique Bible. It is God's inscripturated Word given to Christians for all times and carries with it God's full weight of authority.
    God, the Creator and Father, has given Jesus, the Son, his own full and divine authority (Matt. 28:18). This same Jesus both taught, and by example confirmed, the authority of the Old Testament of the

Bible, even to the minutest detail (Matt. 5:17-19; Luke 16:17; 24:25), and utilized it as an authoritative statement which cannot be broken (Matt. 4:11; John 10:35; Luke 24:32).

In New Testament times, Jesus committed his authority to his Apostles both before his crucifixion and during his post-resurrection appearances (John 14:12-13; John 20:21). The Apostles, guided by the Holy Spirit, proclaimed, taught, and wrote on his authority (Acts 19:11; I Pet. 1:23-25; I Cor. 2:12, 13; I Thess. 1:13). Apostolic authority in the New Testament continues in effect today — a body of truth conveyed first by Apostolic preaching and then by written Apostolic tradition (II Thess. 2:15; I Cor. 15:1-6).

Thus the entire Bible, both the Old Testament and the New Testament, is God's authoritative message to us today. Affirming and accepting the authority of the incarnated and risen Christ, who taught and even submitted himself to the full authority of the Scripture (John 19:28), we too recognize the full authority of the Bible. For the same reason, moreover, we dare not overlook the claims that the Bible makes for itself as to its unique authority since such claims ultimately derive from the commission given to the Apostles by the Lord (II Tim. 3:16-17; II Pet. 1:20, 21; I Pet. 1:25).

2. Relationship to evangelization

We affirm the unique role of the Bible as the indispensable means for world evangelization (Heb. 4:12; Luke 1:1-4; John 20:30, 31; Heb. 3:4; II Tim. 3:14). We cannot know the true divine Christ apart from the Scriptures. Thus, the biblical Gospel must be the foundation for any Christian witness.

The task of world evangelization demands a message from God for all peoples of the world. The experiences of an individual or group cannot be the base for the universal Gospel; rather our message must be based in God's divine Word of revelation, the Bible, which is applicable to all men (Matt. 24:14). It is this Word, not personal opinions (II Tim. 4:2), that we are to preach. Such witness God has promised to bless (Isa. 55:11), and he will not deny his promise (Num. 23:19).

3. Terminology and straw men

We affirm the verbally inspired Bible to be the inerrant Word of God. Perhaps the largest amount of discussion time was devoted to this section. The affirmation is followed by elaborations in some detail in order to refute "straw men" often wrongly labelled as the Evangelical viewpoint.

Some asserted that verbal inspiration implies mechanical dictation as the method employed by God. It does not permit, therefore, an appropriate recognition of the truly human authorship of the books of Scripture. In reply, the consensus was that verbal applies to the extent of God's inspiration of the Scriptures and does not describe a methodology of inspiration. Dictation, especially, is not to be implied. Rather "verbal" denotes that the Holy Spirit so superintended the writers of Scripture that his guidance extended down to all the words used by each writer. This did not, however, inhibit in any sense the free expression of the personality of each biblical author. As thoughts and concepts are conveyed in words, so God conveyed his thoughts to us in the human words of Scripture by means of a verbal guidance very different in nature than human dictation.

The teaching of Scripture itself is clear on this point in many places. References are made to "Isaiah says" (Matt. 15:7; Luke 3:4; John 12:39), "David says" (Matt. 22:23, 24; Luke 20:42, 44; Acts 2:25), "Moses says" (Matt. 22:24; Mark 12:19). Luke examined his sources carefully and wrote in his Gospel what "seemed good to him" (Luke 1:1-4). John organized his Gospel in accordance with his purpose (John 20:30, 31). Such phrases point unambiguously to human authorship. On numerous occasions the historical books of Scripture refer to sources which the author used in preparation of Scripture (Josh. 10:13; I Kings 11:41; II Chron. 24:27).

The Bible is thus a fully divine product in which even the words were guided by God and produced by his inspiration, which is at the same time also a fully human production. Like our Lord, however, who in his divine human person was still free from the taint of human sin, so the Bible, a fully divine and fully human product, is able to speak God's truth in human language but without human falsehood. The words of Paul's Letter to the Galatians, for example, were not calmly copied by an unmoved scribe, but obviously poured forth in white heat from the burning soul of the apostle.

Early in the group discussion periods, some representatives balked at the use of the word "inerrant." One such objection related to scriptural use of exact scientific language. It was pointed out, however, that Scripture was not written in precise technical language. The word "inerrant" simply means "not wandering from the truth in any point." As applied to the Bible, it designates the entire trustworthiness of all Scripture says, without exception. At the same time, Scripture must be interpreted fairly in accord with what each passage in context is really endeavoring to affirm. For example, when the Bible uses the phrase "the sun rises" it is no more in error than twentieth-century man who uses the same phrase in daily conversation. It is not given for scientific description, but makes a true statement about the world in ordinary language.

In a similar misunderstanding, "inerrant" is often criticized as a phrase which demands literal interpretation of every word and phrase. Again this is not the case. Christ referred to King Herod as "that fox," but we are not forced to picture a literal four-footed furry creature.

The un-chronological order of many biblical statements was also raised up as a "straw man" to refute inerrancy. It has been said, for example, that various books of the Bible contradict each other in matters related to chronology. If, however, an author does not claim to be writing in chronological order, as is often the case, his listing of events should not be faulted if it varies from that of another author. Each author was free under God's inspiration to choose any data of special interest and concern to him, and to record it in whatever order best suited the purpose of his writings. As long as the author does not state that he is actually giving the events in a strict chronological order, we too must give him that freedom.

4. *Translations and autographs*

We affirm the verbally inspired Word of God to be inerrant in all of its autographs.

In the discussion regarding the inerrancy of the Bible, some raised the problem of conflicting translations, all of which "certainly could not be inerrant." The response of almost all those present and particularly in the discussion was that absolute inerrancy (freedom from untruth) lay only in the autographs of the prophets and the apostles, not in every extant text or translation.

This does not mean that our present texts are unreliable or without any authority. Most of the words of the original manuscripts we *do* have with us today in our present texts. They share in the divine authority of the originals to the degree that they are faithful renderings of the original texts. Our current texts are generally very trustworthy and, therefore, very authoritative.

The evangelical who knows that the original is absolutely free from error has an objective standard by which he may test all current texts and translations (The value of knowing that the original manuscripts — not now in our hands — were inerrant is clearly evident by comparing how the believing evangelical arrives at truth, contrasted with how one who does not accept an inerrant original must arrive at truth. For the evangelical, the degree of certainty that he has the correct text, plus the degree of certainty that he has the correct interpretation of any biblical passage, is precisely the degree of certainty he may have that he has the truth without error and, in fact, the very truth of God himself. For the person who does not accept an inerrant original, on the other hand, the degree of certainty that he has the correct text and has interpreted that text rightly has only the limited certainty that he has what an ancient prophet or the religious teacher Paul or John believed — which in itself may be true or false!

For the non-evangelical to discover the truth, he must pass Scripture through additional tests; and, unfortunately, in practice most of these additional tests are exceedingly subjective (like "what brings Christ to me," "what speaks to my heart," or "what is of faith"). No objective reasons can be given for such sieves applied to the teaching of Scripture. Certainly our Lord did not enjoin the use of any sieve to divide the good and true from the evil and false in Scripture. His word was to "believe all of it" (Luke 24:25).

5. *The canon*

We affirm the full divine authority of only the thirty-nine books of the Old Testament (twenty-two according to the reckoning of these same books by the Jews) and the twenty-seven books of the New Testament.

The question of additional books in the Roman Catholic Bible compared to the Protestant Bible was raised in the group and brought forth considerable discussion. It was pointed out by various members of the group that the books in dispute are exclusively Old Testament books. There is no disagreement as to which books belong to the New Testament. Neither our Lord nor the New Testament authors cited any of these disputed books (Enoch, referred to by Jude, is not one of them). More importantly, Christ (Matt. 5:17, 23:35; John 5:39) and his apostles (cf. II Tim. 3:14; Rom. 3:2) acknowledge the same Scriptures as did the Jews of their day. It is demonstrable that the Old Testament of the Jews, both of Palestine (cf. Josephus, *Against Apion*, I, 8:41, 42) and of the dispersion (cf. Philo cited by Eusebius, *De Pref. Evang.*, VIII, 6), was precisely the sacred books to which our Lord gave his allegiance. The apocrypha were existent at the time of Christ; but were not part of what he and the Jews considered Holy Scripture. They were gradually introduced into the canon in the Greek and Latin churches and were never insisted upon even by the Roman communion until after the Reformation period. In the light of their rejection by our Lord, evangelicals are obligated not to receive them in the canon of inspired Scripture, however interesting or profitable they may be as human litera- ture and history (and on these points the apocrypha vary greatly from one book to another).

6. *Relation of the Holy Spirit to evangelization*

We affirm the work of the Holy Spirit to be that not only of verbally superintending the writing of the inerrant Bible but also of enabling man to appropriate the objective truth of the Scripture so it becomes subjectively true to individual men in a personal way.

Often the *objective* truth of the Bible, which is that utilized by the Holy Spirit, is ignored, misconstrued, or denied; and the subjective work of the Holy Spirit on the heart is overly emphasized. Such a tendency was exhibited in a portion of our discussion. Consensus, however, em- phasized *both* the past inspiration of the Bible *and* the present work of the Holy Spirit here and now as he illuminates men's understanding of it (Eph. 1:18), so that it is also God's contemporary living Word to men.

Only men regenerated by the Holy Spirit are able to come to a true understanding of what God has inspired by the Spirit (I Cor. 2:14; II Cor. 3:14-16). The Word is to be proclaimed with the assurance that the Spirit of the Living God (Heb. 3:12) will accompany the living Word (Heb. 4:12) in a supernatural way to bring conviction of sin to men and salvation to those who believe (Rom. 10:9, 10).

7. *Desiderata*

Discussants laid special emphasis upon the necessity of keeping the preaching of Christ at the center of our message (Rom. 10:17). In preach- ing we are to submit to the divine authority of the Scripture. Humanly- devised methods are never to take precedence over the authoritative message. Faithfulness to our Lord demands that we preach the whole Christ of the whole of Scripture (John 5:39; Acts 20:27; II Tim. 4:2; Rom. 15:19).

In view of the authoritative and unique nature of the Bible, we urge men not to become a prey to "philosophy and empty deceit, according to human tradition, according to the elemental spirits of the universe and not according to Christ" (Col. 2:8-10). We urge brethren not to succumb to the call of another Christ or another gospel (Gal. 1:8, 9), but to rightly divide (treat) the Word of God (II Tim. 2:15) for it alone is the authoritative truth, provided for us by God and, therefore, profitable for teaching, for rebuking, for correcting and training in righteousness, so that the men of God may be thoroughly equipped for every good work (II Tim. 3:16, 17).

Conclusion

As evangelical Christians we are men and women under divine orders. The Bible, God's unique and authoritative Word, instructs us as to how to carry on the work of evangelization in our world in obedience to Christ. We must constantly strive to conform our actions to that divine Word, our authority, guide, and message (II Tim. 4:2, John 5:31; Heb. 4:12). Amen, alleluia!

HERMENEUTICS: BIBLICAL INTERPRETATION AND EVANGELISM
Saphir Athyal

Dr. Athyal, Yeotmal, Maharashtra,
India, is Principal of the Union
Biblical Seminary in India.

Diversities in Christian theological systems and differences in the teachings and emphases of various Christian groups may be ultimately traced to different methods of interpretation of the Bible. All Christian teachers, preachers, and theologians claim to base their knowledge on the Scripture, but one's presuppositions and methodology of exegesis determine what one "sees" in the text. Theological problems are basically hermeneutical problems. Hence the importance of the theme that is dealt with here.

The relationship between biblical interpretation and evangelism is almost solely the question of the right methods of interpretation by which a biblical theology of evangelism may be developed. Their relationship is not peculiar or different from the relationship between biblical interpretation and any other area of Christian theology and life. Therefore the discussion of this paper will primarily concern itself with proper methods of interpretation.

A concept of evangelism that is biblically founded is supremely concerned with the question of what the biblical record really teaches us about the nature of the evangelistic task entrusted to the Christian Church by its Lord, and what is the real content of the "evangel" or God's news for man. Essentially the same is the task of biblical hermeneutics, namely, to bring out the relevance of the message of the Bible for modern man by certain proper and valid principles of study of the Bible. The foundations of evangelism are not based on the desperate condition of the world and its crying needs, nor on the concern for others and missionary zeal of the church, but rather on the written Word of God, its authority, verdicts, and message. Evangelism is an empty notion if we cannot determine what the Bible does say to us. A right theology of evangelism can be developed only by a right way of "handling the Word of Truth."

The Bible is a mine of riches which was never exhausted by the church's scholarship and study through the last centuries. The more it is investigated and the better it is studied, the richer and newer are the treasures that are found in it. It seems sometimes to hide certain knowledge from the Church for many years and all of a sudden open up new understanding of the Truth with revolutionary effects. Many Old Testament passages were little understood by men during Old Testament times. Biblical scholars and "doctors of the law" during New Testament times spent much of their life time in full-time study and exposition of the Scripture, but concerning them St. Paul remarked, "For until this very day at the reading of the Old Covenant the same veil remains unlifted" (II Cor. 3:14). The Middle Ages had giants in biblical scholarship and outstanding theologians who produced numerous volumes of works interpreting the Scripture, but it was not until the Reformation period that many of the biblical foundational truths were rediscovered. Twentieth-century biblical scholarship gave new light on the developments of the writings and the message of the Bible, but today we feel that we stand at the threshold of a new age of biblical studies. The church seems to rediscover the Word from time to time and the understanding of its message is fresh and dynamic every time.

1. Certain inadequate methods of interpretation

For some considerable time we have seen the development of different methods of biblical interpretation, some of them adequate and most helpful, some not. We may note a few major examples of improper and inadequate methods of interpretation which lead to a false understanding of the teaching of the Scripture.

a. *Allegorical method* — this method of interpretation is based on the assumption that the real message of a biblical passage is not its obvious or natural meaning but rather something hidden and mystical. Bunyan's *Pilgrim's Progress* is an example of allegory. This method of study was applied to Greek myths by ancient Greek thinkers, particularly the Stoics. It was later used by Philo and the Alexandrian Jews to show the superiority of the Jewish Scripture over Greek philosophies, and to harmonize the two wherever desirable.

The early Christians exegetes used this method, especially in their controversy with the Jews to prove that the true hidden meanings of the Old Testament passages are fulfilled in Jesus Christ.

Clement of Alexandria spoke of five meanings or senses of any Scripture passage, namely: the historical sense or the actual event as recorded; the doctrinal sense which is the obvious theological teaching; the prophetic sense, that is to say, the predictive and typological meaning; the philosophical sense, that is the cosmic or psychological values; and finally, the mystical sense which is the deeper spiritual meaning.

Origen, Clement's great successor, following the analogy of the three-fold nature of man, said that each text has three senses: literal sense, compared to man's body and useful for the simple man; moral sense, compared to man's soul and useful for one growing in Christ; and spiritual or mystical sense, compared to the spirit of man and useful for the "perfect man." He held that if the Old Testament is studied only in the literal sense, Christians would be no better than Jews. To give an example of his use of this method, interpreting Joshua chapter two, he considered the spies as the forerunners of Christ, Rahab as representing the publicans and sinners, the scarlet thread signifying the blood of Christ, Rahab's house as the Church, etc., Origen's methods of allegorical interpretation influenced the church for several centuries after him.

The allegorical method was the single major principle of interpretation used by the church during the Middle Ages. While the literal interpretation was not abandoned, both the Old Testament and the New Testament were explained and taught through the allegorical approach to support the many traditions and doctrines of the Roman Church.

Typological interpretation is different from the use of allegory in this, that in typology no foreign meaning, a meaning which is not originally there, is supplied to a passage. In allegory, there is complete freedom in spiritualizing, and one can read into a passage almost anything one wants, while in typology the interpretation is bound to the historical sense of the passage.

There is an innate resemblance between the type and the antitype; type is a "prophetic symbol" which contains promise of a greater fulfillment which is to take place at a later time. We may use typology to the extent justified by the biblical use of it. Our approach ought to be a treatment of the whole and not of details. For example, while the tabernacle may lend itself to a typological explanation, the details of the tabernacle do not. Also, we should not base any fundamental doctrines on typological interpretation.

The basic weakness of allegorical method is that each passage is understood to have several meanings, the literal meaning being the least valuable one. The obvious surface meaning is treated only as the shell that surrounds the truth.

Allegorism brings chaos in biblical study, as each one can bring upon the text the wildest possible explanations according to his ingenuity and imagination. Objectivity of the Word of God is destroyed, and any type of ideas may be read into a text.

Many evangelical expositors delight in this type of fantasy — interpretation rather than obediently studying the text with teachableness, patience, and humility.

b. *Letterism* — the Rabbinic School that gradually developed after Ezra, while it removed idol worship from the Jewish nation, developed a new form of idolatry, namely, the worship of the "letter of the law." Some of its leading exegetes, such as Akiba, held that, as hammering of fire produces many sparks, every word of the Scripture and every letter of each word have many meanings which should be brought out. Hidden special meanings were sought for each word and syllable. They held that a mystical meaning lay in every letter and every "horn of the letter." If a letter was larger or smaller than the rest, inverted or suspended, repeated or omitted, some special meaning was given to it.

In this dominant method of exegesis there was a tendency to worship the very script of the Scripture. A type of hyperliteralism somewhat similar to this is seen in certain circles of the Christian Church today. Undue significance is given to the very script of the Bible and elaborate meanings unwarranted by the context of the text are attributed to it. This tends to develop a form of biblioatry and unhealthy dogmatism. This is based, moreover, on a false view of the inspiration of the Bible.

c. *"Eisegesis"* — often people come to the Scripture with preconceived ideas and doctrines rather than with an open mind, thus arbitrary interpretations are forced on the Scripture. Study of the Scripture for several centuries of Roman supremacy was dominated and shaped by church traditions and dogmas. The church through its official exegetes, whose interpretation alone was accepted, tried to conform the Scripture to the doctrines of the church.

The danger of making the text a servant of the interpretation is a common danger. Eisegesis of the text, or reading into it ideas not there, is seen in various forms. Particular doctrines and distinctive teachings of certain denominations are often based on questionable interpretation of certain unclear and secondary texts taken out of their contexts. In such cases interpretation is placed at the service of denominational doctrines.

How often in pulpit preaching, also, we find that the text is used only as a springboard to preach one's own ideas, subjective experience, and certain petty doctrines. A text is chosen from the Bible purely for its namesake, and the preaching is not subjected to what the text actually says.

Another form of this type of approach is found in the modern existential interpretation which holds that the New Testament taken at its face value is meaningless for modern man, because its images, thought forms, and concepts are restricted to New Testament times. It needs to be "demythologized" to be made relevant. The Bible has to be studied "in conversation with God," and revelation should re-occur in the reader himself. The Bible becomes authoritative to one insofar as it communicates God's claim on him and "Christ event" happens in him. One does not understand history by standing aloof. These emphases, made clear by Bultmann and developed by his followers, raise serious questions with regard to the objective validity of the revelation of God. Interpretation is to be considered as true only if it agrees with truth as understood in one's self-understanding.

Approach to the Scripture with already formulated presuppositions is seen in an extreme manner in the rationalistic interpretation of the Bible. Rejecting the supernatural, the Bible is viewed as representing at best the highest thoughts of the ancient religions. With the refusal to accept the biblical accounts at their face value, a naturalistic and rationalistic interpretation is given to the text whereby it ceases to be God's Word for man.

It is true that none can come to the Bible with absolutely no presuppositions and with a mind devoid of any other influences. When we come to the text with reverence and belief that it is the Word of God, already we come to it in a certain frame of mind. But this type of presupposition is found validated by the text itself, when it is closely studied.

2. Basic principles of interpretation

Now we may examine certain fundamental and cardinal principles of interpretation which are basic to biblically-founded preaching and evangelism as well as to the development of evangelical theology.

a. *The right attitude to Scripture* — an interpreter should have the right approach to Scripture. When he comes to the Word he is at the same time both a "spectator" and a "hearer." As a spectator he objectively studies the text, taking into account the findings of the critical studies, the meaning of the words, historical contexts, etc., but "as a hearer" he comes to the Word with faith and commitment. He takes for granted the supreme authority of the Bible and its character as the revelation of God, and commits himself to its message. He studies it with expectancy and receptiveness.

The interpreter submits himself to the Bible as the authoritative Word of God. He believes that God "inspired" in a special manner certain select men of the Old Testament and the New Testament periods so that they were capable of receiving and communicating God's Word for man through the framework of their own mind and in the context of their life-situations. God, using their knowledge and language as media, uttered his words as authoritative in all matters of faith for all times and binding upon all men. "All Scripture is given by inspiration of God, and *is* profitable for doctrine, for reproof, for correction, for instruction in righteousness: That the man of God may be perfect, thoroughly furnished unto all good works" (II Tim. 3:16-17).

The interpreter believes in the sufficiency of the written Word to guide him in things pertaining to salvation: nothing is to be added or subtracted. He comes to it without the mediatorship of any church or human authority, but believing that with the inward witness and illumination of the Holy Spirit he can understand the Word of God. This is not to say that he will know everything in the Scripture, but that the Scripture can be sufficiently clear to him to serve as "a lamp to his feet and a light to his path."

Only the Holy Spirit, the author of the Word of God, can make it understood to us. Therefore, the reformers considered "faith and prayer" as the first main principle of interpretation. It is said that Thomas Aquinas used to fast and pray when he struggled with the exegesis of difficult passages.

One should also be teachable and ready to be corrected. When the Scripture is not clear there should be a willingness to admit our limitations. An old Rabbinic admonition says, "Teach your tongue to say, 'I do not know'." If we are willing to admit that none of us can expect a knowledge beyond what is clearly taught in the Bible, we would avoid many theological controversies.

As evangelical interpreters of the Bible we may admit that, though our method may seem to be unscientific, our hermeneutics is controlled by our view of, and attitude to, the Scripture, while our attitude to the Scripture is formulated by the teaching of the Scripture itself which we do not understand apart from clear investigation of it. Further study of the Scripture strengthens and confirms our doctrine of Scripture. Thus our hermeneutics and our doctrine of Scripture are, as it were, in some form of dialogical relationship.

b. *Literal sense* — the real meaning of a Scripture passage is its obvious and normal meaning. Perhaps about one hundred Old Testament events are alluded to in the New Testament, and in doing so their historicity is taken for granted, and no hidden or mystical interpretation is ascribed to them. So also the numerous Old Testament quotations in the New Testament are, by and large, understood and used in their obvious and clear sense. This principle of the New Testament writers of preferring the literal sense of the Scripture passages should be the basic principle in our interpretative method.

An abundance of metaphors, symbolisms, and poetic expressions is used in the Bible. Also, different types of literature are found in it. But the natural meaning of these is obvious. Even in a figurative speech as "Lion of Judah" or "Sword coming out of the Lord's mouth," its obvious meaning is what is to be understood as its "literal" meaning. Whatever the writers originally meant or intended to say is the literal sense.

The primary task of the interpreter is to discover what the Scripture accounts meant to the writer and to those for whom they were written. The real meaning of the text is to be found in the grammatical sense of the text in the framework of the style of the particular literature and in the context of the life and times of the writer. Literal sense is the meaning originally intended by him. Imposing upon a text a meaning other than its natural meaning is to do injustice to the text.

In the attempt to find the real meaning of a passage we must remember the fundamental principles of the primacy of the original languages, viewing translations as only second best. Etymological study of the words and phrases on the basis of comparative linguistics and grammatical, syntaxical studies, are basic to interpretation. Also passages should be treated by their literary types, many of which are found in the Bible, namely, poetic, narrative, legal, dramatic, figurative, prophetic, illustrative, biographical, etc., and interpretation should treat each on the basis of its style. For example, in dealing with Old Testament prophecies one ought to make a distinction between the "form" of a prophecy and its "content" or message. While the content of the messanic prophecies finds its fulfillment in Christ, the "form" in which it was presented was superseded and made invalid in its literal sense.

Or again, in the interpretation of a parable one must give attention to the one central truth it signifies and not try to find spiritual meaning for all its details. All parables of Jesus deal with one great subject, namely the Kingdom of God, and interpretation of each should be in harmony with Christ's teachings in general.

c. *Historical and cultural context* — there is an analogy between the Bible and Christ. Christ is both perfect God and perfect man, and so also the written Word is genuinely human while it is genuinely divine in its entirety. When God spoke through men, he spoke through their languages and their frame of mind. Otherwise God's words would not have been intelligible to them. The writers of the biblical books wrote their works to be understood by people of their times. In being inspired, the individuality of the writers was not in any way canceled or even weakened, while God overruled them to keep their utterance from error. Necessarily the Word of God came to man in a mold or form tied up to some particular period of history.

So our study of the Scripture should exegete or lead out the original meaning of the text. For this the interpreter should transpose himself to the times and life-situations of the writers, and try to stand in their shoes. He should understand their historical, cultural, and religious conditions. He should study what their words and phrases meant to them and to their contemporaries.

There is a vast cultural and historical difference between biblical times and our own day. The biblical period itself spans several centuries of great differences and diversities. But today we have numerous data of knowledge coming from many periods of history, throwing much light upon the biblical accounts and languages.

When our understanding of God's Word exceeds the original historical meaning of the text, it should only be a development of the meaning which is already there and application of it to a contemporary situation, in the context of the teaching of the Scripture at large. Therefore it is not adding multiple meaning or imposing a new sense to a text, but rather a drawing out and applying the message in a passage making clear its relevance to a given situation.

d. *Principle of the unity of the Bible* — though the Bible was written during a period of several centuries of greatly diverse circumstances and by many authors, there is a deep harmony and unity among all its books. This is because they all come from one Divine Mind. Therefore a passage which is not clear may be understood in the light of the main ideas of the Bible, or by comparing it with another passage where the question may be dealt with more fully. A later passage may throw light on an earlier passage, and the New Testament may be used to interpret the Old. This is possible because there is a historical development and progress in God's revelation and man's understanding of it.

Because of the unity of the Bible, one passage should not be so interpreted as to contradict the meaning of another passage or be in disharmony with the general biblical emphases. The Word of God is consistent with itself.

The unity of the Bible further means that our main doctrines and theology should be based on the primary and important teachings of the Bible rather than on obscure passages and incidental statements. The Bible is not a source book for proof texts, or a flat ocean beach from which pebbles may be picked up at random. Rather it is to be used as a major work of the mind, every detail understood in the context of the major "thesis" or message of the Bible.

In conclusion, two points of particular interest may be noted where the same underlying principles govern an evangelical biblical interpretation and a theology of evangelism.

First, concept of the sovereignty of God and the authority of his Word. Basic to evangelical hermeneutics is the acceptance of the final authority of the Bible as the Word of God. The interpreter is not the master of the text, and in his "conversation" with the text the Word of God masters him, and he finds the authority of the Word binding on him.

So also evangelism is based on the sovereign plan of God and all the authority under heaven and on earth that is given by him. We are under orders, and not to evangelize is to disregard the authority of the Lord and his Word. We are commissioned by one who has absolute right over us and whose authority is over all the world, all men, and all areas of the life of man. The scope of evangelism should cover all the spheres of the sovereignty of God on earth. It is the authority of the Lord and his sovereignty that fills the evangelist with confidence, courage, and hope in his work.

Second, understanding the nature of God's revelation. One's belief about the place of the biblical records in the concept of God's special revelation determines one's hermeneutical method. For example, the Barthian school would hold that the Scripture bears witness to Christ, the true revelation, and that the hermeneutic task basically is to inquire of each text what does it speak about Christ. To the existential school, the "Christ event," the Word of God, should be experienced by the believers. Faith is not based on historical facts nor on any written words. The importance of Scripture is that through it God "acts" in one who studies it.

Perhaps, the most dominant theory today regarding God's revelation is that God reveals himself through his redemptive acts, the climax of which is the death of Jesus Christ. The place of Scripture is that it bears witness to God's revelatory deeds.

We should say however, that while it is undoubtedly true that God reveals himself through his mighty deeds, the acts of God are meaningless unless God through "spoken" words interprets the significance of his deeds. The so-called redemptive acts in themselves say nothing. A band of slaves escaping from Egypt, the tiny insignificant nation of Israel struggling to survive while always being trodden down by great nations, an unfortunate carpenter from Nazareth getting into trouble with the leaders of the Jews and getting himself crucified: such accounts in themselves taken at their pure scientific historical value say nothing about the great God of the Bible except disprove the audacious claims of the Bible for the God of Israel and his son Jesus Christ.

Moreover, there are major parts of the Bible which come outside the sphere of history, such as most of the Psalms and the book of Proverbs. Also, how can the acts of God apart from revealing the nature of God in some general way speak in particular on some specific truths? Further, the biblical accounts themselves in both Old and New Testaments give central importance to God's communication through spoken words as the real revelation of God's will in these accounts.

All the above representative attitudes to the Bible in contemporary theologies reject the authority of the Bible as God's Word, and they lead to improper methods of interpretation.

One's concept of God's revelation is equally determinative in one's theology of evangelism. The idea of evangelism that denies the possibility of God speaking to communicate his will, has nothing authoritative to proclaim. Unless what is proclaimed is assured as "Thus says the Lord," it carries no power and creates no conviction. No doubt an evangelist should be keenly interested in what God does in history and should be deeply concerned with the development of human conditions and the establishment of justice, if he knows anything of Christian love. But if he has an inadequate understanding of God's revelation and his Word for the contemporary man as seen in the Scripture, he stands on false foundations. A right theology of evangelism is always based on a right view of Scripture.

THE REPORT OF THE STUDY GROUP ON THE ROLE OF HERMENEUTICS IN THE THEOLOGY OF EVANGELIZATION REPORT

Chairman: H. Wilbert Norton
Secretary: Jean Wilson

As a study group of the International Congress on World Evangelization, we have sought to understand the relevance of the Word of God to be heard today. Consequently, we share the following report with our colleagues at the Congress.

Biblical hermeneutics is the science of the interpretation of the Holy Scriptures leading to the understanding of the meaning of God's revelation. Recognition of Jesus Christ as Lord and Savior demands a theology of evangelism based on sound hermeneutics:

—Accepts the unique inspiration, entire trustworthiness and final authority of the Old and New Testaments.

—Accepts the principle that all of man's life and activity is under the judgment of the Word of God, the Bible. Man therefore cannot sit in judgment on the Holy Scriptures. The sciences can aid in interpreting the Holy Scriptures in providing tools to open its meaning.

—Avoids the hermeneutical extremes of allegorism, rabbinical types of literalism, eisegetical tendencies, to conform the teachings of the Scriptures to rigid denominational and sectarian dogma.

—Rejects the principles enunciated by contemporary existential hermeneutics in its efforts to demythologize the Scriptures, to re-reveal revelation subjectively to the reader himself — the authentication of truth by the reader's self-understanding.

—Insists on the principle of the right approach to the Scriptures by the interpreter consciously submitting himself to the message of the Bible in confidence that Scripture aids in the interpretation of Scripture with the help of the Holy Spirit.

—Holds that the primary task of the interpreter is to discover what the scriptural accounts meant to the writer and to those for whom the message was written.

—Stands on the principle of the unity of the Bible.

—Accepts the presence of figurative language (allegory, metaphors, symbols, poetic expressions) in the Bible, the meanings of which are discovered in the historical, cultural, and religious contexts of their times. Scientific methods, if properly used, can help us in interpreting the Scriptures.

—Holds that the redemptive sovereignty of God in the history of the church has led and will lead submissive believers by the Holy Spirit to acts of charity and social concern as the witness is given to forgiveness of sins by Jesus Christ (Acts 6).

—Anticipates the ultimate culmination of the Kingdom of God as the final time-space, socio-political-cultural triumph of redemptive love and the victory of God's justice, the righteousness of Jesus Christ our Savior and Lord, and the peace of God that transcends all knowledge.

Postscript to the report
The group elected to study one passage of Scripture (Luke 24:44-53) to apply the principles presented by Principal Saphir Athyal in his paper. Five members of the group plus the author were elected to speak for five minutes with particular application of the truths of this Scripture to their respective cultures in the Philippines, Great Britain, Australasia, South Africa, the United States, and India.

The suggestion was made that the Lord Jesus himself gave his unique hermeneutic of the Old Testament Scriptures which transformed two groups of frustrated disciples into dynamic witnesses to repentance and forgiveness of sins. It was pointed out that the Lord Jesus affirmed that the traditional divisions of the Jewish Old Testament (Moses, the Psalms, and the Prophets) prophesied the death, resurrection, and evangelization of the ethnic groups of all the world. World evangelization is, therefore, an integral part of the atonement and incorporates the involvement of all true disciples who identify with the living Lord of the harvest in his death and resurrection life.

The message of Peter (Acts 2-4) incorporated the Prophets, Psalms and Moses as he initiated God's program of world evangelization. Stephen based the authority of his message (Acts 7) on Moses, the Psalms, and the Prophets. Philip interpreted Isaiah to the Ethiopian eunuch. Saul approved the execution of Stephen (having heard his "Jesus hermeneutic" in the newly-founded apostolic tradition.) Later he wrote "faith comes by hearing in the Word of God," Rom. 10:17).

Saul collapsed (Acts 9) under the impact of the revealed Word, evangelized in Damascus, integrated the new hermeneutic of Jesus in his three years' desert study program, and evangelized in Antioch of Pisidia through the medium of the Old Testament: Law, Psalms, and Prophets.

He terminated his lifelong ministry of world evangelization in declaring to Agrippa that "the Jesus hermeneutic" was the promise made to the fathers (Acts 26). The basis of all New Testament evangelism is founded on Jesus' identification of himself with the written Word of God's redeeming grace.

THE TRINITARIAN NATURE OF GOD AS CREATOR AND MAN'S AUTHENTIC RELATIONSHIP WITH HIM: THE CHRISTIAN WORLD VIEW

Klaas Runia

Dr. Runia, Netherlands, is Professor of Practical Theology at the University of Kampen.

1. In the years after World War II the *doctrine of God* has gradually become the *focus of attention* for both theologians and ordinary church members. The number of books published on this subject has become staggering, in particular during the last decade. There are several reasons for this special interest in this doctrine.

(a) We find ourselves right in the midst of an accelerating process of *secularization*. In the Western world, but increasingly also in the non-Western world (in particular in the big cities and among the younger generation), belief in God is no longer the natural presupposition of life. More and more people ask themselves the question, "Who is God?" Others go even further and ask, "Is there a God?" Others again have taken the next step and abandoned all faith in God as an antiquated illusion.

(b) Many leading philosophies and ideologies of our time are intentionally and brutally *atheistic*. They not only reject the idea of the existence of God, but also vigorously oppose all religion and in particular the Christian religion. Communism, e.g., which has about one-third of the world population in its iron grip, is based on an atheistic philosophy and tries to eradicate all religion by means of propaganda and persecution. In the so-called "free world" the thinking of many people, both scientists and non-scientists, is deeply influenced by the philosophy of evolutionism, which by definition has no place for the idea of God as the Creator and Supreme Ruler of the universe. One of the main schools of psychology, behaviorism (e.g., B. F. Skinner) not only rejects the idea of God, but also regards man as a being entirely determined by his inherited nature and by his environment.

(c) The encounter of Christianity with the *other world religions* has also brought the doctrine of God into new prominence. Those who live in a pagan country daily rub shoulders with adherents of other religions. But also on a global scale a new "dialogue" has started between Christianity and the other world religions. The latter all have their own conception of the Godhead and increasingly they challenge the Christian view of God, in particular the Christian doctrine of the Triune God.

2. In this paper we take *our starting point in the biblical doctrine of God*. We realize that by doing this we take a fundamental decision. It is not only a personal decision of faith, but also a theological decision of far-reaching significance.

Theoretically we could follow another pathway. We could, by means of an apologetic argument, try to lay a philosophical foundation and then

proceed to discuss the biblical doctrine of God as the building to be erected
on this foundation. We believe, however, that such an approach is contrary
to the nature of the Christian faith. In fact, we must go further and
say that it is excluded by the biblical message itself. Our God is not
the god of the philosophers (Pascal), but the God of Abraham, Isaac,
and Jacob — the God who is the Father of Jesus Christ. Of him one
can speak only from within the circle of faith. Or to put it in another
way: everyone who wants to speak of God has to start with God's
own self-revelation as recorded in Scripture.

This starting point means that we reject every possibility of developing a so-called "natural theology" as a stepping-stone towards a "revealed
theology." Since the Middle Ages, especially since Thomas Aquinas,
the "church father" of the medieval church, such a "natural theology,"
based on the so-called proofs for the existence of God, has been very
popular, not only in Roman Catholic theology, but at times also in
Protestant theology. The Roman Catholic Church even went so far as
to make it the official doctrine of the church, when at the First Vatican
Council (1870) it declared "to hold and teach that God, the beginning
and end of all things, may be certainly known by the natural light of
human reason by means of created things," yes that he can "be known by
every one with facility, with firm assurance, and with no admixture of
error" (*Creeds of Christendom*). This view also explains the generally
favorable attitude of the Roman Catholic Church toward other religions
which are seen as a "preparation" for the Gospel. In some of these other
religions themselves, the proofs for the existence of God also play an
important part, e.g., in Islam.

There is, however, no basis for this approach in Scripture. To be
sure, Scripture does teach that there is a *general self-revelation of God,*
going out to all men through nature, history and man's own conscience
(cf. Psa. 19:1ff.; Rom. 1:8ff.; 2:14, 15; Acts 14:17, 17: 26ff.), but this
general revelation never leads to true knowledge of God on the side of
sinful man. Paul clearly states concerning the Gentiles of his day that
they "suppress the truth" of this revelation (Rom. 1:18), "For although
they knew God they did not honor him as God or give thanks to him,
but they became futile in their thinking and their senseless minds were
darkened. Claiming to be wise, they became fools and exchanged the
glory of the immortal God for images resembling mortal man or birds
or animals or reptiles" (vv. 21-23). This negative view of all human
religion (including the so-called higher religions) is not contradicted by
the words of the same apostle in Acts 17, for even there, although he
approaches his listeners in a very positive way, he clearly states that
they do not know the God who made the world and everything in it
(Acts 17:23, 24). It is only through God's *special revelation* that man can
know God as he really is. Apart from this revelation man gropes in
darkness and all his imaginations, however beautiful in themselves,
are futile and do not lead to true knowledge of the true God.

3. *Who then is God according to the Bible?* In the Scripture of the
Old Testament, Israel's prophets, inspired by the Holy Spirit, have
recorded the revelation of God as it came to the covenant people of
old. The Old Testament, in the form in which it has been handed down

to us, starts with the proclamation: "In the beginning God created the heavens and the earth" (Gen. 1:1). This is not just a general statement about some great architect who stands behind all that is visible to the human eye, but it is the confession Israel makes about him whom it had learned to know as the great Redeemer of his people. Yahweh, the covenant-God of Israel, of whom it confessed in the "Shema" (Israel's Creed), "Hear, O Israel: The Lord our God is one Lord" (Deut. 6:4), is the Creator. Especially in the second part of the book of Isaiah it is emphasized that Yahweh is the Creator. All the other gods are only the products of man's mind and hands (Isa. 40:19ff.). But "the Lord is the everlasting God, the Creator of the ends of the earth" (v. 28). He is the Lord and there is no other (45:6). "Thus says the Lord who created the heavens (He is God!), who formed the earth and made it (He established it . . .), "I am the Lord and there is no other" (v. 18).

In the beginning of all time he created the heavens and the earth. This means first of all that God is in no way dependent on the creation. He is not eternally co-existent with the creation, but he, the eternal God, preceded the creation which he made. He did not need the creation either. The act of creation is not a "necessary" but a "free" act of his divine will and power. He is therefore not in any way limited by the creation, but *transcends* it in his eternal glory. There is in Israel's faith *not a trace of pantheism.* He, the eternal God, is so great, so far beyond his creation that even "heaven and the highest heaven cannot contain" him (I Kings 8:27).

In the Old Testament it is in particular the attribute of God's *holiness* that emphasizes this unique transcendence of God. This attribute not only indicates that God is pure and far removed from all sin (the ethical aspect), but also and primarily that he is wholly other, the Majestic One, before whose face not only sinful men tremble (Exod. 19; Isa. 6:5), but the holy angels as well (Isa. 6:2, 3).

And yet this very same God maintains a continuous relationship with his creation. There is *no trace of deism* either in the Old Testament. God, the transcendent Creator, is from moment to moment involved in the existence and history of his creation. In one of the Reformation confessions, the Belgic Confession of 1563, we read: "We believe that the same good God, after he had created all things, did not forsake them or give them up to fortune or chance, but that he rules and governs them according to his holy will so that nothing happens in this world without his appointment" (article 13, *Creeds of Christendom).*

4. God the Creator of all that exists established *a special relationship with man,* the creature that, according to Genesis, was called into being on the last "day" of creation. Genesis 1 clearly indicates the special place of man within the whole structure of creation by the fact that his creation was preceded by a special "council" of God, in which God decided to create a being "in his own image, after his own likeness" (Gen. 1:26). "So God created man in his own image; in the image of God he created him; male and female he created them" (1:27).

In the course of history many heavy tomes have been written on this topic of *man being in the image of God.* Undoubtedly this expression points to the secret of man's being. But what does it mean?

It has often been explained as indicating the rational and moral nature of man. In other words, it would be indicative of some inherent qualities, which distinguish man from the animals. It is to be questioned, however, whether such an explanation does justice to the expression as it is used in Scripture. The expression is a form of pictorial language which indicates *a special relationship* between God and man, namely, the relationship of a father and his child (cf. Gen. 5:3). To live in such a relationship man does need certain qualities (such as rationality and morality), but these qualities themselves do not constitute the image (cf. the fact that angels, who do possess the same qualities are not children of God, but servants!). The "image" presupposes the qualities but at the same time transcends them. It points to the very special relationship with God, into which man was created: the relationship of a child who may call God his Father.

Here we find also the essential difference between man and the animals. The animals too are called into being by God and thus live in relationship with him, but they are not aware of it. Man is called into being, in order to live consciously "coram Deo," *before the face of God.* Yes, we may even go a step further and say that man is called into being in order to live *with God* and to *respond* to his divine Word. The deepest secret of man is that he is a *"responsive"* and therefore a *"responsible"* being. Or to put it in biblical language: man is created by God to be his *covenant-partner* and to live with God in a *relationship of love.* In order to be able to do this he has to be a rational being. Likewise he has to be a moral being who is free to respond in love to the love of God. This *freedom* is essential to man's being in the image of God. His answer to God's covenant-word has to be more than a mere "echo." A response of love must be a free response. At the same time this freedom cannot be an autonomous freedom. True freedom is a freedom that in childlike obedience listens to the word of the Father. This is clearly the meaning of the story about the tree of knowledge of good and evil in Genesis 2.

Unfortunately man has misused the freedom given to him by God and has chosen the way of autonomous freedom. Listening to the persuasive voice of temptation ("you will be like God," Gen. 3:5), he "grasped the equality with God" (cf. Phil. 2:7) and thus became alienated, not only from his heavenly Father, but also from his fellowman and from his own nature and identity. His heart became so corrupt that he "lives in the passions of his flesh, following the desires of body and mind" (Eph. 2:3; cf. Gen. 6:5-7; Mark 7:21-23). As a sinner he is "dead through the trespasses and sins" (Eph. 2:1) and "by nature a child of wrath" (2:3).

All this does not mean that man, the sinner, is no longer responsible for his thoughts, words, and actions. He has not become an "automaton." The special relationship with God into which he was created still exists, even though it is in a perverted form. Every sinful thought, every sinful word and every sinful action is always a sin against the God in whose image he was created and for this very reason his guilt is so exceedingly great, that without the grace of God there is no escape for man from eternal perdition.

5. The great joy of the Christian message is that God himself did not forsake man, but established a *new covenant relationship*, not based on the fact of creation but on his own gracious love. Immediately after the Fall, God speaks the promise of grace, when in the words of the curse addressed to the serpent he says, "I will put enmity between you and the woman, and between your seed and her seed; he shall bruise your head and you shall bruise his heel" (Gen. 3:15).

The remainder of the Old Testament is the story of this promise as it is worked out by God in the Old Testament history of salvation: the new beginning after the Flood, the calling of Abraham, the Exodus from Egypt and the covenant with Israel at Sinai, the messianic sign as foreshadowed in David, etc.

In the Old Testament, however, it becomes increasingly clear that the new covenant relationship, too, continually founders through Israel's unfaithfulness. Instead of serving their gracious Lord they worship the idols of the nations around them. Israel is as the unfaithful wife of Hosea who gives herself to strange lovers (Hos. 1-3). "A spirit of harlotry has led them astray, and they have left their God to play the harlot" (Hos. 4:12).

The *prophets* therefore foretell a day of wrath in which the unfaithful people shall perish (cf. Amos 5:18). Yet they also know of a "remnant" that will survive out of this total destruction (cf. Amos 3:12, Isa. 1:9, 7:3, 10:20, 11:16, 28:5, 65:8-10; Ezek. 12:16; 14:22-23; Joel 2:32; Zeph. 3:12, 13; etc.). Gradually the picture of the one *"Servant of the Lord"* (the *Ebed Yahweh)* emerges, who will be *the* faithful covenant-partner and who as the suffering Messiah will be the Redeemer of his people (cf. Isa. 53).

But the centuries pass by and nothing seems to happen. Until the day arrives that he appears in the person of *Jesus of Nazareth.*

6. *Who is this Jesus of Nazareth?* According to the New Testament he is the son of Mary, a young virgin from Nazareth. He is a real human being, a being of flesh and blood (cf. John 1:14): "The Word became *flesh";* also Heb. 2:14-18, 5:7-10). Yet he is different from all other human beings. The mystery of his being is his *unique relationship with God.* In the announcement of his birth to Mary by the angel Gabriel it is clearly stated, "He will be called the Son of the Most High...he will be called Holy, the Son of God" (Luke 1:32, 34). These expressions first of all indicate that he is the promised Messiah, for they are used here in a messianic context and refer back to similar indications in the Old Testament (cf. Psa. 2:7, 89:26, 27). But there are also obvious overtones in these expressions. They speak also of a relationship with God which goes beyond anything that ever existed before in the world of men.

When Jesus officially starts his messianic task by submitting himself to the baptism by John the Baptist, the voice from the cloud calls him, "My beloved Son" (cf. Matt. 3:17), words later repeated on the Mount of Transfiguration (Matt. 17:15). Throughout the Gospels we notice that he himself is well aware of this unique relationship. He knows himself to be sent by God (cf. Matt. 10:40; Mark 9:37; Luke 9:48; 10:16). He calls God "Abba," which means "Daddy" (Mark 14:36). He even says, "He who has seen Me, has seen the Father (John 14:9), and: "I am in the Father and the Father is in Me" (John 14:11).

Yet it is not until his resurrection from the dead and the outpouring of the promised Spirit that the disciples fully realize how unique his relationship with God was. This was more than an extra-ordinary *human* relationship with God, his Sonship was even more than a *messianic* Sonship. His Sonship was so unique that he was no less than the *eternal Son* of God who had "come into the flesh" (I John 4:2). He was the revelation of God, because in him we meet with God himself. "What men saw in Jesus is eternally in the Unseen, and he 'who came from God and went to God' is the Son inseparable from the Father."

Likewise the disciples, after Pentecost, when they experienced the presence of the *promised Spirit,* began to realize that in this Spirit they had to do with God himself. He was not just a gift from God, but God himself dwelling in them.

7. In this way the *Christian doctrine of the Triune God* gradually developed. In its full-fledged form it is not yet found in the New Testament. Yet it may be called a *biblical* doctrine. We think here of a useful distinction made by Arthur W. Wrainwright in his excellent book *"The Trinity in the New Testament"* (1962). He points out that the term "doctrine" can be taken in a twofold sense. First, it can be taken as a "formal statement of a position." In this sense the doctrine of the Trinity is not found in the Bible. "There is no formal statement of trinitarian doctrine in the New Testament as there is in the Athanasian Creed or in Augustine's *De Trinitate."* But the term "doctrine" can also be taken as "an answer, however fragmentary, to a problem." In this sense the doctrine does occur in the New Testament, for "the problem of the Trinity was in the minds of certain New Testament writers and . . . they made an attempt to answer it."

But why was there such a *problem*? To state it as briefly and as simply as possible, the New Testament writers, together with their fellow-believers in the Old Testament dispensation, uncompromisingly believed that *God is one.* Yet at the same time they believed also that *Jesus, the Messiah, is the Son of God,* and that in a unique sense. Again and again John speaks of the "only-begotten" Son of the Father. In the Synoptic Gospels we read more than once that he is the "beloved" Son, which is virtually equivalent to John's only-begotten. Afterwards the Nicene Creed stated it thus, "God of God, Light of Light, very God of very God."

In this combination of divine one-ness and messianic Sonship we find the origin of the Trinity in the New Testament itself. As to its origin this doctrine has nothing to do with philosophical speculation, but it was born of the heart of the Christian faith, namely, the Christology. Dr. S. R. Franks points to the fact that there are three fundamental acts of God in history. First, there is God's choice of Israel as his peculiar people. To them he revealed himself under the sacred name of Yahweh. Second, comes the sending of Jesus, who was born of the stock of Israel. And third, is the gift of the Holy Spirit to the Church, which is the Society of those confessing Jesus as Messiah (or Christ). God chose, God sent, God gave: the acknowledgment of these three great moments of divine revelation is the starting point. But it was "the second or central act which was the original disturbing factor that set in motion the transformation of Jewish monotheism into the Christian doctrine of the Trinity."

The same is true of the *historical development* of the doctrine. The church of the first three centuries did not engage in the trinitarian controversies, because it was so fond of speculation (although it must be admitted that the Greek-speaking fathers of the East were not always free from speculation), but the controversy about the Trinity was basically a christological controversy. The basic issue was: Is Jesus Christ God, really and fully God (*vere Deus*)? If so, what does this mean with regard to the Being of God? At a later stage the same question was asked with regard to the Holy Spirit. But at that time the christological issue had already been settled and the controversy about the divinity and personality of the Holy Spirit was more in the nature of a consequence. The *core* of the doctrine of the Trinity was and is the *Christology*.

8. Without any doubt this most basic doctrine of the Christian faith is also *the most incomprehensible one*. It is therefore not surprising to see that all through the centuries it has been *opposed*, even within the Christian Church. In our own days it is again attacked by those who advocate a "new" Christology, namely, the idea that Jesus, the man of Nazareth, is the *perfect human* covenant-partner, raised by God himself. Also from outside the Christian faith this doctrine is continually opposed, especially by orthodox Jews and the followers of Mohammed. They all accuse the Christian Church of advocating a form of polytheism, namely, *tri-theism*.

As Christians we should be very patient with those who lay such charges against us. To those who do not share our faith in Jesus Christ and in the Holy Spirit it must be an insurmountable stumbling-block. As a matter of fact, we ourselves must confess that this doctrine is entirely incomprehensible for us too.

But why then do we believe it? Is it a matter of: *Credo quia absurdum*? (I believe it because it is absurd?) No! It is: *Credo quia revelatum est a Deo* (I believe because it is revealed by God himself). I believe it, because I know that Jesus, my Savior, is God himself redeeming me. I believe it, because I know that the Holy Spirit who dwells in me is God himself dwelling in me. I do not believe some abstract doctrine that satisfies my desire for speculative thinking, but I believe because I have met God in this threefold way: as my Creator, as my Redeemer, as my Renewer.

At the same time it is imperative for Christians in all their thinking and speaking of this doctrine always to realize that *every formulation* of this mystery *remains inadequate*. We should never presume to think that we can grasp the innermost Being of God in our words and thoughts. All formulations, including those of the early Creeds, are only *attempts* to express the unthinkable. It has rightly been said that the doctrine of the Trinity "should not be treated as a self-sufficient description of God, but rather as the framework in which all revelation and our experience of God may be seen as a whole, and be saved from being a jumble of ideas and events."

9. Nevertheless, in spite of all its incomprehensibility and in spite of all the inadequacies of our formulations, this doctrine is the *very foundation of our Christian faith*. We mention the following points.

a. In this doctrine it becomes clear that God is the *truly living God*, the God who has life in himself, the God who is literally *full of life*. Some of the early church fathers used a rather peculiar expression. They said: God is *fertile*. In himself he has the fullness of inter-personal communication. This also makes clear that God in no way needed the world. He was not a lonely God, who therefore caused an emanation from himself, so that he would have an "over against." The doctrine of the Trinity is really and definitely *the end of all pantheism*. According to pantheism the universe is, as it were, God's counterpart, in which God comes to full self-development. In our days similar ideas are very popular in the form of "process" philosophy and theology. Although they reject a full-grown pantheism and prefer to speak of *pan-en-theism* (everything is rooted or grounded in God), they nevertheless maintain that God himself grows and is enriched by his contact with the world. The doctrine of the Trinity excludes all such notions. If God is triune in himself, in the depth of his own Being, then he does not need this world in order to come to a full unfolding of himself. Emil Brunner puts it thus, "Only if, in himself, from all eternity, God *is* the Loving One, no world is needed for him to be the Loving One."

b. At the same time the doctrine of the Trinity is of great importance for a proper understanding of the *doctrine of creation*. Brunner continues as follows, "On the contrary, the world as creation is the work of his Love." There is no necessary correlation between God and the world, at least not from God's side. "The relation between God and the world is one-sided: the world is derived from God, through God; he is its source. The world is determined by God; God is not determined by the world. This statement, however, is only true if it be true that, apart from the world, God is also the One who loves, who loves 'before all worlds.' From all eternity he loves his Son and therefore through his Son he creates the world." Athanasius already said: Because God is "fertile" in himself, i.e., because he is able to communicate himself inwardly, he is also able to communicate himself outwardly. Or to put it in more pictorial language: God is love, overflowing love in himself; God is life, self-giving life in himself; and the creation is the creaturely result of this overflowing love and this self-giving life. But it is this always "through the Son." It is not a natural continuation of the inward self-communication of God. But through the Son, God goes out from himself to create a world, which has both its foundation and its aim in God himself — "For from him and through him and to him are all things" (Rom. 11:36; cf. I Cor. 8:6, where the "from" and "to" are predicated of God the Father, and the "through" of Jesus Christ, the incarnate Son).

c. The doctrine of the Trinity is also of essential significance for the *doctrine of revelation*. Indeed, it is the basis of all revelation. Because God is able to reveal himself within himself as the Father in the Son through the Holy Spirit, he is also able to reveal himself to the world he has made, and again it is the self-revelation of the Father in the Son through the Holy Spirit. In the revelation "in the Son through the Spirit" we do not receive some external information about God, but we have the guarantee that God himself is speaking to us and opening his divine heart to us. Instead of being abstract information (not to speak even of human speculation) revelation is really and fully *self*-communication.

d. But above all, the doctrine of the Trinity is of importance for our *salvation*, for this doctrine is the answer to the question whether or not our salvation is really God's work. In the final analysis this is the reason why the Church is so vitally interested in the divinity of Jesus Christ and of the Holy Spirit. *The* vital question in the Christology is: Do we really meet with God himself in Jesus Christ? This was the concern of Athanasius, the champion of trinitarian orthodoxy over against Arius. Read only the following short quotations from his writings. "Nothing created can unite the creatures with God." "God alone can unite the creature with God." "No one could make us the children of God save he who is the true and essential Son of the Father," Luther said the same when he stated that the Reconciler must be God himself, "Because by no other means than that of an eternal person could we be rescued from our terrible fall into sin and eternal death; such a person alone could have power over sin and death, to expiate our sin and to give us instead righteousness and eternal life; no angel or creature could do this, but it must be done by God himself." The same vital question is at stake in the doctrine of the Holy Spirit. Here too everything depends on the question whether or not we really meet with God himself. Again we quote Athanasius: "If the Holy Spirit were a creature, we would have no fellowship with God in him; in that case we would be alien to the divine nature, so that we in no sense would have fellowship with it." H. Berkhof writes, "If the Spirit is not God himself, but something less, he cannot reconcile us to God nor recreate us according to the image of the Son. In that case our redemption can only be expressed in terms of semi-Pelagianism, or deeper knowledge, or of a moral improvement."

10. Because this doctrine of Father, Son and Holy Spirit, the Tri-une God, is unknown to *all other religions,* it is not surprising to see that none of them knows the *secret of real redemption: redemption by God himself.* In all other religions salvation is always a work of man himself. It is *"auto-soteria."*

This is true even of Judaism and Islam. Although the *Jews* share with us the knowledge of the Old Testament, the book of God's salvation in the old dispensation, their rejection of Jesus as the Messiah bars them from reading the full message of salvation in the Old Testament. The apostle Paul writes: "To this day, when they read the old covenant (The Old Testament), that same veil remains unlifted, because only through Christ is it taken away" (II Cor. 3:14). All they know is the "written code" of the law and in vain they try to attain eternal life by keeping it.

The *followers of Mohammed,* who also claim to be descendants of Abraham, who even recognize Moses and Jesus as great prophets, but at the same time subordinate them to their own, still greater prophet, do not know real salvation either. Their religion too is a religion of *"auto-soteria."* Even though they call Allah "merciful, forgiving and kind," these words do not really function in their doctrine of God. The "theology" of Islam is hard and cruel. It is basically a religion of reward and revenge. In the Koran we read, "So he who has done an atom's weight of good shall see it. And he who has done an atom's weight of evil shall see it." In agreement with these words the author of the *"Letters on Islam"* writes in the introduction, "He who is faithful and performs the good, motivated by the love of good is not afraid of death, and he is happy in this world and the next." Such a man does not need salvation by God. He saves himself.

The same is true of *all other religions,* whether one takes the so-called primitive religions or the so-called higher religions, such as Hinduism, Buddhism, Confucianism, etc. None of them knows of real salvation by God himself. In all these religions, in as far as the idea of God plays a part in them (Confucianism, for instance, is basically a system of moral behavior), the Godhead is always seen, either as the supernatural being whom man has to placate and please by his good works, or as the deepest ground of being, into which (on purpose we use the pronoun "which," for one can hardly speak of this ground of being in personal terms!) all that exists one day will return.

Only the *Christian faith* has a message of real salvation, because it knows that in Jesus Christ God himself came to redeem us and that in the Holy Spirit God himself dwells in us with his grace in Jesus Christ. Redemption is *real* redemption because it is fully and wholly God's work.

11. The foregoing does not mean, however, that therefore man acts only like a puppet, moved by the strings in the divine hand. On the contrary, no religion accords such a *high place to man* as Christianity does. First (as we have seen before) it teaches that man was created "in the image of God," created for a very special relationship with God. This relationship is so essential to man's being, that it is not even destroyed by his fall into sin. Man himself has perverted this relationship. Instead of living before the face of God he lives with his back toward God. But even a perverted relationship still means a relationship. Man cannot escape from God, but even in his worst rebellion remains a *"homo religiosus."* His rebellion, yes, even his denial and rejection of God, is of a religious nature.

And when God in his unfathomable love calls man to a renewed relationship by the preaching of the Gospel, the *Holy Spirit* by this very same Gospel *enables man to respond* to the call. Man is not a robot, mechanically pushed around by the divine engineer, but man is called to respond as man: to respond in faith, in love, in obedience, in worship and adoration.

If some of the *other religions or philosophies* seem to give a more exalted place to man, then this *is* only seeming. For instance, some religions make man semi-divine. All pantheistic religions tell man that he is an aspect of the all-embracing totality, which is God. At the same time these very same religions leave man to his own fate. They offer him no solution for the problem of suffering, nor do they offer him redemption from sin and guilt. In fact, they declare that evil is only a hallucination, which should be recognized as such in order to be delivered from it.

Some philosophies make man autonomous. Their message is that man is the master of his own fate. And thus they leave him with his lonely despair, for the evil powers that rule over this world keep him in bondage and all his so-called autonomy does not offer him any escape from this bondage.

Without the redeeming love of God, man is the most pitiable of all creatures. Without this redeeming love, man knows neither himself nor God. Only when the Gospel of Jesus Christ is preached to him and accepted by him, is he delivered from this terrible ignorance. "In the face of Jesus Christ" (II Cor. 4:6) he not only begins to see the awful guilt of his sin, but he also sees the astonishing light of God's redeeming love. Through the presence of the Holy Spirit in his heart he not only begins to hate and fight against sin, he also wants to offer his whole life as a sacrifice of love to the God who redeemed him at such a price: the death of his own Son. The deepest desire of his heart is to praise the God who created and redeemed and renewed him, and he sings with the church of all ages, yes, with the holy angels in heaven:

"Holy, Holy, Holy, Lord God Almighty,
 All Thy works shall praise Thy name, in earth and sky and sea;
 Holy, Holy, Holy, Merciful and Mighty!
 God in Three Persons, blessed Trinity!"

12. But *how does one preach this Gospel of the Triune God?* How does one preach it to adherents of other faiths in Asia and Africa? How does one preach it to unbelievers in the secularized Western world? Is the message of the Triune God not an insurmountable stumbling block to them all? Will they not reject the message of redemption because of this doctrine that seems to defy all logic?

All through the history of the Christian Church attempts have been made to make this doctrine more acceptable by using *analogies and illustrations,* derived from the creation itself, in particular from the nature of man. Augustine, for instance, likened the relationship of Father, Son, and Holy Spirit to the root, the trunk, and the branches of a tree, or to a river, a fountain, and the draught of water from the fountain, or to man's memory, understanding and will. In recent years Dorothy Sayers tried to find an analogy in the mind of man: the creative idea, the creative energy, and the creative power. Likewise Leonard Hodgson used the analogy of the human self with its three activities of thinking, feeling, and willing.

Although we greatly admire the ingenuity of these authors and also respect their genuinely evangelistic motives, yet we believe that this is not the right way to preach the Gospel of the Triune God. No "trinity" in this created world can ever help us to understand the mystery of God's being. Every analogy falls short. For in this world we either have three separate entities which are not really one, or we have one entity which is not really triune.

The only way to preach this Gospel is *to follow the New Testament pattern.* The New Testament witness begins with the Gospel of

Jesus of Nazareth, who is the Christ. Jesus himself proclaims the coming of the Kingdom which is already present in himself, in his words and deeds (cf. Luke 11:20). When after his death and resurrection and after the outpouring of the Spirit his disciples go into all the world to preach the Gospel to all nations (Mark 16:15; Matt. 28:19; Luke 24:47, 48; Acts 1:8), they proclaim the message of the crucified and risen Savior. In their proclamation, new dimensions are added to the original preaching of Jesus, because they see his life through the prism of the resurrection and they are enlightened by the Paraclete who now has come to guide them into all the truth (John 16:13, 14). Yes, the Holy Spirit himself dwells in them as the guarantee, the first installment (arrabon) of the great inheritance (Eph. 1; 14; cf. II Cor. 1:22).

In this way the richness of the Christian faith *unfolds itself* in the preaching of the early church. The Gospel is not a theological doctrine, which like a philosophical system tries to explain the essence of all reality and in particular of the divine reality, but it is the ever-richer unfolding of *God's self-revelation in the history of salvation,* which has its center in the coming of God's Son and the subsequent coming of God's Spirit.

The only way for us to preach the Christian message of the Triune God is to follow in the footsteps of the New Testament apostles and preachers. As William Fulton puts it, "The Christian faith in the incarnation of the Divine Word...in the man Christ Jesus, with whom the believer is united through the fellowship of the Holy Spirit, constitutes the distinctive basis of the Christian doctrine of the Trinity." Only when we take our starting point in this basis, are we able to preach this Gospel to non-Christians in our day, whether they be adherents of other religions or secularized people in the modern Western world. We have *to confront them with Jesus Christ* and, under the guidance of the Holy Spirit, lead them first to faith in Jesus Christ as their Redeemer. Once they have accepted Jesus Christ and have experienced his presence in their hearts and lives through the indwelling Spirit, the way is open to "explain" to them the mystery of God's Triune Being.

Even then we have to be very careful in our *choice of words and concepts.* We should never, under any circumstances, forget that all that we say about the Triune Being of God is only a matter of "pointing to" the mystery. We should never forget that this doctrine is not an adequate self-sufficient description of God, but only the framework in which all revelation and our experience of God may be seen as a whole. We should also keep in mind that some of the terms and concepts used by the ancient church have changed their meaning and actually had better be avoided in our day. For example, the term *"Person,"* which in the days of the church fathers was a rather neutral word (Greek: *prosopon;* Latin: *persona*), indicative of a *personal relationship,* today means a self-conscious, autonomous *individual.* If therefore we use this term today, we can hardly escape from a kind of tri-theism. Today it might be better to speak of *the one God existing in three different ways.* At the same time, in order to avoid the pitfall of modalism, we must add that *the one God exists in three different personal ways.* Father, Son and Holy Spirit are not three different ways of manifestation only (modalism).

God not only *reveals* himself as Father, Son and Holy Spirit, but God *is* Father, Son, and Holy Spirit.

Again we are at the end of all our thinking and we can only agree with Augustine, when he wrote, "We say three persons, not that we wish to say it, but that we may not be reduced to silence." Indeed, the church may not be reduced to silence at this point. It has to preach the *full* Gospel of salvation and therefore it has to speak of *God the Father* who so loved the world that he gave *his only-begotten Son,* so that every one who believes in him (the work of *the Holy Spirit!*) may not perish, but have eternal life (John 3:16). This one text, the glorious summary of the Christian Gospel of salvation, is at the same time the foundation of the Christian doctrine of the Triune God, a God who not only created us, but who also saves us and through his renewing power leads us to eternal life.

TRINITARIAN NATURE OF GOD REPORT
Chairman: Ian Rennie
Secretary: Ian McDowell

The group supported Dr. Runia's paper. The following paragraphs mention some of its implications for those engaged in evangelization, which the group discussed.

1. The historical revelation of our Lord Jesus Christ in Scripture is the necessary basic doctrinal requirement of evangelism in any religious or cultural environment.

2. It is not imperative for a worker to preach the doctrine of the Trinity at an early stage of evangelism. This may well wait until people become Christians and obtain by the Holy Spirit the capacity to receive the doctrine. This point applies also to the doctrines of the person and work of the Holy Spirit.

3. Though a presentation of the Gospel may be comparatively simple in content, as long as it contains an adequate scriptural explanation of the person and work of Christ, God is well able to reveal himself in the hearts of hearers whom he loves and whom he created.

4. Presentation of Jesus Christ by philosophical arguments, or by reference to God's creation, or by appeal to man's sense of his own need, or by sharing his presence in his church, allows useful points of contact for subsequent preaching of Christ in revelation; but these approaches must be regarded as pre-evangelism and not as a substitute for true Gospel preaching.

5. While the explanation of the doctrine of the Trinity may have a place in apologetic or defensive preaching in order to counter prevailing misconceptions such as pantheism or deism, at some point the speaker must require response to the historic Christ whom the Bible reveals.

Notwithstanding all the foregoing, the group emphasized that only the biblical doctrine of the Trinity as given in orthodox historic confessions of faith implies a full-orbed world view which meets the whole need of man. Therefore all Christians should be taught the doctrine of the Trinity as fully as possible in post-evangelistic ministry both for their own souls' need and to counter the various related heresies current in evangelical spheres today.

MAN'S DILEMMA OF SIN AND SUFFERING
Edmund P. Clowney

*Dr. Clowney, Philadelphia, Pennsylvania,
USA, is President and Professor of Practical
Theology at Westminister Theological Seminary.*

"My God," he cries, "my God, why hast thou forsaken me?" Spiked to a cross-beam on a hilltop, he hangs naked and forsaken in the darkness. Who is he? The tortured man, the abandoned man, choking in the dust of death. He is not nameless, for a sign nailed over his head bears his name, "This is Jesus the King of the Jews" (Matt. 27:37).

Jesus. His name holds the theme of Scripture, "Salvation is of the Lord." "Thous shalt call his name Jesus, for he shall save his people from their sins" (Matt. 1:21). Men gather to mock the sign of his Name. "He saved others," they jeer. "Let him save himself!" (Luke 23:35). But the name of salvation is forever fixed to the Cross.

Man's dilemma of sin and suffering is met at Calvary not with speculation but with anguish, not in symbol but in actuality, for the forsaken Sufferer is the Son of God. The Cross has not lost its offence to worldly wise men. They see only another of those atrocities that men must be saved from, or worse, a savior who *chooses* the way to Calvary and betrays the revolution.

Yet the foolishness of the Cross remains the wisdom of God to salvation. At the Cross God reveals the meaning of the human condition and at the Cross God brings the reality of his salvation. Both the wrath of God and the grace of God at the Cross are a scandal to men. The Cross supports no worldly philosophy, it supplements no worldly religion; it is God's foolishness that is wiser than men (I Cor. 1:18-21).

1. *Man before God: sin and suffering*

In preparation for the recent Bangkok conference on the theme "Salvation Today," a booklet was published that packed together more than a hundred brief verbal grenades, charged with rage against power and privilege, some exploding in agonized blasphemy. This shock therapy was prescribed to challenge not only orthodox theology, but any theology that offers answers from the Bible rather than struggle in encounter.

It is true that the Gospel does not give the answers men are seeking in the rage of their rebellion. But God does speak, and his Word proclaims not only struggle but victory. That victory is his salvation, and only before God can we see either the plight of our lostness or the glory of his saving purpose. The call to salvation is a call to repentance, a call to turn to the living God.

At Calvary, before God, we learn the deepest meaning of human misery. All misery measures to a degree our lostness from God. The cry of Jesus from the Cross is the cry of the final misery, the misery of the God-forsaken man. In the mystery of redemption the Son of God descends into the hell of abandonment and bears the full curse of God's judgment.

In his agony Jesus is identified with the suffering of God's servant in Psalm 22. He endures physical pain (vv. 14-16), but more painful than the tearing of his hands is the crushing of his heart: he is despised and scorned (vv. 6, 7); like snarling dogs his enemies surround him and his friends have fled (*cf.* Psa. 88:8, 31:11, 12).

Yet the supreme agony of the righteous Sufferer is not that he is abandoned by his friends, but that he is forsaken by his Father. Though we cannot imagine what this meant to the Beloved Son of God, we do know in the spiritual depth of human anguish the brokenness of our alienation from God.

The man who looks into the jaws of death knows more than fear. He knows the dread that is the shadow of God's image. Our life is but a breath, a sigh, in contrast to God's eternity. The fascination in Andrew Wyeth's paintings is not simply the nostalgic realism he gives to everyday objects. It is the frightening tension between the familiar window curtain billowing toward us and the nameless immensity of the gray sky from which the sea wind blows.

"Before the mountains were brought forth,
   Or ever thou hadst formed the earth and the world,
   Even from everlasting to everlasting, thou art God" (Psa. 90:2).

Man's misery bears mute witness to his humanity. Agony no less than ecstasy reminds us that God has made us for himself. But humanity is not constituted by misery. We are miserable, not because we are humans, but because we are sinners. Misery is not man's fate but his judgment.

"For we are consumed in thine anger,
   And in thy wrath are we troubled.
   Thou has set our iniquities before thee,
   Our secret sins in the light of thy countenance" (Psa. 90:7, 8).

God's thoughts are not our thoughts when we reflect on misery. Men see themselves as victims and lift proud heads "bloody but unbowed." Man fancies himself as Sisphus, a hero of the absurd who gives meaning to his doom of meaninglessness by his own decision to go on.

If not a hero, man would be a sage, quenching the desire that leads to suffering, and anticipating by the transformation of his consciousness that absorption in the All to which the wheel of existence eternally returns.

Or man would take charge, controlling threats from without and modifying behavior within. Perhaps not at Walden and perhaps not by 1984, but in time, and planetary space, man would engineer the garden of Eden again.

Every human formula for coping with misery sees it as fate: definitive of human existence, necessary to the cosmic process, or perhaps the inevitable price of progress in the dialectic of history. There is no other way men can see it, until they stand before the living God. Then they understand why misery is so miserable, why life that ends in death can never offer rest. All along man's sense of tragedy has betrayed him. Misery is the curse of the *sinner*. Man is not the hapless victim but the willing rebel.

To be sure, not all of a man's suffering is the direct result of his sin. When Jesus was told of Galileans massacred by Pilate he assured his hearers that these were not the worst Galilean sinners singled out for judgment. Only by God's final judgment are all sins justly punished. But Jesus' next words show the gulf between man's view of sin and God's "Except ye repent ye shall all in like manner perish" (Luke 13:3, 5). The tragedy of destruction is not a strange intrusion, but a certain judgment. All men are sinners, and the wages of sin is death.

Sin is not capable of illuminating analysis; it does not offer its own coherent theme to be traced. It is rebellion, self-destructive madness, exploiting the gifts of the Creator to pander to the vain illusions of the apostate heart. Faith is coherent: it is grounded in knowledge of the truth of God, it gives full assent to that truth, and commits the believer to the Lord in whole-hearted trust. Sin is unbelief: it does not escape believing, but chooses to believe the lie; in assenting to the lie it constructs a fabric of illusion and becomes self-deceived. Finally it commits itself to the lie in idolatry.

All the dimensions of sin are determined by its direction against God. As *alienation* it seeks to escape from God — by concealment in the garden, by flight east of Eden, or by setting up a boundary complete with a golden calf (I Kings 12:28f). As *rebellion* sin does not so much seek to escape from God as to defy him. The rebels will take counsel together to cast off God's rule; they will abuse his servants, kill his Son, and divide his inheritance among themselves (Psa. 2:1-3, Matt. 21:35-58). If the alien is driven by fear, the rebel is moved by hate (Rom. 8:7).

As *corruption,* sin seeks revenge. Licentious lust has a theological motif. It is not simple desire, for it rushes past satiety into perversion. It is spite against God, not simply in seizing the objects of desire in violation of God's order, but in profaning God's image, destroying his creation, and defacing the beauty of his glory. Delighting in the abuse of God's good gifts, sin pollutes language with the oaths of blasphemy, love with the vices of lust, and worship with the degradations of idolatry. Sin's corruption assaults the holiness of God: Cain murders Abel because Abel reflects the beauty of God's righteousness (I John 3:12). On the walls of God's holy place the sinner writes his obscene graffiti in blood. When God tabernacles among men in human flesh, sinners mangle, mock, and murder him, delighting to spit in the face of the Holy One of God.

As *guilt,* sin transgresses the law of God. God's goodness gave Adam a paradise dwelling, and a path for living. His commandment was also promise, directing man's steps to the tree of life. By his revealed will, God binds himself to man in personal communion; his *torah* points the way along the path of proving and sonship. Sin is lawlessness, disobedience to the Word of God. The clear and binding authority of God's commandment demonstrates the reality of sin and increases the guilt of disobedience (Rom. 5:20). Both the Old and New Testaments have words for sin that mean "missing the mark," but in biblical use the "mark" is the law of God, established in his covenant with his people.

Jesus teaches the God-centered meaning of the law by showing that the first and great commandment is whole-souled love for God, and further, that the second commandment depends upon the first. Lawlessness in the light of the heart of God's law is *lovelessness* — "He that loveth not, knoweth not God, for God is love" (I John 4:8).

If the revelation of God's law heightens sin by making it "exceeding sinful," then the full and final revelation of God's redeeming love in Jesus Christ gives to sin its ultimate horror: disobedience becomes the apostasy that spurns God's love and tramples under foot the blood of the Cross (Heb. 6:6; 10:29).

In spite of sin's irrational madness and self-destructiveness it remains guilty. The Apostle Paul presents the full wickedness of sin under God's law, "That every mouth may be stopped, and all the world may be brought under the judgment of God" (Rom. 3:19). Part of the judgment that sin merits is the exposure of its guilt. Those who are condemned must confess the justice of that condemnation; at the last judgment the scandal of disobedience must cease.

Sin is also *bondage* — not just through its own deceitfulness and the irreversible drive of its depravity, but through the fatal alliance of the sinner with the power of the devil (Eph. 2:1, 2). God's salvation "delivered us from the power of darkness, and translated us into the kingdom of his dear Son" (Col. 1:13).

The power of evil is not exercised only by the individual and by society, but by principalities and powers. According to the New Testament these are not symbolic designations of such things as imperialism or patterns of economic exploitation. They are, quite simply, the devil and his angels.

Closely linked with the bondage of sin is its deceitfulness: the god of this world has "blinded the minds of the unbelieving" (II Cor. 4:4). If false teachers fashion themselves into apostles of Christ it is no marvel, "for even Satan disguises himself into an angel of light" (II Cor. 11:14). God in judgment abandons those who believe not the truth to the lying wonders of Satan (II Thess. 2:9-12).

The consummate manifestation of sin and evil is therefore not secular but religious. Antichrist sits in the temple of God, setting himself forth as God (II Thess. 2:4). The climax of sin in the world is true to its beginning: the lie by which the creature would usurp the place of the Creator.

From this dominion of sin, because it is against God, there can be no deliverance that does not come from God. Sin has its seat in man's heart (Jer. 17:9) from which all unrighteousness proceeds (Mark 7:21-22). "Proceeding from the heart as center this pollution darkens the understanding (Rom. 1:21), inclines the will to do evil and makes it powerless to do the truly good (John 8:34 and Rom. 8:7), taints or defiles the conscience (Tit. 1:15) and makes of the body with all of its members . . . a weapon for unrighteousness (Rom. 3:13-17 and 6:13)"

The sin that pervades the whole man pervades also the whole of mankind. "There is none righteous, no not one: there is none that understandeth, there is none that seeketh after God" (Rom. 3:10, 11). "There is no distinction; for all have sinned, and fall short of the glory of God" (Rom. 3:22, 23). Not only do all men become sinners in word and deed; they are born in sin (Psa. 51:5). The apostle Paul traces back the course of sin in the world by following the course of death (Rom. 5:12-21). When the death-knell sounds, sin is being judged. At what point did sin enter, and death through sin? Evidently in the sin of the first man, Adam. Through *one* trespass death ruled over many (Rom. 5:19), including those who did not repeat Adam's sin and who could not yet be held accountable by the law given to Moses. How does death pass to the many through the sin of the one? The many bear the judgment because they share in the sin. Paul stresses the representative role of Adam because he wishes to show the parallel in Christ: as one act of sin made men guilty, caused sin to be charged against them — for all men sinned in Adam (Rom. 5:12, 18), so one act of righteousness brought justification and life to the new humanity in Christ. "For as in Adam all die, so also in Christ all shall be made alive . . . Christ the first fruits, after that those who are Christ's at his coming" (I Cor. 15:22, 23).

The sinfulness of all humanity is not a survival of the jungle; it is the result of the fall. It is sin before God. Man's doom springs from his initial rebellion and grows with his multiplied iniquity. Nothing that man is or does remains untainted.

All that God commanded for blessing, man perverts to his destruction. From the earth he draws the metals that give him tools, but he seizes the sword as the tool of power and sings his hymn of vengeance (Gen. 4:23, 24). He forges social and cultural unity in the city and raises a tower for God, a ramp of religion for the descent of the divine (Gen. 11:4). But his religiosity is not obedient devotion but proud rebellion, and God comes down not in blessing but in judgment.

But God is not mocked. The sinner will reap what he sows. Because God is slow to anger and merciful he gives men opportunity to repent (Ex. 34:6; Rom. 2:4, 5). Yet his final judgment is sure, and long before that last reckoning God makes evident his wrath against sin. Indeed the dynamic of sin's development shows how God judges men by making their very sins their punishment. Men give up the glory of the incorruptible God for idols (Rom. 1:23); God gives them up in the lusts of their hearts to uncleanness (1:24). Men give up the truth of God for a lie (v. 25); God gives them up to vile passions (v. 26). Men give up the knowledge of God (v. 28), and God gives them up to a reprobate mind (v. 28). Man's abandonment of natural sexual relations is judged by God's abandonment to the chains of perversion (vv. 26, 27).

Man's sin continually perverts, twists, and destroys what God has given. Whether he tortures God's creatures or worships them he yet assaults God's goodness. Paul emphasizes the continuing witness of God's creation that makes the Gentiles without excuse. Man cannot escape God's revelation of his power and divinity (Rom. 1:20), but he refuses to have God in his knowledge (v. 28), seizes the truth in unrighteousness (v. 18) and exchanges it for a lie (v. 25).

In man's struggle against God there is progressive apostasy, leading to God's abandonment. In the spiritual state of the Gentiles of his day Paul finds a depravity that has progressed far beyond the first beginnings of idolatry. God's truth is not a settled deposit in the thoughts of the nations. Rather it has been increasingly abandoned and continually resisted and twisted. Static models of a natural theology forget the dynamic of the psychology (and, indeed the epistemology) of sin.

J.H. Bavinck puts the right question to the religious systems of the world: "What have you done with God?"

His analysis of some of the motifs of world religions shows the fruitfulness of the question. Men deal with God by promoting him to be the "high god," a heavenly deity of no earthly concern, an otiose god who can be safely ignored in favor of the snake cult. Or men deal with God by identifying him with the cosmos, the great process polarity of *yin* and *yang*. Another religious option is to screen off God by erecting a barrier of legalism. No yoke of codified conduct seems as forbidding to the sinner as a living relationship with God! Yet another "solution" is to de-personalize and vaporize God in the world-ocean of mysticism.

From each of these motifs springs a distinctive view of sin and suffering. Yet each removes the personal depth of sin against the revealed goodness of the living God. All are characterized by the apostle as "weak and beggarly elements" that bring men into bondage to them that are no gods (Gal. 4:8, 9). Gentile corruption and Pharisaical pride, animal lust and heroic asceticism, worldly irreligion and sanctimonious religion — all are expressions of man's sin against God. Indeed, as the ministry of Jesus Christ shows, publicans and harlots go into the kingdom before the righteous religionists, for they may more readily confess their sin, turn from their own ways and cast themselves upon the mercy of God, "God be merciful to me a sinner!" (Luke 18:13).

2. The Gospel of God: salvation and suffering

a. "Salvation is of the Lord" — "For of him, and through him, and to him, *are* all things: to whom be glory for ever" (Rom. 11:36). Paul's doxology springs from reflection on the wonder of God's plan in salvation. Even the burden of Israel's unbelief, so crushing to the Apostle, he has brought to the throne of God's sovereignty; Paul beholds the severity and the goodness of the Lord (11:22) and worships.

Job's complaints were silenced by the overwhelming awe of God's presence (. . . "But now mine eye seeth thee!", Job 42:5). In the revelation of Gospel mysteries, that silence before God becomes a song of praise.

God's salvation goes beyond all imagining; his purposes are hidden in the inaccessible heights of his grace (Jer. 33:2, 3; Isa. 55:8-11). Salvation is more than God's gift: in giving salvation God gives himself. In the *Lord* is the glory that outweighs suffering; in the *Lord* is the design that is accomplished through suffering; in the *Lord* is the grace that transforms suffering. Apart from God men may account suffering and death the greatest evils; they may mock a salvation that *calls* men to suffer. But those who hear the voice of the Son of God are ready to take up a cross and follow him.

God's dealings with Israel focus on the bond of possession between Yahweh as the Lord and the people as his servant. The heart of God's salvation is not the escape from Egypt, as a sign of God's deliverance, or the possession of the land, as a sign of his blessing. It is the trust at Sinai where God claims the people for himself. "Ye have seen what I did unto the Egyptians, and how I bare you on eagles' wings, and brought you unto myself" (Ex. 19:4-6).

Israel is a nation of priests, God's own possession. After the sin of the golden calf, God proposes to go before the people and give them the land, but not to dwell in their midst (Ex. 33:1-3). Moses rejects this proposal with dismay, and pleads for the declaration of God's name of grace. Receiving this assurance of divine favor, Moses prays, not that the people be given *their* inheritance, but that God take them as *his* inheritance (Ex. 34:9). The tabernacle, and later, the temple, are built to be the abiding sign of the dwelling of the Lord in the midst of his people.

Scholars have isolated the themes of redemption and of blessing in the Old Testament; they have contrasted the episodic drama of redemptive history with a continuous experience of life, health and *shalom*. But the Old Testament message is neither a theology of liberation nor a natural theology of prosperity. It is the theology of the covenant: the bond of favor that joins the living God with his chosen people.

Because of that favor God hears the cries of his people, and comes to deliver them. Yet God's presence and even God's deliverance do not at once end Israel's suffering. Instead, God leads his people through the desert to prove and strengthen their faith in him. At Marah, where bitter water mocks their thirst, the people receive the sign and promise of God's healing presence, "I *am* the Lord that healeth thee" (Ex. 15:26).

The Lord who heals also wounds in discipline or in judgment when his people are unfaithful to his covenant. As apostasy in the land of promise leads to destruction and captivity, it is God who judges his people. From God too must come their restoration, a restoration that centers in the knowledge of the Lord (Hos. 6:1-3). God's mercy causes restoration to become renewal. The dry bones in the valley hear the word of the Lord, and live before God with new hearts (Ezek. 36:26; 37:1-14). So great are God's promises that they can be fulfilled only by the coming of God himself. When God's glory shines upon his people, then "nations shall come to your light and kings to the brightness of your rising" (Isa. 60:3). God's glory transforms the city, the land, and the world. The curse even in the animal world is changed to the blessing of God's peace (Isa. 11:6-10).

If in the blessing of that day the very pots of Jerusalem shall be holy and the feeblest citizen as David, then "the house of David shall be as God, as the angel of the Lord before them" (Zech. 12:8). The ensign that God lifts up for the gathering of the nations is the rod that grows from the root of Jesse, the individual "Remnant," God's anointed Servant (Isa. 10:33, 34, 11:1-5, 10). The Servant is God's elect, in whom his soul delights (Isa. 42:1); he bears God's Name (Isa. 9:6) as God's Son (Psa. 2:7) and will share God's rule at his right hand (Psa. 110:1).

The Gospel proclaims the coming of salvation with the birth of the Savior, Christ the Lord (Luke 2:11). Then as now salvation had many meanings. For the slave it meant freedom, for the citizen, prosperity. Emperors stamped the title on their coins as divinized guardians of the "Pax Romana." To the devotee of the mystery cult it meant immortality, to the mystic the transport of ecstasy. To the zealous Israelite, salvation meant military deliverance from Rome.

But the angelic announcement of the Savior came not to zealot captains but to shepherds; the sign of the angel presented a Savior in a feed-bin, despised from his birth (Isa. 1:3, LXX). The angelic hosts did not come to the fields of Bethleham as avengers, but to bless God for giving his peace to the men of his good pleasure, the humble poor made heirs of the kingdom by grace.

All the words and deeds of Jesus Christ fulfill this heavenly plan of salvation. He preached the good news of the kingdom of God, the coming of God's rule of righteousness. But Jesus is more than a herald, he is the Deliverer. In Nazareth he reads Isaiah's prophecy of the great year of jubilee and says, "Today is this scripture fulfilled in your ears" (Luke 4:21).

His miracles are signs of kingdom cleansing and power. He can restore the world of creation and the hearts of men from the pollution of demonic evil. He is Lord over the wind and the sea, life and death, men and demons. Because he has bound the strong man, Satan, in his wilderness ordeal he can free his captives (Luke 11:14-22). He is the second Adam, the Son of Man who has authority to subdue the earth and to fill all things (Gen. 1:28; Eph. 1:21, 23; 4:10; Matt. 14:33). Christ crushes the head of the serpent in the conflict of his life and in the triumph of his death. He is the seeking Shepherd who gathers the "little flock" (Luke 12:32), calling his sheep by name and promising to gather others "not of this fold" (John 10:16). He raises up the afflicted, ministers healing to the suffering, and feeds the fainting crowds in the desert.

Yet he hid himself from those who would make him king by force; he would not lead a march of political liberation to Jerusalem (John 6:15). When he entered the city among the crowds, it was as the meek and lowly king of Zechariah's prophecy (Matt. 21:4-11). He refused Peter's sword in his defense and would not call down from heaven either fire or angels for his vindication (John 18:11, Luke 9:54, 55; Matt. 26:53). Set before Pilate he said, "My kingdom is not of this world, else would my servants fight" (John 18:36).

John the Baptist, his forerunner, sent to him from the prison where he was soon to die, "Art thou he that cometh, or look we for another?" (Luke 7:20). John had preached the coming judgment of the kingdom. Jesus' miracles demonstrated the blessings of the kingdom; but Jesus did not lift the axe of judgment against the oppressors. How could kingdom blessing come without kingdom justice? What could explain the restraint of kingdom power that left John in prison?

Jesus reaffirmed his miracles as the fulfillment of prophecy (Isa. 35:5, 6) and said, "Blessed is he whosoever is not offended in me" (Matt. 11:6). John must accept his refusal to use kingdom power to bring in kingdom judgment. In that refusal lies the mystery of the Gospel: the true purpose and program of the kingdom. Christ did not come to slay the wicked but to be slain for the wicked; not to bring the judgment upon men but to bear the judgment for men. Justice apart from justification is not the blessing that men complacently imagine. Full justice will be brought upon all those that know not God when Christ comes again (II Thess. 1:7-9).

Without God's justifying righteousness, God's justice must bring upon men not what they desire but what they deserve: God's wrath and curse in the day of judgment. Those who speak of "salvations" in the plural deny the Gospel at its heart. Without the salvation of Christ's justifying righteousness and atoning death, there is no other salvation. God's salvation is indeed comprehensive, and includes total justice at the last day, but apart from forgiveness of sins through the Gospel of the Cross of Christ total justice means final doom for every sinner. The kingdom of God is not a composite of personal awareness and political action to be entered individually by conversion or socially by revolution. Rather, God's kingdom is the operation of his power to accomplish his plan through his Savior, Jesus Christ. God's plan includes the withholding of his judgment so that the Gospel may be preached and men may repent and believe in Christ. Neither peace of mind nor peace in society as human achievements can bring in God's kingdom. The rich fool of Jesus' parable was well content and the builders of Babel demonstrated social unity. Neither was prepared for divine judgment. The distinction is not between the individual and society, for the kingdom of God is manifested not only in the individual lives of those who have been born of the Spirit, but also in the corporate life of God's new community, the Church of Christ, set as a light in the world.

The abiding question is the meaning of salvation itself — whether it means deliverance from God's wrath into the blessing of his peace or whether it means whatever personal aspirations or social structures seem desirable or right to men who reject the counsel of God about this purpose and plan of salvation.

b. *The suffering Savior* — Jesus came in the power of the kingdom, yet he did not bring in the judgment of the kingdom. Instead, he sent his apostles to the ends of the earth to disciple the nations. But the time of the mission of the church is not just a worldwide extension of the ministry of John the Baptist, calling men to repentance. Jesus did not simply announce the postponing of judgment; he bore the judgment. At the Cross he gave his life a ransom for many, bearing in their place God's judgment for sin.

The Cross is not merely a sign of judgment, a warning that in spite of delay, God's justice is sure. Rather, it is the execution of judgment. Paul's whole doctrine of salvation rests upon the meaning of union with Christ in his death and resurrection. The believer was chosen in Christ before the world began; when Christ died, he died, too; when Christ rose, he rose in Christ and ascended in Christ. The Holy Spirit brings to the church the fruits of Christ's victory. The new life in Christ is a beginning of the life of the world to come. Further, Christ's triumph has cosmic dimensions. The principalities and powers are defeated; Christ now has all power in heaven and earth. No power can thwart his purpose in gathering all that the Father has given him. Even the final revelation of his power in judgment is not a new victory but the full outcome of the victory of the Cross (Phil. 2:9-11; Col. 2:13-15; Heb. 2:9).

Only in the full meaning of the Cross do we find the Gospel for suffering humanity. The triumph of the Cross forms the hope of the Gospel: the resurrection victory of Jesus Christ that enables the believer to cry, "O death, where is thy sting? O grave where is thy victory?" (I Cor. 15:55). The Gospel does not glorify suffering but promises that God will wipe away every tear . . . "and death shall be no more; neither shall there be mourning, nor crying, nor pain any more" . . . (Rev. 21:4). That consolation of joy in God's presence comes through the Lamb that was slain — the Cross of Christ (Rev. 21:22, 22:3).

The Gospel of the suffering Savior has yet a deeper meaning. The promise of an end to suffering and death would be utterly incredible apart from the God who makes it. The passage that declares "death shall be no more" begins, "Behold the tabernacle of God is with men, and he shall dwell with them, and they shall be his people, and God himself shall be with them, and be their God, and he shall wipe away every tear . . ." (Rev. 21:3).

Only God's power can remove all suffering; but more is declared here — the divine compassion that wipes away the tears of men. The God who "forgiveth all thine iniquities, who healeth all thy diseases" (Psa. 103:3) is the God of mercy. In the Old Testament he reserves healing to himself to show his covenant love. King Hezekiah who cries to the Lord and is healed confesses, ". . . thou hast in love to my soul delivered it from the pit . . ." (Isa. 38:17). To the prayer of anguish, "Heal me O Lord, and I shall be healed; save me and I shall be saved" (Jer. 17:14), God responds, "For I will restore health unto thee, and I will heal thee of thy wounds, saith the Lord" (Jer. 30:17, 33:6).

Only the Lord heals, and it is by the Spirit of the Lord that his anointed will bind up the broken-hearted and comfort the mourning (Isa. 61:1, 2). Not only will the Servant of the Lord comfort those that mourn, he himself "hath borne our griefs, and carried our sorrows . . . but he was wounded for our transgressions, he was bruised for our iniquities: the chastisement of our peace was upon him; and with his stripes we are healed" (Isa. 53:4, 5).

In the background of the Suffering Servant of Isaiah's prophecy is the figure of the righteous sufferer in the Old Testament. ". . . The reproaches of them that reproached thee are fallen upon me" says the psalmist (Psa. 69:9). Beyond the problem of undeserved suffering in the lives of the righteous, the Old Testament perceives the mystery of suffering endured for the sake of righteousness. For his righteousness Abel is killed, Joseph is sold into slavery. Moses is threatened with stoning, and David, the Lord's anointed, is outlawed in the wilderness. The theme finds ritual expression in the sacrifice of a perfect lamb for the sin-offering. The Suffering Servant of Isaiah reflects both the righteous Servant theme (especially with Moses in view) and the theme of the sin-bearing sacrifice.

Yet the wonder of this Suffering Servant theme lies in the union of the Servant with the Lord who sends him. This Servant does not remonstrate with God as Job did; he silently endures outrage and anguish, knowing that it pleased the Lord to bruise him and put him to grief. The Lord and the Servant alike rejoice in the outcome of the travail of his soul "by his knowledge shall my righteous servant justify many; and he shall bear their iniquities" (Isa. 53:11).

How can the disfiguring anguish of the chosen Servant become a hymn of salvation? Because of the wonder of the Servant's consecration; and because of the wonder of God's grace.

When God calls his servants to bear reproach for his sake he reveals also the love of his own longsuffering mercy. From the depths of the Old Testament there flows like a river of life from the throne of God the stream of divine compassion. It shines through the figures of the shepherd, the lover and husband, the father, — and even the vine-dresser as they describe God's care for his people. It appears at Maasah-Meribah where the people charged God with covenant breaking. God himself appears before Moses in the place of the accused and receives the smiting of judgment. The Rock on which God stands and which symbolizes his presence and his name is struck by the rod of Moses to bring forth the water of life to Israel. The people, not the Lord, have broken the covenant, but when they demand a trial, he bears the judgment.

At Mount Moriah, too, God's love is symbolized. Abraham is spared the offering of his beloved son Isaac, for God provides a ram in his place. Yet the oracular ambiguity of the name "Jehovah-Jireh" suggests more. "God will see for himself the lamb for a burnt-offering, my son," says Abraham. "He (God) that spared not his own Son, but delivered him up for us all," testifies the Apostle Paul (Rom. 8:32).

"In all their affliction he was afflicted, and the angel of his presence saved them: in his love and in his pity he redeemed them; and he bare them . . . and carried them all the days of old" (Isa. 63:9).

When Jesus comes as the true shepherd who gives his life for the sheep, he manifests the mystery of the divine love. He is the beloved Son of the Father, the true Isaac; the smitten Rock (I Cor. 10:4).

His compassion joins him with the suffering people; it motivates his healing and teaching ministry. His hand of compassion leads the blind, touches the leper, raises the dead. His eye of compassion sees the multitude as sheep without a shepherd. Ministering among the sick at Capernaum, he "himself took our infirmities, and bare our sicknesses" as the Gospel testifies (Matt. 8:17). His vicarious suffering endured the misery of affliction as well as the judgment of sin, and he endured personally and willingly — "having loved his own which were in the world, he loved them unto the end" (John 13:1)

In the parable of the "Good Samaritan," Jesus taught that the love of the kingdom is the love of compassion. Confronted with the law of love to God and to one's neighbor, the lawyer has asked Jesus, "Who is my neighbor?"

That question revealed the lawyer's misconception of God's law. Love must not draw boundaries to minimize its obligation, for love must be modeled on God's love — the love of compassion by which God sent his only begotten Son into the world. "He that loveth not knoweth not God; for God is love" (I John 4:8). To refuse to minister mercy where God offers opportunity is to deny the saving love of the Father and the compassion of the Son.

At the Cross the love of God triumphs through suffering. The actuality of Christ's atonement excludes sentimental dilution of the love of God. The troubling of Christ's soul as he took the cup of suffering witnesses to the reality of his sin-bearing in his once-for-all sacrifice (John 12:27; Heb. 10:10). In that transaction "he hath made him to be sin for us, who knew no sin; that we might be made the righteousness of God in him" (II Cor. 5:21). His prayer as he came to the Cross was not that he might be delivered from this hour (the prayer of the afflicted psalmists), but rather, "Father, glorify thy name!" (John 12:28). Christ's prayer was heard and answered. God's name was hallowed in the justice of Calvary; God's name was hallowed in the love of Calvary. Beyond our expressing is the price of the Cross — the price the Son paid as he gave his life a ransom for many; the price the Father paid when he gave his only begotten Son. All our problems with suffering are overcome by the mystery of that divine sacrifice. Hear again the cry of the beloved Son from the Cross, "Eloi, Eloi, lama sabachthani?" Hear, too, from the darkness the silence of the Father while the soldiers prepare a sponge of vinegar.

The compassion of Calvary is God's answer to human suffering. The doom of suffering is inevitable and just, for the wages of sin is death, and man is a rebel not a victim. But God provided a victim, the only sufferer without sin, that whoever believes in him should not perish but have everlasting life.

The finished sacrifice of Calvary redeems the people of God, but Calvary does not end Christ's ministry of mercy. The risen Christ remains a priest forever, and because his priesthood is unchanging he continues to be "touched with the feeling of our infirmity" (Heb. 4:15). His heavenly priesthood shows the same compassion that moved him in the streets of Capernaum.

c. *The suffering church* — Only in the perspective of Calvary can the calling of the church to suffer be understood. When James and John asked for places of honor in Christ's glory, Jesus promised them rather a portion of his cup of suffering and his baptism of agony (Mark 10:35-40). He called his disciples to take up a cross and follow him (Luke 9:23) and blessed those who would be persecuted for his name's sake (Matt. 5:11).

The sequence of sufferings first and glory to follow was the pattern of Christ's own ministry (Luke 24:26; I Pet. 1:11; Heb. 2:9, 10), and it must be the pattern for the ministry of his disciples (Rom. 8:17; Phil. 3:10; I Pet. 4:13). The apostle warned new converts that "through many tribulations we must enter the Kingdom of God" (Acts 14:22). Not only is apocalyptic tribulation to precede the return of Christ (Matt. 24:29-31), but suffering marks faithfulness to Christ when "ye shall be hated of all the nations for my name's sake" (Matt. 24:9). "All that will live godly in Christ Jesus shall suffer persecution" (II Tim. 3:12).

The ordeal of suffering is not simply to be endured but received as a means of proving and strengthening. Christ was proved through his passion, and as the Son of God learned obedience through the things that he suffered (Heb. 5:8, 2:10). He endured fiery trial without sin; sinners who have not yet resisted unto blood striving against sin must also be corrected by the chastisement of suffering, the fatherly discipline that proves them to be true sons (Heb. 12:4, 8).

Suffering for the Christian is also a means of witness. Paul's calling includes not only the commission to bear the Lord's name before Gentiles and kings but also "I will show him how great things he must suffer for my name's sake" (Acts 9:16). The apostles rejoice that they are "counted worthy to suffer dishonor for his name" (Acts 5:41). The Old Testament theme of the righteous sufferer, now fulfilled in Jesus Christ, has new meaning and depth. Those who suffer for righteousness' sake sanctify in their hearts Christ as Lord (I Pet. 4:14, 15); they rejoice in their abiding possession (Heb. 10:34) and future glory (Rom. 8:18; II Cor. 4:17); they know that the trial of their faith works patience and hope (I Pet. 1:6, 7; Rom. 5:3, 4). But above all they rejoice with the apostles that they are made a spectacle to the world, both to angels and men (I Cor. 4:9) for Christ's sake (II Cor. 12:10).

At the heart of Christian joy in suffering is the deepening of fellowship with Christ that suffering provides. "We suffer with him, that we may be also glorified together" (Rom. 8:17). Paul also writes, "That I may know him, and the power of his resurrection, and the fellowship of his sufferings, being made conformable unto his death; if by any means I might attain unto the resurrection of the dead" (Phil. 3:10). Here the apostle is thinking of Christ's righteousness that is his by faith (v. 9) and of the application to his own life of the liberation from sin wrought by Christ's death. But he also has in view that his identification with Christ in his death has required that he suffer the loss of all things (v. 8). Because he has died with Christ, he dies daily for Christ (I Cor. 15:31), and desires only that "Christ shall be magnified in my body, whether it be by life, or by death" (Phil. 1:20). Paul speaks of his sufferings as the "sufferings of Christ" in the sense of Christian sufferings, suffering for Christ's sake (II Cor. 1:5-7), but these sufferings are borne in fellowship with Christ. (How close the two themes are appears in I Peter 4:12-16.) The apostle can rejoice in his sufferings as completing that which is lacking in the full amount of affliction for Christ. That is his own calling on behalf of the church (Col. 1:24). Suffering intensifies the bond of fellowship with Christ and with the church. In suffering the love of God is "poured out within our hearts through the Holy Spirit . . . for while we were still helpless, at the right time Christ died for the ungodly..." (Rom. 5:5, 6).

Christ's sufferings and death also transform the ministry of the church. Paul sees his own experiences in suffering as well as his experience of God's comfort as aiding him in ministering comfort to the afflicted (II Cor. 1:3-6). Christians who remember the thirst of Christ's anguish on the Cross are bound by his love to give a cup of cold water in his name (Mark 9:41). The other side of Christian fellowship that Christians have with Christ in his suffering is the fellowship Christ has with Christians in theirs. When Saul persecutes the church he persecutes Christ (Acts 9:4); when men minister to Christ's brethren who are hungry, thirsty, strangers, naked, sick, or imprisoned, they minister to Christ himself (Matt. 25:31-46). The relief of need among the brethren became a distinguishing mark of the apostolic church, binding together rich and poor, Jew and Gentile, bond and free in the sharing of possessions so that none would lack the necessities of life or the ministry of love (Acts 4:32-35; Rom. 15:26, 27).

d. *The Gospel in the suffering world* — In the suffering world the Church of Jesus Christ preaches his passion, his resurrection, and the hope of his *parousia*. To preach the Cross is to reprove the wisdom of men even as they describe their own plight. The Gospel confronts the man made in God's image with the profound depth of his misery before God. That realization comes not from the analysis of suffering but from the revelation of the living God.

Apart from that revelation all the options of human speculation about suffering are fatally flawed. In the Confucian tradition a moralistic theme of due reward and punishment in this life is modified by insight into the educational value of suffering. The law of karma in the Hindu tradition binds suffering to a strict causality operating through successive reincarnations. Buddhism would break the chain of suffering by subduing desires. The ancient dualism of Zoroastrian religion explains suffering in the conflict of the ultimate light and darkness.

Modern mythologies struggle to open a door of hope for the despair of alienated man. Marxists proclaim the economic root of misery, neo-Freudians trace misery to repression, and Darwin still has followers who preach the inevitable agony of the evolutionary process.

All these views of suffering fail to express the seriousness of man's misery before the holy, living God. Far less can they express the mystery of the suffering Savior on the Cross. Paul was resolved to know nothing but Christ crucified, closing his mind against all temptations to lessen the offense of the Gospel by compromising the message of the Cross.

Today we must cling to the Cross to be faithful to men in their misery and to God in his love. The new political gospel takes away the centrality of the Cross. Politically the Cross was foolishness. The theologians of political liberation must therefore leave the Cross behind to discover what the "politician God" is up to as he works in contemporary history to advance the revolution.

We must cling to the Cross, too, when men would destroy its centrality by reducing substitutionary atonement to one theory among many describing reconciliation. The biblical doctrine of the atonement is not a "contextual" theology offering a culture-bound interpretation of an ineffable event. It is the message that "Christ died for our sins according to the Scriptures" (I Cor. 15:3). The God who gave his Son gave the meaning of his sacrifice in the words of his apostles and prophets.

The Gospel of Christ crucified cuts across the theories of the sinner's darkened mind to meet the need of his rebellious heart. It is the power of God to salvation. We must neither conceal it nor minimize it. Our concern must be to proclaim the whole counsel of God, including the "hard sayings" of Jesus about his sacrificial death and the Father's sovereign drawing of men (John 6:26-65). Man-centered theology puts God in debt to man, and demands universalism

if there is to be salvation. God-centered theology bows with the Apostle
Paul before the sovereignty of God in salvation, and marvels at his
grace.

But to preach the Cross in its offense could become a frightening
caricature if the *love* of the Cross were not proclaimed in the compassion of Christ. In a suffering world Christians both proclaim and
manifest present salvation and joy in Christ. The new life that can
rejoice in suffering finds expression in a new community where all
are ministers of mercy in Christ's name. When that ministry fails in
the church its witness to the world is jeopardized.

The vivid reality of the Christian *hope* is equally vital in a world
of war, famine, and despair. The church awaits not the grinding of
cosmic process but the coming of the risen Lord who already fills
all things with his power and will subdue all things to himself. The
cosmic power and purpose of the Lord of glory frees the Christian to
serve God in this groaning creation, even as he tastes in the Spirit
the powers of the age to come. The redeemer is the Creator, the Lord,
the Spirit.

The life of the Spirit is the fountain of joy for the church's ministry
in a suffering world. The comfort and encouragement, the tenderness
and power, the burden-bearing sharing of the Spirit, these are the
spiritual gifts that ministry to suffering requires.

The true comprehensiveness of salvation is the fullness of the
Spirit's work in the church by which the saints are rooted in the love
of Christ and grow to minister in his name, working that which is
good "unto all men, and especially unto them who are of the household of faith" (Gal. 6:10).

As the opportunity is given in our time of famine and need, the
church must show the compassion of Christ to the world. The genuineness of deeds as well as words, of sacrifice to care for the forgotten will manifest the reality of the love of Christ. A renewed diaconate must manifest continuous rather than sporadic concern; the fellowship of the ministry of the Word and of tables reflects the permanent
structure of office in Christ's Church. As the risen Lord bears in his
body the marks of his sufferings, so must the Church, his body, bear
the marks of Jesus (Gal. 6:17) not only by suffering in his name, but
by ministering in his compassion to an afflicted and guilty world.

MAN'S DILEMMA OF SIN AND SUFFERING
Chairman: D. Pantupong
Secretary: D. Penney

1. *Major points of agreement*

 a. The depth and meaning of human suffering can be understood only in terms of man's relation to the living God. The doom and dread of suffering in God's wrath is inescapable and final. Salvation from suffering is God's promise and work, wrought through Christ's atonement. Fellowship with God in Christ transforms suffering both in its experience and its fruit.

 b. The many aspects of suffering are probed in the Bible with profound realism. In prayers of anguish and in meditations of reflection, the experience of suffering is brought before God. Yet all of these aspects are taken up in the unity of God's revelation and the climax of his work of redemption in Christ. The Bible presents the origin of sin and suffering in man's first disobedience. God's initiative in grace promises salvation through suffering (Gen. 3:15). Suffering is related to the divine discipline of the covenant people as well as to the covenant curse. The suffering of the righteous is a growing theme, climaxing in the redemptive suffering of the Servant of the Lord and the promise of a new order without suffering and sin.

 c. Sin must be defined in terms of the right relation to God that it rejects and perverts. Sin is alienation from God, rebellion against him, and the corruption of all of his good gifts. The sinner is in bondage not only to his own error, illusion, and idolatry, but to the powers of darkness. Suffering may be pathetic, but sin is heinous, guilty and damnable. The folly and absurdity of sin can never conceal its guilt.

 No part of man's nature escapes the taint of sin or stands outside the dynamic of sin's direction against God. Only salvation by God's grace can provide the new birth of the Spirit and the total reversal of direction that breaks the dominion of sin in the heart of man.

 e. No part of mankind escapes the condemnation of God's righteousness. All are guilty, deserving God's wrath: the death penalty is pronounced against all. They are guilty in Adam's first transgression; they participate in progressive abandonment of God, and are abandoned by God in judgment.

 f. Religious and cultural achievements reflect to some degree not only that man is made in God's image, but also that God's grace restrains human corruption. But the religion and culture of fallen man do not escape from the apostate direction of his rebellious heart. Indeed, man's spiritual iniquity gives the deepest expression to his sin. Man's religions, in distinction from the true worship of the living God, seek to do away with God, not to seek his face.

 g. Salvation is not only God's gift, but God's own presence and fellowship. It is the bond that joins the redeemed to the Redeemer. Neither a "theology of liberation" nor a "theology of creation" can be isolated from the theocentric core of biblical salvation. God's delivering, healing, leading, proving, chastening, and blessing are all part of the salvation by which he brings men to himself.

h. God's salvation is accomplished by his coming in Jesus Christ, who is God the Son born as a true man of the Virgin Mary. His coming is the fulfillment of his promised salvation. Because Christ is Lord his power and presence accomplish the salvation of God's kingdom decisively in his first coming, even though he will come again to bring the final fullness of his kingdom. Jesus Christ is the only Savior.

i. The "gathering" of Christ's saving rule assembles the Church as the new mankind in Christ. Christ calls his Church to the ministry of worship, edification, and witness in the power of the Holy Spirit. But while the Church has a heavenly life, lives by the heavenly law of love, and is separated from the world to holiness, it is not now taken from the world, but called to follow Christ in suffering now and in glory hereafter.

j. Christ's own work defines the nature and the program of his kingdom of salvation:

    (i) His refusal of political Messiahship

    (ii) His teaching of kingdom righteousness

    (iii) His claim to Lordship in all his ministry

    (iv) His granting of kingdom blessing and withholding judgment

    (v) His sufferings and glory

    (vi) His *parousia*

k. The Gospel of Christ therefore presents both the present and the future of salvation as Christ's own work. Suffering now has an eschatological setting for Christ's Church. "The sufferings of this present time are not worthy to be compared with the glory that is to be revealed in us" (Rom. 8:18).

l. Salvation in Christ is comprehensive and unitary. It includes his work as the last Adam in fulfilling man's original calling, his death for sinners as the Lamb of God who gives his life a ransom for many, his coming again as the judge to bring perfect and eternal justice. The church is now called to have fellowship with Christ in suffering; it is not now called to vindicative retribution. The discipline of the church is spiritual, not physical; the church judges those within, not those without. In the last day only will the church share in Christ's judgment.

m. Christ's triumph is total, his salvation will provide a new heaven and earth; even now he has all authority in heaven and in earth. Christ's authority sets his people free to fulfill his calling in the world, yet his calling includes the limitations imposed by his present purpose of withholding final judgment while the Gospel is preached to the nations.

n. Christ's calling to his Church is to take up the cross to follow him. By suffering his Church is proved and disciplined, in suffering the Church bears witness to the suffering servant Christ; above all, in suffering the Church has deepened fellowship with Christ and with fellow Christians. Joy in suffering marks the obedience of Christ's Church until he comes. God's suffering servants glorify him as all men see their patient confidence as they affirm God's loving faithfulness in every circumstance. God uses tribulation to disciple his people, consuming the dross in the hearts of believers.

o. The power of the Gospel lies in the "foolishness" of the Cross of Christ, where misery of man's sin and majesty of God's love are revealed. In man's weakness, God's grace and power are manifested.

2. *Implications for evangelism: man's dilemma of sin and suffering*

a. The Gospel of Christ crucified must remain central for evangelism.

(i) The Cross reveals the righteousness of God's judgment against sin.

(ii) The Cross reveals the mystery of God's love in Christ's substitutionary atonement for sin.

(iii) The Cross reveals the triumph of Christ over sin, death, and the powers of darkness.

(iv) The Cross puts to shame the wisdom of men as the sublime "foolishness" of God.

(v) The Cross puts to shame the power of men by the victorious "weakness" of God.

b. Evangelism proclaims the Gospel of the Kingdom, a message centered in Christ the King: his present exaltation and Lordship and his future subjecting of all things to himself. This message requires total obedience to Christ in all of life, but obedience to the specific program and will of Christ in the pattern of his own ministry: sufferings and glory. The Gospel cannot promise deliverance from present suffering because of Christ's present victory. Rather it is through suffering that we are called to inherit the kingdom (I Thess. 3:3, 4).

c. The Gospel must be presented boldly in its condemnation of sin and in its call to repentance and conversion. The pattern of the Gospel does not require an inflexible ordering of the message (as though the promise of the Gospel could never precede the Gospel's condemnation of sin), but we are charged with presenting to men the whole Gospel. To understand the grace of God, men must perceive the meaning of the righteous wrath of God.

d. The fearful bondage of men to sin and death requires us to proclaim and trust in God alone as Savior. Trust in the power of God's Spirit and God's Word are indispensable in faithful evangelism.

e. The comprehensivenss of salvation in Christ is not a composite of personal deliverance from the guilt and power of sin and the amelioration of social conditions (or the re-ordering of social structures). It is rather the fullness of God's presence in salvation among his people. The new structure of corporate life in Christ is found among the people of God. Christ said, "I will build my church." The biblical doctrine of the Church must be given its rightful place in the theology and program of evangelism.

f. Fellowship in suffering must include a return to biblical principles of stewardship on the part of those who need to give and those who need to receive.

g. The blessed hope of Christ's return forms a most significant part of the Gospel message in contrast to the illusory promises of humanistic and political utopias.

Summary of further discussion

Question: Modern evangelism seems more suffering conscious than sin conscious. How can we turn this suffering consciousness to the main question, sin? Isn't social action bypassing the main issue?

Conclusion: Natural man sees suffering as the problem and wants to do away with it. He may either accuse God of being unjust or claim that suffering shows that no loving God exists. However, God wants man to stop his rebelling, which is the root cause of the suffering. A doctor does not treat only the symptoms; he must also attack the disease. But serious symptoms must also be treated.

Question: Just what is the diaconal ministry of the Church?

Conclusion: It is the Church showing forth Christ's love among the brethren within and Christ's mercy to all men outside the Church. This must be given an important place. The Christian community has not adequately felt the need to be involved.

Question: How does this diaconal ministry relate to evangelism?

Conclusion: It is a powerful witness to Christ's presence in his Church when men see *truth* being practiced in and from the Christian community.

Question: Do people listen more to the Gospel when they have experienced the diaconal ministry toward themselves?

Conclusion: Sometimes yes, sometimes no.

Question: Then, why help them?

Conclusion: We extend them Christ's mercy for Christ's sake, "We love because he first loved us" (I John 4:19). There should be an evangelistic effect, but not merely an evangelistic purpose. People will know the difference as to whether we have sincerely acted in love for Christ and for them, or merely to gain opportunity to preach to them. Our first priority and act should be to pray for those who are suffering; but we must not stop there. We must then share in their suffering. This may then give opportunity to share our experience of Christ — how he has helped us in our need. The interest we show in them must be real in relation to their felt need. A starving person may need bread in order to be able to listen to the Gospel.

Question: But, if we could relieve all hunger, for example, would there not still be a deeper suffering? Many of those who have the most that this world can offer are among the most desperate and frustrated.

Conclusion: We must keep our main aim on treating the real problem: man's sin, which can only be treated by the full communication of the Gospel of Christ. But at the same time, we must do what we can for the symptoms of suffering. Perhaps the simplest statement of this combination is, "Give a cup of cold water in the name of Christ." The water represents physical ministry to a real need: physical thirst, while the "name of Christ" represents all that Jesus Christ is — the God-man who gave himself for our spiritual need, to free us from the sin that is at the root of mankind's problem; the sin that is the root cause of all suffering, and also the cause in every man's personal frustration, spiritual suffering and separation from God.

JESUS CHRIST, THE UNIQUE SON OF GOD: THE RELATIONSHIP OF HIS DEITY AND HUMANITY WITH REFERENCE TO EVANGELISM

Roger Nicole

Dr. Nicole, South Hamilton, Massachusetts, USA, is Professor of Theology at Gordon-Conwell Theological Seminary.

It is clear beyond challenge that the New Testament identifies the hope of salvation for any human being with the name of Jesus Christ. Peter the Apostle said, "There is salvation in no one else; for there is no other name under heaven that has been given among men, by which we must be saved" (Acts 4:12).

Paul said, "That if you confess with your mouth, 'Jesus is Lord,' and believe in your heart that God raised him from the dead, you will be saved. For it is with your heart that you believe and are justified, and it is with your mouth that you confess and are saved." As the Scripture says, "He who believes in him will not be put to shame." For there is no difference between Jew and Gentile — the same Lord is Lord of all and richly blesses all who call on him, for, "Everyone who calls on the name of the Lord will be saved." How, then, can they call on the one they have not believed in? And how can they believe in the one of whom they have not heard? And how can they hear without someone preaching to them? And how can they preach unless they are sent? As it is written, "How beautiful are the feet of those who bring good news!" (Rom. 10:9-15).

John said "God has given us eternal life, and this life is in his Son. He who has the Son has life; he who does not have the Son of God does not have life" (I John 5:11, 12). And again, "Whoever puts his faith in the Son has eternal life, but whoever rejects the Son will not see that life, for God's wrath remains on him" (John 3:36).

Jesus said, "I am the way, the truth and the life. No one comes to the Father except through me" (John 14:6). "If anyone does not remain in me, he is like a branch that is thrown away and withers; such branches are picked up, thrown into the fire and burned" (John 15:6). "No one knows the Father except the Son and those to whom the Son chooses to reveal him" (Matt. 11:27).

These are only some representative verses from some of the most highly accredited teachers in the New Testament. They could be supplemented by scores of other passages to the same effect as well as by the sense of intense urgency which prompted Jesus Christ to accomplish his work on earth and the apostles to proclaim the salvation which only he could secure for fallen man. In fact, the centrality of Christ for salvation is not found in the New Testament alone, but it is envisioned in prophetic perspective in the Old Testament, "I will put enmity between thee and the woman, and between thy seed and her seed; he shall bruise thy head, and thou shalt bruise his heel" (Gen. 3:15).

"The stone which the builders rejected is become the head of the corner" (Psa. 118:22). "The root of Jesse will spring up, one who will arise to rule over the nations; the Gentiles will hope in him" (Isa. 11:10, quoted in Rom. 15:12).

This approach may appear narrow-minded to some, restricting the opportunity of salvation to a minority of the human race who may have contact with the Gospel. But it lies in the face of the texts quoted that this attitude was that of some of the greatest of inspired writers, of the very ones who in the most moving manner have spoken of God's immeasurable love (cf. for Isa. 42:1-3, 49:15-16, 61:1-3; for Paul, I Cor. 13; for John, I John 3 and 4; for Jesus Christ, John 3:16, 10:11, 13:1, 15:13; Rom. 5:8; etc.). One who seeks to be more generous than God, and on that account does take a stance different from that of these great exponents of revealed truth, places himself in a precarious position. The net effect of this approach is injurious in two respects:

1. In assuming that there are other remedies to sin than Jesus Christ, such visionaries tend to encourage people who are lost to seek for salvation in places where it certainly may not — and quite probably cannot — be found. What kind of charity and concern is this, when a doctor who knows a sure remedy for cancer directs his patient to be satisfied with aspirin? Such a man could be charged with malpractice in the medical profession, but there are those who think that this method should be standard in the Christian ministry!

2. In claiming that there are other sources of salvation beside Jesus Christ, these friends assert by implication that the work of Christ is really not necessary at all. If some can be saved without Christ, why did the Son of God view it as essential that he should come to this earth, and suffer at the hands of sinners, and die on Calvary, and rise from the dead on the third day? The mediatorial career of Jesus Christ is so very spectacular and so very central in God's purpose, that it does not make sense to imagine that men can attain to fellowship with God apart from it. God does not use an atomic bomb in order to kill a mosquito: is it not absurd to think that he would undertake the extreme form of intervention involved in the incarnation and the Cross if there were multitudes that could attain to salvation without Christ? Those who are so glib to speak of a larger hope have not always given sufficient reflection to the havoc which this view wreaks with our understanding of God's purpose in general and of Christ's work in particular.

1. In view of this biblical emphasis upon the centrality of Christ for salvation, it is not surprising that we should note a corresponding emphasis upon the question of who Christ was. The crucial significance of the doctrine of the person of Christ is to be seen in its close inter-relationship with the work of Christ. A Christ who is less than the Scripture asserts could not perform what the Bible teaches he has accomplished. And *vice versa*, a Christ who is seen as the potential "Savior of the World" (John 4:42; I John 4:14; I Tim. 4:10) must be such a superlative person as to be capable of this gigantic task.

The Church in history was therefore not on a wrong track when it kept on discussing christological issues in the period of the great councils (325-451 and also later). While its judgment of heretics appeared sometimes harsh, what was at stake was truly paramount, and we must admire the resoluteness with which the fathers insisted on securing a consensus of faith with respect to the doctrine of Christ. The indifference and laxity frequently characteristic of present-day attitudes in this respect can scarcely be viewed as a virtue, even by those who desire to cultivate charity and compassion at all times and towards all people.

    a. In order that Christ might effect his saving work on a universal scale it is necessary that he should be God. The deity of Christ is not just a fine tenet of the faith developed at a relatively late date in the history of the Church: it is an indispensable prerequisite for a proper understanding of the atonement. In his atoning work Christ took the place of a great multitude of sinful men and women; he bore in their stead the full sanctions of God's holy law against all their sins; in the short time span of his life in the flesh, and particularly in the crucial hours between Gethsemane and his death on the Cross, he endured to the fullest the burden of the eternal wrath of the triune God against all these sins, thus vindicating the full exercise of divine justice while securing the total release of the guilty sinners. What creature is there in the whole universe who is sufficient for such a task? A man, even if he were perfect from his birth to his death, would not be an adequate ransom for more than one life. An angel, even of the highest order, would hardly suffice for the ransom of one soul. We need here a substitute whose offering is literally infinite in value so that the giving of his one life might indeed provide a ransom for the *many*, for the innumerable multitude of those of the human race who will be saved. We need one whose person is so great that the relatively brief time of his torment might be readily seen as equivalent to the eternal punishment and death which sin rightly deserves. No one but God himself satisfies these conditions: the immensity of the work of salvation demands the deity of the Savior. Inversely, whoever claims that Christ is not God undermines by his denial the adequacy of the salvation which he has wrought. It is not surprising therefore that we should find that the New Testament in fact, clearly, repeatedly, and vigorously asserts the deity of Christ (John 1:1, 18, 10:30, 33-36, 20:28; Rom. 9:5; Phil. 2:6; Tit. 2:13; Heb. 1:8, 9; etc.) Even though this truth forced a drastic reinterpretation of the traditional Jewish view of God, the reality of salvation imposed a trinitarian outlook upon the Christian Church. This outlook does indeed not deny the unity and uniqueness of God so strongly taught and apprehended in Old Testament times, but it manifests the distinctness of the persons and recognizes that Jesus Christ and the Holy Spirit are God in the same full sense as the Father. In pressing toward a systematic formulation of this great truth the Council of Nicea did not distort the biblical revelation, but simply manifested its correct apprehension of the scriptural data in their appropriate relationships. Those who fought and died for the *"homo-ousios"* were better than "martyrs" for a "vowel's sake" — they had gained hold of something which is of the very essence of Christianity. No evangelism which fails to acknowledge the deity of Christ can be considered in any sense adequate.

b. In order that proper worship and praise be directed to God on account of our redemption it is also essential that Christ be acknowledged as God. One great marvel of the biblical doctrine of salvation is that it is presented as God's own work (Exod. 6:6, 20:2; Deut. 7:8; II Sam. 7:23; Psa. 49:15, 107:2, 130:8; Isa. 43:1, 14 and repeatedly in Isaiah; Jer. 31:11; Hos. 13:14; Matt. 1:21; Luke 1:68; Eph. 2:4; etc.) as is so forcefully asserted in Jonah 2:9, "Salvation is of the Lord."

Now God does not delegate this work to another. Very specifically he does not permit a third party to intervene and to bear in the place of the sinner the judicial penalty of sin. Where there is a burden to bear, God himself bears it; where there is a price to pay, God himself pays it; where there is an obligation to be met, God himself provides satisfaction. Jehovah will not give his glory to another (Isa. 42:8, 48:11). The saving work of Jesus Christ is emphatically the work of God, which no one but God can perform. Were it otherwise, two very damaging consequences would follow:

(i) If Christ were not God, it would appear that God would have permitted that another should bear man's penalty. God himself would not have done anything to help man in his plight. The one invariable thing in God's character would be his disposition to vent his wrath against sin and in this process he would permit that an innocent third party should die in torment and desperation rather than relent and attenuate the punishment of the wicked. This approach would set before us a picture of God arrayed in judicial rigor and unrelieved by any mercy, a kind of celestial Shylock who will have his revenge no matter who has to bear the cost! But this is deeply unbiblical and disgraceful, for the Scripture represents that in Jesus Christ it is God himself who takes the burden and who satisfies by his own suffering and death the full requirements of divine justice and holiness. No Shylock ever gave his own flesh to meet the obligation of his debtor, but God the Son shed his own blood to redeem the Church (Acts 20:28).

(ii) Since Jesus Christ is the one who in love offered his own life for the redemption of sinners, surely the highest gratitude and allegiance of the redeemed should be directed to him. "We love" him, they would say, "because he first loved us" (cf. I John 4:19). Such a statement would not be made concerning God, whose love, if existent at all, would not have been manifest in action. We would thus be left with an inveterate disposition to relate to Christ in supreme gratitude and love, while our attitude toward God would only be one of fear tempered by the assurance that a third party had borne our punishment. For all practical purposes Christ, although not God, would become our God, and the true God would pale into a star of the second magnitude in the sky of our devotion and worship. This could never be tolerated.

But now Christ is God indeed. There is no disjunction between the Father and the Son. They concur and collaborate in the work of redemption. The love and worship with which we approach Jesus

Christ (John 20:28; Acts 7:59; etc.) is not an act of idolatry, but the worship of the true God, addressed alike to the Father, and to the Son and to the Holy Spirit. This understanding is fundamental to the proper presentation of the evangelistic message. Hesitancy or denial here threatens the very foundations of salvation.

2. Jesus Christ is true God, and he is also true man. The true and full humanity of our Lord is an essential element of the salvific message. It is scarcely less important than his deity.

Surely if Christ is to take our place, and be our representative as Adam once was, it is imperative that he should himself be a human being. The redemption that we need cannot be achieved extrinsically, but must be worked organically, from within the race and as an appropriate satisfaction to God's righteous demands. The reality of the connection of the saving work of Christ with us depends on the reality of his humanity.

"The Word became flesh, and lived for a while among us" (John 1:14).

". . . he made himself nothing, taking the very nature of a servant, being made in human likeness . . ." (Phil. 2:7).

"Since the children have flesh and blood, he too shared in their humanity . . . for surely it is not angels he helps, but Abraham's descendants. For this reason he had to be made like his brothers in every way . . . that he might make atonement for the sins of the people" (Heb. 2:14, 16, 17).

"There is one mediator between God and men, the man Christ Jesus, who gave himself as a ransom for all men . . ." (I Tim. 2:5, 6).

"Just as through the disobedience of the one man the many were made sinners, so also through the obedience of the one man the many will be made righteous" (Rom. 5:19, cf. 5:14-17).

The need to retain a firm hold of Christ's real humanity must put us on our guard against any form of docetism which would tend to obscure or erase the human in Christ. This is a subtle danger about which certain enthusiastic advocates of the deity of Christ have not always been sufficiently watchful. Specifically we must pay close attention to the historical details of the life of Christ on earth, as recorded for us in the Gospel. No ethereal Christ, however divine, could compensate us for the loss of the real, historical Jesus whom the New Testament presents to us. To lose Christ's humanity is to lose the relevancy of Christ's saving work to our race.

It may surprise the observer that frequently people of various races and nations, when making pictorial representations of the life of Christ, have portrayed him and his disciples as members of their own community. Few have attempted to depict a Jewish Galilean artisan, except sometimes in his clothing. Since the historical record is so clear, this may puzzle us at first, but we may well ascribe this phenomenon to an instinctive desire to manifest the close relationship of Christ to any part of our race. It is a good thing that Chinese, Flemish, Hottentots, Arabs, Maoris, Indians, Eskimos, Spaniards as well as Jews could recognize unmistakably that Jesus Christ is one of them, for what he assumed is generic humanity found alike in every member of the race, male or female, child or adult, great or small, Jew or Gentile.

Evangelism needs to feature the humanity no less than the deity of Christ. We need to stress that when the Son was sent by the Father he went all the way to our earth, to make common cause with the outcasts, the downtrodden, the broken-hearted. He was not born in a marble palace in imperial Rome, or in an academic grove in intellectual Athens, but in an ill-favored stable in lowly Bethlehem. He lived a life of humility and poverty; he died the death of a slave or a criminal, although unjustly condemned. There is literally no one, however low on our scale of human values, who can say that Christ cannot or will not sympathize with him (Heb. 2:17, 4:15).

The pattern of the incarnation must be the norm of our evangelistic ministry. "As the Father has sent me, I am sending you" (John 20:21). We must ever learn again to go all the way, sin excepted, to make common cause with those to whom God sends us in order to lead them from where they are to the loving arms of the Savior.

3. Inasmuch as Jesus Christ is both God and man there must be two ways of approaching his person. One is to start with his deity and to descend to his humanity, and the other is to start from his humanity and to ascend to his deity. At first we might expect that the former approach is that of faith, while the latter is that of empirical evidence and of historical ratiocination. But really the issue is not so simple. The starting point is not all that matters, for indeed the orientation and landing point are also of paramount importance. Furthermore, one may start where one wills at any point of the historic incarnation of the Son of God and proceed from there, under the guidance of the Scripture, to the fullness of what Christ is.

The Scripture itself gives us examples of both types of approach. The Gospel of John is largely taking its starting point in heaven from which the Son "came down" (John 3:13), and then it proceeds to present some stages of his career on earth, uncovering for us the meaning of his life. Throughout the development there is the overarching sense of the divine origin and mission of our Lord, not only in his own consciousness, but also in the mind of the reader. This lends special significance to the theme of the struggle between belief and unbelief, characteristic of the whole development of John's Gospel, and culminating in the triumphant confession of Thomas, "My Lord and my God" (John 20:28).

The Synoptic Gospels, on the other hand, appear to take their start in the earthly beginnings of the career of Jesus: Matthew and Luke dealing with his birth and tracing his ancestry by genealogy; Mark beginning with Christ's public ministry. All three Gospels from the outset emphasize strongly the supernatural element in Christ's life and lead us to an understanding of his Messianic mission and claims. In the final analysis, therefore, we may say that the four Gospels differ among themselves in their starting point and in their aim, but all of them have a firm footing in the historical reality of the life of Christ on earth and a recognition of the superhuman dimensions of his whole person.

This balance, so well maintained in Scripture, between the deity and the humanity of Christ, was not always kept by theologians and exegetes. For many centuries the dominant tendency was to place such one-sided emphasis on his deity that his humanity almost vanished from sight. This is the problem which besets the Monophysites and the many schools of christological thought, where a kind of fusion of natures is thought to take place in the incarnation. To start with the divine and to place emphatic stress on it is no guarantee against heresy, and evangelicals need to remember this, for they may face their besetting temptations in this direction.

On the other hand, much study was bestowed upon the so-called "historical Jesus," in which, by virtue of naturalistic presuppositions, the supernatural was expunged or systematically downgraded, so that the picture which emerged was that of a gentle (or not so gentle) human genius who met a tragic end. But this approach fails utterly to explain the prodigious impact of Jesus upon his followers, from the first hour and to the present time. No one can really make good historical sense with Christ unless he is prepared to recognize that here we are truly faced with a visitation from heaven, unique in the annals of mankind, and the ground of the hope of the world.

Christology is fundamentally the study of a bridge: God's bridge, which crosses the whole chasm opened by sin between God and man. It is of the essence of a good bridge that it should have a firm foundation on both sides and carry the traveler all the way across the gap.

Christ, being true God and true man, has his moorings in the very nature of God and of humanity and he is "the one mediator between God and men" (I Tim. 2:5), who alone can safely lead us from the estrangement and misery of our sin into restored fellowship with the triune God. *Salve Christe, spes unica* (We salute you, O Christ, the only hope).

JESUS CHRIST, THE UNIQUE SON OF GOD: THE RELATIONSHIP OF HIS DEITY AND HUMANITY REPORT
Secretary: Ray C. Stedman

In many and various ways the New Testament declares that Jesus Christ combines in his unique person the fullness of the nature of God and the fullness of the nature of man. While this truth is not a required element in every declaration of the Gospel, it is nevertheless the essential and fertile ground out of which the Gospel grows and from which it derives its beauty, strength, and glory. Apart from this truth there would be no Good News at all.

Jesus himself is the one who conveyed this truth to his Apostles and out of their profound conviction of its reality they have taught the church. His humanity was clearly evident to the Apostles in the way he lived, walked, and behaved before them. His essential deity gradually dawned upon them as they observed his doing works attributed in the Old Testament only to God himself; as they became convinced, by the Spirit, and through witnessing his many miracles, that he was the long-expected Messiah whose divine qualities were described by the prophets — eternal Father, mighty God; and by the direct claims of Jesus to identity in nature with the Father and the spoken confirmation of the Father at the baptism and transfiguration.

It is apparent, however, that the Apostles did not proclaim Jesus as the Son of God until after the Holy Spirit came upon them at Pentecost, and when they subsequently preached Jesus they began with statements presenting his humanity and ended with clear declarations of his Lordship, rooted in his essential deity.

We affirm, therefore, that though the preaching of the Gospel in today's world should properly begin wherever man is, taking note of his hurts, his sorrows, his hungers, and dreams it must conclude with declarations, explicit or implicit, that Jesus Christ is Lord, whether men acknowledge it or not, and that all judgment is committed into his hands and from that judgment there is no escape but by means of the Gospel of the forgiveness of sins through calling on the name of the Lord.

We take special note of those working among the 600 million of the Moslem world and urge them to make it clear that the title "Son of God" as applied to Jesus means an essential oneness with the Father and not physical procreation.

As a necessary follow-up of evangelism we urge churches everywhere to make clear that the humanity of Jesus is the pattern for Christian living, both as to what Christians do and also as to the power and resources by which they do these things. As the Father sent the Son into the world to live by means of the Father, so the Son sends us, to live by means of him.

THE THEOLOGY OF THE CROSS AND OF THE RESURRECTION IN OUR UNIQUE SALVATION

Rudy Budiman

Dr. Budiman, Yogyakarta, Indonesia, is a
Professor at the Theological Seminary,
"Sekolah Tinggi Theologia Duta Wacana" in Indonesia

1. *Evidence of the importance of the Cross and the resurrection in Paul's letters.*

The importance of Christ's death and resurrection for our salvation is best demonstrated by the way in which the apostle Paul esteems the two salvation acts with regard to the church's belief as well as to man's conduct. "I delivered to you as of first importance what I also received, that Christ died for our sins in accordance with the Scriptures, that he was buried, that he was raised on the third day in accordance with the Scriptures" (I Cor. 15:3,4). "And he died for all, that those who live might live no longer for themselves but for him who for their sake died and was raised" (II Cor. 5:18).

Besides this combined appearance of the Cross and the resurrection, Paul often mentions the former separately, laying special stress on it, "I decided to know nothing among you except Jesus Christ and him crucified" (I Cor. 2:2), "The word of the Cross is folly to those who are perishing, but to us who are being saved it is the power of God" (I Cor. 1:18); "O foolish Galatians! Who has bewitched you, before whose eyes Jesus Christ was publicly portrayed as crucified?" (Gal. 3:1); "Many, of whom I have often told you and now tell you even with tears, live as enemies of the Cross of Christ" (Phil. 3:18).

On the other hand Paul also attaches great importance to the resurrection, "If you confess with your lips that Jesus is Lord and believe in your heart that God raised him from the dead, you will be saved" (Rom. 10:9); "If Christ has not been raised, your faith is futile and you are still in your sins" (I Cor. 15:17). Further examination (see 4/below) will show that between the Cross and the resurrection there exists a close relation, being one of cause and effect.

2. *The significance of the Cross for our salvation: the forgiveness of sins.*

The apostle Paul once depicts the result of Christ's death on the Cross as the cancellation of an IOU, "And you, (who were dead in trespasses and the circumcision of your flesh), God made alive together with him, having forgiven us all our trespasses, having cancelled the bond which stood against us with its legal demands; this he set aside, nailing it to the Cross" (Col. 2:13,14).

The metaphor of the bond (IOU) Paul derives from the rabbinic thought that God registers all good and bad acts of men. The settlement of their deeds, then, results in an IOU on the part of man. The apostle can borrow the figure without falling into the rabbinic doctrine of merits, because the covenant relation between God and man obliges man to keep the rules of the covenant.

Thus the apostle is also able to say in terms of the New Covenant that the believer "owes" (Greek: *opheilein*) to love his neighbor (Rom. 13:8), to bear with the failing of the weak (Rom. 15:1), to love one's own wife as his body (Eph. 5:28), etc. Every shortcoming in the fulfilling of this obligation means an unpaid *"debt"* (cf. Matt. 6:12 "Forgive us our debts"), or, to stick to our metaphor, a bond, an IOU. Christ's death for the sins of man, then, means the cancellation of that bond. "This he set aside, nailing it to the Cross" (Col. 2:13,14).

Another time Paul describes Christ's salvation act as "redeeming us from the curse of the law" (Gal. 3:13). Back of this conception is the Old Testament thought that "cursed is every one who does not abide by all things written in the book of the law, and do them" (cf. Gal. 3:10 and Deut. 27:26). Christ has come to carry that curse away by bearing the divine wrath in the place of mankind.

In both instances Christ died a vicarious death for man. This is apparent from utterances like Gal. 3:13, "Christ redeemed us from the curse of law, having become a curse for us," and II Cor. 5:21, "For our sake he made him to be sin who knew no sin, so that in him we might become the righteousness of God."

The idea of the vicarious death furthermore occurs with Paul in his conception of the expiation of sins by means of Christ's sacrifice. Compare Rom. 3:25 "(Christ Jesus), whom God put forward as an expiation by his blood," with Lev. 17:11 "The life of the flesh is in the blood; and I have given it for you upon the altar to make atonement for your sake; for it is the blood that makes atonement by reason of the life." This expiation and atonement produces forgiveness of sins, justification for sinners (Rom. 3:23,24).

In short, regarding sin as a *guilt*, a *debt*, the apostle can say that Christ's death brings about the *forgiveness of sins*.

3. *The significance of the Cross for our salvation: the deliverance from the power of sin*

According to Paul, Christ not only delivers us from the guilt of sin, but also from the power of sin. Sin is like a power that dominates man's life and takes him in prison, so that he does not do the good he wants, but the evil he does not want is what he does (Rom. 7:19). Paul bears witness to this situation in the following words, "Wretched man that I am! Who will deliver me from this body of death? Thanks be to God through Jesus Christ our Lord!" (Rom. 7:24,25).

So it is Christ who delivers man from the power of sin. How? He had the power of sin destroyed the flesh, he bore as a representative of man. "For God had done what the law, weakened by the flesh, could not do: sending his own Son in the likeness of sinful flesh and for sin, he condemned sin in the flesh, in order that the just requirement of the law might be fulfilled in us . . . " (Rom. 8:3,4). It means that Jesus came in the likeness of sinful flesh, but he fulfilled the will of his Father during his whole life. Such a life in obedience to God runs counter to the strivings of sinful flesh and can only mean a continuous annihilation of the latter. A definite extermination of the sinful flesh took place on the Cross, where Christ underwent the wrath of God. Through this life of obedience God exterminated the power of sin in the flesh which Jesus bore for mankind (the Greek word for "condemned," viz. *"katekrinen,"* does not so much mean the condemnation as the execution of this condemnation that is to say the punishment (cf. Mark 16:16; I Cor. 11:32; II Pet. 2:6). By this act the power of sin has been put to an end.

To this fact Rom. 6:6 also reminds, "We know that our old self was crucified with him so that the sinful body might be destroyed, and we might no longer be enslaved to sin." It is clear from these words that in Christ the sinful body of man had been destroyed so that it no longer could enslave man (cf. Rom. 7:24,25). Man has been delivered from the power of sin.

4. The genetic relation between the Cross and the resurrection

Christ was not raised from the dead because he finished his task on earth and was allowed to "return home." For that purpose he might return "in the spirit" and need not be raised from the dead. For is God not spirit? (cf. John 4:24). There must, therefore, be another ground.

Rom. 4:25 mentions, "(Jesus our Lord), who was put to death for our trespasses and raised for our justification." Both times the preposition "for" (in Greek *"dia"* with the accusative) should, in fact, be rendered "because of." So Christ was put to death because of our trespasses and was raised because of our justification. The latter means that Christ was raised because he accomplished the righteousness for us.

The idea "trespasses lead to death and righteousness to resurrection" finds its parallel in Rom. 5:18, "Then as one man's trespass led to condemnation for all men, so one man's act of righteousness leads to . . . life for all men." The idea has its background in the Old Testament. God gave his commandments in order that, by fulfilling them, man should have life (cf. Lev. 26). Quoting Lev. 18:5, Paul also says, "He who does them (i.e. the commandments) shall live by them" (Gal. 3:12). The life, in Old Testament times described in this-worldly terms (see Lev. 26), receives in the New Testament eschatological fullness. It includes resurrection and eternal life.

So Christ's resurrection was brought about by his fulfillment of the law. The Cross as the summit of this fulfillment was the reason of his resurrection. In other words: the Cross stands in a genetic relation to the resurrection.

This thought makes us understand an earlier mentioned text, I Cor. 15:17, "If Christ has not been raised, your faith is futile and you are still in your sins" (see 1 above). It should be interpreted as follows: Christ's resurrection is the logical consequence, the proof of your justification; if Christ has not been raised, then it is evident that he failed in accomplishing righteousness for you, and in that case, you are still in your sins.

5. The "inclusive representative" character of Christ's death and resurrection

Christ died and was raised as the representative of mankind. Mankind is understood as a corporate unity. The fate of those who are represented is decided in their representative. Paul does not see representation as an "as-if," but as a reality. This is clear from II Cor. 5:14

". . . one has died for all; therefore all have died." The expression "all have died" must not be interpreted as "all are *regarded* as dead," but as a *reality in Christ.* Those who are represented are *really included* in his death and resurrection. They all *have* died and *have* been raised to such a realistic extent, that Paul draws far-reaching consequences from it.

First of all, He died for all, that those who live might live no longer for themselves but for him "who for their sake died and was raised" (II Cor. 5:15). The words "therefore all have died" and "those who live" are meant as a parallel to "who for their sake (better: in their place) died and was raised." All men have died and have been raised, because they were really included in the representative Jesus Christ. It is therefore impossible that they still live for themselves. The only logical possibility is "that they live for him" according to the new pattern of life (note: "*Might* live" is too weak a rendering of the Greek word).

The same idea is found in Rom. 8:3,4, "....sending his own Son in the likeness of sinful flesh and for sin, he condemned sin in the flesh (which represents our flesh), in order that the just requirement of the law (might) be fulfilled in us." Here again, Paul draws consequences from the inclusive representative death in Christ for our life: the requirement of the law be fulfilled in us. Furthermore, Paul shows the way, in which the new pattern of life is realized in our existence, ". . . in us, who walk not according to the flesh but according to the Spirit." It is the Spirit, who effects the death and resurrection reality-in-the-representative into our existence.

Another instance is Rom. 6:4, "We were buried therefore with him by baptism into death, so that as Christ was raised from the dead by the glory of the Father, we too (might) walk in newness of life." Here our being included in Christ's death and resurrection is symbolized by and effectualized through baptism.

A second, far-reaching consequence of the inclusive representative character of Christ's death and resurrection is drawn by Paul with regard to the Christian's missionary attitude (II Cor. 5:16), "From now on, therefore, we regard no one from a human point of view." The believer does not judge his fellowman any longer with worldly standards as if he is "an ordinary man," but he respects him as a person, who also died and was raised in Christ. That man has the right to know this truth. To keep it from him is a sin. This explains Paul's missionary zeal, "Woe to me if I do not preach the Gospel!" (I Cor. 9:16). The Christian should also behave in his life according to this missionary attitude, "Do not let what you eat cause the ruin of one for whom Christ died" (Rom. 14:15). Moving in its simplicity is Paul's utterance, "The love of Christ controls us, because we are convinced that one has died for all "therefore all have died" (II Cor. 5:14). Here again, Paul's missionary passion is caused by the above idea of all men being included in Christ's death.

6. *The renewal of man through the effectualization of the Cross and the resurrection in his life*

The blessings of Christ's death and resurrection are not confined to the forgiveness of sins. They also comprise the renewal of man's life.

This renewal is brought about by the effectualization of the death and the resurrection in his life. What has been done by Christ — once for all — through his inclusive representation is now *effectualized* in our life *by the Holy Spirit through faith.* The following texts testify to this.

First of all, the Spirit works — through faith — Christ's dwelling is us, (cf. Eph. 3:16,17) "that according to the riches of his glory he may grant you to be strengthened with might through his Spirit in the inner man, that Christ may dwell in your hearts through faith . . ." (see for the idea of "faith - Christ dwelling in us" also Gal. 2:20, II Cor. 13:5, and 8 below).

After Christ dwells in our hearts, something new happens to our life. The old flesh cannot bear his presence. Either Christ has to leave our heart, because our sinful existence cannot stand his holy presence (as happened to the Galatians, to whom Paul writes, "My little children, with whom I am again in travail until Christ be formed in you!", Gal. 4:19), or our flesh will be put to death. The same process we perceive in Rom. 8. After Christ dwells in us (cf. vs. 10, "If Christ is in you"), we put our flesh to death in order that we may live (cf. vs. 13), "For if you live according to the flesh you will die, but if by the Spirit you put to death the deeds of the body you will live." This process is described as effectualizing the Cross and the resurrection in our existence (cf. vs. 17, "provided we suffer with him in order that we may also be glorified with him").

Another instance is Phil. 3. After Paul says "that I may gain Christ and be found in him" (vss. 8,9), he continues, "that I may know him and the power of his resurrection, and may share his sufferings, becoming like him in his death, that if possible I may attain the resurrection from the dead" (vss. 10,11). Only through sharing his sufferings shall we experience the new life in Christ.

A third example is II Cor. 4. First comes the in-dwelling of Christ; cf. vss. 6,7; "For it is the God who said 'Let light shine out of darkness,' who has shone in our hearts to give light of the knowledge of the glory of God in the face of Christ. But we have this treasure in earthen vessels, to show that the transcendent power belongs to God and not to us." Then follow the sufferings in the fellowship of Christ (vs. 8), "We are afflicted in every way, but not crushed; perplexed, but not forsaken; struck down, but not destroyed," which sufferings Paul describes as (vs. 10) "always carrying in the body the death of Jesus, so that the life of Jesus may also be manifested in our bodies. For while we live we are always being given up to death for Jesus' sake, so that the life of Jesus may be manifested in our mortal flesh." Here also the death and resurrection of Christ is effectualized in our existence.

God uses sufferings to bring about the dying of our flesh and the beginning of the new life. These sufferings may be caused by our active combating of sins (cf. Rom. 8:13 "put to death the deeds of the body"), by an illness inflicted upon us for the sake of our sanctification (compare II Cor. 12:9 "but he said to me: My grace is sufficient for you, for my *power* is made perfect in weakness" with II Cor. 13:4 "For he was crucified in weakness, but lives by the power of God. For we are weak in him, but in dealing with you we shall live with him by the power of

God") or by afflictions in the service of the kingdom of God (cf. II Cor. 4:8-10 "we are afflicted in every way . . . perplexed . . . struck down . . . always carrying in the body the death of Jesus"). Anyhow, the above sufferings are considered by Paul as sharing Christ's sufferings to attain the resurrection in our life.

The effectualizing is, according to Paul, also symbolized by baptism, of Rom. 6:4, "We were buried therefore with him by baptism into death, so that as Christ was raised from the dead by the glory of the Father, we too might walk in newness of life," and Col. 2:12: "and you were buried with him in baptism, in which you were also raised with him through faith in the working of God, who raised him from the dead."

7. *The importance of sharing Christ's death and resurrection for evangelism*

This sharing in Christ's death and resurrection not only has its impact on the renewal of man's life, but also on evangelism. The following exposition will prove it.

We start with II Cor. 1:5, "As we share abundantly in Christ's sufferings, so through Christ we share abundantly in comfort too." The word "comfort" has no ordinary meaning here. Already in Old Testament times the word has an eschatological depth, comprising the messianic salvation, cf. Isa. 40:1, 49:13, 51:3, 61:2, 66:11,13. In Luke 2:25ff. we find Simon "looking for the consolation of Israel" in the coming of the Messiah. Paul gives christological contents to "comfort," when he in II Cor. 1:3 crosswise connects the sentence, "Blessed be the God and Father of our Lord Jesus Christ" with "the Father of mercies and God of all comfort." Here "the God of Jesus Christ" covers "the God of all comfort," so that the comfort is Jesus Christ himself.

It is striking to see that, according to the apostle, this comfort comes into being through sharing in Christ's sufferings (II Cor. 1:5). This corresponds with the earlier stated genetic relation between the Cross and the resurrection (see 4). If we ask whereto the comfort is brought about in the life of the believer, the apostle's answer is: not to keep it for himself. "If we are afflicted, it is for *your* comfort and salvation; and if we are comforted, it is for *your* comfort, which you experience when you patiently endure the same suffering that we suffer" (II Cor. 1:6). This comfort keeps the Corinthians not away from sufferings, but enables them to endure sufferings. Their afflictions bring about new comfort and in their turn they will pass it on to others. So the messianic comfort or salvation is passed on from one to another.

The same situation we encounter in II Cor. 4:11,12, "For while we live we are always being given up to death for Jesus' sake, so that the life of Jesus may be manifested in *our* mortal flesh. So death is at work in us, but life in you." In a terse style Paul mentions here that the life of Jesus, experienced by the apostle (after having suffered) is passed on to the Corinthians. In their turn they will continue the process towards others. Paul pictures the course of events as follows: "For it is all for your sake, so that as grace extends *to more and more people* it may increase thanksgiving, to the glory of God" (II Cor. 4:15). It is a continuous action, going through to the end of the world. More and more people will praise the Lord for his salvation, the salvation through his death and his resurrection, accomplished centuries ago and ever since effectualized in the lives of millions of people, who love him and surrender their lives to him.

Not only does "sharing Christ's suffering" play an important role in the renewal of the convert's life. This also does the power of Christ's resurrection. This should be stated clearly, for otherwise the impression is made, as if the only renewing force in the Christian's life is his fellowship with Christ's sufferings.

Paul mentions it clearly in Col. 2:12,13, "You were buried with him in baptism, in which you were also raised with him through faith in the working of God, who raised him from the dead. And you, who were dead in trespasses and the uncircumcision of your flesh, God made alive together with him. . ." This is good news for all men who are in despair because of their wretched lives: there is the power of Christ's resurrection which renews their lives!

As a matter of fact fellowship with Christ's sufferings and the power of his resurrection go hand in hand and work simultaneously in the believer's life. On the one hand the resurrection power gives new life to man; on the other hand that very life brings the believer into sharing Christ's sufferings. For this reason Paul can place each of the two prior to the other in Phil. 3:10,11, "That I may know him and the power of his *resurrection,* and may share his *sufferings,* becoming like him in his *death,* that if possibile, I may attain the *resurrection* from the dead."

In evangelism the church should always keep two aspects of the reconciliation in mind: the *objective aspect* (God's salvation act in the past) cf. Rom. 5:8, "God shows his love for us in that while we were yet sinners Christ died for us": and the *subjective aspect,* viz., the effectualization of reconciliation in human existence. The Bible sees both aspects as a unity, see, e.g., Phil. 3:9, 10 "that I may gain Christ, and be found *in him,* not having righteousness of my own, based on law, but that which is through faith in Christ, the *righteousness from God* that depends on faith (objective aspect), that I may know him and the power of his resurrection, etc. (subjective aspect)." Reducing the reconcilation to one of these aspects would impoverish the richness of our unique salvation in Christ.

8. *Appendix*

There are a few things in the above exposition which may cause misunderstanding and therefore must be clarified. One of them is the idea of Christ dwelling in us (see 6). This may be misinterpreted as a kind of mysticism, whereby the mystic presumes to be one with God to the extent that he is like God. It is certainly not the intention of Paul to teach this!

When he says, "It is no longer I who live, but Christ who lives in me" (Gal. 2:20), he does not mean that the believer ceased to exist and is replaced by Christ, for presently he adds, "And the life I now live in the flesh I live by faith in the Son of God, who loved me and gave himself for me." The believer still exists! He only surrenders to Christ and from now on lets the Lord rule all his doings.

Far from teaching mysticism, Paul tries to make Christians everywhere realize that faith is not simply a matter of intellectual knowledge of salvation facts, but in the first place an existential experiencing of salvation. Through faith Christ dwells in our hearts. When one realizes this, many things in his life will change. The holy presence of the Lord does not bear sinful habits and acts. When Christians manifest offensive behavior, Paul urges, "Examine yourselves, to see whether you are holding to your faith. Test yourselves. Do you not realize that Jesus Christ is in you? — unless indeed you fail to meet the test!" (II Cor. 13:5). Faith is to Paul *existential faith,* a surrender to Christ with one's whole existence.

Second to be cleared is the thought that we have to share in Christ's sufferings in order that we may share in his resurrection; that we have to die to the old man in order that we may partake of the new man. It gives the impression of stressing man's efforts at the expense of the saving grace of God. Does it not contradict Paul's own device of "sola gratia"?

Paul is no doubt the great champion of "sola gratia" and "sola fide." This is evident from utterances like Rom. 3:20,24, "No human being will be justified in his sight by works of the law . . . they are justified by his grace as a gift," and Gal. 2:16, "A man is not justified by works of the law but through faith in Jesus Christ." On the other hand Paul stresses man's active part in this salvation process: "If by the Spirit you put to death the deeds of the body you will live" (Rom. 8:13); "I say, walk by the Spirit and do not gratify the desires of the flesh" (Gal. 5:16).

This contradiction is not understood until we see Paul's view of the inclusive representative character of Christ's death and resurrection. An illustration of it is Rom. 6:10,11, "The death he died he died to sin, once for all, but the life he lives he lives to God. So you also must consider yourselves dead to sin and alive to God in Christ Jesus." It is an impossibility that man who is really included in Christ's death and resurrection still lives his own way of life. So Paul continues, "Let not sin therefore reign in your mortal bodies, to make you obey their passions" (Rom. 6:12), and, "By the Spirit put to death the deeds of the body" (Rom. 8:13), while resuming, "We suffer with him in order that we may also be glorified with him." According to the apostle, our sharing in Christ's sufferings and resurrection is nothing other than the effectualizing of both through the Spirit into our existence, thereby utilizing our own activity.

The same process (viz., inclusive representation — effectualizing through the Spirit) we perceive in Gal. 2:20, "I have been crucified with Christ; it is no longer I who live, but Christ who lives in me;" Gal. 5:16,17, "Walk by the Spirit and do not gratify the desires of the flesh, for the desires of the flesh are against the Spirit;" Gal. 5:24, "Those who belong to Christ Jesus have crucified the flesh with its passions and desires."

This conception does not rob the glory of God's saving grace; on the contrary, it brings that grace to its summit. Every theology that confines the significance of the Cross and the resurrection to the forgiveness of sins without including the renewal of life, does not do full justice to the saving grace of God.

This view also has its implications for mission and evangelism. Paul does not know a style of evangelism that limits the proclamation to the verbal form. To him the proclamation is an *existential proclamation* (an existential kerygma), i.e., a proclamation through the whole (renewed and changed) existence of the believer. We have seen it (cf. 7) in II Cor. 4:11,12, "For while we live we are always being given up to death for Jesus' sake, so that the life of Jesus may be manifested in our mortal flesh. So death is at work in us, but life in you" (also II Cor. 1:6).

We may conclude with II Cor. 3:2,3, "You yourselves are our letter of recommendation, written on your hearts, to be known and read by all men; and you show that you are a letter from Christ delivered by us, written not with ink but with the Spirit of the living God, not on tables of stone but on tables of human hearts." The message of Christ's death and resurrection is first written by the Spirit in Paul's heart, and through Paul in the hearts of the Corinthians. So is it now also in our hearts and through us in those of others. May our lives, therefore, be a real letter from the Lord, who died and was raised for us.

THE THEOLOGY OF THE CROSS AND OF THE RESURRECTION IN OUR UNIQUE SALVATION REPORT

Chairman: Brian H. Butler
Secretary: Barry Moore

The group wishes to thank Dr. Budiman for his paper, which provided a valued introduction to our discussions. We ought to add, however, that we are very conscious that this theme is far larger than we could handle in the time allotted, and with the resources available. With that in mind, we present a summary of our discussion.

1. We note the centrality of the Cross and resurrection of Jesus Christ in the total New Testament witness. It formed the central segment in the apostolic preaching (I Cor. 1:23, Acts 2:23,24).

Christ's death is a propitiatory sacrifice, and produces reconciliation for man in the areas of his need. It deals first with man's alienation and enmity with God, then with the estrangement of man and man; i.e., it is an absolute presupposition for complete personal, social, and international reconciliation; it makes a reconciliation between man and the natural world, and lastly, integrates man himself in his personality. (We are not certain of the implications of the third of these, but ecology, pollution, and the right use of the world's resources directly impinge on world relations, and on evangelization. More study is needed.)

Christ's work is a finished work. We affirm that the greatest strength and blessing that the church can know and experience is the assurance of the personal, continual, and effective intercession of Christ her Lord at the right hand of God. This has relevance to the suffering church: Christ is with his body, the church, and may be said to suffer with his body — not as he suffered on the Cross (for that is *hapax*) but with believers in their afflictions. Christians should share with Christ in this identification with their suffering brethren.

Man was judged representatively in Christ the God-man. He is saved representatively also. This is the Good News which demands a telling to men for whom Christ died.

2. Christ died unto sin once for all. He is the only Mediator (I Tim. 2:5). This we affirm over against all other saviors. The resurrection is God's confirmation of this truth, and therefore must be proclaimed with it.

This truth underscores the urgency of the need to proclaim forgiveness to all, through the death of Christ. The Cross has universal significance but the New Testament is not universalist. It calls for each person to repent and to be saved through faith. Nor is there to be only a recognition of salvation, but appropriation of it. We are not to tell men that they are saved (as some ecumenical theology states), but we are to call them to be reconciled and renounce their rebellion and enmity with God.

3. We came to a new appreciation of the subjective element in re-

demption. Christ has reconciled us to God through his death, but the historic event needs effectualization in our lives and in our world. This occurs in our sanctification, in our identity with the suffering church, through our victory over the world and death.

4. We believe that the emphasis in the New Testament on Christ's victory over the demonic powers which rule the world needs fresh and urgent emphasis. It is especially needed in situations where demon powers, the fear of death, and ignorance are holding men in bondage. Christ is Victor!

5. It is because of the Cross and resurrection that we have hope for the world. Although Christ stands in judgment upon every human system, and particularly man's utopian dreams, his death and resurrection are the means by which the Kingdom of God will be realized.

For world evangelization, this means that, just as Mary weeping at the tomb was given the command "Go and tell," so the church redeemed has still to take the message to a weary, death-ridden humanity.

The resurrection is guarantee that Jesus is Lord. It is the presupposition of his real Lordship over the world which he created and now claims. It is a contradiction, therefore, to affirm his Lordship in our lives without at the same time affirming his Lordship over every personal, social, national, and international structure of society and church.

6. In the church's identification with Christ, evangelization and service for mankind need to be cast in the role of Servant of the Lord, The Cross may be (even unknowingly) an offense to Christians as well as to the world, and we have often sought to evade the call to be servants and to lay aside the cross which Christ would lay upon us. The spirit of this Congress suggests that we may yet awaken to a truer conception of our role. It was through the death of Christ that his life was released to the world — the life of Christ still needs to be released through our death (Col. 3:1ff.).

PERSONAL AND ETERNAL SALVATION AND HUMAN REDEMPTION
C. Emilio Antonio Nunez

*Dr. Nunez, Guatemala City, Guatemala,
is President of the Central American
Theological Seminary.*

The purpose of this paper is simply to expose some ideas which can guide us to reflect on the subject herewith proposed.

Lately the church has been faced with great political-social problems which have become especially aggravated in the so-called countries of the "Third World." As in other epochs of ecclesiastical history, theology has not been immune to the ideas which prevail in the social milieu and in one way or the other it finally reflects these ideas in sizing up the contemporaneous scene.

Finally, we are asked today, is the Gospel extramundane or intramundane? Is Christianity only "vertical," turned towards heaven, or is it "horizontal," at the service of the total man within the context of human society? Is our proclamation fundamentally futuristic or presentistic? Is it a message for here and now, or only a promise for the beyond? Is our attitude one of escape or absenteeism or that of social compromise? Is it true that it is intended to divide man in two or three constitutive parts of his being and only preach the "salvation of the soul" apart from taking any interest in his temporary needs? Is the Christian message redemption, in the widest sense of this term, or is it the opium of the people?

From these and other similar questions we will reflect on the nature of Christian mission and what the church represents in the world of today. Is the church only called to care for souls or should it more and more integrate in the society and fight to radically transform it in its economic and political structures?

In the light of the Scriptures, it is worth our while to study some of the replies to these questions.

Theology of Redemption

No one can ignore the distressed, desperate, and heart-rending drama in which the great majority of mankind is living. There is a great difference between preaching on Sunday morning to a congregation of well-fed and well-clothed Christians and announcing the Gospel to a multitude of persons who hardly succeed in subsisting and covering their nudity. Last year a prominent political leader of South America said that it profoundly touched him to see that among the peasants of his country many toothless mouths cry, "Viva Liberty." When reporting on the Fourth Conference of the Non-Aligned Countries, which took place in Algiers in September 1973, the Madrilenean magazine *Hechos y Dichos* comments:

"There were 76 countries represented as members, twelve more as observers, three (Austria, Sweden and Australia) as guests, and sixteen movements of liberation which still fought against colonialism. And behind these representatives are 2,600 million inhabitants of the earth, 70% of the world population. 16% of the total income of the whole planet comes from capitalist countries which represent only 21% of the population of the world but realizes 66% of the world product. All these countries which met In Algiers were united by the lacerating preoccupation with the abyss which widening, separates the developed countries from the marginal ones."

In the year 2,000, the 4,500 million inhabitants of the "Third World" will receive only $300 of income "per capita" while the 1,500 million of rich nations will enjoy $5,000 to $10,000. These convenors were united by the common humiliations, the gags and the exploitations.

The fact that such a meeting was held is symptomatic of the awakening of the poor nations to their condition of disadvantage as contrasted with the great and mighty of the financial world. Being conscious of these realities, some Catholic and Protestant thinkers have devoted themselves to formulating a theology of liberation.

The term *liberation,* possesses for these theologians a conflicting and political dilemma which suggests the failure of the economic development as a pretended reply to the problem of dependent nations. Hugo Assman, for instance, considers the theology of liberation a Latin American form of political theology which was born in the revolutionary leftism. After denying that the liberating theology had spontaneously arisen with the postconciliar leftist reformism, Assman says:

"The language of the revolutionary leftists (the marxist vocabulary of the "new marxism" latinamerican) discrepant from the reformism of the communist parties of the moscovite line, the language of the student movement, influenced more or less directly. A certain influence, presumably more indirect for Latin America, was exerted by H. Marcust (Un ensayo sobre la liberacion) and by international meetings on the 'dialéctica de la liberacion.' "

There is no time or space for us to make a short study of the currents of theological thinking which open the channel of the theology of liberation. Of course, the liberationist theologians believe they have overcome the theologies commonly called vanguards but which do not originate from the social reality of the under-developed countries. Such would be the case of the "new European theology" of Metz and Moltmann, the theology of "secularization" and the theology of Rahner and Küng, who are considered to be alienated from social praxis, excessively reactionaries on the political level. Assman believes that "the revolution of the Third World exceeds, in its structure of ideas, both the middle class revolution in 1769 and its similar subproducts, and the proletarian revolution of 1917 in Russia."

The theologians of the liberation profess that the origin of the liberating language is due to the fact that the poor nations have become conscious of their being maintained in underdevelopment, as nations dominated by others. To the criticism that in this language some criteria are established that are neither theological nor biblical, they reply that the message of the Scriptures is liberating and that Jesus Christ himself was a sign of protest against the unjust order of his time. They make frequent recourse to the Israelite exodus as being a paradigm of the liberating process although the hermeneutics they employ in the study of this theme leave much to be desired.

In reality, the origin of the theology of liberation is not the Bible but the economical-social-political analysis of the infrahuman situation in which millions of persons are living throughout the world.

According to the liberational theologians, the mission of the church is to compromise with the, political-social liberation. To this end it must denounce every dehumanizing situation, question the *status quo,* and render the masses conscious and political. Gutierrez believes that becoming converted means embracing the cause of the poor and that "in the present Latin American context it should be said that the church must politize when evangelizing."

The call tends more for revolutionary action than for theological reflection. Action comes first, theology afterwards. Gutierrez admits that there are chapters of theology which will be written later, on the way to liberation. In the end, there are no established doctrinal norms for the church. "The Bible," says Assman, "is not a direct text of criterions." However, the theology of liberation is "theology," they say, insofar as it discovers in the revolutionary practice the presence of the Christian faith.

According to P. Blanquart's view of the revolutionary, "Faith does not speak to him about revolution but it is precisely in the heart of his revolutionary action that the Word of God enters in a direct manner." The use of violence is licit in this liberating action.

Another of the main characteristics of theological liberationism is its great emphasis on the social dimension of sin. Much is said about the unjust structures, but very little about sinning individuals. Above all, it is the society which must change.

The injustices of the dominant classes are denounced, but not that of the oppressed classes. The latter must free themselves from their slavery, freeing at the same time their oppressors, by whose agency the devil is acting in the world. However, they do not underline personal or social culpability of which the oppressed must free themselves.

In reality, the theology of liberation is a form of revolutionary humanism and a utopia (in the traditional sense of this term), although now the utopia comes in the name of "scientific analysis" and "social practice."

For the liberationist theologians there exists the danger of looking for the maximum wellbeing in economic prosperity as if man himself were only food and clothing, and did not live for other things apart from material bread. Also, they run the risk of converting the Gospel into a revolutionary ideology, or making sacred a political system (whatever it may be) which, although speaking in the name of the oppressed, is nonetheless imperfect and transitory.

To sum up, the liberationist theology does not have its point of origin in the Bible, but in the economical-social situation of the underdeveloped nations. It lacks adequate hermeneutics for the study and application of the Scriptures. It is radically humanistic in its anthropology. It tends to reduce the mission of the church to political activism and it is in constant danger of sanctifying the social-economical-political system which has given it strength. And it gives way to a leftist triumphalism and constantinism, without permitting any criticism from outside, or other possibilities for the expression of social justice which are demanded by the Gospel.

Liberation in the New Testament

Having examined the theme in the light of the theology described in broad terms in the previous chapter, it is worth our while approaching the New Testament, trying to find at least some code for the study of salvation as the total liberation of man.

a. *Testimony of Christ.* When beginning his ministry in Galilee, Christ said, "The Spirit of the Lord is upon me, because he hath anointed me to preach the gospel to the poor; he hath sent me to heal the broken-hearted, to preach deliverance to the captives, and recovering of sight to the blind, to set at liberty them that are bruised, to preach the acceptable year of the Lord" (Luke 4:18, 19).

The words extracted from the prophecy of Isaiah are definitely messianic (Isa. 61:1,2). Fully conscious of the seriousness of his proclamation, Jesus of Nazareth says that in him all that has been announced by the prophet is fulfilled. He is the Liberator, the *Ruomenos* of Israel (Rom. 11:26) and of all nations. The name of Jesus signifies Savior (*soter*), and the Savior has the function of Liberator.

Proof is abounding that Jesus of Nazareth is what he says he is. For instance, note the reply he gives to the emissaries of John the Baptist (Matt. 11:4,5). The liberation he brings is total. He not only forgives sinners, he also cures the body, snatching it from the clutches of sickness and in some cases even from the power of the devil (Luke 13:16). Even death is defeated by the power of the Messiah.

However, his liberating action is selective. He does not heal all the sick people at the pool of Bethesda, nor even less all those in Palestine who were spiritually and physically slaves of the Evil One. The time of universal health had seemingly not yet come. The ministry of Christ is directed fundamentally to individuals. Even when preaching to multitudes he hints that he expects from any one of his listeners a personal decision. He does not free the masses, but only certain individuals.

It is obvious that the emphasis of his mission and teaching is spiritual. In John 8:31-36 he uses the verb *eleutheroo* (to free), but he uses it above all in relation with the spiritual and moral liberty. "Everybody who sins," is a slave who needs to be freed by the Son of God (v. 34). It is a fact that sin has individual and social dimensions; however, it is not in the sense of "liberation of oppressing structures," that is at once perceived in this passage. The reference to the contrast between the slave and the son in the society of the first century (v. 35) only serves to illustrate the sad condition of him who is slave of sin, but not to fight directly against the institution of slavery as such.

The word translated "liberty" in Luke 4:18, 19, is not *eleutheria* but *aphesis* which is also used with regard to the pardon of sins. According to this last point, Christ would especially announce a spiritual liberation. However, we have already outlined the messianic character of the passage. Jesus does not deny, rather he confirms, the eschatological liberation promised in the Old Testament. It is not necessary to wait for someone else. He is the Messiah announced to Israel. His credentials are authentic and the hope of total freedom is not vain. But to the surprise of those who crave to be freed immediately on the political and social level, Christ does not act as the political Messiah; he does not call for a general rebellion.

We must take into consideration that in those times Palestine was in the orbit of the Roman Empire. Each day the inhabitants of Jerusalem could see in the streets of the holy town the heathen soldiers. The Israelite nation was victim of imperialism and colonialism. The masses were like sheep without a shepherd. There were too many who exploited them, there was no one who was nourishing or defending them. The misfortunes inherent in poverty were many. Slavery was an institution protected by laws and justified by hate. The militant politicians — Herodians, Sadducees — were corrupt, defending their own corrupt interests. Guerrilla zealots formed a gang of desperadoes who could not succeed in uniting the whole nation against the military power of the Romans. The economic, social, and political structures cried for a profound, radical change. The climate seemed most propitious for a popular rebellion and the multitude in Galilee searched for Jesus to proclaim him King. However, he, being conscious of the immediate objective of his mission and of the political consequences of the proposal that the people were making to him, refused to raise the banner of rebellion against the Empire.

What a strange Messiah was this! He even went to the extreme of not opposing payment of the tribute to Caesar.

He did not change unjust structures of society. He did not abolish the thrones of the mighty or raise the humble to royal power. He did not shower good things on the poor or strip the rich of their possessions (Luke 1:52, 53). The powers of the evil of this world seemed to smash him in the dark hours of Calvary. It was certain that he would rise on the third day from the dead. Then he ascended to heaven and left the earthly scene in the same miserable condition in which he had found it. He did not free his people from the oppressor. The legions of Caesar were not vanquished.

There are some who insist that Jesus was a politician who compromised in the cause of the economical-social liberation of the disinherited. They say that his birth had political significance (which would explain the violent reaction of Herod), that his teaching was a challenge to the structures of the political and religious power, that his attitude of criticism of the established order and the presence of at least one publican zealot among his disciples identified him with the Palestine guerrilla, and that his death had a political motive, because the title on the Cross indicated that he was "the King of the Jews."

Neither do we have time nor space to go more thoroughly into these themes which Oscar Cullmann discusses fully in some of his writings. It will be sufficient for now to say that it cannot be proven, on the basis of the New Testament, that Christ incited the masses to violently subvert the political-social order of his time. Cullmann says that Christ does not consider the State "an ultimate divine donation; however, on the other hand, he accepts it and he radically refutes every attempt to destroy it."

Nevertheless, it would not be biblical to say that his incarnation, death, and resurrection did not produce any changes in the march of history. The cross became an instrument of judgment against the prince of this world (John 12:31; Col. 2:14,15). Christ has seated himself at the right hand of the Majesty in heaven such as a king who, after victory, occupies the throne awaiting all his enemies to come and prostrate themselves at his feet (Psa. 110:1; Matt. 22:44, Heb. 1:13, etc.). Furthermore, the presence of his church in the world and the proclamation of the message of reconciliation to all nations are realities which cannot be ignored if there is to be an impartial analysis of this era called Christian.

Also, it is necessary to recall that in the teaching of Christ there exists a ferment of deep social transformation. The principles which speak of the dignity of human being, of the justice, mercy, peace, equality, liberty, and fraternity, did not fail to have repercussions on the conscience of our civilization over nearly two thousand years and, directly or indirectly, they have produced social changes for the benefit of humanity.

In Christian apologetics even the premillenarians frequently resort to the argument that the teaching of Christ has favorably influenced occidental culture and the whole contemporary world. We cite positive examples of this influence, such as the claim of the rights of women and children, the abolition of slavery, and the incorporation of Christian principles in the ideas of the big movements of social transformation. We have repeated that modern science originated from and flourished in the Christian context. In other words, we believe that the doctrine of Christ has exerted clear influences on the historical future of our nations and on the structures of human society. We believe that, in one way or another, the first coming of the Savior also changed the course of history.

However, fearing to be called "horizontalists" or, even worse, "leftists," we do not ask if these principles which produced so good an influence on the people of past generations ought not also to influence our generation in favor of economic-social liberation. We do not ask why we continue to permit others to proclaim, in their own manner, the Christian truths which we, who claim that we follow the living God, ought to proclaim on the strength of his Word and Spirit. It is undeniable that some banners of freedom which we have dropped on the way have been picked up by others, not in the name of God but, sometimes, against God.

On the other hand, it is imperative not to forget that even social changes, inspired sometimes by Christian principles, have not themselves solved the spiritual problem of man. For example, the abolition of slavery in the Western world does not signify that the chains of sin, in the hearts of those who suffered such a shameful yoke or of those who have oppressed them, have been broken. Christ said that all evil comes out of the heart of man, and that he has to be born again.

When citing Isa. 61:1,2, and Luke 4:18,19, Jesus omits the words which speak about judgment. This omission may point to the right way of interpreting the earthly ministry of Christ. He had not come to judge,

but to save (John 3:17). The term *Ruomenos,* liberator (Rom. 11:26)
has strong Old Testament roots, evoking the figure of the *gaal,* the close
parent who redeems, who brings freedom by paying the required ransom. It is suggested in the Old Testament that the liberation of the
Exodus, the type of the future great redemption, was also a ransom
made possible by the divine Gaal, Jehovah of the armies (Exod. 6:6,
Psa. 74:2).

When at the beginning of his ministry Christ declared he was sent
to free the captives, he is aware of the thought of the cross. Some time
afterwards he said, "Even as the Son of man came not to be ministered
unto, but to minister, and to give his life a ransom (lutron) for many"
(Matt. 20:26). There can be no real *eleutheria* (liberation) without the
corresponding *lutron* (ransom). The prophecies relative to the Messiah
suffering had to be fulfilled (Psa. 2; Isa. 53). The objective of God with
regard to redemption would not remain frustrated (Eph. 1:13,14; I Pet.
1:17-21; Rev. 13:8).

The *Ruomenos* had to die on the cross. This is, therefore, the divine
message for man today that Christ died for our sin, that he was resurrected,
and that he will return to establish throughout the world his reign of
justice and peace. All authentically Christian liberation bases itself on
that proclamation. Every actual liberation in Christ confirms to us the
promise of the cosmic liberation which is to come, the regeneration
which the Son of Man will bring (Matt. 19:28), and the restoration of
all things which God has revealed through his prophets (Acts 3:21).
Meanwhile we are called upon to live and serve in the dynamics of this
new and glorious hope.

b. *Testimony of Paul.* One of the prominent themes in Pauline theology is liberty or liberation, the one which the believers in Christ are
enjoying now, and the one which will manifest itself when he comes again.

We have already discussed the concept of *Ruomenos* in Rom. 11:26.
According to this passage, Christ will be the deliverer of Israel, and
that the deliverance will have far-reaching effects is obvious from the
Scriptures. As as example, (i) the Son of God will deliver his church
from the future wrath (I Thess. 1:10); (ii) the body of the believer will
be redeemed finally (Rom. 8:23). The ideas of deliverance and redemption
are closely linked in the Bible.

The believer is redeemed in all dimensions; spiritual, mental, and
physical. In the salvation plan of God there is no antithesis between
the soul and the body such as we generally apply and which has conveyed the impression that our Christianity is, in this aspect, docetic, or
without body. The exegetes and theologians have pointed out that
certain wrong ideas which have been introduced in the church with
respect to the body are Greek, not Christian. Paul highly esteems the
body of the believer; he sees it in its present glory (temple of the Spirit,
instrument of justice), and in its future glory (I Cor. 15:35-38, Phil.
3:20,21).

(iii) The creation itself will be delivered "from the bondage of
corruption into the glorious liberty of the children of God" (Rom. 8:21).
This suggests the cosmic liberation already mentioned above which
cannot include all sinners because many of them will "suffer the punish-

ment of eternal damnation" (II Thess. 1:9). Humanistic and universalistic sentimentalism, which overlooks the justice of God, lacks Biblical backing. It is a fact that God loves the world (John 3:16), and is "not willing that any should perish, but that all should come to repentance" (II Pet. 3:9).

However, there will always be those who prefer to treasure up "unto themselves wrath against the day of wrath and revelation of the righteous judgment of God" (Rom. 2:5). The warning of this judgment should more often accompany the proclamation of the Gospel.

In Christ, liberty is the promise for the remote future and reality for today. Paul teaches that the believer is already fundamentally delivered due to the new relationship he has with Christ and to the new position which he enjoys in him. Identifying himself with Christ in his faith, the sinner is reborn to the liberty of the sons of God. Significantly, the Apostle indicates that the believer has been delivered from the domination of sin (Rom. 6:6, 12, 14-23), from the domination of law (Rom. 7:1-6; Gal. 3:5), from the law of sin and death, and from all damnation (Rom. 8:1, 2).

It is hoped that this deliverance will show reality in the life of the redeemed. It is necessary to leave the servitude of sin and to live justly (Rom. 6:11-13, 19-22) in the private experiences of every day and in all relationships either of family or society. We are called to live "as free, and not using our liberty for a cloak of maliciousness, but as the servants of God" (I Pet. 2:16). Christianity, it is recognized, has a lot of paradoxes.

Paul says, "to be free from everybody," however, he becomes a "servant to everybody" in order to win the greatest number (I Cor. 9:19). Martin Luther has majestically explained this paradox in his famous treatise on Christian liberty.

Christ, "who gave himself for our sins that he might deliver us from this present evil world," (Gal. 1:4) meaning the world system which is full of evil. However, the apostle also affirms that in our personal relationships, we should not avoid the sinners, "for then must ye needs go out of the world" (I Cor. 6:10). This coincides with the teaching of our Master in his holy prayer (John 17). He personified his doctrine when he received sinners and ate with them.

The exhortations of verses such as Rom 12:2, and I John 2:12-17 are still valid. However, Christ will deliver us practically not only before the world but in the world. The dualism "Christian world," which we have underlined without taking into account other aspects of biblical worldliness and which has made the evangelical Church in many places retire from the social scene, may be ascetic but not Christian. Neither is the secularism "Christian" which tries to sacralize the world and make the Church mundane. However, if Christ wishes to deliver us in the world, what are the oppressing forces from which he will deliver us?

When Paul refers to the fight of the Christian, he emphasizes the spiritual. Our battle is not "against flesh and blood" (Eph. 6:10-20), and the weapons of our warfare are not carnal (II Cor. 10:4). However, recognizing the presence and activity of the Satanic world does not mean spiritualizing the problems of man in such a manner that it will make it impossible for him to become conscious of the social reality in which he lives.

We can learn much from the teaching and the example given by the Apostle about the attitude the Christian must assume in the presence of worldly powers. Let us consider three concrete causes: (i) concerning religion, it is evident that from the day of his meeting Christ, Saul of Tarsus chose a path that would lead him always further away from the institutional Judaism of the synagogue, the temple, the sects of the Scribes, Pharisees, Sadducees, and Herodians.

The total breach becomes inevitable. The Jewish leaders declare lethal warfare on Paul. He weeps for the spiritual condition of his Israelite brothers (Rom. 9:1-5), but he does not renounce his liberty in Christ or tolerate the slightest mixture of Judaistic legalism with the Gospel of the grace of God. The epistle to the Galatians has been called "the letter of Christian freedom."

In the case of heathen religions, the attack of Paul is direct without any trace of palliative. According to the letter to the Romans, by not glorifying God the heathen have lost understanding, have fallen into idolatry and the most repugnant immorality (1:18-32). The tumult in Ephesus (Acts 19) gives us an idea of the deep-rootedness of the heathen cult in the mentality of the masses. Some philosophers, such as Seneca, were biting in their criticism of idolatry, but nevertheless, for social convenience sake, they practiced it. The Roman Empire was tolerant of the religions of the conquered nations, but the time came when they were required to give homage to the emperor. It would be impossible to bring into harmony their heathen religion with Paul's gospel. For the apostle, Christ and not Caesar is the Master.

(iv) The mention of Caesar brings us to reflect on the attitude Paul adopted before the civil power. Chapter 13 of Romans has given rise to much controversy. It is certain, moreover, that the apostle was not an anarchist. Neither did he believe that the state was divine in itself, although he confers on the state a certain dignity as having been ordained by God. However, he did not regard civil power as autonomous with the Creator. Caesar is not equal to God, or over God, but underneath God. His authority comes from above (John 19:11). Consequently, the Christian owes obedience to the state as long as the state does not demand what belongs to God. There came a time many Christians had to elect between adoring Caesar or suffering martyrdom.

It is interesting to note that Paul, who did not conspire against civil power or incite others to destroy it, died as if he were an enemy of the state. However capricious the sentence of the empire was, it is undeniable that the apostle had been condemned to die because he was Christian.

(v) One of the most acute social problems in those days was that of slavery. However, in Pauline literature, or in any other part of the New Testament, there does not exist any exhortation to insurrection among the slaves, who were certainly numerous in the Empire. On the contrary, Paul exhorted them to obey in all ways and to serve faithfully their worldly masters (Eph. 6:5-7; Col. 3:22-25; I Pet. 2:18-25).

He told the masters to treat well their slaves because there is a Lord in heaven to whom they would have to give account (Eph. 6:9; Col. 4:1). But he does not ask them to free their slaves for the glory of the Gospel. Apparently Paul's Christ had not come to free the captives, at least not in the form many had hoped for. It is necessary to take into account that Christianity was in constant danger of being confused with the Zealot movement or with some other subversive group. This is a danger harassing us also at the present time. Following the steps of the Lord, with regard to social problems, Paul was not mistaken.

However, in his teaching there are seeds of freedom which in due time, would germinate and give abundant fruit. For example, the idea that the free as well as servants are the slaves of the Master. The strong affirmation that in Christ there are neither slaves nor free men could not help but rouse firm convictions about human dignity and the equality of all men in the presence of God. The letter to Philemon abounds in implications about freedom. Within the framework of the most refined Christian courtesy, this document possesses an enormous abolitionist potential.

The passage in I Cor. 7:20-24 is difficult to translate and to interpret, but it gives enough light on the problem which occupies us. According to A. Biber, the correct translation would be, "Even when you have the possibility of freeing yourself you should rather remain slave." More reasonable seems to be the concept of W. Rees regarding this verse: "It would be better to take it as parenthesis ('However, if you can obtain your liberty, take it'). Others think that Paul recommends that one should continue in the condition of slavery even if one could become emancipated. This seems to be an unreasonable demand because the desire for liberty is innate to man and slavery might constitute an obstacle to the practice of religion."

What Paul seems to teach is that the slave who was a slave before his conversion in Christ should not strive to free himself if it does not seem possible for the moment. However, if the opportunity comes for him to break his chains, he should do so. After all, he is already the Lord's freeman (v. 22). As for the Christian who was found by Christ as a free man, he should not make himself the servant of men (v. 23).

Paul does not sanctify, even less glorify, slavery. It is an evil rather than a good thing for humanity. The recommendation of the apostle that everyone remain "in the state in which he was found" is of a general nature and admits other possibilities. If single women and widows can change their civil status (I Cor. 7:25-40), so the slave cannot be denied the right to free himself from the oppressing yoke when this is within his reach.

In our day there is no biblical basis for a Christian who suffers any form of oppression to resign himself to remain in this without at least asking himself whether there are any possibilities of putting an end to his abject state. In former times a slave had several means of becoming a freeman. Today we do not have to accept blindly the thesis that violence is the only way of liberation.

We who have been delivered in Christ should not become servants of men (I Cor. 7:23), even if they claim to offer deliverance from our economic-social chains. We are bought with the price of the blood of the Lamb of God (John 1:29; I Cor. 6:18-20, I Pet. 1:18, 19). We are the servants of God.

Conclusion

Christ is the Savior; not only the liberator who comes, but the liberator who has already come. Deliverance in Christ is fundamentally related to the sin which is enchaining man in his deepest being. Therefore, the essence of the evangelistic message for every creature in the world is "Christ died for our sins according to the Scriptures, and that he was buried, and that he rose again the third day according to the Scriptures" (I Cor. 15:3, 4). The message of the Gospel points to the total liberation of man, in all dimensions of his personality and all his relations of his life.

Although the Gospel emphasizes the deliverance of the individual, there are evangelical principles that have been influenced and can influence here and now for the good of humanity. Even if the Church fulfills its mission faithfully to proclaim "the entire counsel of God," it cannot avoid either the auto-judgment or the trial of society because of the state of oppression in which millions and millions of human beings are living in different parts of the world.

However, deliverance will not be total until the return of Christ the Lord.

The transformation of this world in a reign of justice and peace for all human beings will not be the work of man but that of God. The Gospel is the message of hope — the hope in Christ, not in man.

THE KINGDOM OF GOD AND THE CHURCH IN CONTEMPORARY PROTESTANTISM AND CATHOLICISM

J. Andrew Kirk

Rev. Kirk, Buenos Aires, Argentina, is Associate Professor of New Testament at the Catholic University of Buenos Aires.

The scope of this study paper is naturally limited: it is based on a selective bibliography, which may not be everyone's choice; it will be largely descriptive, though having an evaluative conclusion; its form will be highly schematic, thus running the risk of exaggerating positions, though with no intention to do so; and the material will be condensed, i.e., presented without much explanatory elaboration. Despite these obvious limitations imposed by space and time, it is to be hoped that the reader will enjoy entering into what is a fascinating contemporary discussion.

1. *The Kingdom and the Church in Jesus' ministry and teaching*

a. Jesus of Nazareth is the Messiah promised in the Old Testament Scriptures. It is the business of the Messiah to establish the Kingdom. Jesus, as Messiah, has therefore come to make actual God's victorious rule over his people (Bright).

b. The Messiah never appears alone. If Jesus is the Messiah there must be a remnant (Bright). There is no Messiah without a community. Those who are called into God's Kingdom form such a community (Ridderbos).

c. Jesus declares his intention to found a Church (not to be confused with the later, hierarchically ordered, structure) when it becomes obvious both that Israel rejects him as Messiah and the disciples accept him as such (Matt. 16:13 ff.) (Padilla).

d. According to some, it is the failure of the preaching of the Kingdom which leads Jesus to pay special attention to instructing his disciples, the *ecclesia designata* (Karrer). According to others, the Church is the calculated result of this preaching, the group of disciples forming the nucleus of the new people of the new covenant (Padilla, *Lumen Gentium*).

e. The rejection of Jesus as Messiah was basically due to his failure to re-establish the Kingdom of David. The new community which he introduced was an unprecedented new reality. The inclusion of the Gentiles within the people of God is already anticipated in Jesus' ministry (especially Luke) (Nunez).

f. Further evidence of Jesus' intention to form a Church is given by the following facts: he gathered men to himself ("follow after me") and instructed his disciples to gather more; he foretold that the gulf between this new community and the Jews would grow and that the Kingdom would be taken away from Israel and given to another people (parable of the vineyard and the tenants) Ridderbos).

g. Summarizing: Jesus did not found an ecclesiastical organization, but as the Messiah he called out a remnant. This remnant is the new Israel, the people of the covenant, symbolized in the Last Supper as the fellowship of the Kingdom (Bright).

2. *The Kingdom and Church in the New Testament after the Resurrection*

a. One of the basic differences between the Gospels and the rest of the New Testament, reflecting the changed historical situation, is that Jesus, the *preacher* of the Kingdom, becomes Christ *preached* as Lord (Kung). God's reign is operative in the reign of Christ. The transition is reflected by an application of Psa. 110:1 to the universal dominion of the ascended Christ.

b. Christ is now proclaimed as head (sovereign) both of the Church and of the universe (especially in Paul's captivity epistles). The exercise of his kingly rule is applied to both spheres, the juxtaposition of his authority over both spheres being seen most clearly in Matt. 28:16-20 (Bosc, Pereira, Grau).

c. Christ's authority over the universe is linked to his mediatorship of the act of creation (Colossians). As mediator he is also the reconciler of all things (Ephesians, Colossians).

d. The fact that Christ is both head of the Church and ruler over the entire creation means that the relationship between the *regnum Christi* and the Church is one aspect of the relationship between redemption and creation (Cullmann).

e. "The actual reign of Christ over the Church and the world is the manner of bringing about the sovereignty of God in the time of salvation (Schnackenburg). The time of salvation is the interim period between the two comings (Padilla). In this period Christ reigns as Lord of his Church and as such he creates it.

f. The Church is created by Christ through the Holy Spirit. Thus it is the result of both the preaching of the Gospel of the Kingdom and the activity of the Spirit (Padilla). "Those who hear the word with faith and become part of the little flock of Christ have received the kingdom" *(Lumen Gentium)*.

g. Paul's particular contribution to the fulfillment of the Church's commitment to Jesus Christ is the development of the meaning and significance of life in the Spirit as the pledge of the full reception of our heritage in the future (Eph. 1, 4; Rom. 8). Life in the Spirit is synonymous with life in Christ. Also, to be transported into the Kingdom of Christ (Col. 1:13) is to participate in the new life of the resurrected Christ (Col 3:1-3) (Schnackenburg). "Christian life is not an effort to conform to a spiritual or moral ideal nor submission to a law, however exalted, but life in Christ" (Bosc).

h. The early Church, following its Lord, rejected the temptation to establish a political kingdom in opposition to the Roman Empire. In this way it rejected the theocratic ideal of Israel (Nunez). "The early Church never imagined it could bring in the Kingdom. It was sent rather into the world as a missionary witness to a Kingdom already set up" (Bright).

3. *Identification and Separation of the Kingdom and the Church*

There are a few authors who make a complete identification between the Church and the Kingdom. A more numerous body make a partial identification. A third group tend toward a radical separation.

a. A study of Matt. 16:18-20 shows us that the Kingdom is organized into the form of the Church. The two do not appear as separate institutions. Jesus' near coming which he foretold (e.g., Mark 9:1) is in his Kingdom-Church (Vos).

b. The Church and the Kingdom are identified in the following passages: Rev. 1:6; Jas. 2:5; Col. 1:13; I Thess. 2:12. The Kingdom will come through the believing people who are the bearers of the Kingdom in the world. "However, the Church cannot just be identified with the Kingdom; at least when the 'Church' is understood as the visible order of the believing community and the Kingdom of God as the divine domain" (Karrer).

c. The Church is the Kingdom already in our midst: that Kingdom which Jesus came to announce and mysteriously inaugurate, which has begun now on earth and is advancing through sufferings to plentitude. The Church constitutes the germ and beginning of that Kingdom. It is the Kingdom veiled and in pilgrimage (Maritain).

d. The possibility of identifying the Church with the Kingdom already inaugurated, though not with the Kingdom finally consummated, is tentatively broached by several authors: the *regnum Christi* was born at Ascension and the Church at Pentecost, which took place at the Ascension for the whole creation took place at Pentecost for the Church. The Church is the heart and center of the *regnum Christi*. It forms the earthly setting of the *regnum Christi* as the body which Christ has chosen (Cullmann) (Cullmann bases his views on a temporal distinction which he makes between the Kingdoms of Christ and of God). "The Church is the expression of Jesus Christ's universal sovereignty, it is the concrete manifestation of the Kingdom" (Padilla). "She (the Church) becomes on earth the initial budding forth of that Kingdom. While she slowly grows, the Church strains toward the consummation of the Kingdom" *(Lumen Gentium).*

e. The third group of writers see the Church and the Kingdom always in strict contrast. Miguez stresses that the history of Israel was that of a prolonged conflict between God and his people. Bright is convinced that there is no hint in the New Testament that "the visible existing Church can either be or produce the Kingdom." According to Grau, the Kingdom cannot be limited to the frontiers of the Church because (i) it takes in the whole of creation, (ii) the believing peoples have not yet reached their fullness. The tendency to identify the Kingdom and the Church arises from an over-emphasis on the present fulfillment of the Kingdom (Kung). The Church, therefore, is neither the fore-runner of the Kingdom, nor does it build it up. There is no question even of continuity, the Kingdom emerging from the Church, for the reign of God is neither a product of organic development nor a process of penetration, but a wholly new work of God (Kung).

4. *The scope of the Kingdom and of the Church*

a. *Definitions of the Kingdom:* The Kingdom of God is God's kingly activity manifested in a breaking into human history and experience to visit and redeem his people in a manner decisive for their salvation" (Perrin); "the Kingdom of God is the active and dynamic exercise of the divine sovereignty" (Schuurman); "the Kingdom is God's active sovereignty over the world, especially and representatively exercised and testified to in Israel, perfected in Jesus Christ and promised in full manifestation in the Parousia of the Lord" (Miguez); "the Kingdom has three meanings: (1) the exercise of power or government; (ii) the sphere or territory governed; (iii) the community of those governed" (Cullmann); "in its present aspect, the Kingdom is the exercise of God's sovereignty over his creation, especially over those who willingly accept his will. It is also the salvific activity of God on behalf of man (Nunez).

b. The notion of *the Kingdom as a personal, internal reality*, strong among theological liberals in the nineteenth-century, though somewhat shattered by Schweitzer and Weiss, still continues in some modern authors. Perrin considers that the offer of the forgiveness of sins is the most characteristic note of the Kingdom. Individual experience thus becomes the sphere in which the Kingdom is manifested. The ethical teaching of the Kingdom is concerned with what the individual must do as he is caught up in the eschatological tension between present and future. There is a strong mystical tradition within the Catholic Church which points in the same direction, "by their prayers and active labors, religious men and women play an indispensable role in rooting and strengthening *the Kingdom of Christ in souls,* and in causing it to grow" (*Ad Gentes,* my italics). Identification of the Kingdom with the "invisible" Church springs from the same internalized interpretation. Also, wherever the Church has become introverted or has separated the material from the spiritual in its mission it testifies to the same interior concept of the Kingdom.

c. *The Kingdom as eschatological.* The kingship of Christ is established in his exaltation. It will become fully manifested when he returns in glory (Bosc). Miguez points out that the testimony of apocalyptic places the consummation of the Kingdom in a cataclysmic future. It underlines the radical discontinuity between present history and the Kingdom and emphasizes the influence of the "mystery of evil" in human affairs. Schnackenburg stresses the continuity of all acts which make up the history of salvation: the eschatological reign, in the form of a visible Kingdom, is already announced in manifestations of power. For him (and Kung), against Cullmann, there is complete identification between the kingdoms of Christ and of God.

d. *The Kingdom as universal.* God's purpose of reconciling to himself the whole of creation gives to the kingship of Christ a universal dimension. The church awaits the new creation which is the manifestation of Christ's universal kingship (Bosc). But even now Christ's victory over disobedient powers and his liberating presence are working, outside the church in human "secular" history (e.g., scientific technology which is alleviating many kinds of suffering) (Schuurman). The new order to be established through Christ is the recovery of the perfect primitive divine order (Schnackenburg).

e. The consummation of the universal and eschatological divine kingdom means *the final and complete victory over all demonic forces.* In the present period of salvation; fear of hostile, demonic powers disappears for all who are united to Christ. Their liberty and their dignity are recovered (Grau). For Cullmann, the title, Lord, means that Jesus Christ rules as king not only over men but also over the invisible powers. Cullmann advances the novel thesis that these powers actually form part of Christ's rule (c.f. 2nd and 3rd above) and they they are therefore entitled to obedience and active support (his interpretation of Rom. 13:1ff.). However, these powers are able to free themselves temporarily, converting themselves into the "beast" (Rom. 13). The self-deification of the state is a sure sign that the powers have broken free from the *regnum Christi.* These enemies will be destroyed in the last stages of Christ's rule (the millenium). Padilla rejects Cullmann's interpretation on the grounds that the Kingdom is a *soteriological* order which is entered only by the *obedience of faith.* Schnackenburg rejects it on the grounds that Christ now exercises as the glorified Lord, a true reign in which he maintains the evil cosmic forces under his feet.

f. *The temporary, provisional nature of the church* is stressed by Kung. For him the church belongs essentially to the present; the Kingdom to the future. The church embraces sinners; the Kingdom is only inherited by the righteous. The church is not a preliminary sign but an anticipation of God's reign which is present in the church in the word which promises forgiveness, new life, and constant renewal. The church exists in the time of salvation as a saving event for sinners.

5. *The Kingdom, the church, and the world*

At this stage we must introduce a new element, the world. If it is true, as the majority of our commentators insist, that the Kingdom extends beyond the church, then it must have some relation to secular human history as well. The nature of this relation is a matter of intense, polemical debate within modern theological thought (Moltmann, Metz, Teilhard de Chardin, the Theology of Liberation, Christian-Marxist encounter, etc.).

a. Almost every writer rejects as untenable the "Constantinian" relationship between the church and the state which arose in the fourth century and was justified *a posteriori*, principally by Augustine, by identifying the church with the Kingdom (a "post-Christian theocracy"). The Christendom notion of the church was carried over into the thought of the Reformers. It influenced their lack of an eschatological perspective, due largely to the too exclusive place given to the sovereignty of Christ over the church and the corresponding relegation of his kingship over the world (Bosc). "Neither the church nor the Christian society is God's Kingdom on earth" (Kung).

b. Equally clear, among most writers, is a rejection of the opposite extreme: i.e., an atemporal negation of interest in the world. If Constantinism is the result, in theological terms, of a strong post-millenialism, withdrawal from the world is due largely to the apocalypticism associated with pre-millenialism. Pre-millenialism also stresses the exclusiveness of Christ's Lordship over the church. Christ, as Lord, defends his church against the attacks of her enemies. Hostility on the part of a decaying world leads to withdrawal. However, negation of the world is not justified, for the Church awaits a new creation (Bosc).

c. If these two views have stressed, from different angles, the place of the church, there is another view which minimizes the church and stresses the correlation between the Kingdom and the world. Maritain characterizes this view (not his own) as portraying a near identification between the Kingdom and the world, "the world is itself the Kingdom in a state of becoming . . . the Kingdom is leaven *in* the world, it is not a reality beyond the world." Miguez calls this view which he does not share, *monistic:* there is only *one* history (i.e., no separate history of salvation) *in* and *from* which God is building his kingdom. Christian faith does not constitute a separate history but gives this one a new motivation and issues a new invitation to transform it.

d. Gutierrez, the most systematic representative of the Theology of Liberation, starts from a clear distinction between the church and the world, and between these and the Kingdom. The church and the world both contribute to the building up of the Kingdom. But the world is totally autonomous, i.e., man is the mature agent of his own destiny. The church meets to celebrate its faith and discuss its political options in the light of God's Word. The church is marked by its attitude to that process of liberation which God is establishing in this world. The struggle for and the construction of a just and free society is equivalent to accepting the Kingdom, even unconsciously; it is written into the history of salvation. The growth of the Kingdom is given in this historic process of liberation, it signifies a greater realization of man. Nevertheless, none of this is equivalent to the complete arrival of the Kingdom nor to a full salvation.

e. For Metz, the problem for the church in its relationship to the world is one of practice: how to find new ways to insert itself critically into society. The church ought not to establish itself as a mini-society on the edge of the macro-society of the secular world. The church lives in the light of the eschatological promises of God concerning a new world. This hope allows it to enter fully into the construction of an eschatological order of justice, humanization, and universal peace. However, it opposes all idols, which spring from utopias, on the grounds that it knows less about the future than the humanists. Its prophetic voice must be raised against the identification of any planned future of man with the coming Kingdom of God. *Guadium et Spes* also raises a cautious but optimistic note concerning the relationship between the world and the Kingdom, "earthly progress must be carefully distinguished from the growth of Christ's Kingdom. Insofar as the former can contribute to a better ordering of human society it is of vital concern to the Kingdom."

f. Miguez also seeks to resolve the conflict between monism and dualism in the relation between salvation history and universal history. The Kingdom is not the elimination of human history but rather of its corruptibility, weakness, and ambiguity. The Kingdom is not an enigma (*where* is it?) but a mission (what ought I *to do*?). We must, therefore, recognize intermediaries between the Kingdom and our *obedience* without identifying them. These intermediaries are the Scriptures and the historical context. Both are necessary for true obedience.

g. Yoder resolves the conflict in a slightly different way. The church must be sufficiently experienced to be able to discern when, where and how God is using the powers (c.f. the sections above on Cullmann). Whether by collaboration or refusal, she is called to the creation of structures more worthy of man. That Christ is Lord, is a proclamation to which only individuals can respond, but it is also a social, political, structural fact which constitutes a challenge to the powers. The position of the New Testament church is not one of withdrawal. The "otherness" of the church consists in her being a herald of liberation and not a community of slaves. The church accepts that she is a new community created by the cross and not the sword. The believer's task is not to bring the powers to their knees but to hold their seduction and enslavement at a distance.

6. *Dangers of identification and of separation between the Kingdom and the church.*

a. When the kingships of Christ over the church and over the world are too closely associated, e.g., when the kingship of Christ over the world is pushed into the background, the church falls into the temptation of idealism and mysticism: it takes refuge in the world of ideas or of religious sentiment (Bosc). An easy identification between the two, says Kung, leads to an unhealthy dissociation. The church is then seen as the enemy of the Kingdom, which tends to use force and/or privilege to defend its own establishment. As a result the opposite reaction of apocalyptic chiliasm is generated which, when allied to social revolution gives rise to secularized imperial utopias (messianisms) using a socialist eschatology as a historical motivation. Kung warns, however, that dissociation from the church does not necessarily lead nearer to the reign of God. Bright suggests that a church which identifies itself with the Kingdom will soon begin to invite God to endorse its own policies — or demand the right to decide on every aspect of a person's life —

(Grau), and will reckon on the advance of the Kingdom in terms of numerical growth. In practice this position has fathered the fatuous conceit that righteousness with God can be gained by external conformity.

b. When there is too great a separation between the Kingdom and the church, e.g., when the kingship of Christ over the church is considered insignificant, the church falls into the temptations of individualism, moralism, rationalism, and utopianism. It is condemned to conceiving the realization of the Kingdom in a semi-magical fashion (Bosc). The danger of moralism is the danger of identifying the Kingdom with one specific culture (e.g., the liberal bourgeois) (Kung). The danger of utopianism, in any of its forms, even that of dialectical materialism, is that of identifying the future Kingdom of the Messiah either with an ideal state or with a particular, identifiable, political-social system (the error of the Zealots) (Munez). According to Trestmontant (and Maritain) biblical thought is equally opposed to idealism and to materialism.

7. The Kingdom and the church today

a. *Relationship between the Kingdom and the church ideally conceived.* (i) The church is the organism where *the Gospel of the Kingdom* (already present) *is preached and obeyed* (Bosc). In its proclamation of the Gospel the church is a sign of the end. It constantly points to the fact that this age is passing away (Padilla). It is not a compromise community for the Kingdom. It exists to proclaim the Kingdom under whose authority it now lives (Kung).

(ii) The church participates by its life and witness to the Kingdom in *the present cosmic struggle.* It cannot escape the tension thus engendered between its present obedience and its future hope, e.g., by living at peace in the secular order, without betraying itself. The church can neither create nor abandon the Kingdom (Bright). The universal Lordship of Jesus Christ (Matt. 28) is exercised through the church in two ways: in the *conquest* of men of all nations as his disciples and in the upbuilding of the community in love in which a lost humanity is restored and the evil cosmic powers are destroyed in its midst (Schnackenburg).

(iii) The church is the community which *receives the gifts of the Kingdom* (Ridderbos, Grau). The gifts are gifts of a grace which is sovereign and thus free (Bosc). The gifts are essentially those — forgiveness (Perrin), new life and constant renewal (Kung) — which keep the church from adopting a self-righteous and uncompassionate attitude to those outside (Kung).

(iv) The church is supremely the community that bears the fruit of the Kingdom. The Kingdom of God is directed towards the formation of a new people that will replace Israel in the history of salvation. A people that will yield the fruits of the Kingdom (Ridderbos). The church must demonstrate in her life and fellowship that man can live freed from the dominion of the powers (i.e., through substantial reconciliation) (Yoder). The moral requirements of the Kingdom are designed to challenge the church to be worthy of her calling (Matt. 7:21). The ethics of the Kingdom preached by Christ were taken over into the catechetical instruction of the early church (ethical sections of Paul's epistles), where there is a particular stress on service ("who is greatest in the Kingdom of God?") and on undiscriminating reception of all into the fellowship (Schnackenburg).

(v) The Kingdom is, at the same time, the goal, limitation, and judgment of the church (Kung). The church is the symbol, sign and announcement of the Kingdom (Schuurman).

b. *The Kingdom, the church, and evangelism.* This final section will be a short, personal, attempt at an evaluation of the contemporary discussion in the light of the church's call to proclaim the Gospel to all people.

(i) Baird suggests that the Kingdom formed for Jesus Christ an integral world-view, i.e., a conceptual framework in which the entire revelation of God finds its focus. In God's universal rule we find included every biblical theme from creation to the new creation.

(ii) The early church used the word infrequently. However, when it did so it occurred in key contexts. The book of Acts, for example, begins and ends with a discussion of the Kingdom (Acts 1:6-8; 28:30-31). The concept is also present in the confession that Christ is Lord; that he reigns.

(iii) He reigns over both the Kingdom and the church. The two find their perfectly harmonious relationship when correctly linked to his Lordship. In theological terms, Christology is the key to understanding the present period of salvation. Thus it is of vital concern to guard closely the content of our proclamation of Christ. Naming Christ (Rom. 15:20), apart from the controlling influence of the full biblical revelation about Christ, is not preaching the Gospel of the Kingdom for, conversely, Christ cannot be understood apart from a proclamation of the Kingdom. From this fact two important consequences for evangelism follow: first, the Gospel cannot be compressed into neat formulas and served up as a "simple Gospel," for the simple Gospel is *no* Gospel unless it includes the dimensions of the Kingdom; Second, *indiscriminate* use of the word Christ in evangelism may be self-defeating. It may convey no more than any political or ideological slogan.

(iv) The Lordship of Christ over the universe means that he is sovereign over the nations. This also has profound implications for evangelism. It is supremely relevant in a world which every day grows politically more conscious and more inclined to invest politics with the mystique of salvation (or liberation). Evangelism should include a prophetic ministry to the nations which is not partial (as in, e.g., the false nationalsim of those evangelicals who refuse to condemn the aggression or oppression of their respective governments or the biased ideology of certain international church leaders who select the kind of racial bigotry they wish to condemn) but which, sumultaneously, denounce the false freedom claimed by autonomous man to distribute his own justice and build his own future and announces the true freedom of the sons of God. Without this prophetic ministry our proclamation of Christ as Lord over the nations and the cosmic powers is devoid of any meaningful context.

(v) The church evangelizes from a place of political weakness. For example, every attempt to reintroduce the Constantinian concept of the church meets with the rebuke of the eschatological Kingdom inauguarated by the Cross (compare Luke 22:25-26; I Cor. 1:23-24; 2:2-5; 4:20 for a christian view of the meaning of real power). The church's methods of evangelism must consistently reflect this weakness. They are not, as some evangelicals claim, only controlled by the success syndrome or their contextual relevance, but also by what the ethic of the Kingdom, based on the Cross, constantly demands. The biblical ideas of the remnant, of discipleship, of fellowship, of the prophetic ministry, of a faithful testimony unto death, warn against the current evangelistic triumphalism of a concern for numbers.

(vi) There is little contemporary interest in the "ontological" relationship between the Kingdom and the church. Suffice it to say, that neither complete identification nor absolute separation is biblically viable. Rather the relationship has been sought for in practical terms: what does it mean for the life of the church that she proclaims and teaches the Gospel of the Kingdom? It means at least two things: First, the church either evangelizes by its life or it erects barriers to the Gospel by its life. The world is quick to judge the authenticity of its message by its courage in allowing that message to transform its *total* outlook. The Kingdom is either a world-view which offers a message which revolutionizes practice or else in today's world, it is spurious. Lenin once said of an ideology which proffers a false expectation, "there is no revolutionary practice without a revolutionary theory." Conversely, revolutionary theory is proved credible, or otherwise, in action. Second, there is less emphasis on what the Gospel offers and more on what it demands. We present it not as an immediate solution to every human problem but as a call to a new life-style. It is true, of course, that the Christian imperative springs from a Christian indicative, and that without this it leads to a destructive legalism. It is equally true, however, that the indicative without the imperative leads to a dead orthodoxy, sentimentality, individualism, or an esoteric mysticism.

(vii) The purpose of evangelism is that of forming a new people who express individually and in community the reality of God's reign. It is thus based on the fulfilment of the Kingdom in the ministry, death, and resurrection of Jesus Christ and on its final consummation in the *eschaton*. All evangelism should reflect this tension between past historical certainty and future historical hope.

THE KINGDOM OF GOD AND ITS RELATIONSHIP TO THE VISIBLE CHURCH IN CONTEMPORARY PROTESTANTISM AND CATHOLICISM REPORT

Chairman: Rev. Chas. Tipp
Secretary: Harry S. D. Robinson

A nationally, denominationally and vocationally varied group were informed that the paper was simply an attempt to glean from contemporary writers both Protestant and Catholic their views of the Kingdom of God in its relationship to the visible church. Strong group support was given to the personal conclusions of the author as expressed in his final section.

The Church. There is a need for a dynamic and charismatic (using that word literally) re-understanding of the church. There can be no evangelism outside of the church since membership in the Body and Bride of Christ is explicitly in response to the faithful hearing of the Gospel. The church is the place where the rule and authority of Christ is to be seen.

The present local institutional churches have to be defined as biologically reproducible, as communities where the Kingdom of God becomes visible and where the Kingdom is encountered. In the New Testament there can be no evangelism except that which comes out of the church and receives converts into the church. Para-church structures are not biblical nor can they in fact preach the full Gospel because the church is part of the Gospel message. What have become known as para-church structures must be recognized and recognize themselves as a part of the church, not in an institutional sense but in a dynamic and charismatic sense.

The Kingdom. The attempt to picture the Kingdom as an essential basis of evangelization raised several different problems:

(i) Can we distinguish between the Kingdom of Christ and the Kingdom of God?

(ii) Is the Kingdom in the world what the reformers called "common goose"?

(iii) Can the Kingdom be seen as a manifestation of the Lordship of Christ outside of and unrelated to the church?

(iv) Is there a model by which we can understand the Kingdom over against the church in the world?

(v) Has confusion between the Kingdom and the church tended to make an easy Gospel and a weak church?

The Kingdom and the world. This subject was treated speculatively because of the shortness of time, diversity in background of the participants, and its own tremendous complexity.

(i) Does the authority of God in government, justice, marriage and family life constitute an area of his Kingdom outside the church?

(ii) Does the Kingdom of God demand that he act independently in the world when the church fails in its responsibility?

(iii) Can God's purpose in his Kingdom transcend his purpose for the church, or is it always an indication of God's larger purpose for his church?

(iv) The confession of the Kingdom demands that no absolute church structure is possible. The local, visible church is that community where the Kingdom of God comes into being.

(v) Triumphalism is when the church loses its consciousness of being a servant (see final section of paper).

The scriptural basis for most of our discussion centered around the John chapter 3 references to seeing and entering the Kingdom; the New Testament references to Psalm 110, Romans 13-15, and Ephesians 4-6; the kingdom parables, Revelation 11:15; and local church references in Acts.

THE KINGDOM OF GOD AMONG THE KINGDOMS OF EARTH

José Grau

"The Lord hath prepared his throne in the heavens, and his kingdom ruleth over all" (Psa. 103:19).

God, the only absolute Ruler

We shall leave it to theologians to decide whether human government belongs or does not belong to the so-called "creation orders." One thing is certain, anyhow, the *ruling of God* over his creation and creatures. His Providence uses different instruments for the ruling of the world, "O Assyrian, the rod of mine anger, and the staff in their hands is mine indignation. Wherefore it shall come to pass, that, when the Lord hath performed his whole work upon Mount Zion and on Jerusalem, I will punish the fruit of the stout heart of the king of Assyria, and the glory of his high looks. And my hand hath found as a nest the riches of the people . . ." (Isa. 10:5, 12, 14a). Here we see that human powers are recognized by all the authors of Scripture, as being parts of the Almighty God's interventions in his Providence.

We should keep in mind that those powers or rulers are acting as God's delegates. They are relative, never absolute, since it is God who "changeth the times and seasons, removeth kings and setteth up kings" (Dan. 2:21, cf. Isa. 40:23,24). Thus, God is not submitted to the order of his creation, nor is he in the realm of nature, in spite of the opinions of certain liberal theologians. But, on the other hand, he is not indifferent to the evolution of civil powers or the order of nature, in spite of the statements of deists of all times. God is sovereign in time, history, and space, i.e., in all his creation (cf. Isa. 40:23,24, 10:1-3).

Ruling powers and sin

As Hans Bürki judiciously remarked, "Earthly powers have to do with the sinful condition of men. One cannot say that the State be sinful in itself, nor that it is a natural or neutral institution. Yet one may affirm that ruling powers are always bound up with the law of God, and this according to the Bible, so that both state and individual have to do in several ways with Divine Law. Even God's law is a grace, a divine mercy. We must never forget that law expresses divine will, and this will is always 'eudekia,' i.e., kindness towards us. Even when it is sentencing, it comes to us as grace, for it kills, so that the Lord may heal us. The authority of God comes to us as a liberating power and not as a threat; for the law is always in favor of man and at his side, as an essential source of true liberty."

In scriptural thinking, *state* and *law* always belong together. And this because powers are ruling by God's delegation, in order to command that which is rightful (Prov. 8:15). And it is God's law that determines what is right and what is not. That is why Hans Bürki, quoting Gal. 3:19,22-24, says that the law was given because of sin and in view of the coming Savior. So, as long as a state is obedient towards the law by means of its political power, it is more or less submitted to the will of God. In this way it becomes a power because of sin, in the same way as the law of Moses was a kind of "school master" leading us to the coming Christ. A fact remains very clear: ruling powers are utterly unable to give life, even when submitted to a certain extent to the law of God; they can only lead and show the way to the saving power. And this because of sin, for the citizens are sinners and the state is made up of sinners. Thus, ruling powers not only have to do with the reality of sin, but are themselves contaminated by sin. This is an evident fact in all realms — not only in politics. It is the same with churches: neither the state, nor the people (not even God's people!) are free from the influences of sin, though Christians should be the clearest example of deliverance from sin's power, for they were constituted a "holy people" (Exod. 19:5; I Pet. 1:13-16; 2:4-5).

Why should one demand so much from God's people? And what are the consequences of that demand, as far as the relation of God's people to the ruling power is concerned? One should not forget that God's interest for this world was manifested in an extraordinary way in forming, in spite of fall and sin, a people of his own. And it will be in their midst, since they are bound with God by a covenant, that the Lord will establish a kingdom entirely of his own (Exod. 19:6). God establishes his kingdom among men's kingdom.

The Kingdom of God

First of all, it is a kingdom of *soteriological origin.* God forms his Old Testament people with Hebrew slaves in Egypt. The New Testament Church is the congregation of saved sinners.

The nature of this kingdom is *eschatological.* The words of Exod. 19:6 are for the future, when the law will be given from Sinai. Yet, from Sinai, the kingdom becomes a reality and, in the same time, *a hope.* It will be the hope of the prophets, who are the mouthpiece of the coming kingdom.

It is a *present and hidden* kingdom at the same time, which fact can already be verified in the Old Testament books. Israel is called to be a holy people of "priests." It is a kingship associated with God's great deeds for his people. Yet this kingship remains brittle and sinful, even apostate. In other words, it is only a shadow of what it ought to be, a "type" of future realities. For there is a future for Jehovah's people, a future in which God himself will be King, Savior, and Lord of his people. From the time of David, the Old Testament people have been living in a present kingdom, but they were mostly expecting a new kingdom with a new king, the Son of David. This expectation was not concerning a kingdom like those of Israel or Judah, but an entirely new and eschatological one.

This kingdom came with Jesus Christ. John the Baptist already announced that it was near at hand (Matt. 3:2). Jesus himself says, "Repent for the kingdom of heaven is near at hand" (Matt. 4:17). The person of Jesus *is* the kingdom among men (Matt. 11:2,6,9,10, 12:28; Luke 11:20). The "good tiding" of the Savior is the *"Gospel of the kingdom,"* which was made present in him and through him. Thus, in Jesus Christ, the future became present.

Jesus is really *"autobasileia"* but, at the same time, *revelation* and *mystery*, for the kingdom is hidden. It comes as a seed, a mustard seed, as leaven, as a hidden treasury, as a hidden pearl of great price. But it is also "like a net that was cast into the sea and gathered of every kind." One should not forget that the Cross is one of the aspects of that kingdom and that it forms the central subject of its preaching.

The kingdom experiences the paradox of its present weakness and of its eschatological greatness; of its revelation and mystery. Paradoxically, too, the king comes under the form of a slave before taking the whole possession of his kingdom (Matt. 28:18) and before the day in which all kingdoms of this world will belong to God and Christ.

Thus, the kingdom came in the past, is coming in the present and will be coming in the future. As O. Cullmann puts it, "We are living the time of the 'already' and of the 'not yet.'" In any case, the kingdom is the only *real absolute*. Therefore, the believer is invited to ask, "Thy kingdom come, thy will be done in earth, as it is in heaven" (Matt. 6:10).

The people of God are living in the *theocentrical* expectation. Their attitude towards the ruling powers can only be understood in the light of that expectation. It is the expectation of the prophets, apostles, and Christian martyrs.

The authors of the Bible and ruling powers

As Martin Buber writes, the Old Testament is theopolitical in its conception of ruling powers. If Israel was a religious and national community, it is not the same as the Church. However, after taking hermeneutic precautions one must not forget that the Christian — as well as the Israelite — is under a theocentric expectation though he is not submitted to a theocratic power. Besides, the Christian belongs to the *earthly dwelling*, as well as to the *civitas Dei*. Christians are being tried in the same way as the Israelites of old, by different forms of ruling powers — some of them entirely idolatrous — who would replace the absolute of God's kingdom by the "absolutes" of this world's kingdoms.

Let us consider a few examples of such trials or temptations.

a. *Samuel* — The situation of Israel at the time of Samuel offers a good illustration of the fact that no form of human government can be idolized. The important fact is the people's attitude towards God's government, as well as the attitude of ruling powers towards divine will. No government system is perfect, compared with the perspective of the sovereign will of the Lord, as revealed in his Word.

For Samuel, the fundamental question was not to know which form of government was the best — the neo-federalism of the judges or the monarchy — but the disposition of the people's heart (governors and governed) towards God's will, whatever the government system. And such a principle is as valid today as it was yesterday.

According to certain modern critical schools, one might find two kinds of texts in I Sam. 8 and 9. The anti-monarchic version would be chapter 8 and also chapter 10:17-24, and chapter 12. The one in favor of the monarchy would be I Sam. 9:1-10,16:11. To ask which is the better system would mean having a mentality very different from the scriptural one. The passages which appear to be "against" monarchy are less against a system than against the motives that make the people want a king. If Samuel appears to be sometimes against monarchy and sometimes in favor of it, there is actually no contradiction. Samuel prayed for God's guidance (I Sam. 8:6). and God revealed to him that he would give Israel a king (I Sam. 9:16). What he was fearing was a *monarchy according to the human pattern,* independent of the will of God. The real problem came from the words the people were using, "Make us a king to judge us *like all the nations*" (15:5,8); "We also may be *like all the nations*" (v. 20). The people were not asking for a king like the one promised in the Torah, but for a ruling power which would be an imitation of heathen powers. And it is that which Samuel could not accept.

True, God used the people's desire in order to choose a king, but according to the prophecy of Deut. 17:14-20. In Israel, the king will be submitted to the law of God as any other citizen, and he will have to respect the life, honor, and possessions of his subjects. He will have to read every day a copy of that law "so that he may learn to fear the Lord, his God" (v. 19). We are very far from the heathen divinization of emperors.

Samuel hastens to show them the kind of monarchy found among other nations (15:8,11); cruelty, lack of righteousness, which the Hebrews well knew. How then can this desire to have a king like that of other nations be explained? History shows us a certain "attraction of the abyss," as was the case at the coming out of Egypt and is the case in many a sector of the twentieth-century Christianity.

One fact is important; Samuel introduces a *principle of critic.* And said principle will manifest itself in all future relations of God's people with ruling powers. Theocracy will assume different expressions: God will no longer be the immediate king he was at the time of the judges. Yet his law and his covenant *remain valid for the king as well as for the people.* The king of Israel will not be prophet and priest (I Sam. 13:8-14,15; I Kings 13:1-10). In spite of theocracy, civil and religious functions have their own particular and distinct form of sovereignty and all of them are placed under the sovereignty of the Lord.

There is no contradiction whatever in the texts of I Sam. If the people want to be prosperous, they will have to do the will of the God of the covenant, whatever the ruling system. The God who gave the judges can also give the kings needed by Israel (Jdg. 2:16, Deut. 17:14, 15; I Sam. 16:1-13). *God's sovereignty* always remains in the foreground. The text informing us of the election of David also tells us about the rejected king. It is still God who "rejects and establishes kings." This divine almightiness made the believers of Israel take an attitude of *obedience* and also of *critic* towards ruling powers.

b. *Wisdom* — Obedience and critic are thus to be found with all the authors of the Bible, for they are convinced that ruling powers come from God and that they themselves might become untrue to their calling. "Keep the king's commandment, and in regard of the oath of God," (Eccl. 8:1-8;cf., Prov. 24:21). The aim of this obedience is "not to stand in an evil thing" (Eccl. 8:3,5, Rom. 13:3). Yet the king may lose his intelligence and no longer be able to listen to others' advice (Eccl. 4:13). Then the people look for another to reign instead of the foolish one.

The example found in Eccl. 4 is rich in teachings. It should be understood in its context, which denounces selfishness and solitude (Eccl. 4:9-16).

Despotism has one of its sources in selfishness and the separating of the ruling power from the people. The foolish king refuses everybody's advice and governs arbitrarily. On the other hand, the young candidate who knows and lives among the people, becomes the interpreter of the latter's will, thus the king becomes afraid of his popularity among the oppressed (Eccl. 3:16,4:1). A change in the ruling — we do not know how it happened — put the imprisoned young man on the throne. This young man was poor, but wise (Eccl. 4:13), for he knew how to draw advantage from listening and discoursing. This passage is praising cooperation in social life, where there is selfishness and the isolation of foolish ruling powers. In this case, the critic of the author is not alluding to structures, but to persons. Wisdom is more important than age; and men are more determining as systems. The lesson is emphasized again at the end of the passage where we find a fundamental scepticism towards the human condition, which is a characteristic of every biblical criticism of men and institutions. In the beginning there is great enthusiasm for the new king; it is the novelty, but let us read verse 16 of chapter 4, "There is no end of all the people, even of all that have been before them: they also that come after shall not rejoice in him. Surely this also is vanity and vexation of spirit."

The mystery of frustration and iniquity, which is inherent in all human activity, will manifest itself in the king's experience with his people. Popularity is not lasting; the people are unconscious. Civic virtues, such as friendship, cooperation, etc., are not usually kept intact by man. That is why there is a time for everything (Eccl. 3:1), a time for popularity, for certain ideologies, and also a time for weariness of that which yesterday was new. "Vox populi, vox Dei" is not a scriptural principle!

Let us add to all this the relativeness of our existence and all its plans (Eccl. 8:6-8). Placed in a "political" context (cf. vv. 2-5) verse 8 teaches us that there are more fundamental questions than those of governmental structures, and more important struggles than those concerning ruling powers and the condition of citizens. Therefore, we should be attentive to God's will and his providence.

c. *The prophets* — The texts we have just been considering convey an aspect of biblical criticism towards ruling powers, which aspect is also present with the prophets who criticized the people as well as the governments.

This is found, among others, in Ezekiel, viz., in chapter 34, which was called one of the most political prophecies of Ezekiel. It is a denunciation of the policy of the country's civil leaders. At that time, the situation was the result of a perverted monarchy which had been lasting for five centuries. Such authorities were incapable of feeding the sheep, i.e., the people. However, Ezekiel is not ringleader or agitator denouncing only the government's faults, he also strongly criticizes the people's sins. He was aware that monarchy was not the only one guilty of the national failure. He knew that "men of the people" had tyrannized other men of the people. Therefore, the Lord will be obliged to judge "between cattle and cattle, between rams and goats, between fat cattle and lean cattle" (Ezek. 34:17-21). Avarice and tyranny were as common among the masses as among the rulers. Ezekiel, as well as Amos, Micah, and other prophets, denounces small towns and villages, etc., who had helped to destroy the country as much as apostate and unworthy kings.

Let us make matters even clearer: What is the prophet's goal? It is the kingdom of God, the Messianic hope, according to the concepts of kingdom and covenant. It is the norm for the judging of the present and the expectation of an eschatological future. This is the subject of verses 23-31. The passage unfolds the blessings of God's covenant with Israel (v. 24,25,31). God's answer to the problems arising from ruling powers is the announcement of the Messianic kingdom. Therefore, the prophet's message is not at all secular or laic but theocentric and even christological.

Amos denounces the sins committed by other nations with the complicity of the Jews (Amos 1:1-2;15) and then also those of Israel, which are worse since Israel had heard the Word of God. He denounces, (i) their forgetting the Word of God (Amos 2:6-8), (ii) their neglecting God's love towards man (Amos 2:9-12), and (iii) their forgetting God's judgment concerning all injustice (Amos 2:13-16). Later on, he denounces the dangers of false prosperity, which today would be called the society of consummation, creating illusions of security and power (Amos 6:1-14). It is a world based on materialism and injustice. All those denunciations are given by Amos in God's name, not in the name of an ideology or system.

We have not sufficient space to consider the other prophets. Let us take only Micah. We have in Micah a man condemning the social injustice of his time, as well as the political unrighteousness of ruling powers (Mic. 2:1-13). But his message is also messianic (Mic. 4:1-13) and even evangelical (Mic. 5:1-15, cf., Isa. 36:19-36). Here again we find the ever present perspective of the kingdom. The prophets had a message concerning eternity (Mic. 6:1-16); they were mouthpieces of God's grace (Mic. 7:5-20), totally engaged with God and his Word (Mic. 1:1-2).

Biblical prophecies and secularization

It has been recently suggested that the result of the biblical message concerning ruling powers is the "desacralizing" of the state, since the latter is considered as absolute and totally sacred. "There exists a real continuity between the prophetic resistance to the sacred pretentions of kings, the Christian resistance against the divinity of emperors, and secular spirit, traditions and official ideology trampling

rights and personal dignity," says Lesslie Newbigin, who rightly emphasizes the fact that such prophetic and Christian protestation is linked
with the conception of absolute divine authority held by prophets
and martyrs. Some of the modern analysts seem to have forgotten
that conception of divine authority, and consequently the true origin
and nature of scriptural protestation, which is always made in the name
of the sovereign God, against any idolatry and sin of men and ruling
powers.

Prophets and martyrs never denounce a king in favor of another
king, or a system in favor of another system, but always in God's
name, because of the sins committed against God. For them, faithfulness towards God is the only guarantee of human rights. They never
take any ideology as their pattern. On the contrary, their pattern is
the divinely revealed conception of the kingdom of God.

The realities of this world are only provisional and anticipating
the manifestation of the kingdom, though in an imperfect and limited
way. Yet this is not an excuse for remaining motionless, but an inspiration to work in favor of the world's renewal, for the Christian
should never be satisfied with the present state of things.

The provisional character of all temporary achievement is a warning against the temptation to deprecate any system or ruling power.
Thus that which is provisional always leads, according to the prophetic
line, to a constant critic of authorities and at the same time, to obeying
the constituted authorities. It is a critical submission of the critic in a
certain obedience.

The New Testament and the ruling powers

All we have said hitherto is found again in the New Testament.
There is no contradiction between Romans 13 and Revelation 13. We
find there the same critical obedience or the same respectful criticism
as in the Old Testament. Thus, the unity of the Bible on that subject is
fundamental.

Ruling powers may prevent evil if the laws are rightful and if the
men in authority have a certain understanding of their calling. But
they can also multiply evil by the sin which is present in every man and
every institution. Therefore, Romans 13 speaks of the God-given authority and of the respect due to it. It is not, as certain theologians noticed,
just plain obedience (this word obedience itself does not appear in
the text), but a serious and responsible obeying on the part of the
citizens.

On the other hand, Revelation 13, as well as Acts 4:19 and 5:29
and other passages, show us the possibility of divinization of ruling
powers, in which case obedience toward the state is disobedience
towards God. Civil disobedience should always be a responsible act
and should not degenerate into anarchy or personal vengeance. Christians should manifest in the same way as the prophets of Israel, that
it is founded on solid biblical reasons. There are several examples of
such disobedience or active criticism among believers in the Bible
including: Moses' mother, Daniel, Jeremiah, and John the Baptist.

The Christian should not forget the theocentric perspective of the kingdom, as well as the covenant to which he belongs and in which he finds the only "absolute program." Any engagement, for or against constituted authorities, which would forget to be entirely loyal to the Gospel or (which is even worse) would betray evangelical doctrine in some way or other, would no longer correspond to a prophetic or Christian attitude.

Prophets and natives never denounce a king in favor of another king or a system in favor of another system, but always in God's name, because of the sins committed against God. For them faithfulness towards God is the only guarantee of human rights. They never take any ideology as their pattern. On the contrary, their pattern is the divinely revealed conception of the kingdom of God.

The realities of this world are only provisional and anticipating the manifestation of the kingdom, though in an imperfect and limited way. Yet this is not an excuse for remaining motionless, but an inspiration to work in favor of the world's renewal, for the Christian should never be satisfied with the present state of things.

The New Testament and the ruling power

All we have said hitherto is found again in the New Testament. There is no contradiction between Romans 13 and Revelation 13. We find there the same critical obedience or the same respectful criticism as in the Old Testament. Thus, the unity of the Bible on that subject is fundamental.

Ruling powers may prevent evil if the laws are rightful and if the men in authority have a certain understanding of their calling. But they can also multiply evil by the sin which is present in every man and every institution. Therefore, Romans 13 speaks of the God-given authority and of the respect due to it. It is not, as certain theologians noticed, just plain obedience (this word obedience itself does not appear in the text), but a serious and reasonable obeying on the part of the citizens.

THE KINGDOM OF GOD AND ITS RELATIONSHIP TO POLITICAL UTOPIANISM AND CULTURAL REVOLUTION REPORT

Chairman: M. Wiggins
Secretary: B. Demarest

The group accepted the paper's view of the Kingdom of God as both part of salvation to be entered into now and as an eschatological hope. In the meantime, the kingdoms of this world, no matter how ideal, can never be given absolute allegiance. In relation to them the Christian exists in a tension: owing obedience, yet necessarily judging the kingdoms by the divine law and at times ready to refuse obedience when "Caesar" demands what is "God's," or when it is necessary to say, "We ought to obey God rather than man." The Christian who, as a citizen, partakes in the power process must take such positive action as lies open to him to set right the situation. The discussion was pinpointed in relation to South Africa, from which some members came. There was a strong feeling that the preaching of the Gospel in that country is greatly hindered by the unjust system maintained by a government, most of the members of which claim to be Christian. The group would like to see a united stand made by all evangelical Christians against the system so that the Gospel may be recognized as "good news to the poor," etc.

A danger at the other end of the spectrum is to be seen in newly independent nations where Christians, as part of the nation and naturally sharing its aspirations and joy, may too long give the uncritical consent to all that is done by the new government which can only be given to the Kingdom of God.

A Christian feeling bound to resist the state should check his conviction with the believers and should have the backing of the fellowship.

There was considerable discussion concerning the affluent society and the Christian's relation to this. For although material blessing is cited in the Old Testament as a token of God's blessing, and a life freed from the bonds of sin becomes more efficient in business and so brings prosperity, yet the dangers and temptations of riches are fully spelled out in the New Testament. While riches themselves are not condemned as sinful, the warnings are so pointed that Christians need to be sensitive not only to their own acquisitive instincts but politically critical of government policies designed to produce evergrowing affluence for their own state, especially when this is at the expense of sub-standard living for trading partners.

The revolution produced by God when a man comes into his kingdom is the revolution of the heart, more radical and essentially different from the revolutions produced in the political world. In a discussion on the use of force, it was doubted by many that this could be justified; others spoke of force as being right in overthrowing an unjust system maintained by force. Revolution by force can never be more than a parital solution. Only the heart revolution of Christ produces a "final solution."

In looking at utopianism, it was noted that all utopias can only be arrangements for organizing fallen men whose sin will break down the systems. Systems depersonalize people; in God's kingdom they become fully personal remade men. Systems only change conditions; God changes men. Utopian systems, such as Marxism, may in fact demand the same action as Christians desire in a given situation. For the Marxist this will be the solution. For the Christian it can only be a step to cope with the present situation; he will not commit himself to it as a solution. Only God's bringing his Kingdom will be the solution.

THE BIBLICAL MISSION OF THE CHURCH IN WORSHIP, WITNESS, AND SERVICE

Hector Espinoza

PART ONE: The present perplexity concerning the mission of the church

The *"sui generis"* character of the church resides in Jesus, its Lord. The authority of this sovereign is found in all circumstances and all the decisions of this living organism. Nevertheless, the church, being a human structure, the realization of its mission has depended on the image or idea that in fixed time it has made of itself. That image was born of a particular historic situation. The consequence is not completely desirable since the church could stay prisoner of the image it has formed of itself.

There exists uncertainty concerning the mission of the church, caused in part by the enormous tasks with which the church is faced in our days; the unrest, the society in which it develops, and the issues with which it communicates. Before her is presented with unavoidable priority the unfinished task of the proclamation of the Gospel to every creature. In its redemptive role the church nourishes the certainty that each task to be fulfilled represents a glorious opportunity; and that as numerous, urgent, and overbearing as are the issues, tasks, and circumstances that demand its immediate attention, so equally as numerous are the opportunities.

This crisis of the church has not been only caused by the characteristics of the society in which we live, but by the church itself. Hans Kung says that we should not think of, "An ideal church in the abstract spheres of a theological theory, but a real church in the middle of this world and in the history of this world." Neither does the New Testament begin with a doctrine concerning the church that later would be realized, but with the reality of the church concerning that which was reflected upon before. The real church is in the first place, a happening, an act, and an historical event." We are living that reality and confront ourselves with certain issues that reflect the enigma that exists in the business of the church.

1. *Rationalism versus faith* God is found bound earthward in an action of salvation to the world. This work in our days is seen hindered by the confrontation of rationalism and faith. In the first place, thinking is more important than being. Meanwhile for the Christian thinkers like Paul, Augustine, and Pascal, reason should be subordinated to faith. For example, "The justice of God by means of faith in Jesus Christ for all that believe in him. Because there is no difference, inasmuch as all have sinned and come short of the glory of God". "It is not understood in order to believe, it is believed in order to understand"; "the heart has reasons that reason does not know. This is what faith is: God perceptible to the heart, not to reason". For them, then, existence which is in the revealed God precedes thinking.

At first we observe a frequent hesitancy in the work of evangelization. Allowing itself to be carried by the rationalism of an incredulous world, many are dedicated to convincing the people, instead of calling them to believe. Nicolas Berdyaev said that the problem of man originates in the fact that not only does he find himself lost on the way, but he has lost the direction. The Gospel is the good news to that lost and disoriented man so that he might believe in the action of God manifested in Jesus Christ and align himself towards him.

2. *Institutionalism versus personal conversion*

There exist many that, like the Roman Church, make synonyms of evangelization and institutionalization, identifying in this way Christ with the organization of the church in an indissoluble way. The idea is communicated that the invisible spiritual church of the believers is equivalent to the juristical-hierarchical organization of the church.

Basing itself on the authority of dogmas and traditions believed by man, institutionalism precedes personal conversion, and submission to human precepts is demanded in place of the radical transformation of man. The individual is made a servant of the institution, instead of the church being an instrument of life for the sinner.

3. *Politics versus worship*

The definition is heard also of the church as a revolutionary ferment of society. Some denounce with evangelistic passion "the scandalous separation between worship and politics," and based on this, say that the elements of worship as the very structures of the church ought to be instruments of conscientiousness in favor of the emancipation of the disinherited. The *Kerygma* has to center around the physical liberation of the person.

Notoriously absent from the mission of the church conceived by these political agents is the Pauline interpretation of worship as a sacrifice of our bodies "alive, holy, pleasing to God" (Rom. 12:1); the practice of worship as the stimulus "to love and good works" (Heb. 10:24); and the church as the "chosen lineage, royal priesthood, holy nation, people purchased by God," whose mission consists in "announcing the virtues of him who called you from darkness into his marvelous light" (I Pet. 2:9).

4. *Body versus spirit*

For others, the church exists with the end of satiating the physical necessities of the individual. They justify their activism with the well known phrase, "No one will be interested in the Gospel if he has an empty stomach." Saying this, they expose the false base over which their reasoning lies: the piece of bread is going to be the conditioning for the spiritual liberation of man.

Even when it is certain that the church should not negate the right of each man to obtain or receive the necessary material sustenance, under no circumstance should it invert priorities or substitute the temporal for the permanent. Before Christ taught his disciples to pray for "daily bread," he taught them to say, "Thy Kingdom come, thy will be done."

5. *Proselytism versus reconciliation*

For those who understand evangelization as proselytism, the emphasis is fixed on convincing men so that they might be members of their culture, ecclesiology, or religion; or on the other hand, the spiritual conflict is understood as a controversy between "church of the good" and "church of the bad," and he wins who carries off to the other side the most initiates.

In this context the biblical concept of the necessity for all men to be reconciled recedes, and the superiority of the forms of government, the dogmas, or the practices of the church are placed before the word of reconciliation.

6. *Universalism versus sacrifice*

Also there have arisen those who consider the possibility of a unique universal message as the solution to the spiritual problem of humanity. Here they endeavor to adapt the message of Christ to the mentalities of the followers of other religions, and find the similar elements and those of a common denominator that could facilitate their coming together to form from all the religious precepts one sole, universal brotherhood. It is obvious that to obtain such an amalgam, the claims concerning the exclusivity of the ministry and the Gospel made by Christ are obscured, and very specially the notion of sacrifice by him.

7. *Moral obligation versus revelation*

With some frequency we listen to even another alternative to the business of the church among humanity. It is interpreted as the task of succeeding in the moral transcedence of the individual. Dr. Bergmann has well warned us against this danger saying, "Kant excercised a strong influence over generations in the east and the west, the north and the south. We are grateful for it. But the Gospel is not a categorical imperative, neither is it a personal moral achievement. The true nature of the Gospel is based on another thing, that is, the 'revelatio dei' the revelation of God. The Gospel is the reflection of this self-communication of God. Owing to this revelation of God, the Gospel is exclusive and unique. This revelation of God culminates in Jesus Christ, He is the theme of the Gospel. The true nature of the Gospel is found then inseparably united with the true nature of Jesus Christ. And the true nature of Jesus Christ is derived at the same time from the fact that he is the eternal Son of God."

8. *Humanism versus transformation*

The conflict between humanism which saturates the mentality of men of this century and the radical transformation that the Gospel can bring about in a man by the Holy Spirit is distinguished today. It is true that man constitutes the principal preoccupation of the Creator and that the love of God has been focused plainly on the human creature, but it is essential to reflect upon the means which that Creator has laid out to liberate the human being from his condition and follow the plan devised for his spiritual and physical liberation.

Obsessed by an exaggerated, superficial humanistic concept, and interpreting society and its structures as the center of the action of God, some Christian thinkers lately have directed their attention from the church towards these secondary objectives, interpreting them as their mission, and not towards the radical transformation of the human being.

9. *Ghettos versus service communities*

One alternative that has captivated the attention of many is the concept of "the church for others." Based on the theological developments of Bonhoeffer, its basic enunciation at simple view seems to embrace the redemptive, social, humanistic, and spiritual elements for a balanced combination. This idea of the German theologian seems to provide us with the necessary formula to finish once and for all with the desperate and egocentric attitude of the church. In effect, it tends to point out a wholesome way to the destruction of the spiritual ghetto and make the people of God a centrifugal rather than a centripetal community, sending the Christian to serve the world and putting him at the disposal of others.

But if it is certain that the church should not be a privileged ghetto for a select minority, it is also certain that it should not be converted into an agency that reduces into a unique mission helping society in its renovation of the economic, social, and political structures. The service of the people of God, ought to be a continuation of the compassion of Christ for men, as he fed the multitudes after preaching to them the Gospel of the Kingdom, and healed the sick during his exhaustive rounds of preaching about the necessity of all men to come to repentance.

10. *Syncretism versus the message of the Cross*

Between a church which focuses its mission and fixes priority in serving humanity in its political, economic, and social unrest, and syncretism, there exists not more than a step. Entangled in a work of this nature, "the church for others," will soon find itself fighting together with Hindus, Marxists, Agnostics, or Muslims in the conquest for the dignity of man. On this plane, its action will allocate Christ to the vanguard of the fight for the transcendence of the individual, together with Buddha, Mohammed, Marx, or Che Guevarra, but stripping him of the Cross, the empty tomb, and the reconciliation with the Father.

"The great temptation of this century, according to Dr. Visser't Hooft, is syncretism: the human soul is not 'naturally Christian, but naturally syncretistic.' The temptation of syncretism is intensified from the moment that the contemporary world searches for a universal faith. This search is totally legitimate. The preoccupation of all those who are interested in the destiny of mankind, says Dr. Radakrishnan, is 'to give a spiritual base to a world unified by human techniques.' Why not unite, then? At least among the four 'greats' of universalism: Buddhism, Islam, Hinduism and Christianity, to promote the universal religion". We should overcome this great temptation.

11. *Ideologies versus Christian message*

There are many powerful or different ideologies that compete for the attention of modern man, demanding priority in action, citing superiority and desiring to impose their own ideas. Such a cause has as an immediate threat the nullification of the Christian message, the incompletion of the genuine mission of the church, and the subordination of the sovereignty of Christ to the demands of human thinking.

12. *World versus supreme calling*

From other circles a dialogue with the world is urgently required. It is insisted that we permit the world to present to the church the plan to follow in communication. Under this, the church should be preoccupied with the conflicts and uncertainties in the world today. Its action should be directed towards the unrest that the world suffers. If society is discussing economic, political, or racial afflictions, the message of the church should be limited to such necessities. Of secondary importance seems to be that which the church has to say to the world. In this case, the supreme calling delivered to the early Church is wanting in force. Nevertheless, it is urgent that the church sustain within itself the character of the circumstances in which it moves as proclaimer-witness-servant.

13. "Isms" versus repentance

The matters of ecumenism, denominationalism, and others "isms" as primary concern and fundamental mission of the church, is another tension today. The people of God should not lose its calling to repentance for all men and busy itself with temporal and secondary goals.

14. Activism versus redemptive proclamation

In accordance with the first concept, the purpose of the Gospel does not reside in persuasive action, but in the presence of the church in society. The proclamation of the Gospel becomes unnecessary upon understanding that the social changes constitute the mission of God, and that in those transformations of the structures is brought about the advent of the Kingdom of God. We ought to recognize also that others have substituted the organizations, projects, and events of an exaggerated activism in place of the redemptive proclamation of the Good News.

15. Unrest in the world versus eschatological vision

In some cases the Christian has been infected with the restlessness of the world which searches out as a chief end, peace, bread, or conveniences and has lost the eschatological vision of the sovereign reign of Jesus Christ. Before the frantic race of the world to obtain pleasures and passing delights, the voice of the people of God should be that of the Irish hymnist, "Be Thou my vision, oh Lord of my heart."

16. Identification with the world versus identification with Christ

We ought not to contribute to the manouvers of those desiring to manipulate the biblical concept of the identification with Christ and transform it into the identification with the world. If the people of God are called to be converted into an "extension of the incarnation" of Christ, it must be remembered that this finds it highest expression in the Christian discipleship described by the Master as a denial of the self, taking the cross, and going after him.

In view of the perplexity of the church's mission manifested in the penetrative crisis that we have tried to touch upon here, it is good to remember that prior to Christ's visit to the world, God had already been involved in the missionary act by sending his angels to announce the good news of a Savior "who is Christ the Lord," who "will save the people from their sins." Orlando Costas says, "The missionary enterprise finds its foundation in the very character of God. God is a missionary God, who from the beginning goes, and therefore chooses and sends. He is at the same time sender and emissary. It is said of him that he stoops over the earth to see the work of men, separates those who he wants to use as messengers and orders them to go as instruments of his justice, love and peace. The Triune God, who goes ahead in accordance with his purpose, is involved in history and recruits messengers to go everywhere to give testimony of his active presence in history."

It is not the church has imposed the task upon itself. The centrifugal movement originated in God and at the same time has its culmination in him. It is God who sends, it is God who achieves, and it is to God that man must return. By heeding the command, the church participates in the divine effort for the reconciliation between God and man. To that end the Father sent the Son to send his people "and by his means reconciliate with himself all things, those on the earth and those in the heavens, making peace by virtue of the blood of the Cross" (Col. 1:20).

The church has been sent clearly and specifically to "all the nations" (Luke 24:47; Matt. 28:19), to "all the world" (Mark 16:15), and "to the ends of the earth" (Acts 1:9). And its distinctive mission consists unmistakably in "making disciples" (Matt. 28:19), "preaching the Gospel," including on its behalf "repentance and pardon of sins in all nations" (Mark 16:15; Luke 24:47), and acting as "witnesses" (Acts 1:8).

PART TWO: The Biblical mission of the church

The Christian church through the centuries has yielded to being under the strict orders of the worldwide evangelistic pronunciation as it is found recorded in the five books (the four Gospels and the book of Acts) of the New Testament which has been given the name of "the Great Commission." We consider this ordinance and the completion that we can give it in the context of the church as a community that worships, evangelizes and serves.

1. *A community of worship*

Whether we think that the five versions of the "Great Commission" represent one occasion on which it was expressed by the Lord, but afterwards narrated differently by the various writers, or whether we think that during the forty days that transpired between the resurrection and the ascension of the Lord, he repeated the same words in different places with small variations, it is certain that in either case the disciples were found reunited and the vision of Christ produced in them a profound feeling of adoration. This adoration seems to be clearly founded in the reality of the bodily resurrection of Jesus Christ. Worship of the Son of God is subject to the reliability of an historical event. John the apostle wrote, "We have seen him, we have seen him with our own eyes, beheld him and felt our hands touching the Word of life" (I John 1:1).

Of the report concerning the activities of the early church, according to its narrative in the book of Acts, we conclude that this original Christian nucleus was a community that worshipped. A.B. McDonald has written, "They possessed nothing more tangible than their congregations of worship. They had no buildings, no sacred book particular to them, neither a definite creed, nor rules or norms, such as those of Benedict or Bernard — they had nothing, except their worshiping congregations, which served as a stimulus for their loyalties."

In these congregations, the early Christians shared the outcomes of their public testimony ("and as soon as they were discharged went back to their friends and told them everything that the chief priests and elders had said," Acts 4:23), and obtained inspiration and courage for their evangelistic work ("and now, Lord, mark their threats and enable thy servants to speak thy Word with all boldness," Acts 4:29).

Worship is an opportunity for evangelistic witness. Through worship we exalt Christ and present him to an unredeemed world. Why proclaim him to the people without explaining to them who he is? The advice of Paul to the Romans was that they confess with their mouths Jesus Christ as the "Lord," and this means worshiping him and proclaiming him. At the same time our approach in being involved in worship constitutes an eloquent testimony of the faith which unites us, the love that we practice, and the pardon that we share. What the world wants to see is not only identification with him in suffering, injustice, and poverty, but the objective demonstration that we are brothers and are disposed to reunite ourselves around one God only and exalt him as our common Father. Bruce Larson has said, "The ministry of all believers doesn't mean that we should do away with ministers, but rather that we ought to convert ourselves into ministers to serve one another." The Christians who worship under a genuine sense of community, evangelize through their words, example and service.

2. An evangelizing brotherhood

The second element that stands out in the "Great Commission," is the order to evangelize that Christ gave his disciples; and this concept appears in the five books already mentioned, through the use of the three main verbs: *kerussein* ("to proclaim"); *euaggelizesthai* ("to tell the good news"), and *marturein* ("to give testimony"). In these three verbs we find the fullness of the significance of the evangelistic work that Christ charges to his church as an inescapable mission.

The order of evangelizing embraces the idea of proclamation. John Strott reminds us that, "If the majority of versions translate 'that it be preached' well, they treat in reality the Greek word *keruchthenai,* which means 'to be publicly known.' It is found fixed at the beginning of the sentence in Greek, which means that over it falls the main emphasis. The intention of Christ is that a definite message 'be preached' throughout the world, and for this he establishes his church as the messenger of his Gospel."

While in one sector of the church preaching is an obsolete method, for another it constitutes a very important method of evangelization. Without underestimating the ministry of healing the sick, helping the poor, being involved in politics, or participation in causes of social justice, the proclamation is the outstanding element of the Great Commission. Jose D. Camacho has written, "From the point of view of the Christian Church we are looking to expand a bridge over the abyss between the church and the world; the sacred and the secular; the public and the private. We are looking for something that gives cohesion and coherence to an unsettled world and man. How can this succeed? If we take seriously the theological implications of the evangelism of Christ; that is, if we take it seriously as we take the structural, organizational and administrative realities of our society — the powerful structures — we will find the answer."

3. *A body that serves*

A third element we encounter in the Great Commission is that act of witnessing (Acts 1:8; Luke 24:47; John 20:21-23). Christ ordered his disciples to walk the whole world giving testimony of that which they had witnessed. To witness does not only mean to make a verbal announcement, but it ought to include as well the proof of the transformation made in the life of the witness.

It is in this living witness that the church lends it services to the world. It is necessary that the element of service be included as an essential part of the mission of the church, as part of the evangelization that has been commended to it to be fulfilled among all men. Rolando Gutierrez-Cortes wrote, "When Jesus said, 'I have not come to be served but to serve', it was totally a revelation of the dimensions of the heart of God for man. In these words Jesus described the more profound intimacies of the divine purposes, and only when we serve in this same dimension is it that we are united in a Christian activity."

In its service to the world the church should be careful that it does not fall in either of these two extremes: one is the ministering of help to the individual with only evangelistic ends. Regeneration should not only be a "religious" subject, but rather a total transformation of the man should occur, including a change in his attitudes towards his fellow man. Ministering service only as an excuse to bring the unconverted to the church, or to make him accept our religious convictions, is not honest. In the missionary fields of the world much has been suffered by the sincere but mistaken efforts of missionaries who distribute clothing, food, and medicine to those who attend the worship, while impartial service assisting those who suffer oppression, injustice, or pain, remains outside their agenda.

The second extreme of which we should be careful, is thinking that we should leave all social action outside of the proclamation of the Gospel so that it can be effective. It indicates that the proclamation itself is social action. When the Gospel is presented completely and correctly, it has a transforming effect, such that men change their relations with others, rectify their conduct, and openly declare themselves in favor of justice and truth. The great revivals of the past had this characteristic. Men having been transformed in their inner lives, society also experienced a notable change in its action and in its structures.

By means of worship, proclamation, and service, the church should recognize that the mission that its Lord put to them was over all things that of the individual obtaining reconciliation with God. The evangelistic command given to the church should be completed and to this work the church should dedicate its best men, its most valuable resources, and its most ardent prayer.

THE BIBLICAL MISSION OF THE CHURCH IN WORSHIP, WITNESS AND SERVICE REPORT

Discussion among the participants of this group based on the paper by Hector Espinoza reflected the fact that uncertainty and perplexity concerning the mission of the church is indeed a problem faced by the church today. This uncertainty, it was recognized, has its roots in a number of unresolved issues, sixteen of which were outlined in Mr. Espinoza's paper.

Any approach to a solution of this problem must be based upon a fresh, widespread response of the Christian community to the Lord of the church, and such a response may well be considered in terms of worship, witness and service, as the paper suggests.

Many aspects of our uncertainty tend to disappear as the people of God gain a more mature understanding of who God really is, especially as they meet him afresh in the risen Christ. Any true response to the risen Christ vibrates with joy and adoration, as well as reverence. Expressions of worship may involve the gathered community in a particular area, either as whole congregations or in small group settings, or may characterize the expression and attitude of the individual believer. In developing our expression of worship, we should be less concerned about the binding elements of tradition, and more concerned about a joyful response to the Word of God and the Lord of the Word.

It was recognized that worship implies certain essential elements including praise and thanksgiving, confession and affirmation, intercession and petition, proclamation and exposition of Scripture, consecration and commitment and the sacramental celebration of the believing body around the table of the Lord.

Worship should also function as the means by which the people of God are built up in the Spirit in order to move out into the unredeemed world with an authentic, effective witness to the reality of God and to his great love made known to us in Jesus Christ. In the course of worship, even though it is primarily directed to the needs of the believers and represents the Godward expression of the Lord's people, the unbeliever may well catch sight of God and thus be brought to faith.

As believers move out into the world, thus refreshed in their witness to Christ by participation in worship, they are called to reflect the love of Jesus Christ, in their attitudes, their behavior and their explicit witness. The Christian community must remember the Scriptural injunction that all men should recognize the believers by their love and, "By this shall all men know that you are my disciples because ye have love one for another" (John 13:35).

Further effective witness on the part of the church will depend heavily on the involvement of the laity — all the people of God — in the total ministry of the church. This in turn suggests the great need for further recognizing authentic gifts and carefully developing those gifts for the benefit of the whole body. In pursuing this goal we must recognize the beautiful balance between unity and diversity which God has designed for his Body both within and among congregations.

Although different forms of witness may imply different particularized gifts, we believe that all Christians must be concerned with the developing of relationships which draw other people into contact with the believing community and thus eventually into a true corporation with the truth of God in Jesus Christ. It is along such lines of personal relationship that the Gospel usually moves.

Service to the world is the natural outgrowth of any attempt to understand Jesus Christ and his attitude toward mankind. It is impossible to be fully true to Christ and not maintain an attitude of concerned service to the world. We find that needs of people around us tend to define the points where we are called in service to the world.

The Christian is called to honest service, not to a manipulative or condescending reaction to people's needs. The Great Commission, to evangelize, must always be understood within the context of the great commandment, to love. In the acting out of our service to Christ, we recognize the opportunity for the Christian community to play a creative role, especially in building models that the world, including the secular state, can follow. We are thus involved in responding to the needs of the whole man, and the needs of all men.

THE NATURE OF THE UNITY OF THE LOCAL AND UNIVERSAL CHURCH IN EVANGELISM AND CHURCH GROWTH

Jonathan T'ien-en Chao

Dr. Chao, currently studying in Philadelphia, Pennsylvania, USA, is Dean of the China Graduate School of Theology in Hong King.

This is a difficult and "loaded" topic. Whatever position emerges out of it will have serious implications for our current understanding of the church and its missionary enterprise. Due to limitations of time I accepted this assignment reluctantly on condition that it be regarded as an Asian interpretive footnote to the crucial issue.

Our topic stands between Howard Snyder's paper on "The Church as God's Agent of Evangelism" and Henri Blocher's paper on "The Nature of Biblical Unity" — for both of which I am grateful. Our task here is to discover the nature of the unity between local and universal church with particular reference to evangelism which, in the Great Commission context, includes church growth.

Implicit in this subject also are such pressing missiological issues confronting evangelicals today as the following: (i) In the light of our understanding of the nature of this unity, what should be the role of the foreign missionary in relation to the emerging national churches in the Third World? (ii) Do foreign missions have the right to operate independently of the local national church, or to bypass it if the latter is not doing a good job in evangelism? (iii) What implications does this study have on the validity or continuity of culture-bound para-church structures such as denominations in the "mission field" today? These and many more related questions demand nothing less than a re-examination of some of the most basic presuppositions of the evangelical missionary enterprise hitherto yet unchallenged.

PART ONE: Local and universal churches: their relationship and unity

The term "local church" is generally understood as the local congregation, whether denominational, state-related, or independent churches. Often it is used correlatively. In the missiological context, local churches refer to the national "younger churches" planted by a sending church which is often called the "universal church." Within a denominational context, the worldwide church of the denomination is regarded as the universal church.

The meaning of "universal church" is further complicated by the term "invisible church," with which it is often used interchangeably. Here the correlative of the invisible church is the "visible church," which refers to the organized institutional church. Augustine was probably the first to introduce the concept of the "invisible church" as "the true body of Christ" to which all believers belong, even though one might not be a member of a "visible" organized church. Reformed theologians since Wycliffe and Calvin have defined it in terms of predestination as "the totality of the predestined," including the saints who died and the elect who are not yet converted. Lutherans since Luther and Melanchthon have defined it in terms of justification as "the total believerhood now living on earth." They are found in the institutional churches, but their identity could not be discovered by man. How then shall we determine the nature of the unity of the local and universal church if we have so many variant definitions for the latter term? Should we regard it as the invisible elect or the unidentifiable believerhood or the sectarian denominational world church or the "sending church" of a particular locality? As our concern is with unity for evangelism, neither the invisible "elect" nor the unidentifiable "faithful" would do. On the other hand, we can hardly be satisfied with regarding denominational world churches or sending churches as our working definition for "universal church." We must, therefore, go to the New Testament for the basic definition of *ecclesia,* the church, and from there deduce the scriptural equivalents to the terms "local church" and "universal church."

1. *Union with Christ: the christological unity of the church*

The most comprehensive New Testament definition of *ecclesia* is simply "the assembly of God in Christ Jesus" (I Thess. 2:14; Gal. 1:22; I Cor. 1:2). Howard Snyder's definition of the church as "the community of God's people" is very close to it. This simple formula has three essential components of the church: (i) the people assembled; (ii) God who assembles them; and (iii) "in Christ," the sphere into which they are assembled.

Howard Snyder has clearly expounded the church as the community of God's people. There is very little controversy on this point. Neither is there any serious argument on the church as the assembly of God, called out from the world by God the Father through the Gospel. It is "in Christ" that the nature of the unity of the church is to be found.

"In Christ" is the richest theological concept and soteric reality in the New Testament. Believers are incorporated into Christ through faith in him and signified by baptism. Thus Paul speaks of all believers as being baptized into Christ, into his death, and into his resurrection (Rom. 6:3-4). To be baptized "into Christ" is also to be baptized "into the body of Christ" (I Cor. 12:13). Thus union with Christ is also union with the body of Christ; for Christ and his body are one. From Romans 5-8 we know clearly that evangelism is essentially the act of God in his transferring his people from "in Adam" to "in Christ" through the

proclamation of the Gospel in the power of the Holy Spirit. This transference takes place on an individual basis, which we call "personal
conversion." Thus first and foremost the people of God stand in covenantal relationship to God "in Christ Jesus." Therein they receive forgiveness of sin, justification, sanctification, and life, which is none
other than the receiving of the Holy Spirit. Union with Christ is, therefore, the basis and nature of the unity of all the people of God.

Although God calls his people into Christ by name, one by one individually, he does not call them to isolated individualistic existence.
In Christ he creates a new humanity; in him he forms a new community,
and fills it with his living Spirit so that the new christological humanity
becomes a living community of his own. They are called from the world
of sin, in time and space. Where they are called, there they are assembled
into a new community in that locality, and he dwells in their midst
through the Holy Spirit. Thus we find Paul addressing the churches in
the New Testament in terms of "to the church of God in Christ Jesus
which is in Galatia, in Corinth, in Philippi, in Colossae, in Rome, etc."
(I Cor. 1:2; II Cor. 1:2; Gal. 1:1; Phil. 1:1; Col. 1:2; Rom. 1:7). Paul
further equates "the church of God in Christ Jesus" with "the saints
in Christ Jesus who are in..." (Phil. 1:1, 4:21; Eph. 1:1; Col. 1:2). Likewise Peter addressed the saints who were exiled in Pontus, Galatia,
Cappadocia, Asia, etc. (I Pet. 1:1-2).

The emphasis in the apostolic usage of the term *ecclesia* is definitely
more God's people-oriented than congregation-oriented. The locality
is rather incidental: wherever the people of God are called and congregated, they are called the assembly of God in that place. New Testament evangelism is God's calling out of his people from the world. It
is not "church planting." Thus the stress is more on a vertical relationship between the God who calls and the people who respond to his
call than on a horizontal relationship of missionary church extension
from one denominational sending church to its "receiving church."

Thus viewed, each local church or local assembly of God in Christ
Jesus is God's possession. Each is on a parity with the other. Each is a
community of God's people, and the totality of the people of God's
people is also God's people. Herein we find the nature of the unity of
the local church and the Body of Christ, which is the biblical equivalent
for the term "universal church." The nature of that unity is basically a
unity of a part in relation to its whole. In other words, the local church
as "the saints who are in Christ" is an integral part of the entire body
of Christ. It appears that the problem is not so much the unity of the
local church in relation to the entire body of Christ as the unity of one
local church to another as fellow group-members of the same body.
The question is not what is the nature of the unity between the church
of Corinth and the Body of Christ, but what is the nature of the unity
between "the Church of God in Christ Jesus which is in Corinth" and
the "Church of God which is in Philippi"? To bring the question closer
to home, the question is, "What is the nature of the unity between the
Presbyterian Church on Third and Walnut Streets and the Methodist
Church on Second and Walnut Streets in hundreds of towns?"

The nature of the unity among local churches is essentially an ontological unity by virtue of their union with Christ as the people of God. It is, therefore, a christological unity. By virtue of their union with Christ, the people of God in these local churches also receive the Spirit of Christ, the Holy Spirit. Hence the nature of the unity among local churches as the people of God is also a pneumatic (spiritual) unity. These are the "given" realities "in Christ Jesus" which believers are urged to preserve and experience as members of the same body.

2. *Solidarity of the Body: the context of pneumatic unity of the church*

The New Testament is very clear that although Christ is one and his body is one, the body has many members (Rom. 12:4-5; I Cor. 12: 12-26, Eph. 4:15-16). This is necessarily so because the people of God are individual "saints." Just as the totality of the people of God in Christ Jesus is regarded as one body, so each local church is also called "the body of Christ" (I Cor. 12:27), and each saint members one of another. Oneness of the body is an ontological unity by virtue of its union with Christ, and the multiplicity of its members provides the diversity of ministry within the body.

The unity of the body is characterized by its unity of purpose: obedience to its head, Jesus Christ, "growing into Christ" (Eph. 4:15), and being transformed into his likeness (II Cor. 3:18). This is done through the mutual ministry of the members through the diverse gifts of the Holy Spirit. All exercises are "for the common good," toward the upbuilding of the body in love. This is why prophecy is regarded as the most desired of all gifts (I Cor. 14:1, 12, 22).

The unity of the body, and hence of the unity of the local churches in relation to each other, finds its functional unity in the Trinity: (i) one Spirit, but diversities of gifts; (ii) one Lord, but diversities of rule; (iii) one God, but diversities of operation (I Cor. 12:4-6). In real practice unity among local churches — whether within the same block or within the same region, or between churches cross-culturally, even "functional unity in evangelism" — can be achieved only through their joint submission to the rule of the Lord Jesus, appreciating the diverse gifts given by the Holy Spirit, and allowing diverse forms of operation as God chooses. God in his sovereignty delights in diversities within his Spirit of unity. This should warn us from desiring any kind of uniformity, for in so doing one might be working against the work of God. Spiritual discernment and spiritual submission seem to be the required guidelines for preserving unity while allowing diversities. Obedience is an art! That art is for all members to discover the mind of Christ and learn to "be of the same mind" (Rom. 12:16, 15:5-6; I Cor. 1:10; II Cor. 13:11; Eph. 4:3; Phil. 1:27, 2:2, 3:16). This identity of mind among so many members, so many different individuals, is an impossibility on the human level, but it is possible when they are governed by love with body-building as their goal in obedience to the Holy Spirit. Thus the unity of one local church with another is a unity of obedience and a unity of love, the real visible manifestation of the Christo-somatic unity of the church with its pneumatic-charismatic diversities.

PART TWO: *The implications of Christo-somatic unity of the church for evangelism and church growth*

1. *The Great Commission: the common task of the church*

Within evangelical Christianity today there is a tendency to separate evangelism and missions. The former usually refers to local evangelism, and that latter to cross-cultural evangelism. There is also a tendency to absolutize missions to the devaluation of the local church, be it the sending church or the "receiving church." This is probably a result of inadequate theological understanding of the Christological and somatic nature of the church on the one hand and the influence of the institutional-ization of foreign missions during the last two hundred years on the other hand. There is also a tendency to dichotomize "evangelism" from "church growth."

Students of the Greek text all know clearly that the command in Matt. 28:19-20 is "make disciples of all nations," a command that is to be carried out by (i) baptism into the name of the Father, Son, and Holy Spirit, and (ii) teaching them to observe all things that Jesus commanded his disciples, the chief of which is the commandment of love. These are nothing less than incorporating the believers into Christ and into his body, and helping them to experience the body life of love as the people of God. "Going" is a necessity in making disciples, but it is not the imperative; it is discipling which unites evangelism and church growth into one united task.

Likewise Peter declares that the people of God as a whole are charged with the great commission responsibility of declaring the mighty deeds of God in his work of salvation (I Pet. 2:9). It is true that in Matt. 28:19-20 Jesus was addressing the disciples who were to become apostles, and it is also true that in the early church Christ gave "lead-ership gifts" (apostles, prophets, teachers, evangelists, pastors, and teachers), but even they carried out their ministry within the context of the body of the church. The church as the people of God and as a whole was to carry out the evangelistic mandate of Christ. These observations point us to the fact that God chose the concrete local church as the body of Christ to carry out his redemptive will. We should, therefore, give more significance to the local church as the basic unit of body life and as the primary base for evangelistic out-reach. All members of the local Body of Christ have this evangelistic mandate, and all local churches as group-members of the total body of Christ have the same evangelistic mandate. Is this not the nature of the unity of the local church and the universal church in evangelism? It is a unity of task based on the unity of nature.

2. *The local church: the focus of challenge for unity in evangelism*

The term local church as used here means "the assembly of God's people in (a specified) place." That means we are referring to some-thing more than a local congregation in its institutional form. What then should be the unity of the people of God in a certain locality in their common evangelistic task? In terms of current Protestant institutional set-up, this would mean, "What should be the unity of the people of God in the twenty-odd congregations that belong to seven or eight different denominations, including the Catholics and the Green Orthodox brethren, in their common task of evangelism in that town?" If members of these congregations recognize their Christo-somatic unity, if they truly love each other as members of the same body, and if they are truly desirous to carry out their missionary responsibility in obedience to Christ, then they would be able to discover the mind of Christ for their evangelistic task. In fact, many churches of differing denominational affiliations do cooperate in joint evangelistic campaigns. But they seldom join together as one body in the exercise of their body life. A disjunction between evangelism and body building is sustained. This example illustrates the tremendous challenge for unity in body-building and evangelism on a limited regional level.

If a Presbyterian, a Methodist, a Baptist, and a Catholic happen to find themselves to be the only four born-again Christians in their neighborhood from which there are no other churches within fifty miles, and they desire to have fellowship as well as evangelism, what should they do? Should they each try to seek commission from their individual denominations and each start a "mission station" named after their denominations and work separately, sending reports to their "home churches?" Or should they join together as the people of God, build up each other, and preach Jesus to their neighbors? The answer seems so obvious, doesn't it? But the history of Protestant missions from the West is filled with agonizing and heartbreaking records of denominational agents trying to carry out their evangelistic task separately, each seeking to "plant" his own denomination churches to the great confusion of both new converts and non-Christians.

The challenge of the hour for effective worldwide evangelization is to work out real spiritual and visible unity among local churches in each locality. In the final analysis the nature of the unity of the people of God in Christ poses an unavoidable challenge to current denominational and other "para-church" divisions on the local level, especially in the mission fields. While denominational boundaries are being justified as "para-church" structures, it cannot be denied that they are not mere cultural wineskins that "aid" the mission of the church, but are actual barriers to a greater realization of the meaning of the somatic unity of the people of God in Christ in their common life and mission.

3. *The local (national) church and foreign missions*

Here we are confronted by the challenge of cross-cultural somatic unity in evangelism. What should be the role of foreign missionaries in a land where local national churches have already been established? How can the continuing role of the foreign missionary be scripturally validated? J. Robertson McQuilkin sought to validate it along traditional and pragmatic lines, "So long as the evangelistic mandate has not been completed, the Church of Jesus Christ has need for representatives with evangelistic ability to which it may delegate this responsibility."

He advocates that a missionary is sent by a sending church, not called by a receiving church. Furthermore, he advocates that missions should bypass the national church if the latter is not an aid in completing the evangelistic mandate.

C. Peter Wagner is even more vocal in advocating that foreign missions should bypass the national church if the latter is not doing a good job. He seems to assume the legitimacy of the independent existence of missions, and he outlines a "mission-world" structure as the nature and ultimate objective of missions. He seems to mean that disciple-making is the same as conversion, "Disciples are made, not in the church, but in the world." He likens the church to an automobile that takes a person from New York to Pennsylvania. If the car runs well, fine. If the carburetor plugs or the transmission goes out "the car turns out to be a hindrance and you realize you would have accomplished your objective of reaching Pennsylvania better if you had taken the train," He seems to regard the church as a *means* to missions and that the church is disposable or may be bypassed. Clearly this is an evidence of the influence of American pragmatism on missionary strategy.

Can foreign missions bypass the national church if we examine this question from the nature of the unity of members of the Body of Christ as developed above? Should we permit a pragmatic approach to cross-cultural missionary strategy, especially when it concerns such a large segment of the Body of Christ in the Third World? Both Wagner and McQuilkin (and probably many others) seem to have failed to recognize the clear biblical teaching that the emerging national churches in the mission field are integral parts of the Body of Christ to which they belong, members who need the ministry of representatives of the churches in the West and whose ministry they need in carrying out an effective evangelistic outreach in that land. McQuilkin identified the sending church as the "church universal." Both failed to see that both the sending church and the receiving church are members of the Body of Christ, the true church universal; both are essentially local churches. As such they are on *a parity* with each other, equal in status and glory. Christ died for both. Does a missionary sent by one local church to a place where another local church is also seeking to serve her Lord have the right to ignore the latter or simply bypass it? Since the Holy Spirit ministers to each local church, would that not also be bypassing the bodily ministry of the Holy Spirit or bypassing the Lordship of Christ? Can the eye say to the foot "I have no need of you?" Should a stronger member of the body ignore the inferior part or the weaker part to whom God has given the greater honor? (I Cor. 12:22-23). The biblical doctrine of the unity of the body and the diversity of its members does not warrant such a pragmatic policy which is contrary to the explicit teachings of Scripture.

The missionary, in addition to his being a missionary, is ontologically and functionally a member of the local Body of Christ. As such he needs the ministry of the body, and wherever he might be, he is obliged to minister to other members of the same body. Although he might be sent by his "home church," he is not an evangelist unless he is given the gift of an evangelist by the Spirit of Christ. All such "leadership gifts" are gifts to the church-at-large for the work of the ministry of the church, including evangelism. If *he* is a *gift* of the Holy Spirit, the local national church, in whom the same Spirit resides, would and should recognize such gift and would welcome such gift from the same Spirit. Thus the national local church as the Body of Christ is the agent for the verification of the missionary's gifts, and hence the validity of his being sent by the Lord. The local national church also has the right to discern whether such a missionary is a true prophet or a false prophet. Therefore it seems proper that when a missionary is sent to a land where there already exists local national churches the sending church should give the local church in the foreign field appropriate introduction of the missionary being sent. The missionary, as a member of the new Body of Christ, should submit himself to the authority of Christ administered through the local national church in love, unless he is sent to a pioneer situation. Apollos submitted himself to the local church at Ephesus and was ministered to and corrected by Priscilla and Aquila. As he departed from Ephesus he was sent away with the blessing and recommendation of the brethren at Ephesus" (Acts 18:25-28). Paul, the missionary, had the intention of evangelizing Rome. So he wrote the saints in Rome expressing his desire to see them, "That I might impart to you some spiritual gift to strengthen you." Then he quickly added, "That is, that we may be mutually encouraged by each other's faith, both yours and mine" (Rom. 1:11-12).

Such is the validity of the role of a missionary in a land where the saints already reside. The missionary has a "right" to go to a land where a national church exists, not on the basis of political treaty rights as in the case of China, but by virtue of his membership in the body of Christ, which entitles him to his membership in the local body of Christ, the national church. He may minister to the saints within the church or he may evangelize outside the church in accordance with the gifts that are given to him by the Spirit and as discerned by the Christ-ordained authority deposited in the local national church. A missionary should not be made responsible only to his sending church, but also, and even more so, to the local national church.

By virtue of a missionary's membership in the body of Christ, and in view of the Christo-somatic unity of all the people of God, the local national church has no right to say to the missionary "Go home!" on account of his racial difference. The national local church should regard the missionary as a brother with certain gifts, and encourage him to exercise his spiritual gifts for the upbuilding of the body and for reaching out to the non-Christians. This Christo-somatic approach to the church mission relationship will also necessarily invalidate C. Peter Wagner's "church development syndrome" theory. As an Asian I welcome any missionary whose gifts from the Spirit of God have been validated by the local national church's verification. I will also welcome him as a brother in Christ in whom we are united and with whom we share a common task and a common destiny.

By the same token of the nature of the unity of local transcultural churches in Christ, I am inclined to say that foreign missions have no right "in Christ" to extend their administrative authorities to the local national churches as in the case of Western administration of younger churches in the mission field. Missions must learn to recognize the rightful rule of Christ over all of his churches. Similarly we may question the right of missions to import para-church structures to the mission field, though this is not the place to discuss it.

The nature of the unity between the local national church and foreign missions/churches is identical with that of fellow local churches within the same culture: members of the body of Christ whose unity is rooted in Christ. Cross-cultural evangelism too, must be carried out as the task of the body.

PART THREE: Visible unity, schism, and evangelism

Visible unity has been often understood in terms of organizational unity. This has marked the history of the ecumenical movement since 1910. It is interesting to observe that the movement began with an evangelistic concern and was successful while it was under the leadership of the International Missionary Council. It was a remarkable expression of modern Protestant search for unity for the purpose of evangelism.

Modern evangelicals of recent years have insisted that unity is not necessarily organizational unity, and certainly not uniformity, but rather a "spiritual unity." Having said that they have done very little to realize a visible functional expression of spiritual unity. For our present purposes, what then is the relation between visible unity and evangelism?

1. Visible unity is the means to evangelism

Jesus, at the eve of his glorification, gave a new covenantal commandment to his disciples, "Love one another . . . by this shall all men know that you are my disciples . . . ." (John 13:34-35). Mutual love among the disciples is to be *the* trade mark of those whose master is Jesus. Love is the expression of unity and, in the believers, love is a fruit of the Holy Spirit. It seems that Jesus wants to attract the world to himself through the disciples' display of a new life style of love. Unity and love in the believers provide the incentives to non-believers for desiring to become disciples of Jesus. Thus unity is the best means to evangelism. Love is a visible expression of unity, which validates the Gospel as authentic.

2. Schism: a visible disunity that hinders evangelism

When I showed Dr. R. Pierce Beaver the assignment letter of this paper he commented: "More and more I am convinced that exported divisiveness is the greatest hindrance to the spread of the Gospel in the non-Christian world." There are currently at least three theories on unity and schism:

a. *That there can be no effective witness to the world without visible organizational unity.* The ecumenical wing of Protestantism is still pushing this form of visible unity. This attempt, however, has created a widening gulf between ecumenicals and evangelicals. We must ask, "To what extent is such form of visible unity warranted by Scripture? Has the resultant hierarchical centralization of authority in some way usurped the Lordship of Christ? How much has this attempt built up the body of Christ as a demonstration of love?"

b. *That there can be no visible unity without doctrinal unity.* This is the Reformed and fundamentalist position. It is a continuation of the Protestant confessional mentality. However, the scriptural teaching is that the church should chase out false teachers rather than withdraw from a fellowship. But many evangelicals have, in American church history, withdrawn from larger churches that tolerated "liberals." Furthermore, doctrinal unity is the *goal* of church growth, not the condition of evangelism and church growth (Eph. 4:3, 13). This priority of doctrinal integrity over mutual love of the body members has been a cause of schism within the body, and thereby weakens both the task force and the witness of the body for evangelism.

c. *That unity in the form of cooperation may be expected in direct proportion to the degree of doctrinal agreement.* This is a kind of compromise of the above two extremes, but still basically adopting a "doctrinal integrity" approach to this problem. May we not ask, "In addition to doctrinal integrity, should we not apply the doctrine of the unity of the Body in Christ which demands love as another criterion for participating in visible forms of unity?"

3. *Schism: a breach of the New Covenant*

Schism is visible disunity. It disrupts the fulfillment of Christo-somatic unity and the love life of the body. As a factious spirit, it is essentially a breach of love, resulting in spiritual separation from other members of the body of Christ. It is a direct contradistinction of Paul's teaching on the interdependence of members of the Body of Christ (I Cor. 12:32). As such it is a denial of the integrity of the body, a rejection of those for whom Christ died. It is an assertion of the autonomous spirit for independent existence away from the other members of the Body of Christ and a usurpation of the Lordship of Christ.

Schism is a self-imposed termination of spiritual fellowship with other parts of the Body of Christ, depriving oneself of the benefits of mutual ministry of members. As a rejection of the ministry of other members it is a form of rejection of the ministry of the Holy Spirit.

Schism is a member or a group of members' declaration to refuse to love the Body of Christ. This breach of love is basically a breach of the new covenant; it is declared disobedience to the new commandment, resulting in self-deprivation of the richer blessings of the new covenant.

Conclusion

The real issue confronting evangelicals worldwide today is not so much finding out the nature of the unity of the local church in relation to the universal church as the body of Christ, but understanding the nature of the unity among local churches within a given locality. The nature of that unity is an ontological, Christological unity by virtue of

believers' union with Christ. It is also a somatic unity within the body of
Christ and with fellow members of the body. The greatest challenge
today is to manifest that unity in the local churches and in the mission
field between missionaries and national churches.

With particular reference to evangelism and church growth, the
nature of the unity among churches is one of common task and common
purpose. Biblical evangelism is both initial evangelism terminating in
conversion and church growth aiming at the upbuilding of the body
through the mutual ministry of its members. This is true for all churches,
cross-cultural situation making no difference.

Mutual love and ministry within the body-life must be sought as
the criterion for the development of visible forms of unity for effective
evangelism. It should also be a deterrent to schism.

The evangelical world must re-examine its para-church structures
in the light of the nature of the unity among local churches. Denominationalism as a significant form of schism is a barrier to the proper
function of the body life for evangelism and church growth.

THE NATURE OF THE UNITY OF THE LOCAL AND UNIVERSAL CHURCH IN EVANGELIZATION AND CHURCH GROWTH REPORT

Chairman: John Reid
Secretary: R. Colenian

Nature of church unity. The church, witnessing to the triumph of God's sovereign grace, comprises a community of the redeemed. In union with Christ every person is related through the Spirit to every other member of his body. Each member is vital to the whole. Clearly the church is one, for Christ cannot be divided against himself.

This unity embraces Christ's world mission. Here was the focal point of his own life and work. There are diversities of gifts, but every part of the body participates in his ministry to the world, sharing the common mandate to "make disciples."

As long as we speak of this in theoretical terms, no one takes offense. Problems become apparent when visibility is given to our unity, both in structure and ministry. This is particularly apparent when viewing the multiplicity of conflicting para-church organizations and forms of ministry.

However, it was stressed that unity is not to be confused with uniformity. Merely having different groupings and procedures does not discredit the unity of the Spirit. God seems to like variety (even in heaven there are twelve kinds of fruits). Let us recognize this diversity and be grateful. Our differences can complement the church and serve to make us all more aware of our interdependence within the body.

The point made was that visible unity is not determined by organizational affiliation but by our inner life in the Spirit. Disunity may exist on any level of corporate life. Still, as an ideal we should seek to maximize the reality of true spiritual unity in the larger expressions of Christian commitment. With this in mind, perhaps we should re-examine our para-church structures, asking whether they frustrate the manifestation of visible unity, body life and evangelism.

The local community in united outreach. Unity of the church finally has its most dynamic focus within a given community, of which the local congregation is the primary base for fellowship, teaching the Word, administering the sacraments, and for evangelistic outreach. Here the love displayed for one another, the exercise of spiritual gifts, and the building up of the body in the stature of Christ creates a compelling witness to the watching world. For this reason, any blemish to this appeal constitutes a serious barrier to communication of the Gospel.

An obvious infraction of this rule, noted by several in the seminar, is to admit into full fellowship persons who evidence no personal conversion. This practice only dilutes the witness of the church and confuses the unbeliever.

The absence of genuine commitment to the work of evangelism was also posed as a real hindrance to unity. Many members of the local church do not understand their priesthood, nor have any personal involvement in fulfilling the Great Commission. Where this is true, the unifying obedience to Christ's command is missing.

What is said here applies to believers from every congregation of the community. The members of the body of Christ need to express their unity across artificial structures of denominations demonstrating in the marketplace of their own world that they are one. Ways can be found by which this can be done, such as public rallies, cooperative efforts in Scripture distribution, joint prayer meetings, singing in the streets, sharing groups in homes and together facing burning social issues.

Probably the greatest need and opportunity for such a united voice comes in the area of evangelism, for it is here that the church confronts the basic problem of lost men. What more practical expression of love can we give to the world? Little wonder that when evangelism becomes a controlling passion, people from widely different confessions and traditions find themselves working together. A number in the seminar cited examples in their own experience where some evangelistic program became the focus around which the community of God's people were unified.

Schism within the church. What about those who find no unifying attraction within a church and leave? Obviously this is a recurring problem. Considerable attention was directed to it by this seminar.

Schism occurs where there is a visible separation from the body fellowship. It demonstrates to the world a basic disharmony within the church and therefore reflects upon her witness. Everyone was agreed that schism should be avoided if at all possible.

Only apostasy was recognized as justification for such drastic action. Where such teaching is suspected, the church should make every effort to correct the erring member. If the matter cannot be resolved, then the body has the obligation to put out the heretic.

The question was raised: What if the majority of the fellowship have sympathy with the false doctrine? At this point, schism may be the only course left for those who remain faithful to this truth. However, let it be clear that the issue is of fundamental substance. Even in this event, others of the same conviction may remain within the apostate para-church in order to continue their witness in evangelism.

Members of the seminar were mindful of their own limited knowledge, particularly in ascertaining the position of divergent parts of the church fellowship. We affirmed that love is the first step toward experiencing greater unity in Christ. For this we prayed that God would give us wisdom tempered with humility in the bonds of Christ, our Lord.

THEOLOGIES OF PRESENCE, DIALOGUE, AND PROCLAMATION

David Gitari

Dr. Gitari, Nairobi, Kenya, is General Secretary of the Bible Society of Kenya.

1. *Presence*

"Christian presence" is a post-World War II term popularized in the mid-60s by publication of a statement entitled "The Christian Community in the Academic World" published by the World Student Christian Federation. The term was originally made current by Roman Catholic priests who tried to find a new approach to evangelize France. The priests sought to engage themselves in the life of the people as workers in industry, etc. The term was later extended to include "involvement in the concrete structure of the society."

The advocates of "Christian presence" believe that this term expresses most satisfactorily the center of Christian faith and our response to it. It is the term which should replace the traditional terms such as mission, evangelism, and witness. Biblical foundations of the term have been formulated, and a theology of presence is in the making.

a. *Biblical roots of presence.*

(i) *Shekinah* is a word used in the Old Testament to describe the Jewish "over-whelming sense" of the presence of God.

(ii) In *Exod. 3:1-14* Yahweh reveals his name as "I am who I am." "Yahweh" means precisely "He who is present" being present, "He will be seen and known for what he is in the situation as men become aware of his presence and act accordingly as Moses did while at work among the thorn bushes."

(iii) In *Psa. 139:7-12* we find that "man cannot run away from the presence of God."

(iv) In *John's Gospel*, Jesus Christ is the Shekinah who became flesh and dwelt among men in grace and truth. He is the "I am" who is also sent to fill men with his presence and send them out to preach the Gospel (20:19-23). The theologians of "Christian presence" find the support of their position in John's thinking. They see in this Gospel a close relationship between "presence" and "witness" or "mission." The incarnation is described by John as the becoming of flesh or as the "word becoming flesh and dwelling among us."

b. *Practice of Christian presence in evangelism.*

(i) The application of Christian presence in evangelism is probably best expressed in the WSCF statement which says:

> "We use the word 'Presence' to describe the adventure of being there in the name of Christ, often anonymously, listening before we speak, hoping that men will recognize Jesus for what he is and stay where they are, involved in their fierce fight against all that dehumanizes, ready to act against demonic powers, to identify

with the outcasts, merciless in ridiculing modern idols and new myths. When we say 'Presence' we say that we have to get in the midst of the things that frighten us. Once we are there, we are to witness fearlessly to Christ if the occasion is given; we may also have to be silent. Presence for us means 'engagement' in the concrete structures of our society.' It indicates a priority. First we have to be there before we can see our task clearly. In one sense of the word presence precedes witness. In another sense, the very presence is witness."

(ii) Closely associated with "Christian presence" is what Gilbert Rist calls "Theology of Silence." He defines silence as the proclamation of the Gospel "without religious vocabulary and without the use of conceptual apparatus which is customary in traditional theology." Rist goes so far as to assert that "the word of God which we must witness is not first of all a collection of Scriptural quotations, nor even of the sayings of Jesus (for this would be a return to fundamentalism): It is Jesus himself. This is why we must often refrain at first from mentioning the name of Jesus Christ . . . this is the silence which Jesus Christ commanded his disciples to keep on the subject of his Messiahship" (cf. Matt. 17:9; Mark 1:43). What is important, according to Rist, is to "preach Christ, without talking about him, to bring him to life for others without imprisoning him in our words."

(iii) Kenneth Cragg in his missionary approach to the Muslims represents a particular emphasis on Christian presence. His approach may be summarized as "unveiling the Presence of Christ." For Cragg, the missionary task is the unveiling of the hidden Christ who is already present in the religious man. This emphasis is derived from the Johannine interpretation of the relationship between Christ the Creator and Christ the Redeemer. Cragg tries to enter into the Muslim experience by being involved in a divine-human relationship. From within Islam he raises the question of what surrender to God really means. This question implies the quest for redemption. Using Islamic symbols, Cragg tries to reinterpret the Christocentric view of human surrender to God. In this way Cragg, who takes the Muslim faith seriously, tries to demonstrate that Christ is not a stumbling-block but a fulfiller of Islam. According to this interpretation of "Christian presence" the missionary is urged to try from within the framework of religious systems to relate the faith of religious man to Christ. The missionary should "unveil Christ who is already present in the religious experience of the man he is trying to reach." Cragg's approach has had a great appeal among many missionaries and scholars.

c. *Critique of the theology of presence*

(i) The word "presence" is rather passive and static. Christian evangelism cannot satisfactorily be expressed by this term. The Hebrew word "Shekinah" which is translated "presence" in English, and the

Greek word "Parousia" (that which is present and is to come) have a more dynamic sense than the English word "presence." God's great word of self-revelation in Exod. 2:13-14 is not a static word. Its Hebrew dynamism was diluted by the Septuagint translators, for God reveals his name not merely as "I am" but as the active God who "shall be what I shall be" or "I shall continue to be what I shall continue to be." God reveals himself as the living God, the active, creative saving God whose presence is always dynamic.

The advocates of "Christian presence" realize the shortcomings of this word and attempt to explain it in terms of "being present does not mean we are merely there." Similarly lengthy definitions are made so as to make the theology of presence sound plausible. "The witness of silence," we are told, "is not one of mutism. We must still speak, but we must not become punch-drunk with words . . . True silence is in speaking." This is merely playing with words.

(ii) John Arthur criticizes "Christian presence" for being "so sure of the righteousness of its social goals but so reticent about any explicit witness to Jesus Christ as Savior of the world." The Christian presence theologians criticize words such as evangelism, witness, and mission because "they suggest certainty of faith and purpose. . . ." Arthur remarks that "if the Christian student of today is supposed to be unsure about his faith and purpose, then he is quite unlike other revolutionaries with whom he is to join to fight against dehumanization and demonic powers."

(iii) Statements about "Christian presence" seem to lack confidence about witness to Christ. We are urged to be present with a hope that "man will recognize Jesus for what he is and we will witness if occasion is given and we will be there in the name of Christ but often anonymously." Whereas the rest of the revolutionaries (be they Marxists, Nazis, hippies, etc.) do not hesitate to be identified with their heroes, the Christian is told not to start by proclaiming the name of Jesus, nor declare that he knows him, lest he sound empirical about his knowledge; but rather "to be present anonymously, for presence precedes witness and in another sense the very presence is witness." The Christian is often advised to be silent, and refrain from mentioning the name of Christ, and to preach Christ without talking about him. Theologians of Christian presence would find it difficult to say with Paul, "I am not ashamed of the Gospel: for it is the power of God for salvation to everyone who has faith. . . ." (Rom. 1:16).

(iv) The practice of Christian presence in evangelism has its value if it is not taken to be an end in itself. As a preliminary towards proclamation it is valuable. It calls the evangelist to remember that he is not necessarily preaching in a vacuum. Cragg's approach of unveiling "the presence of Christ" is not entirely unbiblical. It reminds us of Paul's encounter with the religious Athenians and his effort to "proclaim the God who made the world and everything in it, whom they had hitherto considered as 'the unknown God.'" The Christian message was viewed by Paul as a fulfiller of the Athenians' religious longings. He unveils the God who remains unknown in man's effort to understand him. Cragg's practice of Christian presence is different from the theology of silence. Indeed it is unfortunate that he should call his approach "Christian presence." He chooses to live amid Muslims in order to understand their faith, and using Islamic symbols he courageously proclaims the redeeming power of Jesus Christ.

2. Dialogue

Dialogue is a non-biblical term which has become a key concept in contemporary missionary thought and is regarded as the basis of all ecumenism. It has been defined as "any honest confrontation between adherents of different religions where the participants meet and challenge each other testifying to the depths of their own experiences to what stands forth as being of ultimate concern." Since the 1938 Tambaram controversy centered around Hendrik Kraemer's epoch-making volume *The Christian Message in a Non-Christian World,* dialogue has been brought to the forefront of missionary discussions. Among its chief advocates are Asian Christian thinkers such as Dr. P.D. Devandan and Dr. D.T. Niles who were driven into this concept as a reaction against Kraemer's evangelistic approach and his Barthian emphasis upon revelation from God. In Eastern Europe, J.L. Hromadka's spearheaded dialogue with Marxists; in the West, Bonhoeffer indirectly paved the way for Christian dialogue with secular man.

a. *Need for dialogue.*

(i) *Christians in a pluralistic society.* Dialogue is said to be necessary because Christians everywhere are living in a pluralistic society. It is urgent because all men are under common pressures in search for justice and peace, and are faced with the challenge to live together as human beings. Dialogue is full of opportunity because "Christians can now, as never before, discover the meaning of the Lordship of and the implications for the mission of the church in a truly universal context of common living and common urgency."

(ii) *To save the church from itself.* It has been asserted that "dialogue" with men of other faiths is necessary for renewal of the church. Speaking of the church in India, Frank Whaling says that "dialogue with Hinduism will save the church from itself and its chronic inward lookingness." True dialogue, says Whaling, "would help restore the confidence of the church in India and put her in touch with the real situation rather than one of her own imagining." John Mbiti also asserts that African traditional religiosity can become an enrichment for Christianity in Africa. In a moving statement he says:

"Romanism, Canterburyism and Athenism in Africa are on temporary visas, Christianity is on a permanent term as a Mwananchi (i.e., Swahili for "citizen") in Africa, and it must be enriched from within and not from outside. For too long we have sung borrowed hymns from Europe and America. Now we are beginning to realize that these imported hymns have nearly become theologically all extinct.

The more we continue to sing them, the nearer we draw to extinguishing the freshness of the Christian faith in Africa. We must allow our rich heritage to make a contribution to Christianity."

(iii) *Dialogue will benefit the universal Christian Church.* Christians committed to dialogical approach are convinced that this method of encounter with men of other faiths will be of value to the whole church. For too long the dynamism of the Gospel has been imprisoned in the passive Hellenistic thought forms. The Eastern contributions were virtually swamped by the Greek, Roman, and medieval European elements. Hence the theology of the church has been cradled, nurtured, and formulated within Western Europe. The Western missionary took what he considered to be the legitimate way of expressing the Gospel and church structure as he knew it, and applied this to other countries where it was not necessarily relevant. Following the principles of dialogue, the church can learn a new dynamic way of expressing the Gospel which could release her from the imprisonment of outmoded Greek and medieval thought forms. "By dialogue with Hinduism," says Whaling, "Christians can come to a deeper understanding of their own Gospel and its nature. Not only will this be of value to Christian theology, it will also give insights to the whole world Church." As Radhakrishnan, former president of India has put it, "Perhaps Christianity which arose out of an Eastern background and early in its career got wedded to Graeco-Roman culture may find her rebirth today in the heritage of India." Pursuing a similar theme, John Mbiti makes these provocative remarks:

"We who have been educated in Europe and America sometimes reach a point of despair for Christianity in those continents, when we see what little impact it has on the morals and life of people there; we almost despair when we recall that in spite of Christianity in Germany, some thirty years ago six million Jews were massacred in the most abominable ways; we almost despair when we see that in spite of Christianity in America, such a big nation was engaged in a senseless war with Vietnam, and Negroes are treated as second-class citizens. We almost despair when we see that the apartheid policy in South Africa is backed up and given blessing by at least one brand of Christianity from Europe. What shall we do? Are we to inherit a largely bankrupt Christianity from the West, and cherish it in our bosoms without adding anything valuable to it? I believe that some enrichment can come to Christianity from our African background. We can add nothing to the Gospel, for this is an eternal gift of God; but Christianity is always a beggar seeking food and drink, cover and shelter from the cultures and times it encounters in its never ending journeys and wanderings."

b. *Principles of dialogue.*

(i) *Genuine openness.* The key guiding principle of true dialogue is genuine openness on both sides. The 1970 W.C.C. Zurich Consultation on "Dialogue between Men of Living Faiths" asserts that "the Christian is free to bear witness to what is most important in his own existence." This openness repudiates "not mission as such, but merely certain one-way patterns of mission in which those who spoke and acted in the name of Christ have failed to listen to and learn from those to whom they were sent, about the latter's approach to and apprehension of reality . . . By opening ourselves to other men we may be enabled better to understand what God is saying to us in Christ."

(ii) *A common basis.* To be able to engage in a meaningful dialogue, a common basis is desirable. Without this, dialogue is impossible. Such a basis might be found in the assumption that God is already present and is at work in the lives of religious men.

(iii) *Understanding the other person.* True dialogue cannot be a one-way traffic. It is give and take. Dialogue requires a transparent willingness to listen to what the other is saying, and to recognize whatever truth is in it. Genuine dialogue is "mutually transforming." It therefore involves "the risk of one partner being changed by the other." This implies that there should be willingness to change. Unless there is this willingness, there is no point in engaging in dialogue.

(iv) *Personal encounter.* Whereas "Christian presence" can fulfill its aim without personal encounter, dialogue cannot be impersonal.

(v) *Commitment to one's own faith.* In genuine dialogue there is need for commitment of all parties involved to their own faith.

c. *Theology of dialogue.*

(i) Though "dialogue" is not a biblical word, dialogical approach is not without its biblical equivalent. The meeting of Jesus Christ with Nicodemus in John 3:1-22 has been cited by Dr. G.W. Peters in his paper on contemporary practices of evangelism as "the biblical pattern of dialogue in personal evangelism." Theologians of dialogical approach would, however, not consider this passage as a good guide to genuine dialogue.

Though Nicodemus comes to Jesus with an open mind, he is more of an inquirer who wants to learn as much as possible about Jesus. He is therefore content to ask questions and humbly wait for answers. A genuine dialogue, we are told, is a two-way traffic where the partners engage in a discussion on equal terms and from the position of commitment to their respective faiths. In this instance Nicodemus has little to offer in the dialogue, and indeed does not wish to proceed along those lines.

In a dialogical approach there should be willingness to listen to the other person. This is important in evangelism, but in this instance Jesus does not wait for Nicodemus to finish framing the first question, and answers a question Nicodemus does not ask. He even uses a vocabulary foreign to Nicodemus, "Truly, truly I say to you, unless one is born anew, he cannot see the Kingdom of God." In a genuine dialogical approach, words like "truly, truly" and "we speak what we know" and "unless one is born anew," etc., cannot be accommodated as they would arouse bitter confrontation and make dialogue fruitless.

Finally, though personal meeting with Nicodemus begins as a promising dialogue, it quickly becomes a monologue of a cut-and-dried proclamation. Nicodemus is even challenged to make a decision: "He who does not believe in him is condemned already because he has not believed in the name of the only Son of God" (John 3:18).

(ii) In the Synoptic Gospels there are many examples of people, especially Pharisees, scribes and other groups, who initiate a dialogue with Jesus. Often such dialogues do not develop into what dialogical theologians regard as "give and take." Jesus seems to seize the opportunity to proclaim the Good News in parables or to give specific teaching. A lawyer who wants a dialogue on the legal definition of who a neighbor is is told the story of the Good Samaritan and it ends with a command: "Go and do likewise" (Luke 10:25-37). The rich young man who wants a dialogue on what good deed to do so as to have eternal life is told to sell everything he has (Matt. 19:16-22). Jesus even refuses to engage in a dialogue where the other partner is not a sincere seeker of the truth (e.g., Luke 23:10).

(iii) In the Acts of the Apostles, we have examples of dialogue between Sanhedrin on one hand and John and Peter on the other (Acts 4); the members of the synagogue of freed men dispute with Stephen (Acts 6); Philip has dialogue with the Ethiopian (Acts 7); Paul argues with Epicurean and Stoic philosophers (Acts 17), and there are many instances of his dialogues with Jews. All these encounters of apostles with men of living faiths and ideologies begin as dialogues but always end as proclamation of "Jesus and the resurrection" and invitation to salvation through belief in the name of Jesus and repentance. The great error some of the dialogical theologians make is to assume that dialogue is the only legitimate way of Christian witness to men of living faiths and ideologies. Such a conclusion is unbiblical. The kind of dialogue we are asked to engage in is such that proclamation of Jesus and resurrection, repentance, and acceptance of his Lordship is kept at bay. Whereas the apostles welcomed dialogue, they did not hesitate to proclaim, with no uncertain voice, the whole kerygma.

(iv) The most disturbing thing about dialogical approach as advocated by some theologians is its presuppositions and uncertainty. The Christian is encouraged to enter boldly into dialogue with full openness because of his belief "in the power of the Holy Spirit to lead men into all truth." The Holy Spirit is at work in the Christian Church and outside it. The cosmic Christ is not the Christ of the church, but of the whole world. These presuppositions are "the basis of the quality of dialogue." Granted that the Holy Spirit cannot be confined within the church, it is difficult to assume that he has led all religions and ideologies into all truth. If this were so, then there is no point in our trying to witness to them. "All the truth" (John 16:13) does not mean that the church will be guided into the truth about all subjects. By inserting the definite article, "all the truth" is to be taken to mean the specific truth about the Person of Jesus and all the significance about what he said and did (R.V.G. Tasker). A genuine dialogue "is an attempt on the part of the Christian to find out what is true in the faith of other men, and assimilate such truth in proclamation of the cosmic Christ." This methodology despite its merits veers towards universalism and syncretism. It has potent dangers of "superficial consensus of finding the greatest common factor."

Though one of the basic principles of dialogue is that each person must understand and be committed to his own position, he must nevertheless be willing to change. Hence there is no guarantee of the outcome of the dialogue. It could degenerate into "sophistic intellectualism and dilution of all convictions for the sake of false harmony," as the Zurich aide-memoire admits. If it is the Christian who has to change, then dialogical approach is not the answer to the Great Commission.

(v) Despite its demerits, discussion about dialogical approach has many useful insights for evangelical Christians including missionaries. In the past there has been a tendency by some white missionaries to approach men of other faiths with blunt arrogance and insensitivity and total lack of humility and understanding. Dialogical approach discourages such attitudes and calls us not to assume that other religions are but "a rotten heap of superstitions, taboos and magic." It is a challenge to us to be more loving in our approach to others and to be willing to take seriously the cultural, historical, and religious circumstances of the other person.

(vi) There is much to be said about the value of a dialogue in enriching Christianity. This must not be taken to mean "dialogue" will add anything to the Gospel of Jesus. But the way an African will choose to express Christianity within his cultural set-up will benefit not only the church in Africa but the universal Church. The white missionaries have imported into the church in Africa certain church institutions, characteristics, and mannerisms which are not necessarily Christian and which have tended to imprison the liberty of the Gospel in outmoded medieval thought forms. The Anglican church in Africa inherited a prayer book written four centuries ago in England, and we still follow its archaic liturgy and sing the Te Deum and Jubilate Deo in ancient dull tunes which have no parallel in our musical inspirations. We will preach wearing clerical collars and thick black cassocks even when the temperature is 110 degrees Fahrenheit. This is imprisoning the beauty of Christianity in the traditional dull English expression best fitted to the English snowy winter about which we know nothing. This could be the reason why the African Independent Churches are growing faster than historic churches. They have liberated Christianity from the dull Gothic cathedrals where it has been confined and are now expressing its riches as they trot chanting Christian hymns in African tunes along the city and village streets and the Gospel is often preached in the open-air — the traditional places of assembly. Where dialogue with men of other faiths brings such enrichment to Christian expression, it should be welcomed.

3. Proclamation

Proclamation or preaching may be defined as "the unmistakable communication of the Word of God to men by men under assignment from God" (Baker's Dictionary of Theology). It is "an open and public proclamation of God's redemptive activity in and through Jesus Christ" (New English Dictionary).

a. Biblical terms. In the New Testament, thirty different terms are used to describe the preaching of John the Baptist, Jesus and the apostles. We may single out three of the most important terms.

(i) *Kerysso,* "to be a herald, to proclaim," is used sixty-one times in the New Testament.

(ii) *Kerygma,* "the thing preached, or proclamation," occurs eight times in the New Testament. Six of the occurrences refer specifically to the apostolic proclamation of the death and resurrection of Jesus Christ.

(iii) *Euangelizomai,* "to publish good news," is used over fifty times. The good news to be published almost always refers to "the Son of God as proclaimed in the Gospel." While *kerysso* tells us something about the activity of preaching, *euangelizomai* emphasizes the quality of the message itself. "Proclamation" is not without precedent in the Old Testament. The Hebrew prophets were the forerunners of the apostolic herald. They proclaimed the message of God under divine impulse. The Hebrew word *nagad* is used to describe prophetic proclamation of judgment and future hope of salvation, while *qara* refers to their cry against the iniquities of the people and the leaders. The Septuagint uses *kerysso* more than thirty times, both in the secular sense of official proclamation on behalf of the king and in the religious sense of prophetic utterance. Jonah is told to "preach" (Septuagint *Kerysso*) and Noah is designated a preacher *(keryx)* of righteousness.

b. *Content of the proclamation.*

(i) In the Synoptic Gospels the content of the message is the proclamation of the Kingdom of God. Jesus is portrayed as the one who came "heralding the Kingdom of God." With the coming of Jesus, "God's eternal sovereignty was now invading the realm of the evil powers and winning the decisive victory." This is the basic content of Jesus' *kerygma.*

(ii) In the rest of the New Testament, the content of Kerygma is "Christ." The apostolic message is a declaration of the "redemptive-historical facts of Christ's life, death, resurrection, glorification, and coming again, coupled with a call to repentance and faith. This is expressed variously as proclamation of "Christ Crucified" (I Cor. 1:23); "Christ Raised" (I Cor. 15:12); "Christ Jesus the Lord" (II Cor. 4:5). The change of emphasis from "the kingdom" as the kerygma to "Christ" is simply because the apostles were convinced that Jesus was the Kingdom. To enter the Kingdom one has to make a decision concerning that Kingdom.

C. H. Dodd has made a great contribution to New Testament scholarship in his discussion and crystallization of the primitive kerygma. In his research the content of the apostolic message emerges as "a proclamation of the death, resurrection and exaltation of Jesus that led to an evaluation of his person as both Lord and Christ, confronted man with the necessity of repentance, and promised the forgiveness of sins" (R. H. Mounce). Rudolf Bultmann, however, regards much of the proclamation of the apostles as "myth." This has led him to work out an existentialist kerygma which differs markedly from the apostolic preaching and the historic Christian faith. In the words of Alan Richardson, Bultmann's kerygma "is in fact, 'another gospel,' not the historic Gospel of the resurrection of Jesus Christ from the dead." Richardson warns that much confusion is caused by investing

New Testament words with new philosophical meaning.

c. *Features of the proclamation.*

(i) *Divine impulse.* The Old Testament prophets were prompted to proclaim by irresistible divine impulse — nothing could silence them from declaring their message. Jesus does not allow anything to delay or interfere with his preaching program because the purpose of his coming was to preach (Mark 1:38). Peter and John are compelled to tell the Sanhedrin, "We cannot but speak the things which we have seen and heard" (Acts 4:20), and Paul declares that he is under obligation to preach the Gospel, "How terrible it would be for me if I do not preach the Gospel" (I Cor. 9:16 TEV). He urges Timothy to preach the message "to insist upon telling it whether the time is right or not" (II Tim. 4).

(ii) *Open statement of the truth.* Unlike "Christian presence," apostolic proclamation is open declaration of the content of kerygma. Paul refused to practice cunning or tamper with God's Word, but rather he sought to "commend himself" to every man's conscience by the open statement of the truth (II Cor. 4:2). He does not want the message to be obscured with eloquent wisdom and lofty words (I Cor. 1:17, 2:1-4).

(iii) *Persuasion and patience.* Despite a deep sense of divine compulsion and urgency, apostolic proclamation was not done simply on the basis of "take it or leave it." Although Timothy is to be "urgent in season and out of season," he is also to be "unfailing in patience." Our Lord was ready for an extensive and penetrating dialogue with a Samaritan woman; Paul is his missionary outreach claims to have become "all things to all men that by all means he might win some." In our proclamation, urgency and patience must go together. John Stott's word of advice should be heeded, "We must never resort to the use of human pressure techniques, or attempt to contrive a 'decision.' Our responsibility is to be faithful in preaching the word; the results of the proclamation are the responsibility of the Holy Spirit and we can afford to wait patiently for him to work. . . . However solemn our commission and urgent our message, there can be no possible justification for a brusque and impatient manner."

Conclusion

Christian presence, dialogue, or proclamation? Understood in their biblical context, each of these terms may have a place in evangelism. There can be no hard and fast rules about methods of evangelism other than being faithful to the Scriptures. Some of the "Christian presence" and dialogical theologians, however, have taken these terms as the only legitimate way of witnessing the Gospel to men of other faiths and ideologies. And yet the exposition of the theology of these terms lacks the urgency, the dynamism of the apostolic proclamation, and the certainty of the Good News and the judgment of the Gospel. Apostolic proclamation must be the basis of all true Christian evangelism at all times. We are sent to proclaim Jesus Christ and the resurrection. We must be present to be able to proclaim, and the kind of life we live in the midst of men of other faiths should be a witness to the world. Our presence cannot, however, be the static silence advocated by some. Many times our proclamation will be dialogical, but not a mere intellectual exchange of words and ideas. In the course of the dialogue, the Christian will not hesitate to proclaim "Christ and him crucified," for we are not ashamed of the Gospel. Our proclamation nevertheless is not to be conducted with the arrogance and insensitivity that disregard the cultural and religious background of the other person.

In certain situations, proclamation being a personal way of communicating the Gospel must involve a struggle to achieve understanding and to establish a human relationship. Such was the struggle of Paul to become, "All things to all men, that I might by all means win some" (I Cor. 9:22). Having preached the Gospel, we must let people express its riches from their own cultural background. Evangelical theologians should as a matter of urgency and through inspiration of Lausanne 1974 work out a positive biblical theology of "Christian Presence, Dialogue and Proclamation."

In true biblical evangelism no wedge should be drawn between these terms. The apostolic approach was by and large "dialogical-proclamation." The challenge is for Christian men everywhere to proclaim the whole Gospel faithfully with urgency and patience from Jerusalem to the teeming cities of the world and unto the utmost villages of the earth. "Let the earth hear his voice."

EVANGELISM IN BIBLICAL HISTORY AND CONTEMPORARY LIFE

Chul-Ha Han

Dr. Han, Seoul, Korea, is a Professor at the Presbyterian Theological Seminary.

Old Testament history as the history of Good News

"Evangelism attempts to bring all men into living, active fellowship with God through Jesus Christ as divine Savior and through the regenerating power of the Holy Spirit, and to gather them into the fellowship of the church. It endeavors also to lead them to express their Christian discipleship in every area of human life, that the Kingdom of God may be realized" (Dawson C. Bryan, "Evangelism" in *Twentieth Century Encyclopedia*). In short, evangelism is the act of bringing the good news which God has given through Jesus Christ to all mankind so that the Kingdom of God may be realized. Although in Old Testament times Jesus Christ did not yet appear in the flesh as he did in the New Testament, yet the good news of God was never lacking. The Old Testament good news was given in the form of "promise" and "hope."

Old Testament history is the history of the life of Israel. It has many aspects and must not be simplified. But from the New Testament viewpoint the essential point of that history certainly should be interpreted as a history of good news. Not only the God-chosen people, but also mankind in general was never lacking the good news. To fallen mankind, which deserves only punishment of God, God was always gracious to grant the good news, especially in the form of promise and prophecy. Thus God has prepared the gospel history ever clearer as time progressed.

The calling of Abraham can be considered as the beginning of the good news in the Old Testament, though we can find many examples of good news of God already before the time of Abraham. To Abraham the promise of the blessing of all mankind was given. The blessing of all mankind was indeed good news, even more because it was from God himself. To fallen mankind God granted this good news in the form of promise. God did not stop with this one announcement of good news but was working throughout Old Testament history. God was, of course, the God of justice and judgment. Therefore the history of fallen humanity as well as the history of Israel, can be seen more in terms of divine judgment. Constant misery, wars, captivity, and famine were the characteristic of human history. This human misery can be interpreted in many ways. But at the last analysis the interpretation of human suffering in terms of human responsibility before God is most appropriate to give us hope and courage to face it in the future.

The purpose of the history was not in punishment as such. The true end is seen in the good news which developed gradually. This fact becomes more and more apparent as time progressed. Through Moses the promise of a "good land" is confirmed. Moses is always related to "law." But the positive purpose of law was the blessing of God. Especially the promise of Canaan, already given to Abraham. But it was obvious that Israel's conquering Canaan was not as such the real end of the good news. That went far beyond Israel's Canaanite conquest. At that time the real purpose was not yet so apparent. It was the coming of God himself, and God's reign to be established, namely, the Kingdom of God. To show this fact, God has given Israel the form of the Kingdom of God, namely, the monarchy through Saul and David. When the monarchy was granted to Israel, however, they were warned not to mistake it, or to lose sight of the fact that it was only the form of the kingdom of God. They had to seek the God-chosen Messiah in their kings. God declared, "I have set my king on Zion, my holy hill" (Psa. 2:6).

To this king, all the kings on the earth were to be obedient and make homage. "Now therefore, O kings, be wise: be warned, O rulers of the earth, serve the Lord with fear, with trembling kiss his feet." God has given the promise of the everlasting kingdom on the throne, "Of the increase of his government and peace there shall be no end, upon the throne of David, and upon his kingdom, to establish it, and to uphold it with justice and with righteousness from this time forth and forevermore. (Isa. 9).

But, the end of the good news in connection with this monarchy was not in the Davidic monarchy as such. The earthly kingdoms were to be utterly destroyed and the people of Israel were only to be brought to captivity. It was only at this moment that the Old Testament good news became clearer. The term "good news" in the Old Testament is most frequently used in relation to the post-exilic situation of the people. The good news became prominent only in relation to the post exilic hope.

The eschatological character of the Old Testament Gospel

As the time of destruction of the Davidic monarchy drew near, the Old Testament eschatological hope also became prominent in Old Testament prophecy. Phraseology such as "in that day," "in the last day," "in the day of the Lord" were used more frequently. The final fulfillment of the promise of the Lord would be realized in those days. Naturally this final day is related also to the day of divine judgment. Amos is considered the first to have used the term "the day of the Lord." Though he may be the first one who left the word in written form, in fact, this eschatological hope was the focal point of the mind of the people of God, since the day of Abraham. The people of Israel actually have been living their historical life with this hope.

But, as time passed, it became clearer, that the day must be the day of divine judgment, and that only through this divine judgment would the great forgiveness be given to the repentant remnant. "Woe unto you that desire the day of the Lord! To what end is it for you? The day of the Lord is darkness, and not light" (Amos. 5:18). This day of the Lord was often related to the marching of the invading army and complete desolation and devastation. Shame and humility are the natural results of this violence and destruction. Habakkuk describes very vividly the picture of the invading Chaldeans. Isaiah describes the devastated land. "Your country is desolate, your cities are burned with fire: your land, strangers devour it in your presence, and it is desolate, as overthrown by strangers." Actually, the divine judgment is to bring down all the high things before God. "The lofty looks of man shall be humbled, and the haughtiness of man shall be bowed down; and the Lord alone shall be exalted in that day" (Isa. 2).

In the total judgment and devastation God shows his grace to the remnant of Israel and all the heathen. They shall be gathered from the nations and they shall form the nucleus of a new Israel. "In that day will I raise up the tabernacle of David that is fallen, and close up the breaches thereof, and I will build it as in the day of old: That they may possess the remnant of Edom, and of all the heathen, which are called by my name, saith the Lord that doth this" (Amos 9:11, 12).

This good news is most eminent in Isa. 40-66. It starts with "Comfort ye, comfort ye my people, saith your God. Speak ye comfortably to Jerusalem, and cry unto her, that her warfare is accomplished, that her iniquity is pardoned: for she hath received of the Lord's hand double for all her sins." "O Zion, that bringest good tidings, get thee up into the high mountain: O Jerusalem, that bringest good tidings, lift up thy voice with strength; lift it up, be not afraid; say unto the cities of Judah, Behold your God!" The content of the good news is summarized in these words: "Behold your God!" "Behold, the Lord God will come with strong hand, and his arm shall rule for him" (Isa. 52:7). sings the beauty of one who brings this good news.

"How beautiful upon the mountains are the feet of him that bringeth good tidings, that publisheth peace; that bringeth good tidings of good, that publisheth salvation; that saith unto Zion, "Thy God reigneth!" Break forth into joy, sing together, ye waste places of Jerusalem: for the Lord hath comforted his people, he hath redeemed Jerusalem."

This is the new age, the day which all the prophets have foreseen beyond the horizon of history. That is the new age which is introduced by the day of the Lord's judgment.

The world historical character of Old Testament Good News

This good news of the redemption of Israel, God's coming to reign over his people is not only related to the people of Israel but to all nations. It is the time when all nations come to Jerusalem to honor God. "It shall come to pass in the last days, that the mountain of the Lord's house shall be established in the top of mountains, and shall be exalted above hills." All nations shall come to the house of God, the final peace shall be established in the world. In that day, Israel shall be the third with Egypt and with Assyria. The Lord of hosts shall bless Egypt and Assyria: "Blessed be Egypt my people, and Assyria the work of my hands" (Isa. 19:24, 25). Therefore the psalmist calls all nations to be glad and sing for joy: for God shall judge the people righteously, and govern the nations upon earth (Psa. 67:4).

Summary

(i) Old Testament history is truly the history of the judgment of God over his people and the nations, but it was never lacking in "good news" which was given in the form of "promise" and "hope."

(ii) This "good news" took different forms in different circumstances such as multiplication of family members, deliverance from enemy: but the core content became ever clearer as the time progressed, i.e., it was "Behold, your God," and references to the kingdom of God.

(iii) This was the news of "the last days," "in those days," i.e., the eschatological time.

(iv) It was the day of great judgment of God, and the result is the humiliation of man's part, and the peace of the world, established among all nations.

Evangelism in New Testament history

Old Testament history was the history of the proclamation of good news to Israel as well as to the nations. But it was only in the form of promise and hope. But New Testament history is nothing but a history of the Gospel. The New Testament history starts with the preaching of John the Baptist. All four Gospels introduce him as a forerunner of the Gospel history. The focus of his preaching was to urge people to repent and prepare the approaching Kingdom, "The Kingdom of God is near!" John was considered as the dividing point. Before him it was the age of law and prophets, but thereafter the kingdom of God was preached (Luke 16:16). He stands between the old age and the new age. In fact he was also an evangelist, because he functioned as an organ to introduce this new age. Before the new age was introduced, repentance must be preached. John was preparing the way of the Lord: the Lord of the Good News.

Jesus is the bearer of the good news of the new age. When Jesus heard that John was cast into prison, according to Matthew, he began to preach, "Repent, for the kingdom of heaven is at hand" (Matt 4:12, 17). The content of Jesus' preaching was actually the same as that of John the Baptist. It could not be different. As long as history continues the kingdom can never be fully realized, but can only be at hand. The only difference between Jesus' preaching and John's was in their relationship to the kingdom. One was preparing the kingdom's coming, the other was to give the kingdom. Therefore he could say that the kingdom was at hand and at the same time that the kingdom was already there, as to the women at Sychar (John 4:23) or as in his Beelzebub discussion, "If I with the finger of God cast out devils, no doubt the kingdom of God is come upon you" (Luke 11:20). Therefore the coming kingdom of Jesus is already here and now, but the final coming which is at hand has yet to come. To the question of John the Baptist, he says, "The blind receive their sight, and the lame walk, the lepers are cleansed, and the deaf hear, the dead are raised up, and the poor have the Gospel preached to them" (Matt. 11:5). Jesus declared that the kingdom of heaven belongs to the poor in spirit (Matt. 5:3). With the accompaniment of signs and wonders Jesus preached the kingdom of God. his entire life is characterized as the life of preaching the good news of the kingdom. "And he said unto them, I must preach the kingdom of God to other cities also: for therefore am I sent" (Luke 4:43). He was sent to preach the Gospel which John the Baptist predicted.

Luke 8:11 describes vividly the manner of his life, "He went throughout every city and village, preaching and showing the glad tidings of the kingdom of God; and the twelve were with him."

Jesus did not only himself preach the good news, but also he sent his disciples out to preach the kingdom of God, and to heal the sick (Luke 9:2). After Pentecost, the content of the disciples' preaching was concentrated upon Jesus Christ. According to Acts 5:42, the disciples did not cease to teach and preach Jesus Christ, daily in the temple and in every house.

When the persecution came on Jerusalem the Gospel was spread more widely outside Jerusalem. They were scattered abroad throughout the region of Judaea and Samaria. Philip was the first one who "went down to the city of Samaria, and preached Christ unto them" (Acts 8:5). It was even taken as far as to the Greeks (Acts 11:12). Then Paul became the evangelist to the Gentiles. Everywhere in the world he preached the Gospel (Acts 14:7, 15, 21, 16:10, 17:18; Rom. 15:20; I Cor. 15:1, 2; II Cor. 10:16, 11:7; Gal. 1:8, 11, 4:13). The Gospel is nothing but Jesus Christ himself. They preached "him" (Gal. 1:16), namely Jesus (Acts 8:15, 17:18), Christ Jesus (Acts 5:42), the Lord Jesus (Acts 11:20).

The ultimate source of the Gospel is God himself. In the New Testament two places refer to God himself as the proclaimer of the good news. In Acts 10:36, God is said to preach peace by Jesus Christ. In Rev. 10:7 God declares to his servants the prophets the fulfillment of the mystery of God, namely, the coming of Messiah, the kingdom of God.

Therefore, the same source of the good news in the Old Testament period, namely, to the people of Israel and to the nations, is the source of the New Testament Gospel. The only difference is that in the Old Testament period the good news was given in terms of promise and hope. The good news, namely the Lord's coming, as their God, establishing ultimate peace on earth, was in terms of eschatological hope. The day would come. Now, in the New Testament, was the fulfillment. Jesus *had* come, and his presence is the good news.

The Gospel of the New Testament is "power".

The Gospel of the New Testament is not simply words or news, it is *power,* a living power which introduces a new reality of life. Paul says, "I am not ashamed of the Gospel of Christ; for it is the power of God" (Rom. 1:16). To the Thessalonians he says, "Our Gospel came not unto you in word only, but also in power and in the Holy Ghost, and in much assurance" (I Thess. 1:8). Thus the Gospel could realize a new reality, in which man may find a new life. This is the power of salvation. In this new reality, man is born again, rendered righteous, becomes an obedient nation. The Gospel is the power of God which creates the ecclesiological communion in faith.

Evangelism in the New Testament period is, therefore, the activity of calling both Jews and Gentiles into the communion of this new reality of life which was brought by Jesus and created by the Spirit among mankind, namely, the communion of saints. The apostles labored for the regeneration of new believers. The number must increase, until the fullness of the number (I Cor. 4:15, I Pet. 1:23, I John 1:3; Acts 2:38).

The world historical scope of New Testament evangelism

Old Testament evangelism was of the world historical scale. It was not only related to the final salvation and blessing of the people of Israel, but also to all nations coming to Zion, to exalt and praise the name of God, saying, "Come ye, and let us go up to the mountain of the Lord, to the house of the God of Jacob." Thus the peace of God shall be established on earth, "Nation shall not lift up sword against nation, neither shall they learn war any more." This world historical scope of Old Testament evangelism is visible also in the New Testament evangelism. The Lord commands, "Go therefore and make disciples of all nations." Therefore all nations must become disciples of Jesus Christ. All nations must learn from Jesus: how to live and obey God. From our experience we may interpret this command to make disciples out of all nations as meaning that not each nation as a unit but individuals from each nation may become disciples of the Lord. But the literal meaning is not so, but to make disciples of all nations, namely make every nation his disciple. It is our ideal that each nation should become obedient to the Gospel of the Lord Jesus Christ. Already the walls of partition between Jews and Gentiles were broken open. According to Paul, both the Jews as well as the Gentiles were imprisoned or shut up in unbelief by God, that God might have mercy upon all (Rom. 11:32). This world historical scope of New Testament evangelism must not be neglected, because the doctrine of limited atonement does not conflict with the universal validity of Christ's atonement. Therefore we must take the words, "Make disciples of all nations" literally, with a good hope, because it is also the scope of Old Testament eschatological vision.

This world historical scope of both Old Testament and New Testament evangelism must not be confused with the mistaken idea of "universal salvation." The error in this latter case comes in obliterating the sharp distinction between obedience and disobedience. As we hold firm the world historical scope of our Lord's command, we must not lose sight of human haughtiness and disobedience against the Cross of Jesus Christ. As many as come into the new reality of life become the disciples of Jesus, and as many nations as learn from our Lord how to live harmoniously, taking care of each other with true brotherly love, become the disciple nations of our Lord Jesus. Therefore we must bring this good news, the news of our Lord Jesus Christ and his kingdom, which is already imminent, with good and urgent eschatological hope, boldly and with confidence to all nations!

Revivalism in biblical history

If we define Old Testament evangelism as the prophetic act of bringing the good news to the people of Israel as well as to the nations, Old Testament revivalism can be defined as the event of the renewed realization of the people of God, where they stand. It is the act of the people coming to themselves by returning to God from their fallen state. Therefore, in their external forms, the two, evangelism and revivalism are different from each other. One is through the prophetic preaching of a good news, previously unheard, but the other is the equally prophetic preaching of the good news which had been preached to them in former times. This latter is through anamnesis of God's good news toward them, and through a new realization of their fallen state, so that they can also realize that they have had a promise of God's final salvation and thus recover the hope of the good news.

Though evangelism and revivalism are different from each other in their external forms, in the inner core both have the same aim, i.e., coming back to the promise and hope of the good news. It is through evangelists that men have continually received the good news of God and been brought into the communion of the people of God, but it is only through revivalism that the people of God come to the vivid realization of the good news and recover the courage and confidence in hope. Good examples of Old Testament revivalism are King Josiah's reform movement (II Kings 22:3, 23:25) and Ezra-Nehemiah's revival movement after the exile.

New Testament history is in toto revivalistic, especially in its Spirit filled character. In fact Old Testament history is also nothing but Spirit-led history. Indeed God is Spirit, and where God is concerned, the divine Spirit of truth is prominent. This Spirit-filled movement is most clearly seen in the new birth of the New Testament church at Pentecost. The disciples, scattered after the passover, were brought together one after another by the Risen Lord, and through the presence of the Spirit were now totally renewed and enlightened in spirit and thus arise as a new community: first of all as a preaching community. Since that time, the history of Acts is characterized as Spirit-led history. The Risen Lord himself is the Master of the mission works. Every action and every decision on the part of the disciples are motivated and commanded by the spirit of Jesus.

This gift of the Spirit is interpreted as the sign of the coming of the last days. The Apostle Peter claimed that the prophecy of Joel had been fulfilled. Therefore, spiritually speaking the last days have already come here on earth, but historically — especially eschatologically — speaking, this is the sign and pre-manifestation of the coming kingdom. Therefore the revivalism has an eschatological character. It is the phenomenon of the end-time. According to H. Bavinck, the New Testament foundation of missions is the invitation of Jesus Christ to the eschatological feast. The word of Jesus "everthing is ready" is the real foundation of mission works. At the same time, according to him, the end is imminent. Therefore in this interim period the activity of invitation must be carried out all the more urgently. Therefore the mission of the apostles is nothing but the action of extending this invitation of the Lord Jesus to his kingdom, to all the world.

Evangelism in comtemporary life

In comparison with evangelism in biblical history, evangelism in contemporary life is characterized in the following three points:

    (i) lack of world historical persepctive

    (ii) lack of a sense of urgency

    (iii) the basic philosophical presupposition of Western individualism.

    All these basic defective characteristics of contemporary evange-
lism are rooted in one great and serious historical disease of the West:
secularization. In the West, Christian religion has been always *cultus
publicus* up to the time of Reformation. But after the Reformation,
especially since the rise of modern industrial society, the Western
world became gradually secularized, and religion was pushed out from
essential social relationships, and became a matter of private life. On
the other hand, the various spheres of human life have developed on
the secularistic philosophical bases. The conomic socio-political aspect
became especially prominent. Particularly at the time of World War
II, pagan forms of national integrity in the form of national socialism
and communism, devastated the Western world. In spite of the postwar effort of the rehabilitation of Christian Europe, the deep-rooted
secularism of Western civilization does not seem to have healed quickly.

    It is against this kind of background that evangelism found itself
deficient. Evangelistic programs calculate usually to arouse religious
interest on the part of people who have been leading busy lives in a
secularistic society. But the religion which is aroused in the mind of
the people can hardly have any relationship to this world. The only
possible concentration point of evangelism in the changing, multidimensional, even chaotic world is the concentric center of an individual ego, "I". Since the day of Kierkegaard, and during the two
World War periods, this point has been the only possible area of
identity in the identity crisis. Not only Rudolf Bultmann, but also
Billy Graham have concentrated the whole attention upon the point
of "decision" or "Entscheidung."

    This individualistic tendency in contemporary Christian thinking
has been all the more strengthened because of the biblical interest
of man himself and the personhood of God. Though the biblical ideal
of the kingdom of God aims at the total salvation of man and the
cosmic palingenesis, at the same time the Bible is always concerned
with the condition of an individual heart and therefore the individual
salvation: election, calling, justification, sancitification, and glorification of the individual. At the same time God comes to man in personal
encounter. Our Lord knocks at the door of each individual heart.

    The contemporary dichotomous conflict between humanization
and evangelization is also actually deep-rooted in the inner discrepancy
between the biblical personalism and the sociological character of
modern man's existence.

    In order to solve the religious problems which come from the
secularization of the West, a number of proposals have been made.
Barth's transcendental realism, Bultmann's existentialist interpretation
of the Gospel, Bonhoeffer's non-religious (secular) interpretation of
the Gospel, the various radical theologies: the theology of revolution,
the theologies of counter-culture movements, and finally Moltmann's
reinterpretation of Christianity in terms of hope. All these approaches
have a common methodology, though their contents are different from

each other: they each draw a certain hermeneutical principle from contemporary life which is basically drawn from the biblical source. The hermeneutical principles are prophetic to time in its historical movement, and therefore they speak to modern man's various problems.

The basic problem of these approaches is that they do not attempt to heal the basic disease of the modern time, namely, secularism; on the contrary, they try to conform to it. The result is the impoverishment of biblical content. The churches remain as they are. Only in historical Christianity can the Christian have true satisfaction in life. I do not say that those modern attempts to solve religious problems are useless. In fact they are very meaningful as Christian apologies to modern man. They speak very eloquently to modern man that Christianity is not meaningless even from modern man's perspectives. But, they are too abstract and theoretical to be of much practical value. Take the example of Dietrich Bonhoeffer. Indeed, he was a martyr. He had to fight against Hitler to be faithful to his Lord. In this sense, his theology and his Christianity were very meaningful. But what of many other Christians in Germany at that time? Were all of them who did not or could not fight against Hitler non-Christian? Should the Christianity of that time have been exhausted only in that political action? No, Christ was needed by the numerous Christians even during the time of war, in every moment of daily life, every family gathering, for the reconciliation of various broken human relationship, and for the final comfort of the dying — *ad infinitum,* apart from the matter of war. If any theological system is so arrogant that it tries to be the whole of Christianity, it is trying to limit God too much. We can say that biblical religion alone with its total religious content can give ultimate and full satisfaction to man.

The direction which the contemporary evangelism should take

I find no other solution but the following:

(a) In spite of the irrelevant form of personal evangelism in view of the sociological character of modern man's existence, the billion Christians of the world must engage in a total campaign to win the hearts of the rest of mankind. The irrelevance does not come from the fallacy of biblical religion, but from the secularism of the modern world.

(b). This evangelistic movement must recover the world historical perspective. It is nothing but the biblical kingdom ideal. As we have seen, the good news in the Bible was the prophetic vision of the last days in the history of Israel, and the coming kingdom in the message of Jesus. Jesus Christ our Lord has fulfilled Old Testament prophecy in his power and in his spirit, and therefore in the communion of the church. This communion is to be extended, our Lord commands, to all nations, to the end of the earth. Why should we from the first give up the evangelization of the world? It is the will of God. We pray every day, "Thy kingdom come. Thy will be done on earth!" While the love of God does not forsake the vilest sinner, why do we give up the present generation prematurely? The world historical perspective of the biblical kingdom ideal is nothing but the ideal of world evangelization. It is nothing but the obedience to the great commission, "Make disciples of all nations." This commission itself contains the good news: the vision of the making disciples of all nations, i.e., the vision of the evangelization of the world.

All nations should become disciples of Jesus. It is obvious that a nation can only be happy by becoming a disciple nation of Jesus. Jesus only can fulfill democratic ideals, social justice ideals, and all kinds of cultural ideals. In fact, therefore, all nations are presently striving to become disciples of Jesus, but in wrong ways. We must therefore tell all nations to learn about Jesus our Lord in the right way for only in that way can nations really live.

c. *The sense of urgency* — The work of world evangelization must be accompanied by a sense of urgency. No nation can become happy without Christ. The happiness of mankind depends upon him. As much as he is preached and put into realization in the national life or whatever sphere of life, so much the nation or its people can become happier. Each individual, each group, each nation, indeed all the world, urgently need to learn from Jesus Christ, and to have him as the Lord. His personal presence only can give them true life and new values. At present all mankind is in agony and misery without him. Without him, there remains nothing but power struggles, economic injustice, enmity, wars, corruptions, dehumanizations: in toto, sin! Therefore all the world urgently needs to be saved from all these miseries into the fellowship of Jesus Christ.

The true urgency of world evangelization originates from God himself. God commands all mankind to be obedient to his Son: the Way, the Truth, and the Life! God created man for his own glory. Therefore all mankind is obliged to glorify God, by becoming obedient to him. The coming of the kingdom is nothing but God's recovery of his own sovereignty over his chosen people and all nations and all creatures. "I will sanctify my great name and the heathen shall know that I am the Lord," says God (Ezk. 36:22, 23). God has exalted his great name through the crucified Lord. The kingdom is nothing but the kingdom of the crucified and risen Christ. God urges all the nations of the earth to be obedient to this Christ. Any nation which does not obey this Christ shall be punished by God the Father of Jesus Christ. Therefore God urges the evangelization of the nations.

The Lord Jesus himself urges world evangelization. He is the coming Lord. When we, with uplifted head, look for only him, the coming Lord, to come back again for our perfect comfort, the time seems to be very short. The Lord is truly very near to us. The time of salvation seems to be at hand. In fact we shall see him before long because we shall be with him in heaven. Therefore the souls under the altar cried, "How long, O Lord, holy and true, dost thou not judge?" (Rev. 6:10). Since we look for him, he seems to be coming very soon, yet if we look at the works which are still going on in the earth, his coming seems to be delayed. Those who asked the question cited above are told that they "Shall rest yet for a little season, until their fellow servants also — that should be killed as they were, should be fulfilled." (Verse 11). While this number, namely the number of martyrs increases, they are told they should wait. This New Testament sense of delay of the Lord's coming does not eliminate the sense of urgency of the New Testament evangelism; on the contrary, it enhances the sense of urgency. The clue is to have a clearer vision of the kingdom's coming and of the nearness of the Lord. Only the world historical perspective of the Gospel can provide us with the sense of the urgency of evangelization. This was indeed one of the essential characteristics of evangelism right from the time of Abraham through the prophetic movements and on to the New Testament evangelism.

EVANGELISM IN BIBLICAL HISTORY AND CONTEMPORARY LIFE REPORT

Chairman: Frank A. Horton
Secretary: Peter A. Hicks

Preamble

The title given to Dr. Han for his paper was "Evangelism in Biblical History and Contemporary Life." In the Congress program this was changed to "Methods of Evangelization in Biblical History and Their Contemporary Relevance." This change was unfortunate since the interest of Dr. Han's paper was decidedly theological and not methodological. A number of participants attended the first session expecting the group to deal with methods; when they found it was not doing so they stayed away from the remaining sessions. Conversely a number who wanted to study the theological understanding of evangelism may well have stayed away from the group because of the incorrect title in the program.

The subject is a difficult one, and few of us in this group were in the habit of wrestling with serious theological issues. Lausanne reflected a sad deficiency among evangelicals at large. There were also a certain lack of communication among us in the area of semantics, which was difficult to correct in the short time we had together. In the light of these factors we deliberately tackled only part of the set syllabus.

The members of the group were fairly representative of worldwide Christianity and the different theological emphases of evangelism. We generally welcomed Dr. Han's paper and were grateful to him for tackling the subject in a serious way, and for being willing to raise provocative and difficult issues.

We were particularly grateful for the paper's emphasis on the one overall, worldwide purpose of God revealed in the Old and New Testaments in terms of promise, hope, the Kingdom of God, God working out his purpose in history, and the sure and certain eschatological hope. We welcomed, too, the critique of the basically individualistic preopposition of Western contemporary Christian thinking, feeling that this was an error into which we had all fallen.

Most of the group's time, however, was spent wrestling with the implications of this last point, and trying to find an alternative to an exclusively individualistic approach to evangelism. We were agreed that God's interest in the Old Testament revelation was not just in individuals but in nations, and we traced this element into the New Testament. (e.g. Matt 25:32, Rom. 11, Rev. 22:2). We sought to understand how such prophecies as Micah 4:1-7 and the more eschatological passages of Isaiah 40-66 were to be fulfilled in history. The variety of our theological background and the shortage of time precluded any final agreement on this matter, but among others we made the following four points:

1. We wish to disavow universalism in the sense that all men will be saved whether they personally accept Christ or not. But at the same time we recognize that there is a universal efficacy in Christ's work which will certainly be manifested at the Day of the Lord

(Romans 8:19-21) and which in some ways is already manifested.
2. There is a sense in which the prayer "Thy Kingdom Come" can
be fulfilled in a nation as well as in an individual. This would be
particularly when, for example, the promises of Luke 4:18-19 have
been fulfilled in that nation.
3. To avoid misunderstanding, and with Dr. Han's comment, we
would altar the expression "the irrelevant character of personal
evangelism" to "the irrelevant character of individualistic evangelism."
4. There were mixed feelings over interpreting Matt. 28:19 in the
sense of "make nations my disciples." However, we responded
readily to Dr. Han's call to stop concentrating exclusively on the
individual in our evangelism and widen our horizons.

We felt evangelicals need to give much further thought to these
matters.

Some course was expressed over the last paragraph of page 16.
There is a sense in which "all nations are striving to become disciples
of Jesus Christ" but we must not lose sight of the Bible's doctrine of
man-in-revolt. Dr. Han clarified his statement, "Jesus only can fulfill
democratic ideals" by referring to passages like Luke 1:51-53. He does
not wish to be understood as referring to just one political structure.

It became clear in the group that some did not share fully in the
optimism of Dr. Han regarding the implementation of God's purposes
for the nations in history. We all agreed Christ will ultimately triumph,
but some insisted that the biblical doctrines of the work of Satan and
the Antichrist should be given more prominence in our thinking. Several
references were made to Dr. Beyerhaus' paper and his interpretation
of Matthew 24 in this connection.

Dr. Han had set himself to deal with the biblical doctrine of the
Good News, which in itself is a very positive doctrine. We felt, however,
that it would be unreal to concentrate on that to the neglect of the
others, more negative elements in evangelism-conviction of sin, repentance and forgiveness. One way to correct the balance would be
to add to Dr. Han's concept of the prophetic and kingly elements of the
Old Testament and their fulfillment in Christ, the Levitical emphasis
of the Old Testament and the New Testament doctrine of Christ our
Priest and Atonement. No preaching of the Good News is complete, it
was emphasized, without the element of the substitutionary atonement.

The group tackled the question "What changes in emphasis are
necessary in our modern preaching of the Gospel in the light of this
paper?", and gave three main answers:
1. We need to get back to a message that is as worldwide (or
creation wide) as the message of the Bible. Our preaching must
regain the vision of the eternal purpose of God, firmly grounded
in history. We noted that apostolic preaching contained a clear
commandment that "God's promises have been fulfilled" and we
need to regain this element.
2. The Good News is *God's* Good News. As we prepare ourselves
to preach it, we must guard against the notion that we are the
source of the Good News and that everything depends on our presentation of it. Instead we must remember that the sovereign God goes

before us; we are reapers, not promoters.

3. We need to free ourselves from excessive individualism and get back to the Biblical vision of the community of man. This means that our evangelistic preaching must not isolate a man from his social context, and that we must accept and act upon the truth that when a man becomes a Christian he is linked into a real worldwide community and is given a new and demanding relationship with the whole world.

THE CENTRAL THRUST OF THE MODERN CHARISMATIC MOVEMENT

Harold B. Kuhn

*Dr. Kuhn, Wilmore, Kentucky, USA, is
the Chairman of the Division of Theology and
Philosophy of Religion at Asbury Theological Seminary.*

Among the possible ways of considering the broad charismatic movement in our century, the committee of the congress has suggested the approach of the movement's emphasis be upon the energizing ministry of the Holy Spirit. In harmony with this welcome suggestion, the writer proposes to structure this paper with a vew to acquainting the reader with the origins, growth and dynamics of the broad charismatic movement of our time, particularly as these features relate to its evangelistic and missionary thrust. The paper does not profess to deal with, much less to evaluate, all aspects of Pentecostalism, nor even to mention all of the features which have accompanied its appearance.

Part 1 of the paper will define the movement, and sketch its historical antecedents and its origins, including contributions made to it by both white and black believers. Part 2 will emphasize the manner in which more recent pentecostal movements have affected the Christian world in the last two decades, particularly the Neo-Pentecostal form of the charismatic movement as it has exerted an influence in and through mainline religious bodies. This discussion will deal primarily with American Pentecostalism.

It is the major thesis of the writer that while Pentecostalism has had its vocal manifestations and its "motor movements," its deeper and more characteristic quality has been, and is, its emphasis upon the blessed Third Person of the Trinity, the Holy Spirit. With this in mind, the writer proposes in Part 3 to deal specifically with the manner in which, under the Holy Spirit's guidance, the charismatic movement has found expression in a dynamic contribution to the evangelistic and missionary thrust of evangelical Christianity. This will include an attempted bird's eye view of the outreach of this movement in our world of today.

1. The movement and its origins

The term "charismatic movement" signifies, in its broad usage, that modern expression of activity of the Holy Spirit within Protestant Christendom in our century (and latterly within Roman Catholicism as well) which has for its primary sign or initial evidence of the baptism with (or in) the Holy Spirit the vocal manifestation of glossolalia (sometimes called xenolalia) or speaking in tongues. Like all movements involving the human spirit, the Pentecostal Movement had its origins in earlier historic expressions of the spiritual life. But like all operations of the Holy Spirit, it has had its unpredictable and sometimes baffling qualities. (It might be explained here, that we use the term "charismatic movement," with small letters, to denote the entire range of Pentecostalism, while the use of the same term with capital letters (as, Charismatic Movement) denotes the Neo-Pentecostal Movement of the past fifteen or twenty years among the old-line denominations.)

It needs to be noted at the outset that while Pentecostalism took form as a trend within existing religious bodies, it very soon became institutionalized. Thus, within two decades after its intial appearance, it had given rise to denominations with visible structure and order. These have in general followed the course of development which is typical of such bodies. The largest and best known of denominational or confessional Pentecostal groups is the Assemblies of God, including in 1969 some 8570 congregations and 625,660 members.

About two decades ago, there began to emerge within the non-pentecostal bodies phenomena very similar to those marking the charismatic movement at the beginning of the present century. This movement, perhaps best embodied in the Full Gospel Business Men's Fellowship International, is popularly known as Neo-Pentecostal. It represents a cutting edge of charismatic fervor in the more staid churches. More will be said later concerning this, and the manner in which Neo-Pentecostalism has become a force within Roman Catholic circles.

Religious movements seldom appear upon the stage of history without first being heralded by trends or institutions which bear at least some of the qualities which they themselves come to emphasize. It is generally recognized that the impact of so-called Modernism, and its related movement, that of the Social Gospel, produced or issued in a general neglect of the inner life within the major Protestant bodies. This brought an attending spiritual sterility and aridness which produced an undercurrent of spiritual longing, notably about the turn of the present century. Then, too, institutionalized Protestantism tended, by this same date, to be middle-class, both in membership and in outlook. As a result, many of the so-called lower classes — the urban and rural poor and the socially rejected — began to feel alienated from the mainline churches. Being unable to meet middle-class expectations in such matters as dress, education, and social usages, the working class was prepared to receive a new religious life-style which would afford them a sense of belonging — a place in which they could feel at home and participate without regard to class lines.

It might be noted, as an aside, that it was the same kind of conditions which through the centuries have given rise to "free church" movements. Actually, many of these same social features and trends contributed to the emergence of the Wesleyan revival of the eighteenth century. In other words, this is not the first time in history when such a configuration of situations has produced such a result.

With regard to the classical Pentecostalism of the early twentieth century, it was the coldness produced by the non-Evangelical trends in major church bodies, and the bourgeois tendency within their mentality, which afforded a negative climate within which a more free, less class-oriented form of spiritual life was welcomed. These factors would not, in themselves, dictate the precise form which such a movement of the Spirit would take, except that they would create an expectation of a trend toward freedom and spontaneity.

Of the factors which gave concrete form to the emerging Pentecostal Movement at the turn of the present century, none was more significant than the Wesleyan Perfectionist trend as it took shape in the last three decades of the nineteenth century as the Holiness Movement, whose organizational title was the National Association for the Promotion of Holiness. Especially significant for the rise of Pentecostalism was the shift which came within this Holiness Movement in the late decades of the nineteenth century toward the identification of Entire Sanctification with the Baptism of the Holy Spirit.

The earlier methodistic movement toward Christian Perfection stressed the work of Jesus Christ as Perfecter of the saints; but there came a gradual change as a result of the Camp Meeting movement. Under the strong influence of the Congregational minister and president of Oberlin College, Asa Mahan, the Christian Perfectionist movement came to give increasing attention to the role of the Holy Spirit as the sanctifying force in the "Second Blessing." This gives support to the view of Vinson Synan as expressed in his volume *The Holiness-Pentecostal Movement in the United States,* to the effect that the historical roots of American Pentecostalism are to be found in the Wesleyan-Perfectionist tradition. Further, he traces the rise of Pentecostalism to the specifically Spirit-centered emphasis in this tradition.

This does not mean that the transition from the Spirit-oriented ministry of perfectionist groups, to the classical charismatic movement was a smooth one. Actually there arose a great deal of debate, and there came to be wide differences of opinion. Many regard the rising pentecostalism as being primarily a theological division within the Holiness Movement, centering in the problem of the *evidence* that one had been baptized with the Holy Spirit. But it is clear in any case that the charismatic movement had its roots in Wesleyanism, particularly as articulated by those whose theological base was found in the primacy of the Holy Spirit's role in the sanctification of the believer.

Accounts of the actual origination of the twentieth-century charismatic movement vary on at least one important point. Some writers insist that its primary impetus came from the ministry of the Reverend Charles Fox Parham, a supply pastor in the Methodist Episcopal Church in Kansas. Others disagree, and insist either that the credit for the origination of the movement must be divided between Parham's work and the revival at Azusa Street in Los Angeles, *or* that this latter event was the major factor which contributed to its rise. We will attempt to look at each of these estimates.

Charles Fox Parham opened Bethel Bible School near Topeka, Kansas in October of 1900. From this as a base, Parham held large meetings in towns of the same state, in which participants were reportedly baptized with the Holy Spirit and healed of sickness. Even before his own special awakening in January of 1901, Parham had emphasized the teaching of the Spirit's baptism, evidenced by the speaking in tongues.

Fervency in prayer marked life at Bethel, and prolonged prayer vigils led to an intense feeling of expectancy. A student, Miss Agnes N. Ozman, had been combining fasting with earnest seeking, and on January 1, 1901, she received the Spirit's baptism (following the laying on of hands) and according to her own testimony, "Began to speak in tongues, glorifying God." She reports also having "talked several languages." In days following many others experienced the same manifestation, and as a result meetings were held in other cities in Kansas, and in the states of Texas and Missouri.

One of Parham's pupils, the Reverend W.J. Seymour, was invited to come to Los Angeles by Neelly Terry, the pastor of a black Holiness church in which Baptist preachers Joseph Smale and Frank Bartleman had already preached. (These two men had been influenced profoundly by the Welsh revival.) Finding some of his emphases unacceptable to Mr. Terry, Seymour went to a prayer meeting in Bonnie Brae Street, where on April 9, 1906, a number of believers received the baptism of the Spirit, the first being an eight-year-old black boy. Seymour shortly rented a Methodist Church building at 312 Azusa Street. In this Azusa Street Mission, three years of continuous prayer and evangelistic meetings took place, and significant numbers of believers, both black and white, received the Spirit and spoke in tongues.

By the end of the year 1906, there were no fewer than nine Pentecostal groups meeting in Los Angeles. Whites withdrew from the Azusa Street Mission two years later. Viewing the moving of the Spirit here, some estimate that it was but an extension of what actually began in Topeka in 1900-1901, and that this earlier manifestation was the true beginning of the Pentecostal movement. Others incline to the view that the movement did not really take root in America prior to the Los Angeles revival, and that the meetings in Azusa Street marked the actual founding of Pentecostalism.

It is not the purpose of this writer to take sides; but it is important to note that to our black brethren and sisters must go credit for a significant share in the establishment of the charismatic movement in the United States. Thus Nils Bloch-Hoell can write, "It was in *Los Angeles* (italics his) that the Pentecostal Movement first truly took root and flourished . . . ."

2. *The impact of the movement*

Thus far we have been concerned with the origination of the classical Pentecostal movement in the early part of the present century. It needs to be noted at the outset that while the earlier phase of the modern charismatic movement found its following among those in the levels of society which were alienated from the mainline churches, Neo-Pentecostalism has, on the other hand, appeared from within the established denominations. It has reached members of the major Protestant bodies, and significant elements within the Roman Catholic Church also.

No discussion of the charismatic movement of our day would be complete without special attention to the manner in which it has penetrated the major Protestant denominations. The selection of data at this point will necessarily be limited; it is hoped, however, that the following paragraphs will afford an overview of this penetration, and suggest as well some of the underlying reasons for its success. The extended ministries of men like Oral Roberts began at least two decades ago, to have an impact upon the devout in the mainline denominations. By 1960 there could be found those who witnessed to the baptism of the Holy Spirit, with tongues-speaking as "an initial witness," within the several branches of Lutheranism, the Protestant Episcopal Church, the United Methodist Church, the United Presbyterian Church, and others. Among those having experienced this are both ministers and lay persons.

Significant numbers of clergy are reported to have experienced this manifestation in the American Lutheran Church, the Lutheran Church — Missouri Synod, and the Lutheran Church in America. At the First International Lutheran Conference on the Holy Spirit held in Minneapolis, Minnesota August 8-12, 1972, an unofficial gathering, the extent of charismatic experiences within the Lutheran ministry was reported by Norris L. Wogen of the ALC. He indicated that 1,000 pastors have "received the baptism of the Spirit," 400 in the ALC, 400 in the LC-MS and 200 in the LCA. Laymen were also prominent in this Conference, at which many non-Lutherans were present. The Conference also included, significantly enough, many Lutherans from Europe who witnessed of this same grace.

Similar penetration of other Protestant bodies has occurred. The appearance of Neo-Pentecostalism within the Protestant Episcopal Church seems to have begun with the parish of St. Mark's Church in Van Nuys, California, when the rector, Dennis Bennett, who had earlier professed to be an atheist, received "this baptism" and shortly sixty of his parishoners. Before long, there were at least twelve of the clergy in the diocese of Bishop James A. Pike who had spoken in tongues, so that the Protestant Episcopal Church three years later (i.e., in 1963) sent officials to the headquarters of the Assemblies of God in Sprinfield, Missouri to discuss the question of the baptism of the Holy Spirit.

Similar appearances of Neo-Pentecostalism were found in the early 1960s within the United Methodist and United Presbyterian Churches. Surprisingly, perhaps, the First Presbyterian Church of Hollywood, which is the largest Presbyterian congregation in the world, is said to have had (in 1964) six hundred members professing to have received the gift of tongues. Thus, it could no longer be said that Pentecostalism was exclusively a movement within persons and groups marginal to the life of America.

The appearance of Neo-Pentecostalism among Roman Catholics is another of the surprising phenomena of the past two decades. Again space prevents a detailed tracing of the rise of Catholic Pentecostalism. It did, remarkably enough, appear first in academic circles, beginning at Duquesne University, and shortly spreading to the University of Notre Dame, with an overflow in the direction of the university city of Ann Arbor, Michigan, of Iowa State University at Ames, Iowa, and of Holy Cross in Worcester, Massachusetts. From the beginning there was a significant involvement of professors of theology, of philosophy, of history, and of physics.

The movement spread from university circles to convents, and into the parishes. At least seven conferences have been held to "work out the theology of the Pentecostal experience within the Roman context." Well educated persons unashamedly professed their new-found pentecostal experiences in these gatherings. Recent estimates place the number of Catholic Pentecostals somewhere between 60,000 and 100,000. The movement within the Roman Catholic Church has been greeted with caution but in a basically positive way, by the hierarchy, and the hope is frequently expressed that pentecostalism among its members will be channeled creatively through careful articulation and internal discipline. From time to time, sober counsel is given at this point, both by those outside the charismatic branch of the church, and by those who themselves have espoused it.

3. *The dynamic contribution of the movement*

Having looked at the antecedents, central thrust, and confessional quality of the broad charismatic movement, and having traced briefly its spread and current extent, we turn to an examination of what is felt to be its major emphasis and most significant outreach. While most branches of orthodox Christianity have been "Son-oriented" and thus have been primarily concerned with Christology, the Pentecostal movement (with its neo-pentecostal resurgence) has tended to be Spirit-oriented. The expression(s) of this were frequently misunderstood by most Christian bodies, even evangelical groups, in the decades following Bethel Bible School and the Azusa Street Mission. The tendency was to seize almost exclusively upon the vocal and motor aspects of Pentecostalism, so that its central drive was frequently overlooked.

It is only reasonable, however, to permit charismatics to speak for themselves at the point of their understanding of the major thrust of the movement. Nils Bloch-Hoell observes that the Pentecostal movement would have been dynamic and agressive, "even if the tongues emphasis and eschatology had not been the major motive." It has been characteristic of the charismatic movement to regard itself as the true contemporary representative of original Christianity, whose primary emphasis is regarded to have been upon the person and work of the Holy Spirit as the Endurer, the Enlightener and the Energizer.

Dr. J. Rodman Williams, an astute and sympathetic Presbyterian writer and former professor in Austin Presbyterian Seminary, confirms this view of the primacy of the Holy Spirit, in and of himself, in Pentecostalism. In his perceptive book, *The Pentecostal Reality,* he writes, "...The Pentecostal is essentially talking about something that is deeply existential. Hence the expression used thus far — "baptism," "filling," "gift,"' "reception," and others — though biblical, are not primarily understood by exegeting certain texts. Rather, these terms are helpful ways of defining what has occurred. Others may wonder why the Pentecostal witness makes so much use of this kind of language . . . nonetheless, the person of Pentecostal experience finds in such language the biblical way of expressing what has taken place in his life.

If Christendom in general has not understood the classical pentecostal at this point, it may be due to the fact that Christendom itself has, in general, failed to deal adequately with the biblical teaching concerning the Holy Spirit. To the major confessions, "The Holy Spirit has been recognized as fully God, third person in the Trinity, but his particular field of activity has not stood out with sufficient clarity." Thus the outsider tends not to understand the charismatic believer as one to whom the Holy Spirit has opened up entirely new dimensions, so that it is in reality the Holy Spirit who forms the center and core of his faith.

A representative of the charismatic movement whose interdenominational contacts have been broad expresses the matter in these words, "Finally the essential doctrinal content of pentecostalism and neopentecostalism is not speaking in tongues. Jesus promised power — not tongues . . . the charismatic renewal involves a mighty powerful experiential filling of believers by the Holy Spirit."

It goes without saying that Pentecostals do not sever the Holy Spirit and his work from Jesus Christ. There is full recognition among the doctrininally conscious that the Holy Spirit is given by and through Christ. The baptism of the Holy Spirit is, in the final analysis, Christ's bestowal, Christ's baptism.

The question of the relation of the Spirit's baptism to the ordinance of water baptism has given some concern to charismatics, especially among Roman Catholics and Lutherans. In an article which is in reality a pastoral letter to Catholic pentecostals, Miss J. Massingberd Ford, associate professor of theology in the University of Notre Dame, shows an awareness of this problem. In her excellent little devotional manual for charismatics, *The Pentecostal Experience,* she makes clear the distinction which she feels she must draw between the Spirit's baptism, on the one hand, and the sacrament of Catholic baptism on the other, "One must ever bear in mind that in distinction to the sacrament of baptism, this release (baptism) of the Spirit is not a permanent state, and does not give an indelible character to the individual."

A similar concern is expressed by Paul F. Hutchinson, pastor of Christ Lutheran Church in St. Louis, Missouri, in his "Open Letter to Charismatic Luthers." His words at this point are these, "When the baptism in the Holy Spirit is separated from the initial reception of the Holy Spirit in infant baptism or adult conversion . . . then certain dangers open up."

It is time to take a careful look, in closing, at the evangelistic and missionary activities which Pentecostals have undertaken under the Spirit's impulse. We note, first, that they were from the earliest impelled to go to people where they were. As circuit riders without horses, they sought out the poor, the neglected, the alienated. They afforded, through their meetings, an opportunity to the anonymous and the voiceless to *belong* and to *speak*.

Further, they followed their people into the cities, perhaps sensing before many other groups the trend toward urbanization. If a personal word is permitted here, the writer is a member of a small denomination which is not charismatically oriented, which for years preferred small country or village churches, with burying grounds attached. It required time to persuade the writer's denomination that the future of America lay in urbanization, and to turn its energies toward the building of city congregations. Not so with the pentecostal bodies!

The emphasis upon the Holy Spirit has afforded these churches a powerful impetus toward missions. In his unique way of expressing things, David J. duPlessis explains how the pentecostals have accomplished so much in the past seventy years. He says, "The reason why pentecostals have been so successful in missions is because they are pentecostal."

The annals of the charismatic movement are full of accounts of the way in which persons untrained (by using standards) went forth, without any support from institutions or boards, and planted churches in the most forbidding and unlikely places. Who would have expected, humanly speaking, that T. B. Barratt, son of an English family who settled in Norway so the elder Barratt could manage a small sulphur mine in Hardanger, would have become the European apostle of pentecostalism? Yet from the influence of his Spirit-filled life (and he himself secured a fine education) there proceeded forces by which the message took root in Norway, Sweden, Finland, and Denmark, and shortly in Central Europe also.

Similarly, two Scandinavian-Americans felt called, about 1910, to go to Brazil. They went by naked faith, with no sponsoring board. Within fifty years the assemblies which grew out of their ministries came to number some 1500, with members totaling over a quarter of a million. About the same time an Italian-American from Chicago went to Brazil, alone and without visible support. Today the work which he initiated has about an equal number of congregations and of members. Together the two fellowships include over half of all Protestants in Brazil, and over one-tenth of all pentecostals in the world.

The charismatic movement in Chile had the most modest, even forbidding, origin. An American pastoring a Methodist Church there received the pentecostal blessing, was asked to leave his pastorate, and ventured forth on faith. In the wake of his ministry has come a Chilean pentecostalism including, in four groups (the Iglesia Metodista Pentecostal, the Iglesia Evangelica Pentecostal, the Mision Iglesia Pentecostal, and the Iglesia Pentecostal de Chile), a total membership of 920,000 members. These four bodies include two-thirds of all Protestants in Chile.

Similar illustrations of the evangelical and missionary impetus afforded the charismatic movement by its single-minded emphasis upon the baptism of the Holy Spirit could be brought from Central Africa, South Africa, Colombia, and even the U.S.S.R. It may be said safely that seldom since apostolic days have such single advances within the Christian movement been registered.

Lest it be thought that it is only in the lands just noted that pentecostalism is "on the move," let it be said that in the so-called Western world (including western Europe) the Full Gospel Business Men's Fellowship International (commonly known as the FGBMFI) has opened the charismatic ministry to laymen. This movement has, by enlisting the energies and gifts of men well-placed in the business world, shattered the earlier stereotype by which pentecostalism was regarded as a phenomenon largely confined to the economically deprived. The FGBMFI is an aggressive and effective instrument of evangelism, to all classes, in the U.S. and abroad.

The charismatic movement has also moved into the "highways and byways" of the youth subculture, for example, into the Jesus Revolution. Included among the triumphs registered in this area is the penetration of the victims of drug addiction and of ghetto gang warfare.

Perhaps enough has been said to demonstrate the position, that a single-minded emphasis upon the Holy Spirit as Baptizer, Energizer, and Empowerer has produced an outreach into areas largely neglected by the more conventional and "respectable" branches of the Christian movement which is amazing in its scope. Pentecostalism has always regarded itself as an instrument of church renewal. Its very life has consisted in a thrust toward *persons,* whether near at hand or afar off. Actually, early pentecostalism, taking Acts 1:8 with deadly seriousness, tended to find much of its "Jerusalem and all Judaea" in the region of Samaria. Possibly its ultimate success in "the uttermost parts of the earth" was due to its faithfulness to the call to society's Samaritans — the alienated, the neglected, the persons being bypassed in the march of worldly progress.

It goes without saying that no religious movement which might emerge today would face exactly the same kind of world as the charismatic movement encountered between 1900 and 1974. But if the details of the world of the *2.7 billion who have never heard the name of Jesus Christ* may differ, the demands upon the Church Militant remain very much the same. Could it be that the broad charismatic movement has something exceedingly important to say to any group which takes the Great Commission seriously? If so, that "something" will no doubt focus upon the blessed Holy Spirit — his special ministry within the hearts and the lives of Christian believers who are willing to grant him an utter centrality.

THE HOLY SPIRIT IN THE CHARISMATIC LIFE AND RENEWAL OF THE CHURCH TODAY IN EVANGELIZATION REPORT

Chairman: Larry Christensen
Secretary: S. Damaris

Everyone agrees that world evangelization depends upon the working of the Holy Spirit. However, there are differing views among Christians (i) as to how one "receives" the Holy Spirit, and (ii) as to how the Holy Spirit, once received, manifests himself. The way in which we handle these questions will have an effect upon our expectation and experience of the Holy Spirit's working in world evangelization.

A first step toward gaining understanding and mutual regard among Christians with differing views is to consider the ways in which these questions have been answered historically in the experience of the church. The group devoted about one-half of its time to laying this necessary groundwork. Members of the group who represented different points of view, and different historical traditions, dealt with the basic question: *How do you "receive" the Holy Spirit?*

1. *The classic view of the historic churches.*

The gift of the Holy Spirit is a part of the gift of salvation. The experience of the Holy Spirit comes as one reckons upon this fact and puts it into practice. Three principles underlie this position: (i) all believers participate in the Holy Spirit (I Cor. 12:13, Rom. 8:9); (ii) Pentecost and the other experiences of receiving the Holy Spirit in *Acts* are descriptions of historical, non-repeatable phenomenon; and (iii) believers are called continually to experience more of the fullness of the Spirit. There is no formal second step or stage in Christian maturity.

2. *The "second blessing" view.*

The gift of the Holy Spirit is received through a definite experience subsequent to salvation.

a. *Sanctification-as-experience.* This view developed in Wesleyanism. The emphasis was on holiness. Christians who are genuinely converted nevertheless see great deficiencies in their life, e.g., lack of inward purity, power, consistency. By faith one may appropriate the power of the Holy Spirit, and through an experience of sanctification have the carnal mind cleansed. Three conditions are involved: (i) ask (Luke 11:13), (ii) obey (Acts 5:32), and (iii) believe (Gal. 3:14). Three results may be expected: (i) power to witness (Acts 1:8), (ii) love of God (Rom. 5:5), (iii) purity.

b. *Baptism with the Holy Spirit in the holiness tradition.* This teaching was a historical outgrowth of the foregoing position, developing in the latter half of the nineteenth-century. The Spirit-filled life is deemed the express will of God (Eph. 5:18). That which God commands accords with his will, and one may therefore pray for it with confidence (I John 5:14-15). One appropriates this blessing by faith. Feelings or

special manifestations may come but are not essential; the essential
is to believe and receive. The result is that a life of defeat and carnality
is transformed into a life of fruitfulness.

c. *Baptism with the Holy Spirit in the classical pentecostal tradition.*
The Holy Spirit is received in a way that parallels one's receiving of
Christ. The new birth is called a baptism (I Cor. 12:13). In an exactly
similar manner, one receives the baptism with the Holy Spirit. In
salvation, the Spirit baptizes into Christ's Body, the church; when we
are endued with power, the Lord Jesus Christ baptizes us in the Holy
Spirit. At this baptism (and subsequently) the Holy Spirit manifests
his presence by speaking with unknown tongues (Acts 2:4, 10:44, 19:6).
As a result of this baptism, believers make themselves available to the
Holy Spirit for his "charismata." In the life of the early church these
gifts opened doors of evangelism in an explosive way.

d. *Baptism with the Holy Spirit in the neo-pentecostal movement.*
Around 1960 the experiences which had characterized classical pentecostal churches began to spread into the historical churches; in some
sectors of this new movement, the understanding of the baptism with
the Holy Spirit was similar to that of classical pentecostalism, though
speaking in tongues was not usually considered the "necessary sign"
that one had been baptized in the Holy Spirit. The experience of
tongues, however, has been widespread.

Among churches with more of a sacramental tradition (Anglicans,
Lutherans, Roman Catholic, Orthodox), the baptism with the Holy
Spirit is understood in a more "organic" sense, i.e., the outgrowth or
actualization of the relationship with the Holy Spirit which is established in salvation. In this view there is an appreciation both of the
"crisis" and the "growth" motifs in sanctification, baptism with the
Holy Spirit usually being regarded under the former category. While
there is no doctrine of tongues as initial evidence, the experience of
tongues is common.

The result of this brief historical/theological survey, which was
amplified by several appropriate testimonies, was an appreciation of
the variety of ways in which Christians experience the reality of the
Spirit, and the variety of ways in which they explain or verbally communicate that experience. The group manifested a marked willingness
to listen to one another, and a genuine appreciation for one another's
experience, even where it may have involved points of disagreement.
This formed the background for the most significant area of agreement
in the group. Christians with differing experience and understanding
of the working of the Holy Spirit can and must hold one another in
high regard as they join together in the task of world evangelization;
a spirit of dogmatism and exclusivism will grieve the Spirit, whereas a
spirit of openness to one another will lead to an increase of love and
understanding, which will greatly aid the spread of the Gospel.

The study group not only voiced this kind of an idea, but became a
forum where the members experienced this very thing in a significant
measure through various kinds of action and interaction. While the
ideas presented helped to clarify certain misunderstandings, the more
important outcome was a marked change in *attitudes* which could be
seen as the meetings progressed: Christians of widely differing backgrounds and points of view expressed a fresh appreciation and regard

for one another.

Against the background of such understanding in the study group, the participants were challenged with this question: How does my understanding of the working of the Holy Spirit contribute to the work of world evangelization? Working in a number of small groups, the participants cited various ways in which we should expect and/or are already experiencing the working of the Holy Spirit, as well as areas where problems may exist, or where further work needs to be done.

Prelude

a. All were agreed that there can be no evangelization without the empowering, the guidance, and direction of the Holy Spirit. He sets us free to witness joyously to the Lordship of Jesus Christ. We rejoice that this whole Congress has been characterized by this theme.

b. There was great stress on the need of waiting for the power. This is Jesus' command. The whole church needs to enter into this kind of "waiting prayer" and renewed study of the Scriptures.

c. And one of the missing facts in church life today has been a deep spirit of repentance — not simply vaguely or generally, but specifically and concretely — from hardness of heart, false pride, unbelief, and concern with the wrong priorities. This is a crucial prelude to the "fullness of the Spirit" and evangelization.

Developing strategies

A. We were made keenly aware of what the Spirit is doing among young people. There is a fresh openness and life among many of them. We need to listen and learn from them.

b. Wherever the Spirit has come, every believer becomes a fresh witness, natural and real. Often then there is great need for a teaching, enabling ministry.

c. There is new liberty whenever the Spirit comes, not just in the exercise of the gifts, but in church life and strategy. Notice the richness and diversity in much of the para-church movement.

d. Often hard places have been penetrated when the Spirit has come. Here different situations were spoken of: Jews for Jesus; the evangelization of gypsies in one country; and Christ coming among materialists, the Hindus, Muslims; and even the nominal ones in other places. Impossible without the Holy Spirit.

e. The manifestation of the miraculous through spiritual gifts often become signs in the evangelistic task. We should expect this.

f. There is always a wonderful sense of unity, of being in "one accord," when the Spirit comes. This in itself becomes a powerful way of drawing people to belief.

g. The whole Church needs to take seriously, and learn from, the house church and small group movement. The Lord is doing something very real here.

Further areas for study

a. In view of the resurgence of the pentecostal and neo-pente-

costal movements, we need a "theology of the charismatic life." Not
a polemic, but careful thinking and study of the person and work of
the Holy Spirit.

   b. What is a charismatic church? What is its style of worship and
ministry?

   c. What is an authentic ministry of deliverance, particularly in
view of the heightened manifestation of the occult and demon possession?

   d. There is a great need for understanding. How can we learn from
one another, and speak the truth in love?

GUILT CONVERSION AND MODERN PSYCHOLOGY

Jorge A. Leon

*Dr. Leon, Buenos Aires, Argentina,
is the Director of the Department on
Culture, Education, and Christian
Emphasis of the YMCA in Buenos Aires.*

We do not mean, in such a short report, to make an exhaustive study about such a wide subject. However, within the brief space allotted we shall try to reach the simplest and most concrete form possible.

1. *Critical evaluation of psychological interpretations about guilt*
    a. Sigmund Freud published his book *Totem and Taboo* in 1913. On the basis of Darwin and Alkinson this work gives a peculiar theory, according to which man acquires the feeling of guilt for having "fallen into the sin of parricide" in order to be able to satisfy his sexual needs by means of an incestuous form. According to that theory, primitive men used to live in small tribes, under the domination of a despotic chief: the "father." All the women of the tribe belonged exclusively to him. The father recurred to human sacrifices, castration, or expulsion from the tribe as a means for the maintaining of his sexual monopoly. All this led the young people to rebel against the father's tyranny: they banned together and killed him. Moreoever, they ate his flesh in order to inherit his virility. Once they had thus satisfied their hatred, they got back a feeling of love for the father, which had been suppressed. It is in this kind of ambivalence, *hatred-love*, that the feeling of guilt is expressed.

We agree with Dr. J. H. van der Berg of *Psychology and Faith* when he says that "the accuracy in this ingenious theory becomes a starting point." Surely, the sexual behavior of primitive men — according to the opinion of a few anthropologists — does not fit into Freud's theory. This is clearly demonstrated in Dr. Malinovsky's book, *Sex and Repression in Savage Society*.

Freud published his *Totem and Taboo* before his *Second Topics* on the psychic apparatus. We may accept, on the basis of his second topic, his interpretation of the feeling of guilt as a result of the tension between the I and the Super-I.

Freud distinguishes two causes to the feeling of guilt: the fear and respect for the Super-I. The first obliges us to give up the demands of the "He." Yet the second one, who is much more exigent, leads to seek punishment, since it is impossible for him to hide the constant, forbidden desires from the Super-I. Such Freudian reflection is very important for the preacher of the Gospel, for it shows that the feeling of guilt may be the cause, and not the result of sin. One knows that some become delinquents for they unconsciously seek punishment from society in order to thus quieten their consciences. In my pastoral work, I have come across many cases where the feeling of guilt is not necessarily the result of sin, e.g., a woman feels herself guilty of her mother's death, because of a provoked miscarriage. At the age of fifteen she had an argument with her mother about the birth of a little brother. The mother miscarried and died. The daughter had not sought this, yet she feels herself guilty of that miscarriage and death.

Dr. Rollo May makes a distinction between neurotic and ontologic guilt. I prefer to distinguish between neurotic and existential guilt. Existential guilt is something normal, since we are all sinners. Neurotic guilt is generally depressive. Nervous breakdown expresses itself by a disgust for life, a feeling of illness, a general discouragement which prevents initiative and realization. Such reflections are very important for those who want to evangelize. Most evangelists tend to intensify the feeling of guilt as a way to induce repentance. However, what happens with those who suffer from feelings of guilt which are not the result of sin? Is one not in danger of reaching the opposite result from what one is expecting? Is it possible that sin be converted into a form of self-punishment advocated from the pulpit?

It is also necessary to keep in mind the fact that there is not only a conscious guilt, but also an unconscious one. "Yet, such a feeling of guilt does not always penetrate into the realm of consciousness. On the contrary, it is sometimes entirely suppressed into the unconscious and manifests itself indirectly through irritability, bad temper, apathy, depression, psychosomatic troubles and so on. In other cases, it expresses itself through an interior tension, provoking a deep uneasy feeling with continual suffering and fear of some coming catastrophe. These latter expressions are deeply associated with a necessity for punishment." In my book *Pastoral Psychology for all Christians,* I also mention the following symptoms of unconscious feeling of guilt; susceptibility, insomnia, feeling of insecurity, abnormal activity, tendencies to suicide and sensation of being away from God. The preacher must keep in mind the reality of unconscious guilt, in order to be able to help arrogant and self-satisfied persons who seem to have no feeling of guilt and affirm that they do not need to repent because they haven't offended anyone. Persons with such an attitude are the ones most in need. The feeling of guilt had been hidden in the unconscious, since the conscious mind found it intolerable. It becomes the subconscious mechanism of repression.

b. *Critical evaluation of psychologic interpretations about conversion.* The psychology of religion deals with conversion as a psychological phenomenon. Before going ahead with the different psychological interpretations, we must admit that the endeavors of that science are defeated in advance for the cause producing the effect, i.e., God, cannot be subject to any possibility of scientific examination.

The first work on psychology of religion, by E. D. Starbuch, appeared in 1899. It deals fundamentally with conversion. According to Starbuch's statistics, conversion occurs most frequently at the age of seventeen. It is relatively seldom after forty. Starbuch does not believe in any exclusively human phenomenon, a common experience in the development of adolescence. Though a conversion is claimed to be a relation between God and man, he says, this is purely an assumption.

The converted person thinks he has been transformed, yet he is mistaken.

George A. Coe made statistical studies, seeking to prove that those who are converted are mostly of a temperament where sensitiveness predominates over intellect. Thus the conversion or non-conversion of a person is determined by his or her temperament, not by the action of a transcendental being.

For T. A. Leuba, a psychologist of religion, God exists only as a psychical process. God had only a "subjective existence."

Yet not all psychologists of religion have an atheistic point of view. William James, in his famous work *Varieties of Religious Experience,* dedicates a chapter to "The Reality of the Unseen," which recognizes the existence of a transcendental being. He defines conversion as "the gradual or sudden process by which an I, up to then divided and consciously wicked, inferior and miserable, becomes unified and consciously good, superior and happy, as a consequence of his or her former attachment to religious realities."

For George Gerguer, when the psychologist of religion wants to convert to transcendence in a mere subjective experience, he is trying to eliminate a perturbing element, i.e., the "other side" from which the believer receives his faith and where he directs it.

Dr. William Sargant, a famous English psychiatrist, who, at the same time acknowledges himself as a Christian, has more recently written a study about the psychology of conversion. He writes that he has a deep belief and owes a great deal to the Christian education he received. He adds, "My choosing Wesley for a special study about the technique of religious conversions comes from my own Methodist education."

For him, religious conversion and "brain washing" correspond to the same physiological laws that cannot be controlled by their subject. According to Sargant, the religious technique of conversion basically consists in increasing suggestiveness, in order to then implant new ideas. Under the effects of that hyper-suggestiveness, the said ideas remain engraved in the subject. "An individual or a group may adopt new beliefs or ways of behavior as the result of a sudden and intense interior illumination, generally after a period of strong emotional tension." "In the same way, *brain washing,* having a political object, is aiming at the discovery of a new way of salvation, after calling forth a shock of violent emotions (anger, fear, and others) as a means of disengaging the old "burgess" mental system. If the communist gospel is accepted, love may be replaced by fear; yet, the ones who use such methods must know that an implacable judgment is awaiting them."

In much detail Sargant relates the conversion to communism of Arthur Koestler following a succession of sad events. On the other side, speaking of mass conversions on the day of Pentecost (Acts 2), he shows that the story corresponds to modern physiological observations. He emphasizes the fact that, at Pentecost, Peter was successfully using the methods described in Sargant's book, and he advises using such techniques in evangelization. "Reality demonstrates," he says, "that there cannot be an authentic religious revival of protestantism while other proselytism is mainly based on an appeal to the reason and intellect of adults. A stand must be taken against the emotional barriers which already exist. This would help extirpate previous points of view and make it possible for new and desired ones to be accepted. Even Wesley's efforts were relatively inefficacious until his heart was warmed from the outside."

Sargant's point of view is extremely dangerous for the Christian idea of evangelization. Indigenous preachers may obtain, with Sargant's technique the same results as those obtained by the communists with similar methods. True, we can accept the existence of the physiological mechanism described by Sargant; yet this also means the acceptance of Starbuch's thesis, according to which conversion is an exclusively human phenomenon. Describing some phenomenon does not explain its etiology.

We do not have sufficient space, here, for a more detailed critical analysis. But we offer a possibility of investigation.

2. *Reflections about the psycho-theological aspects of preaching*

We have too little space to elaborate on a psychology of evangelical preaching. We merely want to share a few psycho-theological reflections about the preaching against sin, aiming at conversion.

We think it necessary to establish a clear differentiation between (the) feeling of guilt and sin itself. The first is a psychological concept; the second is theological. The New Testament speaks about sin and not about the feeling of guilt, even if the latter is often implicit, as a consequence of sin. Paul refers to sin as a kind of being abiding in him (Rom. 7:14, 17, 20, 23, 25) producing an emotional state (feeling) of guilt which leads to the statement that he feels miserable. However, as mentioned earlier, a person may feel guilty while his emotional state is not necessarily the consequence of sin. Therefore, the preaching of the Gospel must be positive. When it speaks of sin it must always leave some hope, emphasizing the way leading to liberation in Christ. (Such idea of sin as a being abiding in the Christian would correspond to what is called the "child" in transactional analysis, where the "states" of the I are meant to express themselves as if there were several persons in one. Sometimes one of them is appearing, sometimes another.)

Some are neurotically seeking a pastor who gives them "spiritual lashes," from the pulpit, every Sunday. The "masochism" of certain parishioners needs the "sadism" of certain preachers. Thus a neurotic relation is established between preacher and parishioner, which is a guarantee of faithful attendance. I have often seen that neurotic need for punishment applied by the "messenger of God." Also, some parishioners after making their confession, have asked me, "Don't you despise me, pastor?" Sometimes it takes the form of a pleading, as if they are asking, "Please, despise me." I remember a girl saying to me, "Please, beat me. I feel some trembling in my chest and I can't cry, please give me the strongest possible box on my ear." This is a conscious expression of what some parishioners are unconsciously seeking. To beat them — either with the hand or with words — means nothing else than to satisfy some neurotic necessity similar to some heathen expiation. However, Jesus Christ suffered on the cross for our redemption and therefore we do not need to suffer for our sins. True, the Lord is expecting our repentance. Yet to beat people from the pulpit, instead of being a means for their spiritual growth, is nothing more than to feed their neuroses.

The preacher has to deal with sin as with a theological problem because it separates man from God and from the goal of his existence. He must not try to increase the feeling of guilt as a psychological problem, but always remember that existential guilt is the expression of an emotional break. Berne shows that great troubles in our lives often take the form of games. His disciples have developed his ideas. It seems that a favorite game is "beat me." The pastor should not indulge in that game, neither from the pulpit, nor in private talk. The shepherd carries a stick, but it should be used to rescue the sheep that have fallen into the abyss, and not to beat him.

If the pastor helps to increase the feeling of neurotic guilt — which is not necessarily a consequence of sin — he may paradoxically help the people to fall into sin, one sin feeding the next sin, i.e., a sin that brings the punishment desired by the person in order to get rid of the feeling of guilt for a time.

The preacher ought to take as his basic hypothesis the fact that every human being feels himself a sinner, consciously or not. The forgiveness of God, objectively expressed by the atoning work of Jesus Christ, is, on a psychological level, the greatest healing power that exists. On a theological level it includes redemption.

It is not our intention to eliminate preaching against sin. We only intend to underline the dangers of increasing the feeling of guilt and remind us of the fact that preaching should be positive and liberating. We want to advocate the kind of preaching that contributes to the entire salvation of the believer including mental health. In his last book the famous American psychiatrist Karl Menninger (founder of the Menninger Hospital of Topeka, Kansas) insists upon the necessity of maintaining the preaching against sin. Moreover, he recognizes that psychiatry has helped to create a sort of erosion of the notion of sin. What we need today is balanced, evangelical preaching, based on a valuable exegesis and hermeneutic. Without falling into a cheap psychology we should be conscious of our need of both spiritual and mental health if we want to be channels of grace.

One last reflection about conversion. There are authentic conversions and others that are non-authentic. The latter is a sclerotic experience. Jesus invites us to "follow him on the way" and this makes abundant life possible. Conversion is necessarily lineal. A line is a continuation of dots. New birth is nothing else but one of those dots.

3. *Elements for the elaboration of a theology of evangelization*

Evangelical preaching insists, and so do we, on the new birth. Yet to remain a child is not the ideal Christian; for an ankylosed child becomes a dwarf. That is why the preaching of the Gospel should be supported by a good exegesis and hermeneutic. A Christian is one who is in the process of becoming the Image of God. A Christian is also a pilgrim seeking fullness in Christ. "Till we all come in the unity of the faith, and of the knowledge of the Son of God, unto a perfect man, unto the measure of the stature of the fullness of Christ" (Eph. 4:13-14). We have been developing these ideas in two books.

Biblical anthropology includes an implicit soteriology. The fullness of Christ (second Adam — Rom. 5:12-21; I Cor. 12:21,22 — or image of God — Col. 1:15) is the arrival at the end of the process of salvation, which includes not only the essence of man, but also his existence. A theology of evangelization should be supported by three basic points:

(i) A good exegesis and hermeneutic of the Gospel as proclaimed by Jesus, the gospel of the kingdom, good tidings to the poor and the gospel of salvation.

(ii) Becoming acquainted with the sociology and psychology of the man to whom we want to communicate the Gospel.

(iii) A methodology which, on one hand, must have a biblical foundation and, on the other, should be adjusted to the reality of the man of our time.

Before ending we would give a brief exposition of what we call *Evangelization of Tension* which will be exhaustively explained in my forthcoming book. The basic principles are alluded to in *Psychology of Religious Experience.* We are reproducing three paragraphs of the same. "The conclusions of this work are a call to humility for all evangelists . . . If I am not a living Gospel, but only have a knowledge of the Gospel, I shall only be able to offer biblical education, i.e. a transmission of knowledge, but not *communicate* the Gospel . . . . We evangelists sometimes fall into pride and arrogancy, and this stems from three false presuppositions: 1. that we are a bag full of wisdom and power from God; 2. that the other person is also a bag, but empty of any knowledge of God; 3. that the evangelical task consists in pouring into the other some of our contents, so that he should be filled. We should not be deceived, nor deceive others. If our life is incomplete, why haven't we started to pattern it according to the stature of Jesus Christ. Moreover, the other one is *not* an empty bag, since in the worst of man there is the *Image of God,* asking for completion. That is why our approach should be respectful.

Concerning Evangelization

"I am convinced that the majority of evangelists of our time have tended to fill up bags and not to win men and lead them according to the dimension of Christ.

"The conclusions of said work demonstrate the necessity of a communication of the Gospel aiming at a linear conversion, whereas the technique of the full bag leads to "punctual" conversion. The linear includes the punctual, since a line is a succession of points. True conversion, i.e. the linear one, is the space between two points, the point where one *is and stands* and the point where one *should be.*

"Jesus knew that there is an *Imago Dei* in the worst of men and that, because of sin, this image of God is calling for completion. Hence, what every human being needs is to discover himself as a man and as a perfectible man in the light of Jesus Christ. No man is an empty bag. The problem is not to put new contents into the bag, but to help tidy up that which is already in it, in order to be able to receive, in a harmonious form, that which is missing. It is to show the difference between what one is and what one should be. With a clear vision of his problem, man feels challenged, by his existential emptiness, to seek his ontological vocation. It is a question of trying to reach the fullness of his human condition given in Jesus Christ.

"Evangelization must tend to the "creation" of interior tensions for the discovery of our "to be" and "should be." The *evangelization of tension* goes out from the reality according to which there are, in every man, two deep realities: an *Imago Dei* distorted by sin and, as a logical consequence, the *necessity of completion*. Unfortunately, many are using conscious or unconscious mechanisms in order to ease the interior tension unitl it almost disappears. Yet the existential emptiness remains. The psycho-theological presuppositions developed in the present work determine the method we have called *"evangelization of tension."*

GUILT CONVERSION AND MODERN PSYCHOLOGY REPORT

Chairman: A. Martinez
Secretary: R.N. Nelson

The content of Dr. Leon's paper should be communicated to all who are involved in evangelism. This was the overwhelming conclusion of the participants in the group. The material Leon presented received enthusiastic acceptance in the group. A chief concern of the participants was that his books should be translated into English.

The significance of Leon's ideas lies in the damage that is being done to many members of congregations because of pastors' ignorance of the points covered in the study paper. This makes it imperative, in the opinion of the participants, that the Congress take steps to disseminate this material.

Leon's paper begins with a treatment of guilt as related to evangelization and conversion. Drawing from the works of other psychologists, Leon distinguishes between "existential guilt" and "neurotic guilt." For him, existential guilt is a realistic and healthy recognition by an individual of his own sin. Neurotic guilt, on the other hand, is the sick obsessive preoccupation of a person who has failed to recognize the expiation that the Lord Jesus has made once for all on the Cross. People who are predisposed toward neurotic guilt tend to seek out preachers who will punish them by continually emphasizing their badness. A neurotic interaction *(symbiosis)* can thus be established between neurotically guilt-laden persons and preachers who themselves have a neurotic need to inflict suffering on others. It constitutes a masochistic-sadistic partnership between persons whose problems feed on others' sickness.

This kind of dynamic may seemingly be effective in producing "conversions," states Leon, but cannot be seen as the result of the Holy Spirit's work. It is to be shunned, because instead of producing spiritual healing, it promotes emotional and spiritual sickness.

Quoting from Sargant, Leon points out that some preachers resort to brain-washing techniques to produce conversions, and that this brainwashing corresponds with identifiable physiological laws. Leon insists that brainwashing is not an ethical tool for the evangelist to use in proclaiming the Gospel.

Leon's paper distinguishes between sin as a theological issue and guilt (the subjective awareness, conscious or unconscious, of sin) as a psychological issue. The preacher has to deal with sin because it separates man from God, but he must not resort to tormenting guilt feelings in a neurotic manner.

Evangelical preaching, states Leon, should insist on the new birth as the beginning of a process of perfecting the image of God which is in every man. In order that the newborn Christian experience this perfecting of the divine image that is in him, hermeneutic and exegetical preaching is necessary.

From the lively interaction and contributions of those who participated in the discussion resulting from Dr. Leon's paper, the following recommendations emerged:

1. *See that Leon's books are translated into English.* He has written three books dealing with the subject, thus making an important contribution which should be available to a wider segment of the evangelical world. Partly as a result of the participants' encouragement in this regard, Dr. Leon has taken some preliminary steps to publish his works in the United States.

2. *Discourage all methods of evangelism which violate the message of the Gospel.* These would include, among others, the sadistic stimulation of neurotic guilt and brainwashing methods mentioned above.

3. *Promote training programs for pastors and evangelists, which seek to unify theology and counseling.* Theology is needed for the understanding of God's purpose and message. The principles of counseling are necessary for the sensitive and effective communication of this message to man in his real condition.

4. *Pastoral counseling should be considered as a matter of concern in evangelism.* One participant quoted from Eric Berne the fact that in the United States more than 70 percent of those who seek counseling, consult a pastor or priest. This exemplifies the responsibility which Christian workers have in the area of helping troubled people.

Conclusion

The Gospel and its cause can be enhanced or discredited accordingly as it is proclaimed with integrity or for the satisfaction of an unhealthy or selfish need. Our hearers will be healed or harmed by the announcing of the Gospel compassionately or self-seekingly. Therefore we urge that the points contained in this paper, which identify some distinctions between a wholesome evangelism and a sick parody of our redemptive message, be made known on a wide basis so that all who are concerned with the task of evangelism can benefit by them.

CHRISTIAN PERSONAL AND SOCIAL ETHICS IN RELATION TO RACISM POVERTY, WAR, AND OTHER PROBLEMS

Carl F.H. Henry

*Dr. Henry, Arlington, Virginia, USA, is
theologian-at-large for World Vision in California, and
Professor of Theology at Trinity Evangelical Divinity School in Illinois.*

This essay is "to evaluate current personal and social ethics in hindering and furthering the proclamation of the Gospel; to show the implications of the Gospel for contemporary social ethics including sex (marriage, divorce, promiscuity, pornography), wealth (capital, property, profit, poverty), race (racism, casteism), political power (bribery and corruption), and war."

Within the imposed space limits we can do little more than project a brief exposition and evaluation of current moral theory and practice in relation to the Gospel, and a similarly brief discussion of the Gospel's implications for five central issues which the assignment subdivides into thirteen specific concerns. It seems best, therefore, simply to offer summary statements suitable for consideration and expansion in group discussion.

1. Introduction

a. Civilization is not merely a product of human aspiration, nor solely a by-product of the Gospel; it springs, rather, from God-given gifts of creation and reflects God's creation-mandate that man subdue the world to the ethical and spiritual purposes of the Creator.

b. Human sinfulness pervades all fallen man's motives, and conditions all his works and goals. Man was made not for civilization and culture but for God; man in sin tends to assimilate revelation to civilization, however, so that civilization becomes the channel through which human life is thought to gain meaning and worth.

c. The truth of revelation ranges itself critically alongside all achievements of civilization, and judges these by the Kingdom of God. God's covenant and commandments, set forth intelligibly in the prophetic-apostolic Scriptures and manifested in Jesus Christ, define the content of Christian morality. The Christian's task is not merely to preserve an inherited civilization or culture but to promote the Kingdom of God; only the divinely-given principles of social morality assure public justice and human welfare. Christian mission in the world includes an open declaration of God's purposes and commandments as they relate to sex and marriage, labor and economics, civil government and public life, since these constitute the criteria by which God wills that all men should live in society, and by which men and nations will finally be judged.

d. Because of his revolt against the God of creation and inordinate desires, fallen man represses and distorts the moral claim universally exerted by God in history and in conscience. Since a morality predicated on human expedients cannot ongoingly sustain civilization, its moral foundations inevitably weaken and crumble. The Christian mission in fallen society is one of light and salt; that is, it has illuminating and preserving significance. Christians are duty-bound to exemplify and to promote social justice. Only private and public righteousness can exalt a nation; disobedience to God's will marks nations and civilizations for destruction. For all that, Christians do not advance the personal and public righteousness that God demands merely to Christianize the world or to preserve a dated civilization or parochial national culture. Nor do they becloud their mission into modern utopian ideologies by succumbing to fanciful visions of a new man and a new society. Christians know that God's new man has already been historically manifested in Jesus Christ who is risen from the dead and powerfully alive as the publicly identified judge of the human race. They know, moreover, that the new society is not simply a future expectation but is already here in the redeemed community over which the crucified and risen Jesus rules as Head of the Body. Not only are individual believers, dispersed throughout many nations, to be inwardly conformed by the Spirit to the holy image of God's obedient Son, but also the church as a community is to exemplify that public righteousness which God desires in society. Over against all the uninformed and misleading ideological pledges of alien kingdoms, only the regenerate church approximates the Kingdom of God in history.

e. Much of the positive ingredient in modern secular ethics has been inherited at a distance from earlier Christian insights. When worldings, who lack special revelation and redemption, nonetheless devote themselves in part to certain moral concerns stemming from the biblical view of God and man, while many Christians conspicuously neglect these same concerns, the Gospel is understandably disdained as erosive of ethical earnestness, rather than as singularly promotive of it.

2. *How current personal and social ethics hinders or furthers the proclamation of the Gospel*

While we can make only a very limited survey of recent moral theory here, we can nonetheless ascertain certain trends that are likely to gain worldwide attention in the days ahead.

a. Ancient non-biblical religions are being exported to the West today as an antidote to secular materialism. Zen fascinates young people in quest of a transcendent world beyond the sense-sphere of technocratic science; it attracts them also for its amorality. Islam, Hinduism, and Buddhism, the latter more a moral vision than a religion, offer few ethical hindrances and obstacles to the Gospel markedly different from those attaching to them in the past; in large urban centers, moreover, their own followers are increasingly vulnerable to Western secularization. The fact that Chrisitanity as an ethical religion has already gone through the scientific revolution and survives as a powerful missionary movement and intellectual and moral force gives it an advantage over religions whose followers have yet to undergo the full impact of the scientific age. In mainland China, where Communism has driven Christianity out of church buildings and into homes, the ongoing reformulation and erosion of Confucian teaching could yet become a providential preparation for future evangelical advance; just as modern Chinese scholars praised Confucianism for rejecting religion, so contemporary Communist scholars are rejecting Confucian ethics as well. Nonetheless new indigenous forms are emerging in which Confucianism retains importance. The weakness of ancient religious vis-a-vis Christianity lies in their failure to overcome doubts about the meaning and worth of human life in the present world alongside the lack of persuasive cognitive support for such doctrines as reincarnation or nirvana, while Christianity promises a new quality of life even now and finds its center in the crucified and risen Lord.

b. In the West, radical secularity claims that man himself defines the time and the good. Man's "coming of age" is said to require his repudiation of transcendent moral law, revealed commandments, and fixed principles, and the elaboration of moral action instead on the basis of personal automomy and individual creativity. This commitment to all-embracing contigency and relativity follows fast upon a loss of faith in evolutionary utopianism. Atheistic scientism holds that man himself, and not an inherently or divinely patterned nature or history, determines the present and future, and dismisses as mythological any representation of supernatural being, divine revelation, Scriptural rule of right, and transcendent offer of salvation.

c. For a generation, logical positivism sought to reduce moral and theological claims to nonsense on the ground of their non-verifiability by empirical scientific method. Although positivistic theory collapsed through its own internal contradictions, and was itself reducible to nonsense when judged by the criteria it adduced, it helpfully exposed the vast number of contrary and contradictory ethical theories based on philosophical reasoning (logical positivism being another!); it also publicized the impropriety of readily calling "scientific" the flexible morality companioned by modern viewpoints. Logical positivism focused interest on the meaning and verification of ethical statements. Historic Christianity is able to confront these concerns with far less apprehension than can secular alternatives.

d. It will not do to confront current naturalistic views, e.g., radical secularity, with anything less than the equally radical alternative of the biblical revelation of the will of God and its definition of the good life. All intermediary options, whether Western or Eastern, retain mythologies of nature, of history, or of man, and cannot adduce valid moral norms on the basis of philosophical reasoning, mystical experience, sense observation, or any other indicated alternative to transcendent revelation. Even the "new" morality, because it retains only a vestige of Christianity in its appeal to interpersonal love as the only motivation and criterion of conduct, could not escape a decline to moral relativism. By surrendering the objective revelational content of ethics, sacrificing fixed moral principles, and forfeiting the importance of justice alongside love, the "new" morality could not adjudicate between contrary and contradictory courses of action appealing to love as their motivation. The fact that all the speculative alternatives to revelational ethics have now cancelled each other out to the point of radical secularity creates a situation favorable to a fresh examination of revealed morality.

e. Discerning Christian theologians have long pointed out that a culture predicated on technological scientism inevitably undermines personal values. The church in the twentieth century has not, however, related its preaching effectively to this contemporary phenomenon, nor has it powerfully demonstrated the difference of lifestyle involved in the evangelical alternative. Dramatically and conspicuously the youth counter-culture movement has revolted against a reductive scientistic pursuit of quantitative apart from qualitative and personal concerns took expression. Instead of technocratically tapering external reality to impersonal processes and events, counter-culture youth demands a recognition that personal values belong to the real world. The quest for a realm of reality that transcends scientific-empirical data explains in part their growing interest in Oriental mystery religions, hallucinatory drugs, spritisim, and demon phenomena. Such practices are neither truly mind-expanding, nor are they an unambiguous reflection of "moral" concern; indeed, no logically persuasive case whatever for transcendent morality can be mounted in this way.

f. Through theologically unlettered, the Jesus-movement confidently probes the supernatural world in terms of divine revelation in Christ and in the Bible as the Word of God. While vulnerable to all sorts of charismatic excesses, it is not immune to larger possibilities of authentic spiritual dynamism than that manifested today by many evangelicals; and by elevating scriptural authority above personal experience, this movement can be preserved from cultic deviations. The youth counter-culture outside the Jesus-movement tries to confront the technocratic myth of ultimate impersonal reality by emphasizing mystical consciousness; this, however, merely counters one myth of reality with another. The myth of technocratic scientism cannot be eradicated by a simplistic substitution of the myth of superrational mysticism. The only firm transcendent basis for moral values is God as an intelligible religious reality. As far as values are concerned, moreover, the secular counter-culture concentrates on social values to the neglect of personal righteousness, and despite its emphasis on love for neighbor, neglects the first and great commandment, namely, love for God. In these respects the Jesus-movement provides many refreshing contrasts. From the very first the Christian message has emphasized the need of totally new selfhood, has called men to love of God and fellow man, and has stressed concern for public no less than for private righteousness.

g. For many persons in North America and Western Europe the problem of human meaning and worth turns upon psychological emptiness amid affluence; for untold multitudes elsewhere, it turns rather upon dire poverty and the powerlessness to change one's destiny — upon the search for food and shelter to survive another day. When Christians fail to emphasize that it is morally wicked, that human creatures starve and suffer like animals, and that insensitivity of the rich to the physical needs of those around them is ethically culpable; they, as it were, yield to Marxists the privilege of formulating social criticism; they also nourish the propaganda that only communism or socialism can guarantee a just society. In some areas like Latin America with its vast pockets of poverty, the burden of the *status quo* is so heavy that all existing social structures are deplored as oppressive; the underprivileged and victimized consequently reach for radical alternatives that retrieve hope from some remote nebulous future and insert it into the immediate present and its problems. This is true of both spiritual and social concerns. Roman Catholicism, by far the dominant religion in Latin America, has done little across 400 years to insert hope into the economic plight of the masses; evangelical Protestantism, while inculcating vital personal religion, has similarly done but little to cope with the problem of poverty. To stress that the total human predicament will be solved only if people are personally converted to Christ lacks assurance because even a phenomenal church growth rate of more than five per cent in a single decade would still miss the vast majority, and lacks credibility when one notes the limited reversal of poverty among people even in evangelical churches. In respect of spiritual concerns, the yearning for hope fulfilled in the immediate present accounts for surging interest in charismatic forms of Christianity. In Chile, Pentecostal Christians have outstripped Southern Baptists 60 to one in evangelism, winning many converts among the destitute who are the very targets of the social revolutionaries. Charismatic Christianity promises nothing less than the extension of apostolic gifts into the present and an earnest of the eschatological future right now. But many, notably in Brazil, who seek dynamic relationships to a transcendent world turn as readily to spiritism. The longing for material fulfilment in the face of poverty is widespread among all the masses, however, and the relentless Marxist attack on capitalism promotes socialism as the utopian alternative and revolutionary violence as the way to achieve it. The confiscation and redistribution of wealth becomes more credible as an ideal solution of the human predicament whenever several factors are present:

(i) When Marxists are allowed exclusive rights as a preface to socialist propaganda to fervently indict the moral wrongs of human destitution, suffering, affliction, and oppression.

(ii) When Christian proclamation speaks only of personal spiritual conversion, ignores social criticism attuned to biblical justice, and elaborates no persuasive alternative to a forced redistrubution of wealth either in theory or practice.

(iii) When Marxists are allowed to speak of socialism in romantic terms without being asked either to identify which of its many forms they propose or to explain why socialism, despite tyrannical imposition, has nowhere achieved the just society it propagandizes. Alexander Solzhenitsyn's *The Gulag Archipelago* (1973) is highly illuminatizing of the realities of Soviet life; it indicates that Communist repression in Russia was ten to a thousand times worse than Czarist repression, and that the Soviets destroyed more dissenters than did the Nazis. It is essential to contrast socialist uncertainty about the identity of the ideal man and of the express nature of the new society with Christian certainty about the Second Adam and the regenerate society as a beachhead in history for the coming Kingdom.

(iv) When Christians fail to emphasize that Marxist proposals for utopia do not really, as claimed, overcome human alienation, but in fact perpetuate that alienation by substituting one preferred class for another and deepen it by ignoring man's fundamental spiritual relationships to the living God.

h. If despite utopian promises socialism and materialistic capitalism continue to siphon off the meaning and worth of individual existence for multitudes of moderns, no less is this true of radical secularism which is penetrating the academic centers of the so-called Free World as the theoretical stance of many pseudo-intellectuals. Anyone who tries to live consistently by the creed of atheistic naturalism — to wit, that ultimate reality consists of impersonal processes and events; that the cosmos originated unpurposed and accidentally; that history has no objective pattern or plan; that man is an oddity destined for extinction like the animals, and that distinctions of morality and truth are private preferences only — such a one drains personal existence of everything that makes human survival significant. The secular naturalist lives in fact by strikingly different premises than his vaunted naturalistic creed accommodates. How is one to reconcile his public call for universal human justice, for sensitivity to human welfare, for ecological awareness of the cosmos and a field of ethical responsibility, with the notion that moral distinctions are but autonomous expressions of individual creativity? How is one to square his sense of personal worth, the unyielding desire to guarantee his own individual security and survival, his reluctance to contemplate with tranquility his own ultimate non-being, with the insistence that the cosmic process is wholly purposeless and indifferent to personal concerns? How is one to explain the fact that, when wronged by his neighbor, he refuses to concede that universal ethical obligation is but an adolescent notion happily outgrown by man come of age, and that justice is, rather, a legitimate expectation from others. To the Christian the reason for this refusal to rest in a reductionistic naturalism is clear: it lies in the general revelation of the Creator in the conscience of every man (Rom. 2:14f.), and in the fractured *imago Dei* that survives in the sinner even if he is a radical secularist.

In summary, the hindrances and obstacles to Christian evangelism therefore include:

(i) The uncritical acceptance of inherited religious traditions and moral philosophies.

(ii) The prohibition of public evangelism and restrictions on religious freedom by atheistic totalitarian powers.

(iii) The failure to relate the Christian good news to the material poverty, economic exploitation, and political oppression of masses of people, and the misconception of these same multitudes that the abundant life is assured by material affluence or political panaceas.

(iv) The pervasive regard for empirical scientific methodology as the omnicompetent criterion of reliable knowledge and as the guarantee of immunity from adverse consequences of moral transgression.

(v) The rejection of supernatural reality and revelation by radical secularity, with its relativizing of all claims of truth and morality, and the reduction of all conceptualities of the meaning and worth of human life to cultural mythology.

(vi) The anti-intellectual trend which probes extra-rational and mystical experiences as the roadway to transcendent personal values.

(vii) The neo-Protestant distortion of Christian revelation, theology, and ethics in a manner that nullifies its biblical character and authority.

(viii) The theological superficiality of much evangelical evangelism in respect to the intellectual barriers to belief, seen in anecdotal preaching and in a hurried call for decision which asks converts to leap in faith over problems that, if not confronted and resolved, will return to haunt their experience.

(ix) The experiential shallowness of evangelistic commitment which substitutes a legalistic formula of Christian personal behavior for a Spirit-surrendered life ruled by scriptural teaching applied in good conscience in one's cultural milieu.

(x) The neglect by evangelical Christianity of a corporate exhibition of the content of biblical morality, as well as of theological and apologetic priorities, in a world committed to alien ideas and ideals.

In brief, Christian evangelism must do far more than speak only to the emotional vacuums in the lives of men; it must also help shape the intellectual mood of the day, deal with cultural idolatries and national priorities, confront the problems which erode a sense of human worth and dignity, cope with the moral paralysis that emboldens multitudes to shameless vices, uncover all the subtle and alluring masks that man wears in an age which believed itself at the gates of Paradise only to discover a desolation and a waste. Evangelists must reject the thought that Christianity in the world survives onesidedly through activistic engagement; the truth of the Gospel alone is what establishes evangelistic validity. Evangelism can lay no true claim to success if it obscures or compromises the truth of revelation. In their appeal to the uncommitted masses, cults like Christian Science, Jehovah's Witnesses, and Mormonism all point to Christ while they eclipse the truth of the Gospel. Christians make a serious error if spectacular evangelistic results become the prime criterion or proof of the evangelical authenticity and legitimacy of Christian education and social engagement; evangelism, after all, like all Christian activity, is itself wholly answerable to the truth of God.

3. *Implications of the Gospel for contemporary social issues*

a. *Sex* — The human need of man and woman for each other springs from an original relationship grounded in God's creative act (Gen. 2:18 ff.). The family is a basic natural order of creation and a microcosm of mankind (Eph. 3:14). Parents find new life together in union; children are divinely given as a sacred trust. In Judeo-Christian ethics the origin and norm of all genuine love is God's love for man, a love proffered to undeserving sinners. Because of the wholeness of human personality, what one thinks and does sexually has consequences for the entire self in this life and the next. For Christians, sex involves considerate gratitude, personal devotion, and welcome responsibility under God.

Respect for constituted authority has its earthly center in the familial unit where the problem of authority constantly arises. But modern society increasingly views sex solely in terms of biological gratification and in a context of autonomianism, license, and irresponsibility. Much recent psychiatric theory reinforces this misunderstanding. The Gospel is forgiving and renewing. What Christ forgives must be acknowledged to be sin, however; turning to new life involves recognition of a past lived in violation of God's will, and a self now given over to a radically changed future. The Gospel calls the believer to honor the New Testament disclosure of the will of God.

(i) *Marriage* — The Gospel seeks to restore the sex life of mankind to God's purpose in creation. The biblical revelation of man and woman as one flesh through covenant-responsibility calls for steadfast fidelity of one man and one woman to each other in lifelong relationships that death alone can sever. The New Testament relates total sexual satisfaction with the practice of godliness (I Cor. 6:19, 7:7).

Current sexual ethics lack commitment to permanent monogamous marriage. Many regard the marriage contract as only a temporary probation, and this absence of lasting commitment conditions the relationship in psychically adverse ways. The New Testament does not correlate marital intercourse solely with procreation, which nonetheless is the first creation mandate, but rather with the total personality needs of the marital partners (I Cor. 7:3-5). The prospect of over-population is the more awesome because in respect to the creation-mandate, humans have more conspicuously filled the earth than they have subdued it for good ends. Yet, euthanasia has no biblical support but conflicts with the sixth commandment, while abortion poses grave moral problems, except in certain circumstances. Birth control is admissible, the motivation being an important factor. Morally acceptable techniques prevent the ovum and sperm from uniting (as a barrier to fertilization) rather than attacking the product of conception. Christ can forgive ethical perversions of marriage and its intention; indeed, the Gospel summons marriage partners to Christ's love for the Church as an analogy for the marital relationship (Eph. 5:22 f.).

(ii) *Divorce* — The legal dissolution of the marriage bond involving permanent separation of marriage partners and their lawful right to remarry. Tolerated in certain instances in the Old Testament with a notable safeguard of the woman's rights, Jesus condemned it; he stigmatized remarriage as adultery, unless the original marriage was itself eroded by "sexual impurity" (adultery?).

Although casual sexual intercourse does not of itself link two partners as "one flesh" (I Cor. 6:15 f.), the faithful spouse may on this ground legalize the breach of marriage. But he or she may also forgive and the Gospel provides precedent for the forgiveness of sinners that can reinvigorate and sanctify a violated union. The apostle Paul seems to indicate that a believer deserted by an unbelieving spouse may contract another marriage (I Cor. 7:10 ff.), but here, too, grace works an extended season in hope of reconciliation.

The soaring divorce rate in many lands, snarling multitudes of modern lives in marriage and remarriage complications, is often turned into a plea for relaxation of New Testament principles in the name of "love" as a superior criterion. Situational ethics, championed by liberal Protestants, avers that love of God and neighbor may permit in one relationship what it disallows in another. But this overlooks

the importance of permanent interpersonal commitments at the heart
of true marriage. The psychological damage done by broken homes
to the personalities of parents and children alike is incalculable, since
no member of the family can ever again be what he or she alone was
before the divorce; nor are the consequences for society, additionally
to those of a particular household, to be minimized. Christ and the
apostles lived in a time much like our own, when laxity pervaded the
whole realm of sex and marriage. Precisely in such a cultural context
the New Testament reiterated the revealed purpose of the Creator,
namely, to make them "male and female" and to establish the marriage
bond.

The Gospel indeed covers a multitude of sins, but it does not do
so by disregarding the commands of God or diluting them spuriously
under the banner of *agape* (cf. John 14:15). The Gospel does not
require two persons whose love has died to live in marital hell, but
offers new life and new love that none can scorn in good conscience in
a society where even the secular world ventures probationary relationships.

(iii) *Promiscuity* — This involves indiscriminate sexual union in
which the responsibilities of intercourse are ignored. Modern notions
of liberation often nurture promiscuous sexual attitudes, and the availability of scientific contraceptive techniques and of "abortion on
demand" have fostered a sex-centered generation preoccupied with
genitals. Women's liberation, on the other hand, has protested the
demeaning of women into sex objects. Communal sex seeks to confer
social respectability on promiscuity, yet ignores the special inter-
personal qualities that define monogamous marriage.

Jesus directed some of his most burning indictments against sexual
immorality; the New Testament catalogues of sin repeatedly reproach
sexual deviations. Damaging effects upon the personalities of the
sexually truant are widely emphasized. Many young people themselves
confess that as sex has become free and easy, love has become elusive.
No generation needs to hear Jesus' warning against the lustful look
more than a sex-oriented mass-media age.

Promiscuity berates and denies the basic Christian concept of sex
as a God-given entrustment requiring respectful responsibility, and
of sexual misconduct as sin against God. Forcefully and commendably
the Jesus-movement has reminded many congregations anew of the
need to bring the whole body under the Holy Spirit's control. In a sex-
saturated age the Gospel can break the power of temptation and equip
the human spirit with new motivation and dynamics. Christ-given freedom liberates sexual deviants for true enjoyment of sex as creative
and renewing, rather than enervating and destructive.

(iv) *Pornography* — The term incorporates root words meaning
harlotry and writing; originally it designated a treatise on the subject
of prostitutes. Modern use refers more broadly to literature, photog-
raphy, or art that depicts sexual activity, especially illicit acts and perversions. A tide of pornographic materials floods much of the modern
world. In the United States alone it is a billion-dollar business. Communist lands ban it as culturally debilitating, but do so in a context of

state absolutism that politically defines the good and restrains freedom of the press, contrasted with a free society where some unregenerates will do almost anything for financial gain. Many courts have held that what is "devoid of redeeming social values" may be legally banned, but on this basis works long excluded are now sometimes widely published, and foot-dragging law enforcement and the difficulty of gaining court convictions have accommadated crude and "hard core" pornography that makes no claim whatever to social utility.

The Roman Catholic emphasis on ecclesiastical censorship is hardly an adequate answer. However, as the criterion has shifted increasingly to prevailing community standards, Christians should publicize their views of the moral wrong of degrading sex into a cheap animal commodity. Stragely enough, socially-active churches were so preoccupied with politico-economic issues, and evangelical churches with changing persons, that neither did much to stem the tide of pornography. Women's liberation movements have protested the pornographic depiction of women as mere sex objects stripped of personality for the sake of male gratification; now the nude male centerfold has made its debut in some women's magazines. Christians should enter the arena of public persuasion, emphasizing not only the adverse effects of pornography on the morals of youth, but also its offense to God. The full answer to the problem lies both in an evangelical changing of unregenerate engrossments and in the production of a creative literature of love. The church has *agape* to combat *eros*. The preaching of the Gospel should not only summon sinners to experience *agape,* but also so compellingly publish it to the world that *eros* will seek the altar rail.

b. *Wealth*

(i) *Capital* — Both the terms "wealth" and "capital" are used of economically significant elements existing at any given time. While these elements are very diverse, and included many intangibles, they popularly refer to land, buildings, machines, and equipment, and stocks of goods, especially money. Taken in scriptural context, the wealth of nations surely includes spiritual and ethical features and cultural stability, even though such assets are not negotiable. With an eye on industrialization and gross national product, political experts designate the non-communist world — except for the English-speaking nations, Europe, and Japan — as developing or emerging nations. By the GNP standard, Kuwait is ironically now one of the earth's most highly developed countries.

In past centuries, ethical thought focused on the relation of capital and interest, whereas modern thought is more interested in the correlation of capital and income. Medieval scholastics viewed all interest as usury and condemned it; the Church of Rome later altered this view, however. At the time of the Protestant Reformation capitalists still operated under suspicion of the sin of avarice, although the public mood gradually changed. While the Protestant ethic was not the cause of modern capitalism, it exonerated capitalists from the sin of avarice and by its emphasis on hard work, frugality, sobriety, and efficient fulfillment of one's vocational calling gave stimulus to the new economic order.

Personal attitudes toward debt have been liberalized by the concept that credit contributes to economic prosperity; mass production has lowered prices, and young families have enjoyed numerous comforts through installment buying. But government deficit spending doubtlessly exerts adverse influence upon many people. The morality, at least wisdom, of using credit to finance luxuries, vacation travel, and nonessentials is debatable.

The Protestant emphasis was that accumulated wealth should be invested to produce additional wealth, although the allurements of wealth were to be resisted and the rich no less than the poor were to live frugally. The deceitfulness of riches is a recurring New Testament theme.

(ii) *Property* — While Christ did not dispute the right of personal possessions, but viewed them as a divine entrustment acquired through the use of God-given talents, he noted that they could all too easily become one's prime concern (Matt. 6:24). Since all we possess is held as a divine stewardship, the apostles emphasize that one who has more than others has greater opportunity to bless those who have less (I Pet. 4:14 f.). No true Christian can be rich and use wealth merely for self-gratification (Luke 12:24).

Yet distribution to others was voluntary. New Testament Christianity is often erroneously depicted as normatively communistic. There were times when, for a specific objective, believers voluntarily pooled possessions, but this procedure is never declared to be a Christian moral imperative; private property is not scripturally viewed as evil in itself, and a case can even be made biblically that some property is universally necessary to personal fulfillment. The Eight Commandment establishes the principle of private ownership, "Thou shalt not steal" (Exod. 20:15). Scripture sanctions the acquisition of property by legitimate means only (Deut. 25:4, I Cor. 9:9 ff.), however, whether it be by work, purchase, or inheritance.

The biblical representation of private property nonetheless differs profoundly from the view of ancient Roman jurisprudence and modern secular thought. The right to possession is not absolute and unqualified, for God is the ultimate Creator and owner of all (Lev. 25:23); man holds what he has in trusteeship for God, and even then, Scripture provided safeguards lest accumulation of property permanently disadvantage the underprivileged. The year of Jubilee cancelled automatic possession for perpetuity, and the eighth-century prophets inveighed against amassing land to the detriment of common good (Isa. 5:8, Mic. 2:2). Yet the refusal of Naboth to surrender his legitimate property on demand even of the king (I King 21:3) attested the right of possession and ancestral inheritance.

The Bible's main focus is on the use of possessions, and reflects a consistent concern for the poor. Possessions enable one to support and advance evangelical witness in the world, to minister to the needs of the household of faith (James 2:16), neighbors (Lev. 19:18), and others in need (Gal. 6:10).

(iii) *Profit* — The excess of income over expenditure, or gain over and above cost of acquisition or production. Scripture assumes its legitimacy, using the concept to motivate faithful engagement. Proverbs lays down the principle that labor is properly profitable (14:23). Solomon recognized God as the ultimate source of profit and reward (Prov. 3:9f.) and promoted effort as the road to prosperity (Ecc. 11:6). Yet, illegal acquisition of profit, whether by deceit, false weights, or oppression of usury, is sharply condemned. The Bible repeatedly contrasts the principle of greed with that of gratitude; while it considers fair profit legitimate, the Bible's concern is that riches should not corrupt their possessor by indulgence, misuse, or indifference to the needs of others. A most familiar text is Jesus' classic question, "What does it profit a man if he gain the whole world and lose his own soul?" (Mark 8:36).

(iv) *Poverty* — Scripture focuses on physical, moral, and spiritual poverty. Modern sociology is concerned mainly with the first, whose terrors have been a stark reality for multitudes in all ages. Some basis exists for a distinction between destitution, or lack of bare survival needs, and poverty, or the inability to achieve more than basic daily needs. Poverty is not easily defined (some relate it to minimum income, others to median income, and others to group percentage of national income). The relative condition of the poor in some lands (e.g., America) is vastly superior to that in many others, and the mass media relentlessly accelerates universal aspiration for higher living standards. The blind, lame, and aged poor can hardly escape their poverty by hard work, and the poorly educated often face unrewarding jobs, while race and sex discrimination have impeded opportunity for still others.

The Old Testament prophets and New Testament writers as well thrust the problem of poverty upon the conscience of God's people, although in the Gospels "the poor" becomes also a non-economic designation for a harried remnant of the spiritually faithful. While the concern of Scripture is with spiritual and moral need, it does not gloss over material need. Jesus launched his public ministry with Isaiah's prophecy of good news to the poor, and the Gospel must therefore reach people in need as a message of hope in their total predicament. Jesus unobtrusively gave to the poor (cf. John 13:39) and Paul took up collections for the poor. Distribution to those in need is viewed biblically as evidence of love for God (Lev. 25:55; Matt. 19:21). The first charitable work of the early Christians took the form of gifts to impoverished widows. The classic reminder that "Christ became poor that we might become rich" (II Cor. 8:9) utterly disarms anyone clinging to possessions in the face of need.

Sensitive Christian conscience should support programs responding to needs of the aged, the blind, lame and dying, supplying food for the starving, job-training for adults, and non-discriminatory educational opportunities. Believers should set an example by providing for their own kin and those of the fellowship of faith. Healthy adults should in any event contribute to the well-being of the community; to be temporarily out of work is no necessary mandate for state support (II Thess. 3:10). Christians should resist encouraging parasitism or materialism; poverty should be alleviated as much as possible by self-help. As the Jesus-movement has warned even evangelical believers, the Bible places restraints on consumer-aspirations. It emphasizes the responsibility of all men (even those who have less) in respect to neighbors in need. It should be interesting in this materialistically-oriented society, moreover, that the Song of Hannah depicted poverty and riches alike as the work of God (I Sam. 2:7); it is also interesting that the Mosaic Law, and its concern for the economically deprived, nonetheless forbade partiality because of poverty (Lev. 19:15). But God has an eye for the poor, and divine blessing is promised those who are charitable toward them (Psa. 41:1), and who advance justice in their behalf.

c. *Race.*

(i) *Racism* — Racial variations are a fact of human existence, but they are subordinate to a common humanity. When racial differences are absolutized, racism occurs, e.g., Hitler's premium on Nordic origin, South African apartheid, and white supremacy in American and other societies. The notion that any single race is the special carrier of human destiny involves a demonic pretense of divine election; it thus becomes a prideful revolt against God's creation-purpose for all mankind and his redemption-purpose in Christ.

The Bible assuredly indicates that Yahweh chose the Jews, not however because of their superiority but because of his election, giving them special advantages as a witness to the world of the blessings of serving the living God. Jesus of Nazareth, the promised Son, manifests God's ideal for all humanity; as the Second Adam, he is the true antithesis to racism, breaking down the wall even between Jew and Gentile.

Scripture condemns racism and God judges it in history. The God of grace exalts the humble and topples the proud. The church is a transracial body whose head is known no longer "after the flesh" but as the carrier of a common humanity into the eternal order as firstfruits of a general resurrection. Racism is therefore anti-Christ in spirit, arbitrarily implying an election that Scripture disowns.

Christians should see themselves in the mirror of history whenever any minority is deprived of equal rights before the law, since Christians may themselves always be a minority and may well be the next target of abuse. But more fundamentally, racial injustice to any minority should be considered implicitly a threat not simply to one's own kind but to all humanity. The Christian has double motivation for identifying with the victims of race discrimination; first, he knows that God created all men of one flesh, and second, that Christ died for all and is head of a body transcending racial situations. The evangel is therefore repudiated in principle wherever and whenever the church practices racial exclusion instead of exhibiting the spiritual and moral unity of the whole family of the redeemed.

(ii) *Casteism* — The caste system seems to have arisen among the non-Aryan peoples of India as a means of assimilating different racial, religious, and social groups into Hinduism. Ancient Indian society was divided into four classes: priests and learned (Brahmins), warriors, merchants and peasants, and servants. Through the centuries more than 2,000 castes and subcastes emerged across which or against which no one could marry or even entertain in his home. Although extremes of "untouchability" have been legally abolished, and in larger towns many caste distinctions are being eroded, caste has a religious anchorage

in Hinduism. In view of status evaluations based on the pollution concept, Hinduism considers it possible for persons or groups to be degraded
in behavior yet advanced in religious understanding.

Objections to racism apply also to casteism. The New Testament
doctrine of the priesthood of all believers strikes a death blow at religious caste systems. The Church of Christ is administratively structured,
but not on the basis of personal superiority or ritual purity. The Christian doctrine of creation no less fundamentally precludes casteism.

d. *Political Power.* God is Sovereign Creator and Lord of history;
all other power is therefore derivative. Civil government derives its
power ultimately not from military capability or from the will of the
people but from God (cf. John 19:11). All organs of power can function
properly only in obedience to his will. God purposes civil government
in a fallen society for the promotion and preservation of justice and
order (Rom. 13). Insofar as government arrogates to itself powers and
objectives contrary to its divinely intended purpose it becomes anti-God
and anti-Christ (Rev. 13). Civil government is God's alternative to
anarchy and tyranny alike.

The growing inability of individual nations to assure their own
survival in view of economic and military dependence upon allies increasingly raises the question whether the nation-state concept of civil
government has outlived its usefulness. Yet the difficulty of common
international action in the face of national interests has been repeatedly
demonstrated, first by the League of Nations and now by the United
Nations (which includes some 130 of the 150 nation-states). The need
of transnational commitments is nonetheless simultaneously reflected
in the ongoing alignment of nations into power-blocs (Soviet-sphere,
NATO, European Common Market, etc.).

The vision of global peace is biblical, and as such is irreducibly
messianic (Isa. 9:6). God who judges nations decides their historical
fortunes (Acts 17:26). No durable reconciliation of nations in a fallen
society is possible without their recognition of the God of the nations
and a common commitment to his justice, order, and peace (John 14:27).
To substitute instead merely a world government with transcendent
political authority and military power obscures the principles by which
that body itself is to be judged. In principle the superstate is not inherently more or less superior ethically to a nation-state. But if God
is not clearly owned as the source and stipulator of human rights and
welfare, why should superstate absolutism be thought to promote these
in a legitimate way any more than state absolutism? The book of Revelation notably speaks of world government in the context of antichrist.

Scripture focuses on the Holy Land as a decisive conflict-area for
world destiny, although modern political science attributes geopolitical
significance to the Near East only for economic and not for meta-
political reasons, and one can hardly inject prophecy as a guide for
grounding day-to-day political decisions. With the regathering of Israel
as a modern nation-state, two centers of political controversy have
emerged, one involving Communist, non-Communist, and third-world
countries inside the United Nations, and the other, participants in the
Arab-Israeli conflict. Through the military involvement of the major
powers in the Near East, and the international crisis over energy resources,

virtually all political entities worldwide are now affected and involved through a strip of land where Christ ("the government shall be upon his shoulders") warned of an inescapable final judgment of the nations.

The call for Christian participation in political life is grounded not simply in the moral and spiritual chaos of the modern nations, but in a biblical mandate as well.Christians should be politically active, where they have citizenship, to the limit of their ability and competence. The penalty for failure to lead and to be vocal is that others who misuse and expolit political power for objectionable ends and by objectionable means preempt the field. But Christian witness regarding government also has a transcendent dimension. Christians pray for rulers, knowing that Christ is King of kings. Civil government will pass away, while the rule and reign of Christ in the Kingdom of God remains. The church is to witness to the world of the supremacy of love in the life of the fellowship that endures.

(i) *Bribery* — The general term corruption includes bribery, undue influence, and similar infractions. Bribery is a penal offense involving a gift or receipt of some consideration for official favor. The crime is usually considered a felony, and the guilty official's eligibility to hold office is often forfcited. The law first applied only to officials voting on public matters, and exempted public ("ministerial") servants who could be induced to do their duty more efficiently through tips, fees, or presents. Later bribery legislation in some places covered all public servants. But even here gifts were considered culpable only where they actually secured "any benefit or advantage," and criminal prosecution was rare. Although gifts to civil servants out of friendship or gratitude, and without intent to influence official behavior, are not punishable as bribery, corrupt practices legislation in some places prohibits them.

In many foreign lands, missionaries face the problem on arrival. A ten-dollar bill will expedite in minutes baggage that has been impounded in customs for days. In some Asian lands, after buying property at official prices, missionaries must pay thousands of dollars of additional "key-money" to gain possession. When they subsequently sell the property, are they to charge the buyer for this levy as well? National Christians also face the question of whether to condone and participate in such established bribery routines, especially where public servants expediting customs and mails expect special rewards, or where automobiles may be damaged in public parking lots if one does not tip a self-appointed watchman. Many such practices are not really illegal, but are matters of custom and culture; they would therefore require an enactment of laws if there is to be change for the better. The problem is perhaps best met by encouraging Christians to enter public service and to set higher standards, and to seek political offices with authority to end such questionable practices. Moreover, the Gospel can change lives; in dealing with officials who exact more than they should, one ought never to forget Matthew, the tax collector who learned to give rather than to take.

(ii) *Corruption* — Already in the last century many nations outlawed so-called "corrupt" political practices (such as intimidation and coercion) that interfere with free elections. The secret ballot was introduced to reduce infractions, and soon restrictions were applied on the amount, sources, and uses of money in political campaigns; finally adequate accounting and full public disclosure became law.

In the United States, both state and federal regulations govern campaign practices. Although legislation sometimes was poorly drafted and casually enforced, Americans were proud, at a time when democratic processes were promoted almost worldwide as politically utopian, that political reform had accomplished more in their country than in other nations. The effort to regulate corrupt practices in Britain was widely approved, but considered modest alongside achievements in the United States.

In many lands, entrenched regimes flagrantly violate professedly deomcratic commitments, and the Christian community experiences a sense of futility in any desire for improvement. In some cases, where Christians have entered government service, their lives have been imperiled when resisting the corrupt goals of superiors. In these circumstances the feeling is widespread that political engagement is necessarily corrupt.

Since the United States had championed democratic processes wherever its world influence extended, the Watergate scandals have had a debilitating effect. The Nixon administration had maintained a posture of law-and-order in a world beset by revolutionary violence. But word that the Democratic and Republican parties may have raised $100 million in contributions for the 1972 campaign without adequate accounting; that the Committee to Re-elect the President had rigged a newspaper poll and advertising in order to influence public opinion; and that the president's leading aides had resorted to illegal acts, using even the danger of domestic subversion as a cover, had costly repercussions throughout the Free World and especially in Third World countries. In many Third World countries the tendency was to laugh at American consternation over Watergate, since for the most part they consider politics inherently corrupt. This has been a serious blow to the ideals of democratic government at a time when the fortunes of democracies were already declining worldwide.

The effect of Watergate and related scandals has been to call for more stringent election reforms. But it also has gradually focused attention on the many office-holders of political integrity, and has stimulated competent evangelicals to increased and more aggressive engagement in political matters. When the Christian Church has been strong in society she has no less an interest in law and jurisprudence than in Grace and theology. That fact does not by any means demand a Christian political party, but it does demand Christian political responsibility. In the absence of a will to do the good, no law, however desirable, can assuredly achieve its public objectives. Evangelism can bring to multitudes the good will and moral dynamic necessary to make good laws work.

e, *War* — War is a monstrous evil. The only miscalculation worse than its acceptance as perpetually necessary is the failure to deal with the wickedness of man as the datum that makes war sometimes morally unavoidable in fallen human history.

Civil government is divinely projected as an instrument of justice and order. But because of the recalcitrance of the human will, government cannot be wholly protected against a tyrannical deployment of its power to aggressive warfare. It is not governments that cause war but the lusts and imperial ambitions of leaders and privileged groups (James 4:2).

The early Church during the first three centuries was rather clearly pacifist, in contrast with the relative militarism of the Church in the modern world. The pacifist response has the merit of trying to escape the sad compromises of mainline churches with the armed conflicts of the nations on which they have conferred holy baptism and confirmation almost without exception, and which should stir Christian conscience to critical self-examination. Counter-cultural youth today rightly protest the readiness of nations to sacrifice their young as the best way to achieve international objectives and to settle international grievances.

But, as Reinhold Niebuhr noted, the effort of pacifism to make the peace of the Kingdom of God a present historical possibility places a premium on surrender to evil. It glosses over Christianity's profound insights into the universal sinfulness of man and the fallen nature of human history, and oversimplifies the ethic of Jesus. The New Testament ethic of political justice and peace relies on coercion — the power of the state — to restrain the selfish and sinful impulses of humans. Yet it repudiates militarism, with its exaltation of military virtues to cultural priority, as promotive of war.

Terrible and terrifying as war is — in an atomic age approaching international insanity — its moral necessity derives from the fact that the refusal to challenge an unjust aggressor is an immoral response to wanton injustice, and invites the enslavement and dehumanization of the victims of tyrannical aggression, and the risk of annihilation as the alternative to subjugation. The ever increasing escalation of nuclear destructive potential heightens the criminality of the aggressor, but it does not eliminate the moral duty of potential victims to deny tyrants an unimpeded victory in history.

Against the initiation of war all energies of moral suasion must now be exerted since war, for whatever reason, in a nuclear age may involve such massive disorder that it imperils some goals of civil government as much as it advances others. Christianity is on the side of peace; both its social ethic and its redemptive evangel put the highest premium on peace. But peace among the nations often means little more than the mere cessation of hostilities or "cold war," something not to be belittled in the atomic era; worse yet, in our time, it not infrequently consists of public verbal assurances alongside ongoing covert warfare. For the regenerate church, peace is positive reconciliation between once-alienated man and his God and fellow-man.

The Old Testament prophets warned that trust in military might rather than in God invites national calamity. For Israel as a theocracy, holy war was always a response to the threat and aggression of her foes. The New Testament has no concept of holy war in behalf of the Messianic King (Jesus avoided identification with the Zealots and their revolutionary movement) except in apocalyptic texts centering in the

Lord's return in judgment and glory. But the New Testament, like the Old, takes war for granted as an evil brought on by sin, yet incorporated into God's plan and deployed to his purposes. Nowhere does the New Testament suggest that a soldier should leave military service upon becoming a believer.

In Christian ethics just war criteria aim more to limit the evils of war than to justify it. But the complexities of modern warfare increasingly complicate evaluation by earlier standards, due to the destruction of the lives of non-combatants — whether by guerilla warfare in jungle villages, by conventional warfare in industrial society, or by nucleur warfare. Yet conscientious objectors to all military involvement have their right of non-participation today only because others in the past were willing to bear arms to preserve personal freedom.

The Gospel transforms believers for life in a new society ruled by love and, as such, anticipative of the Kingdom of Heaven. But it does not remove men from the world and the struggle for justice. In the Church, love of God and man is the only adequate norm of human conduct, for it mirrors God's own love. The Church knows the value of human life as a creation of God and as an object of Christ's redemption, and it can and ought fervently to plead the cause of peace and the merit of universal disarmament.

But it is not alone the egoism of others outside the Church that alerts the believer to an awareness that love needs still to be correlated with something that sets itself against selfish and arrogant human ambition. The believer's own struggle against self-regarding impulse, and against that of fellow-believers, tells him that the Kingdom of Heaven has not yet fully dawned. The Gospel can rescue men from the guilt and penalty of sin, and in a remarkable degree from its power. But it does not wholly transform the world into the church, nor wholly transform the church into the Kingdom of God. Only on that day when the King of kings appears will the tyrant and the pacifist lie down together. When the government is upon his shoulders it will confidently be said that war shall be no more, and the counterforce of ungodly powers and the coercive ministry of civil government will fade into oblivion.

CHRISTIAN PERSONAL AND SOCIAL ETHICS IN RELATION TO RACISM, POVERTY, WAR, AND OTHER PROBLEMS REPORT

Chairman: J. Court
Secretary: K. Bockmuhl

The church, under Christ's Lordship is sent into the world to proclaim personal and social righteousness and redemption. We affirm the validity of the Ten Commandments for our time. Personal conversion is of primary importance for the building up of the Body of Christ.

We evangelicals, with all other Christians, are duty bound to exemplify and to promote social justice, both as individuals and in community. It is the very nature of righteousness to act justly. God wills justice and God wills justification.

No man or woman needs to accept as normative oppressive, wicked, and exploitative forces which rob human existence of its God-given worth. Because the crucified Jesus in his resurrection triumphed over the forces of iniquity, they all are now dated and doomed.

We are called to affirm and to exemplify love and justice. There is a need to stand against that which is sinful and corrupt in order to show the good and the creative. Both on the negative and positive side, we should be willing to proclaim and to act within the bounds of fair play and legality.

Evangelism serves as a root in effecting the valid ministry of the church, producing compassionate acts of charity, righteousness, and justice, worship and fellowship and the knowledge of God, and educating people about his will for men. Constructive social reform according to biblical principles is as legitimate an area for Christian action as the compassionate acts of charity, and just as urgent.

We believe that Christian affirmation and exemplification must be within the God-given spheres of family, state, church, economy, and the sphere of free association. There are some areas where it is appropriate for the church to act, but there are many areas where individual Christians or groups coming together for a special purpose may express a Christian conscience in society.

The prophetic voice of the church must always speak creatively to human power structures. It will not use the language of force, but will use the force of language. Regenerate men and women are creative catalysts for social betterment. This is what Christ meant when he spoke of illuminating and preserving elements in the world.

Law is necessary to outlaw evil, but true brotherly love can only be achieved through personal regeneration, not through mere legal obligation.

While we recognize that there are certain immutable structures, there are, nonetheless, some subsidiary structures which need to change in the course of time. Christian social involvement includes not only personal but institutional action. Institutionalized evil requires institutional action for change. We recommend study of the life and work of William Wilberforce and Lord Shaftesbury, who in their time promoted individual and institutional action, and even combined the two. We acknowledge these ventures without expecting or seeking to build utopia this side of the return of Christ.

We stress the importance of the resources entrusted to us. They require stewardship, particularly in view of the fact of waste and inflation. Wealth is entrusted to us in order for us to distribute to the needy, particularly to support them in basic needs of human existence, and is not for selfish advancement. Teaching the underprivileged to use their resources is important; e.g., it is better to teach people how to catch fish rather than to give them fish. We alert Christians to their responsibility to counter the exploitation of disadvantaged groups such as migrant workers, cheap labor, and disabled workers. We urge Christians to be associated with programs that create work for the jobless, particularly in the Third World. We encourage Christians to further education, housing, credit unions, consumer and production cooperatives and land reform.

We dissociate ourselves from any form of racism.

Sex is ordained of God in the context of love, which is essentially a spiritual factor. Christians must not underestimate the damage caused by over-emphasis on sex by adultery and promiscuity to the individuals involved and to society itself. Over-emphasis on sex goes together with the loneliness of the young. There is a preoccupation with physical sexuality and this tends to heighten the loneliness felt by young people. Christians must not let go unchallenged the flood of pornography. which involves the exploitation of the weaknesses of man and the corruption of his spiritual and moral nature. By attacking man in this way he is made an object of lust rather than a person made in the image of God. Pornography in attacking the image of God in man, is an attack upon God himself. In short, pornography is a destructive dehumanizing trade which exploits the weaknesses of consumers.

In observing the breakdown of marriage in many places, we record that in revival on the mission field, renewal of the homes is often a feature. Difficulties are still experienced in understanding the cultural backgrounds of polygamy. We urge further studies in the biblical response to polygamy.

The ideal Christian would do two things: He would promote social betterment in government councils; and at the same time, he would preach the ideal situation. Social engagement is a divine imperative with great opportunities today if only we remain under the control of the Bible.

PRAYER IN EVANGELIZATION
Bruno Herm

We all believe, we all are sure, many of us have often said, and maybe some of us have often preached that prayer plays a vital part in evangelism. It is impossible to think of an evangelical rally without preparation in prayer, without a prayer secretary, without special prayer-meetings. There is no missionary going out without asking those that stay behind to pray for him.

The vital question, however, which I want to put before us is: *What* part does prayer play in evangelism? Is it just one of many other activities that are necessary to bring about what we call "fruitful or successful evangelism?" Or is it *the* activity on which all others and the final results depend? In other words: Is prayer fundamental in evangelism or is it supplemental? Is it essential to evangelism or is it complementary? Is it the primary task in evangelism or is it just one of many others? Is it the decisive factor determining the course and results of our evangelistic efforts, or is it one of many factors which will bring about what we want to see?

I am sure there are many who will be inclined to agree right at the beginning, that prayer is fundamental in evangelism. If this is so — and I will have to try to prove this in my paper — then let us start to examine the foundation on which our evangelistic efforts are built. Is our foundation sound and good? If not, should we not stop building on it? What is better, building a house on a shaky foundation, or postponing building till something has been done to the basic structure? We may all agree here today that prayer is fundamental in our work, but are we also willing and prepared to take the consequences?

What do our activities in evangelism look like today? Is not the primary thing to secure a good speaker? Then there must be good and widespread publicity. Then we have to choose a good location for the meetings. Now we can form our committees and appoint our secretaries for music, prayer, finances, etc.

When we think of "missions today," what comes foremost into our minds? Finances? Well-trained personnel? Open doors, by which we mean countries with political and economic stability? Or is it first and foremost prayer? Prayer that clings to the promises of God and gives him the glory?

I have three headings to our theme.

1. Prayer implied, though not mentioned

If prayer is so important in evangelism, why then is it not mentioned in the Lord's command which we call the Great Commission, "All power is given unto me, go ye therefore and teach all nations, baptizing them in the name of the Father and the Son and the Holy Ghost, teaching them to observe all things, whatsoever I have commanded you, and lo, I am with you, even unto the end of the world"?

Why did not our Lord include prayer in this command to go, teach, baptize? Where does prayer come in? Is it not sufficient that the Lord has said, "All power is given unto me in heaven and on earth, go ye therefore"? Is it not for us to go and to prove and experience that all power does belong to Christ? Is this in fact our daily experience in evangelization and mission-work, that we are working together with an Almighty, All-powerful Lord? Or does it look much more that all power is given unto the Lord in heaven, but on earth other powers are ruling and determining events, against which we are absolutely powerless?

The Greek word for power in our passage means authority or right *(exousia)*. Christ says, "All authority is given unto me in heaven and on earth". Christ has the absolute authority and right to send his disciples into all the world. They and we have the authority and the right to go where he sends us. No authority on earth has the right to forbid us preaching the Gospel! But is this truth and the knowledge of it sufficient to carry out what the Lord has commanded us?

In Acts 1:8 we find another word about power, "Ye shall receive power, after that the Holy Ghost is come upon you and ye shall be my witnesses. . . ." The Greek word used here *(dynamis)* means power to accomplish and fulfill something. Paul calls the Gospel the "dynamis" of God (Rom. 1:16). The preaching of the Cross, which is foolishness to the world, he calls the "dynamis" of God. He writes in the same letter (I Cor. 2:4-5), "My speech was not in enticing words of men's wisdom but in demonstration of the spirit and of power (dynamis) that your faith shall not stand in the wisdom of man but in the power of God." Further he says in I Cor. 4:20, "The kingdom of God is not in word but in power." If we would keep this last passage well in our minds, then many discussions about the priority of word or deeds, preaching or helping, evangelizing or social action would be superfluous. These are not the biblical alternatives, at least as Paul puts it, but rather "words" and "power." One is something from man — "word" no matter how much doing goes with it; the other is something from God — "power", working through words of preaching and through the lives of transformed men and women.

Christ has not only given us authority to preach the Gospel but also the power to do it, and to do it in a way that this power will be manifested in the lives of the believers. Has this anything to do with prayer? Is prayer implied in Matt. 28:20 and in Acts 1:8?

What was the reaction of the disciples after they had received the Great Commission? Christ had said, "You shall be my witnesses," but first of all they became his intercessors. He had said, "Go ye," but first of all they stayed in the upper room. He had said, "Wait ye till ye receive power," but we see them, not sitting and waiting, but kneeling and praying. Who had told them that now was the time for prayer? Did they know what they were in for? We know of course that that prayer meeting lasted just ten days. We also probably would manage, if we really tried, to spend ten days in prayer. But did they know? Yet they were determined to pray till . . . till what . . . till the power would be given. They did not speculate that it might be on the day of Pentecost, and if they did, they still did not know if it was going to be that year or the next. They were set for pryaer, not only for ten days, but if needs be, for twenty, thirty or more, till the Lord would fulfil his promise.

What would have happened to them — to the world — to us, if they had not prayed these ten days? What would have happened if they had done what we evangelicals so often do saying: God has promised to do it anyway, we have no part in it, it will come when God's time is fulfilled! They knew they had authority to preach, but they were praying for the power to come.

We can thus assume that, though unmentioned, the Lord implied that only through and by earnest and persevering prayer could there be a fulfillment and experience of what he had promised his disciples in their lives and in their work.

When we look at the life and work of our Lord himself, we see on the whole that prayer is much more implied than mentioned in the Gospels. I can never but marvel at the fact that our Lord did pray and that he should have needed prayer in order to live the life he lived and to fulfil his task. This is no deviation from our theme. The Lord, though not an evangelist as we know such today, was sent from God to fulfill a task as specific in relation to the world and its needs as ours is today. His whole life was geared to the fulfillment of it. Was prayer fundamental in his life and work or was it just one of his many activities? We have no doctrinal statement about this in the New Testament, but from some passages we can conclude that our Lord not only needed prayer, but that all his words and deeds, his miracles and teachings were answers to prayer and grew out of his continual and perfect inner prayer life.

Matt. 26:53, "Thinkest thou that I cannot pray to my father and he shall presently give me more than twelve legions of angels?" Was it needful for him to pray? Could he not just command and the angels would come?

In John 11:14 we find, "Jesus lifted up his eyes and said, Father, I thank thee that thou hast heard me, and I knew that thou hearest me always, but because of the people that stand by I said it, that they may believe that thou hast sent me."

Who was at work at the raising of Lazarus? Jesus himself said (John 5:19-20), "Verily, verily I say unto you, the Son can do nothing of himself, but what he sees the father do . . . for the father loves the son and shows him all things that he himself doeth." The raising of Lazarus was an answer to the Lord's praying. An answer to his asking, "Father I thank thee, that thou hast heard me!" In his inner prayer life, the Lord was constantly seeing the Father, hearing his word, seeing what the Father was doing. And he did the same. He knew what he could ask according to the Father's will, and he knew that the father would give it to him. Does this not remind us of I John 5:14, "If we ask anything according to his will, he heareth us, and we know that he hears us, whatsoever we ask, we know that we have the petitions, that we desire of him."

Is it implied, though not mentioned, that every word, deed and miracle of our Lord was the result of his inner prayer life, of his seeing the father at all times and his asking of him according to his will. If this was the way the Son was sent by the father, what do these words mean to us? "As my Father has sent me, so send I you." Is then prayer fundamental in our task of evangelizing the world?

We find in the New Testament an unmentioned link between the fact that we have the authority to be or to do something given to us by our Lord and the power to live out what we are and to accomplish what we are authorized to do. This all-important link is prayer. Has it become the "missing link" in our lives and work?

We find this link also in the life of Paul, the greatest missionary of all times. According to Acts 9 he received his call through Ananias right at the time of his conversion in Damascus. In his own words he recalls this experience in Acts 26, "For I have appeared unto thee to make thee a minister and a witness, delivering thee from the people and from the Gentiles unto whom now I send thee to open their eyes and to turn them from darkness to light, from the power of Satan unto God, that they may receive forgiveness of sins. . . ." How many of our candidates and missionaries have been called and encouraged to go to the mission field by these words, spoken by the Holy Ghost! Yet is it sufficient to receive a word like this from the Lord as a personal call for going out as a missionary? Paul did not wait long to fulfill in his way what he had been asked to do. In Damascus "he preached Christ straightway and he confounded the Jews, proving that this is very Christ," and in Jerusalem we find him "disputing against the Grecians" (Acts 9:29). From Jerusalem the brethren brought him down to Ceasarea and from there sent him to Tarsus. Now Paul vanishes for at least seven years. What happened in these few years that are between his conversion and call and his first missionary journey in Acts 13? What happened to his call? Ten full years in Arabia and Tarsus. We read of no converts, of no churches founded by Paul during that time. On his first missionary journey Paul's next stop after Derbe could have been Tarsus had he continued on that road, but he did not. He turns back and visits the newly established churches and returns to Antioch. On his second and third journeys Paul must have passed through Tarsus. We read of no church or converts in that city where Paul had stayed seven years. Is it implied in Acts and other records that these silent ten years were marked by what the Lord told Ananias about Saul of Tarsus: Behold, he prayeth?

Was there any need for Paul to find that link between his call and authority to preach to the Gentiles and deliver them from the powers of evil and to receive the power from on high to do so? And if Paul did, what about us and our work?

2. Prayer exemplified and taught

a. *The example and teaching of Jesus* — It will always remain a mystery how the Lord Jesus himself should be an example for us of what prayer means in the life and work of a servant of God. Luke seems to have observed this side of the Lord's life in a special way. He mentions at the baptism of Jesus, "It came to pass that Jesus also being baptized and praying, the heaven was opened. . . ." Was it essential for Christ to pray in this moment? Would that which followed have happened anyhow? "The Holy Ghost descended in a bodily shape like a dove upon him." When we look at the prayer life of our Lord we can ask again and again: what would have happened if he had not prayed in a certain situation, at a certain moment?

Luke 4:42-43, "And when it was day he departed and went into a desert place." Crowds of people had been listening to the Lord's message, many had been healed and freed from demons. Many were still waiting for him, but he departed and went into a desert place. Can we image a doctor leaving his patients and going off to pray? Can we imagine a preacher leaving those who want to hear going away into a desert place to pray? Jesus shows clearly what has priority in his life and service: prayer and then preaching — "for therefore am I sent." Jesus was not sent — as many want to make us believe today — to just live the Gospel. He was sent to preach it (Luke 5:15-16), "Great multitudes came together to hear and to be healed. And he withdrew himself into the wilderness and prayed. What priceless opportunities for mass evangelism he missed! He went off into the wilderness for prayer. Maybe he needed it just at that point. Is it perchance that in the next verse (17) we read, "And the power of the Lord was present to heal them"?

Then comes the time when he has to choose the twelve disciples from those who followed him (Luke 6;12), ". . . He went out into the mountain to pray and he continued all night in prayer to God." Is it not astounding that the Son of God should have need to do this? "And when it was day he called unto him his disciples and of them he chose twelve. . . ." What does it look like when the Lord tells us, ". . . pray ye the Lord of the harvest that he may thrust out laborers into the harvest"? Does it mean that we take every and any young man or woman who is interested enough to spend three weeks, three months, or two years on a mission station, preferably at the other end of the world so that we might not have to close a clinic or a hospital? The Lord Jesus had to pray a whole night before he knew whom to choose and whom to send. His prayer was answered. Never did he doubt that he had chosen the right people, even in the case of Judas, even after Peter's denial.

Luke 9:18, "He was alone praying. . . ." Out of this prayer comes the first announcement of his suffering, death, and resurrection, on which we cannot touch today. But one thing should be clear from this brief study: Jesus gave prayer the absolute priority in his life. Prayer to him was like breathing is to every one of us. We do not need to exhort ourselves not to forget breathing! I feel in many instances the Holy Ghost treats this matter of prayer in the same way. I say again: the life and work of our Lord Jesus were the result of his prayer life. It is unperceivable what would have happened if Jesus had failed in his prayer life. We can only thank him on our knees that he did live as he lived and follow in his steps, even in the steps of prayer.

It is almost unbelievable, that we should have today the same means and ways to accomplish our task as Jesus had to do his. "As my father sent me, so send I you." We are called to live that same prayer life in constant communion with our Father in heaven, who is prepared to give what we ask. Before Jesus left his disciples, he puts them with regard to their prayers into his own place (John 16:23-24), "Verily I say unto you, whatsoever ye shall ask the Father in my name, he will give it to you"; "in that day ye shall ask the Father in my name and I say not full"; "in that day ye shall ask the Father in my name and I say unto you that I will pray the Father for you, for the Father himself loves you."

Praying in the name of Jesus means standing in his place, having the same open door, the same opportunities, the same listening heart of the Father. It is all ours for the asking. Jesus continues his teachings about prayer (John 14:12, "The works that I do . . . and greater works . . . because I go to my Father and whatsoever ye shall ask in my name that will I do . . . If ye shall ask anything in my name, I will do it." Jesus had taken great pains to make clear to his disciples that the Father was dwelling in him, doing the works, giving the words. Now he extends this relationship to them. The Lord does not look at the task of his disciples to be just telling what someone else had done. In order to accomplish our task we will have to do the same works as he did, indeed we will have to do even greater works than his! This is what he promises us if we would only make the basis of our life and work asking and receiving.

What will happen in the world after this Congress? All what we plan, discuss, decide? Will it all happen — what we have the money, the skills and the personnel for, or what governments and authorities will allow us to do? Or will the outcome of this Congress be: What you will ask! I will do!

In one of his parables, recorded by Luke only, the Lord shows that there is no other way to fulfill our task than by asking. Luke 11:5 — the parable of the importunate friend. Here is a man in his home at night. His cupboard is empty. A knock at the door at midnight. His friend asks for shelter and food. Now in our culture it would be perfectly all right to tell him, "Dear friend, you did not tell me that you were coming, and you arrived at the most unsuitable time, you will understand that I haven't anything to offer you." But not so in the culture in which Jesus lived. I have lived long enough among Arabs to know that if a guest comes — he need not even be a friend — he has to be entertained, he has to be fed. No matter if you will have to give him your last sugar or tea or how much you have to pay to get something. Let us learn one thing here: If the world stands at our doorsteps in utter need, there is one excuse which we just cannot make, "I have nothing!" And the second one also is not valid, "I cannot rise and give thee." Looking at the world in its tremendous need and overwhelming demands on the church, we find two excuses which we cannot use, "I have not" and "I cannot!" Why? Because we have a friend to whom we can go and ask. And if we go and ask, how much will he give us? The Lord says, "And he will give him as many as he needeth." What are our resources for the evangelization of the world? The Lord says, "You have nothing at all that will satisfy the need of the world." Not a thing. Yes, we have lots of things: money, machines, medicines, skills, knowledge, good evangelicals who carry the whole Bible with them. Yet we have to give, we have to feed, we have to satisfy the need of others. We can only give by receiving and we can only receive by asking. The Lord has bound himself to give according to the need of the man at our doorstep, "He will give him as many (or as much) as he needeth."

b. *The example and teachings of the Apostles.* Did they have regular prayer times? Acts 3:1 — Peter and John on their way to prayer at the ninth hour. Acts 10:9 — Peter, climbing onto the roof at the sixth hour to pray. And while he prayed we read he saw . . . he had a vision. Out of this prayer-time and out of this vision there sprang the evangelization of the Gentiles, his visit to Cornelius, the conversion and baptism of his whole household. How does he remember this incident? "I (Peter) was in the city of Joppa, praying" (Acts 11:5). And then it happened. Might we ask here, what would have happened if Peter had not kept this hour of prayer.

There is not time for us now to have a close look at the prayer life of the Apostle Paul, but who can fathom the meaning of all his statements in his letters to different churches, "I am praying for you without ceasing, I am always praying for you, thanking God always on your behalf . . . I cease not to give thanks for you . . . I thank my God always in every prayer for you all . . . we give thanks, praying always for you . . . for this cause we do in prayer . . . we give thanks always for you, remembering without ceasing . . . we are bound to thank God always for you . . . wherefore also we pray always for you . . . ." To his "son" Timothy he writes, "I thank God that without ceasing I have remembered you in my prayers night and day" (Rom. 1:9-10; I Cor. 1:4; Eph. 1:15-16; Phil. 1:3-4; Col. 1:3, 1:9, 4:12; I Thess. 1:2, 2:13; II Thess. 1:3, 1:11; II Tim. 1:3). Are these words just phrases which Paul used to start his letters with? Empty words, or was it true that this man spent most of his days and nights in prayer? Was he condemning himself when he exhorted others to pray, as we so often do, or did he confirm his own practice when he wrote to Timothy, "I exhort therefore that first of all supplications, prayers, intercessions, and giving of thanks be made for all men, for kings and all that are in authority . . . for God will have all men to be saved and to come unto the knowledge of the truth" (I Tim. 2:1-4). Has this anything to do with world evangelization? "God will have all men to be saved and to come to a knowledge of the truth!" What comes first of all, when it comes to fulfilling the will of God for this world, for all men? "I exhort therefore that first of all supplications, prayers, intercessions . . . be made for all men." What comes before prayer if prayer comes first of all?

Paul also covets prayer for himself, because he knows that he can't find the words, he cannot minister as he should, if the Colossians and other churches were not praying for him. "Withal praying also for us that God may open unto us a door of utterance . . ." (Col. 4:3).

We have seen the examples of our Lord and the apostles, we have heard their teachings and exhortations: pray always, pray without ceasing, first of all, prayer should be made. Let us now look briefly at prayer typified and illustrated in the Old Testament.

3. *Prayer typified and illustrated*

Can we find any command in the Old Testament that people should pray? Why did Abraham pray? Why his servant on his way to Laban? It was like breathing to them. They could not live without it. Moses on one occasion was definitely told to pray. The armies of Amalek tried to prevent the children of Israel from fulfilling the task which God had given them: to march into the promised land and occupy it. What was the decisive factor in this battle? The prayer of Moses on the mount, with Aaron and Hur holding his hands. We often think that lack of prayer will just slow down or hinder God's work. This Old Testament type of New Testament prayer for the advance of God's kingdom and for the overthrow of the enemy tell us a different truth: when Moses' arms sank down, Amalek prevailed. Amalek had the victory, Amalek was able to advance. Is there an answer in this truth for many of our problems on the mission fields today?

Let us look at Joshua and the conquest of Jericho: Jericho is the type of a closed land, "Shut up from within and from without" (Josh. 6:1). What about Albania, what about Saudi Arabia, Afghanistan? Which is the decisive moment in this unequal and hopeless battle of Israel against Jericho? Joshua meets the commander of the Lord's army. He tells Joshua, take off your shoes! There on his knees on holy ground Joshua receives God's plan, God's strategy for the conquest of Jericho. Seven days of marching around the city, on the seventh day seven times, till the fullness of God's time has come and the walls tumble. Have we given up marching round the closed lands in faith and prayer? Maybe on the sixth day! Maybe just before God's time has come!

Let us look at Gideon: was there prayer in his life? He had an impossible task before him; he was alone, and yet he should deliver the Israelites out of the hands of the Midianites who were spread out in the valley of Jezreel — 120,000 men. Do we blame Gideon for asking signs of God? What were these signs? He wanted to watch the dew in the early morning hour. He had to get up pretty early, because there is no chance of seeing where the dew has fallen after the sun is up in those lands. In the early morning hours, when in the quietness and stillness God's heavenly dew was falling, Gideon got his assurance that God would be with him and that he would give the enemies into his hands. Do we know this hour of the day before the battle? In this same hour, when the sleep of people is lightest and most dreams are dreamt, God was working in the army of the Midianites: he was giving them dreams, spreading fear and discouragement. Gideon hears it while spying at the enemies' gates. What happens? Judges 7:15, "When Gideon heard it, he worshipped." This is the decisive moment in the battle against the Midianites, who had come upon Israel "like grasshoppers for multitude and with their camels without number as the sand on the seaside." Gideon worshipped. Prayer had turned into worship. The victory was in his hand. The stage was set for God to do for Gideon what he had asked him to do: to deliver his people from their enemies. Did it matter that he had only 32,000, and later 10,000 and finally only 300 men to combat against 120,000? Have we ever seen the multitudes that are like grasshoppers and like the sand of the sea in numbers: in Calcutta, in Tokyo, in Sao Paulo, or the masses in Mecca and Medina during pilgrimage? Uncounted thousands and millions? And each individual of these should — or is it shall — or is it must — hear the Gospel and understand it!

There is only one fitting parallel to Gideon and the host of the

Midianites in the New Testament. Eleven men on the Mount of Olives. They had just come out of their hiding places, they were just recovering from the shock of the execution of their leader and of their own failure to stand by him, remembering their flight and denial. His last words still rang in their ears, "You" . . . Why? "You eleven men" (to be quite sure Luke gives us the names of those eleven men in Acts 1). "You shall be my witnesses in Jerusalem . . . and to the ends of the earth." Now they were alone, just by themselves. The voice had gone, their master had gone. They were left alone, with an unbelievable, impossible task: the evangelization of the world. What was the best they could do? Form a committee to decide who would go where? Take a collection and see how far they could book their tickets? Arrange for prayer meetings for those that were staying behind?

We read, "Then they returned and went up to the upper room, and with one accord devoted themselves to prayer." The upper room, with one accord, devoted to prayer! This is the humble inconspicuous birthplace of world evangelization. And this is its foundation: by prayer! Is our foundation firm? Are our priorities right?

PRAYER IN EVANGELIZATION REPORT
Chairman: Bishop M. M. Jon
Secretary: M. Mpauyei

1. List the points relating to the subject on which most of the study group agrees.

Both English speaking study groups agreed wholeheartedly on the paper. In the French speaking group the same points of disagreement were mentioned.

2. List significant disagreements.

  a. There is no clear definition of what prayer is.

  b. According to the text we cannot say that prayer has absolute priority in the life of Jesus.

  c. Prayer is linked to the major points in the life of Christ.

  d. Jesus had time for everything he did and prayer was included in this.

3. Compile a list of major questions being asked inside and outside the church related to this subject. Seek between five and fifteen questions most encountered and put them in order of relative importance.

  a. If Jesus was God why did he pray? To whom and for whom did he pray?

  b. How can we be sure that the thing we are asking for is according to the will of God?

  c. What is the relationship between prayer and fasting?

  d. How long shall we pray for a specific need?

  e. What is meant by "pray without ceasing"?

4. Compile answers to major questions being asked.

There are various aspects of influencing God in our prayers. It seems that prayer might be used to change God's decision. We have the following examples in Scripture:

  a. unjust judge (Luke 18:1-5)

  b. importunate friend (Luke 11:5)

  c. Abraham's prayer for Sodom (Genesis 18:23-33)

The fact that we are children of God and we can ask the Father to change his mind was not the opinion of the whole group but of some individuals. The paper had stressed the opposite.

Answer to question 3b

If we ask it, if we begin to pray for it, we receive the answer (II Sam. 12:22).

If we are the temple of the Holy Spirit we do not need to ask ourselves if the thing we are praying is according to the will of God. It will be revealed to us as we pray (Rom. 8:26-27). In that sense we are in a situation which is quite different from that of David.

Answer to question 3c
Biblical teaching regarding fasting, Acts 13:1-3, indicates that in the early Church fasting was part of the ministry and was especially employed with prayer and sending out of missionaries (Matt. 17:21).
Another example of fasting is Jesus who fasted for forty days in the wilderness.
Paul's example can be found in II Cor. 11:27.

Answer to question 3d
We should pray till the Lord fulfills his promise and meets the need. The Lord can give us the assurance of the fulfillment of his promise (I John 5:14-15).
Matt. 9:37-38 seeing the great need and possibilities in the world (Whitefield) and the lack of workers the Lord commands us to pray for laborers in the harvest.

Answer to question 3e
To Pray *without ceasing* is only possible when prayer becomes an attitude, not just conversation.

5. Draw up a list of specific attitudes and activities which seem to be necessary as an outgrowth of this theological position, showing the theological support for listing each item.
   a. Praying without ceasing can be accomplished in a community by 24 hour chains of prayer.
   b. The women's world Day of Prayer: observed on the first day of March every year.
   c. Nights of prayer for world revival. These are held on the first of every month throughout the world.
   d. Telephone prayer chains.
   e. Special days of prayer.
   f. Prayer conferences.
   g. Daily family altars.
   h. Daily prayer groups in churches or other Christian bodies.
   i. Prayer lists — providing sufficient and specific prayer items (written or printed for all participants).
   j. Illustrated prayer calendars for missionaries.

APOLOGETICS AND EVANGELIZATION
Kenneth Hamilton

*Dr. Hamilton, Winnipeg, Manitoba,
Canada, is a Professor at the
University of Winnipeg.*

Apologetics and evangelization is my theme. At first sight the two might seem to be very far apart and to have little to do with each other. For apologetics is a branch of theology. It is an activity of the study and of the academic world, an activity concerned with bringing doctrine into relation to philosophy and justifying the truth of the Gospel on the level of theory. Evangelization, on the other hand, is a decidedly practical activity. It is concerned with the proclamation of the Gospel so that lives may be touched and transformed by the power of God's Spirit. Its place is wherever men and women gather together — in the church, the home, the market place, the public hall. Its aim is not abstract justification but concrete conviction. It commends the Gospel, not to the dispassionate intellect, but to the engaged and anxious heart.

Nevertheless, the two are more intimately connected than a superficial view might suppose. Conversion means the turning of *the whole man* to Christ in body, mind, and spirit. It cannot be a wholly emotional matter, just as it cannot be a wholly intellectual matter. An individual does not have to consider himself "an intellectual" in order to be genuinely moved to be able to explain his faith in meaningful, rational terms. Indeed, no one is likely to continue for long confessing a faith which does not seem reasonable to him and which he cannot explain in words that make sense to other people.

Apologetics and evangelism, therefore, are not two wholly separate activities, although they are not one and the same thing. Apologetics may be developed as a distinct branch of Christian theology, one having a special interest for intellectuals and for those wishing to provide a theoretical undergirding to the Gospel. But all evangelism involves some apologetical element — some attempt to explain the Gospel in such a way that it makes sense to the minds of those who hear it proclaimed.

Thus there is a real need for all who are engaged in the task of evangelization to consider what place apologetics may have in the preaching of the Evangel in our day and age. Only after facing the issues involved in relating the two activities can we be sure that we neither overestimate nor underestimate the value of the apologetical emphasis.

With these introductory thoughts I now turn to consider what apologetics can mean to Christians as they proclaim the faith to which they are committed. I shall start by looking at what it has meant in the past for the Christian Church.

1. *Apologetics in the Early Church*

In New Testament times an *apologia* was a technical term for a speech made in defense of an accused person in a court of law. The speech could be made either by the accused himself or by another on his behalf. An *apologia,* then, suggested two things: first, that there was an element of attack — an accusation had been made which raised the necessity for a defense; and second, that a defense was forthcoming — a plea of "not guilty" had been entered, together with the assurance that an adequate demonstration of innocence would be supplied. It followed, very naturally, that the word *apologia* came to be used whenever these two conditions were present, whether or not the setting was an actual court of law.

In the New Testament itself, the technical use of the word was still the main one. Apologetics, in the modern sense, has sometimes been justified by an appeal to I Pet. 3:15, which in the King James' Version reads, "Be ready always to give an answer to every man that asketh you for a reason of the hope that is in you, with meekness and fear." But the context of the verse is given in the previous verse, "And if ye suffer for righteousness' sake, . . ." The young churches soon discovered that the prophecy of Jesus was literally true for them, "Ye shall be brought before governors and kings for my sake" (Matt. 10:18). The fact that the verse refers to a formal trial where Christians were accused because of their faith is seen in Peter's command that they are to answer "in meekness and fear" — not making their defense defiantly or insolently, but with deference to the authority of law, even though they were accused unjustly. (The New English Bible has this context in mind when it translates the verse, "Be always ready with your defense whenever you are called to account for the hope that is in you, but make that defense with modesty and respect.")

Apologetics in the wider sense really entered the scene in the second century of the Christian era, with a group of men who came to be called the Apologists. These were Christians who realized that the Gospel needed to be defended in the world of that time, not only by the strength of Christian faith and the witness of Christian conduct, but also by the skillful presentation of Christian truth. The Apologists had two contemporary audiences in mind when they prepared their defense of the faith. The first consisted of Jews whose rejection of Christianity was made on serious theological grounds. Confession of faith in Jesus as the Son of God seemed to them to imperil the sole Lordship of the One True God, the God of Israel. Here, starting from the common ground of the authority of the Old Testament Scriptures, the Apologists attempted to show that a faithful reading of Scripture pointed to the Messiahship of Jesus and justified his claim that he was one with the Father. The second audience — by this time far the greater — was made up of pagans who were ignorant of the Scriptures and unimpressed by arguments based on scriptural evidence. Yet very many of these pagans were searching for a true philosophy and for a rule of life. The Apologists used their knowledge of Greek philosophy to introduce the teachings of Christ as a viable guide to the good life, and the Scriptures as an inspired revelation of the truths that led to wisdom.

In following their chosen path the Apologists, perforce, emphasized the intellectual aspects of the Christian faith. Yet they did not expound a Gospel that was theoretical merely, or divorced from a call to total commitment to Christ. The name bestowed upon the best-known of the Apologists gives the lie to such an impression. Justin was his name, but we know him as Justin *Martyr*. This converted philosopher defended the Gospel, arguing with both Jews and Gentiles, and finally he sealed his work with his life's blood.

The Apologists never imagined themselves to be introducing anything new when they took upon themselves to give a reasoned defense of the faith. Had not Stephen given to the Jews a Christian exposition of the purposes of God in the history of Israel? Had not Paul stood on Mars Hill and proclaimed Christ in terms adapted to the understanding of Athenian Stoics and Epicureans? Not only that, but Christ in his lifetime had disputed with the Pharisees and Sadducees, and with the Samaritan woman at Jacob's well.

Thus both the motive and the method followed by the Apologists were based on precedents to be found in the New Testament. What was new was the notion that defense of the faith could be a distinct vocation for Christians to take up who were peculiarly suited to undertake this calling. The *apologia* or speech for the defense was now taken out of the narrower context of the court of law and the tribunal and was seen to be an essential part of the ongoing mission of the Christian church. Added to the teachers and preachers who interpreted and expounded the Scriptures for the building up of the Body of Christ, there was now felt to be a need also for specialists in communicating the Gospel to those who found its message so strange and unfamiliar that they were unwilling to listen to it. The Apologist must be someone who, familiar with the outlook of the unbelieving world, was able to build a bridge between that world and the community of believers. So it was that apologetics came to be accepted as essential to the strategy of mission and evangelization.

2. *Apologetics down the centuries*

The acceptance of apologetics within the framework of the church's missionary strategy coincided with the spread of the church through the pagan world. In New Testament times the missionary work of the church was still carried out through centers where there were Jewish communities. Even Paul, "The apostle to the Gentiles," made use of these, and he could assume that the churches felt a particular obligation to help the Christians at Jerusalem (I Cor. 16:1). The situation became entirely different, though, after the fall of Jerusalem and the entire separation between church and synagogue. The Christian mission now had to be carried out wholly in an environment shaped by pagan culture, and converts made of those who knew nothing of Scripture or of the God proclaimed in Scripture. No common *religious* foundation for communication existed at all. If Christian apologists were to build a bridge between the pagan culture surrounding them and the community of faith, it had to be out of elements present in pagan culture.

Here we come to an important aspect of apologetics that I have not yet spelled out, namely, that *it seeks a common ground on which to begin its defense* of the faith. I have already mentioned that an *apologia* assumes two conditions. One condition is that the Gospel is under attack. The other condition is that the attack can be met by an adequate defense. But there is a third condition also. This is that the defense can be understood by those to whom it is addressed — hence the need for a common ground. Unless the apologist can start his defense by stating something to which the prosecution can agree, his defense will fall on deaf ears.

This goal of establishing a common ground is both the strength of apologetics and its weakness. It is its strength, because, once the opponent of the faith has begun to listen to a defense of the faith, he may be persuaded to change his mind. It is its weakness, because the apologist may be so anxious to gain a hearing that he waters down the faith in order to make it acceptable. Now, it is the clear teaching of Scripture that the Gospel is never entirely acceptable to the unbeliever. "But the natural man receiveth not the things of the Spirit of God: for they are foolishness unto him: neither can he know them, because they are spiritually discerned" (I Cor. 2:14). "But we preach Christ crucified, unto the Jews a stumbling block, and unto the Greeks foolishness" (I Cor. 1:23). The apologist, therefore, is impelled through faithfulness to the Gospel "to be able by sound doctrine both to exhort and to convince the gainsayers" (Tit. 1:9). But he must also be careful not to remove the "offence" of the Gospel through trusting in "wisdom of words, lest the Cross of Christ should be made of none effect" (I Cor. 1:17).

It follows that apologetics can never become the sole means of evangelism for the Christian Church. The proclamation of the Gospel is first and foremost a setting forth of what God has done for us in Jesus Christ. It is a preaching of Christ crucified which may seem foolish in the eyes of men but which becomes the means of salvation through the power of God (I Cor. 1:18). It is also an invitation to search the Scriptures, since these make us "wise unto salvation through faith which is in Jesus Christ" (II Tim. 3:15). Worldly wisdom can never be a substitute for the wisdom given us through God's Spirit. And the Spirit is received by the hearing of faith (Gal. 3:2). Arguments, in themselves, do not convert any one or bring about a living faith.

Nevertheless the Christian, who is commanded to keep that which is committed to his trust and to oppose false teachings (I Tim. 6:20) cannot forego argument when the truth of the Gospel is attacked. Although the wisdom of the world is foolishness in God's sight, to despise all wisdom as "worldly" is in direct contradiction to Christ and to Paul. Christ called his followers to be wise as serpents (Matt. 10:16); while Paul warned Christian disciples not to be children in understanding (I Cor. 14:20). Apologetics, one might say, cannot blaze a trail for the Gospel. Instead, it endeavors to keep open those paths that have been cleared and to see that these do not become blocked by the enemies of the Gospel.

Down the centuries, writers of apologetics can be seen engaged in the task of trying to keep open the paths to Christian truth. Sometimes they have tried the way of dialogue, starting from the viewpoint of the non-believer, the apologist seeks to show that the objections raised against the Gospel by the other are really mistaken ones which can easily be answered by a more careful examination of the issues. This was the way taken, for example, by Justin Martyr in the second century when he wrote his *Dialogue with the Jew Trypho.* And it was the way taken at the turn of the nineteenth century by Schleiermacher in his *Speeches on Religion to Its Cultured Despisers.* Sometimes apologists have sharpened dialogue into a frontal attack upon the unbelieving viewpoint, exposing its errors in order to follow with a demonstration of the rational and convincing nature of the Christian's commitment to faith. This was the way taken, for example, by Thomas Aquinas in his *Summa Against the Gentiles,* by Calvin in Book I of the *Institutes of the Christian Religion,* and by Joseph Butler in his *Analogy of Religion.*

When apologists take the way of attacking errors, the "common ground" does not seem to have a place in their arguments. Yet, in fact, it has. For the defense of the faith that they make concentrates upon refuting just those arguments which are in the forefront of the minds of those whom they oppose, and so are live issues for them also. Thus, Thomas Aquinas answered the objections to faith that were current in the thirteenth century; Calvin raised the main points of conflict over doctrine that engaged men of Reformation times; and Butler's arguments all were directed to the Deists of the eighteenth century. One result of the fact that apologists always have in mind this "common ground" is that the most purely *apologetic* parts of their writings have a way of becoming outdated. Live issues turn into dead ones, and other issues take their place. Today, there are few Deists around, so many of Butler's arguments hardly interest us, although the positive claims that he makes for Christian faith are still very worthwhile reading. On the other hand, Calvin's main purpose in writing the *Institutes* was to expound the eternal truths of the Gospel. His attacks upon mistaken beliefs are largely incidental to his main argument. The *Institutes,* therefore, has a "timeless quality" although it is also a work reflecting vividly the times it was written in.

The matter of growing out of date is one that affects the writings of apologists very greatly. Some apologetic works that were extremely popular in their day now seem to us in our day to be of slight value, if any. William Paley's *View of the Evidences of Christianity* seemed thoroughly convincing when it was written at the end of the eighteenth century, and continued to be influential for many years. Who reads it now? Augustine's *City of God* was written in the first place to refute those pagans who argued that the coming of Christianity had brought about the decline and fall of the Roman Empire. Augustine's work is still powerful today, but not because we are particularly interested in the original question but because in it Augustine gave us a vision of God's purposes working continually throughout history, in our own day as well as in Augustine's day.

Some apologetic works that tend to date quickly are those which take up a concern much on people's minds at a particular time, and then try to show that Christianity throws light upon this concern. Henry Drummond's *Natural Law in the Spiritual World,* for example, took its theme because men in the late nineteenth century were much impressed by the scientific view of those days that believed everything to be controlled by the impersonal laws of nature. Drummond argued that spiritual laws are just as real and that the two sets of laws can be compared. Again, what is most lasting in Drummond's book is his positive faith, not the success or failure of his argument. Today the writings of Teilhard de Chardin have a wide appeal to many both inside and outside the churches, because Teilhard argues that the present findings of science are completely compatible with Christian faith, and indeed support rather than undermine faith. Perhaps in a few years' time the arguments used by Chardin may seem completely out of date and quite unconvincing.

If many books of apologetics quickly lose their appeal, and seem to us now of historical interest merely — or even to be merely historical curiosities — that may not matter too much. In their day they showed that Christians believed that they must defend the faith, however well or badly they actually managed their defense. These apologists did their best to keep the paths open so that their contemporaries would not be prevented from walking on them and finding a way to their salvation. If they sometimes trusted in arguments that depended overmuch on worldly wisdom rather than on the truth that is from above, at least they turned those arguments against the world and its ways and sought to point men to Christ. To be faithful in a little is all that the apologist can claim — and not to let the children of the devil do all the talking and all the persuading.

3. Informal apologetics in evangelism

Apologetics supposes there to be a common ground between the Christian and the non-Christian. That common ground is to be found in the culture and thought of the society in which both Christian and non-Christian live. The apologist, for this reason, has to be someone who really knows that common ground well. It follows that apologetics is an area for specialists in thought and culture, for those well-versed in philosophy and ideas and familiar with the thinkers and writers of the day and of other days. Just as a defendant in a law suit will be careful in choosing a lawyer to defend him — requiring a specialist in criminal law, or in company law, and so on, as his case demands — so the defense of the faith requires trained specialists, theologians or informed laymen who will not fail for lack of the proper knowledge required.

So it has been true down the centuries that apologetics has been a field largely given over to experts: particularly to theologians with a professional training in philosophy. There is, indeed, an area in apologetics which requires, more than philosophical knowledge, an ability to communicate. This is the area of defenses of the faith directed to ordinary Christians (or to the uncommitted) who wish to know how to answer some of the common objections made to the credibility of the Gospel message, or who are troubled over the plausibility of modern alternatives to Christianity that are being put forward today, or who simply are perplexed about how to explain their faith to unbelievers. Men such as the late C. S. Lewis or, more recently, Francis A. Schaeffer have met a widespread need in giving such apologetical material in non-technical words. Their popularity reflects the felt need for a popular and readily available apologetic for the ordinary Christian to use. Yet apologists of this kind have to be themselves specialists, though not narrowly academic ones. They have to explain the writings of philosophers, and sociologists, and psychologists, and artists, and a host of other leaders in shaping the ideas abroad in the culture of our times. They simply try to mediate between the specialists and the non-specialists, giving the results of their studies to those who do not have the time or the training to do this for themselves.

There is, however, a further area of apologetics which is quite removed from the control of the expert. This might be called the area of non-specialized or informal apologetics. It is the type of apologetics which every Christian man or woman may be called upon to enter, without preparation, in the ordinary course of his or her Christian witness. Someone asks, "Why should I believe in Christ, in particular?" "I know some worshippers of Krishna and they are obviously sincere." Or someone says, "Last night I was able to talk to my husband through a medium at a seance. Isn't that a better proof of life after death than resurrection of Christ, which happened so long ago and can't be proved?" Or someone else says, "Christians have hang-ups on sex. They talk about eternal life, but they really are afraid of *life*, and they want to take the joy out of living."

The Christian who is told these things and others like them may simply testify to the faith that is in him. But he knows that he is expected to do more than that, and he will probably try to give an opinion, as well as he is able, saying why he believes the alternatives to the Gospel that have been suggested are not the right answers. In other words, he will embark on some informal apologetics.

At such times, the Christian who replies, "Well, I don't know the answer to that, but I still believe in Christ," is giving his witness. But the point is that he can hardly leave it at that. An objection to the faith has been made that requires a defense, an *apologia*. So he is called upon to be an apologist, whether or not he has any special competence to make an adequate defense in relation to this particular issue. Christians engaged in evangelization come to expect questions along a number of lines, because of issues that are topical and are being widely discussed in the newspapers and magazines and books and films — in the secular world. A few years ago, many questions would have concerned religion and science, and the Christian attitude to war and peace. Today, the questions are more likely to be about what Christians believe in connection with ecology, and abortion, and women's liberation, and world hunger and revolution. The Christian who is asked about these things can, of course, refer the questioner to experts. He can suggest that there is Christian literature on these topics, or he can quote what Christian leaders have said about them. But, since the most convincing witness is always a personal one, he will probably speak to more effect if he can speak for himself, even if he stresses that he is giving his own views and not committing all Christians to sharing his viewpoint.

What this adds up to is that the Christian who is engaged in the task of evangelization can never wholly avoid the area of apologetics.

As well as knowing his faith and being concerned to communicate the Gospel effectively, he must know something about the secular world also. He must have a real involvement in contemporary culture, so as to be able to move onto that common ground between believer and non-believer which is the place where apologetics makes its witness.

This common ground is not the chief place where the task of the evangelist is done. That is the Scriptures, on the ground of which all true witness must be made. But the other ground — the ground on which the secular world is familiar — cannot be shunned just because the Christian knows that it is not the ground where his true home is. For the sake of others — and in a real sense for his own sake also — he cannot be ignorant of the world where men move every day without thought of God or of their salvation, the world of secular culture, secular values, secular ideas. When Christ came among us, he worked in the carpenter's shop and talked to all kinds of people where they were. We cannot retire from the common arena.

In this connection, a word from one of the great evangelists of history, John Wesley, is very pertinent. Wesley said to his preachers, "Read the most useful books, and that regularly and constantly. . . . 'but I read only the Bible.' Then you ought to teach others to read only the Bible, and by parity to reason, to hear, only the Bible; but if so, you need preach no more. Just so said George Bell. And what is the fruit? Why, now he neither reads the Bible nor anything else. This is rank enthusiasm. If you need no book but the Bible, you are got above St. Paul. He wanted others too. 'Bring me the books,' says he, but especially the parchments,' those wrote on parchment. 'But I have no taste for reading.' Contract a taste for it by use, or return to your trade."

Wesley was concentrating in this statement upon reading, and he probably had in mind the reading of books that would be of direct edification of preachers. But the principle that he evoked holds true in a much wider field. Unless we keep entirely to the words of Scripture in evangelization — adding no comments whatsoever to those words — we are entering upon the common ground of culture, not simply preaching the faith but also entering upon some type of apologetics by claiming to *explain* the faith. In these days of many modern translations of the Bible, also, we are perhaps more conscious before that every translated word we use, even when it is a word of Scripture, bears some imprint of the culture of the time — is to some small degree an interpretation. So, if we are to be wise stewards of the Gospel in our generation, we will read books and use the other means available to us that link us with the cultural world in which the work of evangelization has to be carried out.

Paul reminds us that we have the treasure of the Gospel only in earthen vessels (II Cor. 4:7). This is true not only of the earthen vessel of the preacher's own personality, which has to serve as the vehicle by means of which the Gospel is communicated, but also of the earthen vessel of the culturally-conditioned words in which the preacher's message is given. We often forget (or do not recognize sufficiently) how greatly we are dependent upon the forms of thought and of speech that rise out of our culture — that common ground which Christians share with non-Christians. How readily, for instance, we appeal to people today to take Christ "as their personal Savior." Yet these words would have had no meaning to men and women in New Testament times and for many centuries after. The concept of "the personal" is a very recent one. It is founded, indeed, upon the value which the New Testament place upon the *person* of Jesus Christ and of relating ourselves through faith to him. In these days of TV "personalities" and the like, the concept has been cheapened. Yet it still remains a valuable one by means of which we can convey to our contemporaries that through committing ourselves to the Son of God we may ourselves become sons of God, or *true persons*. But it was through apologetic witness, through entering upon the common ground of secular culture, that the concept became understandable. You can speak of a "personal Savior" and be understood only when you belong to a culture that also speaks about a "person to person" telephone call!

So, let us understand that the task of evangelization must include, inevitably, the willingness to take up the work of apologetics. Apologetics, like all good things, may be misused and misapplied. Whenever it becomes self-sufficient and is parted from its foundation in the Christ revealed in Scripture, then it can be dangerous and even come to be the enemy of the Gospel. The Word of God cannot be established through the explanations — those limited and culturally-conditioned explanations — that we give of it in terms of "worldly wisdom." The apologist may all too easily fall under the spell of his own cleverness in justifying the ways of God to man that we forget that it is God who justifies, and God alone who can declare that is true. But, in the Providence of God, men also can speak a human word to human beings like themselves that may be used by God to touch the mind and the heart of those who otherwise would not give heed to their salvation. Apologetics, in the service of evangelization, has a humble and subordinate part in breaking the Word of life so that men may partake of it. But it has a part, and we should not neglect that part. Some may find that their calling is to be, in a formal way, apologists in the service of the Gospel. All are called, as the time fits and as the occasion offers, to undertake informal apologetics. Part of the field that is the world to be won for Christ is the common ground where the Christian apologist meets the non-Christians.

APOLOGETICS IN EVANGELISM REPORT
Secretary: V.S.C. Tyndale

Preamble

It was agreed that the most urgent task in apologetics facing evangelicals is the contention of a deeply biblical theology of apologetics. This task could not be undertaken by a discussion convening in four and one-half hours, and remains to be done. The group confesses to its shame, however, that the majority of that time was not spent in that area. The discussion, albeit so, was very profitable. By the nature of things, this report cannot be a definitive statement on apologetics, but is, in fact, a survey of the areas covered by the discussion and of some points on which there was a measure of consensus.

1. After a resumé of the paper by Dr. Kenneth Hamilton, which all who read it agreed that it had been most helpful and profitable, we were faced by a number of issues which might be tackled, and it was thought to be preferable to tackle a selective number. Nevertheless, as this report will indicate, discussion was wide-ranging.

2. The group found the biblical mandates for apologetics in the doctrine of creation. Man being made in the image of God was approachable by the Christian on the basis of mental, physical and emotional needs.

Apologetics has its source in man's creation by God as creatures who have been made in order that they might know their Creator and to see the world as under his sovereign rule. The reconciling Word that is Christ the Redeemer — restoring our sinful nature so that we may once more know God and his love — makes possible our speaking words that point men to the reconciliation of the Cross insofar as our minds can comprehend God's purpose for us.

3. Apologetics is not the same as evangelism, yet it should not be separated from the evangelistic task. It can bring men to understand their fallen nature by admitting the poverty and futility of their lives apart from God and the failure of all human hopes to make a truly human community. It can help the believer to understand more fully the promises offered in the Gospel. Yet the direct preaching of the Gospel in its power can alone open men's hearts to the believing reception of the Good News and deliver them from sin and despair. It stands as a separate discipline, not merely as a tool for evangelism, but it does not stand in isolation. It is important that the dichotomy between prophet, apologist and evangelist should be corrected. If apologetics is related to, and based on, an adequate theological basis, this tension will be resolved.

4. The discussion forced us to begin to face some questions in relation to apologetics, such as: What is the effect of the fall on the unbelieving mind? What is the place of revelation in nature and conscience? What do we mean by a point of contact or common ground?

5. The role of apologetics in the witness of the Christian community is to open the mind to the truth that is in Christ. It should not be thought of narrowly as the presentation of Christian "endeavor" to convince the

unbeliever. The guidance of the Holy Spirit bringing us into all truth is operative in apologetics, confronting us with the realities of faith in such a way that we are able to see our human situation before God and in the light of his Word addressing us.

Apologetics is seeing the whole of life in the context of faith. We cannot take ourselves out of faith, for we stand on the ground of our faith. This will gratify the "commonness" of the ground upon which we stand in apologetics.

The task of apologetics is to give a vision of a world made by God, and redeemed by God, and to illuminate this world in the light of faith. Reason alone will not do this, either that of the speaker or the recipient, but insight given to both by the Holy Spirit.

6. How do we know that an apologetic is going to be "meaningful"? If we walk by faith we do not have finality. If the issue rests on the skill of debate, then our "success" depends upon our skill or lack of it. Furthermore, as C.S. Lewis put it, the danger of the apologist is that his God may become no more real than his defense of his God.

7. The development of an apologetic that shall speak to man's concrete situation is one which must be undertaken anew by each generation of Christians. Apologetics must address men where they are in their cultural and intellectual environment. The unchanging Gospel must be presented in terms of particular times and places, and apologetics have constantly to undertake this task, so that supposed obstacles to belief may be seen to be unimportant or fictitious, and that the Gospel may stand before men's eyes as the saving Truth which it is eternal.

8. The biblical context of the apologia is that of the law court — the setting forth of a defense of the faith, but a defense with a view to prosecution. In later church history the forum shifted to the lecture hall, the debating room and the written Word.

9. For the apologetic to be effective it must take place on common ground so that communication can take place. However, the Christian knows that this is not the same as "neutral ground." It is the ground of God's creation, of God's reality, and, insofar as the debate takes place in the arena of reality, it points to God's truth. However, in seeking to locate the common ground of a man-culture, thought processes and experience — the Christian apologist must avoid compromise. If we can maintain God's truth about God's world, with a total Christian world-and-life view, then there is no subject upon which the Good News of Jesus Christ has no bearing.

10. In Paul, cross-cultural preaching in Lystra and Athens, he starts from the point of a common Creator — "of one blood" — of whomself he has left evidence. Instances were given in the current Third World scene, in the Philippines, Taiwan, Tanzania, and among the Bantu, when an argument from creation is effective. As modern Western "cerebral" civilization breaks down perhaps we can return to Creation as a "common ground."

11. When this is valid, either or both of two lines of reasoning can develop from creation. Firstly, that of from creation to a creator, to One who has spoken, and who has revealed himself. Secondly, that of from

creation to the creatureliness of man, and his nature as neither animal nor God, responsible yet not sovereign (i.e. in the areas of ecology, politics, etc.).

12. What is the place of Scripture in this? The anti-authoritarian stance of many would make an appeal to Scripture qua Scripture unavailing. Yet out of God's revealed truth we can demonstrate its realism by its correspondence with the real world around. The truth of God does not have to be expressed in the enscripturalist form, nor with appeal to its authority, but because it expresses truth. At some point, however, we can well point out what we have been saying is precisely what Scripture says.

13. At this stage of our discussion the differing schools of apologetics were discussed; i.e. those who would argue from evidences (the historicity of the resurrection, etc.) or Ln Montgomery, and those who would follow Van Til in his establishment of the presuppositions of the unbeliever.

If common presuppositions are held concerning sense-perception, the nature of external reality etc., then the evidences can be presented and the issues pressed. If, however, they are not shared, then by questioning the presuppositions of the other can be drawn out, examined and shown to be inadequate or impossible to live by. One of the functions of apologetics is to press the non-Christian to the limit of the logical consequences of his position (as biblical radicalism pushes the Christian to the consistent end of what he holds to be true).

14. But this must be done with loving care so that we do not destroy a man by removing all his props and hiding places, and giving nothing in return. When the autonomy of a man's position collapses he is very vulnerable and we must be gentle while urgently persistent. Preferrably he calls the other to self-analysis rather than carrying him by assault.

Throughout our contact with him, we must remember that apologetics is for the whole man, intellectual, moral, social; and a relationship which is concerned and respectful is essential. It is not just a matter of reasoning, but of presenting and demonstrating the whole of life as a matter of faith.

The Christian apologist has the double task of locating with sensitivity the point of need, and meeting that appropriately, but not resting there, but rather presenting a whole Christian world-and-life view as a satisfying and acceptable concept. The pastoral concern for the other will seek to establish him in a new position, one of having the mind of Christ.

Epilogue

It was maintained that had we an adequate theology of apologetics, then many of the more pragmatic questions would be resolved. Be that as it may, the consensus of those participating underlined the urgent necessity of this theology of apologetics being rigorously and immediately undertaken.

UNIVERSALISM
Harold Lindsell

There are no new heresies, just old ones dressed up in new garb. Universalism, the notion that ultimately all men will be saved and enjoy the eternal bliss of heaven, has antecedents that go back to origin, one of the anti-Nicene fathers. Employing an allegorical hermeneutic, Origen theorized that all men and even fallen angels would be redeemed at last. His was a grand "cosmological salvation" in which nothing was excluded either by divine fiat or human or angelic choice. His view received short shrift in the church and was repudiated in the great creeds of the church and in the pronouncements of church councils. Traditionally, the Roman Catholic church, the Orthodox churches, and Protestantism have rejected universalism.

From Origen's time until the nineteenth-century, universalism was virtually dormant. It became a live option in the United States in New England. It was here that Calvinism had been dominant from the early seventeenth century. And it was here that the notion of a limited atonement in which Christ died only for the elect, all others being subject to reprobation, was passing away. Strangely enough, the new universalism of the nineteenth century in New England really preserved the doctrine of eternal predestination simply by enlarging the scope of election to include all men rather than some. The Universalist churches that were formed went far beyond a renunciation of eternal reprobation and of the doctrine of hell. Within a short time they denied many if not most of the major tenets of the orthodox faith including the Trinity, the deity of Jesus Christ, and the infallibility of the Word of God written. Concurrently with the rise of Universalism, New England was plagued with the advent of Unitarianism, another older heresy that in some measure can be traced back to Arianism. In the twentieth century in the United States the Unitarians and the Universalists joined hands to form one denomination that stood outside the stream of historic Protestantism. The new denomination was literally filled with humanists, agnostics, and atheists whose antecedents had their roots in a theological orthodoxy they had then abandoned in commitment and in principle. The Unitarian-Universalist group was, and is, thoroughly apostate.

We need not dwell on the Universalists who have completely departed from biblical norms. Yet we must recognize that they initiated a return to the teaching that all men will be saved, a teaching that is not limited to this apostate group today. Rather, it has spread widely among churches who have not yet, in their creed and confessions, renounced the basic teachings of the Christian faith nor have any of them officially discarded the doctrine of hell and replaced it with salvation for all. In most of the large churches in Christendom there can still be found those who are more or less orthodox in doctrine who adhere to universalism. There are also those who hold to universalism who have also discarded some or all of the basics of the Christian faith. There are still others who hold to all of the major teachings of historic Protestantism and who also sturdily repudiate universalism, and teach that some men are eternally lost.

Advocates of universalism, or those who refuse to cast a decisive vote against it, are to be found in almost every large denomination and among key leaders from all parts of the world. Universalism is not a Western tenet nor is it limited to the churches of Western Christendom. It is to be found most widely in the modern ecumenical movement and its presence, as we shall see, has altered the concept of mission and wrought extensive damage to the missionary outreach of the church.

D.T. Niles of India was a prominent church leader and very active in the ecumenical movement. He had status as a scholar and was a key speaker at the World Council Assembly at Uppsala in 1968. In his book, *Upon the Earth,* he speaks to the question of universalism. He wrote: "Will all men be reclaimed? That is not our side of the problem. There are those who insist that no genuine and urgent conviction about the mission of the church is possible unless one is able to say positively: some will be saved and others will be damned. It is certainly true that those who are able to state the matter in this way do have a sense of urgency about their evangelistic and missionary responsibility; but the issue must nevertheless be pressed as to whether the whole drift of the teaching of the New Testament allows for so simple and simplified a conviction. Can it be that anyone will reject him even at the last? This is a speculation to which the New Testament does not lend itself." Dr. Niles comes to the conclusion, "The New Testament does not allow us to say either yes or no to the question, 'Will all men be saved?'"

Paul Verghese, a priest of the Syrian Orthodox Church, India, and at the time, Associate General Secretary of the World Council of Churches and Director of its Division of Ecumenical Action, wrote in *The Ecumenical Review* as follows, "Will the unbaptized man be saved? God wills that all men be saved. Christ wills that all men be saved. And he wills as he ought to will. And his will is, 'When the hour of destiny strikes to gather together into one the whole universe in him' (Eph. 1:10). Can that will be thwarted? No, for his will is commensurate with his power. But how is his will to be fulfilled? That is a cosmic question. Our task is to learn the answer slowly, by the tragic method, by laying down our lives for the life of the world."

Bishop James Pike, an Episcopalian now dead, had a word to say about universalism. He wrote, "But as to that which can be saved, it is on this earth broader than any particular historical revelation, even the full revelation in Jesus Christ. But the kind of God I first believed in, who would limit salvation to a select group of people who happen to have heard the news and heard it well, is an impossible God. As to this god I am now an atheist."

American theologian Nels Ferre took a strong stand for universal salvation. He wrote, "The first choice is that the Christian faith alone is true and that all other religions are pagan and false . . . . The final resurrection can mean nothing less than the victory of Christ over all his enemies; the final victory of universal love is universal salvation . . . . The logic of the situation is simple. Either God could not or would not save all. If he could not he is not sovereign; then not all things are possible with God. If he would not, again the New Testament is wrong, for it openly claims that he would have all to be saved. Nor would he be totally good. The total logic of the deepest message of the New Testament, namely that God can and wants to save all, is unanswerable."

Dean Norman Pittenger of the Episcopal General Theological Seminary in New York City said, "I believe that a corollary of the Christian doctrine of God as all all-sovereign love — is that it is God's will, as the New Testament puts it, that all men shall be saved, and that God's will is in the long run bound to accomplish that for which it sets out — that there will be no 'pockets of resistance' left when God has accomplished his final victory over sin, evil, and death. How to hold this 'universalist' doctrine without destroying man's sense of moral responsibility is another question . . . . Barth and Robinson have pointed the way — God's loving self-expression is so subtle and so persuasive that all men and the whole creation will be won (not coerced) into a response to the Creator, so that God will be all in all. Anything less seems to me a blasphemous denial of the central reality of the Christian revelation — God is love — and setting up of a heathen idol who ought not to be worshipped but destroyed."

Dr. Woodbridge O. Johnson, Chairman of the Department of Religion and Biblical Literature at Park College (Presbyterian), Parkville, Missouri, wrote an article in which he said that heaven and hell once stood for absolutely discontinuous states, "everlasting rapture on the one hand and everlasting torture on the other — with faith in Christ as the all-determining factor between them. But since such meanings of 'saved' and 'lost' seem both absurd and immoral to the modern mind, they might well be described as Christian nonsense . . . . No man can be evil enough to deserve hell." He said finally, "Some of us are following the way of Jesus toward eternal life; others the path of Moses, Krishna, the Buddha, Confucius, and Mohammed. But since God invites all men to the one ultimate destination, they ought to share their travel experience in the camaraderie of the journey. If the Christians find their way good and their guide trustworthy, they ought to share with their companions 'the riches of God's grace in Jesus Christ' (Eph. 2:8). But Christians should also be glad to receive any news of divine grace which the others have found, and which still others may find in Zoroaster and Lao-tzu and Mo-tzu, in Plato and Epictetus and Plotinus, in Nanak and Baha'u'llah and Ramakrishna. Jesus has been called 'the light of the world' and the Buddha 'the light of Asia'; but light is good in whatever lamp it burns."

Whatever may be said about the inroads of universalism in Protestantism, the same observations can be made about the Roman Catholic Church. This church is in theological disarray and its problems are perhaps greater than those in Protestantism. The theological spectrum ranges from the far left to the far right. Higher criticism has left an indelible mark on Roman Catholic scholars. The same effects that follow the advent of this criticism are now to be found in the Roman Catholic Church — a diminution of the authority of Scripture, increased emphasis on an errant Bible, radical demythologization, as well as some other consequences not felt within Protestantism. Whereas the Bible was the last court of authority in Protestantism, an infallible pope was the final resort in Roman Catholicism. The same criticism that opposes an infallible Bible is now opposed to an infallible pope. Thus Hans Kung could write that infallibility is to be found only in God and Christ, not in the Bible or in the papacy.

Among Roman Catholic theologians there is to be found the same streak of universalism as within Protestantism. It takes a somewhat different form depending for its orientation upon the Roman Catholic doctrine of the necessity of water baptism for salvation. But this has not hindered the advance of universal salvation once it is stated that intention is an adequate substitute for the actual use of water for baptisms. But this Congress should not add to the theological confusion by considering universalism segmentally by special reference to this or that church. The overarching question is universalism regardless of the setting or church in which it is found. Once the biblical position on the subject has been discerned, application should and must be made to all churches. And the apologetic to counter universalism should be developed for each and every church tradition. But Lausanne will have enough to keep it occupied by doing this for Protestantism whose churches need to be put in order before consideration is given to providing a corrective for the Roman Catholic theologians and missiologists who hold that all men will at last be redeemed.

It cannot be disputed that many voices among Protestants have been raised in the propagation and defense of universalism. Nor can it be denied that as a result of this neo-universalism there has been a radical shift in the definition of the mission of the church. Nowhere has this been more obvious than in the ecumenical movement and particularly in the Commission on World Mission and Evangelism of the World Council of Churches. In the 1963 Mexico City meetings of the Commission, and more recently in Bangkok in December of 1972, it was quite apparent that the central thrust of the conferences was based upon a commitment to changing the social, economic, and political structures of society. This was based, in turn, upon the underlying assumption that all men are now in Christ and only need to be informed of what is already true. Such being the case there is no reason why the mission of the church should not be redefined, personal evangelism neglected, and improving the temporal conditions of men made the focal point of reference. Both at Mexico City and Bankok it was clear, however, that there are some within the World Council of Churches who still believe in a heaven and a hell, that men are not in Christ in their unbelief, and that those who do not experience the new birth are forever lost and undone.

There was every opportunity for the World Council of Churches at Uppsala, or for the Commission on World Mission and Evangelism at Mexico City and Bangkok to clarify their position if what has been said here is inaccurate. But nothing has come from these gatherings, nor has the leadership of the World Council of Churches repudiated universalism. All that would be necessary would be for them to state clearly that some men are lost, that there is a hell, and that those who die without having personally made a profession of faith in Jesus Christ are lost. But this has not been done and it is this failure that, in part, makes the International Congress on World Evangelization necessary, and occasions our discussion about universalism so that some definitive judgment can be rendered for our generation, especially as such a judgment relates to the evangelization of the world.

There are only three possibilities with respect to the question of universalism. They are: (i) nobody is saved; (ii) everybody is saved; (iii) some are saved and some are lost. Option one is obviously false and no further discussion of it is required. That leaves us with but two options: all are saved, or only some are saved. Before we decide which option is biblical and binding we should not overlook some of the important theological questions that underlie such a discussion. These have to do with election, a universal or particular atonement, and free will or the power of contrary choice. Let us see how these relate to universalism.

There can be no doubt that Scripture does teach divine election. The problem connected with it is whether Christ died for all men or only for those who are elect. It is a problem of the particularity or the universality of his death on the Cross. If Christ died only for the elect then those who are non-elect are lost, there is no universalism possible and the doctrine of hell remains intact (that is, the lake of fire as the ultimate destination of those who die without Christ).

If Christ died only for the elect how is it then possible for us to proclaim to any man that Christ died for *him*? Christ did not die for that man unless he was one of the elect. Therefore we would not be able to proclaim a universal call and ask all men to receive Christ as Savior. The best we could do would be to say, "Christ died for sinners such as you." But whether Christ died for him would depend upon whether he was among the elect. This constitutes a problem.

It was Karl Barth who sought a resolution to the problem of election and in the process opened the door wide to universal salvation for all. He combined a belief in the death of Christ for all with a doctrine of election and was left with the choice whether or not this meant that all were elected and all saved. He came perilously close to a full commitment to universalism. It was Berkouwer who commented on Barth's difficulty when he said, "But with Barth, Christ's death touches precisely upon the election of all, which election has become manifest in Christ's death. The universality of the message is no longer at odds with the fact of election, for it is based upon the universality of election." But we must note the conclusions that flow from this standpoint.

If by divine election and universal atonement all are saved, then (i) there is no hell, no lake of fire, and no eternal punishment. (ii) There is no genuine freedom of choice which is no better in principle than any Calvinistic doctrine of election based upon a limited or particular atonement. For if the elect, some or all, must be saved, then it is difficult if not impossible to reconcile this with the power of contrary choice. And if all are saved there is no real power of contrary choice. Thus in universalism the problem of freedom of choice is no less pressing than that problem within the context of a particular atonement efficacious only for the elect. The Arminian does not escape a similar problem.

With great emphasis on freedom of choice, the doctrine of election loses its force and seems to wither away. Election then becomes a negligible wish without the sovereign power of God behind it to make it come to pass.

There are still other implications involved in the belief in universal atonement and universal election. This has to do with the evangelization of the world. (i) Whatever force is connected with the Great Commission is lost when universalism is adopted. If all men are at last to be saved then the urgency of the Commission is gone, and indeed the need for it is dissipated. All men are already in Christ whether they know it or not. They are going to be saved finally. There is no need for haste since death without the knowledge of Christ will not keep them from heaven. Whether they stay in their own religions or not or whether they have no religion at all ceases to be important. Thus Paul Tillich could aver that the denial of God is in fact an affirmation of him. (ii) Why should the people of God suffer and sacrifice in going to the ends of the earth when the best they can hope for is to bring some people to a knowledge of the salvation they already have just a bit sooner? And what difference does a few years make in that regard in the light of the eternal ages? (iii) Indeed, if universalism is true then to change the mission of the church to the improvement of the temporal conditions of men is logical and compelling. (iv) There is no need for a Congress on World Evangelization; we are wasting time and spending money uselessly. (v) But above all we cannot escape the conviction that God forces men into the kingdom against their wills and he thus becomes a capricious being and man a virtual automaton.

It appears that we are led by Scripture and logic, with some element of mystery, to conclude that Christ did die for all, but all are not saved at last. There are abundant evidences in Scripture for this just as there are sufficient evidences to believe in the lake of fire (the doctrine of hell and everlasting punishment): I John 2:2; John 3:16; Rom. 5:6; Rev. 20:10, 11-14; Matt. 25:46, 16:26. Christ's death on the cross was potentially efficacious for all men; it was actually efficacious only for those who believe. But all do not believe and so all are not saved. But those who never hear are lost and unless they hear they will never have a chance of being saved. To believe thus is to make possible the proclamation of a universal Gospel, stating that Christ died for all men, and to follow it with an invitation for men to receive Christ as Savior. In this view the evangelization of the world takes on concrete significance and the church must assume its rightful role in the plan of God to finish the evangelization mandate.

Against the backdrop of the Canons of Dort, G.C. Berkouwer helps us see that freedom of the will and divine election can be reconciled. Speaking of the Canons of Dort he says, "On the one hand we find reference to a universal preaching of the Gospel to all without exception and, on the other, we are confronted with an unmistakable particularity." "The Canons," he says, "speak of the death of Christ as a sufficient sacrifice. If the call of the Gospel is not accepted and many do not repent, this is not owing to any defect or insufficiency in Christ's sacrifice, but to man himself (CD, II, 6, Rejection of Errors). Christ's death is the only and most perfect sacrifice which is of 'infinite

worth and value, abundantly sufficient to expiate the sins of the whole
world' (CD, II, 3). On the basis of this confession it is possible to assure
all men 'that in this sacrifice lies an infinite power and worthiness, so
that in all the world no person could be sunk so deep that Christ's
sacrifice would not be abundantly sufficient for the expiation of his
sins. In this way we reject the dilemma which says that there is either
no general offer of salvation or universal election.'" It is true, says
Berkauwer, that "he who studies the history of doctrine repeatedly
discovers the power of the dilemma between universalism and the
denial of a general offer of salvation."

It is here that some word must be expressed about the eternal
destiny of those who have never heard the Gospel. This is a difficult
and perplexing question that cannot be avoided even if our conclusions
are somewhat tentative and an element of mystery remains. We must
start with the biblical datum of Paul that every man must personally
believe in Christ himself before he can be saved. Paul then asks the
question, "How are men to call upon him in whom they have not
believed? And how are they to believe in him of whom they have
never heard? And how are they to hear without a preacher?" (Rom. 10:14).

Scripture in Romans makes it abundantly clear that there are three
lights that provide guidance for men. One is the light of nature, the
second the light of the law, and the third the light of the Gospel. (See
here Romans 1-3.) There are people who have rejected the Savior
who have heard the Gospel, are familiar with the Ten Commandments (the law) and who have the light of nature or of human conscience.
Yet they are lost. They have rejected the Light. But what about those
who know neither the law of God nor the Gospel? First, let it be said
that anyone who really wants to know God even though he has no
particular knowledge of the law or the Gospel will be given the opportunity to hear of Christ and to receive him as Savior. It is God's
responsibility to make certain that whoever really wants the knowledge
of God will receive it. This has been demonstrated many times in the
missionary situation. Unsaved people have welcomed the advent of
missionaries with the Gospel message and indicated that they have
been looking for them to come. One way or another God in his mercy
will make known what the unsaved need to know if they really wish
to know God.

Let us suppose for a moment that there are those who never received any knowledge of the Gospel or of the law of God. And they
die this way. Are they then lost forever? It is here that we must aver
that the least that anyone ever has by way of the knowledge of God
is the light of nature or the law of conscience written in the hearts of
all men. This indeed may be the light that lighteth every man that
cometh into the world. In Romans I, Paul argues that, "What can be
known about God is plain to them (Gentiles, i.e., people without the
law) because God has shown it to them. Ever since the creation of
the world his invisible nature, namely his eternal power and deity,
has been clearly perceived in the things that have been made. So they
are without excuse." "All who have sinned without the law will also
perish without the law. . . . When Gentiles who have not the law do by

nature what the law requires, they are a law to themselves, even though they do not have the law. They show that the law is written on their hearts, while their conscience also bears witness and their conflicting thoughts accuse or perhaps excuse them. . . . both Jews and Greeks, are under the power of sin . . . none is righteous, no, not one" (from Romans 2 and 3). Whatever may be the human situation, however great our compassion, and however strongly we might wish that things were different, it appears clear that Scripture teaches that even men whose knowledge is limited to the light of nature or of conscience are forever lost if they die without the saving knowledge of Jesus Christ.

Based upon the conviction that some are saved and some are lost, we must conclude:

(i) Universalism cannot be supported from Scripture and is a heresy.

(ii) The Scriptures do make a universal offer of salvation to all men.

(iii) There is a doctrine of election and perhaps election follows atonement in the order of the divine decrees so that those who spurn the offer of salvation because they have not been elected are passed over. But they are responsible and exercise freedom of choice.

(iv) God has ordained that men shall be saved through the proclamation of the Gospel. And they will not be saved if the Gospel is not preached. Therefore it behooves the Church of Jesus Christ to preach the Gospel to all men everywhere so that they may have the opportunity to accept Christ.

(v) Those who die without Christ are lost even if they do not know of the law or hear the Gospel.

(vi) We urge those who believe in universalism to re-examine their position and the evidences, change their opinions, and join us in the global task of reaching all men everywhere with the Good News of salvation.

(vii) Although we reject universalism categorically and say fearlessly that we believe in both heaven and hell, we do not pass judgment upon the eternal destiny of those who may cling to a belief in universalism. It is possible for some universalists to have saving faith in Christ and to have experienced the new birth. But God alone is the judge of the living and the dead.

UNIVERSALISM REPORT
Secretary: Keat Peng Goh

1. List the points relating to the subject on which most of the group agrees.

a. Universalism is sustained by two lines of thinking. For those who adhere to biblical authority, appeal is made to several texts which speak of God's desire for all men to be saved. A second basis of this theory is philosophical, an appeal to the love and justice which rendered unthinkable the idea of hell. The appeal to Scripture is weak on two counts. It uses Scripture relatively, finding the mass of biblical evidence pointing to the lost estate of some (Luke 16:19ff; Matt. 25:31ff; John 3:36; John 6:14; Acts 14:6, etc.). Hermeneutically it fails to take into account the context of those passages which speak of God's desire for all to be saved. In each case the lostness of some is found in the immediate or larger context.

The appeal to the character of God is not usually linked with biblical exposition based on commitment to the authority of Scripture. Therefore we do not find it compelling. However, we do not allow the charge that biblical teaching on the eternal lostness of men is irrational or contrary to God's character in any way. Among many evidences addressing were the following: (i) men are condemned for rejecting the light they have (natural, revelational), not for failing to respond to light they do not have; (ii) punishment would be in line with the amont of light rejected (Luke 12:47a); (iii) the possibility of separation from God is the inevitable result of God's love. He created man in his image with potential to reject his loving fellowship, not as robots programmed for obedience. Forced love is not true love; (iv) those who do respond to God's mercy will receive justice. God will deal justly with all; (v) those who remain disobedient to God cannot be included in the fellowship of the obedient. This would be injustice for the obedient and for the disobedient, loving to neither.

Therefore, we conclude that universalism cannot be supported from Scripture and is heresy.

b. The Scriptures do make a universal offer of salvation to all men. When Jesus Christ took the sins of the world upon himself on the Cross, he made the gift of salvation available to all (I Tim. 4:10; II Pet. 3:9; Rom. 5:18). It is through this salvation and this salvation alone that men can be justified before God and reconciled to God (II Cor. 5:19; Rom. 3:22,26; John 14:6). This does not mean that all men are reconciled to God, but only those who, under the conviction of the Holy Spirit, repent and put their faith in Christ.

c. God has ordained that men shall be saved through the proclamation of the Gospel. And, in our understanding of Scripture, they would not be saved if the Gospel is not preached to them. This is a major reason for the Church of Jesus Christ to go preach the Gospel that men might receive him and become responsible members of his church.

d. We cannot accept the new universalism which stresses that God is reconciled to all men because of Christ's sacrifice and, therefore, saved. Man is regenerated and justified only by faith in Jesus. Without saving faith, man is ignorant of God's righteousness and is separated from God (Romans 3:28; 4:5; 10:4; 10:13; Eph. 2:12). Only through believing in the merits of Christ as Savior can man have eternal life (John 20:31). The Bible teaches that those who neither know God nor obey the Gospel will not experience the glory of God in eternity (I Thess. 1:7-9).

e. We urge those who believe in universalism to re-examine their positions and evidences, change their opinions and join us in the global task of reaching all men everywhere with the Good News of salvation.

f. Although we reject universalism categorically and say fearlessly that we believe in both heaven and hell, we do not hold this view lightly but with deep sorrow and a broken heart. We are aware that it is totally inconsistent to maintain this belief without a deep sense of responsibility to do all in our power to present the Gospel to all men and urge them to believe. We confess before God that evangelicals have been too ready in the past to leave the task of evangelism to the few and not consistently to match faith with deeds. "It is not the will of God that any should perish but that all should be saved, and come to the knowledge of the truth." (II Pet. 3:9). It is urgent that we see that all receive the knowledge of this saving truth.

2. List of major questions being asked relating to this subject.

a. Will everybody be ultimately saved?

b. What about the difficult passages of Scripture that seem to suggest universalism e.g. Philippians 2:10, 11; Romans 5:18; Romans 11:32; I Tim. 4:10; Col. 1:19, 20; Eph. 1:10?

c. What are the implications of universalism to world evangelization — e.g., if all people would ultimately be saved, would we have to preach?

d. What would the nature and form of punishment be? Would it be everlasting, or would it be in the form of annihilation? Can a God of love allow everlasting punishment?

e. What about those who die in infancy?

f. What about those who are mentally retarded?

g. What about those who have never heard or known of Christ in their lifetime?

3. Compile answers to the major questions asked. We feel that some of these questions are covered under section 1 of this report.

THE GOSPEL, CULTURAL CONTEXT AND RELIGIOUS SYNCRETISM
Byang H. Kato

*Dr. Kato, Nairobi, Kenya, is General
Secretary of the Association of
Evangelicals of Africa and Madagascar.*

"If I had a thousand lives I would give them to the service of Christ in Africa." Robert Moffat uttered this passionante cry because he had a clear-cut Gospel to proclaim, and Africa as any other part of the globe, was groping in complete darkness without Christ. This is no denial of God's general revelation through nature, conscience, history, and miracles. But it is an admission that "he who has the Son has life" (I John 5:12 RSV). If there was a time in Africa when there was a need of the clean-cut Gospel it is today. It is, therefore, a great privilege for me to share with God's servants my understanding of the Gospel in Africa and the challenge it faces in the area of syncretism.

1. *The Gospel*

The inspired, inerrant Word of God gives us the Gospel and its working power in a nutshell in I Cor. 15:1-4. It is not a part of any people's culture. It is not indigenous to any soil. It is revealed propositionally and must be declared accordingly. The Jews did not have it. The Germans, the Americans, the Africans, the Europeans, needed to get it revealed through a messenger (Rom. 10:9, 10). The Gospel must be received, and it is impossible to receive it corporately, though each individual recipient becomes a member of a group upon his decisive action. The receiving is described as an act of believing and is evidenced by the fact of holding form to the Lordship of Christ. The outcome of acceptance by faith is salvation. Only a drowning, helpless person needs to be saved. All men, therefore, regardless of their ethnic origin are entirely helpless, in fact, spiritually dead (Eph. 2:1; Rom. 5:6).

The content of the Gospel is the heart of its proclamation and the resulting effectiveness. This is why the Christian faith is not a leap in the dark. When I say I believe, the sentence is meaningless unless I give the object of my belief. The center of the Gospel message is not a philosophical, ever-pervading "logos" of Philo or even Justin Martyr. It is not the cosmic Christ present in all religious aspirations of various faiths in the world. It is a historic person, Jesus the Christ. That he lived and died under Pontius Pilate is verifiable. That he was buried and literally rose again is also a convincing fact of one history. A long list of his contemporaries who saw him after resurrection was unchallenged. The best the religious leaders could do was to bribe the guards to conceal the truth (Matt. 28:11-15). No amount of fraud can destroy the truth of God predicted several millenia earlier. That Jesus died, was buried, and rose again is not only an indisputable fact of history, but it is a fact borne out in the lives of more than half a billion people in the world today. He alone as God-man has made the claims of death, resurrection, and a promise of drawing men to himself, and the claims have been fulfilled. This is the undiluted Gospel for which Christ's sons and daughters in Africa must be prepared to lay down their lives (Matt. 10:34-39).

2. Contextualization

This is a new term imported into theology to express a deeper concept than indigenization ever does. We understand the term to mean making concepts or ideals relevant in a given situation. In reference to Christian practices, it is an effort to express the never changing Word of God in ever changing modes for relevance. Since the Gospel message is inspired but the mode of its expression is not, contextualization of the modes of expression is not only right but necessary. William Barclay, has rightly stated, "But it is not Jesus' purpose that we should turn all men into one nation but that there should be Christian Indians and Christian Africans, whose unity lies in their Christianity. The oneness in Christ is in Christ, and not in any external change. The unity in Christ produces Christians whose Christianity transcends all their local and racial differences; it produces men who are friends with each other because they are friends with God; it produces men who are one, because they meet in the presence of God to whom they have access."

The New Testament has given us the pattern for cultural adaptations. The incarnation itself is a form of contextualization. The Son of God condescended to pitch his tent among us to make it possible for us to be redeemed (John 1:14). The unapproachable Yahweh whom no man has seen and lived has become the Object of seeing and touching through the incarnation (John 14:9, I John 1:1). The moving old hymn on humiliation and exaltation of Jesus Christ, the Lord (Phil. 2:5-8) was evidently an incentive to Apostle Paul in his philosophy of the ministry which was to become "all things to all men." This in turn should motivate us to make the Gospel relevant in every situation everywhere as long as the Gospel is not compromised.

Contextualization can take place in the area of liturgy, dress, language, church service, and any other form of expression of the Gospel truth. Musical instruments such as organ and piano can be replaced or supplemented with such indigenous and easily acquired instruments, as drums, cymbals, and corn-stalk instruments of various descriptions. It must be borne in mind, of course, that the sound of music must not drown the message. Clergy do not have to wear "Geneva" gown or even dog collar. Not only should the message be preached in the language best understood by the congregation, but terminology of theology should be expressed the way common people can understand. But theological meanings must not be sacrificed at the altar of comprehension. Instead of employing terms that would water down the Gospel, the congregations should be taught the meaning of the term as originally meant. One instance is the mustard seed. This is a crop not found in America or Africa. Instead of substituting it with a local grain the term should be employed and the explanation given. While the content of God's Word should remain what it is, the expression of it in teaching, preaching, and singing should be made relevant. Drama and storytelling, for instance, should be considered more seriously in Africa. Any method that helps the advance of Christ's message should be employed.

3. *Religious syncretism*

In a recent talk to church leaders in East Africa, the Rev. John R. W. Stott described syncretism as "a fruit cocktail of religions." Eric Sharpe defines it as denoting "any form of religion in which elements from more than one original religious tradition are combined."

Christianity has gone full circle. Christianity in Africa, or in the Third World for that matter, has come to the stage it was in the second century. Just as syncretism plagued the church in the days of apologists, so it challenges the historic faith in Africa today. Donald McGavran's evaluation is quite fitting with the situation obtained in Africa today. The great missiologist writes, "It seems clear that the next decades, Christians again as in the first two centuries, will fight the long battle against syncretism and religious relativism. And for the same reason — namely, that they are again in intimate contact with multitudes of non-Christian *peers* who believe that many paths lead to the top of the mountain. The concept of the cosmic Christ, some maintain, is a way out of the arrogance which stains the Christian Father. Other Christians believe that the concept of a cosmic Christ operating through many religions sacrifices turth, for if there are, in fact many revelations then each voices approximation of the truth. As hundreds of Christian and non-Christian denominations spring into being across Africa, Asia, and other lands on earth some will inevitably hold biblical views of the Person of Christ.

Incentives for syncretism in Africa are not hard to seek. The incentives for universalism (i.e., the idea that all will be saved in the end) are the same for syncretism since only a thin line separates the two ideologies. The reason for growing syncretisitc tendencies may be summed up briefly as follows:

(i) The prevailing wind of religious relativism in the older churches is carried abroad by the liberal missionaries in person and through literature.

(ii) The crying need for universal solidarity in the world fosters religious respect one for the other.

(iii) Political awareness in Africa carries with it a search for ideological identity. Some theologians seek to find this identity in African traditional religions.

(iv) Emotional concerns for the ancestors who died before the advent of Christianity force some theologians to call for a recognition of religious practices of pre-Christian idol worshipers.

(v) Cultural revolution calls for a return to socio-religio-cultural way of life in Africa. Since it is hard to separate culture from religion, the tendency is to make them identical and cling on to idolatrous practices as being an African authentic way of life.

(vi) Inadequate biblical teaching has left the average Christian with inability to "rightly dividing the Word of truth." Syncretistic or neo-orthodox teachers bring their views, and even Christian leaders fail to discern what is right according to the teaching of God's Word.

(vii) The African loves to get along fine with everybody. He therefore does not offend his neighbor by letting him know what the Bible says about non-Christian religions. That is why liberal ecumenism is thriving in Africa.

(viii) Liberal Christianity has done a thorough job in picking up key brains from the Third World and grooming them in liberal schools in the Western world.

(ix) The study of comparative religions without the effort to assert the uniqueness of Christianity has helped produce theologians of syncretistic persuasion.

(x) The genuine desire to make Christianity truly African has not been matched with the power of discernment not to tamper with the inspired inerrant content of the revealed Word of God.

The spirit of syncretism in Africa is predominant today both inside and outside church circles. Otto Stahlke accurately describes the contemporary situation when he writes, "The syncretistic tendency, the attempt to blend and reconcile various religions, is not new, but never before has it been so prominently espoused by a leading agency for many Christian churches. Promotion of this point of view has come from philosophers, sociologists, anthropologists, comparative religionists, and some avant garde theologians."

An African anthropologist, Okot p'Bitek, advocates, "In my view the student of African religions needs to soak himself thoroughly in the day-to-day life of the people whose thought-systems and beliefs he wishes to study. He must have a deep knowledge of their language. When attending ceremonies, he must not stand apart as a spectator, but join in fully, singing the songs, chanting the chants and dancing the dances."

P'Bitek calls for syncretism not only in matters of pagan religious festivities but also in pagan immoral practices. He considers Christian teaching on sex confined to marriage alone as being Western and that it must be rejected by the African. Realizing that Christian ethical teaching is based on God's Word, the university lecturer condemns the Apostle Paul in a derogatory manner. He writes, "This ex-Pharisee who has been described as the ugly little Jew, was a small man barely five feet tall, bow-legged, a chronic malaria patient with serious eye trouble. We learn from Acts Chapter IX that he became a mental case for a short time, and on recovery, he joined the Christians whom he had formerly persecuted. Paul was a great woman hater." Since the "Western world is still a prisoner of St. Paul's thwarted sexual morality" the African should outgrow that delusion and follow the type of morality which allows free sex. P'Bitek considers that African. He writes, "In most African societies, having sexual intercourse with married women by persons other than their husbands is strictly forbidden; but unmarried women enjoy both unmarried and married men." He suggests, "It is important for African leaders to consider whether sexual ethics in their countries should be based on St. Paul's prejudices against women and sex, or built on the African view-point which takes sex as a good thing."

In political circles, recognition of all religions as being good is ideal for national solidarity. Religious tolerance in almost all African countries is admirable. Christians should continue to pray for men in government that such a peaceful atmosphere may continue. But religious tolerance is quite different from enforced unity or regulated practice against one's religious convictions. The authentic philosophy resulting in enforced unity into one Church of Christ in Zaire would lead on to compromising syncretistic situations. But the worst situation is that which is reported to be taking place in the Republic of Chad. It has been reported that Christians are being forced to undergo circumcision ceremonies which amount to an initiation into pagan rites. It is reported that some Christian leaders have been imprisoned, some churches burnt down, and missionaries expelled because they rejected what would amount to syncretism.

It is rather sad that some Christian leaders are encouraging government interference in religious affairs because they want to encourage ecumenism. The recently appointed head of the Ecumenical Institute, Boisey, Professor John S. Mbiti, writes, "Denominationalism and its proliferation, then, are the product of human selfishness and weakness. Our church leaders in Kenya, present and past, African and expatriate, have made a mess of the church through inheriting and agreeing to accept divisions, through multiplying divisions, and through perpetuating division." The Kenyan theologian continues, "Finally, the information in this Handbook makes one wish to appeal to the Government of Kenya to set up ministry of religious affairs." Situations similar to that of Zaire may not be far away in other African countries. When such

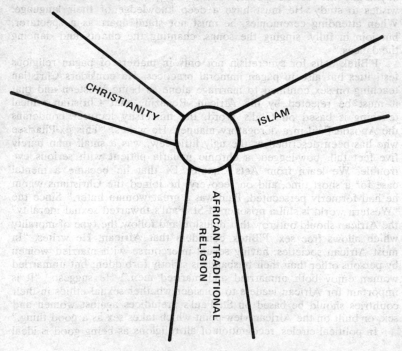

takes place, syncretistic practices of some semi-Christian groups will likely pervade a wider Christian spectrum.

Apart from secular writing and government encouragement for syncretism, the study of comparative religions is another major factor. Most of the universities in Black Africa have departments of religions. The primary goal of these departments, far from being the spiritual growth of individual Christian students, is academic excellence. The tendency is to study Christianity, Islam, and African traditional religions in a detached manner. The journal of the department of religious studies at the University of Ibadan best illustrates this. The journal is called *Orita,* a Yoruba word meaning a junction. It has on its cover this design:

The head of the department is a Christian. But the editor of the journal is a Muslim. One explanation of this mixed situation is that the department seeks only to understand the encounter of these three religions in Africa. One evident fact is that the journal persupposes the validity of all these religions and the silence on declaring the uniqueness of the Christian faith. Thus the seed of syncretism and implication of universalism is planted in the minds of theological students, many of whom become religious teachers in schools and colleges. Some find their way to the pulpit. Admittedly some will survive the test and grow stronger, but not a few will end up proclaiming a syncretistic message.

The teaching of African traditional religions in secondary schools is increasingly becoming popular. It is being suggested in some circles that religious knowledge teachers should present just the objective facts of Islam, African traditional religions, and Christianity without any show of what they believe. The young teenagers should then be left to sort out for themselves what to believe. But since there are some good elements in every religion would it not be easier for an immature student to pick up the good points of each and make up a new religion? This may fulfill the aspirations of some theologians that Africa should come up with a religion that is modern and truly African. As a matter of fact, Dr. J. K. Agbeti of Ghana feels that the survival of Christianity in Africa lies with the traditional religions rather than the prophetic Word of God. He writes, "The true theological interpretation of the traditional African religious experience could be a strong springboard from which the tottering Christianity of Africa today may be rescued and rooted more meaningfully in the African soil." Evidently this is a call for a syncretistic form of Christianity.

Some church leaders today frown at the missionaries for declaring the unique Lordship of Christ as presented in the Scriptures. Criticizing the presentation of the unique Christ who would not share room with idols, Joachim Getonga writes, "To be regarded as a true Christian in those days, a person had to abandon almost all the culture which he had acquired from his own African society. He had to detach himself from virtually all the beliefs of his parents, throw away his native clothes and put on Western dress or ornaments in order to be accepted into the Christian faith. Tribal dances in particular were considered diabolical." Getonga then appeals to "all Christian preachers to rethink the place of their cultural heritage and to reconstruct what was destroyed during those pioneering days of evangelization." One is tempted to ask Getonga what native clothes he has in mind and whether he would honestly like to go back to them. What concerns us here is the question of "the beliefs of his parents." African Christians who have found it necessary to burn up every idol have followed precedents set in the Scriptures (Acts 19). Christianity stands to judge every culture, destroying elements that are incompatible with the Word of God, employing compatible modes of expression for its advance, and bringing new life to its adherents, the qualitative life that begins at the moment of conversion and culminates eternally with the imminent return of our Lord Jesus Christ.

Even some of the most outstanding theologians in Africa have syncretistic and/or universalistic tendencies. Professor John S. Mbiti holds that all men will be saved in the final analysis. He affirms, "There is not a single soul, however debased or even unrepentant, which can successfully 'flee' from the Spirit of God (Psa. 139:1-18). God's patient waiting for the soul's repentance must in the end be surely more potent than the soul's reluctance to repent and turn to him . . . (II Pet. 3:9). The harmony of the heavenly worship would be impaired if, out of the one hundred in the sheepfold, there is one soul which continues to languish in Sheol or 'the lake of fire.'" Incidentally, Mbiti does not believe in the reality of hell or heaven. Christ's teaching on heaven and hell is all symbolic so far as the Kenyan theologian is concerned. Such elements are expected to be a part of the proposed so-called African Theology, which is just a revamping of liberal theology.

Professor E. Bolaji Idowu objects to localizing theology. He would also eschew syncretism. But one wonders where his high view of African traditional religions is leading to. He writes, "To call African traditional religion 'idolatry' is to be grossly unfair to its essence." If pagan gods are not idols, then what are they? Idowu claims with the adherents that these gods are ministers of the Almighty God. To recognize the reality of these man-made gods is to reject the scriptural view of these "dumb idols" (Isa. 2:8, 40:18-20, 41:7; I Thess. 1:9; I Cor. 8:4-6). While it is true that the pagan is conscious of the existence of a Supreme Being through general revelation, his vision of the Supreme Being is distorted because of the original sin. The image of God in man, though not obliterated, is disfigured to the point that he is considered dead in "trespasses and sins" (Eph. 2:1) until he receives new life in Christ. His worship of creatures rather than the Creator can be described adequately only as idolatry. What Africa needs is the unadulterated Gospel of Jesus Christ who declares authoritatively and finally, "I am the Way the Truth, and the Life. No man cometh unto the Father, but by me," (John 14:6).

4. Conclusion

Syncretism, will increasingly become popular in the Third World. The watered down concept of "Salvation Today" hatched at Bangkok in 1972-73 will give impetus to syncretistic and universalistic yearning in the Third World. The persistent urge for cultural revolution in Africa with external influences from communist and Arab worlds will energize the challenging force of syncretism. The days of persecution for the Bible-believing Christian may not be too far away. Christians all over the world should pray for more grace for the Third World followers and heralds of the unique Christ. Meanwhile the Bible-believing Christian should respect and pray "for kings and all who are in high positions, that we may lead a quiet and peaceable life, godly and respectful in every way" (I Tim. 2:2). Christians in Africa should realize that to stand for the uniqueness of Christ will not be popular as ungodliness increases in the world. There may come a time when Christians will have to say, "For we cannot but speak the things which we have seen and heard" (Acts 4:20). They may even have to say, "We ought to obey God rather than men" (Acts 5:29) and face the consequences that Stephen and others after him faced.

The final word for the African Christian is to make Christianity culturally relevant without destroying its ever-abiding message. The subject of cultural relevance belongs to another presentation. But we may conclude the paper with this appropriate observation from Dr. McGavran. "It (Christianity) purges all cultures — Christian, partially Christian, and non-Christian alike. Since it purges twentieth-century Christianity in a way it did not purge seventeenth-century Christianity, it also purges twentieth-century Bantu religion and Marxist religion as their adherents come to believe on Jesus Christ." Another great missiologist, Dr. George Peters, has issued this plea which must not fall into deaf evangelical ears. "Let me plead the cause of the African churches to save them from Christo-paganism which is a real threat to the future evangelical church of that continent."

THE GOSPEL, CONTEXTUALIZATION AND SYNCRETISM REPORT

Chairman: M. Bradshaw
Secretary: P. Savage

The overarching concern to the communication of the Gospel to every person in our generation must seriously take into account the clothing of the Gospel in meaningful terms for the hearer and the adequate response of the hearer, under the guidance of the Holy Spirit, that will take into account both his day-to-day ministry and his life-style. In this attempt to communicate meaningfully, there is an inherent danger of syncretism that must be faced; but fear of it should not distract the evangelist and theologian from rooting their message.

In many minds there exists an ideal model of communication, illustrated in diagram 1, where the once and for all message, clothed in the culture of the Hebrews and Jews, is communicated unchanged into a new culture, taking on the forms of such a culture, but the essential core remaining unchanged.

Diagram 1

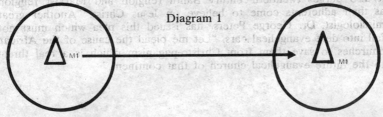

In the real world, however, the ideal model breaks down and diagram 2 better illustrates the communication process. God communicates both by act and word his message — the revealed Word — through the inspiration of the Holy Spirit within the language and culture of the Hebrew and Jew. Jesus Christ, the central focus of the revelation, took on flesh as a human being — a Jew. This message was communicated through the Greek and Roman world to the West; but in the process, the essential core takes an additional substance, which make the lines around the central core fuzzy. This message two, is then clothed in the culture of the West. Examples of this can be best illustrated from the hellenization process, whereby ideas such as substance were incorporated into the trinitarian definitions, or where the concepts of soul and body almost became the basic presentation in evangelism. These concepts were hellenistic and not biblical. The West becomes the carrier, which in turn clothes the message with its own culture and communicates the message to the "receiving people." The essential core, however, is somewhat changed by the presentation of the carrier, and so we may speak of message three. In the core there are elements of the original Hebrew, Greek and Western cultures. While this process occurs, there are basic elements of the Gospel — elements that may well have been retained throughout.

Having stated all this, it should be emphasized that what ensures the final communication of the Gospel from the early Church to the entire world is the constant illumination by the Holy Spirit, so that blind eyes can see, stony hearts are turned to flesh and can respond. This process, however, is not linear, but as illustrated in the model, is triangular, allowing the receiving people to turn directly to the Scripture under the guidance of the Holy Spirit, to search the original message for themselves and in turn rediscover elements of the Gospel lost in the transmission by the carrier. If a truly submissive attitude exists in the carrier, he is willing to drop out of the process and allow the Lord to be sovereign in that missiological context.

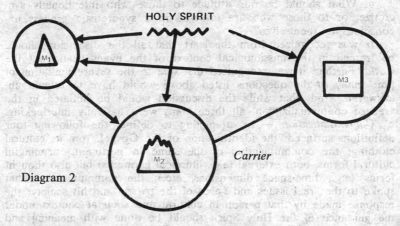

Diagram 2

Thereafter, several crucial questions surfaced:

1. The Gospel

a. What are the key biblical principles of hermeneutics that will help us identify clearly and objectively the Gospel core?

b. What criteria can I use to isolate these elements which I call the Gospel core from other biblical elements?

c. What is the Gospel? Is there an unchangeable core?

2. Contextualization

a. How do we define contextualization? How do we isolate it from indigenization?

b. Does contextualization take in more than the physical expressions of the culture, e.g., musical instruments, liturgical clothings, or does it include thought forms as well?

c. What are the criteria or biblical guidlines we should observe to contextualize the Gospel message in a healthy way to produce a growing church loyal to God and the evangelization of the world?

d. Are contextualization and syncretism the same thing on a continuum, or are they two different things?

e. Should each cultural zone have its own theology?

f. Who should undertake the task of contextualization?

3. *Syncretism*

   a. How do we define syncretism? In what ways can we differentiate it from a contexturalized message?

   b. How does syncretism arise?

   c. What guidelines can we lay down to avoid syncretism, e.g., in translation?

   d. Are there different types of syncretism? What are they?

   e. Is there a similarity between the syncretism found in the USA and that in the Third World?

   f. Is there a time when syncretism can be good (e.g., Christmas in the West)? What is wrong with syncretism?

   g. What should be our attitude to those who intentionally syncretize, or to those who are involved in a syncretistic process unconscious to themselves?

It was recognized from the start that all the discussion should be framed in the missiological context of the evangelization of the world. Further, it was recognized that due to the severe limitation of time many of the questions listed above would have to remain unanswered. And, that while the discussion would be initiated in the area of contextualization, all three areas were basically interlocking.

Contextualization — In attempting to define, the following four definitions surfaced: the identification of the Gospel from its cultural clothing; the communication of the same in pertinent, meaningful cultural forms, both external (e.g., liturgical garments) but also thought forms (e.g., time-space dimensions, etc.); the communication that spoke to the "real issues and needs of the person and his society; the response made by that person in cultural and societal context under the guidance of the Holy Spirit should be done with meaning and integrity. In no way should demands be placed on the person that would dehumanize him or destroy his identify as a person in his culture; as a consequence of his response, he should live an integral Christian life in obedience to the Lord, expressed in cultural forms that are meaningful to him and his community; this life should be expressed in the local community of saints as they together face their call to missions.

We may summarize this statement by identifying the two sides of the coin in this definition: meaningful communication in forms that are real to the person, and his full response to the Lord in repentance and obedience of faith that affects his whole life-style, his attitudes, and his values, etc.

In the discussion to bring out guidelines or criteria in the contextualizing process, two models were studied: one from Bali presented by Dr. Munstra, and a linguistic model by Dr. Loewen. As a result, the following tentative suggestions were made:

1. In the biblical message there is both form and meaning, as we see in I Peter 1:13. In attempting to give a new form, the communicator must ensure that the true meaning is being conveyed. It may contradict the essence of the meaning and so confuse the hearer and destroy the communication. In giving a new form to "Gird up the loins," the meaning found must be fully understood and effectively

communicated in a form meaningful to the receiver.

2. In some cases the form may not have a deep value and can be easily exchanged without the loss of the original meaning; but in some other cases, the form may have a historical value, (e.g., the lamb). The message is essentially tied up with the form and so the form will have to be carried over to the receiver culture. An example of this is the Cross. Here a crass translation has to be undertaken.

3. In a particular message, the types of words must be identified, e.g., "the dead bury the dead." The first dead is not the same as the second. The former has a "teaching" value which contains within it a theological idea, while the latter speaks of the "happening" dead. It is not always easy to separate those words, symbols, analogies, that contain within them the theological idea from a mere description of visible reality.

4. The form that is adopted in the new context must in no way contradict the biblical message.

5. In attempting to contextualize, the focus must not only be on the words, but also in the total message. An attempt to identify the pieces of meaning in the message and their relationship must be made before contextualizing a particular section. The overarching message of pieces of meaning will and must hold in place a particular part of that message.

We may summarize these brief guidelines by underscoring the necessity of knowing the receptor's world view and thought forms. What are they? What are his space-time dimensions? His social structures? His authority patterns? His socio-economic dimensions of class and economy? What are his dimensions of relationships? In this dimension of contextualization there must be a constant concern to bring our "communication theologizing" under the judgment of the Scriptures, so that an effective proclamation of the Gospel under the illumination of the Holy Spirit may ensue. There must be a zeal and a zest in the proclamation, which is accompanied by a fear and trembling in the Holy Spirit.

Syncretism

While there was no final agreement on a definition of syncretism, various elements were brought to light. Syncretism might be said to occur when critical and *basic elements* of the Gospel are lost in the process of contextualization and are replaced by religious elements from the receiving culture; there is a synthesis with this partial Gospel. In some cases syncretism reaches such proportions that a totally new "gospel" appears.

It was noted that there were several stages and factors that could cause syncretism; these are:

a. A conscious and deliberate mixing of the message, in a desire to identify with the people.

b. There is a semi-conscious attempt when the message is partial. The speaker has not fully grasped the Gospel message.

c. Generally the syncretist processes round the world tend to be unconscious to the communicator as in the following cases:

(i) When the speaker gives an unanchored message — a topical message without anchoring it in the Scriptures.

(ii) When the receptor hears the message on the basis of his own presuppositions.

(iii) When the receptor must fall back on an indigenous model for expressing his new life in Christ Jesus.

(iv) When a gradual cultural change leads to a major change of values which is subtle and unconscious to the person living in that culture, as has occurred with much of Western Christianity facing secularism.

It was natural in the discussion to constantly resurface the basic question, "What is the Gospel and how can we find it?" While no final conclusion was reached, Dr. John H. Yoder helpfully presented the following seven hermeneutical guidelines which take the student of the Scriptures down the layers to find the Gospel core. These are as follows:

a. The linguistic layer. A study of words in Scriptures when the two languages are in the same world. A transliteration of the Word can occur through the use of simple lexicographic aids.

b. The quasi-linguistic layer, where a transliteration cannot occur. An interpretation of an idea in a particular historical point of time must be made. An understanding of the particular historical background is critical.

c. Linguistic level, when the two languages are in different worlds, so that all referrents differ.

d. Linguistic level, when the two languages have different basic logics, such as in the cases of the Hebrew and the English. Some of the basic ingredients of the Hebrew thought patterns are not found in the English.

e. Cultural level (e.g., what does the head covering of I Cor. 2 mean?).

f. Ideological. This is the filter that each student of the Scriptures has into his self-consciousness — his world view that imposes itself on his grasp of the biblical message. This is best exemplified by showing how Bultmann has intentionally placed his world view as a filter for the understanding of the biblical message.

g. Existential level — what is the meaningfulness of the Word for a specific subject?

In conclusion, the methodology that must guide both the communication of the Gospel and the theologizing is the missiological concern that the "whole world hear his voice."

HOW TO EVALUATE CULTURAL PRACTICES BY BIBLICAL STANDARDS IN MAINTAINING CULTURAL IDENTIY IN AFRICA

John T. Mpaayei

*Rev. Mpaayei, Nairobi, Kenya, is
Secretary for Translation in the Bible
Society of Kenya.*

"To you who were spiritually dead all the time you drifted along on the stream of this world's ideas of living, and obeyed its unseen ruler (who is still operating in those who do not respond to the truth of God) to you Christ has given life! We all lived like that in the past, and followed the impulses of our evil nature being in fact under the wrath of God by nature, like everyone else" (Eph. 2:1-3, J.B. Phillips).

These words of Paul to the Ephesians should help us in thinking about cultural practices, past or present. Paul, a Jew, liberated by the Lord Jesus Christ, is unafraid in applying the grace of God and his salvation to himself as well as the Ephesians, both Jews and Gentiles. For him the criterion of judging any idea of living is whether it is from God's grace, from God's love in Christ or from the ruler of this world and those still under his control. In union with Christ, Paul is freed from applying the criterion of Judaism to applying only that one, valid for all time, the grace of God in Jesus Christ. We can do no better than follow his example, since we too now belong to the same Lord Jesus Christ as he did and we live in union with him.

During the period of colonialism, much of African culture in all its forms was subjected to extreme pressures of subjection and despised because of the more vigorous and technically advanced forms of the colonizing Western culture, backed by the political power dominant at that time in any particular area. Even in the church there was generally an attitude of looking down on African culture.

With the coming of independence, there has been a strong reaction to all this, and the political liberation forces have played a great part in reasserting African culture in its various forms. For example, African traditional dances and other forms of artistic expression have now been given their rightful place in public entertainment. African handicrafts are now displayed all over the world.

But in church life several generations have grown up largely cut off from traditional forms of worship and the only ways they know are adopted Western models. Educated young people, for example, who are gifted in music will compose tunes for the guitar rather than for drums and flutes or other traditional instruments with which they have lost touch. And yet, what they produce is original and peculiarly their own. Must they go back to drums and other rattles to be African?

Their non-Christian contemporaries produce jazz and other musical forms for secular entertainment and no one grumbles that such music is un-African. It is fully accepted as a new African creation acceptable and welcome to the rest of the world.

The church needs to accept the challenge of African Christian youth today, to be given every opportunity to create new forms of worship peculiarly suited to their needs, and thus give them a chance to blaze the trail for the next generation. The important thing is that such composition is for the glory of the Lord Jesus Christ and none other.

In Africa, as in other parts of the world, there are as many cultures as there are tribes. While certain broad outlines may be similar in many ways, nevertheless there are also fundamental differences, e.g., between sedentary agricultural peoples and nomadic pastoral ones living on livestock. Their focus of worship and attitude to sacrifices also differs from tribe to tribe. But neighboring tribes may share religious leaders at times, provided peaceful conditions exist between the parties. A medicine man may be consulted by people from a very wide area according to his fame and attributed dependability. Traditionally, chiefs too may extend their influence beyond their own language group by mutual consent. This is why opinion makers are so important in spreading ideas as often they are the ones who will determine their rejection or adoption. Key men are often the opinion makers. But occasionally women have assumed that role for considerable periods of time.

In God's own sovereignty, he gives his gifts to men and women for the building of the body of Christ. The greatest of all these gifts is that of knowing the Lord Jesus Christ personally as Savior and Master. When the message of Jesus Christ lives in the language of any people, such dynamic power is released that great things happen as a result of faith in the living Christ, whatever the cultural background. For example, a woman, long troubled by demon possession, hears the Gospel for the first time in a village open air meeting. She cries out, "Is this message for men only or is it also for women?"

"Mother, it is for all of us — mothers, children, and all," answers the evangelist. She follows and hears more of the power of Jesus Christ and is completely and permanently healed. Then the husband, delighted with his wife's cure, tries to take and keep her in the old way of life away from where she can hear and learn more of Jesus Christ. But she is adamant though carefully obedient otherwise. In the end he arranges a contest between his god (a witch doctor) and her new found Lord.

The witch doctor comes and performs all his magic to bind her to the village. But she has prayed to her new Master for deliverance and complete victory so that she can go for more teaching and baptism. She wins and a new congregation of believers soon grows in that village because of the faith of one who was formerly a demoniac.

Second example. Here is a chief. He is troubled by the tribal hatreds and constant fighting and family feuds. He has tried for more than twenty years to end these, all to no avail. Then he is told of one who is God's only Son who came personally into this world to give his own life so that his blood may wash away the sin of mankind. He learns that all the sacrifices he had personally witnessed in his own lifetime never actually took away any sin. Only the blood of Jesus Christ, God's own sacrificial lamb is acceptable for cleansing away sin. Furthermore, he learns that this same Jesus actually rose from the dead and is alive and can give new power and life today to any who believe in him. He has the power to change difficult lives. The chief believes. He himself is changed. He tells his family and they too are changed. New joy and peace spreads to the neighbors. Fighting subsides, quarrels disappear, new congregations of believers are born and multiply. Jesus lives afresh in new hearts, in a new language and culture. New life has been created by the grace of God in Christ Jesus.

Then the elders, traditional helpers and guardians of chieftainship resent departures from tradition especially by the chief. They mobilize to stop it all. They apply traditional methods, they organize a cursing raid on the chief's home in his absence. This is reported to him on arrival. Will he retaliate? No. Like his newly-found Master, he forgives completely with the words, "No, let them alone. They do not yet understand what I am doing. One day they will."

But they organize themselves again to get him officially demoted by the government. But a fellow Christian is sent to settle the dispute and instead of demotion, he is confirmed in his new zeal and given material help to complete an unfinished church building.

A drought comes. Water is short. The new believers are building a new church. They want to stop till after the drought. The chief says, "No. Honor God first. Complete his house. Let him think what he is to do about water."

As they begin roofing the new church, a friend arrives unexpected, uninvited, unknown — a water engineer from another country but a servant of the same Master, Jesus Christ. He builds a dam and pipes water to the wall of the new church. The faith of the new congregation is confirmed. They know now that Jesus Christ is real, he is near.

But the evil one is at work. Three brothers believe. Two brothers love the Lord dearly. One has more understanding than the others. The Lord calls him first. He becomes an evangelist and gives up herding cattle to preach the Gospel. The middle brother believes but is weak. His wife has lost too many babies. He thinks he must try at least one more medicine man for his young wife's sake. She agrees. Before they get to the medicine man, the evangelist hears and stops them. He persuades them to try the prayers of God's people first. They agree and come and spend a couple of days of prayer with other believers. Other Christians help at the clinic and the longed-for baby arrives safely, their first son. Brother Wilson's faith is confirmed; he also becomes an evangelist.

But the older brother is still tradition-bound. His father loves him dearly. He has found him a third girl from a wealthy family, and he is determined that the oldest son must marry a third wife before he accepts these strange new rules of the Christians and be dipped in the water. The man himself is a dutiful, obedient son but *weak*. He is unable to stand on his own like his younger brothers. This particular denomination would have baptized him with his original two wives whom he married before he believed. But he was told quite definitely that after professing faith in Jesus Christ he could not live in the old ways anymore. So he slips back; he never really understood the new Master and his ways. He had just followed his two younger brothers.

His brothers have not given him up. They still teach him and love him for Christ's sake and they hope that one day he will be courageous enough to stand for Jesus Christ on his own. The peculiar thing in this situation is that the emphasis among the believers is not how many wives a man has, but whether he loves the Lord Jesus Christ with all his heart and wishes to obey him above all others. Polygamy is normal in the community and family ties are strong. Clan and extended family relationships are also strong. Even if a man disowns a wife and children, they would still belong to the extended family and clan; hence the problem of believers in dealing with polygamy. In any case, the first believer among them, the chief, still retains his original two wives. Is this un christian?

What is the essence of conversion? Is it not a complete change of direction in one's life and instead of being directed by one's own human motives, to let the Lord Jesus Christ reign supreme? Is it not having a new permanent point of reference, someone loved and trusted, who is consulted whenever any decision has to be made? It is a most revealing thing with new converts that the Lord gives them often a peculiarly sharp perception in spiritual matters which more mature believers seem to have lost. It is the Spirit of Christ who marks people out as belonging to Christ by showing clearly the fruit of the Spirit in their lives. In doing this, any forms of legalism seem peculiarly out of place.

In telling people about the Cross of Jesus Christ and the love of God so revealed to mankind, a rare opportunity is provided for leading men to faith in him. The idea of shedding blood for cleansing away sin is commonly understood. But in the tribal situation the physical elements are uppermost in the mind. There is a necessity to dwell on what are the unique elements in the death of Christ at Calvary. First, that he is the Son of God and always has been. That he came voluntarily to offer himself for our sake according to God's own plan. That he loved us when we did not deserve such love, just as he prayed from the Cross for forgiveness for those who put him there. That his death cannot be repeated and needs no addition of any kind to complete our salvation other than that we accept what he has done for our sake.

In the traditional setting, tribal presuppositions are peculiarly resistant to change. People often talk of sin as synonymous with a curse. They often worry about the consequences of sin in the same way as the result of a curse pronounced on a person by his father. There is great need to teach about the attitude of one's heart to God and his holiness, his righteousness, and his commands as well as his judgment.

The key to much Christian teaching is the Bible which, when available and readable, immediately forms a firm point of reference on all matters of faith and conduct. All customs and social rules are then tested with what the Scriptures say. The Bible also delivers believers from the limitations of tribal ethics which always tend to encourage double or multifaceted standards. For instance, in the tribal situation one is expected to be loyal, truthful, honest, and reliable to one's relative, clansman, and so on. But cheating an outsider is supposed to be clever. Stealing from a relative or a fellow tribesman is definitely frowned upon but robbing a neighboring tribe is adventurous and brave.

From the Bible we learn that the deepest and most precious truth of God is revealed graciously to man and that he could never have attained to such on his own. We also realize that by God's sovereign will some are saved while others may be forever lost. Some are granted gifts of healing, speech, or prophecy by the same sovereign will, just as it pleases him.

In the tribal situations, the worst thing that can be done to a neighbor or a clan is to be declared an "outsider." That means that they cannot enjoy the normal protection from the group. Stolen animals will not be restored, murders will not be paid for, and so on. The Bible teaches us that in Christ God does the opposite and in his grace he makes us through faith in Christ his own children, members of his own household and even heirs of God with Christ.

Reconciliation is a major part of the Christian message. The word used in several tribal languages means, "to make people hear one another" or "to make people obey one another."

In union with Christ, God has enabled us to become his own obedient children instead of rebel subjects. He has also given us his own Spirit who prays for us in groanings which cannot be uttered. He gives us the assurance of answered prayer.

Through the Bible we learn that the truth of God which has become precious to all believers is universal and applies to all mankind through faith in Jesus Christ. Thus we are freed from the tyranny of the tribal mold which would bind and cramp our spirits for time and for eternity. Jesus said, "If the Son makes you free, you will be free indeed" (John 8.36).

When the Bible is well translated we hear the voice of the Lord Jesus Christ in an authentic way as he speaks directly to our own inner being. Matters of outward form, of dress, and at times rituals in worship, become less significant as we commune with him in spirit and learn to love him more. A new relationship is established with the living God. We learn to recognize other Christians, the body of Christ, not by tribal labels which are often derogatory, but by the fruits of the Spirit — love, joy, peace, kindness, etc., as in Galatians 5:22. We do not then cease to belong to our tribes, but we belong to the new universal tribe of Jesus Christ through faith in him. The love of Christ which found us when we were dead in trespasses and sins frees us to tell others that he can do the same for them, too.

It is rare that any language group in Africa fits into a single Christian denomination. Normally, there are several denominations working in any language group. The Bible is the surest unchanging common factor which is universally acceptable for all denominations. In many ways this is providential because there has been a tendency to put doctrinal matters which may be denominational on an equal footing with the Bible. Before political independence, this was largely accepted without question. Many of these old attitudes are bound to be questioned within the next few decades. But the essentials of Scripture will stand. For this reason evangelism should more and more be biblical so that the messages cut across denominational boundaries. Often there has been duplication of effort in evangelism because some denominational requirements must be observed. Training facilities cannot be shared because of doctrinal differences. Is this scriptural among evangelicals?

It must not be imagined that with political independence in Africa there have been secular pressures on the Church of Jesus Christ to conform or to compromise her position. These pressures have come, but on the whole, the church has remained loyal and often the result of such pressures has been remarkable spiritual growth in faithfulness. For instance, faced with the threat of losing one's life for the sake of Jesus Christ, many Christians were able to discover that the gift of enduring pain and suffering for the Master may not be the ultimate reason for the trial. Many were granted the perception that the greater gift was learning to forgive the unrepentant sinner. A word of testimony to the gaoler or persecutor, and an assurance of forgiveness for Jesus' sake, had a much more permanent effect on such individuals than the actual endurance of physical pain and torture.

Christians have discovered under trial that many outward forms of church life are not essential for deep spiritual fellowship in Christ. The secular world also learned that the church of Jesus Christ in Africa is not dependent for survival on any outside group or people, nor on material help however welcome such may be. The power lay in faith in the ever-present help of the Lord of the church and his indwelling Spirit in the believer. This Spirit, of course, they could not see or understand, in accordance with the Scriptures.

And yet, at such times of trial, other members of the body of Christ who looked apparently helpless and could do nothing physically for their suffering brethren were extremely active in praying to God on behalf of his Church Militant here on earth. In other words, it has been during the times of trial that the church has been most active both in deep mutual fellowship and in witnessing to the hostile world around us. We need to remember things so that we may not look for help or encouragement either for the growth or continuing strength of the church of Christ from the wrong direction. The church of Jesus Christ is alive and growing in Africa, perhaps more rapidly than the world realizes. Is this an indication that the Lord's return is near?

HOW TO EVALUATE CULTURAL PRACTICES BY BIBLICAL STANDARDS IN MAINTAINING CULTURAL IDENTITY IN AFRICA REPORT

Chairman: N. Olukimaym
Secretary: J. Dean

Following the reading of the paper by Mr. John Mpaayei the following points were made in general discussion.

1) Things that distinguish the different cultures should not be allowed to divide us.

2) All cultures are corrupted by the fall of man. Wc are all prone to ethnocentricity. We are interested in neither Western culture nor African culture in any of their varied forms but in a life-style based on Scripture.

3) We agreed with the point made by Dr. McGavran that the best thing that can happen to any culture is for it to meet with the Gospel.

4) There is a danger to think in terms of culture being something static and of the past. We must think of it as being dynamic and contemporary.

5) The possibility of certain things being attributable to neither God nor the devil but to a third source, the flesh.

6) The need to distinguish between the essential and the inessential.

Those gathered divided into five groups, three Anglophone and two Francophone. The major questions being asked were then identified.

1) The traditional missionary insistence on monogamy and the prevailing local traditions of polygamy.

2) Whether confession of sin should be public or private.

3) Are certain rhythms intrinsically demonic?

4) Should Bible reading and prayer be individual (Western culture) or communal (African culture)?

5) The question of living standards with reference to sanitation.

6) Involvement in traditional festivals and the eating of food associated with such.

7) The extent of family responsibilities for a Christian in a culture with the extended family system.

8) The problems connected with engagement and marriage, especially those of the ceremony itself.

9) Initiation ceremonies.

10) Dress, including the covering of the head in church.

11) Segregation of men and women in the church and in the home.

12) Naming ceremonies and names.

13) Conditions for baptism.

14) Funerals and funeral rights.

15) Dress for the clergy.

16) Is the African concept of God at loggerheads with the biblical concept?

17) Is a seven-day week to be insisted upon?

18) The problem arising from a leader being a servant in Scripture but a chief in African society.

19) The question of legitimate and illegitimate traditional medicines.

20) Should we either accept or reject offerings from those who are unbaptized or not eligible for baptism.

Some of these questions were considered by the groups. A summary of their findings follows:

Polygamy and monogamy

1) Churches should not condemn polygamous marriages.

2) A person who is polygamous at conversion should be accepted to full Christian (church) membership except for holding office as a bishop or deacon. (Titus 1:6)

3) A polygamous male convert should continue to fulfill all his responsibilities to all his wives.

4) These principles should be administered in such a way as not to encourage polygamy.

5) A polygamous wife on conversion remains faithful to her husband.

6) A convert who voluntarily contracts a polygamous marriage after conversion is disciplined for adultery and normally only re-admitted on full repentance including the discontinuation of the marriage.

It seems that there is an increasing tendency to allow baptism of those involved in longstanding polygamous marriages. Point four above is difficult to implement.

Music–Worship

Africans sing in a minor key. After conversion they sing in a major key. This is only after patient and sustained teaching!

1) Instruments and musical gifts are neither secular nor sacred of themselves, e.g., the organ was originally associated with the massacre of Christians.

2) African culture is richer in gifts of the arts than Western culture.

3) All cultures are vulnerable to the following in their worship:

a. Formalism — concentration on the form and neglect of the content of worship;

b. Love of beauty — leading to cultural arrogance and exclusivism;

c. Hedonism — the substitution of pleasure for sacrifice;

d. Sacerdotalism (spectatorism) — e.g. solos and choirs rather than congregational singing which becomes the pervading life style as laity leave everything else to the clergy;

e. Limiting worship to the mind rather than involving the whole personality.

Only a national can devise his own worship but he must do so in the light of Scripture.

Other points

1) Aspects of African culture should be retained unless and until they are recognized to be specifically non-biblical.

2) To insist on renouncing of local culture erects another barrier to

the Gospel (I Cor. 9:19-23) unless it is specifically non-biblical.

3) There is a need for sustained and systematic teaching on the nature of God. Vagueness on this subject leads to idolatry and tribal deities.

The way ahead

1) The need for African, biblical theologians to meet and give serious consideration to most of the subjects listed items one through twenty, especially the matter of polygamy.

2) The need for regular, sustained and systematic teaching on the nature of God and the law.

3) The need for missionaries to be less ethnocentric and for missionaries and national Christians to investigate the teaching of the Scripture on this whole area.

BIBLICAL FOUNDATIONS AND CULTURAL IDENTITY IN ASIA

Petrus Octavianus

*Dr. Octavianus, Batu, East Java, Indonesia,
is President of the Indonesian Missionary Fellowship
and the Indonesian Evangelical Fellowship.*

My theme is too extensive to be covered thoroughly in this paper. However, I am trying to put forward what I have learned through experience and investigation and observation concerning the Gospel of Jesus Christ in Asia today, even though it be just a dip or two of water from the flowing stream of Asia's cultures.

Geographically, Asia stretches from Turkey in the West to Japan in the East, thereby covering one-third of the world's surface. It is more realistic to speak of sub-regions such as East Asia, South East Asia, Central Asia, North and North East Asia, and West Asia, as has been done increasingly in recent years.

Asia is not culturally uniform, but cultures are as divergent as the geographical areas: from the nomad life of Arabia's desert, to India's caste system, and to China's age-old clan structure with its ancestor worship, on to the manifold variations of Indonesia's adat areas on her 3,000 islands.

It is obvious that we cannot speak of one Asian culture, but must recognize many different cultures in Asia. Another important fact is the influence of religion upon culture, so that often culture and religion are inseparably linked together and can hardly be isolated.

It is the purpose of this paper:
1. to show the place of culture in the Scriptures and to recognize God's desire for communication with man in his culture;
2. to identify the biblical foundations and absolutes which are supracultural, and must be maintained in any given cultural situation;
3. to recognize the cultural-religious setting in Asia with the major religions; and to separate original-cultural factors (which are neutral and can be maintained) from such elements that are opposed to Christian revelation in the Bible, and must therefore be rejected by the Christian;
4. to consider the adaptation of the Christian faith to Asian culture, by studying various patterns of worship in Asia;
5. to make some suggestions for the proclamation of biblical faith in Asia's cultures today.

1. *The place of culture in Scripture and God's desire for communication with man in his culture*
God has given to us two mandates regarding our relationship to the world: the cultural mandate (Gen. 1:26, 28) and the evangelistic mandate (Matt. 28:18-20).

Through the cultural mandate, issued from God the Creator, Sustainer, and Lord of the Universe, man who was made in God's image, was commissioned to multiply, fill the earth and subdue it, exercising dominion over all creatures.

That he was charged with the task of developing all areas of science and human culture, can be seen from Genesis chapter 4. Here, God gave an example how culture and the civilization of man should develop according to specialized fields. Jabal's task was to dwell in tents and care for cattle (Gen. 4:20). This task being further developed, covers all efforts in the area of food and clothing. Jubal's task was to play music (Gen. 4:21). This would apply later to all efforts in the fields of art, drama, and education. Tubal-Cain's task was to forge brass and iron (Gen. 4:22), which later developed into the branches of technics, mechanization, and science.

Though the cultural mandate is given to all mankind, I am in complete agreement with Dr. Glasser's statement concerning its relevancy for the Christian Church, "Despite the Fall, the cultural mandate was never abrogated . . . . Man, even fallen man, continues under the divine obligation and compulsion to unlock and harness the natural forces of his environment and to involve himself in all aspects of human existence . . . . from feeding the hungry and giving water to the thirsty, to laboring for justice in society . . . . A valid missionary strategy for the church dare not overlook or downgrade the cultural mandate."

The purpose of the cultural mandate is to glorify the Creator (Exod. 20:2-6). But man responded with rebellion and disobedience to God's love. Sin has entered his life. Thus, man changed the purpose, and instead of glorifying God, he became proud and took the glory for himself, or for the worship of idols, or for the worship of his own works (Isa. 42:8).

Since God has never withdrawn the cultural mandate, even the non-Christian can still subdue creation, urged by an inner compulsion . . . since he was made in the image of God. However, he has lost fellowship with God, and he has not glorified God: his works and his culture cannot save him. He needs a Savior. There is no other way for reconciling him with God (John 14:6).

The second, the evangelistic mandate, complements the cultural mandate: because the Savior has come, who brings deliverance from sin, the Good News of the Gospel can be preached, and, by faith, man can be reconciled with God and recapture the original purpose for his life, to glorify.

While the Church of Christ is entrusted with the fulfillment of the cultural mandate given by the Creator God, it is supremely committed to observe the evangelistic mandate given by Christ. "All authority has been given to me in heaven and on earth. Go therefore and make disciples of all the nations, baptizing them in the name of the Father and the Son and the Holy Spirit, teaching them to observe all that I commanded you; and lo, I am with you always, even to the end of the age." (Matt. 28:18-20).

How does the Christian now function in his culture and society? Before he answered God's call in Christ, he was lost in his ambitions and desires, in his tradition, community, and in his culture. After experiencing the work of salvation in his own life and being filled with the Holy Spirit, he will consciously and willingly involve himself in the fulfillment of both mandates.

His eyes having been opened to God's special revelation and plan for mankind, yes, for his own culture, his role will be unique. He does not leave his culture behind, but he re-evaluates it in the light of God's Word and its supra-cultural values. From then on, the evangelistic mandate will become of highest urgency and pirority, so that other values of necessity will be subjected to it.

How does God communicate with man through his culture? While in the Old Testament God revealed himself to mankind through the Hebrew nation, language, and culture, the New Testament shows his revelation to the world in the framework of Graeco-Roman language and culture, the latter forming the *soma* for the *kerygma.*

We may therefore conclude that God looks upon cultures as potential channels for his interaction with man. Dr. McGavran expressed it in this way in his paper on "The Dimensions of World Evangelization," "According to the Bible, the Lord has no favorites among cultures. He accepts them all." In Rev. 21:26, we read, "The wealth and splendor of the nations shall be brought into the Holy City." Hour after hour, day after day, the kings of the earth shall bring in all their splendor and beautiful stream of their cultures — on one condition only, verse 27, "But nothing unclean shall enter." Cultures must be cleansed from sin, they must be redeemed and made whole by the Blood of the Lamb. Thus, they may troop into the New Jerusalem, and the Lord will accept them as part of the brilliance and glory of the Heavenly City (Isa. 66:18).

2. *Supra-cultural biblical foundations*

The biblical foundations or universals are those truths that can apply to any culture in any place at any time in history. They are absolute, which God expects and desires all men to know, to believe and to do. For a deeper study I recommend Charles Kraft's discussion in which he explains how Christian Ethnotheology would attempt to carefully distinguish between what in Christian doctrine is supra-cultural revelation from God, and what is the cultural clothing of this revelation in terms meaningful either to those who originally received the revelation, or to those in another culture.

Since the theology of biblical foundations is well known among evangelicals, I need not go into extensive details here, but want to confine myself to a simple listing of those truths that are of immediate importance when confronted with the challenge to share the supra-cultural truths with men in Asia today.

a. *The Bible* is God's revelation to all cultures and the document of supreme and unsurpassed value for the measurement, testing, and correction of all human cultures. It has already been translated in over 1000 tongues and languages and claims to be the inspired Word of God, agent of renewal of the human heart and of human societies, thus changing and refining such cultures that open themselves up to its dynamic influence. All the following truths are revealed in its pages, since the Bible deals with God's revelation concerning man's condition and origin, his purpose for life on earth, the coming of the Savior and his work of salvation on our behalf, as well as the future events still waited for by the Christians and by the world in general.

b. *The Gospel of Jesus Christ* which introduces God's act to save man from sin by sending his only son into the world to die for us, thus making him the center of Old and New Testament revelation. First preached by Jesus himself, the Gospel was summarized by Paul in I Cor. 15:3-4, that he died for our sins, was buried, rose again and, in later writings, would return to earth. The absoluteness of the Gospel is confirmed by Acts 4:12, where Jesus Christ is called the only Savior of men.

c. *Man's condition* as fallen in sin, is described since the days of Adam and Eve in the garden of Eden. Sin's wages became death, and, since then, death has come upon all men. Man cannot redeem himself, his condition is without hope, awaiting eternal judgment.

d. *Salvation* is gained through personal faith in Christ as Savior, Lord and King. An active, personal response is necessary to make salvation valid for any individual or group of individuals, in whatever fashion they choose to decide.

e. *Personal repentance* is necessary in order to be saved, and it denotes an action taken, a turning away from, for example, idol worship, sin, traditions that are connected with dark powers, impurity of living, to a new life in Christ.

f. *Conversion, or the New Birth* is a supra-cultural experience describing man's process of renewal, starting with repentance and faith in Christ, into a new life begun by and lived in the power of the Holy Spirit. The person's confession, his changed life, and his witness to Jesus Christ manifest the change that has taken place.

g. *Baptism* as a sign of the new-found faith in Christ and complete identification with him, is the outward seal on the new relationship, and usually also brings with it the incorporation into a new community.

h. *The church, or fellowship of Christian believers* consists of those who equally have been redeemed by the Blood of Christ, and strive to build up each other in him, strengthened through the Word, prayer, fellowship and the sacrament of the Holy Communion (or the Lord's Supper). United by the Holy Spirit, the church universal knows no boundaries of race, color of skin, nation, cultures, and customs, but continually celebrates the oneness of all in the Body of Christ and with the Head, the Lord Jesus.

i. *The Ten Commandments* ever since given by God to Moses upon the Mount, are basic for individuals and societies, to order men's lives in relationship to God and to each other.

3. *The cultural-religious situation in Asia*

As mentioned earlier, culture and religion are closely linked and often can hardly be separated. All the major religions of the world originated in Asia, such as Hinduism, Buddhism, Confucianism, Shintoism, Islam, and Christianity. They all meet together in today's situation in Asia; they compete with and influence each other. Underneath and inter-mixed are such customs and thought-patterns and practices that have their roots in Animism which has preceded the major religions.

In order adequately to analyze, understand and evaluate Asian cultures, we must know both the religion and its background, as well as the structure of the society we are dealing with. The messenger of the Gospel, who wants to bring Christ to some society or group, must determine such features in that culture that are neutral and can be maintained, these that are definitely opposed and contrary to biblical revelation and must therefore be either eliminated or a functional substitute found and those features that are endorsed by the Scriptures and should be encouraged and strengthened.

Such analysis and evaluation should best be done by one closely acquainted with that culture, even born in it and reared — but, who is renewed through conversion to Jesus Christ and filled with the Holy Spirit who alone can give the needed discernment and understanding.

J.H. Bavinck said, "Christians are to take legitimate possession of customs and cultures, give them new meaning and new contents, and enlist them in the service of Christ . . . . It is never easy to decide whether a custom may be retained or should be rejected . . ."

It is desirable that not only individual Christians, but young churches in Asia themselves consider and judge such matters with concern and urgency, seeing that the foreign missionary cannot do it for them! It will contribute to their growth and maturity to thus interact with their own culture(s), and, though the job be difficult and the process slow, to come up with results that allow them to remain part of their culture, but faithful and true to the Word of God.

The main criteria for the evaluation whether any cultural features are neutral and can be maintained, opposed to Christian truth and must be rejected, or endorsed through Christian revelation, are given in the Bible, the inspired Word of God.

Close acquaintance with its precepts and doctrines in the Spirit of Christ is necessary for anyone attempting an analysis of any given cultural setting. Such passages as refer to the Christian's worship will throw light on the mode and contents of religious practices. Scriptures referring to the Christian's walk in the world and towards his family and fellow men will show them how to live as Christians within their society structure which in itself may be neutral, respecting the authority pattern and using it for the advance of the Gospel. Scriptures clearly teach the ethical standard to be aimed for, and practices that must be abstained from. Thus, the new Christians may stay in their cultural environment, not rejecting their own people, but showing forth the light of Christ within the context of their lives. Human events of life such as birth of a child, marriage, death, give ample opportunity to examine the customs and concepts related to it. I would like to illustrate this by describing and comparing the Asian view of marriage and the biblical view of marriage.

The Asian concept of marriage is that of a garden. Man is viewed as the sower of seed whereas woman is the garden (cultivated ground) which nurtures and gives food to the seed. This theory views man as the owner of woman, because woman is viewed as a possessed thing only (unbiblical).

The biblical concept of marriage is explained on the basis of God's statement concerning marriage, as is found in Genesis 2:24, "For this cause a man shall *leave* his father and his mother, and shall cleave to his wife; and they shall become *one flesh*."

This "triangle" cleave concept is supra-cultural in nature and has three aspects in it:

a. The *legal* aspect: the word "leave," shows that a legal act has to be taken for the marriage to become legal. The marriage is legal according to law, adolescence, and responsibility.

b. The *personal* aspect: the word "cleave," describes love which has come to a decision to remain faithful, faithful to *one* person, and to share one's life with one person only: the monogamy principle.

c. The *physical* aspect: "one flesh" describes the physical unity between husband and wife.

Thus, the Garden concept is unbiblical and must be rejected.

We can divide the countries of Asia into three groups:

(i) The countries in which the process of the growth of one of the religions into a state religion was completed before Christianity came, such as Arabia, China, Burma, Vietnam, Thailand, and Japan. This was the greatest obstacle for the penetration of the Gospel.

(ii) The countries in which the process of the growth of one of the religions into a state religion was still taking place and incomplete when Christianity came, such as Pakistan and Malaysia. The process by which Pakistan, or Malaysia for that matter, became Islamic was almost complete when Christianity came.

(iii) The countries in which the growth of other religions and Christianity took place at the same time, such as Indonesia and the Philippines. The two former reflect a stronger cultural identity and are harder to deal with the Gospel messenger, while the third has shown more openness to the change offered by Christianity.

The question arises: how much of cultural identity should be retained when people become Christians? I like to illustrate this point with reference to my own country, Indonesia. One interesting example is the birth of the Christian Church in East Java in 1842. The roots of this church are in two fellowships which differed greatly from each other and show us two different methods of evangelism, and two ways of dealing with the culture of the people.

Emde, a watchmaker of German descent married to a Javanese, lived and witnessed in the town of Surabaya. He requested his converts to cut their hair, to replace their sarong by western-style trousers, and to wear shoes instead of sandals. The gamelan (Javanese musical instrument), wayang performance (Javanese shadow play), and tembang (Javanese reciting style) were forbidden. Emde in every way replaced Javanese customs through European customs and thereby "westernized" his converts. Thereby he estranged the latter from their own society. His mistake was, that he identified the contents of the Gospel strongly with his own cultural framework, transmitting both to the Javanese, instead of bringing to them the universal truths only! He unknowingly hindered the Gospel from finding its own form in Javanese society.

Coolen, the founder of the second Christian fellowship, started in a village southwest of Surabaya, was the son of a Dutch father and a Javanese mother. Born and raised in Javanese customs and concepts, he carried the religion and independence of his father, while following the Javanese mysticism through his mother. He "Javanized" the Gospel in every way: his converts would sing hymns in the form of tembang, perform Bible stories by the way of the wayang, and the gamelan was freely used in the worship services. Thus he gained much attention and many followers. His meetings resembled Javanese religious gatherings. Membership was attained when people could quote the Lord's Prayer, the Apostles' Creed. Baptism and Holy Communion were not practiced, because Coolen feared they might lose their cultural identity and become "Dutch." Coolen's strength was in his attempt to adapt to the Javanese way of life, so Javanese could become Christians without losing their Javanese identity. His weakness lay in the fact that he overlooked the importance of certain supra-cultural truths of the Bible, like Baptism and Holy Communion, and thereby compromised the contents of the Gospel, for the sake of cultural identity.

However, the witness of both groups was heard, inspiring others to follow Christ and to find their form of Christianity, which finally formed the Christian Church of East Java. Today, this church has the biggest number of converts from a Muslim background in the whole world.

I propose now to give a short list of features from the culture I am best acquainted with, the Indonesian Muslim culture, as to which factors can be maintained, which must be rejected, and which are endorsed by Scriptures.

a. *Neutral features that can be maintained:*

(i) The use of the cap, Kopiah; White cap: used in Palembang (South Sumatra) by those who have not yet gone to Mecca for pilgrimage. Black cap: used in other parts of Indonesia, mainly as a national hat.

(ii) The use of sarong and kebaya, the women's native dress, and not only worn by Muslims.

(iii) Sitting on the floor mat without chairs.

(iv) Ways of greeting one another.

(v) To take off one's sandals or shoes when entering a house or church for worship or fellowship.

(vi) The use of indigenous musical instruments with the preaching of the Gospel or with worship, to make Javanese feel at home.

(vii) The use of Arabic language when approaching educated Muslims, since Arabic is the unifying language of Islam and shows our respect for them.

(viii) Circumcision, a Muslim tradition, is basically a health measure and should be considered as such.

b. *Indonesian Muslim features that are endorsed by Scripture:*

(i) Respect to parents (Exod. 20:12).

(ii) Respect to husband (Eph. 5:22).

(iii) Strict sex regulations: no sex relationships before marriage (Eph. 5:3,5).

(iv) Giving of alms, concern for the poor (Eph. 2:10).

(v) Abstinence from alcohol and drunkenness: in strong Muslim areas, like Aceh, nearly no liquor can be found in the shops (Gal. 5:21).

c. *Features opposed to biblical revelation:*

(i) Polygamy.

(ii) Prayer ceremonies performed for the deceased.

(iii) Other forms of association with the occult, such as spiritualistic practices and animistic observances.

Each of the major religions, with its underlying Animism, has to be carefully examined and evaluated, according to the above pattern, so that Christians may discern which practices and features are neutral, which are opposed to Scripture, and which can be endorsed by Scripture. In this way, e.g., the Gospel messenger to the Chinese will have to introduce a functional substitute that replaces the customs related to Ancestor Worship, in order to fill the social vacuum.

I would also like to give a short list of forms of culture which has Shintoism and Buddhism as its background, as to which factors can be maintained, which ones must be rejected, and which ones are endorsed by Scripture.

a. *Neutral features that can be maintained:*

(i) Ethics on polite manners; e.g., "Sado" (tea ceremony), "Kado" (flower ceremony).

(ii) Way of visiting friends and relatives with gifts after returning home from a long journey (not just because of tradition but with all sincerity!).

(iii) Music and Japanese traditional dance, e.g., using "Kato," a kind of harp, played by women, and "Shakohochi," a kind of flute played by men.

b. *Forms of culture which can be taken from Shintoism/Buddhism and then substituted:*

(i) "Hichi-go-san" Ceremony. Children aged three, five, seven years go to the temple and ask blessing from their gods and then receive cakes. The Christian can take this and give the real meaning of Christianity, e.g., by taking the Christian children to the church to receive the blessing of our God and introduce them to the congregation to pray for them one by one (the pastor can pray for each one of them).

(ii) Self-discipline in Buddhism is stressed in order to gain peace, reading loudly the Buddhist sacred books diligently every day, and copying the words out from the Sacred Books. This custom in Buddhism can also be copied with the Bible: reading it aloud every day and copying it. The Buddhist people lead a self-disciplined life only for their own salvation, but Christians lead a self-disciplined life for the glory of God as people who have been saved.

c. *Forms of culture endorsed by Scripture:*

(i) Monogamy (Matt. 19:5; Mark 10:7; Eph. 5:31).

(ii) Respect to parents (Exod. 20:12).

(iii) Respect and loyalty to the government (Rom. 13).

d. *Forms of culture opposed to biblical revelation:*

(i) To worship the departed ones. Those who think that a departed person still has a living soul and thus must be fed. The food must be prepared on the table with the ashes of the departed upon it.

(ii) Yearly ceremony held during spring and autumn in the temple for the departed. By doing so they think that the soul of the departed will take time to visit their homes ("Higan"-spring; "Bong"-autumn).

(iii) Ceremony for the deceased (Buddhist ceremony).

(iv) Wedding ceremony. "San-san-kudo" ceremony, drinking sake: worshiping the sun god (from Shintoism), also drinking liquor (God's sake, "Syinsyu," a kind of sanctification before marriage).

(v) Birth ceremony. The son must be taken to the temple on the thirty-first day after his birth (a girl on her thirty-second day), to be prayed for and given a sanctification mark to be able to receive the blessing of the sun god. A worship ceremony to the gods in a small temple is held on Children's Celebration Day, every March 5.

(vi) Economic and political matters: economic and political discussion is always accompanied by the presense of women and the serving of alcohol. There is a saying in Japanese, "Machiai seeji" or "The policy of the Japanese government is decided in the bar."

4. *The adaptation of the Christian faith to Asian cultures*

In order to find out which forms the adaptation of the Christian faith to Asian cultures has taken we may study various patterns of worship represented in Asia. The question which may serve as a criterion is simply: are the patterns of worship in Asia today relevant to the culture and social structure of the people?

First of all, we observe, that many an Asian church consciously or unconsciously follows a pattern which has originated in the West. The reason is that often Western missionaries have not only brought the Gospel to Asia, but the structure and form of their own denomination has been brought along with the Gospel. Dr. Ebbie C. Smith has discussed this problem in the following way, "The pervasive temptation of the missionary is to establish a church patterned on his own customary denominational structure. This use of American methods without any real attempt to adapt to national psychology and methods is one of the foremost reasons for failure to establish churches that can live, grow, reproduce and share the life in their own community. The tendency to reproduce cultural factors in missionary churches is called by McGavran 'Cultural Overhang,' and has profound effect on Church Growth."

Dr. J. L. Ch. Abineno, who quotes Dr. Hendrik Kraemer's warning against gradually developing "spiritual domination," calls the "imported forms of worship" an "obstacle in the life and growth of the young churches." Dr. Muller-Kruger, well-known Indonesian church historian, feels that the Indonesian Christians are so used to their imported forms of worship, that they don't recognize their foreign origin and consider them as their very own!

It seems to depend on a people's measure of selfhood and indigenousness, how much or how little of the foreign culture they will accept along with the Gospel. And there are various degrees in which features are adapted or assimilated, accepted, modified, or rejected.

The second point of concern is the fact that Western missions often brought along an over-emphasis on individualism, not being aware of the communal nature of Asian societies. The claims of Christ for conversion and dedication are usually directed to the individual, not to the group, thus encouraging the "one by one against the crowd" conversion pattern. McGavran explains the advantage of the multi-individual mutually interdependent conversion pattern which lies so much closer to the Asian way of making decisions, and thereby allows people to become Christians without social dislocation or separation from their family and society.

If people in this way retain part of their social structure, their worship patterns will also remain relevant to the Asian way of life, and this is desirable for the sake of the growth of the church and for the multiplication of Christians.

Dr. Abineno reminds us that we must pay attention not only to the purity of the *kerygma,* but also to the *soma,* the pattern of worship, so that we might attract and enable the whole of our community to hear the proclamation of the Gospel. Obviously this is not a matter of principle, as some tend to think, but a matter of relevance, which we must emphasize. In this way, the pattern of worship will never be a barrier between the Christians and their surrounding community, but become a useful tool for the *kerygma.*

Dr. W. A. Smalley expresses his opinion in these words, "While the basic need of man and the basic message are the same everywhere, the most effective presentation of the Gospel is that which takes into account the cultural beliefs and fears of the people."

A successful experiment has been carried out by the Rev. Nagakura of Okayama, Japan. He has carried on worship services in forms of "tatami" (a form of assembling) which seems to fit well the Japanese tradition (house church). He felt that, "Japanese must become Japanese Christians, not European or American Christians." About 200 people attend these weekly meetings (the biggest number of worshipers among Japanese churches), and there are about 600 members of his church today. The *Okayama Seisin Kyokai,* as the church is called, emphasize giving, and their offering reached fifteen million yen a year, or about US $60,000. We can see that an indigenous structure encourages the development of an indigenous Christianity, because, as Donald McGavran states, "Men like to become Christians without crossing racial, linguistic or class barriers."

In conclusion, we will summarize some important elements in a form of worship:

a. *The Word of God.* The proclamation of the Word of God *(kerygma)* must have first place.

b. *Relevancy.*

(i) The form of worship must be relevant to a particular community/society in a concrete situation. The culture, social structure, customs, and traditions of that nation/people must be studied, in order that certain methods, forms, cultural tools may be determined to be used in the forms of worship as a tool to communicate the Gospel. A pattern of worship forms is needed here to relate the *kerygma* and the *soma* so that it becomes relevant to the society (local).

(ii) There must be a participation of those worshiping in the service. Usually in Asia, in the ceremonial/traditional feasts, e.g., in reciting a song or poem, the leader recites it or reads it with intonation verse by verse, followed by the audience. Thus it goes alternately until it is finished.

The pattern of the form of worship, as much as possible liberates itself from the form of worship as a rule based upon rites and regulations. Is it not that Christ through his death and resurrection has freed us from the bondages of law, regulations and rites? The patterns of worship, according to the New Testament, are in Christ Jesus freed from rites.

(iii) *The worship element.* In the service, opportunity must be given for its participants to express their worship to God in the liberty of the Spirit.

(iv) *The evangelistic element.* The form of worship must be a two-way channel: In one aspect it is a means of God to express his work of salvation for the world, in another aspect it is an invitation to the world/surrounding community. The pattern of Christ's life, moreoever, is a pattern of a form of worship which covers all aspects of the ministry of the Gospel.

5. *Summary and suggestions*

a. We concluded that there is a place for culture in the Scriptures, and we learned how cultures began. God loves men in their cultures and wants to see them all redeemed through the salvation provided through his Son Jesus Christ. He wants them to hear his voice through his Word in their own cultural setting. We have sought to identify from the Bible such basic truths that are supra-cultural and must be preached and maintained in any cultural situation.

b. Furthermore, we have tried to point to the cultural-religious setting in Asia with its major religions, which present us with the challenge to separate original cultural factors (which are neutral and may be maintained) from such features as are opposed to Christian revelation in the Bible and must therefore be rejected by the Christians, to those features that are endorsed by the Bible and must be strengthened and kept.

c. A thorough study of the cultures, society structures, customs, religions past and present, has been recommended for Asia, so that the Gospel may be proclaimed in a relevant way. A clear separation of essential Christian elements from the "cultural enclothing" is attempted through a biblical ethnotheology, to help the messenger of the Gospel.

d. Adaptation of patterns of worship to those forms that are indigenous and familiar both to the worshipers and to their community, have been recommended as necessary, if barriers are to be kept down.

e. Besides the individual conversion pattern brought over from the West, I recommend the multi-individual mode of conversion which allows people to become Christians within their social structure, so that they need not feel they must become Westerners when they turn to Christ!

f. Let us consider that for the sake of reaching the millions of Asia with the Gospel of Jesus Christ, a clear understanding of *biblical foundations and cultural identity* will be the basis of a new strategy for missions which will bring many not only to hear the Gospel, but also to become Christians in their own cultural setting.

HOW TO EVALUATE CULTURAL PRACTICES BY BIBLICAL STANDARDS IN MAINTAINING CULTURAL IDENTIY IN ASIA REPORT

Chairman: D. Chan
Secretary: G. Samuel

1. *Points of agreement* (with Mr. Octavianus' paper)
   a. The importance of the subject in relation to the evangelization of Asia
   b. The need for further study of the subject
   c. Recognition of the diversity of each culture
   d. The culture itself is not evil
   e. Cultural and religious elements are often inseparable
   f. Culture is to be seen as a channel for communication
   g. The supracultural aspects as set forth in the Bible are more than the nine aspects listed in the paper (e.g., aspects of eschatology are to be included).

2. *Significant disagreements*
   Though Hebrew and Greek cultures are media for revelation, these cultures are not to be considered as superior; however, it was pointed out that these cultures *are* superior.

3. *List of major questions and answers*
   a. Is multi-individual conversion typical in Asia? Often the Asians make their decisions in groups. The Asian society is not that individualistic, so Asians like to make decisions in mutual affection and dependence.
   b. Is Christianity imported to Asia from the West? No. Christianity is not imported from the West. Its origin is in Asia. But the Gospel message was brought back to Asia mainly by Western missionaries.
   c. How much of the cultural element can be retained? Those which are not contradictory to the Bible and those which do not have religious significance.
   d. Is individualism evil? Modern forms of individualism (these are unscriptural) are to be differentiated from individual's integrity before God and man.

4. *Specific attitudes*
   People can become Christians in their own culture with a minimum of social dislocation. Cultural adaptation is acceptable, but should not lead to syncretism of any kind.

5. *New emphasis in evangelization*
   a. Use culture as a channel for communication.
   b. When the particular cultural practice is opposed to biblical revelation, find (or look for) suitable functional substitutes for the social life of the society concerned.

c. Clear the misunderstanding on the part of the listeners toward the Christians (or missionaries) before the Gospel is preached.

7. *More study and research needed*
a. The meaning and cultural implications of customs are to be studied in a particular culture in order to evaluate whether the customs are to be retained or not.
b. In-depth study of various cultures: study must be undertaken to help those working among Muslims, Hindus, followers of Confucius, etc.
c. Study of missionary anthropology for each region.

8. *Resources*
Information is available through the School of World Mission of Fuller Theological Seminary, Pasadena, California.

9. *Steps to share the contents of the paper with others*
a. Study our own church: list those which are cultural, elements of a foreign culture and those which need modification.
b. List practices often questioned in our own society and evaluate them.
c. Share the insights of the paper with other church members.
d. Incorporate the study of cultural aspects in the training programs for evangelists.

BIBLICAL THEOLOGY AND CULTURAL IDENTITY IN LATIN AMERICA

Pablo M. Pérez

The presence of Protestantism in Latin America has been felt in forms which are stereotyped to a certain extent and which have in turn been taken by many to be its distinctive characteristics. In different circles and areas "the brothers" — as believers are known throughout the continent — are identified by their habits, norms of conduct, patterns of social organization, worship forms, as well as one or two works of charity — besides a number of peculiarities which are somewhat inexplicable. Furthermore, a good number of these same believers is in complete agreement with such a description and some even find a special satisfaction with it and do not give any further thought to what it implies.

But when one goes deeper into what is really represented by the Protestant prototype in Latin America, one will discover that in many respects such a "prototype" is nothing more than the somewhat strange amalgamation of customs and habits which were prevalent in other countries some decades ago, and the Latin American character. And it is strange not only because it is out-of-date in those places where it originated and is thus considered a relic of the past, but also because it was from the very beginning a result of imported ideas with but little discernment, and consequently has not taken root in its new habitat. If there are no roots, its fruit has been practically nonexistent; in order to produce it almost every effort has been concentrated in those stereotyped forms mentioned above and in a conformity to them. In other words, an external demonstration of some secondary characteristics has been sought primarily, and it has been made to appear that they in turn are the final goal of every believer.

It is pertinent, then, to raise the question: Should customs and activities as practiced in our Protestant churches in Latin America be discarded? This question at the same time raises some others which help us focus the problem in its true dimension. It is not a case of discarding or accepting, but of the need to place the Protestant church in our continent in a position where new horizons open before it. This will mean on the one hand that the church should be enabled to reach a higher level of discernment concerning its own position, and that she may do so in the light of biblical directives. She should also be able to take the appropriate steps to find her true identity and, consequently, offer a more viable spiritual alternative to the average Latin American. On the other hand, it will also demand a rigorous discipline which should keep her from going back to old practices while allowing her to launch confidently into new undertakings which up to now have been outside her reach. No doubt it will also produce more stable and reliable foundations for the second and third generation Protestants. These in themselves represent a most serious problem in connection with the strengthening of the Protestant witness and the continuity necessary to establish a more solid and visible community of individuals and groups which evidence the control of the Holy Spirit.

Briefly, then, it is urgent now more than ever that the Protestant church in Latin America be confronted with the need to define its own personality and to follow its own path within the will of God. The task in itself is almost impossible and cannot even pretend to find the final word on the subject. But our predicament demands that we at least promote thinking along these lines in order to encourage an ever increasing nucleus of men and women who are concerned about reaching satisfactory conclusions within our own context. As such, the plan suggested by the title of this paper seems to be the most adequate to confront the problem, only following an inverted order. Just the same, it is necessary to point out that the term "evangelical," which will be used from here on, refers to the Protestant community as a whole, as has been used in Latin America for nearly half a century. While it includes the so-called conservatives which make up the majority of the Protestant community, it does not exclusively refer to them. Just the same, it does not include the cults and sects which are very much a part of a religious minority, but have never been an integral part of the Protestant community as such.

1. Cultural dimensions

Latin American culture, just like any other culture, consists of both positive and negative elements in the light of biblical revelation. That is, while some of them lend themselves to be God-approved means, others have been used and continue to be used very effectively by Satan for his own purposes. Now a good many Latin American evangelicals have held that there are really very few positive elements which could be approved by God and consequently used for his glory. They have adopted a mentality which holds that everything that surrounds us is "worldly" and that since it does not contribute anything to a truly "spiritual" development, it has to be eliminated radically.

But a simple examination, even if it is limited, of several aspects of our culture will indicate that there is a great deal of positive values within it that should be used properly. On the one hand we find that much of what is related to the family in our context has a biblical basis. Respect for parents, and effective and inter-dependent relationship among its members, the recognition and effort to keep alive the lasting bonds which unite it, as well as some other latent aspects, reveal a religious if not a strictly biblical background. The Word of God does not hesitate to affirm constantly that respect, love, mutual help are integral parts of the divine ideal for the family. All of this naturally is best expressed in a Christian home, and extension, in that spiritual family which finds its shelter whichin a church building.

However, I believe that we have also shown a lack of discernment when we encourage a tacit separation of the family unit when it reaches our churches. The children go to their respective classes, the young people do the same and seek to be with their friends during worship services. As a result the parents are reunited with their family only at the time to go back home. This means that we do not even perceive that activities and relationships within the church itself tend to go against the positive elements which are a part of the family. Or that, in the best of cases, the church represents an extended family to which a nuclear family incorporates itself in order to function more effectively in society. In any case there is the urgent need to devise and develop those programs which will promote the maximum use of positive elements in our families, together with a proper attention given to age groups and those of common interests. These in turn should be local in origin and development so that local needs are met rather than dependent on suggestions or intervention from the outside.

Closely related to all of this we find respect for human dignity. It is not uncommon to speak of the distinctive characteristics of this concept such as family reputation as a part of our name, the recognition of courageous deeds performed by our national heroes, a due respect for the professional or technical ability of an individual, as well as the place of importance given to mothers and women in general with all that this entails. No doubt we can also discover here some biblical elements which value man in a special way and which allow him to function as an integral and essential part of the society in which he lives. At the same time he is expected to contribute in a unique way without being demanded to act as a specialist who may be detached from the warmth of human relations at different levels.

And undoubtedly this particular aspect has been used effectively in the task of evangelization. The intrinsic value of each individual has been appreciated and he has been given the opportunity to recover his dignity before God through the redeeming power of the Gospel. Nevertheless, in most cases he has been accepted only as he has proved his usefulness to the church and her programs, but not in the way he can show forth his new relationship to God in the secular world where he operates. It is possible that this is one of the results of a kind of evangelization which has been so individualistic and fragmentary as to pay special attention only to the "spiritual" aspects of Salvation while it overlooks other important elements of a believer's life.

In a similar way there has been an appeal to the ethical responsibility of the Christian just because he is a child of God. But generally speaking he has been led to believe that this responsibility can be satisfied by obeying certain norms of behavior; he has learned to think of these as distinctive characteristics of any "consecrated" evangelical. Nevertheless he does not even know that such norms were conceived and practiced in lands and circumstances very different from his own; that they are the result of a culture which has been molded by noble ideals and principles, but quite apart from Latin American reality. It is imperative, then, to face seriously our problems not on the basis of a Puritan context nor on a Victorian era, but within our particular historical heritage. This includes the repressive power of the Holy Office and the indelible marks of moral theology and its canon law — as well as Jesuit casuistry. A biblical ethic with such a background demands a solid basis which is closely dependent on the Holy Spirit rather than an external conformity built merely on "moral" reasonings that are obviously pharisaical.

Finally — as far as this paper is concerned — it is necessary for us to consider several positive aspects of a hierarchical structure inherent in our society, which has in itself vast and profound scope in our culture. It cannot be denied that this has contributed somewhat to social stability and to encourage the degree of respect which we naturally feel for our elders or for people in influential positions in society. It is true that to talk about hierarchical structures and their implications is out of ideological fashion, but we have to recognize that in our society an elite factor still plays a very important part. Whereas before the goal was to be a part of a select, aristocratic group, now it is to be able to have a prestigious position in government and to enlist in a "national liberation army." And without even trying to perpetuate everything this hierarchical structure implies, and not being blind to the evils it involves, it is necessary to examine its dynamics carefully since it still — whether we like it or not — rules most of our relationships.

In connection with this I suggest that besides the multiplicity of inferences which this concept has and will continue to have as to systems of church government, it also has positive results as to its ethical and liturgical implications. All of us know that one of our pressing needs is for the believer to attain a certain degree of stability in his daily life, whether in his personal or in his family life. This is not a case of that type of stability which results from a submission to oppressive structures and systems, but the one which gives stability to character and aids in the control of violent reactions because it obeys a personal discipline based on biblical principles. These point to a system of priorities — or hierarchies — as to our relationship with God and with Christ on the part of men, women, and children. Not far behind we find those where we are exhorted to follow love and peace, both of which are derived from an adequate knowledge and the proper respect for a supreme and sovereign God. All of these and many more have ethical principles of vast reaching significance.

But at the same time a hierarchical structure affects our worship of God in a very direct way. Not only are we speaking here of recognizing a superiority which belongs to him only, but of the habits and principles which govern it. Many times we worship God with too much of a loose attitude as an honest reaction to that cold and ritualistic formalism of the religious tradition which we used to profess. Others worship with imported expressions and under regulations lacking in authenticity and relevance in our context, but yet full of "evangelical tradition." Still others, even though to a lesser degree, employ an elaborate ritualism or an imitation which smacks of servility, of what we can conceive of majesty and splendor. In all of these what really has taken place is that we have convinced ourselves that worship is an esoteric act of highly mystical dimensions and extra-terrestrial language — all of it strictly anthropocentric. Here a hierarchical structure has been inverted for even if we repeatedly declare that God is supreme and is worthy of all our respect, we are really offering him what seems best to us.

Both the contents and context of such passages as John 4:24, all the doxological ones in the New Testament, as well as the unlimited wealth from the Psalms will throw light that will help us appreciate much better this hierarchical mentality we have. By the same token they will help us place it in its proper perspective and cause it to move in the right direction. It should be pleasing to God not only as it is related to worship but also in many other aspects of our daily Christian life.

And what can we say about service to the world? We do admire the spirit of generosity which still persists in one way or another in Latin America. We like to give in order to alleviate burdens of the needy and we are easily moved by tragedy. Moreover, it is not very difficult for us to make room in our home to provide shelter for a relative who wants to strive for a better lot or for one who is experiencing difficulties in his job — all of it in a spirit that is not opposed to biblical principles.

It is unfortunate, however, that when some of these practices are introduced to our churches the picture changes radically. According to our religious tradition, social work has been classified as charity supported by alms or pious gifts. In evangelical circles very little of this background has been changed in principle. But there is now increased reticence to act due to the fear of falling into a type of "social gospel" — a somewhat nebulous concept in the minds of believers, but which has repeatedly been discredited during several decades and is thus rejected without further discussion. And there seems to be no tendency for improvement when some are currently trying to assign it a measure of theological stature and speak with John XXIII, of "serving Christ in the poor" or giving them the power they have been denied. What this has accomplished is that the practice of social benevolence is limited for only those institutions which supposedly have the duty to perform it, while in the meantime neither individual nor collective responsibility has been promoted in certain groups.

It is my conviction that the Word of God allows freedom in this matter without having to specialize or to institutionalize such aid. Those means and avenues of service within the normal flow of human relations should be encouraged under the guidance of Bible study and its imperatives. Thus every form of positive social service will be multiplied in a continent overflowing with outcasts and deprived people. Whatever is being done in the name of the church should also be promoted, but it does not have to be limited to it only.

Now considering the negative aspects of our culture, it is necessary to recognize that many people are thoroughly convinced that we really do not find any positive elements in it. And even though they may not be totally right, note has to be taken of several features which undoubtedly are in need of correction so they may ultimately produce favorable results.

From the very beginning one can detect a marked tendency to imitate. It is observed that from our early history there have been determined efforts to reproduce both practices and models which seem worthy of such an endeavor. Furthermore, a great deal of attention is given to small details so that the impression can be created that the original rather than its copy is being presented. Consequently, no effort seems too big for such a goal in order to get full acceptance.

And perhaps in no other aspect can this same effort be seen than in liturgy. It is not by accident that either German or Anglo-Saxon tunes are heard in our worship services or that North American-style choruses, in all their full splendor, are almost immediately adopted by our young people. The celebration of the Lord's Supper resembles a formal banquet in a European palace much more than a spiritual feast in the Near East. It is only recently that the use of guitars for instrumental accompaniment has been generally accepted, but many of us still prefer the organ. And let no one dare to question these practices because someone will promptly and vigorously declare, "We have always done it this way!"

And the approval that is usually sought for such an imitation is, on the one hand, that which is based on experience and the authority derived from it, which are foundations to which very few can object. Nevertheless, it is usually ignored that they represent circumstances and meanings which are different from those which originally prompted the external forms now being perpetuated; that just the same they evidence an attitude of dependence lacking in discernment. They ultimately produce intellectual and spiritual laziness.

Some others may argue that Paul exhorts us to imitate him since he was trying to introduce new habits to cultures with no biblical base whatsoever. It is well to note that the apostle stated that he was an imitator of Christ, and that he never had the desire to impose static patterns of behavior, worship, or church government on them. This means that, even if it can be accepted that there is nothing spiritual or biblical in our culture, there is no justification for the introduction of rituals and norms from another culture which has transmitted them, already modified, as meaningful as they might have been in the past. It would be well to remember that every symbol has its own individual background and that it must become a living reality to every generation which adopts it. In other words, there is rather a need to assimilate and adapt patterns than to imitate them in a servile manner; to know how to differentiate between the basic principles being represented and their external forms. And a great deal of disciplined effort and rigorous creativity is demanded for this task.

An imitative spirit also gives rise to a tendency to institutionalize and, consequently, sacralize activities and regulations. As has already been pointed out, the weight of experience and tradition is felt here in all its strength. Because of this, such items as time schedules, official posts, groups, and methods for evangelization are institutionalized rather speedily, just as the ones already mentioned. Once this is accomplished, there is the requirement for almost absolute submission in the precise observance of a multiplicity of details, slogans, program outlines, schedules of meetings, etc. In some groups known to this writer no one dares omit a "prayer circle" before opening a meeting, a "talk" with its corresponding "prayer after the talk," as well as "offering and announcements" and the unavoidable "benediction."

But one can also ask, is it not true that Latin Americans like improvisation so that they can express creativity? How can you explain the imitative spirit with the tendency to institutionalize and consequently sacralize everything? On the one hand it can be answered that we like to create items of local art and handcraft which have but little bearing on basic forms and principles; they are rather peripheral. Similarly, that in many instances a practice is approved by the simple statement that it has already been tried elsewhere. Immediately there is an aura of authority over it which requires a minimum time for testing it and subsequently it becomes institutionalized within a community.

Obviously all of this lends itself to a glaring lack of adequate acclimatization which will permit such a practice to be assimilated with proper adaptations, if it is to take root. Unfortunately this becomes an obstacle to the outsider, the person we usually call "an unbeliever," since he cannot even begin to understand us. If he does understand us after some time, he will most likely feel encouraged to join our group or church and he will then use our terminology and speak of salvation, the worship service, the brethren, the offering. But he will go out to face a hostile world just as many members of our churches do, that is with no spiritual power but only with a barren vocabulary. The task would have been completed then: we would have converted him into a "believer" after our likeness, spiritually indolent and utterly dependent on formalism.

Furthermore, we cannot ignore the markedly negative aspects of the hierarchical structure mentioned before. Whereas it provides a certain degree of stability to society, it allows its head almost unlimited freedom and even extreme misuse of authority. It also fosters the idea of class distinctions — that respect of persons which the Scriptures speak about. All of these contribute to maintain conditions of hostility or a rather repugnant type of servility. Several samples of these are to be found in our churches and their structures of government. Ostensibly they may not tolerate the existence of hierarchical degrees with their corresponding titles, but in reality they are zealously guarded and any attempt to achieve a promotion is carefully brought under control. As a result several denominations are in the hands of veritable oligarchies which rule them with an iron fist. In the best of cases they do so with a true zeal and fervor, as guiding lights in defense of doctrine; in the worst, with violence and terrorist tactics which are contrary to a truly evangelical spirit. One can also notice the existence of small chieftains who operate outside of any control. However, they have a great deal of influence in the life and decisions of their parishioners.

Now, all of these elements have to be confronted in the light of reality and not merely idealistically. True, we live in a world where teachings concerning class equality forbid any talk about existing social distinctions, much less does it tolerate any idea which may tend to foster them. But this should not mean that society as such is beyond redemption nor that we should abstain from attempting the improvement of some of its structures, even if we have already labeled them as alienating. There are many examples in the Word of God where we can see a temporary spirit of toleration which eventually results in a different situation to favor the outworking of God's plan, either within a short or a long term. From this vantage point, then, many basic problems can be dealt with as they apply to a variety of circumstances.

And even if some points may not be a direct result of our cultural legacy, we cannot ignore that there are conditions which directly affect the very existence of the evangelical community in Latin America in its own context. One of these is the high rate of illiteracy which still persists despite the efforts of several governments to the contrary. Some experts declare that the problem is even worse due to the fact that while the number of people who learn to read and write increases, there is still a great deal of "functional illiteracy." This takes on an alarming dimension among evangelicals when we recognize the fact that even though we are known as the people of the book, there still prevails what we could call a "biblical functional illiteracy" intimately related to our environment as a very real problem in our churches. In order to solve it we would need a drastic revision of methods and teaching materials so as to find the most effective means to teach the Word of God and its implications for our time. This must be done not only in the light of methods being used by contemporary secular education, but even of other means which have not traditionally been accepted as educational. I am speaking both of mass communication media and of publications with attractive formats, low in intellectual content but immensely popular in every level of the social scale. Many a positive lesson can be learned from Walt Disney stories in comic-book form, as well as from the corresponding local heroes as they relate to tactics and the acknowledgment of mass dynamic factors.

In short, if the evangelical community is to express its true cultural identity all the elements that make up Latin American culture have to be taken into consideration, be they seemingly or notoriously positive or negative. We have to repeat that this is neither a pleasant nor an easy task, but that it is extremely urgent in order to offset a trend toward an indigenous syncretism or, worse than that, to import another syncretism which is original to other places and times. This task demands also the active participation, representative of a cross-section of the Latin American community. This group, with a definite commitment of both spiritual and intellectual discipline, can study conditions and suggest directives to follow. These will then be adapted to any local situation so that they may be real models for adaptation without becoming normative examples for every specific situation. And all of this within the broad but disciplined framework of the ministry of the Holy Spirit and the Holy Word of which he is the author.

2. Biblical dimensions

One of the distinguishing characteristics of biblical revelation is that it uncovers for us a God dynamically and constantly active in his relationship to humanity and his own. He is a being who knows fully the place culture has in the life of man. Thus he does not oppose it automatically, nor does he manipulate it with petty desires, much less does he make it the only expression of his will for all humanity for all times. Thus we can understand that culture can become a means of divine action but that it never becomes an end in itself.

As far as the limits of this paper are concerned it will be necessary once more to restrict our treatment to just a few outstanding points of biblical revelation which have a bearing on Iberian-America at the present time. It is pertinent to state that the present author holds to a position which accepts unreservedly the Bible as the inspired Word of God to the full extent of the term and according to Peter's expression that the biblical authors did not invent their message but that they, "Spoke as they were moved by the Holy Spirit" (II Pet. 1:21).

a. *Introductory remarks* — We have almost forgotten the counter-cultural spirit of early Christianity. In other words, that while it acknowledged that peoples and tribes had a particular life-style expressed in their cultures, it also had a corrective attitude towards them. It brought with itself divine judgment against their negative points as well as radical modification of the positive aspects. The apostles and their followers did not hesitate to condemn idolatry and every type of immorality as well as philosophical doctrines which kept their minds ensnared.

No doubt this was one of the aspects which contributed to the success of the preaching of the Gospel in the early church. It was not simply a "prophetic" task (as it is conceived nowadays), but the simple condemnation of sin and a call to repentance leading to forgiveness and the transforming power which could drive its possessor to a new life. "Repent," said the Lord in his first public message; "Let men repent," reiterated Paul before the Athenians. It was in this way and in many others that those who listened to the Gospel message for the first time were confronted with the fact that there were some negative elements in their culture from which they should turn away. At the same time they were exhorted to take a new stance which would let them establish trends pleasing to God, even if this meant that such a trend would run contrary to the existing order. It can thus be noticed that the door would then be opened for divine intervention in any given culture, obviously governed by biblical directives toward the goal which the Lord himself set.

This naturally demands that discipline of an adequate interpretation of God's Word both as a strict and as a relevant discipline. That is, that it should be a task which serves the scriptural record rather than an ideology or a theological fad with all the limitations inherent to it. Nevertheless, in view of the fact that it originated in a dynamic and living Being, it is necessary to remember that such a Word speaks directly and addresses itself to concrete situations which can assimilate its principles in order to adapt them to our idiosyncrasy. As such, the task of hermeneutics represents a challenge which cannot afford to ignore the genius and characteristics of the culture to which it seeks to transmit the message, nor the seriousness of this same message and its divine origin. This means that every system of interpretation must be examined in the light of the place it has had in history. When it is finally adopted, if it is, it can only be used as a starting point. Every conclusion must be reached methodically and not arbitrarily;

under the strict and conscious control of the Holy Spirit and not slavish-
ly following archaic patterns or high-sounding novelties.

b. *Some basic concepts* — Our present era makes us forget the primary importance of concepts that are basic to cultural activity, as
stated in the Word of God. On the one hand the same God who has
revealed himself in the Scriptures is a personal God who, while he is
merciful and kind, is also hard and jealous of his own name and his
own glory. His intervention may be multifarious, but always within the
limits that he himself has made known in his Word. His glory stands
out unequivocally as the starting point, the moving force, and the
primary goal of his every act as well as those of his creatures in the
universe. Within that same glory we can find his desire to have man
participate with him in all the eternal blessings in his heavenly mansions. For this purpose he has provided the means through which man
can attain this: salvation through faith in the substitutionary work of
his Son Jesus Christ on the Cross. At the same time he desires that
everyone who becomes identified with him through faith may live in
obedience to his will and enjoy an abundant life which pleases him and
affords personal satisfaction to man. Consequently he has given the
Holy Spirit to live in every believer so that he may enable and impel
him to obey his will and thus prepare for life in heaven. And that
same will is found clearly expressed in the Bible, the only rule of
faith and practice for every aspect of a believer's life.

The Lord has also planned for the establishment of a visible body
of believers who encourage one another to love and good works.
They exhibit both corporately and individually God's power, love, and
concern for that part of humanity which is still not committed to his
control. This body, the Church, does not live for itself nor for the
world primarily, but for the Lord and the goals he has established. It
is a community of witness, aggressive proclamation of the praises of
him who called it "from darkness to his marvelous light," and a consuming passion for those who are still far from God and his Christ.
The Church, then, has a mission which is highly spiritual and un-
questionably humanizing in the fullest sense of both terms as part
of one and the same reality. It thus is anxiously expecting its Lord
who will return to establish his kingdom in all its fullness, as a complete
expression of what is now already at work among us.

c. *Contemporary manifestations* — Conditions at present in Latin
America have contributed already to the discussion of several topics
in the realm of biblical theology. It is unfortunate that such a discussion has been limited up to now to socio-political approaches with a
marked socialist and Marxist flavor, heavily spiced with European
theological terminology even if the development has been in Latin
America by Latin Americans. In reality, then, the very same mistake
which has haunted Latin American thinking and practice has been
made again: Both patterns and categories of thought of an old nature
and a foreign origin have been followed.

However, it is imperative that we acknowledge that those topics
merit an in-depth treatment with a thoroughly biblical framework
and contents. There is an urgent need to develop a biblical anthro-

pology that takes into consideration the predicament of every Latin American, not only the poor and the outcasts; one that will also include insights and contributions of those sciences which have carefully analyzed man within the recent past; that will place man in his proper perspective within divine priorities and plans. Just as important are the interpersonal relations in a society which, like ours, is bankrupt but still has redeemable elements in it.

Closely related to all of this we find the concept concerning the Kingdom of God and its application to the Latin American situation. It is no longer considered idle talk to consider socio-political expressions that must be analyzed in the light of the Word of God to determine their relationship with the divine purpose, both temporal and eternal. If socialism with its messianic hopes is one form of that Kingdom, there should be no shadow of a doubt that it must be accepted. Just the same, it cannot be forgotten that the Kingdom of God and of his Christ is not to be submitted to systems or ideologies of human origin, humanizing as their postulates may sound. In the light of the failure of capitalism it cannot afford to embrace the best option to be found in a market place which is still in the experimental stage. If it does so, it is bound to make the same mistake and thus to lose its corrective power definitely.

Another important aspect will be that of proposing a doctrine of the Church in its Latin American expression even before determining its identity. While any true ecclesiology cannot be conceived apart from the biblical principles as the Body of Christ under the absolute control of the Holy Spirit, it is just as valid that it cannot exist in a purely abstract form. But it is precisely at this juncture that little attention has been paid to the theoretical basis in favor of a speedy naturalization and acclimatization in our continent. Furthermore, its evangelistic task has been emphasized while the organization of supporting groups to encourage the development of a truly Christian character in the new believers has been neglected. For this reason it is still hard to determine the true identity of the Latin American evangelical church. And it will continue to be so unless there is a definite effort in every level within itself so that concrete proposals are made to achieve this purpose.

Finally, it is just as important to study every detail that is involved in the doctrine and sanctification. The Word of God does not limit its reach to external patterns of behavior at certain ethical levels, but it extends to what these in turn reflect concerning the relationship of the individual to God. Again, social ethics operates under guidelines of a divine origin rather than because of the pressures of collective needs. Thus the Latin American evangelical church can no longer be at the mercy of pious requirements with a shallow depth and a high pharisaical content, neither is it to have new mystiques with humanistic overtones which ignore divine priorities for the sake of the community. Neither barren legalism nor passionate ideologies are to be allowed as substitutes of biblical concepts to rule the believers' behavior.

What, then, can be done specifically? For the time being it would be good to operate at least under the following general principles:

(i) With a creative attitude which does not depend upon external influences exclusively, but rather in absolute submission to biblical principles.

(ii) With a system of priorities in the light of God's will and according to both his temporal and eternal plan for man and the believer, with awareness at the same time of the totality of Latin American reality.

(iii) With an increasing consciousness of the corrective role of the Gospel in its relationships with society, the structures which make it up, and the prevailing ideologies.

(iv) With all seriousness and earnestness which will not incorporate novelties automatically nor do away with existing principles, as long as nothing which might offend the Lord is discovered.

(v) With a high degree of spiritual discernment which results from the unconditional commitment to the Lord of the Church and to the control of the Holy Spirit in individual as well as in collective matters.

(vi) With special care in order to avoid any unnecessary institutionalization of forms and expressions of a passing nature concerning liturgy, systems of church government, and social concern.

With all of these and many others which can undoubtedly be suggested during the Congress a new trend can be started, one which sooner or later will contribute positively to determine the true identity of the Latin American church in the light of biblical theology.

HOW TO EVALUATE CULTURAL PRACTICES BY BIBLICAL STANDARDS IN MAINTAINING CULTURAL IDENTITY IN LATIN AMERICA REPORT

Chairman: Benjamin Moraes
Secretary: William Taylor

The relationship between culture and the theology of evangelization is a dynamic, living one. It is one which implicates all elements involved in the process of evangelization and the establishment of the local Christian community. If it is a cross-cultural communication, the Good News bearer — if he comes from a foreign culture — must be sensitive to understand both his own culture and the one he works in! The recipient is not expected to share the burden of understanding both. He deserves a pure Gospel. That Gospel essence must not be confused or changed, although it is often jarred out of focus due to verbal and non-verbal communication which comes as part of the Gospel wrappings.

The subject of Latin American cultural identity is a touchy one to some. The Latin American people have suffered from social, political, economic, and ecclesiastical exploitation and control from without. The impact of this search for cultural identity has been felt within the evangelical church also. Most believers from Latin America will readily express appreciation and gratitude for the foreign believers and missionaries who brought the Gospel. At the same time, many of these Latin brethren express their own personal experience of subjugation to inferior status, snubs, and apparently deliberate mistreatment. The fact is that many non-Latin American missionaries are totally unaware of what they have done in the past.

It takes a careful, cool and loving interpersonal relationship to deal with these problems. Over-riding our discussion of Dr. Pérez' paper — in which both Latin American and non-Latin American actively participated — was a sense of common dependence upon the Spirit.

Some pointed questions

Here are some of the interrogatives which stimulated discussion, some without answers. First, what does the Latin American culture have that is positive, and what is negative? Second, are there positive aspects of this culture which we have ignored or even violated as Christians in Latin America? Third, have we biblically judged the negative aspects of the culture? Fourth, what examples illustrate these first three questions? Fifth, what does it mean to be a *Latin American* believer in Jesus Christ? Does it differ from a believer in other cultures? Sixth, since missionaries have committed mistakes, should they all move out and allow the autonomous Latin American church to take over? Seventh, what is our responsibility as foreign missionaries and Latin American believers to the society at large? How do we express a biblical balance between evangelism and social concern, between biblical authority and the loving Christian community?

Some biblical guidelines to evaluate our culture and cultural identity in Latin America

1. The Scriptures must be supreme. Christ is our Lord. The Lausanne Covenant affirms, "The message of the Bible is addressed to all mankind . . ." The Holy Spirit ". . . illumines the minds of God's people in every culture to perceive its truth freshly through their own eyes . . . ." Therefore all culture must be evaluated in the light of, and be subjected to, Scripture. Every culture has its positive and negative aspects. No culture is perfect, regardless of ethnocentrisms. This applies equally to the culture in which one works, as well as the one from which he perhaps has come.

2. All men are created in the image of God (Gen. 1:26, Gal. 3:28, Acts 17:26). Therefore we must recognize cultural diversity as reflecting some of God's image. At the same time we acknowledge that sin has disfigured man and his culture, and God must judge.

3. The form and freedom which the New Testament allows are vast both in the proclamation of the Gospel, as well as within the life of the community of believers. We must not allow cultural traditions, which are found within and outside of the local church, to stifle the life of Christ (Mark 7:8-13).

4. Cultural pressures must not permit a change of emphasis in the purity and demands of the New Testament Gospel and discipleship. The social needs of Latin America call for a Christian response, but the priorities must be sustained. Again the Lausanne Covenant expresses the balance and tension, "Although reconciliation with man is not reconciliation with God, nor is social action evangelism, nor is political liberation salvation, nevertheless we affirm that evangelism and sociopolitical involvement are both part of our Christian duty." The emotional quality of the Latin American appears to cause him to be especially receptive to the Gospel, but this should cause us to be careful in articulating the demands of biblical discipleship.

5. Jesus is the perfect example of one who crossed many cultural barriers. The Word became flesh, and dwelt among us, full of grace and truth. Paul's teaching in Philippians chapter 2 underscores this. Our responsibility in evaluating culture — whether our own or another's — is to do it in love, with an honest desire to learn, identifying with the culture without violating our own personal identity, free to make our critiques in careful love, avoiding the confusion of cultural relatives with biblical absolutes.

Implication in the theology of evangelization

Our theology must not change. The essence of our proclamation is cross-cultural, and has its origins in the Person of God and in the work of the Son. While the diversity of cultural realities must not neutralize the evangelization of the world, we underline the fact that this task must be carried out with an awareness of the culture in which the evangelization is being carried out.

The essential results of evangelization will not change obedience to

Christ, incorporation into a local community of believers, and significant outreach to the world. What *will* change should be local manifestations of both strategy and methodology of evangelization. There will also be biblical freedom in the forms and structures of the new church. The Latin American culture is rich in interpersonal relationships which are both emotionally moving and personally satisfying. These must be studied, cleansed if necessary, and utilized in the church.

Current, and sometimes carelessly imported, methods of evangelization and forms in the local Latin American church must be re-examined. They will change; some may be discarded, but all must be examined in light of the New Testament principles as they apply to Latin America.

Further study and research

We suggest a few examples of imperative research.

1. Careful definitions of "culture" and "biblical absolutes" must be developed as they apply to Latin America. Obviously these are done in a time and space dimension which will change depending on the individual and his place in history. But we need help here.

2. We request study of worship patterns that Scripture encourages, so that these can be developed and incorporated in the matrix of the Latin American cultures — whether Indian or ladino, poor barrio or rising middle classes.

3. We request study into the nature of the Latin American family life and dynamic, and its implication in evangelization and Christian nurture. The roles and hierarchy of the family must be analyzed. The concept of manhood, leadership, must be evaluated. What is present in the Latin family which is biblical — support.

4. We recommend the distribution of Dr. Pérez' paper, and other similar articles, in Christian magazines such as *Decision, Rensamiento Cristiano, Certeza.* This should be just a start in the right direction of positive self-analysis in Latin America.

5. We suggest that centers for theological education in Latin America include studies in the Christian approach of cultural anthropology.

Some immediate needs

1. We must evaluate our attitudes to our own culture, as well as to the culture we may have adopted. How can we learn, change, love?

2. We must discuss the topic of cultural identity and its biblical guidelines with our brethren in Latin America, regardless of their origin.

3. We request that the non-Latin American sending and supporting agencies evaluate their criteria for new missionaries to Latin America. (It is not a matter of not sending them, but of sending the right ones.) We ask them to evaluate their operating methodologies, problem solving processes, and organization leadership structures.

4. We encourage the desperately needed change — gradual and loving — in evangelical churches and leaders in Latin America that will bring life and renewal in proclamation, worship, education, and service in the light of the Latin American cultures and biblical principles.

5. We ask all Christians — Latin American and non-Latin American — to consider carefully what it means to be a Latin American

believer in countries that suffer centuries of injustice and damage to human dignity, or countries which are undergoing significant social and structural changes. Scripture must ultimately judge all social systems.

EUROPEAN CHRISTIANS: THE TENSION BETWEEN BIBLE AND CULTURE

Gunter Wieske

Dr. Wieske, Langesund, Norway, is the Evangelism Secretary in the Norwegian Baptist Union.

1. Problem and task

a. *The situation* — At the present time Europe consists of thirty-three countries. The national frontiers on this continent have shifted rather frequently, and are not identical with linguistic, cultural, and national borders. Today there are even more languages than nations. There are, however, cultural areas with their own distinct characteristics.

Since the early days, Christianity has had an enormous impact on Europe — east, west, north and south. It has influenced through revival periods, through influential institutions, through varying forms of theologies, through spiritual and ecclesiastical life, through constantly changing creative knowledge and actions, as well as the preservation of already existing elements. This century has contributed a number of radical changes within European churches as no century before. Some of these widely varying factors, responsible for this development are as follows: technology, leisure time, political situations and ideologies, opulence, and persecutions.

Even though the mutual cultural influence of nations and churches in Europe was and still is strong, the problem we face can be tackled from various aspects such as the political, cultural, and religious development. We have to confine ourselves to one of the possibilities available.

b. *Problem and task* — In the midst of the rapid changes in our day, many Christians ask themselves how our generation will cope with the problems and yet remain faithful to Jesus Christ and his biblical commands, while at the same time avoiding unnecessary cultural isolation and thus missionary fruitlessness.

It is possible that the characteristic of our European situation with its long history of culture and Christianity, is that our consciousness of problems has become our major preoccupation. This results in a limited capacity to produce solutions. The problems of Europe and the world, of the church and humanity, encumber our minds. In some cases we are able to analyze them and avail ourselves of the latest theological, sociological, etc., helps. The solutions suggested, however, often are of theoretical ideas that were born around conference tables but lack the power and inspiration to become workable projects for the masses.

A number of participants of the Congress have asked beforehand that the tension between true Christianity from the biblical point of view and those cultures surrounding us should be discussed. This question is both comprehensive and old, and I am certain that every one of us will contribute some solutions. Before going on I would like to define the term "culture" to form the basis for a better understanding for our working team.

The term "culture" conveys to us the "embodiment of all human efforts to conquer nature (agriculture, engineering) and to settle inter-human relations (in institutions, law and order, custom, folklore, etc.) as well as the somatic, intellectual and spiritual development of the human being (in language, art, science, philosophy and religion)."

The first diagram (see appendix) with its comparisons of the main terms in our working paper is not completely definitive. The second diagram should further clarify the terms. Even in this diagram the separation of parish and world still remains unsatisfactory. It is correct to say that they represent two different fields. The diagram illustrates both the ancient cultural concepts of God which still exist, and the act of new creation which takes place at conversion via Christ, the Holy Spirit, and the parish. It is of vital importance for us to note that the parish remains in the world, and that therefore its deeds will never be perfect like the deeds of their Lord.

Our question is much more concerned with the proper relation of congregation and world to one another. "Who has more power?" or "In what way should we live as Christians and co-workers of God to pass his Word on to humanity?"

2. *False solutions*

In order not to allow history to repeat itself and the mistakes that were made in the course of 1900 years of church history, I would first draw your attention to those attempted solutions that have to be avoided and also those that do not correspond to the biblical message and the spirit of Jesus Christ.

a. The problem cannot be solved by changing the radical eschatological call for repentance of Jesus Christ into practicable rules of wisdom to facilitate the Christian existence of believers to the protracted return of Christ; for repentance is necessary until the Lord's return. We remain in the tension, we remain imperfect between the Bible and our culture until the Lord himself will accomplish his work that he so wonderfully began in us.

b. The problem cannot be solved by changing the offer of love and sanctification into causistic individual instructions in order to spare those living in a complicated cultural environment the necessity of deciding.

Although I agree with those advocating the idea of assisting young people in their decisions, I consider the opinion totally wrong that maintains that valid decisions can be made for another person. The results of such efforts may have an encouraging effect in their own cultural circle or they may evoke opposition. Christians of other cultural circles, however, might regard these efforts as amusing.

c. The problem cannot be solved by accepting the life-style of a parish or church without examining and propagating it as "the only right one." Although it is both necessary and desirable for a group of Christians to help its members by some form of group ethic, it is never-theless wrong to allow those customs — which in many cases are copies of the life-styles of their founders — to become obligatory and unim-peachable rules for the following generations, nations, races, and social groups.

d. The problem cannot be solved by some Christians withdrawing from the world and leading a holy life because they are dissatisfied with the liberal cultural openness of their parish. Conscience holds the individual responsible, but it is nevertheless wrong and even detrimental to religious welfare when people with spiritual open-mindedness and sensitive consciences let their ideas become the general attitude of the parish. In some cases they may even leave, if their intention does not bring forth immediate results. Withdrawal from the world into a holy life-style has to be an exception which ought to be carefully checked.

e. The problem cannot be solved by some Christians withdrawing from cultural life because they are dissatisfied with the prevailing cultural narrow-mindedness in their parish. Members of a given community come from different backgrounds and different outlooks. It is nevertheless wrong to assume that a Christian with greater intelligence, aesthetic gifts, and dynamic class-consciousness may lead his community to destruction. Denial of one's culture can be avoided in a normally operating parish through patient development of dissimilar forms of living and working under the one and only Lord. Every Christian is only a part of the body of Christ.

f. The problem cannot be solved by regarding the various fields of culture (e.g., natural science, pedagogics, psychology, social science, art) as autonomous and using them uncritically. A Christian may confess God as the creator of the universe, but he cannot ignore sin. He cannot hold that the more clever a thought, the more beautiful the creature, the more obvious it is that they are accepted as good or even "divine." As far as a community is concerned, culture must be seen from God's perspective and how best to serve all people according to his will.

g. The problem cannot be solved by calling every individual Christian to do what he likes in the name of personal freedom or in order to preserve peace. Although every Christian has his personal relationship with Jesus Christ — the one and only head of the body of Christ — this very Lord wants the whole congregation to belong together and to cooperate. Therefore there can neither be an uncontrolled "spiritual" individualism nor an unbalanced moral libertinism. Reason and feelings, determination and conscience, are to be subordinated to the rule of Jesus Christ — and this applies to everybody.

h. The problem cannot be solved when some theologians resign themselves to the immense tensions between the Bible and their culture, and state that "there 'are' no specifically Christian standards that are different from those ideas circulating in their society." Even though God has equipped each individual human being with culturally creative impulses, Jesus Christ has nevertheless come to begin a completely new creation. He does not merely bless the status quo. The relation between the Bible and culture cannot be determined without including sin, redemption, and Jesus Christ.

i. The problem cannot be solved by idealizing a community in the New Testament times and following its footsteps as the one way the biblical commission can be demonstrated. There was not even a perfect community in the first century. Therefore today's generation burdens itself unnecessarily with the idea of trying to copy Jerusalem, Rome, or Corinth. A community of the first or the twentieth-century can only be a model if its members live "in Christ." In this respect we have to learn from one another across cultural boundaries even though 2000 years or whole continents might separate us.

3. *Contributions to the right solution*

I am of the opinion that it should be our task to develop some kind of systematic cultural theology, if the suggested solutions are to be of value to whole communities and not just to a limited number of experts. Therefore I would like to suggest that the term we are aiming to define should be "the Christian life-style." Then the question runs as follows: How can we reach a Christian life-style within our community and for the individual Christian in the light of the tension between Bible and culture?

First, I would make some basic suggestions. Later I will give some examples that will demonstrate the direction that we Europeans might choose.

a. A basic element in Christian life-style is to learn how to distinguish the essential from the unessential from God's point of view. Jesus Christ, the Son of God, the Lord and Redeemer of the world, is the actual point of reference for us. Commitment to Christ must never become a relative relationship of secondary importance. It must remain absolute in all the situations we face. Only then can we be assured of security in existence and certitude in action (See diagram 3).

Whenever another human being, a desire, a trend, etc., gains absolute value in our daily lives and determines our actions there is bound to be conflict, unrest, sin, and loss of spiritual strength. The answer to that can only be repentance.

b. For a Christian life-style it is indispensable to experience the power of the risen Christ through the Holy Spirit. Only then can we expect Jesus Christ to dwell in us as Savior, friend, and Lord. Without experiencing Jesus Christ as a reality in a work-day routine every answer to the tension between Bible and culture becomes a theory and more frequently an oppressive rule. Lives, however, that are in the hands of Christ will basically experience happiness and hope. This applies in any culture.

c. A Christian life-style can only be developed in practical situations. Although it may be influenced by supra-national cultural mores, by the so-called national characteristics of a country, by family and psychological traits, it will still never be possible to establish a uniform Christian life-style on these bases. For example, there is no such thing as uniform European Christian life-style any more than there is a Christian life-style for a phlegmatic person.

God grants man the opportunity of remaining a creative and spiritual individual within the congregation of his Son. He is concerned about people and has a never-ending love for the individual in Jesus Christ. Consequently there is not only one Christian life-style but many variants in the total commitment to Christ. God regards no variant in itself as better or worse than the others. In practical terms this means that a tremendous number of individual tensions between Christ and culture, between the absolute and the relative, can be solved in many different ways. This is Christian freedom which saves us from pharisaism and fanaticism. Like our Lord, we show consideration for social and personal differences and level of spiritual maturity.

d. The individual Christian can only acquire a Christian life-style through careful self-control. This statement refers to a tension mentioned above which is, however, in accordance with the Gospel. I would like to illustrate the tensions mentioned with three related diagrams: cf. diagram 4 a-c, "Aids to self-control," cf. diagram 4 a, "Freedom and commitment." Under the term "freedom" we could put "culture" and on the other side under "conscience" the term "Bible."

First, this diagram is to show the necessity for the tension between two positive values, i.e., freedom and conscience. If this tension does not exist as illustrated on the upper horizontal line in the diagram, overemphasis of one part is bound to come about which will inevitably lead to the loss of harmony. The following diagram is to illustrate that the Christian conscience is mainly concerned with service to one's own neighbor (See diagram 4b).

No matter what the individual solutions with regard to life-style may be, each Christian has to live a life of entireness that exerts a positive influence on others, and influence that leads to God. Service is an essential element in the Christian life-style of any culture and in any generation. When we focus our attention on serving others (that they might have it more abundantly, John 10:10) we will soon discover that we are largely delivered from the search for increasing our personal rights and from the temptation to self-pity.

Nevertheless I would like to add a third partial diagram illustrating the fact that service is to be directed toward regeneration of individual lives (See diagram 4c).

This diagram proceeds from the premise that in this world man possesses a limited quantity of energy reserves to use for all phases of life. He needs recreation to be able to serve permanently. The danger has been indicated. On the other hand, there must not be any doubt that before God our neighbor is so important that one has to make sacrifices to serve — as Jesus Christ did.

A solution to the tensions illustrated in these diagrams can be found in the term good economical management in the context of the culture available to the individual or the congregation. We have to call for Christians to be faithful and good economical managers, and to find joy and satisfaction in their tasks both in view of our neighbor and eternity.

To sum up the picture, it is imperative to call for an active relationship to culture that is dealt with in the final chapter.

4. From cultural fear to cultural creation

In many cases Christians face some aspects of their culture in an insecure manner. It is understandable that in the early stages of revival a young Christian may not be able to experience the intellectual and spiritual strength to live alongside the boundaries of an ambivalent world, from which he has just been delivered. Such Christians may have developed a critical attitude toward culture or even cultural hostility, and cultivated their own forms of living in a parish that had isolated itself. In doing so they forfeited their natural contacts — even here in Europe — and thus their natural ability to tell their neighbors about Christ in word and deed. Their missionary impulse, however, continued to exist, nurtured by their personal experience of salvation and the message of the Bible. This impulse led to the foreign missionary service. Especially in Europe, evangelization particularly under the aspect of one's own country has come to a disastrous standstill.

On the basis of these observations, the final chapter of this paper is to submit only one thesis and to demand it especially for Europe. This thesis runs as follows: The congregations must have the courage to create new forms of living that bear the character of Christ from a biblical point of view regarding God and man, so that everyone can benefit from this service and be won for Jesus Christ. This thesis is to underline the fact that Christians were far too often concerned with questions of consumption in a passive way and discussed in detail to what extent Christians were allowed to make use of them.

Our attitude toward apologetic and creative action and culture as well as our own personal influence on other people and cultural practices, however, have to be completely in harmony with each other. Europe does not have to repulse foreign cultures and then try laboriously to find itself in the position of resistance, i.e., partially accepting foreign cultures. Rather, it is concerned with becoming active with the triune God in its own living situation. This is to be the basic idea of diagram 5.

This creative exerting of influence on the world is also important for another reason. A bored congregation has lots of excess energy which finally is reflected in criticism, flight, opposition, or in the sad attempt of constant increase in consumption.

A congregation with an apologetic relationship to culture, only is a bad economical housekeeper of the gifts of God, the Creator, the Redeemer, the Holy Spirit.

The following may be regarded as examples for the Christian influence on culture today:

a. *Orbit: music* — If we ask for the proper relation between Bible and culture from the consumer's perspective, we would run into a lengthy debate which from the biblical point of view would not be very helpful. Individual trends of taste are bound to collide with each other tending to regard themselves as the yardstick for the whole congregation.

If we ask, however, how to express our joy towards the Father in heaven, our admiration for the great things he has done, our gratitude for Jesus Christ, and our message to today's generation by means of music, it would be possible to combine all different kinds of tastes and use them for his glory. It is unproductive to ask what instruments and rhythms can be used in a Christian congregation. It is, however, extremely productive to ask how best to arouse the interest of other people for Christ through words, melody, and rhythm so that the

Christian Gospel can be proclaimed convincingly. One group, for example, may give a Bach concert, another modern songs of their own country, the third may perform a Christian musical — and all of them will reach different groups of people. Moreover, it would be profitable for latent creative gifts of many Christians to be expressed through new words and new musical arrangements. It has, however, to be observed that the ethical demand does not crush the warm real expression of faith.

b. *Orbit: material goods and their use* — All over Europe, Christians are facing the problem of how to use or misuse in an adequate way the material possibilities that are available in almost unlimited quantities and to keep in mind that there are only few important ethical variants at hand. It is not so much our task to consider this problem in view of foreign missions or development aid, but rather to examine it more closely with regard to our living in our own continent and country.

All of us know of the critical attitude of the Bible towards external or material things. And yet the Bible tells us that material goods in themselves are not abominable, nor do they say something about the character of a person. The decisive factor involves the proper use of these goods.

The constructive question of a wealthy congregation would run as follows. What missionary and diaconal tasks of our generation could be solved by financial means? To be more concrete: how could we make use of our apartments, our cars, our money, our leisure time, and our whole standard of living to the effect that both love and justice can dwell among us?

As soon as the Holy Spirit has opened our eyes to eternal dimensions, he wants our faith to be incarnated in a conspicuously new relation to the things of this world. The European sin, e.g., thoughtless, spoiled spending of money, possessions, and luxury can only be overcome through repentance and a new vision for our task. We would not gain anything if we started a discussion on the various standards of neighboring countries which are better off materially than we are, and therefore naturally obliged to greater asceticism and financial sharing. This is similar to the attitude of a reporter who likes to be regarded as modern and socially minded, calling upon the public for greater social justice but at the same time seeing to it that his own personal life remains unchanged. The use of material goods for the benefit of others has to become part of the Christian program to a greater extent than was evident in the generation of the last twenty-five years which was concerned primarily with the improvement of its standard of living. In our day we should be happy to be able to serve others. God cares for our material progress and an old-age pension through our own nations. It is our task to see to it that people learn about Jesus' opinion of men and that we spread his truth by every means available.

c. *Orbit: planning and future* — It may appear strange at first that in line with the examples of art and prosperity, future planning as part of cultural tension within the body of Christ should be discussed. I am, however, of the opinion that this subject does not only deserve to be mentioned but it is absolutely imperative to be discussed in European churches. Why?

It is a fact that our organizational methods today are largely not missionary-oriented but adhere to present systems. Furthermore, we are too involved with the past and too little with the future. We are the richest continent in historical maturity, in people, and financial resources, but at the same time the only continent where the number of Christians is decreasing constantly.

When the early Church in Jerusalem discovered a detrimental development in their own ranks, they did not hesitate to analyze the situation honestly, and this immediately led to a division of duties and the nomination of new co-workers. They were open to admit the disgrace of wrong leadership and decisions made in the interest of people and man.

Europe's top priority seems to be that we once again discover our forgotten intellectual gifts of cybernetics in our congregations (I Cor. 12:18) and to use them with determination for God's plan, i.e., to reconcile our fellowmen to God and make them his co-workers (Eph. 4:11). Local congregations, church managements, and theo-logical training centers finally have to summon up their courage to break away from their complacent, retrospective view of history and to return to a missionary existence with the risen Christ. In Europe we have lost a tremendous amount of credibility, and our willingness to serve is not taken for granted. Apart from our biblical slogans we have not had confidence in the Holy Spirit to act among the old and young members of the congregation. We have failed to give them at least some adequate training to enable them to face the world. People in key positions are to blame for these huge problems of mounting scepticism and lack of positive experience of the risen Lord, for they failed to plan creatively. In my opinion, most problems that exist can constantly be overcome if we approach our organizing task with confidence and good teamwork in the spirit and "style" of Jesus. It is not a question of more or less involvement with one's culture, but missionary service on our continent in the name of our Creator, the Reconciliator, and the Holy Spirit.

Questions

1. When and through which elements does a cultural advantage turn into sin? The tool of service?

2. Is there a possibility of "cultural practices" within the congregation such as good social relations, preaching, or songs degenerating and becoming sin? Please substantiate your answers briefly. How can a congregation escape such false development?

3. With regard to the term "cultural adaptation" name some biblical motives for cultural adaption and their individual situations.

4. *Main question:* In what way can we contribute to changing the

egocentric handling of the cultural question (abstention or participation) into a serving attitude (creative contribution)? Apart from some general guidelines you may name some examples on which we might report briefly.

Diagram 1. Bible and culture

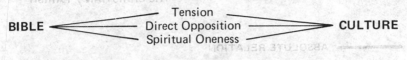

BIBLE ⟨————— Tension —————⟩ CULTURE
Direct Opposition
Spiritual Oneness

Diagram 2. The actual influences

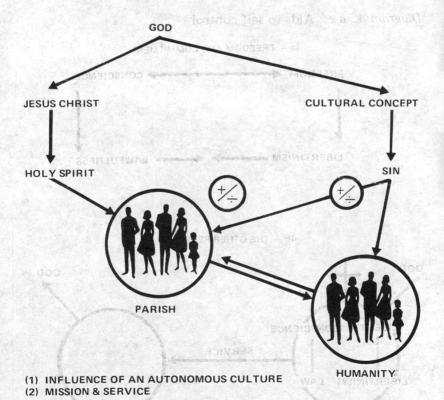

GOD

JESUS CHRIST   CULTURAL CONCEPT

HOLY SPIRIT   SIN

PARISH

HUMANITY

(1) INFLUENCE OF AN AUTONOMOUS CULTURE
(2) MISSION & SERVICE

Diagram 3:

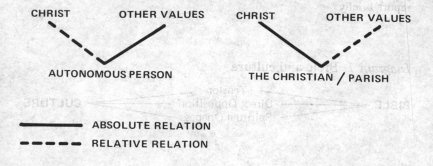

CHRIST   OTHER VALUES   CHRIST   OTHER VALUES

AUTONOMOUS PERSON   THE CHRISTIAN / PARISH

———————— ABSOLUTE RELATION

– – – – – – RELATIVE RELATION

Diagram 4. a-c: Aids to self control

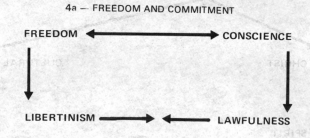

4a — FREEDOM AND COMMITMENT

FREEDOM ⟷ CONSCIENCE

LIBERTINISM → ← LAWFULNESS

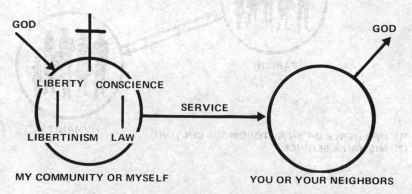

4b — THE OTHER PERSON AND I

GOD

LIBERTY   CONSCIENCE

LIBERTINISM   LAW   SERVICE →   GOD

MY COMMUNITY OR MYSELF   YOU OR YOUR NEIGHBORS

4c — ONE'S OWN LIFE AND SERVICE

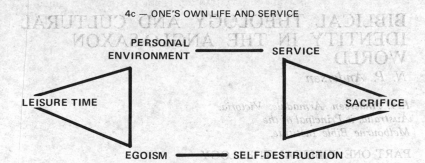

Diagram 5: A constructive relation to culture

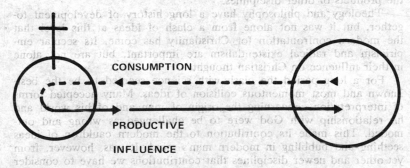

BIBLICAL THEOLOGY AND CULTURAL IDENTITY IN THE ANGLO-SAXON WORLD

N. P. Andersen

Rev. Andersen, Armadale, Victoria,
Australia, is Principal of the
Melbourne Bible Institute.

PART ONE: BIBLICAL THEOLOGY

That biblical theology is at a point of crisis has been stated so often as to have almost lost its vital quality of meaning.

In fact the crisis is no new phenomenon, but the result of powerful intellectual movements stretching back over several centuries. The post-Reformation period of history is bursting with movements of vital importance to the Christian faith, many of which challenge the premise on which biblical theology is built. Some of these movements have arisen within Christian thought and have been theological in content, others have been the outcome of the clash of Christian thought with the products of other disciplines.

Theology and philosophy have a long history of development together, but it was not alone from a clash of ideas at this level that the modern confrontation for Christianity has come. Its secular empiricism and radical existentialism are important, but are not alone in their influence on Christian thought.

For a long period the clash with science seemed to be the best-known and most momentous collision of ideas. Many accepted forms of interpretation concerning the origin of man and of his world and his relationship with God were to be challenged as wrong and outmoded. This made its contribution to the modern cauldron of ideas seething and bubbling in modern man's mind. It was, however, from yet other and newer disciplines that contributions we have to consider flowed.

Psychology, sociology, and perhaps more importantly anthropology brought to the fore ideas concerning man and his life and community which added a whole new section of vocabulary to language and demanded fresh interpretation from biblical scholars. When anthropology moved into the interesting field of study called "cultural anthropology" it brought into sharper focus many problems previously only vaguely sensed.

The interpretation of culture, the new understanding of its role in man's community life, the place of religion in this framework of living so important to primitive or sophisticated man, raised many new issues. How does the doctrine of revelation of God in Scripture relate to the writers of the various books within their own day and to the reader in various cultures in the twentieth-century?

The great upsurge of interest in translation of the Scriptures during the last two centuries has unveiled a great many problems and has brought to light many solutions which have enriched thought, but above all have revealed the accretions of culture to the Gospel. The question

is being asked in so many different ways and demands an answer:
"Is this the message of God in Christ, or is this some Western development that the messenger of the Gospel had best forget?"

While cultural relativism and secularism owe something to this
discipline we ought not to be afraid of the consequences of facing
the issues raised. Some interpreters of culture see faith in God as the
very antithesis of man's effort in his culture; Marxists believe that
men make history and culture and that religion is a sleeping pill, yet
these ideas are only part of the case we examine.

Nowhere in the Gospels do we find Christ dealing specifically
with the problem of culture as such. All he did and said was oriented
to the immediate context of people's lives, it was a continuation of
the message of the Old Testament, and this was culturally oriented.

On the other hand, E. Nida points out, "In Jesus Christ there is a
break with the past, a discontinuity with culture, his followers were
to be in the world but not of it." Richard Niebuhr points up the same
problem when he quotes from Klauser who claims, "Judaism is a national life. . . . In their stead he set up nothing but an ethico-religious
system bound up with his conception of the Godhead."

Niebuhr goes on to draw attention to the difficulty the Graeco/
Roman world faced when it tried to understand Christianity. In some
ways, he declares, the cultural problem was possibly greater than the
political or economic one. Pliny in his letters to Trajan helps make
this point — his query is much more in the field of culture than any
other.

Williams takes up this theme as he describes the early Church
theologians facing the culturing difficulty of Christianity which began
on Jewish soil and had to become part of the cultural milieu of the
Gentile world. Yet he can go on to report the transformation of European thought by this new intruder. For some scholars, Christianity
and Western culture are so inextricably entwined that there is no way
by which a Christian can talk to a member of another civilization. For
others, who do not venture so far, the need is to identify what are
cultural accretions as compared to what are the fundamentals of
God's revelation.

The problem can be stated quite simply as E. Wright has done,
"How are we to outline the present biblical theology? . . . In the Bible
these doctrines are so inter-related in historical context that they
cannot be separated and examined entirely as independent objects
of reflection."

In facing this study we have to accept the problem of terminology.
It is difficult to be certain of the use of words from one scholar to
another; this is particularly the case when we use technical words to
describe some new theory or school of thought. For example: "demythologize" no longer is used simply as a term to describe Bultmann's
development of Form Criticism in his New Testament studies. It is
used more widely and can quite satisfactorily be used in this study —
we can evaluate attempts to demythologize cultural accretions. Whether
this is the best term to use is debatable — it is an emotive word and
would require considerable effort by some to escape their normal

emotional reaction to Bultmann's theory. Further, so much would depend on the definition of "myth." It would seem best, in this study to limit the term to describe one of the modern methods — namely Bultmann's and to summarize other methods by their own chosen terms.

In attempting an evaluation of current theories and then finally to try to determine cultural forms usable by modern man it is essential that we recognize the "reality of God is still the central problem." Sooner or later it is fundamental to all questions about man and society. Man cannot understand himself and answer questions about himself without reference to God.

Michelsen sums up the situation well, "But if he is preoccupied with history and culture, the interpreter can treat the content as secondary to the reconstruction of the original setting. History and culture, then, as secondary elements, are essential for the understanding of content. Out of a complex maze of events and into the agonizing pressures of daily existence, God's message came and confronted men with God himself."

Barr in the search for the real question for theology rejects the "Level of cultural patterns, inherited presuppositions underlying thought forms," and sees it in "relation of groups and individuals as they stand within or without the people of God." This is enough to warn us to use our topic with care, to examine and evaluate modern theories of cultural accretion, and to seek to come to our own concept of the medium of communication from the central position of "God's revelation of himself."

Where do we start in our brief attempt to cope with those who deal with cultural assertions? It could be done by a chronological summary of the details of theology in the twentieth century. However logical this may seem let me lead you in another way and select theories at random. Not select on popularity or danger to a true understanding of biblical theology — but more in the light of the interest they have aroused. Not all theories can be evaluated, the selection may reveal something of the writer's own areas of interest.

1. *Myth and demythologizing*

Many modern theologians are attempting to deal with the problem of the Bible by the use of the world "myth." The assumption is that myth and history are so interwoven that the Bible may be described as mythical. For some the Bible is regarded as essentially untrue and foreign to modern men; for others it is acceptable, provided modern man can unravel the "ultimate questions" behind myth by separating all such from the sequence and causality in empirical data.

Bultmann believes that most of the biblical terms are not usable as they stand, they require re-interpretation. He calls this process of interpretation, hermeneutic, and his method, demythologizing. He does not intend to get rid of mythology, but to reinterpret it to the man of today. W. Nichols believes that the definition of myth is not of great importance to Bultmann, "It would appear that his program of demythologizing would hold good for him, whatever sense of myth were agreed on."

Myth is meant to express man's understanding of himself in the world in which he lives and should be interpreted not cosmologically, but anthropologically, or better still existentially. This is not the way the liberal predecessors of Bultmann dealt with myth — they eliminated it. Bultmann, like Barth, does not; he retains the myth. It cannot be accounted for in terms of culture and yet when the first-century cosmology is removed by Bultmann, are not the objective statements bound up with the cosmology removed also?

The core of his theology is "kerygma," the proclamation as a human event in which God speaks — it is not the product of human culture, but the Word of the transcendent God, and it is here that his existentialist analysis cannot apply. Analogy is used, but not very convincingly.

Bultmann seeks to separate salvation and the Gospel from any sort of world view and the question is immediately apparent: is it possible to be free from such a world view and to see it divorced from faith? Bultmann minimized the importance of the historical aspects of Jesus' life as unimportant for faith, and stressed the importance of the kerygma.

In all of these matters the border between mythological and non-mythological tends in practice to be somewhat blurred. The Bultmannian language may be intelligible when it deals with human experience and existence. But it does not come nearer an explanation of God. Why can the Holy Spirit be demythologized? "Biological man cannot see how a supernatural entity like 'pneuma' can penetrate within the close texture of his natural powers and set to work within him" and yet God can be described as "God is incomprehensible, enigmatic power that surges through my concrete life and sets limits to it."

This has been a continuing problem for Bultmann and he later used analogy as a means of demythologizing God. "He does not show the relationship between the two ways. There is a logical difference between existential language which refers to its proper subject 'human existence,' and its existential language which is said to refer analogically to God as its subject. Bultmann nowhere seems to have paid sufficient attention to this logical difference."

In closing this sub-section, attention needs to be drawn to the danger of subjectivism in the method of existential interpretation of myth. All ideas are taken to refer to elements in our own inner life. Attempts to escape from this conclusion lead to a further idea of myth that then includes a transcendent reference, but only if history is understood as the history that everyone experiences for himself and not world history.

In his small book *Frontiers of Modern Theology*, Carl Henry lists the theological groups who have taken the place of Bultmann — our interest, however, lies in examining other efforts to deal with cultural accretions.

2. *Secular theology*

The glamour word at the moment would seem to be "secular."

Theologies of the secular-Christian type ante-date the Death of God theologies. Its warrant from Bonhoeffer is clearer than the latter.

In secular theologies, Bonhoeffer's concept that God allowed himself to be edged out is the usual starting point. This leaves the initiative with God, in comparison to Christian atheism which demands that the Christian should will the death of God. Secular Christianity flows in two streams: E. Van Buren demands that the word "God" be cut out of the vocabulary and so seems to be one with the Christian atheist; the other stream just remains silent on this issue.

Harvey Cox argues that secularization has its meaning in the first place in "desacralization" first of nature then of politics. The creation and exodus stories show both of these processes in the Bible. Cox does not deal with man's relationship with God. Biblical faith desacralizes the cosmos — to achieve this concept Cox has to place an evolution of religous consciousness in the Bible. This is difficult to sustain from the biblical theme of human response to revelation and also from Andrew Lange's work on "high gods."

Cox reads the Bible in developmental and sociological terms; he identifies the secular city with the Kingdom of God. Here the promise of new life is offered, here conversion offers a hope that cannot fade — outside the secular city there is no salvation for man.

Cox conceives of creation without the fall, he imagines partnership with God to be sufficient Christian description of human existence. The acts of God are what increase "human freedom." For Cox, secular Christianity lays bare the real meaning of Christianity and so is another modern attempt to clear away accretions. The supernatural Christianity fitted the needs of the time of ignorance, secular Christianity is a religion fitting the needs of maturity. This shows an acceptance of Bonhoeffer's world-come-of-age, but not of his willingness to make room for God and the world in the heart.

Professor Saran in *Religion and Society* sets out the aim with great clarity. "Secular theologians feel deeply concerned about making religion (church) individually and socially relevant and significant to the industrial, technological modern man . . . he therefore strives for a reinterpretation of the Christian tradition which will be consistent with modern knowledge and consciousness."

In summing up his opinion of secularism, John Macquarrie writes, "The secular has its legitimate claims and rightly condemns all false religiosity. But we have seen too that the secular has possibilities for exaggeration and distortion that are incompatible with Christian faith." In the final assessment we can record Macquarrie's quotation of Cragg's criticism of Van Leeuen, "We would be either strangely naive or incredibly arrogant if we supposed that a technology of which our hemisphere had been the matrix sufficiently represented the world obligations of Christian faith or fulfilled them in the only feasible contemporary form."

3. *Cultural relativism*

Among the many strands of thought in radicalism is that of cultural relativism. Its importance requires some time and space in our study.

The position has been well presented by Barr, "The Bible, like all other literary works, is dependent on the cultural milieu in which it was written. Our modern culture is different, and it is not possible that the same book, the Bible, can have the same meaning as it had in its own cultural milieu. Any work or text composed in an ancient time and in an ancient culture has its meaning in that time and culture, and in our time and culture may have a different meaning or indeed no meaning at all."

Cultural relativism has no place for biblical authority, that is, at least in its extreme forms. Any effort to update for modern man is a waste of time. Much is made by this school of thought of whether human nature changes, or not, also of what are described as "apparent absurdities," e.g., women wearing hats in church and finally of the problem falling on the translator to show the Bible is right. The accidental nature of much biblical material is also derided.

In trying to assess this movement the following points of criticism seem to be valid:

(i) They encapsulate man in his own culture.

(ii) They assume that cultures do not borrow or adapt.

(iii) They place religion in a one-way traffic with culture, when in fact it is a two-way movement.

(iv) In rejecting the "human nature does not change" thesis, this school of thought overplays the position; there is a degree of similarity. Ancient drama reveals character by its acting with many of the emotions, feelings and problems of modern man.

In conclusion, it would seem that a great deal more thought is needed in examining this thesis, especially in the light of translation success as achieved by Nida, Pyke, Smalley, Larson, and others. Cross-cultural communication is difficult, but achievement by the methods being successfully carried forward to modern man in multiple cultural situations is an indication of a line of development for biblical theological thought by theologians in relationship to the "culture-relativists,"

4. *"Religionless Christianity"*

The above term also is popularly linked with modern man's attempt to analyze accretions in order to rediscover the genuine Gospel. The movement against religion received its emphasis from Barth. Bonhoeffer felt that Barth started in the right direction but did not go far enough. In his *Letters*, Bonhoeffer claims that Barth gives no non-religious interpretation of theological concepts.

His demand is not to do away with false religion, but to do away with religion. Leon Morris quotes from the *Letters* and comments, "'God is teaching us that we must live as men who can get along very well without him,' writes Bonhoeffer. This does not mean that religion must be kept in its place. It means that there is no place for religion."

Bonhoeffer sees Christianity religiously conceived for 1900 years, its view of God conditioned by religious expectations — now the false god of religion must give way to the true God. The *deux ex machina* of false religion is present when men want him, the true God is present through the Cross by suffering and powerlessness. The distinction is one of power and weakness, true transcendence is not a metaphysical notion, it is the presence of a "person who is for others."

In concluding his article on Bonhoeffer in *Interchange*, Klaus Runia writes, "But these exceptional circumstances do not give us the right to posit a religionless Christianity as the ideal situation for our day." He goes on to suggest the need for a radical re-thinking of religious language and Christian activity if we are to present a viable alternative.

In analyzing Bonhoeffer's concept, Leon Morris adds, "But religionless Christianity appears to mean the abandonment of any real emphasis on Christian doctrine and worship. The question then arises, what contribution have Christians to make to the new world that is to arise? It seems to me that the logic of religionless Christianity is that the Christian Church has no great role to play."

5. *The death of God*

This is most dramatically set forth by Altizer and Hamilton in what they call "Christian atheism." Their assertion is that the God who once was alive is now dead — the death of God is an historical event, God died in our time, in our history. Nietzsche's phrase is taken over; Hamilton claims that the difference between a Christian atheist and a secular atheist is "not the absence of the experience of God but the experience of the absence of God."

Van Buren, who belongs in this category although quite far removed in some ways from Hamilton and Altizer, says, "The word 'god' is dead, he goes on to point out that we are no poorer for this loss, all we need we have in the man Jesus Christ." Francis Schaeffer comments, "But Jesus here turns out to be a non-defined symbol. They use the word because it is rooted in the memory of the race. It is humanism with a religious banner called Jesus to which they can give any content they wish." Altizer and Hamilton write of the aim to liberate man from God and from the struggle of faith, "To be free from God as the meeter of needs and solver of problems."

It would seem that this concept of God is far removed from that of the Bible where God is the very ground of freedom and hope, the God through whom men have found themselves. He is the one by whom we make sense of life. The revelation of God in the Scriptures is not tyrannical but creative, who sets life in the context of grace and judgment. The atheist makes himself or human society the measure of all things, and claims that belief is a survival from the past — the sign of immaturity.

Van Buren's use of the sentence analysis of Wittgenstein where meaning is determined by how the phrase functions allows for any amount of religious doctrine. Along with other linguistic positivists this thesis will be difficult for Van Buren to validate and is one of the factors to be examined in assessing the value of this method of dealing with cultural accretions.

One other concept, from Altizer, needs a brief mention. He sees modern man living in the chaos of nihilism, of a new meaninglessness,

"The new humanity lying on our horizon can be reached only by means of a voyage through the darkness which has fallen with the breakdown of our past." Altizer demands that contemporary Christians forsake their faith in order to remain with secular man. "We must recognize that to cling to the Christian God in our time is to evade the human situation in our century and to renounce the unsuitable suffering which is its lot. Already a Kierkegaard and a Dostoevsky knew that no suffering can be foreign to the Christian, not even the anguish that comes with the loss of God, for the way of the Christian is to bear with Jesus all the pain of the flesh."

These theories pervert the essence of New Testament Christianity and make claims that will not bear the test of analyses by true biblical theology. Modern man does not see Christianity becoming respectable by dispensing with God-talk, but is hungry for the reality of the transcendent God.

6. *Ground of being*

The last representative to be added to this list is Tillich who perhaps goes further than any others in trying to give the Christian faith an expression that will render it intelligible to the world while preserving its unique substance.

Tillich interprets man in a religious way — man has a "God-shaped-blank" in his soul, a religious *a priori* assuredly exists. This man is very much in the dark and certainly has not "come of age." His awareness is constantly invaded by despair, finitude, guilt, suffering, loneliness, estrangement, doubt, and meaninglessness. These factors throw man beyond himself to God-being itself. Man is essentially religious, aware of his finitude which drives him towards the infinite.

When we turn to Tillich's teaching on God we find a very radical departure from the doctrine of God as it is set forth in biblical theology. God is that which ultimately or unconditionally concerns us. God is Being itself, he is not a being, consequently God is not a person, but he seems to say God is personal. God's existence is not relevant, being itself does not exist. God as Being — itself and as ultimate concern are the two themes, important to the understanding of God. Tillich objects strongly to supranaturalism, which incidentally is not identical with supernatural; over against supranaturalism he puts "self-transcending" or "ecstatic naturalism."

All descriptions of God, other than "Being itself" he regards as symbolical and non-literal. The central symbolic descriptions are that he is "living," "personal," "creative and abysmal ground of being," "spirit," "love." God is living inasmuch as he is the ground of life. Ground here does not mean "cause" or "substance," but something which underlies all things in some way or other which we can describe only by means of some such symbol as cause. This, of course, led to the popular term "ground of our being," God is creative because he is God and it is meaningless to talk of creation as a necessary or contingent act of God. Creation is not the story of an event, it is identical with God's life.

Tillich employs the symbol of "depth," to indicate that God is in the world, not out beyond it. God as Being itself within which human self and all other beings have their being is Tillich's contribution and yet even he is not certain. He conceives his vocation as "on the boundary," an attempt to explain to modern man the Christian's relation to the reality of God. The tentativeness of the idea surely cuts into the reasonableness of the proposition. "At almost every point, I have to stand between alternative possibilities of existence, to be completely at home in neither and to take no definitive stand against either." Even if this is defined as the meeting point of two dimensions belonging to one world, it still leaves man without the certainty which the biblical teaching implies.

He accepts much crucial biblical material as "myth" which he conceives as the "language of faith," and although he takes a different line of approach to Bultmann, it nevertheless does not help "biblical theology" to bring a true message to modern man. While using biblical terminology, Tillich so changes its meaning as to finish up with another message; or to use the criticism of one modern scholar, "He has interpreted the Gospel into a language nobody is speaking." Modern man cannot be blamed for asking whether he is not left with something nearer Eastern Pantheism than the Christian faith.

These summaries are brief and have been limited to analyses only in relationship to our theme. They could be described as the major, but not the only, attempts by Christian scholars to remove what are called the "cultural accretions" which have caused inquiries in Asia, Africa, and other parts of the world to ask whether Christianity is a "Western" religion.

While these theories have thrown up many ideas worthy of consideration, none are satisfactory as the answer of modern man's dilemma. They do not answer the despair of philosophers like Heidegger, Jaspers, Camus, and Sarte. Nor is the existential experience as attractive to the man on the street as some forms of Eastern transcendentalism, or the charismatic attraction of modern Pentecostalism. The demythologized Bible is no more readable to modern man than the King James version. God as the "ground of my being" falls short of the traditional doctrine behind Christ's prayer, "Our Father." The rediscovery of the Jesus of history gives no brighter light than in the original discovery. A better view of man related to history and of biblical history as part of world history is emerging, but as our second portion of study reveals, evangelical scholarship has an unprecedented opportunity to point man to the true message of God.

We cannot neglect the world in which we live, nor ignore history, nor is it valid to reject the Bible as revelation of God. Other disciplines have contributions to make and can only be assessed against the background of God's initiative towards man.

PART TWO: CULTURAL FORMS AND BIBLICAL PRINCIPLES

In a very stimulating article, "The Relevance of Scripture Today," Montgomery Watt says, "It is the firm conviction of the writer that the Bible does not need to be 'made relevant' to twentieth-century man, any more than it needed to be made relevant to fifth-or seventeenth-century man."

This assertion leaves a lot to be examined: the understanding of God and man and the whole gamut of Christian doctrine as conceived at this point of time is the product of how the various centuries realized the relevance of the Word of God in their own day. Each interpreted and in so doing added its ideas which are part of the tradition which inevitably we have to examine. While the evidence Montgomery Watt adduces is correct, in each case the message has come to each recipient and has been decoded in the light of his own day and environment. When twentieth-century man reads God's Word, how does he decode?

We have reviewed what the writer believes are the failures of some Christian scholars to decode correctly the Eternal Word in the light of current disciplines of thought. Does this mean there is no alternative? Certainly not! Many evangelical scholars are producing material which interprets for modern man the timelessness of God's Word. At times, in so doing, some disciplines have been shown to be the victims of defective logic or of incomplete scientific truth, or of unproven theses. But frequently the interpreter of the Christian message has to recognize and point out that certain concepts held to be Christian are not part of the "core" of Christian truth. The alleged infallibility of the bishop of Rome, denominational emphases in the sacraments, methods of church government, all drawn from Scripture plus, are but a few of the cases that could be compiled. Modern man asks the question Montgomery Watt answers later in his article, "Is the Bible relevant today?" Can a fully authoritative Scripture, as attested by historic evangelical Christianity, speak as clearly to the needs of the present and the future as it evidently did to the needs of the past?

The attempt to answer this question is made in four areas of life: the church's worship, ethical behavior, evangelism, and service in the world. Before we deal with each of these, a few thoughts at a general level are called for.

Our world is a place of rapid change and due to the spread of the mass media one area of change is that brought about by the impact of various cultures on other cultural groups. Our title restricts us to the Anglo-Saxon world, but it could legitimately be asked if this is clearly identifiable today. For this reason the writer is thinking more in terms of the "West" as that is loosely understood today.

Who could adequately measure the influence of radical thought on the university campuses of the West and in the forms of the trade union movement, the effect of rock music, and the drug culture? How can we assess the influence on twentieth-century man of some modern theological catch-cries? "God is dead!" "The Church is an Anachronism." "The influence of situation ethics for man come of age."

What is the result of modern man's thinking about problems of ecology and the growing wave of brutality and violence? Or perhaps more important, the vast effect of theories of education now permeating secondary schools? Population explosion, racism, urbanization, are further pressures molding the thought patterns of modern man. Many other movements, political, economic, sociological, and religious could be added to the above. All reveal the complex culture patterns of the modern man to whom we are seeking to reveal the core of the Christian faith as given by God.

a. *The church's worship* — This is a vital area of Christian life and experience, and yet one in which the vitality of reality seems to have disappeared and "form" or "tradition" have taken control.

The role of worship must be to reflect the believer's response to the truth of God. It must be vertical before it can be horizontal. Marx wrote of man's alienation from man (the Scripture talks of man's alienation from God), and worship, irrespective of its liturgical pattern must first give opportunity to express man's gratitude and joy that God has taken the initiative in the restoration of this relationship. It must be objective before it can be subjective. It must also give expression to the wonder of faith, i.e., the personal trust of the individual in God through Christ.

Further, worship must be intimate enough to develop the "fellowship" of the Gospel in the way that bridges race, social status, education, and even language. The church has failed lamentably at this point.

Cultural forms become the by-product of these basic essentials. The form a service takes will vary from culture to culture. So long as it helps the worshiper in the problem of values and meaning in life, and helps him to relate to the only source whereby these can be evaluated, it is functioning as it is meant to do.

Worship can bring to man the recovery of the dimension of transcendence, and this helps man find the significance of faith in its cognitive, emotional, and volitional aspects. Certain sociological trends indicate a new place for worship (see Henry Rach and his *Twentieth-century Spirituality,* where the author discusses the significance for worship of the sociological trend noted from communal groups to associational groups).

In a study of the history of worship it is noteworthy that there was a radical change from Middle Ages to the post-Reformation era. Changes in music in response to changing times have left the church with a vast heritage by which to praise God in worship. The music which is popular in the secular world today is having its influence on sacred music, not however without conflict and controversy. The question is raised, "What is wrong with it if it speaks to the modern man as older forms of music no longer do?" The confusion of thought here is intensified because frequently the champions of old versus new sit on either side of a generation gap. Do those who cling to the conservative ways represent a cultural phenomenon? We have to recognize that the music of the early twentieth-century church is very different from that of the church of five hundred years ago. Is change then wrong, or does it merely represent change in culture reflecting itself into our emotional response to God? Do we need to discriminate between "beat" and ordinary music forms?

Does a change in architecture reflect anything for worship, or are we simply in the hand of the technician? Is the sermon-centered form of worship viable for our day, or is it a relic of an age now gone? These thoughts only begin to reflect the immensity of the question.

When a Christian worships, he is expressing in community action the corporate nature of all spirituality. The people of God are not simply a collection of individuals, but a gathered people needing to meet together to break bread and to pray. Christ took flesh to become the head of the body, the new people of God, and at worship we have an encounter in faith with Christ and with each other. If this experience is to be real to the member and the outsider, somehow the expression of its "worth" must be clear. It must say what we know about the meaning of life and what we are trying to be because we are the people of God.

The so-called "symbol collapse," whether referring to verbal symbols or ordinary ones, can be reversed by interpreting afresh in the language of our day the depth of meaning in the original. This will come about by careful research linguistically oriented along with a renewal of spiritual power. The Holy Spirit, as teacher, awaits in each generation those believers through whom he can bring the newness of wonder — this must be in the pew as well as in the pulpit. Thus worship would precede evangelism and evangelism would be the fruit of worship (Acts 2:47). Always the vertical must bring about the time-line for the horizontal, then the form of the horizontal can change from group to group, age to age, and remain vital and relevant.

b. *Ethical behavior* — Joseph Fletcher's book *Situation Ethics* is a typical example of modern attempts to find an answer to behavior questions when the authority of God is removed. Nothing is universally right or wrong; goodness and badness are not built in, essential, unchangeable qualities of anything; only one thing is intrinsically good — love, and it is the same as justice.

A very clear statement about this relating of Christian ethics to the secular world is set out by Professor Barclay in his book *Ethics in A Permissive Society*. The issues are dealt with by Lutzer in his *The Morality Gap*. There are others who have written on this theme, perhaps the small book by Martyn Lloyd-Jones should be added as it is a book of "biblical theology" — a study of Romans, *The Plight of Man and the Power of God*.

In this section there is not the simplicity noted in the previous study. Here we have biblical principles as a cogent part of revelation and no amount of cultural relativity can be used to escape the implications of the revelation. The marked change in behavior patterns of the last fifty years can be traced back to the movements of thought which have reduced the Word of God to an outmoded piece of literature, to theories which have put man at the center of religion and ethics. Instead of religion being the source of behavior, it became an appendage. Godliness is essential to ethics — this is the message of both Old Testament and New Testament.

Biblical principles leave us no choice — we are absolutists and can have no relationship with either the situationalists or the hierarchialist. Having said this, we have dealt with an issue of vital importance. However, another issue remains to be considered: are all the codes of behavior, dress, etc., always related to these absolutes? Once again we will be called on to note a variety of answers from different cultural groups. Many patterns of behavior are good; they are the oil that helps the machinery of a society to continue to function — but they are not essential and can be changed. Study needs to be carried out to try to show where certain matters are fundamental and where others are cultural and can be done away with. Too often biblical truth is saddled with concepts which are purely social and yet people cling to them eagerly.

Many people have been turned away from God's Word because its message has been encumbered with cultural and social shibboleths. The intrinsic value of the moral laws of Scripture needs to be made clear to our contemporaries and given the opportunity to be seen for what they are.

The true nature of God must be proclaimed along with the following great themes to rescue them from becoming lost as appendages of prior cultures. To attempt a list is to invite criticism and yet to fail to do so robs this portion of the study of its realism.

(i) The right of life (homicide, euthanasia, abortion, suicide.)

(ii) Sex as God-given in marriage (homosexuality, adultery, premarital intercourse, prostitution, lust).

(iii) Freedom (racism, slavery, worship, expression of opinion).

(iv) Truth, honesty (stealing, false witness).

(v) Envy, jealousy, hatred (the sins of the spirit and of motive).

(vi) The community responsibility, the strong help the weak, place no cause of stumbling.

(vii) Marriage, divorce.

It must be admitted that some of these are open to interpretation (e.g., when does life come to the foetus?), but the basic norms are there and relate to the being of God and man's relationship to God.

c. *Evangelism* — The vehicle which carries God's truth to man is evangelism, the proclamation of God's existence, of man's relationship to God, of man's destruction of that relationship, of God's initiative to deal with man's revolt, of God's offer to man of his salvation.

Christ told his disciples that he was "truth," he taught that the Holy Spirit was the "Spirit of truth" and would lead his followers into truth; this is part of the Bible's testimony to God as the source of all truth. But today man is busy trying to forget that this is so.

Modern theologians say God is dead, truth is relative, the masters of propaganda, both political and commercial, have taken words and twisted and warped their meaning. George Marsden entitled an article on this problem "Evangelicals in Wonderland." He sets forth the danger of the attack on words. We have to use them for the message of evangelism, we can convey truth, even its ultimate truth about God. Carl Henry takes this up trenchantly, "Nothing is more foundationally important for the world and for the church in the twentieth-century than a recovery of truth. Truth-famine is the ultimate and worst of all famines. Unless modern culture recovers the truth of truth and the truth of God, civilization is doomed to oblivion and the spirit of man to nihilism."

It is against this backdrop of a cultural state of worldwide confusion of terms and truth that evangelism must stand and declare God as the judge of culture and as ultimate truth.

The task of evangelism is greater than ever; it must declare the whole truth of God, on a world scale. Man must be given back a new clarity which only God can give. The forces arrayed against such a project are immense; the powers of evil see man in their grasp and have the media to increase this hold and will yield nothing in the battle for man. Evangelism is God's weapon of proclamation (I nearly wrote counter-proclamation, but that would be wrong). It is the purveyors of "untruth" who make the counter-proclamation. The confusion on this arises because

at present these forces seem to have all before them and the church
seems unable to compete. But this is an illusion — among the confusions
of the twentieth-century nothing is worse than the confused state of
man's own thought about himself, his destiny, and his relationship to
ultimate authority.

Evangelism has power at its disposal, "But you shall receive power
when the Holy Spirit comes upon you" (Acts 1:8); "the Gospel is God's
dynamis (dynamite) unto salvation" (I Cor. 15:3-4); "so that your faith
might be built, not upon human wisdom, but on the power of God" (I Cor.
2:1-5).

These comments do not relate to the "methodology" of evangelism —
it is here that culture can and should play a part. Some time ago Bishop
Chandu Ray reported on the new life which was coming to evangelism
in Asian countries when the concept of using Western patterns was no
longer regarded as binding. This is the result of the Congress on Evangelism held in Singapore in 1968. Proclamation in some areas became a
"family" matter, because the family was the basic unit of the community.

There is a lesson here at a wider level; the sub-culture of every community will respond to the evangel if it is brought in meaningful ways.
The content of the message has an amazing capacity to be translated
to different cultures, the methodology needs to recognize the cultural
challenge. When this is accepted, the timeless, God-given message begins
to pulsate with life — the spoken and written word becomes potent.
When this is allied with the biblical requirement of demonstration of
the truth in life, then the deadness of orthodoxy is circumvented and
faith has the opportunity to demonstrate its power.

Man has the right to stand by God, made in the image of God, justified by faith in what God has done for him, to stand over and against
all else in nature, and thus to find God's purpose and satisfaction.

Francis Schaeffer has recently published *He Is There and He Is Not
Silent.* This is evangelism's message. The words may be updated to bring
meaning to modern man, but the centrality of this message must be
flung out to mankind. Os Guiness in his *Dust of Death* calls for evangelism that takes the message of the Bible to man in its totality — what
God says in the world, what God says in man, what God says in the
Bible, what God says in Christ. Put these concepts together and we
have evangelism expressed in biblical concepts in a way understandable
by modern man.

d. *Service in the world* — Biblical theology shows both individual
conversion and social justice to be indispensable; personal holiness
of living and social responsibility are closely linked.

The Bible reveals "a new man" who is immediately committed to
love of neighbor. The biblical doctrine of man, made in the image of
God, and of God's ceaseless activity of redemption, opens up an area
of responsibility which the early church accepted. Gibbon, the historian,
acknowledges the importance of Christian benevolence in the triumph
of Christianity. The continuing history of the church saw this line of
practice fluctuate a great deal, but always there was the evidence of
concern for the needy.

Marsden lists the nineteenth-century concern of evangelicals in his article "Dusting off the Heritage" in *Christianity Today*. That this declined during the twentieth-century, probably due to the influence of the "social gospel," is a factor which needs to be recognized as we examine the present confrontation. We have also to check and assess the claim of the radicals that even at its best this is "a doctor at the bedside of capitalism."

Is service in the world to be restricted to the individual, to treating social symptoms rather than removing the causes of the ills of society? David Claydon writes, "But in this generation the absence of a developed strategy on the community front stands out in stark contrast to the highly geared programs for ministering to individuals."

That problems of race, poverty, war, over-population, ecology, and many others need overall strategy is only just being rediscovered. The area to be researched is vast. Max Weber claimed that Protestantism was largely responsible for the birth of capitalism and the shape of the modern world. Marx, Engels, and Lenin had proclaimed a similar thesis when they attacked the one-dimensional society largely shaped by Christian authoritarianism. Whether such claims can stand investigation, whether the process of preparing a Christian strategy for true service in the world is feasible — these are areas for discussion and thought.

Evangelicals in education face a herculean task as they face the challenge of service in their own field. *The Journal of Christian Education* has shown that positive and fruitful work goes on. This is true also in other disciplines. However, it seems that any concept of a concerted attack is far from being realized.

Our task then, rests in both areas of activity mentioned above. "The cup of cold water" must be given in greatly increased ways to meet the need of the individual at the moment of suffering. The greater strategy to help eradicate or reduce evil calls for vision and planning of those trained to see the need and capable of response. This must not be separated from the fact of man's greatest need — the vertical must be proclaimed before the horizontal can be projected, "Thou shalt love the Lord thy God . . . and thy neighbor as thyself."

Bangkok is a symbol of failure because true concern for strategy and achievement at a world level has been rooted in man and his ability. To ignore the biblical pattern, or to select out of context, as so often was the case, biblical material to give an air of biblical faith and theory presents man with as great a source of future disappointment as can be imagined.

Carl Henry writes, "Social action must not be viewed as an independent and detachable concern, nor may the preaching of the Gospel be aborted from the whole counsel of God. Fundamental to biblical theology is the revelation of the true and living God, the God both of justice and justification."

J. N. D. Anderson has set out seven points to develop broad biblical principles in the matter of social responsibility:

"(1) That God originally created man in his 'image' and after his likeness' (Gen. 1:26). It is this which gives man his initial worth.

(2) That when man had fallen into sin Christ died to save him.

(3) That God made the material world, and must have a purpose

for it as such. 'Everything created by God is good' (I Tim. 4:4), and we must accept all that God has given with gratitude, even where it is ministered through unbelievers. One way in which we give glory to God is by using created things rightly, that is in accordance with the creator's revealed will (I Cor. 10:31).

(4) That in the new creation all things are to be summed up in Christ as head (Eph. 1:10), for his Cross has somehow reconciled not only the world of men but the whole material and spiritual universe (Col. 1:20).

(5) That in the meanwhile the world is still under God's government and is still the object of his love and concern.

(6) That Christ taught that every man is our 'neighbor' whom we must love and serve; that the prophets passionately proclaimed God's demand for social justice; and that the apostles unequivocally stated that such human institutions as the family and the state are God-ordained, designed to fulfill particular functions and purposes for the welfare of the race.

(7) That Christ said that his servants were not only to be the 'light' of society but also its 'salt' — presumably in the sense of a preservative from evil."

There can be no Christian doctrine of service in the world which is not God-centered, which does not reach out to meet total man's total need, which is not empowered by the Holy Spirit, which does not express true compassion. This grows out of true understanding, out of outrage that sees wrong and evil as God sees it, out of identification fired by love, forceful, practical, effective.

THEOLOGY IMPLICATIONS OF RADICAL DISCIPLESHIP

A number of issues have thrust themselves upon us from papers delivered in this Congress and, from the subsequent wrestling with them under the authority of God's Word, a number of us have felt the compulsion of his Spirit to share this response.

We affirm that . . .

The *evangel* is God's Good News in Jesus Christ; it is Good News of the reign he proclaimed and embodies; of God's mission of love to restore the world to wholeness through the Cross of Christ and him alone; of his victory over the demonic powers of destruction and death; of his Lordship over the entire universe; it is Good News of a new creation of a new humanity, a new birth through him by his life-giving Spirit; of the gifts of the messianic reign contained in Jesus and mediated through him by his Spirit; of the charismatic community empowered to embody his reign of shalom here and now before the whole creation and make his Good News seen and known. It is Good News of liberation, of restoration, of wholeness, and of salvation that is personal, social, global and cosmic. Jesus is Lord! Alleluia! Let the earth hear his voice!

The *communication of the evangel* in its fullness to every person worldwide is a mandate of the Lord Jesus to his community. There is no biblical dichotomy between the Word spoken and the Word made visible in the lives of God's people. Men will look as they listen and what they see must be at one with what they hear. The Christian community must chatter, discuss and proclaim the Gospel; it must express the Gospel in its life as the new society, in its sacrificial service of others as a genuine expression of God's love, in its prophetic exposing and opposing of all demonic forces that deny the Lordship of Christ and keep men less than fully human; in its pursuit of real justice for all men; in its responsible and caring trusteeship of God's creation and its resources.

There are times when our communication may be by attitude and action only, and times when the spoken Word will stand alone; but we must repudiate as demonic the attempt to drive a wedge between evangelism and social action.

The *response demanded by the evangel* is that men and women repent of their sin and every other lordship than that of Jesus Christ, and commit themselves to him to serve him in the world. Men are not already reconciled to God and simply awaiting the realization of it. Nor can biblical authority be found for the false hope of universalism; the reality of the eternal destruction of evil and all who cling to it must be solemnly affirmed, however humbly agnostic the Bible requires us to be about its nature.

Salvation is by God's grace on the sole ground of Christ's death and resurrection and is received by obedient faith. Repentance is demanded; men must experience a change of understanding, attitude and orientation. But the new birth is not merely a subjective experience of forgiveness. It is a placement within the messianic community, God's new order which exists as a sign of God's reign to be consummated at the end of the age.

Methods in evangelization must center in Jesus Christ who took our humanity, our frailty, our death and gave himself in suffering servant-hood for others. He sends his community into the world, as the Father sent him, to identify and agonize with men, to renounce status and demonic power, and to give itself in selfless service of others for God. Those who proclaim the Cross must be continually marked by the Cross. With unashamed commitment to Jesus Christ we must engage in the mutual listening of dialogue, the reward of which is understanding. We need to meet men on their own ground and be particularly attentive to the powerless. We must use the language, thought-forms and imagery appropriate to differing cultures. As Christians, we must live in such unity and love that men may believe. We must allow God to make visible in the new humanity the quality of life that reflects Christ and demonstrates his reign. We must respect cultural integrity while being free from all that denies or distorts the Lordship of Christ. God's Spirit overcomes all barriers of race, color and culture.

Strategy for world evangelization in our generation is with God, from whom we eagerly anticipate the renewal of his community, equipping us with love and power so that the whole Christian community may make known the whole Gospel to the whole man throughout the whole world. We believe God to be calling us into greater unity and partnership throughout the earth to fulfill the commission of our Lord Jesus Christ.

We confess that . . .

We have been failing in our obedience to the Lordship of Christ and have been refusing to submit to his Word and be led by his Spirit.

We have failed to incarnate the Gospel and to come to men as servants for Christ's sake.

Our testimony has often been marred by triumphalism and arrogance, by lack of faith in God and by diminished love for his people.

We have often been in bondage to a particular culture and sought to spread it in the name of Jesus.

We have not been aware of when we have debased and distorted the Gospel by acceptance of a contrary value system.

We have been partisan in our condemnation of totalitarianism and violence and have failed to condemn societal and institutionalized sin, especially that of racism.

We have sometimes so identified ourselves with particular political systems that the Gospel has been compromised and the prophetic voice muted.

We have frequently denied the rights and neglected the cries of the underprivileged and those struggling for freedom and justice.

We have often separated Jesus Christ the Savior from Jesus Christ the Lord.

We have sometimes distorted the biblical understanding of man as a total being and have courted an unbiblical dualism.

We have insulated new Christians from life in the world and given simplistic responses to complex problems.

We have sometimes manipulated our message, used pressure techniques and been unduly pre-occupied with statistics.

We have allowed eagerness for qualitative growth to render us silent about the whole counsel of God. We have been usurping God's Holy Spirit of love and power.

We rejoice . . .

In our membership by his Spirit in the Body of Christ and in the joy and love he has given us in each other.

In the openness and honesty with which we have met each other and have experienced mutual acceptance and forgiveness.

In the possibilities for men to read his Word in their own languages through indigenous translations.

In the stimulation of mind and challenge to action that has come to us from his Word as we have placed the needs of our generation under its judgment and light.

In the prophetic voices of our brothers and sisters in this Congress, with whom we go forth in humility and hope.

In the certainty that the kingdoms of this world shall become the Kingdom of our God and of his Christ. He shall reign forever. Alleluia!

We resolve . . .

To submit ourselves afresh to the Word of God and to the leading of his Spirit, to pray and work together for the renewal of his community as the expression of his reign, to participate in God's mission to his world in our generation, showing forth Jesus as Lord and Savior, and calling on all men everywhere to repent, to submit to his Lordship, to know his salvation, to identify in him with the oppressed and work for the liberation of all men and women in his name.

LET THE EARTH HEAR HIS VOICE!

Section VIII:
Functional Reports

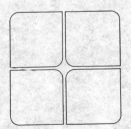

REPORT ON FUNCTIONAL GROUPS

Jan J. van Capelleveen

Mr. van Capelleveen, The Hague,
Netherlands, is the Secretary for Publishing
for Netherlands Bible Society in
Amsterdam.

Lausanne '74 is about to die. People from some 150 countries will leave and return to their home church, home office, home base, or homestead. Lausanne '74 is about to be born again. Born across borders, oceans, culture gaps, to bear fruit.

What I had to say I have said on this platform, in the Congress paper, and in the various groups. What the men behind me had to say, they have said time and time again in the meetings. Now we are standing here not to speak for ourselves but to convey the mind of this Congress, to repeat in as few words as possible what was said in the functional groups. This is what you said:

We leave with deeper insights into the magnitude of the task. The world is more than the total number of geographical areas. Though in the wilds of Latin America and in the valleys of Papua some tribes are still to be reached, the Gospel has reached the ends of the world, if not by men, certainly by radio waves.

But there are new worlds that lie before us to proclaim the Gospel. There are the worlds of Europe and America. It has been impressed upon us that in these worlds many millions of people live who have never heard the Gospel. Maybe their fathers had, or their grandfathers. My own wife was a fifth generation non-Christian when she was reached for Christ. Our task has not been accomplished until they too have heard that Christ has come to give us life and give it more abundantly than materialism can.

There is the world of youth. Whereas in a city of Austria some 50 per cent of the people are older than sixty, in many cities of the South 50 per cent of the population is under 25 years of age. In our Western world a better expression may be the worlds of the North and also the extreme South, youth are disillusioned by material affluence. They must hear the message of the Lord who can fill their hearts with real satisfaction. In the rest of the South youth are entering a new world but are hampered by lack of schools and lack of work. They enter a world without a future. They must hear the message about the Lord of the future.

There is the world of growing cities. Jakarta, Bombay, Rio de Janeiro, Lagos, Nairobi. People flock there to start a new life, and finding no jobs settle in the dirt and dust to vegetate instead of live. They have turned their backs upon their families, their traditions, and their religions. And they find themselves deserted in a world without hope. They must hear the message of the Lord, our hope. Only united evangelistic endeavors can reach them.

There is the world of children, millions of them. Of the two thousand million people yet unreached, some 500 million are children. Most of them will never get a chance to go to school. They must hear that Christ said: "Let all the children come to me."

In this Congress we have wrestled with cultural and racial differences. When we preach the Gospel the Word becomes flesh in a cultural situation. But cultures change. In our Northern world they change rapidly. We have learned that we have again and again to reconsider our beliefs, and out of our cultures we have to return to the Christ of the Scriptures. We are not called to carry a culture to the ends of the world. We must preach Christ.

We have learned that we have to reconsider carefully our training programs both in the North and in the South, both of pastors and laymen. Do we really teach them to go out and present Christ in their own situations, or do we prepare them for a world which is not their own, be it the world of the white man, or the world of yesteryear?

We have learned that the Word must become flesh in other cultures. But we have also learned that Christ calls us together. As never before there is a need to work, to evangelize together, to learn the beauty of a real community across cultural and race differences, to proclaim the Gospel in word and deed together as partners white and black, yellow and red, that the vision of John may come true: "They were from every race, tribe, nation and language and they stood in front of the throne and the Lamb."

We go home with a definite calling not to forget the social implications of the Gospel. We refuse to believe that our grandfathers forgot them, when they went out to newly discovered areas to proclaim the Gospel. Languages were reduced to writing, schools were started, hospitals were built. And we refuse to believe that the newest evangelistic groups who reach the hippies and drug addicts do forget them. But we were reminded of the need not to separate the word from the deed. And rightly so, for in the Hebrew the expression for word means also deed. God spoke, and it was. God wants us to apply the Gospel to the whole man, body, soul, and spirit. New life in Christ means a new life, a new way of life on earth, recognizing God as the Lord of the world. One way to implement this is to send out teams that minister to both the needs of the heart and the body.

We have discovered too that there are new methods to carry the Gospel into all the world. Exciting possibilities lie before us. Look up and see the satellites hurling through space. There are already agricultural mapping satellites. And next year it will be possible to reach every little village of India by satellite. A simple antenna made of a few bars and chickenwire which can be made by the local village blacksmith will be enough to catch the electronic waves which can be transferred into sound and vision.

But we do not have to turn to the dreams of Jules Verne which have become reality. In the various groups we have considered methods of the past, which in a new way can be used in the future.

However, we must carry home with us the exhortation that new methods cannot be planned, but are born out of new circumstances. We must give them a chance to be born. Therefore, every church and every evangelistic organization should, in the coming years, try to reach out for a new group of people in a new way.

I have tried to formulate trends, possibilities, new or renewed insights which have come out of the groups. But let us become specific. I call upon Walter Angst, executive secretary of the Swiss Missionary Fellowship to tell us what we can do to evangelize through Western Missions.

The churches of the Third World are rapidly discovering their missionary calling. Here is Stephen Akangbe from Nigeria, the former president of Evangelical Churches of West Africa, now student at Gordon Conwell Theological Seminary, to report on Third World Missions.

It is time to spell out our social responsibilities. George Hoffman of London, England, director of TEAR Fund, gives us the feedback from his group.

Evangelism will soon become extinct without the right theological education. Saphir Athyal, Principal of Union Biblical Seminary, Yeotmal, India, and general coordinator of Asia Theological Assocation reports.

The task will never be accomplished without the laymen accepting their responsibilities. Dr. John Court, senior lecturer in psychology at Flinders University in South Australia, spells out what his group discovered.

The word to be heard must be communicated. Phil Butler, director of Intercristo, a communications consultant, tells us what our 300 communication men come up with.

Half the population of the world is youth. They want to accept their responsibility. John Ray, who has been involved in student work, now studying in Britain, speaks for them.

We had another functional group, a huge one, touching upon all we have heard: Evangelism, plain and not so simple. Michael Cassidy, team leader of Africa Enterprise, an interdenominational and interracial evangelistic team with ministries in East and South Africa, gives us his committee's soundings.

Thus you spoke. Charting the way of the Gospel. Giving guidelines for the days before us.

Hurry home for the days are short and the task is immense. Hurry home to find time to stop to think. Hurry home, to inspire your congregations and your organizations, for without their involvement the task cannot be accomplished.

Hurry home, not just to evangelize but to make disciples who can teach others also.

Hurry home, for the population clock ticks on.

Hurry home, for someone is waiting to hear you speak.

Hurry home.

But do not forget what you have learned.

Do not forget the friends you have made.

Do not forget that they need your prayers.

Do not forget that this is not your task alone, but our task.

Do not forget that he who has called you will do it because he is faithful.

THIRD WORLD MISSIONS

Stephen J. Akangbe

1. Strategic goals

It is of primary importance that the goals for Third World missions are set by the church and not by the Western missions. The evangelization of the entire world must be the scope of her strategy. All the regional evangelical missions should be integrated and mobilized for a jointly supported operation and quick achievement of objectives. Strategies should be indigenous and not foreign but advice should not be refused. There should be a wholesome relationship between the church and the mission for effective working of the mission programs. National and international Third World mission cooperation is needed for the purpose of sharing of ideas, fellowship, prayer support, and financial assistance wherever the need arises. The spirit of domination or authoritarianism must not be allowed in the inter-mission relations. The structure should be formulated and directed by the national mission church people and should not be a carbon copy of Western mission structure.

2. Actions recommended

There must be proper preparation and orientation of national missionaries to be sent out in order to avoid unnecessary casualties. An effective missionary-minded board should be set up for the proper coordination. The regular dissemination of information to member bodies and missionaries should not be ignored. There must be schools of missions, evangelism, church growth, and constant study of the Scriptures in order to equip missionaries who will be sent to new areas. Revival of in-depth evangelistic campaigns in urban and rural areas is a matter of urgency in all Third World constituencies.

If any fund is to be given for the support of the mission by Western mission agencies, it is wise to channel it through the existing church board and not directly to individuals in order to avoid the spirit of divided loyalties on the part of individual missionaries.

The social ministries of medicine, food supplies, clothing, and rehabilitation of nationals into business life will increase their income and advance their social status. There ought to be specific concentration on helping nominal Christians, the conversion of Muslims, neglected ethnic groups, adherents of traditional religions, prisoners, the Armed Forces, the handicapped, street-beggars, the shut-ins, and the aged.

Christian endeavors, e.g., camping, missionary conferences, daily devotion Bible schools, boys' and girls' brigades, youth meetings, Scripture Union, family evangelism, body life ministry, and Campus Crusade for Christ programs are very essential to mission strategy. The importance of tent-making missionaries who earn their living in other areas of their own country or across the borders cannot be over-emphasized. Duplication of efforts and unnecessary multiplicity of mission societies must be eliminated.

3. Plans for follow-up

Regular joint meetings will assist the church in keeping up the resolutions made on mission strategy. Regular Bible study groups will increase the involvement of individual churches and missions. The provision and distribution of literature always has lasting and effective results. The assignment of individual Christian workers for visitation and production of progress reports will stimulate action and produce better results. Regular prayer meetings and repeated spiritual cooperative activities of all types can easily unite mission bodies, strengthen individuals, generate zeal, and inspire action. The use of available resources of men and materials can improve the mission program.

Hindrances to mission strategy are inconsistent Christian living, lack of Bible understanding, Westernization of Christianity, syncretism, Islam, and other cults which are growing at high rates today. The manipulation of people for selfish purposes and exploitation of fellow workers must be stamped out if we want to work together to evangelize our generation with the Gospel of Christ.

MISSION-THE THIRD WORLD REPORT

Chairman: Dr. Petrus Octavianus
Secretary: Dr. Samuel I. Kim

The committee meeting has been called three times and discussed the major questions. The following are brief reports of our discussions and approvals.

I. Priority Targets and Goals in Next Decade

I) *Asian's Priority Targets* for Third World Mission

a. Before the Christmas of 1975, Asia Mission Association will be formed. Prior to this convention, each country in Asia should form their national Missions Association.

b. Before the end of December, 1974, 200 Asian missionaries will be sent out, as the All-Asia Mission Consultation, Seoul '73 already proclaimed.

c. "Seoul '73" also set a goal to establish East-West Center for Missionary Research and Development which will be located in Seoul by 1975, with the goal to train 10,000 Asian missionaries by the year 2000. And individual countries are also being encouraged to start their own missionary training institutes.

d. The Continuation Committee Meeting of Asia Mission Consultation which was held in Hong Kong in April,1974, decided to send 100 missionaries to Borneo (Kalimantan) Island and Northern Thailand, as a united effort.

e. It was proposed by the Rev. David J. Cho that the First Third World Mission Consultation be convened before the end of 1977.

2) The Priority Targets of *African Missions*

The Rev. Akangbe gave a report that there are some missionary societies in various countries in Africa, and yet, they have not formed any Association of Missions in Africa. Most of the African Churches have worked together for the Evangelism-in-Depth and set their goals to reach unevangelized people within two decades.

Evangelical Churches in West Africa have sent out 115 missionaries beyond their regions, and promoted cooperative missionary efforts throughout the entire African continent. Rev. Akangbe also stressed that African Churches would welcome missionaries from Asia and mutual assistance among the Third World churches.

3) The Rev. Juan Isais *from Mexico (representing Latin America)* expressed the opinion that the churches in Latin America would welcome mutual exchange preaching-mission between Latin America and rest of the Third World. He also pointed out that as far as Latin America is concerned there are no indigenous organized missionary societies, however, some churches inspired by foreign organizations send their missionaries to other regions.

II. Strategy

a. To encourage the National Missions Associations to hold short-term seminars or institutes for missionary promotion and orientation.

b. To study the East-West cooperative channels for the united efforts of the worldwide outreach.

c. Third World Mission leaders should be encouraged to conduct fact-finding surveys to ascertain needs and establish priorities.

d. To study feasibility of establishing a system whereby all resources, human and financial, could be shared together.

e. To encourage the exchange of missiologists and other specialists in missions between East-West in order to provide Third World Mission Societies with Third World missiologists.

III. Specific Action

a. Immediately upon return from the Congress, several feedback seminars will be held in Korea for the further study and implementation of the Third World mission involvement.

b. All the churches in the Third World must be encouraged to have mission messages at least once a month so that the Christians will give more for world mission.

c. Encourage to inaugurate mission courses at theological schools to promote general mission works among pastors and church leaders.

d. Mexican church leaders will organize mission-tour groups to Indonesia in order to provide inspiration for the missionary outreach.

e. Encourage the local churches to organize prayer groups for the worldwide mission.

f. Encourage the churches in Latin America to send missionary offerings to Indonesia.

IV. Beyond Your Own Resources

a. It is desirable to exchange technicians and specialists mutually between East-West and from one country to another for training and communication study.

b. In initial stage of projects (of Kalimantang) the Asian missions may need outside assistance in the form of Western lay technicians and specialists supported at least in part by Western funds.

V. Continual Efforts

After this Congress, the Lafricasia Missionary Organizations will continually expend mission philosophy, strategy and general operation among the Third World mission. We also have desire to form a Third World Mission Consultation before the end of 1977, as a result of our joint efforts.

THE SOCIAL RESPONSIBILITIES OF EVANGELIZATION

George Hoffman

Rev. Hoffman, Teddington, England, is the Director of TEAR Fund (The Evangelical Alliance Relief Fund).

We would like to reaffirm that the meeting of human need in whatever form it confronts us is simply obedience to the command of God and, as Paul says: "A faithful confession of the Gospel of Christ."

We do not believe therefore in evangelization *through* social service. We recognize that social service must be an integrated part of our evangelization. It is in itself an essential expression of the love of God for his world.

We deplore the disparities and uneven distribution of the resources in God's world. And we repent of our corporate and individual identification with a status quo which exploits, perpetuates, or at best ignores the factors which create conditions that dehumanize our fellowmen and degrade the image of God in which they were made. And we must devote ourselves to a far greater measure of sacrificial involvement in society in the Name and for the sake of our Lord Jesus Christ.

We recognize that much of the poverty in the world is poverty of opportunity and not just poverty *per se.* We acknowledge therefore the need to devote more thought and action to helping those who are unable to help themselves and are the victims of injustice and exploitation. We were rebuked by Prov. 31:8, "To speak up for the poor and the needy and see they get justice." And unless we are to act like ostriches in the face of the overwhelming teaching of Scripture, we must fulfill our rights and responsibilities on behalf of those whose rights and responsibilities are proscribed or denied.

However, we saw a danger of being preoccupied with world problems in terms of impersonal facts and figures remembering that "statistics don't bleed — humans do." Surely we are called in the words of a popular song to be "people who love people." As Jesus did. As Eliza Doolittle said to Prof. Higgins in the musical *My Fair Lady,* the world is saying to us as Christians, "Don't just tell me you love me — show me."

There has been much talk here about our being all one in Christ Jesus. The time has come, we believe, to stop just professing it and to start practicing it. In this connection we will never learn to bear one another's burdens until we start to care for one another as brothers. As the Living Bible translates I John 3:18, "Let us stop just saying that we love people: let us really love them and show it by our actions."

To fulfill our respective goals we desire to forsake our overt identification as agencies and organizations for the good of the people we are seeking to serve. We must cooperate for Christ's sake. So often the only reason for an organization's independence is to promote its own program as a fund-raising flag. And we must beware of capitalizing on the plight of those who suffer for the sake of the funds we are seeking to raise.

We call therefore upon evangelicals worldwide to cooperate more effectively and to coordinate more efficiently as we assist those we seek to serve. This could prevent the scandal of unnecessary duplication and wasted time, energy, and limited resources.

We recognize only too well that the heart of all our society's problems is the problem of the human heart. Nevertheless we urge evangelicals to think through the basic principles that relate to our social responsibilities. Let us face up to the commands of Scripture in meeting human need and tackling the social problems that confront us at local, national, and international levels.

Finally we recall the words of Dr. Josip Horak of Yugoslavia speaking at the Berlin Congress: "The most important thing for Christians today is not simply to talk about their opportunities but to use them."

PROGRESSIVE REPORT ON FUNCTIONAL GROUP

Saphir Athyal

*Dr. Athyal, Yeotmal, Maharashta, India, is
Principal of the Union Biblical Seminary in
India.*

I. *Primary Goals or Priorities*
    The priorities in theology and theological education for the rest of this decade are:
    1. *Training leadership* with respect to the Third World Church training of national leaders and teachers.
    2. *Post-graduate level training* to strengthen the teaching program of theological seminaries and Bible schools. This training should be done in one's own country or continent if at all possible.
    3. *Research* in particular issues of relevance and a few *centers* should be established with needed resource materials. Related to this is the greatly needed publication of books in the Third World; books written in one's own cultural context.
    4. *Training of the total church* in the mobilizing of the church for the task of evangelization.
    5. *Development of theology* which will be wholly true to the teachings of the Bible and at the same time will speak to contemporary issues in meaningful terms.
    6. *Specific goals* to be spelled out from time to time.

II. *Strategy To Be Followed*
    1. One or two *key centers* already existing to be selected from each continent especially within Third World, to be *developed* and *strengthened*. This is much preferable to having one such center only in the world. These centers may be developed to offer master and doctoral level training and provide resources for creative and contextual research.
    2. *United effort* wherever and whenever possible in the areas of developing theology and theological education. Evangelicals have often fragmentalized their efforts which has hurt our cause.
    3. *To develop creative theology,* relevant issues should be carefully studied on national and continental or regional levels. Because churches on the continents of the Third World face certain common problems and issues, even a *Third World Theological Consultation* may prove to be a catalyst in developing contextual theology. Theology always should have a missiological task and not just be the pastime exercise of a few intellectuals.

4. For the training of the whole church, some lay-training programs should be implemented on a local congregational level. Theological education by extension may be of great service in the area and may help in training pastors also.

5. Many sections of the Congress raised serious questions on the traditional patterns of theological training. New patterns of training should be experimented with and any structure for theological education should be servant to the goals or purpose of theological education. Theological teachers should be given training in *teaching methodology*.

III. *Post-Congress Coordination*

1. There is need for national level coordination, with an international network of fellowship, passing of information, etc. An international commission of four or five members may be appointed to help the national bodies in their theological concerns.

2. W.C.E. and T.E.F. have helped to strengthen theology and theological education in the Third World. An international committee for the coordination of raising finances and lending assistance where needed, may be set up.

LAITY GROUP REPORT

J.H. Court

We start from a biblical view of the laity as the people of God with no distinction of status before God between ordained and lay people. Nonetheless, clergy and laity can fulfill different functions both in expressing community within the church and in witness to the world. Without being anti-clerical we emphasize that the laity must play a strategic part in effective evangelism.

Insofar as a distinction may be made, we see the pastor training the congregation to fulfill its responsibilities, more than the congregation supporting the pastor in evangelism.

It is important to train lay people to think and act evangelistically through home and family.

The training and skills of lay people must be harnessed at all levels to complement those of the pastor so that each is free to do that for which he is equipped.

The talents of women are all too often confined by convention and tradition; their personal worth must be respected and fostered. We remember that in most places women represent more than half of the evangelistic force.

Christian witness is not completed in faithful church attendance and preservation of existing organizational structures of the church. There must be an encouragement to become involved in the social structures of the community — in secular organizations and political bodies at all levels so that opportunities to create a specifically Christian life-style will be taken. Young people should be encouraged to explore their Christian calling in terms of involvement in the media, in politics, in the world of the arts and culture. A call to E-1 evangelism is no less a call than one to E-3 evangelism.

Lay people can challenge the *life-style* of the world by living in fellowship with one another, proclaiming God's love by both word and deed; a self-critical humility in relation to wealth, race, and personal morality are necessary prerequisites to chattering the Gospel.

The *thought-forms* of the world must also be challenged. The expertise of lay people can be harnessed to insure an informed witness in controversial areas of personal and social ethics. We reiterate the call of C.S. Lewis for more books by Christians as well as more Christian books. Ideally these should not only be distributed through Christian bookshops.

Three more detailed recommendations are made —

(i) That minority groups be reached through bi-lingual or bi-cultural Christians, e.g., the second generation migrant in such places as Britain or Australia who becomes a Christian. He should be encouraged to witness to the migrant group rather than withdraw from it.

(ii) That the ways in which lay people are witnessing effectively around the world be made known through literature for the purpose.

(iii) That regional conferences across denominations bring lay people together for training in evangelism.

MASS COMMUNICATIONS REPORT

Phil Butler

An unusually high number of Congress participants indicated an interest in the field of mass communications as it relates to evangelism. Over 300 participants took part in six days of strategy sessions and demonstrations. From these meetings came the following priorities.

First, we feel there is a need for a genuinely biblical, theological basis for our use of the mass communications media. Writing on the subject is needed as well as teaching in Christian schools and training centers throughout the world.

Then, there is a need for truly professional training and experience in Christian use of the media. Fewer than ten per cent of those attending the mass communications sessions here at the Congress had ever worked for five years outside the parochial field. Regional training centers must be established to provide this badly needed emphasis.

Christian use of all media is essential — secular as well as church-related. This will require our realization of the strategic role of Christians in commercial and state media. It necessitates our bringing these men and women into fellowship and planning for evangelism through all levels of media.

There must be a local-church centeredness to our use of the media. Coordinated integration of the media is a priority. And the local church must be seen as a part of that integrated plan — playing its unique and vital role in the total task of evangelism and discipleship.

We must encourage the proliferation of Christian publishing, broadcasting, and film production units throughout the world.

Cooperative communications entities must be developed in each country. These fellowships of communicators can provide encouragement and practical assistance for evangelism through the media.

Evangelicals must make an energetic effort to find what media are already available in their countries — many opportunities are often lost due to lack of awareness and action on our part.

An international communications resource center is needed which will provide for the exchange of information, ideas, *and* provide directories of people and materials available in the field.

The church must grasp *new* media. Satellites, computer networks, data transmission, and other remarkable media forms are already reshaping world commerce and political structures. They must be considered and used for evangelism.

Communications conferences are needed in each country as early as possible, allowing Christians to explore methods, share ideas, and provide focus for media, fellowship and strategy.

An international communications congress needs to be convened within two years. This congress would provide full display of current hardware; exhibition of Christian communications output from around the world — including the field of films, audio-visuals, literature, television, radio, and other media.

Finally, we feel a radical change is necessary in the church's view of mass communications media. There must be a totally new awareness of how completely the media presently dominate our lives, and their awesome potential for evangelism. Power, communication, and action are available if the church, under God's Spirit, takes hold of this remarkable field with vision and an aggressive spirit.

YOUTH REPORT

John Ray

This Congress has been and is going to continue to be an important event in the ongoing task of evangelization among that ever-increasing proportion of our world's population — those under 30. This is not a youth congress as shown by just one example: a national group from a country with more than half of its church membership under 30 has not included a single young person in its contingent. Even so, the importance of reaching youth must be emphasized. In an extraordinary way, the problems and situations of young people mean that we constitute a more uniquely homogenous group than almost any other. It is therefore urged that serious thought be given to a strategy for the evangelization of youth which focuses on how to reach the millions of those under 30 on every continent, especially Asia. If we who have gathered here do not take decisive action, there are others who most definitely will and indeed already are. We thank God for the various worldwide church and parachurch youth organizations, but the challenge of the evangelization of youth in this generation must be faced squarely by us and a more concerted effort made to reach them with the Gospel that deals with the whole man.

One consistent message has come through from young people at the Congress. More than ever before, young people must be given and indeed are ready to shoulder their full and responsible share in the continuing task of world evangelization. We want increasingly to be part of the many teams that God by his Spirit is raising up in various parts of the world. In country after country, he is uniting, preparing and equipping to make us more useful and useable members of his body. We young people say: Your experience and our enthusiasm consecrated to the service of the living God can achieve great things for him.

We have begun to discover each other as partners in our common task at this Congress. This has been partly through listening and listening and listening. But also by singing, sharing, and praying together. Many of us felt the lack of praising the Lord together but the Holy Spirit himself has allowed us in these last few days to experience something of the "beautiful community." We will return encouraged by and supportive of each other. Many have voiced the need for sound evangelical theology based unequivocally on Holy Scripture as vital to our evangelistic and disciple-making strategy. In the years ahead, I can see many of us going to each other's countries, especially in the Third World, as evangelists and disciple-makers with a renewed understanding of the Gospel in its fullest dimension because we have been here at Lausanne.

EVANGELISM FUNCTIONAL COMMITTEE REPORT

Michael Cassidy

Mr. Cassidy, Pietermaritzburg, Natal, South Africa, is President and Director of African Enterprise.

Introduction

The rhythm of Jesus' life in which one sees him "going apart" before "going out," and "withdrawing" before "advancing," was seen by our evangelism committee as having real relevance in terms of our assigned task. This was to "listen" for practical suggestions concerning the immediate follow-up activities for individual participants as they arrive home. It was noted that the factors of fatigue, information overload, and spiritual indigestion necessitated that the first thing for participants to do after returning is to:

1. Stop

a. *To rest:* most will need to take time to rest and catch their breath. Someone said we are to work ourselves to death for the Lord — but slowly! This vital rest process will also give time —

b. *To pray:* having heard such a range of ideas and statistics, each of us needs to pray that the Lord will distil out for us those one or two special insights or initiatives which will represent the Holy Spirit's immediate strategy for us as individuals. Pausing to pray will also relieve indigestion and pave the way for digestion. We must stop —

c. *To digest:* the written material. This process will take time and we must each make time to do it. Pausing to rest, pray and digest will prepare us for the next three steps.

2. Share

Our sharing process should happen at at least three levels:

a. *With our immediate colleagues and co-workers:* this should lead first into a serious *re-evaluation* of our own churches, missions, and organizations in the light of Lausanne's insights and models, secondly into a *re-examination* of our respective situations, so that individually and corporately we make our message contextual, in the biblical sense, and relevant.

b. *With our local churches:* this can be done by teamlets of two who will share the Lausanne experience, tools, and resources.

c. *With our denominations and denominational leaders:* this will necessitate scheduling time to see key denominational leaders and write articles for denominational magazines, urging all to give pride of place to evangelism in denominational programs.

Transition: having stopped, having shared, we will then want to *gear up* for action.

3. Gear Up

The gearing up process can likewise happen at three levels:

a. *In prayer cells.*

b. *In brainstorming and planning sessions* (so that we pound out tailor-made strategies for our respective situations).

c. *In maintaining links* by correspondence and thereby maintaining an exchange of ideas, resources, tools and even troubles.

Finally, having stopped, shared, and geared up for action, we are then to *go* out in obedient evangelistic witness.

4. Go

This once again is at three levels:

a. *The personal level:* God help each of us to become gossipers of the Gospel.

b. *The local church level:* this latter can be done through renewed initiatives of *laytraining* and through encouraging our local churches to aim for *measurable growth.*

c. *The community, city and regional level:* many of our communities or regions are perhaps ready for concerted evangelistic endeavors. If so, let's go.

5. Conclusion

In short, it has been recommended by many of you, as we return, that — WE STOP — WE SHARE — WE GEAR UP — WE GO.

Section IX:
Geographical Reports

REGIONAL GROUP SUMMARY REPORT

Ian Rennie

The purpose of this session is to attempt to give a summary report of the work of the regional groups. My task is to attempt to give a general world-wide interpretation. The task of my colleagues, representing the respective regions, is briefly to highlight one or two distinctive points from their region which will be primarily illustrative.

1. Renewal of the church

As one listens in this Congress to what has been done in the name of Jesus Christ in many parts of the world, and as one reads the projected plans contained in the regional reports, one cannot help but ask: are we entering a new period of Christian renewal and revival? Renewal or revival is a sovereign, wide-spread, deep and surprising work of the Holy Spirit which makes Jesus Christ real, and has profound effects upon every aspect and activity of the Christian church. These movements, I would suggest, have been the most important movements of Christian history. As I see it, there have been five such eras preceding our day.

a. *The movement of the early church to 450 A.D.,* when the Christian Church evangelized the Roman Empire, in an obvious way triumphed over the empire, and came to profound theological understanding about the Trinity, the nature and person of our Lord, sin and grace.

b. *The movement of the dark ages from 550-750 A.D.,* when the Irish and British missionaries evangelized much of Western Europe, using at times a peculiarly contextualized form of the people movement approach.

c. *The movement of the high middle ages from 1100-1300 A.D.,* with its emphasis on the atonement in thought and experience, its profound search for Christian culture, and the peripatetic street ministry of St. Francis.

d. *The movement of the reformation from 1517-1648 A.D.,* with its theological and spiritual renewal of so much of Christendom, and its gloriously positive proclamation of the justification of the ungodly by faith, its impelling persuasion of the authority of the Bible, and its overwhelming confidence in the work of the Holy Spirit in regeneration, union with Christ and sanctification.

e. *The movement of the evangelical awakening from 1738-1908 A.D.,* with its stress on decisive conversion, and that of which this Congress is such an evidence, the founding and building of a world-wide church in the modern missionary movement.

I would like to present the evidence as I see it, and allow you to draw your own conclusions.

2. Today we are the inheritors of a number of relatively recent and still vital movements of revival

The movement of the evangelical awakening had several phases, the last known, in the West, as the Welsh revival of 1904-1908. But this western movement was only, as the English say, a damp squib, in comparison with the movements overseas. The powerful churches, so well represented here, of Korea, Assam, Chile, and Brazil all received their baptism at that time, and by God's grace have continued in remarkable health at this hour. Then there were the Chinese movements of the nineteen-thirties, typified for so many by the name of John Sung, and the Ruanda revival of the same period, now rightly called the East African revival because of its geographic extension. Are these movements of sovereign and surprising grace overspilling their bounds so that even the dry bones of the western churches are being revived?

3. The renaissance of evangelical theology

Twenty years ago, when I began my theological training, evangelical theology was in a perilous state indeed. The change in the last two decades has been phenomenal. The Inter Varsity Fellowship productions of Britain, the works of Henry, Ramm, and Cornell in the U.S., Leon Morris in Australia, and now of a host of younger evangelical exegetes throughout the western world are all evidence. Evangelical seminaries and Bible schools have proliferated world-wide, and in many places are filled to overflowing with young Christians eager to engage in the serious and demanding study of the Bible in the original languages. The churches of the Third World are calling for increased top-level theological education, and also for that which will equip those whose ministries are of a part-time nature. The Eastern churches are careful to guard against syncretism in theology and one even hears on occasion the suggestion being whispered that some European theological students, laboring in stifling atmospheres, might find a considerable relief in cross-registration for a year at a Third World theological school. Has this movement been laying a foundation? For every great time of renewal has had a theological stress.

4. The small group movement

Days of revival have always been accompanied by small groups — those preaching earnestly, praying and studying the Bible, and those during the period of life being a time of expressing and sharing the love and life in Jesus Christ. Historians tell us that cities such as Paris and Edinburgh were laced with such groups in the Reformation, while the evangelical awakening produced the Methodist class-meetings in England, men in the Highlands of Scotland, and the prayer huts in Norway. Such groups have become a commonplace of much church life in the last two decades, and various regional groups in this Congress are planning strategy which gives a significant place to these groups which in the past have been either harbingers or signs of life.

5. Evangelism and missions

These related emphases have always been present in and from renewed churches, except where churches may have been faced with walls of intransigent hostility or untraversable geography. Preaching evangelism, to large crowds, to use the colloquial, never seems to have had it so good. In every region plans are being laid. Eurofest will take place in Belgium in '75. There is a renewed interest in city-wide endeavors in Asia, and Dr. Graham will be in Rio in a few months. New creativity is being shown in mass evangelism as stereotypes fall to the ground. Further methods are also being stressed; evangelism-in-depth in all its adaptations, the use of homes, camps, medicine and the media. National and cultural points of contact are being probed, and there are requests for help — requests combined with dignity—from churches in less fertile areas, so that they may accomplish their evangelistic mandate. And the churches of the Third World are becoming missionary sending bodies, with Asian churches projecting a goal of 10,000 cross-cultural missionaries by the year 2000.

6. New emphasis

There are certain new movements, at least for evangelical Protestantism, which may also be signs of renewal. I see these as gathering around two foci: the church in its inner life and experience, and the community of Christians in relation to society and culture. For centuries the church has been studied by Christians in its external and organizational life, but today the emphasis is on the inner life of the gifts of the Spirit and the ministry of all members. This seems to have come from two sources. On the one hand there is the charismatic movement which, I humbly believe, in addition to its power to penetrate the strongholds of entrenched Roman Catholicism and Protestant liberalism, will, in the end of the day, be most remembered for the contribution of its stress on the gifts of the Body. And then, in part, I am sure, to remind us that the Body of Christ is always greater than anything we can engineer on earth, is the contribution of an undoubtedly unrepresented part of the Body — the Exclusive Plymouth Brethren, as the teaching of John Nelson Darley and other chief men among the brethren have been communicated to us in our generation by the inimitable Chinese author, Watchman Nee. With the new emphasis on the Body of Christ being abroad in many parts of the church, it is natural that regional groups should stress the congregation, calling on para-church groups to relate to it, and urging the congregation to fulfill its ministry of training those young in the faith in a living way, as far from institutionalism as possible.

The other emphasis relates Christians to society and culture. The evangelical movement of the eighteenth and nineteenth centuries was usually profoundly indifferent to the issues of culture in their widest dimensions. But today Christians are concerned to separate what is anti-Christian from what is merely ethnic in their culture. Others are imbued with a new sense of social justice, while yet others, often following the guidance of Kuyper, Dooyerveerd and the Dutch school, stress the Lordship of Jesus Christ over all culture. Not for centuries, I would argue, have we had so many young biblical Christians arising with both academic and theological competence, who are set to relate positively their faith to the disciplines and areas of culture. Is God doing a new thing? Is he leading us into a revival with dimensions, to most of us, almost unimagined?

Closely allied with these two dealt with, are another two which can only be mentioned: the stress and plan in some quarters of types of communal living: and the rediscovery of authentic musical forms of worship, including a return to the Psalter, which has always been characteristic of the praise of God's people at its best — but not necessarily with Bourgeois' Genevan tunes — and various forms of folk and classical music.

7. Youth

And we cannot avoid the fact that on every continent youth are responding to Jesus Christ. In some areas the response is unparalleled and in many the cutting edge of the church is obviously among the under-30's. This has always been the story of renewal. Luther was just over thirty when the Reformation began, while his right-hand man, Melanchthon, occupied that place at the age of twenty-two, at which time he also had a European reputation as a Hebraist. Calvin was only twenty-six when he completed the first draft of the greatest work of Protestant theology, the *Institutes,* and twenty-seven when he began his ministry at Geneva, which soon turned it, at least in John Knox's estimation, into the veriest school of Christ since the apostles. Jonathan Edwards was thirty when revival came to Northampton, Massachusetts, and George Whitefield was an international evangelist at twenty-six. When God does a new thing he has always used the young — and he is using them in our day.

And how can we overlook the young Jews for Jesus? Is this the generation when converted Israel shall be as life from the dead to the Gentiles according to Romans 11? I do not know, but at least we should contemplate the signs of the times.

Do the signs point to the return of Jesus Christ or an unprecedented revival, to be accompanied and followed by great and increasing apostasy before he comes? Once again, I do not know. But as I sit here day by day with my brothers from the Third World I have less and less assurance in an eschatology which sees scores of millions from the Western world in the rapture, but is quite satisfied with half a dozen from Abi Dhabu, the Trucial States and Afghanistan combined. In the light of this Congress, that looks more like chauvinism than eschatology. If the Gospel is to be preached to all peoples before Jesus returns, perhaps we are being given the opportunity and promise of helping to prepare that beautiful Bride out of every people, nation, tribe, and tongue, which is so glorious and great that no man can number it.

REGIONAL STRATEGY REPORT ON EAST ASIA

by James Wong

East Asia is perhaps the most populated region in the world which is the least evangelized. China alone, with its 800 million people is within this region. Even in countries like Thailand, Japan, Laos, Cambodia and others the proportion of Christians over the total population is not more than 2 per cent.

Asia is a continent of great cultural, ethnic, linguistic, political and economic diversities. Unlike other continents, the witness faced by the Asian church is compounded with the difficulty of penetrating a large segment of its population which has embraced major religions like Buddhism, Confucianism, Taoism, Shintoism, Hinduism and Islam for centuries before the arrival of Christianity into these countries.

Steady church growth — Yet for all these seeming difficulties and obstacles there have been signs of encouragement, in recent years, pointing towards the possibility of significant evangelistic break-through. This is seen in Indonesia (traditionally a Muslim stronghold) and North Thailand (a Buddhist country) and in parts of Vietnam and Burma (amongst the animistic tribes). Beginning from the early part of the twentieth century, the churches in Korea, Taiwan, the Philippines, Malaysia-Singapore, Indonesia, Hong Kong and even in Burma have all been experiencing growth rates in excess of the population growth. The momentum is gathering in these East Asian countries. At this Congress, it has been clearly expressed by all the Asian national strategy groups that they have been encouraged and that many of them are setting the sights high — aiming towards a rate of at least 10 per cent church growth.

Areas of effectiveness — No single method of evangelism can be said to be the most effective for Asia. Because of great cultural diversities it is important to warn Western agencies not to be insensitive and impose their style of evangelism into Asia. Presently the church in East Asia is experiencing great responsiveness from the youth and students. Hence, school works and campus ministries carried out by the various church and para-church groups should be encouraged and supported. This area of evangelism should be given priority seeing that in many Asian countries, between 50 and 60 per cent of the total population is said to be under twenty-five years. In Korea and Singapore the work among the armed forces personnel and factory workers is reaping a spiritual harvest. Mass evangelism in rural areas and small evangelistic Bible study groups in urban centers have also been effective. In many of the densely populated metropolises city-wide evangelistic campaigns have recorded responses to the Gospel.

New opportunities — The church in East Asia is optimistic in its goal towards world evangelization. This Congress has encouraged our participants and has given them new insights into strategies and possibilities for evangelizing the whole of Asia. We believe that we are going to see the beginning of a vast missionary enterprise in the hands of Asian leadership. For us it is the sunrise of missions. Asians are beginning to assume the major responsibility of evangelizing Asians across cultural, ethnic and geographical boundaries. The greatest challenge and need is not to motivate them for evangelism but to train them in the know-how of evangelism. The training of Asian Christian leadership (beyond the formal academic program at theological seminaries) for evangelism and church planting should be given top priority of attention.

Distinctive contribution towards world evangelization — The churches in Asia do not feel that, even though the people in their own country have not yet been fully evangelized, they should not engage in overseas missions. The Gospel must be taken to all nations and here we can see the beginning of a new set of relationships between the older Western missions and the younger indigenous Asian missions. Over the past thirty years it is estimated that eighteen Asian countries have founded over 100 mission-sending agencies for cross-cultural evangelism. Japan, Korea, Hong Kong and the Philippines have sent many of their ambassadors for Christ overseas, while Taiwan, Vietnam, Singapore, Malaysia and Indonesia have also started. Presently more than 1,000 cross-cultural missionaries engaging in E-2 and E-3 evangelism are found not only among Asian countries but also in Europe, the United States, the Middle East, Africa and Latin America. Efforts are being made to coordinate and train more Asian missionaries to be recruited each year. The projection is that, by the end of this century, the churches in Asia will train and send 10,000 missionaries to reach the unevangelized areas of the world. Thus, we in Asia are encouraged and excited, that in these last days, we have a part to play in obedience to the Lord's command to preach the Gospel to every creature.

SOUTHERN ASIA NATIONAL STRATEGY GROUP REPORT

Samuel Kamaleson

Dr. Kamaleson, Madras, India, is the District Superintendent for the Methodist Church in Southern Asia.

Prayer — The church in Southern Asia cannot depend upon herself in terms of numerical or economic strength. To be the dependent community that she must be should come naturally to her. Hence many significant thrusts stem from prayer. The efforts that are city-wide and state-wide and the cross-cultural efforts all stem from grass-root-level prayer groups. Great accent has been laid upon prayer-cell movements in terms of planning for the future.

Bible Message — South Asia is the spawning ground for many virile world faiths. The church which is like "the little flock" must be careful to avoid the temptation of syncretism when she seeks to identify in order to communicate. A merely dogmatic, philosophical, or emphatical theology will not remain Christian within this context too long. It will be swallowed up into the philosophical matrix of these other faiths. The message of the church has to be Jesus Christ — the person himself. No system can swallow the biblical Jesus Christ without suffering indigestion. There is no other message. Small groups, theological training for ministry as well as laity, are all planned accordingly.

Authority — Authority is his. In cross-cultural communication, as in the days of the earliest Christians, this aspect is the same still. The church knows this authority in her "being sent." The church in South Asia presents the message not with arrogance, but with the certainty of faith, and the quality of the servant. She confidently plans strategic evangelism, as well as finding the freedom to participate in the great programs of social uplift that the secular governments of this area have planned such as family planning, uplift of the socially injured, voluntary limitation of personal property ownership, care of the uncared-for (like children and other destitutes), increase of food production, etc.

So far, even within conditions that are new and unexpected the church has found the possibility of "pasture" and the freedom to "go in and out" because of this authority of the person of Jesus Christ. The new innovations that emerge from South Asia in this context are numerous. A supreme court judge in reading his verdict in the case accusing a Christian pastor's act of baptizing converts into the believers' community said: "If Christianity is a recognized religion, then conversion is part of it because the Christian is under obligation by mandate to do so." The case was dismissed.

Faith — Unity demands courage — unusual courage — and faith is the basis for such courage. The dependent community exhibits such faith-born courage in many acts of united effort in proclamation and cross-cultural expression of mission. Avoiding the word "crusade" and "campaign" because of their unusual historic connotations, the church in a large city in Southern Asia called the effort of united proclamation of Jesus Christ as "the festival of joy unquenchable." Held on the clear white sands of the beach, the proclamation was made from a platform which previously had been used for political rallies only. Enormous crowds of non-Christians listened and responded. In the closing meeting the archbishop of the Catholic church presided while a Methodist minister and a layman of the church of South India did the proclamation. Men from all denominations were on the platform. There was a great response. The same courage in unity is expressed in mission as in interdenominational mission agencies. Well-planned action with and for youth is a primary accent. There are "in depth" plans like the "India Penetration Program" available for use. The lorry drivers' union in Meldram, a Northeastern state in India, had a vision for reaching the people of their state and launched forth into a very successful preaching mission in which all the denominations cooperated.

There is rich reward in Southern Asia.

CENTRAL ASIA

Background
Muslim countries in Central Asia have been closed both politically and socially for centuries, preventing official missionary work right up to the present time. Following World War II, some countries began to admit an increasing number of foreigners to pursue technical, educational, medical, and social programs. A number of Christians have taken advantage of this opportunity, and as they have shown a genuine interest in the area's general advancement, and in its people and their welfare, they have been blessed in their relationship to the people and to each other. A church developed for foreigners in the capital city. A beautiful building was constructed for the worship of the Christian foreigners and for a visible testimony to all who might see it and inquire. The summer of 1973 saw its destruction by a hostile government.

Present situation
The political situation is changing, and a pro-Russian and pro-Indian course is being pursued. The Western personnel connected with technical, educational, social, and medical projects are being phased out. Possible trouble with Pakistan has been forecast. There is a small number of believers in the land.

Strategy
Realizing that God often uses changing events to forward his purposes, Christians around the world are encouraged to pray for this land, its government, and its people. Pray for the small group of believers, some of whom were converted inside the country through their friendships with Christian foreigners and others outside the country.

Radio broadcasts into the country from the Seychelles and Sri Lanka in the languages of the country are being contemplated, and should be encouraged to move forward. Literature should be made available to respondees in the languages. Gospel recordings should be spotted on certain broadcasts for lesser-used languages and could also be sent into the country with the literature to respondees. Christian nationals outside the country are helping with the preparation of the broadcasts. This is to be encouraged and assisted. Correspondence courses should be prepared for follow up from Iran and India.

Mail
It was noted that one organization is to send Scriptures to everyone in Central Asia who is a telephone subscriber. This is excellent. They will be encouraged to include a Gospel recording provided by another organization. It is also possible to encourage Christians of other nations to use the phone directory list to write personal letters to establish friendships and contacts for others to pursue personally.

Self-support opportunities

Christians are asked to seek self-supporting ways of entering from other countries such as U.N., embassy staff, technical and other forms of employment.

Expatriates

Christians in other countries should contact students, teachers, workers, government officials, etc., who are in their countries. An organized effort is needed in Europe (Germany, France, Britain) and in U.S.A.). The U.S. group reports it is endeavoring long-term training and discipleship of groups of converts, as opposed to letting converts struggle back one at a time without having extensive fellowship with other believers. (If they do not have extensive contact/fellowship with other converts before returning, the difficulties of fellowship and worship after returning retard the establishment of a strong witness.) A transplant of the church is needed, such as the one from Jerusalem to Antioch recorded in Acts 11.

NORTH AMERICA

David Hubbard

The commitment that brought us from Canada and the United States to Lausanne, has been strengthened by our study and our fellowship here — a commitment to the truth of the Gospel as proclaimed in the Scripture and effected by Jesus Christ in his incarnation, his death, his resurrection, his ascension, his outpouring of his Holy Spirit on his people — a commitment to the urgency of the task of evangelism across the broad sweep of our states and provinces. It is a commitment to cooperative endeavors beyond the lines of a single denomination, congregation or parachurch agency.

May I focus on three areas of concern that we have in North America, and particularly in the United States. The first is the bi-centennial of American independence coming up in 1976. The eyes of the nation will be on the legacy which our founding fathers bequeathed to us. It becomes an appropriate time to remind our fellow citizens of the spiritual aspects of our heritage and to call them to repentance and faith in the Christ who is Lord of all nations. We are recommending then, that Christian churches and agencies consider ways that they can use the events of the bicentennial for Christian witness, observing national holidays as days of prayer, focusing Bible study and preaching on the meaning of Christian freedom, pointing out the way in which human rights are rooted in a biblical view of creation, stressing the contribution that personal renewal will make to the stability of the nation. There will be special efforts made to distribute the Bible to every home. There is some talk of a day or week of national witness to be set aside during which every Christian will be urged to share his or her faith with another Christian person, perhaps the period between Ascension Day and Pentecost. Interdenominational rallies are planned; denominations have bicentennial programs that they are seeking to implement; Bible studies and prayer groups are being asked to put special emphasis on the needs of our fellow citizens for repentance and faith; and the Forum for Evangelism, which is an informal organization continuing the fellowship and cooperative spirit begun with "Key '73," may be used as a clearinghouse for the sharing of plans and the developing of strategy in 1976.

A second area of emphasis has to do with lay witness. We feel that when we get to the heart of what is going on in evangelism around the world, it is the role of the lay person in the sharing of faith which becomes crucial. We feel that pastors have to come to grips with the nature of their ministry as teacher, coach, and enabler. We feel that lay people need to understand their own spiritual gifts, their role within the body, and the service that Christ is calling them to perform.

Now I come to a little bit of meddling. We feel that theological seminaries, Bible schools and colleges ought to provide on-the-job training for pastors in future generations, and make, as a basic part of that training, an emphasis on preparing men and women to equip lay persons to carry on the task of evangelism. We are wondering if the time has come when there ought to be a great national or continent-wide congress on lay evangelism.

LAY WITNESS

When most evangelistic plans are reduced to fundamental dimensions they involve the layman, nourished by the Word of God, sensitized by prayer and controlled by the Holy Spirit. We sense, therefore, the vital importance of lay responsibility in evangelism and discipleship.

In the United States we feel that the great hindrances to enthusiastic lay witness are (1) a widespread misunderstanding of spiritual gifts (2) pastors who are not interested in and/or not equipped for the training of lay evangelists. The pastor, however, is the product of his own past. Often he has had no preparation for one-on-one or small-group training in evangelism.

We, therefore, recommend (1) that our Bible schools and theological seminaries provide "on the job" training for our future pastors and missionaries (2) that our pastors, now in ministry, seek training in the mobilization and preparation of lay evangelists (3) that our local churches adopt some program of lay evangelism in order to implement the purposes of this Congress, namely world evangelization (4) that a national or even international Congress on proven approaches to witnessing be considered.

N.A.E.

For three decades the National Association of Evangelicals has provided a forum for evangelical discussion and a structure for cooperative evangelical ministries. It has not achieved the breadth of association nor the depth of support many leaders of NAE desire. Yet it continues as a significant (major) channel for the implementation of evangelistic strategies.

We, therefore, recommend to evangelical organizations and local churches serious consideration of the projected programs of NAE including the NAE convention in Washington, D.C., during the approaching bicentennial year and the projected rally at the Washington monument in Washington, D.C., on Sunday, July 4, 1976.

The last emphasis that we have is an emphasis on para-church cooperation. We are calling for para-church organizations to get together for concerted strategy, for corporate planning in recruiting and training of leadership. We are calling those organizations to form closer relationships with pastors, with local churches and with denominational officials. We are trusting that a directory of para-church organizations will be published periodically which will list the purposes, the resources and the staffs of each of these organizations.

We will go home from Lausanne to a continent that has been stained by scandal, rocked by inflation, and that is riddled by feelings of identity crises in terms of what is our role in the world in the last half of our decade. But, we will go back with a concerted effort to push the cause of evangelism, that these countrymen of ours in the United States and Canada may learn, in the midst of all our uncertainty, to confess that liberating word, "Jesus is Lord."

EUROPE REPORT

Dr. Harold John Ockenga once said: "In many sections of Europe an individual has about as little chance of receiving an evangelical Christian witness as he would have in many better known mission fields of the world." Dr. Robert Evans stated: "Over a quarter of a million towns and villages in Europe do not have an adequate Gospel witness."

In the Dutch National Strategy Group it was pointed out that only 57 per cent of the Dutch people have a Bible and only 12 per cent read the Bible regularly. In France, with its 54 million inhabitants there are only 40 thousand evangelicals. In other European countries the proportion is worse. Thus it can be said that Europe has become a pagan continent.

What can we do as Europeans to bring about a change to the positive? Among the many items that have been suggested and discussed in several of the European national strategy groups, let me touch on only two — and both of them concern the youth.

It is the youth that is more open to the Gospel than any other age group. In the last four to five years all of us noticed a great revival of interest for spiritual things. It seems that more young people are turning to Christ today than what we experienced some years ago. Many of these young people come out of non-Christian and unchurched homes. They do not understand the church and want to have very little to do with it. However, we want to see them established in the church and therefore training at the grass root level within the churches has to take place first, for the dormant members of the church to make them receptive to the new young members; second, for the young people to make *them* understand the situation of the church, and to keep them hot for evangelism. They must be taught the concept of a balanced life which includes the physical, mental, social, and spiritual areas of their lives in order to keep them on even keel and to eventually let them become pillars of the church. Thus training a basis within the church is needed and also, thank God, planned.

The second thing I want to touch on has to do with the practical side of what is going to happen for young people in Europe *now*. Ever since the large youth happening in England called SPREE took place, hundreds of young people across Europe have been waiting for such a youth event to take place on the continent of Europe. The Germans have taken up the challenge, and a large youth congress is being planned for German young people to take place in the city of Essen in 1976. The European Student Missionary Association is organizing "Mission '76" to take place in Lausanne over New Year 75/76 — a conference to challenge young European Christians to do missionary work abroad. But already next summer the largest Christian youth festival ever attempted on the continent of Europe is going to take place in Brussels, Belgium, from August 24 to September 2. It is called EUROFEST '75. Ten thousand young people or more are going to come together for Bible teaching, witness and international Christian fellowship.

We as European evangelicals have a great burden for our continent. We have sat in shame when we heard about the many blessings and advancement of the church in the Third World countries. Our conscience has been pricked; some of us have met in prayer groups to repent. With it we have been challenged and we are determined to leave Lausanne to do better in evangelizing our people and to let them know that Christ our Lord is alive. We are deeply grateful to our brethren from the Third World and we want to thank you for having opened our eyes.

A VIEW OF LATIN AMERICA

Dan Nuesch

Latin America is a continent of contrasts. Its climate varies from the humid tropical heat of Equatorial Amazonas, to the frozen wastes of Tierra del Fuego. To present the continent as monolithic is a mistake. The Republics have only two things in common: the Spanish language and the Roman Catholic faith (Brazil is an exception as the language is Portuguese, and French is spoken in some of the Antilles).

An example of the racial differences became evident in the members of the strategy groups. In the Argentine group all the members were of European or Near Eastern extraction. In the neighboring Republic of Paraguay on the other hand, 90 per cent of the population is a homogenous mixture of Spanish and Guarany.

Contrasts are also evident with regard to the Protestant population. While Chile claims to have a 12 per cent Protestant population its next door neighbor, Argentina, has only 2 per cent, and the remaining republics are some place between these figures.

Some interesting statements about Latin America, heard during the national group meetings, were:

In *Bolivia* an interesting revival based on indigenous principles and practices is taking place among the Aymara Indians.

In *Brazil* 204 cross-cultural missionaries are supported by the Southern Baptists.

A new openness of the Catholic church was reported in *Argentina* and *Brazil*. *Brazil* has the first Protestant president in its history and a new interest in religion on the part of government and military leaders is reported.

In a continent of young people, *Ecuador* would seem to beat the record, with a 47 per cent population less than fifteen years old.

The report of the *Central American and Dominican Republics* mentions an awakening among young people which provides many opportunities for the use of mass media.

It is interesting to note that in spite of the differences mentioned above, the *definitions* given by the different groups on *world evangelism*, all include the note of *urgency* in their respective areas.

Successful methods

It is obvious from the reports given by the different groups, that the mass media are the most successful methods to reach the unreached people of the areas. Mentions were made of the tremendous impact of the television programs shown, and regrets were expressed that there are not more programs available for general use.

Brazil reports that the Sunday School continues to be the outstanding means of reaching and teaching people, a subject on which the *Central America and Dominican Republics* agreed with added emphasis.

Costa Rica reported a good response from young people, students and the poorer classes, probably because these sections of the population received the greater attention from the churches.

Less spectacular, but yet significant methods were reported in other areas, such as the School Evangelism in *Argentina,* a mobile workshop in *Columbia* which spreads the Gospel while teaching manual arts to rural people, and the use of folklore musical groups in *Paraguay.*

Needs

The needs of Latin America, according to the reports given by the groups, appear to be twofold: *outside* the church, and *in* the church. Outside the church, the most evident need is the evangelization of unreached tribes in many countries. Also a prominent need is to reach the young people, students and children. Several countries mention the present influx of migrant workers. It was stated that in the past God has used these migrant groups for his purposes and to move history. It could happen again.

Inside the church, the most prominent needs appear to be: to emphasize the theological concept of evangelism; the absolute necessity to stimulate aggressive evangelism; lack of transcultural means — mission societies, funds, interest; training of leaders (this need was strongly underlined); to evangelize the second and third generations of evangelicals; a better usage of radio for evangelization; and a more widespread and efficient use of schools for evangelization.

Resources available

The "coming of age" of the church in Latin America appears to provide the possibility of sending missionaries to other parts of the world. *Brazil* thinks in terms of Portugal and Portuguese-speaking Africa; *Mexico* in terms of its neighbors in Central America and the USA, while *Argentina* feels that she might help with human resources for Italy, the Arab-speaking countries, and some countries of Latin America.

Goals

Many of the goals are mentioned under the heading of Needs. It was felt by most of the participants, and strongly recommended by *Colombia,* that the church needs to be mobilized for it to evangelize in every way it can.

Another need emphasized during the Congress was the raising of local leaders who are motivated for evangelism. It was unanimously felt that the continuing committee should be in close contact with the national churches.

Strategy

Mention was made of the necessity to form groups of study on personal evangelism with people of different churches. The Paraguay delegation asked that the booklet "The Church Around the World" be translated into Spanish.

Action for participants

All the countries emphasized the need that every participant take the responsibility of carrying the Congress to his or her area of activity. *Argentina* formed a committee with some of the participants in the Congress to take immediate action upon arriving back home. One of the goals of this committee is the realization of a great united campaign by 1977.

Help beyond resources

Many participants expressed the need of human and financial help to put certain programs into action. *Peru* mentioned the need of help in order to study the real situation of the evangelical churches in the country. Many other countries mentioned the need of help for the organization of national congresses and retreats to promote evangelism.

Forms of continuing association

The general idea was that this Congress should be followed by national groups that would take the emphasis on evangelization into every country of every area. The feeling of practically all of the Latin American participants was that *national* congresses and pastors' retreats should be organized as soon after the Congress as possible in order to make further studies on the needs of each region.

Mention was also made of the need of having a system of sharing *information* regarding crusades and methods of evangelization between the different countries of the area. The hope was expressed that the continuing committee will not become an international super-structure, but a functional body to help the churches fulfill their task of evangelism.

MIDDLE EAST AND NORTH AFRICA REPORT

Antoina Deeb

We who are convening here at the International Congress on World Evangelization from the Middle East and North African countries are deeply moved by the extraordinary occasion of being here at the invitation of the Congress. We are most grateful for the golden opportunity afforded us and for the generosity and hospitality in providing so many scholarships to our people.

Those of us who have come from our respective countries have been greatly blessed and more enlightened regarding the evangelization of our own areas and the world in general. Our hearts were greatly stirred up and challenged to move forward with fixed determination to take the Good News of God's love, life and light to the regions beyond.

Due to the conflicting and touchy situation politically and religiously, we deemed it wise to mention nothing regarding the details of our strategy; however, please find here below the decisions which we made at our discussion group:

1. To form a fellowship for Evangelistic Outreach throughout the Middle East and North Africa.

2. To make a thorough study of the existing resources (personnel, literature, and finances) which could be attained and utilized for the purpose of fulfilling the vision.

3. To spread and impart the vision of the Congress and share its evangelistic and missionary burden.

To involve all in sharing the Good News with their neighbors.

To reach laborers and students who have left their own countries to work and study in foreign lands.

To strengthen and encourage those who are evangelizing through medical work. Since more people pass through the hospitals of the area than through its churches, the need is urgent for more dedicated medical personnel to fill such strategic positions.

4. Adequate materials adaptable by our people in order to help educate and train laymen. The establishing of a center library to be used as a resource for reference on evangelization and missions.

There is a desperate need in all of our churches and among our ministers for leadership training seminars, geared especially toward subjects related to evangelization and missions.

Since some of the churches are poor and some do lack teaching on Scriptural giving, its privileges and its blessings, there is a need for financing the program for its realization at the beginning until it matures.

5. We need to form an evangelistic fellowship which comprises all of these countries mentioned above, as much as possible in order to:

a. maintain the common vision;

b. fall in line with what is happening in the Asian, Latin, American, and African churches;

c. determine the proper course of action to be taken regarding holding a Congress on Evangelization for Christians from said countries.

(This subject was discussed after the Amsterdam Congress with the Billy Graham Evangelistic Association but never materialized due to the much needed preparation which this present Congress demanded).

d. participants in this Congress from all areas mentioned above eagerly desire and long to continue in fellowship with the fellowship of evangelical Christians who share the same vision of worldwide evangelization in our generation.

We do appreciate your sharing the burden of intercession with us for our area, for divine intervention and visitation upon the lives of teaming millions who live in gross darkness and the shadow of death.

Since action speaks louder than words, we are looking to the Lord to divinely enable us to act according to our newfound convictions and see God in action in our midst for his glory.

AFRICA AREA REPORT

G. Osei-Mensah

Individuals and national groups testify to a new and widened vision of world evangelization. For some (especially from franco-phone areas where evangelical work is relatively young) this has been their first exposure to the evangelistic vision. For others who have grappled longer with the evangelistic task and seen much fruit for their labors, the Congress has opened their eyes to greater possibilities. There is genuine desire to translate resolution into action back home, and every encouragement must be given to see this happen.

1. National groups have identified geographical, ethnic, social, and cultural groups in their own country as yet unreached with the Good News. The obstacles that stand in the way have been studied, as well as ways of penetrating them with God's help.

2. Evangelical cooperation at national, grass roots level is recommended overwhelmingly as the first step in mobilizing our efforts for outreach.

3. Participants should form the core of this cooperation in every place. Small teams should report back to churches and fellowships (using the tools and kits from the Congress), every member reporting on one aspect of the skills and insights gathered at Lausanne. Some recommend this to be done within two weeks of return home, while memory is still fresh. Personal objectives should include implementing some skill or model studied at the Congress in the individual's home context. In all this, others who could not attend the Congress should be involved so that the vision and know-how may be spread through sharing.

4. From a modest beginning, there could be evaluation and expansion, using local resources and tools and skills gathered from the Congress, calling on those fellowships and agencies to provide specific help and resources needed for expansion.

5. There is need for an information and resource center which will also give functional expression to the inspiring sense of our worldwide fellowship in evangelization.

ANGOLA NATIONAL STRATEGY GROUP REPORT

Secretary: Eliseu Simeão

The national strategy group of Angola met every scheduled day, holding two sessions with Mozambique and Guiné Bissau, and one with Portugal. In this last session various cross-cultural problems were discussed in the light of the Congress's work and in the light of the new freedom of Angola.

1. Goals for the next decade.

Cooperation between evangelical churches had to be greatly developed.

Radio work which is already being done must be more developed, also in African languages.

Literature has to be greatly developed. Evangelical bookshops are very necessary. Various evangelistic leaflets must be adapted to local conditions.

The work among young people, being of paramount importance, should be developed. A special effort is to be made among young intellectuals.

Biblical training is to be developed and Bible study papers for village evangelists prepared by a central agency. Training of laymen must be started on a larger scale.

An inventory or directory of all evangelical workers and agencies of Angola should be prepared.

A special effort to reach the last unreached tribes in South and East must be made.

Reconstruction of the evangelical churches — spiritually and materially — which have been wiped out in all northern Angola must be started. There many faithful Christians remain, without being able to meet.

2. Basic strategy

Evangelistic campaigns are essential on a local or regional basis for uniting the evangelicals of various groups. Spiritual preparation of the teams is essential. Personal evangelism remains fundamental.

Evangelization of towns is a great priority, as little is being done.

Laymen working on various levels is emphasized.

In modern Angola it is more important than ever to bring a *pure Gospel,* without western cultural adjuncts and without any superiority attitudes.

3. Special action recommended for participants

To communicate the aims and the inspiration of this Congress, deeply and in all areas of our various fields of work.

To convince the leaders of our various churches and denominations of the importance of these aims and of evangelical unity.

To begin without delay evangelization and development of the social activities, and do this in a spirit of prayer, communicating the importance of prayer.

To promote the mutual visitation of various church leaders in other churches. To promote the beginning of little Bible study groups and love for the Word of God.

To help in the alphabetization of primitive groups.

To obey the vision and the personal strategy received in these days, speaking of Christ and winning souls.

4. Help needed

Visits are needed from other evangelicals to the Angola churches. Financial means to be able to send delegates of Angola to regional and other evangelical meetings and conventions is needed.

Technical help for radio work.

Financial help for literature, for evangelistic leaflets, etc.

Literature of the Congress to be made available in Portuguese.

5. Continuing association

The members of the Angola group unanimously decided to found an EVANGELICAL FELLOWSHIP of Angola. The doctrinal basis is the same as the one of the Association of Evangelicals of Africa and Madagascar.

The need of such an association had been felt years ago, but has not been possible because of the tight political situation of the old regime. Now with the new freedom evangelicals should all join together and work in close spiritual unity.

The Angola group is to meet to study the details of this association of Evangelicals.

The prospect of the Evangelistic campaign of Rev. Fanini of Brazil, in Angola, for 1975 could be the means of cooperation; and it is considered that an invitation could be arranged for some meetings in southern Angola.

In conclusion we can say that the vision of this Congress and the new and great freedom of Angola, are for us signs of God for a new and promising period of proclamation of God's message in that country.

AUSTRALIA NATIONAL STRATEGY GROUP REPORT

Secretary: David Claydon

Mr. Claydon, Sydney, New South Wales, Australia, is Federal Secretary of Scripture Union of Australia.

1. Attitudes

As Australians who have prayed and talked together at the Lausanne Congress, we express our gratitude to God for the renewed vision he has given us for world and home evangelism.

We acknowledge the unique opportunities which the Congress has provided to examine in fellowship our committal to a full-orbed biblical evangelism. This has resulted in our being deeply concerned to see the church in Australia in all its manifoldness, confront and penetrate the nation with the Gospel, in the context of the whole counsel of God.

We unreservedly affirm both the entire trustworthiness of Scripture and our need to submit ourselves to it, as governing our total life-style. We affirm that it is through the Word of God that the Spirit teaches the meaning of the Lordship of Christ.

We acknowledge with pain the existence of superficiality and complacency in our attitude towards the Gospel, and lack of openness and patience towards each other's structures and methods.

We acknowledge the use by the Holy Spirit of many and diverse methods. We recognize the danger that all methods tend to become stereotyped and that the Spirit is continually reshaping and transcending our methods.

We recognize our responsibilities to share in world evangelization, but especially our need to enter more deeply into partnership with the church in Asia and Oceania. We desire this partnership because we are conscious that we share some problems and believe that we can learn from each other. In particular, we believe that the Australian church can renew its missionary vision through closer contact with the vigorous church life evident in parts of Asia and Oceania.

While we would like to express our goals and strategies precisely, we feel we can only attempt to sketch a framework of some of the things we have begun to learn.

2. Goals

As we return to Australia, we set before ourselves the following goals:

a. To promote and maintain the unity of the Spirit in the bond of peace (Eph. 4:3) and in the practice of evangelism. We believe that this will come with renewal through the constant and prayerful submission to Scripture of our message, our methods, and our structures (Rev. 2:7).

b. To implement Christ's new commandment (John 13:34,35) so that it will be more obvious in our lives. As this happens we expect to see a deeper penetration of society and a more dynamic proclamation of the Gospel by every member of the church.

3. *Strategy*

a. *Australia-wide.* We see the need to have a national initiating group, both to provide a channel of communication enabling ideas, needs, and resources to be shared, and to set up study groups and conferences as desired. We request that the Evangelical Alliance be invited to take immediate action thus: (i) to initiate discussions with the leaders of the Aboriginal church, (ii) to seek advice from the Co-ordinating Office of Evangelism in Singapore concerning partnership with Asia; (iii) to initiate discussions with leaders in the new emerging youth movements; (iv) to set up study groups on the following issues: the meaning and content of the Gospel in relationship to such areas as ethics, social concern, and apologetics; the ministry of women; the nature of the Church; our responsibility in social action; the need for hermeneutics today; the ministry of youth; our ministry among ethnic minorities in Australia; the need for evangelism, and for an understanding of problems in industry and commerce; and (v) to examine the possibility of a national study and evaluation conference in one year's time.

b. *The local church.* We recognize the absolute necessity for the local church to be excited with the vision for world evangelization. We therefore: (i) call all ministers to a renewed teaching expository ministry designed to renew and reawaken the body of Christ and to give leadership to a deeper evangelistic and missionary involvement; (ii) commend the use of the Congress study booklets, cassettes, and tapes by local congregations so that members might focus on the message of the Congress and be challenged by the call for renewal in our evangelistic mission; (iii) commend the use of Christian publications to examine the issues highlighted by the Congress; and (iv) commend church members to open their homes to Asian students and new migrants as an expression of Christian love.

4. *Educational institutions*

We are convinced of the profound importance of teaching, arising out of biblical exegesis in the life of the church in the growth of zeal to be obedient to the Lord's command to be his witnesses. We therefore will give priority to assist in whatever way possible:

a. theological and Bible colleges as they impart to students an enthusiastic concern for evangelism;

b. denominational departments of Christian education as they teach the Gospel in the context of the whole counsel of God;

c. churches near the campuses of tertiary institutions as they seek to develop as teaching centers to students.

5. *Association*

We recommend the development of autonomous regional fellowships rather than an international association.

BANGLADESH

Secretary: Phil Parshall

Gratitude was expressed to God for the miraculous way in which he opened the door for the eleven national participants to attend the Congress. An appeal for permission to leave the country had to go all the way to the Home Minister. It was only four hours prior to the plane's departure that all the obstacles were finally removed. Seven missionaries joined the delegation, making a total of eighteen Christian leaders.

One of the sessions was devoted to an overview of the challenges and opportunities existent among the 72 million people in Bangladesh. Particularly significant was the response received to the Gospel among certain Hindu groups. Tribespeople in the north and south of the country are also turning responsively. Muslims are coming to Christ on an individual basis, but as yet there is no indication of a move of the Spirit of God among them.

There was a unanimous feeling that church renewal and evangelistic emphasis are imperatives for the situation current in Bangladesh. There was, however, diversity of opinion on the options open for the initiation of such schemes for forward thrust. After a great deal of frank and lucid discussion the following was unanimously adopted:

1. Church renewal

a. A call to each church to engage in daily prayer for revival.

b. A new emphasis on personal Bible study to be made through church leaders.

c. Pastors and lay leaders are to be requested to give systematic Bible studies from the pulpit.

d. A prayer bulletin is to be initiated in the Bengali language. The purpose of this bulletin will be to inform, as well as to call Bengali Christians to fervent intercessory prayer.

2. Evangelistic emphasis

a. A fellowship of spiritual partnership for prayer and proclamation of the Word of God was formed, and is to be known as the "Bangladesh Prayer and Preaching Fellowship." The Rev. Subash Sangma and the Rev. Simon Sircar will serve as coordinators for this group. They will seek to supply preachers and Gospel teams for churches which request their assistance.

b. Asian Christian teams are cordially invited to minister within the Bangladesh Christian scene.

c. It is hoped that national Christians can meet all expenses from their own resources in regard to the above-mentioned projects. If this proves impossible, however, outside assistance may be required.

3. Ten-year goals

a. Importune prayer for spiritual renewal in every church in the nation.

b. Provide evangelistic help to those churches or groups who request it.

c. *Double the number of Christians in Bangladesh.* The people of Bangladesh have received millions of dollars in aid from the Christians of the world in the past two years. We now fervently request their prayerful attention and involvement in the tremendous task of reaching a nation for Christ — a nation that is over 99 1/2% unevangelized. To the end of making our Savior known, we humbly rededicate our lives, and we will, by God's grace, seek to redouble our efforts in the vital areas of prayer and evangelism. "Where there is no vision the people perish" (Prov. 29:18).

BRAZIL NATIONAL STRATEGY GROUP REPORT

Secretaries: Russell Shedd and Paul Landrey

Wed. July 17, 1974

1. Definition: World evangelism is the communication of the good news of Jesus Christ through all means with the purpose of reconciling men from all nations, peoples and tongues to God by faith in Christ and integrating them into the life of the church. Evangelization constitutes the responsibility of each believer and local church in obedience to the great commission.

2. For the execution of this work, evangelical pastors and leaders must teach and train the members of their churches to bring each member to a level of effective witness, living and active on all the frontiers where God places them.

3. Among the areas which most demand the work of evangelism, we emphasized the following: youth, military, professional classes, intellectuals, the middle and upper classes of the great urban centers as well as the Indian tribes.

4. Areas in which Brazil is heading the challenge to missions are at this time the Portuguese-and-Spanish speaking people of Latin America, Africa, Europe and Asia.

July 18, 1974

1. The most receptive areas to the Gospel are: (1) North and central-west and particularly the great urban centers of Rio and Sâo Paulo. (2) From the sociological viewpoint the most receptive people are the working classes, youth, urban populations arising from migrations, children and farm workers.

2. New opportunities are: (1) greater accessibility to the mass media of communications — radio, newspaper, and TV; (2) literature distribution — especially Bible distribution among Roman Catholics; (3) receptivity of the Gospel message through music presented by youth in a youthful style like Vencedores por Cristo; (4) openness of military leaders and high government administrators to eternal values of the Gospel.

3. Obstacles to the Gospel presentation: (1) Many Christians' preoccupation with material values; (2) increasing secularization of society beginning with the child's education; (3) lack of authenticity and enthusiasm for the Gospel as well as the lack of a vital testimony on the part of many Christians; (4) the new vitality of all forms of spiritism.

July 19, 1974

1. The most efficient means of evangelization at the present time is the personal invitation of non-christians to a church meeting, where they are evangelized and won. Other means are: radio, TV, literature, camps, child-evangelism, evangelism through youth music groups in schools, personal evangelism in homes, hospitals and prisons.

2. New methods of evangelism learned here by group members are: audio-visual presentation, evangelism-in-depth, house cell groups,

mobilization of the church for evangelism, evangelism explosion, coffee-house evangelism, youth with a mission, operation mobilization. These all presented basic principles which could be useful with convenient adaptation to certain areas and ministries in Brazil.

3. Old means which can be profitable in the future — with improved effectiveness are: the Sunday school, open-air evangelism, evangelistic conferences.

July 20, 1974

1. Among the different cultural groups which need evangelization in Brazil, we note particularly the unreached tribes of the country, as well as ethnic populations of Asiatic (Japanese, Chinese, Korean), European (German, Italian, Portuguese) origin. It was noted that various denominations maintain missionary work among these ethnic peoples who have immigrated to Brazil.

2. The Brazilian churches have sent missionaries to five continents, with workers evangelizing in the following countries: Paraguay, Bolivia, Colombia, Argentina, Uruguay, Chile, Venezuela, Peru, Equador, United States, Portugal, Spain, France, Macau, Timor, Guinea, Mozambique, Angola, South Africa, India and Madagascar.

3. We understand that the greatest opportunity and responsibility in terms of *Brazilian missionary work* is in relation to those people with whom we have racial and linguistic affinity (Latin America, Africa and other Portuguese-speaking peoples).

4. More than 150 foreign mission agencies with over 3,000 missionaries are working in all areas of evangelization and social concern.

5. New forms of collaboration to realize an increased transcultural missionary effort can well be discovered and developed in the light of research and consultation with other denominations and groups.

July 22, 1974

1. The primary objectives for the evangelization of the diverse areas of Brazil vary according to the vision and resources of the church bodies. We can point out some of the goals: an integrated vision of the needs of evangelization in Brazil and of the work during the following decade passed on to leaders and pastors, an interchange of information on the strategies and programs of the various evangelical denominations in Brazil. The same interchange would share the greatest needs still awaiting evangelistic concern as well as possible sources of personnel and finances.

2. There is an expressed desire on the part of older denominations to not depend on financial resources outside Brazil, intensifying Christian stewardship.

3. An increased emphasis on the evangelization of youth under 25 (more than 50% of Brazil's population).

4. Greater use of mass media, especially radio.

5. Intensification of the missionary work beyond the national borders of Brazil.

6. Mobilization and training of laymen for neighborhood and home evangelism as well as opening preaching points and missionary stations. To this end we seek to greatly increase the use of programmed instructional materials.

7. Teach by means of workshops, principles of church growth and methods of evangelization learned at this Congress, to the leadership of Brazilian churches (both pastors and laymen).

Resources needed

1. Trained personnel in communications

2. Motorized boats to reach the thousands of riverside settlements along the immense rivers of Brazil. Campers for aiding roving evangelists to take the Gospel to people along the newly opened interior roads of Brazil.

3. Missionary personnel especially trained to reach indigenous tribes.

4. Missionary personnel and short-term specialists to train leaders in Christian nurture and Christian education.

CANADA NATIONAL STRATEGY GROUP REPORT

Secretary: Mariano Di Gangi

According to the Scriptures, we clearly see our goal as the glory of the Triune God, through the building up of the church, as persons are evangelized and disciples are made for our Lord Jesus Christ in the power of the Holy Spirit.

1. Considering afresh the needs of Canada in the light of God's Word, we discern the following as primary objectives in our service and witness:

a. The evangelization of the whole of Canada by this generation of committed disciples. Our Canadian mosaic includes Indians, Eskimos, those whose ancestry is British, immigrants from the Mediterranean and central regions of Europe as well as other parts of the world. It also includes six million Canadians whose main language and culture is French. All must be called to repentance toward God and faith in Christ for salvation. The fact that many of these may have a superficial connection with some form of religion but no vital relationship to the living Lord only intensifies the challenge to confront our country with the Gospel's demand for radical renewal and personal commitment. We do so in the apostolic tradition, unashamed of the Gospel of Christ, believing it to be God's saving power in the lives of all who receive it, whether Jews or Gentiles (Rom. 1:16).

b. Youth constitutes a significant cultural grouping of increasing importance in our nation. Young people need to be understood through sensitive listening, and evangelized as the Gospel truth is spoken and demonstrated in love. Identification with the legitimate aspirations of youth for justice in the social order, together with the frank confession of our own dependence on grace as sinners, can serve as points of contact in youth evangelization.

c. Internationals who visit Canada as tourists, businessmen, or students should be exposed to the beneficent contagion of the Gospel so that through them it may bring wholeness to the people of the lands to which they return. The place of Christian hospitality, especially with reference to international students, deserves to be highlighted in this connection. And the 1976 Olympics, to be held in Montreal, offer a most strategic opportunity for Christian witness.

d. Genuine social concern expresses the passion of Christ for justice and his compassion for those in need. It also authenticates the word of witness, and thus has a vital role in the furtherance of the Gospel.

2. For the realization of these priorities, we propose the following steps:

a. We call the Christian community of Canada to earnest prayer. While evangelism requires research and resources, it also demands repentance and renewal in the church. Our intercessions should also remember the millions who have never received the Savior in this land, as well as those billions who have never heard of Christ — especially in countries where repressive regimes restrict direct evangelization.

b. We encourage our theological seminaries and Bible colleges to emphasize the content and communication of the Gospel with passionate intensity no less than doctrinal integrity and verbal clarity. Courses should reflect the biblical priorities of making disciples and building up the church in preparing servants for their several ministries.

c. We encourage the recruitment and disciplined training of personnel to undertake cross-cultural Gospel communication to the various linguistic groups in Canada. We commend the possibility of involving fellow-believers from other francophone countries to assist in the evangelization of French Canada.

d. We support the development of an efficient referral service through which prospective candidates for short-term and career service in Canada and overseas can be put in touch with such opportunities and sponsoring agencies.

e. We commend the convening of conferences particularly (though not exclusively) for youth, focusing on Christian vocations and world evangelization. These may be held regionally or nationally, supplementing and complementing the triennial gathering at Urbana. It is not only desirable but advisable that the leadership of agencies active in youth ministries pray and plan with mission executives to this end, so that the unique position open to Canadian citizens internationally may be more fully utilized for committed service abroad.

f. We encourage believers not only to support aid to developing countries through governmental programs, but to share in both emergency relief and self-help projects through Christian agencies in the name of the compassionate Christ.

g. While mindful of global needs, we would also focus attention on the economic disparities between the various regions of Canada and ask the federal and provincial levels of government to give more practical expression to national unity in this regard.

h. We commend programs of orientation for students, travelers, business people, and members of the armed forces, who would let their presence overseas count more effectively for Christ.

i. We recommend the use of camps, conferences, radio, film, television, literature, visitation programs, and preaching missions for the promotion of the Gospel. In this connection we encourage the involvement of emerging Canadian leadership. Joint campaigns of evangelism, concentrating on the great centralities of the evangel, provide a valued opportunity for the articulation of the faith and the demonstration of our fellowship in the Gospel before the world.

Conclusion

We wish to share this fresh vision, arising from our participation in the International Congress on World Evangelization at Lausanne, with the Christian community of Canada. Our priority concern is that the words carved in stone above the Peace Arch at Ottawa, "He shall have dominion from sea to sea" (Psa. 72:8) may become flesh in the personal and national life of our land.

CARIBBEAN NATIONAL STRATEGY GROUP REPORT

Secretary: Ernest Cousins

Countries represented were: Jamaica, Barbados, Trinidad, Surinam, Guyana, Bahamas, U.S. Virgin Islands, St. Lucia and Grenada.

A. Priority Goals for the next decade

1. Evangelization of the area.

a. Survey of the area was considered necessary as a lack of information was a very real problem. No definite plans were laid for this survey, but participants pledged to gather and submit information to the chairman, who was appointed coordinator for the area.

b. Participants identified special groups and people within the area in need of particular attention, such as the Bush Negroes in Surinam, Haitians who are in the Bahamas and the Rastafarians in Jamaica. Minority racial and professional groups were also stressed, such as the Chinese, businessmen, et al.

2. Contributing to world evangelization beyond the area.

a. Specific areas and people were identified, for which it was felt the Caribbean people were best suited to do missionary work — the American Blacks, West Indians in the United Kingdom, Panama and Cuba, Surinam community in Holland, Africa and Brazil. It should be pointed out that West Indians were willing to evangelize people of all races and color but that this report was dealing mainly with a particular slant.

B. A basic strategy for the area to attain goals

1. An urgent and important need is a survey and description of the area called the Caribbean for which there would be cooperation on any organized basis.

2. A central information office is thought essential. In addition, agreement was reached to supply the existing media, secular and Christian, with as much information as possible about evangelism in the Caribbean.

Consideration was given to having a separate and independent medium for the promotion of evangelization, but cost and attendant problems made us defer any plan for immediate implementation, while not shelving the idea.

3. The churches should seek to produce and disseminate literature which tackles social issues, yet which has spiritual thrusts. Advantage should also be taken of the literacy programs of any government, and serious efforts made to supply the new literates with material to read. Much emphasis was put on the matter of churches giving active support to governmental schemes to improve the lot of the people, e.g., literacy and agriculture.

4. For evangelistic crusades, more use should be made of local speakers on an exchange basis among the various Caribbean territories.

C. Specific action recommended to participants as they return to their area

1. Keep in touch with each other on a regular correspondence basis and if possible by visits.

2. Stimulate evangelism in our own churches and denominations by initial and continuing reports and promotion of discussion, seminars, crusades, etc.

3. Work towards a National Congress on Evangelization within the next three years and a regional congress within the next five years.

4. Utilize existing news media for spreading information about what is happening in missions and evangelism.

5. Set in motion a training program in local churches to produce indigenous leadership. Mention was made of Men in Action, an organization which exists for this purpose.

6. Promote ways and means of helping the local church be more dynamic and sensitive towards the needs of young people.

D. Help needed from beyond the resources of the area

Time was not available to discuss this point as a group but from other discussions with Caribbean participants the following recommendations or observations are passed on:

1. Personnel are needed who could offer technical services for carrying out a survey, helping with printing and publishing and distribution, academic institutions, etc.

2. Financial help is needed to defray traveling expenses, which are very great in our scattered geographic areas.

E. What kind of continuing association or cooperation on a regional or world basis is recommended to achieve these goals?

1. On a regional basis we intend to set up a clearinghouse of dates of crusades and information center to supply certain statistical information, etc.

2. A loose link with an international body to keep us in touch with developments in world evangelization.

The Group's definition of "World Evangelization"

The Church fulfilling its supreme and biblical responsibility under the direction of the Holy Spirit; communicating the Good News of salvation through personal faith in Jesus Christ alone; by every available means, and with urgency, to all people of every nation, race, ethnic and social or other grouping in every part of the world. It was further suggested that any definition of World Evangelization should embody the principles of:

a. Authority - The Word
b. Geography - World-Tongues-Peoples
c. Theology - Personal Faith in Jesus Christ alone
d. Methodology - Proclamation by Word and Deed
e. Urgency - Now
f. Agency - The Church

CENTRAL AMERICA, DOMINICAN REPUBLIC, AND CUBA NATIONAL STRATEGY GROUP REPORT

Secretary: John Bueno

Coming to grips with the task and opportunities that our Lord has given us demands a conscious, heart-searching analysis of the dimensions, obstacles, and possibilities before us. Evangelism is the communication of the Gospel (Good News) so that each individual has the opportunity to accept or reject Jesus Christ as his Lord.

PRIORITIES

In order to establish priorities in accomplishing the commission of Christ we made a careful survey of areas in our region that most need our attention. We discovered that response has generally followed the emphasis given by the messenger. The great response of the laboring and less-privileged classes has come as a direct response to our emphasis to that social grouping. The fact that young people are now responding to the message of Christ is due to the fact that, in recent years we have focused on this age-group with specialized ministries geared to reach them. This would imply necessity to focus our attention on other socioeconomic and age groups that are virtually unreached in our area.

The main concern in our area is the professional, upper-class citizens who have not, as a whole, been reached. We propose focusing our attention on these people so that they will have a chance to respond to the Gospel message.

Another area that concerns us is the second generation Christians who seem to have lost their evangelistic fervor and in some cases dropped out of the Christian sphere altogether. We also considered the fact that in many cases evangelical Christians seem to be caught up in a rivalry that instead of reaching the lost, promotes friction and fighting in the Body of Christ. Competition over the Christians in one small area of a city or town has dissipated energies, talent, and finances that could have been better occupied reaching areas that still have no Gospel witness. Churches seem to be indifferent to the challenge of the hour and need to be stimulated to greater action.

OBJECTIVES

Our first order of business upon our return to our respective countries will be to communicate the spirit of this Congress to our leaders and constituents. We want Christians to be aware of the opportunities that beckon at our doors and invite them to do something about it. We don't mean simple reporting, but rather a clear communication of the task before us. This will be followed by a definite plan of action.

First of all, we aim to go back to our local churches and infuse renewed vision in the members of Christ's Church on that level. We feel the real battlefield is not on national or international levels, but at the local church level. World evangelization will never be a reality until we first mobilize at the local level. We intend to do this through *renewed vision of the real purpose of our Sunday schools*. Instead of introverted, child-care sessions, we aim to have real evangelism through Sunday schools, reaching new children and adults for Christ. Both in the church building and out in the various communities we want Sunday schools that are evangelizing. In a systematic, prayerful, and enthusiastic fashion, we propose reaching every community and neighborhood with a Christian witness.

We also want to make better use of the communications media, such as television, radio, the press, etc. Massive literature distribution programs and house-to-house witness will be given careful consideration and emphasis. This will be done through the cooperative effort of the evangelical churches to defray costs and present a united witness.

Through special dinners, cell meetings, television programs, and personal witness in business and government offices, we intend to penetrate the upper-class levels that so desperately need to be reached. With youth teams and youth-oriented programs we want to take advantage of the receptiveness of this element of society. We shall promote family prayer and Bible study in our messages so as to preserve second generation Christians for the Church. With definite, family-oriented programs and studies we intend to conserve young people and children, as well as inspire them to evangelize their peers.

By specialized training of lay leaders we aim to develop house-to-house visitation programs, cell prayer meetings, and church extensions sponsored by the mother church. Giving our lay leaders more latitude in their expression and ministry we intend to multiply rather than add.

On the national level a survey of unreached areas, such as communities, towns, cities and socio-economic strata that are unreached will be made. We will endeavor to select these areas of need and make concentrated efforts to reach them for Christ.

On the international scale we would like to promote an exchange of evangelistic teams from country to country and develop a viable evangelistic effort that would be fomented by a pastoral retreat on evangelism for the region. After the necessary groundwork has been laid we will promote major evangelistic efforts in each country to be culminated by one main effort in a site to be selected at the appointed time.

In all of our considerations we were reminded of the fact that evangelism is born not out of programs and strategies, but when God's people are ready to pay the price in prayer, finances, and talent. Revival will come when Christians everywhere are led by pastors and leaders with real faith and vision who by their example lead their flock into a consciousness of a lost world which desperately needs the message of Christ.

EAST AFRICA REGIONAL STRATEGY REPORT

Secretary: David M. Gitari

About eighty Christians from East Africa participated in the Lausanne '74 Congress on World Evangelization. The Congress gave us the opportunity of meeting for six sessions during which we shared our burdens and made an attempt to apply the messages of the Congress to our local situations. The reports of what God was doing in other parts of the world did not only widen our vision but they warmed our hearts and challenged us to become effectively involved in world evangelization.

1. Priority goals for the next decade

a. It is a matter of great concern to us that there are more than thirty tribes which have not yet been evangelized in East Africa. It is our determination during the next decade to evangelize these areas.

b. We are also determined to preach the Gospel in the new opportunities which God is opening in East Africa, e.g., Ujamaa Villages in Tanzania, refugees and immigrant communities. We shall also intensify our evangelism in schools and universities which are now wide open for the Gospel.

c. It is our determination to consolidate Christianity in East Africa by challenging nominal Christianity with the Gospel of salvation. To this end, we shall seek ways and means of reaching people in all sectors of society (e.g., civil servants, businessmen, members of armed forces, etc.) who have heard the Gospel but have denied its power in their lives.

d. Lausanne '74 has challenged us to take a greater part in the task of worldwide evangelization. We shall endeavor to send East African Christians as ambassadors of Christ not only to the neighboring countries but also to the other parts of the earth.

2. Basic strategy to attain these goals

a. We believe that evangelistic zeal begins with spiritual renewal in the lives of individual Christians and revival within the body of Christ. East Africa has been blessed by the effect of the revival movement for more than forty years. We are, however, concerned that the evangelistic zeal of the revival movement has grown cold due to internal squabbles and divisions among the brethren brought about by unbiblical emphasis. Unity among brethren will be essential in our evangelism during the next decade. We praise God that we are already witnessing a real spirit of reconciliation, brokenness, and repentance among the brethren.

b. We praise the Lord that indigenous denominational evangelistic missions have already been initiated in some parts of East Africa. These, however, have been marred by the spirit of competition and lack of coordination. It is our prayer that the motive for outreach shall primarily be to bring men to the saving power of Jesus Christ rather than to extend denominational empires. We feel there is a great need for a coordination of fellowship on regional and national levels. Those of us who have had the experience of Lausanne '74 shall take upon ourselves the promotion of such a fellowship.

c. We praise the Lord for the evangelistic zeal of the young people in the charismatic renewal movement. We confess that we have tended to look at this movement with suspicion. It is our wish to seek to understand this revival among the young people, to correct any unbiblical emphases and experiences with love, and to encourage its evangelistic and missionary zeal.

d. We shall continue to organize conventions for revival, city, town, and village crusades for evangelism, camps, and conferences for up-building the Christians. We shall also continue to make full use of mass media (radio, TV, visual aids, literature, etc.) and other methods which we may find suitable in evangelizing East Africa.

e. We realize the great need there is of teaching the people the depths of the Christian message. We confess that in emphasizing soul-winning we have neglected the ministry of teaching. As a result the faith of many believers has remained superficial. We are convinced that the ministry of preaching must go side by side with the ministry of teaching. To this end, we shall encourage group Bible studies, faithful expositions of God's Word, and follow-up teaching of young believers. We shall also seek ways and means of encouraging sound religious teaching in our schools and colleges.

f. It is our prayer and concern that the superficial dichotomy which exists between proclamation of the Gospel and social concern should be removed. In our evangelism, we shall be fully involved in the welfare of our respective nations so as to become truly "the salt of the earth" and the "light of the world."

3. Association on world basis

a. Our presence at Lausanne '74 and our encounter with Christians from every nation has powerfully shown us that we are members of a big world family called to "proclaim the Gospel of Jesus Christ." It is our determination to join hands with others in the fulfillment of our Lord's Commission.

b. We are also of the opinion that in many parts of East Africa there is great potential in manpower and other resources needed for evangelism and church growth. Many times we have failed to make full use of our potential resources because of our over-dependence on Western personnel and finances.

c. Although the idea of moratorium has been recommended to the churches in Africa, the churches have not yet discussed the recommendation. Therefore the impression that the churches in Africa have already either declared or rejected moratorium is misleading. It is, however, important to recognize that the idea behind moratorium is concern about over-dependence upon foreign resources, both personnel and finances, which sometimes hinder initiative and development of local responsibility. The East African group felt that the application of the concept behind moratorium might be considered for specific situations rather than generally.

4. Specific action recommended

a. The East African participants felt that immediate action must be taken to spread the spirit and the vision of Lausanne '74 among Christians. To this end, the following decisions and recommendations were made:

(i) *Kenya.* A follow-up committee of six participants was appointed. The committee, which will be convened by Rev. John Mpaayei, will meet as soon as possible to plan a national get-together of Christian leaders in Kenya so that the Kenya participants can share the experience of Lausanne '74 with them. As far as possible the message of Lausanne '74 will be communicated to church groups by making available the cassettes, papers, and sending participants to speak in various congregations. On return to Kenya, the committee will also make arrangements for informing the public about the Congress through mass media.

(ii) *Tanzania.* A follow-up committee under the chairmanship of Bishop Madinda was appointed. The committee was charged with the responsibility of drawing up a document on evangelism which shall be presented to the next meeting of the Christian Council of Tanzania. The document will attempt to relate the message of Lausanne '74 to the Tanzanian situation. The Lausanne '74 participants will be sent to various parts of Tanzania to share the vision of the Congress.

(iii) *Uganda.* The Uganda participants resolved to call church leaders, so as to share with them the vision of Lausanne '74, who in turn should be able to spread the message to their respective churches. Plans to reach the tribes not yet reached with the Gospel will also be made. The participants also resolved to strengthen the Africa Evangelistic Enterprise and to let it be the major organ of evangelism in Uganda. The Ugandans recommended that the National Church Magazine be revived which shall regularly communicate the evangelistic zeal in Uganda. The participants are determined to spread the vision of Lausanne '74 as widely as possible through the use of mass media and visual aids and personal communication. Serious study of the Bible will also be encouraged in every diocese at least once a week.

5. Conclusion

We praise the Lord for enabling us to have the moving experience of Lausanne '74. We return to East Africa determined to join hands together (and in fellowship with the universal church) in the proclamation of the Good News so as to "Let the earth hear His voice."

EASTERN EUROPE NATIONAL STRATEGY GROUP REPORT

Secretary: Judy Norman

Due to the political climate in which the church of each of these countries functions, this group did not always address itself to the questions established by the Congress. Instead, each day, a report was heard from one country regarding the actual state of the church in that nation. The entire strategies group was then restructured into small groups by nationality for consideration of the day's questions. These small groups included Hungary, Rumania, Poland and Yugoslavia, with Russia meeting one day only. A synthesis of each individual country's report is given below.

Then, rather than to synthesize the responses to the daily question, it was decided that the most helpful procedure for evaluation would be to simply state the question and follow it by each country's own response. This report then follows the synthesis of the national reports.

The responses to the daily questions are followed by the entire group's response to the general evaluation questions set for the last day, and this response concludes the report.

Group thinking after four days followed by synthesis of national reports

Evangelization is the confrontation of the world with the Gospel. Since it is the work of the Holy Spirit to draw men, evangelization is completed as members of the living Church listen for and obey the voice of the Holy Spirit.

Particular needs in these countries include the opportunity for fellowship with other believers, encouragement, and prayer. A strong opportunity for evangelism exists among the over one million Yugoslavians working in countries of Western Europe and the United States. Organization of this work and workers are needed. People in the south and east of Poland, especially women and students, are receptive to the Gospel message.

Major obstacles to the spread of the Gospel seem to be *a lack of sound teaching* to develop the knowledge of the practical application of the faith to life, so believers can better evangelize, and the working principles of the Christian faith can be universalized among the existing denominations. To further this goal, there is a need for Christian literature, for more radio programs which are one of the better means of evangelization, and for audio-visual materials of all kinds, coupled with interdenominational workshops to teach their use. These technological techniques are mostly new to these countries.

In some of the countries, the typical methods of evangelization are still possible and effective. They should be supplemented with the new technological techniques mentioned above. In countries where witness is officially restricted, the Gospel is being preached at weddings, funerals, and through the organization of Christian concerts.

Yugoslavia suggested the organization of a Yugoslav Conference on Cooperation to develop techniques presented at Lausanne. The recently organized Board of Protestant Publishers should be further inter-denominationally extended. An evangelical interdenominational Protestant faculty of theology was suggested.

Cultural groups to be reached include Gypsies, Jews, Croatians, Rumanians, Germans, Mohammedans and Slavs.

Churches in the past have sent missionaires outside their countries, but are largely restricted from this activity under present conditions.

Synthesis of national reports

RUSSIA: Despite the political situation, the Word is going out by preaching, at weddings and funerals. Russia has a great need for prayer for the persecuted, prayer for those preaching in the Russian language, and for Bibles. Russia has need of a presentation of the plight of the persecuted to the Western world, but *in general terms, not in specifics,* as specifics bring immediate control from the government.

YUGOSLAVIA: In Yugoslavia, restrictions and opportunities exist. Yugoslavians need to organize themselves to better use the opportunities they do have. These opportunities include: education and baptism of children, preaching inside buildings, the spread of Christian literature, the use of radio, development of Christian schools.

Yugoslavia gives opportunity for the church, acting as a publisher, to publish Christian literature which can be printed in other European languages for Yugoslavian national minorities.

POLAND: All activity in Poland requires official permission. It is necessary to proceed with circumspection. Within these restrictions, the Polish Church functions in the areas of baptism, Bible schools, editorial activities, youth work, and especially radio, which is a most effective ministry. Programs aired through TWR in Monte Carlo are produced in Poland where use of government studios is permitted.

HUNGARY: In Hungary the government wants to know what is happening. Pastors must request permission for travel and for any guests one year ahead. Pastors' salaries must be reported. However churches are open, meetings can be held at any time, but one must be careful whom one invites. Inside the church, anything can be done. Ministers are paid partly by the church, but mostly by the State, and churches are renovated with church money. The Pentecostals have a beautiful church in the heart of Budapest.

Church activities include:

Publication: "Peace Message" edited by Baptists, contains Bible studies and plans for a hymn book publication, although paper supply from the government is uncertain. A New Testament has been published by both the Catholic and the Reformed Churches.

Education: There is a Bible school, although the ratio is five professors and only ten students; some people are in the United States studying.

Cooperation: there is cooperation between evangelical churches. The main problem is lack of an adequate number of missionaries and pastors.

BULGARIA: As no representative from Bulgaria could secure travel permission, a brother from Yugoslavia reported for the Bulgarian church. He has recently traveled in Bulgaria and visited a number of churches.

Before a Bulgarian representative could come to the Congress, he had to be officially invited by the Congress through the Bulgarian consulate in Berne. This was done, but he was not given travel documents. In Bulgaria, there are Baptists, Methodists, Congregationalists, Pentecostals and there used to be a Gypsy church.

Travel is precarious, due to difficulty getting passports.

RUMANIA: We owe a debt of gratitude to God concerning the Gospel which has come to our country. In Rumania there are fourteen denominations. The Orthodox church is the biggest, then there are four Neo-Protestant churches (Evangelical), Baptists, Seventh-Day Adventists, Christian Evangelicals and Pentecostals. In our country all parts have been reached with the Gospel. Nearly everywhere there are Christian congregations. In the past years, many of the church buildings in the cities have become too small. There is permission from the government to enlarge church premises, even to establish new buildings. Aid from other brethren could help considerably by sending a bank draft designated officially for this purpose.

We thank God for the freedom we have in our country, though it is not completely used. In our services we have evangelizing, doctrine, prayer hours with fasting; we have also Sunday schools and youth meetings, choirs and orchestras. In several denominations there is a lack of printed doctrines of faith as explained by a number of brothers. Prayer and help are needed so that the congregations may grow to full maturity. Another area of difficulty is the identification of false teachings from visiting brothers. Therefore we only allow them to preach when we are sure that they will preach a sound biblical doctrine.

Altogether the church is growing. The relations between church and state are good, because the churches take part in the socio-political organization in the interest of the whole country.

ENGLAND NATIONAL STRATEGY GROUP REPORT

Secretary: Gordon Landreth

The England group spent the first two days in general discussion (in small groups with reporting back to full session) of the plenary session papers, and of the national strategy issues suggested by the Congress. It was found however that this led to a superficial and frustrating skimming of issues. The group also agreed that it was not competent to work out a national strategy, because it was insufficiently representative or comprehensive.

Therefore it was decided to spend the second half of the national group sessions working on those issues which members had been hearing in the Congress and which they believed should be reported to the churches, societies and individual Christians back in England as being relevant to evangelism in our country. Small groups looked at those issues under general headings such as the renewal of the church, the analysis of our culture and its needs, the various methods of evangelism, the cross-cultural problems in our society, and the content of the Gospel. A further group is considering how the various issues, or some major ones among them, can be effectively conveyed to British Christians, possibly by means of an audio-visual sequence. It is recognized as important that this communication should reach the grass roots.

Significant lessons from the Congress

One note that became clear to the England group was that we face a situation of a declining church. For most of our countrymen the institutional church, of whatever denomination, is regarded with a degree of affection, but felt to be essentially irrelevant to ordinary life. For better or for worse, the Christian faith is closely identified with the church, and this deepening divide between the church and the world calls us to penitence. Penitence should also lead to prayer.

The Congress has taught us also that a country with a declining church has much to learn from churches overseas where renewal and growth are strikingly evident. Our former "missionary" concepts must be revised so that we recognize the mutual interdependence of the worldwide church not only to which we give but also from which we receive and learn. Our former missionary paternalism must be replaced by a penitent willingness to hear from the church in other countries as well as to promote mission overseas. Pastors from Latin America and other parts of the Third World have a message that can inspire and restore vision and confidence among English leaders.

The church in England has also been seen as representing no more than a small slice of the whole of society, a rigid, middle-class group from which it *must* break out into other sub-cultures of our country. This demands a real honesty in recognizing our true situation, repenting of our failures, and being open to change in both attitudes and methods. We must find ways of overcoming British reserve. We must encourage and express a deepening love in each Christian fellowship which then develops living relationships with other fellowships. Together we must undertake practical service in our neighborhood.

We have also seen how often our own church has developed its own English brand of "cultural Christianity," to use Padilla's phrase. Christians have become infected with the "welfare state" mentality of getting rather than giving; we share society's current malaise and complacency; we have a selective gospel of the things we like rather than the whole biblical truth for our life. We need to work on a biblical understanding of culture in the English context that takes in the whole of life and challenges the unbiblical assumptions of our relativist society. Our lifestyle as Christians must accord with New Testament principles of loving concern for others. We must be involved in society, not just evangelistic technicians.

The cell or small group system was seen as one means of breaking out of our cultural bonds and demonstrating a Christian life-style. Its use in other parts of the world — New Life for All in Africa, Lay Evangelistic Group Studies in Chad and in the Philippines, Christian ashrams in India were examples noted in the Congress. These could be paralleled in England by further development of house groups and home hospitality. Lay initiative and sympathetic involvement with one another and with the world can best be developed in this context.

The cell group has the advantage of flexibility and can thus be more readily relevant to a local situation. Many of the recommended areas of evangelistic method were of the "small group" type — house-to-house visiting, evangelistic house groups, witness in pubs and clubs, in coffee bars, institutions, schools and colleges, in industry. At the same time certain traditional methods were not to be discarded but evaluated in the light of their cultural appropriateness and their ability to mobilize people to work together: mass crusades and evangelistic church services were not necessarily "out." Evangelistic methods must concentrate on mobilizing lay people, starting with the willing nucleus, continuously training them, training the clergy to train, and concentrating on the natural contacts with others in society that Christians have already.

Alongside these practical ways of proceeding now, we also heard from the Congress the value of some kinds of study and research regarding evangelism in our own situation. Case studies and statistics can identify areas of special need and of special opportunity and point up the ways in which the church is failing to communicate with society. Various receptive areas were suggested — some parts of the Roman Catholic church, places where people take their leisure, youth and the student world. Problem areas included the "post literate" world that relied on TV or tabloid rather than heavier reading for all communication, and of course the whole "working class" culture. The "personality" emphasis of much evangelical Protestantism had also been a possible obstacle to the involvement of Christians in society.

In all this analysis there were those who also stressed the importance of communicating the whole content of the Gospel to Christians through expository preaching, especially on the person and work of Christ. Then the churches must themselves reflect as well as preach a life-style that expresses his Kingdom in their local context.

Wider relationships

The England group felt that existing structures, especially the Evangelical Alliance, provided adequate channels for communication and mutual exchange after the Congress, though it was agreed that all English participants would be invited by the Evangelical Alliance to a day conference in six months' time to review the situation and pray together. International relationships were left for discussion in the wider Europe group at the end of the Congress.

FINLAND NATIONAL STRATEGY GROUP REPORT

Secretary: Raimo Harjula

We Finnish evangelical Christians attending the Lausanne Congress realize with gratitude that God, in his mercy and through his Holy Spirit, is continuing to call and renew his people throughout the world for a more concerted and effective evangelization. In particular, we would like to single out one of the main emphases of the whole Congress: no matter what the geographical or social area of our work, no matter how it is traditionally called ("evangelism," "mission," or so on), we do have a common task to evangelize the world, to reach the unreached wherever they are.

We are grateful for the opportunity to attend this Congress. One has been strengthened here and given many new and inspiring ideas. At the same time, however, one would have hoped that the list of the main speakers and lecturers could have included more names from the Northern European countries. In this way, the experience of these countries — the evangelical groups which do send out quite a number of workers to all parts of the world — would have enriched our common coming together.

We realize the significance of global and regional congresses to evangelical leaders and workers. We need to come together to discuss our common strategy, to exchange experiences, to be strengthened in our common faith and witness, and so on. At the same time, we do point out the urgent need for a growing cooperation of various evangelical groups at a national level.

A Congress of Evangelism in Helsinki, Finland, was held in 1973 as a follow-up to the Amsterdam Congress in 1971. The Finnish Congress was attended by some 1000 participants and observers coming from about 65 different Christian congregations, churches, organizations and groups. As a result of this Congress, a growing and renewed understanding and activity is being experienced in many Christian groups regarding the evangelization work at home.

In the Lausanne Congress, we have been met by God's inspiring call to widen, strengthen and deepen the cooperation of various evangelical groups in Finland in the spirit of mutual Christian love and respect. The functional objectives of this continuous cooperation could be for example:

— to identify the common biblical basis of what is traditionally called "evangelism" and "mission"; to bring into and to keep in focus the fact that these are two aspects of the one and the same world evangelization taking place throughout the Six Continents with the aim of proclaiming the Gospel to all people, to bring them into faith, and to make them disciples of Christ and responsible members of local congregations and the universal people of God;

— to bring into the focus of Christian leaders and workers and all Christians the fact that world evangelization is the common task of the people of God with local congregations as the decisive key; this task cannot be fulfilled through isolated groups;

— to keep people informed through various means about what the Christians in Finland are already doing for world evangelization;

— to identify new challenges, resources and practical aims both within and outside Finland;

— to plan for and to materialize common strategies on how to evangelize the nations.

We furthermore propose that a common Ev-73-like event be arranged in Helsinki in 1976 on World Evangelization. The planning of this event should start immediately after the Lausanne Congress and the aims outlined above be kept in mind from the first steps of this planning.

FRANCE NATIONAL STRATEGY GROUP REPORT

Secretary: A. Kuen

The French strategy group is grateful to God for the liberty enjoyed in their country to preach the Gospel, and for the interest which is evident in several new sectors: youth (especially students), Roman Catholics, migrant workers (Portuguese, Brazilian, Antillese).

New possibilities for evangelization open up to us: radio, beach and holiday center evangelism, public testimony in the universities, Bible study groups in secondary schools.

Older methods remain valid and efficacious: open-air singing in the courtyards below high-rise apartments, followed by the distribution of literature; simultaneous evangelistic campaigns in different local churches of a given city, or even nation-wide.

Our greatest obstacles today are concerned with the small number of Christian workers (their percentage one of the smallest in the world). Their training is not sufficient to cope with all the new sectors opening up, such as evangelism among intellectuals, foreigners, youth, etc. In addition, the means available are insufficient for the tens of thousands of evangelicals, who come primarily from the poorer and middle classes, to sustain missionary activity in France and in Third World French-speaking countries.

The areas towards which our evangelistic efforts must give priority in the years to come seem to be: France and French-speaking territories overseas. The large number of foreigners residing in France (North Africans, Portuguese, Brazilians, etc.) are a receptive missionary field on our very doorstep. The example of Liberia and Reunion Island teaches us that we must sow the Word of God extensively in our country by all available means (radio, tract, newpapers) before we can expect abundant harvests. Badly needed is a body of apologetic literature at different intellectual levels, starting with the principle of the Creating God.

Varied methods need to be used to reach first those who have never heard the Gospel, and after the use of film, vocal groups, etc., to bring them progressively to meetings where the verbal communication of the message has a more important place (Moody films followed by discussion, audio-visual presentation, conferences).

Several suggestions were made: a good strategy for evangelization of our country should begin with a complete inventory of what exists (radio work, training, correspondence courses, tracts, literature, audio-visuals). Evangelistic efforts should as far as possible be channeled through the local church which can best assure the follow-up of new converts.

Since there are various evangelical churches, it is important that they should exhibit their unity in Christ to the world, not only by cooperative evangelistic efforts, but also by occasional worship services and common meetings for edification and for deeper teaching, to be held alternately in different locations and church buildings. Prayer meetings grouping a number of families of different denominations should also be held. Experiences in various places show that regular meetings between leaders of various churches and Christian communities help to create and develop a climate of unity and cooperation between God's children.

Three points were particularly stressed:

(i) The necessity of firmly resting on the foundation of our common faith, as expressed, for example, in the profession of faith of the French Evangelical Alliance (inspiration and authority of the Bible, necessity of personal conversion).

(ii) The importance of the deeper training of Christians with an eye to evangelization, and to the sharing of all means of instruction now available, so as to be able to give honest answers to the honest questions that are being put to us.

(iii) The wish expressed to see French evangelical Christianity create and further works with a social thrust, oriented, for example, toward the needs of migrant workers, the problems of unwed mothers, etc.

At the level of *concrete decision* it was suggested that :

(i) Two associations representative of French evangelicalism (the French Evangelical Alliance and the Evangelical Federation of France) should jointly invite the evangelical Christians of our land to meet to examine together what practical implementation to give to these suggestions.

(ii) In view of the evangelization of foreigners residing among us, we request our Portuguese and Brazilian friends, and also missions specializing in work among Arabs, if they could lend to us for several years ten or fifteen evangelists to enlarge the work among these peoples from abroad.

(iii) So as not to limit our horizon to what is going on in France, it would be well to make up a yearbook giving a list of those members of our churches working in missionary lands. This list could serve as a prayer list and strengthen the bonds between Christians of all lands.

Finally, one observer was moved to underline the spirit, unity and brotherhood which has characterized the gatherings of our strategy group. This could augur well for a closer and more effective cooperation aimed at the evangelization of our country.

NATIONAL STUDY GROUP — FRENCH AFRICA: MADAGASCAR, MAURITIUS, REUNION, MALI, UPPER VOLTA, DAHOMEY, NIGER, TOGO, MAURITANIA, GUINEA, GABON, CONGO, CENTRAL AFRICAN REPUBLIC, CHAD, CAMEROON, RWANDA, BURUNDI.

Chairman: Rene Daidanso

Secretary: Paul S. White

It is obvious that with such a great number of countries represented in our group, and because of the great diversity of these nations, only general ideas can be given about our respective goals and strategies for evangelism: national, regional and worldwide. The one human factor that unifies us is our use of the French language. During this Congress, it has been universally felt among us that much more should be done by us as a language unit.

Working first in small national groups, then as four major regions (Indian Ocean, Central Africa, West Africa and Rwanda/Burundi) and finally as one united group, we formulated the following objectives in order to assure that "the world hear his voice."

We will strive to set up *national evangelism committees* in each of our respective nations. Where a committee on evangelism already exists we will endeavor to work with and through that committee. In each of the four major geographical areas represented by our strategy group, we have noted the names of persons willing to act as correspondents. It will be our goal to share information and projects concerning evangelism in our different countries with one another in order to foster a climate of evangelistic activity throughout French Africa. It was suggested that the Association of Evangelicals of Africa and Madagascar establish an evangelistic co-ordination office for the purpose of keeping national and regional evangelism correspondents up to date on evangelistic resources throughout French Africa. It was definitely felt that greater communication with one another and the mutual sharing of our evangelistic resources could help and encourage us all as we seek to evangelize.

While we saw these evangelism committees as essential, we felt two important remarks were necessary:

1. We must avoid "committeemania" (the establishment of committees for committees' sake);

2. The great need to pray intensively for these committees so that they will function efficiently and effectively.

One important aspect of our proposed evangelism committees will be to study the sending of men from our countries to other places as missionaries. All of our countries are interested in this possibility but with one accord recognize that the major problems are financing and know-how. Several countries indicated that they have men with evangelistic talents and gifts who could be sent to other countries if proper organizational and financial help could be found. It was suggested that information and encouragement from Asian and Latin American countries involved in this kind of ministry would be greatly appreciated. This would be one way in which Asia and Latin America could help advance world evangelization.

This Congress, by means of the national strategy groups, has forced us to think about ethnic groups within our countries that desperately need to be evangelized. Our attention has been particularly directed to the following:

1. We suggest that teams of evangelists be formed to follow the nomadic pygmies in Central African forests and present Christ to them.

2. Nomadic peoples, in general, are very numerous in our countries and we must make every effort to reach these people even if their nomadic ways make it difficult.

3. Chinese and Hindu people live in Mauritius, Reunion and Madagascar and form a definite ethnic unit to be evangelized.

4. The same is true of the Muslim populations in our countries.

One major emphasis in the next decade will definitely be evangelism in depth. This concept has been gaining influence among all our nations, with the general conviction that we all need to get involved in continuous *evangelism-in-depth* programs. This will be a major concern of our national evangelism committees. Our desire is that the total church in our entire region will be mobilized for in-depth evangelism on a continuing basis.

Many of our countries are "Bible poor." We have the New Testament but desperately need the Old Testament. We want to use our influence to encourage the translation of the Old Testament in our major languages so that our evangelism can be really Bible-centered. We see this as a "must" during the next decade.

We have been sensitized to the need of our cities. It is our goal to work out from the cities, seeking first to concentrate on them so that a greater impact can be made upon them, and from there spread to the rural areas until our whole country knows about the Lord Jesus in a vital way.

We do have national and denominational evangelists already. We feel a great need to stimulate these men to cooperate together nationally, regionally and even on an international scale.

Finally, it is our desire that as our momentum grows from national to regional to international dimensions, we may be able to then join in worldwide evangelism, at the same time cooperating with other international evangelistic efforts, so that truly the earth may hear his voice.

"Que La Terre Entende Sa Voix!"

GERMANY NATIONAL STRATEGY GROUP REPORT

Secretary: W. Burklin

Expectations on the part of the German group were manifold. The members wanted to come to know each other in a better way and to arrive at a greater unity of spirit. One of the objectives was to achieve an integration of evangelization abroad and at home, another the furthering of cooperation among the various evangelizing groups in the future.

The existing institutions were explored and attempts were made to find a basis wide enough to encompass all evangelizing agencies in Germany. There were four groups interested in advanced cooperation: the evangelizing agencies of the state church, the free churches, confessing congregations, and free agencies. A common theological basis was not found, owing to one group judging the basis of the German Evangelical Alliance together with the Lausanne Covenant to be not sufficient. This must be seen as a result of their specific church situation. There were several additional meetings held pertaining to this question.

The differences between the groups were frankly discussed and led to a spirit of repentance.

One session was dedicated to the discussion of the draft of the Lausanne Covenant and several corrections and supplements were agreed upon by the German, Austrian and Swiss national groups to be presented to the drafting committee.

Although no definite organization was set up for coordinating evangelistic efforts, many positive suggestions for the proceeding in the future were made, e.g., to unite in having a national youth congress in Essen in 1976, in holding several conferences for specialized evangelistic strategies, and various nation and citywide evangelism-in-depth efforts by 1980. Other objectives were the evangelization of migrant workers, a more intensive use of TWR facilities, intensifying and coordinating of evangelical theological training, and the training of many more young evangelists. Further suggestions were made to form a fellowship of evangelical religious instructors in primary and high schools. Several seminars and conferences with guest speakers from Latfricasia have been planned.

All of the German participants expressed their deep gratitude for having the opportunity to take part in the Congress and for receiving most valuable impulses from all parts of the world where the Gospel is preached. They became aware of the urgency of the task and underlined their willingness to cope with the new challenges.

GHANA NATIONAL STRATEGY GROUP REPORT

Secretary: T.B. Dankwa

I. Specific action recommended to participants as they return to Ghana.

A rededication of our whole being to the Lord so as to be available to Him at all times and for all things. Participants were encouraged to be pioneers in new ventures in evangelism. Participants have said that they will share the vision and insights gained in Lausanne with their churches, organizations and other Christians.

A small booklet on the Lausanne Congress is to be written and circulated in Ghana. It is proposed that a Mini-Congress on Evangelism should be held in Ghana after the publication of this booklet.

A committee made up of Rev. T.A. Kumi, Rev. Joseph Egyir-Paintsil, Rev. Joseph Gyanfosu, Rev. Peter Barker and Mr. Theophilus B. Dankwa was nominated. The Committee was asked to convene a meeting with heads of churches on their return to Ghana for a discussion on a report from Lausanne. The Ghana Evangelism Committee represents both evangelical and World Council oriented churches and is launching New Life For All in 1975.

II. Priority goals for the next decade.

A. *For the evangelization of Ghana.*
   1. Church Renewal.
   2. Leadership Training.
   3. Total Evangelization through New Life For All and other denominational programs from 1975.
   4. Research leading to production of information on unevangelized areas and groups in Ghana.
   5. Setting up the means of taking the Gospel to specified groups: e.g. youth, Muslims, non-Ghanaian pagans.

B. *For contributing to world evangelization beyond Ghana.*

There are Ghanaian missionaries serving presently in Togo, Dahomey, Ivory Coast, Upper Volta, Sierra Leone, Liberia and Cameroon. A special responsibility was felt for Togo, Ivory Coast and Upper Volta.

Goal. To train and send out Christians of different backgrounds and professions to other countries in Africa and elsewhere.

III. Basic strategy for the attainment of goals.

A. *Evangelization of Ghana.*
1. Church Renewal.
   — Congresses, conferences and retreats.
   — Regular church Bible study classes.
2. Leadership training.
   — Training of Sunday school teachers.
   — Training of youth leaders.
   — Training of people to train others.

— Provision of schools for the teaching of strong, evangelical biblical theology.

— Provision of a center to train people on reaching different groups.

3. Total evangelization.

New Life For All strategy.

    a.   Preparation.
    b.   Information.
    c.   Intercession instruction.
    d.   Evangelism.
    e.   Consolidation.
    f.   Evaluation.

4. Research. The Christian Outreach Fellowship is about to conduct research leading to the production of information on unevangelized areas and groups in Ghana.

5. Means of taking the Gospel to specified groups. The setting up of a center to train people on reaching different evangelized groups.

B.   *World evangelization.*

The Christian Outreach Fellowship has facilities for the training of Christians with a view to sending them out as missionaries.

IV. *Help needed beyond resources of Ghana.*

— Evangelical radio and television agency.

— Finances to produce material for Ghana on ICOWE. As plans develop, a lot of expenditure will be involved, but it will be premature to state how much will be needed at the moment.

— Help is needed in the production of evangelical literature. Strategy manuals on what is happening in world evangelization in Third World countries.

V. *Continuing association.*

We would prefer to see post-Congress developments channeled through existing organizations.

The publication of a periodical newsletter after the Congress was suggested. This will be mailed to participants. In it participants will share what the Lord is doing in their part of the world after the Lausanne Congress, with special emphasis on strategies and methods adopted or learned at Lausanne.

GREECE NATIONAL STRATEGY GROUP REPORT

Secretary: D. Katsarkas

The discussion in the meetings followed the suggested agenda prepared by the Congress Committee. Thus the first day's discussion focused on the responsive and unresponsive areas of Greece; the second day, new opportunities for evangelism were discussed; the third day was spent talking about the various possibilities for cross-cultural evangelization; the fourth day dealt with goals for the future, and the final day was dedicated to talking about the needs of personnel and resources.

Particularly responsive areas were noted, these being: Macedonia and northern Greece, the Peloponnesus and the islands which are more resistant to the Gospel than the mainland; age, young people, especially boys, seem to have broken through the conservative religious mentality of the Greeks, and are willing to overlook tradition and give consideration to the Gospel. Attention was drawn to what the newspapers called the decline of *Zoi*, a so-called "renewal" group within the Greek Orthodox Church, considered to be the stronghold of fanaticism. The fall of this organization may have pushed some of the sincere individuals from this movement to find spiritual reality through the Bible alone. It was thought that the decline of *Zoi* may signal a new day for Evangelicals and religious freedom.

Hindrances to the Gospel work were listed, beginning with legal difficulties encountered by Protestants, who have less freedom than Roman Catholics, Moslems, and Jews, who are at least recognized as minority religions and tolerated. Fanaticism and religious prejudice were also listed as very significant barriers to the progress of the Gospel, but several stressed that the internal problems are far more destructive than the external ones. Other problems peculiar to Greece were mentioned, including the fact that a work in a given area may progress until the point of formalizing the work and obtaining legal permission, at which time the work tends to remain stagnant for a long time. Also, foreign groups working in Greece have sometimes been insensitive to local idiosyncracies, and hence have worked in ways which some consider detrimental to the overall work.

In the discussion of cross-cultural evangelization, it was apparent that most missionary activity has been confined to E-1 evangelism, both with that coming into Greece from abroad, as well as that going out from the Greek church. Most missionary organizations having a work in Greece are supporting nationals or have sent Greek-Americans to carry on their work, and most Greeks leaving their homeland for ministry abroad have gone to serve among their fellow countrymen who have emigrated to Germany, Australia, and South Africa. Notable exceptions to the former are several North American families with Greater Europe Mission serving at the Greek Bible Institute, and to the latter are Kostas Makris who is serving in New Guinea, Jean and Soula Leck in Africa, and others who are taking advantage of the new open doors among Yugoslavian tourists who come down to vacation in Macedonia.

All the participants expressed the wish to have reciprocal relationships with the church abroad, and with the International Committee of I.C.O.W.E.

Of great significance is the move towards an Evangelical Alliance for Greece. Such a dream for unity among Evangelicals in Greece began at Berlin, was strengthened at Amsterdam, and finally evidenced a step towards realization on April 16th, 1974, when leaders from the Greek Evangelical Church and the Fellowship of Free Evangelical Churches of Greece as well as representatives of other denominations (about 200) met for a one-day congress at the Free Church camp at Sounion, to talk about the possibilities for evangelistic cooperation. This move presumably will lead to a wider union, including Pentecostals, independent churches, and foreign missionary personnel. It was an historical event. We had Dr. Donald E. Hoke with us.

Greek participants expressed a unanimous desire to hold a Billy Graham crusade in Greece, and unofficially resolved to look into the possibilities, both legal and ecclesiastical, and to find facilities. The desire was also expressed to establish a contact in Greece to follow up this Congress, so that local churchmen could see what is happening in other countries.

HAITI NATIONAL STRATEGY GROUP REPORT

Secretary: Rony Joseph

The participants from Haiti have discussed the following points:
1. The identification of the social groups and the places which are not reached by the Gospel.
2. The means for the total evangelization of Haiti.
3. The most effective methods for the evangelization of Haiti.
4. The possibility of collaboration for the evangelization of Haiti.

Generally speaking, the preaching of the Gospel has spread to the entire country by one means or another. Nevertheless the participants have reached the conclusion that professional men, businessmen and the intellectuals are not yet really touched, and that there exist unidentified places where the Gospel is not preached.

The participants propose the following means for the conversion of the professional men, businessmen and intellectuals:
1. The mass media
2. Personal contacts
3. Home Bible studies
4. Associations of Christian professional men
5. Cooperation with associations already organized and working in this direction

According to the participants, if there exist places in Haiti where the Gospel is not preached, the best way to reach them is to encourage the churches to enlarge their field of action to establish in these places what is called in Haiti "stations."

The participants from Haiti have indicated, according to the order of their importance, the following methods as being the most effective for the evangelization of Haiti:
1. Personal evangelism
2. The stations (evangelistic posts where services are held regularly by members of the churches, either under a shelter or in the home of a Christian).
3. Evangelism by mobile, interconfessional groups of laymen (COHORTE)
4. Evangelism by the mass media
5. Bible correspondence courses

As for the help Haiti can bring to the evangelization of other nations, missionaries from Haiti work in Africa, in the United States, in Guadeloupe, in the Dominican Republic, in the Bahamas and in Canada.

Finally, all the participants from Haiti are unanimous in recognizing that a better collaboration between all those who are engaged in the task of evangelism is necessary.

The participants from Haiti have also suggested an exchange of pastors between the French-speaking countries of the Caribbean for the purpose of evangelistic campaigns. They have also mentioned the necessity of organizing a mini-congress among the French-speaking countries of the Caribbean.

INDIA NATIONAL STRATEGY GROUP REPORT

Secretary: Samuel Kamaleson

With over two hundred accepting the invitation extended by the ICOWE to be participants, India had the second largest national group attending the ICOWE. This group met for six days to discuss a national strategy for the evangelization of India. The discussion was conducted on the plenary level as well as on the small group level. The small groups were organized on the basis of geographic areas for one session and then on the basis of interest groups at other sessions. They were told of the recommended areas of discussion but were given the freedom to handle the areas that seemed most relevent to the group itself, even to the point of disregarding the recommendations.

Participation in the discussions went very well and interest was high. In this paper the strategy that each interest group reported as it's recommendation to the final plenary group is recorded.

A statement of national strategy was read to the group on the last day. The group then participated in suggesting some changes in this statement. It did not have time to study it and discuss the various points in detail. This statement is also recorded here.

Youth Evangelism

Realizing that the task of youth evangelism is urgent we strongly feel that emphasis on the training of personnel for evangelism on various levels of youth work is necessary. These workers must specialize at least in the following levels: work with children, high school youth, university youth, and youth who are already gainfully employed.

1. This training should be top priority during the next five years.

2. Youth centers must be established where young people can come and have their honest questions answered as well as enjoy acceptance and fellowship.

3. Suitable material must be published to tackle the problems of youth relating to sex, marriage, etc.

4. The content of the preaching that is aimed to reach youth and the training program for youth should include the relationship of the claims of Christ to the political, scientific issues of the time as well as the vital claims of other religions of India.

5. In addition to training leaders, it is necessary to train young people to effectively communicate their faith to other youth.

6. A list of resource personnel must be made available to the Christian youth.

7. EFI could coordinate the youth work of evangelical organizations.

8. Interdenominational youth work organizations should cooperate with churches and give every help that is possible to them.

9. We felt that the Sunday schools were not meeting the needs of the youth now. They serve the children up to the age of 12 years only. We suggest that naming the Sunday school "Church school" would attract the older youth.

10. Feeling the burden for the sophisticated modern youth of India in the major cities, we feel that the ministry of Cliff Richard would be a great help. We, therefore, unanimously agree to invite him to India for such a ministry.

The use of mass communication in Evangelism

The following means of mass communication were suggested.

1. Literature: tracts, magazines and books are being used. We suggest the organization of an institute for the training of writers. The theological seminaries should include journalism in their curriculum. It is our feeling that the local congregations should encourage Scripture and Christian literature distribution. Resources: tract societies, India Every Home Crusade, Bible Society, Scripture Gift Mission, Bibles for the World Organization. We recommend that the churches include Scripture distribution in their program.

2. Films: since the non-Christian public is attracted by films, we consider this as one of the most effective means of communication. We feel that the church in India should produce feature films which can be shown in cinema houses. The first attempts at this effort could be made in the medium of the Hindi language.

3. Radio: there may be better results through the radio ministry if there is greater coordination. We think that a school of research center should be established where the radio program speakers could learn to speak effectively and learn to communicate through this medium to the non-Christians. The training should be in all the languages of India. The duration of the program should be at least a half-hour.

4. Correspondence courses: There is a tremendous response to this means of communication. Young people and non-Christians are greatly drawn to them. Here again there is need for coordination on an all-India level. Ways and means should be found to put all those who finish their course in touch with the local pastors. Resources: many agencies are doing this job.

They need financial support. Congregations who know and appreciate their work must endeavor to take an offering for their financial support.

5. Scripture distribution: The local congregation may make this a part of their program. Selling agencies like the congregation or other groups may print their addresses on the Scripture so that the purchaser may know whom to contact in his effort to further inquiry.

6. Tape and cassette ministry: It will be advantageous to have a regional library. We feel that available tapes and recordings should be used according to the needs of the local situation.

Recommendations

1. Coordination in the area of each one of these mass media is necessary in order to avoid repetition and waste.

2. Training of radio script writers is necessary.

3. Training is necessary for the writers of Christian literature. Translators of original works need training in their field.

4. We may use our private radio set in our homes, hospitals, and schools to let the public hear Christian broadcasts. They may be located in a proper place for this effort.

5. There must be a proper follow-up program for every one of these means of communication.

6. There may be an agency set up to clear the movies available from outside India through the customs in India.

7. More adequate reading-room facilities may be set up in the cities and towns in India.

Christian nurture

Goal: The goal is to train the laity and organize the average Christian to share the task of world evangelization.

A. Strategy: Evangelistic materials: they fall under two catagories:
1. the reach-out tools.
2. the follow-up tools. These must be locally produced. The material produced at Lausanne may be adapted, translated and mass-produced in India.

B. Lay training:
1. One day conferences may be held to study the Lausanne Covenant and seek ways to implement it.
2. One-day local conferences may be arranged to train laymen in specific areas of lay evangelism such as home-evangelism, cell-group evangelism, etc.
3. Nucleus groups may be started in every local congregation.
4. Sunday school teachers may be trained theologically. Such training may be extended to teachers in public schools so that they may witness more effectively.
5. Each member of the group may pledge to teach and witness to at least one other person every day in India.

Resources Available:
1. TAFTEE.
2. Summer schools of evangelism.
2. Refresher courses in seminaries.
4. CEEFI.
5. The Christian press in India.

Recommendations: Committees may be constituted at the regional level and at the national level to: (a) examine, select, compile and publish materials for evangelism. These materials may be drawn from the Lausanne publications or from other available sources. (b) compile and coordinate all available data and resources.

Mission outside

1. Specific goals: our goal as members of Christ's church, is the same as expressed in the words of the Master: "Other sheep have I which are not of this fold; them also I must bring in." His note of urgency is our goal. He calls them sheep, not goats or wolves. They are all made in the image of God even though they are outside the fold. "As the Father has

sent me, so send I you." We all are sent by Christ Jesus to bring other sheep into the fold — even Christians who are nominal.

2. Strategy and action: evangelism through our medical and educational institutions can always go on. They are institutions with a difference! Industrial evangelism has already started and there are many opportunities in this field. Committed Christians too need training and guidance to do this specialized work.

3. Personal evangelism: this is going on and quality is being emphasized rather than quantity. Everyone has a social circle within which they are active. This social situation must be made an evangelistic opportunity. Ashrams can be great instruments in evangelism; patience, love and fortitude are the prerequisites of ashram evangelists.

4. Christian homes: these must be opened to the non-Christians for fellowship, and each social function can end with prayer and a short message.

5. Counseling centers for those who accept Christ may be established. For this, Christians need special training for action and must understand the line of progress that the new entrants must follow in the Faith.

6. How do we cooperate in our common endeavor? Christianity must become an integral part of our national-cultural stream and not remain alien and foreign in our own country. However, care must be taken to differentiate what is Indian in our culture from what is incompatible with Christianity.

There must be unity of faith and aim by creating one common platform of evangelistic effort, forgetting denominational differences.

7. Quality of life: most important since Christianity is not merely a Sunday morning business, but also Monday to Saturday living. Everyday life and evangelism cannot be contradictory.

We have our common heritage, the Church's one foundation — Jesus Christ. We can unite in this great task if we want others to become inheritors of everlasting salvation.

Evangelism — Crusade type

1. Specific Goals in the coming 5 years:

We feel that the harvesting time in India is now and the time is short. With this due sense of urgency, we have to press to two major goals, revival of the churches, reaching the unevangelized. During the next five years reach every church in India with the message of revival. This should be a definite program of revival ministry to churches. We need to cover the whole of India by campaigns in the next five years. This is a great task but this is our goal. *Note:* The campaigns should be through cooperation of all churches and para-church organizations in this area.

In reaching the non-Christians we should exercise the greatest wisdom so that we do not make the campaigns ineffective and inoperative.

2. Training.

Prayer preparation, planning, counselor training etc. Use all materials that are available in training programs for evangelists; courses for students in seminaries; institutes on evangelism to involve and train leaders in churches for evangelism; programs directed to training of evangelists old and new; conferences for evangelists in India which will give opportunities for fellowship, cooperation, and planning and also inspiration and challenge.

3. Implementation.

Planning should be made on the regional basis in full cooperation. Churches and para-church organizations must be fully involved for this definite goal. Communication of information and events of crusades, campaigns, penetration plans, etc., must be made to the whole country.

We recommend an India edition of *Decision* magazine:

A very close sense of cooperation and national interdependence among the evangelists and evangelical groups and *not* competition.

4. Resources.

Finance should come from the local churches. But in areas where churches are not able to do this, the surplus from the collections in other areas where crusades have been held should be passed on to these needy areas. Churches in India should find the finances.

All churches and missions should budget for evangelism and treat this as priority No. 1 in their budget.

Strategic Evangelism

In order to help build the country and the church we need to give priority to reaching strategic groups of people for Christ. The following recommendations are made for our consideration as we seek to evolve a national strategy.

1. Crucial areas identified.

Politicians, businessmen, administrators, and artists, the educators and members who make up the news media must be reached.

2. Survey needed.

There are Christians in the above mentioned professional groups. We need to discover them, help them through fellowship and remind them of their responsibility.

3. Training needed.

Christians who will work with specialized people need specialized training. Particularly they need to develop a Christian world view, in relation to their jobs and the people they seek to evangelize. Thus we need to develop a biblical theology of politics, economics, authority, education, entertainment, etc. It was proposed that a month-long seminar be held in the summer of 1975 for this purpose.

4. Trained people to be sent into the world.

Along with challenging people to "full-time" work we must also challenge people to enter the secular strategic places of influence, such as the IAS and other administrative services. These people must be trained to relate their faith to their field.

a. Needed more "Christians" in New Delhi — Josephs, Daniels and Esthers.

b. ICL (Prayer Breakfast Fellowship) for key people is needed.

c. All peoples in India must be befriended and reached.

d. The 25 "Christian" M.P.s need prayer support and help.

e. A theological research and communication institute has been formed already and this could help in these areas if it is strengthened and its services used.

f. TV must be used as a medium now.

g. More Christian journalists are required.

h. Apologetic literature is an *urgent must.*

Unreached areas

1. Goal: Identify the unreached peoples and devise plans to reach them.

2. Strategy: *Task* — there are about 38 million tribal peoples in India, and out of these, 17 million are in Central India. The task is to reach these tribes. In addition, priority must be given to those in Rajasthan, Jammu and Kashmir, M.P., N.E. India regions.

It is highly important to find information on these tribes. Christians are to be trained to reach these tribes. Additional training must be given to those Bible school graduates who intend to work among the tribes by way of short-term special courses in missions and evangelism. Then we must keep on looking for dedicated young men to go as pioneer missionaries to these tribes. Christian young men and women must be challenged to go to the needy areas.

3. Implementation: send such trained men as mentioned above to the needy areas. Use hospitals, schools, adult literacy programs and the like as means to reach the unreached. Community living of small groups by dedicated Christians and families must be encouraged, to form as "Ashrams" in various areas of the country, in order that they may come in contact with the people and thus evangelize them. Encourage non-professional ministry. Give ample training to those involved in various kinds of secular employment and trades, and put these people in needy areas; assist them to find employment or business contacts. They can serve as missionaries to the tribes along with their secular employment. Examples given of a tailor who settled in a village, and of Christian students who started a laundry.

As the medical need is great in Indian villages, train committed Christians in medicine and encourage them to settle in villages.

4. Cooperation: great cooperation from churches is needed. Educate the congregations in their need to reach the unreached. Set apart one Sunday a month as "Mission Sunday" and explain the needs and possibilities and encourage the formation of prayer cells to pray for people. Formulate information of needy areas and circulate such information among the missionary and evangelistic agencies of churches and other groups. Make a directory of sending agencies such as different evangelistic bodies of churches and other evangelistic groups.

The National Missionary Society was requested to call a consultation of representatives from the evangelistic bodies and associations and boards of denominations and sending agencies. The purpose of this consultation is to discuss and plan programs for the above proposals. Addresses of such sending agencies are to be given to Rev. Durairaj of the NMS. A study group must be formed to understand "people's movements." Special social action groups may be devised and put into action.

Conclusion

After these group reports were read and accepted "A National Strategy Statement" was read to the group. A brief discussion resulted in some alterations of the first document so read. The group expressed their wish for more discussion time. The following statement was then accepted:

"We who belong to various churches and denominations of the Church of Christ in India, and are participating here at Lausanne in the ICOWE feel convinced that the Lord is calling the Church in the world to revival and unity in order to reach the unreached millions with the Gospel of Jesus Christ. We are led to adopt the following statement for the evangelization of our country in this decade and commend the same to our churches and denominations in India:

"(1) Recognizing that the local congregations are the base for evangelization we would encourage them to form small Koinonia groups which will meet at least once a week for study of the Bible, prayer, and fellowship and then purpose to witness through word and deed.

"(2) We will heartily cooperate and work in united endeavors for evangelization with all such local congregations and denominations in our cities, states and country which subscribe to the historical Apostles' and Nicean Creeds.

"(3) We will, in every city, draw up united plans for revival and evangelization, in addition to what each of us may already be doing by himself.

"(4) We will join hands with all regional and national evangelistic bodies which may be seeking renewal of the church and evangelization of the nation and may be sending out missionaries.

"(5) We will encourage our people to be actively supporting and to be personally involved in all endeavors of evangelistic bodies.

"(6) We will seek to implement the India Penetration Plan of the EFI or any other similar plan to reach the cities of India as was done in the cities of M.P., Maghalaya, etc.

"(7) We desire to have another Indian Congress of Evangelization by the year 1976."

The National Strategy Group from India expressed its desire to invite Dr. Billy Graham to visit India to help in evangelization and revival of the Indian Church in the year 1976 or thereafter.

In the matter of city wide evangelization endeavors, the group felt that the terms "Crusade" and other militaristic terms may be avoided and the local vernacular terms descriptive of love and joy may be used.

Within the world in which we live, and the context of man as we know it, and the understanding of God through his only Son, our Lord Jesus Christ, distinctions between the "spiritual" and "material" are not "mutually exclusive."

We will endeavor to extend the beauty of community to the whole spectrum of man. We will, in this endeavor, work in full cooperation with the intentions and purposes of the governmental agencies. We will also seek to devise programs of similar nature to supplement and complement those already in existence.

INDONESIA NATIONAL STRATEGY GROUP REPORT

Secretary: Stephanus Damaris

Introduction

I. To determine a national strategy for world and Indonesian evangelism for the next decade we need to define first what world evangelism is. World evangelism is the proclamation of Jesus Christ as Savior of the world to all men, and to make them his disciples.

II. To evangelize Indonesia we need to determine goals, basic principles and steps, considering the main obstacles.

    A. External obstacles:
        -opposition from non-Christians;
        - social-political situation and condition.

    B. Internal obstacles:
        - the church leaders are not sufficiently responsive toward the Great Commission;
        - lack of facilities, finances, materials, effective methods, trained personnel, and vision.

III. We need to determine specific responsive areas as targets for evangelism.

IV. We need to find new forms of cooperation, coordination, and systematic follow-up.

The following results were obtained by the Indonesian strategy group through interaction in nine small groups.

Priority goals for the next decade

I. *For the evangelization of Indonesia*

    A. Preach the Gospel to every unreached segment and people of Indonesian society.

        1. According to location:
        - Sumatra (Aceh, West Sumatra, Batak-Karo, Lampung)
        - Java (Jacarta, West Java, Central Java, East Java Madura)
        - Bali, Lombok
        - Kalimantan (West Kalimantan, East Kalimantan, Central Kalimantan)
        - Sulawesi (Southeast Sulawesi)
        - Selayar Island
        - Sumbawa
        - Irian Jaya

        2. According to age level:
        - children
        - youth
        - adult

3. According to profession:
   - labor
   - government employees, teachers, medical personnel
   - businessmen
   - farmers
   - armed forces
4. Special groups:
   - prostitutes
   - unemployed
   - the blind
   - slum areas

B. To train church members for active evangelism
   - lay evangelism training courses
   - evangelist up-grading courses
   - pastors up-grading courses
   - religious teachers up-grading courses

C. Prepare the infrastructure:
   - literature
   - audio-visual aids (cassette recorder, film, slides, over-head projector, radio, TV, flannel-board, tracts, survey and research report, bulletins and magazines)
   - fund-raising and other material resources available in Indonesia

II. *Contribution for world evangelization*

A. Cooperate with evangelistic institutions throughout the world.
   1. O.M.F.
   2. C.M.A.
   3. Overseas Crusade Inc.
   4. Partner churches
   5. Campus Crusade for Christ
   6. Evangelism International
   7. Salvation Army
   8. TEAM
   9. R.B.M.A.
   10. W.E.C.
   11. Baslen Mission, etc.

B. Participate in cross-cultural evangelism to send out Indonesian missionaries to:
   1. Suriname
   2. Netherlands
   3. Pakistan
   4. Malaysia
   5. Hong Kong
   6. Bangladesh
   7. Serawak (North Borneo)
   8. U.S.A.
   9. Singapore
   10. Brazil
   11. Switzerland
   12. Philippines

13. Cambodia
14. Australia
15. Thailand
16. Japan
17. Korea
18. New Zealand

Basic strategy to attain stated goals

I. Mobilize local congregations to carry out the task of evangelism, and coordinate interaction of the local evangelistic bodies.
II. Establish training centers for evangelism of church members.
III. Carry out several kinds of evangelistic approaches:
   A. Ecological approach
      - ethnical
      - anthropological
      - phenomenal
   B. Comprehensive approach
      - medical
      - agricultural
      - economical
      - vocational
IV. Carry out evangelism to:
   A. Areas still closed to the Gospel — Aceh, West Sumatra, South Kalimantan, West Java, Madura, Sumbawa.
   B. Animistic areas — Bali, Central Kalimantan, Kubu, Irian Jaya.
   C. Rural and urban areas — Lampung, (rural) Jacarta, Surabaya, Yogya, Medan, Ujung Pandang (urban).
V. Intensify specific actions:
   A. personal evangelism
   B. small group evangelism
   C. mass evangelism
   D. home meetings
   E. prayer fellowships
   F. cell-groups
   G. air evangelism (Radio, TV)
   H. river evangelism
   I. drama, music, arts, film
   J. community organizing
   K. house churches

Assistance needed from outside Indonesia

I. *Personnel*
   A. Qualified and dedicated personnel to assist in training Indonesian personnel for evangelism.
   B. Scholarships to assist Indonesian leaders to be trained abroad

II.   *Material*
   A.   Literature
   B.   Audio-visual aids, supplies (cassette units, film units, slide units, radio, TV, flannel-boards, tracts, bulletins etc.)

Continuing association

The national strategy group of Indonesia suggests the formation of a national concern committee for world evangelization on a worldwide and national level.

IRAN NATIONAL STRATEGY GROUP REPORT

Secretary: David Thomas

The Iranian strategy group after prayerful discussion of their possibilities and needs, have presented the following report. This report shows some of the main burdens that the participants have upon their hearts for the evangelization of Iran, and the areas surrounding Iran.

I. Priority Goals

Mobilization and wakening of the church in Iran is the main goal for evangelization of the country. In order to accomplish this goal, we need to find and train potential leaders in various areas. Also we must train lay Christians for evangelism. Unreached people are a challenge to us.

We have discovered potential possibilities in contributing to the evangelization of the Persian Gulf and surrounding countries. We believe that the Persian Christians have a unique contribution to make in the region.

II. Basic Strategy to Reach Our Goals

We consider fervent, continuous prayer to be the foremost effective strategy for the preparation of the ground. Then finding key men that God is calling for the work in different areas constitutes a major step in the success of the work. Also, we must encourage strong members of the church to move out into various cities and areas where there are no churches, or where there is need for help.

We believe that new churches will be planted in this way.

Formation of an evangelistic team to strengthen local churches and to reach unevangelized areas is another proposed effective strategy.

Reaching the nation through free correspondence courses has proven to be an effective method. We encourage this medium and would invite those in charge to cooperate with us in the follow up work.

The possibility of radio ministry from within the country, requesting time on national radio, was also suggested.

It seemed to the Iranian group that Christian conventions held in Tehran, and other centers would be of great encouragement to Christians.

III. Specific Action Recommended to Participants

We recommend that our group form themselves into an Evangelical Fellowship to implement actively the proposals of the Congress. We would encourage other evangelical Christian individuals to join this fellowship on a personal basis.

We would encourage prayer and Bible study groups to strengthen converts.

We would encourage special evangelistic efforts among ancient Christian, Jewish and other communities as the Lord directs.

Summer camps for children and young people will be emphasized more than before.

IV. Help Needed

Prayer of all God's people is needed in the first place.

Our people need good Christian literature in Persian in the areas of theology and reference books such as Bible dictionaries, concordances and commentaries; teaching materials for children. We need funds for this project.

V. Continuing Cooperation

As mentioned above, we think the formation of an evangelical fellowship is the first step toward the continued cooperation and implementation of these goals. This would help to coordinate the activities of various Christian groups who work in Iran.

IRELAND NATIONAL STRATEGY GROUP

Secretary: B. Kingsmore

During the Congress, the Irish delegation has been listening to speakers, sharing with one another and endeavoring to find a way to go back and help the Irish churches to become more evangelistic in spirit and play a positive part in the evangelization of the world.

The problems discussed were numerous and included:
1. How to evangelize
    a. a society in conflict.
    b. a society of nominal Christians.
    c. a predominantly Roman Catholic community.
2. Cooperation at all levels in evangelism.

Our discussions were colored by the conflict in Ireland, so much that the following statement was issued:

In view of the reference to the situation in Belfast (The Highest Priority: Cross Cultural Evangelism, p. 3, col. 2, para. 2) and the personal reactions encountered here by Irish Congress participants we wish categorically to state:
1. That the tragic state of affairs in Ireland must not be described as "Christians at War." The issues at stake are not religious but historical and political. We emphatically declare that to our knowledge the perpetrators of the violence are not committed Christians, though they may claim some nominal denominational adherence.
2. We deplore the distortion of the facts of the situation by the mass media, which so often has not only exaggerated but aggravated the difficulties.
3. There is undoubted evidence of foreign subversive elements whose influence is of a totally anti-Christian character and who are exploiting the local religious situation for political ends.
4. We therefore urge the Congress to share this burden for Ireland and join with us in prayer for national repentance and revival; that Ireland may no longer be a burden to world evangelization and that all Ireland may hear his voice.

We named three priorities:
1. Prayer and expository preaching.
2. Creation of Christian community so that the "beauty of community" can be seen in action.
3. To fully evangelize Ireland.

In order to achieve these goals the whole area of the training and mobilizing of the church was discussed. Specific action was requested with regard to information, continued contact with each other, and the possibility of wider involvement.

It is hoped that each participant will share the knowledge acquired during the Congress with all other interested persons; also that another meeting of participants will take place in Ireland in September, 1974.

A further project to be discussed is the production of a newspaper which will inform the Christian public of what God is doing in Ireland.

Cross-cultural evangelism has indicated new awareness of the problems and the use of indigenous workers that are produced by "church-based" strategies. This could be one way used by God to overcome the great barrier of prejudice in Ireland, and the great problem which Ireland is causing to world evangelization.

ISRAEL NATIONAL STRATEGY GROUP REPORT

Secretary: M. Benhayim

The central issue before the Israeli national group was to face up to the many problems which are unique to the Messianic Jews (or Hebrew Christians) living in a situation dissimilar in many respects to the general situation elsewhere confronting believing Christians. In addition to the normal biblical division between the committed believer and the unbelieving world in which he lives, the Messianic Jew faces a problem of identity within the framework of the revived Jewish national life in Israel. What may only seem like semantic preferences, e.g., usages of terms like Messianic in place of Christian, represent serious psychological, social, and intellectual concerns. They express his determination to maintain and nourish his native Jewish identity within as normal an Israeli context as possible.

While this determination is no doubt similar to the desire of various other groups to maintain their own cultural identity apart from the cultural wrappings (usually Western) in which Christian faith has been presented to them, it is even more extreme in its expression in Israel for one simple reason: The Jewish identity of those Jews who confess Christ is often immediately called into question by misguided Christians on the one hand inappropriately citing Galatians (There is neither Jew nor Greek, male nor female...) and by Jewish compatriots who from an often tragic historical perspective view Jewishness and Christianity as mutually exclusive.

In the light of the above, all discussion of strategy of evangelization is overshadowed by existential problems which have affected and continue to affect each participant...and doubtlessly influenced the Arab participant of the Israeli group to unite with other Arabic participants (except for two meetings during which exchange of views was sought in a completely friendly spirit). What emerged from the Lausanne meetings on this level was a determination to crystallize the situation, which the participants are convinced is absolutely necessary if a genuine move of God is to be channeled through them, and through any of their efforts.

To this end a meeting in the homeland was agreed upon, to which would be invited those persons in the believing community there, who manifest a lively and concerned interest in the furtherance of the Messianic cause among our people. Time, place, and the names of such persons were all spelled out, and one of the participants centrally located undertook to initiate the steps necessary in order to effect such a conference...which would last for approximately two days.

It is expected that such a conference will lead to some kind of framework, the Lord leading, whereby basic issues affecting the community of all believers in Israel can be clarified and hopefully acted upon where necessary. Some such issues which it was felt require such clarification and action were generally discussed at these meetings, and are herewith listed:

1. Basic Theology. What is the basic message of the Gospel, and what is the relation to peripheral issues, if they can be so designated: e.g., prophecy, especially as it relates to the Jewish people, Israel and the Middle East...personal immortality and the Kingdom of Heaven...ethics and cultural standards as they affect individual and corporate life-style.

2. The identity of the Messianic Jew (or Hebrew Christian) within the life of Israel, the life of the Jewish people at large, and within the life of the believing Christian church. The specialness of this issue of identity derives from both biblical considerations and extrabiblical considerations (historical and cultural).

3. The problems and challenges of community or fellowship among the believers in Israel. These may be subdivided into three main categories: those involving Hebrew believers, those of Arabic background, and those from Western backgrounds.

4. The need to review some of the programs and methods employed to further the Gospel in terms of effectiveness, ethics, and relevance.

5. The need to convey something of the wider vision and experience that Lausanne has provided the Israeli participants for the benefit of believers in the homeland...i.e., the thrust of the Word of God to the four corners of the earth and the varigated dynamics (whether personal or technical) exhibited by participants and staff.

Negatively, there was a consensus that in the light of the tremendous impact of Jewry upon human history, and most conspicuously in its biblical expression, there was an astonishing lack of reference to this factor at the Congress (apart from the specific local reference of the Israeli group and individual Jews participating with other groups). Eschatological considerations or commitments may be too hazardous for a Congress of this type to enter into. Yet the involvement of Jewish communities and individuals in the mainstreams of history from ancient times to modern times would suggest a more than casual approach to the Jewish people. Accordingly, the following statement was offered to the draft committee of the Lausanne Covenant with the approval of the Hebrew Israeli participants.

IT WAS THROUGH THE JEWISH PEOPLE THAT THE ORACLES OF GOD WERE GIVEN (ROMANS 3:2). THEIRS ARE THE FATHERS AND OF WHOM (CONCERNING THE FLESH) MESSIAH CAME (ROMANS 9:5). WHILE GOD HAS BEEN CALLING OUT TO HIMSELF A HOLY PEOPLE FROM AMONG ALL NATIONS AND PEOPLES, HE HAS BY NO MEANS CAST OFF HIS ANCIENT PEOPLE (ROM. 11:1,2). IT THEREFORE BEHOOVES CHRISTIANS EVERYWHERE TO KEEP IN VIEW THOSE WHO ARE BELOVED FOR THE FATHERS' SAKES (ROM. 11:28). AMONG WHOSE NATURAL BRANCHES MULTITUDES OF GENTILES HAVE BEEN GRAFTED IN.

ITALY NATIONAL STRATEGY REPORT

Secretary: Franco A. Bono

After preliminaries, the discussion centered first of all on the formation of the Evangelical Alliance of Italy.

The need for an Alliance was unanimously felt. How to achieve this was subject to various views. It was decided that the idea should be developed after and not during the Congress.

An honest strategical analysis was then undertaken. An assessment of the Italian delegation and evangelical scene showed that the total spectrum of Italian Evangelicalism was represented; this included literature evangelism, radio evangelism, church-based evangelism and evangelistic campaigns.

A regional analysis and evaluation of each aspect of evangelism revealed that Southern Italy is being evangelized more than the north; proportionally, however, the response to the Gospel seemed about the same throughout the country. As one of us said: "The Spirit blows where it wills, but mainly where Christians are at work." The major response seems to be from young people and elderly people. Middle-aged men seem hardest to reach. Some felt that it is difficult for youth to be integrated into the local church.

The problem was raised as to where to mass our forces. It was thought that we should begin with the easier areas with the view of marching towards the more difficult ones.

A study of the problems and the opportunities connected with evangelism showed that these are mainly having to do with the church. There is a basic lack of unity and cooperation as well as communication and interaction among the Italian evangelicals. Some fear to lose their own religious identity. We suffer from a lack of love and our vision is too often localized even denominationally instead of looking at the vast field of the 55 million Italians. The need therefore arises for visible fellowship and coordinated efforts in evangelism.

External factors were then considered briefly. We must cope with a Roman Catholicism which is in crisis. This breeds fear and suspicion of any religious message and paradoxically it creates a spirit of openness and research. There is therefore a unique opportunity to preach the Gospel. There is also a breakdown of social patterns. Often evangelical organizations and the church have not kept up with the changes. Economic problems and pressures have caused a near mass-migration from South to North. This has both positive and negative implications. Southern churches are weakened but a wider testimony in the North occurred. One problem here is that new northern churches tend to remain southern ghettos and do not reach their northern environment.

There is a dire need for trained believers. Economic problems often discourage young people from going to a Bible school. Laymen will then have to be trained in evening Bible classes or extension seminary programs, but churches need to encourage their young people to be trained.

In order to do this there must be more cooperation and coordination between local churches.

In conclusion we must say that the problem is not with the methods of evangelism as much as with local churches. These must be geared to meet the total sphere of man's need. There must not be a competitive spirit but one of unity. It has been decided that the Congress spirit and materials *must* be shared with urgency and a committee has been nominated to organize a national conference on evangelism.

IVORY COAST REGIONAL STRATEGY REPORT

Without a doubt Ivory Coast faces the same needs as other countries of Africa. In general one could say that it is a country where the Gospel has not deeply penetrated even though missionaries have worked in the metropolitan centers for several decades. Recently several retreats and workshops have been held with the goal of advancing the evangelization of our country. At the end of this Congress and national strategy meetings, we present our plans and future projects for the evangelization of Ivory Coast.

I. *We see the following priorities for the evangelization of our country:*

   a)   Train lay people and Christian workers
   b)   Reach students and children
   c)   Conduct literacy programs among Christians with a view to helping them read the Bible
   d)   Translate the Bible into the principal vernacular languages of the country
   e)   Evangelize by all means possible: campaigns, door-to-door, personal, etc.
   f)   Establish churches for and with new converts
   g)   Utilize mass media : radio, literature, cassettes, films, etc.

As our contribution to the evangelization of the world, we will particularly increase our efforts in the production and distribution of evangelistic literature throughout Francophone Africa. In the future, perhaps we could help with money and some personnel.

II. *To reach these goals we propose the following strategy:*

   a)   To train servants of God and lay people we propose strengthening the Bible Institute and Bible schools as well as holding retreats and training sessions.
   b)   To reach the students and children we will place the accent on Bible teaching in public schools (a program authorized by the Government).
      We will continue youth camps, Sunday schools, and other programs already underway.
   c)   In the literacy efforts it will be necessary to teach illiterate peoples and encourage them to reach their brothers and sisters.
   d)   Missions and local churches will continue their cooperation with the Bible Society and Wycliffe for the translation of the Bible.
   e)   In order to use all the means possible we see the necessity of a national plan and campaign of evangelism. This would necessitate the call of a full-time African evangelist.
   f)   In order to provide literature it will be necessary to train more writers by organizing journalism, workshops and courses in Bible Institutes.

g) To reach the various neighborhoods in large cities, we will utilize the following:
- open air film-showings followed by evangelistic messages.
- Door-to-door visitation and literature evangelism.
- Bible study groups in homes.

III. *Practical applications*

This strategy will be put into practice after our return from Lausanne. Our first action will be to present a report from the Congress in which we will underline those things we feel necessary to the evangelization of our country. This report will be presented first in our local churches, then in the Evangelical Federation of Churches and missions or a Conference which we will hold for that purpose.

The Federation and/or the Conference must encourage churches to pray and to launch evangelistic efforts in such a way that this action will be spread through all the country.

JAPAN NATIONAL STRATEGY GROUP REPORT

Secretary: Rev. Samel K. Arai

INTRODUCTION

1. All members were divided into five groups, each having fair representation of special area; pastoral, specialized ministerial and educational, etc.

2. Five topics for discussion proposed by the Congress Committee were accepted as such and other points were added as sessions proceeded.

3. It is of course impossible to gather all things discussed, proposed, and decided on during 4 days, but they may be summarized as follows:

I. Goal setting for this decade

A. A basic attitude toward the idea of "goal setting" for evangelism. It is noted that there are at least two basic attitudes which seem to stand in opposition. One stresses a need of goal setting and of making strategy to achieve that goal and another emphasizes the dependence on the Spirit's guidance to lead only to the next step.

These attitudes are also apparent among Japanese participants. Therefore, it is agreed not to set a numerical goal right off, but rather to have a general goal of saturating Japan with the Gospel, and each one should make his own practical goal at which to aim.

B. Areas of goal. It is advised to have a goal in the following area since each one has a different viewpoint based upon his past and present involvement in Evangelism:

1. Goal for an individual life as called of God.
2. Goal for each respective area of ministry.
3. Goal for a group denominational, inter-denominational.
4. Goal for national scale in cooperation of all.
5. Goal for the world evangelization in conjunction of Japan's role in it.

C. Practical proposals expressed. Though it is not a general consensus, but is expressed with zeal to aim toward multiplication of the number of present congregation by 3 times in this decade; to move on toward increasing baptized members to 10% of whole population whereas we have now only less then 1%.

II. Activities planned

A. In the light of the past.

1. To review Christian activities, ministries, and works done in the past century, both by foreigners and nationals in the light of the Bible.
2. To clarify the nature and contents of the Gospel, essence of "evangelization," and actual carrying out of evangelism, both theoretically and practically; both individual life and

community as church, and also church-society relationship.

3. To re-evaluate secular education, and theological education in relationship to evangelization.

B. In the projection to the future.

1. To formulate biblical but peculiarly Japanese strategy based upon actual data of contemporary Japan, avoiding to copy the Western one in order to better serve him and Japanese.

2. To set up some type of agency to promote this kind of research and planning and to provide opportunities for mutual consideration of the ministry.

3. To promote an establishing of theology of evangelism by theologians.

4. To provide similar opportunities for discussion and study between pastors and workers of specialized ministries.

5. To encourage participation of laymen with provision for their needed training.

6. To take seriously a responsibility of Japanese Christians in relationship to the world evangelization.

III. Practical proposals for implementation

A. Production of materials. Many expressed their concerns and desires for material production in Japanese. Since materials produced at Berlin and Singapore were not made available to those who could not be there, it is strongly recommended for the central committee of Japanese delegation to study the possibility of this production.

B. Request to J.E.A. for promotion of follow-up of this Congress. It is desired that J.E.A., an evangelical fellowship already in existence, would make plans and promote our future fellowship among participants welcoming those of the same persuasion.

C. Determination of each participant to implement his program. Though all the participants may not be able to work collectively as an organized group, each one determines in his/her respective ministry with his power always to reach the world in view.

KOREA NATIONAL STRATEGY GROUP REPORT

Secretary: Everett N. Hunt, Jr.

The Korean delegation to the Congress is a representative cross-section of the major elements of the Korean Church. These are both laymen and clergy, pastors and theological professors, men and women, men in government and ordinary citizens, denominational and interdenominational, old and young, western missionary and Korean.

This diversity made for some interesting dynamics in the first meetings of the strategy session and indeed continued to provide creative tension in the group through all sessions. This diverse group would probably not have had a similar occasion to meet in Korea. Thus the very fact of bringing together representatives of such diverse segments of Korean church life for concern with world evangelization was an important result of this Congress.

In early discussions it was easily agreed that Korea does have a strong church. It is hard to find in Asia a stronger church than Korea. Thus in relation to potential in manpower, resources, training, and spiritual vitality, the Korean church is not lacking.

Moreover as a result of God's special blessing at the time of the Billy Graham crusade, 1973, the world has come to be aware of the greatness of our church. The anticipation and expectation building for Explo '74 — Campus Crusade — is adding to this worldwide awareness of the Korean Church.

A negative factor in recent weeks has added all the more to world awareness of Korean Christianity. The distorted impression created by various news media that Christians in Korea are presently being persecuted, though false, has added to the interest and focus on Korean Christians.

In light of both the actual strength of the Korean Church and the world awareness of that strength, the Korean delegation recognizes a responsibility for interpretation as well as the need for practical action both within our country, and in the world. To these practical matters the group continued to address itself.

Early discussions centered around areas of opportunity within Korea. These were perceived to include university students, the military, women, family units, and the large percentage of the general population who appear indifferent to religion of any sort.

In the face of the opportunities there was a corollary recognition of hindrances in seeking to evangelize. From the perspective of the church, these may be characterized as both internal and external.

Internally there was recognition that our divisions have hindered evangelization. Denominational differences, legalistic presentations of Christianity while at the same time hypocritical lives of Christians, too large a gap between lay and ordained, a lack of cooperation between denominational and interdenominational organizations and activities, a lack of objective planning for evangelization, and an attitude of indifference to Christianity fostered by "Christian" institutions which have lost their evangelistic concern, such as Christian hospitals, schools, etc.

External hindrances to the Gospel in Korea are not those of religious or political oppressions and persecutions. Rather the greatest hindrance appears to be a widespread indifference to the need for a personal faith of any sort, least of all Christianity. This indifference to Christianity is perhaps most widespread among university students, a group agreed by all to be most alienated from the church.

In light of these hindrances, discussions turned to strategy. A recognized emphasis was that the internal hindrances to evangelization mentioned above must be repented of and overcome before we make any attempt to plan for reaching Korea, Asia, or this world for Christ.

An important first agreement was that the local church must be at the heart of our evangelization. The best evangelistic activities will come to nothing if those brought to faith in Christ are not brought into the local church fellowship.

There was a strong feeling that before a concern with methods we must have a clear understanding of the content of our message. All agreed that Dr. Billy Graham's and John Stott's messages helped to clarify the theological understanding and implications of the Gospel we preach. This is an emphasis needed in our Korean situation as well.

Following this agreement a concern was expressed to find the point of contact with those not yet evangelized. It was agreed that the church must make an effort to bridge the gap between its own community and the world of unbelievers.

A specific area of emphasis was the need for small groups. The church needs to train leaders of these small groups, teaching them such practical matters as how to conduct such a meeting, how to lead an inductive Bible study and such practical matters. The women felt this was an especially relevant strategy for women who represent the majority of Christians in Korea. Because Korea is a family-centered society this near-neighbor evangelism is still the most fruitful area for evangelization.

Beyond Korea's borders it was recognized that with all the strengths of the Korean Church — cross-cultural evangelism is our weakest area. There is agreement as to the vision for, the urgency of, and the necessity of this kind of evangelization. However, it is regrettably true that among those who have gone there have been a considerable number who have stayed only a year or two and then have gone on to other places to live and work. There is a need for a stronger program of training academically, practically, and spiritually for cross-cultural evangelization.

In conclusion, our concerns in the Korean strategy group may be summarized as content, methods, motivation, and perseverance.

Believing that God has richly blessed our Korean Church and that he has given us the potential and thus the responsibility to play an important role in the evangelization of our own country, of Asia, and of the world, this Congress has increased our awareness of needs, helped us to consider ways to meet them, and strengthened our dedication and determination to do, under God, all we can to "let the earth hear his voice."

LAOS NATIONAL STRATEGY GROUP REPORT

Definition of World Evangelization: "The preaching of the good news of salvation to the peoples of the world and the discipling of these into Christian maturity."

1. Goal for next decade

    a.   Evangelization of the area

    b.   To reach:
1. The student population (10,000 persons per year)
2. The workers (16,000 persons per year)
3. The farmers (50,000 persons per year)

    c.   To train these new converts and send them as missionaries (E-1, E-2, E-3) to Thailand and Burma. We aim to win 75,000 persons in a year. And that in ten years we would have 9% (of the 3,000,000) Christians in Laos.

2. Basic strategy

    a.   To convince the mission boards and church organizations to focus on the urban population, a field of evangelization newly arisen. Therefore personnel and resources must be directed to this new need.

    b.   To form training bases after careful study and creation of a training program. To achieve this, we would resort to seminars and conventions for Christian leadership and witnessing training, yearly so each Christian would be equipped and be adequate to witness to students, workers, and farmers. Some of these leaders will be Christian students already studying in the different institutions.

    c.   To persuade the church to set a budget for this work. To raise funds, the church leaders must emphasize tithing and stewardship: Besides we will try to solicit help from International organizations wherever possible.

    d.   To let the mission boards and churches see the need and importance of "Unity in diversity." To evangelize the Christians must therefore take into consideration cultural, sociological values of each group of people, whether E-1, E-2, or E-3 evangelism is suitable.

    e.   We suggest that a permanent work with students be established by inviting organizations such as IVCF, Youth for Christ, Campus Crusade, etc...to come to our land. This will help reach the young which are the cream of the land and the church. It will also give encouragement for the Christian students in living for the Lord. Laos has about 20,000 high schoolers. So we also propose that 2 youth centers be established in 2 key, strategic centers, each with 2 expert foreign youth workers, and a staff of 10 and 5 in Vieuhave and Savannaklet or Pakse. We could expand as the work progresses.

   f.   This is, therefore, the suggestion: that each participant try his best to put this plan and strategy to the knowledge of his overseers by making a report and by taking the necessary measures.

LIBERIA EVANGELISTIC STRATEGY GROUP REPORT

Secretary: George W. Thomas

Liberia has long been blessed by religious liberty. Its government has maintained an openness to the Christian witness of both nationals and missionaries from beyond its borders. Notwithstanding, evangelization remains — in Liberia as in the world — as an urgent need and an unfinished task.

The 1.5 million people of the Republic of Liberia comprise two major groups — the urban populace and the rural populace. All must be confronted with the claims of the Gospel; every man must be given the opportunity to become a disciple of Jesus Christ.

The task is dual in scope:
— to proclaim the Gospel in clear and simple language for all to hear;
— to mobilize and encourage the Christians in Liberia to become active in an evangelistic outreach and a discipling ministry — at the personal level and to the masses.

This task will not be completed until there is evidence of an evangelical, witnessing body of believers in each of the constituent groups of the country's populace.

The work of evangelizing must take into account the varied nature of the populace. Thus, the message of eternal life — by faith in Jesus Christ — must be geared to reach each group within the framework of their own felt needs and distinctive characteristics. Thus, among the urban populace, the guidance of the Holy Spirit is needed in reaching particularly the:
— Professionals: educators, doctors, lawyers, government leaders, business men;
— Non-professionals: civil servants, semi-skilled laborers, office workers;
— Unskilled laborers;
— Students.

Wisdom and perseverance, as only God can give, is needed in reaching the rural populace of chiefs and farmers.

Complicating this task is the multiplicity of language groups and the remote locations of many. Illiteracy and disunity pose further hurdles in communicating and making Christ known.

Accepting, then, the mandate of Scripture to reach and to teach all men everywhere; and recognizing the urgency of the task and the complexities inherent therein; and being desirous of taking full advantage of the opportunities for the evangelization of the people of Liberia, it was the conclusion of this group of Congress participants that:

A. The Primary Needs — and thus objectives — in the evangelization of Liberia are as follows:

1. Spiritual renewal among established churches — so that the body of Christ will be vibrant in its witness;
2. Discipling instruction — so that all may be challenged by God's Word;
3. Recruitment and training of youth for the ministry — so that the church may have strong and continuing leadership;
4. Religious instruction among students coupled with training of religious instruction teachers — to reach the emergent populace;
5. Bible translation in every major language group — so that all may have God's Word;
6. Greater evangelistic outreach by the pastors of evangelical churches in the urban centers;
7. Concerted effort in an evangelistic witness to every village;
8. Literacy instruction — so that all may read God's Word;
9. Development of new approaches in reaching each major tribal group and particularly the Mandingo people.

B. *The Approaches* for evangelization should be related to specific target groups. Thus, it was recommended that consideration be given:

1. for the Professionals — to
   . Prayer Breakfasts — for men,
   . Prayer Band Fellowship — for women,
   . Home Bible Studies — for the professionals and elite,
   . Radio and TV Programming;
2. for the Non-Professionals — to
   . Radio and TV Programming,
   . Area Evangelistic Campaigns,
   . Film Showings,
   . Newspaper Articles,
   . Retreat and Camping Programs,
   . Home Bible Studies;
3. for the Student populace — to collective effort of existing groups — i.e.,
   . Campus Crusade for Christ — in leadership training,
   . Inter-Varsity Christian Fellowship — at the college level,
   . Scripture Union — for Bible study groups,
   . Youth for Christ — among high schoolers,
   . Youth Centers — for the unchurched,
   . Child Evangelism Fellowship — for children;
4. for the farmers — through
   . Pastors going to unevangelized areas for month-long periods of special assignment,
   . Radio programming — integrating with local church and/or other evangelization programs and agencies,
   . Cassette distribution.

C. *Mobilization* of the evangelical clergy — beginning at the highest level — was thought *essential* to an accelerated outreach for Christ. This relates to both national pastors and missionaries. It was concluded that there was value in concerted effort:

— demonstrating a unity in Christ,

— encouraging all groups to participate,

— engaging all resources effectively.

Cooperation within the evangelical community was recognized as both valuable and desirable. It was also recognized that mutual endeavor could be effective in the measure that there was clear commitment to serve unitedly. It was recommended that the heads of evangelical church groups and related agencies meet at an early date to establish a basis for a national thrust.

D. *World Evangelization* will involve Liberian participation, particularly through

— the outreach of Christian radio from Liberia to many countries in Africa;

— the spreading of the Gospel through tribal groups resident on both sides of Liberia's geographical borders — as in Ivory Coast, Sierre Leone and Guinea;

— Liberians reaching the Arabs of Africa for Christ.

MALAYSIA NATIONAL STRATEGY GROUP REPORT

Secretary: Thomas Heng

Fifteen participants and observers meeting together in the Malaysian National Strategy Group began by applying what was so ably said by the speakers of the day to the situation of the church in Malaysia. We recognized our lack of love, urgency, and understanding of the meaning of evangelism. We have not taken seriously the practice of evangelism, much less maintained a united national witness for Christ in the land. We have been put to shame by the zealousness of our fellow Christians from countries where the Gospel has only recently been introduced. We were led to repent of our attitudes and in the spirit of this Congress, by God's grace, we resolve to rectify the defects and to pursue the goals of the evangelization of our nation.

In discussing the opportunities that God has presented to us, there was general agreement that we may have placed too much emphasis on the English- and Chinese-speaking sectors of the population to the neglect of other language groups. We must recognize the responsive peoples whom God has given and make every effort to reach them in the first place. These have by and large been identified in the country profile on Malaysia.

We also recognized that tribal people and Malays are largely unreached, the former due to a severe shortage of personnel (e.g., there is no pastor for 10,000 Kadazan believers), the latter because of governmental restrictions. Present opportunities must not be lost and new opportunities need to be seized for the sake of the Gospel. Among these opportunities are the following:

1) Tribal work — in Sarawak and Sabah and in particular the work among Senoi Aborigines.
2) P.O. Box Mission — where evangelism by mail is particularly useful in reaching Muslims.
3) Literature evangelism — particularly among students.
4) Ship evangelism — similar to the mission to seamen.
5) Industrial mission.
6) Radio evangelism — if the broadcast is made from outside the country.
7) Evangelism among school drop-outs.
8) Evangelism among the elderly.

We recognize that in the evangelization of Malaysia there are obstacles and hindrances some of which have already been mentioned. These are summarized below.

1) *Adverse governmental policies* which restrict the area of work (Muslims are protected against proselytization by other religions) and discourage the missionary enterprise (missionaries may only stay up to 10 years and when they leave, are seldom replaceable by new missionaries).

2) *Racial attitudes* which psychologically prevent an effective
    transmission of the Gospel from believers of *one* race to un-
    believers of another within the country.
3) There has been little effort on the part of national Chris-
    tians to transcend *cultural* barriers.
4) *Theological dilution* as a result of a careless proclamation of
    the Gospel or a deliberate twisting of biblical truths in turn
    has bred *nominalism*.
5) The *lack of full-time personnel* has slowed down the process
    of evangelization.

Turning to the question of missionary output we confess our failure
to send and support even one missionary overseas. To the participants'
knowledge there is only one Malaysian foreign missionary and her support has not even come from the Malaysian church! This lack of missionary interest and vision may be traced to the following factors:

1) Too much dependence on foreign missionaries.
2) The failure of foreign missionaries to teach missions and to
    relinquish their positions of leadership in favor of national
    replacements.
3) The lack of know-how and precedence.
4) The lack of manpower.

There is a tremendous need for the church to be taught the redemptive purposes of God for the world, not just our own nation. We need to
supply our people with specific information regarding the needs of others
around us. In any future follow-up activity, it was decided, *missions*
should occupy a prominent place in the prayer and thinking of the participants. It was also proposed that participants present at this Congress
will, individually and collectively, encourage churches to set aside a part
of their budget for the *support* of missions. We agreed too that we should
encourage a *trans-denominational* movement of missionaries. We noted
that although there is the Chinese-speaking "Malaysian Home and World
Missionary Fellowship" this body has as yet not sent a single missionary
outside Malaysia.

All present felt the need of a follow-up to what we have learned here
in Lausanne. It was agreed that the following steps be taken upon return:

1) *Small prayer groups* would be started by each participant
    throughout the country. Through these groups, participants
    will share the spirit of Lausanne, study the covenant, use
    the tapes and study booklets and call our people to repen-
    tance and the evangelization of Malaysia.
2) *Small teams of participants* will travel from town to town
    and from church to church to inspire, inform and deter-
    mine whether a national congress on mission and evange-
    lism could be held.
3) Mr. Gordon Scott, elected convenor, will call a meeting of
    all interested in 6 months for prayer and those present will
    then decide whether a congress should be held.

It was stressed that all who participate in any future activities will
participate in their individual capacity.

We are grateful to God for his graciousness in enabling us to join with so many others from all parts of the world. Now we pray that we may be channels through which Malaysia may hear his voice.

THE NETHERLANDS NATIONAL STRATEGY GROUP REPORT

Secretary: Oswin Ramaker

Unfortunately the group did not really represent a major portion of Dutch evangelical Christians. Most participants were involved in the ministries of various movements such as Navigators, Inter-Varsity Fellowship, Campus Crusade for Christ, Youth With a Mission. Others represented "In de Ruimte" (working with children and Bible-training), the Dutch Bible Society, Evangelische Omroep (Evangelical Broadcasting, radio and television), Trans World Radio, Jesus People, etc. No church was represented and this was regretted by the group.

The reason why the group had a difficult start in its discussions was that some had different opinions relating to the so-called "charismatic issue." It seemed that the group was divided. One of the reasons for the division was that some did not know each other too well and it was felt that it was really necessary that we should listen to each other and pray together. We shared how the Lord had called us to the various ministries and what our vision was for reaching men and women for Christ. We regularly prayed for each other's ministries and the result was a more open discussion and love and concern for each other. This is not only the result of listening to each other but also because of a real work of the Holy Spirit, through the various other aspects of the Congress.

All participants were very encouraged by the progress of the Congress and what they heard of God's work in other parts of the world. All felt a genuine desire to be used of God to bring the Spirit of Lausanne to The Netherlands, using all that has been shared, all that has been learned, to help encourage Dutch Christians to become involved in reaching every Dutchman for Christ.

The participants were encouraged to hear from each other about what God is doing in our country. Some heard of developments that they were not aware of. Some examples of what was shared: some years ago there were very few students witnessing for Christ; today the Navigators have about 1,500 students and other young people involved in a regular program for Bible study and evangelism.

Campus Crusade for Christ has established a solid ministry on one university campus, and a group of 60 students have trusted Christ and continue to grow spiritually. This movement will now start at a second university. Besides working with students, this movement also trained several thousand young people and adults in how to share their faith.

CNI-Nederland (Inter-Varsity Fellowship) works with 600-700 students in different groups, a majority having a strong Calvinistic background.

Youth for Christ is well-known all over the country through coffeebars, literature, music tours, etc. Tens of thousands of young people are reached for Christ.

Youth With a Mission is actively involved in reaching internationals and Dutch young people through different projects. In Amsterdam they have two boats where these people are welcome.

There is an active work among children: Stichting Timotheus works with approximately 1,500 clubs for children and vacation Bible schools, providing them with materials and ideas through regular workshops in different parts of the country.

"In de Ruimte" also works with children (1,400 this year in youth camps) and with a special magazine for children. This organization also provides training for Christian workers for evangelism and missions. This year 50 students are expected to enroll for the three-year course.

The Bible Society is very active in getting the Bible in the hands of the people. Through a poll they found out that only 57 percent of the Dutch people have a Bible or Scripture portion or have access to a Bible in their home.

Trans World Radio has a competely indigenous work in The Netherlands. A total of 22 programs per week are produced and financed through the involvement of Dutch Christians. The Evangelische Omroep (evangelical radio and television) has 2 1/2 hours of television (prime time) per week available and 11 hours of radio. Another organization NCRV has also a good number of Christian programs. Pentecostal Christians are heavily involved in evangelism and have gatherings where thousands of people meet. Most active is "Opwekking" (magazine, crusades, literature and a yearly gathering, attended by approximately 8,000 last year).

The charismatic movement is attracting a lot of interest, regular conferences are conducted, and more and more Christians are mobilized by this movement. Throughout the country there are different groups of so-called Jesus People, attracting the interest of hundreds of young people.

Many more groups are active and we should not forget that the Baptist Churches are involved in Operation Agape, a church building plan, originally from England but adapted to the Dutch situation. Last year baptisms were increased by 100 per cent.

It all looks like a puzzle, but the Dutch group discovered that some of the parts of this puzzle are coming together and are more and more forming a picture. In some ways it is already looking like a mosaic.

The future:

It was found impossible to draft a proposal for a unified effort for reaching The Netherlands with the Gospel of Jesus Christ. The group needs more time and a serious effort should be undertaken to involve as many evangelical Christians within the various churches as possible.

The group decided to form a working committee of at least four people. They will work on a proposal and will contact other interested people in the meantime.

The group is very much aware of the need to give maximum attention to the follow-up of the Congress and urges Congress organizers to make the compendium available as soon as possible. Attention will be given to the translation needs for various materials and the proposed covenant.

Responsibility towards other parts of the world:

Most missionary agencies in Holland are represented in the Evangelical Missionary Alliance (E.Z.A.). There is no problem in involving all of these groups in the future planning. The group feels a special responsibility for those who live in Holland but are from other countries, such as Chinese, Surinam and Antillian people, Arab-speaking people, Greeks, Turks, Italians, Spaniards, etc. All of these matters will be carefully discussed in the future meetings of the working committee.

The Dutch group is going home, rejoicing for what God did in Lausanne, encouraged and confident that God will do it again...also in The Netherlands.

NEW ZEALAND NATIONAL STRATEGY GROUP REPORT

Secretary: Brian Carrell

Evangelism in New Zealand today

A number of special opportunities for evangelism were noted. There is a marked thirst for the Gospel among youth, an unprecedented openness to the Scriptures and to deep Christian fellowship among Roman Catholics, a sharp rise in demand for evangelical Christian literature, and increasing use of private homes for small Christian fellowship gatherings with an evangelistic edge. The charismatic renewal, especially in mainstream churches, has contributed much to this situation but these opportunities for evangelism are by no means restricted to such areas. The churches of New Zealand are working towards a "Year of Evangelism," similar in broad concept to Key '73, possibly in '76. A recent visit by Tom Skinner exceeded all expectations in response and has shown that the day of mass evangelism is not past.

But we see certain major obstacles to evangelism in our country. There is the rigidity and narrowness of current church structures. Can the old wineskins hold the new wine? Evangelical Christians are not all in a position to communicate the Gospel to society with sensitivity and relevance because they confine their lives to evangelical ghetto-like areas. A characteristic of the life-style of New Zealanders as a whole is an attitude of complacency and even apathy towards all deeper issues of life, induced by our comparative isolation, affluence and security from crisis on the world scene.

The most effective approaches to evangelism in our country we believe include these considerations. New Zealanders have an aversion to any approach which suggests "programming people." Therefore flexibility of style is imperative. To break through complacency and apathy the element of surprise is essential. Yet some felt there was still a place for various forms of "canned evangelism."

There are certain special areas which need attention when considering evangelism in New Zealand. Our multi-racial situation calls for different approaches. Besides Europeans, there are large proportions of Maoris and Polynesian peoples in our country. In the universities there is a high proportion of overseas students, most of whom come to this country from a non-Christian background. There is also an increasing number of children untouched by the churches or by religious teaching in any way as attendances at Sunday Schools decline and the coverage of primary schools with Bible teaching diminishes. While New Zealand does not possess a distinct "working class" in the European sense of the term, Christian contact and church membership is weakest in this area.

One problem which concerned us and which is possibly unique to New Zealand is the question of the relationship of evangelism to service in a welfare state such as we have. The conclusion was that the distinctive contribution Christians have to make when so much is undertaken by the

State is in the area of the quality of personal relationships in social service, whether through secular, charitable or church agencies.

Our contribution to evangelization overseas.

As we looked at our present missionary commitments overseas we found that we were involved in evangelization on every continent of the world, including Europe. It was pointed out that we have the highest proportion per population of any country in the world serving in overseas missionary work. But we still believed that the potential for cross-cultural evangelization from New Zealand is not being fully tapped.

We noted the special strengths our country had to draw upon in cross-cultural evangelism. There is our advantage in being a small country, threatening to nobody, increasingly adopting an independent and unaligned position in world politics, and no longer identified closely with the former colonial power of Great Britain. This makes our missionaries persona grata where others are less acceptable.

The example of good race relations in our country and our ability to fuse Maori and Pakeha together in one team also stands us in good stead overseas. As a young, pioneering nation with limited resources we have developed over the years a "do-it-yourself" mentality and approach to problems, which is useful to communicate to churches in underdeveloped countries who cannot afford the "buy-it-packaged" approach of some other Westerners with greater resources. One distinct contribution we have found we have been able to make (so far largely limited to Southeast Asia) is in the area of music where we seem to have encouraged creativity beyond what we see in most other Western nations.

Two directions in which New Zealand could diversify and develop its missionary outreach were noted. Our government is undertaking more and more development aid programs in underdeveloped countries and we feel a responsibility to see that more committed Christians take up opportunities for appointments abroad with these (paralleling these schemes are also increasing opportunities for appointments abroad with commercial firms). Secondly, it was felt that we could develop a Christian youth volunteer service abroad scheme.

The home base of our overseas missionary work is in need of refurbishing. Our churches and supporters of missionary societies need educating in a modern concept of missions. Along with this there is a need to improve the missionary image in the home church. Part of the answer will lie in a critical reappraisal of the pattern and purpose of missionary deputation.

Over the next decade certain priorities were identified for our country's contribution to world evangelization. First there needs to be some self-scrutiny in the areas of our race relations within New Zealand (because this is an ever-changing scene), and of our accumulated wealth. There was even a strong suggestion that Christians in our country should lobby for a holding, if not a lowering, of our standard of living. Only then might we have an authentic Gospel to share with others. Our past and present record as a missionary-sending nation could well be lost if the secularizing tendencies in our contemporary society are not checked. The principal answer to this process is seen as lying in the encouragement of more Christian youth seeing their vocation within the mass media and within areas of community service such as school teaching. It is in these two areas that secularism in New Zealand is making its greatest impact. If the needs and opportunities for cross-cultural evangelism overseas are to come alive for Christians in New Zealand, there needs to be a much better feeding of information about what the Holy Spirit is doing in other parts of the world. This Congress has opened our eyes to dimensions of the work of God in the world today which have not previously been revealed to us. Must we await another Congress to learn more? We also saw the need to look more closely at the possibility of providing greater facilities for training indigenous church leaders and for developing specialized gifts of ministry.

How are we to share the vision of Lausanne?

Three lines of communication for getting the message of Lausanne through to the churches and Christians of our own country were suggested. There will be the normal denominational channels of synods, church newspapers, committees, etc. But there is also the need to call together in less formal home gatherings carefully selected Christians who are vital links of communication in the body of Christ. Finally, what has been learned at Lausanne must find its way into the embryonic groups now being formed to promote the "Year of Evangelism" in New Zealand.

Postscript: It was agreed, as a method of procedure:

1. That Rev. David Stewart write a comprehensive report for all denominational heads in New Zealand.
2. That National Strategy Group members provide copies to one another of any reports written by them for the home constituency.
3. That areas of tension and uncertainty discerned at the Congress not be concealed in any such reporting.

NIGERIA NATIONAL STRATEGY GROUP REPORT

Secretary: Isaac George

1. Definition of world evangelization

This is narrowly defined as the faithful proclamation of the Gospel by individuals or groups of persons till *all* have heard.

2. The unreached

The "unreached" in Nigeria does not reflect wide geographical areas. Rather this is viewed in terms of "pockets" in various locations. These include ethnic groups such as the Izi-speaking people, Fulani, and some groups in Mid-West; Muslims, nominal Christians, adherents of traditional religions, urban areas, armed forces, prisons, students, the intellectuals, the handicapped, and beggars in the street.

In view of these "pockets," therefore, the task of evangelization in Nigeria is regarded as urgent.

3. Hindrances

Obviously serious obstacles stand in the way of evangelization. Some of them, on the one hand, are internal. These include: lack of concern among many Christians, inconsistent Christian living, the dogmas of certain churches, ecumenical movements, westernization of the Gospel, lack of understanding and conviction on the part of many Christians, nominal Christianity, liberal theology, and materialism. On the other hand external forces against evangelization include: Islam, so-called cultural revival, nationalistic aspirations, linguistic barriers. These hindrances are real, but there are no known serious evangelistic activities without obstacles. Therefore the group is of the opinion that, in spite of these problems, intensive plans for a nation-wide evangelization must be undertaken.

4. Methods and strategy

Among various approaches to evangelization which are considered desirable and also applicable in the situation in Nigeria (some of them learned at Lausanne, 1974) are: city-wide evangelization, neighborhood evangelism, hotel evangelism, dialogue, helping the needy, crusades, and mass media. The goal is total mobilization. It follows then that cooperative efforts must be sought among all evangelicals in the country. These will, among other things, involve holding a post-Lausanne Congress, encouraging and supporting already existing evangelical organizations such as Scripture Union, Nigerian Fellowship of Evangelical Students, Fellowship of Christian Students, Boys/Girls Brigade, etc. It is also suggested that a School of Evangelism is desirable.

5. Resolution

After a prayerful consideration a unanimous decision was taken regarding a post-Lausanne Congress to be held in Nigeria in the near future. Some participants suggested before the end of 1975, but the question of date was not seriously discussed. Two proposals were put before the gathering regarding the procedures to be adopted. One was to request one or more of the already existing evangelical bodies to be convenors. The other was to set up an ad hoc committee drawn from among the Nigerians attending the Lausanne Congress. The problems and implication of each proposal were carefully considered and weighed against those of the other. It was very clearly emphasized that under no circumstance would convenors regard the proposed Congress as their "possession." It was also stressed that no evangelical groups should be left out in the task. The financial implication of such a Congress was also discussed. Faith and sacrifice are the answer.

In the process of deliberations several participants who are leaders in various evangelical groups put on record the fact that their organizations are willing to cooperate and do all that they can in being involved with the proposal. These leaders and their organizations are as follows:

Rev. D.I. Olatayo — Nigerian Evangelical Fellowship

Mr. Tony Wilmot — Tuesday Evening Bible Study Group, Yaba, Lagos

Rev. Benson Idahosa — Christ for the National International

Rev. M. Ariye — Gospel Light Ministry, Ilorin

Dr. Byang Kato — Association of Evangelicals in Africa and Madagascar

Finally, Dr. J. Ayorinde, Rev. J. Ameh, and Mr. S. Odunaike were requested to be convenors. They all accepted the responsibility.

6. Other Points

a. The group commented on the sad phenomenon described as "The Church is out, the Bible is in."

To some extent, it obtains in Nigeria, and is most undesirable. Participants hope that it is only a temporary incident, and efforts must be made to correct the situation immediately.

b. Strategy

The group observed that the early Church did not lack strategy in that they followed plans, but their plans resulted from their being in touch with the Holy Spirit. The lesson learned from that situation is that praying and planning are not alternatives, perhaps not complementary to each other either; rather they are concomitant in that they are jointly undertaken, one does not precede, nor follow, the other.

c. Powers of the age to come

The following quote from Michael Green, ICOWE 1974, was discussed: "When the people saw that in the society of Jesus the powers of the age to come were really exercised (prophecy, tongues, healing, alongside teaching, administration and works of mercy) then they listened to the message of Jesus, who alone accounted for such a remarkable situation." The discussion was brief, but it was argued that prophecy, etc., do not constitute the totality of the basis of evangelization; the main thing is the message.

Whenever and wherever God chooses to demonstrate the powers of the age to come, those who might be his instruments must exercise such powers lovingly, but they should never be to impress people.

d. Evangelism — the church's life-style

It was observed that no efforts should be spared in teaching and stressing the fact that evangelization should be church's life-style. It should be taught from the pulpit. It should be encouraged. Everybody should be talking about Jesus. This implies that those that are within must be fully convinced about who Jesus is and what he means to them. Evangelical Christians in Nigeria look beyond their frontiers. Already they have sent missionaries to other African countries. This trend, it was noted, must be intensified.

NORTH AFRICA AND MIDDLE EAST GROUP REPORT

Secretary: F. E. Allad

After prayer and reading part of Bishop Dain's letter on the subject, the committee moved to draw the attention of the Congress Responsibles to the three following matters which they felt themselves, and also heard from others of their people, to be very important to be followed up before the closing of the Congress if possible:

1) That a *Mini-congress* comprising the Middle East, North Africa and Turkey (mainly Arab countries of North Africa, Egypt, the Sudan, the Arabian Gulf states and peninsula, Nag, Syria, Jordan, Lebanon, Turkey, Iran, Pakistan, Bangladesh and countries of same interest) be sponsored as soon as possible in order to study the ways and possibilities of the quick evangelization of the area, and to take and help in carrying out the decisions that will be made in this Congress.

2) That *a follow-up committee* or organization be formed before the close of the Lausanne Congress in order to follow up evangelization and mission in the above area until the mini-congress has taken place.

3) That a *study and evangelization center* be set up in the Arab world in order to further the work in that area. It was felt that there already exist some similar centers in other Muslim non-Arab countries. That because most of the original and modern books on Islam are written in Arabic, a well-furnished library be attached to the center. That church people from all the Arab and Muslim world may be able to get from this center the help they need for their research work, for their study and plans to reach the Muslim world. Such a center to handle also mass media, literature, etc., and anything that will further its aims in reaching the Muslim.

1) What are the priority targets or goals for your area or group in the next decade?

    a. Put the Scriptures in the hands of every possible person in the Middle East and North Africa and let them bear the message of the Cross.

    b. Reach the unreached areas and people there.

2) What basic strategy do you propose should be followed for the attainment of these goals?

    a. Establish a study center where it is possible and safe in the Middle East. To be attached to this center: a library of most of the resource books needed for the understanding of the area; a studio for radio programming; audio-visual materials; Christian literature especially written for the area.

    b. Establish different specialized study centers in the different countries of the Middle East.

c. Train at least 1,000 of the church members in the task of
    evangelizing the area.
d. Establish an outreach and mission committee or fellowship
    in each country under the name of "Markag Al Kirazah"
    (Outreach Center) with a link of coordination between
    them.

What specific action is recommended for participants as they return
to their own country?

Form a committee of coordination and follow-up of the aims of
the Congress with special emphasis on prayer and action.

4) What help from beyond your own resources will you need, if any,
for the realization of these goals?

Personnel and funds to share in the realization of above
plan will be welcome.

5) What, if any, form of continuing association or cooperation do
you recommend for the realization of these goals?

A world fellowship with local representatives in each country
of the Middle East and North Africa.

OCEANIA REPORT

Secretary: Reverend John Reid

We have received two things. We have received *fellowship and vision*.

Fellowship — Never before have we been exposed to such a fellowship of the people of God. It has been an anticipation of heaven. We long to maintain the unity of the Spirit.

Particularly, the delegates from New Zealand have expressed that they have been excited and stretched by the extraordinary diversity and variety of the work of God in our generation; we see a need for such information to regularly reach us and our people.

Vision — We have responded to a fresh vision of the Gospel and the world. We want time to pray and we want the fresh awareness of large areas of the world without Christ to stab us into prayer and action.

Fellowship and vision lead to action.

Action — Our actions will be varied. They range from:

a. New Zealand sees a need for fresh evaluation of their attitude to race relations and accumulated wealth.

b. Fiji sees a new concern for the Hindu and Muslim immigrants.

c. Papua, New Guinea, sees the need for a small conference to share and interpret this conference to those in their country.

d. Australia sees its greatest asset as the network of congregations which cover the country. It is the minister with the Word of God who regularly engages in systematic and expository preaching who is the key to motivating and equipping his people. People, motivated by the Word and the Spirit are God's instruments. Theological students and ministers are our key and we wish to encourage and challenge them.

We have been amazed at the great variety of methods which we can use. The motivation will come alone from the Word and the Spirit. This is what we long for. We long for an evangelistic thrust at the grass root level, and this is what we will work for.

e. West Irian, which is to the north of Australia and adjoining to Papua, New Guinea, contained large areas which were completely untouched by the Gospel until after 1945. European, North American, New Zealand and Australian missionaries entered that country. They entered valleys and mountains which were idyllic in their beauty. Those valleys were gardens of violence.

Unrestrained savagery, murder and cannibalism reigned without control. Today there is a Dani church. I was there on a recent Sunday after the full moon. I saw hundreds of Christian men and women coming down the mountain to meet for the monthly celebration of the Lord's supper. You could see the brownness of their almost naked bodies as they came to the little church building. I stood with 400 first generation Christians. They were supporting forty full-time missionaries in adjoining valleys where danger and violence still reign. In our sophisticated country, we need to move from this Congress with a fresh vision of the Lordship of Christ and the Gospel and allow him to revolutionize us just like that.

PAKISTAN NATIONAL STRATEGY GROUP REPORT

Secretary: Daniel Bakhsh

The Pakistani participants in the International Congress on World Evangelization will return to their cities, villages and homes imbued with a new zeal to share Christ with the people of that land, with new insights as to how to go about that task, and a new sense of urgency to do the job.

A fresh and fuller understanding of the church and the meaning of evangelization has captured our imaginations. We realize that the church is a fellowship, a community called out by God to witness and to serve. Every member has a part to play even as a member of a body. And we have come to realize that the Gospel of Jesus Christ is not a dichotomy, that faith and the evidences of faith are inseparable. While proclaiming Jesus as the Savior we should manifest his love in practical ways.

We are more keenly aware of dangers along the way: compromise on basic issues of biblical authority, the nature of salvation and man's lostness aside from Christ.

We have been shocked to realize the enormity of the task before us by the relentless flickering of numerals on the population clock.

Very early in the Congress our group organized to insure that maximum help would be gained, as well as inspiration, from the Congress. A findings committee, and evaluation committee and a librarian were appointed to collect, collate and sift the mountains of data and to suggest the most relevant things on which to concentrate. A final report was to be prepared. We took note of our distribution in the various small groups to be able later on to share information. Bishop Wm. Young, Church of Pakistan, Sialbot Diocese, served as chairman and Daniel Bakhsh as secretary of our group.

As *participants* of the Congress we came as individuals, but from a variety of backgrounds, experiences, churches, Christian organizations. It was admitted that we could not establish ourselves as a formal organization. Then, how is the benefit gained to be made available to our people and how is a *co-ordinated* strategy to be evolved for evangelization?

To help understand our role we refer to three figures:

Catalyst — generally speeds up an action but is not itself changed;

Salt — seasons, improves quality;

Yeast — leavens the whole by quiet working.

By implication we are to work in our various circumstances to bring about a new zeal for evangelization and outreach. This is to be done with a low-profile.

As a strategy for evangelization of Pakistan we set the following priority objectives:

I — The evangelization of the existing nominal Christians and Churches.

II — The evangelization of responsive non-Christian groups.

III — The evangelization of resistant non-Christian groups.

These are to be engaged concurrently although in the light of limitation of resources emphasis would be in the order listed but would shift as time goes on.

What goals are to be set to be achieved with God's help in the decade to come?

I. Evangelization of nominal Christians and churches

A. Within three years concentrated efforts would be made among all groups of Christians to call all to repentance and faith in Christ.

B. Particular areas of effort would be:
   a.)   Child evangelism
   b.)   Youth and student evangelism
   c.)   Women's evangelism
   d.)   Family evangelism

C. The work would be conducted in urban and rural areas among educated and illiterate people with methods adapted to suit each situation.

To this end resources of the churches and Christian organizations will be sought to engage in literacy programs, Bible and literature publication, correspondence (Bible) work among other ways *and* through existing institutions and organizations which are concerned with the aforementioned groups to help in planning and training workers as God directs and provides opportunities.

II. Evangelization of responsive non-Christian people

A. Concurrently with the previous efforts work will continue and be expanded to reach responsive people in particular with the Gospel.
   1.   The scheduled castes of Sindh
   2.   Punjabi non-Muslim groups as the Balmiki and Gagre.
   New churches will be planted among them.

B. Within the next three to five years new tribal evangelists will be sought of God and trained.

C. The New Testament will be translated into principal tribal languages.

D. Research on church growth and evangelization will be done. A Church Growth Institute and Training Center would be opened at the Hyderabad Bible Training Institute, Lord willing.

III. Evangelization of resistant non-Christian peoples

A. Along with the other two priorities, effort will be extended to reach resistant people with the Gospel and to establish convert churches.

B. In the next three years evangelists will be trained and commissioned.

C. Research is to be conducted to locate lesser degrees of resistance to evangelization.

D. Effort will be made to disciple whole families.

To best utilize and conserve the results of this Congress, a co-ordination center or secretariat will be established in Pakistan. The group nominated Dr. Robert F. Tebbe as first secretary to be superseded within a year by a Pakistan national to be named.

The Pakistan participants will continue to meet together, to correspond, to share reports and experiences as God leads — and always to pray for the evangelization of the land. Through the secretariat the group would make itself available, as individuals or collectively, to assist in programs in training seminars to any seeking assistance in the task of evangelism. The secretariat would seek co-ordination in all such work going on and would endeavor to evaluate it in the light of stated objectives and goals.

A mini-Congress will be arranged within a year to share the fruits of this Congress. For this project a planning session is contemplated for September, 1974.

In the light of the more general objectives and goals each Pakistani participant is asked to chalk out a specific plan of operation for himself or for his organization or church, whereby serious attention will be given to evangelistic work.

As well as establishing priorities for the nation, it is also projected that in the next decade Pakistani missionaries will be sent to countries where ex-patriate Pakistani communities exist and to plant churches there. A high priority is given to the sending of missionaries to Sri Lanka and to Nepal. Conversations with these countries' participants have already occurred.

A continuing committee of the International Congress on World Evangelization could assist the Pakistani participants in a number of ways depending on how the follow-up is organized.

Suggestions offered are:

1. Publish a periodic news letter;
2. Assist in forming multi-national resource teams (regional basis) to respond to invitations to assist in any of the aspects of evangelization;
3. Provide resource materials;
4. Render guidance in evaluation.

We are greatly excited by our discovery of new methods and techniques of presenting the Gospel. With God's help these will be adapted and used in our task of evangelization. As God may bless our efforts with success it is our prayer that we never stray from the path of his will nor never cease to depend on His Holy Spirit. May all the glory be his alone!

We go to Pakistan from Lausanne in obedience to the words of Jesus, our Lord, "As the Father has sent me, even so send I you...."

PAPUA, NEW GUINEA NATIONAL STRATEGY GROUP REPORT

Chairman: Galleo McArthur

1) We recognize that our Melanesian and Polynesian culture with its animistic religions has evidenced a general revelation of God within the context of Romans 1:19.

2) From this our people have always known the need for a supernatural authority to control life and destiny.

3) Belief in the gods of our forefathers provided a system of spiritual authority.

4) We feared these gods but found no reason to love or respect them.

5) We know that within ourselves and within our culture the Evil one has been doing his own work of deception and that this has resulted in a great spiritual blindness.

6) The coming of the Holy Spirit of Truth with the preaching of the Gospel of our Lord Jesus Christ has revealed how great was our darkness.

7) We humbly acknowledge that while there is much in our culture that we cherish and want to see continued yet there is very little that has provided any foundation for a meaningful experience of the true God.

8) As those who have now been delivered from idols to serve the living and true God (I Thess. 1:9-10), we are convinced that there is only one meaningful authority for life and that is the redeeming love of our Lord and Savior Jesus Christ.

9) We also affirm that from our own experience we have found there is only one sure guide for life and that this is the revealed will of God as recorded in his Word, the Bible.

10) The new spiritual perception so graciously given to the believer in Christ enables us to see certain things of our old religious beliefs for what they really are, namely, strange gods and idols.

11) Humbly, yet willingly and joyfully, do we place ourselves under the sole authority of Christ and his holy Word. And in so doing we affirm that this allegiance is the only real way to both preserve and enrich the values of our cultural heritage.

THE PHILIPPINES NATIONAL STRATEGY GROUP REPORT

Secretary: Fred Magleanua

Introduction

We, fifty-seven participants from the Republic of the Philippines in the International Congress on World Evangelization at Lausanne are thankful to God and the leadership of the Congress for giving us the privilege to participate and enjoy the wonderful fellowship with co-workers from other parts of the world. We are learning many things and are greatly challenged by the many reports of the various ways that God is at work around the world.

Biblical Evangelism

We are thankful to God for the emphasis in the Congress on the need for a clear understanding of the biblical theology of evangelism. We affirm our agreement with the major thrust evident in all the strategy and biblical foundation papers presented during the Congress.

Lausanne Covenant

We wholeheartedly accept the Lausanne Covenant. We are adopting this as the basis of our national fellowship for the purpose of cooperative evangelistic endeavors. We believe that the Covenant constitutes the basic minimum in terms of areas of agreement for a strong and continuing cooperation in evangelism.

Priority in evangelization of the Philippines

We believe that if we are to evangelize the Philippines in our generation, we must endeavor under God to do the following:

1. Ask God for a genuine spiritual revival of the total evangelical community.
2. Mobilize every believer in Christ for the task of witnessing.
3. Establish a local congregation in every barrio in the country.
4. All para-church organizations must coordinate their efforts in helping the believers in evangelism and such endeavors be church-based.
5. All Bible schools and seminaries must revise the curriculum to include a strong emphasis on evangelism and church growth.
6. Encourage every local church to start daughter churches.
7. Strengthen the ministry of "Christ the Only Way Movement" (COWN) in establishing CORE & LEGS groups.

Concern for the unreached

This gathering has helped us to focus our attention to the unreached people of our country. We are determined to increase our efforts in evangelizing the following neglected areas:

1. The four million Muslims of Mindanao, Sulu and Palaevan.

2. The cultural communities and tribal people.

3. The students, young people and children which constitute the majority of our population.

Sending missionaries abroad

We are thankful to God that we have about 170 Filipino missionaries serving the Lord in other countries, especially in Southeast Asia. We, however, believe that we can do more in this area inasmuch as we have been blessed with many years of Christian training and exposed to various types of Christian ministries. In order to be more effective in our missionary program we need to have a deliberate effort in uniting those that are now sending missionaries abroad into a single missionary sending agency.

Social concern

We realize that we have emphasized the proclamation of the Gospel and neglected our social responsibilities. We affirm that evangelism and social concern are both parts of the mission of the church and must be carried out without sacrificing one for the other.

The urgency of our task

Our Philippine population is growing at the rate of 3.2 per cent yearly. With our present population of forty-two million, this means that every year 1,344,000 more souls need to be reached with the message of the Gospel. We are, therefore, committed to utilize all available means and methods that God is using in other parts of the world.

We are all aware that God is opening doors for evangelism such as the unprecedented receptiveness of Roman Catholics to the Word of God. More than ever before this is harvest time in the Philippines and such a ripened harvest may not last long.

Hindrances to evangelism in the Philippines

We recognize that there are still some crucial issues that need to be clarified in the context of evangelism in the Philippines. Some of these issues are definitely affecting the progress of cooperative evangelism in the country. One of the issues concerns Roman Catholic converts and what to do with them. Should they remain in the Roman Catholic church or join the Protestant church? To complicate the situation there are some who believe that it is not our task to convert Roman Catholics but to help them become better Catholics. We have agreed to have dialogues among ourselves to resolve these issues. We resolved to emphasize content in the presentation of the Gospel and to educate our people on the biblical theology of evangelism.

Conclusion

We go back to the Philippines with deeper appreciation and commitment to the uniqueness of our biblical faith and Christ's mandate for its proclamation with all its social and ethical implication. As participants in this Congress we wholeheartedly accept and adopt the Lausanne Covenant and under the guidance and leadership of the Holy Spirit dedicate ourselves to carry out the Great Commission of our Lord and Master Jesus Christ.

This is our national strategy for the evangelization of the Philippines. We shall endeavor to employ whatever tactics the Holy Spirit will direct and pool whatever capabilities we can in order to attain this national goal.

PORTUGAL NATIONAL STRATEGY GROUP REPORT

Secretary: Moises S. Gomes

In Portugal at the moment, we are going through an historical period of political transition. The military coup of April 25, 1974, brings to us the promise of a democratic order in the country. At the time we meet in this Congress at Lausanne, we cannot foretell how much freedom and opportunity the evangelical Christians will have once a duly elected government is instituted in Portugal.

It is our sincere prayer and hope that Portugal will become a free and democratic country. Thus, we feel that new perspectives and opportunities for evangelization will result.

The participants from Continental Portugal, though not representing officially any church, denomination, or Christian organization, met during the Congress to pray and discuss ideas for the advancement of the Gospel in Portugal.

From the group of Portuguese participants at Lausanne '74, an "ad hoc" committee was indicated to present the following suggestions to the evangelical field in Portugal:

1) Call the attention of all the evangelical Christians in Portugal as to their responsibility in being the bearers and proclaimers of the Gospel of Christ by word and action to all those who as yet do not know it in an experiential way.

2) Inform the Portuguese Evangelical Alliance of these suggestions and seek a renewed action by the Alliance for the good of the evangelical community in Portugal.

3) Seek to create an interest among pastors and workers of all denominations to fellowship in Christian unity through the means of pastoral retreats, biblical conferences, and other encounters.

4) Develop the idea of an Iberian Congress on Evangelism to take place in Portugal as a sequence to the one held in Madrid, Spain, in June, 1974. This congress should be preceded by contacts and retreats with all the interested pastors and evangelical workers.

5) Try to develop contact and dialogue between the conservative evangelicals and the ecumenical groups to study points of unity with the objective of realizing the task of evangelization at all levels.

6) Based on the New Testament record and present experience of some evangelical churches in Portugal, promote the idea of evangelizing through family groups and meetings in the homes so as to have a greater impact and penetration of the Gospel in Portuguese society at all levels.

7) Explore all possibilities for presenting the Gospel through the mass media — television, radio, and the press. Prepare a series of pilot programs to present as suggestions of what we have in mind. In this regard we could receive much assistance and help from brethren in other countries who could provide adequate materials.

8) Bring together the suggestions for evangelistic action resulting from the Iberian Congress on Evangelism held in Madrid, Spain (June, 1974), and those resulting from the Lausanne Congress, in order that there might be an efficient study and effectivation of the proposed ideas.

9) Promote interest for in-depth evangelization through local campaigns.

10) Study the possibility of publishing a journal or bulletin as an aid in promoting evangelistic action. The idea is that it should be issued four times a year, giving all possible information about programs for evangelization. One of the issues should be used totally as an evangelistic tool in the form of a pass-along edition. Articles explaining the Gospel of Christ and portions of Scripture will be used. The Bible Society in Portugal is ready to support this project as a means of giving a larger expansion to the Word of God.

11) Promote closer ties and fraternal relationships with Spain, Brazil, Mozambique, Angola, Guine, and other Portuguese territories as an incentive to greater evangelistic involvement and cooperation.

12) Support the projected campaign with Dr. Billy Graham in the fall of 1975.

All the Portuguese participants at the Lausanne Congress are grateful for the opportunity of being a part of this great event in the Christian world.

PUERTO RICO NATIONAL STRATEGY GROUP REPORT

Secretary: Antonio Rodriguez

Following our desire for action, we are very glad to report the following:

1. To express our sincere gratitude to the sponsors of the International Congress on World Evangelization for the invitation extended to us to participate in this historical event for the evangelization of the world.

2. We expressed our concern for the profile on Puerto Rico, where we found many errors about the evangelical work in our country. The matter was considered and after a meeting with Rev. Edward Pentecost, we decided to appoint a committee to review the profile and send it as soon as possible to Mr. Pentecost.

3. We believe that this is a great opportunity for evangelization in Puerto Rico. After considering all the possibilities, we decided to appoint a committee under the leadership of Rev. Florentino Santana and Rev. Lester T. Hershey, to plan a general strategy for the evangelization of all Puerto Rico. The group will meet on Saturday, August 17, 1974.

4. We considered the possibility of establishing a seminary for evangelism and leadership training in Puerto Rico. This idea will continue to be studied in order to see its viability. This may serve other Latin American countries.

5. We voted to explore all the possibilities in terms of leadership, finances, and orientation for all our plan of evangelization, in Puerto Rico and in organizations like the Billy Graham Evangelistic Association.

6. One of our immediate plans is to organize a congress for evangelization in Puerto Rico, under the theme, "Let (all) Puerto Rico hear His Voice." For this we will invite all evangelical churches.

7. We decided to share with all our evangelical people in Puerto Rico not only information, but also all the implications of the presentations made here in Lausanne.

SCANDINAVIA NATIONAL STRATEGY GROUP REPORT

Introduction: The Scandinavian group consisted of participants and observers from Sweden, Denmark, Norway, Iceland and Greenland.

Although there might be differences among the Scandinavian countries, some similar trends might be outlined. In all Scandinavian countries there are Lutheran State Churches covering more than 90% of the population.

In addition to the formation of free churches, in the last century many free-will organizations for missions, home and abroad, have developed inside the state church. This pertains especially to Norway.

I. *Analyzing the present situation in Scandinavia*

In all the Nordic countries there has been a growing number of saved young people. This is astonishing, because in the first 10-15 years after World War II there was little interest among young people for Christ.

During the same time-space the cities have grown much. The great cities and their suburban districts tend to be very secularized and need our attention. This secularization may have reached farthest in Copenhagen. According to a report, only 50% of the state church population continues to baptize their children.

According to their population, the Scandinavian countries have been sending scores of missionaries all over the world. A new challenge within the Nordic countries is the great amount of working people from other nations (some far off) who are immigrating. In Sweden there are as many as 6,000,000 new worker immigrants.

The charismatic movement, as well as the Jesus movement, has in recent years made its impression. A greater awareness of the work of the Spirit has in many cases developed out of this.

The Nordic people reached by evangelism the last century tend to be mostly in the middle class, and geographically mostly in the rural areas.

II. *Strategy in our present situation in Scandinavia*

The first point would be the renewal of the individual Christian and his spiritual life and the personal responsibility everyone has to do evangelization. Secondly, family worship life should be encouraged and revived. Thirdly, out of this should develop house meetings of the small groups trying to reach out with the Gospel to the neighbors.

In addition to this it is noted that only 25% of the children of today go to Sunday school. In addition to this, the influence of the state church throughout the public school system is diminishing. This creates a great challenge to start more evangelizing work among the children, especially in Denmark. This leads to establishing private primary schools.

For secondary and graduate schools one is encouraged by a greater openness to the Gospel. This should challenge us to intensify the evangelizing work among students at all levels.

Through mission agencies for missions home and abroad, and

through free churches we want to encourage participants, out of the inspiration from Lausanne, to write to all their contacts and churches about more personal evangelizing. This might be especially developed through the thousands of small group women's missionary societies. The individual Lausanne participant is urged to do his part in this job of inspiration and information.

As rich countries and as countries where we are politically free to further the work of missions, we think we have a great responsibility to accelerate the evangelizing work in the world. In some cases this has been done over the last years in new countries that have been contacted and where missions in some cases got started. This pertains to Latin America, Indonesia, Guinea-Bissau, and countries like Spain and France in Europe. Likewise in the late years, there has been a fast growing work of missions behind the iron curtain with help in evangelizing, spreading of Bibles and radio mission.

On many other mission fields radio work has been expanded through Trans World Radio, Voice of the Gospel, and Voice of Peace.

III. Cooperation among evangelicals of Scandinavia

In all the Scandinavian countries there has been the work of national committees of the Evangelical Alliance since the end of the 19th century. All evangelicals within and outside the state churches have been represented.

Through the Nordic Missionary Council (as well as each national missionary council) all sending agencies of evangelicals have been represented except for some few agencies of Denmark. The Nordic Missionary Council is not integrated with WCC (not even the national councils of Finland and Norway and half the Swedish council).

On the Scandinavian level the IFES work has bound evangelical students together in a fine way.

It is thought that the post-Lausanne work might be continued on a personal basis as an organ of contact on national and international levels with the participants until eventual further steps may be taken. The post-Lausanne cooperation, now loosely connected, may in the future have a clear and firm theological, biblical basis if it is going to be of any use. If the Lausanne Covenant is not strengthened, the Norwegian group will recommend a closer study of the Frankfurt and Berlin Declarations as such a bibilical basis.

In addition it is mentioned that the Lausanne Covenant should have a chapter (a paragraph) about all men nowadays being persecuted because of their faith. It has to be a balanced, but prophetic word.

Practical implements of the work of Lausanne to Scandinavia would be:

1. The material of Lausanne should come to our Christians through weekly papers, periodicals, theological seminaries, publishing houses and study agencies through books, study materials and cassettes.
2. In Sweden they will try to influence the special week for U-lands.
3. Concerning missions we think that as we should not forget the social work we are doing and will do to meet material needs, the

greatest need is to give the Gospel to the masses.

4. It is considered especially important that a (loose) fellowship of evangelicals after Lausanne might be the information center of evangelicals, and the agency of information for further theological studies and scholarships in sound institutions.

SCOTLAND GROUP REPORT

Secretary: Jeffrey Grogan

The sixteen people in the group, drawn from several Scottish churches, would first of all wish to state their gratitude to God for having brought them to the Lausanne Congress. It has been an experience of great inspiration and challenge. One person said of the Billy Graham evangelistic meeting on Sunday, at the Olympic Stadium, "I just wished it was Scotland," and that sentiment no doubt applies to much that we have heard God is doing in other countries. We go home to Scotland with the prayer that God will bless and heal our land with the unchanging Gospel.

The background to our group discussions on evangelizing Scotland has been the great need of modern Scotland for the Gospel, despite all our history and reputation, and of the steady decline of the churches. And yet the very weakening of the churches is leading to a new openness to evangelical emphasis, and affluence has not satisfied the deep needs of Scotland's people, so that the opportunity for the Gospel is greater than ever.

How best may Scotland now be evangelized, and what may we who go home from Lausanne have to contribute? In our concluding meeting as a group we have thought of many methods and we have discussed the possibility of a Year of Saturation Evangelism, using all methods, in 1976 or 1977. We have agreed to meet again in Glasgow on September 4, to consider what more we can do.

Some of the points which have arisen in our discussion have been these:

There is particular need, and opportunity, among the young people of Scotland. They are often not to be found in churches, but they are in the schools. There is, therefore, need to encourage young Christians to become school teachers as their witnessing vocation, and there is particular need for committed Religious Education teachers. The colleges of education are strategic points for evangelical witness. Scripture Union's long-standing work in schools should be strongly supported. And, as well as this witness in schools, there is need for new approaches such as are typified in the ministry of Mr. Nigel Goodwin.

The group discussed recurring themes of the Congress such as the need for all Christians to evangelize, and it was recognized that the Scottish tradition of the minister's role sometimes raises special problems. On the other hand, when discussing the value of house groups, and frankly recognizing the danger of splintering a congregation, the group saw that the minister can be the necessary bridge and unifier between groups and congregation.

It was recognized that no one method is sufficient to evangelize Scotland. There are no facile solutions. One discussion was on the possibility and validity of city-wide crusades. There would seem to have been a cooling toward this method among evangelicals as well as others, compared with 1955 when Billy Graham conducted his historic crusade in Glasgow. But even after recognizing this, and while failing to see any others apart from Billy Graham who could conduct such a massive crusade effectively, the group felt that mass evangelism is still in the will of God a powerful way of reaching the people, and this conviction was strengthened after Sunday's meeting in the Olympic Stadium.

Concern was expressed that evangelicals are given few opportunities to appear on religious television in Scotland (as contrasted with the opportunities on sound radio) and it was felt that, in the interests of proclamation of the Gospel, representation about this should be made to the B.B.C. religious advisory committee and to the independent television company (Scottish Television).

In all consideration of methods of evangelism, it was recognized that a priority is prayer, and that there is need to restore the old-fashioned congregational prayer meeting. A day of prayer which is being observed in some countries on August 17 this year may be an example which we can consider in our further discussions in Scotland. We know that Scotland needs revival, that revival in Scotland will have worldwide repercussions, and we are grateful to God for letting us learn from his people in so many other parts of the world, here gathered at Lausanne.

SINGAPORE

Chairman: Dr. G.D. James
Secretary: Paul Szeto

The participants from Singapore attempted to identify the problems, opportunities, and obstacles to the evangelization of Singapore. Some recommendations and applications were also offered at the end of our discussion.

A. Opportunity and responsive areas

We attempted to identify the people who are most responsive to the Gospel and where opportunities should be capitalized. These groups of people are:

1. Secondary school students;
2. University and students of teaching educational institution;
3. Young working adults including secretary workers;
4. Military personnel;
5. High rent flat dwellers.

The participants felt that we should make a greater effect to capitalize the opportunities among groups three and four.

B. Obstacles and problems

The problems and obstacles to the evangelization of Singapore were also identified:

1. Secularism;
2. Restitution to the evangelization of certain segments of the population;
3. High drop-out rates of young adults.
   This was seen as a real problem. The reason for this drop-out rate was suggested to be, first of all, due to the lack of communication between the church leaders and the young adults. Little opportunities were also offered for the growth and development of these young adults and in some churches there is a lack of real spiritual food.
4. Insufficient amount of high caliber men going into full-time ministry.
5. A lack of communication between the different para-church organizations and the various local churches.

C. Recommendations and applications

The participants suggested solutions and applications under six major issues:

1. The recommitment of men of quality into the ministry.

This can be accomplished by the personal examples and encouragement of our local full-time workers. A clearer challenge to our young people is also needed. The Christians in Singapore should also come together to provide both prayer and financial support to our workers and to allocate clear responsibilities to them on the completion of their training.

2. A material sStrategy for the evangelization of Spain.
    a. A series of nation-wide evangelistic meetings.
    b. A congress in evangelization for both Singapore and Malaysia.
    c. A combined strategy mobilizing all the various church and para-church groups to present the Good News to the people in Singapore.
3. Fostering of closer ties between-the different church and para-church groups. Two suggestions have been given:
    a. A common prayer meeting
    b. A central information center and a Christian newspaper to keep the Christian community up to date with the Lord's work in Spain and the rest of the world.
4. Prevention of Christian drop-outs from all levels. Individual pastors and Christian workers are to work out this problem.
5. The need to contribute to other regions of the world.
    a. Offering Singapore as a base for training and the preparation for the evangelization of Asia.
    b. Providing committed Christians — professional qualifiers to needy areas of the world.
    c. Sending Gospel teams to other areas for evangelism.
    d. To emerge and develop a wider missionary vision through the distribution of information.
6. The Christian concern for national affairs.
    Christians should be encouraged to meet together and think through the issues arising out of modern society and the life it produces, with a view to contribute to the welfare of the nation. We should also attempt to provide a form where Christians can meet together to discuss national issues for the benefit of Singapore.

D. Follow-up at Congress

The participants discuss how we can best follow up the results of the Congress and spread the spirit of Lausanne 1974 to the other Christians.

1. There is a common agreement to the suggestion given by the Congress committee of forming a continuing committee.
2. We plan to organize a prayer fellowship for worldwide evangelization in Singapore.
    All the Singapore Christian leaders will be invited and besides praying, what is being taught in Lausanne will be discussed. It is our hope that this will develop into a combined effort of evangelism in Singapore.

SOUTH AFRICAN GROUP REPORT

Secretary: Michael Cassidy

1. It proved impossible to meet most of the goals set by the Congress committee with respect to national planning and strategy, because the latent pressures of South African conditions, which arrived with the participants, could not be kept out of the national group meeting. Thus, before the group was able to begin the established agenda, questions arose regarding the reasons underlying the disposition of accommodation for participants. It was also agreed that during the second meeting, the opportunity should be taken to talk with a Billy Graham team member concerning an invitation for Mr. Graham to revisit South Africa. A series of crusades in three or four cities in South Africa had been suggested. Since this would require a widely representative platform the question of an invitation was an essential issue in any proposed national strategy.

2. These two issues acutely surfaced some of the fundamental issues raised in all forms of evangelization in South Africa. The matter of Congress accommodation raised the bona fides and credibility, of first, the Congress Hospitality Committee (though this was later cleared up very satisfactorily), and then of evangelists and evangelistic organizations in South Africa generally. Underlying the Billy Graham invitation, over and above the sheer purpose of evangelism, was the question whether the importation of an evangelist from outside South Africa was an escape from the realities within the country or an important factor in cooperation in order to aid South African Christianity in some of its racial dilemmas.

3. When the large group divided into smaller groups, the following fundamental concerns emerged from individual sub-groups:

   a. A deep concern was expressed for the emergence of black initiatives in evangelization and dialogue, and the acceptance of this on the part of whites. It should be possible for all to participate fully in the process of change, of which evangelism is one. This would require whites to learn to listen to blacks much more than they do, particularly when blacks are saying uncomfortable truths. The sub-group noted the considerable frustration blacks felt because of the limited occasions afforded back home for such frank speaking.

   b. The extent of the change encompassed by "conversion" was debated: was this confined to individual attitudes or did it have a wider application? Several people stressed that the extent of "repentance" and "conversion" has political and social dimensions that cannot be avoided anywhere, least of all in South Africa. Evangelization cannot avoid this issue.

   c. Related to this is the question of the credibility of the Gospel: without clear changes in attitude towards one another on the part of those who claim to be converted, the Gospel itself is partially discredited. Hence even if conversion does not immediately involve all the political and social dimensions of a "new creation," there must at least be a new attitude towards fellow-members of the body.

   d. While it was felt that some form of fellowship should be

formed to insure that the spirit and lessons of this conference would be clearly heard and applied, there was no decision regarding the form this should take, except that a small convening committee was elected to consider how best to follow-up the Lausanne Congress in South Africa.

e. It was suggested that regular evangelistic meetings be organized regionally, but who should do this or what forms the meeting should take were not decided.

4. While the issue of cross-cultural evangelism was implicated in most of the discussion, it surfaced when the group considered the possibilities and obstacles within South Africa. The essential ambivalence of the South African context showed in the inability of the group to agree whether there were legal obstacles to cross-cultural evangelism and contact as well as psychological ones. Since the experience of participants was diverse and contradictory, it became evident that the state clearly encouraged some forms of contact and discouraged others. At the same time, participants stressed the value of such contact. All stood to learn from it, though how much and how quickly were debated. So also was the matter whether such contact should be considered the norm for evangelization. No one contested that the social climate of South Africa added difficulties to the normal obstacles of such contact. But it was also admitted that most did not use to the limit the opportunities that presently existed, and that the reasons for this were not so much legal as social sanctions. The emergence of black power has proved a further deterrent to cross-cultural contact; however much it may be regarded by some as a necessary tactic for the present time. One delegate stressed that the essential requirement for "evangelization" was a "humanization" that would give blacks liberty to treat whites without servility, and whites liberty to listen to blacks without arrogance or patronage. Such humanization was the sign of the presence of the Gospel in the evangelist, as well as a consequence of the Gospel in the lives of those of his hearers who respond. In the South African situation, it is essential that any evangelistic message make clear that the wrongs of the present situation are the consequence of sin, and not of race or color. A man is not sinful because he is white or black, but because he is a sinner by nature.

5. In the final session, a plea was made for a more costly talking and listening process to begin among all South Africa Christians. Unless the South African nation sees "the prints of the nails" in the life of the South African church, it will not believe. Communication and dialogue in an atmosphere of trust and fellowship was considered to be as important between English and Afrikaans-speaking Christians as between blacks and whites. A true "community" of all believers was indispensable to authenticate the Gospel to our country. A costly process would probably be involved for this to emerge.

6. A measure of crisis was created for the group with the request from a number of blacks that the entire South African group be requested to sign a statement which they themselves had drawn up. This was considered by some blacks as the least we could do, but

most of the group seemed to feel that this was too rushed and a precipitate request. Glibly or lightly signed statements could be no substitute for dialogue back home. For some of the brethren, signing could also have "complicating and unforeseen consequences."

7. The idea of a symposium back in South Africa to discuss the "potential and problematics" of evangelism in our sub-continent was mooted. It was decided to leave this to be considered by the continuing committee referred to under number 3d.

8. The matter of an invitation to Billy Graham for a country-wide visit was discussed and a majority of participants indicated openness to "the possibility of such an invitation being investigated." There was uncertainty as to who should initiate such a discussion, but participants felt it should not be tied down to a given organization. Under pressure of time and inability to settle the issue clearly, the rather unsatisfactory expedient was adopted of leaving whoever was prepared to take the initiative to pursue the matter.

9. The entire group felt that this had been a most valuable time, and they thanked God for the opportunities offered by Lausanne. While the group acknowledged the problematic realities of our situation, it was realized that the removal of all socio-political problems would not in itself guarantee revival. While the ultimate sovereignty of the Holy Spirit was recognized, there was also a strong measure of resolution among all to continue that which Lausanne has begun in our lives and thinking.

SPAIN NATIONAL STRATEGY GROUP REPORT

Secretary: Juan Gili

The national strategy group for Spain has reaffirmed, in all its deliberations, the concepts that were studied in the recent Iberian Congress on Evangelization held in Madrid. To these concepts have been added the results of the daily experiences and ideas which have been received in the Lausanne Congress.

A. Keeping in mind the fact that Spain is a country with thirty-four million inhabitants and only 40,000 evangelicals of all denominations, and that there are in our country 9,000 towns and only 500 evangelical churches, we have established the following order of priority goals for the following decade.

1. Establish the basis of a Gospel witness in centers with a minimum of 20,000 inhabitants.
2. Plan evangelistic campaigns at the local, regional and national level.
3. Form training teams for follow-up.
4. Promote a greater interaction between established churches and organizations, movements and missions that work in Spain.
5. Use all possible means of communication, which in accord with the new Religious Liberty Law are now made possible: radio over commercial broadcast stations, use of the secular press, house-to-house distribution of literature, renting of public buildings, film showings, etc.
6. The contribution that Spain can make to the evangelization of other areas are, for the time being, primarily two: an evangelistic ministry in various European and Spanish-speaking countries, and the contribution of Spanish editors and writers, especially in Spanish-speaking countries.

B. A basic strategy for these goals:

1. It is suggested that we give our support to the specialized organizations and movements that are working in the different spheres of evangelism and that, in general, are amply accepted.
2. We contemplated the possibility of joining our efforts, gifts and money in order to attain the above-mentioned goals.

C. Recommendations to the Congress participants for their specific action when returning to our area:

1. That the national evangelical press diffuse, as widely as possible, the spirit of the Lausanne Congress.
2. We recommend that the churches invite one, or several in a team, of the participants of the Congress to share their experiences at different levels: pastors, leaders and specialists in different ministries and to the entire congregation.

D. Help needed apart from the resources of the area in order to fulfill our goals: We consider it difficult at present to outline the relationship between needs and resources. We point out that, because of the characteristics of the evangelical history in Spain, there is not a vast experience of methods and means. For the same reason it is difficult to evaluate the resources that are available and those that are necessary in order to carry out this strategy. Some interesting observations were made however:

1. We need help for the promotion, training and support of national workers.

2. Technical and economic help is needed in order to take advantage of the almost unique opportunity in Europe of using commercial radio stations.

3. Resources are needed to establish schools, camps, hospitals, etc.

4. Promotional literature, Bible courses, follow-up materials, etc., are needed.

5. A need for evangelistic efforts of one to two years in concentrated areas and with a view to establishing churches.

6. A need for a more effective work among the three million Spanish immigrants that work in Europe.

The type of association or continual cooperation — Due to the recent celebration of the Iberian Congress and the experiences of this Lausanne Congress, we are studying such possibilities.

SRI LANKA NATIONAL STRATEGY GROUP REPORT

Secretary: S. Peiris

As we have met together we have reported verbally and these have been recorded. It is not our intention to record all of those remarks, but we wish to share the concerns of the Sri Lanka delegation.

1. We are deeply grateful to God and the ones who planned this Congress, especially Dr. Billy Graham, for the opportunity given to us to participate in this assembly.

2. We are thankful that it was a working Congress and that our vision has been stretched to encompass the whole world.

3. We are thankful that the needs of our own land have become more evident to us and we have been able to plan to reach our people.

4. We accept the responsibility to:
   a. Pray for world evangelization
   b. Mobilize prayer for the fulfillment of the Great Commission
   c. Training and mobilizing of the Christians
   d. The sharing of the vision of Lausanne in our country

In order to do this we need the assistance of the Congress and the Christians in other parts of the world. We believe that with this combination the Lord will honor our faith in Him and we will see revival.

We submit herewith a plan for the implementation of the purpose we have outlined in our reports verbally.

It is certainly evident that there should be a closer unity between Nepal, Pakistan, and Sri Lanka. It may be that India should be included. But even though India is left out due to problems of free movement of people between India and Pakistan the closer unity is needed. Bangladesh could also be included.

A. It is needed for the following reasons:

1. We need the assistance of each in dealing with pockets of those who are culturally and religiously similar to our own areas.

2. We need to widen our vision and the vision of our people.

3. We can use the open door to Asians to visit each country and be available to serve the believing community — evangelistically, theologically, and methodologically.

4. With the Asians moving together expenses would be minimal.

5. There is need for an inter-change of books, studies, etc. between these nations.

6. The opportunity to provide a clearing house to contact and follow-up veridents of one country coming to another.

7. To exchange data and statistics and contacts for those in Christian work in each country.

B. Possibilities of how this could be done:

1. Through a close regional association of the E.F.G. of each country.

2. Through a committee affronted at this Congress and this group representing one or two from each country who would conduct their business by letter but meet once a year in each country in rotation to plan, and implement the goals.

3. That all assistance in this venture goes through the appointed fellowship not so much to restrict the movement of people but rather to prevent or avoid unwanted activity which would undermine rather than help the churches in each country.

4. The one coming from one country to another should come at the expense of the sending country as far as travel is concerned. From the time of arrival to departure they should be given hospitality by the host church. This would build both sides, cross cultural evangelism and indigenous support.

5. This exchange be from a month to three months as and when possible and needed.

6. That a newsletter and a directory of services and ministry needed by each country be made available and the offers of help possible. All such service to be under a Code of Ethics or Job Description.

REPORT OF THE NATIONAL STRATEGY GROUP — FRENCH SPEAKING SWITZERLAND

Secretary: Claire Lise de Benoit

The participants of French Switzerland first tried to formulate a definition of evangelization in the context of the whole church life: "The mission of the Church for the world is to manifest Jesus Christ as Savior and Lord by evangelization, service and testimony of transformed lives in the personal communal realms. By evangelization we mean a proclamation of the Good News in the power of the Holy Spirit through word and deed, aiming at leading men to put their trust in Jesus Christ."

To give practical content to this definition we attempted to clarify our goals. Although there were many shades of opinion regarding the main Congress papers, we were one in our desire and prayer that the ministry of evangelization be promoted in our part of the country, and that we personally be found more faithful in a total and humble obedience to Christ, and that we also fulfill the spiritual conditions which are the prerequisite to any successful evangelization: humility, prayer, sacrifice, sharing. To achieve this end we discerned certain goals, suggested ways to reach them and made one main decision.

The general concensus was that our goals should be:

1. *New spiritual life in our communities.* Evangelization being the responsibility of every Christian and every church, whatever its label, each Christian must become a living witness of Jesus Christ with a genuine, fresh and relevant testimony. This live fellowship in which the pressence of the Lord is manifested and seen by the world in an outflowing of love, is the work of the Holy Spirit, but we can unite in prayer by saying to the God of Elijah, "Lord, do it again!"

Well over 3,000 Christians in French Switzerland prayed regularly for the Congress. Through them and their prayer cells we intend to stimulate a continual flow of intercession based on the promise of II Chronicles 7:14, with a view to carrying on the varied evangelistic enterprises which will take place as a result of this Congress. Christians made a great effort in prayer, personal propaganda and sacrificial giving for the big public meeting of the Congress in the Lausanne stadium called LAUSTADE. The stadium was full to utmost capacity on July 21st, 1974. All the high expenses were covered by gifts beforehand, so that the entire offering could be devoted to evangelical enterprises in the Third World to give both bread for the body and the Bread of Life.

2. *A better inter-relationship between Christians and communities for a better witness.* Many ways of doing this were suggested:

   a. Occasional gatherings of Christians in cities or regions not so much to evangelize as to manifest the presence of the body of Christ.
   b. Days when members of two communities meet, share and have fellowship to stimulate common action.

    c.   Exchange of pulpit speakers.

    d.   Organization of evangelistic campaigns simultaneously in different places.

    e.   Development of house cells, both for children and adults.

    f.   Coordination between leaders at different levels: children's work, young people's work, etc.

    g.   Cooperation on the local level in view of total and continuous evangelization.

    h.   House-to-house crusades throughout the country.

    i.   Reaching whole families, for instance through family camps.

    j.   Reaching old people (the third age) with the Gospel.

    k.   Evangelizing holiday-goers on camping grounds.

    l.   Intensifying the evangelization of foreign workers in Switzerland.

3. *Teaching Christians and training leaders.* To avoid shallowness in the testimony and the lives of Christians, there must be a development of Bible seminars, of Bible correspondence courses, of training classes and week-ends, especially for children's and young people's workers. Being a rich country with many privileges, Switzerland ought to be a great missionary sending country. Churches, movements like "Les Groupes Bibliques Universitaires" and "La Ligue pour la lecture de la Bible" (Scripture Union) ought continually to remind and inform Christians of the unfinished missionary task.

    a.   In addition, certain concerns were expressed:

        1)   The lack of fruitful dialogue with those engaged in the so-called "Social Gospel," although we all feel that soteriology and ethics are inseparable;

        2)   The tendency today to blur the distinction between Christian and non-Christian, which takes the urgency out of evangelism and even makes it totally irrelevant.

        3)   The misrepresentation by the mass media, sometimes including those of the official church, of our activities and news reports.

        4)   The danger in a congress like this of temporary enthusiasm which veils the reality, i.e. theological differences, opposition, indifference, few people to do the job.

    b.   In view of all these considerations we made the decision not to create a new organization, but to use the one already existing, that is "L'Action Commune d'Evangelisation de Lausanne" (ACEL). To the ACEL was delegated the responsibility for the time being:

        1)   To gather all participants of the International Congress on World Evangelization and of the Mini-Congress (organized prior to the big one especially for the French-speaking countries of Europe) to further discuss the practical implications of the papers of the Congress.

        2)   To help put into action the decisions made towards the goals above mentioned.

        3)   To stimulate, if possible, the creation of similar "Action Commune d'Evangelisation" in other parts of French

Switzerland (one exists already in Geneva).

To be involved in the evangelistic thrust planned in 1975 for the 700th anniversary of the foundation of the Lausanne Cathedral. The wish has been expressed to ask a team from Africa to come and help in the land of Farel and Calvin! After sending missionaries to Africa, we welcome missionaries from Africa bringing back the Gospel to us.

"Who is adequate for such a task as this?...Our competency comes from God."

GERMAN-SPEAKING SWITZERLAND NATIONAL STRATEGY GROUP REPORT

During the days we could observe that the participants came more and more to similar attitudes. Though we cannot say that there was unananimous agreement on many issues, the following convictions and vision seemed to have taken hold of most of the participants during the week.

1. The focus of spiritual renewal is with the church. Our churches have to become organic units with cooperation in love of all believers and members. The role of the pastor as helper and trainer of the believers has newly been seen. He should learn to refrain from deciding and acting for his church while only expecting the members to follow him. The fellowship of the church should be brought about through the establishment of small living cells.

2. If the church is alive it will want to expand. Here personal witness was first stressed. We will have to consider in a new way extension growth. How can new churches be founded in Switzerland. This thought seems to be very alien in our thoughts.

3. We have to see the lostness of the souls around us. This will create the compassion to save them through the power of our Savior. For that we have to see the mosaic of Switzerland: a. The vast amount of nominal Christians which wander about like lost sheep; b. The unreached parts of Switzerland which call for research: whole valleys which did not have an evangelical witness for scores of years; c. The foreign workers from all of Europe (one million out of six million inhabitants!). This is a mission field which is at our doorstep. What are we doing about it? Are there no people to learn their language in order to win them for Christ? d. This could lead to a new understanding of a mission to Europe, especially to Spain, Italy and France; e. Our responsibility for the Christians in Russia and the evangelization of Russia was seen too. Could not the Swiss evangelicals see their responsbility especially for that vast country and identify with the suffering church? f. For social needs and helps in catastrophes, it was suggested that money should be channelled to the Tearfund and cooperation with this organization established.

A plan for the next ten years was not established, but it was decided that "SAFE" (Swiss cooperation for Evangelism) should be entrusted with executing the thoughts expressed for German-speaking Switzerland, and that the participants should be encouraged to enlist in that society for cooperation in one of her eight sections to ensure that the vision of Lausanne would be carried out on a national level.

The participants were further encouraged to foster fellowship between the different denominations and local churches in their respective areas. Pastors should regularly have their meetings for spiritual fellowship and perhaps once in a while go away for some days in a retreat to study the implications of what we have heard in Lausanne. Each pastor should aim at the renewal of his church so that different kinds of growth may occur. It was stressed again and again, however, that activism is not the answer to this. The basis is spiritual life which will manifest itself in biblical witnessing, loving fellowship, and good works. The last without the former is at all cost to be avoided. Reconciliation with God is what is needed foremost. This will lead to reconciliation between men. This establishes Christian fellowship. Here is a great field which should not be overlooked. Let us be ambassadors for Christ, helping people and Christians reconcile themselves to the Lord and to each other. The oneness in Christ must come to new expression on the local level. Congregations of different denominations should learn to cooperate in evangelistic undertakings. This attitude and the resulting actions have been suggested to the participants in their own areas.

Many feel that we do not need help from outside. But others have suggested that while we need no material help we should be humble enough to admit that spiritual help and advice in matters of church renewal and witness are needed.

We are aware of the difficulties in SAFE itself and of the danger that this organization is not able to realize and implement the "vision of Lausanne". It would be necessary that all those who are turned on with this vision volunteer for cooperation. The lostness of Switzerland must grip our hearts. Switzerland, hear his voice!

TAIWAN — HONG KONG — OTHER OVERSEAS CHINESE NATIONAL STRATEGY GROUP REPORT

Secretary: Theodore Hsueh

The responsibility of Chinese Christians for world evangelization is not just to our own country, to our own people. The whole world is our mission field. And this commission is given by God to all Christians and should be started as early as possible, no matter how young the church. Overseas mission is not something that we should put off until the church is strong, it should be done along with local evangelism. One Chinese church in Philippines started the overseas mission even before they had their own church building.

To many Chinese, Christianity is still regarded as a foreign religion. We should not repeat the mistake of the Western missionaries, equating their culture with Christianity. We need to recognize the area of culture attached to Christian faith. We should not preach the Gospel with Western or our own culture, but only in the context of local culture. We ought not fight against the culture which has no contradictory teaching against the Christian faith, and ought not compromise the Christian faith with any culture, no matter how good it seems to us. This is because culture is something that is always changing, but the Truth is always the same.

A. In any kind of evangelism, there are several areas which should be noticed.

1. We must not over-emphasize our own organization regardless of its purpose and contribution. The overall and total aim should be taken into full consideration.
2. New methods and approaches should be absorbed. This should be done with careful study and research, so that any method, whether it should be accepted or rejected, will receive serious consideration.
3. We must not blindly follow any traditional approaches. The older generation should open their eyes and ears for new ideas.
4. We must not overlook the value and opportunities of social welfare services.
5. Specialized training and survey is needed in all kinds of ministry; the programs should be studied and incorporated in a most careful way.
6. We must try to mobilize as many people as possible, uniting as many workers and organizations as possible in order to accomplish the great task of world evangelization.

B. Chinese churches are already involved in many kinds of mass media programs, like literature, radio and television. Since the geographic area that can absorb and receive these is limited at present, we ought to be careful not to start any new programs without trying to support the existing ones, and ought not duplicate the work already going on. Understanding one another is vital. All the mass media programs still need greater church support. The involvement of Chinese churches is still very limited and weak. The church needs to realize the value of mass media, learn to use them and support them fully, and mass media people should involve the church at the earliest stage when at all possible.

C. The basic need of overseas mission for Chinese churches is the basic teaching of missions. Some regard this as a Western belief and a waste of both money and personnel. A very encouraging sign is that a few Chinese churches are sending and supporting missionaries overseas. Even the tribal churches in Taiwan, with 190,000 Christians among 260,000, have sent eight missionaries to North Borneo.

The problems that Chinese churches are facing in overseas missions are:

1. Nationality — passport and visa may be problems in quite a few cases.

2. Lack of total working plan, including methods, approaches and organizations.

3. Not enough understanding of the teaching of world evangelization. This should start at a very early stage.

D. Though finance is important, personnel and training are more needed. In some countries Chinese missionaries are more welcome than Western missionaries, since Chinese churches are located in most areas of the world. It is beneficial to have a coordinating office for all. The function of this office should be:

1. To study and research the Western and biblical mission programs to avoid previously made mistakes.

2. To encourage seminaries and Bible schools to teach courses on missions.

3. To exchange information among churches and mission organizations to avoid duplication, and to strengthen one another's programs.

4. To provide opportunities for missionary training, either on a short term or long term basis.

5. To encourage the churches to hold mission conventions.

Before an office for all Chinese churches is set up, regional offices should be formed. Churches, mission organizations and seminaries should support it fully. Hong Kong already has one, and Taiwan, Singapore, and the Philippines offices are in the discussion stage. While churches are realizing the importance of overseas missions, careful planning should be thought of concerning use of funds for direct support of missionaries, pre-mission programs, and the support and use of mass media. Though it is impossible to preach the Gospel openly in mainland China today, we can still do it through the contact of Chinese workers in Africa. This should be done in cooperation with the local churches and missions. Of course, prayer is vital for opening the door of China. Radio is the means to reach Chinese people there now. There are a number of research centers working in this area and the church should be behind them. These centers should be careful not to exaggerate the information nor to incorporate the promotion of their own organizations in the reports. And, we encourage those groups to be more cooperative.

After returning to Hong Kong from this Congress, teams should be formed to go to different churches for reporting and recommendation. Specialized work like youth work, television, literature work and radio work should be held. Our goal is that churches may recognize the tools available, be challenged by testimonies and sharing and that all Chinese churches may unite a bit closer, with greater concern for one another. In this way we are able to take the challenge of world evangelization from the West and fulfill the calling of Christ's Great Commission.

UNITED STATES NATIONAL STRATEGY GROUP REPORT

Introduction

The commitment that brought us to Lausanne has been strengthened by our study and fellowship here. 1) It is a commitment to the truth of the Gospel as proclaimed in the Scripture and effected by Jesus Christ in his incarnation, his death, his resurrection, his ascension, and his outpouring of the Holy Spirit on his people. We pledge our allegiance afresh to the Christ who has commanded us to serve his kingdom, and to the Scriptures which alone can instruct and empower our mission. 2) It is a commitment to the urgency of the task of evangelization across and beyond the broad sweep of our fifty states. We are pledged to spare no effort to herald and practice the lordly claims of Jesus Christ, as Son of God and Savior. 3) It is a commitment to cooperative endeavor beyond the lines of a single denomination, congregation, or para-church agency. We pledge ourselves to seek ways to demonstrate the oneness of Christ's people, to reduce the level of competition, and to pool information, resources, and energies to increase the effectiveness of our part in God's mission.

The bicentennial

The two-hundredth anniversary of the Declaration of Independence in 1976 gives us a rallying point for evangelical witness. The eyes of our nation will be on the legacy which our founding fathers bequeathed to us. It is an appropriate time to remind our fellow citizens of the spiritual aspects of our heritage and to call them to repentance and faith in the Christ who is Lord of all nations.

We, therefore, recommend that:

1) All Christian churches and agencies consider ways that they can use the events of the bicentennial for Christian witness. For example by:
   a. observing national holidays as days of prayer;
   b. focusing Bible study and preaching on the meaning of Christian freedom;
   c. pointing out the way in which human rights are rooted in a biblical view of creation; and
   d. stressing the contribution that personal renewal will make to the stability of the nation.
2) Special effort be made to distribute the Bible to every home.
3) A day or a week of national witness be set aside during which every Christian would be urged to share his or her faith with another Christian person.
4) Interdenominational rallies be planned for ascension day in every city as testimony to the power of the risen Christ.
5) Bible studies and prayer groups put special emphasis on the needs of our fellow citizens for repentance and faith.

6) The Forum for Evangelism, an informal organization continuing the activities began with Key '73, be considered as a clearing house for sharing of plans and the developing of strategy.

Communications strategy

The importance of the media in our national life, the complexity and expense of broadcasting and advertising, and the shortness of our stay in Lausanne conspire to make it impossible for us to do more than pass on recommendations to the appropriate agencies for study and implementation.

We, therefore, recommend that:

1) The National Religious Broadcasters be requested to do an in-depth study of Christian radio and television, especially as they relate to the non-Christian listener. It is further recommended that the NRB solicit samples of exemplary programs to present as part of the 1975 convention.

2) The Evangelical Press Service be asked for recommendations as to how we may be more effective in our approach to non-Christians through journalism and literature.

3) Both National Religious Broadcasters and Evangelical Press Service be asked to consider establishing a clearing house where broadcasters and writers may keep abreast of what others are doing in their fields.

4) Local churches and agencies consider the following avenues of communication:
   a. use of billboards in their local communities;
   b. use of local television and radio stations, especially in smaller communities where public service time may be available;
   c. protest to sponsors, station managers, and elected representatives when programming is derogatory toward the faith or questionable in morality;
   d. encourage Christians in business and the professions to make evangelical literature available in shop and office;
   e. place ads in local papers, especially in sports or amusement sections;

5) All media ministry be preceeded by careful analysis of the audience to be reached and the purposes to be served.

Para-church cooperation

For over a century voluntary agencies, usually interdenominational or non-denominational in character, have been seeking to advance some aspect of Gospel witness or Christian nurture in the United States. The years since World War II have proved unusually fruitful in the founding and development of para-church ministries, especially among young people: Youth for Christ, Young Life, Campus Crusade, InterVarsity Christian Fellowship and Navigators, to name just a few.

The ultimate goal of this type of ministry is to add disciples of Jesus Christ to local congregations in regions where the para-church youth ministries are active in witness. It would be hard to overestimate the contribution organizations like these have made to Christ's body in the United States.

We, therefore, recommend:

1) that para-church organizations seek greater cooperation with agencies of similar ministry in recruiting and training of staff, in service to congregations and denominations, and in developing of specialized strategies of ministry;

2) that para-church organizations strengthen their ties to local congregations by their own participation, by encouraging their converts to participate, and by putting their resources at the service of the local pastors;

3) that pastors be sensitive to the needs of students and staff of para-church organizations in their preaching (expository preaching seems especially helpful), teaching, and counseling;

4) that a directory of para-church organizations be published periodically listing the purposes, resources, and staff of each organization.

WALES NATIONAL STRATEGY GROUP REPORT

Secretary: Philip D. Hill

INTRODUCTION

The group consisted of a cross-section of evangelical life in Wales, both theologically and culturally. Very quickly, however, a sense of oneness came about from the following considerations. Firstly, the Congress exhibited a genuine spirit of fellowship remarkable in so large a group. Secondly, our fears that we would have to be subjected to high-pressure techniques and lack of doctrinal awareness were quickly removed. The Congress has been deeply aware of the failures in missionary and evangelistic work as well as the success stories. Thus the Welsh delegates found their own spirit of concern — and their burden for God's work — clearly reflected on the platform. In the third place we shared a burden for evangelization being wholly biblical and solid, aiming to be faithful both to God and his Word and also to the unsaved of our land. Fourthly, we found a common yearning for our land; indeed, this was such a burden that as we met day by day we were compelled to devote a whole morning session to intercessory prayer. This, then, was the general reaction of the group to the Congress as a whole. Naturally, it was felt that there were some men whose wisdom exceeded others — but it did not alter this general feeling!

Against the background the following issues seemed to the group of particular significance.

The content of the Congress

The Congress came to terms with great issues under the guidance of men of real stature, theologically and spiritually. We have been called to be both more biblical, doctrinally-aware evangelicals and on this basis, more evangelistic. Out of this proclamation of God's Word we felt that certain issues in particular have arisen. Some areas of evangelical attitudes betray a sad lack of concern for truly biblical thinking. By contrast, evangelical life in Wales is comparatively strong here and has a contribution to make in the example it has set. However, it was felt that we must build on this foundation with a greater warmth of fellowship and a deep love for one another —without over-simplifying conscientious differences. A sharing in prayer for Wales was thought to be a wholesome and important part of encouraging this. Perhaps even repentance for lovelessness is necessary. Another area of concern arising from the content of the Congress is in the realm of evangelization across cultures. Much emphasis was laid on the bilingual situation of Wales (60% of the group was Welsh-speaking as a first language). It was felt that the evangelization of Wales must take into account this situation in such a way as to respect language and culture in Wales. This must both promote love and respect within God's people and prevent the alienation of people from the Gospel on purely cultural grounds. Finally in this section, we felt that there was a tendency for the local church to be remote from the immediate community both in evangelism and other concerns for people. Since it was unanimously felt that evangelism ought to be founded on the local church this was deeply regretted. Divine compassion and the movement of the Holy Spirit were seen as desperately needed in Wales.

The aim of the Congress

The aim of the Congress is *not* to create an activist reaction in a burst of hysteria. This realization brought us great relief! Rather, we have been informed about the world situation, the openness or otherwise of different lands to the Gospel, the theological issues, political issues, and social issues involved in world evangelization. Above all, a sense of deepest concern for the glory of God and our responsibility before him for men has been impressed on us not by men but by God himself. We came with a burden for the people of Wales. By its aim we feel the Congress has respectfully yet convictingly spoken to that burden.

Consequently, the group felt it faced a dilemma of sorts. What could it do as a group of individuals not even purporting to be representative of any specific groups? Yet the very burden shared compelled the consideration of some kind of implementation. Thus the following proposals were agreed on, with an openness to other suggestions.

    a.   A comprehensive report with no overtones of "propositions to Wales" to simply pass on reactions and the facts as accurately as possible.

    b.   Some kind of gathering to open the way for different groups of evangelicals in Wales to share together as far as possible a common burden for evangelization in Wales; since only firstly by fidelity to the truth and then by prayer and an awareness of the real situation in Wales did the group believe that God's will can be best discerned for Wales. It was the group's feeling that the Congress has posed vitally relevant questions, but that it would be presumptuous to think that answers could be given for the many different situations represented there. Rather, as the people of God in Wales bring their burden to their God, and themselves as instruments of his will, then, and only then, could the aims of the Congress have any impact at all of real worth. "Not by might, nor by power, but by my Spirit, saith the Lord" (Zech. 4:6).

ZAIRE NATIONAL STRATEGY GROUP REPORT

Introduction: The Zaire group wants first to express its thankfulness to God who permitted such a gathering to take place. Thanks to the organizers who united a substantial representation coming from Zaire. It is a privilege to have been able to work and think together about the problems which are posed by the evangelization of our country and of the world.

During the six meetings, the group studied different questions proposed by the organizers of the Congress. Here are some of our recommendations:

I. Priority for the coming decade.

A. National evangelization.

1. We ask God for an awakening, a spiritual deepening of the actual Church. It is important that our efforts should be on a solid base and that the church become a community capable of receiving the fruits which result from all efforts in evangelization.

2. We must apply ourselves to make all the circles of the church conscious of the necessity to turn to the lost world, the necessity to evangelize.

3. We ask each community (denomination) to make a catalogue of the ethnics belonging to it and to undertake the evangelization of unreached or rejected groups.

   We quote for example:
   — the Bazimba tribes, the Bango-bango, the Banyamonda which concern the community of Grace in Zaire.
   — the Balanja, Banutuku (near Kambabarc) which are the concern of the Baptist community near-by.

4. Some areas have been abandoned by their missionaries and face grave lack of leaders and of finances. The nearby communities are asked to help. When there are no other possibilities we ask the ECZ (Church of Christ in Zaire), department of Evangelization and Church life to find a solution.

5. Zaire has many refugees from Angola, Soudan, Uganda, Rwanda, Burundi, etc. The communities should plan a special program when it doesn't exist yet, and should ask for the collaboration of the Department of Evangelization of ECZ, so that this population could be reached by the message of the love of Christ.

6. The construction of the Inga dam, the development (implantation) of new industries are creating new possibilities for evangelization.

B. Evangelization of the World

Already before the independance of our country we have sent missionaries in the near countries (Gabon, Sordan, Kenya).

Our contribution is and shall remain poor as our first objective is the evangelization in our own country. But, we want, in the 10 years to come, sensitize our members, so that they would contribute financially with a view to send a few missionaries from Zaire. We wonder also if it would be possible for the developed countries to invite some pastors from Zaire and organize for a short time, international exchange. It would contribute to widen our common vision for the evangelization of the world.

II.   Our strategy to reach our aims.

We are thankful for the fact that there exists already in our country a Department of Evangelization on the national level. It coordinates already all the different activities betwee the communities. We all want to collaborate with this department so as to reach our national objectives. Through this department also, the information of this Congress could reach the communities which are not represented here.

To facilitate our work, we foresee the following strategy:

A.   Formation of a mobile squad who would visit all the communities, organizing seminaries for pastors and evangelists. This is a period of five years.

B.   The pastors in their turn would make their parishioners aware of:
1.   necessity of evangelization
2.   individual contacts
3.   financial help for the whole program

C.   The evangelization of the masses could take place through open-air crusades, tent-church, etc. with the aid of national and foreign evangelists.
The realization of these projects depends to a great extent on the possibilities in personnel and finances!

III. A specific action is recommended to participants when they go back to their country.

Each participant should start an evangelization program in his own community, following our strategy and the information received during the Congress.

IV. Help and means needed for these objectives which cannot be taken care of by local resources.

A.   Our thankfulness goes to different communities in Zaire, and also to all the help from foreign countries, which has been coming to support the work of the department of evangelization. This help is far from enough because this department should face the following budget:

National evangelist salary	Z 3.000
Evangelist's travel expense	1.500
Salary for 3 secretaries	1.500
Office expenses	1.200
Families	1.200
Women - girls	1.200
Evangelist for the town of Kin	1.800
Evangelization material (tent)	2.500
Zaire	13.900

The help for this section can come only from those who have the vision of evangelization. We believe we all have a responsbility in this work. Aid can come in money or goods.

B. One strategy foresees a mobile squad of three persons over a period of five years and that would ask for an annual budget of approximately Z 5.000 (Z. 1.00 = $2.00). We count on a 50% participation from the communities in Zaire. The other 50% might be offered by foreign organizations.

C. Our strategy foresees a training seminar. To go there the delegates who are poor or who come from a poor community, should receive financial aid (the distances are great). A local seminar would need about 500 to 1,000 Zaires.

D. Personnel — Our objectives need reinforcement from the personnel of the Evangelization Department. The people required should be from Zaire and could be sent by the communities.

V. Cooperation or association recommended on the local region or world level to reach these objectives:

A. On the local level, we want to support our existing department in personnel and financially.

B. On the world level, we must encourage a cooperation with the Christians of the African continent and those of the whole world.

VI. Some remarks

A. The Christian world should recognize the existence in Africa of two different cultures: Anglophone and Francophone. The influence of this difference in cultures is felt in as far as the forms and practices of the Church! That is why one group regrets that so few participants from the Francophone Africa could express their view during this Congress.

In the choice of the 25 members of the "Follow-up Committee," we wish, considering what was mentioned before, a larger delegation from Africa so as to be able to represent more clearly these two points of view.

B. We regret too that the Zaire people didn't really represent all the different regions of Zaire. Most of the participants came from Haut-Zaire and from Kinshasa.

C. In the next Congress (!) we would wish more time for discussion on the national level.

We are happy that this Lausanne Congress 1974 shows the evidence of a step forward toward the manifestation of the kingdom of God which we are waiting for!

ZAMBIA NATIONAL STRATEGY GROUP REPORT

The main feature of our study was the desire to isolate the essential components of the needs, objectives for future work, and steps for the implementation of these objectives.

The needs

1. The greatest need was found to be a Bible-based Christianity with a clearly defined faith. This is essential in order that a) the believers may be established in the faith "that we may no longer be children tossed to and fro and carried about with every wind of doctrine, by the cunning of men, by their craftiness in deceitful wiles," (Eph. 4:13,14); and b) the many adherents to the faith may be freed from the bondage of sin which continues to manifest itself in excessive drunkeness, vice, the disintegration of the family unit and society. Also in order that the believers may be released from the power and fear of Satan and be released from fear of witchcraft and Satan's other techniques.

2. Another great need is that God may move mightily through us all: a) creating a body of Christ burning with evangelistic zeal; b) raising up more evangelists and Bible expositors that the Gospel may be clarified and truthfully proclaimed; c) making us submissive and sensitive to his Sovereignty and Lordship so we may hear and follow his guidance in areas of social justice and concern, and may have a positive attitude to our culture but make every effort to oppose syncretism; d) the local believers may find a sense of responsibility to support the work God has assigned to us from the resources he has given us. This is not to affirm the moratorium but an expressive on deeper commitment of the local believers in the work of God.

Objectives

In trying to formulate our objectives we have tried to be conscious of the Lordship of Jesus and the power of the Holy Spirit. We humble ourselves to him asking that he may add or subtract from these objectives according to his will.

1. The first objective is to communicate the findings of the Lausanne Congress to our brethren and to enable them to study the implications of these findings to the Zambian situation. The strategy of evangelization can and will best be formulated after such a study. This is because we feel that we are not a representative body capable of formulating an evangelism policy for the whole country.

2. We would recommend however that:

   a. the appropriate church and para-church organizations explore, in the light of the Lausanne Congress, how the church may be mobilized for the task of letting Zambia hear his voice;

   b. that evangelistic techniques be surveyed and appropriated, and that the existing ones be strengthened to reach the urban masses of Zambia; the rural masses; the expatriate communities such as the English, Italian, Chinese, Yugoslavs and many others currently working amongst us; the Zambian youth in all its diversity including students, organized youth in the Zambia Youth Service, the unorganized/unemployed youth in urban and rural areas; and the immigrant workers from Rhodesia and refugees from Angola, Mozambique and other neighboring countries;

c. to consider seriously whether God is calling us to be a missionary church to the Moslem world in view of warmer relationships between this world and our regions, China for similar reasons, any other unreached areas of the world. (Both 1 and 3 present real challenge and cost, calling for careful consideration and much prayer);

d. to consider ways and means whereby the existing work among the youth could be consolidated. We have recognized that the Zambian youth is hungry for truth, reality, meaning, and purpose. Because they cannot find it they turn to alcohol, sex, vandalism, and crime. A strategy of youth work and evangelism comprising all the Zambian youth needs to be developed. *All* includes students, Zambia Youth Service, and the unorganized youth in urban and rural areas.

Steps in implementation of our objectives

1. Sending out preliminary information soon after the Congress to evangelical churches through the evangelical fellowship which has ties with about twenty-three churches.
2. The Evangelical Fellowship of Zambia, whose secretary is a participant in the Congress, should study the plenary papers when they are published.
3. The EFZ should hold special seminars to formulate strategy for evangelism either before, on or after the 10th of July, 1975, when they have a special seminar on church growth.
4. The participants have pledged to apply what they have learned from the Congress under guidance and inspiration of the Holy Spirit in situations and areas where they are working.
5. The greatest step of all is that the participants are burdened with dedication in prayer for more evangelists and Bible expositors, for more teachers and others with the task of the upbuilding of the church, for training and sending out into the world to make disciples of all men.

In the one week of the Lausanne Congress the population of the world increased by 1.5 million. There should be a sense of urgency to let Zambia and the world "hear his voice."

Section X:
Closing Address

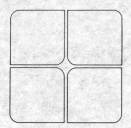

THE KING IS COMING

Billy Graham

The Gospel of the Kingdom, according to Jesus, is to be "preached in all the world for a witness," after which "shall the end come."

There are many things about this that go beyond my understanding. I cannot grasp exactly when a nation can be said to be evangelized, even though I heard it explained at Lausanne several times. I do not understand why God himself did not do the evangelizing. Why did he select instruments like us to do it? Why did he not choose the angels? Why did he give us this awesome responsibility? Why did Christ issue this tremendous command, "Go into all the world and proclaim the Gospel"? I do not understand all of that.

But we are like the Apostle Paul — we know something of the terror of the Lord and the love of Christ on the Cross. We feel compassion for fellow human beings who are lost in the darkness of this world. We accept this command of our Lord Jesus Christ, and today we are closer to fulfilling it than ever before in the history of the Christian church.

We came to Lausanne as messengers, as proclaimers, as evangelists, as teachers, as pastors, as professors, as theologians, but in a sense we are all evangelists. Paul told Timothy, "Do the work of an evangelist." And as we leave Lausanne I say to each person the same words: "Do the work of an evangelist."

We leave here with a vast array of knowledge about different aspects of theology. One of the participants was overheard to say, "I have theological indigestion." Our vision of the world has been enlarged. We have been astonished at the ability of the "third world" participants. We have learned something about the areas of our ministry. We have wept together, we have debated together, we have laughed together.

We have not always agreed on everything, but that brings us to the word in 2 Peter 3:11, "Since all these things are thus to be dissolved, what sort of persons ought you to be in lives of holiness and godliness..." In view of the world in which we live, and the return of the King, what kind of persons should you and I be? Psalm 12 reads in *The Living Bible,* "Lord, Help! Godly men are fast disappearing. Where in all the world can dependable men be found?" Are you a godly man, a godly woman? Are you dependable?

Our world is in a crisis of leadership. We want some person to step onto the stage of events with a formula for world peace. The human race is waiting for a hero, a leader, and some day that leader will appear. Jesus Christ will come with the solution to our complex problems.

Yes, the King is coming. Some day we will see the Son of man seated at the right hand of God and coming in the clouds of heaven. J.B. Phillips translates Colossians 3:4 to read, "One day Christ, the secret center of our lives, will show himself openly, and you will all share in that magnificent glory."

One day Jesus Christ will show himself openly and you who have come to Lausanne from Malawi, from Chad, from Sikkim, from China, from America, from the Soviet Union, from everywhere — you will all share in his magnificent glory on *that day*. But our expectation of what is coming does not make us complacent in the meantime.

Critics of those who believe in the Second Advent claim that such a belief causes Christians to lose their incentive for work. It has been my experience that those who believe in the return of the Lord are the hardest workers, the most zealous and the most dedicated. We do not know that Christ is coming back in this century. We do not know the day or the hour of his return. But even if he were coming tonight, and we were certain of it, we would be busy about our Lord's business.

At this Congress we have heard the groan of the world – groans for justice, groans for freedom, groans for wholeness, groans for salvation, groans for the redemption of the physical order. The agnostic asks, "If there is a God, why doesn't he show?" Well, he is going to show himself. The King is on the way. In the twinkling of an eye, in a thousandth of a second, he will come. That leaves no opportunity for the Christian to recommit his life. It leaves no opportunity for the thief to repent, or for the prodigal to return home.

Now is the moment. Professor George Duffield has pointed out that in the New Testament epistles 22 verses call for purity, patience and service in the light of the glorious return of Jesus Christ. I don't know whether or not we shall hold another congress. We certainly will never meet together again like this; but we will see each other again in *that day*. All the groanings, the sufferings, the tears, the death, will be gone.

Peter Beyerhaus said that the human race has three principal enemies: sin, Satan, and death; and that on the Cross our Lord Jesus Christ nullified all three. We are now awaiting the climactic moment and the total fulfillment of what was done on the Cross.

I believe there are two strains in prophetic Scripture. One leads us to understand that as we approach the latter days and the Second Coming of Christ, things will become worse and worse. Joel speaks of "multitudes, multitudes, in the valley of decision!" The day of the Lord is near in the valley of decision. He is speaking of judgment.

But I believe as we approach the latter days and the coming of the Lord, it could be a time also of great revival. We cannot forget the possibility and the promise of revival, the refreshing of the latter days ("the latter rains" of Hosea), or the outpouring of the Spirit promised in Joel 2:28, and repeated in Acts 2:17. That will happen right up to the advent of the Lord Jesus Christ. James seems to associate the "latter rains" with the return of Christ.

Evil will grow worse, but God will be mightily at work at the same time. I am praying that we will see in the next months and years the "latter rains," a rain of blessings, showers falling from heaven upon all the continents before the coming of our Lord. There is a mystery of iniquity, but there is also a mystery of righteousness, and both are working simultaneously.

A Chinese proverb says, "The journey of a thousand miles begins with the first step." Your journey home from Lausanne begins today; and the first step should be one of rededication and recommitment. You know what God has been saying to you these past ten days; I know what he has convicted me of, and what I must do.

Sam P. Jones was a Methodist evangelist in America 100 years ago. A woman came forward in one of his meetings and said, "Dr. Jones, God is speaking to me about sin in my life, but I don't know exactly which one or what." And Sam Jones said, "Kneel down and guess at it." As he told the story, "The moment she knelt down she hit it right on the head."

If you are to be an instrument prepared by the hand of God as you go home, I would say to you first, you must have had an experience with Christ. John Wesley once said, "What a dreadful thing it would be for me if I should be ignorant of the power of the truth I am preparing to proclaim." Jesus had twelve men who traveled with him, and no one suspected that something was wrong with one of them. No one suspected Judas. Before you leave here, make sure of your personal relationship with Jesus Christ.

Second, you will leave Lausanne to go back, in some cases, to dangerous situations. You may be in physical danger; you may be misunderstood, misquoted, misused. Paul lived in suffering and danger all the time. Yet he declared that he would glory in tribulation, and he seemed to become stronger and bolder in danger because he knew God was with him. There is nothing bolder than a righteous man. In the midst of danger God will be there.

Third, as messengers of God we will often lead lonely lives. "All men forsook me," said Paul. It is a price we have to pay; there is a loneliness in the Gospel. Yet you will not be alone, because you will be ministered to by the Spirit of God, as Elijah was ministered to at the brook Cherith.

Fourth, a true messenger lives a burdened life. If he is the Lord's vessel, he carries in his heart a burden for souls none can share but those who know it firsthand.

Fifth, there is an urgency to his message. Jeremiah said, "His word was in my heart a burning fire." Is God's Word in our hearts today a burning fire?

Sixth, the messenger needs a devotional life. The prayers of Abraham, Jacob, Moses, Nehemiah and Daniel marked a turning point in the history of nations. If our Lord Jesus Christ felt the need to spend nights praying, how much more do we need to spend time in prayer!

Seventh, the messenger of God will be a bold man. "Be filled with the Spirit," says Paul. My experience has been that it is a continuing thing, like a perpetual spring. There have been times of flood, times of revival and renewal in our lives and churches and communities; but there is also that continual flowing spring. The fruits of the Spirit are not present just at floodtide. Love, joy, peace, patience, kindness, generosity, fidelity, power, self-control, should characterize our lives all the time.

Finally, the messenger will lead a disciplined life. The Lausanne Covenant says we are to adopt a simpler life-style. Every area is to be brought under the Lordship of Jesus Christ, so that he might be the disciplinarian.

The problems with which we wrestle as we go back to our places of service are in many cases not intellectual. They lie deep down within the will. Are we willing to deny self and to take up the cross and follow the Lord? Are you willing? Am I willing?

The King is coming!

PRAISE THE LORD, SING HALLELUJAH

E. Margaret Clarkson

(Tune:Regent Square) Angels From the Realms of Glory

Copyright 1974

1. Praise the Lord, sing hallelujah!
Children of God's gracious choice;
Let His praises rise as thunder,
Let the whole earth hear His voice;
Till the song of His salvation
Makes His broken world rejoice!
2. Man's imprisoning night is shattered
At the impact of His Word;
Light and life spring forth eternal
Where that mighty voice is heard;
Let the powers of death and darkness
Own the triumph of their Lord!
3. Praise the Lord until His glory
Floods the farthest realms of earth,
Till from every tribe and nation
Souls rise up in glad rebirth;
Haste the day of His appearing
When all creatures own His worth.
4. Praise the Lord, sing hallelujah!
Sound His sovereign grace abroad,
Till His Word is loved and honored
Everywhere man's feet have trod;
Till His ransomed family gathers
Safely round the throne of God!

Section XI:

AUTHOR INDEX

OTHER LAUSANNE CONGRESS MATERIAL AVAILABLE:

REACHING ALL Study Book. A study book designed for individual or group use. Developed as a tool to be used for exploring the means and methods which can be used in reaching the world for Christ. **W-0118 –$4.95**

Each chapter is also available in individual booklet form for $.95 each.

1. All the World — exploring the message of evangelism
2. All Together — determining the church's role in evangelism
3. All People — examining how to reach people in many different cultural settings
4. All Needs — studying the adequacy of Christ to meet the needs of the whole person
5. By All Means — considering the methods and ways to do the work of evangelism today
6. All Power — exploring the place of prayer, devotional life and the work of the Holy Spirit in evangelism

LAUSANNE COVENANT: An exposition and Commentary by John Stott. This small book explains the significance of the Lausanne Covenant paragraph by paragraph. **STOTT, $.95**

LAUSANNE COVENANT, brochure edition at $.10 each, copies suitable for framing at $1.50 each

CONGRESS ADDRESSES on cassette. $3.95 each

DTL-LA01	Opening Ceremonies
DTL-LA02	Why Lausanne? by Billy Graham
DTL-LA03	"God at Work Through Men: Stephen" Nilson Fanini
	"Biblical Authority and Evangelism" John Stott
DTL-LA04	"The Biblical Basis of Evangelism" John Stott
	"The Dimensions of World Evangelism" Donald McGavran
DTL-LA05	"The Suicide of Man" Harold Lindsell
DTL-LA06	"God at Work Through Men: Ananias & Paul" Philip Teng
	"Positive & Negative Forces for Evangelization" Jan van Capelleveen
DTL-LA07	"Evangelism and the World" C. René Padilla
DTL-LA08	"God at Work Through Men: Peter & a Roman Officer" Branko Lovrec
	"Methods & Strategy of the Early Church" Michael Green
DTL-LA09	"Contemporary Evangelistic Methods" George Peters
	"In-Depth Evangelism Throughout the World" Panel Discussion
DTL-LA10	"Acts of the Holy Spirit" (2 cassettes) Stanley Mooneyham
DTL-LA11-1	"God at Work Through Men: Paul & the Philosophers" Samuel Kamaleson
DTL-LA11-2	"Highest Priority: Cross-Cultural Evangelism" Ralph Winter
DTL-LA12	"God at Work in Circumstances" Fouad Accad
	"The Holy Spirit in World Evangelism" Gottfried Osei-Mensah
DTL-LA13	"Personal Testimonies on Acts of the Holy Spirit" of Larry Christenson, Juan Ortiz, Thomas Houston, Festo Kivengere, Corrie ten Boom
DTL-LA14	Personal Testimonies of K. N. Nambudripad, Festo Kivengere Crusade Address at Laustade by Billy Graham
DTL-LA15	"God at Work in Areas of Unknown Possibilities" Manuel Scott
	"World Evangelization in the Kingdom of God" Peter Beyerhaus

Order the above listed materials from:

WORLD WIDE PUBLICATIONS
1313 Hennepin Avenue
Minneapolis, MN 55403